Morality in Practice

SIXTH EDITION

Edited by
JAMES P. STERBA
University of Notre Dame

Wadsworth
Thomson Learning™

Australia • Canada • Mexico • Singapore • Spain • United Kingdom • United States

Philosophy Editor: Peter Adams
Assistant Editor: Kara Kindstrom
Editorial Assistant: Mark Andrews
Marketing Manager: Dave Garrison
Print Buyer: April Reynolds
Permissions Editor: Joohee Lee

Production Service: Matrix Productions Inc.
Copy Editor: Vicki Nelson
Cover Designer: Yvo Riezebos
Compositor: ColorType, San Diego
Cover and Text Printer: Von Hoffman/
Custom Printing

Printed in the United States of America
2 3 4 5 6 7 04 03 02 01

For permission to use material from this text,
contact us by:
   Web: http://www.thomsonrights.com
   Fax: 1-800-730-2215
   Phone: 1-800-730-2214

For more information, contact
Wadsworth/Thomson Learning
10 Davis Drive
Belmont, CA 94002-3098
USA
http://www.wadsworth.com

International Headquarters
Thomson Learning
International Division
290 Harbor Drive, 2nd Floor
Stamford, CT 06902-7477
USA

UK/Europe/Middle East/South Africa
Thomson Learning
Berkshire House
168-173 High Holborn
London WC1V 7AA
United Kingdom

Asia
Thomson Learning
60 Albert Street, #15-01
Albert Complex
Singapore 189969

Canada
Nelson Thomson Learning
1120 Birchmount Road
Toronto, Ontario M1K 5G4
Canada

**Library of Congress
Cataloging-in-Publication Data**

Morality in practice / edited by James P. Sterba,—6th ed.
      p. cm.
   Includes bibliograhical references
   ISBN 0-534-52111-8
      1. Social ethics. I. Sterba, James P.

HM665 .M67   2000
303.3'72—dc21   00-036795

♲ This book is printed on acid-free recycled paper.

*This book is again dedicated
to Sonya, now 20,
who now knows her understanding
of at least some moral problems
far exceeds my own.*

Contents

Preface

Moral problems courses tend to teach themselves. It takes a really bad teacher to mess them up. Teachers can mess up a moral problems course in at least three ways:

1. By presenting just one set of views on various topics. Students appreciate the need for fair play here.

2. By encouraging students to hold a crude relativism. Students know that all moral stances are not equally good.

3. By not being relevant to student concerns. Students can reasonably expect that at least an ethics course will be relevant to their lives.

This text enables teachers to avoid (1) by presenting radically opposed selections on all topics. It enables teachers to avoid (2) by suggesting, through the introductions and through the ordering and selection of topics, how some views turn out to be more defensible than others. It enables teachers to avoid (3) by being the only moral problems text to provide in-depth coverage of a broad range of new and standard moral problems. In fact, no other moral problems text combines such breadth and depth. In addition, it has to recommend it the following:

New Features

1. Eighteen new readings overall

2. Two almost totally new sections: affirmative action and gun control

3. New readings included in sections on near and distant peoples, sexual equality, sexual harassment, gay and lesbians rights, animal liberation and environmental concern, and war and humanitarian intervention

Retained Features

1. A General Introduction that provides a background discussion of traditional moral approaches to ethics as well as an accessible answer to the question: Why be moral?

2. Section introductions that help to establish the framework for the discussion and criticism of the articles in each section

3. Brief summaries at the beginning of each article that enable students to test and improve their comprehension

4. One or more articles discussing specific practical applications at the end of each section of the anthology

5. Suggestions for further reading at the end of each section

In putting together this sixth edition, I have again benefited enormously from the advice and help of many different people. Very special thanks go to Preston Covey of Carnegie Mellon University, Louis Pojman of the U.S. Military Academy, my colleagues John Robinson and

Raimo Vayrynen, and my long-time partner and fellow philosopher Janet Kourany. I would also like to thank the following reviewers for their suggestions: Eric Gampel, California State University, Chico; Martin Andic, University of Massachusetts, Boston; Donald Blakeley, California State University, Fresno; Michael Byron, Kent State University; Heidi Grasswick, Middlebury College; Paulette Kidder, Seattle University; Deborah Barnbaum, Kent State University; Charles Taliaferro, New York University.

General Introduction

Most of us like to think of ourselves as just and moral people. To be truly such, however, we need to know something about the demands of justice and how they apply in our own particular circumstances. We should be able to assess, for example, whether our society's economic and legal systems are just—that is, whether the ways income and wealth are distributed in society as well as the methods of enforcing that distribution give people what they deserve. We should also consider whether other societal institutions, such as the military defense system, the education system, and the foreign aid program, are truly just. Without investigating these systems and coming to an informed opinion, we cannot say with any certainty that we are just and moral persons rather than perpetrators or beneficiaries of injustice.

This anthology has been created to help you acquire some of the knowledge you will need to justify your belief that you are a just and moral person. For this purpose, the anthology contains a wide spectrum of readings on thirteen important, contemporary, practical problems:

1. The problem of the distribution of income and wealth. (Who should control what resources within a society?)

2. The problem of near and distant peoples. (What obligations do we have to near and distant peoples?)

3. The problem of abortion and euthanasia. (Do fetuses have a right to life, and what should we do for the dying and those requiring life-sustaining medical treatment?)

4. The problem of sex equality. (Should the sexes be treated equally, and what constitutes equal treatment?)

5. The problem of affirmative action. (What specific policies are required to remedy discrimination and prejudice?)

6. The problem of sexual harassment. (What is sexual harassment and how can it be avoided?)

7. The problem of pornography. (Should pornography be prohibited because it promotes violence against women?)

8. The problem of hate speech. (What restrictions, if any, should there be on speech in society?)

9. The problem of gay and lesbian rights. (What rights should gays and lesbians have?)

10. The problem of gun control. (What restrictions should be placed on a citizen's right to own and carry guns?)

11. The problem of animal liberation and environmental justice. (What should our policies

be for the treatment of animals and the environment?)

12. The problem of punishment and responsibility. (Who should be punished and of what should their punishment consist?)

13. The problem of war and humanitarian intervention. (What are the moral limits to the international use of force?)

Before you get into these problems, however, you should know what it means to take a moral approach to these issues and how such an approach is justified.

The Essential Features of a Moral Approach to Practical Problems

To begin with, a moral approach to practical problems must be distinguished from various nonmoral approaches. Nonmoral approaches to practical problems include the *legal approach* (what the law requires with respect to this practical problem), the *group* or *self-interest approach* (what the group interest or self-interest is for the parties affected by this problem), and the *scientific approach* (how this practical problem can best be accounted for or understood). To call these approaches nonmoral, of course, does not imply that they are immoral. All that is implied is that the requirements of these approaches may or may not accord with the requirements of morality.

What, then, essentially characterizes a moral approach to practical problems? I suggest that there are two essential features to such an approach:

1. The approach is prescriptive—that is, it issues in prescriptions, such as "do this" and "don't do that."

2. The approach's prescriptions are acceptable to everyone affected by them.

The first feature distinguishes a moral approach from a scientific approach because a scientific approach is not prescriptive. The second feature distinguishes a moral approach from both a legal approach and a group or self-interest approach because the prescriptions that accord best with the law or serve the interest of particular groups or individuals may not be acceptable to everyone affected by them.

Here the notion of *acceptable* means "ought to be accepted" or "is reasonable to accept" and not simply "is capable of being accepted." Understood in this way, certain prescriptions may be acceptable even though they are not actually accepted by everyone affected by them. For example, a particular welfare program may be acceptable even though many people oppose it because it involves an increased tax burden. Likewise, certain prescriptions may be unacceptable even though they have been accepted by everyone affected by them. For example, it may be that most women have been socialized to accept prescriptions requiring them to fill certain social roles even though these prescriptions are unacceptable because they impose second-class status on them.

Alternative Moral Approaches to Practical Problems

Using the two essential features of a moral approach to practical problems, let us consider three principal alternative moral approaches to practical problems: a *utilitarian approach,* an *Aristotelian approach,* and a *Kantian approach.*[1] The basic principle of a utilitarian approach is:

Do those actions that maximize the net utility or satisfaction of everyone affected by them.

A utilitarian approach qualifies as a moral approach because it is prescriptive and because it can be argued that its prescriptions are acceptable to everyone affected by them since they take the utility or satisfaction of all those individuals equally into account.

To illustrate, let's consider how this approach applies to the question of whether nation A should intervene in the internal affairs of nation B when nation A's choice would have the following consequences:

	Nation A's Choice	
	Intervene	*Don't Intervene*
Net utility to A	4 trillion units	8½ trillion units
Net utility to B	2 trillion units	−2 trillion units
Total utility	6 trillion units	6½ trillion units

Given that these are all the consequences that are relevant to nation A's choice, a utilitarian approach favors not intervening. Note that in this case, the choice favoring a utilitarian approach does not conflict with the group interest of a nation A, although it does conflict with the group interest of nation B.

But are such calculations of utility possible? Admittedly, they are difficult to make. At the same time, such calculations seem to serve as a basis for public discussion. Once President Reagan, addressing a group of black business leaders, asked whether blacks were better off because of the Great Society programs, and although many disagreed with the answer he gave, no one found his question unanswerable.[2] Thus, faced with the exigencies of measuring utility, a utilitarian approach simply counsels that we do our best to determine what maximizes net utility and act on the result.

The second approach to consider is an Aristotelian approach. Its basic principle is:

Do those actions that would further one's proper development as a human being.

This approach also qualifies as a moral approach because it is prescriptive and because it can be argued that its prescriptions are acceptable to everyone affected by them.

There are, however, different versions of this approach. According to some versions, each person can determine through the use of reason his or her proper development as a human being. Other versions disagree. For example, many religious traditions rely on revelation to guide people in their proper development as human beings. However, although an Aristotelian approach can take these various forms, I want to focus on what is probably its philosophically most interesting form. That form specifies proper development in terms of virtuous activity and understands virtuous activity to preclude intentionally doing evil that good may come of it. In this form, an Aristotelian approach conflicts most radically with a utilitarian approach, which requires intentionally doing evil whenever a *greater* good would come of it.

The third approach to be considered is a Kantian approach. This approach has its origins in seventeenth- and eighteenth-century social contract theories, which tended to rely on actual contracts to specify moral requirements. However, actual contracts may or may not have been made, and, even if they were made, they may or may not have been moral or fair. This led Immanuel Kant and contemporary Kantian John Rawls to resort to a hypothetical contract to ground moral requirements. A difficulty with this approach is in determining under what conditions a hypothetical contract is fair and moral. Currently, the most favored Kantian approach is specified by the following basic principle:

Do those actions that persons behind an imaginary veil of ignorance would unanimously agree should be done.[3]

This imaginary veil extends to most particular facts about oneself—anything that would bias one's choice or stand in the way of a unanimous agreement. Accordingly, the imaginary veil of ignorance would mask one's knowledge of one's social position, talents, sex, race, and religion, but not one's knowledge of such general information would be contained in political, social, economic, and psychological theories. A Kantian approach qualifies as a moral approach because it is prescriptive and because it can be argued that its prescriptions would be acceptable to everyone affected by them since they would be agreed to by everyone affected behind an imaginary veil of ignorance.

To illustrate the approach, let's return to the example of nation A and nation B used earlier. The choice facing nation A was the following:

Nation A's Choice		
	Intervene	Don't Intervene
Net utility to A	4 trillion units	8½ trillion units
Net utility to B	2 trillion units	−2 trillion units
Total utility	6 trillion units	6½ trillion units

Given that these are all the consequences relevant to nation A's choice, a Kantian approach favors intervention because persons behind the imaginary veil of ignorance would have to consider that they might turn out to be in nation B, and in that case, they would not want to be so disadvantaged for the greater benefit of those in nation A. This resolution conflicts with the resolution favored by a utilitarian approach and the group interest of nation A, but not with the group interest of nation B.

Assessing Alternative Moral Approaches

Needless to say, each moral approach has its strengths and weaknesses. The main strength of a utilitarian approach is that once the rele-

vant utilities are determined, there is an effective decision-making procedure that can be used to resolve all practical problems. After determining the relevant utilities, all that remains is to total the net utilities and choose the alternative with the highest net utility. The basic weakness of this approach, however, is that it does not give sufficient weight to the distribution of utility among the relevant parties. For example, consider a society equally divided between the Privileged Rich and the Alienated Poor, who face the following alternatives:

Nation A's Choice		
	Alternative A	Alternative B
Net utility to Privileged Rich	5½ trillion units	4 trillion units
Net utility to Alienated Poor	1 trillion units	2 trillion units
Total utility	6½ trillion units	6 trillion units

Given that these are all the relevant utilities, a utilitarian approach favors alternative A even though alternative B provides a higher minimum payoff. And if the utility values for two alternatives were:

Nation A's Choice		
	Alternative A	Alternative B
Net utility to A Privileged Rich	4 trillion units	5 trillion units
Net utility to Alienated Poor	2 trillion units	1 trillion units
Total utility	6 trillion units	6 trillion units

A utilitarian approach would be indifferent between the alternatives, even though alternative A provides a higher minimum payoff. In this way, a utilitarian approach fails to take into account the distribution of utility among the relevant parties. All that matters for this approach is maximizing total utility, and the distribution of utility among the affected parties is taken into account only insofar as it contributes toward the attainment of that goal.

By contrast, the main strength of an Aristotelian approach in the form we are considering is that it limits the means that can be chosen in pursuit of good consequences. In particular, it absolutely prohibits intentionally doing evil that good may come of it. However, although some limit on the means available for the pursuit of good consequences seems desirable, the main weakness of this version of an Aristotelian approach is that the limit it imposes is too strong. Indeed, exceptions to this limit would seem to be justified whenever the evil to be done is:

1. Trivial (e.g., stepping on someone's foot to get out of a crowded subway).

2. Easily reparable (e.g., lying to a temporarily depressed friend to keep her from committing suicide).

3. Sufficiently outweighed by the consequences of the action (e.g., shooting one of 200 civilian hostages to prevent in the only way possible the execution of all 200).

Still another weakness of this approach is that it lacks an effective decision-making procedure for resolving practical problems. Beyond imposing limits on the means that can be employed in the pursuit of good consequences, the advocates of this approach have not agreed on criteria for selecting among the available alternatives.

The main strength of a Kantian approach is that like an Aristotelian approach it seeks to limit the means available for the pursuit of good consequences. However, unlike the version of the Aristotelian approach we considered, a Kantian approach does not impose an absolute limit on intentionally doing evil that good may come of it. Behind the veil of ignorance, persons would surely agree that if the evil were trivial, easily reparable, or sufficiently outweighed by the consequences, there would be an adequate justification for permitting it. On the other hand, the main weakness of a Kantian approach is that although it provides an effective decision-making procedure for resolving some practical problems, such as the problem of how to distribute income and wealth and the problem of near and distant peoples, a Kantian approach cannot be applied to all problems. For example, it will not work for the problems of animals rights and abortion unless we assume that animals and fetuses should be behind the veil of ignorance.

So far, we have seen that prescriptivity and acceptability of prescriptions by everyone affected by them are the two essential features of a moral approach to practical problems, and we have considered three principal alternative approaches that qualify as moral approaches to these problems. Let's now examine what reasons there are for giving a moral approach to practical problems precedence over any nonmoral approach with which it conflicts.

The Justification for Following a Moral Approach to Practical Problems

To begin with, the ethical egoist, by denying the priority of morality over self-interest, presents the most serious challenge to a moral approach to practical problems. Basically, that challenge takes two forms: *individual ethical egoism* and *universal ethical egoism*. The basic principle of individual ethical egoism is:

Everyone ought to do what is in the overall self-interest of just one particular individual.

The basic principle of universal ethical egoism is:

Everyone ought to do what is in his or her overall self-interest.

Obviously, the prescriptions deriving from these two forms of egoism would conflict significantly with prescriptions following from a moral approach to practical problems. How then can we show that a moral approach is preferable to an egoist's approach?

In individual ethical egoism, all prescriptions are based on the overall interests of just one particular individual. Let's call that individual Gladys. Because in individual ethical egoism Gladys's interest constitute the sole basis for determining prescriptions, there should be no problem of inconsistent prescriptions, assuming, of course, that Gladys's own particular interests are in harmony. The crucial problem for individual ethical egoism, however, is justifying that only Gladys's interests count in determining prescriptions. Individual ethical egoism must provide at least some reason for accepting that view. Otherwise, it would be irrational to accept the theory. But what reason or reasons could serve this function? Clearly, it will not do to cite as a reason some characteristic Gladys shares with other persons because whatever justification such a characteristic would provide for favoring Gladys's interests, it would also provide for favoring the interests of those other persons. Nor will it do to cite as a reason some unique characteristic of Gladys, such as knowing all of Shakespeare's writings by heart, because such a characteristic involves a comparative element, and consequently others with similar characteristics, like knowing some or most of Shakespeare's corpus by heart, would still have some justification, although a proportionally lesser justification, for having their interests favored. But again the proposed characteristic would not justify favoring only Gladys's interests.

A similar objection could be raised if a unique relational characteristic were proposed as a reason for Gladys's special status—such as that Gladys is Seymour's wife. Because other persons would have similar but not identical relational characteristics, similar but not identical reasons would hold for them. Nor will it do to argue that the reason for Gladys's special status is not the particular unique traits that she possesses, but rather the mere fact that she has unique traits. The same would hold true of everyone else. Every individual has unique traits. If recourse to unique traits is dropped and Gladys claims that she is special simply because she is herself and wants to further her own interests, every other person could claim the same.[4]

For the individual ethical egoist to argue that the same or similar reasons do *not* hold for other people with the same or similar characteristics to those of Gladys, she must explain *why* they do not hold. It must always be possible to understand how a characteristic serves as a reason in one case but not in another. If no explanation can be provided, and in the case of individual ethical egoism none has been forthcoming, the proposed characteristic either serves as a reason in both cases or does not serve as a reason at all.

Universal Ethical Egoism

Unfortunately, these objections to individual ethical egoism do not work against universal ethical egoism because universal ethical egoism does provide a reason why the egoist should be concerned simply about maximizing his or her own interests, which is simply that the egoist is herself and wants to further her own interests. The individual ethical egoist could not recognize such a reason without giving up her view, but the universal ethical egoist is willing and able to universalize her claim and recognize that everyone has a similar justification for adopting universal ethical egoism.

Accordingly, the objections that typically have been raised against universal ethical egoism are designed to show that the view is fundamentally inconsistent. For the purpose of evaluating these objections, let's consider the case of Gary Gyges, an otherwise normal human being who, for reasons of personal gain, has embezzled $300,000 while working at People's National Bank and is in the process of escaping to a South Sea island where he will have the good fortune to live a pleasant life protected by the local authorities and untroubled by any qualms of conscience. Suppose that Hedda Hawkeye, a fellow employee, knows that Gyges has been embezzling money from the bank and is about to escape. Suppose, further, that it is in Hawkeye's overall self-interest to prevent Gyges from escaping with the embezzled money because she will be generously rewarded for doing so by being appointed vicepresident of the bank. Given that it is in Gyges's overall self-interest to escape with the embezzled money, it now appears that we can derive a contradiction from the following:

1. Gyges ought to escape with the embezzled money.

2. Hawkeye ought to prevent Gyges from escaping with the embezzled money.

3. By preventing Gyges from escaping with the embezzled money, Hawkeye is preventing Gyges from doing what he ought to do.

4. One ought never to prevent someone from doing what he or she ought to do.

5. Thus, Hawkeye ought not to prevent Gyges from escaping with the embezzled money.

Because premise 2 and conclusion 5 are contradictory, universal ethical egoism appears to be inconsistent.

The soundness of this argument depends, however, on premise 4, and defenders of universal ethical egoism believe there are grounds for rejecting this premise. For if "preventing an action" means "rendering the action possible," it would appear that there *are* cases in which a person is justified in preventing someone else from doing what he or she ought to do. Consider, for example, the following case. Suppose Irma and Igor are both actively competing for the same position at a prestigious law firm. If Irma accepts the position, she obviously renders it impossible for Igor to obtain the position. But surely this is *not* what we normally think of as an unacceptable form of prevention. Nor would Hawkeye's prevention of Gyges's escape appear to be unacceptable. Thus, to sustain the argument against universal ethical egoism, one must distinguish between acceptable and unacceptable forms of prevention and then show that the argument succeeds even for forms of prevention that a universal ethical egoist would regard as unacceptable. This requires elucidating the force of "ought" in universal ethical egoism.

To illustrate the sense in which a universal ethical egoist claims that other persons ought to do what is in their overall self-interest, defenders often appeal to an analogy of competitive games. For example, in football a defensive player might think that the opposing team's quarterback ought to pass on third down with five yards to go, while not wanting the quarterback to do so and planning to prevent any such attempt. Or to use Jesse Kalin's example:

> I may see how my chess opponent can put my king in check. This is how he ought to move. But believing that he ought to move his bishop and check my king does not commit me to wanting him to do that, nor to persuading him to do so. What I ought to do is sit there quietly, hoping he does not move as he ought.[5]

The point of these examples is to suggest that a universal ethical egoist may, like a player in a game, judge that others ought to do what is in their overall self-interest while simultaneously attempting to prevent such actions or at least refraining from encouraging them.

The analogy of competitive games also illustrates the sense in which a universal ethical egoist claims that she herself ought to do what is in her overall self-interest. For just as a player's judgment that she ought to make a particular move is followed, other things being equal, by an attempt to perform the appropriate action, so likewise when a universal ethical egoist judges that she ought to do some particular action, other things being equal, an attempt to perform the appropriate action follows. In general, defenders of universal ethical egoism stress that because we have little difficulty understanding the implications of the use of "ought" in competitive games, we should also have little difficulty understanding the analogous use "ought" by the universal ethical egoist.

To claim, however, that the "oughts" in competitive games are analogous to the "oughts" of universal ethical egoism does not mean there are no differences between them. Most important, competitive games are governed by moral constraints such that when everyone plays the game properly, there are acceptable moral limits as to what one can do. For example, in football one cannot poison the opposing quarterback in order to win the game. By contrast, when everyone holds self-interested reasons to be supreme, the only limit to what one can do is the point beyond which one ceases to benefit. But this important difference between the "oughts" of universal ethical egoism and the "oughts" found in publicly recognized activities like competitive games does not defeat the appropriateness of the analogy.

That the "oughts" found in publicly recognized activities are always limited by various moral constraints (what else would get publicly recognized?) does not preclude their being a suggestive model for the unlimited action-guiding character of the "oughts" of universal ethical egoism.[6]

From Rationality to Morality

Although the most promising attempts to show that universal ethical egoism is inconsistent have failed, the challenge the view presents to a moral approach to practical problems can still be turned aside. It can be shown that, although consistent, the egoist acts contrary to reason in rejecting a moral approach to practical problems.

To show this, let us begin by imagining that we are members of a society deliberating over what sort of principles governing action we should accept. Let us assume that each of us is capable of entertaining and acting on both self-interested and moral reasons and that the question we are seeking to answer is what sort of principles governing action it would be rational for us to accept.[7] This question is not about what sort of principles we should publicly affirm since people will sometimes publicly affirm principles that are quite different from those they are prepared to act on, but rather it is a question of what principles it would be rational for us to accept at the deepest level—in our hearts of hearts.

Of course, there are people who are incapable of acting on moral reasons. For such people, there is no question about their being required to act morally or altruistically. But the interesting philosophical question is not about such people, but about people, like ourselves, who are capable of acting self-interestedly or morally and are seeking a rational justification for following one course of action over the others.

In trying to determine how we should act, let us assume that we would like to be able to construct a *good* argument favoring morality over egoism, and given that good arguments are non–question-begging, we accordingly would like to construct an argument that does not beg the question as far as possible. The question at issue here is what reasons each of us should take as supreme, and this question would be begged against egoism if we propose to answer it simply by assuming from the start that moral reasons are the reasons that each of us should take as supreme. But the question would be begged against morality as well if we proposed to answer the question simply by assuming from the start that self-interested reasons are the reasons that each of us should take as supreme. This means, of course, that we cannot answer the question of what reasons we should take as supreme simply by assuming the following principle of universal ethical egoism:

> Each person ought to do what best serves his or her overall self-interest.

We can no more argue for egoism simply by denying the relevance of moral reasons to rational choice than we can argue for pure altruism simply by denying the relevance of self-interested reasons to rational choice and assuming the following general principle of pure altruism:

> Each person ought to do what best serves the overall interest of others.

Consequently, in order not to beg the question, we have no other alternative but to grant the prima facie relevance to both self-interested and moral reasons to rational choice and then try to determine which reasons we would be rationally required to act upon, all things considered. Notice that in order not to beg the question, it is necessary to back off from both the general principle of egoism and the general principle of pure altruism, thus granting the prima facie relevance of both self-interested and moral reasons to rational choice. From this standpoint, it is still an open question whether either egoism or pure altruism will be rationally preferable, all things considered.

In this regard, there are two kinds of cases that must be considered. First, there are cases in which there is a conflict between the relevant self-interested and moral reasons.[8] Second, there are cases in which there is no such conflict.

Now it seems obvious that where there is no conflict, and both reasons are conclusive reasons of their kind, both reasons should be acted on. In such contexts, we should do what is favored both by morality and by self-interest.

Consider the following example. Suppose you accepted a job marketing a baby formula in underdeveloped countries where the formula was improperly used, leading to increased infant mortality.[9] Imagine that you could just as well have accepted an equally attractive and rewarding job marketing a similar formula in developed countries, where the misuse does not occur, so that a rational weighing of the relevant self-interested reasons alone would not have favored your acceptance of one of these jobs over the other.[10] At the same time, there were obviously moral reasons that condemned your acceptance of the first job—reasons that you presumably are or were able to acquire. Moreover, by assumption in this case, the moral reasons do not clash with the relevant self-interested reasons; they simply made a recommendation where the relevant self-interested reasons are silent. Consequently, a rational weighing of all the relevant reasons in this case could not but favor acting in accord with the relevant moral reasons.[11]

Yet it might be objected that in cases of this sort there would frequently be other reasons significantly opposed to these moral reasons— other reasons that you are or were able to acquire. Such reasons would be *malevolent* reasons seeking to bring about the suffering and death of other human beings, or *benevolent* reasons concerned to promote nonhuman welfare even at the expense of human welfare, or *aesthetic* reasons concerned to produce valuable results irrespective of the effects on human or nonhuman welfare. But assuming that such malevolent reasons are ultimately rooted in some conception of what is good for oneself or others,[12] these reasons would have already been taken into account, and by assumption outweighed by the other relevant reasons in this case. And although neither benevolent reasons (concerned to promote nonhuman welfare) nor aesthetic reasons would have been taken into account, such reasons are not directly relevant to justifying morality over universal ethical egoism.[13] Consequently, even with the presence of these three kinds of reasons, your acceptance of the first job can still be seen to be contrary to the relevant reasons in this case.

Needless to say, defenders of universal ethical egoism cannot but be disconcerted with this result since it shows that actions that accord with rational egoism are contrary to reason at least when there are two equally good ways of pursuing one's self-interest, only one of which does not conflict with the basic requirements of morality. Notice also that in cases where there are two equally good ways of fulfilling the basic requirements of morality, only one of which does not conflict with what is in a person's overall self-interest, it is not at all disconcerting for defenders of morality to

admit that we are rationally required to choose the way that does not conflict with what is in our overall self-interest. Nevertheless, exposing this defect in universal ethical egoism for cases where moral reasons and self-interested reasons do not conflict would be but a small victory for defenders of morality if it were not also possible to show that in cases where such reasons do conflict, moral reasons have priority over self-interested reasons.

Now when we rationally assess the relevant reasons in such conflict cases, it is best to cast the conflict not as a conflict between self-interested reasons and moral reasons but instead as a conflict between self-interested reasons and altruistic reasons.[14] Viewed in this way, three solutions are possible. First, we could say that self-interested reasons always have priority over conflicting altruistic reasons. Second, we could say just the opposite, that altruistic reasons always have priority over conflicting self-interested reasons. Third, we could say that some kind of a compromise is rationally required. In this compromise, sometimes self-interested reasons would have priority over altruistic reasons and sometimes altruistic reasons would have priority over self-interested reasons.

Once the conflict is described in this manner, the third solution can be seen to be the one that is rationally required. This is because the first and second solutions give exclusive priority to one class of relevant reasons over the other, and only a completely question-begging justification can be given for such an exclusive priority. Only the third solution, by sometimes giving priority to self-interested reasons and sometimes giving priority to altruistic reasons, can avoid a completely question-begging resolution.

Consider the following example. Suppose you are in the waste disposal business and you decided to dispose of toxic wastes in a manner that was cost efficient for you but predictably caused significant harm to future generations. Imagine that there were alternative methods available for disposing of the waste that were only slightly less cost efficient and which did not cause any significant harm to future generations.[15] In this case, you are to weigh your self-interested reasons favoring the most cost-efficient disposal of the toxic wastes against the relevant altruistic reasons favoring the avoidance of significant harm to future generations. If we suppose that the projected loss of benefit to yourself was ever so slight and the projected harm to future generations was ever so great, then a nonarbitrary compromise between the relevant self-interested and altruistic reasons would have to favor the altruistic reasons in this case. Hence, as judged by a non–question-begging standard of rationality, your method of waste disposal was contrary to the relevant reasons.

Notice also that this standard of rationality would not support just any compromise between the relevant self-interested and altruistic reasons. The compromise must be a nonarbitrary one, for otherwise it would beg the question with respect to the opposing egoistic and altruistic views. Such a compromise would have to respect the rankings of self-interested and altruistic reasons imposed by the egoist and altruistic views, respectively. Since for each individual there is a separate ranking of that individual's relevant self-interested and altruistic reasons, we can represent these rankings from the most important reasons to the least important reasons, as shown in the following diagram.

Accordingly, any nonarbitrary compromise among such reasons in seeking not to beg the question against egoism or altruism will have to give priority to those reasons that rank highest in each category. Failure to give priority to the highest-ranking altruistic or self-interested

Individual A	
Self-Interested Reasons	*Altruistic Reasons*
1	1
2	2
3	3
•	•
•	•
•	•
N	N

Individual B	
Self-Interested Reasons	*Altruistic Reasons*
1	1
2	2
3	3
•	•
•	•
•	•
N	N

reasons would, other things being equal, be contrary to reason.

Of course, there will be cases in which the only way to avoid being required to do what is contrary to your highest-ranking reasons is by requiring someone else to do what is contrary to her highest-ranking reasons. Such cases are sometimes called "lifeboat cases." But while such cases are surely difficult to resolve (maybe only a chance mechanism can offer a reasonable resolution), they surely do not reflect the typical conflict between the relevant self-interested and altruistic reasons that we are or were able to acquire. For typically one or the other of the conflicting reasons will rank higher on its respective scale, thus permitting a clear resolution.

Now it is important to see how morality can be viewed as just such a nonarbitrary compromise between self-interested and altruistic reasons. First of all, a certain amount of self-regard is morally required or at least morally acceptable. Where this is the case, high-ranking self-interested reasons have priority over low-ranking altruistic reasons. Second, morality obviously places limits on the extent to which people should pursue their own self-interest. Where this is the case, high-ranking altruistic reasons have priority over low-ranking self-interested reasons. In this way, morality can be seen to be a nonarbitrary compromise between self-interested and altruistic reasons, and the "moral reasons" which constitute that compromise can be seen as having an absolute priority over the self-interested or altruistic reasons that conflict with them.

Of course, exactly how this compromise is to be worked out is a matter of considerable debate. A utilitarian approach favors one sort of resolution, an Aristotelian approach another, and a Kantian approach yet another. However, irrespective of how this debate is best resolved, it is clear that some sort of a compromise view or moral solution is rationally preferable to either ethical egoism or pure altruism when judged from a non–question-begging standpoint.[16]

The Interconnectedness of Moral Solutions to Practical Problems

Given this justification for following a moral approach to practical problems, we are in a good position to begin examining the thirteen practical problems covered in this anthology. Each section contains readings defending radically opposing solutions to the problem at hand as well as one or more readings discussing specific practical applications. Working through these readings should give you a more informed view about the demands morality places on us with respect to each of these practical problems.

Even if you do not cover all of these practical problems, you should still come to appreciate why a solution to any one of them requires solutions to the others as well. That is to say, the readings on the distribution of income and wealth (in Section I) may help you to characterize a morally defensible system for distributing income and wealth within a society, but you would still not know fully how to apply such a system in a particular society without also inquiring how just that society is with respect to the other problem areas covered by this anthology.

Or suppose justice requires us to provide for the basic nutritional needs of distant peoples as well as for people within our own society. (See the readings in Section II.) Such a requirement would at least restrict the use of nonrenewable resources to satisfy the non-basic or luxury needs of persons within our society—a use that might otherwise be permitted by a morally defensible system for distributing income and wealth within our society.

Further moral restrictions on the satisfaction of nonbasic or luxury needs could arise from a correct determination of who has a right to life. For example, if fetuses have a right to life, many of us may be morally required to sacrifice the satisfaction of certain nonbasic or luxury needs to bring fetuses to term. If, by contrast, euthanasia can be morally justified, scarce resources that are now used to sustain human life could be freed for other purposes. (See the readings in Section III.)

Justice also may demand that we sacrifice some nonbasic or luxury needs to satisfy the requirements of sex equality and remedy past discrimination, prejudice, and harassment. For example, at the cost of considerable redistribution, we may be required to provide women with the same opportunities for self-development that are now open to men. (See the readings in Sections IV and VI.) We may also be required to turn away qualified candidates for medical schools and law schools so that other candidates who have suffered past injustices may be compensated by admission to these schools. (See the readings in Section V.) Obviously, a radical solution to the problem of pornography prohibiting its distribution would affect those who derive their income from that $8-billion-a-year industry. (See the readings in Section VII.) In addition, restrictions on who can own and carry a gun would affect those who derive their income from the sale of weapons to the civilian population. (See the readings in Section X.)

Moral restrictions on the satisfaction of nonbasic needs and even on the way basic needs are satisfied could arise from a determination of what obligations, if any, we have to animals and the environment. For example, if vegetarianism were morally required, and recognized as such, the impact on our lives would be far reaching. (See the readings in Section XI.)

Similarly, the legitimate costs of legal enforcement must ultimately enter into any calculation of who gets to keep what in society. This will require a solution to the problem of punishment and responsibility. (See the readings in Section XII.)

A solution to the problem of punishment and responsibility, in turn, presupposes solutions to the other practical problems discussed in this anthology. Suppose that in a society with a just distribution of income and wealth, persons who put forth their best efforts receive a yearly income of at least $15,000. (If you think a just distribution of income would provide some other amount, plug that amount in and make the corresponding adjustments in subsequent figures.) Further suppose that the society in which you and I live has an unjust distribution of income and wealth because, although there are enough resources for a just distribution, many persons who put forth their best efforts receive no more than $8,000 a year, whereas others receive as much as $500,000. Let's say that your income is $500,000 and mine is only $8,000, even though I have tried every legal way to increase my income. Assume also that any resort to civil disobedience or armed revolution would be ineffectual and too costly for me personally. If I then rob you of $7,000, thus bringing my yearly income up to the just allotment of $15,000, what would a morally defensible system of punishment and responsibility do to me if I were caught? To require a punishment equal in severity to the $7,000 I took simply reinforces an unjust distribution of income and wealth. So it seems that only a fairly light punishment or no punishment at all should be required.[17] This example shows that the application of a morally defensible solution to the problem of punishment and responsibility depends on a solution to the problem of the distribution of income and wealth in a society. To know, therefore, how to apply a morally defensible system of punishment and responsibility in a particular society, you must know to what degree that society incorporates a morally defensible distribution of income and wealth.

Finally, as we in the United States are painfully aware at the present time, proposed allocations for distributing income and wealth through social welfare programs can come into conflict with proposed allocations for defense and humanitarian intervention. Many people have argued that when this happens we must sacrifice social welfare programs to meet the requirements of defense and humanitarian intervention, but many other people have disagreed. Obviously, then, to know exactly how your solutions to the other problem areas treated in this anthology should be applied in a particular society, you also need to know the moral limits to the international use of force. (See the readings in Section XIII.)

Many of these practical problems are also interconnected because they deal with the general question of how free people should be. Specifically, the practical problems address the following questions: Should people be free to keep for themselves all they produce? (See the readings in Sections I and II.) Should people be free to enjoy pornography? (See the readings in Section VII.) Should people be free to engage in (not be punished for) hate speech? (See the readings in Section VIII.) Should people be free from legal penalty and from moral condemnation to engage in sodomy? (See the readings in Section IX.) Should people be free to possess guns for self-defense? (See the readings in Section X.)

Put briefly, what is required (or permitted) by a morally defensible solution to the problem of the distribution of income and wealth within a society will depend on what is required (or permitted) by morally defensible solutions to the problems of near and distant peoples, abortion and euthanasia, sex equality, affirmative action, sexual harassment, pornography, hate speech, gay and lesbian rights, gun control, animal liberation and environmental justice, punishment and responsibility, and war and humanitarian intervention. This means that any solution you might devise to one of these problems is only provisional until you can determine solutions to the others as well. And even if you are unable at the moment to devise solutions to all of these practical problems (because, for example, the course you are now taking is only considering some of them), you must still acknowledge that in the final analysis your solutions to these practical problems will have to be interconnected.

Note, too, that acknowledging the interconnectedness of the solutions to these practical problems does not presuppose a commitment to any particular political or moral ideal. For example, whether you tend to be a libertarian, a welfare liberal, a socialist, or anything else, the interconnectedness of the solutions to the practical problems we are discussing still holds true. Individuals who endorse different political and moral ideals will presumably devise different solutions to these practical problems, but the solutions will still be interconnected.

Working through the readings in this anthology will not always be an easy task. Some articles will be clear on the first reading, whereas others will require closer scrutiny. You should also make sure you give each selection a fair hearing, because although some will accord with your current views, others will not. It is important that you evaluate the latter with an open mind, allowing for the possibility that after sufficient reflection you may come to view them as the most morally defensible. Indeed, to approach the selections of this anthology in any other way would surely undermine the grounds you have for thinking you are a just and moral person.

Endnotes

1. Obviously, other moral approaches to practical problems could be distinguished, but I think the three I consider reflect the range of possible approaches that are relevant to the resolution of these problems.
2. In fact, the debate over whether blacks are better off now because of the programs of the Great Society has taken a more scholarly turn. See Charles Murray, *Losing Ground* (New York: Basic Books, 1984), and Christopher Jencks, "How Poor Are the Poor?" *New York Review of Books,* May 9, 1985.
3. See Section II of this text and my book, *The Demands of Justice* (Notre Dame: University of Notre Dame Press, 1980), especially Chapter 2.

4. For further argument on this point, see Marcus Singer, *Generalization in Ethics* (New York: Alfred A. Knopf, 1961), Chapter 2, and Alan Gewirth, "The Non-Trivializability of Universalizability," *Australasian Journal of Philosophy* (1969), pp. 123–131.

5. Jesse Kalin, "In Defense of Egoism," in *Morality and Rational Self-Interest*, ed. David Gauthier (Englewood Cliffs, NJ: Prentice-Hall, 1970), pp. 73–74.

6. For additional reasons that ethical egoism is a consistent view, see my article, "Ethical Egoism and Beyond," *Canadian Journal of Philosophy* (1979), pp. 91–108.

7. "Ought" presupposes "can" here. Unless the members of the society have the capacity to entertain and follow both self-interested and moral reasons for acting, it does not make any sense to ask whether they ought or ought not to do so.

8. For an account of what counts as *relevant* self-interested or moral reasons, see my *How to Make People Just* (Totowa, NJ: Rowman and Allanheld, 1988), pp. 165–166.

9. For a discussion of the causal links involved here, see *Marketing and Promotion of Infant Formula in Development Countries*. Hearing before the Subcommittee of International Economic Policy and Trade of the Committee on Foreign Affairs, U.S. House of Representatives, 1980. See also Maggie McComas et al., *The Dilemma of Third World Nutrition* (Geneva: Nestlé S.A., 1983).

10. Assume that both jobs have the same beneficial effects on the interests of others.

11. I am assuming that acting contrary to reason is an important failing with respect to the requirements of reason, and that there are many ways of not acting in (perfect) accord with reason that do not constitute acting contrary to reason.

12. Otherwise, they would really fall under the classification of aesthetic reasons.

13. Of course, such reasons would have to be taken into account at some point in a complete justification for morality, but the method of integrating such reasons into a complete justification of morality would simply parallel the method already used for integrating self-interested and altruistic reasons.

14. This is because, as I shall argue, morality itself already represents a compromise between egoism and altruism. So to ask that moral reasons be weighed against self-interested reasons is, in effect, to count self-interested reasons twice—once in the compromise between egoism and altruism and then again when moral reasons are weighed against self-interested reasons. But to count self-interested reasons twice is clearly objectionable.

15. Assume that all these methods of waste disposal have roughly the same amount of beneficial effects on the interests of others.

16. For further argument, see my article, "Justifying Morality: The Right and the Wrong Ways" [Kurt Baier Festschift] *Syntheses* (1987), vol. 1, pp. 45–70.

17. For further argument, see my article, "Is There a Rationale for Punishment?" *Philosophical Topics* (1990), pp. 105–125.

Section I

The Distribution of Income and Wealth

◇

Introduction

Basic Concepts

The problem of the distribution of income and wealth within a society has traditionally been referred to as the problem of *distributive justice.* Less frequently, this problem has included the distribution of other social goods (for example, political freedoms such as speech and press) and sometimes distribution on a worldwide scale. Most philosophers, however, agree that the distribution of income and wealth within a specific society is at the heart of the problem of distributive justice.

Just as traditionally, a variety of solutions have been proposed to the problem of distributive justice. Before examining some solutions, let's observe what they all have in common.

First, even though the solutions may differ as to exactly how much income and wealth people deserve or should rightfully possess, they all purport to tell us what people deserve or have a right to possess. For example, some solutions propose that people deserve to have their needs fulfilled, whereas others state that what people deserve or should rightfully possess is what they can produce by their labor.

Second, all solutions to the problem of distributive justice distinguish between justice and charity. *Justice* is what we should do as a matter of obligation or duty, whereas *charity* is what we should do if we want to choose the morally best possible action available. Accordingly, the demands of charity go beyond duty. In addition, failure to fulfill the demands of justice is blameworthy, violates someone's rights, and can legitimately be punished. By contrast, failure to fulfill the demands of charity, although not ideal, is not blameworthy, does not violate anyone's rights, and cannot legitimately be punished. Some solutions to the problem of distributive justice give more scope to justice and less to charity, whereas others do just the opposite.

Turning from common ground to disputed territory, solutions offered to the problem of distributive justice have appealed to many political ideals. In our own time, libertarians have appealed to an ideal of liberty, socialists to an ideal of equality, and welfare liberals to an ideal of contractual fairness.

Libertarianism

Libertarians such as John Hospers (see Selection 1) take liberty as the ultimate political ideal and typically define liberty as "the state of being unconstrained by other persons from doing what one wants." This definition limits the scope of liberty in two ways. First, not all constraints, whatever the source, count as a restriction of liberty; the constraints must come from other persons. For example, people who are constrained by natural forces from getting to the top of Mount Everest do not lack liberty in this regard. Second, the constraints must run counter to people's wants. Thus, people who do not want to hear Beethoven's Fifth Symphony do not feel their liberty is restricted when other people forbid its performance, even though the proscription does in fact constrain what they are able to do.

Of course, libertarians may argue that these constraints do restrict a person's liberty because people normally want to be unconstrained by others. But other philosophers have claimed that such constraints point to a serious defect in the libertarian's definition of liberty, which can only be remedied by defining liberty more broadly as "the state of being unconstrained by other persons from doing what one is able to do." If we apply this revised definition to the previous example, we find that people's liberty to hear Beethoven's Fifth Symphony would be restricted even if they did not want to hear it (and even if, perchance, they did not want to be unconstrained by others), because other people would still be constraining them from doing what they are able to do.

Confident that problems of defining liberty can be overcome in some satisfactory manner, libertarians go on to characterize their political ideal as requiring that each person should have the greatest amount of liberty commensurate with the same liberty for all. From this ideal, libertarians claim that several more specific requirements—in particular, a right to life; a right to freedom of speech, press, and assembly; and a right to property—can be derived.

It is important to note that the libertarian's right to life is not a right to receive from others the goods and resources necessary for preserving one's life; it is simply a right not to be killed. So understood, the right to life is not a right to welfare. In fact, there are no welfare rights in the libertarian view. Accordingly, the libertarian's understanding of the right to property is not a right to receive from others the goods and resources necessary for one's welfare, but rather a right to acquire goods and resources either by initial acquisition or by voluntary agreement.

Obviously, by defending rights such as these, libertarians can only support a limited role for government. That role is simply to prevent and punish initial acts of coercion—the only wrongful actions for libertarians.

Libertarians do not deny that it is a good thing for people to have sufficient goods and resources to meet at least their basic nutritional needs, but libertarians do deny that government has a duty to provide for such needs. Some good things, such as the provision of welfare to the needy, are requirements of charity rather than justice, libertarians claim. Accordingly, failure to make such provisions is neither blameworthy nor punishable.

A basic difficulty with the libertarian solution to the problem of distributive justice as defended by Hospers is the claim that rights to life and property (as the libertarian understands these rights) derive from an ideal of liberty. Why should we think that an ideal of liberty requires a right to life and a right to property that excludes a right to welfare? Surely a right to property might well justify a rich person's depriving a poor person of the liberty to acquire the goods and resources necessary for meeting his or her basic nutritional needs. How then could we appeal to an ideal of liberty to justify such a deprivation? In Selection 4, James P. Sterba argues that we cannot.

Socialist Justice

In contrast with libertarians, socialists take equality to be the ultimate political ideal and contend that the fundamental rights and duties in a society are determined by this ideal. More specifically, socialists defend an ideal that calls for equality of need fulfillment. As Kai Nielson contends (Selection 2), radical egalitarianism is justified because it produces the conditions for the most extensive satisfaction of everyone's needs.

At first hearing, this ideal might sound simply crazy to someone brought up in a capitalist society. The obvious problem is how to get persons to put forth their best effort if income will be distributed on the basis of individual need rather than individual contribution.

The socialist answer is to make work that must be done as enjoyable in itself as possible. Thus, people will want to do the work they are capable of doing because they find it intrinsically rewarding. For a start, socialists might try to convince workers to accept lower salaries for existing jobs that are intrinsically rewarding. For example, they might ask top executives to work for $300,000 a year rather than $600,000. Yet socialists ultimately hope to make all jobs intrinsically as rewarding as possible so that, after people no longer work primarily for external rewards when making their best contributions to society, distribution can proceed on the basis of need.

Socialists propose to implement their ideal of equality by giving workers democratic control over the workplace: If workers have more to say about how they do their work, they will find their work intrinsically more rewarding. As a consequence, they will be more motivated to work, because their work itself will be meeting their needs. Socialists believe that extending democracy to the workplace will necessarily lead to socialization of the means of production and the end of private property.

However, even with democratic control of the workplace, some jobs, such as collecting garbage or changing bedpans, probably can't be made intrinsically rewarding. What socialists propose to do with respect to such jobs is to divide them up in some equitable manner. Some people might, for example, collect garbage one day a week and then work at intrinsically rewarding jobs the rest of the week. Others would change bedpans or do some other slop job one day a week and then work at an intrinsically rewarding job the other days of the week. By making jobs intrinsically as rewarding as possible, in part through democratic control of the workplace and an equitable assignment of unrewarding tasks, socialists believe people will contribute according to their abilities even when distribution proceeds according to need.

Finally, it is important to note that the socialist ideal of equality does not accord with what existed in the Soviet Union or Eastern Europe under Communism. Judging the acceptability of the socialist ideal of equality by what took place in those countries would be as unfair as judging the acceptability of the libertarian ideal of liberty by what took place in Chile under Pinochet or South Africa under apartheid, where citizens were arrested and imprisoned without cause. By analogy, it would be like judging the merits of college football by the way Vanderbilt's or Northwestern's teams play rather than by the way Miami's or Notre Dame's teams play. Actually, a fairer comparison would be to judge the socialist ideal of equality by what takes place in countries like Sweden and to judge the libertarian ideal of liberty by what takes place in the United States. Even these comparisons, however, are not wholly appropriate because none of these countries fully conforms to those ideals.

To justify the ideal of equality, Kai Nielson argues that it is required by liberty or at least by a fair distribution of liberty. By "liberty" Nielson means both "positive liberty to receive certain goods" and "negative liberty not to be interfered with," so his argument for liberty will not have much weight with libertarians, who only value negative liberty. Rather, his argument is directed primarily at welfare liberals, who value both positive and negative liberty as well as a fair distribution of liberty.

Another basic difficulty with Nielson's socialist solution to the problem of distributive justice is the proclaimed necessity of abolishing private property and socializing the means of production. It seems possible to give workers more control over the workplace while at the same time allowing the means of production to remain privately owned. Of course, private ownership would have a somewhat different character in a society with democratic control of the workplace, but it need not cease to be private ownership. After all, private ownership would also have a somewhat different character in a society where private holdings, and hence bargaining power, were distributed more equally than is found in most capitalist societies, yet it would not cease to be private ownership. Accordingly, we could imagine a society where the means of production are privately owned but where—because ownership is so widely dispersed throughout the society (e.g., nearly everyone owns ten shares of major industrial stock and no one more than twenty shares) and because of the degree of democratic control of the workplace—many of the valid criticisms socialists make of existing capitalist societies would no longer apply.

Welfare Liberalism

In contrast with libertarians and socialists, welfare liberals, such as John Rawls (Selection 3), take contractual fairness to be the ultimate political ideal and contend that the fundamental rights and duties in a society are those that people would agree to under fair conditions.

Note that welfare liberals do not say that the fundamental rights and duties in a society

are those to which people actually do agree, because these might not be fair at all. For example, people might agree to a certain system of fundamental rights and duties because they have been forced to do so or because their only alternative is starving to death. Thus, actual agreement is neither sufficient nor necessary for determining an adequate conception of justice. According to welfare liberals, what is necessary and sufficient is that people would agree to such rights and duties under fair conditions.

But what are fair conditions? According to John Rawls, fair conditions can be expressed by an "original position" in which people are concerned to advance their own interests behind a "veil of ignorance." The effect of the veil of ignorance is to deprive people in the original position of the knowledge they would need to advance their own interests in ways that are morally arbitrary.

Rawls presents the principles of justice he believes would be derived in the original position in two successive formulations. The first formulation is as follows:

(I) Special conception of justice
   (1) Each person is to have an equal right to the most extensive basic liberty compatible with a similar liberty for others.
   (2) Social and economic inequalities are to be arranged so that they are (a) reasonably expected to be to everyone's advantage and (b) attached to positions and offices open to all.

(II) General conception of justice
   All social values—liberty and opportunity, income and wealth, and the bases of self-respect—are to be distributed equally unless an unequal distribution of any or all of these values is to everyone's advantage.

Later these principles are more accurately formulated as:

(I) Special conception of justice
   (1) Each person is to have an equal right to the most extensive total system of equal basic

liberties compatible with a similar system of liberty for all.

(2) Social and economic inequalities are to be arranged so that they are (a) to the greatest benefit of the least advantaged, consistent with the just savings principle, and (b) attached to offices and positions open to all under conditions of fair equality of opportunity.

(II) General conception of justice

All social goods—liberty and opportunity, income and wealth, and the bases of self-respect—are to be distributed equally unless an unequal distribution of any or all of these goods is to the advantage of the least favored.

Under both formulations, the general conception of justice differs from the special conception of justice by allowing tradeoffs between liberty and other social goods. According to Rawls, persons in the original position would want the special conception of justice to be applied in place of the general conception of justice whenever social conditions allowed all representative persons to exercise their basic liberties.

Rawls holds that these principles of justice would be chosen in the original position because persons so situated would find it reasonable to follow the conservative dictates of a "maximin strategy" and thereby secure for themselves the highest minimum payoff.

Rawls's defense of a welfare liberal conception of justice has been challenged in a variety of ways. Some critics have endorsed his contractual approach while disagreeing with him over what principles of justice would be thereby derived. These critics usually attempt to undermine the use of a maximin strategy in the original position.[1] Others, however, have found fault with the contractual approach itself. Libertarians, for example, challenge the moral adequacy of the very ideal of contractual fairness.

This second challenge to the ideal of contractual fairness is potentially more damaging because, if valid, it would force supporters to embrace some other political ideal. This challenge, however, fails if it can be shown, as James P. Sterba argues in Selection 4, that the libertarian's own ideal of liberty, when correctly interpreted, leads to a universal right to welfare usually associated with the welfare liberal's ideal of contractual fairness. But Sterba's argument also raises a problem for the welfare liberal because he shows that recognition of this universal right to welfare leads to the equalization of resources that is characteristic of a socialist state.

Practical Applications

The application of the ideals of libertarianism, socialism, or welfare liberalism to a particular society obviously has basic and far-reaching effects. These ideals have implications for constitutional structure, the control of industry, taxing policy, social welfare programs, property law, and much more. The next two readings in this section are from important U.S. Supreme Court decisions to which our three political ideals can be usefully related.

The Supreme Court, of course, does not view itself as directly applying one or the other of these political ideals to the laws of the land. Rather the Court views itself as deciding whether particular laws accord with the provisions of the U.S. Constitution. However, most people, including Supreme Court justices, do not clearly separate their views about what are the practical applications of the political ideal they take to be the most morally defensible from their views about what sort of laws accord with the U.S. Constitution. Hence, it is frequently possible to see how commitment to a political ideal is decisive in judicial decision making.

Beyond coming to appreciate how political ideals and their presumed applications function in judicial decision making, it is important that you examine Supreme Court decisions to determine to what degree the laws of your society accord with the political ideal you take to be the most morally defensible. To have good reasons to believe that you are a just and moral person, you need to assess to what degree the laws and institutions of your society are just—in this case, to what degree they accord with the requirements of distributive justice. Examining the two U.S. Supreme Court decisions included in this section should serve this purpose well.

In the first decision (*Wyman v. James*), the majority of the Court decided that the rights of welfare recipients are limited in various ways and in particular that recipients are not protected against mandatory visits by caseworkers. Such a decision would surely seem justified if one believed, as libertarians do, that the provision of welfare is, at best, only a requirement of charity. Welfare liberals and socialists, however, would have difficulty accepting this decision, as did the dissenting justices of the Court.

In the second decision (*Plyler v. Doe*), the majority of the Court determined that although public education is not a right, it still cannot be denied to the children of illegal aliens because of the pivotal role of education in sustaining our political and cultural heritage. This decision has some affinity with the way welfare liberals and socialists would understand the practical requirements of their ideals; libertarians would probably find themselves persuaded by the arguments of the dissenting justices.

Notice that you can also work backward from your considered judgments about these Supreme Court cases to the political ideal you should favor. Frequently, we can only clarify our views about a morally defensible position by considering the practical applications of alternative political ideals.

Notice, too, that any fully adequate solution to the problem of distributive justice within a society presupposes a solution to the other moral problems presented in this anthology. In particular, the problem of near and distant peoples, which is discussed in the following section, seems to be clearly connected with the problem of distributive justice. We cannot know for sure what resources particular persons within a society should receive unless we also know what obligations persons within that society have to distant peoples.

Endnote

1. See, for example, my article, "Distributive Justice," *American Journal of Jurisprudence* (1977), pp. 55–79, and John C. Harsanyi, *Essays on Ethics, Social Behavior, and* *Scientific Explanation* (Boston: D. Reidel Publishing Co., 1976), pp. 37–85.

1. The Libertarian Manifesto

John Hospers

John Hospers explores various ways of understanding the basic libertarian thesis that every person is the owner of his or her own life. According to Hospers, such ownership entails rights to life, liberty, and property. Since these rights are violated by an initial use of force, the proper role of government is said to be limited to the retaliatory use of force against those who have initiated its use. All other possible roles for government, such as protecting individuals against themselves or requiring people to help one another, are regarded as illegitimate by the libertarian.

The political philosophy that is called libertarianism (from the Latin *libertas*, liberty) is the doctrine that every person is the owner of his own life, and that no one is the owner of anyone else's life—and that consequently every human being has the right to act in accordance with his own choices, unless those actions infringe on the equal liberty of other human beings to act in accordance with their choices.

There are several other ways of stating the same libertarian thesis:

1. *No one is anyone else's master, and no one is anyone else's slave.* Since I am the one to decide how my life is to be conducted just as you decide about yours, I have no right (even if I had the power) to make you my slave and be your master, nor have you the right to become the master by enslaving me. Slavery is *forced* servitude, and since no one owns the life of anyone else, no one has the right to enslave another. Political theories past and present have traditionally been concerned with who should be the master (usually the king, the dictator, or government bureaucracy) and who should be the slaves, and what the extent of the slavery should be. Libertarianism holds that no one has the right to use force to enslave the life of another, or any portion or aspect of that life.

2. *Other men's lives are not yours to dispose of.* I enjoy seeing operas; but operas are expensive to produce. Opera-lovers often say, "The state (or the city, etc.) should subsidize opera, so that we can all see it.

From "What Libertarianism Is," in *The Libertarian Alternative*, edited by Tibor Machan (1974). Reprinted by permission of the author, the editor, and Nelson-Hall Inc.

Also it would be for the people's betterment, cultural benefit, etc." But what they are advocating is nothing more or less than legalized plunder. They can't pay for the productions themselves, and yet they want to see opera, which involves a large number of people and their labor; so what they are saying in effect is, "Get the money through legalized force. Take a little bit more out of every worker's paycheck every week to pay for the operas we want to see." But I have no right to take by force from the workers' pockets to pay for what I want.

Perhaps it would be better if he *did* go to see opera—then I should try to convince him to go voluntarily. But to take the money from him forcibly, because in my opinion it would be good for *him*, is still seizure of his earnings, which is plunder.

Besides, if I have the right to force him to help pay for my pet projects, hasn't he equally the right to force me to help pay for his? Perhaps he in turn wants the government to subsidize rock-and-roll, or his new car, or a house in the country? If I have the right to milk him, why hasn't he the right to milk me? If I can be a moral cannibal, why can't he too?

We should beware of the inventors of utopias. They would remake the world according to their vision—with the lives and fruits of the labor of *other* human beings. Is it someone's utopian vision that others should build pyramids to beautify the landscape? Very well, then other men should provide the labor; and if he is in a position of political power, and he can't get men to do it voluntarily, then he must *compel* them to "cooperate"—i.e., he must enslave them.

A hundred men might gain great pleasure from beating up or killing just one insignificant human being; but other men's lives are not theirs to dispose of. "In order to achieve the worthy goals of the next five-year plan, we must forcibly collectivize the peasants. . ."; but other men's lives are not theirs to dispose of. Do you want to occupy, rent-free, the mansion that another man has worked for twenty years to buy? But other men's lives are not yours to dispose of. Do you want operas so badly that everyone is forced to work harder to pay for their subsidization through taxes? But other men's lives are not yours to dispose of. Do you want to have free medical care at the expense of other people, whether they wish to provide it or not? But this would require them to work longer for you whether they want to or not, and other men's lives are not yours to dispose of. . . .

3. *No human being should be a nonvoluntary mortgage on the life of another.* I cannot claim your life, your work, or the products of your effort as mine. The fruit of one man's labor should not be fair game for every freeloader who comes along and demands it as his own. The orchard that has been carefully grown, nurtured, and harvested by its owner should not be ripe for the plucking for any bypasser who has a yen for the ripe fruit. The wealth that some men have produced should not be fair game for looting by government, to be used for whatever purposes its representatives determine, no matter what their motives in so doing may be. The theft of your money by a robber is not justified by the fact that he used it to help his injured mother.

It will already be evident that libertarian doctrine is embedded in a view of the rights of man. Each human being has the right to live his life as he chooses, compatibly with the equal right of all other human beings to live their lives as they choose.

All men's rights are implicit in the above statement. Each man has the right to life: Any attempt by others to take it away from him, or even to injure him, violates this right, through the use of coercion against him. Each man has the right to liberty: to conduct his life in accordance with the alternatives open to him without coercive actions by others. And every man has the right to property: to work to sustain his life (and the lives of whichever others he chooses to sustain, such as his family) and to retain the fruits of his labor.

People often defend the rights of life and liberty but denigrate property rights, and yet the right to property is as basic as the other two: Indeed, without property rights no other rights are possible. Depriving you of property is depriving you of the means by which you live. . . .

I have no right to decide how *you* should spend your time or your money. I can make that decision for myself, but not for you, my neighbor. I may deplore your choice of life-style, and I may talk with you about it provided you are willing to listen to me. But I have no right to use force to change it. Nor have I the right to decide how you should spend the money you have earned. I may appeal to you to give it to the Red Cross, and you may prefer to go to prize-fights. But that is your decision, and however much I may chafe about it I do not have the right to interfere forcibly with it, for example by robbing you in order to use the money in accordance with *my* choices. (If I have the right to rob you, have you also the right to rob me?)

When I claim a right, I carve out a niche, as it were, in my life, saying in effect, "This activity I must be able to perform without interference from others. For you and everyone else, this is off limits." And so I put up a "no trespassing" sign, which marks off the area of my right. Each individual's right is his "no trespassing" sign in relation to me and others. I may not encroach upon his domain any more than he upon mine, without my consent. Every right entails a duty, true—but the duty is only that of *forbearance*—that is, of *refraining* from violating the other person's right. If you have a right to life, I have no right to take your life; if you have a right to the products of your labor (property), I have no right to take it from you without your consent. The nonviolation of these rights will not guarantee you protection against natural catastrophes such as floods and earthquakes, but it will protect you against the aggressive activities *of other men.* And rights, after all, have to do with one's relations to other human beings, not with one's relations to physical nature.

Nor were these rights created by government; governments—some governments, obviously not all—*recognize* and *protect* the rights that individuals already have. Governments regularly forbid homicide and theft; and, at a more advanced stage, protect individuals against such things as libel and breach of contract. . . .

The *right to property* is the most misunderstood and unappreciated of human rights, and it is one most constantly violated by governments. "Property" of course does not mean only real estate; it includes anything you can call your own—your clothing, your car, your jewelry, your books and papers.

The right of property is not the right to just *take* it from others, for this would interfere with *their* property rights. It is rather the right to work for it, to obtain noncoercively, the money or services you can present in voluntary exchange.

The right to property is consistently underplayed by intellectuals today, sometimes even frowned upon, as if we should feel guilty for upholding such a right in view of all the poverty in the world. But the right to property is absolutely basic. It is your hedge against the future. It is your assurance that what you have worked to earn will still be there and be yours, when you wish or need to use it, especially when you are too old to work any longer.

Government has always been the chief enemy of the right to property. The officials of government, wishing to increase their power, and finding an increase of wealth an effective way to bring this about, seize some or all of what a person has earned—and since government has a monopoly of physical force within the geographical area of the nation, it has the power (but not the right) to do this. When this happens, of course, every citizen of that country is insecure: He knows that no matter how hard he works the government can swoop down on him at any time and confiscate his earnings and possessions. A person sees his life savings wiped out in a moment when the tax-collectors descend to deprive him of the fruits of his work; or, an industry which has been fifty years in the making and cost millions of dollars and millions of hours of time and planning, is nationalized overnight. Or the government, via inflation, cheapens the currency, so that hard-won dollars aren't worth anything any more. The effect of such actions, of course, is that people lose hope and incentive: If no matter how hard they work the government agencies can take it all away, why bother to work at all, for more than today's needs? Depriving people of property is *depriving them of the means by which they live*—the freedom of the individual citizen to do what he wishes with his own life and to plan for the future. Indeed only if property rights are respected is there any point to planning for the future and working to achieve one's goals. *Property rights are what makes long-range planning possible*—the kind of planning which is a distinctively human endeavor, as opposed to the day-by-day activity of the lion who hunts, who depends on the supply of game tomorrow but has no real insurance against starvation in a day or a week. Without the right to property, the right to life itself amounts to little: How can you sustain your life if you cannot plan ahead? and how can you plan ahead if the fruits of your labor can at any moment be confiscated by government? . . .

Indeed, the right to property may well be considered second only to the right to life. Even the freedom of speech is limited by considerations of property. If a person visiting in your home behaves in a way undesired by you, you have every right to evict him; he can scream or agitate elsewhere if he wishes, but not in your home without your consent. Does a person have a right to shout obscenities in a cathedral? No, for the owners of the cathedral (presumably the Church) have not allowed others on their property for that purpose; one may go there to worship or to visit, but not just for any purpose one wishes. Their property right is prior to your or my wish to scream or expectorate or write graffiti on their building. Or, to take the stock example, does a person have a right to shout "Fire!" falsely in a crowded theater? No, for the theater owner has permitted others to enter and use his property only for a specific purpose, that of seeing a film or watching a stage show. If a person heckles or otherwise disturbs other members of the audience, he can be thrown out. (In fact, he can be removed for any reason the owner chooses, provided his admission money is returned.) And if he shouts "Fire!" when there is no fire, he may be endangering other lives by causing a panic or a stampede. The right to free speech doesn't give one the right to say anything anywhere; it is circumscribed by property rights.

Again, some people seem to assume that the right to free speech (including written speech) means that they can go to a newspaper publisher and demand that he print in his newspaper some propaganda or policy statement for their political party (or other group). But of course they have no right to the use of his newspaper. Ownership of the newspaper is the product of his labor, and he has a right to put into his newspaper whatever he wants, for whatever reason. If he excludes material which many readers would like to have in, perhaps they can find it in another newspaper or persuade him to print it himself (if there are enough of them, they will usually do just that). Perhaps they can even cause his newspaper to fail. But as long as he owns it, he has the right to put in it what he wishes; what would a property right be if he could not do this? They have no right to place their material in his newspaper without his consent—not for free, nor even for a fee. Perhaps other newspapers will include it, or perhaps they can start their own newspaper (in which case they have a right to put in it what they like). If not, an option open to them would be to mimeograph and distribute some handbills.

In exactly the same way, no one has a right to "free television time" unless the owner of the television station consents to give it; it is his station, he has the property rights over it, and it is for him to decide how to dispose of his time. He may not decide wisely, but it is his right to decide as he wishes. If he makes enough unwise decisions, and courts enough unpopularity with the viewing public or the sponsors, he may have to go out of business; but as he is free to make his own decisions, so is he free to face their consequences. (If the government owns the television station, then government officials will make the decisions, and there is no guarantee of *their* superior wisdom. The difference is that when "the government" owns the station, you are forced to help pay for its upkeep through your taxes, whether the bureaucrat in charge decides to give you television time or not.)

"But why have *individual* property rights? Why not have lands and houses owned by everybody together?" Yes, this involves no violation of individual rights, as long as everybody consents to this arrangement and no one is forced to join it. The parties to it may enjoy the communal living enough (at least for a time) to overcome certain inevitable problems: that some will work and some not, that some will achieve more in an hour than others can do in a day, and still they will get the same income. The few who do the most will in the end consider themselves "workhorses" who do the work of two or three or twelve, while the others will be "freeloaders" on the efforts of these few. But as long as they can get out of the arrangement if they no longer like it, no violation of rights is involved. They got in voluntarily, and they can get out voluntarily; no one has used force.

"But why not say that everybody owns everything? That we *all* own everything there is?"

To some this may have a pleasant ring—but let us try to analyze what it means. If everybody owns everything, then everyone has an equal right to go everywhere, do what he pleases, take what he likes, destroy if he wishes, grow crops or burn them,

trample them under, and so on. Consider what it would be like in practice. Suppose you have saved money to buy a house for yourself and your family. Now suppose that the principle, "everybody owns everything," becomes adopted. Well then, why shouldn't every itinerant hippie just come in and take over, sleeping in your beds and eating in your kitchen and not bothering to replace the food supply or clean up the mess? After all, it belongs to all of us, doesn't it? So we have just as much right to it as you, the buyer, have. What happens if we *all* want to sleep in the bedroom and there's not room for all of us? Is it the strongest who wins?

What would be the result? Since no one would be responsible for anything, the property would soon be destroyed, the food used up, the facilities nonfunctional. Beginning as a house that *one* family could use, it would end up as a house that *no one* could use. And if the principle continued to be adopted, no one would build houses any more—or anything else. What for? They would only be occupied and used by others, without remuneration.

Suppose two men are cast ashore on an island, and they agree that each will cultivate half of it. The first man is industrious and grows crops and builds a shelter, making the most of the situation with which he is confronted. The second man, perhaps thinking that the warm days will last forever, lies in the sun, picks coconuts while they last, and does a minimum of work to sustain himself. At the time of harvest, the second man has nothing to harvest, nor does he assist the first man in his labors. But later when there is a dearth of food on the island, the second man comes to the first man and demands half of the harvest as his right. But of course he has no right to the product of the first man's labors. The first man may freely choose to give part of his harvest to the second out of charity rather than see him starve; but that is just what it is—charity, not the second man's right.

How can any of man's rights be violated? Ultimately, only by the use of force. I can make suggestions to you, I can reason with you, entreat you (if you are willing to listen), but I cannot *force* you without violating your rights; only by forcing you do I cut the cord between your free decisions and your actions. Voluntary relations between individuals involve no deprivation of rights, but murder, assault, and rape do, because in doing these things I make you the unwilling victim of my actions. A man's beating his wife involves no violation of rights if she *wanted* to be beaten. *Force is behavior that requires the unwilling involvement of other persons.*

Thus the use of force need not involve the use of physical violence. If I trespass on your property or dump garbage on it, I am violating your property rights, as indeed I am when I steal your watch; although this is not force in the sense of violence, it *is* a case of your being an unwilling victim of my action. Similarly, if you shout at me so that I cannot be heard when I try to speak, or blow a siren in my ear, or start a factory next door which pollutes my land, you are again violating my rights (to free speech, to property); I am, again, an unwilling victim of your actions. Similarly, if you steal a manuscript of mine and publish it as your own, you are confiscating a piece of my property and thus violating my right to keep what is the product of my labor. Of course, if I give you the manuscript with permission to sign your name to it and keep the proceeds, no violation of rights is involved—any more than if I give you permission to dump garbage on my yard.

According to libertarianism, the role of government should be limited to the retaliatory use of force against those who have initiated its use. It should not enter into any other areas, such as religion, social organization, and economics.

Government

Government is the most dangerous institution known to man. Throughout history it has violated the rights of men more than any individual or group of individuals could do: It has killed people, enslaved them, sent them to forced labor and concentration camps, and regularly robbed and pillaged them of the fruits of their expended labor. Unlike individual criminals, government has the power to arrest and try; unlike individual criminals, it can surround and encompass a person totally, dominating every aspect of one's life, so that one has no recourse from it but to leave the country (and in totalitarian nations even that is prohibited). Government throughout history has a much sorrier record than any individual, even that of a ruthless mass murderer. The signs we see on bumper stickers are chillingly accurate: "Beware: The Government Is Armed and Dangerous."

The only proper role of government, according to libertarians, is that of the protector of the citizen against aggression by other individuals. The government, of course, should never initiate aggression; its proper role is as the embodiment of the *retaliatory* use of force against anyone who initiates its use.

If each individual had constantly to defend himself against possible aggressors, he would have to spend a considerable portion of his life in target practice, karate exercises, and other means of self-defenses, and even so he would probably be helpless against groups of individuals who might try to kill, maim, or rob him. He would have little time for cultivating those qualities which are essential to civilized life, nor would improvements in science, medicine, and the arts be likely to occur. The function of government is to take this responsibility off his shoulders: The government undertakes to defend him against aggressors and to punish them if they attack him. When the government is effective in doing this, it enables the citizen to go about his business unmolested and without constant fear for his life. To do this, of course, government must have physical power—the police, to protect the citizen from aggression within its borders, and the armed forces, to protect him from aggressors outside. Beyond that, the government should not intrude upon his life, either to run his business, or adjust his daily activities, or prescribe his personal moral code.

Government, then, undertakes to be the individual's protector; but historically governments have gone far beyond this function. Since they already have the physical power, they have not hesitated to use it for purposes far beyond that which was entrusted to them in the first place. Undertaking initially to protect its citizens against aggression, it has often itself become an aggressor—a far greater aggressor, indeed, than the criminals against whom it was supposed to protect its citizens. Governments have done what no private citizen can do: arrest and imprison individuals without a trial and send them to slave labor camps. Government must have power in order to be effective—and yet the very means by which alone it can be effective make it vulnerable to the abuse of power, leading to managing the lives of individuals and even inflicting terror upon them.

What then should be the function of government? In a phrase, the *protection of human rights*.

1. *The right to life:* Libertarians support all such legislation as will protect human beings against the use of force by others, for

example, laws against killing, attempting killing, maiming, beating, and all kinds of physical violence.

2. *The right to liberty:* There should be no laws compromising in any way freedom of speech, of the press, and peaceable assembly. There should be no censorship of ideas, books, films, or anything else by government.

3. *The right to property:* Libertarians support legislation that protects the property rights of individuals against confiscation, nationalization, eminent domain, robbery, trespass, fraud and misrepresentation, patent and copyright, libel, and slander.

Someone has violently assaulted you. Should he be legally liable? Of course. He has violated one of your rights. He has knowingly injured you, and since he has initiated aggression against you he should be made to expiate.

Someone has negligently left his bicycle on the sidewalk where you trip over it in the dark and injure yourself. He didn't do it intentionally; he didn't mean you any harm. Should he be legally liable? Of course; he has, however unwittingly, injured you, and since the injury is caused by him and you are the victim, he should pay.

Someone across the street is unemployed. Should you be taxed extra to pay for his expenses? Not at all. You have not injured him, you are not responsible for the fact that he is unemployed (unless you are a senator or bureaucrat who agitated for further curtailing of business, which legislation passed, with the result that your neighbor was laid off by the curtailed business). You may voluntarily wish to help him out, or better still, try to get him a job to put him on his feet again; but since you have initiated no aggressive act against him, and neither purposely nor accidentally injured him in any way, you should not be legally penalized for the fact of his unemployment. (Actually, it is just such penalties that increase unemployment.)

One man, A, works hard for years and finally earns a high salary as a professional man. A second man, B, prefers not to work at all, and to spend wastefully what money he has (through inheritance), so that after a year or two he has nothing left. At the end of this time he has a long siege of illness and lots of medical bills to pay. He demands that the bills be paid by the government—that is, by the taxpayers of the land, including Mr. A.

But of course B has no such right. He chose to lead his life in a certain way—that was his voluntary decision. One consequence of that choice is that he must depend on charity in case of later need. Mr. A chose not to live that way. (And if everyone lived like Mr. B, on whom would he depend in case of later need?) Each has a right to live in the way he pleases, but each must live with the consequences of his own decision (which, as always, fall primarily on himself). He cannot, in time of need, claim A's beneficence as his right.

If a house-guest of yours starts to carve his initials in your walls and break up your furniture, you have a right to evict him and call the police if he makes trouble. If someone starts to destroy the machinery in a factory, the factory-owner is also entitled to evict him and call the police. In both cases, persons other than the owner are permitted on the property only under certain conditions, at the pleasure of the owner. If those conditions are violated, the owner is entitled to use force to set things straight. The case is exactly the same on a college or university campus: If a campus demonstrator starts breaking windows, occupying the president's office, and setting fire to a dean, the college authorities are certainly within their rights to evict him forcibly; one is permitted on the college grounds only under specific conditions, set by the administration: study, peaceful student activity, even political activity if those in charge choose to permit it. If they do not choose to permit peaceful political activity on campus, they may be unwise, since a campus is after all a place where all sides of every issue should get discussed, and the college that doesn't permit this may soon lose its reputation and its students. All the same, the college official who does not permit it is quite within his rights; the students do not own the campus, nor do the hired troublemakers imported from elsewhere. In the case of a privately owned college, the owners, or whoever they have delegated to administer it, have the right to make the decisions as to who shall be permitted on the campus and under what conditions. In the case of a state university or college, the ownership problem is more complex: One could say that the "government" owns the campus or that "the people" do, since they are the taxpayers who support it. But in either case, the university administration has the delegated task of keeping order, and until they are removed by the state administration or the taxpayers, it is theirs to decide who shall be permitted on campus, and what nonacademic activities will be permitted to their students on the premises.

Property rights can be violated by physical trespass, of course, or by anyone entering on your property for any reason without your consent. (If you *do* consent to having your neighbor dump garbage on your yard, there is no violation of your rights.) But the physical trespass of a person is only a special case of violation of property rights. Property rights can be violated by sound-waves, in the form of a loud noise, or the sounds of your neighbor's hi-fi set while you are trying to sleep. Such violations of property rights are of course the subject of action in the courts.

But there is another violation of property rights that has not thus far been honored by the courts; this has to do with the effects of *pollution* of the atmosphere.

> From the beginnings of modern air pollution, the courts made a conscious decision not to protect, for example, the orchards of farmers from the smoke of nearby factories or locomotives. They said, in effect, to the farmers: Yes, your private property is being invaded by this smoke, but we hold that "public policy" is more important than private property, and public policy holds factories and locomotives to be good things. These goods were allowed to override the defense of property rights—with our consequent headlong rush into pollution disaster. The remedy is both "radical" and crystal clear, and it has nothing to do with multibillion dollar palliative programs at the expense of the taxpayers, which do not even meet the real issue. The remedy is simply to enjoin anyone from injecting pollutants into the air, and thereby invading the rights of persons and property. Period. The argument that such an injunction prohibition would add to the costs of industrial production is as reprehensible as the pre–Civil War argument that the abolition of slavery would add to the costs of growing cotton, and therefore should not take place. For this means that the polluters are able to impose the high costs of pollution upon those whose property rights they are allowed to invade with impunity.[1]

What about automobiles, the chief polluters of the air? One can hardly sue every automobile owner. But one can sue the manufacturers of automobiles who do not install anti-smog devices on the cars which they distribute—and later (though this is more difficult), owners of individual automobiles if they discard the equipment or do not keep it functional.

The violation of rights does not apply only to air-pollution. If someone with a factory upstream on a river pollutes the river, anyone living downstream from him, finding his water polluted, should be able to sue the owner of the factory. In this way the price of adding the anti-pollutant devices will be the owner's responsibility, and will probably be added to the cost of the products which the factory produces and thus spread around among all consumers, rather than the entire cost being borne by the users of the river in the form of polluted water, with the consequent impossibility of fishing, swimming, and so on. In each case, pollution would be stopped at the source rather than having its ill effects spread around to numerous members of the population.

What about property which you do not work to earn, but which you *inherit* from someone else? Do you have a right to that? You have no right to it until someone decides to give it to you. Consider the man who willed it to you; it was his, he had the right to use and dispose of it as *he* saw fit; and if he decided to give it to you, this is a windfall for you, but it was only the exercise of *his* right. Had the property been seized by the government at the man's death, or distributed among numerous other people designated by the government, it *would* have been a violation of his rights: for he, who worked to earn and sustain it, would not have been able to dispose of it according to his own judgment. If he doesn't have the right to determine who shall have it, who does?

What about the property status of your intellectual activity, such as inventions you may devise and books you write? These, of course, are your property also; they are the products of your mind; you worked at them, you created them. Prior to that, they did not exist. If you worked five years to write a book, and someone stole it and published it as his own, receiving royalties from its sales, he would have stolen your property just as surely as if he had robbed your home. The same is true if someone used and sold without your permission an invention which was the product of your labor and ingenuity.

The role of government with respect to this issue, at least most governments of the Western world, is a proper one: Government protects the products of your labor from the moment they materialize. Copyright law protects your writings from piracy. In the United States, one's writings are protected for a period of twenty-seven years, and another twenty-seven if one applies for renewal of the copyright. In most other countries, they are protected for a period of fifty years after the author's death, permitting both himself and his surviving heirs to reap the fruits of his labor. After that they enter the "public domain"—that is, anyone may reprint them without your or your heirs' permission. Patent law protects your inventions for a limited period, which varies according to the type of invention. In no case are you forced to avail yourself of this protection; you need not apply for patent or copyright coverage if you do not wish to do so. But the protection of your intellectual property is there, in case you wish to use it.

What about the property status of the airwaves? Here the government's position is far more questionable. The government now claims ownership of the airwaves, leasing them to individuals and corporations. The government renews leases or refuses them depending on whether the programs satisfy authorities in the Federal Communications Commission. The official position is that "we all own the airwaves": But since only one party can broadcast on a certain frequency at a certain time without causing chaos, it is simply a fact of reality that "everyone" cannot use it. In fact the government decides who shall use the airwaves and one courts its displeasure only at the price of a revoked license. One can write without government approval, but one cannot use the airwaves without the approval of the government.

What policy should have been observed with regard to the airwaves? Much the same as the policy that was followed in the case of the Homestead Act, when the lands of the American West were opening up for settlement. There was a policy of "first come, first served," with the government parcelling out a certain acreage for each individual who wanted to claim the land as his own. There was no charge for the land, but if a man had not used it and built a dwelling during the first two-year period, it was assumed that he was not homesteading and the land was given to the next man in line. The airwaves too could have been given out on a "first come, first served" basis. The first man who used a given frequency would be its owner, and the government

would protect him in the use of it against trespassers. If others wanted to use the same frequency, they would have to buy it from the first man, if he was willing to sell, or try to buy another, just as one now does with the land.

Laws may be classified into three types: (1) laws protecting individuals against themselves, such as laws against fornication and other sexual behavior, alcohol, and drugs; (2) laws protecting individuals against aggressions by other individuals, such as laws against murder, robbery, and fraud; (3) laws requiring people to help one another; for example, all laws which rob Peter to pay Paul, such as welfare.

Libertarians reject the first class of laws totally. Behavior which harms no one else is strictly the individual's own affair. Thus, there should be no laws against becoming intoxicated, since whether or not to become intoxicated is the individual's own decision: But there should be laws against driving while intoxicated, since the drunken driver is a threat to every other motorist on the highway (drunken driving falls into type 2). Similarly, there should be no laws against drugs (except the prohibition of sale of drugs to minors) as long as the taking of these drugs poses no threat to anyone else. Drug addiction is a psychological problem to which no present solution exists. Most of the social harm caused by addicts, other than to themselves, is the result of thefts which they perform in order to continue their habit—and then the *legal* crime is the theft, not the addiction. The actual cost of heroin is about ten cents a shot; if it were legalized, the enormous traffic in illegal sale and purchase of it would stop, as well as the accompanying proselytization to get new addicts (to make more money for the pusher) and the thefts performed by addicts who often require eighty dollars a day just to keep up the habit. Addiction would not stop, but the crimes would: It is estimated that 75 percent of the burglaries in New York City today are performed by addicts, and all these crimes could be wiped out at one stroke through the legalization of drugs. (Only when the taking of drugs could be shown to constitute a threat to *others* should it be prohibited by law. It is only laws protecting people against *themselves* that libertarians oppose.)

Laws should be limited to the second class only: aggression by individuals against other individuals. These are laws whose function is to protect human beings against encroachment by others; and this, as we have seen, is (according to libertarianism) the sole function of government.

Libertarians also reject the third class of laws totally: No one should be forced by law to help others, not even to tell them the time of day if requested, and certainly not to give them a portion of one's weekly paycheck. Governments, in the guise of humanitarianism, have given to some by taking from others (charging a "handling fee" in the process, which, because of the government's waste and inefficiency, sometimes is several hundred percent). And in so doing they have decreased incentive, violated the rights of individuals, and lowered the standard of living of almost everyone.

All such laws constitute what libertarians call *moral cannibalism*. A cannibal in the physical sense is a person who lives off the flesh of other human beings. A *moral* cannibal is one who believes he has a right to live off the "spirit" of other human beings—who believes that he has a moral claim on the productive capacity, time, and effort expended by others.

It has become fashionable to claim virtually everything that one needs or desires as one's *right*. Thus, many people claim that they have a right to a job, the right to free medical care, to free food and clothing, to a decent home, and so on. Now if one asks, apart from any specific context, whether it would be desirable if everyone had these things, one might well say yes. But there is a gimmick attached to each of them: *At whose expense?* Jobs, medical care, education, and so on, don't grow on trees. These are goods and services *produced only by men*. Who then is to provide them, and under what conditions?

If you have a right to a job, who is to supply it? Must an employer supply it even if he doesn't want to hire you? What if you are unemployable, or incurably lazy? (If you say "the government must supply it," does that mean that a job must be created for you which no employer needs done, and that you must be kept in it regardless of how much or little you work?) If the employer is forced to supply it at his expense even if he doesn't need you, then isn't *he* being enslaved to that extent? What ever happened to *his* right to conduct his life and his affairs in accordance with his choices? If you have a right to free medical care, then, since medical care doesn't exist in nature as wild apples do, some people will have to supply it to you for free: That is, they will have to spend their time and money and energy taking care of you whether they want to or not. What ever happened to *their* right to conduct

their lives as they see fit? Or do you have a right to violate theirs? Can there be a right to violate rights?

All those who demand this or that as a "free service" are consciously or unconsciously evading the fact that there is in reality no such thing as free services. All man-made goods and services are the result of human expenditure of time and effort. There is no such thing as "something for nothing" in this world. If you demand something free, you are demanding that other men give their time and effort to you without compensation. If they voluntarily choose to do this, there is no problem; but if you demand that they be *forced* to do it, you are interfering with their right not to do it if they so choose. "Swimming in this pool ought to be free!" says the indignant passerby. What he means is that others should build a pool, others should provide the material, and still others should run it and keep it in functioning order, so that *he* can use it without fee. But what right has he to the expenditure of *their* time and effort? To expect something "for free" is to expect it *to be paid for by others* whether they choose to or not.

Many questions, particularly about economic matters, will be generated by the libertarian account of human rights and the role of government. Should government have a role in assisting the needy, in providing social security, in legislating minimum wages, in fixing prices and putting a ceiling on rents, in curbing monopolies, in erecting tariffs, in guaranteeing jobs, in managing the money supply? To these and all similar questions the libertarian answers with an unequivocal no.

"But then you'd let people go hungry!" comes the rejoinder. This, the libertarian insists, is precisely what would not happen; with the restrictions removed, the economy would flourish as never before. With the controls taken off business, existing enterprises would expand and new ones would spring into existence satisfying more and more consumer needs; millions more people would be gainfully employed instead of subsisting on welfare, and all kinds of research and production, released from the stranglehold of government, would proliferate, fulfilling man's needs and desires as never before. It has always been so whenever government has permitted men to be free traders on a free market. But *why* this is so, and how the free market is the best solution to all problems relating to the material aspect of man's life, is another and far longer story.

Endnote

1. Murray Rothbard, "The Great Ecology Issue," *The Individualist*, 2, no. 2 (February 1970): p. 5.

2. *Radical Egalitarianism*

KAI NIELSON

The fundamental requirement of radical egalitarianism is equality of basic condition for everyone. Kai Nielson justifies this requirement on the grounds that it produces the conditions for the most extensive satisfaction of everyone's needs. He also contends that radical egalitarianism is required by the moral point of view and would lead to two specific principles of justice. Finally, he defends radical egalitarianism on the grounds that it is required by liberty or at least its fair distribution.

I

I have talked of equality as a right and equality as a goal. And I have taken, as the principal thing, to be able to state what goal we are seeking when we say equality is a goal. When we are in a position actually to achieve that goal, then that same equality becomes a right. The goal we are seeking is an equality of basic condition for everyone. Let me say a bit what this is: Everyone, as far as possible, should have equal life prospects, short of genetic engineering and the like and the rooting out of any form of the family and the undermining of our basic freedoms. There should, where this is possible, be an equality of access to equal resources over each person's life as a whole, though this should be qualified by people's varying needs. Where psychiatrists are in short supply only people who are in need of psychiatric help should have equal access to such help. This equal access to resources should be such that

Abridged from *Equality and Liberty* (1985), pp. 283–292, 302–306, 309. Reprinted by permission of Rowman & Allanheld, Publishers. Notes renumbered.

it stands as a barrier to there being the sort of differences between people that allow some to be in a position to control and to exploit others; such equal access to resources should also stand as a barrier to one adult person having power over other adult persons that does not rest on the revokable consent on the part of the persons over whom he comes to have power. Where, because of some remaining scarcity in a society of considerable productive abundance, we cannot reasonably distribute resources equally, we should first, where considerations of desert are not at issue, distribute according to stringency of need, second according to the strength of unmanipulated preferences, and third, and finally, by lottery. We should, in trying to attain equality of condition, aim at a condition of autonomy (the fuller and more rational the better) for everyone and at a condition where everyone alike, to the fullest extent possible, has his or her needs and wants satisfied. The limitations on the satisfaction of people's wants should be only where that satisfaction is incompatible with everyone getting the same treatment. Where we have conflicting wants, such as where two persons want to marry the same person, the fair thing to do will vary with the circumstances. In the marriage case, freedom of choice is obviously the fair thing. But generally, what should be aimed at is having everyone have their wants satisfied as far as possible. To achieve equality of condition would be, as well, to achieve a condition where the necessary burdens of the society are equally shared, where to do so is reasonable, and where each person has an equal voice in deciding what these burdens shall be. Moreover, everyone, as much as possible, should be in a position—and should be equally in that position—to control his own life. The goals of egalitarianism are to achieve such equalities.

Minimally, classlessness is something we should all aim at if we are egalitarians. It is necessary for the stable achievement of equalities of the type discussed in the previous paragraph. Beyond that, we should also aim at a statusless society, though not at an undifferentiated society or a society which does not recognize merit. . . . It is only in such a classless, statusless society that the ideals of equality (the conception of equality as a very general goal to be achieved) can be realized. In aiming for a statusless society, we are aiming for a society which, while remaining a society of material abundance, is a society in which there are to be no extensive differences in life prospects between people because some have far greater income, power, authority or prestige than others. This is the *via negativia* of the egalitarian way. The *via positiva* is to produce social conditions, where there is generally material abundance, where well-being and satisfaction are not only maximized (the utilitarian thing) but, as well, a society where this condition, as far as it is achievable, is sought equally for all (the egalitarian thing). This is the underlying conception of the egalitarian commitment to equality of condition.

II

Robert Nozick asks "How do we decide how much equality is enough?[1] In the preceding section we gestured in the direction of an answer. I should now like to be somewhat more explicit. Too much equality, as we have been at pains to point out, would be to treat everyone identically, completely ignoring their differing needs. Various forms of "barracks equality" approximating that would also be too much. Too little equality would be to limit equality of condition, as did the old egalitarianism, to achieving equal legal and political rights, equal civil liberties, to equality of opportunity, and to a redistribution of gross disparities in wealth sufficient to keep social peace; the rationale for the latter being that such gross inequalities if allowed to stand would threaten social stability. This Hobbesist stance indicates that the old egalitarianism proceeds in a very pragmatic manner. Against the old egalitarianism I would argue that we must at least aim at an equality of whole life prospects, where that is not read simply as the right to compete for scarce positions of advantage, but where there is to be brought into being the kind of equality of condition that would provide everyone equally, as far as possible, with the resources and the social conditions to satisfy their needs as fully as possible compatible with everyone else doing likewise. (Note that between people these needs will be partly the same but will still often be importantly different as well.) Ideally, as a kind of ideal limit for a society of wondrous abundance, a radical egalitarianism would go beyond that to a similar thing for wants. We should, that is, provide all people equally, as far as possible, with the resources and social conditions to satisfy their wants, as fully as possible compatible with everyone else doing likewise. (I recognize that there is a slide between wants and needs. As the wealth of a society increases and its structure changes, things that started out as wants tend to become needs, e.g., someone in the Falkland Islands might merely reasonably want an auto while someone in Los Angeles might not only want it but need it as well. But this does not collapse the distinction between wants and needs. There are things in any society people need, if they are to survive at all in anything like a commodious condition, whether they want them or not, e.g., they need food, shelter, security, companionship and the like. An egalitarian starts with basic needs, or at least with what are taken in the cultural environment in which a given person lives to be basic needs, and moves out to other needs and finally to wants as the productive power of the society increases.)

I qualified my above formulations with "as far as possible" and with "as fully as possible compatible with everyone else doing likewise." These are essential qualifications. Where, as in societies that we know, there are scarcities, even rather minimal scarcities, not everyone can have the resources or at least all the resources necessary to have their needs satisfied. Here we must first ensure that, again as far as possible, their basic needs are all satisfied and then we move on to other needs and finally to wants. But sometimes, to understate it, even in very affluent societies, everyone's needs cannot be met, or at least they cannot be equally met. In such circumstances we have to make some hard choices. I am thinking of a situation where there are not enough dialysis machines to go around so that everyone who needs one can have one. What then should we do? The thing to aim at, to try as far as possible to approximate, if only as a heuristic ideal, is the full and equal meeting of needs and wants of everyone. It is when we have that much equality that we have enough equality. But, of course, "ought implies can," and where we can't achieve it we can't achieve it. But where we reasonably can, we ought to do it. It is something that fairness requires.

The "reasonably can" is also an essential modification: We need situations of sufficient abundance so that we do not, in going for such an equality of condition, simply spread the misery around or spread very Spartan conditions around. Before we can rightly aim for the equality of condition I mentioned, we must first have the productive capacity and resource conditions to support the institutional means that would make possible the equal satisfaction of basic needs and the equal satisfaction of other needs and wants as well.

Such achievements will often not be possible; perhaps they will never be fully possible, for, no doubt, the physically handicapped will always be with us. Consider, for example, situations where our scarcities are such that we cannot, without causing considerable misery, create the institutions and mechanisms that would work to satisfy all needs, even all basic needs. Suppose we have the technology in place to develop all sorts of complicated life-sustaining machines all of which would predictably provide people with a quality of life that they, viewing the matter clearly, would rationally choose if they were simply choosing for themselves. But suppose, if we put such technologies in place, we will then not have the wherewithal to provide basic health care in outlying regions in the country or adequate educational services in such places. We should not, under those circumstances, put those technologies in place. But we should also recognize that where it becomes possible to put these technologies in place without sacrificing other more pressing needs, we should do so. The underlying egalitarian rationale is evident enough: Produce the conditions for the most extensive satisfaction of needs for everyone. Where A's need and B's need are equally important (equally stringent) but cannot both be satisfied, satisfy A's need rather than B's if the satisfaction of A's need would be more fecund for the satisfaction of the needs of others than B's, or less undermining of the satisfaction of the needs of others than B's. (I do not mean to say that that is our only criterion of choice but it is the criterion most relevant for us here.) We should seek the satisfaction of the greatest compossible set of needs where the conditions for compossibility are (a) that everyone's needs be considered, (b) that everyone's needs be *equally* considered and where two sets of needs cannot both be satisfied, the more stringent set of needs shall first be satisfied. (Do not say we have no working criteria for what they are. If you need food to keep you from starvation or debilitating malnutrition and I need a vacation to relax after a spate of hard work, your need is plainly more stringent than mine. There would, of course, be all sorts of disputable cases, but there are also a host of perfectly determinate cases indicating that we have working criteria.) The underlying rationale is to seek compossible sets of needs so that we approach as far as possible as great a satisfaction of needs as possible for everyone.

This might, it could be said, produce a situation in which very few people got those things that they needed the most, or at least wanted the most. Remember Nozick with his need for the resources of Widner Library in an annex to his house. People, some might argue, with expensive tastes and extravagant needs, say a need for really good wine, would never, with a stress on such compossibilia, get things they are really keen about.[2] Is that the kind of world we would reflectively want? Well, *if* their not getting them is the price we have to pay for everyone having their basic needs met, then it is a price we ought to pay. I am very fond of very good wines as well as fresh ripe mangos, but if the price of my having them is that people starve or suffer malnutrition in the Sahel, or indeed anywhere else, then plainly fairness, if not just plain human decency, requires that I forego them.

In talking about how much equality is enough, I have so far talked of the benefits that equality meant to provide. But egalitarians also speak of an equal sharing of the necessary burdens of the society as well. Fairness requires a sharing of the burdens, and for a radical egalitarian this comes to an equal sharing of the burdens where people are equally capable of sharing them. Translated into the concrete this does *not* mean that a child or an old man or a pregnant woman are to be required to work in the mines or that they be required to collect garbage, but it would involve something like requiring every able-bodied person, say from nineteen to twenty, to take his or her turn at a fair portion of the necessary unpleasant jobs in the world. In that way we all, where we are able to do it, would share equally in these burdens—in doing the things that none of us want to do but that we, if we are at all reasonable, recognize the necessity of having done. (There are all kinds of variations and complications concerning this—what do we do with the youthful wonder at the violin? But, that notwithstanding, the general idea is clear enough.) And, where we think this is reasonably feasible, it squares with our considered judgments about fairness.

I have given you—in effect appealing to my considered judgments, but considered judgments I do not think are at all eccentric—a picture of what I would take to be enough equality, too little equality, and not enough equality. But how can we know that my proportions are right? I do not think we can avoid or should indeed try to avoid an appeal to considered judgments here. But working with them there are some arguments we can appeal to get them in wide reflective equilibrium. Suppose we go back to the formal principle of justice, namely that we must treat like cases alike. Because it does not tell us *what* are like cases, we cannot derive substantive criteria from it. But it may, indirectly, be of some help here. We all, if we are not utterly zany, want a life in which our needs are satisfied and in which we can live as we wish and do what we want to do. Though we differ in many ways, in our abilities, capacities for pleasure, determination to keep on with a job, we do not differ about wanting our needs satisfied or being able to live as we wish. Thus, *ceterus paribus*, where questions of desert, entitlement, and the like do not enter, it is only fair that all of us should have our needs equally considered and that we should, again *ceterus paribus*, all be able to do as we wish in a way that is compatible with others doing likewise. From the formal principle of justice and a few key facts about us, we can get to the claim that *ceterus paribus* we should go for this much equality. But this is the core content of a radical egalitarianism.

However, how do we know that *ceterus* is *paribus* here? What about our entitlements and deserts? Suppose I have built my house with my own hands, from materials I have purchased, and on land that I have purchased and that I have lived in it for years and have carefully cared for it. The house is mine and I am entitled to keep it even if by dividing the house into two apartments greater and more equal satisfaction of need would obtain for everyone. Justice requires that such an entitlement be respected here. (Again, there is an implicit *ceterus paribus* clause. In extreme situations, say after a war with housing in extremely short supply, that entitlement could be rightly overridden.)

There is a response on the egalitarian's part similar to a response utilitarianism made to criticisms of a similar logical type made of utilitarians by pluralistic deontologists. One of the things that people in fact need, or at least reflectively firmly want, is to have such entitlements respected. Where they are routinely overridden to satisfy other needs or wants, we would *not* in fact have a society in which the needs of everyone are being maximally met. To the reply, but what if more needs for everyone were met by ignoring or overriding such entitlements, the radical egalitarian should respond that that is, given the way we are, a thoroughly hypothetical situation and that theories of morality cannot be expected to give guidance for all logically possible worlds but only for worlds which are reasonably like what our actual world is or plausibly could come to be. Setting this argument aside for the moment, even if it did turn out that the need satisfaction linked with having other things—things that involved the overriding of those entitlements—was sufficient to make it the case that more need satisfaction all around for *everyone* would be achieved by overriding those entitlements, then, for reasonable people who clearly saw that, these entitlements would not have the weight presently given to them. They either would not have the importance presently attached to them or the need for the additional living space would be so great that their being overridden would seem, everything considered, the lesser of two evils (as in the example of the postwar housing situation).

There are without doubt genuine entitlements and a theory of justice must take them seriously, but they are not absolute. If the need is great enough we can see the merit in overriding them, just as in law as well as morality the right of eminent domain is recognized. Finally, while I have talked of entitlements here, parallel arguments will go through for desert.

III

I want now to relate this articulation of what equality comes to my radically egalitarian principles of justice. My articulation of justice is a certain spelling out of the slogan proclaimed by Marx "From each according to his ability, to each according to his needs." The egalitarian conception of society argues for the desirability of bringing into existence a world, once the springs of social wealth flow freely, in which everyone's needs are as fully satisfied as possible, and in which everyone gives according to his ability. Which means, among other things, that everyone, according to his ability, shares the burdens of society. There is an equal giving and equal responsibility here according to ability. It is here, with respect to giving according to ability and with respect to receiving according to need, that a complex equality of result, i.e., equality of condition, is being advocated by the radical egalitarian. What it comes to is this: Each of us, where each is to count for one and none to count for more than one, is to give according to ability and receive according to need.

My radical egalitarian principles of justice read as follows:

1. Each person is to have an equal right to the most extensive total system of equal basic liberties and opportunities (including equal opportunities for meaningful work, for self-determination and political and economic participation) compatible with a similar treatment of all. (This principle gives expression to a commitment to attain and/or sustain equal moral autonomy and equal self-respect.)

2. After provisions are made for common social (community) values, for capital overhead to preserve the society's productive capacity, allowances made for differing unmanipulated needs and preferences, and due weight is given to the just entitlements of individuals, the income and wealth (the common stock of means) is to be so divided that each person will have a right to an equal share. The necessary burdens requisite to enhance human well-being are also to be equally shared, subject, of course, to limitations by differing abilities and differing situations. (Here I refer to different natural environments and the like and not to class position and the like.)

Here we are talking about equality as a right rather than about equality as a goal as has previously been the subject matter of equality in this chapter. These principles of egalitarianism spell out rights people have and duties they have under *conditions of very considerable productive abundance.* We have a right to certain basic liberties and opportunities and we have, subject to certain limitations spelled out in the second principle, a right to an equal share of the income and wealth in the world. We also have a duty, again subject to the qualifications mentioned in the principle, to do our equal share in shouldering the burdens necessary to protect us from ills and to enhance our well-being.

What is the relation between these rights and the ideal of equality of condition discussed earlier? That is a goal for which we can struggle now to bring about conditions which will some day make its achievement possible, while these rights only become rights when the goal is actually achievable. We have no such rights in slave, feudal, or capitalist societies or such duties in those societies. In that important way they are not natural rights for they depend on certain social conditions and certain social structures (socialist ones) to be realizable. What we can say is that it is always desirable that socioeconomic conditions come into being which would make it possible to achieve the goal of equality of condition so that these rights and duties I speak of could obtain. But that is a far cry from saying we have such rights and duties now.

It is a corollary of this, if these radical egalitarian principles of justice are correct, that capitalist societies (even capitalist welfare state societies such as Sweden) and statist societies such as the Soviet Union or the People's Republic of China cannot be just societies or at least they must be societies, structured as they are, which are defective in justice. (This is not to say that some of these societies are not juster than others. Sweden is juster than South Africa, Canada than the United States, and Cuba and Nicaragua than Honduras and Guatemala.) But none of these statist or capitalist societies can satisfy these radical egalitarian principles of justice, for equal liberty, equal opportunity, equal wealth or equal sharing of burdens are not at all possible in societies having their social structure. So we do not have such rights now but we can take it as a goal that we bring such a society into being with a commitment to an equality of condition in which we would have these rights and duties. Here we require first the massive development of productive power.

The connection between equality as a goal and equality as a right spelled out in these principles of justice is this. The equality of condition appealed to in equality as a goal would, if it were actually to obtain, have to contain the rights and duties enunciated in those principles. There could be no equal life prospects between all people or anything approximating an equal satisfaction of needs if there were not in place something like the system of equal basic liberties referred to in the first principle. Furthermore, without the rough equality of wealth referred to in the second principle, there would be disparities in power and self-direction in society which would render impossible an equality of life prospects or the social conditions required for an equal satisfaction of needs. And plainly, without a roughly equal sharing of burdens, there cannot be a situation where everyone has equal life prospects or has the chance equally to satisfy his needs. The principles of radical egalitarian justice are implicated in its conception of an ideally adequate equality of condition.

IV

The principles of radical egalitarian justice I have articulated are meant to apply globally and not just to particular societies. But it is certainly fair to say that not a few would worry that such principles of radical egalitarian justice, if applied globally, would force the people in wealthier sections of the world to a kind of financial hari-kari. There are millions of desperately impoverished people. Indeed millions are starving or malnourished and things are not getting any better. People in the affluent societies cannot but worry about whether they face a bottomless pit. Many believe that meeting, even in the most minimal way, the needs of the impoverished is going to put an incredible burden on people—people of all classes—in the affluent societies. Indeed it

will, if acted on nonevasively, bring about their impoverishment, and this is just too much to ask. Radical egalitarianism is forgetting Rawls' admonitions about "the strains of commitment"—the recognition that in any rational account of what is required of us, we must at least give a minimal healthy self-interest its due. We must construct our moral philosophy for human beings and not for saints. Human nature is less fixed than conservatives are wont to assume, but it is not so elastic that we can reasonably expect people to impoverish themselves to make the massive transfers between North and South—the industrialized world and the Third World—required to begin to approach a situation where even Rawls' principles would be in place on a global level, to say nothing of my radical egalitarian principles of justice.[3]

The first thing to say in response to this is that my radical egalitarian principles are meant to actually guide practice, to directly determine what we are to do, only in a world of extensive abundance where, as Marx put it, the springs of social wealth flow freely. If such a world cannot be attained with the undermining of capitalism and the full putting into place, stabilizing, and developing of socialist relations of production, then such radical egalitarian principles can only remain as heuristic ideals against which to measure the distance of our travel in the direction of what would be a perfectly just society.

Aside from a small capitalist class, along with those elites most directly and profitably beholden to it (together a group constituting not more than 5 percent of the world's population), there would, in taking my radical egalitarian principles as heuristic guides, be no impoverishment of people in the affluent societies, if we moved in a radically more egalitarian way to start to achieve a global fairness. There would be massive transfers of wealth between North and South, but this could be done in stages so that, for the people in the affluent societies (capitalist elites apart), there need be no undermining of the quality of their lives. Even what were once capitalist elites would not be impoverished or reduced to some kind of bleak life though they would, the incidental Spartan types aside, find their life styles altered. But their health and general well-being, including their opportunities to do significant and innovative work, would, if anything, be enhanced. And while some of the sources of their enjoyment would be a thing of the past, there would still be a considerable range of enjoyments available to them sufficient to afford anyone a rich life that could be lived with verve and zest.

A fraction of what the United States spends on defense spending would take care of immediate problems of starvation and malnutrition for most of the world. For longer range problems such as bringing conditions of life in the Third World more in line with conditions of life in Sweden and Switzerland, what is necessary is the dismantling of the capitalist system and the creation of a socio-economic system with an underlying rationale directing it toward producing for needs—everyone's needs. With this altered productive mode, the irrationalities and waste of capitalist production would be cut. There would be no more built-in obsolescence, no more merely cosmetic changes in consumer durables, no more fashion roulette, no more useless products and the like. Moreover, the enormous expenditures that go into the war industry would be a thing of the past. There would be great transfers from North to South, but it would be from the North's capitalist fat and not from things people in the North really need. (There would, in other words, be no self-pauperization of people in the capitalist world.) . . .

V

It has been repeatedly argued that equality undermines liberty. Some would say that a society in which principles like my radical egalitarian principles were adopted, or even the liberal egalitarian principles of Rawls or Dworkin were adopted, would not be a free society. My arguments have been just the reverse. I have argued that it is only in an egalitarian society that full and extensive liberty is possible.

Perhaps the egalitarian and the anti-egalitarian are arguing at cross purposes. What we need to recognize, it has been argued, is that we have two kinds of rights, both of which are important to freedom but to rather different freedoms and which are freedoms which not infrequently conflict.[4] We have rights to *fair terms of cooperation* but we also have rights to *noninterference*. If a right of either kind is overridden our freedom is diminished. The reason why it might be thought that the egalitarian and the anti-egalitarian may be arguing at cross purposes is that the egalitarian is pointing to the fact that rights

to fair terms of cooperation and their associated liberties require equality while the anti-egalitarian is pointing to the fact that rights to noninterference and their associated liberties conflict with equality. They focus on different liberties.

What I have said above may not be crystal clear, so let me explain. People have a right to fair terms of cooperation. In political terms this comes to the equal right of all to effective participation in government and, in more broadly social terms, and for a society of economic wealth, it means people having a right to a roughly equal distribution of the benefits and burdens of the basic social arrangements that affect their lives and for them to stand in such relations to each other such that no one has the power to dominate the life of another. By contrast, rights to noninterference come to the equal right of all to be left alone by the government and more broadly to live in a society in which people have a right peacefully to pursue their interests without interference.

The conflict between equality and liberty comes down to, very essentially, the conflicts we get in modern societies between rights to fair terms of cooperation and rights to noninterference. As Joseph Schumpeter saw and J. S. Mill before him, one could have a thoroughly democratic society (at least in conventional terms) in which rights to noninterference might still be extensively violated. A central anti-egalitarian claim is that we cannot have an egalitarian society in which the very precious liberties that go with the rights to noninterference would not be violated.

Socialism and egalitarianism plainly protect rights to fair terms of cooperation. Without the social (collective) ownership and control of the means of production, involving with this, in the initial stages of socialism at least, a workers' state, economic power will be concentrated in the hands of a few who will in turn, as a result, dominate effective participation in government. Some right-wing libertarians blind themselves to that reality, but it is about as evident as can be. Only an utter turning away from the facts of social life could lead to any doubts about this at all. But then this means that in a workers' state, if some people have capitalistic impulses, they would have their rights peacefully to pursue their own interests interfered with. They might wish to invest, retain, and bequeath in economic domains. In a workers' state these capitalist acts in many circumstances would have to be forbidden, but that would be a violation of an individual's right to noninterference and the fact, if it was a fact, that we by democratic vote, even with vast majorities, had made such capitalist acts illegal would still not make any difference because individuals' rights to noninterference would still be violated.

We are indeed driven, by egalitarian impulses of a perfectly understandable sort, to accept interference with laissez-faire capitalism to protect nonsubordination and nondomination of people by protecting the egalitarian right to fair terms of cooperation and the enhanced liberty that that brings. Still, as things stand, this leads inevitably to violations of the right to noninterference and this brings with it a diminution of liberty. There will be people with capitalist impulses and they will be interfered with. It is no good denying, it will be said, that egalitarianism and particularly socialism will . . . lead to interference with very precious individual liberties, namely with our right peacefully to pursue our interests without interference.[5]

The proper response to this, as should be apparent from what I have argued throughout, is that to live in any society at all, capitalist, socialist or whatever, is to live in a world in which there will be some restriction or other on our rights peacefully to pursue our interests without interference. I can't lecture in Albanian or even in French in a standard philosophy class at the University of Calgary, I can't jog naked on most beaches, borrow a book from your library without your permission, fish in your trout pond without your permission, take your dog for a walk without your say so, and the like. At least some of these things have been thought to be things which I might peacefully pursue in my own interests. Stopping me from doing them is plainly interfering with my peaceful pursuit of my own interests. And indeed it is an infringement on liberty, an interference with my doing what I may want to do.

However, for at least many of these activities, and particularly the ones having to do with property, even right-wing libertarians think that such interference is perfectly justified. But, justified or not, they still plainly constitute a restriction on our individual freedom. However, what we must also recognize is that there will always be some such restrictions on freedom in any society whatsoever, just in virtue of the fact that a normless society, without the restrictions that having norms imply, is a contradiction in terms.[6] Many restrictions are hardly felt as

restrictions, as in the attitudes of many people toward seat-belt legislation, but they are, all the same, plainly restrictions on our liberty. It is just that they are thought to be unproblematically justified.

To the question would a socialism with a radical egalitarianism restrict some liberties, including some liberties rooted in rights to noninterference, the answer is that it indeed would; but so would laissez-faire capitalism, aristocratic conceptions of justice, liberal conceptions or any social formations at all, with their associated conceptions of justice. The relevant question is which of these restrictions are justified.

The restrictions on liberty proffered by radical egalitarianism and socialism, I have argued, are justified for they, of the various alternatives, give us both the most extensive and the most abundant system of liberty possible in modern conditions with their thorough protection of the right to fair terms of cooperation. Radical egalitarianism will also, and this is central for us, protect our civil liberties and these liberties are, of course, our most basic liberties. These are the liberties which are the most vital for us to protect. What it will not do is to protect our unrestricted liberties to invest, retain, and bequeath in the economic realm and it will not protect our unrestricted freedom to buy and sell. There is, however, no good reason to think that these restrictions are restrictions of anything like a basic liberty. Moreover, we are justified in restricting our freedom to buy and sell if such restrictions strengthen, rather than weaken, our total system of liberty. This is in this way justified, for only by such market restrictions can the rights of the vast majority of people to effective participation in government and an equal role in the control of their social lives be protected. I say this because if we let the market run free in this way, power will pass into the hands of a few who will control the lives of the many and determine the fundamental design of the society. The actual liberties that are curtailed in a radically egalitarian social order are inessential liberties whose restriction in contemporary circumstances enhances human well-being and indeed makes for a firmer entrenchment of basic liberties and for their greater extension globally. That is to say, we here restrict some liberty in order to attain more liberty and a more equally distributed pattern of liberty. More people will be able to do what they want and have a greater control over their own lives than in a capitalist world order with its at least implicit inegalitarian commitments.

However, some might say I still have not faced the most central objection to radical egalitarianism, namely its statism. (I would prefer to say its putative statism.) The picture is this. The egalitarian state must be in the redistribution business. It has to make, or make sure there is made, an equal relative contribution to the welfare of every citizen. But this in effect means that the socialist state or, for that matter, the welfare state, will be deeply interventionist in our personal lives. It will be in the business, as one right-winger emotively put it, of cutting one person down to size in order to bring about that person's equality with another person who was in a previously disadvantageous position.[7] That is said to be morally objectionable and it would indeed be deeply morally objectionable in many circumstances. But it isn't in the circumstances in which the radical egalitarian presses for redistribution. (I am not speaking of what might be mere equalizing upwards.) The circumstances are these: Capitalist A gets his productive property confiscated so that he could no longer dominate and control the lives of proletarians B, C, D, E, F, and G. But what is wrong with it where this "cutting down to size"—in reality the confiscation of productive property or the taxation of the capitalist—involves no violation of A's civil liberties or the harming of his actual well-being (health, ability to work, to cultivate the arts, to have fruitful personal relations, to live in comfort, and the like) and where B, C, D, E, F, and G will have their freedom and their well-being thoroughly enhanced if such confiscation or taxation occurs? Far from being morally objectionable, it is precisely the sort of state of affairs that people ought to favor. It certainly protects more liberties and more significant liberties than it undermines.

There is another familiar anti-egalitarian argument designed to establish the liberty-undermining qualities of egalitarianism. It is an argument we have touched upon in discussing meritocracy. It turns on the fact that in any society there will be both talents and handicaps. Where they exist, what do we want to do about maintaining equal distribution? Egalitarians, radical or otherwise, certainly do not want to penalize people for talent. That being so, then surely people should be allowed to retain the benefits of superior talent. But this in some circumstances will lead to significant inequalities in resources and in the meetings of needs. To sustain

equality there will have to be an ongoing redistribution in the direction of the less talented and less fortunate. But this redistribution from the more to the less talented does plainly penalize the talented for their talent. That, it will be said, is something which is both unfair and an undermining of liberty.

The following, it has been argued, makes the above evident enough.[8] If people have talents they will tend to want to use them. And if they use them they are very likely to come out ahead. Must not egalitarians say they ought not to be able to come out ahead no matter how well they use their talents and no matter how considerable these talents are? But that is intolerably restrictive and unfair.

The answer to the above anti-egalitarian argument is implicit in a number of things I have already said. But here let me confront this familiar argument directly. Part of the answer comes out in probing some of the ambiguities of "coming out ahead." Note, incidentally, that (1) not all reflective, morally sensitive people will be so concerned with that, and (2) that being very concerned with that is a mentality that capitalism inculcates. Be that as it may, to turn to the ambiguities, note that some take "coming out ahead" principally to mean "being paid well for the use of those talents" where "being paid well" is being paid sufficiently well so that it creates inequalities sufficient to disturb the preferred egalitarian patterns. (Without that, being paid well would give one no relative advantage.) But, as we have seen, "coming out ahead" need not take that form at all. Talents can be recognized and acknowledged in many ways: First, in just the respect and admiration of a fine employment of talents that would naturally come from people seeing them so displayed where these people were not twisted by envy; second, by having, because of these talents, interesting and secure work that their talents fit them for and they merit in virtue of those talents. Moreover, having more money is not going to matter much—for familiar marginal utility reasons—where what in capitalist societies would be called the welfare floors are already very high, this being made feasible by the great productive wealth of the society. Recall that in such a society of abundance everyone will be well off and secure. In such a society people are not going to be very concerned about being a little better off than someone else. The talented are in no way, in such a situation, robbed to help the untalented and handicapped or penalized for their talents. They are only prevented from amassing wealth (most particularly productive wealth), which would enable them to dominate the untalented and the handicapped and to control the social life of the world of which they are both a part. . . .

I think that the moral authority for abstract egalitarianism, for the belief that the interests of everyone matters and matters equally, comes from its being the case that it is *required by the moral point of view.*[9] What I am predicting is that a person who has a good understanding of what morality is, has a good knowledge of the facts, is not ideologically mystified, takes an impartial point of view, and has an attitude of impartial caring, would, if not conceptually confused, come to accept the abstract egal-

itarian thesis. I see no way of arguing someone into such an egalitarianism who does not in this general way have a love of humankind.[10] A hard-hearted Hobbesist is not reachable here. But given that a person has that love of humankind—that impartial and impersonal caring—together with the other qualities mentioned above, then I predict that that person would be an egalitarian at least to the extent of accepting the abstract egalitarian thesis. What I am claiming is that if these conditions were to obtain (if they ceased to be just counterfactuals), then there would be a consensus among moral agents about accepting the abstract egalitarian thesis. . . .

Endnotes

1. See the debate between Robert Nozick, Daniel Bell, and James Tobin, "If Inequality Is Inevitable What Can Be Done About It?" *The New York Times,* January 3, 1982, p. E5. The exchange between Bell and Nozick reveals the differences between the old egalitarianism and right-wing libertarianism. It is not only that the right and left clash but sometimes right clashes with right.

2. Amartya Sen, "Equality of What?" *The Tanner Lectures on Human Values,* vol. 1 (1980, ed. Sterling M. McMurrin (Cambridge, England: Cambridge University Press, 1980), pp. 198–220.

3. Henry Shue, "The Burdens of Justice," *The Journal of Philosophy 80,* no. 10 (October 1983): 600–601; 606–608.

4. Richard W. Miller, "Marx and Morality," in *Marxism,* eds. J. R. Pennock and J. W. Chapman, Nomos 26 (New York: New York University Press, 1983), pp. 9–11.

5. Ibid., p. 10.

6. This has been argued from both the liberal center and the left. Ralf Dahrendorf, *Essays in the Theory of Society* (Stanford, Calif.: Stanford University Press, 1968), pp. 151–178; and G. A. Cohen, "Capitalism, Freedom and

the Proletariat" in *The Idea of Freedom: Essays in Honour of Isaiah Berlin,* ed. Alan Ryan (Oxford: Oxford University Press, 1979).

7. The graphic language should be duly noted. Jan Narveson, "On Dworkinian Equality," *Social Philosophy and Policy 1,* no. 1 (Autumn 1983): 4.

8. Ibid., 1–24.

9. Some will argue that there is no such thing as a moral point of view. My differences with him about the question of whether the amoralist can be argued into morality not withstanding, I think Kurt Baier, in a series of articles written subsequent to his *The Moral Point of View,* has clearly shown that there is something reasonably determinate that can, without ethnocentrism, be called "the moral point of view."

10. Richard Norman has impressively argued that this is an essential background assumption of the moral point of view. Richard Norman, "Critical Notice of Rodger Beehler's *Moral Life," Canadian Journal of Philosophy 11,* no. 1 (March 1981): 157–183.

3. A Social Contract Perspective

JOHN RAWLS

John Rawls believes that principles of justice are those on which free and rational persons would agree if they were in an original position of equality. This original position is characterized as a hypothetical position in which persons are behind an imaginary veil of ignorance with respect to most particular facts about themselves. Rawls claims that persons in this original position would choose principles requiring equal political liberty and opportunity and the highest possible economic minimum because they would be committed to the maximin rule, which requires maximizing the minimum payoff.

My aim is to present a conception of justice which generalizes and carries to a higher level of abstraction the familiar theory of the social contract as found, say, in Locke, Rousseau, and Kant.[1] In order to do this we are not to think of the original contract as one to enter a particular society or to set up a particular form of government. Rather, the guiding idea is that the principles of justice for the basic structure of society are the object of the original agreement. They are the principles that free and rational persons concerned to further their own interests would accept in an initial position of equality as defining the fundamental terms of their association. These principles are to regulate all further agreements; they specify the kinds of social cooperation that can be entered into and the forms of government that can be established. This way of regarding the principles of justice I shall call justice as fairness.

Thus we are to imagine that those who engage in social cooperation choose together, in one joint act, the principles which are to assign basic rights and duties and to determine the division of social benefits. Men are to decide in advance how they are to regulate their claims against one another and what is to be the foundation charter of their society. Just as each person must decide by rational reflec-

tion what constitutes his good—that is, the system of ends which it is rational for him to pursue—so a group of persons must decide once and for all what is to count among them as just and unjust. The choice which rational men would make in this hypothetical situation of equal liberty, assuming for the present that this choice problem has a solution, determines the principles of justice.

In justice as fairness the original position of equality corresponds to the state of nature in the traditional theory of the social contract. This original position is not, of course, thought of as an actual historical state of affairs, much less as a primitive condition of culture. It is understood as a purely hypothetical situation characterized so as to lead to a certain conception of justice.[2] Among the essential features of this situation is that no one knows his place in society, his class position or social status, nor does any one know his fortune in the distribution of natural assets and abilities, his intelligence, strength, and the like. I shall even assume that the parties do not know their conceptions of the good or their special psychological propensities. The principles of justice are chosen behind a veil of ignorance. This ensures that no one is advantaged or disadvantaged in the choice of principles by the outcome of natural chance or the contingency of social circumstances. Since all are similarly situated and no one is able to design principles to favor his particular condition, the principles of justice are the result of a fair agreement or bargain. For given the circumstances of the original position, the symmetry of everyone's relations to each other, this initial situation is fair between individuals as moral persons;

Abridged from *A Theory of Justice* (1971), pp. 11–22, 60–65, 150–156, 302–303. Excerpted by permission of the publishers from *A Theory of Justice* by John Rawls. Cambridge, Mass.: The Belknap Press of Harvard University Press. Copyright © 1971 by the President and Fellows of Harvard College.

that is, as rational beings with their own ends and capable, I shall assume, of a sense of justice. The original position is, one might say, the appropriate initial status quo, and thus the fundamental agreements reached in it are fair. This explains the propriety of the name "justice as fairness"; it conveys the idea that the principles of justice are agreed to in an initial situation that is fair. The name does not mean that the concepts of justice and fairness are the same, any more than the phrase "poetry as metaphor" means that the concepts of poetry and metaphor are the same.

Justice as fairness begins, as I have said, with one of the most general of all choices which persons might make together, namely, with the choice of the first principles of a conception of justice which is to regulate all subsequent criticism and reform of institutions. Then, having chosen a conception of justice, we can suppose that they are to choose a constitution and a legislature to enact laws, and so on, all in accordance with the principles of justice initially agreed upon. Our social situation is just if it is such that by this sequence of hypothetical agreements we would have contracted into the general system of rules which defines it. Moreover, assuming that the original position does determine a set of principles (that is, that a particular conception of justice would be chosen), it will then be true that whenever social institutions satisfy these principles those engaged in them can say to one another that they are cooperating on terms to which they would agree if they were free and equal persons whose relations with respect to one another were fair. They could all view their arrangements as meeting the stipulations which they would acknowledge in an initial situation that embodies widely accepted and reasonable constraints on the choice of principles. The general recognition of this fact would provide the basis for a public acceptance of the corresponding principles of justice. No society can, of course, be a scheme of cooperation which men enter voluntarily in a literal sense; each person finds himself placed at birth in some particular position in some particular society, and the nature of this position materially affects his life prospects. Yet a society satisfying the principles of justice as fairness comes as close as a society can to being a voluntary scheme, for it meets the principles which free and equal persons would assent to under circumstances that are fair. In this sense its members are autonomous and the obligations they recognize self-imposed.

One feature of justice as fairness is to think of the parties in the initial situation as rational and mutually disinterested. This does not mean that the parties are egoists; that is, individuals with only certain kinds of interests, say in wealth, prestige, and domination. But they are conceived as not taking an interest in one another's interests. They are to presume that even their spiritual aims may be opposed, in the way that the aims of those of different religions may be opposed. Moreover, the concept of rationality must be interpreted as far as possible in the narrow sense, standard in economic theory, of taking the most effective means to given ends. I shall modify this concept to some extent . . . , but one must try to avoid introducing into it any controversial ethical elements. The initial situation must be characterized by stipulations that are widely accepted.

In working out the conception of justice as fairness one main task clearly is to determine which principles of justice would be chosen in the original position. To do this we must describe this situation in some detail and formulate with care the problem of choice which it presents. It may be observed, however, that once the principles of justice are thought of as arising from an original agreement in a situation of equality, it is an open question whether the principle of utility would be acknowledged. Offhand it hardly seems likely that persons who view themselves as equals, entitled to press their claims upon one another, would agree to a principle which may require lesser life prospects for some simply for the sake of a greater sum of advantages enjoyed by others. Since each desires to protect his interests, his capacity to advance his conception of the good, no one has a reason to acquiesce in an enduring loss for himself in order to bring about a greater net balance of satisfaction. In the absence of strong and lasting benevolent impulses, a rational man would not accept a basic structure merely because it maximized the algebraic sum of advantages irrespective of its permanent effects on his own basic rights and interests. Thus it seems that the principle of utility is incompatible with the conception of social cooperation among equals for mutual advantage. It appears to be inconsistent with the idea of reciprocity implicit in the notion of a well-ordered society. Or, at any rate, so I shall argue.

I shall maintain instead that the persons in the initial situation would choose two rather different principles: The first requires equality in the assignment of basic rights and duties, while the second holds that social and economic inequalities, for example, inequalities of wealth and authority, are just only if they result in compensating benefits for everyone, and in particular for the least advantaged members of society. These principles rule out justifying institutions on the grounds that the hardships of some are offset by a greater good in the aggregate. It may be expedient but it is not just that some should have less in order that others may prosper. But there is no injustice in the greater benefits earned by a few provided that the situation of persons not so fortunate is thereby improved. The intuitive idea is that since everyone's well-being depends upon a scheme of cooperation without which no one could have a satisfactory life, the division of advantages should be such as to draw forth the willing cooperation of everyone taking part in it, including those less well situated. Yet this can be expected only if reasonable terms are proposed. The two principles mentioned seem to be a fair agreement on the basis of which those better endowed, or more fortunate in their social position, neither of which we can be said to deserve, could expect the willing cooperation of others when some workable scheme is a necessary condition of the welfare of all.[3] Once we decide to look for a conception of justice that nullifies the accidents of natural endowment and the contingencies of social circumstance as counters in quest for political and economic advantage, we are led to these principles. They express the result of leaving aside those aspects of the social world that seem arbitrary from a moral point of view.

The problem of the choice of principles, however, is extremely difficult. I do not expect the answer I shall suggest to be convincing to everyone. It is, therefore, worth noting from the outset that justice as fairness, like other contract views, consists of two parts: (1) an interpretation of the initial situation and of the problem of choice posed there, and (2) a set of principles which, it is argued, would be agreed to. One may accept the first part of the theory (or some variant thereof), but not the other, and conversely. The concept of the initial contractual situation may seem reasonable although the particular principles proposed are rejected. To be sure, I want to maintain that the most appropriate conception of this situation does lead to principles of justice contrary to utilitarianism and perfectionism, and therefore that the contract doctrine provides an alternative to these views. Still, one may dispute this contention even though one grants that the contractarian method is a useful way of studying ethical theories and of setting forth their underlying assumptions.

Justice as fairness is an example of what I have called a contract theory. Now there may be an objection to the term *contract* and related expressions, but I think it will serve reasonably well. Many words have misleading connotations which at first are likely to confuse. The terms *utility* and *utilitarianism* are surely no exception. They too have unfortunate suggestions which hostile critics have been willing to exploit; yet they are clear enough for those prepared to study utilitarian doctrine. The same should be true of the term *contract* applied to moral theories. As I have mentioned, to understand it one has to keep in mind that it implies a certain level of abstraction. In particular, the content of the relevant agreement is not to enter a given society or to adopt a given form of government, but to accept certain moral principles. Moreover, the undertakings referred to are purely hypothetical: A contract view holds that certain principles would be accepted in a well-defined initial situation.

The merit of the contract terminology is that it conveys the idea that principles of justice may be conceived as principles that would be chosen by rational persons, and that in this way conceptions of justice may be explained and justified. The theory of justice is a part, perhaps the most significant part, of the theory of rational choice. Furthermore, principles of justice deal with conflicting claims upon the advantages won by social cooperation; they apply to the relations among several persons or groups. The word *contract* suggests this plurality as well as the condition that the appropriate division of advantages must be in accordance with principles acceptable to all parties. The condition of publicity for principles of justice is also connoted by the contract phraseology. Thus, if these principles are the outcome of an agreement, citizens have a knowledge of the principles that others follow. It is characteristic of contract theories to stress the public nature of political principles. Finally there is the long tradition of the contract doctrine. Expressing the tie with this line of thought helps to define ideas and accords with natural piety. There are then several advantages in the use of the term *contract*. With due precautions taken, it should not be misleading.

A final remark. Justice as fairness is not a complete contract theory. For it is clear that the contractarian idea can be extended to the choice of more or less an entire ethical system; that is, to a system including principles for all the virtues and not only for justice. Now for the most part I shall consider only principles of justice and others closely related to them; I make no attempt to discuss the virtues in a systematic way. Obviously if justice as fairness succeeds reasonably well, a next step would be to study the more general view suggested by the name "rightness as fairness." But even this wider theory fails to embrace all moral relationships, since it would seem to include only our relations with other persons and to leave out of account how we are to conduct ourselves toward animals and the rest of nature. I do not contend that the contract notion offers a way to approach these questions, which are certainly of the first importance; and I shall have to put them aside. We must recognize the limited scope of justice as fairness and of the general type of view that it exemplifies. How far its conclusions must be revised once these other matters are understood cannot be decided in advance.

The Original Position and Justification

I have said that the original position is the appropriate initial status quo which insures that the fundamental agreements reached in it are fair. This fact yields the name "justice as fairness." It is clear, then, that I want to say that one conception of justice is more reasonable than another, or justifiable with respect to it, if rational persons in the initial situation would choose its principles over those of the other for the role of justice. Conceptions of justice are to be ranked by their acceptability to persons so circumstanced. Understood in this way the question of justification is settled by working out a problem of deliberation: We have to ascertain which principles it would be rational to adopt given the contractual situation. This connects the theory of justice with the theory of rational choice.

If this view of the problem of justification is to succeed, we must, of course, describe in some detail the nature of this choice problem. A problem of rational decision has a definite answer only if we know the beliefs and interests of the parties, their relations with respect to one another, the alternatives

between which they are to choose, the procedure whereby they make up their minds, and so on. As the circumstances are presented in different ways, correspondingly different principles are accepted. The concept of the original position, as I shall refer to it, is that of the most philosophically favored interpretation of this initial choice situation for the purposes of a theory of justice.

But how are we to decide what is the most favored interpretation? I assume, for one thing, that there is a broad measure of agreement that principles of justice should be chosen under certain conditions. To justify a particular description of the initial situation one shows that it incorporates these commonly shared presumptions. One argues from widely accepted but weak premises to more specific conclusions. Each of the presumptions should by itself be natural and plausible; some of them may seem innocuous or even trivial. The aim of the contract approach is to establish that taken together they impose significant bounds on acceptable principles of justice. The ideal outcome would be that these conditions determine a unique set of principles; but I shall be satisfied if they suffice to rank the main traditional conceptions of social justice.

One should not be misled, then, by the somewhat unusual conditions which characterize the original position. The idea here is simply to make vivid to ourselves the restrictions that it seems reasonable to impose on arguments for principles of justice, and therefore on these principles themselves. Thus it seems reasonable and generally acceptable that no one should be advantaged or disadvantaged by natural fortune or social circumstances in the choice of principles. It also seems widely agreed that it should be impossible to tailor principles to the circumstances of one's own case. We should ensure further that particular inclinations and aspirations, and persons' conceptions of their good, do not affect the principles adopted. The aim is to rule out those principles that it would be rational to propose for acceptance, however little the chance of success, only if one knew certain things that are irrelevant from the standpoint of justice. For example, if a man knew that he was wealthy, he might find it rational to advance the principle that various taxes for welfare measures be counted unjust; if he knew that he was poor, he would most likely propose the contrary principle. To represent the desired restrictions one imagines a situation in which everyone is deprived of this sort of information. One excludes the knowledge of those contingencies which sets men at odds and allows them to be guided by their prejudices. In this manner the veil of ignorance is arrived at in a natural way. This concept should cause no difficulty if we keep in mind the constraints on arguments that it is meant to express. At any time we can enter the original position, so to speak, simply by following a certain procedure; namely, by arguing for principles of justice in accordance with these restrictions.

It seems reasonable to suppose that the parties in the original position are equal. That is, all have the same rights in the procedure for choosing principles; each can make proposals, submit reasons for their acceptance, and so on. Obviously the purpose of these conditions is to represent equality between human beings as moral persons, as creatures having a conception of their good and capable of a sense of justice. The basis of equality is taken to be similarity in these two respects. Systems of ends are not ranked in value; and each man is presumed to have the requisite ability to understand and to act upon whatever principles are adopted. Together with the veil of ignorance, these conditions define the principles of justice as those which rational persons concerned to advance their interests would consent to as equals when none are known to be advantaged or disadvantaged by social and natural contingencies.

There is, however, another side to justifying a particular description of the original position. This is to see if the principles which would be chosen match our considered convictions of justice or extend them in an acceptable way. We can note whether applying these principles would lead us to make the same judgments about the basic structure of society which we now make intuitively and in which we have the greatest confidence; or whether, in cases where our present judgments are in doubt and given with hesitation, these principles offer a resolution which we can affirm on reflection. There are questions which we feel sure must be answered in a certain way. For example, we are confident that religious intolerance and racial discrimination are unjust. We think that we have examined these things with care and have reached what we believe is an impartial judgment not likely to be distorted by an excessive attention to our own interests. These convictions are provisional fixed points which we presume any conception of justice must fit. But we have much less assurance as to what is the correct distribution of wealth and authority. Here we may be looking for a way to remove

our doubts. We can check an interpretation of the initial situation, then, by the capacity of its principles to accommodate our firmest convictions and to provide guidance where guidance is needed.

In searching for the most favored description of this situation we work from both ends. We begin by describing it so that it represents generally shared and preferably weak conditions. We then see if these conditions are strong enough to yield a significant set of principles. If not, we look for further premises equally reasonable. But if so, and these principles match our considered convictions of justice, then so far well and good. But presumably there will be discrepancies. In this case we have a choice. We can either modify the account of the initial situation or we can revise our existing judgments, for even the judgments we take provisionally as fixed points are liable to revision. By going back and forth, sometimes altering the conditions of the contractual circumstances, at others withdrawing our judgments and conforming them to principle, I assume that eventually we shall find a description of the initial situation that both expresses reasonable conditions and yields principles which match our considered judgments duly pruned and adjusted. This state of affairs I refer to as reflective equilibrium.[4] It is an equilibrium because at last our principles and judgments coincide; and it is reflective since we know to what principles our judgments conform and the premises of their derivation. At the moment everything is in order. But this equilibrium is not necessarily stable. It is liable to be upset by further examination of the conditions which should be imposed on the contractual situation and by particular cases which may lead us to revise our judgments. Yet for the time being we have done what we can to render coherent and to justify our convictions of social justice. We have reached a conception of the original position.

I shall not, of course, actually work through this process. Still, we may think of the interpretation of the original position that I shall present as the result of such a hypothetical course of reflection. It represents the attempt to accommodate within one scheme both reasonable philosophical conditions on principles as well as our considered judgments of justice. In arriving at the favored interpretation of the initial situation there is no point at which an appeal is made to self-evidence in the traditional sense either of general conceptions or particular convictions. I do not claim for the principles of justice proposed that they are necessary truths or derivable from such truths. A conception of justice cannot be deduced from self-evident premises or conditions on principles; instead, its justification is a matter of the mutual support of many considerations, of everything fitting together into one coherent view.

A final comment. We shall want to say that certain principles of justice are justified because they would be agreed to in an initial situation of equality. I have emphasized that this original position is purely hypothetical. It is natural to ask why, if this agreement is never actually entered into, we should take any interest in these principles—moral or otherwise. The answer is that the conditions embodied in the description of the original position are ones that we do in fact accept. Or if we do not, then perhaps we can be persuaded to do so by philosophical reflection. Each aspect of the contractual situation can be given supporting grounds. Thus what we shall do is to collect together into one conception a number of conditions on principles that we are ready upon due consideration to recognize as reasonable. These constraints express what we are prepared to regard as limits on fair terms of social cooperation. One way to look at the idea of the original position, therefore, is to see it as an expository device which sums up the meaning of these conditions and helps us to extract their consequences. On the other hand, this conception is also an intuitive notion that suggests its own elaboration, so that led on by it we are drawn to define more clearly the standpoint from which we can best interpret moral relationships. We need a conception that enables us to envision our objective from afar: The intuitive notion of the original position is to do this for us. . . .

Two Principles of Justice

I shall now state in a provisional form the two principles of justice that I believe would be chosen in the original position. In this section I wish to make only the most general comments, and therefore the first formulation of these principles is tentative. As we go on I shall run through several formulations and approximate step by step the final statement to be given much later. I believe that doing this allows the exposition to proceed in a natural way.

The first statement of the two principles reads as follows:

> First: Each person is to have an equal right to the most extensive basic liberty compatible with a similar liberty for others.

> Second: Social and economic inequalities are to be arranged so that they are both (a) reasonably expected to be to everyone's advantage, and (b) attached to positions and offices open to all.

There are two ambiguous phrases in the second principle, namely "everyone's advantage" and "open to all." Determining their sense more exactly will lead to a second formulation of the principle. . . .

By way of general comment, these principles primarily apply, as I have said, to the basic structure of society. They are to govern the assignment of rights and duties and to regulate the distribution of social and economic advantages. As their formulation suggests, these principles presuppose that the social structure can be divided into two more or less distinct parts, the first principle applying to the one, the second to the other. They distinguish between those aspects of the social system that define and secure the equal liberties of citizenship and those that specify and establish social and economic inequalities. The basic liberties of citizens are, roughly speaking, political liberty (the right to vote and to be eligible for public office) together with freedom of speech and assembly; liberty of conscience and freedom of thought; freedom of the person along with the right to hold personal property; and freedom from arbitrary arrest and seizure as defined by the concept of the rule of law. These liberties are all required to be equal by the first principle, since citizens of a just society are to have the same basic rights.

The second principle applies, in the first approximation, to the distribution of income and wealth and to the design of organizations that make use of differences in authority and responsibility, or chains of command. While the distribution of wealth and income need not be equal, it must be to everyone's advantage, and at the same time, positions of authority and offices of command must be accessible to all. One applies the second principle by holding positions open, and then, subject to this constraint, arranges social and economic inequalities so that everyone benefits.

These principles are to be arranged in a serial order with the first principle prior to the second. This ordering means that a departure from the institutions of equal liberty required by the first principle cannot be justified by, or compensated for, by greater social and economic advantages. The distribution of wealth and income, and the hierarchies of authority, must be consistent with both the liberties of equal citizenship and equality of opportunity.

It is clear that these principles are rather specific in their content, and their acceptance rests on certain assumptions that I must eventually try to explain and justify. A theory of justice depends upon a theory of society in ways that will become evident as we proceed. For the present, it should be observed that the two principles (and this holds for all formulations) are a special case of a more general conception of justice that can be expressed as follows:

> All social values—liberty and opportunity, income and wealth, and the bases of self-respect—are to be distributed equally unless an unequal distribution of any, or all, of these values is to everyone's advantage.

Injustice, then, is simply inequalities that are not to the benefit of all. Of course, this conception is extremely vague and requires interpretation.

As a first step, suppose that the basic structure of society distributes certain primary goods, that is, things that every rational man is presumed to want. These goods normally have a use whatever a person's rational plan of life. For simplicity, assume that the chief primary goods at the disposition of society are rights and liberties, powers and opportunities, income and wealth. (Later on . . . the primary good of self-respect has a central place.) These are the social primary goods. Other primary goods such as health and vigor, intelligence and imagination, are natural goods; although their possession is influenced by the basic structure, they are not so directly under its control. Imagine, then, a hypothetical initial arrangement in which all the social primary goods are equally distributed: Everyone has similar rights and duties, and income and wealth are evenly shared. This state of affairs provides a benchmark for judging improvements. If certain inequalities of wealth and organizational powers would make everyone better off than in this hypothetical starting situation, then they accord with the general conception.

Now it is possible, at least theoretically, that by giving up some of their fundamental liberties men are sufficiently compensated by the resulting social and economic gains. The general conception of justice imposes no restrictions on what sort of inequalities are permissible; it only requires that everyone's position be improved. We need not suppose anything so drastic as consenting to a condition of slavery. Imagine instead that men forgo certain political rights when the economic returns are significant and their capacity to influence the course of policy by the exercise of these rights would be marginal in any case. It is this kind of exchange which the two principles as stated rule out; being arranged in serial order they do not permit exchanges between basic liberties and economic and social gains. The serial ordering of principles expresses an underlying preference among primary social goods. When this preference is rational so likewise is the choice of these principles in this order.

In developing justice as fairness I shall, for the most part, leave aside the general conception of justice and examine instead the special case of the two principles in serial order. The advantage of this procedure is that from the first the matter of priorities is recognized and an effort made to find principles to deal with it. One is led to attend throughout to the conditions under which the acknowledgment of the absolute weight of liberty with respect to social and economic advantages, as defined by the lexical order of the two principles, would be reasonable. Offhand, this ranking appears extreme and too special a case to be of much interest; but there is more justification for it than would appear at first sight. Or at any rate, so I shall maintain. . . . Furthermore, the distinction between fundamental rights and liberties and economic and social benefits marks a difference among primary social goods that one should try to exploit. It suggests an important division in the social system. Of course, the distinctions drawn and the ordering proposed are bound to be at best only approximations. There are surely circumstances in which they fail. But it is essential to depict clearly the main lines of a reasonable conception of justice; and under many conditions, anyway, the two principles in serial order may serve well enough. When necessary we can fall back on the more general conception.

The fact that the two principles apply to institutions has certain consequences. Several points illustrate this. First of all, the rights and liberties referred to by these principles are those that are defined by the public rules of the basic structure. Whether men are free is determined by the rights and duties established by the major institutions of society. Liberty is a certain pattern of social forms. The first principle simply requires that certain sorts of rules, those defining basic liberties, apply to everyone equally and that they allow the most extensive liberty compatible with a like liberty for all. The only reason for circumscribing the rights defining liberty and making men's freedom less extensive than it might otherwise be is that these equal rights as institutionally defined would interfere with one another.

Another thing to bear in mind is that when principles mention persons, or require that everyone gain from an inequality, the reference is to representative persons holding the various social positions, or offices, or whatever, established by the basic structure. Thus in applying the second principle I assume that it is possible to assign an expectation of well-being to representative individuals holding these positions. This expectation indicates their life prospects as viewed from their social station. In general, the expectations of representative persons depend upon the distribution of rights and duties throughout the basic structure. When this changes, expectations change. I assume, then, that expectations are connected: By raising the prospects of the representative man in one position we presumably increase or decrease the prospects of representative men in other positions. Since it applies to institutional forms, the second principle (or rather the first part of it) refers to the expectations of representative individuals. As I shall discuss below, neither principle applies to distributions of particular goods to particular individuals who may be identified by their proper names. The situation where someone is considering how to allocate certain commodities to needy persons who are known to him is not within the scope of the principles. They are meant to regulate basic institutional arrangements. We must not assume that there is much similarity from the standpoint of justice between an administrative allotment of goods to specific persons and the appropriate design of society. Our common sense intuitions for the former may be a poor guide to the latter.

Now the second principle insists that each person benefit from permissible inequalities in the basic structure. This means that it must be reasonable for each relevant representative man defined by this structure, when he views it as a going concern, to prefer his prospects with the inequality, to his prospects without it. One is not allowed to justify differences in income or organizational powers on the ground that the disadvantages of those in one position are outweighed by the greater advantages of those in another. Much less can infringements of liberty be counterbalanced in this way. Applied to the basic structure, the principle of utility would have us maximize the sum of expectations of representative men (weighted by the number of persons they represent, on the classical view); and this would permit us to compensate for the losses of some by the gains of others. Instead, the two principles require that everyone benefit from economic and social inequalities.

The Reasoning Leading to the Two Principles of Justice

It will be recalled that the general conception of justice as fairness requires that all primary social goods be distributed equally unless an unequal distribution would be to everyone's advantage. No restrictions are placed on exchanges of these goods and therefore a lesser liberty can be compensated for by greater social and economic benefits. Now looking at the situation from the standpoint of one person selected arbitrarily, there is no way for him to win special advantages for himself. Nor, on the other hand, are there grounds for his acquiescing in special disadvantages. Since it is not reasonable for him to expect more than an equal share in the division of social goods, and since it is not rational for him to agree to less, the sensible thing for him to do is to acknowledge as the first principle of justice one requiring an equal distribution. Indeed, this principle is so obvious that we would expect it to occur to anyone immediately.

Thus, the parties start with a principle establishing equal liberty for all, including equality of opportunity, as well as an equal distribution of income and wealth. But there is no reason why this acknowledgment should be final. If there are inequalities in the basic structure that work to make everyone better off in comparison with the benchmark of initial equality, why not permit them? The immediate gain which a greater equality might allow can be regarded as intelligently invested in view of its future return. If, for example, these inequalities set up various incentives which succeed in eliciting more productive efforts, a person in the original position may look upon them as necessary to cover the costs of training and to encourage effective performance. One might think that ideally individuals should want to serve one another. But since the parties are assumed not to take an interest in one another's interests, their acceptance of these inequalities is only the acceptance of the relations in which men stand in the circumstances of justice. They have no grounds for complaining of one another's motives. A person in the original position would, therefore, concede the justice of these inequalities. Indeed, it would be shortsighted of him not to do so. He would hesitate to agree to these regularities only if he would be dejected by the bare knowledge or perception that others were better situated; and I have assumed that the parties decide as if they are not moved by envy. In order to make the principle regulating inequalities determinate, one looks at the system from the standpoint of the least advantaged representative man. Inequalities are permissible when they maximize, or at least all contribute to, the long-term expectations of the least fortunate group in society.

Now this general conception imposes no constraints on what sorts of inequalities are allowed, whereas the special conception, by putting the two principles in serial order (with the necessary adjustments in meaning), forbids exchanges between basic liberties and economic and social benefits. I shall not try to justify this ordering here. . . . But roughly, the idea underlying this ordering is that if the parties assume that their basic liberties can be effectively exercised, they will not exchange a lesser liberty for an improvement in economic well-being. It is only when social conditions do not allow the effective establishment of these rights that one can concede their limitation; and these restrictions can be granted only to the extent that they are necessary to prepare the way for a free society. The denial of equal liberty can be defended only if it is necessary to raise the level of civilization so that in due course these freedoms can be enjoyed. Thus in adopting a serial order we are in effect making a special assumption in the original position, namely, that the parties know that the conditions of their society, whatever they are, admit the effective realization of the equal liberties. The serial ordering of the two principles of justice eventually comes to be rea-

sonable if the general conception is consistently followed. This lexical ranking is the long-run tendency of the general view. For the most part I shall assume that the requisite circumstances for the serial order obtain.

It seems clear from these remarks that the two principles are at least a plausible conception of justice. The question, though, is how one is to argue for them more systematically. Now there are several things to do. One can work out their consequences for institutions and note their implications for fundamental social policy. In this way they are tested by a comparison with our considered judgments of justice. . . . But one can also try to find arguments in their favor that are decisive from the standpoint of the original position. In order to see how this might be done, it is useful as a heuristic device to think of the two principles as the maximin solution to the problem of social justice. There is an analogy between the two principles and the maximin rule for choice under uncertainty.[5] This is evident from the fact that the two principles are those a person would choose for the design of a society in which his enemy is to assign him his place. The maximin rule tells us to rank alternatives by their worst possible outcomes: We are to adopt the alternative the worst outcome of which is superior to the worst outcomes of the others. The persons in the original position do not, of course, assume that their initial place in society is decided by a malevolent opponent. As I note below, they should not reason from false premises. The veil of ignorance does not violate this idea, since an absence of information is not misinformation. But that the two principles of justice would be chosen if the parties were forced to protect themselves against such a contingency explains the sense in which this conception is the maximin solution. And this analogy suggests that if the original position has been described so that it is rational for the parties to adopt the conservative attitude expressed by this rule, a conclusive argument can indeed be constructed for these principles. Clearly the maximin rule is not, in general, a suitable guide for choices under uncertainty. But it is attractive in situations marked by certain special features. My aim, then, is to show that a good case can be made for the two principles based on the fact that the original position manifests these features to the fullest possible degree, carrying them to the limit, so to speak.

Consider the gain-and-loss table in the next column. It represents the gains and losses for a situation which is not a game of strategy. There is no one playing against the person making the decision; instead he is faced with several possible circumstances which may or may not obtain. Which circumstances happen to exist does not depend upon what the person choosing decides or whether he announces his moves in advance. The numbers in the table are monetary values (in hundreds of dollars) in comparison with some initial situation. The gain (g) depends upon the individual's decision (d) and the circumstances (c). Thus $g = f(d,c)$. Assuming that there are three possible decisions and three possible circumstances, we might have this gain-and-loss table.

	Circumstances		
Decisions	c_1	c_2	c_3
d_1	−7	8	12
d_2	−8	7	14
d_3	5	6	8

The maximin rule requires that we make the third decision. For in this case the worst that can happen is that one gains five hundred dollars, which is better than the worst for the other actions. If we adopt one of these we may lose either eight or seven hundred dollars. Thus, the choice of d_3 maximizes $f(d,c)$ for the value of c which for a given d, minimizes f. The term *maximin* means the maximum minimorum; and the rule directs our attention to the worst that can happen under any proposed course of action, and to decide in the light of that.

Now there appear to be three chief features of situations that give plausibility to this unusual rule.[6] First, since the rule takes no account for the likelihoods of the possible circumstances, there must be some reason for sharply discounting estimates of these probabilities. Offhand, the most natural rule of choice would seem to be to compute the expectation of monetary gain for each decision and then to adopt the course of action with the highest prospect. (This expectation is defined as follows: Let us suppose that g_{ij} represents the numbers in the gain-and loss table, where i is the row index and j is the column index; and let p_i, j = 1, 2, 3, be the likelihoods of the circumstances, with $\Sigma p_j = 1$. Then the expectation for the ith decision is equal to $\Sigma p_j g_{ij}$.) Thus it must be, for example, that the situation is one in which a knowledge of likelihoods is impossible, or at best extremely insecure. In this case it is unreasonable not to be skeptical of probabilistic calculations unless there is no other way out, particularly if the decision is a fundamental one that needs to be justified to others.

The second feature that suggests the maximin rule is the following: The person choosing has a conception of the good such that he cares very little, if anything, for what he might gain above the minimum stipend that he can, in fact, be sure of by following the maximin rule. It is not worthwhile for him to take a chance for the sake of a further advantage, especially when it may turn out that he loses much that is important to him. This last provision brings in the third feature; namely, that the rejected alternatives have outcomes that one can hardly accept. The situation involves grave risks. Of course these features work most effectively in combination. The paradigm situation for following the maximin rule is when all three features are realized to the highest degree. This rule does not, then, generally apply, nor of course is it self-evident. Rather, it is a maxim, a rule of thumb, that comes into its own in special circumstances. Its application depends upon the qualitative structure of the possible gains and losses in relation to one's conception of the good, all this against a background in which it is reasonable to discount conjectural estimates of likelihoods.

It should be noted, as the comments on the gain-and-loss table say, that the entries in the table represent monetary values and not utilities. This difference is significant since for one thing computing expectations on the basis of such objective values is not the same thing as computing expected utility and may lead to different results. The essential point, though, is that in justice as fairness the parties do not know their conception of the good and cannot estimate their utility in the ordinary sense. In any case, we want to go behind de facto preferences generated by given conditions. Therefore expectations are based upon an index of primary goods and the parties make their choice accordingly. The entries in the example are in terms of money and not utility to indicate this aspect of the contract doctrine.

Now, as I have suggested, the original position has been defined so that it is a situation in which the maximin rule applies. In order to see this, let us review briefly the nature of this situation with these three special features in mind. To begin with, the veil of ignorance excludes all but the vaguest knowledge of likelihoods. The parties have no basis for determining the probable nature of their society, or their place in it. Thus they have strong reasons for being wary of probability calculations if any other course is open to them. They must also take into account the fact that their choice of principles should seem reasonable to others, in particular their descendants, whose rights will be deeply affected by it. There are further grounds for discounting that I shall mention as we go along. For the present it suffices to note that these considerations are strengthened by the fact that the parties know very little about the gain-and-loss table. Not only are they unable to conjecture the likelihoods of the various possible circumstances, they cannot say much about what the possible circumstances are, much less enumerate them and foresee the outcome of each alternative available. Those deciding are much more in the dark than the illustration by a numerical table suggests. It is for this reason that I have spoken of an analogy with the maximin rule.

Several kinds of arguments for the two principles of justice illustrate the second feature. Thus, if we can maintain that these principles provide a workable theory of social justice, and that they are compatible with reasonable demands of efficiency, then this conception guarantees a satisfactory minimum. There may be, on reflection, little reason for trying to do better. Thus much of the argument . . . is to show, by their application to the main questions of social justice, that the two principles are a satisfactory conception. These details have a philosophical purpose. Moreover, this line of thought is practically decisive if we can establish the priority of liberty, the lexical ordering of the two principles. For this priority implies that the persons in the original position have no desire to try for greater gains at the expense of the equal liberties. The minimum assured by the two principles in lexical order is not one that the parties wish to jeopardize for the sake of greater economic and social advantages. . . .

Finally, the third feature holds if we can assume that other conceptions of justice may lead to institutions that the parties would find intolerable. For example, it has sometimes been held that under some conditions the utility principle (in either form) justifies, if not slavery or serfdom, at any rate serious infractions of liberty for the sake of greater social benefits. We need not consider here the truth of this claim, or the likelihood that the requisite conditions obtain. For the moment, this contention is only to illustrate the way in which conceptions of justice

may allow for outcomes which the parties may not be able to accept. And having the ready alternative of the two principles of justice which secure a satisfactory minimum, it seems unwise, if not irrational, for them to take a chance that these outcomes are not realized.

So much, then, for a brief sketch of the features of situations in which the maximin rule comes into its own and of the way in which the arguments for the two principles of justice can be subsumed under them. . . .

The Final Formulation of the Principles of Justice

. . . I now wish to give the final statement of the two principles of justice for institutions. For the sake of completeness, I shall give a full statement including earlier formulations.

First Principle
Each person is to have an equal right to the most extensive total system of equal basic liberties compatible with a similar system of liberty for all.

Second Principle
Social and economic inequalities are to be arranged so that they are both:
(a) to the greatest benefit of the least advantaged, consistent with the just savings principle, and
(b) attached to offices and positions open to all under conditions of fair equality of opportunity.

The First Priority Rule (The Priority of Liberty)
The principles of justice are to be ranked in lexical order and therefore liberty can be restricted only for the sake of liberty. There are two cases:
(a) a less extensive liberty must strengthen the total system of liberty shared by all;
(b) a less than equal liberty must be acceptable to those with the lesser liberty.

Second Priority Rule (The Priority of Justice over Efficiency and Welfare)
The second principle of justice is lexically prior to the principle of efficiency and to that of maximizing the sum of advantages; and fair

opportunity is prior to the difference principle. There are two cases:

(a) an inequality of opportunity must enhance the opportunities of those with the lesser opportunity;

(b) an excessive rate of saving must on balance mitigate the burden of those bearing this hardship.

General Conception

All social primary goods—liberty and opportunity, income and wealth, and the bases of self-respect—are to be distributed equally unless an equal distribution of any or all of these goods is to the advantage of the least favored.

By way of comment, these principles and priority rules are no doubt incomplete. Other modifications will surely have to be made, but I shall not further complicate the statement of the principles. It suffices to observe that when we come to nonideal theory, we do not fall back straightway upon the general conception of justice. The lexical ordering of the two principles, and the valuations that this ordering implies, suggest priority rules which seem to be reasonable enough in many cases. By various examples I have tried to illustrate how these rules can be used and to indicate their plausibility. Thus the ranking of the principles of justice in ideal theory reflects back and guides the application of these principles to nonideal situations. It identifies which limitations need to be dealt with first. The drawback of the general conception of justice is that it lacks the definite structure of the two principles in serial order. In more extreme and tangled instances of nonideal theory there may be no alternative to it. At some point the priority of rules for nonideal cases will fail; and indeed, we may be able to find no satisfactory answer at all. But we must try to postpone the day of reckoning as long as possible, and try to arrange society so that it never comes. . . .

Endnotes

1. As the text suggests, I shall regard Locke's *Second Treatise of Government*, Rousseau's *The Social Contract*, and Kant's ethical works beginning with *The Foundations of the Metaphysics of Morals* as definitive of the contract tradition. For all of its greatness, Hobbes's *Leviathan* raises special problems. A general historical survey is provided by J. W. Gough, *The Social Contract*, 2nd ed. (Oxford, The Clarendon Press, 1957), and Otto Gierke, *Natural Law and the Theory of Society*, trans. with an introduction by Ernest Barker (Cambridge, The University Press, 1934). A presentation of the contract view as primarily an ethical theory is to be found in G. R. Grice, *The Grounds of Moral Judgment* (Cambridge, The University Press, 1967).

2. Kant is clear that the original agreement is hypothetical. See *The Metaphysics of Morals*, pt. I (*Rechtslehre*), especially §§ 47, 52; and pt. II of the essay "Concerning the Common Saying: This May Be True in Theory but It Does Not Apply in Practice," in *Kant's Political Writings*, ed. Hans Reiss and trans. by H. B. Nisbet (Cambridge, The University Press, 1970), pp. 73–87, See Georges Vlachos, *Le pensée politique de Kant* (Paris, Presses Universitaires de France, 1962), pp. 326–335; and J. G. Murphy,

Kant: The Philosophy of Right (London, Macmillan, 1970), pp. 109–112, 133–136, for a further discussion.

3. For the formulation of this intuitive idea I am indebted to Allan Gibbard.

4. The process of mutual adjustment of principles and considered judgments is not peculiar to moral philosophy. See Nelson Goodman, *Fact, Fiction, and Forecast* (Cambridge, Mass., Harvard University Press, 1955), pp. 65–68, for parallel remarks concerning the justification of the principles of deductive and inductive inference.

5. An accessible discussion of this and other rules of choice under uncertainty can be found in W. J. Baumol, *Economic Theory and Operations Analysis*, 2nd ed. (Englewood Cliffs, N.J., Prentice-Hall, 1965), ch. 24. Baumol gives a geometric interpretation of these rules, including the diagram used . . . to illustrate the difference principle. See pp. 558–562. See also R. D. Luce and Howard Raiffa, *Games and Decisions* (New York, John Wiley and Sons, 1957), ch. XIII, for a fuller account.

6. Here I borrow from William Fellner, *Probability and Profit* (Homewood, Ill., Richard D. Irwin, 1965), pp. 140–142, where these features are noted.

4. From Liberty to Equality

JAMES P. STERBA

James P. Sterba argues that when a libertarian ideal of liberty is interpreted in the manner favored by libertarians as the absence of interference by other people from doing what one wants or is able to do, it leads to a universal right to welfare. He further argues that the recognition of this universal right to welfare leads to the equalization of resources characteristic of a socialist state. He considers a number of objections to these arguments and finds them wanting.

The central contrast between libertarians and socialists is usually put this way: Libertarians take the ideal of liberty to be the ultimate political ideal from which they think it follows that only a minimal or night watchman state can be justified, whereas socialists take the ideal of equality to be the ultimate political ideal from which they think it follows that only a state that socializes the means of production can be justified. Libertarians, however, tend to agree with socialists that when the ideal of equality is interpreted in the manner favored by socialists, it would justify a socialist state. Libertarians simply contend that the socialist interpretation of the ideal of equality is morally contestable. Why not interpret the ideal in the manner favored by libertarians as equality before the law or equality of basic rights so that the ideal is at least consistent with, if not required by, the libertarian's own ideal of liberty? Why not indeed! But obviously an analogous question could be directed at libertarians. Why not interpret the ideal of liberty in the manner favored by socialists as a positive rather than a negative ideal so that it would justify the greater equality in the distribution of goods and resources that is characteristic of a socialist state?

To either of these questions, no convincing answer seems forthcoming. Both the interpretations of the ideals of liberty and equality favored by libertarians and those favored by socialists appear morally contestable. Consequently, the dispute between libertarians and socialists seems irresolvable. I wish to argue, however, that this is not the case. I will show that the dispute can be resolved, for all practical purposes, by proceeding from premises that libertarians endorse to a conclusion that socialists endorse. Specifically, I will argue that libertarians, given their ideal of liberty, must be socialists because they must endorse the equality in the distribution of goods and resources required by a socialist state.

I

To see that this is the case, suppose we interpret the ideal of liberty as a negative ideal in the manner favored by libertarians, rather than as a positive ideal in the manner favored by socialists.[1] So understood, liberty is the absence of interference by other people from doing what one wants or is able to do. Interpreting their ideal in this way, libertarians claim to derive a number of more specific requirements, in particular, a right to life; a right to freedom of speech, press, and assembly; and a right to property. Here it is important to observe that the libertarian's right to life is not a right to receive from others the goods and resources necessary for preserving one's life; it is simply a right not to be killed unjustly. Correspondingly, the libertarian's right to property is not a right to receive from others the goods and resources necessary for one's welfare, but rather a right to acquire goods and resources either by initial acquisition or by voluntary agreement.

Of course, libertarians would allow that it would be nice of the rich to share their surplus goods and

A longer version of this article appeared as "Reconciling Liberty and Equality or Why Libertarians Must Be Socialists" in *Liberty and Equality,* edited by Larry May and Jonathan Schonsheck (MIT, 1996).

resources with the poor. Nevertheless, according to libertarians, such acts of charity should not be coercively required. For this reason, libertarians are opposed to coercively supported welfare programs. By contrast, socialists would certainly interpret their ideal of equality to require not only coercively supported welfare programs, but also considerable equality in the distribution of goods and resources as well.

In order to see why libertarians are mistaken about what their ideal requires, consider a typical conflict situation between the rich and the poor. In this situation, the rich have more than enough goods and resources to satisfy their basic needs.[2] By contrast, the poor lack the goods and resources to meet their most basic needs even though they have tried all the means available to them that libertarians regard as legitimate for acquiring such goods and resources. Under such circumstances, libertarians usually maintain that the rich should have the liberty to use their resources to satisfy their luxury needs if they so wish. Libertarians recognize that this liberty might well be enjoyed at the expense of the satisfaction of the most basic needs of the poor; they just think that liberty always has priority over other political ideals, and since they assume that the liberty of the poor is not at stake in such conflict situations, it is easy for them to conclude that the rich should not be required to sacrifice their liberty so that the basic needs of the poor may be met.

Of course, libertarians allow that it would be nice of the rich to share their surplus goods and resources with the poor. Nevertheless, according to libertarians, such acts of charity cannot be required because the liberty of the poor is not thought to be at stake in such conflict situations.

In fact, however, the liberty of the poor *is* at stake in such conflict situations. What is at stake is the liberty of the poor not to be interfered with in taking from the surplus possessions of the rich what is necessary to satisfy their basic needs.[3]

Needless to say, libertarians would want to deny that the poor have this liberty. But how could they justify such a denial? As this liberty of the poor has been specified, it is not a positive right to receive something but a negative right of noninterference. Nor will it do for libertarians to appeal to a right to life or a right to property to rule out such a liberty because on the view under consideration liberty is basic and all other rights are derived from a right to liberty.[4] Clearly, what libertarians must do is recog-

nize the existence of such a liberty and then claim that it conflicts with other liberties of the rich. But when libertarians see that this is the case, they are often genuinely surprised—one might even say rudely awakened—for they had not previously seen the conflict between the rich and the poor as a conflict of liberties.[5]

When the conflict between the rich and the poor is viewed as a conflict of liberties, either we can say that the rich should have the liberty not to be interfered with in using their surplus goods and resources for luxury purposes, or we can say that the poor should have the liberty not to be interfered with in taking from the rich what they require to meet their basic needs. If we choose one liberty, we must reject the other. What needs to be determined, therefore, is which liberty is morally preferable: the liberty of the rich or the liberty of the poor.

Two Principles

In order to see that the liberty of the poor not to be interfered with in taking from the surplus resources of the rich what is required to meet their basic needs is morally preferable to the liberty of the rich not to be interfered with in using surplus goods and resources for luxury purposes, we need to appeal to one of the most fundamental principles of morality, one that is common to all political perspectives. This is the "Ought" Implies "Can" Principle:

> People are not morally required to do what they lack the power to do or what would involve so great a sacrifice that it would be unreasonable to ask them to perform such an action, and/or in the case of severe conflicts of interest, unreasonable to require them to perform such an action.

For example, suppose I promised to attend a departmental meeting on Friday, but on Thursday I am involved in a serious car accident that leaves me in a coma. Surely it is no longer the case that I ought to attend the meeting, now that I lack the power to do so. Or suppose instead that on Thursday I develop a severe case of pneumonia for which I am hospitalized. Surely, I could legitimately claim that I cannot attend the meeting, on the grounds that the risk to my health involved in attending is a sacrifice that it would be unreasonable to ask me to bear. Or suppose the risk to my health from having pneumonia is not so serious that it would be unreasonable to ask me to attend the meeting (a supererogatory request), it might still be serious enough to be unreasonable to require my attendance at the meeting (a demand that is backed up by blame or coercion).

Now applying the "ought" implies "can" principle to the case at hand, it seems clear that the poor have it within their power willingly to relinquish such an important liberty as the liberty not to be interfered with in taking from the rich what they require to meet their basic needs. Nevertheless, it would be unreasonable to ask or require them to make so great a sacrifice. In the extreme case, it would involve asking or requiring the poor to sit back and starve to death. Of course, the poor may have no real alternative to relinquishing this liberty. To do anything else may involve worse consequences for themselves and their loved ones and may invite a painful death. Accordingly, we may expect that the poor would acquiesce, albeit unwillingly, to a political system that denies them the right to welfare supported by such a liberty, at the same time that we recognize that such a system imposes an unreasonable sacrifice upon the poor—a sacrifice that we cannot morally blame the poor for trying to evade.[6] Analogously, we might expect that a woman whose life was threatened would submit to a rapist's demands, at the same time that we recognize the utter unreasonableness of those demands.

By contrast, it would not be unreasonable to ask and require the rich to sacrifice the liberty to meet some of their luxury needs so that the poor can have the liberty to meet their basic needs.[7] Naturally, we might expect that the rich, for reasons of self-interest and past contribution, might be disinclined to make such a sacrifice. We might even suppose that the past contribution of the rich provides a good reason for not sacrificing their liberty to use their surplus for luxury purposes. Yet, unlike the poor, the rich could not claim that relinquishing such a liberty would involve so great a sacrifice that it would be unreasonable to ask and require them to make it; unlike the poor, the rich could be morally blameworthy for failing to make such a sacrifice.

Notice that by virtue of the "ought" implies "can" principle, this argument establishes that:

1a) Because it would be unreasonable to ask or require the poor to sacrifice the liberty not to be interfered with when taking from the surplus goods and resources of the rich what is necessary to meet their basic needs, 1b) it is

not the case that the poor are morally required to make such a sacrifice.

2a) Because it would not be unreasonable to ask and require the rich to sacrifice the liberty not to be interfered with when using their surplus goods and resources for luxury purposes, 2b) it may be the case that the rich are morally required to make such a sacrifice.

What the argument does not establish is that it is the case that the rich are *morally required* to sacrifice (some of) their surplus so that the basic needs of the poor can be met. To clearly establish that conclusion, we need to appeal to a principle, which is, in fact, simply the contrapositive of the "ought" implies "can" principle. It is the Conflict Resolution Principle:

What people are morally required to do is what is either reasonable to ask them to do, or in the case of severe conflicts of interest, reasonable to require them to do.

While the "ought" implies "can" principle claims that if any action is *not reasonable to ask or require* a person to do, all things considered, that action is *not morally required* for that person, all things considered [$-R(A \lor Re) \longrightarrow -MRe$], the conflict resolution principle claims that if any action is *morally required* for a person to do, all things considered, that action is *reasonable to ask or require* that person to do, all things considered [$MRe \longrightarrow R(A \lor Re)$].

This conflict resolution principle accords with the generally accepted view of morality as a system of reasons for resolving interpersonal conflicts of interest. Of course, morality is not limited to such a system of reasons. Most surely it also includes reasons of self-development. All that is being claimed by the principle is that moral resolutions of interpersonal conflicts of interest cannot be contrary to reason to ask everyone affected to accept or, in the case of severe interpersonal conflicts of interest, unreasonable to require everyone affected to accept. The reason for the distinction between the two kinds of cases is that when interpersonal conflicts of interest are not severe, moral resolutions must still be reasonable to ask everyone affected to accept but they need not be reasonable to *require* everyone affected to accept. This is because not all moral resolutions can be justifiably enforced; only moral resolutions of severe interpersonal conflicts of interest can and *should* be justifiably enforced. Furthermore, the reason moral resolutions of severe interpersonal conflicts of interest should be enforced is that if the parties are simply asked but not required to abide by a moral resolution in such cases of conflict, then it is likely that the stronger party will violate the resolution and that would be unreasonable to ask or require the weaker party to accept.

When we apply the conflict resolution principle to our example of severe conflict between the rich and the poor, there are three possible moral resolutions:

I. A moral resolution that would require the rich to sacrifice the liberty not to be interfered with when using their surplus goods and resources for luxury purposes so that the poor can have the liberty not to be interfered with when taking from the surplus resources of the rich what is necessary to meet their basic needs.

II. A moral resolution that would require the poor to sacrifice the liberty not to be interfered with when taking from the surplus goods and resources of the rich what is necessary to meet their basic needs so that the rich can have the liberty not to be interfered with when using their surplus resources for luxury purposes.

III. A moral resolution that would require the rich and the poor to accept the results of a power struggle in which both the rich and the poor are at liberty to appropriate and use the surplus goods and resources of the rich.

Applying our previous discussion of the "ought" implies "can" principle to these three possible moral resolutions, it is clear that 1a (it would be unreasonable to ask or require the poor. . .) rules out II, but 2a (it would not be unreasonable to ask and require the rich . . .) does not rule out I. But what about III? Some libertarians have contended that III is the proper resolution of severe conflicts of interest between the rich and the poor.[8] But a resolution, like III, that sanctions the results of a power struggle between the rich and the poor, is a resolution that, by and large, favors the rich over the poor. So all things considered, it would be no more reasonable to require the poor to accept III than it would be to require them to accept II. This means that only I satisfies the conflict resolution principle

by being a resolution that is reasonable to require everyone affected to accept. Consequently, if we assume that, however else we specify the requirements of morality, they cannot violate the "ought" implies "can" principle or the conflict resolution principle, it follows that, despite what libertarians claim, the basic right to liberty endorsed by them, as determined by a weighing of the relevant competing liberties according to these two principles, actually favors the liberty of the poor over the liberty of the rich.[9]

Yet couldn't libertarians object to this conclusion, claiming that it would be unreasonable to require the rich to sacrifice the liberty to meet some of their luxury needs so that the poor could have the liberty to meet their basic needs? As has been pointed out, libertarians don't usually see the situation as a conflict of liberties. But suppose they did. How plausible would such an objection be? Not very plausible at all.

Consider: What are libertarians going to say about the poor? Isn't it clearly unreasonable to require the poor to sacrifice the liberty to meet their basic needs so that the rich can have the liberty to meet their luxury needs? Isn't it clearly unreasonable to require the poor to sit back and starve to death? If it is, then there is no resolution of this conflict that would be reasonable to require both the rich and the poor to accept. But that would mean that libertarians could not be putting forth a moral resolution, because according to the conflict resolution principle, in cases of severe conflict of interest, a moral resolution resolves conflicts of interest in ways that it would be reasonable to require everyone affected to accept. Therefore, as long as libertarians think of themselves as putting forth a moral resolution for cases of severe conflict of interest, they cannot allow that it would be unreasonable *both* to require the rich to sacrifice the liberty to meet some of their luxury needs in order to benefit the poor and to require the poor to sacrifice the liberty to meet their basic needs in order to benefit the rich. But I submit that if one of these requirements is to be judged reasonable, then, by any neutral assessment, it must be the requirement that the rich sacrifice the liberty to meet some of their luxury needs so that the poor can have the liberty to meet their basic needs. There is no other plausible resolution if libertarians intend to be putting forth a moral resolution.

It should also be noted that this case for restricting the liberty of the rich depends upon the willingness of the poor to take advantage of whatever opportunities are available to them to engage in mutually beneficial work, so that failure of the poor to take advantage of such opportunities would normally cancel or at least significantly reduce the obligation of the rich to restrict their own liberty for the benefit of the poor.[10] In addition, the poor would be required to return the equivalent of any surplus possessions they have taken from the rich once they are able to do so and still satisfy their basic needs. Nor would the poor be required to keep the liberty to which they are entitled. They could give up part of it, or all of it, or risk losing it on the chance of gaining a greater share of liberties or other social goods.[11] Consequently, the case for restricting the liberty of the rich for the benefit of the poor is neither unconditional nor inalienable.

Of course, there will be cases in which the poor fail to satisfy their basic needs, not because of any direct restriction of liberty on the part of the rich but because the poor are in such dire need that they are unable even to attempt to take from the rich what they require to meet their basic needs. In such cases, the rich would not be performing any act of commission that would prevent the poor from taking what they require. Yet, even in such cases, the rich would normally be performing acts of commission that would prevent other persons from taking part of the rich's own surplus possessions and using it to aid the poor. And when assessed from a moral point of view, restricting the liberty of these allies or agents of the poor would not be morally justified for the very same reason that restricting the liberty of the poor to meet their own basic needs would not be morally justified: It would not be reasonable to require all of those affected to accept such a restriction of liberty.

In brief, I have argued that a libertarian ideal of liberty can be seen to support a right to welfare through an application of the "ought" implies "can" principle and the conflict resolution principle to conflicts of liberty between the rich and the poor. In this interpretation of libertarianism, these principles support a right to welfare by favoring the liberty of the poor over the liberty of the rich. In another interpretation of libertarianism (developed elsewhere), these principles support this right to welfare by favoring a conditional right to property over an unconditional right to property.[12] In either interpretation, what is crucial to the derivation of this right is the claim that it would be unreasonable to require the poor to deny their basic needs and accept anything

less than this right to welfare as the condition for their willing cooperation.

Now it might be objected that the right to welfare that this argument establishes from libertarian premises is not the same as the right to welfare endorsed by socialists. This is correct. We could mark this difference by referring to the right that this argument establishes as "a negative welfare right" and by referring to the right endorsed by socialists as "a positive welfare right." The significance of this difference is that a person's negative welfare right can be violated only when other people through acts of commission interfere with its exercise, whereas a person's positive welfare right can be violated not only by such acts of commission but by acts of omission as well. Nonetheless, this difference will have little practical import. For in recognizing the legitimacy of negative welfare rights, libertarians will come to see that virtually any use of their surplus possessions is likely to violate the negative welfare rights of the poor by preventing the poor from rightfully appropriating (some part of) their surplus goods and resources. So in order to ensure that they will not be engaging in such wrongful actions, it will be incumbent on them to set up institutions guaranteeing adequate positive welfare rights for the poor. Only then will they be able to legitimately use any remaining surplus possessions to meet their own nonbasic needs. Furthermore, in the absence of adequate positive welfare rights, the poor, either acting by themselves or through their allies or agents, would have some discretion in determining when and how to exercise their negative welfare rights.[13] In order not to be subject to that discretion, libertarians will tend to favor the only morally legitimate way of preventing the exercise of such rights: They will set up institutions guaranteeing adequate positive welfare rights that will then take precedence over the exercise of negative welfare rights. For these reasons, recognizing the negative welfare rights of the poor will ultimately lead libertarians to endorse the same sort of welfare institutions favored by socialists.

II

Now it is possible that libertarians convinced to some extent by the previous argument might want to accept a right to welfare but then deny that this would lead to anything like a socialist state. After all, the fundamental rights recognized by libertarians are universal rights, that is, rights possessed by all people, not just those who live in certain places or at certain times. Of course, to claim that these rights are universal rights does not mean that they are universally recognized. Obviously, the fundamental rights that flow from the libertarian ideal have not been universally recognized. Rather, to claim that they are universal rights, despite their spotty recognition, implies only that they ought to be recognized at all times and places by people who have or could have had good reasons to recognize these rights, whether or not they actually did or do so. Nor need these universal rights be unconditional. This is particularly true in the case of the right to welfare, which, I have argued, is conditional on people doing all that they legitimately can to provide for themselves. In addition, this right is conditional on there being sufficient goods and resources available so that everyone's welfare needs can be met. So where people do not do all that they can to provide for themselves or where there are not sufficient goods and resources available, people simply do not have a right to welfare. Still, libertarians might grant that there are universal rights, even a right to welfare, that can be supported by the libertarian ideal of liberty but still deny that such rights lead to a socialist rather than a welfare state. But to see why this is not the case, consider what would be required to recognize a universal right to welfare.

Consider that at present there is probably a sufficient worldwide supply of goods and resources to meet the normal costs of satisfying the basic nutritional needs of all existing persons. According to former U.S. Secretary of Agriculture, Bob Bergland:

> For the past 30 years, if the available world food supply had been evenly divided and distributed, each person would have received more than the minimum number of calories.[14]

Other authorities have made similar assessments of the available world food supply.

Needless to say, the adoption of a policy of supporting a right to welfare for all existing persons would necessitate significant changes, especially in developed countries. For example, the large percentage of the U.S. population whose food consumption clearly exceeds even an adequately adjusted poverty index would have to substantially alter their eating habits. In particular, they would have to reduce their consumption of beef and pork in order to make more grain available for direct human consumption. (Presently the amount of grain fed to American livestock is as much as all the people of China and India eat in a year.) Thus, at least the satisfaction of some of the nonbasic needs of the more advantaged in developed countries would have to be foregone if the basic nutritional needs of all existing persons in developing and underdeveloped countries are to be met. Of course, meeting the long-term basic nutritional needs of these societies will require other kinds of aid including appropriate technology and training and the removal of trade barriers favoring developed societies.[15] Furthermore, to raise the standard of living in developing and underdeveloped countries will require substantial increases in the consumption of energy and other resources. But such an increase would have to be matched by a substantial decrease in the consumption of these goods in developed countries; otherwise, global ecological disaster would result from increased global warming, ozone depletion, and acid rain, lowering virtually everyone's standard of living.[16]

In addition, once the basic nutritional needs of future generations are also taken into account, the satisfaction of the nonbasic needs of the more advantaged in developed countries would have to be further restricted in order to preserve the fertility of cropland and other food-related natural resources for the use of future generations. Obviously, the only assured way to guarantee the energy and resources necessary for the satisfaction of the basic needs of future generations is to set aside resources that would otherwise be used to satisfy the nonbasic needs of existing generations.

Once basic needs other than nutritional needs are taken into account as well, still further restrictions would be required. For example, it has been estimated that presently a North American uses fifty times more goods and resources than a person living in India. This means that in terms of resource consumption the North American continent's population is the equivalent of 12.5 billion Indians. So unless we assume that basic goods and resources—such as arable land, iron, coal, oil, and so forth—are in unlimited supply, then this unequal consumption would have to be radically altered if the basic needs of distant peoples and future generations are to be met. Accordingly, recognizing a universal right to welfare applicable both to distant peoples and to future generations would lead to an equal sharing of goods and resources over place and time. In short, socialist equality is the consequence of recognizing a universal libertarian right to welfare.

In brief, I have argued that when a libertarian ideal of liberty is correctly interpreted, it leads to a universal right to welfare, and further that the recognition of this universal right to welfare leads to the equality in the distribution of goods and resources that is characteristic of a socialist state. Of course, the libertarian ideal, unlike the socialist ideal, does not directly pursue the goal of (substantive) equality.[17] Nevertheless, I contend that the practical effect of both ideals is much the same.

◇

Endnotes

I would like to thank Joan Callahan, David Duquette, Joseph Ellin, Sidney Geldin, Carol Gould, Larry May, Jan Narveson, David Phillips, Jonathan Schonsheck, and Carl Wellman for helpful comments on earlier versions of this paper.

1.   See John Hospers, *Libertarianism* (Los Angeles: Nash Press, 1971).

2.   Basic needs, if not satisfied, lead to significant lacks or deficiencies with respect to a standard of mental and physical well-being. Thus, a person's needs for food, shelter, medical care, protection, companionship, and self-development are, at least in part, needs of this sort. For a discussion of basic needs, see *How to Make People Just* (Totowa: Rowman and Littlefield, 1988), pp. 45–48.

3.   It is not being assumed here that the surplus possessions of the rich are either justifiable or unjustifiably possessed by the rich. Moreover, according to the libertarians, it is an assessment of the liberties involved that determines whether the possession is justifiable or not.

4.   There is another interpretation of libertarianism according to which a particular set of rights are basic and liberty is interpreted as the absence of interference with these rights. But, as I have argued elsewhere, the same sort of argument works against both forms of libertarianism. For this other interpretation, see "From Liberty to Welfare," *Ethics* (1994), and my *How to Make People Just,* Chapter 5.

5.   See John Hospers, *Libertarianism* (Los Angeles: Nash Publishing, 1971), Chapter 7, and Tibor Machan, *Human Rights and Human Liberties* (Chicago: Nelson-Hall, 1975), pp. 231ff.

6.   See James P. Sterba, "Is There a Rationale for Punishment?" *American Journal of Jurisprudence* 29 (1984), 29–43.

7.   By the liberty of the rich to meet their luxury needs I continue to mean the liberty of the rich not to be interfered with when using their surplus possessions for luxury purposes. Similarly, by the liberty of the poor to meet their basic needs I continue to mean the liberty of the poor not to be interfered with when taking what they require to meet their basic needs from the surplus possessions of the rich.

8.   See, for example, Eric Mack, "Individualism, Rights and the Open Society," *The Libertarian Alternative,* edited by Tibor Machan (Chicago: Nelson-Hall, 1974).

9.   Since the conflict resolution principle is the contrapositive of the "ought" implies "can" principle, whatever logically follows from the one principle logically follows from the other; nevertheless, by first appealing to the one principle and then the other, as I have here, I maintain that the conclusions that I derive can be seen to follow more clearly.

10.   The employment opportunities offered to the poor must be honorable and supportive of self-respect. To do otherwise would be to offer the poor the opportunity to meet some of their basic needs at the cost of denying some of their other basic needs.

11.   The poor cannot, however, give up the liberty to which their children are entitled.

12.   For this other interpretation, see note #4.

13.   When the poor are acting collectively in conjunction with their agents and allies to exercise their negative welfare rights, they will want, in turn, to institute adequate positive welfare rights to secure a proper distribution of the goods and resources they are acquiring.

14.   Bob Bergland, "Attacking the Problem of World Hunger," *The National Forum* (1979), Vol. 69, No. 2, p. 4.

15.   Henry Shue, *Basic Rights* (Princeton University Press, 1980), Chapter 7.

16.   For a discussion of these causal connections, see Cheryl Silver, *One Earth One Future* (Washington, D.C.: National Academy Press, 1990); Bill McKibben, *The End of Nature* (New York: Anchor Books, 1989); Jeremy Leggett, ed., *Global Warming* (New York: Oxford University Press, 1990); Lester Brown, ed., *The World Watch Reader* (New York: Nelson, 1991).

17.   Here I agree with Narveson that there are formal notions of equality, like equality before the law and equality of basic rights, that libertarians will frequently aim to achieve.

5. Wyman, Commissioner of New York Department of Social Services v. James

SUPREME COURT OF THE UNITED STATES

The issue before the Supreme Court of the United States was whether the Fourth Amendment prohibition of unreasonable searches applies to visits by welfare caseworkers to recipients of Aid to Families with Dependent Children. The majority of the Court held that the Fourth Amendment does not apply in this case because the visitation is not forced or compelled, and even if it were, the visitation serves the state's overriding interest in the welfare of dependent children. Dissenting Justices Douglas and Marshall argued that the Fourth Amendment prohibition does apply because the visitation is forced and compelled (although not normally by a threat of a criminal penalty) and because there are other ways of protecting the state's interest in this case. Justices Douglas and Marshall also argued that the decision of the majority is inconsistent with the Supreme Court's rulings with respect to the allocation of benefits in other cases.

Mr. Justice *Blackmun* delivered the opinion of the Court.

This appeal presents the issue whether a beneficiary of the program for Aid to Families with Dependent Children (AFDC) may refuse a home visit by the caseworker without risking the termination of benefits.

The New York State and City social services commissioners appeal from a judgment and decree of a divided three-judge District Court. . . .

The District Court majority held that a mother receiving AFDC relief may refuse, without forfeiting her right to that relief, the periodic home visit which the cited New York statutes and regulations prescribe as a condition for the continuance of assistance under the program. The beneficiary's thesis, and that of the District Court majority, is that home visitation is a search and, when not consented to or when not supported by a warrant based on probable cause, violates the beneficiary's Fourth and Fourteenth Amendment rights. . . .

Plaintiff Barbara James is the mother of a son, Maurice, who was born in May 1967. They reside in New York City. Mrs. James first applied for AFDC assistance shortly before Maurice's birth. A caseworker made a visit to her apartment at that time without objection. The assistance was authorized.

Two years later, on May 8, 1969, a caseworker wrote Mrs. James that she would visit her home on May 14. Upon receipt of this advice, Mrs. James telephone the worker that, although she was willing to supply information "reasonable and relevant" to her need for public assistance, any discussion was not to take place at her home. The worker told Mrs. James that she was required by law to visit in her home and that refusal to permit the visit would result in the termination of assistance. Permission was still denied. . . .

A notice of termination [was] issued on June 2.

Thereupon, without seeking a hearing at the state level, Mrs. James, individually and on behalf of Maurice, and purporting to act on behalf of all other persons similarly situated, instituted the present civil rights suit. . . .

When a case involves a home and some type of official intrusion into that home, as this case appears to do, an immediate and natural reaction is one of concern about Fourth Amendment rights and the protection which that Amendment is intended to afford. Its emphasis indeed is upon one of the most precious aspects of personal security in home: "The right of the people to be secure in their persons, houses, papers, and effects. . . ." This Court has characterized that right as "basic to a free society. . . ." And over the years the Court consistently has been most protective of the privacy of the dwelling. . . .

This natural and quite proper protective attitude, however, is not a factor in this case, for the seemingly obvious and simple reason that we are not concerned here with any search by the New York social service agency in the Fourth Amendment meaning of that term. It is true that the governing statute and regulations appear to make mandatory the initial home visit and the subsequent periodic "contacts" (which may include home visits) for the inception and continuance of aid. It is also true that the caseworker's posture in the home visit is perhaps, in a sense, both rehabilitative and investigative. But this latter aspect, we think, is given too broad a character and far more emphasis than it deserves if it is equated with a search in the traditional criminal law context. We note, too, that the visitation in itself is not forced or compelled, and that the beneficiary's denial of permission is not a criminal act. If consent to the visitation is withheld, no visitation takes place. The aid then never begins or merely ceases, as the case may be. There is no entry of the home and there is no search.

If, however, we were to assume that a caseworker's home visit, before or subsequent to the beneficiary's initial qualification for benefits, somehow (perhaps because the average beneficiary might feel she is in no position to refuse consent to the visit), and despite its interview nature, does possess some of the characteristics of a search in the traditional sense, we nevertheless conclude that it does not fall within the Fourth Amendment's proscription. This is because it does not descend to the level of unreasonableness. It is unreasonableness which is the Fourth Amendment's standard.

There are a number of factors that compel us to conclude that the home visit proposed for Mrs. James is not unreasonable.

The public's interest in this particular segment of the area of assistance to the unfortunate is protection and aid for the dependent child whose family requires such aid for that child. . . . The dependent child's needs are paramount, and only with hesitancy would we relegate those needs, in the scale of comparative values, to a position secondary to what the mother claims as her rights.

The agency, with tax funds provided from federal as well as from state sources, is fulfilling a public trust. The State, working through its qualified welfare agency, has appropriate and paramount interest and concern in seeing and assuring that the intended and proper objects of that tax-produced assistance are the ones who benefit from the aid it dispenses. . . .

One who dispenses purely private charity naturally has an interest in and expects to know how his charitable funds are utilized and put to work. The public, when it is the provider, rightly expects the same. . . .

We therefore conclude that the home visitation as structured by the New York statutes and regulations is a reasonable administrative tool; that it serves a valid and proper administrative purpose for the dispensation of the AFDC program; that it is not an unwarranted invasion of personal privacy; and that it violates no right guaranteed by the Fourth Amendment.

Reversed and remanded with directions to enter a judgment of dismissal.

It is so ordered. . . .

Mr. Justice *Douglas*, dissenting. . . .

In 1969 roughly 127 billion dollars were spent by the federal, state, and local governments on "social welfare." To farmers alone almost four billion dollars were paid, in part for not growing certain crops. . . .

Yet almost every beneficiary whether rich or poor, rural or urban, has a "house"—one of the places protected by the Fourth Amendment against "unreasonable searches and seizures." The question in this case is whether receipt of largesse from the government makes the *home* of the beneficiary subject to access by an inspector of the agency of oversight, even though the beneficiary objects to the intrusion and even though the Fourth Amendment's procedure for access to one's *house* or *home* is not followed. The penalty here is not, of course, invasion of the privacy of Barbara James, only her loss of federal or state largesse. That, however, is merely rephrasing the problem. Whatever the semantics, the central question is whether the government by force of its largesse has the power to "buy up" rights guaranteed by the Constitution. But for the assertion of her constitutional right, Barbara James in this case would have received the welfare benefit. . . .

The applicable principle, as stated in *Camara* as "justified by history and by current experience" is that "except in certain carefully defined classes of cases, a search of private property without proper consent is 'unreasonable' unless it has been authorized by a valid search warrant."

In *See* we [decided] that the "businessman, like the occupant of a residence, has a constitutional right to go about his business free from unreasonable official entries upon his private commercial property." There is not the slightest hint in *See* that the Government could condition a business license on the "consent" of the licensee to the administrative searches we held violated the Fourth Amendment. It is a strange jurisprudence indeed which safeguards the businessman at his place of work from the warrantless searches but will not do the same for a mother in her *home*.

Is a search of her home without a warrant made "reasonable" merely because she is dependent on government largesse?

Judge Skelly Wright has stated the problem succinctly:

> Welfare has long been considered the equivalent of charity and its recipients have been subjected to all kinds of dehumanizing experiences in the government's effort to police its welfare payments. In fact, over half a billion dollars are expended annually for administration and policing in connection with the Aid to Families with Dependent Children program. Why such large sums are necessary for administration and policing has never been adequately explained. No such sums are spent policing the government subsidies granted to farmers, airlines, steamship companies, and junk mail dealers, to name but a few. The truth is that in this subsidy area society has simply adopted a double standard, one for aid to business and the farmer and a different one for welfare. (Poverty, Minorities, and Respect for Law, 1970 Duke L. J. 425, 437–438.)

If the welfare recipient was not Barbara James but a prominent, affluent cotton or wheat farmer receiving benefit payments for not growing crops, would not the approach be different? Welfare in aid of dependent children, like social security and unemployment benefits, has an aura of suspicion. There doubtless are frauds in every sector of public welfare whether the recipient be a Barbara James or someone who is prominent or influential. But constitutional rights—here the privacy of the *home*—are obviously not dependent on the poverty or on the affluence of the beneficiary. It is the precincts of the *home* that the Fourth Amendment protects; and their privacy is as important to the lowly as to the mighty.

I would sustain the judgment of the three-judge court in the present case.

Mr. Justice *Marshall*, whom Mr. Justice *Brennan* joins, dissenting.

. . . The record plainly shows . . . that Mrs. James offered to furnish any information that the appellants desired and to be interviewed at any place other than her home. Appellants rejected her offers and terminated her benefits solely on the ground that she refused to permit a home visit. In addition, appellants make no contention that any sort of probable cause exists to suspect appellee of welfare fraud or child abuse.

Simply stated, the issue in this case is whether a state welfare agency can require all recipients of AFDC benefits to submit to warrantless "visitations" of their homes. In answering that question, the majority dodges between constitutional issues to reach a result clearly inconsistent with the decisions of this Court. We are told that there is no such search involved in this case; that even if there were a search, it would not be unreasonable; and that even if this were an unreasonable search, a welfare recipient waives her right to object by accepting benefits. I emphatically disagree with all three conclusions. . . .

. . . In an era of rapidly burgeoning governmental activities and their concomitant inspectors, caseworkers, and researchers, a restriction of the Fourth Amendment to "the traditional criminal law context" tramples the ancient concept that a man's home is his castle. Only last Term, we reaffirmed that this concept has lost none of its vitality. . . .

. . . [I]t is argued that the home visit is justified to protect dependent children from "abuse" and "exploitation." These are heinous crimes, but they are not confined to indigent households. Would the majority sanction, in the absence of probable cause, compulsory visits to all American homes for the purpose of discovering child abuse? Or is this Court prepared to hold as a matter of constitutional law that a mother, merely because she is poor, is substantially more likely to injure or exploit her children? Such a categorical approach to an entire class of citizens would be dangerously at odds with the tenets of our democracy. . . .

Although the Court does not agree with my conclusion that the home visit is an unreasonable search, its opinion suggests that even if the visit were unreasonable, appellee has somehow waived her right to object. Surely the majority cannot believe that valid Fourth Amendment consent can be given under the threat of the loss of one's sole means of support. . . .

In deciding that the homes of AFDC recipients are not entitled to protection from warrantless searches by welfare caseworkers, the Court declines to follow prior case law and employs a rationale that, if applied to the claims of all citizens, would threaten the validity of the Fourth Amendment.... Perhaps the majority has explained why a commercial warehouse deserves more protection than does this poor woman's home. I am not convinced; and, therefore, I must respectfully dissent.

6. *Plyler v. Doe*

SUPREME COURT OF THE UNITED STATES

The issue before the Supreme Court was whether a Texas statute that withholds from local school districts any state funds for the education of children who were not "legally admitted" into the United States and that authorizes local school districts to deny enrollment to such children violates the Equal Protection Clause of the Fourteenth Amendment. Justice Brennan, delivering the opinion of the Court, argued that the Texas statute did violate the Equal Protection Clause. He contended that although public education is not a right granted to individuals by the Constitution (Marshall dissenting), given the "pivotal role of education in sustaining our political and cultural heritage" and the economic benefits that accrue to Texas from the presence of illegal aliens, petitioners had failed to establish a legitimate state interest in denying an education to illegal aliens. In dissent, Chief Justice Burger with whom Justices White, Rehnquist, and O'Connor joined, argued that although the Texas statute is unwise and unsound, it is not unconstitutional. Burger contended that although illegal aliens are included within the category of persons protected by the Equal Protection Clause, the Texas statute does bear "a relation to a legitimate state purpose," especially in view of the fact that the federal government sees fit to exclude illegal aliens from numerous social welfare programs.

... In May 1975, the Texas Legislature revised its education laws to withhold from local school districts any state funds for the education of children who were not "legally admitted" into the United States. The 1975 revision also authorized local school districts to deny enrollment in their public schools to children not "legally admitted" to the country.... These cases involve constitutional challenges to those provisions.

[*Plyler v. Doe*] is a class action, filed in the United States District Court for the Eastern District of Texas in September 1977, on behalf of certain school-age children of Mexican origin residing in Smith County, Tex., who could not establish that they had been legally admitted into the United States. The action complained of the exclusion of plaintiff children from the public schools of the Tyler Independent School District. The Superintendent and members of the Board of Trustees of the School District were named as defendants; the State of Texas intervened as a party-defendant. After certifying a class consisting of all undocumented school-age children of Mexican origin residing within the School District, the District Court preliminarily enjoined defendants from denying a free education to members of the plaintiff class. In December 1977, the court conducted an extensive hearing on plaintiffs' motion for permanent injunctive relief....

The District Court held that illegal aliens were entitled to the protection of the Equal Protection Clause of the Fourteenth Amendment, and that [this section] violated that Clause....

The Court of Appeals for the Fifth Circuit upheld the District Court's injunction....

The Fourteenth Amendment provides that "[n]o State shall ... deprive any person of life, liberty, or property, without due process of law; nor deny to *any person within its jurisdiction* the equal protection of the laws.". . . [Emphasis added.] Appellants argue at the outset that undocumented aliens, because of their immigration status, are not "persons within the jurisdiction" of the State of Texas, and that they therefore have no right to the equal protection of Texas Law. We reject this argument. . . .

. . . The Equal Protection Clause was intended to work nothing less than the abolition of all caste-based and invidious class-based legislation. That objective is fundamentally at odds with the power the State asserts here to classify persons subject to its laws as nonetheless excepted from its protection.

Although the congressional debate concerning . . . the Fourteenth Amendment was limited, that debate clearly confirms the understanding that the phrase "within its jurisdiction" was intended in a broad sense to offer the guarantee of equal protection to all within a State's boundaries, and to all upon whom the State would impose the obligations of its laws. Indeed, it appears from those debates that Congress, by using the phrase "person within its jurisdiction," sought expressly to ensure that the equal protection of the laws was provided to the alien population. Representative Bingham reported to the House the draft resolution of the Joint Committee of Fifteen on Reconstruction (H.R. 63) that was to become the Fourteenth Amendment. . . . Two days later, Bingham posed the following question in support of the resolution:

> Is it not essential to the unity of the people that the citizens of each State shall be entitled to all the privileges and immunities of citizens in the several States? Is it not essential to the unity of the Government and the unity of the people that all persons, *whether citizens or strangers, within this land,* shall have equal protection in every State in this Union in the rights of life and liberty and property?

. . . Our conclusion that the illegal aliens who are plaintiffs in these cases may claim the benefit of the Fourteenth Amendment's guarantee of equal protection only begins the inquiry. The more difficult question is whether the Equal Protection Clause has been violated by the refusal of the State of Texas to reimburse local school boards for the education of children who cannot demonstrate that their presence within the United States is lawful, or by the imposition by those school boards of the burden of tuition on those children. It is to this question that we now turn. . . .

. . . In applying the Equal Protection Clause to most forms of state action, we thus seek only the assurance that the classification at issue bears some fair relationship to a legitimate public purpose.

Of course, undocumented status is not irrelevant to any proper legislative goal. Nor is undocumented status an absolutely immutable characteristic since it is the product of conscious, indeed unlawful, action. But [this statute] is directed against children, and imposes its discriminatory burden on the basis of a legal characteristic over which children can have little control. It is thus difficult to conceive of a rational justification for penalizing these children for their presence within the United States. Yet that appears to be precisely the effect of [this statute].

Public education is not a "right" granted to individuals by the Constitution. *San Antonio Independent School Dist. v. Rodriguez* . . . (1973). But neither is it merely some governmental "benefit" indistinguishable from other forms of social welfare legislation. Both the importance of education in maintaining our basic institutions, and the lasting impact of its deprivation on the life of the child, mark the distinction. The "American people have always regarded education and [the] acquisition of knowledge as matters of supreme importance." *Meyer v. Nebraska* . . . (1923). We have recognized "the public schools as a most vital civic institution for the preservation of a democratic system of government," *Abington School District v. Schempp* . . . (1963) . . . and as the primary vehicle for transmitting "the values on which our society rests." *Ambach v. Norwick* . . . (1979). "[A]s . . . pointed out early in our history, . . . some degree of education is necessary to prepare citizens to participate effectively and intelligently in our open political system if we are to preserve freedom and independence." *Wisconsin v. Yoder* . . . (1972). And these historic "perceptions of the public schools as inculcating fundamental values necessary to the maintenance of a democratic political system have been confirmed by the observations of social scientists." *Ambach v. Norwick* . . . In addition, education provides the basic tools by which individuals might lead economically productive lives to the benefit of us all. In sum, education has a fundamental role in maintaining the fabric of our society. We cannot ignore the significant social costs borne by our Nation when select groups are denied the means to absorb the values and skills upon which our social order rests.

In addition to the pivotal role of education in sustaining our political and cultural heritage, denial of education to some isolated group of children poses an affront to one of the goals of the Equal Protection Clause: the abolition of governmental barriers presenting unreasonable obstacles to advancement on the basis of individual merit. Paradoxically, by depriving the children of any disfavored group of an education, we foreclose the means by which that group might raise the level of esteem in which it is held by the majority. But more directly, "education prepares individuals to be self-reliant and self-sufficient participants in society." *Wisconsin v. Yoder*. . . . Illiteracy is an enduring disability. The inability to read and write will handicap the individual deprived of a basic education each and every day of his life. The inestimable toll of that deprivation on the social, economic, intellectual, and psychological well-being of the individual, and the obstacle it poses to individual achievement, make it most difficult to reconcile the cost or the principle of a status-based denial of basic education with the framework of equality embodied in the Equal Protection Clause. What we said 28 year ago in *Brown v. Board of Education*, . . . (1954), still holds true:

> Today, education is perhaps the most important function of state and local governments. Compulsory school attendance laws and the great expenditures for education both demonstrate our recognition of the importance of education to our democratic society. It is required in the performance of our most basic public responsibilities, even service in the armed forces. It is the very foundation of good citizenship. Today it is a principal instrument in awakening the child to cultural values, in preparing him for later professional training, and in helping him to adjust normally to his environment. In these days, it is doubtful that any child may reasonably be expected to succeed in life if he is denied the opportunity of an education. Such an opportunity, where the state has undertaken to provide it, is a right which must be made available to all on equal terms. . . .

. . . [A]ppellants appear to suggest that the State may seek to protect itself from an influx of illegal immigrants. While a State might have an interest in mitigating the potentially harsh economic effects of sudden shifts in population, [this statute] hardly offers an effective method of dealing with an urgent demographic or economic problem. There is no evidence in the record suggesting that illegal entrants impose any significant burden on the State's economy. To the contrary, the available evidence suggests that illegal aliens underutilize public services, while contributing their labor to the local economy and tax money to the state fisc. . . . The dominant incentive for illegal entry into the State of Texas is the availability of employment; few if any illegal immigrants come to this country, or presumably to the State of Texas, in order to avail themselves of a free education. Thus, even making the doubtful assumption that the net impact of illegal aliens on the economy of the State is negative, we think it clear that "[c]harging tuition to undocumented children constitutes a ludicrously ineffectual attempt to stem the tide of illegal immigration," at least when compared with the alternative of prohibiting the employment of illegal aliens. . . .

Accordingly, the judgment of the Court of Appeals in each of these cases is

Affirmed.

Justice *Marshall*, concurring.

While I join the Court's opinion, I do so without in any way retreating from my opinion in *San Antonio Independent School District v. Rodriguez*. . . . I continue to believe that an individual's interest in education is fundamental, and that this view is amply supported "by the unique status accorded public education by our society, and by the close relationship between education and some of our most basic constitutional values." . . . Furthermore, I believe that the facts of these cases demonstrate the wisdom of rejecting a rigidified approach to equal protection analysis, and of employing an approach that allows for varying levels of scrutiny depending upon "the constitutional and societal importance of the interest adversely affected and the recognized invidiousness of the basis upon which the particular classification is drawn." . . . It continues to be my view that a class-based denial of public education is utterly incompatible with the Equal Protection Clause of the Fourteenth Amendment.

Justice *Blackmun*, concurring.

I join the opinion and judgment of the Court.

Like Justice Powell, I believe that the children involved in this litigation "should not be left on the streets uneducated." . . . I write separately, however, because in my view the nature of the interest at stake is crucial to the proper resolution of these cases.

The "fundamental rights" aspect of the Court's equal protection analysis—the now-familiar concept that governmental classifications bearing on certain interests must be closely scrutinized—has been the subject of some controversy. . . .

[This controversy], combined with doubts about the judiciary's ability to make fine distinctions in assessing the effects of complex social policies, led the Court in *Rodriguez* to articulate a firm rule: Fundamental rights are those that "explicitly or implicitly [are] guaranteed by the Constitution." . . . It therefore squarely rejected the notion that "an ad hoc determination as to the social or economic importance" of a given interest is relevant to the level of scrutiny accorded classification involving that interest, . . . and made clear that "[i]t is not the province of this Court to create substantive constitutional rights in the name of guaranteeing equal protection of the laws." . . .

I joined Justice Powell's opinion for the Court in *Rodriguez*, and I continue to believe that it provides the appropriate model for resolving most equal protection disputes. Classifications infringing substantive constitutional rights necessarily will be invalid, if not by force of the Equal Protection Clause, then through operation of other provisions of the Constitution. Conversely, classifications bearing on nonconstitutional interests—even those involving "the most basic economic needs of impoverished human beings" . . . —generally are not subject to special treatment under the Equal Protection Clause, because they are not distinguishable in any relevant way from other regulations in "the area of economics and social welfare."

With all this said, however, I believe the Court's experience has demonstrated that the *Rodriguez* formulation does not settle every issue of "fundamental rights" arising under the Equal Protection Clause. Only a pedant would insist that there are *no* meaningful distinctions among the multitude of social and political interests regulated by the States, and *Rodriguez* does not stand for quite so absolute a proposition. To the contrary, *Rodriguez* implicitly acknowledged that certain interests, though not constitutionally guaranteed, must be accorded a special place in equal protection analysis. Thus, the Court's decisions long have accorded strict scrutiny to classifications bearing on the right to vote in state elections, and *Rodriguez* confirmed the "constitutional underpinnings of the right to equal treatment in the voting process." . . . Yet "the right to vote, *per se,* is not a constitutionally protected right." . . . Instead, regulation of the electoral process receives unusual scrutiny because "the right to exercise the franchise in a free and unimpaired manner is preservative of other basic civil and political rights." . . . In other words, the right to vote is accorded extraordinary treatment because it is, in equal protection terms, an extraordinary right: A citizen cannot hope to achieve any meaningful degree of individual political equality if granted an inferior right of participation in the political process. Those denied the vote are relegated, by state fiat, in a most basic way to second-class status. . . .

In my view, when the State provides an education to some and denies it to others, it immediately and inevitably creates class distinctions of a type fundamentally inconsistent with those purposes, mentioned above, of the Equal Protection Clause. Children denied an education are placed at a permanent and insurmountable competitive disadvantage, for an uneducated child is denied even the opportunity to achieve. And when those children are members of an identifiable group, that group—through the State's action—will have been converted into a discrete underclass. Other benefits provided by the State, such as housing and public assistance, are of course important; to an individual in immediate need, they may be more desirable than the right to be educated. But classifications involving the complete denial of education are in a sense unique, for they strike at the heart of equal protection values by involving the State in the creation of permanent class distinctions. . . . In a sense, then, denial of an education is the analogue of denial of the right to vote: The former relegates the individual to second-class social status; the latter places him at a permanent political disadvantage.

This conclusion is fully consistent with *Rodriguez*. The Court there reserved judgment on the constitutionality of a state system that "occasioned an absolute denial of educational opportunities to any of its children," noting that "no charge fairly could be made that the system . . . fails to provide each child with an opportunity to acquire . . . basic minimal skills." . . . And it cautioned that in a case "involv[ing] the most persistent and difficult questions of educational policy, . . . [the] Court's lack of specialized knowledge and experience counsels against premature interference with the informed judgments made at the state and local levels." . . . Thus *Rodriguez* held, and the Court now reaffirms, that "a State need not justify by compelling necessity every variation in the manner in which education is provided to its population." . . . Similarly, it is undeniable that education is not a "fundamental right" in the sense that it is constitutionally guaranteed. Here, however, the State has undertaken to provide an education to most of the children residing within its borders. And, in contrast to the situation in *Rodriguez*, it does not take an advanced degree to predict the effects of a complete denial of education upon those children targeted by the State's classification. In such circumstances, the voting decisions suggest that the State must offer something more than a rational basis for its classification. . . .

Chief Justice *Burger*, with whom Justice *White*, Justice *Rehnquist*, and Justice *O'Connor* join, dissenting.

Were it our business to set the Nation's social policy, I would agree without hesitation that it is senseless for an enlightened society to deprive any children—including illegal aliens—of an elementary education. I fully agree that it would be folly—and wrong—to tolerate creation of a segment of society made of illiterate persons, many having a limited or no command of our language. However, the Constitution does not constitute us as "Platonic Guardians" nor does it vest in this Court the authority to strike down laws because they do not meet our standards of desirable social policy, "wisdom," or "common sense." . . . We trespass on the assigned function of the political branches under our structure of limited and separated powers when we assume a policy-making role as the Court does today.

The Court makes no attempt to disguise that it is acting to make up for Congress's lack of "effective leadership" in dealing with the serious national problems caused by the influx of uncountable millions of illegal aliens across our borders. . . . The failure of enforcement of the immigration laws over more than a decade and the inherent difficulty and expense of sealing our vast borders have combined to create a grave socioeconomic dilemma. It is a dilemma that has not yet even been fully assessed, let alone addressed. However, it is not the function of the Judiciary to provide "effective leadership" simply because the political branches of government fail to do so.

The Court's holding today manifests the justly criticized judicial tendency to attempt speedy and wholesale formulation of "remedies" for the failures—or simply the laggard pace—of the political processes of our system of government. The Court employs, and in my view abuses, the Fourteenth Amendment in an effort to become an omnipotent and omniscient problem solver. That the motives for doing so are noble and compassionate does not alter the fact that the Court distorts our constitutional function to make amends for the defaults of others. . . .

The Court acknowledges that, except in those cases when state classifications disadvantage a "suspect class" or impinge upon a "fundamental right," the Equal Protection Clause permits a state "substantial latitude" in distinguishing between different groups of persons. . . . Moreover, the Court expressly—and correctly—rejects any suggestion that illegal aliens are a suspect class, . . . or that education is a fundamental right. . . . Yet by patching together bits and pieces of what might be termed quasi-suspect-class and quasi-fundamental-rights analysis, the Court spins out a theory custom-tailored to the facts of these cases.

In the end, we are told little more than that the level of scrutiny employed to strike down the Texas law applies only when illegal alien children are deprived of a public education. . . . If ever a court was guilty of an unabashedly result-oriented approach, this case is a prime example. . . .

Once it is conceded—as the Court does—that illegal aliens are not a suspect class, and that education is not a fundamental right, our inquiry should focus on and be limited to whether the legislative classification at issue bears a rational relationship to a legitimate state purpose. . . .

It is significant that the Federal Government has seen fit to exclude illegal aliens from numerous social welfare programs, such as the food stamp program, . . . the old-age assistance, and aid to families with dependent children, aid to the blind, aid to the permanently and totally disabled, and supplemental security income programs, . . . the Medicare hospital insurance benefits program, . . . and the

Medicaid hospital insurance benefits for the aged and disabled program. . . . Although these exclusions do not conclusively demonstrate the constitutionality of the State's use of the same classification for comparable purposes, at the very least they tend to support the rationality of excluding illegal alien residents of a state from such programs so as to preserve the state's finite revenues for the benefit of lawful residents. . . .

Denying a free education to illegal alien children is not a choice I would make were I a legislator. Apart from compassionate considerations, the long-range costs of excluding any children from the public schools may well outweigh the costs of educating them. But that is not the issue; the fact that there are sound *policy* arguments against the Texas Legislature's choice does not render that choice an unconstitutional one. . . .

The Constitution does not provide a cure for every social ill, nor does it vest judges with a mandate to try to remedy every social problem. . . . Moreover, when this Court rushes in to remedy what it perceives to be the failings of the political processes, it deprives those processes of an opportunity to function. When the political institutions are not forced to exercise constitutionally allocated powers and responsibilities, those powers, like muscles not used, tend to atrophy. Today's cases, I regret to say, present yet another example of unwarranted judicial action, which in the long run tends to contribute to the weakening of our political processes.

Congress, "vested by the Constitution with the responsibility of protecting our borders and legislating with respect to aliens," . . . bears primary responsibility for addressing the problems occasioned by the millions of illegal aliens flooding across our southern border. Similarly, it is for Congress, and not this Court, to assess the "social costs borne by our Nation when select groups are denied the means to absorb the values and skills upon which our social order rests." . . . While the "specter of a permanent caste" of illegal Mexican residents of the United States is indeed a disturbing one, . . . it is but one segment of a larger problem, which is for the political branches to solve. I find it difficult to believe that Congress would long tolerate such a self-destructive result—that it would fail to deport these illegal alien families or to provide for the education of their children. Yet instead of allowing the political processes to run their course—albeit with some delay—the Court seeks to do Congress's job for it, compensating for congressional inaction. It is not unreasonable to think that this encourages the political branches to pass their problems to the Judiciary.

The solution to this seemingly intractable problem is to defer to the political processes, unpalatable as that may be to some.

Suggestions for Further Reading

Anthologies

Arthur, John, and William Shaw. *Social and Political Philosophy.* Englewood Cliffs: Prentice-Hall, 1992.

Sterba, James P. *Social and Political Philosophy: Classical Western Tests in Feminist and Multicultural Perspectives.* Belmont: Wadsworth Publishing Co., 1994.

———. *Justice: Alternative Political Perspectives.* Belmont: Wadsworth Publishing Co., 3rd ed. 1999.

Basic Concepts

Aristotle. *Nicomachean Ethics.* Translated by Martin Ostwald. Indianapolis: Bobbs-Merrill, 1962.

Plato. *The Republic.* Translated by Francis Cornford. New York: Oxford University Press, 1945.

Pieper, Joseph. *Justice.* London: Faber and Faber, 1957.

Libertarianism

Hospers, John. *Libertarianism.* Los Angeles: Nash Publishing, 1971.

Kelly, David. *A Life of One's Own.* Washington, D.C.: The Cato Institute, 1998.

Machan, Tibor. *Individuals and Their Rights.* LaSalle: Open Court, 1989.

Nozick, Robert. *Anarchy, State and Utopia.* New York: Basic Books, 1974.

Welfare Liberalism

Mill, John Stuart. *On Liberty.* Indianapolis: Bobbs-Merrill Co., 1956.

Rawls, John. *Political Liberalism.* New York: Columbia University Press, 1993.

————. *A Theory of Justice.* Cambridge: Harvard University Press, Revised Edition, 1999.

Singer, Peter. *Practical Ethics.* Cambridge: Cambridge University Press, 1979.

Sterba, James P. *Justice for Here and Now.* New York: Cambridge University Press, 1998.

Socialism

Fisk, Milton. *Ethics and Society: A Marxist Interpretation of Value.* New York: New York University Press, 1980.

Harrington, Michael. *Socialism Past and Future.* New York: Arcade Publishing, 1989.

Howard, Michael. *Self-Management and the Crisis of Socialism.* Lanham, Rowman Littlefield, 2000.

Marx, Karl. *Critique of the Gotha Program.* Edited by C. P. Dutt. New York: International Publishers, 1966.

Schweickart, David. *Against Capitalism.* Cambridge: Cambridge University Press, 1993.

Practical Applications

Friedman, David. *The Machinery of Freedom.* 2nd edition. LaSalle: Open Court, 1989.

Haslett, D. W. *Capitalism with Morality.* Oxford: Clarendon Press, 1994.

Timmons, William. *Public Ethics and Issues.* Belmont: Wadsworth Publishing Co., 1990.

Section II

Near and Distant Peoples

Introduction

Basic Concepts

The moral problem of near and distant peoples has only recently begun to be discussed by professional philosophers. There are many reasons for this neglect, not all of them complimentary to the philosophical profession. Suffice it to say that once it became widely recognized how modern technology could significantly benefit or harm distant peoples, philosophers could no longer ignore the importance of this moral problem.

With respect to this problem, the key question that must be answered first is: Can we meaningfully speak of distant peoples as having rights against us or of our having obligations to them? Few philosophers have thought that the mere fact the people are at a distance from us precludes our having any obligations to them or their having any rights against us. Some philosophers, however, have argued that our ignorance of the specific membership of the class of distant peoples does rule out these moral relationships. Yet this cannot be right, given that in other contexts we recognize obligations to indeterminate classes of people, such as a police officer's obligation to help people in distress or the obligation of food processors not to harm those who consume their products.

What does, however, seem to be a necessary requirement before distant peoples can be said to have rights against us is that we are capable of acting across the distance that separates us. (This is simply an implication of the widely accepted philosophical principle that "ought" implies "can.") As long as this condition is met—as it typically is for people living in most technologically advanced societies—there seems to be no conceptual obstacle to claiming that distant peoples have rights against us or that we have obligations to them. Of course, showing that it is conceptually possible does not yet prove that these rights and obligations actually exist. Such proof requires a substantial moral argument.

It used to be argued that the welfare rights of distant peoples would eventually be met as a byproduct of the continued economic growth of the technologically developed societies of the world. It was believed that the transfer of investment and technology to the less developed societies of the world would eventually, if not make everyone well off, at least satisfy everyone's basic needs. Now we are not so sure. Presently more and more evidence points to the conclusion that without some substantial sacrifice on the part of the technologically developed societies of the world, many of the less developed societies will never be able to provide their members with even the basic necessities for survival. How else are we going to meet the basic needs of the 1.2 billion people who are living today in conditions of absolute poverty without some plausible policy of redistribution? Even those, like Herman Kahn, who argue that an almost utopian world situation will obtain in the distant future, still would have to admit that unless some plausible policy of redistribution is adopted, malnutrition and starvation will continue in the less developed societies for many years to come. Thus, a recognition of the welfare rights of distant peoples would appear to have significant consequences for developed and underdeveloped societies alike.

Of course, there are various senses in which distant peoples can be said to have welfare rights and various moral grounds on which those rights can be justified. First of all, the welfare rights of distant peoples can be understood to be either negative rights or positive rights. A negative right is a right not to be interfered with in some specific manner. For example, a right to liberty is usually understood to be a negative right; it guarantees each person the right not to have her liberty interfered with provided that she does not unjustifiably interfere with the liberty of any other person. On the other hand, a positive right is a right to receive some specific goods or services. Typical positive rights are the right to have a loan repaid and the right to receive one's just earnings. Second, the welfare rights of distant peoples can be understood to be either *in personam* rights or *in rem* rights. *In personam* rights are rights that hold against some specific nameable person or persons, while *in rem* rights hold against everyone who is in a position to abide by the rights in question. A right to liberty is usually understood to be an *in rem* right while the right to have a loan repaid or the right to receive one's just earnings are typical *in personam* rights. Finally, the rights of distant peoples can be understood to be either legal rights, that is, rights that *are enforced* by coercive sanctions, or moral rights, that is, rights that *ought to be enforced* either simply by noncoercive sanctions (for example, verbal condemnations) or by both coercive and noncoercive sanctions. Accordingly, what distinguishes the moral rights of distant peoples from the requirements of supererogation (the nonfulfillment of which is never blameworthy) is that the former but not the latter can be justifiably enforced either by noncoercive or by coercive and noncoercive sanctions.

Of the various moral grounds for justifying the welfare rights of distant peoples, quite possibly the most evident are those that appeal either to a right to life or a right to fair treatment. Libertarians interpret a person's right to life as a negative right. Welfare liberals and socialists interpret it as a positive right.

Thus, suppose we interpret a person's right to life as a positive right. So understood, the person's right to life would most plausibly be interpreted as a right to receive those goods and resources that are necessary for satisfying her basic needs. For a person's basic needs are those which must be satisfied in order not to seriously endanger her health or sanity. Thus, receiving the goods and resources that are necessary for satisfying her basic needs would preserve a person's life in the fullest sense. And if a person's positive right to life is to be universal in the sense that it is possessed by every person (as the right to life is generally understood to be) then it must be an *in rem* right. This is because an *in rem* right, unlike an *in personam* right, does not require for its possession the assumption by other persons of any special roles or contractual obligations. Interpreted as a positive *in rem* right, therefore, a person's right to life would clearly justify the welfare rights of distant peoples to have their basic needs satisfied.

Suppose, on the other hand, that we interpret a person's right to life as a negative right. Here again, if the right is to be universal in the sense that it is possessed by all persons then it must also be an *in rem* right. So understood, the right would require that everyone who is in a position to do so not interfere in certain ways with a person's attempts to meet her basic needs.

But what sort of noninterference would this right to life justify? If one's basic needs have not been met, would a person's right to life require that others not interfere with her taking the goods she needs from the surplus possessions of those who already have satisfied their own basic needs? As it is standardly interpreted, a person's negative right to life would not require such noninterference. Instead, a person's negative right to life is usually understood to be limited in such circumstances by the property rights of those who have more than enough to satisfy their own basic needs. Moreover, those who claim property rights to such surplus goods and resources are usually in a position effectively to prohibit those in need from taking what they require. For surely most underdeveloped nations of the world would be able to sponsor expeditions to the American Midwest or the Australian plains for the purpose of collecting the grain necessary to satisfy the basic needs of their citizens if they were not effectively prohibited from doing so at almost every stage of the enterprise.

But are persons with such surplus goods and resources normally justified in so prohibiting others from satisfying their basic needs? Admittedly, such persons may have contributed greatly to the value of the surplus goods and resources they possess, but why should that give them power over the life and death of those less fortunate? Even though their contribution may well justify favoring their nonbasic needs over the nonbasic needs of others, how could it justify favoring their nonbasic needs

over the basic needs of others? After all, a person's negative right to life, being an *in rem* right, does not depend on the assumption by other persons of any special roles or contractual obligations. By contrast, property rights that are *in personam* rights require the assumption by other persons of the relevant roles and contractual obligations that constitute a particular system of acquisition and exchange, such as the role of a neighbor and the obligations of a merchant. Consequently, with respect to such property rights, it would seem that a person could not justifiably be kept from acquiring the goods and resources necessary to satisfy her basic needs by the property rights of others to surplus possessions, unless the person herself had voluntarily agreed to be so constrained by those property rights. But obviously few people would voluntarily agree to have such constraints placed upon their ability to acquire the goods and resources necessary to satisfy their basic needs. For most people, their right to acquire the goods and resources necessary to satisfy their basic needs would have priority over any other person's property rights to surplus possessions, or alternatively, they would conceive of property rights such that no one could have property rights to any surplus possessions which were required to satisfy their own basic needs.

Even if some property rights could arise, as *in rem* rights by a Lockean process of mixing one's labor with previously unowned goods and resources, there would still be a need for some sort of a restriction on such appropriations. For if these *in rem* property rights are to be *moral rights* then it must be reasonable for every affected party to accept such rights, since the requirements of morality cannot be contrary to reason. Accordingly, in order to give rise to *in rem* property rights, the appropriation of previously unowned goods and resources cannot justifiably limit anyone's ability to acquire the goods and resources necessary to satisfy her basic needs, unless it would be reasonable for the person voluntarily to agree to be so constrained. But obviously it would not be reasonable for many people, particularly those whose basic needs are not being met, voluntarily to agree to be so constrained by property rights. This means that whether property rights are *in personam* rights and arise by the assumption of the relevant roles and contractual obligations or are *in rem* rights and arise by a Lockean process of mixing one's labor with previously unowned goods and resources, such rights would rarely limit a negative right to life, interpreted as an *in rem* right to noninterference with one's attempts to acquire the goods and resources necessary to satisfy one's basic needs. So interpreted, a negative right to life would clearly justify the welfare rights of distant people.

If we turn to a consideration of a person's right to fair treatment, a similar justification of the welfare rights of distant peoples emerges. To determine the requirements of fair treatment, suppose we employ a decision procedure analogous to the one John Rawls developed in *A Theory of Justice*. Suppose, that is to say, that in deciding upon the requirements of fair treatment, we were to discount the knowledge of which particular interests happen to be our own. Since we obviously know what our particular interests are, we would just not be taking that knowledge into account when selecting the requirements for fair treatment. Rather, in selecting these requirements, we would be reasoning from our knowledge of all the particular interests of everyone who would be affected by our decision but not from our knowledge of which particular interests happen to be our own. In employing this decision procedure, therefore, we (like judges who discount prejudicial information in order to reach fair decisions) would be able to give a fair hearing to every-

one's particular interests. Assuming further that we are well-informed of the particular interests that would be affected by our decision and are fully capable of rationally deliberating with respect to that information, then our deliberations would culminate in a unanimous decision. This is because each of us would be deliberating in a rationally correct manner with respect to the same information and would be using a decision procedure leading to a uniform evaluation of the alternatives. Consequently, each of us would favor the same requirements for fair treatment.

But what requirements would we select by using this decision procedure? Since by using this decision procedure we would not be using our knowledge of which particular interests happen to be our own, we would be quite concerned about the pattern according to which goods and resources would be distributed throughout the world. By using this decision procedure, we would reason as though our particular interests might be those of persons with the largest share of goods and resources as well as those of persons with the smallest share of goods and resources. Consequently, we would neither exclusively favor the interests of persons with the largest share of goods by endorsing an unlimited right to accumulate goods and resources nor exclusively favor the interests of persons with the smallest share of goods and resources by endorsing the highest possible minimum for those who are least advantaged. Rather, we would compromise by endorsing a right to accumulate goods and resources that was limited by the guarantee of a minimum sufficient to provide each person with the goods and resources necessary to satisfy his or her basic needs. It seems clear, therefore, that a right to fair treatment as captured by this Rawlsian decision procedure would also justify the welfare rights of distant people.

So it would seem that the welfare rights of distant peoples can be firmly grounded either in each person's right to life or each person's right to fair treatment. As a result, it would be impossible for one to deny that distant peoples have welfare rights without also denying that each person has a right to life and a right to fair treatment, unless, that is, one drastically reinterprets the significance of a right to life and a right to fair treatment.

Alternative Views

Not surprisingly, most of the solutions to the problem of near and distant peoples that have been proposed are analogous to the solutions we discussed with regard to the problem of the distribution of income and wealth within a society. (See Section I.)

As before, there is a libertarian solution. According to this view, distant peoples have no right to receive aid from persons living in today's affluent societies, but only a right not to be harmed by them. As before, these requirements are said to be derived from a political ideal of liberty. And, as before, we can question whether such an ideal actually supports these requirements.

Garrett Hardin endorses a "no aid" view in his essay (Selection 7). However, Hardin does not support his view on libertarian grounds. Without denying that there is a general obligation to help those in need, Hardin argues that helping those who live in absolute poverty in today's world would not do any good, and *for that reason* is not required. Hardin justifies this view on empirical grounds, claiming that the giving of aid would be ineffective and even counterproductive for controlling population growth.

In some of his earlier work, Peter Singer has challenged the empirical grounds on which Hardin's view rests. Singer claims that Hardin's view accepts the certain evil of unrelieved poverty in underdeveloped countries—for instance, Bangladesh and Somalia—so as to avoid the fu-

ture possibility of still greater poverty in underdeveloped countries together with deteriorating conditions in developed and developing countries. Singer argues, however, that with a serious commitment to aid from developed countries, there is a "fair chance" that underdeveloped countries will bring their population growth under control, thus avoiding the greater evil Hardin fears. Given the likelihood of this result, Singer argues that we have no moral justification for embracing, as Hardin does, the certain evil of unrelieved poverty in underdeveloped countries by denying them aid.

In Selection 8, Singer provides his own solution to the problem of near and distant peoples, which can be characterized as a welfare liberal solution. Singer at some point would want to defend his "pro-aid" view on utilitarian grounds, but here he tries to ground his view on moral judgments most of us would all make about analogous cases of giving or withholding aid. In this fashion, he argues for the conclusion that whatever money we are spending on luxuries, not necessities, should be given away. However, Singer's argument would not succeed in convincing libertarians, because they take the needs of the poor to be imposing only obligations of charity, not justice, on those who are well off. Accordingly, to convince libertarians that the well-off have an obligation in justice to help the poor, we would need a stronger argument than the one Singer has provided—possibly the one Sterba develops in Selection 4, which appeals to the libertarian's own ideal of liberty.

Unlike Singer, Lawrence Blum supports only a "minimal aid" view grounded not on impartiality but beneficence (Selection 9). This view, Blum claims, accounts better for the role that friendships and special relationships have in our lives. In Selection 10, however, James Rachels questions whether the degree to which we tend to favor those special relations who are our children can really be morally justified. Although Rachels does not draw the same distinction between impartiality and beneficence that Blum does, he argues on grounds of what Blum would call beneficence that we have an obligation to provide basic necessities for needy children rather than provide luxuries for our own.

A socialist solution to the problem of near and distant peoples would place considerable stress on the responsibility of developed countries for the situation in underdeveloped countries. Socialists claim that much of the poverty and unemployment found in underdeveloped countries is the result of the disruptive and exploitative influence of developed countries. For example, it is claimed that arms supplied by developed countries enable repressive regimes in underdeveloped countries to remain in power when they would otherwise be overthrown. Under these repressive regimes, small groups of landowners and capitalists are allowed to exploit the resources in underdeveloped countries for export markets in developed countries. As a result, most people in underdeveloped countries are forced off the land that their forebears have farmed for generations and are required to compete for the few, frequently low-paying jobs that have been created to serve the export markets.

Nevertheless, even if socialists are right about the responsibility of developed countries for poverty in underdeveloped countries, it is still a further question whether the socialization of the means of production and the abolition of private property are the only viable moral responses to this situation. It certainly seems possible that some form of restricted private property system that provides for the meeting of everyone's basic needs, justified either on welfare liberal grounds or on libertarian grounds, would serve as well.

Practical Application

There does not seem to be as much of a gap between the "alternative views" and the "practical applications" with respect to the problem of near and distant peoples as there is in the problem of the distribution of wealth and income. This is because most of the discussions of the alternative views have already taken up the question of practical application (e.g., Singer suggests as a practical application a 10 percent tithe on income in developed countries). The merit of Michael Maren's article (Selection 11), which was originally presented to a group of Cornell University graduate students who were preparing to work in international development, is that it raises a significant challenge to foreign aid programs. Maren argues that food relief projects often hurt the very people they are meant to help. He also argues that private volunteer organizations and their employees have a vested interest in keeping Third World countries dependent on aid. In Selection 12, Mary B. Anderson agrees with Maren that humanitarian assistance programs can have negative side effects, but she argues that there are options for delivering aid without those negative side effects.

Nevertheless, whatever solution to the problem of near and distant peoples you favor, you will still not know how goods and resources should ultimately be distributed in society unless you have a solution to the problems of abortion and euthanasia. If abortion is morally justified, perhaps we should be funding abortions so that every woman, rich or poor, can have an abortion if she wants one. And if euthanasia is morally justified, perhaps we should be reallocating resources that are now being used for the purpose of sustaining life. Appropriately, the next section of this book takes up the problem of abortion and euthanasia.

7. Lifeboat Ethics:
The Case against Helping the Poor

GARRETT HARDIN

Garrett Hardin argues that our first obligation is to ourselves and our posterity. For that reason, he contends, it would be foolish for rich nations to share their surplus with poor nations, whether through a World Food Bank, the exporting of technology, or unrestricted immigration. In view of the growing populations and improvident behavior of poor nations, such sharing would do no good—it would only overload the environment and lead to demands for still greater assistance in the future.

Environmentalists use the metaphor of the earth as a "spaceship" in trying to persuade countries, industries, and people to stop wasting and polluting our natural resources. Since we all share life on this planet, they argue, no single person or institution has the right to destroy, waste, or use more than a fair share of its resources.

But does everyone on earth have an equal right to an equal share of its resources? The spaceship metaphor can be dangerous when used by misguided idealists to justify suicidal policies for sharing our resources through uncontrolled immigration and foreign aid. In their enthusiastic but unrealistic generosity, they confuse the ethics of a spaceship with those of a lifeboat.

A true spaceship would have to be under the control of a captain, since no ship could possibly survive if its course were determined by committee. Spaceship Earth certainly has no captain; the United Nations is merely a toothless tiger, with little power to enforce any policy upon its bickering members.

If we divide the world crudely into rich nations and poor nations, two thirds of them are desperately poor, and only one third comparatively rich, with the United States the wealthiest of all. Metaphorically each rich nation can be seen as a lifeboat full of comparatively rich people. In the ocean outside each lifeboat swim the poor of the world, who would like to get in, or at least to share some of the wealth. What should the lifeboat passengers do?

First we must recognize the limited capacity of any lifeboat. For example, a nation's land has a limited capacity to support a population and as the current energy crisis has shown us, in some ways we have already exceeded the carrying capacity of our land.

Adrift in a Moral Sea

So here we sit, say fifty people in our lifeboat. To be generous, let us assume it has room for ten more, making a total capacity of sixty. Suppose the fifty of us in the lifeboat see one hundred others swimming in the water outside, begging for admission to our boat or for handouts. We have several options: We may be tempted to try to live by the Christian ideal of being "our brother's keeper," or by the Marxist ideal of "to each according to his needs." Since the needs of all in the water are the same, and since they can all be seen as "our brothers," we could take them all into our boat, making a total of 150 in a boat designed for sixty. The boat swamps, everyone drowns. Complete justice, complete catastrophe.

From "The Case against Helping the Poor," *Psychology Today* (1974), pp. 38–43, 123–126. Reprinted with permission from *Psychology Today* magazine. Copyright © 1974 Sussex Publishers, Inc. Addendum 1989. Reprinted by permission of the author.

Since the boat has an unused excess capacity of ten more passengers, we could admit just ten more to it. But which ten do we let in? How do we choose? Do we pick the best ten, the neediest ten, "first come, first served"? And what do we say to the ninety we exclude? If we do let an extra ten into our lifeboat, we will have lost our "safety factor," an engineering principle of critical importance. For example, if we don't leave room for excess capacity as a safety factor in our country's agriculture, a new plant disease or a bad change in the weather could have disastrous consequences.

Suppose we decide to preserve our small safety factor and admit no more to the lifeboat. Our survival is then possible, although we shall have to be constantly on guard against boarding parties.

While this last solution clearly offers the only means of our survival, it is morally abhorrent to many people. Some say they feel guilty about their good luck. My reply is simple: "Get out and yield your place to others." This may solve the problem of the guilt-ridden person's conscience, but it does not change the ethics of the lifeboat. The needy person to whom the guilt-ridden person yields his place will not himself feel guilty about his good luck. If he did, he would not climb aboard. The net result of conscience-stricken people giving up their unjustly held seats is the elimination of that sort of conscience from the lifeboat.

This is the basic metaphor within which we must work out our solutions. Let us now enrich the image, step by step, with substantive additions from the real world, a world that must solve real and pressing problems of overpopulation and hunger.

The harsh ethics of the lifeboat become even harsher when we consider the reproductive differences between the rich nations and the poor nations. The people inside the lifeboats are doubling in number every eighty-seven years; those swimming around outside are doubling, on the average, every thirty-five years, more than twice as fast as the rich. And since the world's resources are dwindling, the difference in prosperity between the rich and the poor can only increase.

As of 1973, the United States had a population of 210 million people, who were increasing by 0.8 percent per year. Outside our lifeboat, let us imagine another 210 million people (say the combined populations of Colombia, Ecuador, Venezuela, Morocco, Pakistan, Thailand, and the Philippines), who are increasing at a rate of 3.3 percent per year. Put differently, the doubling time for this aggregate population is twenty-one years, compared to eighty-seven years for the United States.

Multiplying the Rich and the Poor

Now suppose the United States agreed to pool its resources with those seven countries, with everyone receiving an equal share. Initially the ratio of Americans to non-Americans in this model would be one-to-one. But consider what the ratio would be after eighty-seven years, by which time the Americans would have doubled to a population of 420 million. By then, doubling every twenty-one years, the other group would have swollen to 354 billion. Each American would have to share the available resources with more than eight people.

But, one could argue, this discussion assumes that current population trends will continue, and they may not. Quite so. Most likely the rate of population increase will decline much faster in the United States than it will in the other countries, and there does not seem to be much we can do about it. In sharing with "each according to his needs," we must recognize that needs are determined by population size, which is determined by the rate of reproduction, which at present is regarded as a sovereign right of every nation, poor or not. This being so, the philanthropic load created by the sharing ethic of the spaceship can only increase.

The Tragedy of the Commons

The fundamental error of spaceship ethics, and the sharing it requires, is that it leads to what I call "the tragedy of the commons." Under a system of private property, the men who own property recognize their responsibility to care for it, for if they don't they will eventually suffer. A farmer, for instance, will allow no more cattle in a pasture than its carrying capacity justifies. If he overloads it, erosion sets in, weeds take over, and he loses the use of the pasture.

If a pasture becomes a commons open to all, the right of each to use it may not be matched by a corresponding responsibility to protect it. Asking everyone to use it with discretion will hardly do, for the considerate herdsman who refrains from overloading the commons suffers more than a selfish one who says his needs are greater. If everyone would restrain himself, all would be well; but it takes only one less than everyone to ruin a system of voluntary restraint. In a crowded world of less than perfect human beings, mutual ruin is inevitable if there are no controls. This is the tragedy of the commons.

One of the major tasks of education today should be the creation of such an acute awareness of the dangers of the commons that people will recognize its many varieties. For example, the air and water have become polluted because they are treated as commons. Further growth in the population or per-capita conversion of natural resources into pollutants will only make the problem worse. The same holds true for the fish of the oceans. Fishing fleets have nearly disappeared in many parts of the world; technological improvements in the art of fishing are hastening the day of complete ruin. Only the replacement of the system of the commons with a responsible system of control will save the land, air, water, and oceanic fisheries.

zine *Forbes* revealed the real power behind it: "Feeding the World's Hungry Millions: How It Will Mean Billions for U.S. Business."

And indeed it did. In the years 1960 to 1970, U.S. taxpayers spent a total of $7.9 billion on the Food for Peace program. Between 1948 and 1970, they also paid an additional $50 billion for other economic-aid programs, some of which went for food and food-producing machinery and technology. Though all U.S. taxpayers were forced to contribute to the cost of P.L. 480, certain special interest groups gained handsomely under the program. Farmers did not have to contribute the grain; the Government, or rather the taxpayers, bought it from them at full market prices. The increased demand raised prices of farm products generally. The manufacturers of farm machinery, fertilizers, and pesticides benefited by the farmers' extra efforts to grow more food. Grain elevators profited from storing the surplus until it could be shipped. Railroads made money hauling it to ports, and shipping lines profited from carrying it overseas. The implementation of P.L. 480 required the creation of a vast Government bureaucracy, which then acquired its own vested interest in continuing the program regardless of its merits.

The World Food Bank

In recent years there has been a push to create a new commons called a World Food Bank, an international depository of food reserves to which nations would contribute according to their abilities and from which they would draw according to their needs. This humanitarian proposal has received support from many liberal international groups, and from such prominent citizens as Margaret Mead, U.N. Secretary General Kurt Waldheim, and Senators Edward Kennedy and George McGovern.

A world food bank appeals powerfully to our humanitarian impulses. But before we rush ahead with such a plan, let us recognize where the greatest political push comes from, lest we be disillusioned later. Our experience with the "Food for Peace program," or Public Law 480, gives us the answer. This program moved billions of dollars worth of U.S. surplus grain to food-short, population-long countries during the past two decades. But when P.L. 480 first became law, a headline in the business maga-

Extracting Dollars

Those who proposed and defended the Food for Peace program in public rarely mentioned its importance to any of these special interests. The public emphasis was always on its humanitarian effects. The combination of silent selfish interests and highly vocal humanitarian apologists made a powerful and successful lobby for extracting money from taxpayers. We can expect the same lobby to push now for the creation of a World Food Bank.

However great the potential benefit to selfish interests, it should not be a decisive argument against a truly humanitarian program. We must ask if such a program would actually do more good than harm, not only momentarily but also in the long run. Those who propose the food bank usually refer to a current "emergency" or "crisis" in terms of world food supply. But what is an emergency? Although they may be infrequent and sudden, everyone knows that emergencies will occur from time to time. A well-run family, company, organization, or country prepares for the likelihood of accidents and emergencies. It expects them, it budgets for them, it saves for them.

Learning the Hard Way

What happens if some organizations or countries budget for accidents and others do not? If each country is solely responsible for its own well-being, poorly managed ones will suffer. But they can learn from experience. They may mend their ways and learn to budget for infrequent but certain emergencies. For example, the weather varies from year to year, and periodic crop failures are certain. A wise and competent government saves out of the production of the good years in anticipation of bad years to come. Joseph taught this policy to Pharaoh in Egypt more than 2,000 years ago. Yet the great majority of the governments in the world today do not follow such a policy. They lack either the wisdom or the competence, or both. Should those nations that do manage to put something aside be forced to come to the rescue each time an emergency occurs among the poor nations?

"But it isn't their fault!" some kindhearted liberals argue. "How can we blame the poor people who are caught in an emergency? Why must they suffer for the sins of their governments?" The concept of blame is simply not relevant here. The real question is, what are the operational consequences of establishing a world food bank? If it is open to every country every time a need develops, slovenly rulers will not be motivated to take Joseph's advice. Someone will always come to their aid. Some countries will deposit food in the world food bank, and others will withdraw it. There will be almost no overlap. As a result of such solutions to food shortage emergencies, the poor countries will not learn to mend their ways and will suffer progressively greater emergencies as their populations grow.

Population Control the Crude Way

On the average, poor countries undergo a 2.5 percent increase in population each year; rich countries, about 0.8 percent. Only rich countries have anything in the way of food reserves set aside, and even they

do not have as much as they should. Poor countries have none. If poor countries received no food from the outside, the rate of their population growth would be periodically checked by crop failures and famines. But if they can always draw on a world food bank in time of need, their population can continue to grow unchecked, and so will their "need" for aid. In the short run, a world food bank may diminish that need, but in the long run it actually increases the need without limit.

Without some system of worldwide food sharing, the proportion of people in the rich and poor nations might eventually stabilize. The overpopulated poor countries would decrease in numbers, while the rich countries that had room for more people would increase. But with a well-meaning system of sharing, such as a world food bank, the growth differential between the rich and the poor countries will not only persist, it will increase. Because of the higher rate of population growth in the poor countries of the world, 88 percent of today's children are born poor, and only 12 percent rich. Year by year the ratio becomes worse, as the fast-reproducing poor outnumber the slow-reproducing rich.

A world food bank is thus a commons in disguise. People will have more motivation to draw from it than to add to any common store. The less provident and less able will multiply at the expense of the abler and more provident, bringing eventual ruin upon all who share in the commons. Besides, any system of "sharing" that amounts to foreign aid from the rich nations to the poor nations will carry the taint of charity, which will contribute little to the world peace so devoutly desired by those who support the idea of a world food bank.

As past U.S. foreign-aid programs have amply and depressingly demonstrated, international charity frequently inspires mistrust and antagonism rather than gratitude on the part of the recipient nation.

Chinese Fish and Miracle Rice

The modern approach to foreign aid stresses the export of technology and advice, rather than money and food. As an ancient Chinese proverb goes: "Give a man a fish and he will eat for a day; teach him how to fish and he will eat for the rest of his days." Acting on this advice, the Rockefeller and Ford Foundations have financed a number of programs for improving agriculture in the hungry nations. Known as the "Green Revolution," these programs have led to the development of "miracle rice" and "miracle wheat," new strains that offer bigger harvests and greater resistance to crop damage. Norman Borlaug, the Nobel Prize–winning agronomist who, supported by the Rockefeller Foundation, developed "miracle wheat," is one of the most prominent advocates of a world food bank.

Whether or not the Green Revolution can increase food production as much as its champions claim is a debatable but possibly irrelevant point. Those who support this well-intended humanitarian effort should first consider some of the fundamentals of human ecology. Ironically, one man who did was the late Alan Gregg, a vice-president of the Rockefeller Foundation. Two decades ago he expressed strong doubts about the wisdom of such attempts to increase food production. He likened the growth and spread of humanity over the surface of the earth to the spread of cancer in the human body, remarking that "cancerous growths demand food; but, as far as I know, they have never been cured by getting it."

Overloading the Environment

Every human born constitutes a draft on all aspects of the environment: food, air, water, forests, beaches, wildlife, scenery, and solitude. Food can, perhaps, be significantly increased to meet a growing demand. But what about clean beaches, unspoiled forests, and solitude? If we satisfy a growing population's need for food, we necessarily decrease its per capita supply of the other resources needed by men.

India, for example, now has a population of 600 million, which increases by 15 million each year. This population already puts a huge load on a relatively impoverished environment. The country's forests are now only a small fraction of what they were three centuries ago, and floods and erosion continually destroy the insufficient farmland that remains. Every one of the 15 million new lives added to India's population puts an additional burden on the environment and increases the economic and social costs of crowding. However humanitarian our intent, every Indian life saved through medical or nutritional assistance from abroad diminishes the quality of life for those who remain, and for sub-

sequent generations. If rich countries make it possible, through foreign aid, for 600 million Indians to swell to 1.2 billion in a mere twenty-eight years, as their current growth rate threatens, will future generations of Indians thank us for hastening the destruction of their environment? Will our good intentions be sufficient excuse for the consequences of our actions?

My final example of a commons in action is one for which the public has the least desire for rational discussion—immigration. Anyone who publicly questions the wisdom of current U.S. immigration policy is promptly charged with bigotry, prejudice, ethnocentrism, chauvinism, isolationism, or selfishness. Rather than encounter such accusations, one would rather talk about other matters, leaving immigration policy to wallow in the crosscurrents of special interests that take no account of the good of the whole, or the interests of posterity.

Perhaps we still feel guilty about things we said in the past. Two generations ago the popular press frequently referred to Dagos, Wops, Polacks, Chinks, and Krauts, in articles about how America was being "overrun" by foreigners of supposedly inferior genetic stock. But because the implied inferiority of foreigners was used then as justification for keeping them out, people now assume that restrictive policies could only be based on such misguided notions. There are other grounds.

A Nation of Immigrants

Just consider the numbers involved. Our Government acknowledges a net inflow of 400,000 immigrants a year. While we have no hard data on the extent of illegal entries, educated guesses put the figure at about 600,000 a year. Since the natural increase (excess of births over deaths) of the resident population now runs about 1.7 million per year, the yearly gain from immigration amounts to at least 19 percent of the total annual increase, and may be as much as 37 percent if we include the estimate for illegal immigrants. Considering the growing use of birth-control devices, the potential effect of educational campaigns by such organizations as Planned Parenthood Federation of America and Zero Population Growth, and the influence of inflation and the housing shortage, the fertility rate of American women may decline so much that immigration could account for all the yearly increase in population. Should we not at least ask if that is what we want?

For the sake of those who worry about whether the "quality" of the average immigrant compares favorably with the quality of the average resident, let us assume that immigrants and native-born citizens are of exactly equal quality, however one defines that term. We will focus here only on quantity; and since our conclusions will depend on nothing else, all charges of bigotry and chauvinism become irrelevant.

Immigration versus Food Supply

World food banks *move food to the people,* hastening the exhaustion of the environment of the poor countries. Unrestricted immigration, on the other hand, *moves people to the food,* thus speeding up the destruction of the environment of the rich countries. We can easily understand why poor people should want to make this latter transfer, but why should rich hosts encourage it?

As in the case of foreign-aid programs, immigration receives support from selfish interests and humanitarian impulses. The primary selfish interest in unimpeded immigration is the desire of employers for cheap labor, particularly in industries and trades that offer degrading work. In the past, one wave of foreigners after another was brought into the United States to work at wretched jobs for wretched wages. In recent years the Cubans, Puerto Ricans, and Mexicans have had this dubious honor. The interests of the employers of cheap labor mesh well with the guilty silence of the country's liberal intelligentsia. White Anglo-Saxon Protestants are particularly reluctant to call for a closing of the doors to immigration for fear of being called bigots.

But not all countries have such reluctant leadership. Most educated Hawaiians, for example, are keenly aware of the limits of their environment, particularly in terms of population growth. There is only so much room on the islands, and the islanders know it. To Hawaiians, immigrants from the other forty-nine states present as great a threat as those from other nations. At a recent meeting of Hawaiian government officials in Honolulu, I had the ironic delight of hearing a speaker, who like most of his audience was of Japanese ancestry, ask how the country might practically and constitutionally close

its doors to further immigration. One member of the audience countered: "How can we shut the doors now? We have many friends and relatives in Japan that we'd like to bring here some day so that they can enjoy Hawaii too." The Japanese-American speaker smiled sympathetically and answered: "Yes, but we have children now, and someday we'll have grandchildren too. We can bring more people here from Japan only by giving away some of the land that we hope to pass on to our grandchildren some day. What right do we have to do that?"

At this point, I can hear U.S. liberals asking: "How can you justify slamming the door once you're inside? You say that immigrants should be kept out. But aren't we all immigrants, or the descendants of immigrants? If we insist on staying, must we not admit all others?" Our craving for intellectual order leads us to seek and prefer symmetrical rules and morals: a single rule for me and everybody else; the same rule yesterday, today, and tomorrow. Justice, we feel, should not change with time and place.

We Americans of non-Indian ancestry can look upon ourselves as the descendants of thieves who are guilty morally, if not legally, of stealing this land from its Indian owners. Should we then give back the land to the now living American descendants of those Indians? However morally or logically sound this proposal may be, I, for one, am unwilling to live by it and I know no one else who is. Besides, the logical consequence would be absurd. Suppose that, intoxicated with a sense of pure justice, we should decide to turn our land over to the Indians. Since all our wealth has also been derived from the land, wouldn't we be morally obliged to give that back to the Indians too?

Pure Justice versus Reality

Clearly, the concept of pure justice produces an infinite regression to absurdity. Centuries ago, wise men invented statutes of limitations to justify the rejection of such pure justice, in the interest of preventing continual disorder. The law zealously defends property rights, but only relatively recent property rights. Drawing a line after an arbitrary time has elapsed may be unjust, but the alternatives are worse.

We are all the descendants of thieves, and the world's resources are inequitably distributed. But we must begin the journey to tomorrow from the point where we are today. We cannot remake the past. We cannot safely divide the wealth equitably among all peoples so long as people reproduce at different rates. To do so would guarantee that our grandchildren, and everyone else's grandchildren, would have only a ruined world to inhabit.

To be generous with one's own possessions is quite different from being generous with those of posterity. We should call this point to the attention of those who, from a commendable love of justice and equality, would institute a system of the commons, either in the form of a world food bank, or of unrestricted immigration. We must convince them if we wish to save at least some parts of the world from environmental ruin.

Without a true world government to control reproduction and the use of available resources, the sharing ethic of the spaceship is impossible. For the foreseeable future, our survival demands that we govern our actions by the ethics of a lifeboat, harsh though they may be. Posterity will be satisfied with nothing less.

Addendum 1989

Can anyone watch children starve on television without wanting to help? Naturally sympathetic, a normal human being thinks that he can imagine what it is like to be starving. We all want to do unto others as we would have them do unto us.

But wanting is not doing. Forty years of activity by the U.S. Agency for International Development, as well as episodic nongovernmental attempts to feed the world's starving, have produced mixed results. Before we respond to the next appeal we should ask, "Does what we call 'aid' really help?"

Some of the shortcomings of food aid can be dealt with briefly. Waste is unavoidable: Because most poor countries have wretched transportation systems, food may sit on a dock until it rots. Then there are the corrupt politicians who take donated food away from the poor and give it to their political supporters. In Somalia in the 1980s, fully 70 percent of the donated food went to the army.

We can school ourselves to accept such losses. Panicky projects are always inefficient: Waste and corruption are par for the course. But there is another kind of loss that we cannot—in fact, we should not—

accept, and that is the loss caused by the boomerang effects of philanthropy. Before we jump onto the next "feed-the-starving" bandwagon we need to understand how well-intentioned efforts can be counterproductive.

Briefly put, it is a mistake to focus only on starving people while ignoring their surroundings. Where there is great starvation there is usually an impoverished environment: poor soil, scarce water, and wildly fluctuating weather. As a result, the "carrying capacity" of the environment is low. The territory simply cannot support the population that is trying to live on it. Yet if the population were much smaller, and if it would stay smaller, the people would not need to starve.

Let us look at a particular example. Nigeria, like all the central African countries, has increased greatly in population in the last quarter-century. Over many generations, Nigerians learned that their farmlands would be most productive if crop-growing alternated with "fallow years"—years in which the land was left untilled to recover its fertility.

When modern medicine reduced the death rate, the population began to grow. More food was demanded from the same land. Responding to that need, Nigerians shortened the fallow periods. The result was counterproductive. In one carefully studied village, the average fallow period was shortened from 5.3 to 1.4 years. As a result, the yearly production (averaged over both fallow and crop years) fell by 30 percent.

Are Nigerian farmers stupid? Not at all! They know perfectly well what they are doing. But a farmer whose family has grown too large for his farm has to take care of next year's need before he can provide for the future. To fallow or not to fallow translates into this choice: zero production in a fallow year or a 30 percent shortfall over the long run. Starvation cannot wait. Long-term policies have to give way to short-term ones. So the farmer plows up his overstressed fields, thus diminishing long-term productivity.

Once the carrying capacity of a territory has been transgressed, its capacity goes down, year after year. Transgression is a one-way road to ruin. Ecologists memorialize this reality with an Eleventh Commandment: "Thou shalt not transgress the carrying capacity."

Transgression takes many forms. Poor people are poor in energy resources. They need energy to cook their food. Where do they get it? Typically, from animal dung or trees and bushes. Burning dung deprives the soil of nitrogen. Cutting down trees and bushes deprives the land of protection against eroding rain. Soil-poor slopes cannot support a crop of fuel-plants. Once the soil is gone, water runs off the slopes faster and floods the valleys below. First poor people deforest their land, and then deforestation makes them poorer.

When Americans send food to a starving population that has already grown beyond the environment's carrying capacity, we become a partner in the devastation of their land. Food from the outside keeps more natives alive; these demand more food and fuel; greater demand causes the community to transgress the carrying capacity more, and transgression results in lowering the carrying capacity. The deficit grows exponentially. Gifts of food to an overpopulated country boomerang, increasing starvation over the long run. Our choice is really between letting some die this year and letting more die in the following years.

You may protest, "That's easy enough for a well-fed American to say, but do citizens of poor countries agree?" Well, wisdom is not restricted to the wealthy. The Somali novelist Nuruddin Farrah has courageously condemned foreign gifts as being not truly aid, but a poison, because (if continued) such gifts will make Africans permanently dependent on outside aid.

The ethicist Joseph Fletcher has given a simple directive to would-be philanthropists: "Give if it helps, but not if it hurts." We can grant that giving makes the donor feel good at first—but how will he feel later when he realizes that he has harmed the receiver?

Only one thing can really help a poor country: population control. Having accepted disease control the people must now accept population control.

What the philosopher-economist Kenneth Boulding has called "lovey-dovey charity" is not enough. "It is well to remember," he said, "that the symbol of Christian love is a cross and not a Teddy bear." A good Christian should obey the Eleventh Commandment, refusing to send gifts that help poor people destroy the environment that must support the next generation.

---

8. *The Solution to World Poverty*

PETER SINGER

Using a number of examples to make his case, Peter Singer argues that whatever money we are spending on luxuries, not necessities, should be given away.

In the Brazilian film *Central Station*, Dora is a retired schoolteacher who makes ends meet by sitting at the station writing letters for illiterate people. Suddenly she has an opportunity to pocket $1,000. All she has to do is persuade a homeless 9-year-old boy to follow her to an address she has been given. (She is told he will be adopted by wealthy foreigners.) She

delivers the boy, gets the money, spends some of it on a television set and settles down to enjoy her new acquisition. Her neighbor spoils the fun, however, by telling her that the boy was too old to be adopted—he will be killed and his organs sold for transplantation. Perhaps Dora knew this all along, but after her neighbor's plain speaking, she spends a troubled night. In the morning Dora resolves to take the boy back.

Suppose Dora had told her neighbor that it is a tough world, other people have nice new TV's too, and if selling the kid is the only way she can get one,

From "The Singer Solution to World Poverty." *The New York Times Magazine* (1999). Reprinted by permission of the *New York Times*.

well, he was only a street kid. She would then have become, in the eyes of the audience, a monster. She redeems herself only by being prepared to bear considerable risks to save the boy.

At the end of the movie, in cinemas in the affluent nations of the world, people who would have been quick to condemn Dora if she had not rescued the boy go home to places far more comfortable than her apartment. In fact, the average family in the United States spends almost one-third of its income on things that are no more necessary to them than Dora's new TV was to her. Going out to nice restaurants, buying new clothes because the old ones are no longer stylish, vacationing at beach resorts—so much of our income is spent on things not essential to the preservation of our lives and health. Donated to one of a number of charitable agencies, that money could mean the difference between life and death for children in need.

All of which raises a question: In the end, what is the ethical distinction between a Brazilian who sells a homeless child to organ peddlers and an American who already has a TV and upgrades to a better one—knowing that the money could be donated to an organization that would use it to save the lives of kids in need?

Of course, there are several differences between the two situations that could support different moral judgments about them. For one thing, to be able to consign a child to death when he is standing right in front of you takes a chilling kind of heartlessness; it is much easier to ignore an appeal for money to help children you will never meet. Yet for a utilitarian philosopher like myself—that is, one who judges whether acts are right or wrong by their consequences—if the upshot of the American's failure to donate the money is that one more kid dies on the streets of a Brazilian city, then it is, in some sense, just as bad as selling the kid to the organ peddlers. But one doesn't need to embrace my utilitarian ethic to see that, at the very least, there is a troubling incongruity in being so quick to condemn Dora for taking the child to the organ peddlers while, at the same time, not regarding the American consumer's behavior as raising a serious moral issue.

In his 1996 book, *Living High and Letting Die,* the New York University philosopher Peter Unger presented an ingenious series of imaginary examples designed to probe our intuitions about whether it is wrong to live well without giving substantial amounts of money to help people who are hungry, malnourished or dying from easily treatable illnesses like diarrhea. Here's my paraphrase of one of these examples:

Bob is close to retirement. He has invested most of his savings in a very rare and valuable old car, a Bugatti, which he has not been able to insure. The Bugatti is his pride and joy. In addition to the pleasure he gets from driving and caring for his car, Bob knows that its rising market value means that he will always be able to sell it and live comfortably after retirement. One day when Bob is out for a drive, he parks the Bugatti near the end of a railway siding and goes for a walk up the track. As he does so, he sees that a runaway train, with no one aboard, is running down the railway track. Looking farther down the track, he sees the small figure of a child very likely to be killed by the runaway train. He can't stop the train and the child is too far away to warn of the danger, but he can throw a switch that will divert the train down the siding where his Bugatti is parked. Then nobody will be killed—but the train will destroy his Bugatti. Thinking of his joy in owning the car and the financial security it represents, Bob decides not to throw the switch. The child is killed. For many years to come, Bob enjoys owning his Bugatti and the financial security it represents.

Bob's conduct, most of us will immediately respond, was gravely wrong. Unger agrees. But then he reminds us that we, too, have opportunities to save the lives of children. We can give to organizations like UNICEF or Oxfam America. How much would we have to give one of these organizations to have a high probability of saving the life of a child threatened by easily preventable diseases? (I do not believe that children are more worth saving than adults, but since no one can argue that children have brought their poverty on themselves, focusing on them simplifies the issues.) Unger called up some experts and used the information they provided to offer some plausible estimates that include the cost of raising money, administrative expenses and the cost of delivering aid where it is most needed. By his calculation, $200 in donations would help a sickly 2-year-old transform into a healthy 6-year-old—offering safe passage through childhood's most dangerous years. To show how practical philosophical argument can be, Unger even tells his readers that they can easily donate funds by using their credit card and calling one of these toll-free numbers: (800) 367-5437 for UNICEF; (800) 693-2687 for Oxfam America.

Now you, too, have the information you need to save a child's life. How should you judge yourself if you don't do it? Think again about Bob and his Bugatti. Unlike Dora, Bob did not have to look into the eyes of the child he was sacrificing for his own material comfort. The child was a complete stranger to him and too far away to relate to in an intimate, personal way. Unlike Dora, too, he did not mislead the child or initiate the chain of events imperiling him. In all these respects, Bob's situation resembles that of people able but unwilling to donate to overseas aid and differs from Dora's situation.

If you still think that it was very wrong of Bob not to throw the switch that would have diverted the train and saved the child's life, then it is hard to see how you could deny that it is also very wrong not to send money to one of the organizations listed above. Unless, that is, there is some morally important difference between the two situations that I have overlooked.

Is it the practical uncertainties about whether aid will really reach the people who need it? Nobody who knows the world of overseas aid can doubt that such uncertainties exist. But Unger's figure of $200 to save a child's life was reached after he had made conservative assumptions about the proportion of the money donated that will actually reach its target.

One genuine difference between Bob and those who can afford to donate to overseas aid organizations but don't is that only Bob can save the child on the tracks, whereas there are hundreds of millions of people who can give $200 to overseas aid organizations. The problem is that most of them aren't doing it. Does this mean that it is all right for you not to do it?

Suppose that there were more owners of priceless vintage cars—Carol, Dave, Emma, Fred and so on, down to Ziggy—all in exactly the same situation as Bob, with their own siding and their own switch, all sacrificing the child in order to preserve their own cherished car. Would that make it all right for Bob to do the same? To answer this question affirmatively is to endorse follow-the-crowd ethics—the kind of ethics that led many Germans to look away when the Nazi atrocities were being committed. We do not excuse them because others were behaving no better.

We seem to lack a sound basis for drawing a clear moral line between Bob's situation and that of any reader of this article with $200 to spare who does not donate it to an overseas aid agency. These readers seem to be acting at least as badly as Bob was acting when he chose to let the runaway train hurtle toward the unsuspecting child. In the light of this conclusion, I trust that many readers will reach for the phone and donate that $200. Perhaps you should do it before reading further.

Now that you have distinguished yourself morally from people who put their vintage cars ahead of a child's life, how about treating yourself and your partner to dinner at your favorite restaurant? But wait. The money you will spend at the restaurant could also help save the lives of children overseas! True, you weren't planning to blow $200 tonight, but if you were to give up dining out just for one month, you would easily save that amount. And what is one month's dining out, compared to a child's life? There's the rub. Since there are a lot of desperately needy children in the world, there will always be another child whose life you could save for another $200. Are you therefore obliged to keep giving until you have nothing left? At what point can you stop?

Hypothetical examples can easily become farcical. Consider Bob. How far past losing the Bugatti should he go? Imagine that Bob had got his foot stuck in the track of the siding, and if he diverted the train, then before it rammed the car it would also amputate his big toe. Should he still throw the switch? What if it would amputate his foot? His entire leg?

As absurd as the Bugatti scenario gets when pushed to extremes, the point it raises is a serious one: only when the sacrifices become very significant indeed would most people be prepared to say that Bob does nothing wrong when he decides not to throw the switch. Of course, most people could be wrong; we can't decide moral issues by taking opinion polls. But consider for yourself the level of sacrifice that you would demand of Bob, and then think about how much money you would have to give away in order to make a sacrifice that is roughly equal to that. It's almost certainly much, much more than $200. For most middle-class Americans, it could easily be more like $200,000.

Isn't it counterproductive to ask people to do so much? Don't we run the risk that many will shrug their shoulders and say that morality, so conceived, is fine for saints but not for them? I accept that we are unlikely to see, in the near or even medium-term future, a world in which it is normal for wealthy Americans to give the bulk of their wealth to strangers. When it comes to praising or blaming people for what they do, we tend to use a standard that is relative to some conception of normal behavior. Comfortably off Americans who give, say, 10 percent of their income to overseas aid organizations are so far ahead of most of their equally comfortable fellow citizens that I wouldn't go out of my way to chastise them for not doing more. Nevertheless, they should be doing much more, and they are in no position to criticize Bob for failing to make the much greater sacrifice of his Bugatti.

At this point various objections may crop up. Someone may say: "If every citizen living in the affluent nations contributed his or her share I wouldn't have to make such a drastic sacrifice, because long before such levels were reached, the resources would have been there to save the lives of all those children dying from lack of food or medical care. So why should I give more than my fair share?" Another, related, objection is that the Government ought to increase its overseas aid allocations, since that would spread the burden more equitably across all taxpayers.

Yet the question of how much we ought to give is a matter to be decided in the real world—and that, sadly, is a world in which we know that most people do not, and in the immediate future will not, give substantial amounts to overseas aid agencies. We know, too, that at least in the next year, the United States Government is not going to meet even the very modest United Nations–recommended target of 0.7 percent of gross national product; at the moment it lags far below that, at 0.09 percent, not even half of Japan's 0.22 percent or a tenth of Denmark's 0.97 percent. Thus, we know that the money we can give beyond that theoretical "fair share" is still going to save lives that would otherwise be lost. While the idea that no one need do more than his or her fair share is a powerful one, should it prevail if we know that others are not doing their fair share and that children will die preventable deaths unless we do more than our fair share? That would be taking fairness too far.

Thus, this ground for limiting how much we ought to give also fails. In the world as it is now, I can

see no escape from the conclusion that each one of us with wealth surplus to his or her essential needs should be giving most of it to help people suffering from poverty so dire as to be life-threatening. That's right: I'm saying that you shouldn't buy that new car, take that cruise, redecorate the house or get that pricey new suit. After all, a $1,000 suit could save five children's lives.

So how does my philosophy break down in dollars and cents? An American household with an income of $50,000 spends around $30,000 annually on necessities, according to the Conference Board, a nonprofit economic research organization. Therefore, for a household bringing in $50,000 a year, donations to help the world's poor should be as close as possible to $20,000. The $30,000 required for necessities holds for higher incomes as well. So a household making $100,000 could cut a yearly check for $70,000. Again, the formula is simple: whatever money you're spending on luxuries, not necessities, should be given away.

Now, evolutionary psychologists tell us that human nature just isn't sufficiently altruistic to make it plausible that many people will sacrifice so much for strangers. On the facts of human nature, they might be right, but they would be wrong to draw a moral conclusion from those facts. If it is the case that we ought to do things that, predictably, most of us won't do, then let's face that fact head-on. Then, if we value the life of a child more than going to fancy restaurants, the next time we dine out we will know that we could have done something better with our money. If that makes living a morally decent life extremely arduous, well, then that is the way things are. If we don't do it, then we should at least know that we are failing to live a morally decent life—not because it is good to wallow in guilt but because knowing where we should be going is the first step toward heading in the direction.

When Bob first grasped the dilemma that faced him as he stood by that railway switch, he must have thought how extraordinarily unlucky he was to be placed in a situation in which he must choose between the life of an innocent child and the sacrifice of most of his savings. But he was not unlucky at all. We are all in that situation.

9. Impartiality, Beneficence, and Friendship

Lawrence Blum

Lawrence Blum argues that our duty to be impartial is limited to certain institutional roles we occupy such as that of a judge, a teacher, or a doctor. Outside those roles, Blum argues that we may have a duty of beneficence, but not impartiality, to concern ourselves with the well-being of strangers, but this duty does not rule out special treatment for our friends.

I

I will argue . . . that impartiality is a moral requirement only in certain restricted sorts of situations. It is not a morally incumbent perspective to take up in every situation. In particular, friendship does not typically involve us in situations in which impartiality between the interests of our friends and those of others is a moral requirement; hence in acting beneficently towards our friends we do not typically violate a duty of impartiality.

Certainly attachments to particular persons can lead us to violate impartiality, and thus to be unfair to others. Someone in an official position to dispense jobs can use his position to get jobs for his friends and relatives, independent of their qualification for the jobs. And we may imagine a doctor who because he likes a particular patient devotes too much of his consulting time to this patient, neglecting the others who are waiting to see him.

But such situations do not point to a general conflict between helping one's friends and helping others. It is no violation of impartiality if I phone my friend to see if he is feeling better, knowing that he has been ill. Such a situation of acting from concern for a friend does not impose on me the obligation to take into account the interests of all the people whom I *might* help at that point in time, and to choose according to some impartial criterion whom to benefit. The examples so far given point to one of the primary sorts of situations in which such impartiality is demanded—namely, an official capacity within some public institution or practice.

A judge, a captain of a ship, a doctor, a nurse, a teacher, all occupy roles or positions in which a certain kind of impartiality is demanded of them regarding the interests of certain parties whom they serve or for whom they have some responsibility. This impartiality extends to persons to whom they have special attachments. The benefits or burdens dispensed by these persons are to accrue to persons not on the basis of some personal attachment of the holder of the role to them, but on the basis of some impersonal criterion, connected with need, qualification for a position, established and rational procedure, or the like.

Thus, to take the most obvious case, a judge is meant to dispense justice impartially. He is meant to make his decision on the merits of the case and not according to his attachment to one of the parties involved. A teacher is not supposed to grade a student higher because he likes him or has a special attachment to him. A nurse is supposed to help his patients according to their individual needs, not according to his own personal likings and attachments.

It is an important part of our understanding of the duties of impartiality attaching to these roles that persons who assume the roles are aware of what those duties entail; in particular, aware of how they might impinge on the interests of those to whom they are attached. Thus a doctor or nurse knows that by virtue of his position he is forbidden from attempting to secure for a friend or relative some drugs or other medical care which are properly meant for others, or which fair procedures would allot to others.

A person might refuse to (or not be allowed to) put himself in a position in which he would be required to dispense a benefit or a burden according

From *Friendship, Altruism, and Morality* (1980), Routledge. Used with the permission of the author and the publisher.

to an impartial rule, where a friend would be one of the candidates for the benefit or burden. This could be either because he did not feel he would be capable of such impartiality, or because, if he were, he would find it too difficult or painful to be required to dispense the benefit to someone other than his friend.

For this sort of reason it is a general policy that judges not sit in cases in which they have some special connection to one of the parties (or in which they have a self-interest in the outcome). The temptations of conflict between their impersonal duties and their personal attachments would be too great and would place an extraordinary personal burden on the role-occupiers and on the friendships; so for the good of everyone such a situation is best avoided.

Institutional roles and positions are an obvious arena of life in which a certain kind of impartiality between the interests of all, including those to whom we are personally connected and attached, is demanded of us. Equally obvious is the fact that situations covered by such roles are very untypical of those in which we interact with and benefit our friends. And so the existence of such roles does not betoken a common, much less a fundamental, moral problem regarding the beneficence dispensed to our friends.

This conclusion is strengthened by the fact that even within these institutionalized roles there is a limit to the demand of impartiality, and in most cases a scope outside of that limit for benefiting those whom we choose for whatever reason (e.g., personal attachment or liking) to benefit. Thus if a doctor, having fulfilled his obligations to his patients, spends extra time on the case of a friend, this would not be a violation of impartiality, but on the contrary would be admirable behavior on his part. A teacher is permitted to give more attention to some students than to others (not merely on pedagogical grounds), as long as he gives full and adequate attention to all. The criterion here, vague though it may be, of when it is morally permissible to depart from strict impartiality, has to do with what is regarded as the duties of one's role, in contrast to what is regarded as going beyond those duties (and is in that sense supererogatory). In the latter situations, what one does for those one chooses to help is regarded as giving something of oneself, rather than as depriving others of what one owes to them by virtue of one's institutional relationship with them. The line between these is extremely dif-

ficult to draw, is not in general fixed but is subject to change (e.g., redefinition of what constitutes the responsibilities of a role), and is not applicable in all situations. But that it exists is significant for our argument. For what it shows is that even in contexts in which impartiality between the interests of one's friends and those of others is demanded, this demand is limited in its scope, and there remains an area in which we are able to express our natural care and concern for our friends, our desire to do what is good for them, outside of the constraint of impersonal considerations.

It should be noted that this argument applies not only to actual friends and personal relationships but also to people whom we like but have no substantial or developed relationship with; i.e., it applies to beneficence from personal feelings. Here too we are morally permitted to benefit them, and this benefiting is not in general required to be justified through an impartial perspective or procedure. Morality does not in most situations demand of us that we justify such beneficence with regard to the interests of others whom we could have served but did not.

<hr>

II

I have claimed that institutional-role contexts are ones in which impartiality is demanded of us. What I have not yet done is to show that the demand of impartiality is limited to such institutional-role contexts. Nor, related to this, have I given a general characterization of the conditions in which such a demand is an appropriate one, from a moral point of view.

To help gain some clarity regarding the non-institutional contexts in which impartiality is incumbent upon us, it is necessary to make an important distinction. The fact that impartiality does not demand that we constantly appraise our potential beneficence to our friends by an impartial standard does not mean that we are justified in totally disregarding the interests of others when the good of our friends is at stake, even outside contexts in which strict impartiality is demanded. To take an extreme example, suppose that I am in a train crash in which many people are injured, including my best friend (but not myself). I am certainly justified in giving my first attention to my friend. But it seems also required for me to give some attention to others. Some weighing is evidently called for here. The point is that strict impartiality is not required or appropriate, but neither is ignoring the interests of others simply because the weal and woe of one's friend is at stake.

Suppose I pass two persons on the street digging their cars out of the snow, and one of them is my friend. Surely I am justified in choosing to help my friend in preference to helping the stranger, though it would also perhaps be the decent thing to do to attempt to help both of them. But if, say, the friend could very easily dig the car out by himself, and in fact had almost finished doing so (though there was still room for assistance from someone else), and the other person obviously could not do so without some assistance, then another factor will have been introduced which must be weighed against the desire to help the friend. Here it might be more appropriate that one help the other person. (One would imagine that the friend would agree that this was appropriate.)

We then have three different sorts of situations. In the first we are required to treat the interests of the relevant parties from a strictly impartial perspective, even if one of the parties is our friend. Personal attachments must be entirely overlooked (though only up to a certain point). In the second, we are required to give some attention to the interests of others, but are not required to regard those interests strictly impartially or as having equal weight to the interests of friends who are involved. In the third type of situation consideration to the interests of others is not at all appropriate or relevant. In such situations it is morally permissible to act solely for the benefit of one's friend.

The existence of the second category helps to define the limits of impartiality, while giving credence to our sense that in some situations the presence of friends does not or should not preclude attention to the interests of others. For we see that in some situations there is some moral constraint on us to attend to the weal and woe of others, even though the weal and woe of friends is also at stake; and yet the grounding of such moral constraint need not be located in a demand for impartiality. In the train crash example just described, I have claimed that one ought to give some help to injured persons who are not one's friends, though one's first concern is properly with one's own friend. Some might see this help as a strict duty (of beneficence) on the ground that great harm to others can be avoided with little sacrifice to myself (or to a person to whom I am at-

tached). But even if one does not see this as an actual duty, it is possible to recognize some element of moral constraint in the consideration that my ability to help the injured persons ought to weigh with me in my actions.

Thus, that I ought to help the injured persons seems in many contexts to stem not from a general demand of impartiality between the interests of all concerned (including myself or my friends) but from something like a duty of beneficence. That this is so can be seen if we imagine the situation without the friend's being injured. There would still be moral constraint for us to help the other persons; yet this moral constraint cannot stem from a demand that we treat the interests of everyone, including those to whom we have a special attachment, impartially. What the presence of the friend does to the moral configuration of this situation is not so much to undercut this moral quasi-demand of attention to the weal and woe of others, but to bring into play another consideration against which it is to be balanced. It is still true that we ought to attend to the interests of the injured strangers, but it is entirely proper for us to attend first to our friend. It would be inappropriate for us to give our entire attention to our friend, when further attention to him would produce minimal good to him compared to the much greater good which could be produced by attention to others. But, on the other side, it is also inappropriate for us at the outset to apportion our help impartially—solely according to need—ignoring the fact that one of the persons is our friend.

It could be responded here that this argument applies only to situations where the interests of others are substantially threatened—such as in a train crash—so that attention to their interests is urgent enough to be morally incumbent upon us. The same argument would not seem to hold for the case of digging the car out of the snow (above . . .), where there would seem no demand that we attend to the interests of the person who is not our friend merely because he could use some help.

Yet it seems that whatever consideration is appropriate regarding the weal and woe of the stranger is unaffected by the presence of the friend, and so is not connected to impartiality. Though these is no *duty* to help the stranger, perhaps there is some moral deficiency or inadequacy in failing to do so, if one has nothing very important to do and could help fairly readily. Yet whatever force of "oughtness" one attributes to the consideration of the man's weal and woe (regarding digging his car out) exists independently of whether the friend is present in the situation or not.

The presence of the friend merely interjects another factor which changes the overall moral configuration of the situation. We might properly not help the other, choosing instead to help the friend (assuming we cannot do both). But we do not thereby repudiate the moral consideration of helping the other.

Thus even in cases (involving friends) in which there is nothing like a duty of beneficence, a consideration to the interests of others does not stem from a requirement of impartiality; for, first, that consideration exists even when the friendship issue does not, and second, impartiality between the interests of the friend and of the other(s) is not actually required.

III

If the argument of the previous section is right, then in noninstitutional contexts at least some of the morally appropriate regard to the interests of others can be accounted for without appeal to the principle of impartiality. This is a step towards defining the scope of the principle of impartiality in noninstitutional contexts.

I suggest that we can learn something of that scope by asking in what the nature of impartiality, justice, and fairness consists, as virtues or traits of character exhibited in one's noninstitutional (as well as institutional) life. Here the definition given by Sidgwick seems to me close to the mark:

> What then do we mean by a just man in matters where law-observance does not enter? It is natural to reply that we mean an impartial man, one who seeks with equal care to satisfy all claims which he recognizes as valid and does not let himself be unduly influenced by personal preferences.

This definition brings out that impartiality or justice has to do with overlooking personal preferences in circumstances which have to do with according burdens and benefits to persons.

For example, suppose I am helping to settle a dispute between two persons, one of whom is a friend. Both persons are looking to me for mediation in the quarrel. This is a circumstance where justice or impartiality is required, or appropriate. We are not to favor the friend simply because he is our friend. Rather we are to overlook our personal attachment and consider only the factors relevant to the dispute. Hearing the claims made on both sides, it might turn out that I feel that the nonfriend's claim has more merit, and that he is more deserving of the benefit regarding which there is a dispute.

Sidgwick's definition suggests why impartiality is not always required of us, nor required in every situation in which our actions are of a potential benefit to someone. For the application of impartiality depends on the pre-existence of claims on the part of persons involved (though the claim need not actually be made, or even recognized as existing, by the person who has it). It is only when someone has a certain claim on a benefit that it is a matter of impartiality to give due regard to his interest in that benefit. If he has no claim to it then such regard is no longer a matter relevant to impartiality. (These claims can be grounded in a person's meeting the criteria relevant for relegating a certain benefit within a certain procedure—e.g., the criteria for producing the soundest argument in a dispute, or the criteria for meeting a certain job specification.) A just person is one who can be counted on to overlook personal interest and preference, where others might tailor their views of the claims involved to their own preferences.

It is thus not impartiality regarding interest *per se* which defines impartiality, as it is impartiality regarding interests in which the parties involved have some claim, the honoring of which might require the overlooking of personal ties and preferences. This claim is not itself grounded in impartiality but is rather the grounds of it.

This is why it is not a violation of impartiality if I help my friend in preference to the other person also digging his car out of the snow. For this other person has no claim to my help. It may be good or decent of me to help him; to do so may be something which one could expect of a decent person. But it is not a claim. It is thus not a violation of impartiality if I fail to help, preferring to help my friend.

In the train-crash case the other injured persons also have no claim on my beneficence; or, rather, if one wants to argue that a duty of beneficence exists, which is thus correlative to a right or claim on the part of the injured persons, this is not the kind of claim which demands that we overlook or abstract ourselves from our personal attachments, apportioning our attention and help purely on the basis of need. (If this is so, then not every claim can be a basis for impartiality.)

Impartiality is appropriate therefore only in certain situations. It is not a perspective which defines what it is for us to act morally, to take up a moral point of view on our actions (regarding our friends). To refer to an example from Telfer, if I choose to visit a pensioner (to help decorate his flat) rather than my friend, determining that the pensioner is in greater need of my visiting, this behavior is not in accordance with the virtues of justice of fairness; for the pensioner has no claim on my visit, which requires me to overlook my relationship with my friend and make my decision purely on the basis of which one will benefit more from my visit. Depending on other factors in the situation, my visit to the pensioner can evidence a commendable concern for a particular person to whom I have no relation; and, again depending on the situation, my friend may be able to acknowledge that it was a good thing for me to visit the pensioner rather than him. But if there is some virtue here it is not the virtue of justice or impartiality. (In other circumstances the visit to the pensioner can show an insufficient regard to the friend and to the friendship.)

The same can be said of impartiality in noninstitutional contexts as was said above about institutional ones, namely that in most cases in which we can act to benefit our friends, but in which it is also within our power to benefit someone else, there are no claims on our beneficence the honoring of which requires us to overlook our personal ties. Thus there is no general demand of impartiality.

In fact Sidgwick's definition could be taken to apply to institutional as well as noninstitutional contexts. Institutional contexts can be seen as an application of the general definition to a certain category of situation. For we can look at institutional contexts as helping to define the claims which some persons have, with regard to their interests, on other persons. For example, the claim which a patient has to be treated in a certain way by a doctor; or the student to be graded according to certain procedures by his teacher; or an applicant to be given a certain kind of consideration by the personnel officer. Part of what characterizes such institutional contexts is that they define more precisely than is often done in ordinary life what the relevant considerations are for allocating benefits to persons. This is why institutional contexts seem so appropriate for impartiality.

Finally, it should be remembered that even in contexts in which impartiality is demanded, there is almost always some room for the person of whom impartiality is demanded to benefit the friend in a way appropriate to friendship. For example, in the case of the quarrel mentioned above . . . , suppose I feel that the nonfriend's claim to benefit is greater than that of my friend. Impartiality requires me to overlook my attachment to the friend in deciding that the benefit properly goes to the nonfriend. But impartiality does not prevent me from showing special attention to my friend if he is disappointed, trying to do something to cheer him up, comforting him, etc., while not doing the same for the other person.

Thus impartiality is limited not only to certain sorts of situations. In addition, even within the situations in which it applies, it applies, so to speak, only up to a point, and generally there will be room left over for extra beneficence to be shown to the friend.

To summarize the argument so far: According to one important strain of thought within the Kantian view, a principle definitive of morality is impartiality. To take up a perspective of impartiality regarding any of one's actions which impinge on the interests of others is to take up, and act from, the moral point of view. To fail to do this is to fail to act morally. A corollary is that it is contrary to morality—because contrary to impartiality—to favor the interests of oneself to one's friends simply as such, i.e., simply because they are one's own or one's friends.

Against this I have argued that it is not in general contrary to the demands of morality to prefer our friends' interests as such, i.e., to act for the sake of R's good simply because R is my friend, even if there are other persons whom it is in my power to help and who are in greater need than R. In fact it is entirely morally appropriate to do so. Such action does not typically violate the demands of impartiality; for that perspective is appropriate only in certain contexts, which do not include most friendship situations. There is no general demand of impartiality. Rather the demand of impartiality rests on prior claims to some benefit, the acknowledging of which requires the overlooking of personal preferences and attachments.

Thus acting morally is not always or fundamentally a matter of equality or impartiality towards all. For this is not what it is to act morally within friendship.

Thus in one sense it is actually misleading to say that we are necessarily or typically partial to our friends, if this is meant to imply a deviation from a morally requisite norm of impartiality. For such a norm is not typically in force in regard to our benefiting our friends. In another sense, however, we are partial to our friends, in that we benefit our friends without testing that benefiting against a norm of impartiality with respect to others; and we are not morally remiss for doing so.

If this argument is right, then impartiality does not define "the moral point of view." Rather, it defines a moral viewpoint appropriate in certain circumstances but not in others. When acting from friendship it is neither required nor appropriate (normally) to look to impartial or impersonal considerations to guide our actions. Impartiality, fairness, and justice are personal virtues, but they are merely some virtues among others. They are not definitive of moral virtue altogether.

---

10. Morality, Parents, and Children

JAMES RACHELS

James Rachels argues that the idea of morality as impartiality allows for the idea of special parental obligations particularly with regard to the day-to-day care of our own children. Nevertheless, he contends that we are not justified in providing our own children with luxuries while other children lack necessities.

The Problem

At about the same time Socrates was being put to death for corrupting the youth of Athens, the great Chinese sage Mo Tzu was also antagonizing his community. Unlike the Confucianists, who were the social conservatives of the day, Mo and his followers were sharply critical of traditional institutions and practices. One of Mo's controversial teachings was that human relationships should be governed by an "all-embracing love" that makes no distinctions between friends, family, and humanity at large. "Partiality," he said "is to be replaced by universality." To his followers, these were the words of a moral visionary. To the Confucianists, however, they were the words of a man out of touch with moral reality. In particular, Mo's doctrine was said to subvert the family, for it recommended that one have as much regard for strangers as for one's own kin. Meng Tzu summed up the complaint when he wrote that "Mo Tzu, by preaching universal love, has repudiated the family." Mo did not deny it. Instead, he argued that universal love is a higher ideal than family loyalty, and that obligations within families can be properly understood only as particular instances of obligations to all mankind.

This ancient dispute has not disappeared. Do parents have special obligations to their own children? Or, to put the question a bit differently: Do they have obligations to their own children that they do not have to other children, or to children in general? Our instincts are with the Confucianists. Surely, we think, parents do have a special obligation to care for their own. Parents must love and protect their children; they must feed and clothe them; they must see to their medical needs, their education, and a hundred other things. Who could deny it? At the same time, we do not believe that we have such duties toward strangers. Perhaps we do have a general duty of beneficence toward them, but that duty is not nearly so extensive or specific as the duties we have toward our own young sons and daughters. If faced with a choice between feeding our own children and sending food to orphans in a foreign country, we would prefer our own, without hesitation.

Yet the Mohist objection is still with us. The idea that morality requires us to be impartial, clearly articulated by Mo Tzu, is a recurring theme of Western

From "Morality, Parents, and Children," in *Person to Person*, ed. George Grahan and Hugh LaFollette (1989), Temple University Press.

moral philosophy. Perhaps the most famous expression of this idea was Bentham's formula, "Each to count for one and none for more than one." Mill's formulation was less memorable but no less emphatic: He urged that, when weighing the interests of different people, we should be "as strictly impartial as a disinterested and benevolent spectator." Utilitarianism of the kind espoused by Bentham and Mill has, of course, often been criticized for conflicting with common-sense morality, and so it will probably come as no great surprise that utilitarian notions clash with the common-sense idea of special parental obligations. However, the idea that morality requires impartiality is by no means exclusively a utilitarian doctrine. It is common ground to a considerable range of theories and thinkers.[1]

The problem, in its most general form, is this. As moral agents, we cannot play favorites—at least, not according to the conception of morality as impartiality. But as parents, we do play favorites. Parental love is partial through and through. And we think there is nothing wrong with this; in fact, we normally think there is something wrong with the parent who is *not* deeply partial where his own children are concerned. Therefore, it would seem, one or the other of these conceptions has to be modified or abandoned.

Of course, exactly the same is true of our relations with friends, spouses, and lovers. All these relationships, and others like them, seem to include, as part of their very nature, special obligations. Friends, spouses, and lovers are not just members of the great crowd of humanity. They are all special, at least to the one who loves them. The problem is that the conception of morality as impartiality seems to conflict with *any* kind of loving personal relationship. Mo Tzu notwithstanding, it seems to conflict with love itself. In this essay I discuss only the question of parental obligations to children, but it should be kept in mind that the deeper issue has to do with personal relationships in general.

Possible Solutions

There are three obvious approaches to solving our problem: First, we might reject the idea of morality as impartiality; second, we might reject the idea of special parental obligations; or third, we might try to find some way of understanding the two notions that would make them consistent. The first approach

has recently attracted some support among philosophers, who think that although the conception of morality as impartiality seems plausible when stated abstractly, it is refuted by such counterexamples as parental obligation. Their thought is that we should reject this conception and look for a new theory of morality, one that would acknowledge from the outset that personal relationships can be the source of special obligations.

Rejecting the idea of impartiality has a certain appeal, for it is always exciting to learn that some popular philosophical view is no good and that there is interesting work to be done in formulating an alternative. However, we should not be too quick here. It is no accident that the conception of morality as impartiality has been so widely accepted. It seems to express something deeply important that we should be reluctant to give up. It is useful, for example, in explaining why egoism, racism, and sexism are morally odious, and if we abandon this conception we lose our most natural and persuasive means of combating those doctrines. (The idea of morality as impartiality is closely connected to modern thoughts about human equality. That humans are in some sense equals would never have occurred to the Confucianists, which perhaps explains why they saw nothing plausible in Mo's teaching.) Therefore, it seems desirable to retain the notion of moral impartiality in some form. The question is, can we find some way of keeping both ideas—morality as impartiality, and special parental obligations? Can we understand them in a way that makes them compatible with one another?

As it turns out, this is not a difficult task. It is fairly easy to interpret impartiality in such a way that it no longer conflicts with special parental obligations. We can say, for example, that impartiality requires us to treat people in the same way *only when there are no relevant differences between them*. This qualification is obviously needed, quite apart from any considerations about parents and children. For example, it is not a failure of impartiality to imprison a convicted criminal, while innocent citizens go free, because there is a relevant difference between them (one has commited a crime; the others have not) to which we can appeal to justify the difference in treatment. Similar examples come easily to mind. But once we have admitted the need for this qualification, we can make use of it to resolve our problem about parental obligations: We can say that there is a relevant difference between one's own children and other children that justifies treating one's own children better. The difference will have something to do with the fact that they are one's own.

We might call this the compromise view. It is appealing because it allows us to retain the plausible idea of morality as impartiality, without having to give up the equally plausible idea that we have special obligations to our own children. Having found this solution to our problem, we might be tempted to stop here. That, however, would be premature. There is a further issue that needs to be addressed, and when we do, the compromise view will begin to look less attractive.

We are not free to call just any differences between individuals relevant. Suppose a racist claimed that there is a relevant difference between blacks and whites that justifies treating whites better—the difference being that they are members of different races. We would think this mere bluster and demand to know why *that* difference should count for anything. Similarly, it is only hand-waving to say that there is a relevant difference between one's own children and others that justifies treating one's own better—the difference being that they are one's own. We need to ask why *that* difference matters.

◇

Why Should It Matter That a Child Is One's Own?

Why should it matter, from a moral point of view, that a child is one's own? Our natural tendency is to assume that it *does* matter and to take it as a mere philosophical puzzle to figure out why. Why should anyone want to resist this tendency? The feeling that our own children have a superior natural claim on our attention is among the deepest moral instincts we have. Can it possibly be doubted? I believe there is a powerful reason for doubting that this feeling is morally legitimate—the fact that a child is one's own may *not* matter, or at least it may not matter nearly as much as we usually assume. That reason has to do with luck.

The point about luck can be brought out like this. Suppose a parent believes that, when faced with a choice between feeding his own children and feeding starving orphans, he should give preference to his own. This is natural enough. But the orphans need the food just as much, and they are no less deserving. It is only their bad luck that they were not born to affluent parents; and why should luck count, from a moral point of view? Why should we think that a moral view is correct, if it implies that some children should be fed, while others starve, for no better reason than that some were unlucky in the circumstances of their birth? This seems to me to be an extremely important matter—important enough, perhaps, that we should take seriously the possibility that a child's being one's own does not have the moral importance that we usually assume it has.

With this in mind, let us look at some of the arguments that support the Compromise View. The idea that one's own children have a superior claim to one's care might be defended in various ways. Let us consider the three arguments that seem most important.

1. The Argument from Social Roles

The first line of reasoning begins with some observations about social roles. It is not possible for an isolated individual to have anything resembling a normal human life. For that, a social setting is required. The social setting provides roles for us to fill—thus in the context of society we are able to be citizens, friends, husbands and wives, hospital patients, construction workers, scientists, teachers, customers, sports fans, and all the rest. None of us (with rare heroic exceptions) creates the roles we play; they have evolved over many centuries of human life, and we encounter them as simply the raw materials out of which we must fashion our individual lives.

These roles define, in large measure, our relations with other people. They specify how we should behave toward others. Teachers must wisely guide their students; friends must be loyal; husbands should be faithful; and so on. To the extent that you fail in these respects, you will be an inferior teacher, a bad friend, a poor husband. You can avoid these obligations by declining to enter into these roles: Not everyone will be a teacher, not everyone will marry, and some unfortunate people will not even have friends. But you can hardly avoid *all* social roles, and you cannot fill a social role without at the same time acknowledging the special responsibilities that go with it.

Now, parenthood is a social role, and like other such roles it includes special duties as part of its very nature. You can choose not to have children, or, having had a child, you may give it up for adoption. But if you *are* a parent, you are stuck with the responsibilities that go with the role. A parent who doesn't see to his children's needs is a bad parent, just as a disloyal friend is a bad friend, and an unfaithful husband is a poor husband. And that is why (according to this argument) we have obligations to our own children that we do not have to other children.

The argument from social roles is plausible; but how far should we be persuaded by it? The argument has at least four apparent weaknesses.

(i) We need to distinguish two claims: first, that our obligations to our own children *have a different basis* from our obligations to other children; and second, that our obligations to our own children *are stronger than* (take precedence over) our obligations to other children. If successful, the argument from social roles would show only that our obligations to our own children are based on different considerations than are our obligations to other children. We have a social relationship with our own children that is the basis of our obligation to them, while our obligations to other children are based on a general duty of beneficence. The argument would not show that the former obligations are *stronger*. Thus a critic of the idea of special parental obligations could continue the dispute at another level. It could be argued that, even if one's duties to one's own children have a different basis, they nevertheless are *no stronger than* one's duties to other children.

(ii) The second point is related to the first. The argument from social roles trades on the notion of what it means to be a bad father or a bad mother. Now, suppose we admit that a man who ignores the need of his own children is a bad father. It may also be observed that a man who ignores the cries of orphans, when he could help, is a bad *man*—a man lacking a proper regard for the needs of others. While it is undesirable to be a bad father (or mother), it is also undesirable to be a bad man (or woman). So, once again, the argument from social roles does nothing to show that our obligations to other children are weaker.

(iii) Third, there is the point about luck that I have already mentioned. The system of social roles acknowledged in our society makes special provision for children lucky enough to live in homes with parents. This system favors even more those lucky enough to have affluent parents who can provide more for them than less affluent parents are able to provide. Even granting this, we can still ask: Is it a morally decent system? The system itself can be subject to criticism.

We do not have to look far to find an obvious objection to the system. The system does well enough in providing for some children; but it does miserably where others are concerned. There is no social role comparable to the parent-child relationship that targets the interests of orphans, or the interests of children whose parents are unable or unwilling to provide for them. Thus in this system luck plays an unacceptably important part.

(iv) Finally, students of social history might find the argument from social roles rather naive. The argument draws much of its strength from the fact that contemporary American and European ideals favor families bound together by love. Anyone who is likely to read these words will have been influenced by that ideal—consider how the reader will have passed over the second paragraph of this essay, with its easy talk of parents loving and protecting their children, without a pause. Yet the cozy nuclear family, nourished by affectionate relationships, is a relatively recent development. The norm throughout most of Western history has been very different.

In his acclaimed book *The Family, Sex and Marriage in England 1500–1800,* Lawrence Stone points out that as recently as the seventeenth century affectionate relations between husbands and wives were so rare as to be virtually nonexistent, and certainly were not expected within normal marriages. Among the upper classes, husbands and wives occupied separate stations within large households and rarely saw one another in private. Children were sent away immediately after birth to be looked after by wet-nurses for 12 to 18 months;

then, returning home, they would be raised largely by nurses, governesses, and tutors. Finally they would be sent away to boarding school when they were between 7 and 13, with 10 the most common age. The children of the poor were of course worse off: They would leave home at an equally early age, often to go and work in the houses of the rich. Stone writes,

> About all that can be said with confidence on the matter of emotional relations within the sixteenth- and early seventeenth-century family at all social levels is that there was a general psychological atmosphere of distance, manipulation, and deference. . . . Family relationships were characterized by interchangeability, so that substitution of another wife or another child was easy. . . . It was a structure held together not by affective bonds but by mutual economic interests.

And what of parental duties? Of course there has always been a recognition of *some* special parental duties, but in earlier times these were much more restricted and were not associated with bonds of affection. Until some time in the eighteenth century, it seems, the emphasis in European morals was almost entirely on the duties owed by children to parents, rather than the other way around. Children were commonly said to owe their parents absolute obedience, in gratitude for having been given life. The French historian Jean Flandrin notes that "In Brittany the son remained subject to the authority of his father until the age of sixty, but marriage contracted with the father's consent emancipated him." Pity the man whose father lived to a ripe old age and refused consent for marriage—his only emancipation would be to flee. Both Stone and Flandrin make it clear that, while parental *rights* is an old idea, the idea of extensive parental *obligations* is a notion of much more recent vintage. (The debate between Mo Tzu and the Confucianists was also conducted in such terms—for them, the primary issue was whether children had special duties to their fathers, not the other way around.)

These observations about social history should be approached with care. Of course they do not refute the idea of special parental obligations. However, they do go some way toward undermining our easy confidence that present-day social arrangements only institutionalize our natural duties. That is the only moral to be drawn from them, but it is an important one. In this area, as in so many others, what seems natural just depends on the conventions of one's society.

2. The Argument from Proximity

The second argument goes like this: It is reasonable to accept a social arrangement in which parents are assigned special responsibility for their own children because parents are *better situated* to look after their own. Granted, all children need help and protection. But other children are remote, and their needs are less clear, while a parent's own children live in the same house, and the parent is (or ought to be) intimately familiar with their needs. Other things being equal, it makes sense to think that A has a greater responsibility for helping B than for helping C, if A is better situated to help B. This is true in the case of helping one's own children versus helping other children; therefore, one's obligation in the first instance is greater.

This argument is plausible if we concentrate on certain kinds of aid. Children wake up sick in the middle of the night; someone must attend to them, and that someone is usually Mother or Father. The parents are in a position to do so, and (most of the time) no one else is. The complaint that you nursed your own children, but you didn't help the other children who woke up sick elsewhere in the world is obviously misguided. The same goes for countless other ways that parents assist their children, by making them take their medicine, by stopping them from playing in the roadway, by bundling them up against the cold, and so on. These are all matters of what we might call *day-to-day care.*

Day-to-day care involves a kind of personal attention that a parent *could not* provide for many others, because it is physically impossible. The importance of physical proximity is that it makes these kinds of caring behaviors possible; the impossibility of doing the same for other children is just the impossibility of being in two places at once. So if there is partiality here, it is a partiality that we need not worry about because it cannot be avoided. There is little doubt, then, that parents are normally in a better position to provide day-to-day care for their own children than for others.

This type of argument is less plausible, however, when we consider more general, fundamental needs, such as food. Is a parent in a better position to feed his own children than to provide for others? At one time this might have been the case. Before the advent of modern communications and transportation, and before the creation of efficient relief agencies, people might have been able to say that while they could feed their own, they were unable to do much about the plight of children elsewhere. But that is no longer true. Today, with relief agencies ready to take our assistance all over the world, needing only sufficient resources to do so, it is almost as easy to provide food for a child in Africa as to provide for one's own. The same goes for providing basic medical care: International relief agencies carry medical assistance around the world on the same basis.

Therefore, the argument from proximity is, at best, only partially successful. Some forms of assistance (such as getting up in the middle of the night to attend to sick children) do require proximity but others (such as providing food) do not. The argument might show that, where day-to-day care is concerned, parents have special duties. But the same cannot be said for the provision of fundamental needs.

3. The Argument from Personal Goods

The third argument hinges on the idea that loving relationships are personal goods of great importance: To love other people and be loved in return are part of what is involved in having a rich and satisfying human life. A loving relationship with one's children is, for many parents, a source of such happiness that they would sacrifice almost anything else to preserve it. But as we have already observed, love necessarily involves having a special concern for the well-being of the loved one, and so it is not impartial. An ethic that required absolute impartiality would therefore require forgoing a great personal good.

The intuitive idea behind this argument may seem plain enough. Nevertheless, it is difficult to formulate the argument with any precision. Why, exactly, is a loving relationship with another person such a great good? Part of the answer may be that pacts of mutual assistance enable all of us to fare better. If A and B have this sort of relationship, then A can count on B's assistance when it is needed, and vice versa. They are both better off. Of course, deals of this kind could be made between people who are not joined by bonds of affection, but affection makes the arrangement more dependable: People who love one another are more apt to remain faithful when the going is hard. But there is more. Bonds of affection are more than just instrumentally

good. To be loved is to have one's own value affirmed; thus it is a source of self-esteem. This is important for all of us, but especially for children, who are more helpless and vulnerable than adults. Moreover, there is, at a deep level, a connection between love and the meaning of life (although I cannot go into this very deeply here). We question whether our lives have meaning when we find nothing worth valuing, when it seems to us that "all is vanity." Loving relationships provide individuals with things to value, and so give their lives this kind of meaning. That is why parents who love their children, and who strive to see that they do well, can find in this meaning for their lives.

These are important points, but they do not prove as much as they are sometimes taken to prove. In the first place, there is a lot about parental love that *is* consistent with a large measure of impartiality. Loving someone is not only a matter of preferring their interests. Love involves, among other things, intimacy and the sharing of experiences. A parent shows his love by listening to the child's jokes, by talking, by being a considerate companion, by praising, and even by scolding when that is needed. It may be objected that these kinds of behavior also show partiality, since the parent does not do these things for all children. But these are only further instances of the day-to-day care that requires proximity; again, if this is partiality, it is partiality that cannot be avoided. And there is another difference between these kinds of support and such things as providing food and medical care. The companionship, the listening, the talking, and the praising and scolding are what make personal relationships *personal*. That is why the psychic benefits that accompany such relationships are more closely associated with these matters than with such relatively impersonal things as being fed.

Moreover, it is not necessary, in order to have a loving relationship with one's children and to derive from it the benefits that the argument from personal goods envisions, to regard their interests as *always* having priority, especially when the interests in question are not comparable. One could have a loving relationship that involves all the intimacies of day-to-day care and the provision of life's necessities, while acknowledging at the same time that when it comes to choosing between luxuries for them and food for orphans, the orphans' needs should prevail. At the very least, there is nothing in the argument from personal goods that rules out such an approach.

The Moral Point of Utopian Thinking

There is another approach to our problem, favored by the Mohists, that we have not yet considered: Clinging to the ideal of impartiality, we could simply reject the idea of special parental duties. This goes against our intuitions, and it is opposed by the (partially successful) arguments we have just examined. Nevertheless, we may ask whether there is anything to be said in favor of this approach.

In fact, there is a lot that might be said in its favor. Suppose we forget, for a moment, the imperfections of actual human life, and try to imagine what it would be like if everyone behaved in a morally blameless manner. What would relations between adults and children be like in such a utopia? Here is one plausible picture of such a world. In it, children with living parents able to provide for them would be raised by their parents, who would give them all the love and care they need. Parents who through no fault of their own were unable to provide for their children would be given whatever assistance they need. Orphans would be taken in by families who would raise and love them as their own. The burdens involved in such adoptions would be shared by all.

It is fair to say that, in such a world, the ideal of impartiality is realized. In this world people do not act as if any child is more deserving than any other: One way or another, equal provision is made for the needs of all. Moreover, luck plays no part in how children will fare: The orphans' needs are satisfied too. When it is said by the Mohists that "love is universal," or by their modern counterparts, the utilitarians, that we should "promote impartially the interests of everyone alike," this might be the point: In the morally best world, we would not recognize many of the distinctions that we do recognize in the real world we inhabit.

Practical Implications

How should parents, living not in utopia but in our society, who are concerned to do what is morally best, conceive of the relation between their obligations to their own children and their obligations to other children? Here are three contrasting views; each is implausible, but for different reasons.

1. *Extreme Bias.* On this view, parents have obligations to provide for their own children, but they have *no obligations at all* to other children. Anything done for other children is best supererogatory—good and praiseworthy if one chooses to do it, but in no way morally mandatory. On this view, parents may provide not only necessities but also luxuries for their own children, while other children starve, and yet be immune from moral criticism.

Extreme bias is not plausible, because it makes no provision whatever for a duty of general beneficence. It is hard to believe that we do not have some obligation to be concerned with the plight of the starving, whoever they are, even if that obligation is less extensive than our obligations to our own kin.[2] Thus it will not be surprising if this view turns out to be unacceptable.

2. *Complete Equality.* The opposite view seems to be implied by the idea of morality as impartiality—the view that all children are equal and that there is no difference at all between one's moral obligations toward one's own children and one's moral obligations toward other children. This view denies that there are any good moral grounds for preferring to feed one's own child rather than an orphan in a foreign country. In our society anyone who accepted and acted on such a view would seem to his neighbors to be morally deranged, for doing so would seem to involve a rejection of one's children—a refusal to treat them with the love that is appropriate to the parent–child relationship.

3. *The Most Common View.* What, in fact, do people in our society seem to believe? Most people seem to believe that one has an obligation to provide the necessities of life for other children only after one has already provided a great range of luxuries for one's own. On this view, it is permissible to provide one's own children with virtually everything they need in order to have a good start in life—not only food and clothing, but, if possible, a good education, opportunities for travel, opportunities for enjoyable leisure, and so forth. In the United States children of affluent families often have TV sets, stereos, and now computers, all laid out in their own rooms. They drive their own cars to high school. Few people seem to think there is anything wrong with this—parents who are unable to provide their children with such luxuries nevertheless aspire to do so.

The most common view imposes *some* duty regarding other children, but not much. In practical terms, it imposes a duty only on the very rich, who have resources left over even after they have provided ample luxuries for their own children. The rest of us, who have nothing left after doing as much as we can for our own, are off the hook. It takes only a little reflection to see that this view is also implausible. How can it be right to spend money on luxuries for some children, even one's own—buying them the latest trendy toys, for example—while others do not have enough to eat?

Perhaps, when confronted with this, many people might come to doubt whether it is correct. But certainly most affluent people act as if it were correct.

Is there a better alternative? Is there a view that escapes the difficulties of extreme bias, complete equality, and the most common view, and is consistent with the various other points that have been made in our discussion? I suggest the following.

4. *Partial Bias.* We might say that, while we do have a substantial obligation to be concerned about the welfare of all children, our own nevertheless come first. This vague thought needs to be sharpened. One way of making it more precise is this: When considering similar needs, you may permissibly prefer to provide for the needs of your own children. For example, if you were faced with a choice between feeding your own children or contributing the money to provide food for other children, you could rightly choose to feed your own. But if the choice were between some relatively trivial thing for your own and necessities for other children, preference should be given to helping the others. Thus if the choice were between providing trendy toys for your own already well-fed children or feeding the starving, you should feed the starving.

This view will turn out to be more or less demanding, depending on what one counts as a "relatively trivial thing." We might agree that buying trendy toys for some children, even for one's own, while other children starve is indefensible. But what about buying them nice clothes? Or a college education? Am I justified in sending my children to an ex-

pensive college? Clearly, the line between the trivial and the important can be drawn at different places. (One will be pushed toward a more demanding interpretation as one takes more seriously the point about the moral irrelevance of luck.) Nevertheless, the intuitive idea is plain enough. On this view, you may provide the necessities for your own children first, but you are not justified in providing them luxuries while other children lack necessities. Even in a fairly weak form, this view would still require much greater concern for others than the view that is most common in our society.

From the point of view of the various arguments we have considered, partial bias clearly stands out as the superior view. It is closer to the utopian ideal than either extreme bias or the most common view; it is morally superior in that it makes greater provision for children who have no loving parents; it is consistent with the arguments we have considered concerning the benefits to be derived from loving relationships; and it is perhaps as much as we could expect from people in the real world. It is not, in fact, very far from the utopian ideal. If we begin with Complete Equality, and then modify it in the ways suggested in our discussion of utopia, we end up with something very much like partial bias.

What would the adoption of partial bias mean for actual families? It would mean that parents could continue to provide loving day-to-day care for their own children, with all that this involves, while giving them preferential treatment in the provision of life's necessities. But it would also mean preferring to provide the necessities for needier children, rather than luxuries for their own. Children in such families would be worse off, in an obvious sense, than the children of affluent parents who continued to live according to the dictates of extreme bias or the most common view. However, we might hope that they would not regard themselves as deprived, for they might learn the moral value of giving up their luxuries so that the other children do not starve. They might even come to see their parents as morally admirable people. That hope is itself utopian enough.

Endnotes

1. "The good of any one individual is of no more importance, from the point of view (if I may say so) of the Universe, than the good of any other," says Sidgwick (1907, 382). "We [must] give equal weight in our moral deliberations to the like interests of all those affected by our actions," says Singer (1971, 197). "Moral rules must

be for the good of everyone alike," says Baier (1958, 200). "A rational and impartial sympathetic spectator is a person who takes up a general perspective: He assumes a position where his own interests are not at stake and he possesses all the requisite information and powers of reasoning. So situated, he is equally responsive and sympathetic to the desires and satisfactions of everyone affected by the social system. . . . Responding to the interests of each person in the same way, an impartial spectator gives free rein to his capacity for sympathetic identification by viewing each person's situation as it affects that person," says Rawls (1971, 186). In an interesting discussion, R. M. Hare argues that virtually all the major moral theories incorporate a requirement of impartiality and adds that his own "universal prescriptivism" is no exception.

2. For arguments concerning the extensiveness of our obligations towards others, see Singer (1972) and Rachels (1979).

References

Baier, Kurt. 1958. *The Moral Point of View.* Ithaca: Cornell University Press.

Fung Yu-lan. 1960. *A Short History of Chinese Philosophy.* New York: Macmillan.

Hare, R. M. 1972. "Rules of War and Moral Reasoning." *Philosophy and Public Affairs, 1,* 166–181.

Mill, John Stuart. 1957. *Utilitarianism.* Indianapolis: Bobbs-Merrill. This work, first published in 1861, is today available in many editions.

Rachels, James. 1979. "Killing and Starving to Death." *Philosophy, 54,* 159–171.

Rawls, John. 1971. *A Theory of Justice.* Cambridge: Harvard University Press.

Rubin, Vitaly A. 1976. *Individual and State in Ancient China.* New York: Columbia University Press.

Sidgwick, Henry. 1907. *The Methods of Ethics,* 7th ed. London: Macmillan.

Singer, Peter. 1972. "Famine, Affluence, and Morality." *Philosophy and Public Affairs, 1,* 229–243.

———. 1978. "Is Racial Discrimination Arbitrary?" *Philosophia, 8,* 185–203.

Stone, Lawrence. 1979. *The Family, Sex and Marriage in England 1500–1800.* New York: Harper & Row.

11. The Food-Aid Racket

MICHAEL MAREN

Former development worker Michael Maren argues that food relief projects are often damaging to the people they are meant to help. He also argues that private volunteer organizations and their employees have a vested interest in keeping Third World countries dependent on aid.

As you prepare for and look forward to careers in international development, I am compelled to issue a warning. With the hindsight of someone who spent five years in the development business, I'm going to tell you that the development industry hurts people in the developing world. Its greatest success has been to provide good jobs for Westerners with graduate degrees from institutions like this one [Cornell]. I don't expect that any of you will take my advice and start looking for careers elsewhere. And I'm in no position to criticize you for going ahead and working in development even after you hear me out. You see, I had a pretty wonderful career in the aid business. I can't remember ever having more fun. In fact, I was having so much fun that I didn't want to stop, even after I realized that our programs were hurting the very people they were supposed to help.

Reprinted from *Harper's Magazine* (1993) with permission.

In 1980, when I was twenty-five years old, I was hired by Catholic Relief Services (CRS) to administer food-for-work programs—programs that feed people in exchange for their work on local development projects—in Kenya. I was given a beautiful garden apartment in a nice neighborhood in Nairobi, a brand-new Land Cruiser, a great office, and almost a million dollars in a U.S. Agency for International Development (AID) grant to oversee the programs. As I began the job, shiploads of U.S. government surplus rice were leaving a port in Texas and heading to Mombasa.

Meanwhile, CRS notified the country's parish priests and government officials that this rice was available. All they had to do to receive it was fill out a one-page application describing their proposed project and specifying the number of "recipients"— the number of the project's workers who would receive sacks of rice in exchange for their labor. Thousands of applications were submitted.

I took some of the U.S. AID money and customized the Land Cruiser, adding extra-large fuel tanks and a really nice stereo system, and then I set off across Kenya to inspect the proposed projects. It was a dream come true. I was driving absolutely free across one of the world's most beautiful landscapes. I was so awestruck by my own good luck that sometimes I'd stop in the middle of a huge empty wilderness, or beside a herd of giraffes or elephants, and just yelp with delight.

I was having so much fun running around starting food-for-work projects—water projects, agriculture projects, forestry projects—that I completely overlooked the most obvious problem: I knew nothing about agriculture, forestry, road building, well digging, dam building, or any of the projects I was approving. But nobody seemed to care. Only once did anyone in authority at CRS ever go and look at a project. When I'd return to Nairobi every few weeks, my boss, who let me work completely unsupervised, had only one question: How many more recipients did you sign on? More recipients meant more government grant money, which meant we could buy more vehicles and hire more assistants.

When I slowed down for a moment to consider what was happening, it became clear: aid distribution is just another big, private business that relies on government contracts. Private voluntary organizations (PVOs) such as CRS are paid by the U.S. government to give away surplus food produced by subsidized U.S. farmers. The more food CRS gave

away, the more money they received from the government to administer the handouts. Since the securing of grant money is the primary goal, PVOs rarely meet a development project they don't like.

Of all the aid programs, those involving food delivery are especially prized by PVOs because they generate income, are easy to administer, and are warmly received by the public. Yet most food aid has little to do with need and everything to do with getting rid of surplus food. Kenya was not a country facing starvation when I worked there. Many of the projects I started were in the rich agricultural land of the central and western parts of the country. In fact, around the world, only about 10 percent of food aid is targeted at emergency situations. PVOs publicize situations such as the one in Somalia in order to raise money from the public, but most of their work is done in areas where there is plenty to eat, because there are simply not enough starving people to absorb all of our surplus food. Also, it's easier to distribute large quantities of food in more developed areas.

Harmless as this might at first sound, sending food to areas where there is already food creates serious problems. It decreases demand for locally produced commodities, subsidizes the production of cash crops, and fosters dependence among those who receive the aid. Since PVOs can only operate with the approval of the host government, they typically end up supporting the government leaders' political goals, rewarding the government's friends, punishing its enemies, and providing fodder for a vast system of political patronage.

That's exactly what happened in Somalia, where the government and the generals had been playing games with food aid for more than a decade before the Marines arrived. I was working for U.S. AID in Somalia in 1981, when we started pumping food into that country. It was clear to many of us, even then, that the program was working to prop up a corrupt dictator and turn nomads into relief junkies. Refugees poured over the borders and into camps, where they were fed day after day, year after year, by PVOs, while little effort was made to break their growing dependence. In 1987 a World Food Program report stated that Somalia had actually produced a surplus of food that year, yet PVOs continue to distribute free food and collect U.S. government money for administering the delivery. Inevitably, indigenous food-distribution networks withered and died. The country's economy adapted to foreign aid—not to production. Meanwhile, the PVOs and corrupt government officials got fat and rich.

No one questions private voluntary organizations. Not the U.S. government, which needs to get rid of the food and wants to keep its aid bureaucracy functioning. Not the host government, whose officials often profit from the aid racket. Not the public, which sees aid workers as so many Mother Teresas. And not the press—especially not the press—which has, in recent years, become an integral part of the aid system.

The press's role in that system is to convey to the West the PVOs' view of Africa. And because the distribution of food aid is first and foremost a business, it is not surprising that the priorities of aid organizations dominate the West's image of the continent—an image of helpless nations in need of our support.

This is not a new phenomenon. Aid workers are simply the latest in a series of recent western vanguards in Africa, each of whom put forward the image of Africa that best suited its own interests. The first Europeans to form a vanguard in Africa were the naturalists. Because of them, early European views of Africa emphasized the continent's natural history. Later, as missionaries began to outnumber explorers, Europe began to see the continent through the eyes of those who were out to save its soul. And as Europe developed political and mercantile interests in Africa, merchants and traders were at the vanguard. At that time, Europeans were concerned with turning Africans into loyal subjects, workers, producers, and citizens of empires. No one really worried about feeding them.

Historically, the press has been willing to uncritically accept whatever image of Africa the western vanguard has been selling. In the case of the PVOs, the press has bought their line because reporters are as dependent on aid organizations as the organizations are on them. It would have been impossible, for example, for the press to cover Somalia without the assistance of PVOs. There's no Hertz counter at the Mogadishu airport, and no road maps available at gas stations. If a journalist arrives in Africa from Europe or the United States and needs to get to the interior of the country, PVOS are the only ticket. Journalists sleep and eat with PVO workers.

When they want history and facts and figures, they turn to the PVOs. In press coverage of Somalia or almost any other crisis in Africa, it is always the PVOs who are most often quoted and are regarded as the neutral and authoritative sources—as if they have no vested interest in anything but the truth.

A typical example of the connection between journalism and the aid system is this analysis from a February 22, 1993 story about Africa in the *New York Times*:

> The greatest danger now to Mozambique's tranquillity, almost everyone agrees, is Mozambique's tranquillity. Lacking scenes of carnage and starvation to disturb Western television audiences, Mozambique is having trouble competing for attention with Somalia and the former Yugoslavia.

The article goes on to quote numerous CARE officials whose primary concern is to raise more money to give more aid to Mozambique. The article never considers any alternatives to aid. No aid worker raises the possibility, for example, that Mozambique's economy might improve if the country focused on exporting goods. No one mentions that in the absence of carnage, Mozambique might be a good place to invest. No one is talking about creating permanent employment for Africans. The only discussion is about raising more money to send experts there and preserve the jobs of expatriates and create more jobs for graduate students from programs like this one. The people who are called upon to diagnose and comment on Africa's problems are the very people who stand to profit from the diagnoses.

I know that you don't want to be part of this problem. You'll tell me that you can change all of this, that you want to work within the bureaucracy to reform the bureaucracy. But in a couple of years you're going to be in Ouagadougou or Gaborone making a very good salary. The years will pass and you'll find yourself with two kids in an expensive private school in New England, and you're going to have perfected skills that aren't very useful outside of the Third World. You're going to think about quitting, about raising hell, but you won't be able to. Because by then you, too, will have become part of the never-ending cycle of aid.

12. Some Moral Dilemmas of Humanitarian Aid

MARY B. ANDERSON

Mary B. Anderson admits that humanitarian assistance programs can have negative side effects and she discusses three responses to this problem. The response that she favors is to find options for delivering aid without those negative side effects, and she gives a number of examples of where this was done.

There can be little doubt that humanitarian assistance is under challenge. Time after time, aid that was meant as simple, neutral, and pure "act of mercy" becomes tainted by subsequent negative ramifications in the complex settings of today's war-induced crises. We have lost our innocence about the impacts of aid. We know that, even as it saves lives and reduces human suffering, humanitarian assistance can also lead to dependency on the part of those who receive it. We know that aid provided in conflict settings can feed into and exacerbate the conflicts that cause the suffering it is meant to alleviate. And we know that aid too often does nothing to alter—and very often reinforces—the fundamental circumstances that produced the needs it temporarily meets.

Faced with strong evidence that emergency aid has negative side effects and too little systemic positive effect, and faced with the moral conundrum that these realities entail, aid providers have several responses.

Some affirm their commitment to "the primacy of the humanitarian imperative" and conclude that, despite aid's negative consequences, it is imperative to respond to others' urgent needs as a matter of conscience. They feel that if they can save a life and do not do so, they do wrong. They are concerned that accepting responsibility for potential side effects of their actions may immobilize them entirely. These providers of aid accept the negative side effects of aid but believe that the good they succeed in doing still outweighs the harm they unintentionally do.

Reprinted from *Hard Choices* (1998) edited by Jonathan Moore by permission of Rowman & Littlefield.

A second response to the negative effects of aid comes as direct criticism. After each major outpouring of assistance in response to a crisis, another book or television special appears that reports on the multiple problems caused by aid. The critics tell true stories. They assemble evidence familiar to every field-based worker.

They conclude that no aid would be preferable to the aid that does such harm. This position, however, entails a logical and moral fallacy. Demonstrating that aid does harm is not the same as demonstrating that no aid would do no harm. Nor does the conclusion that aid does harm justify the additional conclusion that providing no aid would result in good. If there is moral ambiguity in providing aid, there is also moral ambiguity in providing no aid.

Are providers of humanitarian assistance morally trapped between giving aid with its bad outcomes or not giving aid with other probable negative effects? I will argue here that the answer is no. Citing field experience of aid workers who have found ways to avoid the most commonly accepted negative outcomes of aid, I argue that this evidence suggests that it is possible for all aid workers to do so if they learn and employ the lessons of experience.

This point does not mean that providers of emergency assistance can altogether escape moral uncertainty. The same experience that suggests it is possible to avoid aid's negative impacts that have been considered virtually inevitable also suggests that other areas are emerging in which aid raises new moral challenges.

I first discuss two areas in which most observers locate the moral *problematique* presented by the negative impacts of emergency humanitarian assistance: (1) the tendency for humanitarian aid to result in long-term dependency of recipients on donors and (2) the tendency for humanitarian aid that is provided in conflict settings to feed into, worsen, and prolong wars that cause the suffering it is intended to alleviate. I shall also consider how these tendencies are linked to the failure of emergency aid to address the fundamental problems that underlie and cause emergencies.

Having considered these dilemmas, I shall then cite evidence that shows them to be more apparent than real. As aid workers incorporate the lessons learned from experience in many settings, they can avoid repeating these past wrongs. These two dilemmas, often considered inevitable, can be averted. . . .

I turn first to the two areas in which aid providers and critics have traditionally thought the difficult moral challenges lie.

The Tendency for Aid to Result in Long-Term Dependency of Recipients on Donors

When humanitarian aid workers rush into a crisis to save lives and reduce human suffering, they do so with bravery and goodwill. They very often achieve significant success. However, they also often adopt a mode of operation that assumes that victims of crises can do little or nothing for themselves.

Aid providers adopt what they believe to be efficient delivery systems. To provide food, shelter, sanitation, and/or medical services, assistance agencies import or rent fleets of trucks and other equipment, they hire drivers and experts (also often imported), and they set up warehousing facilities and communications systems. They set up large-scale, centrally managed delivery systems focused on getting a product from donors to recipients, usually managed by expatriate staff. Aid is focused on meeting the needs of the "poorest of the poor." Learning from past experience that crisis victims received goods they could not use or did not need or that aid had been received by advantaged rather than disadvantaged people, aid providers now begin interventions with "needs assessments." These concentrate on physical lacks that are easily enumerated. Donors know how to respond to requests for a given tonnage of food or for specific quantities of housing materials or medical supplies.

The criteria for effectiveness of centrally managed, materials-focused aid systems include speed, accountability to outside donors, and, of course, receipt by individuals and groups deemed to be most needy.

The role for local people—those seen as "victims"—to manage any aspects of this aid system is minimal or nonexistent. Concentration on the delivery of things *to* these people, rather than on problem solving *with* them, places the beneficiaries of aid in a passive, accepting role.

Experience shows that such aid, by failing to recognize and connect with existing decision-making, management, distributional, or other productive and psychological capacities of the people affected by crises, undermines and weakens these capacities. More and more, recipients of aid accept what is given from outside as their due, their right. The experience of having needs met by outsiders produces a belief that outside aid is necessary for survival. Not only does aid thus disrupt existing decision-making and marketing systems that represented strengths in recipient economies, it also undermines networks and relationships on which the social order rests and any sense of efficacy that individuals had prior to their crisis.[1]

In addition, emergency aid usually ignores the causes of the emergency that prompted it. Often, responders focus on "getting things back to normal." However, it is the conditions of "normalcy" that gave rise to the emergency in the first place. That is, the disastrous impacts of emergencies (whether initiated by a natural event such as a flood, cyclone, or earthquake or by a political event such as a riot or war) fall on different groups of people with varying weight. Who suffers and who does not suffer reflect differences in economic, social, and political status. The vulnerability of people to disasters varies.

Emergency aid too often fails to address the circumstances that cause people to be vulnerable to the disasters from which they suffer. When aid is provided only to address the symptoms of crises, it leaves in place the causative factors of the crises. Thus, aid may reinforce vulnerabilities and even lead to new areas of vulnerability through creating privileged groups, undercutting coping systems, or encouraging unwarranted expectations about the availability of outside resources.

Aid does not have to be given in this way. Field-based experience from many sites shows that it is possible to avoid creating dependency among aid recipients and to provide even short-term emergency aid in ways that address the underlying root causes of an emergency. I shall return to this point later after examining the ways in which aid provided in war settings worsens conflict.

The Tendency for Aid Provided in Conflict Settings to Exacerbate the Conflict

A second area in which experience shows that well-intentioned assistance often has negative consequences is in relation to conflict. When aid is provided in war settings, even when it is effective in saving lives and alleviating human suffering, it very often, at the same time, inadvertently feeds into, worsens, and prolongs the conflict that prompted the need for aid. Again, many observers have written about these effects.[2]

The most obvious way that aid feeds conflict is through the direct misappropriation of goods by warring parties. Aid workers frequently report that the goods they deliver are routinely "taxed" as they pass through military checkpoints to reach intended beneficiaries. Aid goods are often stolen, diverted, and manipulated to serve the interests of those at war. Warriors also use aid in indirect ways. By controlling the locations where aid may be delivered, commanders manipulate population movements. By negotiating with aid agencies for the safe delivery of goods, commanders gain legitimacy in the eyes of those who depend on aid for survival and, sometimes, in the eyes of the international community.

When aid agencies assume the responsibility for supporting civilian survival during wars, fighters can use available internal resources for the purposes of battle. This approach also allows the warring leaders to define their responsibilities solely in military terms. Local so-called leaders are able to abdicate their responsibility for civilian life because it is adequately handled by the international aid community.

Aid goods represent both an economic resource and a source of power and control for people at war. It is neither surprising nor mysterious that aid, provided in a context of conflict, becomes an active part of that context.

Avoiding the Moral Dilemmas of Creating Dependency and Exacerbating Conflict

Concerned about the negative impacts of humanitarian aid, donors and aid providers have undertaken concerted efforts to understand, analyze, and find ways to avoid them. From examination of field-based experience, lessons have been learned about how to provide aid in ways that reinforce its positive impacts rather than lead to negative outcomes.[3]

The lessons learned point to a central principle of non–dependency-creating aid: providers should always start from the recognition that "victims" have capacities and that they are already coping with their own crisis before aid arrives.[4] Even very poor people have materials, social systems, attitudes, and beliefs that enable them to survive and on which their future lives and livelihoods must be based. When aid providers begin from a recognition of local capacities and supply aid in ways that support these, they help people both survive immediate life-threatening circumstances and strengthen and build a foundation on which their future independent development can occur.

Rather than doing "needs assessments" as the basis for designing interventions, aid providers should (and some do) focus on assessing capacities. A capacities assessment communicates respect for people's competence, their skills in life management, and their minds and spirits. It also lessens the need for imported supplies and management so that it costs less than outsider-managed aid and can be more easily withdrawn when internal recovery becomes possible.

In addition, aid providers should recognize that the needs they address are only manifestations of deeper circumstances that cause people to be vulnerable. It is important that they analyze the circumstances that underlie the crisis and identify the ways that their aid either reinforces and worsens these circumstances or reduces or overcomes them.

Many illustrations show that this approach can work. For example, during a postvolcano relief effort in the Philippines, one nongovernmental organization (NGO) placed community development workers in emergency shelters to live with displaced disaster victims. These NGO workers not only supplied food, blankets, and other things needed for survival but also helped the disaster sufferers plan future community projects to be undertaken when they returned to their villages. During the long days and nights during which they had nowhere to go and nothing else to do, the disaster victims got to know each other, organized committees, and laid the groundwork for community enterprises that they launched later when they returned to their homes.

Recognizing the "capacities" of idle time and an opportunity for daily community interaction and planning, aid workers helped local people use these to good advantage. They assisted these people to assess the underlying circumstances that kept them in poverty, and they supported their development of new systems for organizing to address these circumstances. These aid workers recognized and strengthened the victims' capacities and helped them reduce their long-term vulnerabilities.[5]

In Ethiopia, during the major famine of 1983–1984, many international NGOs helped feed the thousands of people at risk of starvation. Most set up feeding camps along the roadsides where hungry people gathered. They shipped food into these settings and established systems for ensuring that those in the greatest need were fed first. The result was that many people received food who needed it.

At the same time, disease was a constant threat (and reality) in the overcrowded camps, and aid recipients had nothing to do but wait for food to be delivered, measured, and meted out to them. Because some people became weakened by hunger earlier than others, families were often separated by aid workers who determined that only those in greatest need could enter the feeding centers. The concentration of food in camps enticed people to gather around them, waiting until their need was great enough to justify their admission. Vulnerability to disease and dependency increased. When the famine ended, people in feeding camps were often far from their homes and thus not able to take advantage of rains in time to plant a new crop. Their vulnerability and dependence on others was thus extended for another season.

Another NGO, in the same crisis, gave people gathered at roadsides sufficient rations to survive and told them to return home. This agency promised to deliver food "as close as possible" to villages. The people who were still sufficiently healthy organized crews to build roads to reach remote villages. The NGO provided an engineer to advise them on road grades, and the people used their own tools and the abundant stones scattered across the countryside for building. Others organized donkey trains to carry food to even more remote villages. Some organized warehousing in community buildings. Everyone was able to stay at home, families and communities remained together, and when the rains began, people were on their fields and ready to plant. Recovery was quickly possible. Idle time, stones, tools, community structures, and donkeys all represented indigenous capacities that, when coupled with outside food, allowed people to survive the emergency and to be ready for recovery and development.[6]

In Central America after an earthquake destroyed many homes, an NGO sent a representative to the area to survey the needs. This man arrived in a village that was particularly badly hit and was met by villagers asking how much aid he planned to give them. He responded that, before he could decide, he needed to see what had happened, and he invited people to take him on a walking tour of the town. As they walked (and larger and larger crowds of people joined the entourage), the aid provider asked the community to explain "why this building is still standing" and "why that building fell down." By the time the tour was finished, he told the community that they had answered his questions with great knowledge. He pointed out that they knew what made a building earthquake-resistant and why some structures were vulnerable. He then offered to provide just enough aid to assist them in rebuilding their homes, using their own knowledge and local materials to ensure greater security against future earth tremors. Local knowledge and local building materials provided capacities that, when coupled with minimal external aid, allowed a large number of people in this community to rebuild stronger, less vulnerable houses. They also recognized that their knowledge of the area was superior to that of any outsider.[7]

These illustrations of how aid may build on and support capacities and address vulnerabilities are from areas in which the crisis was based on a natural event—volcano, drought, and earthquake. When aid is delivered in a context of war, former close associates, friends, neighbors, and coworkers are in conflict, and commanders rule over contiguous and conflicting regions. Experience shows that in such a context, identification of legitimate local capacities and the design of aid to address deep-seated causes of the crisis are more difficult.

For example, in 1994, as refugees poured from Rwanda into eastern Zaire and the humanitarian assistance community wished to preserve life in this unhealthy setting, international aid workers report that the circumstances seemed to be "an aid provider's dream."[8] Whole villages arrived together with leadership structures intact so that early decisions about how to allocate and distribute food seemed easy. Relying on apparent local capacities in order to avoid dependency, aid providers accepted these leaders as the appropriate conduit for food distributions. It is now well known that the camp "leadership" was the Hutu militia who had committed the genocide in Rwanda. They were able to use the resources provided by international humanitarian aid to control civilian populations and to rearm and prepare for a return battle in Rwanda.

As this example shows, reliance on local capacities in war settings can reinforce existing power structures that are a part of the conflict. From experience, we are now learning that avoiding the negative impacts on conflict while giving aid in conflict settings requires two distinct levels of analysis and planning.[9]

On the one hand, aid providers must recognize that some indigenous capacities in war settings are capacities for war. They need to analyze the ways that warriors may misappropriate aid resources and develop strategies for avoiding these. On the other hand, aid providers need also to develop skills for identifying—and supporting—local capacities that are, genuinely, capacities for peace.

Though experience is still being assembled, evidence indicates that negative impacts can be avoided and positive peace-supporting activities can be linked to the provision of life-saving humanitarian aid in war situations.

For example, to avoid theft or misappropriation of aid goods by warring commanders, aid providers have been inventive in adopting different, locally effective strategies. In some areas, they have relied on broad publicity of scheduled delivery times and quantities to enable local people to control the aid resources and hold potential thieves accountable if losses occur. In other places, aid agencies have relied on secrecy, delivering goods without prior announcement of times or locations to avoid theft.

Dispersal techniques have proven effective in some places. For example, a cargo plane landing in Siem Riep, Cambodia, loaded with bags of cash to pay local aid staff, was met on the runway by a series of small vehicles. A few bags of cash were loaded into the trunk of a car, and it sped away. Another bag went in the back of a truck, and it left. Others went into carts, Jeeps, and a variety of vehicles. As aid providers explained, each of these transports took a different route to the aid office. It would hardly be worth the effort of thieves to stop any one of them because each carried an insignificant amount of money.[10]

To avoid caring for civilian needs in ways that allow commanders to abdicate their responsibilities for civilian survival, aid agencies have also tried a variety of approaches. Some establish a pattern of regular, "friendly" meetings with a local commander to discuss civilian needs and activities and encourage the commander to recognize the interests of his people. Oddly, sometimes a commander has been completely unaware of this aspect of leadership and has appreciated being helped to gauge public opinion on civilian affairs as well as on military issues.[11] In Sudan, aid workers report that the military personnel assigned to work in the humanitarian wings of the Southern Movements indicate that they value the opportunity to be something other than fighters. They feel that circumstances have trapped them into constant warfare; they need and want space to act in non-war ways.[12]

Experience shows that, in every civil war situation, no matter how violent and divisive, certain systems, structures, attitudes, and actions that connect people continue to exist. It is these "connectors" that we call capacities for peace because they represent the base (albeit inadequate!) on which past peace rested and on which future peace must, in part, be reconstructed. Warriors are good at identifying connectors and intentionally destroying them in pursuit of victory. For example, communications systems that allow people to keep in touch and share information across factional lines are often targeted by fighters who control media as a weapon. In spite of this problem, people find ways to maintain systems for staying in touch throughout wars. For example, in Tusla, Bosnia and Herzegovina, one local group maintained E-mail contact with colleagues in Serbia when all other contact was severed. In many war zones, people report that they rely on the BBC for impartial information rather than only on the information beamed to them by war propagandists. In some areas, drivers of aid truck convoys state that they keep radio contact with drivers "on the other side" to share information about areas of danger and safety in a kind of "underground fraternity."

In war zones, many people continue to trade with designated "enemies." This enterprise may occur on the riverbank one afternoon a week, or it may involve formal contracts and bank accounts. When markets are seen to be effective in binding people in mutual interdependence, they may become targets of warriors intent on destroying mutuality. However, more often people on different sides of wars continue to trade with each other in spite of fighting.

Aid workers who enter a war context to provide emergency assistance very often fail to see such continuing connectors. Because they have come in response to war, and because they are themselves in danger from the prevalent violence, they are dramatically aware of societal divisions. Experience shows that they therefore deliver assistance in relation to obvious divisions rather than in relation to (and support of) connectors. The question arises, If humanitarian assistance were channeled to reinforce the things that connect people rather than divide them, could it not only meet immediate needs but also help buttress and enlarge the "connecting space" and "voice" for people to disengage from war?

Isolated Good Luck or Generalizable Experiences?

Some might argue that the stories told here are no more than isolated examples or just good luck. They might feel that, in the face of the complexities of today's war-rent societies, such examples are puerile, insignificant, and misleading.

I would argue that easy dismissal of inventive field approaches that have avoided what were considered "inevitable" negative impacts of aid is misleading. The challenge posed by the stories told here (and they are only a small sampling of a much larger collection of positive and promising experiences) is that options for the delivery of aid without negative outcomes are available.[13] Business-as-usual that accepts aid's negative impacts as justified by positive outcomes is no longer acceptable because experience shows that negative impacts are not inevitable.

So, although moral ambiguity is not yet entirely vanquished in the areas of dependency and conflict, there is hope. More careful analysis and more concerted learning from experience that builds on the progress that has been made can free us from entrapment in these particular moral webs. . . .

Endnotes

The quotation in the title of this chapter comes from a personal communication by a man from Sierra Leone where international aid was being delivered by many nongovernment organizations at the time, fall 1996.

1. These tendencies are reported in many analyses of aid. Several of the earliest documentation of these impacts are found in Fred Cuny, *Disasters and Development* (Oxford: Oxford University Press, 1983); Gunner Hagman (with Henrik Beer, Marten Bend, and Anders Wijkman), *Prevention Better Than Cure: Report on Human and Environmental Disasters in the Third World* (Stockholm: Swedish Red Cross, 1984); and Barbara E. Harrell-Bond, *Imposing Aid: Emergency Assistance to Refugees* (Oxford: Oxford University Press, 1986). The International Relief/Development Project also documented and classified the negative effects of relief aid on development, published in Mary B. Anderson and Peter J. Woodrow, *Rising from the Ashes: Development Strategies at Times of Disaster* (Boulder, Colo. and Paris: Westview and UNESCO Presses, 1989).

2. See, for example, Robert Miller, ed., *Aid as Peacemaker: Canadian Development Assistance and Third World Conflict*

(Ottawa: Charlatan University Press, 1992); Mary B. Anderson, "International Assistance and Conflict: An Exploration of Negative Impacts" (Cambridge, Mass.: Local Capacities for Peace Project, Collaborative for Development Action, 1994); and John Prendergast, *Frontline Diplomacy: Humanitarian Aid and Conflict in Africa* (Boulder, Colo.: Lynne Rienner, 1996).

3. In the pages that follow, I cite examples found through two projects that I have directed that were aimed, specifically, at collecting from field experience lessons learned on how to avoid negative impacts of aid. These are (1) the International Relief/Development Project (IR/DP), which Peter Woodrow and I codirected at Harvard University between 1987 and 1989 and which resulted in the publication of *Rising from the Ashes* cited earlier; and (2) the Local Capacities for Peace Project, run from the Collaborate for Development Action, Inc., in Cambridge, Massachusetts, which involves a number of donor governments and multilateral agencies, NGOs, and individuals involved in aid delivery in conflict settings.

4. Again, the IR/DP assembled this evidence and put forward a Capacities and Vulnerabilities Analytical Framework for the use of aid workers in planning and running aid projects in ways that avoid long-term dependency. See Anderson and Woodrow, *Rising from the Ashes.* Further, the Canadian Council for International Cooperation has published a series of studies using the framework of the IR/DP to assess and plan aid interventions.

5. Local Resource Management Project, Santo Domingo, Albay, Bicol Region, Philippines, reported in Anderson and Woodrow, *Rising from the Ashes,* 241–58.

6. Ethiopia Emergency Program, Yifat na Timuga, Ethiopia, reported in Anderson and Woodrow, *Rising from the Ashes,* 135–56.

7. Reported from his own experience by Ronald J. Parker in personal communication.

8. Personal communication from an aid worker who requested anonymity. However, I since asked others who

were present who concurred with this individual's judgment that it appeared that the circumstances were ideal in terms of relying on local capacities.

9. Finding of the Local Capacities for Peace Project, reported in Mary B. Anderson, *Do No Harm: Supporting Local Capacities for Peace through Aid* (Cambridge, Mass.: Collaborative for Development Action, 1996).

10. Reported in Anderson, *Do No Harm,* 22–23.

11. Personal communication from a staff member of CARE/Canada who had worked in parts of Liberia.

12. From discussions at a Local Capacities for Peace Feedback Workshop held in Nairobi, Kenya, January 1997, for aid agency personnel working in southern Sudan.

13. One person who has examined how to avoid negative impacts of aid on conflict *and* the potential for aid to lead toward peace building is John Prendergast; see his *Frontline Diplomacy.*

Suggestions for Further Reading

Anthologies

Brown, Peter, and Henry Shue. *Boundaries.* Totowa, NJ: Rowman and Littlefield, 1981.

Crocker, David and Toby Linden, *The Ethics of Consumption.* Lanham, NJ: Rowman & Littlefield, 1998.

Lucas, George R., Jr., and Thomas W. Ogletree. *Lifeboat Ethics.* New York: Harper & Row, 1976.

Luper-Foy, Steven. *Problems of International Justice.* Boulder, CO: Westview, 1988.

Partridge, Ernest. *Responsibilities to Future Generations.* Buffalo, NY: Prometheus, 1981.

Sikora, R. I., and Brian Barry. *Obligation to Future Generations.* Philadelphia: Temple University Press, 1978.

Basic Concepts

Parfit, Derek. *Reasons and Persons.* Oxford: Oxford University Press, 1985.

Alternative Views

Amur, Samir. *Unequal Development.* New York: Monthly Review Press, 1976.

Barbieri, William. *The Ethics of Citizenship.* Durham: Duke University Press, 1998.

Bauer, P. T. *Equality, the Third World and Economic Delusion.* Cambridge: Harvard University Press, 1981.

Bayles, Michael D. *Morality and Population Policy.* Birmingham: University of Alabama Press, 1980.

Beitz, Charles R. *Political Theory and International Relations.* Princeton: Princeton University Press, 1979.

Elfstrom, Gerald. *Ethics for a Shrinking World.* New York: St. Martin's Press, 1990.

Hardin, Garrett. *Promethean Ethics.* Seattle: University of Washington Press, 1980.

Renner, Michael. *Fighting for Survival.* New York: Norton, 1996.

Shue, Henry. *Basic Rights.* Princeton: Princeton University Press, 1980.

Practical Applications

Lappé, Frances Moore. *World Hunger: Twelve Myths.* New York: Grove Press, 1986.

Russett, Bruce, and Harvey Starr. *World Politics: The Menu for Choice.* San Francisco: W. H. Freeman and Co., 1981.

Schumacher, E. F. *Small Is Beautiful.* New York: Harper & Row, 1973.

Section III

Abortion and Euthanasia

Introduction

Basic Concepts

The problem of abortion and euthanasia has been as thoroughly discussed as any contemporary moral problem. As a result, the conceptual issues have been fairly well laid out, and there have been some interesting attempts to bridge the troublesome normative and practical disagreements that remain.

First of all, almost everyone agrees that the fundamental issue in justifying abortion is the moral status of the fetus, although considerable disagreement exists as to what that status is.[1] Conservatives on the abortion question, like Don Marquis (Selection 14), contend that from conception the fetus has full moral status and hence a serious right to life. Liberals like Mary Anne Warren (Selection 15) hold that, at least until birth, the fetus has almost no moral status whatsoever and lacks a serious right to life.[2] Moderates on the question adopt some position in between these two views. And still others, like Judith Jarvis Thompson (Selection 13), adopt for the sake of argument either the conservative or the liberal view on moral status of the fetus and then try to show that such a view does not lead to the consequences its supporters assume.[3]

Second, almost everyone agrees that the position one takes on the moral status of the fetus influences whether one considers either the distinction between killing and letting die or the doctrine of double effect to be relevant to the abortion question. For example, conservatives are quite interested in whether the kill-ing and letting die distinction can be used to show that it is permissible to let the fetus die in certain contexts, even when it would be impermissible to kill it. However, liberals find the use of this distinction in such contexts to be completely unnecessary: They hold that the fetus has almost no moral status, so they do not object to either killing it or letting it die. Similarly, although conservatives are quite interested in whether the doctrine of double effect can be used to permit the death of the fetus as a foreseen but unintended consequence of some legitimate course of action, liberals find no use for the doctrine of double effect in such contexts.

Third, almost everyone agrees that either the killing and letting die distinction or the doctrine of double effect could prove useful in cases of euthanasia. Agreement is possible because most of the subjects of euthanasia are humans who, in everyone's view, have full moral status and hence a serious right to life. Accordingly, despite the disagreement as to where it is useful to apply the killing and letting die distinction and the doctrine of double effect, everyone agrees that both conceptual tools deserve further examination.

The distinction between killing and letting die has its advocates and its critics. Advocates maintain that, other things being equal, killing is morally worse than letting die, with the consequence that letting die is justified in cases where killing is not. The critics of this distinction maintain that, other things being equal, killing is not morally worse than letting die, with the consequence that killing is morally justified whenever letting die is. Both advocates and critics agree that other things would not be equal if the killing were justified or deserved while the letting die unwanted and undeserved. They tend to disagree, however, over whether other things would be equal if the killing were in response to a patient's request to die while the letting die involved a prolonged and excruciatingly painful death, or if the killing resulted in the death of just a few individuals while the letting die resulted in the death of many people.

Yet whatever view one adopts as to when other things are equal, it is hard to defend the moral preferability of letting die over killing when both are taken to be intentional acts. As James Rachels so graphically illustrates (Selection 17), it seems impossible to judge the act of A, who intentionally lets Z die while standing ready to finish Z off if that proves necessary, as being morally preferable to the act of B, who with similar motive and intention kills Y. But it is far from clear whether advocates of the killing and letting die distinction are claiming that the distinction holds when the killing and the letting die are both intentional acts because it is unlikely in such cases that the letting die would be morally justified when the killing is not. Rather, as Bonnie Steinbock argues (Selection 18), advocates of the distinction seem to have in mind a contrast between *intentional* killing and *unintentional* letting die, or more fully stated, a contrast between intentional killing and unintentional letting die when the latter is the foreseen consequence of an otherwise legitimate course of action.

Steinbock maintains that there are at least two types of cases in which letting die, distinguished in this way from killing, seems justified. In the first, a doctor ceases treatment at the patient's request, foreseeing that the patient will die or die sooner than otherwise, yet not intending that result. In the second, a doctor's intention is to avoid employing treatment that is extremely painful and has little hope of benefiting the patient, even though she foresees that this may hasten the patient's death. In addition, conservatives have argued that letting die, distinguished in this way from killing, can be justified in cases of ectopic pregnancy and cancer of the uterus because in such cases the fetus's death is the foreseen but unintended consequence of medical treatment that is necessary to preserve the basic well-being of the pregnant woman.

When the killing and letting die distinction is interpreted in this way, it has much in common with the doctrine of double effect. This doctrine places four restrictions on the permissibility of acting when some of the consequences of one's action are evil. These restrictions are as follows:

1. The act is good in itself or at least indifferent.

2. Only the good consequences of the act are intended.

3. The good consequences are not the effect of the evil.

4. The good consequences are commensurate with the evil consequences.

The basic idea of the killing and letting die distinction, as we have interpreted it, is expressed by restrictions 2 and 3.

When conservatives apply the doctrine of double effect to a case in which a pregnant woman has cancer of the uterus, the doctrine is said to justify an abortion because:

1. The act of removing the cancerous uterus is good in itself.

2. Only the removal of the cancerous uterus is intended.

3. The removal of the cancerous uterus is not a consequence of the abortion.

4. Preserving the life of the mother by removing the cancerous uterus is commensurate with the death of the fetus.

The doctrine is also said to justify unintentionally letting a person die, or "passive euthanasia," at least in the two types of cases described by Steinbock.

In recent moral philosophy, the main objection to the doctrine of double effect has been to question the necessity of its restrictions. Consider the following example. Imagine that a fat person who is leading a party of spelunkers gets herself stuck in the mouth of a cave in which flood waters are rising. The trapped party of spelunkers just happens to have a stick of dynamite with which they can blast the fat person out of the mouth of the cave; either they use the dynamite or they all drown, the fat person with them. It appears that the doctrine of double effect would *not* permit the use of the dynamite in this case because the evil consequences of the act are intended as a means to securing the good consequences in violation of restrictions 2 and 3. Yet it is plausible to argue in such a case that using dynamite would be justified on the grounds that (a) the evil to be avoided (i.e., the evil of failing to save the party of spelunkers except for the fat person) is considerably greater than the evil resulting from the means employed (i.e., the evil of intentionally causing the death of the fat person) and/or that (b) the greater part of evil resulting from the means employed (i.e., the death of the fat person) would still occur regardless of whether those means were actually employed.

Some people might want to defend the doctrine of double effect against this line of criticism by maintaining that the spelunkers need not intend the death of the fat person, but only that "she be blown into little pieces" or that "the mouth of the cave be suitably enlarged." But how is the use of dynamite expected to produce these results except by way of killing the fat person? Thus, the death of the fat person is part of the means employed by the spelunkers to secure their release from the cause, and thus would be impermissible according to the doctrine of double effect. If, however, we think that bringing about the death of the fat person could be morally justified in this case, because, for example, (a) and/or (b) obtain, we are left with a serious objection to the necessity of the restrictions imposed by the doctrine of double effect for acting morally.

Given these objections to the doctrine of double effect, Philippa Foot has suggested that we might more profitably deal with the moral questions at issue by distinguishing between negative and positive duties. *Negative duties* are said to be duties to refrain from doing certain sorts of actions. Typically, these are duties to avoid actions that inflict harm or injury on others. Thus, the duties not to kill or assault others are negative duties. By contrast, *positive duties* are duties to do certain actions, usually those that aid or benefit others. The duties to repay a debt and help others in need are positive duties. This distinction is used to resolve practical disputes by claiming that negative duties have priority over positive duties; accordingly, when negative and positive duties conflict, negative duties always take precedence over positive duties.

Applying this distinction, Foot claims that a doctor is justified in performing an abortion when nothing can be done to save the lives of both child and mother, but the life of the mother can be saved by killing the child. Obviously, this case is quite similar to the example of the fat person stuck in the mouth of the cave. But it is not clear how the distinction between positive and negative duties can help us in either situation. Since both the doctor and the group of spelunkers trapped by the fat person have a negative duty not to kill that takes precedence over any positive duty to help either themselves or others, it would seem that neither aborting the fetus nor blowing up the fat person could be justified on the basis of this distinction. Thus, the distinction between negative and positive duties no more justifies evil consequences in such cases than does the doctrine of double effect. Accordingly, if we want to provide such a justification, we need to find some morally acceptable way of going beyond both of these requirements.

Alternative Views

As we mentioned earlier, conservatives hold that the fetus has full moral status and hence a serious right to life. As a consequence, they oppose abortion in a wide range of cases. Hoping to undercut this antiabortion stance, Judith Jarvis Thomson adopts, for the sake of argument, the conservative position on the moral status of the fetus (Selection 13). She then tries to show that abortion is still justified in a wide range of cases. She asks us to imagine that we are kidnapped and connected to an unconscious violinist who now shares the use of our kidneys. The situation is such that if we detach ourselves from the violinist before nine months transpire, the violinist will die. Thomson thinks it obvious that we have no obligation to share our kidneys with the violinist in such a case, and hence that, in analogous cases, abortion can be justified. Thomson's view has provoked so much discussion that the authors of the four following selections feel compelled to consider her view in developing their own positions.

In this selection, Don Marquis begins by assuming what Thomson argues against— namely, that if fetuses have the same moral status as adult human beings, then the presumption that any particular abortion is immoral is exceedingly strong (Selection 14). What Marquis wants to defend is the conservative claim that fetuses have the same moral status as adult humans. He argues that what is wrong with killing adults is that it deprives them of "all the experience, activities, projects, and enjoyments that would otherwise have constituted (their) future." Because abortion deprives a typical fetus of a "future like ours," Marquis contends that the moral presumption against abortion is as strong as the moral presumption against killing adult human beings. But there are at least two problems with Marquis's argument. First, his argument would seem to suggest that it would be less wrong to kill an older rather than a younger person and maybe not wrong at all to kill a person who doesn't have much of a future, say only a year or two left to live. Second, Marquis tries to distinguish contraception from abortion on the grounds that only abortion deprives *something* of a "future like ours." But it is not clear why, given that abortion and contraception both prevent a "future like ours," the fact that only abortion deprives something of a "future like ours" suffices to render it morally prohibited while contraception remains morally permissible.

Like Marquis, Mary Anne Warren also distinguishes her view from Thomson's (Selection 13). In particular, she objects to Thomson's violinist example, claiming that, at most, the example justified abortion in cases of rape and hence will not provide the desired support for abortion on demand. Thomson, however, did provide additional examples and arguments in an attempt to show that abortion is justified in cases other than rape.

Like Marquis, Warren wants to build a consensus on the abortion question. To achieve this, she proposes a set of criteria for being a person with full moral status that she thinks proabortionists and antiabortionists alike could accept. The criteria are (1) consciousness; (2) developed reasoning; (3) self-motivated activity; (4) a capacity to communicate; and (5) the presence of self-concepts and self-awareness. But although most people would certainly agree that these criteria are met in paradigm cases, conservatives would still reject them as necessary requirements for being a person. But it is not clear that the concept of a person is sharp or decisive enough to bear the weight of a solution to the abortion controversy.

Those who find both the conservative and liberal views on abortion unattractive might be inclined toward the moderate view. This view attempts to draw a line—typically at implantation, or at quickening, or at viability—for the purpose of separating those who do not have full moral status from those who do. The U.S. Supreme Court in *Roe v. Wade* (1973) has frequently been understood as supporting a moderate view on abortion. In this decision, the Court, by a majority of 7 to 2, decided that the constitutional right to privacy, protected by the due process clause of the Fourteenth Amendment to the Constitution, entails that (1) no law may restrict the right of a woman to be aborted by a physician during the first three months (trimester) of her pregnancy; (2) during the second trimester abortion may be regulated by law only to the extent that the regulation is reasonably related to the preservation and protection of maternal health; and (3) when the fetus becomes viable (not before the beginning of the third trimester) a law may prohibit abortion, but only subject to an exception permitting abortion whenever necessary to protect the woman's life or health (including any aspects of her physical or mental health). But regardless of whether the Court's decision was intended to support the moderate view on abortion, some have argued that in the absence of reasonable constraints, the Court's decision has led to abortion on demand.

In Selection 16, Sally Markowitz provides what she regards as a specifically feminist argument for abortion; that is, one that is grounded on awareness of women's oppression and a commitment to a more egalitarian society. She distinguishes her view from other approaches to abortion, which focus either on the moral status of the fetus or on a woman's right to autonomy. Accordingly, Markowitz assumes for the sake of argument that the fetus has a serious right to life. She bases her defense of abortion on two principles: the Impermissible Sacrifice Principle and the Feminist Proviso. According to the Impermissible Sacrifice Principle, when one social group in a society is systematically oppressed by another, it is impermissible to require the oppressed group to make sacrifices that will exacerbate or perpetuate the oppression. According to the Feminist Proviso, women are, as a group, sexually oppressed by men, and this oppression can neither be completely understood in terms of, nor otherwise reduced to, oppressions of other sorts. From these two principles, Markowitz derives the conclusion that, because in the sexist society in which we live women are denied the equality to which they are entitled, a right to abortion is justified. It is interesting to note, however, that Markowitz's stance on abortion might turn out to be reconciled in practice with the conservative stance on abortion, provided that those who support the conservative stance on abortion are willing to first institutionalize the feminist agenda for equality between men and women.

Although most of the contemporary discussion of abortion has focused on the moral status of the fetus, most of the discussion of euthanasia has focused on the killing and letting die distinction and the doctrine of double effect. As we noted before, advocates of the killing and letting die distinction and the doctrine of double effect tend to justify only passive euthanasia (i.e., letting a person die as a foreseen but unintended consequence of an otherwise legitimate course of action). In contrast, critics of the killing and letting die distinction and the doctrine of double effect tend also to justify active euthanasia (i.e., intentional killing) on the basis of its consequences. Rachels (Selection 17) cites the case of a person suffering from cancer of the throat who has three options: (1) with continued treatment she will have a few more days of pain and then die; (2) if treatment is stopped but nothing else is done, it will be a few more hours; or (3) with a lethal injection she will die at once. In such a case, Rachels thinks, the third option—active euthanasia—is justified on the grounds that the person would be better off dying immediately.

But euthanasia is not only passive or active, it is also voluntary or involuntary. Voluntary euthanasia has the (informed) consent of the person involved. Involuntary euthanasia lacks such consent, usually but not always because the person involved is incapable of providing it. This means that at least four different types of euthanasia are possible: voluntary passive euthanasia, involuntary passive euthanasia, voluntary active euthanasia, and involuntary active euthanasia. Of the four types, voluntary passive euthanasia seems easiest to justify, involuntary active euthanasia the most difficult. But voluntary euthanasia, both passive and active, would seem more justifiable if it could be shown that there were a fundamental moral right to be assisted in bringing about one's own death if one so desired. Even if such a right could be supported, however, it would presumably only have force when one could reasonably be judged to be better off dead.

Practical Applications

It is not at all difficult to see how the various proposed solutions to the problem of abortion and euthanasia could be applied in contemporary societies. In *Planned Parenthood v. Casey* (Selection 19), the U.S. Supreme Court reaffirmed its commitment to what they took to be the essential holding of *Roe v. Wade*, which is a woman's right to terminate her pregnancy before viability, while rejecting *Roe V. Wade*'s trimester analysis in favor of an undue burden standard, which only the spousal notification requirement of Pennsylvania's Abortion Control Act violated. In *Cruzan v. Director, Missouri Department of Health* (Selection 20) the majority of the Supreme Court held that the state of Missouri was exercising a legitimate interest in protecting and preserving human life by requiring clear and convincing evidence of an incompetent's wishes concerning the withdrawal of life-sustaining medical treatment. . . .

But even as you begin to formulate the laws and social institutions, with their demands on social goods and resources, that are needed to enforce what you take to be the most morally defensible solution to the problem of abortion and euthanasia, you will still need to take into account the demands on social goods and resources that derive from solutions to other practical moral problems—such as the problem of sex equality, which is taken up in the next section.

Endnotes

1. The term "fetus" is understood to refer to any human organism from conception to birth.
2. Note that liberals on the abortion question need not be welfare liberals, although many of them are. Likewise, conservatives on the abortion question need not be libertarians or political conservatives.

3. Henceforth liberals, conservatives, and moderates on the abortion question are simply referred to as liberals, conservatives, and moderates.

13. A Defense of Abortion

JUDITH JARVIS THOMSON

Judith Jarvis Thomson begins by assuming, for the sale of argument, that the fetus is a person. Using a series of examples, she then argues that even granting this assumption, a woman has a right to abortion in cases involving rape, where her life is endangered, and when she has taken reasonable precautions to avoid becoming pregnant. In these cases, Thomson claims, the fetus's assumed right not to be killed unjustly would not be violated by abortion. Thomson further distinguishes between cases in which it would be a good thing for a woman to forego an abortion and cases in which a woman has an obligation to do so.

Most opposition to abortion relies on the premise that the fetus is a human being, a person, from the moment of conception. The premise is argued for, but, as I think, not well. Take, for example, the most common argument. We are asked to notice that the development of a human being from conception through birth into childhood is continuous; then it is said that to draw a line, to choose a point in this development and say "before this point the thing is not a person, after this point it is a person" is to make an arbitrary choice, a choice for which in the nature of things no good reason can be given. It is concluded that the fetus is, or anyway we had better say it is, a person from the moment of conception. But this conclusion does not follow. Similar things might be said about the development of an acorn into an oak tree, and it does not follow that acorns are oak trees or that we had better say they are. Arguments of this form are sometimes called "slippery slope arguments"—the phrase is perhaps self-explanatory—and it is dismaying that opponents of abortion rely on them so heavily and uncritically.

I am inclined to agree, however, that the prospects for "drawing a line" in the development of the fetus look dim. I am inclined to think also that we shall probably have to agree that the fetus has already become a human person well before birth. Indeed, it comes as a surprise when one first learns how early in its life it begins to acquire human characteristics. By the tenth week, for example, it already has a face, arms and legs, fingers and toes; it has internal organs, and brain activity is detectable.[1] On the other hand, I think that the premise is false, that the fetus is not a person from the moment of conception. A newly fertilized ovum, a newly implanted clump of cells, is no more a person than an acorn is an oak tree. But I shall not discuss any of this. For it seems to me to be of great interest to ask what happens if, for the sake of argument, we allow the premise. How, precisely, are we supposed to get from there to the conclusion that abortion is morally impermissible? Opponents of abortion commonly spend most of their time establishing that the fetus is a person, and hardly any time explaining the step from there to the impermissibility of abortion. Perhaps they think the step too simple and obvious to require much comment. Or perhaps instead they are simply being economical in argument. Many of those who defend abortion rely on the premise that the fetus is not a person, but only a bit of tissue that will become a person at birth; and why pay out more arguments than you have to? Whatever the explanation, I suggest that the step they take is neither easy nor obvious, that it calls for closer examination than it is commonly given, and that when we do give it this closer examination we shall feel inclined to reject it.

I propose, then, that we grant that the fetus is a person from the moment of conception. How does the argument go from here? Something like this, I take it. Every person has a right to life. So the fetus has a right to life. No doubt the mother has a right to decide what shall happen in and to her body;

Abridged from Judith Jarvis Thomson, "A Defense of Abortion," *Philosophy & Public Affairs 1,* no 1 (Fall 1971). Copyright 1971 by Princeton University Press. Excerpts, pp. 47–62, 65–66, reprinted by permission of Princeton University Press everyone would grant that. But surely a person's right to life is stronger and more stringent than the mother's right to decide what happens in and to her body, and so outweighs it. So the fetus may not be killed; an abortion may not be performed.

It sounds plausible. But now let me ask you to imagine this. You wake up in the morning and find yourself back to back in bed with an unconscious violinist. A famous unconscious violinist. He has been found to have a fatal kidney ailment, and the Society of Music Lovers has canvassed all the available medical records and found that you alone have the right blood type to help. They have therefore kidnapped you, and last night the violinist's circulatory system was plugged into yours, so that your kidneys can be used to extract poisons from his blood as well as your own. The director of the hospital now tells you, "Look, we're sorry the Society of Music Lovers did this to you—we would never have permitted it if we had known. But still, they did it, and the violinist now is plugged into you. To unplug you would be to kill him. But never mind, it's only for nine months. By then he will have recovered from his ailment, and can safely be unplugged from you." Is it morally incumbent on you to accede to this situation? No doubt it would be very nice of you if you did, a great kindness. But do you *have* to accede to it? What if it were not nine months, but nine years? Or longer still? What if the director of the hospital says, "Tough luck, I agree, but you've now got to stay in bed, with the violinist plugged into you, for the rest of your life. Because remember this. All persons have a right to life, and violinists are persons. Granted you have a right to decide what happens in and to your body, but a person's right to life outweighs your right to decide what happens in and to your body. So you cannot ever be unplugged from him." I imagine you would regard this as outrageous, which suggests that something is really wrong with that plausible-sounding argument I mentioned a moment ago.

In this case, of course, you were kidnapped; you didn't volunteer for the operation that plugged the violinist into your kidneys. Can those who oppose abortion on the ground I mentioned make an exception for a pregnancy due to rape? Certainly. They can say that persons have a right to life only if they didn't come into existence because of rape; or they can say that all persons have a right to life, but that some have less of a right to life than others, in particular, that those who came into existence be-

cause of rape have less. But these statements have a rather unpleasant sound. Surely the question of whether you have a right to life at all, or how much of it you have, shouldn't turn on the question of whether or not you are the product of a rape. And in fact the people who oppose abortion on the ground I mentioned do not make this distinction, and hence do not make an exception in case of rape.

Nor do they make an exception for a case in which the mother has to spend the nine months of her pregnancy in bed. They would agree that would be a great pity, and hard on the mother; but all the same, all persons have a right to life, the fetus is a person, and so on. I suspect, in fact, that they would not make an exception for a case in which, miraculously enough, the pregnancy went on for nine years, or even the rest of the mother's life.

Some won't even make an exception for a case in which continuation of the pregnancy is likely to shorten the mother's life; they regard abortion as impermissible even to save the mother's life. Such cases are nowadays very rare, and many opponents of abortion do not accept this extreme view. All the same, it is a good place to begin: A number of points of interest come out in respect to it.

1. Let us call the view that abortion is impermissible even to save the mother's life "the extreme view." I want to suggest first that it does not issue from the argument I mentioned earlier without the addition of some fairly powerful premises. Suppose a woman has become pregnant, and now learns that she has a cardiac condition such that she will die if she carries the baby to term. What may be done for her? The fetus, being a person, has a right to life, but as the mother is a person too, so has she a right to life. Presumably they have an equal right to life. How is it supposed to come out that an abortion may not be performed? If mother and child have an equal right to life, shouldn't we perhaps flip a coin? Or should we add to the mother's right to life her right to decide what happens in and to her body, which everybody seems to be ready to grant—the sum of her rights now outweighing the fetus's right to life?

The most familiar argument here is the following. We are told that performing the abortion would be directly killing[2] the child, whereas doing nothing would not be killing the mother, but only letting her die. Moreover, in killing the child, one would be killing an innocent person, for the child has committed no crime, and is not aiming at his mother's death. And then there are a variety of ways in which this might be continued. (1) But as directly killing an innocent person is always and absolutely impermissible, an abortion may not be performed. Or, (2) as directly killing an innocent person is murder, and murder is always and absolutely impermissible, an abortion may not be performed.[3] Or, (3) as one's duty to refrain from directly killing an innocent person is more stringent than one's duty to keep a person from dying, an abortion may not be performed. Or, (4) if one's only options are directly killing an innocent person or letting a person die, one must prefer letting the person die, and thus an abortion may not be performed.[4]

Some people seem to have thought that these are not further premises which must be added if the conclusion is to be reached, but that they follow from the very fact that an innocent person has a right to life.[5] But this seems to me to be a mistake, and perhaps the simplest way to show this is to bring out that while we must certainly grant that innocent persons have a right to life, the theses in (1) through (4) are all false. Take (2), for example. If directly killing an innocent person is murder, and thus is impermissible, then the mother's directly killing the innocent person inside her is murder, and thus is impermissible. But it cannot seriously be thought to be murder if the mother performs an abortion on herself to save her life. It cannot seriously be said that she *must* refrain, that she *must* sit passively by and wait for her death. Let us look again at the case of you and the violinist. There you are, in bed with the violinist, and the director of the hospital says to you, "It's all most distressing, and I deeply sympathize, but you see this is putting an additional strain on your kidneys, and you'll be dead within the month. But you *have* to stay where you are all the same. Because unplugging you would be directly killing an innocent violinist, and that's murder, and that's impermissible." If anything in the world is true, it is that you do not commit murder, you do not do what is impermissible, if you reach around to your back and unplug yourself from that violinist to save your life.

The main focus of attention in writings on abortion has been on what a third party may or may not do in answer to a request from a woman for an abortion. This is in a way understandable. Things being as they are, there isn't much a

woman can safely do to abort herself. So the question asked is what a third party may do, and what the mother may do, if it is mentioned at all, is deduced, almost as an afterthought, from what is concluded that the third parties may do. But it seems to me that to treat the matter in this way is to refuse to grant to the mother that very status of person which is so firmly insisted on for the fetus. For we cannot simply read off what a person may do from what a third party may do. Suppose you find yourself trapped in a tiny house with a growing child. I mean a very tiny house, and a rapidly growing child—you are already up against the wall of the house and in a few minutes you'll be crushed to death. The child on the other hand won't be crushed to death; if nothing is done to stop him from growing he'll be hurt, but in the end he'll simply burst open the house and walk out a free man. Now I could well understand it if a bystander were to say, "There's nothing we can do for you. We cannot chose between your life and his, we cannot be the ones to decide who is to live, we cannot intervene." But it cannot be concluded that you too can do nothing, that you cannot attack it to save your life. However innocent the child may be, you do not have to wait passively while it crushes you to death. Perhaps a pregnant woman is vaguely felt to have the status of a house, to which we don't allow the right of self-defense. But if the woman houses the child, it should be remembered that she is a person who houses it.

I should perhaps stop to say explicitly that I am not claiming that people have a right to do anything whatever to save their lives. I think, rather, that there are drastic limits to the right of self-defense. If someone threatens you with death unless you torture someone else to death, I think you have not the right, even to save your life, to do so. But the case under consideration here is very different. In our case there are only two people involved, one whose life is threatened, and one who threatens it. Both are innocent: The one who is threatened is not threatened because of any fault, the one who threatens does not threaten because of any fault. For this reason we may feel that we bystanders cannot intervene. But the person threatened can.

In sum, a woman surely can defend her life against the threat to it posed by the unborn child, even if doing so involves its death. And this shows not merely that the theses in (1) through (4) are false; it shows also that the extreme view of abortion is false, and so we need not canvass any other possible ways of arriving at it from the argument I mentioned at the outset.

2. The extreme view could of course be weakened to say that while abortion is permissible to save the mother's life, it may not be performed by a third party, but only by the mother herself. But this cannot be right either. For what we have to keep in mind is that the mother and the unborn child are not like two tenants in a small house which has, by an unfortunate mistake, been rented to both: The mother *owns* the house. The fact that she does adds to the offensiveness of deducing that the mother can do nothing from the supposition that third parties can do nothing. But it does more than this: It casts a bright light on the supposition that third parties can do nothing. Certainly it lets us see that a third party who says "I cannot choose between you" is fooling himself if he thinks this is impartiality. If Jones has found and fastened on a certain coat, which he needs to keep him from freezing, but which Smith also needs to keep him from freezing, then it is not impartiality that says "I cannot choose between you" when Smith owns the coat. Women have said again and again "This body is *my* body!" and they have reason to feel angry, reason to feel that it has been like shouting into the wind. Smith, after all, is hardly likely to bless us if we say to him, "Of course it's your coat, anybody would grant that it is. But no one may choose between you and Jones who is to have it...."

3. Where the mother's life is not at stake, the argument I mentioned at the outset seems to have a much stronger pull. "Everyone has a right to life, so the unborn person has a right to life." And isn't the child's right to life weightier than anything other than the mother's own right to life, which she might put forward as ground for an abortion?

This argument treats the right to life as if it were unproblematic. It is not, and this seems to me to be precisely the source of the mistake.

For we should now, at long last, ask what it comes to, to have a right to life. In some views having a right to life includes having a right to be given at least the bare minimum one needs for continued life. But suppose that what in fact *is* the bare minimum a man needs for continued life is something he has no right at all to be given? If I am sick

unto death, and the only thing that will save my life is the touch of Henry Fonda's cool hand on my fevered brow, then all the same, I have no right to be given the touch of Henry Fonda's cool hand on my fevered brow. It would be frightfully nice of him to fly in from the West Coast to provide it. It would be less nice, though no doubt well meant, if my friends flew out to the West Coast and carried Henry Fonda back with them. But I have no right at all against anybody that he should do this for me. Or again, to return to the story I told earlier, the fact that for continued life that violinist needs the continued use of your kidneys does not establish that he has the right to be given the continued use of your kidneys. He certainly has no right against you that *you* should give him continued use of your kidneys. For nobody has any right to use your kidneys unless you give him such a right; and nobody has the right against you that you shall give him this right—if you do allow him to go on using your kidneys, this is a kindness on your part, and not something he can claim from you as his due. Nor has he any right against anybody else that *they* should give him continued use of your kidneys. Certainly he had no right against the Society of Music Lovers that they should plug him into you in the first place. And if you now start to unplug yourself, having learned that you will otherwise have to spend nine years in bed with him, there is nobody in the world who must try to prevent you, in order to see to it that he is given something he has a right to be given.

Some people are rather stricter about the right to life. In their view, it does not include the right to be given anything, but amounts to, and only to, the right not to be killed by anybody. But here a related difficulty arises. If everybody is to refrain from killing that violinist, then everybody must refrain from doing a great many different sorts of things. Everybody must refrain from slitting his throat, everybody must refrain from shooting him—and everybody must refrain from unplugging you from him. But does he have a right against everybody that they shall refrain from unplugging you from him? To refrain from doing this is to allow him to continue to use your kidneys. It could be argued that he has a right against us that *we* should allow him to continue to use your kidneys. That is, while he had no right against us that we should give him the use of your kidneys, it might be argued that he anyway has a right against us that we shall not now intervene and deprive him of the use of your kidneys. I shall come back to third-party interventions later. But certainly the violinist has no right against you that *you* shall allow him to continue to use your kidneys. As I said, if you do allow him to use them, it is a kindness on your part, and not something you owe him.

The difficulty I point to here is not peculiar to the right to life. It reappears in connection with all the other natural rights; and it is something which an adequate account of rights must deal with. For present purposes it is enough just to draw attention to it. But I would stress that I am not arguing that people do not have a right to life—quite to the contrary, it seems to me that the primary control we must place on the acceptability of an account of rights is that it should turn out in that account to be a truth that all persons have a right to life. I am arguing only that having a right to life does not guarantee having either a right to be given the use of or a right to be allowed continued use of another person's body—even if one needs it for life itself. So the right to life will not serve the opponents of abortion in the very simple and clear way in which they seem to have thought it would.

4. There is another way to bring out the difficulty. In the most ordinary sort of case, to deprive someone of what he has a right to is to treat him unjustly. Suppose a boy and his small brother are jointly given a box of chocolates for Christmas. If the older boy takes the box and refuses to give his brother any of the chocolates, he is unjust to him, for the brother has been given a right to half of them. But suppose that, having learned that otherwise it means nine years in bed with that violinist, you unplug yourself from him. You surely are not being unjust to him, for you gave him no right to use your kidneys, and no one else can have given him any such right. But we have to notice that in unplugging yourself, you are killing him; and violinists, like everybody else, have a right to life, and thus in the view we were considering just now, the right not to be killed.

So here you do what he supposedly has a right you shall not do, but you do not act unjustly to him in doing it.

The emendation which may be made at this point is this: The right to life consists not in the right not to be killed, but rather in the right not to be killed unjustly. This runs a risk of circularity, but never mind: It would enable us to square the fact that the violinist has a right to life with the fact that you do not act unjustly toward him in unplugging yourself, thereby killing him. For if you do not kill him unjustly, you do not violate his right to life, and so it is no wonder you do him no injustice. But if this emendation is accepted, the gap in the argument against abortion stares us plainly in the face: It is by no means enough to show that the fetus is a person, and to remind us that all persons have a right to life—we need to be shown also that killing the fetus violates its right to life, i.e., that abortion is unjust killing. And is it?

I suppose we may take it as a datum that in a case of pregnancy due to rape the mother has not given the unborn person a right to the use of her body for food and shelter. Indeed, in what pregnancy could it be supposed that the mother has given the unborn person such a right? It is not as if there were unborn persons drifting about the world, to whom a woman who wants a child says "I invite you in."

But it might be argued that there are other ways one can have acquired a right to the use of another person's body than by having been invited to use it by that person. Suppose a woman voluntarily indulges in intercourse, knowing of the chance it will issue in pregnancy, and then she does become pregnant; is she not in part responsible for the presence, in fact the very existence, of the unborn person inside her? No doubt she did not invite it in. But doesn't her partial responsibility for its being there itself give it a right to the use of her body? If so, then her aborting it would be more like the boy's taking away the chocolates, and less like your unplugging yourself from the violinist—doing so would be depriving it of what it does have a right to, and thus would be doing it an injustice.

Then, too, it might be asked whether she can kill it even to save her own life: If she voluntarily called it into existence, how can she now kill it, even in self-defense?

The first thing to be said about this is that it is something new. Opponents of abortion have been so concerned to make out the independence of the fetus, in order to establish that it has a right to life, just as its mother does, that they have tended to overlook the possible support they might gain from making out that the fetus is *dependent* on the mother, in order to establish that she has a special kind of responsibility for it, a responsibility that gives it rights against her which are not possessed by any independent person—such as an ailing violinist who is a stranger to her.

On the other hand, this argument would give the unborn person a right to its mother's body only if her pregnancy resulted from a voluntary act, undertaken in full knowledge of the chance a pregnancy might result from it. It would leave out entirely the unborn person whose existence is due to rape. Pending the availability of some further argument, then, we would be left with the conclusion that unborn persons whose existence is due to rape have no right to the use of their mothers' bodies, and thus that aborting them is not depriving them of anything they have a right to and hence is not unjust killing.

We should also notice that it is not at all plain that this argument really does go as far as it purports to. For there are cases and cases, and the details make a difference. If the room is stuffy, and I therefore open a window to air it, and a burglar climbs in, it would be absurd to say, "Ah, now he can stay, she's given him a right to the use of her house—for she is partially responsible for his presence there, having voluntarily done what enabled him to get in, in full knowledge that there are such things as burglars, and that burglars burgle." It would be still more absurd to say this if I had had bars installed outside my windows, precisely to prevent burglars from getting in, and a burglar got in only because of a defect in the bars. It remains equally absurd if we imagine it is not a burglar who climbs in, but an innocent person who blunders or falls in. Again, suppose it were like this: People seeds drift about in the air like pollen, and if you open your windows, one may drift in and take root in your carpets or upholstery. You don't want children, so you fix up your windows with fine mesh screens, the very best you can buy. As can happen, however, and on very, very rare occasions does happen, one of the screens is defective; a seed drifts in and takes root. Does the person-plant who now develops have a right to the use of your house? Surely not—despite the fact that you voluntarily opened your windows, knowingly kept carpets and upholstered furniture, and knew that screens were sometimes defective. Someone may

argue that you are responsible for its rooting, that it does have a right to your house, because after all you *could* have lived out your life with bare floors and furniture, or with sealed windows and doors. But this won't do—by the same token anyone can avoid a pregnancy due to rape by having a hysterectomy, or anyway by never leaving home without a (reliable!) army.

It seems to me that the argument we are looking at can establish at most that there are *some* cases in which the unborn person has a right to the use of its mother's body, and therefore *some* cases in which abortion is unjust killing. There is room for much discussion and argument as to precisely which, if any. But I think we should sidestep this issue and leave it open, for at any rate the argument certainly does not establish that all abortion is unjust killing.

5. There is room for yet another argument here, however. We surely must all grant that there may be cases in which it would be morally indecent to detach a person from your body at the cost of his life. Suppose you learn that what the violinist needs is not nine years of your life, but only one hour: All you need do to save his life is to spend one hour in that bed with him. Suppose also that letting him use your kidneys for that one hour would not affect your health in the slightest. Admittedly you were kidnapped. Admittedly you did not give anyone permission to plug him into you. Nevertheless it seems plain to me you *ought* to allow him to use your kidneys for that hour— it would be indecent to refuse.

Again, suppose pregnancy lasted only an hour, and constituted no threat to life or health. And suppose that a woman becomes pregnant as a result of rape. Admittedly she did not voluntarily do anything to bring about the existence of a child. Admittedly she did nothing at all which would give the unborn person a right to the use of her body. All the same it might well be said, as in the newly emended violinist story, that she *ought* to allow it to remain for that hour—that it would be indecent of her to refuse.

Now some people are inclined to use the term "right" in such a way that it follows from the fact that you ought to allow a person to use your body for the hour he needs, that he has a right to use your body for the hour he needs, even though he has not been given that right by any person or act.

They may say that it follows also that if you refuse, you act unjustly toward him. This use of the term is perhaps so common that it cannot be called wrong; nevertheless it seems to me to be an unfortunate loosening of what we would do better to keep a tight rein on. Suppose that box of chocolates I mentioned earlier had not been given to both boys jointly, but was given only to the older boy. There he sits, stolidly eating his way through the box, his small brother watching enviously. Here we are likely to say "You ought not to be so mean. You ought to give your brother some of those chocolates." My own view is that it just does not follow from the truth of this that the brother has any right to any of the chocolates. If the boy refuses to give his brother any, he is greedy, stingy, callous—but not unjust. I suppose that the people I have in mind will say it does follow that the brother has a right to some of the chocolates, and thus that the boy does act unjustly if he refuses to give his brother any. But the effect of saying this is to obscure what we should keep distinct, namely the difference between the boy's refusal in this case and the boy's refusal in the earlier case, in which the box was given to both boys jointly, and in which the small brother thus had what was from any point of view clear title to half.

A further objection to so using the term "right" stems from the fact that A ought to do a thing for B, it follows that B has a right against A that A do it for him, is that it is going to make the question of whether or not a man has a right to a thing turn on how easy it is to provide him with it; and this seems not merely unfortunate, but morally unacceptable. Take the case of Henry Fonda again. I said earlier that I had no right to the touch of his cool hand on my fevered brow, even though I needed it to save my life. I said it would be frightfully nice of him to fly in from the West Coast to provide me with it, but that I had no right against him that he should do so. But suppose he isn't on the West Coast. Suppose he has only to walk across the room, place a hand briefly on my brow—and lo, my life is saved. Then surely he ought to do it, it would be indecent to refuse. Is it to be said "Ah, well, it follows that in this case she has a right to the touch of his hand on her brow, and so it would be an injustice of him to refuse"? So that I have a right to it when it is easy for him to provide it, though no right when it's hard? It's rather a shocking idea that anyone's rights should fade away and

disappear as it gets harder and harder to accord them to him.

So my own view is that even though you ought to let the violinist use your kidneys for the one hour he needs, we should not conclude that he has a right to do so—we should say that if you refuse, you are, like the boy who owns all the chocolates and will give none away, self-centered and callous, indecent in fact, but not unjust. And similarly, that even supposing a case in which a woman pregnant due to rape ought to allow the unborn person to use her body for the hour he needs, we should not conclude that he has a right to do so; we should conclude that she is self-centered, callous, indecent, but not unjust, if she refuses. The complaints are no less grave; they are just different. However, there is no need to insist on this point. If anyone does wish to deduce "he has a right" from "you ought," then all the same he must surely grant that there are cases in which it is not morally required of you that you allow that violinist to use your kidneys, and in which he does not have a right to use them, and in which you do not do him injustice if you refuse. And so also for mother and unborn child. Except in such cases as the unborn person has a right to demand it—and we were leaving open the possibility that there may be such cases—nobody is morally *required* to make large sacrifices, of health, of all other interests and concerns, of all other duties and commitments, for nine years, or even for nine months, in order to keep another person alive. . . .

6. My argument will be found unsatisfactory on two counts by many of those who want to regard abortion as morally permissible. First, while I do argue that abortion is not impermissible, I do not argue that it is always permissible. I am inclined to think it a merit of my account precisely that it does *not* give a general yes or a general no. It allows for and supports our sense that, for example, a sick and desperately frightened fourteen-year-old schoolgirl, pregnant due to rape, may *of course* choose abortion, and that any law which rules this out is an insane law. And it also allows for and supports our sense that in other cases resort to abortion is even positively indecent. It would be indecent of the woman to request an abortion, and indecent of a doctor to perform it, if she is in her seventh month, and wants the abortion just to avoid the nuisance of postponing a trip

abroad. The very fact that the arguments I have been drawing attention to treat all cases of abortion, or even all cases of abortion in which the mother's life is not at stake, as morally on a par ought to have made them suspect at the outset.

Secondly, while I am arguing for the permissibility of abortion in some cases, I am not arguing for the right to secure the death of the unborn child. It is easy to confuse these two things in that up to a certain point in the life of the fetus it is not able to survive outside the mother's body; hence removing it from her body guarantees its death. But they are importantly different. I have argued that you are not morally required to spend nine months in bed, sustaining the life of that violinist; but to say this is by no means to say that if, when you unplug yourself, there is a miracle and he survives, you then have a right to turn round and slit his throat. You may detach yourself even if this costs him his life; you have no right to be guaranteed his death, by some other means, if unplugging

yourself does not kill him. There are some people who will feel dissatisfied by this feature of my argument. A woman may be utterly devastated by the thought of a child, a bit of herself, put out for adoption and never seen or heard of again. She may therefore want not merely that the child be detached from her, but more, that it die. Some opponents of abortion are inclined to regard this as beneath contempt—thereby showing insensitivity to what is surely a powerful source of despair. All the same, I agree that the desire for the child's death is not one which anybody may gratify, should it turn out to be possible to detach the child alive.

At this place, however, it should be remembered that we have only been pretending throughout that the fetus is a human being from the moment of conception. A very early abortion is surely not the killing of a person, and so is not dealt with by anything I have said here.

Endnotes

1. Daniel Callahan, *Abortion: Law, Choice and Morality* (New York, 1970), p. 373. This book gives a fascinating survey of the available information on abortion. The Jewish tradition is surveyed in David M. Feldman, *Birth Control in Jewish Law* (New York, 1968), Part 5, the Catholic tradition in John T. Noonan, Jr., "An Almost Absolute Value in History," in *The Morality of Abortion*, ed. John T. Noonan, Jr. (Cambridge, Mass., 1970).
2. The term "direct" in the arguments I refer to is a technical one. Roughly, what is meant by "direct killing" is either killing as an end in itself, or killing as a means to some end, for example, the end of saving someone else's life. See note 5, below, for an example of its use.
3. Cf. *Encyclical Letter of Pope Pius XI on Christian Marriage*, St. Paul Editions (Boston, n.d.), p. 32: "however much we may pity the mother whose health and even life is gravely imperiled in the performance of the duty allotted to her by nature, nevertheless what could ever be a sufficient reason for excusing in any way the direct murder of the innocent? This is precisely what we are dealing with here." Noonan (*The Morality of Abortion*, p. 43) reads

this as follows: "What cause can ever avail to excuse in any way the direct killing of the innocent? For it is a question of that."
4. The thesis in (4) is an interesting way weaker than those in (1), (2), and (3): They rule out abortion even in cases in which both mother *and* child will die if the abortion is not performed. By contrast, one who held the view expressed in (4) could consistently say that one needn't prefer letting two persons die to killing one.
5. Cf. the following passage from Pius XII, *Address to the Italian Catholic Society of Midwives:* "The baby in the maternal breast has the right to life immediately from God.— Hence there is no man, no human authority, no science, no medical, eugenic, social, economic, or moral 'indication' which can establish or grant a valid juridical ground for a direct deliberate disposition of an innocent human life, that is a disposition which looks to its destruction either as an end or as a means to another end perhaps in itself not illicit.—The baby, still not born, is a man in the same degree and for the same reason as the mother" (quoted in Noonan, *The Morality of Abortion*, p. 45).

14. Why Abortion Is Immoral

DON MARQUIS

Marquis argues that fetuses have the same moral status as adult human beings on the grounds that what is wrong with killing an adult human being and what is wrong with killing a fetus are the same. Both are deprived of a "future like ours." On this account, Marquis contends that the moral presumption against abortion is as strong as the moral presumption against killing adult human beings.

The view that abortion is, with rare exceptions, seriously immoral has received little support in the recent philosophical literature. No doubt most philosophers affiliated with secular institutions of higher education believe that the anti-abortion position is either a symptom of irrational religious dogma or a conclusion generated by seriously confused philosophical argument. The purpose of this essay is to undermine this general belief. This essay sets out an argument that purports to show, as well as any argument in ethics can show, that abortion is, except possibly in rare cases, seriously immoral, that it is in the same moral category as killing an innocent adult human being.

This argument is based on a major assumption: If fetuses are in the same category as adult human beings with respect to the moral value of their lives, then the *presumption* that any particular abortion is immoral is exceedingly strong. Such a presumption could be overridden only by considerations more compelling than a woman's right to privacy. The defense of this assumption is beyond the scope of this essay.[1]

Furthermore, this essay will neglect a discussion of whether there are any such compelling considerations and what they are. Plainly there are strong candidates: abortion before implantation, abortion when the life of a woman is threatened by a pregnancy, or abortion after rape. The casuistry of these hard cases will not be explored in this essay. The purpose of this essay is to develop a general argument for the claim that, subject to the assumption

above, the overwhelming majority of deliberate abortions are seriously immoral. . . .

A necessary condition of resolving the abortion controversy is a . . . theoretical account of the wrongness of killing. After all, if we merely believe, but do not understand, why killing adult human beings such as ourselves is wrong, how could we conceivably show that abortion is either immoral or permissible? . . .

In order to develop such an account, we can start from the following unproblematic assumption concerning our own case: It is wrong to kill *us*. Why is it wrong? Some answers can be easily eliminated. It might be said that what makes killing us wrong is that a killing brutalizes the one who kills. But the brutalization consists of being inured to the performance of an act that is hideously immoral; hence, the brutalization does not explain the immorality. It might be said that what makes killing us wrong is the great loss others would experience due to our absence. Although such hubris is understandable, such an explanation does not account for the wrongness of killing hermits, or those whose lives are relatively independent and whose friends find it easy to make new friends.

A more obvious answer is better. What primarily makes killing wrong is neither its effect on the murderer nor its effect on the victim's friends and relatives, but its effect on the victim. The loss of one's life is one of the greatest losses one can suffer. The loss of one's life deprives one of all the experiences, activities, projects, and enjoyments that would otherwise have constituted one's future. Therefore, killing someone is wrong, primarily because the killing inflicts (one of) the greatest possible losses on the victim. To describe this as the loss of life can be misleading, however. The change in my biological

---

Reprinted, as slightly modified by the author, with permission of the author and the publisher from the *Journal of Philosophy*, vol. 86 (April 1989).

state does not by itself make killing me wrong. The effect of the loss of my biological life is the loss to me of all those activities, projects, experiences, and enjoyments which would otherwise have constituted my future personal life. These activities, projects, experiences, and enjoyments are either valuable for their own sake or are means to something else that is valuable for its own sake. Some parts of my future are not valued by me now, but will come to be valued by me as I grow older and as my values and capacities change. When I am killed, I am deprived both of what I now value, which would have been part of my future personal life, but also what I would come to value. Therefore, when I die, I am deprived of all of the value of my future. Inflicting this loss on me is ultimately what makes killing me wrong. This being the case, it would seem that what makes killing *any* adult human being prima facie seriously wrong is the loss of his or her future.[2]

How should this rudimentary theory of the wrongness of killing be evaluated? It cannot be faulted for deriving an "ought" from an "is," for it does not. The analysis assumes that killing me (or you, reader) is prima facie seriously wrong. The point of the analysis is to establish which natural property ultimately explains the wrongness of the killing, given that it is wrong. A natural property will ultimately explain the wrongness of killing, only if (1) the explanation fits with our intuitions about the matter and (2) there is no other natural property that provides the basis for a better explanation of the wrongness of killing. This analysis rests on the intuition that what makes killing a particular human or animal wrong is what it does to that particular human or animal. What makes killing wrong is some natural effect or other of the killing. Some would deny this. For instance, a divine-command theorist in ethics would deny it. Surely this denial is, however, one of those features of divine-command theory which renders it so implausible.

The claim that what makes killing wrong is the loss of the victim's future is directly supported by two considerations. In the first place, this theory explains why we regard killing as one of the worst of crimes. Killing is especially wrong, because it deprives the victim of more than perhaps any other crime. In the second place, people with AIDS or cancer who know they are dying believe, of course, that dying is a very bad thing for them. They believe that the loss of a future to them that they would otherwise have experienced is what makes their premature death a very bad thing for them. A better theory of the wrongness of killing would require a different natural property associated with killing which better fits with the attitudes of the dying. What could it be?

The view that what makes killing wrong is the loss to the victim of the value of the victim's future gains additional support when some of its implications are examined. In the first place, it is incompatible with the view that it is wrong to kill only beings who are biologically human. It is possible that there exists a different species from another planet whose members have a future like ours. Since having a future like that is what makes killing someone wrong, this theory entails that it would be wrong to kill members of such a species. Hence, this theory is opposed to the claim that only life that is biologically human has great moral worth, a claim which many anti-abortionists have seemed to adopt. This opposition, which this theory has in common with personhood theories, seems to be a merit of the theory.

In the second place, the claim that the loss of one's future is the wrong-making feature of one's being killed entails the possibility that the futures of some actual nonhuman mammals on our own planet are sufficiently like ours that it is seriously wrong to kill them also. Whether some animals do have the same right to life as human beings depends on adding to the account of the wrongness of killing some additional account of just what it is about my future or the futures of other adult human beings which makes it wrong to kill us. No such additional account will be offered in this essay. Undoubtedly, the provision of such an account would be a very difficult matter. Undoubtedly, any such account would be quite controversial. Hence, it surely should not reflect badly on this sketch of an elementary theory of the wrongness of killing that it is indeterminate with respect to some very difficult issues regarding animal rights.

In the third place, the claim that the loss of one's future is the wrong-making feature of one's being killed does not entail, as sanctity-of-human-life theories do, that active euthanasia is wrong. Persons who are severely and incurably ill, who face a future of pain and despair, and who wish to die will not have suffered a loss if they are killed. It is, strictly speaking, the value of a human's future which makes killing wrong in this theory. This being so, killing does not necessarily wrong some persons who are sick and dying. Of course, there may be other reasons for a prohibition of active euthanasia, but that is another matter. Sanctity-of-human-life theories seem to hold that active euthanasia is serious wrong even in an individual case where there seems to be good reason for it independently of public policy considerations. This consequence is most implausible, and it is a plus for the claim that the loss of a future of value is what makes killing wrong that it does not share this consequence.

In the fourth place, the account of the wrongness of killing defended [here] does straightforwardly entail that it is prima facie seriously wrong to kill children and infants, for we do presume that they have futures of value. Since we do believe that it is wrong to kill defenseless little babies, it is important that a theory of the wrongness of killing easily account for this. Personhood theories of the wrongness of killing, on the other hand, cannot straight-forwardly account the wrongness of killing infants and young children. Hence, such theories must add special ad hoc accounts of the wrongness of killing the young. The plausibility of such ad hoc theories seems to be a function of how desperately one wants such theories to work. The claim that the primary wrong-making feature of killing is the loss to the victim of the value of its future accounts for the wrongness of killing young children and infants directly; it makes the wrongness of such acts as obvious as we actually think it is. This is a further merit of this theory. Accordingly, it seems that this value of a future-like-ours theory of the wrongness of killing shares strengths of both sanctity-of-life and personhood accounts, while avoiding weaknesses of both. In addition, it meshes with a central intuition concerning what makes killing wrong.

The claim that the primary wrong-making feature of killing is the loss to the victim of the value of its future has obvious consequences for the ethics of abortion. The future of a standard fetus includes a set of experiences, projects, activities, and such which are identical with the futures of adult human beings and are identical with the futures of young children. Since the reason that is sufficient to explain why it is wrong to kill human beings after the time of birth is a reason that also applies to fetuses, it follows that abortion is prima facie seriously morally wrong.

This argument does not rely on the invalid inference that, since it is wrong to kill persons, it is wrong to kill potential persons also. The category that is morally central to this analysis is the category of having a valuable future like ours; it is not the category of personhood. The argument to the conclusion that abortion is prima facie seriously morally wrong proceeded independently of the notion of person or potential person or any equivalent. Someone may wish to start with this analysis in terms of the value of a human future, conclude that abortion is, except perhaps in rare circumstances, seriously morally wrong, infer that fetuses have the right to life, and then call fetuses "persons" as a result of their having the right to life. Clearly, in this case, the category of person is being used to state the *conclusion* of the analysis rather than to generate the *argument* of the analysis.

The structure of this anti-abortion argument can be both illuminated and defended by comparing it to what appears to be the best argument for the wrongness of the wanton infliction of pain on animals. This latter argument is based on the assumption that it is prima facie wrong to inflict pain on me (or you, reader). What is the natural property associated with the infliction of pain which makes such infliction wrong? The obvious answer seems to be that the infliction of pain causes suffering, and that suffering is a misfortune. The suffering caused by the infliction of pain is what makes the wanton infliction of pain on me wrong. The wanton infliction of pain on other adult humans causes suffering. The wanton infliction of pain on animals causes suffering. Since causing suffering is what makes the wanton infliction of pain wrong and since the wanton infliction of pain on animals causes suffering, it follows that the wanton infliction of pain on animals is wrong.

This argument for the wrongness of the wanton infliction of pain on animals shares a number of structural features with the argument for the serious prima facie wrongness of abortion. Both arguments start with an obvious assumption concerning what it is wrong to do to me (or you, reader). Both then look for the characteristic or the consequence of the wrong action which makes the action wrong. Both recognize that the wrong-making feature of these immoral actions is a property of actions sometimes directed at individuals other than postnatal human beings. If the structure of the argument for the wrongness of the wanton infliction of pain on animals is sound, then the structure of the argument for the prima facie serious wrongness of abortion is also sound, for the structure of the two arguments is the same. The structure common to both is the key to the explanation of how the wrongness of abortion can be demonstrated without recourse to the category of person. In neither argument is that category crucial. . . .

Of course, this value of a future-like-ours argument, if sound, shows only that abortion is prima facie wrong, not that it is wrong in any and all circumstances. Since the loss of the future to a standard fetus, if killed, is, however, at least as great a loss of the loss of the future to a standard adult human being who is killed, abortion, like ordinary killing, could be justified only by the most compelling reasons. The loss of one's life is almost the greatest misfortune that can happen to one. Presumably abortion could be justified in some circumstances, only if the loss consequent on failing to abort would be at least as great. Accordingly, morally permissible abortions will be rare indeed unless, perhaps, they occur so early in pregnancy that a fetus is not yet definitely an individual. Hence, this argument should be taken as showing that abortion is presumptively very seriously wrong, where the presumption is very strong—as strong as the presumption that killing another adult human being is wrong. . . .

In this essay, it has been argued that the correct ethic of the wrongness of killing can be extended to fetal life and used to show that there is a strong presumption that any abortion is morally impermissible. If the ethic of killing adopted here entails, however, that contraception is also seriously immoral, then there would appear to be a difficulty with the analysis of this essay.

But this analysis does not entail that contraception is wrong. Of course, contraception prevents the actualization of a possible future of value. Hence, it follows from the claim that futures of value should be maximized that contraception is prima facie immoral. This obligation to maximize does not exist, however; furthermore, nothing in the ethics of killing in this paper entails that it does. The ethics of killing in this essay would entail that contraception is wrong only if something were denied a human future of value by contraception. Nothing at all is denied such a future by contraception, however.

Candidates for a subject of harm by contraception fall into four categories: (1) some sperm or other, (2) some ovum or other, (3) a sperm and an ovum separately, and (4) a sperm and an ovum together. Assigning the harm to some sperm is utterly arbi-

trary, for no reason can be given for making a sperm the subject of harm rather than an ovum. Assigning the harm to some ovum is utterly arbitrary, for no reason can be given for making an ovum the subject of harm rather than a sperm. One might attempt to avoid these problems by insisting that contraception deprives both the sperm and the ovum separately of a valuable future like ours. On this alternative, too, many futures are lost. Contraception was supposed to be wrong, because it deprived us of one future of value, not two. One might attempt to avoid this problem by holding that contraception deprives the combination of sperm and ovum of a valuable future like ours. But here the definite article misleads. At the time of contraception, there are hundreds of millions of sperm, one (released) ovum, and millions of possible combinations of all of these. There is no actual combination at all. Is the subject of the loss to be a merely possible combination? Which one? This alternative does not yield an actual subject of harm either. Accordingly, the immorality of contraception is not entailed by the loss of a future-like-ours argument simply because there is no nonarbitrarily identifiable subject of the loss in the case of contraception. . . .

The purpose of this essay has been to set out an argument for the serious presumptive wrongness of abortion subject to the assumption that the moral permissibility of abortion stands or falls on the moral status of the fetus. Since a fetus possesses a property, the possession of which in adult human beings is sufficient to make killing an adult human being wrong, abortion is wrong. This way of dealing with the problem of abortion seems superior to other approaches to the ethics of abortion, because it rests on the ethics of killing which is close to self-evident, because the crucial morally relevant property clearly applies to fetuses, and because the argument avoids the usual equivocations on "human life," "human being," or "person." The argument rests neither on religious claims nor on Papal dogma. It is not subject to the objection of "speciesism." Its soundness is compatible with the moral permissibility of euthanasia and contraception. It deals with our intuitions concerning young children.

Finally, this analysis can be viewed as resolving a standard problem—indeed, *the* standard problem—concerning the ethics of abortion. Clearly, it is wrong to kill adult human beings. Clearly, it is not wrong to end the life of some arbitrarily chosen single human cell. Fetuses seem to be like arbitrarily chosen human cells in some respects and like adult humans in other respects. The problem of the ethics of abortion is the problem of determining the fetal property that settles this moral controversy. The thesis of this essay is that the problem of the ethics of abortion, so understood, is solvable.

Endnotes

1. Judith Jarvis Thomson has rejected this assumption in a famous essay, "A Defense of Abortion," *Philosophy and Public Affairs 1*, 1 (1971), 47–66.
2. I have been most influenced on this matter by Jonathan Glover, *Causing Death and Saving Lives* (New York: Penguin, 1977), ch. 3; and Robert Young, "What Is So Wrong with Killing People?" *Philosophy*, LIV, 210 (1979): 515–528.

15. On the Moral and Legal Status of Abortion

MARY ANNE WARREN

Mary Anne Warren argues that if the fetus is assumed to be a person, there is a wide range of cases in which abortion cannot be defended. To provide such a defense, Warren sets out five criteria for being a person she feels should be acceptable to anti-abortionists and pro-abortionists alike. Appealing to these criteria, she contends that fetuses, even when their potentiality is taken into account, do not sufficiently resemble persons to have a significant right to life. In a "Postscript" to her article, Warren defends her view against the objection that it would justify infanticide. Although by her criteria newborn infants would not have a significant right to life, she claims that infanticide would still not be permissible, so long as there are people willing to care and provide for the well-being of such infants.

We will be concerned with both the moral status of abortion, which for our purposes we may define as the act which a woman performs in voluntarily terminating, or allowing another person to terminate, her pregnancy, and the legal status which is appropriate for this act. I will argue that, while it is not possible to produce a satisfactory defense of a woman's right to obtain an abortion without showing that a fetus is not a human being, in the morally relevant sense of that term, we ought not to conclude that the difficulties involved in determining whether or not a fetus is a human make it impossible to produce any satisfactory solution to the problem of the moral status of abortion. For it is possible to show that, on the basis of intuitions which we may expect even the opponents of abortion to share, a fetus is not a person, and hence not the sort of entity to which it is proper to ascribe full moral rights.

Of course, while some philosophers would deny the possibility of any such proof,[1] others will deny that there is any need for it, since the moral permissibility of abortion appears to them to be too obvious to require proof. But the inadequacy of this attitude should be evident from the fact that both the friends and the foes of abortion consider their position to be morally self-evident. Because pro-abortionists have never adequately come to grips with the conceptual issues surrounding abortion, most if not all of the arguments which they advance in opposition to laws restricting access to abortion fail to refute or even weaken the traditional anti-abortion argument, i.e., that a fetus is a human being, and therefore abortion is murder.

These arguments are typically of one of two sorts. Either they point to the terrible side effects of the restrictive laws, e.g., the deaths due to illegal abortions, and the fact that it is poor women who suffer the most as a result of these laws, or else they state that to deny a woman access to abortion is to deprive her of her right to control her own body. Unfortunately, however, the fact that restricting access to abortion has tragic side effects does not, in itself, show that the restrictions are unjustified, since murder is wrong regardless of the consequences of prohibiting it; and the appeal to the right to control one's body, which is generally construed as a property right, is at best a rather feeble argument for the permissibility of abortion. Mere ownership does not give me the right to kill innocent people whom I find on my property, and indeed I am apt to be held responsible if such people injure themselves while on my property. It is equally unclear that I have any moral right to expel an innocent person from my property when I know that doing so will result in his death.

Furthermore, it is probably inappropriate to describe a woman's body as her property, since it seems natural to hold that a person is something distinct from her property but not from her body. Even those who would object to the identification of a person with his body, or with the conjunction of his body and his mind, must admit that it would be very odd to describe, say, breaking a leg, as damaging one's property, and much more appropriate to describe it as injuring one*self*. Thus it is probably a mistake to argue that the right to obtain an abortion is in any way derived from the right to own and regulate property.

But however we wish to construe the right to abortion, we cannot hope to convince those who consider abortion a form of murder of the existence of any such right unless we are able to produce a clear and convincing refutation of the traditional anti-abortion argument, and this has not, to my knowledge, been done. With respect to the two most vital issues which that argument involves, i.e., the

humanity of the fetus and its implication for the moral status of abortion, confusion has prevailed on both sides of the dispute.

Thus, both pro-abortionists and anti-abortionists have tended to abstract the question of whether abortion is wrong to that of whether it is wrong to destroy a fetus, just as though the rights of another person were not necessarily involved. This mistaken abstraction has led to the almost universal assumption that if a fetus is a human being, with a right to life, then it follows immediately that abortion is wrong (except perhaps when necessary to save the woman's life), and that it ought to be prohibited. It has also been generally assumed that unless the question about the status of the fetus is answered, the moral status of abortion cannot possibly be determined. . . . John Noonan is correct in saying that "the fundamental question in the long history of abortion is, How do you determine the humanity of a being?"[2] He summarizes his own anti-abortion argument, which is a version of the official position of the Catholic Church, as follows:

> . . . it is wrong to kill humans, however, poor, weak, defenseless, and lacking in opportunity to develop their potential they may be. It is therefore morally wrong to kill Biafrans. Similarly, it is morally wrong to kill embryos.[3]

Noonan bases his claim that fetuses are human on what he calls the theologians' criterion of humanity: Whoever is conceived of human beings is human. But although he argues at length for the appropriateness of this criterion, he never questions the assumption that if the fetus is human then abortion is wrong for exactly the same reason that murder is wrong.

Judith Thomson is, in fact, the only writer I am aware of who has seriously questioned this assumption; she has argued that, even if we grant the anti-abortionist his claim that a fetus is a human being, with the same right to life as any other human being, we can still demonstrate that, in at least some and perhaps most cases, a woman is under no moral obligation to complete an unwanted pregnancy.[4] Her argument is worth examining, since if it holds up it may enable us to establish the moral permissibility of abortion without becoming involved in problems about what entitles an entity to be considered human, and accorded full moral rights. To be able to do this would be great pain in the power and simplicity of the pro-abortion position, since, although I will argue that these problems can be solved at least as decisively as can any other moral problems, we should certainly be pleased to be able to avoid having to solve them as part of the justification of abortion.

On the other hand, even if Thomson's argument does not hold up, her insight—that it requires argument to show that if fetuses are human then abortion is properly classified as murder—is extremely valuable. The assumption she attacks is particularly invidious, for it amounts to the decision that it is appropriate, in deciding the moral status of abortion, to leave the rights of the pregnant woman out of consideration entirely, except possibly when her life is threatened. Obviously, this will not do; determining what moral rights, if any, a fetus possesses is only the first step in determining the moral status of abortion. Step two, which is at least equally essential, is finding a just solution to the conflict between whatever rights the fetus may have, and the rights of the woman who is unwillingly pregnant. While the historical error has been to pay far too little attention to the second step, Ms. Thomson suggests that if we look at the second step first we may find that a woman has a right to obtain an abortion *regardless* of what rights the fetus has.

Our own inquiry will also have two stages. In Section I, we will consider whether or not it is possible to establish that abortion is morally permissible even on the assumption that a fetus is an entity with a full-fledged right to life. I will argue that in fact this cannot be established, at least not with the conclusiveness which is essential to our hopes of convincing those who are skeptical about the morality of abortion, and that we therefore cannot avoid dealing with the question of whether or not a fetus really does have the same right to life as a (more fully developed) human being.

In Section II, I will propose an answer to this question, namely, that a fetus cannot be considered a member of the moral community, the set of beings with full and equal moral rights, for the simple reason that it is not a person, and that it is personhood, and not genetic humanity, i.e., humanity as defined by Noonan, which is the basis for membership in this community. I will argue that a fetus, whatever its stage of development, satisfies none of the basic criteria for personhood, and is not even enough *like* a person to be accorded even some of the same rights on the basis of this resemblance. Nor, as we will see, is a fetus's *potential* personhood a threat to the morality of abortion, since, whatever the rights of potential people may be, they are invariably overridden in any conflict with the moral rights of actual people.

◇

I

We now turn to Professor Thomson's case for the claim that even if a fetus has full moral rights, abortion is still morally permissible, at least sometimes, and for some reasons other than to save the woman's life. Her argument is based upon a clever, but I think faulty, analogy. She asks us to picture ourselves waking up one day, in bed with a famous violinist. Imagine that you have been kidnapped, and your bloodstream hooked up to that of the violinist, who happens to have an ailment which will certainly kill him unless he is permitted to share your kidneys for a period of nine months. No one else can save him, since you alone have the right type of blood. He will be unconscious all that time, and you will have to stay in bed with him, but after the nine months are over he may be unplugged, completely cured; that is, provided that you have cooperated.

Now then, she continues, what are your obligations in this situation? The anti-abortionist, if he is consistent, will have to say that you are obligated to stay in bed with the violinist: for all people have a right to life, and violinists are people, and therefore it would be murder for you to disconnect yourself from him and let him die. But this is outrageous, and so there must be something wrong with the same argument when it is applied to abortion. It would certainly be commendable of you to agree to save the violinist, but it is absurd to suggest that your refusal to do so would be murder. His right to life does not obligate you to do whatever is required to keep him alive, nor does it justify anyone else in forcing you to do so. A law which required you to say in bed with the violinist would clearly be an unjust law, since it is no proper function of the law to force unwilling people to make huge sacrifices for the sake of other people toward whom they have no such prior obligation.

Thomson concludes that, if this analogy is apt, then we can grant the anti-abortionist claim that a fetus is a human being and still hold that it is at least sometimes the case that a pregnant woman has the right to refuse to be a Good Samaritan towards the fetus, i.e., to obtain an abortion. For there is a great gap between the claim that X has a right to life, and the claim that Y is obligated to do whatever is necessary to keep X alive, let alone that he ought to be forced to do so. It is Y's duty to keep X alive only if he has somehow contracted a *special* obligation to do so; and a woman who is unwillingly pregnant, e.g., who was raped, has nothing which obligates her to make the enormous sacrifice which is necessary to preserve the conceptus.

This argument is initially quite plausible, and in the extreme case of pregnancy due to rape is probably conclusive. Difficulties arise, however, when we try to specify more exactly the range of cases in which abortion is clearly justifiable even on the assumption that the fetus is human. Professor Thomson considers it a virtue of her argument that it does not enable us to conclude that abortion is *always* permissible. It would, she says, be "indecent" for a woman in her seventh month to obtain an abortion just to avoid having to postpone a trip to Europe. On the other hand, her argument enables us to see that "a sick and desperately frightened schoolgirl pregnant due to rape may *of course* choose abortion, and that any law which rules this out is an insane law" (p. 65). So far, so good; but what are we to say about the woman who becomes pregnant not through rape but as a result of her own carelessness, or because of contraceptive failure, or who gets pregnant intentionally and then changes her mind about wanting a child? With respect to such cases, the violinist analogy is of much less use to the defender of the woman's right to obtain an abortion.

Indeed, the choice of a pregnancy due to rape, as an example of a case in which abortion is permissible even if a fetus is considered a human being, is extremely significant; for it is only in the case of pregnancy due to rape that the woman's situation is adequately analogous to the violinist case for our intuitions about the latter to transfer convincingly. The crucial difference between a pregnancy due to rape and the *normal* case of unwanted pregnancy is that in the normal case we cannot claim that the woman is in no way responsible for her predicament; she could have remained chaste, or taken her pills more faithfully, or abstained on dangerous days, and so on. If, on the other hand, you are kidnapped by strangers, and hooked up to a strange violinist, then you are free of any shred of responsibility for the situation, on the basis of which it could be argued that you are obligated to keep the violin-

ist alive. Only when her pregnancy is due to rape is a woman clearly just as nonresponsible.[5]

Consequently, there is room for the anti-abortionists to argue that in the normal case of unwanted pregnancy, a woman has, by her own actions, assumed responsibility for the fetus. For if X behaves in a way which he could have avoided, and which he knows involves, let us say, a 1 percent chance of bringing into existence a human being, with a right to life, and does so knowing that if this should happen then that human being will perish unless X does certain things to keep him alive, then it is by no means clear that when it does happen X is free of any obligation to what he knew in advance would be required to keep that human being alive.

The plausibility of such an argument is enough to show that the Thomson analogy can provide a clear and persuasive defense of a woman's right to obtain an abortion only with respect to those cases in which the woman is in no way responsible for her pregnancy [e.g., rape]. In all other cases, we would almost certainly conclude that it was necessary to look carefully at the particular circumstances in order to determine the extent of the woman's responsibility, and hence the extent of her obligation. This is an extremely unsatisfactory outcome, from the viewpoint of the opponents of restrictive abortion laws, most of whom are convinced that a woman has a right to obtain an abortion regardless of how or why she got pregnant.

Of course, a supporter of the violinist analogy might point out that it is absurd to suggest that forgetting her pill one day might be sufficient to obligate a woman to complete an unwanted pregnancy. And indeed it *is* absurd to suggest this. As we will see, the moral right to obtain an abortion is not in the least dependent upon the extent to which the woman is responsible for her pregnancy. But unfortunately, once we allow the assumption that a fetus has full moral rights, we cannot avoid taking this absurd suggestion seriously. Perhaps we can make this point more clear by altering the violinist story just enough to make it more analogous to a normal unwanted pregnancy and less to a pregnancy due to rape, and then seeing whether it is still obvious that you are not obligated to stay in bed with the fellow.

Suppose, then, that violinists are peculiarly prone to the sort of illness the only cure for which is the use of someone else's bloodstream for nine months, and that because of this there has been formed a society of music lovers who agree that whenever a violinist is stricken they will draw lots and the loser will, by some means, be made the one and only person capable of saving him. Now then, would you be obligated to cooperate in curing the violinist if you had voluntarily joined this society, knowing the possible consequences, and then your name had been drawn and you had been kidnapped? Admittedly, you did not promise ahead of time that you would, but you did deliberately place yourself in a position in which it might happen that a human life would be lost if you did not. Surely this is at least a *prima facie* reason for supposing that you have an obligation to stay in bed with the violinist. Suppose you had gotten your name drawn deliberately; surely *that* would be quite a strong reason for thinking that you had such an obligation.

It might be suggested that there is one important disanalogy between the modified violinist case and the case of an unwanted pregnancy, which makes the woman's responsibility significantly less, namely, the fact that the fetus *comes into existence* as the result of the woman's actions. This fact might give her a right to refuse to keep it alive, whereas she would not have had this right had it existed previously, independently, and then as a result of her actions become dependent upon her for its survival.

My own intuition, however, is that X has no more right to bring into existence, either deliberately or as a foreseeable result of actions he could have avoided, a being with full moral rights (Y), and then refuse to do what he knew beforehand would be required to keep that being alive, than he has to enter into an agreement with an existing person, whereby he may be called upon to save that person's life, and then refuse to do so when so called upon. Thus, X's responsibility for Y's existence does not seem to lessen his obligation to keep Y alive, if he is also responsible for Y's being in a situation in which only he can save him.

Whether this intuition is entirely correct, it brings us back again to the conclusion that once we allow the assumption that a fetus has full moral rights it becomes an extremely complex and difficult question whether and when abortion is justifiable. Thus, the Thomson analogy cannot help us produce a clear and persuasive proof of the moral permissibility of abortion. Nor will the opponents of the restrictive laws thank us for anything less; for their conviction (for the most part) is that abortion is obviously *not* a morally serious and extremely unfortunate, even though sometimes justified, act comparable to killing in self-defense or to letting the violinist die, but rather is closer to being a morally neutral act like cutting one's hair.

The basis of this conviction, I believe, is the realization that a fetus is not a person, and thus does not have a full-fledged right to life. Perhaps the reason why this claim has been so inadequately defended is that it seems self-evident to those who accept it. And so it is, insofar as it follows that what I take to be perfectly obvious claims about the nature of personhood and about the proper grounds for ascribing moral rights, claims which ought, indeed, to be obvious to both the friends and foes of abortion. Nevertheless, it is worth examining these claims, and showing how they demonstrate the moral innocuousness of abortion, since this apparently has not been adequately done before.

◇

II

The question we must answer in order to produce a satisfactory solution to the problem of the moral status of abortion is this: How are we to define the moral community, the set of beings with full and equal moral rights, such that we can decide whether a human fetus is a member of this community or not? What sort of entity, exactly, has the inalienable rights to life, liberty, and the pursuit of happiness? Jefferson attributed these rights to all *men*, and it may or may not be fair to suggest that he intended to attribute them *only* to men. Perhaps he ought to have attributed them to all human beings. If so, then we arrive, first, at Noonan's problem of defining what makes a being human, and, second, at the equally vital question which Noonan does not consider, namely: What reason is there for identifying the moral community with the set of all human beings, in whatever way we have chosen to define that term?

1. On the Definition of "Human"

One reason why this vital second question is so frequently overlooked in the debate over the moral status of abortion is that the term *human* has two distinct, but not often distinguished, senses. This fact results in a slide of meaning, which serves to conceal the fallaciousness of the traditional argument that since (1) it is wrong to kill innocent human beings and (2) fetuses are innocent human beings, then (3) it is wrong to kill fetuses. For if *human* is used in the same sense in both (1) and (2) then, whichever of the two senses is meant, one of these premises is question-begging. And if it is used in two different senses then of course the conclusion doesn't follow.

Thus, (1) is a self-evident moral truth[6] and avoids begging the question about abortion, only if "human being" is used to mean something like "a full-fledged member of the moral community." (It may or may not also be meant to refer exclusively to members of the species *Homo sapiens*.) We may call this the *moral* sense of "human." It is not to be confused with what we will call the *genetic* sense, i.e., the sense in which *any* member of the species is a human being, and no member of any other species could be. If (1) is acceptable only if the moral sense is intended, (2) is nonquestion-begging only if what is intended is the genetic sense.

In "Deciding Who Is Human," Noonan argues for the classification of fetuses with human beings by pointing to the presence of the full genetic code, and the potential capacity for rational thought (p. 135). It is clear that what he needs to show, for his version of the traditional argument to be valid, is that fetuses are human in the moral sense, the sense in which it is analytically true that all human beings have full moral rights. But, in the absence of any argument showing that whatever is genetically human is also morally human, and he gives none, nothing more than genetic humanity can be demonstrated by the presence of the human genetic code. And, as we will see, the *potential* capacity for rational thought can at most show that an entity has the potential for *becoming* human in the moral sense.

2. Defining the Moral Community

Can it be established that genetic humanity is sufficient for moral humanity? I think that there are very good reasons for not defining the moral community in this way. I would like to suggest an alternative way of defining the moral community, which I will argue for only to the extent of explaining why it is, or should be, self-evident. The suggestion is simply that the moral community consists of all and only *people,* rather than all and only human beings,[7] and probably the best way of demonstrating its self-evidence is by considering the concept of personhood, to see what sorts of entity are and are not persons, and

what the decision that a being is or is not a person implies about its moral rights.

What characteristics entitle an entity to be considered a person? This is obviously not the place to attempt a complete analysis of the concept of personhood, but we do not need such a fully adequate analysis just to determine whether and why a fetus is or isn't a person. All we need is a rough and approximate list of the most basic criteria of personhood, and some idea of which, or how many, of these an entity must satisfy . . . to properly be considered a person.

In searching for such criteria, it is useful to look beyond the set of people with whom we are acquainted, and ask how we would decide whether a totally alien being was a person or not. (For we have no right to assume that genetic humanity is necessary for personhood.) Imagine a space traveler who lands on an unknown planet and encounters a race of beings utterly unlike any he has ever seen or heard of. If he wants to be sure of behaving morally toward these beings, he has to somehow decide whether these are people, and hence have full moral rights, or whether they are the sort of thing which he need not feel guilty about treating as, for example, a source of food.

How should he go about making this decision? If he has some anthropological background, he might look for such things as religion, art, and the manufacturing of tools, weapons, or shelters, since these factors have been used to distinguish our human from our prehuman ancestors, in what seems to be closer to the moral than the genetic sense of "human." And no doubt he would be right to consider the presence of such factors as good evidence that the alien beings were people and morally human. It would, however, be overly anthropocentric of him to take the absence of these things as adequate evidence that they were not, since we can imagine people who have progressed beyond, or evolved without ever developing, these cultural characteristics.

I suggest that the traits which are most central to the concept of personhood, or humanity in the moral sense, are, very roughly, the following:

1. consciousness (of objects and events external and/or internal to the being), and in particular the capacity to feel pain;

2. reasoning (the *developed* capacity to solve new and relatively complex problems);

3. self-motivated activity (activity which is relatively independent of either genetic or direct external control);

4. the capacity to communicate, by whatever means, messages of an indefinite variety of types, . . . not just with an indefinite number of possible contents, but on indefinitely many possible topics;

5. the presence of self-concepts, and self-awareness, either individual or racial, or both.

Admittedly, there are apt to be a great many problems involved in formulating precise definitions of these criteria, let alone in developing universally valid behavioral criteria for deciding when they apply. But I will assume that both we and our explorer know approximately what (1)–(5) mean, and that he is also able to determine whether or not they apply. How, then, should he use his findings to decide whether . . . the alien beings are people? We needn't suppose that an entity must have *all* of these attributes to be properly considered a person; (1) and (2) alone may well be sufficient for personhood, and quite probably (1)–(3) are sufficient. Neither do we need to insist that any one of these criteria is necessary for personhood, although once again (1) and (2) look like fairly good candidates for *necessary* conditions, as does (3), if "activity" is construed to include the activity of reasoning.

All we need to claim, to demonstrate that a fetus is not a person, is that any being which satisfies *none* of (1)–(5) is certainly not a person. I consider this claim to be so obvious that I think anyone who denied it, and claimed that a being which satisfied none of (1)–(5) was a person all the same, would thereby demonstrate that he had no notion of all of what a person is—perhaps because he had confused the concept of a person with that of genetic humanity. If the opponents of abortion were to deny the appropriateness of these five criteria, I do not know what further arguments would convince them. We would probably have to admit that our conceptual schemes were indeed irreconcilably different, and that our dispute could not be settled objectively.

I do not expect this to happen, however, since I think that the concept of a person is one which is very nearly universal (to people), and that it is common to both pro-abortionists and anti-abortionists, even though neither group has fully realized the relevance of this concept to the resolution of their dispute. Furthermore, I think that on reflection even the anti-abortionists ought to agree not only that (1)–(5) are central to the concept of personhood, but also that it is a part of this concept that all and only people have full moral rights. The concept of a person is in part a moral concept; once we have admitted that X is a person, we have recognized, even if we have not agreed to respect, X's right to be treated as a member of the moral community. It is true that the claim that X is a *human being* is more commonly voiced as part of an appeal to treat X decently than is the claim that X is a person, but this is either because "human being" is here used in the sense which implies personhood, or because the genetic and moral senses of "human" have been confused.

Now if (1)–(5) are indeed the primary criteria of personhood, then it is clear that genetic humanity is neither necessary nor sufficient for establishing that an entity is a person. Some human beings are not people, and there may well be people who are not human beings. A man or woman whose consciousness has been permanently obliterated but who remains alive is a human being which is no longer a person; defective human beings, with no appreciable mental capacity, are not and presumably never will be people; and a fetus is a human being which is not yet a person, and which therefore cannot coherently be said to have full moral rights. Citizens of the next century should be prepared to recognize highly advanced, self-aware robots or computers, should such be developed, and intelligent inhabitants of other worlds, should such be found, as people in the fullest sense, and to respect their moral rights. But to ascribe full rights to an entity which is not a person is as absurd as to ascribe moral obligations and responsibilities to such an entity.

3. Fetal Development and the Right to Life

Two problems arise in the application of these suggestions for the definition of the moral community to the determination of the precise moral status of a human fetus. Given that the paradigm example of a person is a normal adult human being, then (1) How like this paradigm, in particular how far advanced since conception, does a human being need to be before it begins to have a right to life by virtue, not of being fully a person as of yet, but of being *like* a person? And (2) To what extent, if any, does the fact that a fetus has the *potential* for becoming a person endow it with some of the same rights? Each of these questions requires some comment.

In answering the first question, we need not attempt a detailed consideration of the moral rights of organisms which are not developed enough, aware enough, intelligent enough, etc., to be considered people, but which resemble people in some respects. It does seem reasonable to suggest that the more like a person, in the relevant aspects, a being is, the stronger is the case for regarding it as having a right to life, and indeed the stronger its right to life is. Thus we ought to take seriously the suggestion that, insofar as "the human individual develops biologically in a continuous fashion . . . the rights of a human person might develop in the same way."[8] But we must keep in mind that the attributes which are relevant in determining whether or not an entity is enough like a person to be regarded as having some of the same moral rights are no different from those which are relevant to determining whether or not it is fully a person—i.e., are no different from (1)–(5)—and that being genetically human, or having recognizably human facial and other physical features, or detectable brain activity, or the capacity to survive outside the uterus, is simply not among those relevant attributes.

Thus it is clear that even though a seven- or eight-month fetus has features which make it apt to arouse in us almost the same powerful protective instinct as is commonly aroused by a small infant, nevertheless it is not significantly more personlike than a very small embryo. It is *somewhat* more personlike; it can apparently feel and respond to pain, and it may even have a rudimentary form of consciousness, insofar as its brain is quite active. Nevertheless, it seems safe to say that it is not fully conscious, in the way that an infant of a few months is, and that it cannot reason, or communicate messages of indefinitely many sorts, does not engage in self-motivated activity, and has no self-awareness. Thus, in the *relevant* respects, a fetus, even a fully developed one, is considerably less personlike than is the average mature mammal, indeed the average fish. And I think that a rational person must conclude that if the right to life of a fetus is to be based upon its resemblance to a person, then it cannot be said to have any more right to life than, let us say, a newborn guppy (which also seems to be capable of feeling pain), and that a right of that magnitude could never override a woman's right to obtain an abortion, at any stage of her pregnancy.

There may . . . be other arguments in favor of placing legal limits on the stage of pregnancy in which abortion may be performed. Given the relative safety of the new techniques of artificially inducing labor during the third trimester, the danger to the woman's life or health is no longer such an argument. Neither is the fact that people tend to respond to the thought of abortion in the later stages of pregnancy with emotional repulsion, since mere emotional responses cannot take the place of moral reasoning in determining what ought to be permitted. Nor, finally, is the . . . argument that legalizing abortion, especially late in the pregnancy, may erode the level of respect for human life, leading perhaps, to an increase in unjustified euthanasia and other crimes. For this threat . . . can be better met by educating people to the kinds of moral distinctions which we are making here than by limiting access to abortion (which limitation may, in its disregard for the rights of women, be just as damaging to the level of respect for human rights).

Thus, since the fact that even a fully developed fetus is not personlike enough to have any significant right to life on the basis of its personlikeness shows that no legal restrictions upon the stage of pregnancy in which an abortion may be performed can be justified on the grounds that we should protect the rights of the older fetus; and since there is no other apparent justification for such restrictions, we may conclude that they are entirely unjustified. Whether or not it would be *indecent* (whatever that means) for a woman in her seventh month to obtain an abortion just to avoid having to postpone a trip to Europe, it would not, in itself, be *immoral*, and therefore it ought to be permitted.

4. Potential Personhood and the Right to Life

We have seen that a fetus does not resemble a person in any way which can support the claim that it has even some of the same rights. But what about its *potential*, the fact that if nurtured and allowed to develop naturally it will very probably become a person? Doesn't that alone give it at least some right to life? It is hard to deny that . . . an entity is a potential person is a strong *prima facie* reason for not destroying it; but we need not conclude from this that a potential person has a right to life, by virtue of that potential. It may be that our feeling that it is better, other things being equal, not to destroy a potential person is better explained by the fact that potential people are still (felt to be) an invaluable resource, not to be lightly squandered. Surely, if every speck of dust were a potential person, we would be much less apt to conclude that every potential person has a right to become actual.

Still, we do not need to insist that a potential person has no right to life whatever. There may well be something immoral, and not just imprudent, about wantonly destroying potential people, when doing so isn't necessary to protect anyone's rights. But even if a potential person does have some prima facie right to life, such a right could not possibly outweigh the right of a woman to obtain an abortion, since the rights of any actual person invariably outweigh those of any potential person, whenever the two conflict. Since this may not be immediately obvious in the case of a human fetus, let us look at another case.

Suppose that our space explorer falls into the hands of an alien culture, whose scientists decide to create a few hundred thousand or more human beings by breaking his body into component cells and using these to create fully developed human beings with, of course, his genetic code. We may imagine that each of these newly created men will have all of the original man's abilities, skills, knowledge, and so on, and also have an individual self-concept, in short that each of them will be a bona fide (though hardly unique) person. Imagine that the whole project will take only seconds, and that its chances of success are extremely high, and that our explorer knows all of this, and also knows that these people will be treated fairly. I maintain that in such a situation he would have every right to escape if he could, and thus to deprive all of these potential people of their potential lives; for his right to life outweighs all of theirs together, in spite of the fact that they are all genetically human, all innocent, and all have a very high probability of becoming people very soon, if only he refrains from acting.

Indeed, I think he would have a right to escape even if it were not his life which the alien scientists planned to take, but only a year of his freedom, or, indeed, only a day. Nor would he be obligated to stay if he had gotten captured (thus bringing all of these people potentials into existence) because of his own carelessness, or even if he had done so deliberately, knowing the consequences. Regardless of how he got captured, he is not morally obligated to remain in captivity for *any* period of time for the sake of permitting any number of potential people to

come into actuality, so great is the margin by which one actual person's right to liberty outweighs whatever right to life even a hundred thousand potential people have. And it seems reasonable to conclude that the rights of a woman will outweigh by a similar margin whatever right to life a fetus may have by virtue of its potential personhood.

Thus, neither a fetus's resemblance to a person, nor its potential for becoming a person provides any basis whatever for the claim that it has any significant right to life. Consequently, a woman's right to protect her health, happiness, freedom, and even her life[9] by terminating an unwanted pregnancy, will always override whatever right to life it may be appropriate to ascribe to a fetus, even a fully developed one. And thus, in the absence of any overwhelming social need for every possible child, the laws which restrict the right to obtain an abortion, or limit the period of pregnancy during which an abortion may be performed, are a wholly unjustified violation of a woman's most basic moral and constitutional rights.[10] . . .

Postscript on Infanticide

Since the publication of this article, many people have [pointed out] that my argument appears to justify not only abortion, but also infanticide. For a newborn infant is not significantly more personlike than an advanced fetus, and consequently it would seem that if the destruction of the latter is permissible so too must be that of the former. Inasmuch as most people, regardless of how they feel about the morality of abortion, consider infanticide a form of murder, this might appear to represent a serious flaw in my argument.

Now, if I am right in holding that it is only people who have a full-fledged right to life, and who can be murdered, and if the criteria of personhood are as I have described them, then it obviously follows that killing a newborn infant isn't murder. It does *not* follow, however, that infanticide is permissible, for two reasons. In the first place, it would be wrong, at least in this country and this period of history, and other things being equal, to kill a newborn infant, because even if its parents do not want it and would not suffer from its destruction, there are other people who would like to have it and would, in all probability, be deprived of a great deal of pleasure by its destruction. Thus, infanticide is wrong for reasons analogous to those which make it wrong to wantonly destroy natural resources, or great works of art.

Second, most people, at least in this country, value infants and would much prefer that they be preserved, even if foster parents are not immediately available. Most of us would rather be taxed to support orphanages than allow unwanted infants to be destroyed. So long as there are people who want an infant preserved, and who are willing and able to provide the means of caring for it, under reasonably humane conditions, it is, *ceteris paribus*, wrong to destroy it.

But, it might be replied, if this argument shows that infanticide is wrong, at least at this time and in this country, doesn't it also show that abortion is wrong? After all, many people value fetuses, are disturbed by their destruction, and would much prefer that they be preserved, even at some cost to themselves. Furthermore, as a potential source of pleasure to some foster family, a fetus is just as valuable as an infant. There is, however, a crucial difference between the two cases: So long as the fetus is unborn, its preservation, contrary to the wishes of the pregnant woman, violates her rights to freedom, happiness, and self-determination. Her rights override the rights of those who would like the fetus pre-

served, just as if someone's life or limb is threatened by a wild animal, his right to protect himself by destroying the animal overrides the rights of those who would prefer that the animal not be harmed.

The minute the infant is born, however, its preservation no longer violates any of its mother's rights, even if she wants it destroyed, because she is free to put it up for adoption. Consequently, while the moment of birth does not mark any sharp discontinuity in the degree to which an infant possesses the right to life, it does mark the end of its mother's right to determine its fate. Indeed, if abortion could be performed without killing the fetus, she would never possess the right to have the fetus destroyed, for the same reasons that she has no right to have an infant destroyed.

On the other hand, it follows from my argument that when an unwanted or defective infant is born into a society which cannot afford and/or is not willing to care for it, then its destruction is permissible. This conclusion will, no doubt, strike many people as heartless and immoral; but remember that the very existence of people who feel this way, and who are willing and able to provide care for unwanted infants, is reason enough to conclude that they should be preserved.

Endnotes

1. For example, Roger Wertheimer, who in "Understanding the Abortion Argument" (*Philosophy and Public Affairs*, 1, no. 1 [Fall, 1971], 67–95), argues that the problem of the moral status of abortion is insoluble, in that the dispute over the status of the fetus is not a question of fact at all, but only a question of how one responds to the facts.

2. John Noonan, "Abortion and the Catholic Church: A Summary History," *Natural Law Forum*, 12 (1967), 125.

3. John Noonan, "Deciding Who Is Human," *Natural Law Forum*, 13 (1968), 134.

4. "A Defense of Abortion."

5. We may safely ignore the fact that she might have avoided getting raped, e.g., by carrying a gun, since by similar means you might likewise have avoided getting kidnapped, and in neither case does the victim's failure to take all possible precautions against a highly unlikely event (as opposed to reasonable precautions against a rather likely event) mean that he is morally responsible for what happens.

6. Of course, the principle that it is (always) wrong to kill innocent human beings is in need of many other modifications, e.g., that it may be permissible to do so to save a greater number of innocent human beings, but we may safely ignore these complications here.

7. From here on, we will use "human" to mean genetically human, since the moral sense seems closely connected to, and perhaps derived from, the assumption that genetic humanity is sufficient for membership in the moral community.

8. Thomas L. Hayes, "A Biological View," *Commonweal*, 85 (March 17, 1967), 677–78; quoted by Daniel Callahan, in *Abortion, Law, Choice, and Morality* (London: Macmillan & Co., 1970).

9. That is, insofar as the death rate, for the woman, is higher for childbirth than for early abortion.

10. My thanks to the following people, who were kind enough to read and criticize an earlier version of this paper: Herbert Gold, Gene Glass, Anne Lauterbach, Judith Thomson, Mary Mothersill, and Timothy Binkley.

16. A Feminist Defense of Abortion

SALLY MARKOWITZ

Sally Markowitz provides what she regards as a specifically feminist argument for abortion, that is, one that is grounded on awareness of women's oppression and a commitment to a more egalitarian society. She argues that because in the sexist society in which we live women are denied the equality to which they are entitled, a right to abortion is justified until that equality is guaranteed.

In the past few decades, the issue of abortion, long of concern to women, has gained a prominent place in the platforms of politicians and a respectable, if marginal, one in the writings of moral philosophers. It is natural to speculate that the rise of and reactions to the women's liberation movement explain the feverish pitch of the recent debate, and no doubt there is much to this speculation. And yet, philosophical analyses of abortion have had surprisingly little to say directly about either women or feminism. Instead, their primary concern has been to decide whether or not the fetus is a person, with a right to life like yours or mine. That this question deserves philosophical attention becomes especially clear when we consider the frightening (if fanciful) ways it is asked and answered by those in power. Nevertheless, as many feminists and some philosophers have recognized, the way we respond to the problem of personhood will not necessarily settle the dispute over abortion once and for all. On some views, a full account must deal with the rights of pregnant women as well.

In fact, one popular defense of abortion is based on the woman's right to autonomy and avoids the personhood issue altogether. The central claim of the autonomy defense is that anti-abortion policies simply interfere in an impermissible way with the pregnant woman's autonomy. In what has become the classic philosophical statement of this view, Judith Jarvis Thomson ingeniously argues that even if the fetus has a right to life, it need not also have

the right to use its mother's body to stay alive. The woman's body is her own property, to dispose of as she wishes.[1] But autonomy theorists need not rest their case on the vaguely disturbing notion of the pregnant woman's property rights to her own body. For example, Jane English, in another version of the view, argues that a woman is justified in aborting if pregnancy and childbearing will prevent her from pursuing the life she wants to live, the expression of her own autonomy.[2]

Philosophers have come to call this strategy the "feminist" or "woman's liberation" approach, and some version of it seems to be favored by many feminists.[3] This is no surprise since such a view may seem to be quite an improvement over accounts that regard personhood as the only essential issue. At least it recognizes women as bearers of rights as well as of babies. In what follows, however, I suggest that this defense may fall short of the feminist mark. Then I shall offer another defense, one derived not from the right to autonomy, but from an awareness of women's oppression and commitment to a more egalitarian society.

I will assume throughout that the fetus has a serious right to life. I do so not because I believe this to be true, but rather because a feminist defense of abortion rights should be independent of the status of the fetus. For if, as many feminists believe, the move toward a sexually egalitarian society requires women's control of their reproductive lives, and if the permissibility of this control depends ultimately upon the status of the fetus, then the future of feminism rests upon how we resolve the personhood issue. This is not acceptable to most feminists. No doubt many feminists are comforted by arguments

Reprinted from *Social Theory and Practice* 16, no. 1 (Spring 1990) by permission.

against the fetus's personhood. But regardless of the fetus's status, more must be said.

———————◇———————

1.

What, then, from a feminist point of view, is wrong with an autonomy defense? Feminists should be wary on three counts. First, most feminists believe not only that women in our society are oppressed, but also that our failure to face the scope and depth of this oppression does much to maintain it. This makes feminists suspicious of perspectives, often called humanist or liberal, that focus only on the individual and deemphasize the issue of gender by either refusing to acknowledge that women have less power than men or denying that this inequity is worth much attention. While liberals and humanists may try to discuss social issues, including abortion, with as little mention as possible of gender, feminists tend to search for the hidden, unexpected, and perhaps unwelcome ways in which gender is relevant. From this perspective, defenses of abortion that focus only on the personhood of the fetus are not essentially or even especially feminist ones since they completely avoid any mention of gender. Autonomy arguments, though, are not much of an improvement. They may take into account the well-being of individual women, but they manage to skirt the issue of women's status, as a group, in a sexist society.

Second, the autonomy defense incorporates a (supposedly) gender-neutral right, one that belongs to every citizen; there's nothing special about being a woman—except, of course, for the inescapable fact that only women find themselves pregnant against their wills. Some feminists have become disillusioned with this gender-neutral approach. They reject it both on principle, because it shifts attention away from gender inequality, and for practical reasons, because it often works against women in the courts.[4] Instead, feminists have come to realize that sometimes gender should be relevant in claiming rights. Some of these rights, like adequate gynecological care, may be based on women's special physiology; others may stem from the special needs experienced by female casualties of a sexist society: the impoverished, divorced, or unwed mother, the rape victim, the anorexic teen, the coed who has been convinced that she lacks (or had better

lack) mathematical aptitude. A thoroughly feminist analysis, then, will not hesitate, when appropriate, to claim a right on the basis of gender, rather than in spite of it.[5] To do otherwise in the case of abortion may be not only to deny the obvious, but also to obscure the relation of reproductive practices to women's oppression.

The third problem feminists might have with an autonomy defense involves the content of the human ideal on which the right to autonomy rests. Some feminists, influenced by Marxist and socialist traditions, may reject an ideal that seems to be so ultimately connected with the individualistic ideology of capitalism. Others may suspect that this ideology is not just capitalist but male-biased. And if feminists hesitate to justify abortion by appeal to a gender-neutral right derived from a gender-neutral ideal, they are even more suspicious of an ideal that seems to be gender-neutral when really it's not. Increasingly, feminists reject the ideals of older feminists, like Simone de Beauvoir, who, in promoting for women what appeared to be an androgynous human ideal, unwittingly adopted one that was androcentric, or male-centered. Instead, feminists seek to free themselves from the misogynist perspective that sees women as incomplete men and ignores, devalues, or denies the existence of particularly female psychologies, values, and experiences. On this view, to fashion a feminist human ideal we must look to women's values and experiences—or at least we must not look only to men's.[6]

This re-evaluation has important implications for the abortion issue, since many feminists consider an overriding right to autonomy to be a characteristically male ideal, while nurturance and responsibility for others (the paradigmatic case of which is motherhood) to be characteristically female ones. Indeed, in the name of such women's values, some women who call themselves feminists have actually joined the anti-abortionist camp.[7] Most feminists, of course, don't go this far. But, paradoxically, many seem to find the ideal of autonomy less acceptable than the right to abortion it is supposed to justify. Clearly, something is awry. (I shall have more to say in section 4 about how autonomy is important to feminists.)

Feminists, therefore, need another argument. Instead of resting on an ideal many feminists reject, a feminist defense of abortion should somehow reflect an awareness of women's oppression and a commitment to ending it.

2.

Of all the philosophers, feminist and otherwise, who have discussed abortion, Alison Jaggar seems to be the only one to address the problem from this perspective. Jaggar argues that in societies where mothers bear the responsibility for pregnancy, birth, and childrearing, women should control abortion decisions. Women who live in other, more cooperative social communities (wherever they are), where members of both sexes share such responsibilities, cannot claim a right of the same force. The strength of a woman's say about whether or not to abort, then should be relative to the amount of support (financial, emotional, physical, medical, and otherwise) she can expect from those around her.[8]

It is disheartening that the philosophical community has not paid Jaggar's paper the attention it merits in the decade and a half since its publication, but this lapse is hardly surprising. The notion of the individual's right to autonomy is so firmly entrenched that we have difficulty even entertaining other approaches. We find ourselves invoking such rights perhaps without realizing it even when we neither want nor need to. And Jaggar is no exception; despite the promising intuition with which she starts, Jaggar finally offers us another, albeit more sophisticated, version of the autonomy argument. Quite simply, her argument implies that if abortion ought to be permissible in some societies but not in others, this is only because pregnancy and motherhood create obstacles to personal autonomy in some societies but not in others.

Jaggar bases her argument for abortion rights in our society on two principles. The first, or Right to Life Principle, holds that

> the right to life, when it is claimed for a human being, means the right to a full human life and to whatever means are necessary to achieve this. . . . To be born, then, is only one of the necessary conditions for a full human life. The others presumably include nutritious food, breathable air, warm human companionship, and so on. If anyone has a right to life, she or he must be entitled to all of these.[9]

According to the second, or Personal Control Principle, "Decisions should be made by those, and only by those, who are importantly affected by them."[10]

In our society, then, the state cannot legitimately set itself up as the protector of the fetus's right to life (as Jaggar has characterized it) because the mother and not the state will be expected to provide for this right, both during pregnancy and afterwards. But since, by the Personal Control Principle, only those whose lives will be importantly affected have the right to make a decision, in our society the pregnant woman should determine whether to continue her pregnancy.

Jaggar's argument incorporates both liberal and feminist perspectives, and there is a tension between them. Her argument is feminist rather than merely liberal because it does not rest exclusively on a universal right to autonomy. Instead, it takes seriously the contingent and socially variable features of reproduction and parenting, their relationship to women's position in a society, and the effect of antiabortion policy on this position. But her argument is also a liberal one. Consider, for example, the Personal Control Principle. While Jaggar doesn't explicitly spell out its motivation, she does state that the principle "provides the fundamental justification for democracy and is accepted by most shades of political opinion."[11] Surely this wide acceptance has something to do with the belief, equally widely held, that citizens should be able to decide for themselves what courses their lives should take, especially when some courses involve sacrifices or burdens. This becomes clear when Jaggar explains that an individual or organization has no moral claim as a protector of the right to life "that would justify its insistence on just one of the many conditions necessary to a full human life, in circumstances where this would place the burden of fulfilling all the other conditions squarely on the shoulders of some other individual or organization."[12] Once again we have an appeal to a universal right to personal autonomy, indeed a right based on an ideal which not only might be unacceptable to many feminists, but may cast the net too widely even for some liberals. For example, one might claim that taxation policies designed to finance social programs interfere with personal choices about how to spend earnings, a matter that will have important consequences for one's life. Such a view also permits a range of private actions which some liberals may believe are immoral: For example, an adult grandchild may decide to stop caring for a burdensome and senile grandparent if such care places a heavy burden on the grandchild.

I shall not attempt to pass judgment here on the desirability of either redistributing income through taxation or passing laws requiring us to be Good Samaritans in our private lives. Nor do I want to beg the question, which I shall discuss later, of whether reproductive autonomy is, in all circumstances, over-ridingly important in a way other sorts of autonomy may not be. I can leave these matters open because a feminist defense of abortion need not depend on how we settle them. For there is a significant difference between the sacrifices required by restrictive abortion policies and those required by enforcing other sorts of Good Samaritanism: Taxes and laws against letting the aged or handicapped starve to death apply to everyone; those prohibiting abortion apply only to women. While anyone might end up with a helpless, cantankerous grandparent and most of us end up paying taxes, only women end up pregnant. So anti-abortion laws require sacrifice not of everyone, but only of women.

3.

This brings us to what I regard as the crucial question: When, if ever, can people be required to sacrifice for the sake of others? And how can feminists answer this question in a way that rests not on the individual right to personal autonomy, but on a view of social reality that takes seriously power relations between genders? I suggest the following principle, which I shall call the Impermissible Sacrifice Principle: *When one social group in a society is systematically oppressed by another, it is impermissible to require the oppressed group to make sacrifices that will exacerbate or perpetuate this oppression.* (Note that this principle does not exempt the members of oppressed groups from *all* sorts of sacrifices just because they are oppressed; they may be as morally responsible as anyone for rendering aid in some circumstances. Only sacrifices that will clearly perpetuate their oppression are ruled out.)

The Impermissible Sacrifice Principle focuses on power relationships between groups rather than on the rights of individuals. This approach will suit not only feminists but all who recognize and deplore other sorts of systematic social oppression as well. Indeed, if we take our opposition to oppression seriously, this approach may be necessary. Otherwise, when policy decisions are made, competing goals and commitments may distract us from the

conditions we claim to deplore and encourage decisions that allow such conditions to remain. Even worse, these other goals and commitments can be used as excuses for perpetuating oppression. Testing policies against the Impermissible Sacrifice Principle keeps this from happening.

Feminists should welcome the applicability of the Impermissible Sacrifice Principle to groups other than women. Radical feminists are sometimes accused of being blind to any sort of oppression but their own. The Impermissible Sacrifice Principle, however, enables feminists to demonstrate solidarity with other oppressed groups by resting the case for abortion on the same principle that might, for example, block a policy requiring the poor rather than the rich to bear the tax burden, or workers rather than management to take a pay cut. On the other hand, feminists may worry that the Impermissible Sacrifice Principle, taken by itself, may not yield the verdict on abortion feminists seek. For if some radical feminists err by recognizing only women's oppression, some men err by not recognizing it at all. So the Impermissible Sacrifice Principle must be supplemented by what I shall call the Feminist Proviso: *Women are, as a group, sexually oppressed by men; and this oppression can neither be completely understood in terms of, nor otherwise reduced to, oppressions of other sorts.*

Feminists often understand this oppression to involve men's treating women as breeding machines, sexual or aesthetic objects, nurturers who need no nurturance. Women become alienated from their bodies, their sexuality, their work, their intellect, their emotions, their moral agency. Of course, feminists disagree about exactly how to formulate this analysis, especially since women experience oppression differently depending on their class, race, and ethnicity. But however we decide to understand women's oppression, we can be sure an anti-abortion policy will make it worse.

Adding the Feminist Proviso, then, keeps (or makes) sexism visible, ensuring that women are one of the oppressed groups to which the Principle applies. This should hardly need saying. Yet by focusing on other sorts of oppression the Principle might cover, men often trivialize or ignore feminists' demands and women's pain. For example, someone (perhaps a white male) who is more sympathetic to the claims of racial minorities or workers than to those of women might try to trivialize or deny the sexual oppression of a white, affluent woman (perhaps his wife) by reminding her that she's richer than an unemployed black male and so should not complain. The Feminist Proviso also prevents an affluent white woman who rejects the unwelcome sexual advances of a minority or working class male from being dismissed (or dismissing herself) as a racist or classist. She may well be both. But she also lives in a world where, all things being equal, she is fair sexual game, in one way or another, for any male.[13] Finally, the Impermissible Sacrifice Principle in conjunction with the Feminist Proviso might be used to block the view that a black or Third World woman's first obligation is to bear children to swell the ranks of the revolution, regardless of the consequences of maternity within her culture. Having children for this reason may be a legitimate choice; but she also may have independent grounds to refuse.

I have added the Feminist Proviso so that the Impermissible Sacrifice Principle cannot be used to frustrate a feminist analysis. But I must also emphasize that the point is not to pit one oppressed group against another, but to make sure that the men in otherwise progressive social movements do not ignore women's oppression or, worse, find "politically correct" justifications for it. Women refuse to wait until "after the revolution" not just because they are impatient, but also because they have learned that not all revolutions are feminist ones.

The Impermissible Sacrifice Principle and the Feminist Proviso together, then, justify abortion on demand for women *because they live in a sexist society.* This approach not only gives a more explicitly feminist justification of abortion than the autonomy defense; it also gives a stronger one. For autonomy defenses are open to objections and qualifications that a feminist one avoids. Consider the ways the feminist approach handles these four challenges to the autonomy defense.

First, some philosophers have dismissed autonomy defenses by suggesting blithely that we simply compensate the pregnant woman.[14] Of what, though, will such compensation consist? Maternity leave? Tax breaks? Prenatal healthcare? Twenty points added to her civil-service exam score? Such benefits lighten one's load, no doubt. But what women suffer by being forced to continue unwanted pregnancies is not merely a matter of finances or missed opportunities; in a sexist society, there is reason to expect that an anti-abortion policy will reinforce a specifically *sexual* oppression, whatever sorts of compensation are offered. Indeed, even talk of compensation may be misguided, since it implies a prior state when things were as they should be; compensation seeks to restore the balance after a temporary upset. But in a sexist society, there is no original balance; women's oppression is the status quo. Even if individual women are compensated by money, services, or opportunities, sexual oppression may remain.

Second, an autonomy defense may seem appropriate only in cases where a woman engages in "responsible" sex: It is one thing to be a victim of rape or even contraceptive failure, one might argue; it is quite another voluntarily to have unprotected intercourse. A feminist defense suggests another approach. First, we might question the double standard that requires that women pay for "irresponsible" sex while men don't have to, even though women are oppressed by men. More importantly, if we focus on the *way* women are oppressed, we may understand many unwanted pregnancies to result from fear and paralysis rather than irresponsibility. For in a sexist society, many women simply do not believe they control the conditions under which they have sex. And, sad to say, often they may be right.[15]

Third, what about poor women's access to abortion? The sort of right the autonomy theorists invoke, after all, seems to be a right to noninterference by the state. But this negative right seems to be in tension with a demand for state-funded abortions, especially since not everyone supports abortions. At any rate, we will need another argument to justify the funding of abortion for poor women. The defense I suggest, however, is clearly committed to providing all women with access to abortion, since to allow abortions only for those who can afford them forces poor women, who are doubly oppressed, to make special sacrifices. An egalitarian society must liberate all women, not just the rich ones.

Finally, autonomy defenses allow, indeed invite, the charge that the choice to abort is selfish. Even Thomson finds abortion, while not unjust, often to be "selfish" or "indecent." Although she has deprived nothing of its rights, the woman who aborts has chosen self-interested autonomy over altruism in the same way one might choose to watch while a child starves. Of course, one is tempted to point out that the (largely male) world of commerce and politics thrives on such "morally indecent" but legal actions. But then feminists are reduced to claiming a right to be as selfish as men are. Moreover, once the specter of selfishness is raised, this defense does not allow feminists to make enough of male anti-abortionists' motives. On an autonomy defense, these motives are simply not relevant, let alone damning, and feminists who dwell on them seem to be resorting to *ad hominem*s. From a feminist perspective, however, abortion is a political issue, one which essentially concerns the interests of and power relations between men and women. Thus, what women and men can expect to gain or lose from an abortion policy becomes the point rather than the subject of *ad hominem* arguments.[16]

The approach I propose does well on each of these important counts. But its real test comes when we weigh the demands of the Impermissible Sacrifice Principle against fetal rights; for we have required that a feminist analysis be independent of the status of the fetus. Indeed, we may even be tempted to regard fetuses as constituting just the sort of oppressed group to whom the principle applies, and surely a fetus about to be aborted is in worse shape than the woman who carries it.

However, it may not make sense to count fetuses as an oppressed group. A disadvantaged one, perhaps. But the Impermissible Sacrifice Principle does not prescribe that more disadvantaged groups have a right to aid from less disadvantaged ones; it focuses only on the particular disadvantage of social oppression. That the fetus has a serious right to life does not imply that it's the sort of being that can be oppressed, if it cannot yet enter into the sorts of social relationships that constitute oppression. I cannot argue for this here; in any case, I suspect my best argument will not convince everyone. But feminists have another, more pointed response.

Whether or not we can weigh the disadvantage of fetuses against the oppression of women, we must realize what insisting on such a comparison does to the debate. It narrows our focus, turning it back to the conflict between the rights of fetuses and of women (even if now this conflict is between the rights of groups rather than of individuals). This is certainly not to deny that fetal rights should be relevant to an abortion policy. But feminists must insist that the oppression of women should be relevant too. And it is also relevant that unless our society changes in deep and global ways, anti-abortion policies, intentionally or not, will perpetuate women's oppression by men. This, then, is where feminists must stand firm.

Does this mean that instead of overriding the fetus's right to life by women's right to autonomy, I am proposing that feminists override the fetus's right by the right of women to live in a sexually egalitarian society? This is a difficult position for feminists but not an impossible one, especially for feminists with utilitarian leanings. Many feminists, for example, see sexism as responsible for a culture of death: war, violence, child abuse, ecological disaster. Eradicate sexism, it might be argued, and we will save more lives than we will lose. Some feminists might even claim that an oppressed woman's fate can be worse than that of an aborted fetus. Although I will not argue for such claims, they may be less implausible than they seem. But feminists need not rest their case on them. Instead, they must simply insist that society must change so that women are no longer oppressed. Such changes, of course, may require of men sacrifices unwelcome beyond their wildest dreams. But that, according to a feminist analysis, is the point.

So we should not see the choice as between liberating women and saving fetuses, but between two ways of respecting the fetus's right to life. The first requires women to sacrifice while men benefit. The second requires deep social changes that will ensure that men no longer gain and women lose through our practices of sexuality, reproduction, and parenthood. To point out how men gain from women's compulsory pregnancy is to steal the misplaced moral thunder from those male authorities—fathers, husbands, judges, congressmen, priests, philosophers—who, exhorting women to do their duty, present themselves as the benevolent, disinterested protectors of fetuses against women's selfishness. Let feminists insist that the conditions for refraining from having abortions is a sexually egalitarian society. If men do not respond, and quickly, they will have indicated that fetal life isn't so important to them after all, or at least not important enough to give up the privileges of being male in a sexist society. If this makes feminists look bad, it makes men look worse still.

Endnotes

1.   Judith Jarvis Thomson, "A Defense of Abortion," *Philosophy and Public Affairs* 1 (1971): 47–66.
2.   Jane English, "Abortion and the Concept of a Person," in *Today's Moral Problems,* ed. by Richard A. Wasserstrom (New York: Macmillan, 1985), pp. 448–457.
3.   Peter Singer, *Practical Ethics* (Cambridge: Cambridge University Press, 1979), p. 113.
4.   Catherine A. MacKinnon, *Feminism Unmodified: Discourses on Life and Law* (Cambridge: Harvard University Press, 1987), pp. 35–36.

5. See, for example, Alison Jaggar, *Feminism Politics and Human Nature* (Totowa, New Jersey: Rowman & Allanheld, 1983), especially Parts 1 and 2; and Catherine A. MacKinnon, *Feminism Unmodified: Discourses on Life and Law.*
6. See Sara Ruddick, "Maternal Thinking," *Feminist Studies 6* (1980): 345–346; Nancy Chodorow, *The Reproduction of Mothering: Psychoanalysis and the Sociology of Gender* (Berkeley and Los Angeles: University of California Press, 1978); Carol Gilligan, *In a Different Voice: Psychological Theory and Women's Development* (Cambridge: Harvard University Press, 1982).
7. Sidney Callahan, "A Pro-Life Feminist Makes Her Case," *Commonweal* (April 25, 1986), quoted in the *Utne Reader 20* (1987); 104–108.
8. Alison Jaggar, "Abortion and a Woman's Right to Decide," in *Philosophy and Sex*, ed. Robert Baker and Frank Elliston (Buffalo: Prometheus Press, 1975), pp. 324–337.
9. "Abortion and a Woman's Right to Decide," p. 328.
10. "Abortion and a Woman's Right to Decide," p. 328.
11. "Abortion and a Woman's Right to Decide," p. 329.
12. For classic discussions of sexism in the civil rights movement, see Susan Brownmiller, *Against Our Will: Men, Women, and Rape* (New York: Simon and Schuster, 1975), especially pp. 210–255; and Michelle Wallace, *Black Macho and the Myth of the Superwoman* (New York: Dial Press, 1978).
13. [This reference, apparently to Jaggar, is missing in the original—Ed.]
14. Michael Tooley, "Abortion and Infanticide," in Joel Feinberg, ed., *The Problem of Abortion* (Belmont, California: Wadsworth, 1983).
15. MacKinnon, *Feminism Unmodified*, p. 95.
16. This approach also allows us to understand the deep division between women on this issue. For many women in traditional roles fear the immediate effects on their lives of women's liberation generally and a permissive abortion policy in particular. On this, see Kristen Luker, *Abortion and the Politics of Motherhood* (Berkeley: University of California Press, 1984), especially pp. 158–215.

---

17. *Euthanasia, Killing, and Letting Die*

JAMES RACHELS

James Rachels criticizes a policy statement of the American Medical Association on the grounds that it endorses the doctrine that there is an important moral difference between active and passive euthanasia. Rachels denies that there is any moral difference between the two. He argues that once we judge a patient would be better off dead, it should not matter much whether that patient is killed or let die. He points out that both killing and letting die can be intentional and deliberate and can proceed from the same motives; further, that when killing and letting die are similar in these and other relevant respects, our moral assessment of these acts is also similar. Rachels concludes by considering a number of counterarguments to his view and finds them all wanting. In particular, Rachels rejects the idea that the killing and letting die distinction can be supported on the grounds that our duty to refrain from harming people is much stronger than our duty to help people in need. Rather, he contends that when conditions are similar our duty to refrain from harming people and our duty to help people in need have a similar moral force.

Dr. F. J. Ingelfinger, former editor of *The New England Journal of Medicine*, observes that

> this is the heyday of the ethicist in medicine. He delineates the rights of patients, of experimental subjects, of fetuses, of mothers, of animals, and even of doctors. (And what a far cry it is from the days when medical "ethics" consisted of condemning economic improprieties such as fee splitting and advertising!) With impeccable logic—once certain basic assumptions are granted—and with graceful prose, the ethicist develops his arguments. . . . Yet his precepts are essentially the products of armchair exercise and remain abstract and idealistic until they have been tested in the laboratory of experience.[1]

From *Ethical Issues Relating to Life and Death*, edited by John Ladd, pp. 146–161. Copyright 1979 Oxford University Press, Inc. Reprinted by Permission.

One problem with such armchair exercises, he complains, is that in spite of the impeccable logic and the graceful prose, the result is often an absolutist ethic which is unsatisfactory when applied to particular cases, and which is therefore of little use to the practicing physician. Unlike some absolutist philosophers, "the practitioner appears to prefer the principles of individualism. As there are few atheists in fox holes, there tend to be few absolutists at the bedside."[2]

I must concede at the outset that this chapter is another exercise in "armchair ethics" in the sense that I am not a physician but a philosopher. Yet I am no absolutist; and my purpose is to examine a doctrine that is held in an absolute form by many doctors. The doctrine is that there is an important moral difference between active and passive euthanasia, such that even though the latter is sometimes permissible, the former is always forbidden. This is an absolute which doctors hold "at the bedside" as well as in the seminar room, and the "principles of individualism" make little headway against it. But I will argue that this is an irrational dogma, and that there is no sound moral basis for it.

I will not argue, simply, that active euthanasia is all right. Rather, I will be concerned with the *relation* between active euthanasia and passive euthanasia: I will argue that there is no moral difference between them. By this I mean that there is no reason to prefer one over the other as a matter of principle—the fact that one case of euthanasia is active, while another is passive, is not *itself* a reason to think one morally better than the other. If you already think that passive euthanasia is all right, and you are convinced by my arguments, then you may conclude that active euthanasia must be all right, too. On the other hand, if you believe that active euthanasia is immoral, you may want to conclude that passive euthanasia must be immoral, too. Although I prefer the former alternative, I will not argue for it here. I will only argue that the two forms of euthanasia are morally equivalent—either both are acceptable or both are unacceptable.

I am aware that this will at first seem incredible to many readers, but I hope that this impression will be dispelled as the discussion proceeds. The discussion will be guided by two methodological considerations, both of which are touched on in the editorial quoted above. The first has to do with my "basic assumptions." My arguments are intended to appeal to all reasonable people, and not merely to those who already share my psychological preconceptions. Therefore, I will try not to rely on any assumptions that cannot be accepted by any reasonable person. None of my arguments will depend on morally eccentric premises. Second, Dr. Ingelfinger is surely correct when he says that we must be as concerned with the realities of medical practice as with the more abstract issues of moral theory. As he notes, the philosopher's precepts "remain abstract and idealistic until they are tested in the laboratory of experience." Part of my argument will be precisely that, when "tested in the laboratory of experience," the doctrine in question has terrible results. I believe that if this doctrine were to be recognized as irrational, and rejected by the medical profession, the benefit to both doctors and patients would be enormous. In this sense, my paper is not intended as an "armchair exercise" at all.

The American Medical Association Policy Statement

"Active euthanasia," as the term is used, means taking some positive action designed to kill the patient; for example, giving him a lethal injection of potassium chloride. "Passive euthanasia," on the other hand, means simply refraining from doing anything to keep the patient alive. In passive euthanasia we withhold medication or other life-sustaining therapy, or we refuse to perform surgery, etc., and let the patient die "naturally" of whatever ills already afflict him.

Many doctors and theologians prefer to use the term *euthanasia* only in connection with active euthanasia, and they use other words to refer to what I am calling "passive euthanasia"—for example, instead of "passive euthanasia" they may speak of "the right to death with dignity." One reason for this choice of terms is the emotional impact of the words: It *sounds* so much better to defend "death with dignity" than to advocate "euthanasia" of any sort. And of course if one believes that there is a great moral difference between active and passive euthanasia—as most doctors and religious writers do—then one may prefer a terminology which puts as much psychological distance as possible between them. However, I do not want to become involved in a pointless dispute about terminology, because nothing of substance depends on which label is used. I will stay with the terms *active euthanasia* and *passive euthanasia* because they are the most convenient; but if the reader prefers a different terminology he may substitute his own throughout, and my arguments will be unaffected.

The belief that there is an important moral difference between active and passive euthanasia obviously has important consequences for medical practice. It makes a difference to what doctors are willing to do. Consider, for example, the following familiar situation. A patient who is dying from incurable cancer of the throat is in terrible pain that we can no longer satisfactorily alleviate. He is certain to die within a few days, but he decides that he does not want to go on living for those days since the pain is unbearable. So he asks the doctor to end his life now; and his family joins in the request. One way that the doctor might comply with this request is simply by killing the patient with a lethal injection. Most doctors would not do that, not only because of the possible legal consequences, but because they think such a course would be immoral. And this is understandable: The idea of killing someone goes against very deep moral feelings; and besides, as we are often reminded, it is the special business of doctors to save and protect life, not to destroy it. Yet, even so, the physician may sympathize with the dying patient's request and feel that it is entirely reasonable for him to prefer death now rather than after a few more days of agony. The doctrine that we are considering tells the doctor what to do: It says that although he may not administer the lethal injection—that would be "active euthanasia," which is forbidden—he *may* withhold treatment and let the patient die sooner than he otherwise would.

It is no wonder that this simple idea is so widely accepted, for it seems to give the doctor a way out of his dilemma without having to kill the patient, and without having to prolong the patient's agony. The idea is not a new one. What *is* new is that the idea is now being incorporated into official documents of medical ethics. What was once unofficially done is now becoming official policy. The idea is expressed, for example, in a 1973 policy statement of the American Medical Association, which says (in its entirety):

The intentional termination of the life of one human being by another—mercy killing—is contrary to that for which the medical profession stands and is contrary to the policy of the American Medical Association.

The cessation of the employment of extraordinary means to prolong the life of the body when there is irrefutable evidence that biological death is imminent is the decision of the patient and/or his immediate family. The advice and judgment of the physician should be freely available to the patient and/or his immediate family.[3]

This is a cautiously worded statement, and it is not clear *exactly* what is being affirmed. I take it, however, that at least these three propositions are intended:

1. Killing patients is absolutely forbidden; however, it is sometimes permissible to allow patients to die.

2. It is permissible to allow a patient to die if (a) there is irrefutable evidence that he will die soon anyway; (b) "extraordinary" measures would be required to keep him alive; and (c) the patient and/or his immediate family requests it.

3. Doctors should make their own advice and judgments available to the patient and/or his immediate family when the latter are deciding whether to request that the patient be allowed to die.

The first proposition expresses the doctrine which is the main subject of this paper. As for the third, it seems obvious enough, provided that 1 and 2 are accepted, so I shall say nothing further about it. I do want to say a few things about 2. Physicians often allow patients to die; however, they do *not* always keep to the guidelines set out in 2. For example, a doctor may leave instructions that if a hopeless, comatose patient suffers cardiac arrest, nothing be done to start his heart beating again. "No-coding" is the name given to this practice, and the consent of the patient and/or his immediate family is not commonly sought. This is thought to be a medical decision (in reality, of course, it is a moral one) which is the doctor's affair. To take a different sort of example, when a Down's syndrome infant is born with an intestinal blockage, the doctor and parents may agree that there will be no operation to remove the blockage, so that the baby will die.[4] (If the same infant were born without the obstruction, it certainly would not be killed. This is a clear application of the idea that "letting die" is all right even though killing is forbidden.) But in such cases it is clear that the baby is *not* going to die soon anyway. If the surgery were performed, the baby would proceed to a "normal" infancy—normal, that is, for a mongoloid. Moreover, the treatment required to save the baby—abdominal surgery—can hardly be called "extraordinary" by today's medical standards.

Therefore, all three conditions which the AMA statement places on the decision to let die are commonly violated. It is beyond the scope of this paper to determine whether doctors are right to violate those conditions. But I firmly believe that the second requirement—2b—is not acceptable. Only a little reflection is needed to show that the distinction between ordinary and extraordinary means is not important. Even a very conservative, religiously oriented writer such as Paul Ramsey stresses this. Ramsey gives these examples:

> Suppose that a diabetic patient long accustomed to self-administration of insulin falls victim to terminal cancer, or suppose that a terminal cancer patient suddenly develops diabetes. Is he in the first case obliged to continue, and in the second case obliged to begin, insulin treatment and die painfully of cancer, or in either or both cases may the patient choose rather to pass into diabetic coma and an earlier death? . . . Or an old man slowly deteriorating who from simply being inactive and recumbent gets pneumonia: Are we to use antibiotics in a likely successful attack upon this disease which from time immemorial has been called "the old man's friend"?[5]

I agree with Ramsey, and with many other writers, that in such cases treatment may be withheld even though it is not "extraordinary" by any reasonable standard. Contrary to what is implied by the AMA statement, the distinction between heroic and nonheroic means of treatment *cannot* be used to determine when treatment is or is not mandatory.

◇

Killing and Letting Die

I return now to the distinction between active and passive euthanasia. Of course, not every doctor believes that this distinction is morally important.

Over twenty years ago Dr. D. C. S. Cameron of the American Cancer Society said that "Actually the difference between euthanasia [i.e., killing] and letting the patient die by omitting life-sustaining treatment is a moral quibble."[6] I argue that Cameron was right.

The initial thought can be expressed quite simply. In any case in which euthanasia seems desirable, it is because we think that the patient would literally be better off dead—or at least, no worst off dead—than continuing the kind of life available to him. (Without this assumption, even *passive* euthanasia would be unthinkable.) But, as far as the main question of ending the patient's life is concerned, it does not matter whether the euthanasia is active or passive: *In either case,* he ends up dead sooner than he otherwise would. And if the results are the same, why should it matter so much which method is used?

Moreover, we need to remember that, in cases such as that of the terminal cancer patient, the justification for allowing him to die, rather than prolonging his life for a few more hopeless days, is that he is in horrible pain. But if we simply withhold treatment, it may take him *longer* to die, and so he will suffer *more* than he would if we were to administer the lethal injection. This fact provides strong reason for thinking that, once we have made the initial decision not to prolong his agony, active euthanasia is actually preferable to passive euthanasia rather than the reverse. It also shows a kind of incoherence in the conventional view: To say that passive euthanasia is preferable is to endorse the option which leads to more suffering rather than less, and is contrary to the humanitarian impulse which prompts the decision not to prolong his life in the first place.

But many people are convinced that there is an important moral difference between active and passive euthanasia because they think that, in passive euthanasia, the doctor does not really *do* anything. No action whatever is taken; the doctor simply does nothing, and the patient dies of whatever ills already afflict him. In active euthanasia, however, we *do something* to bring about the patient's death. We kill him. Thus, the difference between active and passive euthanasia is thought to be the difference between doing something to bring about someone's death, and not doing anything to bring about anyone's death. And of course if we conceive the matter in *this* way, passive euthanasia seems preferable. Ramsey, who denounces the view I am defending as "extremist" and who regards the active/passive distinction as one of the "flexibly wise categories of traditional medical ethics," takes just this view of the matter. He says that the choice between active and passive euthanasia "is not a choice between directly and indirectly willing and doing something. *It is rather the important choice between doing something and doing nothing,* or (better said) ceasing to do something that was begun in order to do something that is better because now more fitting."[7]

This is a very misleading way of thinking, for it ignores the fact that in passive euthanasia the doctor *does* do one thing which is very important. Namely, he lets the patient die. We may overlook this obvious fact—or at least, we may put it out of our minds—if we concentrate only on a very restricted way of describing what happens: "The doctor does not administer medication or any other therapy; he does not instruct the nurses to administer any such medication; he does not perform any surgery"; and so on. And of course this description of what happens is correct, as far as it goes—these are all things that the doctor does not do. But the point is that the doctor *does* let the patient die when he could save him, and this must be included in the description, too.

There is another reason why we might fall into this error. We might confuse *not saving* someone with *letting him die.* Suppose a patient is dying, and Dr. X could prolong his life. But he decides not to do so and the patient dies. Now it is true of everyone on earth that he did not save the patient. Dr. X did not save him, and neither did you, and neither did I. So we might be tempted to think that all of us are in the same moral position, reasoning that since neither you nor I are responsible for the patient's death, neither is Dr. X. None of us did anything. This, however, is a mistake, for even though it is true that none of us saved the patient, it is *not* true that we all let him die. In order to let someone die, one must be *in a position* to save him. You and I were not in a position to save the patient, so we did not let him die. Dr. X, on the other hand, was in a position to save him, and did let him die. Thus the doctor is in a special moral position which not just everyone is in.

Here we must remember some elementary points, which are so obvious that they would not be worth mentioning except for the fact that overlooking them is a source of so much confusion in this area. The act of letting someone die may be intentional and deliberate, just as the act of killing someone may be intentional and deliberate. Moreover,

the doctor is *responsible* for his decision to let the patient die, just as he would be responsible for giving the patient a lethal injection. The decision to let a patient die is subject to moral appraisal in the same way that a decision to kill is subject to moral appraisal: It may be assessed as wise or unwise, compassionate or sadistic, right or wrong. If a doctor deliberately let a patient die who was suffering from a routinely curable illness, then he would be to blame for what he did, just as he would be to blame if he had needlessly killed the patient. It would be no defense at all for him to insist that, *really,* he didn't "do anything" but just stand there. We would all know that he did do something very serious indeed, for he let the patient die.

These considerations show how misleading it is to characterize the difference between active and passive euthanasia as a difference between doing something (killing), for which the doctor may be morally culpable; and doing nothing (just standing there while the patient dies), for which the doctor is not culpable. The real difference between them is, rather, the difference between *killing* and letting die, both of which are actions for which a doctor, or anyone else, will be morally responsible.

Now we can formulate our problem more precisely. If there is an important moral difference between active and passive euthanasia, it must be because *killing someone is morally worse than letting someone die.* But is it? Is killing, in itself, worse than letting die? In order to investigate this issue, we may consider two cases which are exactly alike except that one involves killing where the other involves letting die. Then we can ask whether this difference makes any difference to our moral assessments. It is important that the cases be *exactly* alike except for this one difference, since otherwise we cannot be confident that it is *this* difference which accounts for any variation in our assessments.

1. Smith stands to gain a large inheritance if anything should happen to his six-year-old cousin. One evening while the child is taking his bath, Smith sneaks into the bathroom and drowns the child, and then arranges things so that it will look like an accident.

2. Jones also stands to gain if anything should happen to his six-year-old cousin. Like Smith, Jones sneaks in planning to drown the child in his bath. However, just as he enters the bathroom Jones sees the child slip, hit his head, and fall face down in the water. Jones is delighted; he stands by, ready to

push the child's head back under if it is necessary, but it is not necessary. With only a little thrashing about, the child drowns all by himself, "accidentally," as Jones watches and does nothing.

Now Smith killed the child, while Jones "merely" let the child die. That is the only difference between them. Did either man behave better, from a moral point of view? Is there a moral difference between them? *If the difference between killing and letting die were itself a morally important matter, then we should say that Jones's behavior was less reprehensible than Smith's.* But do we actually want to say that? I think not, for several reasons. In the first place, both men acted from the same motive, personal gain, and both had exactly the same end in view when they acted. We may infer from Smith's conduct that he is a bad man, although we may withdraw or modify that judgment if we learn certain further facts about him; for example, that he is mentally deranged. But would we not also infer the very same thing about Jones from his conduct? And would not the same further considerations also be relevant to any modification of that judgment? Moreover, suppose Jones pleaded in his defense," After all, I didn't kill the child. I only stood there and let him die." Again, if letting die were in itself less bad than killing, this defense should have some weight. But—morally, at least—it does not. Such a "defense" can only be regarded as a grotesque perversion of moral reasoning.

Thus, it seems that when we are careful not to smuggle in any further differences which prejudice the issue, the mere difference between killing and letting die does not itself make any difference to the morality of actions concerning life and death.[8]

Now it may be pointed out, quite properly, that the cases of euthanasia with which doctors are concerned are not like this at all. They do not involve personal gain or the destruction of normal, healthy children. Doctors are concerned only with cases in which the patient's life is of no further use to him, or in which the patient's life has become or soon will become a positive burden. However, the point is the same in those cases: The difference between killing or letting die does not, *in itself*, make a difference, from the point of view of morality. If a doctor lets a patient die, for humane reasons, he is in the same moral position as if he had given the patient a lethal injection for humane reasons. If his decision was wrong—if, for example, the patient's illness was in fact curable—then the decision would be equally regrettable no matter which method was used to carry it out. And if the doctor's decision was

the right one, then the method he used is not itself important.

The AMA statement isolates the crucial issue very well: "the intentional termination of the life of one human being by another." But then the statement goes on to deny that the cessation of treatment *is* the intentional termination of a life. This is where the mistake comes in, for what is the cessation of treatment, in those circumstances, if it is not "the intentional termination of the life of one human being by another"? Of course it is exactly that; if it were not, there would be no point to it.

Counterarguments

Our argument has now brought us to this point: We cannot draw any moral distinction between active and passive euthanasia on the grounds that one involves killing while the other only involves letting someone die, because that is a difference that does not make a difference, from a moral point of view. Some people will find this hard to accept. One reason, I think, is that they fail to distinguish the question of whether killing is, in itself, worse than letting die, from the very different question of whether most actual cases of killing are more reprehensible than most actual cases of letting die. Most actual cases of killing are clearly terrible—think of the murders reported in the newspapers—and we hear of such cases almost every day. On the other hand, we hardly ever hear of a case of letting die, except for the actions of doctors who are motivated by humanitarian reasons. So we learn to think of killing in a much worse light than letting die; and we conclude, invalidly, that there must be something about killing which makes it *in itself* worse than letting die. But this does not follow for it is not the bare difference between killing and letting die that makes the difference in these cases. Rather, it is the other factors—the murderer's motive of personal gain, for example, contrasted with the doctor's humanitarian motivation, or the fact that the murderer kills a healthy person while the doctor lets die a terminal patient racked with disease—that account for our different reactions to the different cases.

There are, however, some substantial arguments that may be advanced to oppose my conclusion. Here are two of them:

The first counterargument focuses specifically on the concept of *being the cause of someone's death.* If we kill someone, then we are the cause of his death. But if we merely let someone die, we are not the cause; rather, he dies of whatever condition he already has. The doctor who gives the cancer patient a lethal injection will have caused his patient's death, and will have this on his conscience; whereas if he merely ceases treatment, the cancer and not the doctor is the cause of death. This is supposed to make a moral difference. This argument has been advanced many times. Ramsey, for example, urges us to remember that "In omission no human agent causes the patient's death, directly or indirectly."[9] And, writing in the *Villanova Law Review* for 1968, Dr. J. Russell Elkinton said that what makes the active/passive distinction important is that in passive euthanasia, "the patient does not die from the act [e.g., the act of turning off the respirator] but from the underlying disease or injury."[10]

This argument will not do, for two reasons. First, just as there is a distinction to be drawn between being and not being the cause of someone's death, there is also a distinction to be drawn between letting someone die and not letting anyone die. It is certainly desirable, in general, not to be the cause of anyone's death; but it is also desirable, in general, not to let anyone die when we can save them. (Doctors act on this precept every day.) Therefore, we cannot draw any special conclusion about the relative desirability of passive euthanasia just on these grounds. Second, the reason we think it is bad to be the cause of someone's death is that we think that death is a great evil—and so it is. However, if we have decided that euthanasia, even passive euthanasia, is desirable in a given case, then we have decided that in *this* instance death is no greater an evil than the patient's continued existence. And if this is true, then the usual reason for not wanting to be the cause of someone's death simply does not apply. To put the point just a bit differently: There is nothing wrong with being the cause of someone's death if his death is, all things considered, a good thing. And if his death is *not* a good thing, then *no* form of euthanasia, active or passive, is justified. So once again we see that the two kinds of euthanasia stand or fall together.

The second counterargument appeals to a favorite idea of philosophers, namely that our duty not to harm people is generally more stringent than our duty to help them. The law affirms this when it forbids us to kill people, or steal their goods, but does not require us in general to save people's lives or give them charity. And this is said to be not merely a point about the law, but about morality as well. We do not have a strict moral duty to help some poor man in Ethiopia—although it might be kind and generous of us if we did—but we *do* have a strict moral duty to refrain from doing anything to harm him. Killing someone is a violation of our duty not to harm, whereas letting someone die is merely a failure to give help. Therefore, the former is a more serious breach of morality than the latter; and so, contrary to what was said above, there is a morally significant difference between killing and letting die.

This argument has a certain superficial plausibility, but it cannot be used to show that there is a morally important difference between active and passive euthanasia. For one thing, it only seems that our duty to help people is less stringent than our duty not to harm them when we concentrate on certain sorts of cases: cases in which the people we could help are very far away, and are strangers to us; or cases in which it would be very difficult for us to help them, or in which helping would require a substantial sacrifice on our part. Many people feel that, in *these* types of cases, it may be kind and generous of us to give help, but we are not morally required to do so. Thus it is felt that when we give money for famine relief we are being especially big-hearted, and we deserve special praise—even if it would be immodest of us to seek such praise—because we are doing more than, strictly speaking, we are required to do.[11]

However, if we think of cases in which it would be very easy for us to help someone who is close at hand and in which no great personal sacrifice is required, things look very different. Think again of the child drowning in the bathtub: *Of course* a man standing next to the tub would have a strict moral duty to help the child. Here the alleged asymmetry between the duty to help and the duty not to do harm vanishes. Since most of the cases of euthanasia with which we are concerned are for this latter type—the patient is close at hand, it is well within the professional skills of the physician to keep him alive—the alleged asymmetry has little relevance.

It should also be remembered, in considering this argument, that the duty of doctors toward their patients *is* precisely to help them; that is what doctors are supposed to do. Therefore, even if there were a general asymmetry between the duty to help and the duty not to harm—which I deny—it would not apply in the special case of the relation between doctors and their patients. Finally, it is not clear that killing such a patient *is* harming him, even though in other cases it certainly is a great harm to someone to kill him, for as I said before, we are going under the assumption that the patient would be no worse off dead than he is now; if this is so, then killing him is not harming him. For the same reason we should not classify letting such a patient die as failing to help him. Therefore, even if we grant that our duty to help people is less stringent than our duty not to harm them, nothing follows about our duties with respect to killing and letting die in the special case of euthanasia.

◇

Practical Consequences

This is enough, I think, to show that the doctrine underlying the AMA statement is false. There is no general moral difference between active and passive euthanasia; if one is permissible, so is the other. Now if this were merely an intellectual mistake, having no significant consequences for medical practice, the whole matter would not be very important. But the opposite is true: The doctrine has terrible consequences for, as I have already mentioned—and as doctors know very well—the process of being "allowed to die" can be relatively slow and painful, while being given a lethal injection is relatively quick and painless. Dr. Anthony Shaw describes what happens when the decision has been made not to perform the surgery necessary to "save" a Down's syndrome infant:

> When surgery is denied [the doctor] must try to keep the infant from suffering while natural forces sap the baby's life away. As a surgeon whose natural inclination is to use the scalpel to fight off death, standing by and watching a salvageable baby die is the most emotionally exhausting experience I know. It is easy at a conference, in a theoretical discussion, to decide that such infants should be allowed to die. It is altogether different to stand by in the nursery and watch as dehydration and infection wither a tiny being over hours and days. This is a terrible ordeal for me and the hospital staff—much more so than for the parents who never set foot in the nursery.[12]

Why must the hospital staff "stand by in the nursery and watch as dehydration and infection wither a tiny being over hours and days"? Why must they merely "try" to reduce the infant's suffering? The doctrine that says the baby may be allowed to dehydrate and wither but not be given an injection that would end its life without suffering is not only irrational but cruel.

The same goes for the case of the man with cancer of the throat. Here there are three options: With continued treatment, he will have a few more days of pain, and then die; if treatment is stopped, but nothing else is done, it will be a few more hours; and with a lethal injection, he will die at once. Those who oppose euthanasia in all its forms say that we must take the first option, and keep the patient alive for as long as possible. This view is so patently inhumane that few defend it; nevertheless, it does have a certain kind of integrity. It is at least consistent. The third option is the one I think best. But the *middle* position—that, although the patient need not suffer for days before dying, he must nevertheless suffer for a few more hours—is a "moderate" view which incorporates the worst, and not the best, features of both extremes.

Let me mention one other practice that we would be well rid of if we stopped thinking that the distinction between active and passive euthanasia is important. About one in six hundred babies born in the United States is mongoloid. Most of these babies are otherwise healthy—that is, with only the usual pediatric care, they will proceed to a "normal" infancy. Some however, are born with other congenital defects such as intestinal obstructions which require surgery if the baby is to live. As I have already mentioned, sometimes the surgery is withheld and the baby dies. But when there is no defect requiring surgery, the baby lives on.[13] Now surgery to remove an intestinal obstruction is not difficult; the reason it is not performed in such cases is, clearly, that the child [has Down's syndrome] and the parents and doctor judge that because of *this* it is better for the child to die.

But notice that this situation is absurd, no matter what view one takes of the lives and potentials of such babies. If you think that the life of such an infant is worth preserving, then what does it matter if it needs a simple operation? Or, if you think it better that such a baby not live on, then what difference does it make if its intestinal tract is *not* blocked? In either case, the matter of life or death is being decided on irrelevant grounds. It is the mongolism, and not the intestine, that is the issue. The matter should be decided, if at all, on *that* basis, and not be allowed to depend on the essentially irrelevant question of whether the intestinal tract is blocked.

What makes this situation possible, of course, is the idea that when there is an intestinal obstruction we can "let the baby die," but when there is no such defect there is nothing we can do, for we must not "kill" it. The fact that this idea leads to such results as deciding life or death on irrelevant grounds is another good reason it should be rejected.

Doctors may think that all of this is only of academic interest, the sort of thing which philosophers may worry about but which has no practical bearing on their own work. After all, doctors must be concerned about the legal consequences of what they do, and active euthanasia is clearly forbidden by the law. They are right to be concerned about this. There have not been many prosecutions of doctors in the United States for active euthanasia, but there have been some. Prosecutions for passive euthanasia, on the other hand, are virtually nonexistent, even though there are laws under which charges could be brought, and even though this practice is much more widespread. Passive euthanasia, unlike active euthanasia, is by and large tolerated by the law. The law may sometimes compel a doctor to take action which he might not otherwise take to keep a patient alive,[14] but of course this is very different from bringing criminal charges against him after the patient is dead.

Even so, doctors should be concerned with the fact that the law and public opinion are forcing upon them an indefensible moral position, which has a considerable effect on their practices. Of course, most doctors are not now in the position of being coerced in this matter, for they do not regard themselves as merely going along with what the law requires. Rather, in statements such as the AMA statement that I quoted, they are endorsing the doctrine as a central point of medical ethics. In that statement, active euthanasia is condemned not merely as illegal but as "contrary to that for which the medical profession stands," while passive euthanasia is approved. However, if my arguments have been sound, there really is no intrinsic moral difference between them (although there may be morally important differences in their consequences, varying from case to case); so while doctors may have to discriminate between them to satisfy the law, they should not do any *more* than that. In particular, they should not give the distinction any added authority and weight by writing it into official statements of medical ethics.

Endnotes

1. F. J. Ingelfinger, "Bedside Ethics for the Hopeless Case," *New England Journal of Medicine 289* (25 October 1973), p. 914.
2. Ibid.
3. This statement was approved by the House of Delegates of the AMA on December 4, 1973. It is worth noting that some state medical societies have advised *patients* to take a similar attitude toward the termination of their lives. In 1973 the Connecticut State Medical Society approved a "background statement" to be signed by terminal patients which includes this sentence: "I value life and the dignity of life, so that I am not asking that my life be directly taken, but that my life not be unreasonably prolonged or the dignity of life be destroyed." Other state medical societies have followed suit.
4. A discussion of this type of case can be found in Anthony Shaw, "'Doctor, Do We Have a Choice?'" *The New York Times Magazine*, 30 January 1972, pp. 44–54. Also see Shaw's "Dilemmas of 'Informed Consent' in Children." *New England Journal of Medicine 289* (25 October 1973), pp. 885–990.
5. Paul Ramsey, *The Patient as Person* (New Haven, Conn.: Yale University Press, 1970), pp. 115–116.
6. D. C. S. Cameron, *The Truth About Cancer* (Englewood Cliffs, N.J.: Prentice-Hall, 1956), p. 116.
7. Ramsey, *The Patient as Person*, p. 151.
8. Judith Jarvis Thomson has argued that this line of reasoning is unsound. Consider, she says, this argument which is parallel to the one involving Smith and Jones.:

Alfrieda knows that if she cuts off Alfred's head he will die, and wanting him to die, cuts it off; Bertha knows that if she punches Bert in the nose he will die—Bert is in peculiar physical condition—and, wanting him to die, punches him in the nose. But what Bertha does is surely every bit as bad as what Alfrieda does. So cutting off a man's head isn't worse than punching a man in the nose. ("Killing, Letting Die, and the Trolley Problem," *The Monist 59* [1976], p. 204.)

She concludes that, since this absurd argument doesn't prove anything, the Smith/Jones argument doesn't prove anything either.

However, I think that the Alfrieda/Bertha argument is not absurd, as strange as it is. A little analysis shows that it is a sound argument and that its conclusion is true. We need to notice first that the reason it is wrong to chop someone's head off is, obviously, that this causes death. The act is objectionable because of its consequences.

Thus, a different act with the same consequences may be equally objectionable. In Thomson's example, punching Bert in the nose has the same consequences as chopping off Alfred's head; and indeed, the two actions are equally bad.

Now the Alfrieda/Bertha argument presuppose a distinction between the act of chopping off someone's head, and the results of this act, the victim's death. (It is stipulated that, except for the fact that Alfrieda chops off someone's head, while Bertha punches someone in the nose, the two acts are "in all other respects alike." The *other* respects include the act's consequence, the victim's death.) This is not a distinction we would normally think to make, since we cannot in fact cut off someone's head without killing him. Yet in thought the distinction can be drawn. The question raised in the argument, then, is whether, *considered apart from their consequences,* head-chopping is worse than nose-punching. And the answer to *this* strange question is No, just as the argument says it should be.

The conclusion of the argument should be construed like this: The bare fact that one act is an act of head-chopping, while another act is an act of nose-punching, is not a reason for judging the former to be worse than the latter. At the same time—and this is perfectly compatible with the argument—the fact that one act causes death, while another does not, *is* a reason for judging the former to be worse. The parallel construal of my conclusion is: The bare fact that one act is an act of killing, while another act is an act of letting die, is not a reason

for judging the former to be worse than the latter. At the same time—and this is perfectly compatible with my argument—the fact that an act (of killing, for example) prevents suffering, while another act (of letting die, for example) does not, *is* a reason for preferring one over the other. So once we see exactly how the Alfrieda/Bertha argument *is* parallel to the Smith/Jones argument, we find that Thomson's argument is, surprisingly, quite all right.

9. Ramsey, *The Patient as Person,* p. 151.
10. J. Russell Elkinton, "The Dying Patient, the Doctor, and the Law," *Villanova Law Review 13* (Summer 1968), p. 743.
11. For the purposes of this essay we do not need to consider whether this way of thinking about "charity" is justified. There are, however, strong arguments that it is morally indefensible: see Peter Singer, "Famine, Affluence, and Morality," *Philosophy and Public Affairs 1* (Spring 1972), pp. 229–243. Also see James Rachels, "Killing and Letting People Die of Starvation," *Philosophy 54* (1979), pp. 159–171, for a discussion of the killing/letting die distinction in the context of world hunger, as well as further arguments that the distinction is morally unimportant.
12. Shaw, "'Doctor, Do We Have a Choice?'" p. 54.
13. See the articles by Shaw cited in note 4.
14. For example, in February 1974 a Superior Court judge in Maine ordered a doctor to proceed with an operation to repair a hole in the esophagus of a baby with multiple deformities. Otherwise the operation would not have been performed. The baby died anyway a few days later. "Deformed Baby Dies Amid Controversy," *Miami Herald,* 25 February 1974, p. 4-B.

18. The Intentional Termination of Life

BONNIE STEINBOCK

Bonnie Steinbock defends the policy statement of the American Medical Association on euthanasia against James Rachels's critique. She argues that the statement does not rest on the belief that there is a moral difference between active and passive euthanasia. Rather, she contends that the statement rejects both active and passive euthanasia but permits "the cessation of the employment of extraordinary means," which she claims is not the same as passive euthanasia. She points out that doctors can cease to employ extraordinary means to respect the wishes of the patient or because continued treatment is painful and has little chance of success, without intending to let the patient die. She allows, however, that in some cases, ceasing to employ extraordinary means does amount to intending to let the patient die and also that in other cases, killing may even be morally preferable to letting die.

According to James Rachels[1] a common mistake in medical ethics is the belief that there is a moral difference between active and passive euthanasia. This is a mistake, [he] argues, because the rationale underlying the distinction between active and passive euthanasia is the idea that there is a significant moral difference between intentionally killing and letting die. . . . Whether the belief that there is a significant moral difference (between intentionally killing and intentionally letting die) is mistaken is not my concern here. For it is far from clear that this distinction is the basis of the doctrine of the American Medical Association which Rachels attacks. And if the killing/letting die distinction is not the basis of the AMA doctrine, then arguments showing that the distinction has no moral force do not, in themselves, reveal in the doctrine's adherents either "confused thinking" or "a moral point of view unrelated to the interests of individuals." Indeed, as we examine the AMA doctrine, I think it will become clear that it appeals to and makes use of a number of overlapping distinctions, which may have moral significance in particular cases, such as the distinction between intending and foreseeing, or between ordinary and extraordinary care. Let us then turn to the statement, from the House of Delegates of the AMA, which Rachels cites:

> The intentional termination of the life of one human being by another—mercy-killing—

is contrary to that for which the medical profession stands and is contrary to the policy of the AMA.

> The cessation of the employment of extraordinary means to prolong the life of the body when there is irrefutable evidence that biological death is imminent is the decision of the patient and/or his immediate family. The advice and judgment of the physician should be freely available to the patient and/or his immediate family.[2]

Rachels attacks this statement because he believes that it contains a moral distinction between active and passive euthanasia. . . .

I intend to show that the AMA statement does not imply support of the active/passive euthanasia distinction. In forbidding the intentional termination of life, the statement rejects both active and passive euthanasia. It does allow for ". . . the cessation of the employment of extraordinary means . . ." to prolong life. The mistake Rachels makes is in identifying the cessation of life-prolonging treatment with passive euthanasia, or intentionally letting die. If it were right to equate the two, then the AMA statement would be self-contradictory, for it would begin by condemning, and end by allowing, the intentional termination of life. But if the cessation of life-prolonging treatment is not always or necessarily passive euthanasia, then there is no confusion and no contradiction.

Why does Rachels think that the cessation of life-prolonging treatment is the intentional termination of life? He says:

Reprinted with permission from *Ethics in Science and Medicine*, pp. 59–64, Bonnie Steinbock, "The Intentional Termination of Life." Copyright 1979, Pergamon Press, Ltd.

The AMA policy statement isolates the crucial issue very well: The crucial issue is "the intentional termination of the life of one human being by another." But after identifying this issue, and forbidding "mercy-killing," the statement goes on to deny that the cessation of treatment is the intentional termination of a life. This is where the mistake comes in, for what is the cessation of treatment, in these circumstances, if it is not "the intentional termination of the life of one human being by another"? Of course it is exactly that, and if it were not, there would be no point to it.[3]

However, there *can* be a point (to the cessation of life-prolonging treatment) other than an endeavor to bring about the patient's death, and so the blanket identification of cessation of treatment with the intentional termination of a life is inaccurate. There are at least two situations in which the termination of life-prolonging treatment cannot be identified with the intentional termination of the life of one human being by another.

The first situation concerns the patient's right to refuse treatment. Rachels gives the example of a patient dying of an incurable disease, accompanied by unrelievable pain, who wants to end the treatment which cannot cure him but can only prolong his miserable existence. Why, they ask, may a doctor accede to the patient's request to stop treatment, but not provide a patient in a similar situation with a lethal dose? The answer lies in the patient's right to refuse treatment. In general, a competent adult has the right to refuse treatment, even where such treatment is necessary to prolong life. Indeed, the right to refuse treatment has been upheld even when the patient's reason for refusing treatment is generally agreed to be inadequate.[4] This right can be overridden (if, for example, the patient has dependent children) but, in general, no one may legally compel you to undergo treatment to which you have not consented. "Historically, surgical intrusion has always been considered a technical battery upon the person and one to be excused or justified by consent of the patient or justified by necessity created by the circumstances of the moment. . ."[5]

At this point, it might be objected that if one has the right to refuse life-prolonging treatment, then consistency demands that one have the right to decide to end his life, and to obtain help in doing so. The idea is that the right to refuse treatment some-how implies a right to voluntary euthanasia, and we need to see why someone might think this. The right to refuse treatment has been considered by legal writers as an example of the right to privacy or, better, the right to bodily self-determination. You have the right to decide what happens to your own body, and the right to refuse treatment is an instance of that more general right. But if you have the right to determine what happens to your body, then should you not have the right to choose to end your life, and even a right to get help in doing so?

However, it is important to see that the right to refuse treatment is not the same as, nor does it entail, a right to voluntary euthanasia, even if both can be derived from the right to bodily self-determination. The right to refuse treatment is not itself a "right to die"; that one may choose to exercise this right even at the risk of death, or even *in order to die*, is irrelevant. The purpose of the right to refuse medical treatment is not to give persons a right to decide whether to live or die, but to protect them from the unwanted interferences of others. Perhaps we ought to interpret the right to bodily self-determination more broadly so as to include a right to die: But this would be a substantial extension of our present understanding of the right to bodily self-determination, and not a consequence of it. Should we recognize a right to voluntary euthanasia, we would have to agree that people have the right not merely to be left alone, but also the right to be killed. I leave to one side that substantive moral issue. My claim is simply that there can be a reason for terminating life-prolonging treatment other than "to bring about the patient's death."

The second case in which termination of treatment cannot be identified with intentional termination of life is where continued treatment has little chance of improving the patient's condition and brings greater discomfort than relief.

The question here is what treatment is appropriate to the particular case. A cancer specialist describes it in this way:

> My general rule is to administer therapy as long as a patient responds well and has the potential for a reasonably good quality of life. But when all feasible therapies have been administered and a patient shows signs of rapid deterioration, the continuation of therapy can cause more discomfort than the cancer. From that time I recommend surgery, radiotherapy,

or chemotherapy only as a means of relieving pain. But if a patient's condition should once again stabilize after the withdrawal of active therapy and if it should appear that he could still gain some good time, I would immediately reinstitute active therapy. The decision to cease anticancer treatment is never irrevocable, and often the desire to live will push a patient to try for another remission, or even a few more days of life.[6]

The decision here to cease anticancer treatment cannot be construed as a decision that the patient die, or as the intentional termination of life. It is a decision to provide the most appropriate treatment for that patient at that time. Rachels suggests that the point of the cessation of treatment is the intentional termination of life. But here the point of discontinuing treatment is not to bring about the patient's death but to avoid treatment that will cause more discomfort than the cancer and has little hope of benefiting the patient. Treatment that meets this description is often called "extraordinary."[7] The concept is flexible, and what might be considered "extraordinary" in one situation might be ordinary in another. The use of a respirator to sustain a patient through a severe bout with a respiratory disease would be considered ordinary; its use to sustain the life of a severely brain-damaged person in an irreversible coma would be considered extraordinary.

Contrasted with extraordinary treatment is ordinary treatment, the care a doctor would normally be expected to provide. Failure to provide ordinary care constitutes neglect, and can even be construed as the intentional infliction of harm, where there is a legal obligation to provide care. The importance of the ordinary/extraordinary care distinction lies partly in its connection to the doctor's intention. The withholding of extraordinary care should be seen as a decision not to inflict painful treatment on a patient without reasonable hope of success. The withholding of ordinary care, by contrast, must be seen as neglect. Thus, one doctor says, "We have to draw a distinction between ordinary and extraordinary means. We never withdraw what's needed to make a baby comfortable, we would never withdraw the care a parent would provide. We never kill a baby. . . . But we may decide certain heroic intervention is not worthwhile."[8]

We should keep in mind the ordinary/extraordinary care distinction when considering an example given by Rachels to show the irrationality of the active/passive distinction with regard to infanticide. The example is this: A child is born with Down's syndrome and also has an intestinal obstruction which requires corrective surgery. If the surgery is not performed, the infant will starve to death, since it cannot take food orally. This may take days or even weeks, as dehydration and infection set in. Commenting on this situation, Rachels says:

> I can understand why some people are opposed to all euthanasia, and insist that such infants must be allowed to live. I think I can also understand why other people favor destroying these babies quickly and painlessly. But why should anyone favor letting "dehydration and infection wither a tiny being over hours and days"? The doctrine that says that a baby may be allowed to dehydrate and wither, but may not be given an injection that would end its life without suffering, seems so patently cruel as to require no further refutation.[9]

Such a doctrine perhaps does not need further refutation; but this is not the AMA doctrine. For the AMA statement criticized by Rachels allows only for the cessation of extraordinary means to prolong life when death is imminent. Neither of these conditions is satisfied in this example. Death is not imminent in this situation, any more than it would be if a normal child had an attack of appendicitis. Neither the corrective surgery to remove the intestinal obstruction, nor the intravenous feeding required to keep the infant alive until such surgery is performed, can be regarded as extraordinary means, for neither is particularly expensive, nor does either place an overwhelming burden on the patient or others. (The continued existence of the child might be thought to place an overwhelming burden on its parents, but that has nothing to do with the characterization of the means to prolong its life as extraordinary. If it had, then *feeding* a severely defective child who required a great deal of care could be regarded as extraordinary.) The chances of success if the operation is undertaken are quite good, though there is always a risk in operating on infants. Though the Down's syndrome will not be alleviated, the child will proceed to an otherwise normal infancy.

It cannot be argued that the treatment is withheld for the infant's sake, unless one is prepared to argue that all mentally retarded babies are better off dead. This is particularly implausible in the case of Down's syndrome babies who generally do not suffer and are capable of giving and receiving love, of learning and playing, to varying degrees.

In a film on this subject entitled, "Who Should Survive?," a doctor defended a decision not to operate, saying that since the parents did not consent to the operation, the doctor's hands were tied. As we have seen, surgical intrusion requires consent, and in the case of infants, consent would normally come from the parents. But, as their legal guardians, parents are required to provide medical care for their children, and failure to do so can constitute criminal neglect or even homicide. In general, courts have been understandably reluctant to recognize a parental right to terminate life-prolonging treatment.[10] Although prosecution is unlikely, physicians who comply with invalid instructions from the parents and permit the infant's death could be liable for aiding and abetting, failure to report child neglect, or even homicide. So it is not true that, in this situation, doctors are legally bound to do as the parents wish.

To sum up, I think that Rachels is right to regard the decision not to operate in the Down's syndrome example as the intentional termination of life. But there is no reason to believe that either the law or the AMA would regard it otherwise. Certainly the decision to withhold treatment is not justified by the AMA statement. That such infants have been allowed to die cannot be denied; but this, I think, is the result of doctors misunderstanding the law and the AMA position.

Withholding treatment in this case is the intentional termination of life because the infant is deliberately allowed to die; that is the point of not operating. But there are other cases in which that is not the point. If the point is to avoid inflicting painful treatment on a patient with little or no reasonable hope of success, this is not the intentional termination of life. The permissibility of such withholding of treatment, then, would have no implications for the permissibility of euthanasia, active or passive.

The decision whether or not to operate, or to institute vigorous treatment, is particularly agonizing in the case of children born with spina bifida, an opening in the base of the spine usually accompanied by hydrocephalus and mental retardation. If left unoperated, these children usually die of meningitis or kidney failure within the first few years of life. Even if they survive, all affected children face a lifetime of illness, operations, and varying degrees of disability. The policy used to be to save as many as possible, but the trend now is toward selective treatment, based on the physician's estimate of the chances of success. If operating is not likely to improve significantly the child's condition, parents and doctors may agree not to operate. This is not the intentional termination of life, for again the purpose is not the termination of the child's life but the avoidance of painful and pointless treatment. Thus, the fact that withholding treatment is justified does not imply that killing the child would be equally justified.

Throughout the discussion, I have claimed that intentionally ceasing life-prolonging treatment is not the intentional termination of life unless the doctor has, as his or her purpose in stopping treatment, the patient's death.

It may be objected that I have incorrectly characterized the conditions for the intentional termination of life. Perhaps it is enough that the doctor intentionally ceases treatment, foreseeing that the patient will die; perhaps the reason for ceasing treatment is irrelevant to its characterization as the intentional termination of life. I find this suggestion implausible, but am willing to consider arguments for it. Rachels has provided no such arguments: Indeed, he apparently shares my view about the intentional termination of life. For when he claims that the cessation of life-prolonging treatment *is* the intentional termination of life, his reason for making the claim is that "if it were not, there would be no point to it." Rachels believes that the point of ceasing treatment, "in these cases," is to bring about the patient's death. If that were not the point, he suggests, why would the doctor cease treatment? I have shown, however, that there can be a point to ceasing treatment which is not the death of the patient. In showing this, I have refuted Rachels's reason for identifying the cessation of life-prolonging treatment with the intentional termination of life, and thus his argument against the AMA doctrine.

Here someone might say: Even if the withholding of treatment is not the intentional termination of life, does that make a difference, morally speaking? If life-prolonging treatment may be withheld, for the sake of the child, may not an easy death be provided, for the sake of the child, as well? The unoperated child with spina bifida may take months or even years to die. Distressed by the spectacle of children "lying around waiting to die," one doctor has written, "It is time that society and medicine stopped perpetuating the fiction that withholding treatment is ethically different from terminating a life. It is time that society began to discuss mechanisms by which we can alleviate the pain and suffering for those individuals whom we cannot help."[11]

I do not deny that there may be cases in which death is in the best interests of the patient. In such cases, a quick and painless death may be the best thing. However, I do not think that, once active or vigorous treatment is stopped, a quick death is always preferable to a lingering one. We must be cautious about attributing to defective children *our* distress at seeing them linger. Waiting for them to die may be tough on parents, doctors, and nurses—it isn't necessarily tough on the child. The decision not to operate need not mean a decision to neglect, and it may be possible to make the remaining months of the child's life comfortable, pleasant, and filled with love. If this alternative is possible, surely it is more decent and humane than killing the child. In such a situation, withholding treatment, foreseeing the child's death, is not ethically equivalent to killing the child, and we cannot move from the permissibility of the former to that of the latter. I am worried that there will be a tendency to do precisely that if active euthanasia is regarded as morally equivalent to the withholding of life-prolonging treatment.

Conclusion

The AMA statement does not make the distinction Rachels wishes to attack, i.e., that between active and passive euthanasia. Instead, the statement draws a distinction between the intentional termination of life, on the one hand, and the cessation of the employment of extraordinary means to prolong life, on the other. Nothing said by Rachels shows that this distinction is confused. It may be that doctors have misinterpreted the AMA statement, and that this has led, for example, to decisions to allow defective infants slowly to starve to death. I quite agree with Rachels that the decisions to which they allude were cruel and made on irrelevant grounds. Certainly it is worth pointing out that allowing someone to die can be the intentional termination of life, and that it can be just as bad as, or worse than, killing someone. However, the withholding of life-prolonging treatment is not necessarily the intentional termination of life, so that if it is permissible to withhold life-prolonging treatment, it does not follow that, other things being equal, it is permissible to kill. Furthermore, most of the time, other things are not equal. In many of the cases in which it would be right to cease treatment, I do not think that it would also be right to kill.

Endnotes

1. James Rachels, "Active and passive euthanasia." *New England Journal of Medicine*, 292, 78–80, 1975.
2. Rachels, p. 78.
3. Rachels, p. 79–80.
4. For example, *In re Yetter*, 62 Pa. D. & C. 2d 619, C.P., Northampton County Ct., 1974.
5. David W. Meyers. "Legal aspects of voluntary euthanasia." In *Dilemmas of Euthanasia* (edited by John Behnke and Sissela Bok), p. 56. Anchor Books, New York, 1975.
6. Ernest H. Rosenbaum. *Living with Cancer*, p. 27. Praeger, New York, 1975.
7. Cf. Tristam Engelhardt, Jr. "Ethical issues in aiding the death of young children." In *Beneficent Euthanasia* (edited by Marvin Kohl), Prometheus Books, Buffalo, N.Y., 1975.
8. B. D. Colen, *Karen Ann Quinlan: Living and Dying in the Age of Eternal Life*, p. 115. Nash, 1976.
9. Rachels, p. 79.
10. Cf. Norman Cantor. "Law and the termination of an incompetent patient's life-preserving care." *Dilemmas of Euthanasia*, op. cit., pp. 69–105.
11. John Freeman, "Is there a right to die—quickly?" *Journal of Pediatrics 80*, p. 905.

19. *Planned Parenthood v. Casey*

SUPREME COURT OF THE UNITED STATES

The issue before the Supreme Court was whether the Pennsylvania Abortion Control Act as amended in 1988 and 1989 violated the due process clause of the U.S. Constitution by requiring informed consent, a twenty-four-hour waiting period, parental consent in the case of a minor, spousal notification, and certain reporting and record keeping by facilities that provide abortion services. While reaffirming its commitment to the essential holding of Roe v. Wade, the Court allowed that the state had a legitimate interest in imposing all of the above requirements except spousal notification.

Justices *O'Connor, Kennedy,* and *Souter* announcing the judgment of the Court in which Justices *Blackmun* and *Stevens* concurred in part:

Liberty finds no refuge in a jurisprudence of doubt. Yet nineteen years after our holding that the Constitution protects a woman's right to terminate her pregnancy in its early stages, *Roe v. Wade* . . . (1973), that definition of liberty is still questioned. . . .

At issue in these cases are five provisions of the Pennsylvania Abortion Control Act of 1982 as amended in 1988 and 1989. . . . The Act requires that a woman seeking an abortion give her informed consent prior to the abortion procedure, and specifies that she be provided with certain information at least 24 hours before the abortion is performed. . . . For a minor to obtain an abortion, the Act requires the informed consent of one of her parents, but provides for a judicial bypass option if the minor does not wish to or cannot obtain a parent's consent. . . . Another provision of the Act requires that, unless certain exceptions apply, a married woman seeking an abortion must sign a statement indicating that she has notified her husband of her intended abortion. . . . The Act exempts compliance with these three requirements in the event of a "medical emergency." . . . In addition to the above provisions regulating the performance of abortions, the Act imposes certain reporting requirements on facilities that provide abortion services. . . .

It must be stated at the outset and with clarity that *Roe*'s essential holding, the holding we reaffirm, has three parts. First is a recognition of the right of the woman to choose to have an abortion before viability and to obtain it without undue interference from the State. Before viability, the State's interests are not strong enough to support a prohibition of abortion or the imposition of a substantial obstacle to the woman's effective right to elect the procedure. Second is a confirmation of the State's power to restrict abortions after fetal viability, if the law contains exceptions for pregnancies which endanger a woman's life or health. And third is the principle that the State has legitimate interests from the outset of the pregnancy in protecting the health of the woman and the life of the fetus that may become a child. These principles do not contradict one another; and we adhere to each.

Constitutional protection of the woman's decision to terminate her pregnancy derives from the Due Process Clause of the Fourteenth Amendment. It declares that no State shall "deprive any person of life, liberty, or property, without due process of law." The controlling word in the case before us is "liberty." . . .

Men and women of good conscience can disagree . . . about the profound moral and spiritual implications of terminating a pregnancy, even in its earliest stage. Some of us as individuals find abortion offensive to our most basic principles of morality, but that cannot control our decision. Our obligation is to define the liberty of all, not to mandate our own moral code. The underlying constitutional issue is whether the State can resolve these philosophic questions in such a definitive way that a woman lacks all choice in the matter, except perhaps in those rare circumstances in which the pregnancy is itself a danger to her own life or health, or is the result of rape or incest.

It is conventional constitutional doctrine that where reasonable people disagree, the government can adopt one position or the other. . . . That theorem, however, assumes a state of affairs in which the choice does not intrude upon a protected liberty. Thus, while some people might disagree about whether or not the flag should be saluted, or disagree about the proposition that it may not be defiled, we have ruled that a State may not compel or enforce one view or the other. . . .

Our law affords constitutional protection to personal decisions relating to marriage, procreation, contraception, family relationships, child rearing, and education. . . . Our cases recognize "the right of the *individual,* married or single, to be free from unwarranted governmental intrusion into matters so fundamentally affecting a person as the decision whether to bear or beget a child." . . . Our precedents "have respected the private realm of family life which the state cannot enter." . . . These matters, involving the most intimate and personal choices a person may make in a lifetime, choices central to personal dignity and autonomy, are central to the liberty protected by the Fourteenth Amendment. At the heart of liberty is the right to define one's own concept of existence, of meaning, of the universe, and of the mystery of human life. Beliefs about these matters could not define the attributes of personhood were they formed under compulsion of the State.

These considerations begin our analysis of the woman's interest in terminating her pregnancy but cannot end it, for this reason: Though the abortion decision may originate within the zone of conscience and belief, it is more than a philosophic exercise. Abortion is a unique act. It is an act fraught with consequences for others: for the woman who must live with the implications of her decision; for the persons who perform and assist in the procedure; for the spouse, family, and society which must confront the knowledge that these procedures exist, procedures some deem nothing short of an act of violence against innocent human life; and, depending on one's beliefs, for the life or potential life that is aborted. Though abortion is conduct, it does not follow that the State is entitled to proscribe it in all instances. That is because the liberty of the woman is at stake in a sense unique to the human condition and so unique to the law. The mother who carries a child to full term is subject to anxieties, to physical constraints, to pain that only she must bear. That these sacrifices have from the beginning of the human race been endured by woman with a pride that ennobles her in the eyes of others and gives to the infant a bond of love cannot alone be grounds for the State to insist she make the sacrifice. Her suffering is too intimate and personal for the State to insist, without more, upon its own vision of the woman's role, however dominant that vision has been in the course of our history and our culture. The destiny of the woman must be shaped to a large extent on her own conception of her spiritual imperatives and her place in society.

It should be recognized, moreover, that in some critical respects the abortion decision is of the same character as the decision to use contraception, to which *Griswold v. Connecticut, Eisenstadt v. Baird,* and *Carey v. Population Services International* afford constitutional protection. We have no doubt as to the correctness of those decisions. They support the reasoning in *Roe* relating to the woman's liberty because they involve personal decisions concerning not only the meaning of procreation but also human responsibility and respect for it. As with abortion, reasonable people will have differences of opinion about these matters. One view is based on such reverence for the wonder of creation that any pregnancy ought to be welcomed and carried to full term no matter how difficult it will be to provide for the child and ensure its well-being. Another is that the inability to provide for the nurture and care of the infant is a cruelty to the child and an anguish to the parent. These are intimate views with infinite variations, and their deep, personal character underlay our decisions in *Griswold, Eisenstadt,* and *Carey.* The same concerns are present when the woman confronts the reality that, perhaps despite her attempts to avoid it, she has become pregnant.

It was this dimension of personal liberty that *Roe* sought to protect, and its holding invoked the reasoning and the tradition of the precedents we have discussed, granting protection to substantive liberties of the person. *Roe* was, of course, an extension of those cases and, as the decision itself indicated, the separate States could act in some degree to further their own legitimate interests in protecting pre-natal life. The extent to which the legislatures of the States might act to outweigh the interests of the woman in choosing to terminate her pregnancy was a subject of debate both in *Roe* itself and in decisions following it.

While we appreciate the weight of the arguments made on behalf of the State in the case before us, arguments which in their ultimate formulation conclude that *Roe* should be overruled, the reservations any of us may have in reaffirming the central holding of *Roe* are outweighed by the explication of individual liberty we have given combined with the force of *stare decisis*. We turn now to that doctrine.

The obligation to follow precedent begins with necessity, and a contrary necessity marks its outer limit. With Cardozo, we recognize that no judicial system could do society's work if it eyed each issue afresh in every case that raised it. . . . Indeed, the very concept of the rule of law underlying our own Constitution requires such a continuity over time that a respect for precedent is, by definition, indispensable. . . . At the other extreme, a different necessity would make itself felt if a prior judicial ruling should come to be seen so clearly as error that its enforcement was for that very reason doomed. . . .

So in this case we may inquire whether *Roe's* central . . . rule's limitation on state power could be removed without serious inequity to those who have relied upon it or significant damage to the stability of the society governed by the rule in question. . . .

Abortion is customarily chosen as an unplanned response to the consequence of unplanned activity or to the failure of conventional birth control, and except on the assumption that no intercourse would have occurred but for *Roe's* holding, such behavior may appear to justify no reliance claim. Even if reliance could be claimed on that unrealistic assumption, the argument might run, any reliance interest would be *de minimis*. This argument would be premised on the hypothesis that reproductive planning could take virtually immediate account of any sudden restoration of state authority to ban abortions.

To eliminate the issue of reliance that easily, however, one would need to limit cognizable reliance to specific instances of sexual activity. But to do this would be simply to refuse to face the fact that for two decades of economic and social developments, people have organized intimate relationships and made choices that define their views of themselves and their places in society, in reliance on the availability of abortion in the event that contraception should fail. The ability of women to participate equally in the economic and social life of the nation has been facilitated by their ability to control their reproductive lives. . . .

We have seen how time has overtaken some of *Roe's* factual assumptions: Advances in maternal health care allow for abortions safe to the mother later in pregnancy than was true in 1973. . . . But these facts go only to the scheme of time limits on the realization of competing interests, and the divergences from the factual premises of 1973 have no bearing on the validity of *Roe's* central holding, that viability marks the earliest point at which the State's interest in fetal life is constitutionally adequate to justify a legislative ban on nontherapeutic abortions. The soundness or unsoundness of that constitutional judgment in no sense turns on whether viability occurs at approximately 28 weeks, as was usual at the time of *Roe*, at 23 to 24 weeks, as it sometimes does today, or at some moment even slightly earlier in pregnancy, as it may if fetal respiratory capacity can somehow be enhanced in the future. Whenever it may occur, the attainment of viability may continue to serve as the critical fact, just as it has done since *Roe* was decided; which is to say that no change in *Roe's* factual underpinning has left its central holding obsolete, and none supports an argument for overruling it.

The sum of the precedential inquiry to this point shows *Roe's* underpinnings unweakened in any way affecting its central holding. While it has engendered disapproval, it has not been unworkable. An entire generation has come of age free to assume *Roe's* concept of liberty in defining the capacity of women to act in society, and to make reproductive decisions; no erosion of principle going to liberty or personal autonomy has left *Roe's* central holding a doctrinal remnant; *Roe* portends no developments at odds with other precedent for the analysis of personal liberty; and no changes of fact have rendered viability more or less appropriate as the point at which the balance of interests tips. Within the bounds of normal *stare decisis* analysis, then, and subject to the considerations on which it customarily turns, the stronger argument is for affirming *Roe's* central holding, with whatever degree of personal reluctance any of us may have, not for overruling it. . . .

From what we have said so far it follows that it is a constitutional liberty of the woman to have some freedom to terminate her pregnancy. We conclude that the basic decision in *Roe* was based on a constitutional analysis which we cannot now repudiate. The woman's liberty is not so unlimited, however, that from the outset the State cannot show its concern for the life of the unborn, and at a later point in fetal development the State's interest in life has sufficient force so that the right of the woman to terminate the pregnancy can be restricted.

That brings us, of course, to the point where much criticism has been directed at *Roe*, a criticism that always inheres when the Court draws a specific rule from what in the Constitution is but a general standard. We conclude, however, that the urgent claims of the woman to retain the ultimate control over her destiny and her body, claims implicit in the meaning of liberty, require us to perform that function. Liberty must not be extinguished for want of a line that is clear. And it falls to us to give some real substance to the woman's liberty to determine whether to carry her pregnancy to full term.

We conclude the line should be drawn at viability, so that before that time the woman has a right to choose to terminate her pregnancy. Any judicial act of line-drawing may seem somewhat arbitrary, but *Roe* was a reasoned statement, elaborated with great care. We have twice reaffirmed it in the face of great opposition. . . . The woman's right to terminate her pregnancy before viability is the most central principle of *Roe v. Wade*. It is a rule of law and a component of liberty we cannot renounce.

On the other side of the equation is the interest of the State in the protection of potential life. The *Roe* Court recognized the State's "important and legitimate interest in protecting the potentiality of human life." . . . The weight to be given this state interest, not the strength of the woman's interest, was the difficult question faced in *Roe*. We do not need to say whether each of us, had we been Members of the Court when the valuation of the State interest came before it as an original matter, would have concluded, as the *Roe* Court did, that its weight is insufficient to justify a ban on abortions prior to viability even when it is subject to certain exceptions. The matter is not before us in the first instance, and coming as it does after nearly 20 years of litigation in *Roe*'s wake we are satisfied that the immediate question is not the soundness of *Roe*'s resolution of the issue, but the precedential force that must be accorded to its holding. And we have concluded that the essential holding of *Roe* should be reaffirmed.

Yet it must be remembered that *Roe v. Wade* speaks with clarity in establishing not only the woman's liberty but also the State's "important and legitimate interest in potential life." . . . That portion of the decision in *Roe* has been given too little acknowledgement and implementation by the Court in its subsequent cases. Those cases decided that any regulation touching upon the abortion decision must survive strict scrutiny, to be sustained only if drawn in narrow terms to further a compelling state interest. . . . Not all of the cases decided under that formulation can be reconciled with the holding in

Roe itself that the State has legitimate interests in the health of the woman and in protecting the potential life within her. In resolving this tension, we choose to rely upon *Roe*, as against the later cases.

Roe established a trimester framework to govern abortion regulations. Under this elaborate but rigid construct, almost no regulation at all is permitted during the first trimester of pregnancy; regulations designed to protect the woman's health, but not to further the State's interest in potential life, are permitted during the second trimester; and during the third trimester, when the fetus is viable, prohibitions are permitted provided the life or health of the mother is not at stake. . . . Most of our cases since *Roe* have involved the application of rules derived from the trimester framework. . . .

The trimester framework no doubt was erected to ensure that the woman's right to choose not become so subordinate to the State's interest in promoting fetal life that her choice exists in theory but not in fact. We do not agree, however, that the trimester approach is necessary to accomplish this objective. A framework of this rigidity was unnecessary and in its later interpretation sometimes contradicted the State's permissible exercise of its powers.

Though the woman has a right to choose to terminate or continue her pregnancy before viability, it does not at all follow that the State is prohibited from taking steps to ensure that this choice is thoughtful and informed. Even in the earliest stages of pregnancy, the State may enact rules and regulations designed to encourage her to know that there are philosophic and social arguments of great weight that can be brought to bear in favor of continuing the pregnancy to full term and that there are procedures and institutions to allow adoption of unwanted children as well as a certain degree of state assistance if the mother chooses to raise the child herself. " '[T]he Constitution does not forbid a State or city, pursuant to democratic processes, from expressing a preference for normal childbirth' " . . . It follows that States are free to enact laws to provide a reasonable framework for a woman to make a decision that has such profound and lasting meaning. This, too, we find consistent with *Roe*'s central premises, and indeed the inevitable consequence of our holding that the State has an interest in protecting the life of the unborn.

We reject the trimester framework, which we do not consider to be part of the essential holding of *Roe*. . . . Measures aimed at ensuring that a woman's choice contemplates the consequences for the fetus do not necessarily interfere with the right recognized in *Roe,* although those measures have been found to be inconsistent with the rigid trimester framework announced in that case. A logical reading of the central holding in *Roe* itself, and a necessary reconciliation of the liberty of the woman and the interest of the State in promoting prenatal life, require, in our view, that we abandon the trimester framework as a rigid prohibition on all previability regulation aimed at the protection of fetal life. The trimester framework suffers from these basic flaws: In its formulation it misconceives the nature of the pregnant woman's interest; and in practice it undervalues the State's interest in potential life, as recognized in *Roe.* . . .

The very notion that the State has a substantial interest in potential life leads to the conclusion that not all regulations must be deemed unwarranted. Not all burdens on the right to decide whether to terminate a pregnancy will be undue. In our view, the undue burden standard is the appropriate means of reconciling the State's interest with the woman's constitutionally protected liberty. . . .

An undue burden exists, and therefore a provision of law is invalid, if its purpose or effect is to place a substantial obstacle in the path of a woman seeking an abortion before the fetus attains viability. . . . The Court of Appeals applied what it believed to be the undue burden standard and upheld each of the provisions except for the husband notification requirement. We agree generally with this conclusion. . . .

Studies reveal that family violence occurs in two million families in the United States. This figure, however, is a conservative one that substantially understates (because battering is usually not reported until it reaches life-threatening proportions) the actual number of families affected by domestic violence. In fact, researchers estimate that one of every two women will be battered at some time in their life. . . .

In well-functioning marriages, spouses discuss important intimate decisions such as whether to bear a child. But there are millions of women in this country who are the victims of regular physical and psychological abuse at the hands of their husbands. Should these women become pregnant, they may have very good reasons for not wishing to inform their husbands of their decision to obtain an abortion. Many may have justifiable fears of physical abuse, but may be no less fearful of the consequences of reporting prior abuse to the Commonwealth of Pennsylvania. Many may have a reasonable fear that notifying their husbands will provoke further instances of child abuse. . . . Many may fear devastating forms of psychological abuse from their husbands, including verbal harassment, threats of future violence, the destruction of possessions, physical confinement to the home, the withdrawal of financial support, or the disclosure of the abortion to family and friends. . . . And many women who are pregnant as a result of sexual assaults by their husbands will be unable to avail themselves of the exception for spousal sexual assault . . . because the exception requires that the woman have notified law enforcement authorities within 90 days of the assault, and her husband will be notified of her report once an investigation begins. . . . If anything in this field is certain, it is that victims of spousal sexual assault are extremely reluctant to report the abuse to the government; hence, a great many spousal rape victims will not be exempt from the notification requirement. . . .

The spousal notification requirement is thus likely to prevent a significant number of women from obtaining an abortion. It does not merely make abortions a little more difficult or expensive to obtain; for many women, it will impose a substantial obstacle. We must not blind ourselves to the fact that the significant number of women who fear for their safety and the safety of their children are likely to be deterred from procuring an abortion as surely as if the Commonwealth had outlawed abortion in all cases. . . .

We recognize that a husband has a "deep and proper concern and interest . . . in his wife's pregnancy and in the growth and development of the fetus she is carrying." . . . With regard to the children he has fathered and raised, the Court has recognized his "cognizable and substantial" interest in their custody. . . . If this case concerned a State's ability to require the mother to notify the father before taking some action with respect to a living child raised by both, therefore, it would be reasonable to conclude as a general matter that the father's interest in the welfare of the child and the mother's interest are equal.

Before birth, however, the issue takes on a very different cast. It is an inescapable biological fact that state regulation with respect to the child a woman is carrying will have a far greater impact on the mother's liberty than on the father's. The effect of state regulation on a woman's protected liberty is doubly deserving of scrutiny in such a case, as the

State has touched not only upon the private sphere of the family but upon the very bodily integrity of the pregnant woman. . . . The Court has held that "when the wife and the husband disagree on this decision, the view of only one of the two marriage partners can prevail. Inasmuch as it is the woman who physically bears the child and who is the more directly and immediately affected by the pregnancy, as between the two, the balance weighs in her favor." . . . This conclusion rests upon the basic nature of marriage and the nature of our Constitution: "[T]he marital couple is not an independent entity with a mind and heart of its own, but an association of two individuals each with a separate intellectual and emotional makeup. If the right of privacy means anything, it is the right of the *individual,* married or single, to be free from unwarranted governmental intrusion into matters so fundamentally affecting a person as the decision whether to bear or beget a child." . . . The Constitution protects individuals, men and women alike, from unjustified state interference, even when that interference is enacted into law for the benefit of their spouses. . . .

The husband's interest in the life of the child his wife is carrying does not permit the State to empower him with this troubling degree of authority over his wife. The contrary view leads to consequences reminiscent of the common law. A husband has no enforceable right to require a wife to advise him before she exercises her personal choices. If a husband's interest in the potential life of the child outweighs a wife's liberty, the State could require a married woman to notify her husband before she uses a postfertilization contraceptive. Perhaps next in line would be a statute requiring pregnant married women to notify their husbands before engaging in conduct causing risks to the fetus. After all, if the husband's interest in the fetus's safety is a sufficient predicate for state regulation, the State could reasonably conclude that pregnant wives should notify their husbands before drinking alcohol or smoking. Perhaps married women should notify their husbands before using contraceptives or before undergoing any type of surgery that may have complications affecting the husband's interest in his wife's reproductive organs. And if a husband's interest justifies notice in any of these cases, one might reasonably argue that it justifies exactly what the *Danforth* Court held it did not justify—a requirement of the husband's consent as well. A State may not give to a man the kind of dominion over his wife that parents exercise over their children. . . .

Our Constitution is a covenant running from the first generation of Americans to us and then to future generations. It is a coherent succession. Each generation must learn anew that the Constitution's written terms embody ideas and aspirations that must survive more ages than one. We accept our responsibility not to retreat from interpreting the full meaning of the covenant in light of all of our precedents. We invoke it once again to define the freedom guaranteed by the Constitution's own promise, the promise of liberty.

20. Cruzan v. Director, Missouri Department of Health

SUPREME COURT OF THE UNITED STATES

The issue before the Supreme Court was whether the state of Missouri's requirement of clear and convincing evidence of an incompetent's wishes concerning the withdrawal of life-sustaining medical treatment conflicts with the U.S. Constitution. Justice Rehnquist, speaking for the majority of the Court, held that the state of Missouri had a legitimate interest in protecting and preserving human life in imposing its clear and convincing evidence requirement. He further held that in imposing this requirement the state of Missouri need not make any judgment about the quality of human life.

Justice *Rehnquist* delivered the majority opinion:

Petitioner Nancy Beth Cruzan was rendered incompetent as a result of severe injuries sustained during an automobile accident. Co-petitioners Lester and Joyce Cruzan, Nancy's parents and co-guardians, sought a court order directing the withdrawal of their daughter's artificial feeding and hydration equipment after it became apparent that she had virtually no chance of recovering her cognitive faculties. The Supreme Court of Missouri held that because there was no clear and convincing evidence of Nancy's desire to have life-sustaining treatment withdrawn under such circumstances, her parents lacked authority to effectuate such a request. We . . . now affirm.

On the night of January 11, 1983, Nancy Cruzan lost control of her car as she traveled down Elm Road in Jasper County, Missouri. The vehicle overturned, and Cruzan was discovered lying face down in a ditch without detectable respiratory or cardiac function. Paramedics were able to restore her breathing and heartbeat at the accident site, and she was transported to a hospital in an unconscious state. An attending neurosurgeon diagnosed her as having sustained probable cerebral contusions compounded by significant anoxia (lack of oxygen). The Missouri trial court in this case found that permanent brain damage generally results after 6 minutes in an anoxic state; it was estimated that Cruzan was deprived of oxygen from 12 to 14 minutes. She remained in a coma for approximately three weeks and then progressed to an unconscious state in which she was able to orally ingest some nutrition. In order to ease feeding and further the recovery, surgeons implanted a gastrostomy feeding and hydration tube in Cruzan with the consent of her then husband. Subsequent rehabilitative efforts proved unavailing. She now lies in a Missouri state hospital in what is commonly referred to as a persistent vegetative state: generally, a condition in which a person exhibits motor reflexes but evinces no indications of significant cognitive function.[1] The State of Missouri is bearing the cost of her care.

After it had become apparent that Nancy Cruzan had virtually no chance of regaining her mental faculties her parents asked hospital employees to terminate the artificial nutrition and hydration procedures. All agree that such a removal would cause her death. The employees refused to honor the request without court approval. The parents then sought and received authorization from the state trial court for termination. The court found that a person in Nancy's condition had a fundamental right under the State and Federal Constitutions to refuse or direct the withdrawal of "death prolonging procedures." The court also found that Nancy's "expressed thoughts at age twenty-five in somewhat serious conversation with a housemate friend that if sick or injured she would not wish to continue her life unless she could live at least halfway normally suggests that given her present condition she would not wish to continue on with her nutrition and hydration." The Supreme Court of Missouri reversed by a divided vote. The court recognized a right to refuse treatment embodied in the common-law doctrine of informed consent, but expressed skepticism about the application of that doctrine in the circumstances of this case. The court also declined to read a broad right of privacy into the State Constitution which would "support the right of a person to refuse medical treatment in every circumstance," and expressed doubt as to whether such a right existed under the U.S. Constitution. It then decided that the Missouri Living Will statute (1986) embodied a state policy strongly favoring the preservation of life. The court found that Cruzan's statements to her roommate regarding her desire to live or die under certain conditions were "unreliable for the purpose of determining her intent," "and thus insufficient to support the co-guardians' claim to exercise substituted judgment on Nancy's behalf." It rejected the argument that Cruzan's parents were entitled to order the termination of her medical treatment, concluding that "no person can assume that choice for an incompetent in the absence of the formalities required under Missouri's Living Will statutes or the clear and convincing, inherently reliable evidence absent here." . . .

We granted certiorari to consider the question of whether Cruzan has a right under the U.S. Constitution that would require the hospital to withdraw life-sustaining treatment from her under these circumstances.

At common law, even the touching of one person by another without consent and without legal justification was a battery. Before the turn of the century, this Court observed that "[n]o right is held more sacred, or is more carefully guarded, by the common law, than the right of every individual to the possession and control of his own person, free from all restraint or interference of others, unless by clear and unquestionable authority of law." This notion of bodily integrity has been embodied in the requirement that informed consent is generally required for medical treatment. Justice Cardozo, while on the Court of Appeals of New York, aptly described this doctrine: "Every human being of adult years and sound mind has a right to determine what shall be done with his own body; and a surgeon who performs an operation without his patient's consent commits an assault, for which he is liable in damage." The informed consent doctrine has become firmly entrenched in American tort law.

The logical corollary of the doctrine of informed consent is that the patient generally possesses the right not to consent, that is, to refuse treatment. Until about 15 years ago and the seminal decision [of the New Jersey Supreme Court] in *In re Quinlan* (1976), the number of right-to-refuse-treatment decisions were relatively few. Most of the earlier cases involved patients who refused medical treatment forbidden by their religious beliefs, thus implicating First Amendment rights as well as common law rights of self-determination. More recently, however, with the advance of medical technology capable of sustaining life well past the point where natural forces would have brought certain death in earlier times, cases involving the right to refuse life-sustaining treatment have burgeoned.

In the *Quinlan* case, young Karen Quinlan suffered severe brain damage as the result of anoxia, and entered a persistent vegetative state. Karen's father sought judicial approval to disconnect his daughter's respirator. The New Jersey Supreme Court granted the relief, holding that Karen had a right of privacy grounded in the Federal Constitution to terminate treatment. Recognizing that this right was not absolute, however, the court balanced it against asserted state interests. Noting that the State's interest "weakens and the individual's right to privacy grows as the degree of bodily invasion increases and the prognosis dims," the court concluded that the state interests had to give way in that case. The court also concluded that the "only practical way" to prevent the loss of Karen's privacy right due to her incompetence was to allow her guardian and family to decide "whether she would exercise it in these circumstances."

After *Quinlan,* however, most courts have based a right to refuse treatment either solely on the common law right to informed consent or on both the common law right and a constitutional privacy right. . . .

State courts have available to them for decision a number of sources—state constitutions, statutes, and common law—which are not available to us. In this Court, the question is simply and starkly whether the U.S. Constitution prohibits Missouri from choosing the rule of decision which it did. This is the first case in which we have been squarely presented with the issue of whether the U.S. Constitution grants what is in common parlance referred to as a "right to die." We follow the judicious counsel . . . that in deciding "a question of such magnitude and importance . . . it is the [better] part of wisdom not to attempt, by any general statement, to cover every possible phase of the subject."

The Fourteenth Amendment provides that no State shall "deprive any person of life, liberty, or property, without due process of law." The principle that a competent person has a constitutionally protected liberty interest in refusing unwanted medical treatment may be inferred from our prior decisions. In *Jacobson v. Massachusetts* (1905), for instance, the Court balanced an individual's liberty interest in declining an unwanted smallpox vaccine against the State's interest in preventing disease.... Just this Term, in the course of holding that a State's procedures for administering antipsychotic medication to prisoners were sufficient to satisfy due process concerns, we recognized that prisoners possess "a significant liberty interest in avoiding the unwanted administration of antipsychotic drugs under the Due Process Clause of the Fourteenth Amendment." Still other cases support the recognition of a general liberty interest in refusing medical treatment.

But determining that a person has a "liberty interest" under the Due Process Clause does not end the inquiry;[2] "whether respondent's constitutional rights have been violated must be determined by balancing his liberty interests against the relevant state interests."

Petitioners insist that under the general holdings of our cases, the forced administration of life-sustaining medical treatment, and even of artificially delivered food and water essential to life, would implicate a competent person's liberty interest. Although we think the logic of the cases [referred to] above would embrace such a liberty interest, the dramatic consequences involved in refusal of such treatment would inform the inquiry as to whether the deprivation of that interest is constitutionally permissible. But for purposes of this case, we assume that the U.S. Constitution would grant a competent person a constitutionally protected right to refuse life-saving hydration and nutrition.

Petitioners go on to assert that an incompetent person should possess the same right in this respect as is possessed by a competent person.... The difficulty with petitioners' claim is that in a sense it begs the question: An incompetent person is not able to make an informed and voluntary choice to exercise a hypothetical right to refuse treatment or any other right. Such a "right" must be exercised for her, if at all, by some sort of surrogate. Here, Missouri has in effect recognized that under certain circumstances a surrogate may act for the patient in electing to have hydration and nutrition withdrawn in such a way as to cause death, but it has established a procedural safeguard to assure that the action of the surrogate conforms as best it may to the wishes expressed by the patient while competent. Missouri requires that evidence of the incompetent's wishes as to the withdrawal of treatment be proved by clear and convincing evidence. The question, then, is whether the U.S. Constitution forbids the establishment of this procedural requirement by the State. We hold that it does not.

Whether or not Missouri's clear and convincing evidence requirement comports with the U.S. Constitution depends in part on what interests the State may properly seek to protect in this situation. Missouri relies on its interest in the protection and preservation of human life, and there can be no gainsaying this interest. As a general matter, the States—indeed, all civilized nations—demonstrate their commitment to life by treating homicide as serious crime. Moreover, the majority of States in this country have laws imposing criminal penalties on one who assists another to commit suicide. We do not think a State is required to remain neutral in the face of an informed and voluntary decision by a physically able adult to starve to death.

But in the context presented here, a State has more particular interests at stake. The choice between life and death is a deeply personal decision of obvious and overwhelming finality. We believe Missouri may legitimately seek to safeguard the personal element of this choice through the imposition of heightened evidentiary requirements. It cannot be disputed that the Due Process Clause protects an interest in life as well as an interest in refusing life-sustaining medical treatment. Not all incompetent patients will have loved ones available to serve as surrogate decision makers. And even where family members are present, "[t]here will, of course, be some unfortunate situations in which family members will not act to protect a patient." A State is entitled to guard against potential abuses in such situations. Similarly, a State is entitled to consider that a judicial proceeding to make a determination regarding an incompetent's wishes may very well not be an adversarial one, with the added guarantee of accurate fact finding that the adversary process brings with it. Finally, we think a State may properly decline to make judgments about the "quality" of life that a particular individual may enjoy, and simply assert an unqualified interest in the preservation of human life to be weighed against the constitutionally protected interests of the individual.

In our view, Missouri has permissibly sought to advance these interests through the adoption of a "clear and convincing" standard of proof to govern such proceedings. "The function of a standard of proof, as that concept is embodied in the Due Process Clause and in the realm of fact finding, is to 'instruct the fact finder concerning the degree of confidence our society thinks he should have in the correctness of factual conclusions for a particular type of adjudication.'" . . .

We think it self-evident that the interests at stake in the instant proceedings are more substantial, both on an individual and societal level, than those involved in a run-of-the-mill civil dispute. But not only does the standard of proof reflect the importance of a particular adjudication, it also serves as "a societal judgment about how the risk of error should be distributed between the litigants." The more stringent the burden of proof a party must bear, the more that party bears the risk of an erroneous decision. We believe that Missouri may permissibly place an increased risk of an erroneous decision on those seeking to terminate an incompetent individual's life-sustaining treatment. An erroneous decision not to terminate results in a maintenance of the status quo; the possibility of subsequent developments such as advancements in medical science, the discovery of new evidence regarding the patient's intent, changes in the law, or simply the unexpected death of the patient despite the administration of life-sustaining treatment, at least create the potential that a wrong decision will eventually be corrected or its impact mitigated. An erroneous decision to withdraw life-sustaining treatment, however, is not susceptible of correction. . . .

In sum, we conclude that a State may apply a clear and convincing evidence standard in proceedings where a guardian seeks to discontinue nutrition and hydration of a person diagnosed to be in a persistent vegetative state. . . .

The Supreme Court of Missouri held that in this case the testimony adduced at trial did not amount to clear and convincing proof of the patient's desire to have hydration and nutrition withdrawn. In so doing, it reversed a decision of the Missouri trial court which had found that the evidence "suggest[ed]" Nancy Cruzan would not have desired to continue such measures, but which had not adopted the standard of "clear and convincing evidence" enunciated by the Supreme Court. The testimony adduced at trial consisted primarily of Nancy Cruzan's statements made to a housemate about a year before her accident that she would not want to live should she face life as a "vegetable," and other observations to the same effect. The observations did not deal in terms with withdrawal of medical treatment or hydration and nutrition. We cannot say that the Supreme Court of Missouri committed constitutional error in reaching the conclusion that it did.[3]

Petitioners alternatively contend that Missouri must accept the "substituted judgment" of close family members even in the absence of substantial proof that their views reflect the views of the patient. . . .

No doubt is engendered by anything in this record but that Nancy Cruzan's mother and father are loving and caring parents. If the State were required by the U.S. Constitution to repose a right of "substituted judgment" with anyone, the Cruzans would surely qualify. But we do not think the Due Process Clause requires the State to repose judgment on these matters with anyone but the patient herself. Close family members may have a strong feeling—a feeling not at all ignoble or unworthy, but not entirely disinterested, either—that they do not wish to witness the continuation of the life of a loved one which they regard as hopeless, meaningless, and even degrading. But there is no automatic assurance that the view of close family members will necessarily be the same as the patient's would have been had she been confronted with the prospect of her situation while competent. All of the reasons previously discussed for allowing Missouri to require clear and convincing evidence of the patient's wishes lead us to conclude that the State may choose to defer only to those wishes, rather than confine the decision to close family members.

The judgment of the Supreme Court of Missouri is *Affirmed.*

Endnotes

1. The State Supreme Court, adopting much of the trial court's findings, described Nancy Cruzan's medical condition as follows: ". . . In sum, Nancy is diagnosed as in a persistent vegetative state. She is not dead. She is not terminally ill. Medical experts testified that she could live another thirty years." . . .

2. Although many state courts have held that a right to refuse treatment is encompassed by a generalized constitutional right of privacy, we have never so held. We believe this issue is more properly analyzed in terms of a Fourteenth Amendment liberty interest. See *Bowers v. Hardwick* (1986).

3. The clear and convincing standard of proof has been variously defined in this context as "proof sufficient to persuade the trier of fact that the patient held a firm and settled commitment to the termination of life supports under the circumstances like those presented," and as evidence which "produces in the mind of the trier of fact a firm belief or conviction as to the truth of the allegations sought to be established, evidence so clear, direct, and weighty and convincing as to enable [the fact finder] to come to a clear conviction, without hesitancy, of the truth of the precise facts in issue.". . .

Suggestions for Further Reading

Anthologies

Brody, Baruch, and Tristan Engelhardt. *Bioethics*. Englewood Cliffs, NJ: Prentice-Hall, 1987.

Cohen, Marshall, et al. *The Rights and Wrongs of Abortion*. Princeton: Princeton University Press, 1974.

Feinberg, Joel. *The Problem of Abortion*, 2nd ed. Belmont, CA: Wadsworth Publishing Co., 1984.

Ladd, John. *Ethical Issues Relating to Life and Death*. New York: Oxford University Press, 1979.

Moreno, Jonathan. *Arguing Euthanasia*. New York: Simon and Schuster, 1995.

Munson, Ronald. *Interventions and Reflections*. Belmont, CA: Wadsworth Publishing Co., 1979.

Basic Concepts

Devine, Philip. *The Ethics of Homicide*. Ithaca, NY: Cornell University Press, 1978.

Glover, Jonathan. *Causing Death and Saving Lives*. New York: Penguin Books, 1977.

Steinbock, Bonnie, ed. *Killing and Letting Die*. Englewood Cliffs, NJ: Prentice-Hall, 1980.

Alternative Views

Battin, Margaret Pabst. *The Least Worst Death*. New York: Oxford University Press, 1994.

Bungsjord, Selmer. *Abortion: A Dialogue*. Indianapolis: Hackett Publishing, 1997.

Crum, Gary, and Thelma McCormack. *Abortion: Pro-Choice or Pro-Life*. Washington, DC: American University Press, 1992.

Garber, Mark. *Rethinking Abortion*. Princeton: Princeton University Press, 1996.

Grisez, Germain, and Joseph Boyle. *Life and Death with Liberty and Justice*. Notre Dame: University of Notre Dame Press, 1979.

Luker, Kristin. *Abortion and the Politics of Motherhood*. Berkeley: University of California Press, 1984.

Pojman, Louis P. *Life and Death*. Boston: Jones and Bartlett Publishers, 1992.

Rachels, James. *The End of Life*. New York: Oxford University Press, 1986.

Summer, L. W. *Abortion and Moral Theory*. Princeton: Princeton University Press, 1981.

Tribe, Lawrence. *Abortion: The Clash of Absolutes*. Norton: New York, 1990.

Practical Applications

Denes, Magda. *In Necessity and Sorrow: Life and Death in an Abortion Hospital*. New York: Penguin Books, 1977.

Law Reform Commission of Canada. *Euthanasia, Aiding Suicide and Cessation of Treatment*. Working Paper 28, 1982.

Supreme Court of Michigan, *People v. Kevorkian*, 1994.

Section IV

Sex Equality

Introduction

Basic Concepts

The problem of sex equality concerns the question of whether the sexes should be treated equally, and, if so, what constitutes equal treatment. This question was at the heart of the decade-long public debate on the Equal Rights Amendment to the Constitution (the ERA), which began in March 1972, when the Senate passed the amendment with a vote of 84 to 8, and ended in June 1982, when the extended deadline for the ERA expired—three states short of the 38 required for ratification.

The complete text of the ERA was as follows:

1. Equality of rights under the law shall not be denied or abridged by the United States or by any state on account of sex.

2. The Congress shall have the power to enforce by appropriate legislation the provisions of this article.

3. This amendment shall take effect two years after the date of ratification.

Public support for the ERA over this period, judging from opinion polls, hovered between 55 and 60 percent, but in key states anti-ERA forces were able to mount sufficient resistance to prevent its passage. In the end, Alabama, Arizona, Arkansas, Florida, Georgia, Illinois, Louisiana, Mississippi, Missouri, Nevada, North Carolina, Oklahoma, Utah, and Virginia failed to ratify the amendment.

Anti-ERA forces were able to block ratification because they successfully shifted the debate from equal rights to the substantive changes the ERA might bring about. This strategy was effective because support for the amendment generally came from individuals sympathetic to the notion of "equal rights" but not necessarily committed to substantive changes in women's roles.[1] For example, in one national survey, 67 percent of the people who claimed to have heard or read about the ERA favored it, 25 percent were opposed to it, and 8 percent had no opinion. Many people in the sample, however, had quite traditional views about women's roles. Two-thirds of the respondents thought that preschool children would suffer if their mothers worked, 62 percent thought married women should not hold jobs when jobs were scarce and their husbands could support them, and 55 percent thought it was more important for a woman to advance her husband's career than to have one of her own.

But what substantive changes would the ERA have brought about if it had been ratified in 1982? The surprising answer is not many, at least in the short run.[2] In 1970, when the ERA first reached the floor of Congress, a significant number of laws and official practices denied women "equality of rights under the law." For example, in 1970, eight states treated all property that a couple bought with their earnings during marriage as "community property," and these states normally gave the husband managerial control over such property. By 1976, most of these laws had been voluntarily changed or struck down by the Supreme Court's interpretation of the equal protection clause of the Fourteenth Amendment. Of course, supporters of the ERA did attempt to argue for the amendment on the grounds that it would bring about equal pay for equal work. Lobby-ists for the ERA in state capitols wore buttons that said "59¢" to remind legislators that women who worked full-time outside the home still typically earned only 59 cents for every dollar men earned—a ratio that has changed little since the federal government first began publishing such statistics in the 1950s. But the passage of the ERA would have had little immediate impact on that inequality. The ERA would have kept the federal or state governments from legally denying or abridging "equality of rights under the law." However, to help workers, the ERA would have had to do more than just make the law gender blind. It would have had to forbid wage discrimination by *private* organizations and individuals. And this it did not do.

Moreover, the ERA would have had few of the effects its opponents predicted. For example, Phyllis Schlafly frequently claimed that the ERA would require unisex public toilets and combat duty for women, but the Supreme Court would have found the first requirement an infringement of the right to privacy and the second would have run afoul of the war powers clause of the Constitution, which gives military commanders the freedom to decide how best to use their forces. Yet despite the fact that the immediate impact of the passage of the ERA would have been largely symbolic, neither proponents nor opponents sufficiently recognized this or, if they did, were not willing to surrender their exaggerated claims about the effects the amendment would have. Leaders on both sides of this debate may have feared the difficulty of motivating their followers if these exaggerated claims were abandoned.

Alternative Views

Susan Okin argues (Selection 21) that women have not achieved equality in society. Most of the unpaid labor in the family is done by women. Most jobs assume that workers have wives at home, and traditional gender-structured families make women vulnerable in ways that men are not vulnerable. Okin points out that contemporary political philosophers have ignored all this. They have assumed without argument the justice of traditional gender-structured families. Okin contends that this is a morally unacceptable state of affairs. Families are the first school of justice, and they must be shown to be just if we are to have a just society.

In Selection 22, James P. Sterba argues that if family structures are to be just they must meet the requirements of feminist justice, which he identifies with an ideal of androgyny. This ideal of androgyny requires that traits that are truly desirable and distributable in society be equally available to both women and men, or in the case of virtues, equally expected of both women and men. He considers attempts to derive the ideal of androgyny either from a right to equal opportunity that is a central requirement of a welfare liberal conception of justice or from an equal right of self-development that is a central requirement of a socialist conception of justice. He argues that although the ideal of androgyny is compatible with the requirements of both of these two conceptions of justice, it also transcends them by requiring that all virtues be equally expected of both women and men. Sterba further argues that the ideal of androgyny would require (1) that all children irrespective of their sex must be given the same type of up-bringing consistent with their native capabilities, and (2) that mothers and fathers must also have the same opportunities for education and employment consistent with their native capabilities. He then considers how achieving equal opportunity for women and men requires vastly improved day-care facilities and flexible (usually part-time) work schedules for both women and men.

In Selection 23, Christina Hoff Sommers criticizes the attack by feminist philosophers like Okin and Sterba on traditional family structures. She distinguishes liberal feminists from radical feminists and contends that liberal feminists like herself want equal opportunity in the workplace and politics, but would leave marriage and motherhood "untouched and unimpugned." By contrast, Sommers contends that radical feminists are committed to an assimilationist or androgynous ideal that would destroy the (traditional) family and deny most women what they want. Sommers, however, never explains how it is possible to secure for women equal opportunity in the workplace and politics while rejecting androgyny in favor of traditional gender roles. For example, how could women be passive, submissive, dependent, indecisive, and weak and still enjoy the same opportunities in the workplace and politics that are enjoyed by aggressive, dominant, independent, decisive, and strong men?

Marilyn Friedman (Selection 24) does not challenge Sommers's contention that radical feminists are committed to an assimilationist or androgynous ideal. There is, however, an important distinction between these two ideals. According to an assimilationist ideal, "one's sex should be no more noticeable than one's eye color," but according to an androgynous ideal, this need not be the case, as long as all desirable traits are equally open to both women and men, and all virtues equally expected of both women and men.

Friedman does, however, question whether what Sommers supports is really what most women want. She quotes a 1983 survey which indicated that 63 percent of women preferred nontraditional family relationships, and points out that in 1977 only 16 percent of American households were traditional families consisting of a legally married heterosexual couple and their children, in which the man is the sole breadwinner and "head" of the household, and the woman does the domestic work and child-care. In responding to Friedman, Sommers explains that what she means by a traditional family is one that consists of two heterosexual parents and one or more children in which the mother plays a distinctive gender role in caring for the children.[3] This definition obviously broadens the class of families to which Sommers is referring. But in her response, Sommers goes on to renounce any attempt to be promoting even the traditional family—even as she defines it. What she claims to be promoting is simply "the right and liberty to live under the arrangement of one's choice." According to Sommers, if people want to live in nontraditional families, they should be free to do so.

Friedman further disagrees with Sommers, contending that no woman should "swoon at the sight of Rhett Butler carrying Scarlett O'Hara up the stairs to a fate undreamt of in feminist philosophy." According to Friedman, what Rhett Butler is doing in *Gone With the Wind* is raping Scarlett O'Hara. In a subsequent response to Sommers, Friedman, noting that Scarlett O'Hara, although initially unwilling, later appears to be a willing sexual partner, defines "rape" as "any very intimate sexual contact which is *initiated* forcefully or against the will of the recipient."[4] Friedman allows that others might want to define such activity as sexual domination rather than rape, but under either definition, Friedman condemns it, whereas Sommers does not. In her response, Sommers cites approvingly the following passage from

Scarlett's Women: Gone with the Wind and Its Female Fans.

> The majority of my correspondents (and I agree) recognize the ambiguous nature of the encounter and interpret it as a scene of mutually pleasurable rough sex. . . . By far the majority of women who responded to me saw the episode as erotically exciting, emotionally stirring and profoundly memorable. Few of them referred to it as "rape."[5]

In Selection 25, Warren Farrell argues that while the various ways that women lack power in society have been noted, the various ways that men lack power have not been similarly recognized. In this selection, Farrell chronicles many of the ways that he thinks men lack power in society. For example, Farrell notes that men must fight in wars, but women do not; that the suicide rate of boys and men is much higher than that of girls and women; that 99 percent of volunteer firefighters are men; and that most men are unpaid bodyguards of the women they are with. Farrell concludes from this that there is a high degree of equality between the sexes, or as he puts it, "both sexes make themselves 'slaves' of the other sex in different ways."

In Selection 26, Virginia Valian seeks to explain the factors that have kept women from being equal with men. Valian thinks that once these factors have been exposed and corrected, fair and accurate evaluations of men and women will become possible. She argues that the existence of successful women only shows that *some* women are evaluated positively *some* of the time. It does not show what fairness requires, which is that there be no consistent advantage for men relative to women.

Practical Applications

Turning to practical applications, we can see that, at least in the statement of the National Organization for Women (NOW) Bill of Rights (Selection 27), there was never any confusion that the ERA would achieve all the goals of the organization. In this Bill of Rights, the ERA is one of eight goals to be achieved.

The Beijing Declaration of Platform for Action (Selection 28), which emerged from the Fourth World Congress on Women sponsored by the United Nations in 1995, expresses in an international context many of the same sentiments found in the NOW statement. Through this declaration, the Congress also reaffirmed a commitment to the equal rights and inherent human dignity of women and men enshrined in the Charter of the United Nations, the Declaration of Human Rights, the Convention on the Elimination of All Forms of Discrimination against Women, and the Declaration on the Elimination of Violence against Women.

Endnotes

1. Jane J. Mansbridge, *Why We Lost the ERA* (Chicago: University of Chicago Press, 1986), Chapter 3.
2. Ibid., Chapters 5–7.
3. Christina Hoff Sommers, "Do These Feminists Like Women?" *Journal of Social Philosophy* (1991), pp. 66–74.
4. Marilyn Friedman, "Does Sommers Like Women?" *Journal of Social Philosophy* (1991), pp. 75–90.
5. Ibid., p. 72.

21. Justice and Gender

SUSAN OKIN

Susan Okin points out that in the face of the radical inequality that exists between women and men in our society, there is still a widespread failure of political philosophers to address gender issues in their political theories. She claims that this is true even among those philosophers who have seen the need to adopt gender-neutral language. Okin argues that no theory of justice can be adequate until it addresses these issues.

We as a society pride ourselves on our democratic values. We don't believe people should be constrained by innate differences from being able to achieve desired positions of influence to improve their well-being; equality of opportunity is our professed aim. The Preamble to our Constitution stresses the importance of justice, as well as the general welfare and the blessings of liberty. The Pledge of Allegiance asserts that our republic preserves "liberty and justice for all."

Yet substantial inequalities between the sexes still exist in our society. In economic terms, full-time working women (after some very recent improvement) earn on average 71 percent of the earnings of full-time working men. One-half of poor and three-fifths of chronically poor households with dependent children are maintained by a single female parent. The poverty rate for elderly women is nearly twice that for elderly men. On the political front, two out of one hundred U.S. senators are women, one out of nine justices seems to be considered sufficient female representation on the Supreme Court, and the number of men chosen in each congressional election far exceeds the number of women elected in the entire history of the country. Underlying and intertwined with all of these inequalities is the unequal distribution of the unpaid labor of the family.

An equal sharing between the sexes of family responsibilities, especially child care, is "the great revolution that has not happened." Women, including mothers of young children, are, of course, working outside the household far more than their mothers did. And the small proportion of women who reach high-level positions in politics, business, and the professions command a vastly disproportionate amount of space in the media, compared with the millions of women who work at low-paying, dead-end jobs, the millions who do part-time work with its lack of benefits, and the millions of others who stay home performing for no pay what is frequently not even acknowledged as work. Certainly, the fact that women are doing more paid work does not imply that they are more equal. It is often said that we are living in a postfeminist era. This claim, due in part to the distorted emphasis on women who have "made it," is false, no matter which of its meanings is intended. It is certainly not true that feminism has been vanquished, and equally untrue that it is no longer needed because its aims have been fulfilled. Until there is justice within the family, women will not be able to gain equality in politics, at work, or in any other sphere.

... The typical current practices of family life, structured to a large extent by gender, are not just. Both the expectation and the experience of the division of labor by sex make women vulnerable. As I shall show, a cycle of power relations and decisions pervades both family and workplace, each reinforcing the inequalities between the sexes that already exist within the other. Not only women, but children of both sexes, too, are often made vulnerable by gender-structured marriage. One-quarter of children in the United States now live in families with only one parent—in almost 90 percent of cases, the mother. Contrary to common perceptions—in which the situation of never-married mothers looms largest—65 percent of single-parent families are a result of marital separation or divorce. Recent research in a number of states has shown that, in the average case, the standard of living of divorced women and the children who live with them plummets after divorce, whereas the economic situation of divorced men tends to be better than when they were married.

A central source of injustice for women these days is that the law, most noticeably in the event of divorce, treats more or less as equals those whom custom, workplace discrimination, and the still conventional division of labor within the family have made very unequal. Central to this socially created inequality are two commonly made but inconsistent presumptions: that women are primarily responsible for the rearing of children; and that serious and committed members of the work force (regardless of class) do not have primary responsibility, or even shared responsibility, for the rearing of children. The old assumption of the workplace, still implicit, is that workers have wives at home. It is built not only into the structure and expectations of the workplace but into other crucial social institutions, such as schools, which make no attempt to take account, in their scheduled hours or vacations, of the fact that parents are likely to hold jobs.

Now, of course, many wage workers do not have wives at home. Often, they *are* wives and mothers, or single, separated, or divorced mothers of small children. But neither the family nor the workplace has taken much account of this fact. Employed wives still do by far the greatest proportion of unpaid family work, such as child care and housework. Women are far more likely to take time out of the workplace or to work part-time because of family responsibilities than are their husbands or male partners. And they are much more likely to move because of their husbands' employment needs or opportunities than their own. All these tendencies, which are due to a number of factors, including the sex segregation and discrimination of the workplace itself, tend to be cyclical in their effects: Wives advance more slowly than their husbands at work and thus gain less seniority, and the discrepancy between their wages increases over time. Then, because both the power structure of the family and what is regarded as consensual "rational" family decision-making reflect the fact that the husband usually earns more, it will become even less likely as time goes on that the unpaid work of the family will

be shared between the spouses. Thus the cycle of inequality is perpetuated. Often hidden from view within a marriage, it is in the increasingly likely event of marital breakdown that the socially constructed inequality of married women is at its most visible.

This is what I mean when I say that gender-structured marriage *makes* women vulnerable. These are not matters of natural necessity, as some people would believe. Surely nothing in our natures dictates that men should not be equal participants in the rearing of their children. Nothing in the nature of work makes it impossible to adjust it to the fact that people are parents as well as workers. That these things have not happened is part of the historically, socially constructed differentiation between the sexes that feminists have come to call *gender*. We live in a society that has over the years regarded the innate characteristic of sex as one of the clearest legitimizers of different rights and restrictions, both formal and informal. While the legal sanctions that uphold male dominance have begun to be eroded in the past century, and more rapidly in the last twenty years, the heavy weight of tradition, combined with the effects of socialization, still works powerfully to reinforce sex roles that are commonly regarded as of unequal prestige and worth. The sexual division of labor has not only been a fundamental part of the marriage contract, but so deeply influences us in our formative years that feminists of both sexes who try to reject it can find themselves struggling against it with varying degrees of ambivalence. Based on this linchpin, "gender"—by which I mean *the deeply entrenched institutionalization of sexual difference*—still permeates our society.

The Construction of Gender

Due to feminism and feminist theory, gender is coming to be recognized as a social factor of major importance. Indeed, the new meaning of the word reflects the fact that so much of what has traditionally been thought of as sexual difference is now considered by many to be largely socially produced. Feminist scholars from many disciplines and with radically different points of view have contributed to the enterprise of making gender fully visible and comprehensible. At one end of the spectrum are those whose explanations of the subordination of women focus primarily on biological difference as causal in the construction of gender, and at the other end are those who argue that biological difference may not even lie at the core of the social construction that is gender; the views of the vast majority of feminists fall between these extremes. The rejection of biological determinism and the corresponding emphasis on gender as a social construction characterize most current feminist scholarship. Of particular relevance is work in psychology, where scholars have investigated the importance of female primary parenting in the formation of our gendered identities, and in history and anthropology, where emphasis has been placed on the historical and cultural variability of gender. Some feminists have been criticized for developing theories of gender that do not take sufficient account of differences *among* women, especially race, class, religion, and ethnicity. While such critiques should always inform our research and improve our arguments, it would be a mistake to allow them to distract our attention from gender itself as a factor of significance. Many injustices are experienced by women *as women,* whatever the differences among them and whatever other injustices they also suffer from. The past and present gendered nature of the family, and the ideology that surrounds it, affects virtually all women, whether or not they live or ever lived in traditional families. Recognizing this is not to deny or de-emphasize the fact that gender may affect different subgroups of women to a different extent and in different ways.

The potential significance of feminist discoveries and conclusions about gender for issues of social justice cannot be overemphasized. They undermine centuries of argument that started with the notion that not only the distinct differentiation of women and men but the domination of women by men, being natural, was therefore inevitable and not even to be considered in discussions of justice. As I shall make clear . . . , despite the fact that such notions cannot stand up to rational scrutiny, they not only still survive but flourish in influential places.

During the same two decades in which feminists have been intensely thinking, researching, analyzing, disagreeing about, and rethinking the subject of gender, our political and legal institutions have been increasingly faced with issues concerning the injustices of gender and their effects. These issues are being decided within a fundamentally patriarchal system, founded in a tradition in which "individuals" were assumed to be male heads of households. Not surprisingly, the system has demonstrated a limited capacity for determining what is just, in many cases involving gender. Sex discrimination, sexual harassment, abortion, pregnancy in the workplace, parental leave, childcare, and surrogate mothering have all become major and well-publicized issues of public policy, engaging both courts and legislatures. Issues of family justice, in particular—from child custody and divorce terms to physical and sexual abuse of wives and children—have become increasingly visible and pressing, and are commanding increasing attention from the police and court systems. There is clearly a major "justice crisis" in contemporary society arising from issues of gender.

◇

Theories of Justice and the Neglect of Gender

During these same two decades, there has been a great resurgence of theories of social justice. Political theory, which had been sparse for a period before the late 1960s except as an important branch of intellectual history, has become a flourishing field, with social justice as its central concern. Yet, remarkably, major contemporary theorists of justice have almost without exception ignored the situation just described. They have displayed little interest in or knowledge of the findings of feminism. They have largely bypassed the fact that the society to which their theories are supposed to pertain is heavily and deeply affected by gender, and faces difficult issues of justice stemming from its gendered past and present assumptions. Since theories of justice are centrally concerned with whether, how, and why persons should be treated differently from one another, this neglect seems inexplicable. These theories are *about* which initial or acquired characteristics or positions in society legitimize differential treatment of persons by social institutions, laws, and customs. They are *about* how and whether and to what extent beginnings should affect outcomes. The division of humanity into two sexes seems to provide an obvious subject for such inquiries. But, as we shall see, this does not strike most contemporary theorists of justice, and their theories suffer in both coherence and relevance because of it. This piece is . . . an attempt to rectify [this neglect], to point the way toward a more fully humanist theory of justice by confronting the question, "How just is gender?"

Why is it that when we turn to contemporary theories of justice, we do not find illuminating and positive contributions to this question? How can theories of justice that are ostensibly about people in general neglect women, gender, and all the inequalities between the sexes? One reason is that most theorists *assume*, though they do not discuss, the traditional, gender-structured family. Another is that they often employ gender-neutral language in a false, hollow way. Let us examine these two points.

The Hidden Gender-Structured Family

In the past, political theorists often used to distinguish clearly between "private" domestic life and the "public" life of politics and the marketplace, claiming explicitly that the two spheres operated in accordance with different principles. They separated out the family from what they deemed the subject matter of politics, and they made closely related, explicit claims about the nature of women and the appropriateness of excluding them from civil and political life. Men, the subjects of the theories, were able to make the transition back and forth from domestic to public life with ease, largely because of the functions performed by women in the family. When we turn to contemporary theories of justice, superficial appearances can easily lead to the impression that they are inclusive of women. In fact, they continue the same "separate spheres" tradition, by ignoring the family, its division of labor, and the related economic dependency and restricted opportunities of most women. The judgment that the family is "nonpolitical" is implicit in the fact that it is simply not discussed in most works of political theory today. In one way or another . . . almost all current theorists continue to assume that the "individual" who is the basic subject of their theories is the male head of a fairly traditional household. Thus the application of principles of justice to relations between the sexes, or within the household, is frequently, though tacitly, ruled out from the start. In the most influential of all twentieth-century theories of justice, that of John Rawls, family life is not only assumed, but is assumed to be just—and yet the prevalent gendered division of labor within the family is neglected, along with the associated distribution of power, responsibility, and privilege. . . .

Moreover, this stance is typical of contemporary theories of justice. They persist, despite the wealth of feminist challenges to their assumptions, in their refusal even to discuss the family and its gender structure, much less to recognize the family as a political institution of primary importance. Recent theories that pay even less attention to issues of family justice than Rawls's include Bruce Ackerman's *Social Justice in the Liberal State*, Ronald Dworkin's *Taking Rights Seriously*, William Galston's *Justice and the Human Good*, Alasdair MacIntyre's *After Virtue* and *Whose Justice? Whose Rationality?*, Robert Nozick's *Anarchy, State, and Utopia*, and Roberto Unger's *Knowledge and Politics and The Critical Legal Studies Movement*. Philip Green's *Retrieving Democracy* is a welcome exception. Michael Walzer's *Spheres of Justice* is exceptional in this regard, but the conclusion that can be inferred from his discussion of the family—that its gender structure is unjust—does not sit at all easily with his emphasis on the shared understandings of a culture as the foundation of justice. For gender is one aspect of social life about which clearly, in the United States in the latter part of the twentieth century, there are no shared understandings.

What is the basis of my claim that the family, while neglected, is *assumed* by theorists of justice? One obvious indication is that they take mature, independent human beings as the subjects of their theories without any mention of how they got to be that way. We know, of course, that human beings develop and mature only as a result of a great deal of attention and hard work, by far the greater part of it done by women. But when theorists of justice talk about "work," they mean paid work performed in the marketplace. They must be assuming that women in the gender-structured family continue to do their unpaid work of nurturing and socializing the young and providing a haven of intimate relations—[or] there would be no moral subjects for them to theorize about. But these activities apparently take place outside the scope of their theories. Typically, the family itself is not examined in the light of whatever standard of justice the theorist arrives at.

The continued neglect of the family by theorists of justice flies in the face of a great deal of persuasive feminist argument. . . . Scholars have clearly revealed the interconnections between the gender structure inside and outside the family and the extent to which the personal is political. They have shown that the assignment of primary parenting to women is crucial, both in forming the gendered identities of men and women and in influencing their respective choices and opportunities in life. Yet, so far, the simultaneous assumption and neglect of the family has allowed the impact of these arguments to go unnoticed in major theories of justice.

False Gender Neutrality

Many academics . . . have become aware of the objectionable nature of using the supposedly generic male forms of nouns and pronouns. As feminist scholars have demonstrated, these words have most often *not* been used, throughout history and the history of philosophy in particular, with the intent to include women. *Man, mankind,* and *he* are going out of style as universal representations, though they have by no means disappeared. But the gender-neutral alternatives that most contemporary theorists employ are often even more misleading than the blatantly sexist use of male terms of reference. They serve to disguise the real and continuing failure of theorists to confront the fact that the human race consists of persons of two sexes. They are by this means able to ignore the fact that there are *some* socially relevant physical differences between women and men, and the even more important fact that the sexes have had very different histories, very different assigned social roles and "natures," and very different degrees of access to power and opportunity in all human societies up to and including the present.

False gender neutrality is not a new phenomenon. Aristotle, for example, used *anthropos*—"human being"—in discussions of "the human good" that turn out not only to exclude women but to depend on their subordination. Kant even wrote of "all rational beings as such" in making arguments that he did not mean to apply to women. But it was more readily apparent that such arguments or conceptions of the good were not about all of us, but only about male heads of families. For their authors usually gave at some point an explanation, no matter how inadequate, of why what they were saying did not apply to women and of the different characteristics and virtues, rights, and responsibilities they thought women ought to have. Nevertheless, their theories have often been read as though they per-

tain (or can easily be applied) to all of us. Feminist interpretations of the last fifteen years or so have revealed the falsity of this "add women and stir" method of reading the history of political thought.

The falseness of the gender-neutral language of contemporary political theorists is less readily apparent. Most, though not all, contemporary moral and political philosophers use "men and women," "he or she," "persons," or the increasingly ubiquitous "self." Sometimes they even get their computers to distribute masculine and feminine terms of reference randomly. Since they do not explicitly exclude or differentiate women, as most theorists in the past did, we may be tempted to read their theories as inclusive of all of us. But we cannot. Their merely terminological responses to feminist challenges, in spite of giving a superficial impression of tolerance and inclusiveness, often strain credulity and sometimes result in nonsense. They do this in two ways: by ignoring the irreducible biological differences between the sexes, and/or by ignoring their different assigned social roles and consequent power differentials, and the ideologies that have supported them. Thus gender-neutral terms frequently obscure the fact that so much of the real experience of "persons," so long as they live in gender-structured societies, *does* in fact depend on what sex they are.

False gender neutrality is by no means confined to the realm of theory. Its harmful effects can be seen in public policies that have directly affected large numbers of women adversely. It was used, for example, in the Supreme Court's 1976 decision that the exclusion of pregnancy-related disabilities from employers' disability insurance plans was "not a gender-based discrimination at all." In a now infamous phrase of its majority opinion, the Court explained that such plans did not discriminate against women because the distinction drawn by such plans was between pregnant women and "non-pregnant *persons.*"

. . . I will illustrate the concept [of false gender neutrality in contemporary political theory] by citing just two examples. Ackerman's *Social Justice in the Liberal State* is a book containing scrupulously gender-neutral language. He breaks with this neutrality only, it seems, to *defy* existing sex roles; he refers to the "Commander," who plays the lead role in the theory, as "she." However, the argument of the book does not address the existing inequality or role differentiation between the sexes, though it has the potential for doing so. The full impact of Ackerman's gender-neutral language without attention to gender is revealed in his section on abortion: a two-page discussion written, with the exception of a single "she," in the completely gender-neutral language of fetuses and their "parents." The impression given is that there is no relevant respect in which the relationship of the two parents to the fetus differs. Now it is, of course, possible to imagine (and in the view of many feminists, would be desirable to achieve) a society in which differences in the relation of women and men to fetuses would be so slight as to reasonably play only a minor role in the discussion of abortion. But this would have to be a society without gender—one in which sexual difference carried no social significance, the sexes were equal in power and interdependence, and "mothering" and "fathering" a child meant the same thing, so that parenting and earning responsibilities were equally shared. We certainly do not live in such a society. Neither is there any discussion of one in Ackerman's theory, in which the division of labor between the sexes is not considered a matter of social (in)justice. In such a context, a "gender-neutral" discussion of abortion is almost as misleading as the Supreme Court's "gender-neutral" discussion of pregnancy.

A second illustration of false gender neutrality comes from Derek Phillips's *Toward a Just Social Order.* Largely because of the extent of his concern—rare among theorists of justice—with how we are to *achieve and maintain* a just social order, Phillips pays an unusual amount of attention to the family. He writes about the family as the locus for the development of a sense of justice and self-esteem, of an appreciation of the meaning of reciprocity, of the ability to exercise unforced choice, and of an awareness of alternative ways of life. The problem with this otherwise admirable discussion is that, apart from a couple of brief exceptions, the family itself is presented in gender-neutral terms that bear little resemblance to actual, gender-structured life.[1] It is because of "parental affection," "parental nurturance," and "child rearing" that children in Phillips's families become the autonomous moral agents that his just society requires its citizens to be. The child's development of a sense of identity very much depends on being raised by "parental figures who themselves have coherent and well-integrated personal identities," and we are told that such a coher-

ent identity is "ideally one built around commitments to work and love." This all sounds very plausible. But it does not take into account the multiple inequalities of gender. In gender-structured societies—in which the child rearers are women, "parental nurturance" is largely mothering, and those who do what society regards as "meaningful work" are assumed *not* to be primary parents—women in even the best of circumstances face considerable conflicts between love (a fulfilling family life) and "meaningful work." Women in less fortunate circumstances face even greater conflicts between love (even basic care of their children) and any kind of paid work at all.

It follows from Phillips's own premises that these conflicts are very likely to affect the strength and coherence in women of that sense of identity and self-esteem, coming from love and meaningful work, that he regards as essential for being an autonomous moral agent. In turn, if they are mothers, it is also likely to affect their daughters' and sons' developing senses of their identity. Gender is clearly a major obstacle to the attainment of a social order remotely comparable to the just one Phillips aspires to—but his false gender-neutral language allows him to ignore this fact. Although he is clearly aware of how distant in some other respects his vision of a just social order is from contemporary societies, his falsely gender-neutral language leaves him quite unaware of the distance between the type of family that might be able to socialize just citizens and typical families today.

The combined effect of the omission of the family and the falsely gender-neutral language in recent political thought is that most theorists are continuing to ignore the highly political issue of gender. The language they use makes little difference to what they actually do, which is to write about men and about only those women who manage, in spite of the gendered structures and practices of the society in which they live, to adopt patterns of life that have been developed to suit the needs of men. The fact that human beings are born as helpless infants—not as the purportedly autonomous actors who populate political theories—is obscured by the implicit assumption of gendered families, operating outside the range of theories. To a large extent, contemporary theories of justice, like those of the past, are about men with wives at home.

Gender as an Issue of Justice

For three major reasons, this state of affairs is unacceptable. The first is the obvious point that women must be fully included in any satisfactory theory of justice. The second is that equality of opportunity, not only for women but for children of both sexes, is seriously undermined by the current gender injustices of our society. And the third reason is that, as has already been suggested, the family—currently the linchpin of the gender structure—must be just if we are to have a just society, since it is within the family that we first come to have that sense of ourselves and our relations with others that is at the root of moral development.

Counting Women In

When we turn to the great tradition of Western political thought with questions about the justice of the treatment of the sexes in mind, it is to little avail. Bold feminists like Mary Astell, Mary Wollstonecraft, William Thompson, Harriet Taylor, and George Bernard Shaw have occasionally challenged the tradition, often using its own premises and arguments to overturn its explicit or implicit justification of the inequality of women. But John Stuart Mill is a rare exception to the rule that those who hold central positions in the tradition almost never question the justice of the subordination of women. This phenomenon is undoubtedly due in part to the fact that Aristotle, whose theory of justice has been so influential, relegated women to a sphere of "household justice"—populated by persons who are not fundamentally equal to the free men who participate in political justice, but inferiors whose natural function is to serve those who are more fully human. The liberal tradition, despite its supposed foundation of individual rights and human equality, is more Aristotelian in this respect than is generally acknowledged. In one way or another, almost all liberal theorists have assumed that the "individual" who is the basic subject of the theories is the male head of a patriarchal household. Thus they have not usually considered applying the principles of justice to women or to relations between the sexes.

When we turn to contemporary theories of justice, however, we expect to find more illuminating and positive contributions to the subject of gender

and justice. [But as] the omission of the family and the falseness of their gender-neutral language suggest . . . mainstream contemporary theories of justice do not address the subject any better than those of the past. Theories of justice that apply to only half of us simply won't do; the inclusiveness falsely implied by the current use of gender-neutral terms must become real. Theories of justice must apply to all of us, and to all of human life, instead of *assuming* silently that half of us take care of whole areas of life that are considered outside the scope of social justice. In a just society, the structure and practices of families must afford women the same opportunities as men to develop their capacities, to participate in political power, to influence social choices, and to be economically as well as physically secure.

Unfortunately, much feminist intellectual energy in the 1980s has gone into the claim that "justice" and "rights" are masculinist ways of thinking about morality that feminists should eschew or radically revise, advocating a morality of care. The emphasis is misplaced, I think, for several reasons. First, what is by now a vast literature on the subject shows that the evidence for differences in women's and men's ways of thinking about moral issues is not (at least yet) very clear; neither is the evidence about the source of whatever differences there might be. It may well turn out that any differences can be readily explained in terms of roles, including female primary parenting, that are socially determined and therefore alterable. There is certainly no evidence—nor could there be, in such a gender-structured society—for concluding that women are somehow naturally more inclined toward contextuality and away from universalism in their moral thinking, a false concept that unfortunately reinforces the old stereotypes that justify separate spheres. The capacity of reactionary forces to capitalize on the "different moralities" strain in feminism is particularly evident in Pope John Paul II's recent Apostolic Letter, "On the Dignity of Women," in which he refers to women's special capacity to care for others in arguing for confining them to motherhood or celibacy.

Second . . . I think the distinction between an ethic of justice and an ethic of care has been overdrawn. The best theorizing about justice . . . has integral to it the notions of care and empathy, of thinking of the interests and well-being of others who may be very different from ourselves. It is, therefore, misleading to draw a dichotomy as though they were two contrasting ethics. The best theorizing about justice is not some abstract "view from nowhere," but results from the carefully attentive consideration of *everyone's* point of view. This means, of course, that the best theorizing about justice is not good enough if it does not, or cannot readily be adapted to, include women and their points of view as fully as men and their points of view.

Gender and Equality of Opportunity

The family is a crucial determinant of our opportunities in life, of what we "become." It has frequently been acknowledged by those concerned with real equality of opportunity that the family presents a problem. But though they have discerned a serious problem, these theorists have underestimated it because they have seen only half of it. They have seen that the disparity among families in terms of the physical and emotional environment, motivation, and material advantages they can give their children has a tremendous effect upon children's opportunities in life. We are not born as isolated, equal individuals in our society, but into family situations: some in the social middle, some poor and homeless, and some superaffluent; some to a single or soon-to-be-separated parent, some to parents whose marriage is fraught with conflict, some to parents who will stay together in love and happiness. Any claims that equal opportunity exists are therefore completely unfounded. Decades of neglect of the poor, especially of poor black and Hispanic households, accentuated by the policies of the Reagan years, have brought us farther from the principles of equal opportunity. To come close to them would require, for example, a high and uniform standard of public education and the provision of equal social services—including health care, employment training, job opportunities, drug rehabilitation, and decent housing—for all who need them. In addition to redistributive taxation, only massive reallocations of resources from the military to social services could make these things possible.

But even if all these disparities were somehow eliminated, we would still not attain equal opportunity for all. This is because what has not been recognized as an equal opportunity problem, except in feminist literature and circles, is the disparity *within* the family, the fact that its gender structure is itself a major obstacle to equality of opportunity. This is very important in itself, since one of the factors with

most influence on our opportunities in life is the social significance attributed to our sex. The opportunities of girls and women are centrally affected by the structure and practices of family life, particularly by the fact that women are almost invariably primary parents. What nonfeminists who see in the family an obstacle to equal opportunity have *not* seen is that the extent to which a family is gender-structured can make the sex we belong to a relatively insignificant aspect of our identity and our life prospects or an all-pervading one. This is because so much of the social construction of gender takes place in the family, and particularly in the institution of female parenting.

Moreover, . . . with the increased rates of single motherhood, separation, and divorce, the inequalities between the sexes have *compounded* the first part of the problem. The disparity among families has grown largely because of the impoverishment of many women and children after separation or divorce. The division of labor in the typical family leaves most women far less capable than men of supporting themselves, and this disparity is accentuated by the fact that children of separated or divorced parents usually live with their mothers. The inadequacy—and frequent nonpayment—of child support has become recognized as a major social problem. Thus the inequalities of gender are now directly harming many children of both sexes as well as women themselves. Enhancing equal opportunity for women, important as it is in itself, is also a crucial way of improving the opportunities of many of the most disadvantaged children.

As . . . the parts of this problem [are connected, so are] some of the solutions: Much of what needs to be done to end the inequalities of gender, and to work in the direction of ending gender itself, will also help to equalize opportunity from one family to another. Subsidized, high quality day-care is obviously one such thing; another is the adaptation of the workplace to the needs of parents. . . .

The Family as a School of Justice

One of the things that theorists who have argued that families need not or cannot be just, or who have simply neglected them, have failed to explain is how, within a formative social environment that is *not* founded upon principles of justice, children can learn to develop that sense of justice they will require as citizens of a just society. Rather than being one among many co-equal institutions of a just society, a just family is its essential foundation.

It may seem uncontroversial, even obvious, that families must be just because of the vast influence they have on the moral development of children. But this is clearly not the case. I shall argue that unless the first and most formative example of adult interaction usually experienced by children is one of justice and reciprocity, rather than one of domination and manipulation or of unequal altruism and one-sided self-sacrifice, and unless they themselves are treated with concern and respect, they are likely to be considerably hindered in becoming people who are guided by principles of justice. Moreover, I claim, the sharing of roles by men and women, rather than the division of roles between them, would have a further positive impact because the experience of *being* a physical and psychological nurturer—whether of a child or of another adult—would increase that capacity to identify with and fully comprehend the viewpoints of others that is important to a sense of justice. In a society that minimized gender this would be more likely to be the experience of all of us.

Almost every person in our society starts life in a family of some sort or other. Fewer of these families now fit the usual, although not universal, standard of previous generations, that is, wage-working father, homemaking mother, and children. More families these days are headed by a single parent; lesbian and gay parenting is no longer so rare; many children have two wage-working parents, and receive at least some of their early care outside the home. While its forms are varied, the family in which a child is raised, especially in the earliest years, is clearly a crucial place for early moral development and for the formation of our basic attitudes to others. It is, potentially, a place where we can *learn to be just*. It is especially important for the development of a sense of justice that grows from sharing the experiences of others and becoming aware of the points of view of others who are different in some respects from ourselves, but with whom we clearly have some interests in common.

The importance of the family for the moral development of individuals was far more often recognized by political theorists of the past than it is by those of the present. Hegel, Rousseau, Tocqueville, Mill, and Dewey are obvious examples that come to mind. Rousseau, for example, shocked by Plato's proposal to abolish the family, says that it is

as though there were no need for a natural base on which to form conventional ties; as though the love of one's nearest were not the principle of the love one owes the state; as though it were not by means of the small fatherland which is the family that the heart attaches itself to the large one.

Defenders of both autocratic and democratic regimes have recognized the political importance of different family forms for the formation of citizens. On the one hand, the nineteenth-century monarchist Louis de Bonald argued against the divorce reforms of the French Revolution, which he claimed weakened the patriarchal family, on the grounds that "in order to keep the state out of the hands of the people, it is necessary to keep the family out of the hands of women and children." Taking this same line of thought in the opposite direction, the U.S. Supreme Court decided in 1879 in *Reynolds v. Nebraska* that familial patriarchy fostered despotism and was therefore intolerable. Denying Mormon men the freedom to practice polygamy, the Court asserted that it was an offense "subversive of good order" that "leads to the patriarchal principle, . . . [and] when applied to large communities, fetters the people in stationary despotism, while that principle cannot long exist in connection with monogamy."

However, while de Bonald was consistent in his adherence to an hierarchical family structure as necessary for an undemocratic political system, the Supreme Court was by no means consistent in promoting an egalitarian family as an essential underpinning for political democracy. For in other decisions of the same period—such as *Bradwell v. Illinois*, the famous 1872 case that upheld the exclusion of women from the practice of law—the Court rejected women's claims to legal equality, in the name of a thoroughly patriarchal, though monogamous, family that was held to require the dependence of women and their exclusion from civil and political life. While bigamy was considered patriarchal, and as such a threat to republican, democratic government, the refusal to allow a married woman to employ her talents and to make use of her qualifications to earn an independent living was not considered patriarchal. It was so far from being a threat to the civil order, in fact, that it was deemed necessary for it, and as such was ordained by both God and nature. Clearly in both *Reynolds* and *Bradwell*, "state authorities enforced family forms preferred by those in

power and justified as necessary to stability and order." The Court noticed the despotic potential of
polygamy, but was blind to the despotic potential
of patriarchal monogamy. This was perfectly acceptable to them as a training ground for citizens.

Most theorists of the past who stressed the importance of the family and its practices for the wider
world of moral and political life by no means insisted on congruence between the structures or practices of the family and those of the outside world.
Though concerned with moral development, they
bifurcated public from private life to such an extent
that they had no trouble reconciling inegalitarian,
sometimes admittedly unjust, relations founded
upon sentiment within the family with a more just,
even egalitarian, social structure outside the family.
Rousseau, Hegel, Tocqueville—all thought the family was centrally important for the development of
morality in citizens, but all defended the hierarchy
of the marital structure while spurning such a degree of hierarchy in institutions and practices outside the household. Preferring instead to rely on
love, altruism, and generosity as the basis for family
relations, none of these theorists argued for *just* family structures as necessary for socializing children
into citizenship in a just society.

The position that justice within the family is
irrelevant to the development of just citizens was
not plausible even when only men were citizens.
John Stuart Mill, in *The Subjection of Women*, takes an
impassioned stand against it. He argues that the inequality of women within the family is deeply subversive of justice in general in the wider social
world, because it subverts the moral potential of
men. Mill's first answer to the question, "For whose
good are all these changes in women's rights to be
undertaken?" is: "the advantage of having the most
universal and pervading of all human relations
regulated by justice instead of injustice." Making
marriage a relationship of equals, he argues, would
transform this central part of daily life from "a school
of despotism" into "a school of moral cultivation."
He goes on to discuss, in the strongest of terms, the
noxious effect of growing up in a family not regulated by justice. Consider . . . "the self-worship, the
unjust self-preference," nourished in a boy growing
up in a household in which "by the mere fact of
being born a male he is by right the superior of all
and every one of an entire half of the human race."
Mill concludes that the example set by perpetuating

a marital structure "contradictory to the first principles of social justice" must have such "a perverting
influence" that it is hard even to imagine the good
effects of changing it. All other attempts to educate
people to respect and practice justice, Mill claims,
will be superficial "as long as the citadel of the enemy is not attacked." Mill felt as much hope for
what the family might be as he felt despair at what
it was not. "The family, justly constituted, would be
the real school of the virtues of freedom," primary
among which was "justice, . . . grounded as before
on equal, but now also on sympathetic association."
Mill both saw clearly and had the courage to address what so many other political philosophers either could not see, or saw and turned away from.

Despite the strength and fervor of his advocacy
of women's rights, however, Mill's idea of a just
family structure falls far short of that of many feminists even of his own time, including his wife,
Harriet Taylor. In spite of the fact that Mill recognized both the empowering effect of earnings on
one's position in the family and the limiting effect of
domestic responsibility on women's opportunities,
he balked at questioning the traditional division of
labor between the sexes. For him, a woman's choice
of marriage was parallel to a man's choice of a profession: Unless and until she had fulfilled her obligations to her husband and children, she should
not undertake anything else. But . . . however equal
the legal rights of husbands and wives, this position
largely undermines Mill's own insistence upon the
importance of marital equality for a just society. His
acceptance of the traditional division of labor, without making any provision for wives who were
thereby made economically dependent on their husbands, largely undermines his insistence on family
justice as the necessary foundation for social justice.

Thus even those political theorists of the past
who have perceived the family as an important
school of moral development have rarely acknowledged the need for congruence between the family
and the wider social order, which suggests that families themselves need to be just. Even when they
have, as with Mill, they have been unwilling to push
hard on the traditional division of labor within the
family in the name of justice or equality.

Contemporary theorists of justice, with few
exceptions, have paid little or no attention to the
question of moral development—of how we are to
become just. Most seem to think, to adapt slightly

Hobbes's notable phrase, that just men spring like mushrooms from the earth. Not surprisingly, then, it is far less often acknowledged in recent than in past theories that the family is important for moral development, and especially for instilling a sense of justice. As already noted, many theorists pay no attention at all to either the family or gender. In the rare case that the issue of justice within the family is given any sustained attention, the family is not viewed as a potential school of social justice. In the rare case that a theorist pays any sustained attention to the development of a sense of justice or morality, little if any attention is likely to be paid to the family. Even in the rare event that theorists pay considerable attention to the family *as* the first major locus of moral socialization, they do not refer to the fact that families are almost all still thoroughly gender-structured institutions.

Among major contemporary theorists of justice, John Rawls alone treats the family seriously as the earliest school of moral development. He argues that a just, well-ordered society will be stable only if its members continue to develop a sense of justice. And he argues that families play a fundamental role in the stages by which this sense of justice is acquired. From the parents' love for their child, which comes to be reciprocated, comes the child's "sense of his own value and the desire to become the sort of person that they are." The family, too, is the first of that series of "associations" in which we participate, from which we acquire the capacity, crucial for a sense of justice, to see things from the perspectives of others. . . . This capacity—the capacity for empathy—is essential for maintaining a sense of justice of the Rawlsian kind. For the perspective [needed to maintain] a sense of justice is not that of the egoistic or disembodied self, or of the dominant few who overdetermine "our" traditions or "shared understandings," or (to use Nagel's term) of "the view from nowhere," but rather the perspective of every person in the society for whom the principles of justice are being arrived at. . . . The problem with Rawls's rare and interesting discussion of moral development is that it rests on the unexplained *assumption* that family institutions are just. If gendered family institutions are *not* just, but are . . . a relic of caste or feudal societies in which responsibilities, roles, and resources are distributed, not in accordance with the principles of justice he arrives at or with any other commonly respected values, but

in accordance with innate differences that are imbued with enormous social significance, then Rawls's theory of moral development would seem to be built on uncertain ground. This problem is exacerbated by suggestions in some of Rawls's most recent work that families are "private institutions," to which it is not appropriate to apply standards of justice. But if families are to help form just individuals and citizens, surely they must be *just families*.

In a just society, the structure and practices of families must give women the same opportunities as men to develop their capacities, to participate in political power and influence social choices, and to be economically secure. But in addition, families must be just because of the vast influence they have on the moral development of children. The family is the primary institution of formative moral development. And the structure and practices of the family must parallel those of the larger society if the sense of justice is to be fostered and maintained. [M]any theorists of justice, both past and present, appear to have denied the importance of at least one of these factors, [but] my own view is that both are absolutely crucial. A society that is committed to equal respect for all of its members, and to justice in social distributions of benefits and responsibilities, can neither neglect the family nor accept family structures and practices that violate these norms, as do current gender-based structures and practices. [C]hildren who are to develop into adults with a strong sense of justice and commitment to just institutions [must] spend their earliest and most formative years in an environment in which they are loved and nurtured, *and* in which principles of justice are abided by and respected. What is a child of either sex to learn about fairness in the average household with two full-time working parents, where the mother does, at the very least, twice as much family work as the father? What is a child to learn about the value of nurturing and domestic work in a home with a traditional division of labor in which the father either subtly or not so subtly uses the fact that he is the wage earner to "pull rank" on or to abuse his wife? What is a child to learn about responsibility for others in a family in which, after many years of arranging her life around the needs of her husband and children, a woman must provide for herself and her children but is totally ill-equipped for the task by the life she agreed to lead, has led, and expected to go on leading?

Endnote

1. He points out the shortcomings of the "earlier ethic of sacrifice," especially for women. He also welcomes the recent lessening of women's dependence on their husbands, but at the same time blames it for tending to weaken family stability. The falseness of Phillips's gender neutrality in discussing parenting is clearly confirmed later in the book, where paid work is "men's" and it is "fathers" who bequeath wealth or poverty on their children.

22. *Feminist Justice and the Family*

James P. Sterba

James P. Sterba sets out and defends an ideal of androgyny that he identifies with feminist justice. This ideal requires that traits that are truly desirable in society be equally available to both women and men, or in the case of virtues, equally expected in both women and men. He considers attempts to derive the ideal of androgyny either from a right to equal opportunity that is a central requirement of a welfare liberal conception of justice or from an equal right of self-development that is a central requirement of a socialist conception of justice. Sterba further argues that the ideal of androgyny would require (1) that all children irrespective of their sex must be given the same type of upbringing consistent with their native capabilities and (2) that mothers and fathers must also have the same opportunities for education and employment consistent with their native capabilities.

Contemporary feminists almost by definition seek to put an end to male domination and to secure women's liberation. To achieve these goals, many feminists support the political ideal of androgyny. According to these feminists, all assignments of rights and duties are ultimately to be justified in terms of the ideal of androgyny. Since a conception of justice is usually thought to provide the ultimate grounds for the assignment of rights and duties in a society, I shall refer to this ideal of androgyny as "feminist justice."

The Ideal of Androgyny

But how is this ideal of androgyny to be interpreted? In a well-known article, Joyce Trebilcot dis-

tinguishes two forms of androgyny. The first form postulates the same ideal for everyone. According to this form of androgyny, the ideal person "combines characteristics usually attributed to men with characteristics usually attributed to women." Thus, we should expect both nurturance and mastery, openness and objectivity, compassion and competitiveness from each and every person who has the capacities for these traits.

By contrast, the second form of androgyny does not advocate the same ideal for everyone but rather a variety of options from "pure" femininity to "pure" masculinity. As Trebilcot points out. this form of androgyny shares with the first the view that biological sex should not be the basis for determining the appropriateness of gender characterization. It differs in that it holds that "all alternatives with respect to gender should be equally available to and equally approved for everyone, regardless of sex."

It would be a mistake, however, to sharply distinguish between these two forms of androgyny. Properly understood, they are simply two different facets of a single ideal. For, as Mary Ann Warren has

From *Perspectives on the Family* (1990), edited by Robert Moffat, Joseph Grcic, and Michael Bayles. Reprinted with revisions by permission.

argued, the second form of androgyny is appropriate *only* "with respect to feminine and masculine traits which are largely matters of personal style and preference and which have little direct moral significance." However, when we consider so-called feminine and masculine *virtues,* it is the first form of androgyny that is required because, then, other things being equal, the same virtues are appropriate for everyone.

We can even formulate the ideal of androgyny more abstractly so that it is no longer specified in terms of so-called feminine and masculine traits. We can, for example, specify the ideal as requiring no more than that the traits that are truly desirable and distributable in society be equally available to both women and men, or in the case of virtues, equally expected of both women and men.

There is a problem, of course, in determining which traits of character are virtues and which traits are largely matters of personal style and preference. To make this determination, Trebilcot has suggested that we seek to bring about the second form of androgyny, where people have the option of acquiring the full range of so-called feminine and masculine traits. But surely when we already have good grounds for thinking that certain traits are virtues, such as courage and compassion, fairness and openness, there is no reason to adopt such a laissez-faire approach to moral education. Although, as Trebilcot rightly points out, proscribing certain options will involve a loss of freedom, nevertheless, we should be able to determine, at least with respect to some character traits, when a gain in virtue is worth the loss of freedom. It may even be the case that the loss of freedom suffered by an individual now will be compensated for by a gain of freedom to that same individual in the future once the relevant virtue or virtues have been acquired.

So understood, the class of virtues will turn out to be those desirable traits that can be reasonably expected of both women and men. Admittedly, this is a restrictive use of the term virtue. In normal usage, "virtue" is almost synonymous with "desirable trait." But there is good reason to focus on those desirable traits that can be justifiably inculcated in both women and men, and, for present purposes, I will refer to this class of desirable traits as virtues.

Unfortunately, many of the challenges to the ideal of androgyny fail to appreciate how the ideal can be interpreted to combine a required set of virtues with equal choice from among other desirable traits. For example, some challenges interpret the ideal as attempting to achieve "a proper balance of moderation" among opposing feminine and masculine traits and then question whether traits like feminine gullibility or masculine brutality could ever be combined with opposing gender traits to achieve such a balance. Other challenges interpret the ideal as permitting unrestricted choice of personal traits and then regard the possibility of Total Women and Hells Angels androgynes as a *reductio ad absurdum* of the ideal. But once it is recognized that the ideal of androgyny can not only be interpreted to expect of everyone a set of virtues (which need not be a mean between opposing extreme traits), but can also be interpreted to limit everyone's choice to desirable traits, then such challenges to the ideal clearly lose their force.

Actually the main challenge raised by feminists to the ideal of androgyny is that [it] is self-defeating in that it seeks to eliminate sexual stereotyping of human beings [while] it is formulated in terms of the very same stereotypical concepts it seeks to eliminate. Or as Warren has put it, "Is it not at least mildly paradoxical to urge people to cultivate both 'feminine' and 'masculine' virtues, while at the same time holding that virtues ought not to be sexually stereotyped?"

But in response to this challenge, it can be argued that to build a better society we must begin where we are now, and where we are now people still speak of feminine and masculine character traits. Consequently, if we want to easily refer to such traits and to formulate an ideal with respect to how they should be distributed in society it is plausible to refer to them in the way that people presently refer to them, that is, as feminine or masculine traits.

Alternatively, to avoid misunderstanding altogether, the ideal could be formulated in the more abstract way I suggested earlier so that it no longer specifically refers to so-called feminine or masculine traits. So formulated, the ideal requires that the traits that are truly desirable and distributable in society be equally available to both women and men or in the case of virtues equally expected of women and men. So formulated, the ideal would, in effect, require that men and women have in the fullest sense an equal right of self-development. The ideal would require this because an equal right to self-development can only be effectively guaranteed by expecting the same virtues of both women and men and by making other desirable traits that are distributable equally available to both women and men.

So characterized, the ideal of androgyny represents neither a revolt against so-called feminine virtues and traits nor their exaltation over so-called masculine virtues and traits. Accordingly, the ideal of androgyny does not view women's liberation as *simply* the freeing of women from the confines of traditional roles thus making it possible for them to develop in ways heretofore reserved for men. Nor does the ideal view women's liberation as *simply* the revaluation and glorification of so-called feminine activities like housekeeping or mothering or so-called feminine modes of thinking as reflected in an ethic of caring. The first perspective ignores or devalues genuine virtues and desirable traits traditionally associated with women while the second ignores or devalues genuine virtues and desirable traits traditionally associated with men. By contrast, the ideal of androgyny seeks a broader-based ideal for both women and men that combines virtues and desirable traits traditionally associated with women with virtues and desirable traits traditionally associated with men. Nevertheless, the ideal of androgyny will clearly reject any so-called virtues or desirable traits traditionally associated with women or men that have been supportive of discrimination or oppression against women or men.

Defenses of Androgyny

Now there are various contemporary defenses of the ideal of androgyny. Some feminists have attempted to derive the ideal from a Welfare Liberal Conception of Justice. Others have attempted to derive the ideal from a Socialist Conception of Justice. Let us briefly consider each of these defenses in turn.

In attempting to derive the ideal of androgyny from a Welfare Liberal Conception of Justice, feminists have tended to focus on the right to equal opportunity, which is a central requirement of a Welfare Liberal Conception of Justice. Of course, equal opportunity could be interpreted minimally as providing people only with the same legal rights of access to all advantaged positions in society for which they are qualified. But this is not the interpretation given the right by welfare liberals. In a Welfare Liberal Conception of Justice, equal opportunity is interpreted to require in addition the same prospects for success for all those who are relevantly similar, where relevant similarity involves more than simply present

qualifications. For example, Rawls claims that persons in his original position would favor a right to "fair equality of opportunity," which means that persons who have the same natural assets and . . . willingness to use them would have the necessary resources to achieve similar life prospects. The point feminists have been making is simply that failure to achieve the ideal of androgyny translates into a failure to guarantee equal opportunity to both women and men. The present evidence for this failure to provide equal opportunity is the discrimination that exists against women in education, employment, and personal relations. Discrimination in education begins early in a child's formal educational experience as teachers and school books support different and less desirable roles for girls than for boys. Discrimination in employment has been well documented. Women continue to earn only a fraction of what men earn for the same or comparable jobs and although women make up almost half of the paid labor force in the U.S., 70 percent of them are concentrated in just twenty different job categories, only five more than in 1905. Finally, discrimination in personal relations is the most entrenched of all forms of discrimination against women. It primarily manifests itself in traditional family structures in which the woman is responsible for domestic work and childcare and the man's task is "to protect against the outside world and to show how to meet this world successfully." In none of these areas, therefore, do women have the same prospects for success as compared with men with similar natural talents and similar desires to succeed.

Now the support for the ideal of androgyny provided by a Socialist Conception of Justice appears to be much more direct than that provided by a Welfare Liberal Conception of Justice. This is because the Socialist Conception of Justice and the ideal of androgyny can be interpreted as requiring the very same equal right of self-development. What a Socialist Conception of Justice purports to add to this interpretation of the ideal of androgyny is an understanding of how the ideal is best to be realized in contemporary capitalist societies. For according to advocates of this defense of androgyny, the ideal is best achieved by socializing the means of production and satisfying people's nonbasic as well as their basic needs. Thus, the general idea behind this approach to realizing the ideal of androgyny is that a cure for capitalist exploitation will also be a cure for women's oppression.

Yet despite attempts to identify the feminist ideal of androgyny with a right to equal opportunity endorsed by a Welfare Liberal Conception of Justice or an equal right of self-development endorsed by a Socialist Conception of Justice, the ideal still transcends both of these rights by requiring not only that desirable traits be equally available to both women and men but also that the same virtues be equally expected of both women and men. Of course, part of the rationale for expecting the same virtues in both women and men is to support such rights. And if support for such rights is to be fairly allocated, the virtues needed to support such rights must be equally expected of both women and men. Nevertheless, to hold that the virtues required to support a right to equal opportunity or an equal right to self-development must be equally expected of both women and men is different from claiming, as the ideal of androgyny does, that human virtues, sans phrase, should be equally expected of both women and men. Thus, the ideal of androgyny clearly requires an inculcation of virtues beyond what is necessary to support a right to equal opportunity or . . . self-development. What additional virtues are required by the ideal obviously depends upon what other rights should be recognized. In this regard, the ideal of androgyny is somewhat open-ended. Feminists who endorse the ideal would simply have to go along with the best arguments for additional rights and corresponding virtues. In particular, I would claim that they would have to support a right to welfare that is necessary for meeting the basic needs of all legitimate claimants given the strong case that can be made for such a right from welfare liberal, socialist, and even libertarian perspectives.

Now, in order to provide all legitimate claimants with the resources necessary for meeting their basic needs, there obviously has to be a limit on the resources that will be available for each individual's self-development, and this limit will definitely have an effect upon the implementation of the ideal of androgyny. Of course, some feminists would want to pursue various possible technological transformations of human biology in order to implement their ideal. For example, they would like to make it possible for women to inseminate other women and for men to lactate and even to bring fertilized ova to term. But bringing about such possibilities would be very costly indeed. Consequently, since the means selected for meeting basic needs must be provided to all legitimate claimants including distant peoples and future generations, it is unlikely that such costly means could ever be morally justified. Rather it seems preferable radically to equalize the conventionally provided opportunities to women and men and wait for such changes to have their ultimate effect on human biology as well. Of course, if any "technological fixes" for achieving androgyny should prove to be cost-efficient as a means for meeting people's basic needs, then obviously there would be every reason to utilize them.

Unfortunately, the commitment of a Feminist Conception of Justice to a right of equal opportunity raises still another problem for the view. Some philosophers have contended that equal opportunity is ultimately an incoherent goal. As Lloyd Thomas has put the charge, "We have a problem for those who advocate competitive equality of opportunity: The prizes won in the competitions of the first generation will tend to defeat the requirements of equality of opportunity for the next." The only way to avoid this result, Thomas claims, "is by not permitting persons to be dependent for their self-development on others at all," which obviously is a completely unacceptable solution.

But this is a problem, as Thomas points out, that exists for competitive opportunities. They are opportunities for which, even when each person does her best, there are considerably more losers than winners. With respect to such opportunities, the winners may well be able to place themselves and their children in an advantageous position with respect to subsequent competitions. But under a Welfare Liberal Conception of Justice, and presumably a Feminist Conception of Justice as well, most of the opportunities people have are not competitive opportunities at all, but rather noncompetitive opportunities to acquire the resources necessary for meeting their basic needs. These are opportunities with respect to which virtually everyone who does her best can be a winner. Of course, some people who do not do their best may fail to satisfy their basic needs, and this failure may have negative consequences for their children's prospects. But under a Welfare Liberal Conception of Justice, and presumably a Feminist Conception of Justice as well, every effort is required to insure that each generation has the same opportunities to meet their basic needs, and as long as most of the opportunities that are available are of the noncompetitive sort, this goal should not be that difficult to achieve.

Now it might be objected that if all that will be accomplished under the proposed system of equal opportunity is, for the most part, the satisfaction of people's basic needs, then that would not bring about the revolutionary change in the relationship between women and men that feminists are demanding. For don't most women in technologically advanced societies already have their basic needs satisfied, despite the fact that they are not yet fully liberated?

In response, it should be emphasized that the concern of defenders of the ideal of androgyny is not just with women in technologically advanced societies. The ideal of androgyny is also applicable to women in Third World and developing societies, and in such societies it is clear that the basic needs of many women are not being met. Furthermore, it is just not the case that all the basic needs of most women in technologically advanced societies are being met. Most obviously, their basic needs for self-development are still not being met. This is because they are being denied an equal right to education, training, jobs, and a variety of social roles for which they have the native capabilities. In effect, women in technologically advanced societies are still being treated as second-class persons, no matter how well-fed, well-clothed, well-housed they happen to be. This is why there must be a radical restructuring of social institutions even in technologically advanced societies if women's basic needs for self-development are to be met.

Androgyny and the Family

Now the primary locus for the radical restructuring required by the ideal of androgyny is the family. Here two fundamental changes are needed. First, all children irrespective of their sex must be given the same type of upbringing consistent with their native capabilities. Second, mothers and fathers must also have the same opportunities for education and employment consistent with their native capabilities.

Surprisingly, however, some welfare liberals have viewed the existence of the family as imposing an acceptable limit on the right to equal opportunity. Rawls, for example, claims the principle of fair opportunity can be only imperfectly carried out, at least as long as the institution of the family exists. The extent to which natural capacities develop and

reach fruition is affected by all kinds of social conditions and class attitudes. Even the willingness to make an effort, to try, and so to be deserving in the ordinary sense is itself dependent upon happy family and social circumstances. It is impossible in practice to secure equal chances of achievement and culture for those similarly endowed, and therefore we may want to adopt a principle which recognizes this fact and also mitigates the arbitrary effects of the natural lottery itself.

Thus, according to Rawls, since different families will provide different opportunities for their children, the only way to fully achieve "fair equality of opportunity" would require us to go too far and abolish or radically modify traditional family structures.

Yet others have argued that the full attainment of equal opportunity requires that we go even further and equalize people's native as well as their social assets. For only when everyone's natural and social assets have been equalized would everyone have exactly the same chance as everyone else to attain the desirable social positions in society. Of course, feminists have no difficulty recognizing that there are moral limits to the pursuit of equal opportunity. Accordingly, feminists could grant that other than the possibility of special cases, such as sharing a surplus organ like a second kidney, it would be too much to ask people to sacrifice their native assets to achieve equal opportunity.

Rawls, however, proposes to limit the pursuit of equal opportunity still further by accepting the inequalities generated by families in any given sector of society, provided that there is still equal opportunity between the sectors or that the existing inequality of opportunity can be justified in terms of its benefit to those in the least-advantaged position. Nevertheless, what Rawls is concerned with here is simply the inequality of opportunity that exists between individuals owing to the fact that they come from different families. He fails to consider the inequality of opportunity that exists in traditional family structures, especially between adult members, in virtue of the different roles expected of women and men. When viewed from the original position, this latter inequality of opportunity clearly is sufficient to require a radical modification of traditional family structures, even if the former inequality, for the reasons Rawls suggests, does not require any such modifications.

Yet at least in the United States this need radically to modify traditional family structures to guarantee equal opportunity confronts a serious problem. Given that a significant proportion of the available jobs are at least 9 to 5, families with preschool children require day-care facilities if their adult members are to pursue their careers. Unfortunately, for many families such facilities are simply unavailable. In New York City, for example, more than 144,000 children under the age of six are competing for 46,000 full-time slots in day-care centers. In Seattle, there is licensed day-care space for 8,800 of the 23,000 children who need it. In Miami, two children, 3 and 4 years old, were left unattended at home while their mother worked. They climbed into a clothes dryer while the timer was on, closed the door and burned to death.

Moreover, even the available day-care facilities are frequently inadequate either because their staffs are poorly trained or because the child/adult ratio in such facilities is too high. At best, such facilities provide little more than custodial care; at worst, they actually retard the development of those under their care. What this suggests is that at least under present conditions if preschool children are to be adequately cared for, frequently, one of the adult members of the family will have to remain at home to provide that care. But since most jobs are at least 9 to 5, this will require that the adult members who stay at home temporarily give up pursuing a career. However, such sacrifice appears to conflict with the equal opportunity requirement of Feminist Justice.

Now families might try to meet this equal opportunity requirement by having one parent give up pursuing a career for a certain period of time and the other give up pursuing a career for a subsequent (equal) period of time. But there are problems here too. Some careers are difficult to interrupt for any significant period of time, while others never adequately reward latecomers. In addition, given the high rate of divorce and the inadequacies of most legally mandated child support, those who first sacrifice their careers may find themselves later faced with the impossible task of beginning or reviving their careers while continuing to be the primary caretaker of their children. Furthermore, there is considerable evidence that children will benefit more from equal rearing from both parents. So the option of having just one parent doing the child-rearing for any length of time is, other things being equal, not optimal.

It would seem, therefore, that to truly share child-rearing within the family, what is needed is flexible (typically part-time) work schedules that also allow both parents to be together with their children for a significant period every day. Now some flexible job schedules have already been tried by various corporations. But if equal opportunity is to be a reality in our society, the option of flexible job schedules must be guaranteed to all those with preschool children. Of course, to require employers to guarantee flexible job schedules to all those with preschool children would place a significant restriction upon the rights of employers, and it may appear to move the practical requirements of Feminist Justice closer to those of Socialist Justice. But if the case for flexible job schedules is grounded on a right to equal opportunity then at least defenders of Welfare Liberal Justice will have no reason to object. This is clearly one place where Feminist Justice with its focus on equal opportunity within the family tends to drive Welfare Liberal Justice and Socialist Justice closer together in their practical requirements.

Recently, however, Christina Hoff Sommers has criticized feminist philosophers for being "against the family." Her main objection is that feminist philosophers have criticized traditional family structures without adequately justifying what they would put in its place. In this paper, I have tried to avoid any criticism of this sort by first articulating a defensible version of the feminist ideal of androgyny which can draw upon support from both Welfare Liberal and Socialist Conceptions of Justice and then by showing what demands this ideal would impose upon family structures. Since Sommers and other critics of the feminist ideal of androgyny also support a strong requirement of equal opportunity, it is difficult to see how they can consistently do so while denying the radical implications of that requirement (and the ideal of androgyny that underlies it) for traditional family structures.

23. Philosophers against the Family

CHRISTINA HOFF SOMMERS

Christina Hoff Sommers distinguishes liberal feminists from radical feminists. She contends that liberal feminists, like herself, want equal opportunity in the workplace and politics, but would leave marriage and motherhood "untouched and unimpugned." By contrast, Sommers contends that radical feminists are committed to an assimilationist or androgynous ideal that would destroy the (traditional) family and deny most women what they want.

Much of what commonly counts as personal morality is measured by how well we behave within family relationships. We live our moral lives as son or daughter to this mother and that father, as brother or sister to that sister or brother, as father or mother, grandfather, granddaughter to that boy or girl or that man or woman. These relationships and the moral duties defined by them were once popular topics of moral casuistry; but when we turn to the literature of recent moral philosophy, we find little discussion on what it means to be a good son or daughter, a good mother or father, a good husband or wife, a good brother or sister.

Modern ethical theory concentrates on more general topics. Perhaps the majority of us who do ethics accept some version of Kantianism or utilitarianism, and these mainstream doctrines are better designed for telling us about what we should do as persons in general than about our special duties as parents or children or siblings. We believe, perhaps, that these universal theories can fully account for the morality of special relations. In any case, modern ethics is singularly silent on the bread and butter issues of personal morality in daily life. But silence is only part of it. With the exception of marriage itself, the relationships in the family are biologically given. The contemporary philosopher is, on the whole, actively unsympathetic to the idea that we have *any* duties defined by relationships that

we have not voluntarily entered into. We do not, after all, choose our parents or siblings, and even if we do choose to have children, this is not the same as choosing, say, our friends. Because the special relationships that constitute the family as a social arrangement are, in this sense, not voluntarily assumed, many moralists feel bound in principle to dismiss them altogether. The practical result is that philosophers are to be found among those who are contributing to an ongoing disintegration of the traditional family. In what follows I expose some of the philosophical roots of the current hostility to family morality. My own view that the ethical theses underlying this hostility are bad philosophy is made evident throughout the discussion.

The Moral Vantage

Social criticism is a heady pastime to which philosophers are professionally addicted. One approach is Aristotelian in method and temperament. It is antiradical, though it may be liberal, and it approaches the task of needed reform with a prima facie respect for the norms of established morality. It is conservationist and cautious in its recommendations for change. It is therefore not given to such proposals as abolishing the family or abolishing private property and, indeed, does not look kindly on such proposals from other philosophers. The antiradicals I am concerned about are not those who would be called Burkean. I call them liberal but this use of the term is somewhat perverse since, in my stipulative use, a liberal is a philosopher who advocates social reform

From "Philosophers against the Family," in *Person to Person*, George Graham and Hugh LaFollette, eds. (1989). Reprinted with permission of Temple University Press. All Rights Reserved.

but always in a conservative spirit. My liberals share with Aristotle the conviction that the traditional arrangements have great moral weight and that common opinion is a primary source of moral truth. A good modern example is Henry Sidgwick with his constant appeal to common sense. But philosophers like John Stuart Mill, William James, and Bertrand Russell can also be cited. On the other hand, since no radical can be called a liberal in my sense, many so-called liberals could be perversely excluded. Thus when John Rawls toys with the possibility of abolishing the family because kinship bias is a force inimical to equality of opportunity, he is no liberal.

The more exciting genre of social criticism is not liberal-Aristotelian but radical and Platonist in spirit. Its vantage is external or even supernal to the social institutions it has placed under moral scrutiny. Plato was as aware as anyone could be that what he called the cave was social reality. One reason for calling it a cave was to emphasize the need, as he saw it, for an external, objective perspective on established morality. Another point in so calling it was his conviction that common opinion was benighted, and that reform could not be accomplished except by a great deal of consciousness raising and enlightened social engineering. Plato's supernal vantage made it possible for him to look on social reality in somewhat the way the Army Corps of Engineers looks upon a river that needs to have its course changed and its waywardness tamed. In our own day much social criticism of a Marxist variety has taken this radical approach to social change. And of course much of contemporary feminist philosophy is radical. . . .

Feminism and the Family

I have said that the morality of the family has been relatively neglected. The glaring exception to this is, of course, the feminist movement. This movement is complex, but I am primarily confined to its moral philosophers, of whom the most influential is Simone de Beauvoir. For de Beauvoir, a social arrangement that does not allow all its participants the scope and liberty of a human subjectivity is to be condemned. De Beauvoir criticizes the family as an unacceptable arrangement since, for women, marriage and childbearing are essentially incompatible with their subjectivity and freedom:

> The tragedy of marriage is not that it fails to assure woman the promised happiness . . . but that it mutilates her: It dooms her to repetition and routine. . . . At twenty or thereabouts mistress of a home, bound permanently to a man, a child in her arms, she stands with her life virtually finished forever (1952, 534).

For de Beauvoir the tragedy goes deeper than marriage. The loss of subjectivity is unavoidable as long as human reproduction requires the woman's womb. De Beauvoir starkly describes the pregnant woman who ought to be a "free individual" as a "stockpile of colloids, an incubator of an egg." And as recently as 1977 she compared childbearing and nurturing to slavery.

It would be a mistake to say that de Beauvoir's criticism of the family is outside the mainstream of Anglo-American philosophy. Her criterion of moral adequacy may be formulated in continental existentialist terms, but its central contention is generally accepted: Who would deny that an arrangement that systematically thwarts the freedom and autonomy of the individual is *eo ipso* defective? What is perhaps a bit odd to Anglo-American ears is that de Beauvoir makes so little appeal to ideals of fairness and equality. For her, it is the loss of autonomy that is decisive.

De Beauvoir is more pessimistic than most feminists she has influenced about the prospects for technological and social solutions. But implicit in her critique is the ideal of a society in which sexual differences are minimal or nonexistent. This ideal is shared by many contemporary feminist philosophers: . . . Richard Wasserstrom (1980), Ann Ferguson (1977), and Alison Jaggar (1977; 1983; 1986) are representative.

Wasserstrom's approach to social criticism is Platonist in its use of a hypothetical good society. The ideal society is nonsexist and "assimilationist": "In the assimilationist society in respect to sex, persons would not be socialized so as to see or understand themselves or others as essentially or significantly who they were or what their lives would be like because they were either male or female" (1980, 26). Social reality is scrutinized for its approximation to this ideal, and criticism is directed against all existing norms. Take the custom of having sexually segregated bathrooms: Whether this is right or wrong "depends on what the good society would look like in respect to sexual differentiation." The key question in evaluating any law or arrangement in which sex difference figures is: "What would the good or just society make of [it]?"

Thus the supernal light shines on the cave revealing its moral defects. *There,* in the ideal society, gender in the choice of lover or spouse would be of no more significance than eye color. *There* the family would consist of adults but not necessarily of different sexes and not necessarily in pairs. *There* we find equality ensured by a kind of affirmative action which compensates for disabilities. If women are somewhat weaker than men, or if they are subject to lunar disabilities, then this must be compensated for. (Wasserstrom compares women to persons with congenital defects for whom the good society makes special arrangements.) Male-dominated sports such as wrestling and football will . . . be eliminated, and marriage as we know it will not exist.

Other feminist philosophers are equally confident about the need for sweeping change. Ann Ferguson (1977) wants a "radical reorganization of child rearing." She recommends communal living and a de-emphasis on biological parenting. In the ideal society "love relationships would be based on the meshing together of androgynous human beings." Carol Gould (1983) argues for androgyny and for abolishing legal marriage. She favors single parenting, co-parenting, and communal parenting. The only arrangement she emphatically opposes is the traditional one where the mother provides primary care for the children. Janice Raymond (1975) is an assimilationist who objects to the ideal of androgyny, preferring instead to speak of a genderless ideal free of male or female stereotypes. Alison Jaggar's ideal is described in a science-fiction story depicting a society in which "neither sex bears children, but both sexes, through hormone treatments, suckle them . . . thus [the author] envisions a society where every baby has three social 'mothers,' who may be male or female, and at least two of whom agree to breast-feed it" (1983). To those of us who find this bizarre, Jaggar replies that this shows the depth of our prejudice in favor of the natural family.

Though they differ in detail, these feminists hold to a common social ideal that is broadly assimilationist in character and inimical to the traditional family. Sometimes it seems as if the radical feminist simply takes the classical Marxist eschatology of the *Communist Manifesto* and substitutes "gender" for "class."

Indeed, the feminist and the old-fashioned Marxist do have much in common. Both see their caves as politically divided into two warring factions: one oppressing, the other oppressed. Both see the need of raising the consciousness of the oppressed group to its predicament and to the possibility of removing its shackles. Both look forward to the day of a classless or genderless society. And both are zealots, paying little attention to the tragic personal costs to be paid for the revolution they wish to bring about. The feminists tell us little about that side of things. To begin with, how can the benighted myriads in the cave who do not wish to mesh together with other androgynous beings be reeducated? And how are children to be brought up in the genderless society? Plato took great pains to explain his methods. Would the new methods be as thoroughgoing? Unless these questions can be given plausible answers, the supernal attack on the family must always be irresponsible. The appeal to the just society justifies nothing until it can be shown that the radical proposals do not have monstrous consequences. That has not been shown. Indeed, given the perennially dubious state of the social sciences, it is precisely what *cannot* be shown.

Any social arrangement that falls short of the assimilationist ideal is labeled sexist. It should be noted that this characteristically feminist use of the term differs significantly from the popular or literal sense. Literally, and popularly, sexism connotes unfair discrimination. But in its extended philosophical use it connotes discrimination, period. Wasserstrom and many feminists trade on the popular pejorative connotations of sexism when they invite us to be antisexist. Most liberals are antisexist in the popular sense. But to be antisexist in the technical, radical philosophical sense is not merely to be opposed to discrimination against women; it is to be *for* what Wasserstrom calls the assimilationist ideal. The philosopher antisexist opposes any social policy that is nonandrogynous, objecting, for example, to legislation that allows for maternity leave. As Alison Jaggar remarks: "We do not, after all, elevate 'prostate leave' into a special right of men" (1977). From being liberally opposed to sexism, one may in this way insensibly be led to a radical critique of the family whose ideal is assimilationist and androgynous. For it is very clear that the realization of the androgynous ideal is incompatible with the survival of the family as we know it.

The neological extension of labels such as "sexism," "slavery," and "prostitution" is a feature of radical discourse. The liberal too will sometimes call for radical solutions to social problems. Some institutions are essentially unjust. To reform slavery or totalitarian systems of government is to eliminate them. The radical trades on these extreme practices in characterizing other practices—for example, characterizing low wages as "slave" wages and the worker who is paid them as a "slave" laborer. Taking these descriptions seriously may put one on the way to treating a system of a free labor market as a "slave system," which, in simple justice, must be overthrown and replaced by an alternative system of production.

Comparing mothers and wives to slaves is a common radical criticism of the family. Presumably most slaves do not want to be slaves. In fact, the majority of wives and mothers want to be wives and mothers. Calling these women slaves is therefore a pejorative extension of the term. To be slaves in the literal sense these women would have to be too dispirited and oppressed or too corrupt even to want freedom from slavery. Yet that is how some feminist philosophers look upon women who opt for the traditional family. It does seem fanciful and not a little condescending to see them so, but let us suppose that it is in fact a correct and profound description of the plight of married women and mothers. Would it now follow that the term "slave" literally applies to them? Not quite yet. Before we could call these women slaves, we should have to have made a further assumption. Even timorous slaves too fearful of taking any step to freedom are under no illusion that they are not slaves. Yet it is a fact that most women and mothers do not *think* of themselves as slaves, so we must assume that the majority of women have been systematically deluded into thinking they are free. And that assumption, too, is often explicitly made. Here the radical feminist will typically explain that, existentially, women, being treated by men as sex objects, are especially prone to bad faith and false consciousness. Marxist feminists will see them as part of an unawakened and oppressed economic class. Clearly we cannot call on a deluded woman to cast off her bonds before we have made her *aware* of her bondage. So the first task of freeing the slave woman is dispelling the thrall of a false and deceptive consciousness. One must raise her consciousness to the reality of her situation. (Some feminists acknowledge that it may in fact be too late for many of the women who have fallen too far into the delusions of mar-

riage and motherhood. But the educative process can save many from falling into the marriage and baby trap.)

In this sort of rhetorical climate nothing is what it seems. Prostitution is another term that has been subjected to a radical enlargement. Alison Jaggar believes that a feminist interpretation of the term "prostitution" is badly needed and asks for a "philosophical theory of prostitution" (1986). Observing that the average woman dresses for men, marries a man for protection, and so on, she says" "For contemporary radical feminists, prostitution is the archetypal relationship of women to men" (1986, 115).

Of course, the housewife Jaggar has in mind might be offended at the suggestion that she herself is a prostitute, albeit less well paid and less aware of it than the professional street prostitute. To this the radical feminist reply is, to quote Jaggar:

> Individuals' intentions do not necessarily indicate the true nature of what is going on. Both man and woman might be outraged at the description of their candlelit dinner as prostitution, but the radical feminist argues this outrage is due simply to the participants' failure or refusal to perceive the social context in which the dinner occurs (1986, 117).

Apparently, this failure or refusal to perceive affects most women. Thus we may even suppose that the majority of women who have been treated by a man to a candlelit dinner prefer it to other dining alternatives they have experienced. To say that these preferences are misguided is a hard and condescending doctrine. It would appear that most feminist philosophers are not overly impressed with Mill's principle that there can be no appeal from a majority verdict of those who have experienced two alternatives.

The dismissive feminist attitude to the widespread preferences of women takes its human toll. Most women, for example, prefer to have children, and few of those who have them regret having them. It is no more than sensible, from a utilitarian standpoint, to take note of the widespread preference and to take it seriously in planning one's own life. But a significant number of women discount this general verdict as benighted, taking more seriously the idea that the reported joys of motherhood are exaggerated and fleeting, if not altogether illusory. These women tell themselves and others that having babies is a trap to be avoided. But for many women childlessness has become a trap of its own, somewhat lonelier than the more conventional traps of marriage and babies. Some come to find their childlessness regrettable; this sort of regret is common to those who flout Mill's reasonable maxim by putting the verdict of ideology over the verdict of human experience.

It is a serious defect of American feminism that it concentrates its zeal on impugning femininity and feminine culture at the expense of the grassroot fight against economic and social injustices to which women are subjected. As we have seen, the radical feminist attitude to the woman who enjoys her femininity is condescending or even contemptuous. Indeed, the contempt for femininity reminds one of misogynist biases in philosophers such as Kant, Rousseau, and Schopenhauer, who believed that femininity was charming but incompatible with full personhood and reasonableness. The feminists deny the charm, but they too accept the verdict that femininity is weakness. It goes without saying that an essential connection between femininity and powerlessness has not been established by *either* party.

By denigrating conventional feminine roles and holding to an assimilationist ideal in social policy, the feminist movement has lost its natural constituency. The actual concerns, beliefs, and aspirations of the majority of women are not taken seriously *except* as illustrations of bad faith, false consciousness, and successful brainwashing. What women actually want is discounted and reinterpreted as to what they have been led to *think* they want (a man, children). What most women *enjoy* (male gallantry, candlelit dinners, sexy clothes, makeup) is treated as an obscenity (prostitution).

As the British feminist Jennifer Radcliffe Richards says:

> Most women still dream about beauty, dress, weddings, dashing lovers, domesticity, and babies . . . but if feminists seem (as they do) to want to eliminate nearly all of these things— beauty, sex conventions, families, and all—for most people that simply means the removal of everything in life which is worth living for (1980, 341–342).

Radical feminism creates a false dichotomy between sexism and assimilation, as if there were nothing in between. This is to ignore completely the middle ground in which it could be recognized that a woman can be free of oppression and nevertheless feminine in the sense abhorred by many feminists. For women are simply not waiting to be freed from the particular chains the radical feminists are trying to sunder. The average woman enjoys her femininity. She wants a man, not a roommate. She wants fair economic opportunities, and she wants children and the time to care for them. These are the goals that women actually have, and they are not easily attainable. But they will never be furthered by an elitist radical movement that views the actual aspirations of women as the product of a false consciousness. There is room for a liberal feminism that would work for reforms that would give women equal opportunity in the workplace and in politics, but would leave untouched and unimpugned the basic institutions that women want and support: marriage and motherhood. Such a feminism is already in operation in some European countries. But it has been obstructed in the United States by the ideologues who now hold the seat of power in the feminist movement (Hewlett, 1986).

In characterizing and criticizing American feminism, I have not taken into account the latest revisions and qualifications of a lively and variegated movement. There is a kind of feminism-of-the-week that one cannot hope to keep abreast of, short of giving up all other concerns. The best one can do for the present purposes is attend to central theses and arguments that bear on the feminist treatment of the family. Nevertheless, even for this limited purpose, it would be wrong to omit discussion of an important turn taken by feminism in the past few years. I have in mind the recent literature on the idea that there is a specific female ethic that is more concrete, less rule-oriented, more empathetic and caring, and more attentive to the demands of a particular context. The kind of feminism that accepts the idea that women differ from men in approaching ethical dilemmas and social problems from a care perspective is not oriented to androgyny as an ideal. Rather it seeks to develop this special female ethic and give it greater practical scope.

The stress on context might lead one to think these feminists are more sympathetic to the family as the social arrangement that shapes the moral development of women and is the context for many of the moral dilemmas that women actually face. However, one sees as yet no attention being paid to the fact that feminism itself is a force working against the preservation of the family. Psychologists like Carol Gilligan and philosophers like Lawrence

Blum concentrate their attention on the moral quality of the caring relationships, but these relationships are themselves not viewed in their concrete embeddedness in any formal social arrangement.

It should also be said that some feminists are moving away from earlier hostility to motherhood (Trebilcot, 1984). Here, too, one sees the weakening of the assimilationist ideal in the acknowledgment of a primary gender role. However, childrearing is not primarily seen within the context of the family but as a special relationship between mother and daughter or—more awkwardly—between mother and son, a relationship that effectively excludes the male parent. And the often cultist celebration of motherhood remains largely hostile to traditional familial arrangements.

It is too early to say whether a new style of non-assimilationist feminism will lead to a mitigation of the assault on the family or even on femininity. In any case, the recognition of a female ethic of care and responsibility is hardly inconsistent with a social ethic that values the family as a vital, perhaps indispensable, institution. And the recognition that women have their own moral style may well be followed by a more accepting attitude to the kind of femininity that the more assimilationist feminists reject.

References

De Beauvoir, Simone. 1952. *The Second Sex.* H. M. Parshley, trans. New York: Random House.

———. 1977. "Talking to De Beauvoir." In *Spare Rib.*

Ferguson, Ann. 1977. "Androgyny as an Ideal for Human Development." In M. Vetterling-Braggin, F. Elliston, and J. English, eds. *Feminism and Philosophy,* pp. 49–69. Totowa, N.J.: Rowman and Littlefield.

Gould, Carol. 1983. "Private Rights and Public Virtues: Woman, the Family and Democracy." In Carol Gould, ed. *Beyond Domination,* pp. 3–18. Totowa, N.J.: Rowman and Allanheld.

Hewlett, Sylvia Ann. 1986. *A Lesser Life: The Myth of Woman's Liberation in America.* New York: Morrow.

Jaggar, Alison. 1977. "On Sex Equality." In Jane English, ed. *Sex Equality.* Englewood Cliffs, N.J.: Prentice-Hall.

———. 1983. "Human Biology in Feminist Theory: Sexual Equality Reconsidered." In Gould, ed. *Beyond Domination.*

———. 1986. "Prostitution." In Marilyn Pearsell, ed. *Women and Values: Readings in Recent Feminist Philosophy,* pp. 108–121. Belmont, Calif.: Wadsworth.

Raymond, Janice. 1975. "The Illusion of Androgyny." *Quest: A Feminist Quarterly,* 2.

Richards, Jennifer Radcliffe. 1980. *The Sceptical Feminist.* Harmondsworth: Penguin.

Trebilcot, Joyce, ed. 1984. *Mothering: Essays in Feminist Theory.* Totowa, N.J.: Rowman and Allanheld.

Wasserstrom, Richard. 1980. *Philosophy and Social Issues.* Notre Dame, Ind.: University of Notre Dame Press.

24. They Lived Happily Ever After: Sommers on Women and Marriage

Marilyn Friedman

Marilyn Friedman questions whether what Christina Sommers supports is really what most women want. She quotes a 1983 survey which indicated that 63 percent of women preferred nontraditional family relationships. She points out that in 1977 only 16 percent of American households were traditional families. She argues that femininity as slavishly deferring to men is not good for women and contends that no woman should "swoon at the sight of Rhett Butler carrying Scarlett O'Hara up the stairs to a fate undreamt of in feminist philosophy."

1. In a series of papers which has recently appeared in several philosophical and general academic publications,[1] Christina Sommers mounts a campaign against feminist philosophers (1989a, 85; 1989b, B2) and "American feminism" in general (1989a, 90–91). Sommers blames feminists for contributing to the current divorce rate and the breakdown of the traditional family, and she repudiates feminist critiques of traditional forms of marriage, family, and femininity. In this paper, I explore Sommers's views in some detail. My aim is not primarily to defend her feminist targets, but to ferret out Sommers's own views of traditional marriage, family, and femininity, and to see whether or not they have any philosophical merit.

2. In her writings, Sommers generally defends what she claims that feminists have challenged. Whether or not she is actually discussing the same things is often open to question since she fails to define the key terms behind which she rallies. Sommers, for example, endorses "the family," the "traditional family," and "the family as we know it" (1989a, 87–88). These are not equivalent expressions. The so-called traditional family—a nuclear family consisting of a legally married heterosexual couple and their children, in which the man is the sole breadwinner and "head" of the household, and the woman does the domestic work and childcare— comprised only 16% of all U.S. households in 1977, according to the U.S. Census Bureau.[2] Hence, the "traditional family" is no longer "*the* family" or "*the* family as we know it" (italics mine) but is only one sort of family that we know.

Sommers also rallies behind "femininity," "feminine culture," "conventional feminine roles," and "a primary gender role" (1989a, 90, 92). These expressions, as well, call for clarification; they do not necessarily refer to the same practices. In recent years, many feminists have defended various aspects of what might also be called "feminine culture." Sommers notes a few of these authors and works (Carol Gilligan, for example), but finds one reason or another for repudiating each one that she cites.[3]

3. To see what Sommers is promoting under the banner of "feminine culture," we should look to Sommers's claims about what women value, want, and enjoy.[4] First, there are wants, values, and enjoyments pertaining to men.[5] Sommers claims that women want "a man," "marriage," and "to marry good providers."[6] She asserts that "most women" enjoy "male gallantry," that the "majority of women" enjoy being "treated by a man to a candlelit dinner," and that "many women . . . swoon at the sight of Rhett Butler carrying Scarlett O'Hara up the stairs to a fate undreamt of in feminist philosophy."[7]

Second, there are wants, values, and enjoyments having to do with children. Women, Sommers tells us, want children, motherhood, "*conventional* motherhood," "family," and "the time to care for children."[8] In a revealing turn of phrase, Sommers also asserts that women are "willing to pay the price" for family and motherhood (1989b, B2). Sommers does not say, however, what she thinks the price is.

From "They Lived Happily Ever After: Sommers on Women and Marriage," *Journal of Social Philosophy* (1990). Reprinted with permission.

Third, there are wants, values, and enjoyments having to do with femininity. Women are said to enjoy their "femininity," makeup, "sexy clothes," and, even more specifically, "clothes that render them 'sex objects.'"[9] On the topic of femininity, Sommers also quotes approvingly (1989a, 90–91) the words of Janet Radcliffe Richards who wrote that, "Most women still dream about beauty, dress, weddings, dashing lovers," and "domesticity," and that, for "most people," "beauty, sex conventions, families, and all" comprise "everything in life which is worth living for."[10]

4. A very few of the wants which Sommers attributes to women do not fit into my three-part classification scheme (men, children, femininity). Sommers claims that women want "fair economic opportunities" (1989a, 91), and that they are "generally receptive to liberal feminist reforms that enhance their political and economic powers" (1989b, B2). Sommers, ironically, does not recognize that the enhanced economic and political power of women makes them less needful of traditional marriage to a "good provider," and when they are married, makes them less afraid to resort to divorce to solve marital and family problems. The economic concerns of liberal feminism directly threaten one colossal support for the "traditional family," namely, the extreme economic vulnerability of the non–income-earning woman and her concomitant material dependence on a "good provider."

Under traditional arrangements, most women not only *wanted* marriage, they *needed* it. It was by far a woman's most socially legitimate option for economic survival. Take away the need, as liberal feminism seeks to do, and at least some of the want also disappears. One otherwise very traditional aunt of mine became a wealthy widow in her late fifties when my rich uncle died. She never remarried. Now a dynamic woman of 82 who travels widely and lives well, she confesses that no man has interested her enough to make it worthwhile to give up her freedom a second time. "I'm lucky," she confides, "I don't need a meal-ticket." Even a nonfeminist can understand what she is getting at.

5. Before assessing Sommers's overall views, let us rescue Scarlett O'Hara. Sommers's remark that Scarlett O'Hara's rape by Rhett Butler is a fate undreamt of in feminist philosophy is . . . simply stunning. (Note that Sommers does not use the word *rape* here—one of many omissions in her writings.) Even a passing knowledge of feminist philosophy

reveals that rape is hardly undreamt of in it.[11] Rape, of course, is not a dream; it is a nightmare. Any form of sexual aggression can involve coercion, intimidation, degradation, physical abuse, battering, and, in extreme cases, death.

The reality of rape is rendered invisible by the many novels and films, such as *Gone With the Wind*, which romanticize and mystify it. They portray the rapist as a handsome man whose domination is pleasurable in bed, and portray women as happy to have their own sexual choices and refusals crushed by such men. In a culture in which these sorts of portrayals are routine, it is no surprise that this scene arouses the sexual desire of some women. However, the name of Richard Speck,[12] to take one example, can remind us that real rape is not the pleasurable fantasy intimated in *Gone With the Wind*. To put the point graphically: Would "many women" still swoon over Butler's rape of O'Hara if they knew that he urinated on her? When you're the victim of rape, you don't have much choice over what goes on.

6. Let us move on to femininity. Sommers never spells out exactly what she means by femininity. For guidance on this topic, we could turn to literature in social psychology which identifies the important traits of femininity and which explores the social devaluation of the feminine (Eagly, 1987). However, it might be more revealing to turn to a different sort of "expert." By a lucky coincidence, I recently acquired a gem of a cultural artifact, a 1965 book entitled *Always Ask a Man: Arlene Dahl's Key to Femininity*, written by a rather well-known actress and model of the 1960s, Arlene Dahl. I have learned a great deal from this femininity manifesto.

As you might guess from the title, one guiding theme of the book, and of the femininity it aims to promote, is utter deference to the opinions of men. Dahl instructs the female reader: "Look at Yourself Objectively (try to see yourself through a man's eyes)" (p. 2). In Dahl's view, the "truly feminine" woman works "instinctively" at pleasing men and making men feel important. "When [a man] speaks to her, she listens with rapt attention to every word" (p. 5). Dahl believes that every woman has the capacity to measure up to men's ideals of femininity. This is because "Every woman is an actress. (Admit it!) Her first role is that of a coquette. (If you have any doubts just watch a baby girl with her father)" (p. 6).

Dahl's book is laced with quotations from male celebrities who are treated as incontrovertible authorities on what women should be like. Yul Brynner, for example, wants women to be good listeners who are not particularly logical (p. 3). Richard Burton likes women who are "faintly giggly" (p. 3). Tony Perkins thinks that a "girl should act like a girl and not like the head of a corporation—even if she is" (p. 8). The most revealing observation comes from George Hamilton: "A woman is often like a strip of film—obliterated, insignificant—until a man puts a light behind her" (pp. 5–6).

Surprisingly, some of the traits advocated for women by these male celebrities are actually valuable traits: honesty, straightforwardness, maturity, ingenuity, understanding, dignity, generosity, and humor. These traits are not distinctively feminine, however, and that may be the reason why they quickly disappear from Dahl's discussion. The twin themes that resound throughout this femininity manual are that of cultivating one's physical attractiveness and slavishly deferring to men. Instead of a chapter on honesty, a chapter on dignity, and so on, the book features chapters on every aspect of bodily grooming and adornment, including a separate chapter on each of the four basic categories of Caucasian hair color: blonde, redhead, "brownette," and brunette.

The slavish deference to men is crucial, since the whole point of the enterprise is to get a man. Thus, Dahl explains in the introduction that this book is written to counteract a tendency for women to dress to please other women, and it is also not for "women who want to be beautiful for beauty's sake. Such beauty serves no purpose, other than self-satisfaction, if that can be considered a purpose" (pp. x–xi).

The quintessential prohibition involved in femininity seems to be this: "NEVER upstage a man. Don't try to top his joke, even if you have to bite your tongue to keep from doing it. Never launch loudly into your own opinion on a subject—whether it's petunias or politics. Instead, draw out his ideas to which you can gracefully add your footnotes from time to time" (p. 12). Dahl is less sanguine than Sommers that the role of motherhood fits comfortably into a feminine life; she advises, "...don't get so involved with your role of MOTHER that you forget to play WIFE" (p. 9). Once married, your own interests should never override your husband's interests, job, and even hobbies, and, "There should be nothing that takes precedence in your day's schedule over making yourself

attractive and appealing for the man in your life," not even your "children's activities" (p. 175)!

Voila, femininity. Such servility shows the dubiousness of Sommers's claim that "a woman can be free of oppression and nevertheless feminine in the sense abhorred by many feminists" (1989a, 91).

7. Let us turn now to Sommers's overall philosophical defense of traditional marriage, family, and femininity. Having asserted that most women value or want all of these traditions, Sommers charges feminist views with a serious defect: They either dismiss or disparage these popular feminine wants and values.[13] Sommers herself defers to these alleged views of most women as if they were as such authoritative: Because "most women" (as she alleges) want traditional marriage and family, therefore these practices must be better than any alternatives. It is important to note that Sommers does not argue that traditional marriage and so on, on balance, promote important moral values better than any feminist alternatives.[14] No comprehensive moral comparisons appear in her writings. Her argument begins (and ends, as I will argue) with an appeal to popular opinion.

8. Is Sommers right about what "most women" think? She refers to no studies, no representative samples whatsoever to support her generalizations. Whole categories of women are patently excluded from her reference group and are invisible in her writings. This is a fitting moment to mention the "L" word—and I don't mean "liberal." Obviously, no lesbians, unless seriously closeted, are among Sommers's alleged majority of women who want "a man," conventional marriage, or a traditional family.

Even among nonlesbians, [many] women these days do not want a *traditional* marriage or a *traditional* family. Some heterosexual women simply do not want to marry or to have children at all, and many others want *nontraditional* marriages and *nontraditional* families. Surveys show that this attitude, and not the preference for tradition alleged by Sommers, is actually in the majority. In one 1983 study, 63 percent of women surveyed expressed preferences for nontraditional family arrangements (Sapiro, 1990, 355). Sommers's factual claims are, thus, debatable.

Even apart from questions of popularity, the wants, values, and enjoyments which Sommers attributes to "most women" are frankly suspicious as an ensemble. Candlelit dinners do not combine easily with babies. Dashing lovers (extramarital!) can be disastrous for a marriage. This list of wants and values seems to show a failure to separate what is idealized and mythic from what is (to put it very advisedly) authentic and genuinely possible in the daily reality of marital and family relationships over the long haul. To hear Sommers tell it, women are blandly unconcerned about wife-battering, incest, marital rape, or the profound economic vulnerability of the traditional non–income-earning wife. This is hard to believe. What is more likely is that, for many women, "... they got married and lived happily ever after" is only a fairy tale—especially for those who have been married for awhile. Even the most traditional of women, I am convinced, has some sense of the risks involved in traditional heterosexual relationships. As an old saying goes, "When two hearts beat as one, someone is dead."[15]

Sommers's list of women's wants and values is also woefully short. It suggests that this is *all* that "most women" want, that women's aspirations extend no farther than to being "feminine," getting a man—any man—and having babies. On the contrary, many women want meaningful and fulfilling work apart from childcare and domestic labor. Many women aspire to making a social contribution, or they have artistic impulses seeking expression, spiritual callings, deep friendships with other women, and abiding concerns for moral value and their own integrity.[16] One foundational motivation for feminism has always been the aim to overcome the *constraints* on women's genuinely wide-ranging aspirations posed by traditional marital and family arrangements.

9. What philosophical difference would it make if Sommers were right about women's wants and values in general? The popularity of an opinion is hardly an infallible measure of its empirical or moral credibility. Even popular opinions may be based on misinformation, unfounded rumor, and so on. Sommers ignores these possibilities and recommends that we defer to popular opinion on the basis of "... Mill's principle that there can be no appeal from a majority verdict of those who have experienced two alternatives" (1989a, 89–90). Sommers is evidently suggesting that feminist critiques of traditional family, marriage, and femininity should be judged by whether or not they conform to the "majority verdict of those who have experienced" the relevant alternatives. Now, carefully understood, this is actually not such a bad idea. However, rather than supporting Sommers's

deference to popular opinion, this principle repudiates it.

First, there are more than just "two" feminist alternatives to any of the traditions in question. Consider, for example, the traditionally married, heterosexual couple comprised of dominant, breadwinning male and domestic, childrearing female. Feminists have recommended various alternative family arrangements, including egalitarian heterosexual marriage, communal living, lesbian relationships, and single parenting when economic circumstances are favorable.[17] To decide the value of traditional marriage and family, one would have to try all the relevant alternatives—or at least *some* of them. And on Mill's view, merely experiencing alternatives is not enough; one must also be capable of "appreciating and enjoying" them (Mill, 1979, 9). If Sommers is right, however, most women want and choose traditional family, traditional marriage, and traditional femininity, and, thus, do not either experience or enjoy living according to any feminist alternatives. Women such as these are not what Mill calls "competent judges" of the value of those traditions since "they know only their own side of the question" (p. 10). And it is only from the verdict of *competent judges* that Mill believes that "there can be no appeal" (p. 11).

Second, of the "competent judges," in Mill's sense, that is, of the women who *have* experienced and enjoyed feminist alternatives to traditional marriage and family, most (I would wager) *prefer the feminist alternatives.* I am referring, among others, to women in lesbian relationships, and women in genuinely egalitarian heterosexual relationships. If I am right about this, then by Mill's principle, we must reject "popular opinion" along with traditional marriage and the rest.

10. The truth of the matter is that, in the end, Sommers does not rest her case on Mill's principle. Apparently without realizing that she changes her argument, she ends by appealing to something less vaunted than the majority verdict of those who have experienced and enjoyed *both* traditional family, etc., and various feminist alternatives. Her final court of appeal is simply to "what most people think," "common sense," and "tradition" itself (1989a, 95, 97). Sommers urges that "A moral philosophy that does not give proper weight to the customs and opinions of the community is presumptuous in its attitude and pernicious in its consequences" (1989a, 103). She speaks warmly of the Aristotelian conviction that

"traditional arrangements have great moral weight and that common opinion is a primary source of moral truth" (1989a, 83). When it comes to tradition, Sommers would do well to consider Mill again. Mill often deferred to tradition, but it was not a deference from which he thought there was "no appeal," as he amply demonstrated in the important *indictment* of nineteenth century marital traditions on which he collaborated with Harriet Taylor (Mill & Taylor, 1970). (It would be interesting to know what "pernicious . . . consequences," to use Sommers's phrase, flowed from Mill's and Taylor's critique.)

Tradition is a fickle husband. He is constantly changing his mind. On the grounds of tradition, eighty years ago, Sommers would have opposed women's suffrage. One hundred and fifty years ago, she would have opposed women speaking in public (She would have had to do so in private!), opposed the rights of married women to property in their own names, opposed the abolition of slavery, and so on. She would have supported wife-battering since it was permitted by legal tradition—so long as the rod was no bigger around than the size of the husband's thumb.

Not only is tradition ever-changing, it is also plural, both within our own society and globally. Which tradition shall we follow when there is more than one from which to choose? Islam is the world's most widely practiced religion. Shall we non-Islamic women heed the most globally numerous of our sisters' voices and don the veil, retire from public life, and allow husbands to marry up to four wives? Within our own society, marital traditions also vary. Shall we follow the traditions of orthodox Jewish and orthodox Catholic women and avoid all contraceptives? My maternal grandmother did so; she had fourteen births. At nine months per gestation, she spent ten and a half years of her life being pregnant. Although she lingered to the age of eighty-seven, she seemed even older than her age for the final sixteen, worn-out years in which I knew her. Doubtless, that too was part of her tradition.

Why suppose that there is special merit to any of the alternative traditions that we happen to have at this historical moment in this particular geopolitical location? Why suppose that any of our current traditions are better or more deserving of loyalty and support than the traditions toward which we are evolving? And how will we ever evolve if we remain deadlocked in loyalty to all of the traditions we happen to have today?

11. Sommers allows that our traditions may need reform and even recommends "piecemeal social engineering" to deal with "imperfections" in the family (1989a, 97)—although it is noteworthy that she never specifies what these imperfections are, and, in a different passage, she inconsistently calls upon American feminism to leave marriage and motherhood simply "untouched and unimpugned" (1989a, 91).[18] Nevertheless, she insists that her arguments are directed only against those radical feminists who seek the abolition of the family and the "radical reform of preferences, values, aspirations, and prejudices" (1990, 151, 148).

A serious concern to reform imperfections in the family should lead someone to consider the views of nonradical feminist reformers who also criticize marital and family traditions. Many feminists would be content with piecemeal family reform—so long as it was genuine reform (Thorne & Yalom, 1982; Okin, 1987, 1989). Anyway, this issue is a red herring. A dispute over the pace of reform does not show that radical feminist critiques of family traditions are wrong in substance. Most important, by allowing that change is *needed* in family traditions, Sommers effectively concedes that we should not automatically defer to tradition. To admit that reform of tradition is morally permissible is to reject tradition *per se* as an incontestable moral authority. The controversy can only be decided by directly evaluating the conditions of life established by marital and family traditions—and their alternatives.

12. Sommers has one final twist to her argument which we should consider. She notes briefly—all too briefly—that traditions "have *prima facie* moral force" so long as they are not "essentially unjust" (1989a, 97). Sommers does not explain what she means by "essential injustice." Just how much injustice makes a traditional practice "essentially unjust?"

Despite its vagueness, this concession to injustice is critically important. It makes the merit of Sommers's own appeal to tradition contingent on the essential noninjustice of the particular traditions in question. Sommers, however, provides no argument to establish that traditional marriage practices and so forth are not essentially unjust. Nor does she respond substantively to those feminist arguments which claim to locate important injustices in these traditional practices. She rejects all feminist criticisms of the traditional family because they do not coincide with "popular opinion," "common sense," or tradition. Traditional marriage and family are not essentially unjust, in Sommers's view, simply because most people allegedly do not *think* they are.

We seem to have come full circle. Sommers rejects feminist critiques of traditional marriage and so on because they are inconsistent with popular opinion, common sense, and tradition. Tradition is to be relied on, in turn, so long as it is not essentially unjust. But Sommers rejects feminist arguments to show injustices in marital and family traditions simply on the grounds that those arguments are inconsistent with popular opinion, common sense, and tradition itself. Sommers's defense of traditional marriage and family is, in the final analysis, circular and amounts to nothing more than simple *deference to tradition*—indeed, to particular traditions which are no longer so pervasive or popular as Sommers thinks.

13. One final concern: Sommers blames feminists for contributing to the growing divorce rate and the "disintegration of the traditional family."[19] However, feminism could only contribute to the divorce rate if married women ended their marriages as a result of adopting feminist ideas. If Sommers is right, however, in thinking that "most women" reject nonliberal feminist values, then nonliberal feminists could not be having a significant impact on the divorce rate. Sommers cannot have it both ways. Either feminism *is* significantly contributing to the growing divorce rate, in which case it must be in virtue of the wide appeal of feminist ideas about marriage and family, or feminist ideas do *not* have wide appeal, in which case they cannot be significantly contributing to the growing divorce rate.

14. To conclude: My overall assessment of Sommers's views on marriage, family, and femininity is grim.[20] Most important, Sommers rejects feminist views of marriage, family, and femininity ultimately on the basis of her own simple deference to (allegedly) popular opinion, common sense, and tradition. This deference is defensible only if feminist views about injustices in those traditions can be shown, on *independent* grounds, to be misguided— and Sommers never provides this independent argument.

Endnotes

1. Sommers: 1988, 1989a, 1989b, and 1990.
2. Cited in Thorne & Yalom, 1982, 5.
3. Sommers repudiates the feminist literature which explores the value of mothering (e.g., Trebilcot, 1984) on the grounds that it "remains largely hostile to traditional familial arrangements.' She also claims that this literature focuses only on an abstracted mother–child relationship, especially the mother–daughter relationship—a focus that "effectively excludes the male parent" (1989a, 92). Aside from inaccurately summarizing a body of literature, this latter comment, ironically, ignores the fact that under "traditional familial arrangements," the male parent plays a *negligible role* in day-to-day, primary childcare, especially in a child's early years.

The comment also ignores the work of Dorothy Dinnerstein (1977) and, especially, of Nancy Chodorow (1978), which precisely urges *shared parenting* and a prominent role for the male parent. This work has been extremely influential and widely cited among feminists. I suspect, however, that shared parenting is not the way in which Sommers wants to include the male parent, since this arrangement is not "traditional" and it challenges the idea of a "primary gender role" that Sommers appears to support (1989a, 92). Sommers, herself, thus fails to clarify the role of the male parent in her account.

4. Sommers complains that feminist philosophers have not been entrusted by ordinary women with a mission of speaking on behalf of those ordinary women (1989b, B3). Sommers, however, appears to think that she is thus entrusted, since she does not hesitate to make claims about what "most women . . . prefer," what "women actually want," and what "most women *enjoy*" (1989a, 90).
5. The following classification scheme is my own. The categories are not meant to be mutually exclusive.
6. Quotations are, respectively, from: 1989a, 90; 1989a, 91; and 1990, 150.
7. Quotations are, respectively, from: 1989a, 90; 1989a, 89; and 1989b, B3.
8. Quotations are, respectively, from: 1989a, 90; 1989a, 91; 1990, 150, italics mine; 1989b, B2; and 1989a, 91.
9. Quotations are, respectively, from: 1989a, 90; 1989a, 90; 1989a, 90; and 1990, 150.
10. Richards, 1980, 341–342. Quoted in Sommers, 1989a. 90–91.
11. Some important early papers are anthologized in: Vetterling-Braggin et al., 1977, Part VI. Another important, relatively early study is Brownmiller, 1976.
12. In 1966, Richard Speck stunned the city of Chicago and the nation by raping, killing, and, in some cases, mutilating the bodies of eight out of nine nursing students

who shared a house together on Chicago's South Side. The nurse who survived did so by hiding under a bed until Speck left the house after having apparently lost count. That woman might well swoon over Scarlett O'Hara's rape, but it would not be a swoon of ecstasy.

13. 1989a, 88–91. Sommers writes: "It is a serious defect of American feminism that it concentrates its zeal on impugning femininity and feminine culture at the expense of the grass root fight against economic and social injustices to which women are subjected" (p. 90). American feminism has hardly neglected the fight against economic or social injustice against women. Apart from that, the *Philosopher's Index* back to 1970 contains no citations of writings by Sommers herself on "the economic and social injustices to which women are subjected." In the essays reviewed here, she does not even identify the injustices she has in mind.

14. Sommers does warn that "many women" who avoid motherhood find themselves lonely (1989a, 90), and she suggests that those who avoid or divorce themselves from the patriarchal family "often" suffer harm and "might" feel "betrayed by the ideology" which led them to this state (1989b, B3). These faintly threatening suggestions are left unexplained and unsupported.

15. I was reminded of this old saying by an article by Janyce Katz (1990, 88) in which Dagmar Celeste, then the "First Lady of Ohio," is quoted as mentioning it.

16. Raising children involves awesome moral responsibilities, as Sommers herself emphasizes when lamenting the increasing divorce rate. These profound moral responsibilities entail that we should not casually reinforce the cultural ideology which declares that the only hope of women's fulfillment in life depends on their *having* chil-

dren. Sommers complains about divorce because of the harm it inflicts on children (1989a, 98–102), but she never cautions women to consider these moral obligations before marrying or having children in the first place.

17. Cf. Hunter College Women's Studies Collective, 1983, Ch. 9.

18. My worry is that Sommers's occasional, reasonable call for piecemeal family reform disguises a hidden agenda that aims to deadlock us in certain family traditions as we know them now (or knew them three decades ago). This appearance might be dispelled if she were to identify the imperfections she recognizes in the family.

19. 1989a, 82–83, 99–102. Sommers admits that "no reliable study has yet been made comparing children of divorced parents to children from intact families who [sic] parents do not get on well together." She claims cavalierly that "any such study would be compromised by some arbitrary measures of parental incompatibility and one could probably place little reliance on them" (1989a, 101). However, she ignores her own claims of limited evidence on this issue and argues as if it were fact that children of divorced parents are invariably worse off than if their parents had remained married.

When Sommers discusses the problem of divorce, she tends to assimilate the philosophical culprits onto one model: They are all wrong for disregarding "special duties" to family members, especially to children. This latter accusation is simply irrelevant in regard to feminists; no serious feminist literature suggests that responsibilities toward children should be disregarded.

20. Overall, her presentations are marred by ambiguities, inconsistencies, dubious factual claims, misrepresentations of feminist literature, and faulty arguments.

References

Brownmiller, Susan 1976. *Against Our Will: Men, Women and Rape.* New York: Bantam.

Chodorow, Nancy. 1978. *The Reproduction of Mothering.* Berkeley: University of California Press.

Dahl, Arlene. 1965. *Always Ask a Man: Arlene Dahl's Key to Femininity.* Englewood Cliffs, N.J.: Prentice-Hall.

Dinnerstein, Dorothy. 1977. *The Mermaid and the Minotaur: Sexual Arrangements and Human Malaise.* New York: Harper & Row.

Eagly, Alice.1987. *Sex Differences in Social Behavior.* Hillsdale, N.J.: Erlbaum.

Hunter College Women's Studies Collective. 1983. *Women's Realities, Women's Choices. New York: Oxford University Press.*

Katz, Janyce. 1990. "Celestial Reasoning: Ohio's First Lady Talks About Love and Feminism." *Ms: The World of Women,* 1, 2 (September/October), p. 88.

Mill, John Stuart. 1979. *Utilitarianism.* George Sher, ed. Indianapolis: Hackett.

Mill, John Stuart and Harriet Taylor. 1970. *Essays on Sex Equality.* Alice S. Rossi, ed. Chicago: University of Chicago Press.

Okin, Susan Moller. 1987. "Justice and Gender." *Philosophy & Public Affairs,* 16 (Winter), pp. 42–72.

———. 1989. *Justice, Gender, and the Family.* New York: Basic Books.

Richards, Janet Radcliffe. 1980. *The Sceptical Feminist.* Harmondsworth: Penguin.

Sapiro, Virginia. 1990. *Women in American Society.* Mountain View, Calif.: Mayfield Publishing Co.

Sommers, Christina. 1988. "Should the Academy Support Academic Feminism?" *Public Affairs Quarterly, 2,* 3 (July), 97–120.

———. 1989a. "Philosophers Against the Family." In: George Graham and Hugh LaFollette, eds. *Person to Person.* Philadelphia: Temple University Press, 82–105.

———. 1989b. "Feminist Philosophers Are Oddly Unsympathetic to the Women They Claim to Represent." *Chronicle of Higher Education,* October 11, pp. B2–B3.

———. 1990. "The Feminist Revelation," *Social Philosophy and Policy Center, 8,* 1 (Autumn), 141–158.

Thorne, Barrie, with Marilyn Yalom, eds. 1982. *Rethinking the Family.* New York: Longman.

Trebilcot, Joyce, ed. 1984. *Mothering: Essays in Feminist Theory.* Totowa, N.J.: Rowman and Allanheld.

Vetterling-Braggin, Mary, Frederick A. Elliston, and Jane English, eds. 1977. *Feminism and Philosophy.* Totowa, N.J.: Littlefield, Adams & Co.

---

25. Is Male Power Really a Myth?

WARREN FARRELL

Warren Farrell argues that the various ways that men lack power in society have not been recognized. He chronicles many ways in which he thinks that men lack power in society and concludes that there is a high degree of equality between the sexes.

The weakness of men is the facade of strength; the strength of women is the facade of weakness.[1]

There are many ways in which a woman experiences a greater sense of powerlessness than her male counterpart: the fears of pregnancy, aging, rape, date rape, and being physically overpowered; less socialization to take a career that pays enough to support a husband and children; less exposure to team sports and its blend of competitiveness and cooperation that is so helpful to career preparation; greater parental pressure to marry and interrupt career for children without regard for her own wishes; not being part of an "old boys" network; having less freedom to walk into a bar without being bothered. . . .

Fortunately, most industrialized nations have acknowledged these female experiences. Unfortunately, they have acknowledged only the female experiences—and concluded that women *have* the problem, men *are* the problem. Men, though, have a different experience. A man who has seen his marriage become alimony payments, his home become his wife's home, and his children become child-support payments for those who have been turned against him psychologically feels he is spending his life working for people who hate him. He feels desperate for someone to love but fears another marriage might ultimately leave him with another mortgage payment, another set of children turned against him, and deeper desperation. When called "commitment phobic," he doesn't feel understood.

When a man tries to keep up with payments by working overtime and is told he is insensitive, or tries to handle the stress by drinking and is told he is a drunkard, he doesn't feel powerful, but powerless. When he fears a cry for help will be met with "stop whining," or that a plea to be heard will be met with "yes, buts," he skips past *attempting* suicide as a cry for help, and just *commits* suicide. Thus men have remained the silent sex and increasingly become the suicide sex.

A Man's Gotta Do What a Man's Gotta Do

ITEM. Imagine: Music is playing on your car radio. An announcer's voice interrupts: "We have a special bulletin from the president." (For some reason, you decide not to switch stations.) The president announces, "Since 1.2 million American men have been killed in war, as part of my new program for equality, we will draft only women until 1.2 million American women have been killed in war."

In post offices throughout the United States, Selective Service posters remind men that only they must register for the draft. If the post office had a poster saying "A Jew's Gotta Do What a Jew's Gotta Do." . . . Or if "A Woman's Gotta Do . . ." were written across the body of a pregnant woman. . . .

The question is this: How is it that if any other group were singled out to register for the draft based merely on its characteristics at birth—be that group blacks, Jews, women, or gays—we would immediately recognize it as genocide, but when men are singled out based on their sex at birth, men call it power?

The single biggest barrier to getting men to look within is that what any other group would call powerlessness, men have been taught to call power. We don't call "male-killing" sexism; we call it "glory." We don't call the one *million* men who were killed or maimed *in one battle* in World War I (the Battle of the Somme[2]) a holocaust, we call it "serving the country." We don't call those who selected only men to die "murderers." We call them "voters."

Our slogan for women is "A Woman's Body, A Woman's Choice"; our slogan for men is "A Man's Gotta Do What a Man's Gotta Do."

The Power of Life

ITEM. In 1920 women in the United States lived one year longer than men.[3] Today women live *seven* years longer.[4] The male–female life-span gap increased 600 percent.

We acknowledge that blacks dying six years sooner than whites reflects the powerlessness of blacks in American society.[5] Yet men dying seven years sooner than women is rarely seen as a reflection of the powerlessness of men in American society.

Is the seven-year gap biological? If it is, it wouldn't have been just a one-year gap in 1920.

If men lived seven years *longer* than women, feminists would have helped us understand that life expectancy was the best measure of who had the power. And they would be right. Power is the ability to control one's life. Death tends to reduce control. Life expectancy is the bottom line—the ratio of our life's stresses to our life's rewards.

If power means having control over one's own life, then perhaps there is no better ranking of the impact of sex roles and racism on power over our lives than life expectancy. Here is the ranking:

Life Expectancy[6] as a Way
of Seeing Who Has the Power

Females (white)	79
Females (black)	74
Males (white)	72
Males (black)	65

The white female outlives the black male by almost fourteen years. Imagine the support for affirmative action if a 49-year-old woman were expected to die sooner than a 62-year-old man.

Suicide as Powerlessness

Just as life expectancy is [a good indicator] of power, suicide is one of the best indicators of powerlessness

ITEM. Until boys and girls are 9, their suicide rates are identical;

- from 10 to 14, the boys' rate is twice as high as the girls';

- from 15 to 19, four times as high; and

- from 20 to 24, six times as high.[7]

ITEM. As boys experience the pressures of the male role, their suicide rate increases 25,000 percent.[8]

ITEM. The suicide rate for men over 85 is 1,350 percent higher than for women of the same age group.

Here is the breakdown:

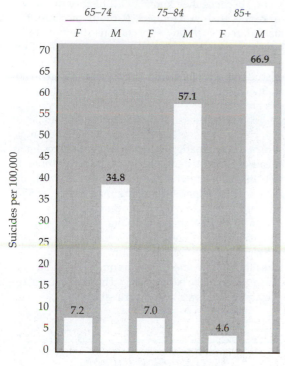

Suicide Rates: Men vs. Women
(per 100,000 Population). Source: National Center
for Health Statistics.[9]

The Invisible Victims of Violence

ITEM. When Rodney King was beaten by police, we called it violence against blacks, not violence against men. Had *Regina* King been beaten, would no one have mentioned violence against women?

Myth. Elderly women are the most susceptible to violent crime.

Fact. Elderly women are the *least* susceptible to violent crime. The U.S. Department of Justice finds that a woman over 65 is less likely to be a victim of violent crime than anyone else in any other category. And she is less than half as vulnerable as a man her own age.[10]

Myth. Women are more likely than men to be victims of violence.

Fact. Men are almost twice as likely as women to be victims of violent crimes (even when rape is *in-*

cluded).[11] Men are three times more likely to be victims of murder.[12]

When *Time* magazine ran a cover story of each of the 464 people shot in a single week, it concluded: "The victims were frequently those most vulnerable in society: the poor, the young, the abandoned, the ill, and the elderly."[13] When you read that, did you think of men? One had to count the pictures to discover that 84 percent of the faces behind the statistics were those of men and boys. In fact, the victims were mostly poor men, young men, abandoned men, ill men, and elderly men. Yet a woman—and only a woman—was featured on the cover. Men are the invisible victims of America's violence.

Net Worth Power

ITEM. The U.S. Census Bureau finds that women who are heads of households have a net worth that is 141 percent of the net worth of men who are heads of households.[14]

(The value of the net worth statistic is that it allows us to see what he and she have left when their different liabilities are subtracted from the different assets. The women's average net worth is $13,885; the men's is $9,883. This is because although male heads of households have higher gross incomes and assets, they have much higher spending obligations. They are much more likely to support wives [or ex-wives] than wives are to support them and thus their income is divided among themselves, a wife, and children—not only for food and housing but for tuition, insurance, vacations. Divorces often mean the woman receives the home the man pays for and also gets custody of the children the man pays for. A woman's obligation to spend more time with the children leaves her earning less and the man earning more but paying out more.)

ITEM. Among the wealthiest 1.6 percent of the U.S. population (those with assets of $500,000 or more), women's net worth is *more* than men's.[15]

How can so many of the wealthiest people be women when women hold none of the top corporate jobs? In part, by selecting the men who do and outliving them. And in part by having greater spending power and lower spending power obligations....

Spending Power

In my own examination of large shopping malls (including men's shops and sporting goods stores) I found that seven times as much floor space is devoted to women's personal items as to men's.[16] *Both* sexes buy more for women. The key to wealth is not in what someone earns: It is in what is spent on ourselves, at our discretion—or in what is spent on us, at our hint.

Overall, women control consumer spending by a wide margin in virtually every consumer category.[17] With spending power comes other forms of power. Women's control over spending gives them control over TV programs because TV is dependent on sponsors. When this is combined with the fact that women watch more TV in every time slot,[18] shows can't afford to bite the hand that feeds them. Women are to TV what bosses are to employees. The result? Half of the 250 made-for-TV movies in 1991 depicted women as victims—subjected to "some form of physical or psychological mistreatment."[19]

The "Spending Obligation Gap"

In restaurants, men pay for women about ten times as frequently as women pay for men—the more expensive the restaurant, the more often the man pays.[20] Women often say, "Well, men earn more." But when two women go to a restaurant, they don't assume that the woman who earns more will pay the bill. The expectation on men to spend more on women creates the "Spending Obligation Gap."

I got a sense of this "Spending Obligation Gap" as soon as I thought about my first date. As a teenager, I loved babysitting. (I genuinely loved kids, but it was also the only way I could get paid for raiding a refrigerator!) But then I got to the dating age. Alas, babysitting paid only fifty cents an hour. Lawn mowing, though, paid two dollars an hour. I hated lawn mowing. (I lived in New Jersey, where bugs, humidity, and noonday sun made mowing a lawn less pleasant than raiding a refrigerator.) But as soon as I started dating, I started mowing lawns.

For boys, lawn mowing is a metaphor for the way we soon learn to take jobs we like less because they pay more. Around junior year of high school, boys begin to repress their interest in foreign lan-guages, literature, art history, sociology, and anthropology because they know an art history major will make less than an engineer. Partially as a result of his different spending expectations (the possibility he might have to support a woman but cannot expect a woman to support him), more than 85 percent of students who take engineering as a college major are men; more than 80 percent of the art history majors are women.[21]

The difference in the earnings of the female art historian vs. the male engineer appears to be a measure of discrimination, when in fact both sexes knew ahead of time that engineering would pay more. In fact, the woman who enters engineering with the same lack of experience as the man averages $571 per year *more* than her male counterpart.[22]

In brief, the spending obligation that leads a man to choose a career he likes less that pays more is a sign of powerlessness, not power. But when he takes that job, women often assume he will pay because "after all, he earns more." Thus both sexes' expectations reinforce his powerlessness.

Influence Power

The Catholic church is often quoted as acknowledging, "Give us a child the first five years and we will shape its life." We acknowledge the influence power of the church over its youth; we often ignore the influence of a mother over her children—including her sons. But it is the mother who can make the child's bedtime earlier, take away desserts, or ground the child if it doesn't obey. It is the hand that rocks the cradle that creates the child's everyday heaven or hell.

Few men have a comparable amount of influence. While theoretically the man was "the master of the house," most men felt they were visitors in their wives' castle in the same way a woman would have felt like a visitor had she entered her husband's place of work. From a woman's perspective, a man's home is his castle; from a man's perspective, a woman's home is his mortgage.

Almost every woman had a primary role in the "female-dominated" family structure; only a small percentage of men had a primary role in the "male-dominated" governmental and religious structures. Many mothers were, in a sense, the chair of the board of a small company—their family. Even in

Japan, women are in charge of the family finances—a fact that was revealed to the average American only after the Japanese stock market crashed in 1992 and thousands of women lost billions of dollars that their husbands never knew they had invested.[23] Conversely, most men were on their company's assembly line—either its physical assembly line or its psychological assembly line.

Control-Over-Life Power

Influence power, though, is not real power. If we told mothers, "The more children you have, the more power you will have," they would laugh. If we then said, "The more children you have, the more everyone will love you and respect you," the mother would feel pressured, not empowered. But when we tell men, "The more people you supervise, the more power you will have," they buy it. Real power does not come from caving in to pressure to expand obligations, it comes from controlling our own life.

Historically, a husband spent the bulk of his day under the eye of his boss—his source of income; a wife did not spend the bulk of her day under the eye of her husband—her source of income. She had more control over her work life than he had over his.

Security Power

The prohibition against divorce gave a woman security in her workplace. Nothing gave a man security in his workplace. His source of income could fire him; her source of income could not fire her. Even today, if he quits his job, he doesn't get severance pay; if she initiates divorce, she takes half the "corporate stock."

"My Body, My Choice" Power

In the 1990s, if a woman and man make love and she says she is using birth control but is not, she has the right to raise the child without his knowing he even has a child, and then to sue him for retroactive child support even ten to twenty years later (depending on the state). This forces him to take a job with more pay and more stress and therefore earlier death. Although it's his body, he has no choice. He has the option of being a slave (working for another without pay or choice) or being a criminal. *Roe v. Wade* gave women the vote over their bodies. Men still don't have the vote over theirs—whether in love or war.

The Power of Appreciation

ITEM. The Mike Tyson trial. The hotel in which the jury is sequestered goes ablaze. Two firefighters die saving its occupants.

The trial of Mike Tyson made us increasingly aware of men-as-rapists. The firefighters' deaths did not make us increasingly aware of men-as-saviors. We were more aware of one man doing harm than of two men saving; of one man threatening one woman who is still physically alive than of dozens of men saving hundreds of people and two of those men being dead. In the United States, almost one million municipal firefighters *volunteer* to risk their lives to save strangers. Ninety-nine percent of them are men.[24] In exchange they ask only for appreciation. In exchange they are ignored.

The "Work Obligation Gap"

The media popularizes studies reporting women's greater amount of time spent on housework and childcare, concluding, "Women work two jobs; men work one." But this is misleading. Women do work more hours inside the home, but men work more hours outside the home. And the average man commutes farther and spends more time doing yardwork, repairs, painting. . . . What happens when all of these are combined? The University of Michigan's study (reported in the *Journal of Economic Literature* in 1991) found the average man worked sixty-one hours per week, the average woman fifty-six.[25]

Is this just a recent change in men? No. In 1975, the largest nationwide probability sampling of households found that when all childcare, all housework, all work outside the home, commuting, and gardening were added together, husbands did 53 percent of the total work, wives 47 percent.[26]

The Unpaid Bodyguard

ITEM. Steve Petrix was a journalist who lived near me in San Diego. Every day he returned home to have lunch with his wife. Recently, as he got near his door, he heard his wife screaming. She was being attacked with a knife. Steve fought the assailant off his wife. His wife ran to call the police. The intruder killed Steve. Steve was 31.[27]

A friend of mine put it this way: "What would you pay someone who agreed that, if he was ever with you when you were attacked, he would intervene and try to get himself killed slowly enough to give you time to escape? What is the hourly wage for a bodyguard? You know that is your job as a man—every time you are with a woman . . . any woman, not just your wife."[28]

What do men as women's personal bodyguards and men as volunteer firefighters have in common besides being men? They are both unpaid. Men have not yet begun to investigate their unpaid roles. . . .

Man as "Nigger"?

In the early years of the women's movement, an article in *Psychology Today* called "Women as Nigger" quickly led to feminist activists (myself included) making parallels between the oppression of women and blacks.[29] Men were characterized as the oppressors, the "master," the "slaveholders." Black congresswoman Shirley Chisholm's statement that she faced far more discrimination as a woman than as a black was widely quoted.

The parallel allowed the hard-earned rights of the civil rights movement to be applied to women. The parallels themselves had more than a germ of truth. But what none of us realized was how each sex was the other's slave in different ways and therefore *neither* sex was the other's "nigger" ("nigger" implies a *one-sided* oppressiveness).

If "masculists" had made such a comparison, they would have had every bit as strong a case as feminists. The comparison is useful because it is not until we understand how men were *also* women's servants that we get a clear picture of the sexual *division* of labor and therefore the fallacy of comparing either sex to "nigger." For starters . . .

Blacks were forced, via slavery, to risk their lives in cotton fields so that whites might benefit economically while blacks died prematurely. Men were forced, via the draft, to risk their lives on battlefields so that everyone else might benefit economically while men died prematurely. The disproportionate numbers of blacks and males in war increases both blacks' and males' likelihood of experiencing posttraumatic stress, of becoming killers in postwar civilian life as well, and of dying earlier. Both slaves and men died to make the world safe for freedom—someone else's.

Slaves had their own children involuntarily taken away from them; men have their own children involuntarily taken away from them. We tell women they have the right to children and tell men they have to fight for children.

Blacks were forced, via slavery, into society's most hazardous jobs; men are forced, via socialization, into society's most hazardous jobs. Both slaves and men constituted almost 100 percent of the "death professions." Men still do.

When slaves gave up their seats for whites, we called it subservience; when men give up their seats for women, we call it politeness. Similarly, we called it a symbol of subservience when slaves stood up as their master entered a room; but a symbol of politeness when men stand up as a woman enters the room. Slaves bowed before their masters; in traditional cultures, men still bow before women.[30] The slave helped the master put on his coat; the man helped the woman put on her coat. He still does. These symbols of deference and subservience are common with slaves to masters and with men to women.

Blacks are more likely than whites to be homeless; men are more likely than women to be homeless. Blacks are more likely than whites to be in prison; men are about twenty times more likely than women to be in prison. Blacks die earlier than whites; men die earlier than women. Blacks are less likely than whites to attend college or graduate from college. Men are less likely than women to attend college (46 percent versus 54 percent) and less likely to graduate from college (45 percent versus 55 percent).[31]

Apartheid forced blacks to mine diamonds for whites; socialization expected men to work in different mines to pay for diamonds for women. Nowhere in history has there been a ruling class working to afford diamonds they could give to the oppressed in hopes the oppressed would love them more.

Blacks are more likely than whites to volunteer for war in the hopes of earning money and gaining skills; men are more likely than women to volunteer for war for the same reasons. Blacks are more likely than whites to subject themselves to the child abuse of boxing and football in the hopes of earning money, respect, and love; men are more likely than women to subject themselves to the child abuse of boxing and football, with the same hopes.

Women are the only "oppressed" group to systematically grow up having their own private member of an "oppressor" class (called fathers) in the field, working for them. Traditionally, the ruling class had people in the field, working for them—called slaves.

Among slaves, the field slave was considered the second-class slave; the house slave, the first-class slave. The male role (out in the field) is akin to the field slave—or the second-class slave; the traditional female role (homemaker) is akin to the house slave—the first-class slave.

Blacks who are heads of households have a net worth much lower than heads of households who are white; men who are heads of households have a net worth much lower than heads of households who are women.[32] No oppressed group has ever had a net worth higher than the oppressor.

It would be hard to find a single example in history in which a group that cast more than 50 percent of the vote got away with calling itself the victim. Or an example of an oppressed group which chooses to vote for their "oppressors" more than it chooses to have its own members take responsibility for running. Women are the only minority group that is a majority, the only group that calls itself "oppressed" that is able to control who is elected to every office in virtually every community in the country. Power is not in who holds the office, power is in who chooses who holds the office. Blacks, Irish, and Jews never had more than 50 percent of America's vote.

Women are the only "oppressed" group to share the same parents as the "oppressor"; to be born into the middle class and upper class as frequently as the "oppressor"; to own more of the culture's luxury items than the "oppressor"; the only "oppressed" group whose "unpaid labor" enables them to buy most of the fifty billion dollars' worth of cosmetics sold each year; the only "oppressed" group that spends more on high fashion, brand-name clothing than their "oppressors"; the only "oppressed" group that watches more TV during every time category than their "oppressors."[33]

Feminists often compare marriage to slavery—with the female as slave. It seems like an insult to

women's intelligence to suggest that marriage is female slavery when we know it is 25 million American females[34] who read an average of *twenty* romance novels per *month*,[35] often with the fantasy of marriage. Are feminists suggesting that 25 million American women have "enslavement" fantasies because they fantasize marriage? Is this the reason Danielle Steele is the best-selling author in the world?

Never has there been a slave class that has spent a lot of time dreaming about being a slave and purchasing books and magazines that told them "How to Get a Slavemaster to Commit." Either marriage is something different from slavery for women or feminists are suggesting that women are not intelligent.

The difference between slaves and males is that African-American blacks rarely thought of their slavery as "power," but men were taught to think of their slavery as "power." If men were, in fact, slavemasters, and women slaves, then why did men spend a lifetime supporting the "slaves" and the "slaves'" children? Why weren't the women supporting the men instead, the way kings were supported by their subjects? Our understanding of blacks' powerlessness has allowed us to call what we did to blacks "immoral," yet we still call what we do to males "patriotism" and "heroism" when they kill on our behalf, but "violence," "murder," and "greed" when they kill the wrong people the wrong way at the wrong time.

By understanding that what we did to blacks was immoral, we were willing to assuage our guilt via affirmative action programs and welfare. By thinking of men as the dominant oppressors who do what they do for power and greed, we feel little guilt when they die early in the process. By believing that women were an oppressed slavelike class, we extended privileges and advantages to women that had originally been designed to compensate for our immorality to blacks. For women—and only women—to take advantage of this slavery compensation was its own brand of immorality. For men to cooperate was its own brand of ignorance.

Did men do all this because they were more altruistic, loving, and less power-hungry than women? No. *Both* sexes made themselves "slaves" to the other sex in different ways. Let's look at why both sexes did that; at why *neither* sex can accurately be called oppressed; at why we should be celebrating rather than blaming; and at why institutions that don't understand their new opportunities are adapting divisively because they don't understand how to adapt lovingly.

Endnotes

1. Lawrence Diggs, *Transitions*. Nov./Dec. 1990, p. 10.
2. The Battle of the Somme was in 1916. British casualties were 420,000; French were 195,000; German were 650,000. See John Laffin, *Brassey's Battles: 3,500 Years of Conflict, Campaigns, and Wars from A–Z* London: A. Wheaton & Co., 1986), p. 399.
3. 1920 statistics from the National Center for Health Statistics, *Monthly Vital Statistics Report*, vol. 38, no. 5, supplement, September 26, 1989, p. 4. In 1920, the life expectancy for men was 53.6 years; for women, 54.6 years.
4. Ibid., vol. 39, no. 13, August 28, 1991, p. 17. In 1990, women's average length of life was 78.8 years; men's, 72.0.
5. Ibid., vol. 38, no. 5, op. cit.
6. Ibid. The exact life span difference is 6.9 years between men and women. The life span for white females is 78.9; for black females, 73.6; for white males, 72.2; and for black males, 65.2.
7. U.S. Bureau of Health and Human Services, National Center for Health Statistics (hereinafter USBH&HS/NCHS), *Vital Statistics of the United States* (Washington, D.C.: USGPO, 1991), vol. 2, part A, "Mortality," p. 51, tables 1–9, "Death Rates for 72 Selected Causes by 5-Year Age Groups, Race, and Sex: U.S., 1998." The exact rates are:

Suicide Rates by Age and Sex per 100,000 Population

Age	Male	Female
5–9	0.1	0.0
10–14	2.1	0.8
15–19	18.0	4.4
20–24	25.8	4.1

8. The 25,000 percent figure is derived by comparing the 0.1 suicides per 100,000 boys under the age of nine to the 25.8 suicides per 100,000 boys between ages 20–24 in the table in the endnote above, from ibid.
9. Latest data available as of 1992. From USBH&HS/NCHS, *Vital Statistics of the United States*, vol. 2, "Mortality," part A, 1987.
10. Among those over the age of 65, 2.7 women per 1,000 and 6.2 men per 1,000 are victims of crimes of violence. U.S. Bureau of Justice Statistics, Office of Justice Programs, Bureau of Justice Statistics, *Criminal Victimization in the United States, 1988*, National Crime Survey Report NCJ-122024, December 1990, p. 18, table 5.
11. Ibid., *1987*, publication NCJ-115524, June 1989, p. 16, table 3, "Personal Crimes, 1987."
12 Ibid.
13. "7 Deadly Days," *Time*, July 17, 1989, p. 31.
14. These are the latest data available (as of 1992). It is from U.S. Department of Commerce, Bureau of the Census, *Statistical Abstracts of the United States, 1989,* 109th edition, p. 459, table 747—"Household Net Worth—Median Value of Holdings: 1984." Their source is U.S. Department of Commerce, Bureau of the Census, *Current Population Reports,* ser. P-70, no. 7. Since women's income has *increased* relative to men's since 1985, the gap is likely to be even greater when the next data are released. The Census Bureau defines head of household (or householder) as any person in whose name a home is owned or rented. Prior to 1980, this used to be the husband in married couple households. Now it is either the husband or wife, doubtless more often still the husband in homes where the man is earning *more.*
15. The wealthiest women's net worth averages $1.17 million; the wealthiest men's averages $1.11 million. Bases on the latest data available from the Internal Revenue Service as of 1990. See the *Los Angeles Times,* August 23, 1990.
16. My examination of large shopping malls was in the San Diego area in 1985. I did a rough measurement of the approximate floor space of departments and special "boutiques" that offered male personal items (men's suits, sporting goods, etc.) vs. female personal items, on the assumption that if women's or men's departments were not creating enough profit per foot, they would be forced to give way to general departments or those of the other sex. In addition, I found that the more valuable floor space (e.g., perfume counters immediately as we enter a department store) was devoted to women's items.
17. See Diane Crispell, "The Brave New World," *American Demographic*, January 1992, p. 38. The article concludes that women dominate consumer spending in personal items, cleaning supplies and housewares, and food. In the category of furniture/cars, it is close to even—men have only a technical dominance.
18. A. C. Nielsen ratings, 1984.
19. Harry F. Waters, "Whip Me, Beat Me, and Give Me Great Ratings," *Newsweek,* November 11, 1991.
20. This is based on my own informal discussions with waiters in restaurants around the country in cities where I speak.
21. Also, 86 percent of engineering *graduates* are men; 83 percent of art history graduates are women. Unpublished information, U.S. Department of Education, Office of Educational Research and Improvement, National Center for Education Statistics, "IPEDS Completions Study," 1989, 1990. Interview on June 1, 1992, with Norman Brandt of the U.S. Office of Education.

22. The starting salary for a female engineer exceeds that for a man by $571 per year. See the Engineering Manpower Commission's *Women in Engineering* (Washington, D.C.: American Association of Engineering Society [AAES]), EMC Bulletin no. 99, December 1989, table 5.

23. Sonni Effron, "Honey, I Shrunk the Nest Egg," *Los Angeles Times,* June 20, 1992, front page.

24. In an interview on February 11, 1992, John Oddison of the Government's United States Fire Administration reported that *99 percent of volunteer municipal firefighters are men.* Of all municipal firefighters, 964,000 are volunteers and 240,000 are career.

25. F. Thomas Juster and Frank P. Stafford, "The Allocation of Time: Empirical Findings, Behavioral Models, and Problems of Measurement," *Journal of Economic Literature,* vol. 29, June 1991, p. 477. Her average hours both inside and outside the home add up to fifty-six; his, to sixty-one.

26. Martha Hill, *Patterns of Time Use in Time, Goods, and Well-Being* (Ann Arbor: Institute for Social Research, University of Michigan, 1985), ed. F. Thomas Juster and Frank P. Stafford. See also Joseph H. Pleck, *Working Wives/Working Husbands* (Beverly Hills: Sage Publications, 1985), p. 41, table 2.3.

27. Carol J. Castañeda, *San Diego Union,* May 21, 1988.

28. Frederic Hayward, "The Male's Unpaid Role: Bodyguard and Protector," as reprinted in Francis Baumli, Ph.D., *Men Freeing Men* (Jersey City, N.J.: New Atlantis Press, 1985), p. 238.

29. Naomi Weisstein, "Women as Nigger," *Psychology Today,* vol. 3, no. 5, October 1969, p. 20. This article is considered a classic of feminist literature. See, for example, Wendy Martin, *The American Sisterhood: Writings of the Feminist Movement from Colonial Times to the Present* (New York: Harper & Row, 1972), pp. 292–98.

30. Credit to Lawrence Diggs for some of these ideas related to symbols of deference, contained in his audiotape called "Introduction to Men's Issues" (P.O. Box 41, Roslyn, SD 57261).

31. U.S. Department of Education, National Center for Education Statistics, *Digest of Education Statistics 1991,* p. 167, table 161, "Total Enrollment in Institutions of Higher Education" shows that women are 54 percent of those enrolled in college; p. 234, table 228, "Earned Degrees Conferred by Institutions of Higher Education," shows that women are 55 percent of those receiving bachelors' degrees from college.

32. Women who are heads of households have a net worth 141 percent greater than that of men who are heads of households. This is the latest data available from the Bureau of the Census as of 1992. See U.S. Department of Commerce, Bureau of the Census, *Statistical Abstracts of the United States, 1989,* op. cit.

33. A. C. Nielsen ratings, 1984.

34. Interview, February 18, 1985, with John Markert, independent researcher and contributor to *Romantic Times* and author of "Marketing Love," dissertation in progress.

35. *Forbes* reports that the average romance novel buyer spent $1,200 in 1991. The average romance costs about $5 in 1991, leading to the purchase of approximately 240 books a year, or 20 books per month. For women who also read their friends' books, the number of books they read is more than 20 per month; for women who do not do this but buy some hardcovers, the figure is less than 20 per month. See Dana Wechsler Linden and Matt Rees, "I'm hungry. But not for food," *Forbes,* July 6, 1992, pp. 70–75.

26. Why So Slow?

Virginia Valian

Virginia Valian seeks to explain the nearly invisible factors, which she calls gender schemas, that retard women's progress. Valian thinks that once these factors have been exposed and corrected, fair and accurate evaluations of men and women will, for the first time, become possible. She argues that the existence of successful women does no more than show that some women are evaluated positively some of the time. It does not show what fairness requires, which is that there be no consistent advantage for men relative to women.

The term *glass ceiling* has become a popular way of referring to the scarcity of women at the top levels of organizations. The phrase suggests that invisible factors—as much as, or more than, overt discrimination—keep women from rising to the top. It also assumes that those hidden influences are unlikely simply to disappear over time; a ceiling is not a structure that evanesces. Finally, the term suggests that women's job performance is at least the equal of their male peers'; a ceiling is something that keeps people down despite their competence. All three assumptions, I will argue, are correct. There *are* invisible barriers; they will not go away on their own; any objective differences in performance are insufficient to explain existing sex differences in salary, rank, and rates of promotion.

There are also, of course, visible problems for women in the workplace, of which sexual assault and harassment are the most obvious examples. I do not discuss those abuses, despite their importance, because I want to explain women's lack of achievement in situations where nothing seems to be wrong. Even in apparently egalitarian environments, women do not advance as far or as rapidly as men. Something invisible limits their progress.

But if there are invisible factors at work, what are they, and how do they operate? My goal is to make the invisible visible: to show what retards women's progress, so that fair and accurate evaluations of men and women will become possible. To do so, I draw on concepts and data from psychology, sociology, economics, and biology.

Reprinted from *Why So Slow?* (1998) by permission of MIT Press.

What Holds Up the Glass Ceiling?

Gender Schemas

[My] central thesis . . . is that a set of implicit, or nonconscious, hypotheses about sex differences plays a central role in shaping men's and women's professional lives. These hypotheses, which I call *gender schemas*, affect our expectations of men and women, our evaluations of their work, and their performance as professionals.[1] Both men and women hold the same gender schemas and begin acquiring them in early childhood. Their most important consequence for professional life is that men are consistently overrated, while women are underrated. Whatever emphasizes a man's gender gives him a small advantage, a plus mark. Whatever accentuates a woman's gender results in a small loss for her, a minus mark.

We are accustomed to calling our conceptions of certain groups *stereotypes*. The word is misleading, for it implies that something is fundamentally wrong with having such concepts. But hypothesis formation is a natural and essential human activity; it is the way we make sense of the world. We all form hypotheses about social groups. Such hypotheses may contain primarily positive characteristics, mostly negative ones, only neutral ones, or some combination of all three. The word *stereotype* refers to one kind of hypothesis, but *schema* is a better, more inclusive, term. It is not the attempt to develop schemas that is wrong, but the errors that can inadvertently creep into the formation, maintenance, and application of schemas.

Gender schemas are usually unarticulated. Their content may even be disavowed. Most men and women in the professions and academia explicitly, and sincerely, profess egalitarian beliefs. Conscious beliefs and values do not, however, fully control the operation of nonconscious schemas. Egalitarian beliefs help, but they do not guarantee accurate, objective, and impartial evaluation and treatment of others. Our interpretations of others' performance are influenced by the unacknowledged beliefs we all—male and female alike—have about gender differences.

Although most people want to judge fairly, genuine fairness demands that we understand that our reactions to an individual are, inevitably, affected by the group the person belongs to. Our implicit ideas about men and women as a whole condition our reactions to men and women as individuals. Only by recognizing how our perceptions are skewed by nonconscious beliefs can we learn to see others, and ourselves, accurately. Fairness requires a more sophisticated understanding of social perception than most of us acquire in the ordinary course of life. To be really fair, we need to know what perceptual distortions are likely and what steps we can take to perceive others more accurately.

Thus, although this [reading] is about a particular set of schemas, it can also be seen as a case study of the more general problem of ensuring fair evaluations for members of any group. Schemas based on sex, age, race, class, or sexual orientation have different contents, but all schemas influence how we perceive and treat group members. Only by discovering a schema's content and mode of operation can we make our evaluations of individuals fairer.

Accumulation of Advantage

The long-term consequences of small differences in the evaluation and treatment of men and women also hold up the glass ceiling. A useful concept in sociology is the accumulation of advantage and disadvantage (J. Cole & Singer 1991; Fox 1981, 1985; Long 1990; Merton 1968).[2] It suggests that, like interest on capital, advantages accrue, and that, like interest on debt, disadvantages also accumulate. Very small differences in treatment can, as they pile up, result in large disparities in salary, promotion, and prestige. It is unfair to neglect even minor instances of group-based bias, because they add up to major inequalities.

A computer model of promotion practices at a hypothetical corporation convincingly demonstrates the cumulative effects of small-scale bias (Martell, Lane, & Emrich 1996). The simulation created an organization with an eight-level hierarchy staffed at the bottom level by equal numbers of men and women. The model assumed that over time a certain percentage of incumbents would be promoted from one level to the next. It also assumed a tiny bias in favor of promoting men, a bias accounting for only 1 percent of the variability in promotion. The researchers ran the simulation through a series of promotions. After many series, the highest level in the hierarchy was 65 percent male. The model shows clearly that even minute disadvantages can have substantial long-term effects.

In fact, the simulation *under*estimates the problem women have in rising to the top, for it reflects only what occurs at the stage of promotion. At every point along the path to the first promotion possibility, however, advantages or disadvantages can accumulate. If conditions for women are only very slightly unfavorable along the way, they are less likely even to be considered for promotion.

One example of how advantage and disadvantage can accrue occurs in a common professional setting—the meeting. Let's say I am attending a meeting with a group of people who know each other but whom I have never met. I notice that some people's comments are taken seriously by the group, while other people's are ignored. Although my assessment of individual participants is formed in part by my own evaluation of the content of their remarks, I cannot always independently evaluate that content. Further, I am likely to be influenced by the reactions of others in the group. Through observing the group dynamics, I learn who has high status and who does not. By the time the meeting ends, people who were equal in my eyes when it began are unequal.

Those whose remarks were ignored have suffered a small loss in prestige, and their contributions have been labeled, implicitly, as low in value. Because they now have less prestige, they will be listened to less in the future; they will carry their previously earned labels into the next professional encounter, losing a little more standing with each negative experience. The gap between them and people who are gaining attention for their remarks will widen as their small initial failures accrue and make future failures more likely.

Successful people seem to recognize that one component of professional advancement is the ability to parlay small gains into bigger ones. Ambitious people worry if their comments are ignored and are pleased if they are taken seriously. A series of disregarded comments can signal failure, while remarks discussed by superiors and coworkers contribute to success. If everyone understood explicitly what some people understand implicitly—that success comes from creating and consolidating small gains—no one would counsel women to ignore being ignored. The concept of the accumulation of advantage lets us see that the well-meaning advice often given to women—not to make a mountain out of a molehill—is mistaken. That advice falls to recognize that mountains *are* molehills, piled one on top of the other. Fairness requires appreciating the importance of each molehill of advantage and disadvantage and taking steps to ensure that molehills do not accrue to individuals on the basis of their group membership.

But even that is not enough. Everyone must also understand that in most organizations women begin at a slight disadvantage. A woman does not walk into the room with the same status as an equivalent man, because she is less likely than a man to be viewed as a serious professional. Moreover, since her ideas are less likely to be attended to than a male peer's, she is correspondingly less likely to accumulate advantage the way he might. A woman who aspires to success *needs* to worry about being ignored; each time it happens she loses prestige and the people around her become less inclined to take her seriously.

The concept of the accumulation of advantage explains another, otherwise puzzling, difference between men and women: women talk less in public and professional settings than men do (see discussion in Haslett, Geis, & Carter 1992).[3] Let us assume that women know—through experience—that their remarks are likely to be ignored. They may then correctly infer that they are better off not speaking and staying at their current level than making a comment and accruing a disadvantage. Saying nothing exacts its own toll, for no one acquires prestige through silence. Still, the tacit loss brought about by saying nothing is smaller than the explicit loss of prestige incurred by speaking and being ignored. A slower accumulation of disadvantage is, on a rational analysis, preferable to a faster accumulation of disadvantage. I am not suggesting that women explicitly or consciously formulate such a policy, only that it *is* rational: women risk less disadvantage overall by remaining silent. (We can

also interpret women's behavior more simply: being ignored is painful and humiliating, and people seek to avoid pain.)

This may be a good time to emphasize that, although I speak of *women,* I am not claiming that what is true of women in general is true of every woman on every occasion. Nor do I argue that men are never ignored in favor of women. At a recent faculty meeting, in fact, I observed a reversal of the usual effect. The chair of my department gave me the credit for an excellent comment that a junior male colleague had made earlier in the meeting. (I was so bemused and amused by the reversal that I failed to correct him.) The exceptions should not, however, obscure the rule. The existence of an exceptional woman who frequently speaks out in public settings and whose contributions are acknowledged and valued does not invalidate the rule that women in general have lower professional status than men and are less likely than men to profit from their positive contributions.

Schemas, Exceptions, and Fairness

Several problems are encountered in efforts to ensure fairness. One of them is convincing ourselves that our judgments really are prone to error. We all want to believe we are unbiased and unaffected by stereotypes we have consciously rejected. We are convinced that we know quality when we see it. Even people who are overtly prejudiced think they can judge others impartially; the facts, they believe, speak for themselves.

A compelling laboratory experiment, however, demonstrates that people are unable to evaluate others accurately, even when a completely straightforward quality like height is involved (Biernat, Manis, & Nelson 1991). In this experiment, college students were shown photographs of various people and asked to guess their heights in feet and inches (including shoes). The photos always contained a reference item, such as a desk or a doorway, to help students with their estimates.

Without telling the students, the experimenters chose the test items so that every photograph of a male student of a given height was matched by a picture of a female student of the same height. Here, then, was an easily visible characteristic that could be measured in objective units—feet and inches—rather than in subjective terms like *short* and *tall.* The students' judgments should have been accurate.

They were not. They were affected by one component of gender schemas—the knowledge that men are, on average, taller than women. When exposed to a sample contrary to the general rule, the students saw the women as shorter and the men as taller than they actually were.

Using a scale marked in objective units does not, therefore, prevent error. (Of course, if the students had had an actual ruler they could have estimated the heights more accurately.) If people have a schema about gender differences, that schema spills over into their judgments. The problem is exacerbated when the schema is accurate—as it is in the case of height differences—because erroneous judgments of individuals are supported by real overall differences between groups. Individuals who diverge from the schema are perceived in the light of the observers' schemas. The implications for judgments of professional competence are clear. Employers faced with a man and a woman matched on the qualities relevant to success in a particular field may believe they are judging the candidates objectively. Yet, if their schemas represent men as more capable than women, they are likely to overestimate the male's qualifications and underestimate the female's.

A second problem in the attempt to ensure fair evaluations is that people find creative ways to justify their perceptions. To take one example, to reassure themselves—and others—that they have rejected stereotypical attitudes or can judge fairly in spite of them, people point to professional women they admire and respect. For another example, people point to women who are successful as evidence that hiring and promotion practices are based on merit. Finally, people use examples of incompetent women to explain women's overall lack of success.

Such examples, however, are irrelevant if they are not representative of the general population. My claim is that they are not. They are atypical—exceptions to a general rule confirmed by the preponderance of the evidence. Examples that represent exceptions do not refute general findings. For instance, on Wall Street in 1996 only 8 percent of the managing directors were women (Truell 1996). Each of the women in that 8 percent is an exception someone might cite as evidence that women can succeed in the investment business. Invalidation of a general rule, however, requires proof that the rule typically does not hold; it is not good enough to show that it occasionally fails to apply. The existence of successful women shows that *some* women are evaluated positively *some* of the time. Fairness demands much more: the guarantee that there is no consistent advantage for members of one group relative to another.

Gender Schemas at Work

Keeping in mind the obstacles to ensuring fairness, we can consider the story of a university department. During the past ten years fifteen men and three women were added to the faculty. When he is queried about the ratio, the chair of the department explains that his only interest is to hire the best, most able, people in order to build the strongest possible department. He makes it clear to search committees that quality is the only issue, and informs them of his views of the candidates. He is sincere in his belief that he is gender-blind and confident of his ability to judge others' competence. And, since the people he chooses *are* able, he has no reason to doubt his judgment or leadership. Even if he were to track the careers of the women he failed to hire, he would probably not question his decisions. Those women are likely to have been undervalued by other prospective and actual department chairs and to have, as a result, careers that are on average less stellar than those of the men he hired.

For the chair to see that the facts call for more self-doubt, he needs an education in social cognition and gender. He needs, first, to learn that people are likely to misperceive men and women in professional settings, to overrate the former and underrate the latter. Clear marks of prestige, ranging from having a degree from an elite institution to sitting at the head of a table, are interpreted differently, depending on whether the person is a man or a woman. Even judgments of height, as described earlier, are affected by the person's gender.

Second, the chair needs to understand how errors of evaluation mount up over time and affect the career trajectories of young professionals and Ph.D.s. Data suggesting that women must meet higher standards than men to gain promotion, partnership, or tenure demonstrate the detrimental consequences of the accumulation of disadvantage, showing for example, that only a few years after earning their degrees, young men and women with the same on-paper qualifications have different professional lives. Finally, the chair needs to learn how expectations of men's and women's achievements can affect their actual performance, as well as their aspirations.

He needs, in short, to see that his confidence is misplaced, that it is the product of ignorance. He is unlikely to be exempt from the processes that affect everyone else, unlikely to have equally high expectations of men and women, and unlikely to know how to change his perceptions and decisions to adjust for the advantages men have incorrectly received. He believes he is different, but that is what everyone thinks—just as we all think we are above average. Even those who are actively concerned about gender equality are affected by gender schemas; the odds are that he is, too. As a good scholar, he should entertain the possibility that his judgments are skewed and consider what steps he can take to make them more accurate. He needs, in sum, a better theory and better data. Then he can be more alert to the pitfalls inherent in making judgments about ability.

Not long ago, a new grandfather happened to read a draft of chapter 2, "Gender Begins—and Continues—at Home" [of *Why So Slow?*], just before meeting his infant granddaughter for the first time. As he held her in his arms he said automatically, "You're so soft"—which of course she was. As the words reverberated in his ear, they reminded him of the data he had just read about fathers' misperceptions of infants' characteristics. He paused, squeezed the baby gently, and added, "and firm"—which of course she also was. There is nothing like observing yourself in the act of an inaccurate or partial perception to engender humility about your freedom from gender schemas and to help you change your perceptions. . . .

The Origins and Effects of Gender Schemas
Childhood Learning

Where do ideas about sex differences come from? Expectations about gender differences, and plans to inculcate them, occur even before children are born. Here's a conversation between a man and a woman who are thinking of having a baby:

SHE: If we have a girl, I'll get her a truck.

HE: Of course.

SHE: If we have a boy, I'll get him a doll.

HE: Well, . . . if he *asks* for one.

Infancy and childhood are a critical period for the development of implicit hypotheses and expectations about the self and others. Small children observe unequal divisions of labor between men and women—both in the home and in the wider world—and notice that adults treat girls and boys differently. Like adults, children search for explanations of the differences they observe, aided by what they are implicitly—and sometimes explicitly—taught. As the conversation quoted above suggests, children are provided with data that require an explanation, such as paternal readiness to give a girl a truck and paternal reluctance to give a boy a doll. The explanation suggested to children, and the one they arrive at themselves, is that there is a causal link between their biology (about which they understand very little) and their talents, interests, preferences, attitudes, and behaviors. Children learn very early that they are not simply children, they are boys and girls. . . .

Saying that children *learn* to be boys and girls does not deny the possibility there are biologically based differences above and beyond reproductive capacity and the organs that mediate reproductive behavior. In some domains, such as rough-and-tumble play and skill at mentally rotating three-dimensional figures, there is good evidence that hormonal differences are important. But in every domain—including those with a clear hormonal influence—there is good evidence for social and cultural influences. Neither biology nor society act alone, nor could they. . . .

Sex, Gender, and Schemas

The terms *male/female, man/woman,* and *boy/girl* distinguish people on the basis of their reproductive role, but do not imply that the characteristics of those groups are due to that role. If, for example, I refer to the superior spelling skills of females, I am not implying a link between the female reproductive role and spelling, though there may conceivably be one. Rather, I am saying that the people we single out on the basis of their having XX chromosomes are superior at spelling to those we single out on the basis of their having XY chromosomes. The difference in spelling skill may be partly influenced by chromosomal status, or it may be solely influenced by differences in how we treat people with XX status versus XY status; females may be especially good at spelling for reasons that have no direct link to their chromosomes. The term *sex difference,* then, refers to a difference between males and females, with no implication that the difference noted is directly linked to chromosomal or reproductive status.

When I speak of *gender,* on the other hand, I am highlighting our psychological and social conceptions of what it means to be a man or a woman. Thus, the term *gender schemas* refers to our intuitive hypotheses about the behaviors, traits, and preferences of men and women, boys and girls. Correspondingly, the term *gender roles* refers to our ideas about how men and women are expected to behave. In sum, *sex* is used to categorize people into two groups, and *gender* is used to describe our beliefs about sex-based categories.[4]

In discussing the contents of gender schemas I sometimes use the adjectives masculine and feminine. When I mention *masculine* characteristics, I refer to the characteristics we traditionally associate with men. I do not mean to suggest that only men have those characteristics. Similarly, if I talk about *feminine* toys, I am referring to toys seen as appropriate for girls to play with. I do not intend to suggest that there is anything inherently suitable for girls or unsuitable for boys about feminine toys. I am indicating only that those toys are seen as the "right" toys for girls. Although I am sometimes tempted to put quotation marks around the words feminine and masculine—to indicate that I do not believe such traits are inherently more natural for women or men—I do not do so. In my terminology, the words are part of gender schemas, part of our belief systems, not a description of the way things are.

Expressions in popular culture, such as "Real men don't eat quiche," are not intended as biological claims. Instead, they are comments about our notions of masculinity and femininity. The idea of a really good example of something—a "real" man or "real" woman—occurs with other concepts as well. For example, people judge the number 2 as a "better" even number than the number 736. At the same time, people agree that both numbers are even numbers and that it is ridiculous to talk of one even number being better than another (Armstrong, Gleitman, & Gleitman 1983). But 2 is psychologically a better example of evenness than 736 is; it is closer to our prototype of what even numbers are. Similarly, at least in North America, men who don't eat quiche are closer to our prototype of what men are than men who do.

The Cognition of Gender

Reproductive status is one way of distinguishing people. It is a distinction most cultures find psychologically compelling, and around which they form the implicit hypotheses I call gender schemas. As I mentioned earlier, all humans form implicit hypotheses to explain their social world.[5] Whenever there is an observable difference between social groups, people develop hypotheses to explain the difference and look for data to support their hypotheses. Hypothesis-formation and hypothesis-testing are natural and valuable human activities. Human cognition seeks explanations of physical and social phenomena. . . .

The sexual division of labor is one example of a social phenomenon. One way to explain and justify it is to appeal to differences in men's and women's natures (Eagly 1987; Hoffman & Hurst 1990). To explain and justify the fact, for example, that almost all engineers are men and almost all homemakers are women, people may say that men have traits and abilities that fit them to be engineers and cause them to choose engineering over homemaking, and women have traits and abilities that fit them to be homemakers and cause them to choose homemaking over engineering.

Such an explanation is an implicit appeal to the deterministic power of built-in, essential differences. . . . [T]here is no evidence in favor of such a picture and considerable evidence against it. There are built-in differences, but biology is not destiny. Biology is one factor in a multifactor equation. In considering the role of hormones in physical and cognitive differences between males and females . . . , I try to avoid both extremes of an increasingly polarized discussion. Biology is not destiny, but neither is the social environment. Neither determines behavior; both influence it.

Our cognitions—how we interpret information, store it in memory, reason with it, draw inferences from it—are yet another important factor. The role of cognition in our everyday understanding of sex differences has not, I think, been adequately examined. In this [reading] I am proposing that cognitive processes are at the heart of our conception of sex differences and help to create and maintain the inequalities among us.

Expectations and Gender Traits

Having attributed different traits and behaviors to men and women to explain the sexual division of labor, people then treat men and women in accordance with their expectations about those characteristics, setting in motion a self-fulfilling prophecy (Merton

1948; Rosenthal & Jacobson 1968). All of us—boys and girls, men and women—become in part what others expect us to become, thereby confirming hypotheses about the different natures of males and females. While no one is infinitely malleable, no one is completely indifferent to others. One way we learn who we are is through others' responses to us. As men and women, we also develop expectations for our own behavior, based on characteristics we believe we possess. We then explain our successes and failures in terms of those abilities and traits. . . .

In white, western, middle-class society, the gender schema for men includes being capable of independent, autonomous action (agentic, in short), assertive, instrumental, and task-oriented. Men act. The gender schema for women is different; it includes being nurturant, expressive, communal, and concerned about others. (Bakan 1966; Spence & Helmreich, 1978; Spence & Sawin 1985). Women nurture others and express their feelings. Men who are nurturant and emotionally expressive are perceived as feminine; women who are agentic and assertive are seen as masculine. Schemas are not wholly inaccurate: on the whole, men have more masculine traits than feminine ones; women have more feminine traits than masculine ones.

But gender schemas oversimplify. Masculine and feminine traits are not opposites of each other; they are not contradictory. Everyone has both to some degree and expresses different traits in different situations. Differences exist, but the sexes are more alike than they are different. It is easy to lose sight of that reality, even though most differences between the sexes are small.

In college I took a vocational-interests test in a psychology course. This test supposedly matched people's dominant interests and traits with different occupations. At the time, I was planning to become a clinical psychologist—not that I knew exactly what that meant—and I had a male friend, Richard, who wanted to be a psychoanalyst. I had learned that women tended to score higher on social and aesthetic traits and that men tended to score higher on, as I recall, scientific and analytic traits. Because the test items pitted the traits against each other, I had to express preferences I often didn't have. I found myself splitting the difference from answer to answer. Richard, half teasing and half taunting, said he could guess what my profile looked like. When I showed it to him, he pounced on how high my so-

cial traits were compared to his. "But look at my analytic traits," I insisted.

I now look at the test and my reactions rather differently. First, I should have said, "Richard, you're a jerk. You want to be a psychoanalyst and your social traits are low?" Second, I see that the test is based on misguided assumptions: it portrays occupations as unidimensional, and it forces people to be one thing *or* another. I now know that being a scientist is a social activity, as well as a solitary activity, as well as an analytic activity, as well as an aesthetic activity. Indeed, what I find wonderful about science is how many different parts of myself are satisfied in the doing of it. Third, I see that I accepted the assumptions of the test and felt correspondingly trapped by my feminine traits: I felt that if I acknowledged them, I would be condemned to a feminine future, always acting in the service of others, never acting for myself. I did not see a way to be nurturant *and* agentic. The either-or implication of gender schemas ruled out the self I wanted to be.

Schemas and Professional Evaluations

People and occupations are multidimensional, but our schemas simplify both. They portray the professions as suitable for men, and men as suitable for the professions. Without exception, every prestigious or high-paying profession in the United States is dominated by men, dominated numerically and in terms of who wields power (Gutek 1993).[6] A man or woman who goes into law or business or academia is entering a field in which positions at the highest levels are disproportionately occupied by men and those at the lowest levels are disproportionately occupied by women. All prestigious professions are professions for men, not simply professions.

The immediate consequence for a woman entering a profession is that those around her, both men and other women, perceive her as at least slightly unsuited to that profession, because her gender doesn't fit in. The schema for women is incompatible with the schema for a successful professional, resulting in lower expectations of a woman's potential achievement. Those low expectations will, in turn, affect evaluations of her work. There is usually room for disagreement about the quality of someone's work. Observers of women will lean in a negative direction, in line with their low expectations. If she performs badly, that will confirm their expectations. If she performs well, she may still fail to receive her due, because her achievement runs counter to expectation. Or, she may be appropriately rewarded, but be seen as an exception to the general rule that women do not make good professionals.

There are a number of potential pitfalls for women professionals that originate in the perceived discordance between the two schemas. Women must appear neither too feminine nor too masculine. At either extreme they make others uncomfortable. A woman who is very feminine runs the risk of seeming less competent; the more she typifies the schema for a woman, the less she matches the schema for the successful professional. On the other hand, a woman with masculine traits runs the risk of appearing unnatural and deviant. The more she typifies the schema for the successful professional, the less she matches the schema for a woman.

Some women—such as the subject of the following admiring description—manage to appear both competent and feminine: "She is a tough, tough lady. She has a soft, genteel way about her, but she is an adversary of steel." That characterization of Janet Reno was offered shortly after her 1993 nomination for U.S. Attorney General (Rohter 1993, quoting a former judge and prosecutor who had hired Reno as state attorney in Florida). Former British Prime Minister Margaret Thatcher, with her sobriquet "The Iron Lady," has been described in similar terms. It is possible, then, to be perceived to be simultaneously as "tough" (masculine) and a "lady" (feminine), as having a "soft" and "genteel" manner while being "an adversary of steel." Although such a blending of opposites may appear almost impossible, observation suggests that it is reasonably common among successful women.

Less common is the woman who concentrates on competence and ignores femininity. It is the rare woman who is completely unconcerned about whether she is perceived as feminine, and the rare environment that is similarly unconcerned. Women who do not have a "soft, genteel way" about them may be told—despite their manifest competence—that they should wear more make-up and go to charm school. That was what Ann Hopkins's evaluators wrote about her when, despite her outstanding record, they rejected her bid for a partnership at Price Waterhouse, an accounting firm (Fiske, Bersoff, Borgida, Deaux & Heilman 1991).

The partners were openly critical of a woman who didn't act like a prototypical woman. Other people's overt beliefs in equality may cause them to avoid making such stereotypic statements, but their nonconscious schemas may not prevent them from making stereotypic judgments. People who eschew statements such as, "Women do not command respect from their subordinates," may nevertheless feel comfortable saying, "Lee does not command respect from her subordinates." The latter comment is just a "fact" about Lee, arrived at through impartial and fair observation. In their laudable resolutions to judge fairly, people may be unaware that their perceptions are guided not only by someone's objective performance, but in addition by their nonconscious expectations of the person's performance.

Lee, then, may be misperceived due to the influence of gender schemas. She might genuinely have her subordinates' respect but be perceived otherwise because of a gender schema that says women do not command respect. Or, her subordinates might express their respect for her somewhat differently than they would for a man. Onlookers, failing to see traditional marks of deference and tacitly believing that women are poor authority figures, might conclude that respect is absent. Finally, Lee might lack her subordinates' respect, not because of her behavior but because her subordinates resent having a woman superior and therefore refuse to grant her the respect they would give a man exhibiting the same behavior. Observers, because of their expectations about women, could mistakenly locate the problem in Lee's performance, rather than in her subordinates' schemas.

A story about a science department at a prestigious university, circa 1990, illustrates how expectations stemming from gender schemas can affect a woman's career. A young Ph.D. who has just been hired has a conference with her department chair about what courses she will teach. She is eager to teach a large introductory lecture course. The chair refuses, saying that students won't accept a woman instructor in that format. The woman presses a bit, saying she thinks she can do it and would like to try. The chair doesn't want to take a chance and instead assigns her to a laboratory course. The woman is not happy with the substitution, because laboratory courses are extremely time-consuming. As a young faculty member, she needs to spend as much time as she can developing her research and getting it published, in order to earn promotion and tenure. She will now have less time for research than will her male peer who is assigned to the lecture course.

The example nicely captures the many different factors—especially gender expectations—that intersect to place a woman in a poor position. The chair believes he is being objective about the students' preferences and is minimizing any risk to an important course. Nothing about the conference causes him to consider the possibility that his decision is guided by gender schemas or might be unfair. The conference has also set a bad precedent. In the conference, the chair activated his nonconscious views of women and attached them to the new faculty member. He explicitly articulated the view that, as a woman, she would not do a good job as a lecturer. In the future, he is likely to reactivate his views about women when he is evaluating her. In a way, she has already failed, because he has already labeled her to himself as an unacceptable lecturer.

What might the chair have done if he had been aware of gender schemas and committed to gender equality? He would still have been concerned about the students' reception of a woman lecturer, but he could have tried to work out with her some techniques to ease her acceptance. He could have recommended that the woman speak to experienced colleagues to learn what has worked well in the past and to plan her response to the authority-challenging events that large lecture classes are prone to no matter who is teaching—newspaper reading, whispered conversations, snoring, and so on. He could have suggested that, to solidify her authority, she schedule several moderately rigorous quizzes early in the semester. Finally, he could have been prepared with statements of full support for her, were students to bring complaints to him. As things stand, however, the chair has put the woman at an objective disadvantage: he has taken time away from her on the basis of her gender.

Statistics on women's progress in the professions . . . back up the idea that a succession of small events, such as not getting a good assignment, results in large discrepancies in advancement and achievement. They also suggest that gender schemas work to women's disadvantage in other ways. Women generally benefit less from their positive achievements than men do. In their first academic appointment, for example, men benefit more than women do from the prestige of the institution where they received their training. Men get better jobs. Men are promoted more quickly. Men are tenured more quickly. Men make more money. Men are overrepresented at senior levels. . . . [T]he differences hold even when men and women are equated on performance (to the extent that they can be).

What is true for academia holds even more strongly in the corporate world. A 1990 *Fortune* magazine survey of 799 of the largest U.S. industrial and service companies found that only nineteen women—less than one-half of 1 percent—were listed among the more than four thousand highest-paid officers and directors (Fierman 1990). In business, as in academia, women earn less than men (two of those nineteen women had cash compensation under $85,000 per year), are promoted more slowly, and work in less prestigious firms. Women's salaries have improved. In a 1996 survey of the twenty most highly paid women, the lowest salary was $152,977 (Greene & Greene 1996). But 615 men earned more than the twentieth woman on the list. Again, as in academia, to the extent that performance can be accurately measured, men and women appear to perform equally well.

Independent of all other factors, gender appears to play a major role in people's ability to get ahead. Gender schemas are objectively costly for women. Relative to women, men have a leg up. Men look right for the job.

Qualifications and Responsibilities

In the same way that some theorists have suggested a deterministic role for biology, others have suggested a deterministic role for educational and professional qualifications. In both cases, women's lower professional status is attributed to something they lack. There often are sex differences in qualifications. But, often like biology, qualifications are not destiny. They too are but one factor in a multifactor equation, as is evident from the fact that men and women with equal qualifications do not advance at the same rate. In evaluating the role of qualifications, I conclude that qualifications influence people's ability to advance but do not fully determine advancement. Gender schemas play an important role in disadvantaging women.

Men's lack of responsibilities outside of work may also contribute to their faster professional advancement. Men accept less responsibility than women do for the day-to-day operation of their households. Men are less likely than women to work part-time in order to raise their children. Inequities at home reverberate in the work place. But men's advantages and women's disadvantages on the job are not solely a function of their differing participation in family life. Men receive a greater reward for their performance than do women, independent of all other factors.

Self-Perception

Subjective costs add to the objective costs of gender schemas. Consider again the young professor who has not been permitted to teach a large lecture course. If she is rational, she must now wonder what other jobs she will be perceived as unable to fill. She may reaffirm to herself that she is competent and willing to work hard. Or she may begin to question her competence and motivation. Either way, she has borne and continues to bear an emotional cost that a comparable man will not have had.

Everyone experiences successes and failures and must then explain to themselves just why they succeeded or failed. A somewhat oversimplified description of men's reactions to success and failure is that they take the credit for their successes but do not accept the blame for their failures. A similarly oversimplified description of women's reactions is that women take the blame for their failures but do not take the credit for their successes.

Because the professions are perceived as requiring masculine abilities and traits, a successful man can reasonably credit himself with the abilities and traits that are necessary for success—and feel masculine into the bargain. A man's success and his masculinity reinforce each other. A man's failure is incompatible with his masculinity. Since people want to feel compatible with their gender—and to perceive others the same way—a man will attempt to interpret his failures in terms that leave his masculinity intact (and others will attempt to do the same for him). One response is to try to escape the blame. Paradoxically, another response is "the-buck-stops-here": the man shoulders the responsibility. Tone seems to be everything here. By taking responsibility in the right way, a man can actually seem more masculine and more in control. Although he acknowledges his failure, he also manages to reduce its overall importance.

For a woman, success and failure work differently. If a woman is professionally successful, she must either see herself as having masculine traits—and thereby run the risk of seeming unfeminine to herself and others—or as having compensated in some way—through luck or extraordinary effort—

for a lack of masculine characteristics. Unlike a successful man, a woman has something to lose from success: her gender identity or belief in her ability. Conversely, failure and femininity reinforce each other. Women are expected to fail and potentially have something to salvage from failure, namely, reinforcement of their femininity. A woman who fails is more of a woman than one who succeeds.

For men, then, there is complete congruence between professional goals and the need to feel like a good example of their gender. For women there is a potential conflict. Naturally, not every woman, on every occasion, will perceive herself or be perceived in terms of a conflict between competence and femininity. But even a small dilemma of that sort, occasionally experienced, will accrue disadvantage for a woman relative to a man, who never has to choose between competence and masculinity.

In experimental investigations, people are asked to apportion the reasons for their success or failure at a task among four different factors: ability, effort, luck, and easiness or difficulty of the task. . . . Women and men contrast most in how they view the role of luck. Women see luck as more important for both their successes and their failures than men do.

"Luck" may be a grab-bag category in such experiments—a reason people use when they don't know exactly why something happened, when they cannot establish a clear cause-and-effect relation. Because luck is by its nature unstable and uncontrollable, attributing outcomes to it is deleterious. If you see a success or failure as due to luck, you cannot learn anything from it. There is no point in trying to figure out what went wrong or right, no point in developing a plan for the future based on the past, no point in putting forth a lot of effort the next time. Chance undoubtedly enters into every result, but consistent success demands competence, strategic analysis, and effort.

Although an emphasis on luck is detrimental to achievement, it is also a rational response for women. Luck, in the guise of an unstable and uncontrollable set of external circumstances, plays an unwarranted role in women's professional lives. Women do not reliably profit from their competence, strategic analysis, and effort to the same extent men do. . . . Yet no professional woman can succeed without those qualities. One might even argue that they are more important for women than for men, because women's objective circumstances are more difficult than men's. But individual effort is insufficient.

Trailing behind every successful woman are the un-successful women—who knows how many?—who were equally competent, strategic, and hardwork-ing, but not lucky.

Women would have to close their eyes to the facts to deny the role of factors outside their control and to insist on the potential efficacy of their own actions. Yet how effective can women be unless they act as if luck were irrelevant? Here is another small dilemma women face that men do not—one that, over time, takes its toll.

I remember a heated discussion with my mother when I was a young teenager. I showed her a poem I had read about being the captain of one's ship. To me the poem was a validation of what I most deeply believed: that my longing and determination to achieve something significant would make reality conform to my will. Here was a poem—a voice from the outside world I planned to succeed in—to lend authority to my certainty that I could control my future. I wanted my mother to have the same opinion, not just about me, but about herself. I wanted her to have high aspirations as well.

But she argued with me. "No," she said, "it isn't so." One wasn't the captain of one's ship, one couldn't do exactly what one wanted.

I was upset and angry. Of course you couldn't be the captain of your ship if you didn't *believe* you could be, if you didn't *try* to be. I rejected my mother's defeatism and took comfort from the poem.

It is of course true that the race is not always to the swift. But women, as a group, do not experience as tight a fit between cause and effect as men do. Women enjoy fewer successes and suffer more fail-ures than comparable men. Men and women live in different environments, environments that are the same only on the surface. Women have puzzles to solve that men do not. Some women decide that they are exceptional and will succeed where others have failed. Others ignore the unstable relationship between cause and effect, action and result. Still oth-ers forgo professional ambition, perhaps without re-alizing why.

Remedies

What can we do to foster equality? Affirmative ac-tion policies, legislation, and recourse to the courts remain important avenues to change in the work-place. The courts make it harder for employers to use gender schemas to justify denying women ad-vancement in the form of salary, promotion, part-nership, and tenure.

But the unexpressed and nonconscious nature of gender schemas and their subterranean mode of action require more subtle remedies as well. The first, and most important, remedy is learning about gender schemas: how they develop, how they work, how they are maintained, and how they in-fluence aspirations and expectations. Using this knowledge, organizations and individuals can de-vise procedures and programs to neutralize gender schemas. . . .

Endnotes

1. Bem (1993) and others have used the expression *gender schema* in a different way. In her usage, people who are *gender schematic* tend both to typify the expectations held of their gender (e.g., males have many stereotypically masculine traits and few stereotypically feminine traits) and to apply those expectations strongly in their percep-tion of others. For gender schematics, gender is a very important category in evaluating the self and others. By contrast, *aschematic* individuals do not markedly conform to the expectations of their gender (e.g., males may be either high or low on both masculinity and femininity); nor do they impose gender conformity on others.

In my usage, gender schemas refer to the implicit hy-potheses that almost all of us share about the nature of men and women. Gender schemas are beliefs about the sexes that we hold in common—whether we want to or not.

I use the term *schemas* rather than *schemata* because the former is the norm in the psychological literature.
2. Merton (1968) dubbed the phenomenon the Matthew effect, after the following passage in one version of Matthew 13:12: "For whosoever hath, to him shall be given, and he shall have more abundance: but whoso-ever hath not, from him shall be taken away even that which he hath."
3. Our usual notion of women is that they talk more than men. In fact, there is little evidence for that claim. Two academic women have mentioned to me their impression that women in academia often seem either to say nothing or say too much. One explanation for this phenomenon, if it is one, is suggested in chapter 7. My own impression, however, is that an equal, if not larger, proportion of aca-demic men say too much.

4. Deaux (1985) and Unger (1990) draw the distinction between sex and gender in a similar way. Terminology concerning sex and gender varies from field to field and front author to author. The following view is typical of work in psychology in the 1990s: ". . . in discussing behavioral differences between human males and females, some authors reserve the term *sex* for distinctions that are biological in origin and *gender* for those thought to have psychosocial origins. . . . However, this convention assumes a great deal more knowledge than actually exists regarding the sources of male-female differences; also, it falsely dichotomizes potential influences, ignoring the possibility that behavior is shaped by a complex interplay between social and biological factors . . . . . Therefore, we view the terms as interchangeable, but generally use the term *sex*" (Collaer & Hines 1995).

5. Fiske and Taylor (1991) contrast three different models of the social perceiver: the naive theorist, the cognitive miser, and the motivated tactician. In their division, the *naive theorist* acts normatively, that is, correctly weighs and analyzes the information available in order to draw accurate conclusions. The *cognitive miser*, in contrast, takes shortcuts, fails to consider all the data and sometimes fails to correctly analyze the data he or she has collected. The *motivated tactician*'s analyses depend on his or her goals. Under some conditions the tactician correctly analyzes the range of data but under others uses shortcuts or reasons incorrectly.

My own use of the analogy of the perceiver as a theorist cuts across Fiske and Taylor's tripartite division. In my usage, the naive theorist does not consistently obey normative reasoning procedures (nor does the individual scientist). The "lapses" are related both to demands for cognitive economy—as suggested by the cognitive miser model—and to the need for cognition to serve different motivational goals—as suggested by the motivated tactician model. The virtue of emphasizing that social perceivers are theorists is the focus it places on people's need to understand and predict their social world. People do not approach their social world with a set of pre-established heuristics or strategies; they attempt to develop a coherent picture.

6. The performing arts are a possible exception: women earn high salaries as performers.

References

Armstrong, S. L., Gleitman, L. R., & Gleitman, H. 1983. What some concepts might not be. *Cognition* 13:263–308.

Bakan, D. 1966. *The duality of human existence.* Chicago: Rand McNally.

Biernat, M., Manis, M., & Nelson, T. 1991. Stereotypes and standards of judgment. *Journal of Personality and Social Psychology* 60:5–20.

Bem, S. 1993. *The lenses of gender: Transforming the debate on sexual inequality.* New Haven: Yale University Press.

Cole, J., & Singer, B. 1991. A theory of limited differences: Explaining the productivity puzzle in science. In *The outer circle: Women in the scientific community,* H. Zuckerman, J. R. Cole, & J. T Bruer, eds., pp. 277–310. New York: W. W. Norton.

Collaer, M. L., & Hines, M. 1995. Human behavioral sex differences: A role for gonadal hormones during early development? *Psychological Bulletin* 118:55–107.

Deaux, K. 1985. Sex and gender. *Annual Review of Psychology* 36:49–81.

Eagly, A. H. 1987. *Sex differences in social behavior: A social-role interpretation.* Hillsdale, N.J.: Erlbaum.

Fierman, J. 1990. Why women still don't hit the top. *Fortune,* 30 July, pp. 40–66.

Fiske, S. T., Bersoff, D. N., Borgida, E., Deaux, K., & Heilman, M. 1991. Social science research on trial: Use of sex stereotyping research in *Price Waterhouse v. Hopkins. American Psychologist* 46:1049–60.

Fiske, S. T., & Taylor, S. E. 1991. *Social cognition,* 2nd ed. New York: McGraw-Hill.

Fox, M. F. 1981. Sex, salary and achievement: Reward-dualism in academia. *Sociology of Education* 54:71–84.

Fox, M. F. 1985. Publication, performance, and reward in science and scholarship. In *Higher education: Handbook of theory and research,* J. Smart, ed., pp. 255–82. New York: Agathon.

Greene, K., & Greene, R. 1996. The 20 top-paid women in corporate America. *Working Woman,* February, pp. 40–44.

Gutek, B. A. 1993. Changing the status of women in management. *Applied Psychology: An International Review* 42:301–11.

Haslett, B., Geis, F. L., & Carter, M. R. 1992. *The organizational woman: Power and paradox.* Norwood, N.J.: Ablex.

Hoffman, C., & Hurst, N. 1990. Gender stereotypes: Perception or rationalization? *Journal of Personality and Social Psychology* 58:197–208.

Long, J. S. 1990. The origins of sex differences in science. *Social Forces* 68:1297–1315.

Martell, R. F., Lane, D. M., & Emrich, C. 1996. Male-female differences: A computer simulation. *American Psychologist* 51:157–58.

Merton, R. K. 1948. The self-fulfilling prophecy. *Antioch Review* 8:193–210.

Merton, R. K. 1968. The Matthew Effect in science. *Science* 159:56–63.

Rohter, L. 1993. Tough "front-line warrior": Janet Reno. *New York Times*, 12 February, pp. 1, 22.

Rosenthal, R. & Jacobson, L. 1968. *Pygmalion in the class-room*. New York: Holt, Rinehart & Winston.

Spence, J. T., & Helmreich, R. L. 1978. *Masculinity and femininity: Their psychological dimensions, correlates, and antecedents*. Austin: University of Texas Press.

Spence, J. T., & Sawin, L. L. 1985. Images of masculinity and femininity: A reconceptualization. In *Women, gender,* *and social psychology*, V. F. O'Leary, R. K. Unger , & B. S. Wallston, eds., pp. 35–66. Hillsdale, N.J.: Erlbaum.

Truell, P. 1996. Success and sharp elbows: One woman's path to lofty heights on Wall Street. *New York Times*, 2 July, pp. D1 and D4.

Unger, R. K. 1990. Imperfect reflections of reality: Psychology constructs gender. In *Making a difference: Psychology and the construction of gender*, R. T. Hare-Mustin & J. Marecek, eds., pp. 102–49. New Haven: Yale University Press.

27. National Organization for Women (NOW) Bill of Rights (1995)

I   Equal Rights Constitutional Amendment
II Enforce Law Banning Sex Discrimination in Employment
III Maternity Leave Rights in Employment and in Social Security Benefits
IV Tax Deduction for Home and Childcare Expenses for Working Parents
V   Childcare Centers
VI Equal and Unsegregated Education
VII Equal Job Training Opportunities and Allowances for Women in Poverty
VIII The Right of Women to Control Their Reproductive Lives

We Demand:

I That the United States Congress immediately pass the Equal Rights Amendment to the Constitution to provide that "Equality of rights under the law shall not be denied or abridged by the United States or by any State on account of sex," and that such then be immediately ratified by the several States.

II That equal employment opportunity be guaranteed to all women, as well as men, by insisting that the Equal Employment Opportunity Commission enforce the prohibitions against sex discrimination in employment under Title VII of the Civil Rights Act of 1964 with the same vigor as it enforces the prohibitions against racial discrimination.

III That women be protected by law to ensure their rights to return to their jobs within a reasonable time after childbirth without loss of seniority or other accrued benefits, and be paid maternity leave as a form of social security and/or employee benefit.

IV Immediate revision of tax laws to permit the deduction of home and childcare expenses for working parents.

V That childcare facilities be established by law on the same basis as parks, libraries, and public schools, adequate to the needs of children from the preschool years through adolescence, as a community resource to be used by all citizens from all income levels.

VI That the right of women to be educated to their full potential equally with men be secured by Federal and State Legislation, eliminating all discrimination and segregation by sex, written and unwritten, at all levels of education, including colleges, graduate and professional schools, loans and fellowships, and Federal and State training programs such as the Job Corps.

VII The right of women in poverty to secure job training, housing, and family allowances on equal terms with men, but without prejudice to a parent's right to remain at home to care for his or her children; revision of welfare legislation and poverty programs which deny women dignity, privacy, and self-respect.

VIII The right of women to control their own reproductive lives by removing from penal codes laws limiting access to contraceptive information and devices and laws governing abortion.

28. The Beijing Declaration and Platform for Action (1995)

1. We, the Governments participating in the Fourth World Conference on Women,

2. Gathered here in Beijing in September 1995, the year of the fiftieth anniversary of the founding of the United Nations,

3. Determined to advance the goals of equality, development and peace for all women everywhere in the interest of all humanity,

4. Acknowledging the voices of all women everywhere and taking note of the diversity of women and their roles and circumstances, honouring the women who paved the way and inspired by the hope present in the world's youth,

5. Recognize that the status of women has advanced in some important respects in the past decade but that progress has been uneven, inequalities between women and men have persisted and major obstacles remain, with serious consequences for the well-being of all people,

6. Also recognize that this situation is exacerbated by the increasing poverty that is affecting the lives of the majority of the world's people, in particular women and children, with origins in both the national and international domains,

7. Dedicate ourselves unreservedly to addressing these constraints and obstacles and thus enhancing further the advancement and empowerment of women all over the world, and agree that this requires urgent action in the spirit of determination, hope, cooperation and solidarity, now and to carry us forward into the next century.

We reaffirm our commitment to:

8. The equal rights and inherent human dignity of women and men and other purposes and principles enshrined in the Charter of the United Nations, to the Universal Declaration of Human Rights and other international human rights instruments, in particular the Convention on the Elimination of All Forms of Discrimination against Women and the Convention on the Rights of the Child, as well as the Declaration on the Elimination of Violence against Women and the Declaration on the Right to Development;

9. Ensure the full implementation of the human rights of women and of the girl child as an inalienable, integral and indivisible part of all human rights and fundamental freedoms;

10. Build on consensus and progress made at previous United Nations conferences and summits—on women in Nairobi in 1985, on children in New York in 1990, on environment and development in Rio de Janeiro in 1992, on human rights in Vienna in 1993, on population and development in Cairo in 1994 and on social development in Copenhagen in 1995 with the objective of achieving equality, development and peace;

11. Achieve the full and effective implementation of the Nairobi Forward-looking Strategies for the Advancement of Women;

12. The empowerment and advancement of women, including the right to freedom of thought, conscience, religion and belief, thus contributing to the moral, ethical, spiritual and intellectual needs of women and men, individually or in community with others and thereby guaranteeing them the possibility of realizing their full potential in society and shaping their lives in accordance with their own aspirations.

We are convinced that:

13. Women's empowerment and their full participation on the basis of equality in all spheres of society, including participation in the decision-making process and access to power, are fundamental for the achievement of equality, development and peace;

14. Women's rights are human rights;

15. Equal rights, opportunities and access to resources, equal sharing of responsibilities for the family by men and women, and a harmonious partnership between them are critical to their well-being and that of their families as well as to the consolidation of democracy;

16. Eradication of poverty based on sustained economic growth, social development, environmental protection and social justice requires the involvement of women in economic and social development, equal opportunities and the full and

equal participation of women and men as agents and beneficiaries of people-centered sustainable development;

17. The explicit recognition and reaffirmation of the right of all women to control all aspects of their health, in particular their own fertility, is basic to their empowerment;

18. Local, national, regional and global peace is attainable and is inextricably linked with the advancement of women, who are a fundamental force for leadership, conflict resolution and the promotion of lasting peace at all levels;

19. It is essential to design, implement and monitor, with the full participation of women, effective, efficient and mutually reinforcing gender-sensitive policies and programmes, including development policies and programmes, at all levels that will foster the empowerment and advancement of women;

20. The participation and contribution of all actors of civil society, particularly women's groups and networks and other non-governmental organizations and community-based organizations, with full respect for their autonomy, in cooperation with Governments, are important to the effective implementation and follow-up of the Platform for Action;

21. The implementation of the Platform for Action requires commitment from Governments and the international community. By making national and international commitments for action, including those made at the Conference, Governments and the international community recognize the need to take priority action for the empowerment and advancement of women.

We are determined to:

22. Intensify efforts and actions to achieve the goals of the Nairobi Forward-looking Strategies for the Advancement of Women by the end of this century;

23. Ensure the full enjoyment by women and the girl child of all human rights and fundamental freedoms and take effective action against violations of these rights and freedoms;

24. Take all necessary measures to eliminate all forms of discrimination against women and the girl child and remove all obstacles to gender equality and the advancement and empowerment of women;

25. Encourage men to participate fully in all actions towards equality;

26. Promote women's economic independence, including employment, and eradicate the persistent and increasing burden of poverty on women by addressing the structural causes of poverty through changes in economic structures, ensuring equal ac-

cess for all women, including those in rural areas, as vital development agents, to productive resources, opportunities and public services;

27. Promote people-centred sustainable development, including sustained economic growth, through the provision of basic education, lifelong education, literacy and training, and primary health care for girls and women;

28. Take positive steps to ensure peace for the advancement of women and, recognizing the leading role that women have played in the peace movement, work actively towards general and complete disarmament under strict and effective international control, and support negotiations on the conclusion, without delay, of a universal and multilaterally and effectively verifiable comprehensive nuclear-test-ban treaty which contributes to nuclear disarmament and the prevention of the proliferation of nuclear weapons in all its aspects;

29. Prevent and eliminate all forms of violence against women and girls;

30. Ensure equal access to and equal treatment of women and men in education and health care and enhance women's sexual and reproductive health as well as education;

31. Promote and protect all human rights of women and girls;

32. Intensify efforts to ensure equal enjoyment of all human rights and fundamental freedoms for all women and girls who face multiple barriers to their empowerment and advancement because of such factors as their race, age, language, ethnicity, culture, religion, or disability, or because they are indigenous people;

33. Ensure respect for international law, including humanitarian law, in order to protect women and girls in particular;

34. Develop the fullest potential of girls and women of all ages, ensure their full and equal participation in building a better world for all and enhance their role in the development process.

We are determined to:

35. Ensure women's equal access to economic resources, including land, credit, science and technology, vocational training, information, communication and markets, as a means to further the advancement and empowerment of women and girls, including through the enhancement of their capacities to enjoy the benefits of equal access to these resources, *inter alia,* by means of international cooperation;

36. Ensure the success of the Platform for Action, which will require a strong commitment on

the part of Governments, international organizations and institutions at all levels. We are deeply convinced that economic development, social development and environmental protection are interdependent and mutually reinforcing components of sustainable development, which is the framework for our efforts to achieve a higher quality of life for all people. Equitable social development that recognizes empowering the poor, particularly women living in poverty, to utilize environmental resources sustainably is a necessary foundation for sustainable development. We also recognize that broad-based and sustained economic growth in the context of sustainable development is necessary to sustain social development and social justice. The success of the Platform for Action will also require adequate mobilization of resources at the national and international levels as well as new and additional resources to the developing countries from all available funding mechanisms, including multilateral, bilateral and private sources for the advancement of women; financial resources to strengthen the capacity of national, subregional, regional and international institutions; a commitment to equal rights, equal responsibilities and equal opportunities and to the equal participation of women and men in all national, regional and international bodies and policy-making processes; and the establishment or strengthening of mechanisms at all levels for accountability to the world's women;

37. Ensure also the success of the Platform for Action in countries with economies in transition, which will require continued international cooperation and assistance;

38. We hereby adopt and commit ourselves as Governments to implement the following Platform for Action, ensuring that a gender perspective is reflected in all our policies and programmes. We urge the United Nations system, regional and international financial institutions, other relevant regional and international institutions and all women and men, as well as non-governmental organizations, with full respect for their autonomy, and all sectors of civil society, in cooperation with Governments, to fully commit themselves and contribute to the implementation of this Platform for Action. . . .

Critical Areas of Concern

41. The advancement of women and the achievement of equality between women and men are a matter of human rights and a condition for social justice and should not be seen in isolation as a women's issue. They are the only way to build a sustainable, just and developed society. Empowerment of women and equality between women and men are prerequisites for achieving political, social, economic, cultural and environmental security among all peoples.

42. Most of the goals set out in the Nairobi Forward-looking Strategies for the Advancement of Women have not been achieved. Barriers to women's empowerment remain, despite the efforts of Governments, as well as non-governmental organizations and women and men everywhere. Vast political, economic and ecological crises persist in many parts of the world. Among them are wars of aggression, armed conflicts, colonial or other forms of alien domination or foreign occupation, civil wars and terrorism. These situations, combined with systematic or de facto discrimination, violations of and failure to protect all human rights and fundamental freedoms of all women, and their civil, cultural, economic, political and social rights, including the right to development and ingrained prejudicial attitudes towards women and girls are but a few of the impediments encountered since the World Conference to Review and Appraise the Achievements of the United Nations Decade for Women: Equality, Development and Peace, in 1985.

43. A review of progress since the Nairobi Conference highlights special concerns—areas of particular urgency that stand out as priorities for action. All actors should focus action and resources on the strategic objectives relating to the critical areas of concern which are, necessarily, interrelated, interdependent and of high priority. There is a need for these actors to develop and implement mechanisms of accountability for all the areas of concern.

44. To this end, Governments, the international community and civil society, including non-governmental organizations and the private sector, are called upon to take strategic action in the following critical areas of concern:

- The persistent and increasing burden of poverty on women

- Inequalities and inadequacies in and unequal access to education and training

- Inequalities and inadequacies in and unequal access to health care and related services

- Violence against women

- The effects of armed or other kinds of conflict on women, including those living under foreign occupation

- Inequality in economic structures and policies, in all forms of productive activities and in access to resources

- Inequality between men and women in the sharing of power and decision-making at all levels

- Insufficient mechanisms at all levels to promote the advancement of women

- Lack of respect for and inadequate promotion and protection of the human rights of women

- Stereotyping of women and inequality in women's access to and participation in all communication systems, especially in the media

- Gender inequalities in the management of natural resources and in the safeguarding of the environment

- Persistent discrimination against and violation of the rights of the girl-child

Suggestions for Further Reading

Anthologies

Bishop, Sharon, and Marjorie Weinzweig. *Philosophy and Women*. Belmont, CA: Wadsworth Publishing Co., 1979.

Frazer, Elizabeth, Jennifer Hornsby and Sabina Lovibond. *Ethics: A Feminist Reader*. Oxford: Blackwell, 1992.

Freeman, Jo. *Women: A Feminist Perspective*. 4th ed. Palo Alto: Mayfield Publishing Co., 1989.

Gould, Carol C., and Marx W. Wartofsky. *Women and Philosophy*. New York: G. P. Putnam & Sons, 1976.

Jaggar, Alison, and W. Iris Young. *A Companion to Feminist Philosophy*. Oxford: Blackwell, 1998.

Kourany, Janet, James Sterba and Rosemarie Tong. *Feminist Philosophies*. 2nd ed. 1999. Englewood Cliffs, NJ: Prentice-Hall.

Pearsall, Marilyn. *Women and Values*. 3rd ed. Belmont, CA: Wadsworth Publishing Co., 1999.

Basic Concepts

Jaggar, Alison M. *Feminist Politics and Human Nature*. Totowa, NJ: Rowman & Allanheld, 1983.

Tong, Rosemarie. *Feminist Thought*. Boulder: Westview Press, 1989.

Tuana, Nancy, and Rosemarie Tong. *Feminism and Philosophy*. Boulder: Westview, 1995.

Alternative Views

DeCrow, Karen. *Sexist Justice*. New York: Vintage, 1975.

Eisenstein, Zellah. *Feminism and Sexual Equality*. New York: Monthly Review, 1984.

Friedan, Betty. *The Feminine Mystique*. New York: W. W. Norton & Co., 1963.

Frye, Marilyn. *The Politics of Reality*. New York: The Crossing Press, 1983.

Held, Virginia. *Feminist Morality*. Chicago: University of Chicago Press, 1993.

Okin, Susan. *Justice, Gender and the Family*. New York: Basic Books, 1989.

Pateman, Carole. *The Sexual Contract*. Stanford: Stanford University Press, 1988.

Sommers, Christina Hoff. *Who Stole Feminism?* New York: Simon and Schuster, 1994.

Young, Iris. *Justice and the Politics of Difference*. Princeton: Princeton University Press, 1990.

Practical Applications

Irving, John. *The World According to Garp*. New York: Dutton, 1978.

United States Commission on Civil Rights. *Statement on the Equal Rights Amendment*. Washington, DC: U.S. Government Printing Office, 1978.

Section V

Affirmative Action

Introduction

Basic Concepts

Solutions to the problem of discrimination and prejudice tend to be either backward looking or forward looking. The former seek to rectify and compensate for past injustices caused by discrimination or prejudice. Forward-looking solutions seek to realize an ideal of a society free from discrimination and prejudice. To justify a backward-looking solution to the problem of discrimination and prejudice, it is necessary to determine (1) who has committed or benefited from a wrongful act of discrimination or prejudice, and (2) who deserves compensation for that act. To justify a forward-looking solution to the problem, it is necessary to determine (1) what a society free from discrimination and prejudice would be like, and (2) how such a society might be realized. Solutions of both types have been proposed to deal with racism and sexism, the dominant forms of discrimination and prejudice in our times.

One useful way of approaching the topic of discrimination and prejudice is to note what particular solutions to the problem are favored by the political ideals of libertarianism, welfare liberalism, and socialism. (See Section I.)

Libertarians, for whom liberty is the ultimate political ideal, are not likely to recognize any need to rectify acts of discrimination and prejudice. Bad as these acts may be, they usually do not—according to libertarians—violate anyone's rights, and hence do not demand rectification. In particular, because no one can demand a right to equal basic educational opportunities (a person's educational opportunities being simply a function of the property he or she controls), no one can justify affirmative action or comparable worth on the basis that such a right was previously denied.

Socialists, for whom equality is the ultimate political ideal, recognize a need to correct for discrimination and prejudice. However, the corrective measures they favor are not limited to affirmative action; socialists ultimately want to socialize the means of production and do away with private property.

Finally, affirmative action is a central requirement of the political program of welfare liberals, whose ultimate political ideal is contractual fairness.

Proposed solutions to the problem of discrimination and prejudice usually involve favoring or compensating certain qualified individuals when there has been a wrongful denial of opportunities or benefits in the past. This practice is called affirmative action, preferential treatment, or reverse discrimination when what is provided are jobs or other desirable positions. *Affirmative action* and *preferential treatment* are designations usually employed by proponents of the practice. *Reverse discrimination* is a designation employed by opponents of the practice.

Alternative Views

In Selection 29, Louis Pojman defines affirmative action as the effort to rectify the injustice of the past by special policies. He distinguishes a weak and a strong form of affirmative action. The weak form involves such measures as the elimination of segregation, widespread advertisement to underrepresented groups, and special scholarships for the disadvantaged classes. The strong form involves such actions as hiring on the basis of race or gender to reach proportionate representation. Pojman argues that neither form of affirmative action can be justified. He begins by considering a number of arguments in favor of affirmative action, such as the argument that role models are required, that compensation is required, and that diversity is needed, and he finds all these arguments wanting. He then considers a few arguments against affirmative action, such as that affirmative action requires discrimination against a different group; and that it encourages mediocrity and incompetence; and he finds merit in each of these arguments. He concludes that the case against affirmative action applies not only to strong affirmative action but also to a lesser degree to weak affirmative action because the weak form slides easily into the strong form.

In Selection 30, Albert Mosley argues that Louis Pojman's main arguments against affirmative action hold only against straw positions that defenders of affirmative action, like himself, have never held. Mosley defends affirmative action as a policy designed to facilitate the inclusion of blacks and women and is not meant as an expression of racial or sexual superiority. Mosley contends that this form of affirmative action is quite different from Pojman's strong affirmative action, which is a

form of reverse racism that would be wrong even if it were meant to correct a wrong.

In Selection 31, Charles Murray argues that affirmative action has actually worked against the interests of blacks by encouraging a new form of racism. The old racism openly held that blacks are permanently less competent than whites. The new racism holds that blacks are temporarily less competent than whites. The main problem with the new racism, according to Murray, is that it tends to perpetuate the racial inequalities it purports to remedy. However, the examples of this new racism that Murray discusses are all composites drawn from personal observations and, hence, as even he seems to realize, do not by themselves support generalizations. At the same time, Murray wants to conclude from his discussion that there is no such thing as good racial discrimination.

In opposition to Pojman and Murray, James P. Sterba argues in Selection 32 that once affirmative action is appropriately defined and the conditions for its morally justifiable application are set out, we can answer the main objections that have been raised against it. He also relates his defense to the Hopwood decision, accepting its defense of color- and gender-blindness but rejecting its limitation on affirmative action.

Practical Applications

Assuming that we accept the need for affirmative action programs to compensate for past injustices, there remains the question of what form such programs should take.

In a recent influential decision, *Hopwood v. Texas* (Selection 33), the issue before the U.S. Court of Appeals for the Fifth Circuit is whether the Fourteenth Amendment permits the University of Texas Law School to discriminate in favor of African Americans and Mexican Americans by using race as a factor in its admissions. The Court of Appeals ruled that it does not, maintaining that achieving diversity is not a sufficient reason to justify an affirmative action program. According to the court, only the goal of remedying proven past racial discrimination at the law school itself would provide an adequate reason in this case for an affirmative action program. In July 1996, the U.S. Supreme Court announced that it would not hear an appeal of the Hopwood decision.

Reva B. Siegel challenges the Hopwood Court in Selection 34, arguing that it endorses two contradictory conceptions of race in reaching its decision. In arguing that diversity is not a sufficient justification for affirmative action, the court maintained that race is a morphological accident, of no more significance than a person's physical size or blood type. In this view, race correlates with nothing than would be relevant to legitimate choice of applicants. But in arguing for limiting affirmative action to correct for the proven past discrimination of the particular social agents, the court allows that there can be significant racial differences in the absence of discrimination with which it would be illegitimate to interfere. In this view, racial differences can be quite relevant to legitimate choice.

To say the least, this recent court decision raises serious questions about the legal justification for many current affirmative action programs. Nevertheless, a moral justification for such programs will still turn on a comparative evaluation of the political ideals of libertarianism, welfare liberalism, and socialism and their practical requirements.

---

29. *The Case against Affirmative Action*

LOUIS POJMAN

Louis Pojman distinguishes between a weak and a strong form of affirmative action. The weak form involves such measures as the elimination of segregation, widespread advertisement to underrepresented groups, and special scholarships for the disadvantaged classes. The strong form involves taking such actions as hiring on the basis of race or gender to reach proportionate representation. Pojman considers a number of arguments both for and against affirmative action and concludes that strong affirmative action, at least, cannot be justified.

Hardly a week goes by but that the subject of Affirmative Action does not come up. Whether in the form of preferential hiring, nontraditional casting, quotas, "goals and time tables," minority scholarships, race-norming, reverse discrimination, or employment of members of underutilized groups, the issue confronts us as a terribly perplexing problem.

Reprinted from the *International Journal of Applied Philosophy* 12:1 (1998), pp. 97–115, by permission.

Affirmative Action was one of the issues that divided the Democratic and Republican parties during the 1996 election, the Democrats supporting it ("Mend it don't end it") and the Republicans opposing it ("affirmative action is reverse racism"). During the last general election (November 7, 1996) California voters by a 55% to 45% vote approved Proposition 209 (called the "California Civil Rights Initiative") which made it illegal to discriminate on the basis of race or gender, hence ending Affirmative Action in public institutions in California. The

Supreme Court recently refused to rule on the appeal, thus leaving it to the individual states to decide how they will deal with this issue. Both sides have reorganized for a renewed battle. Meanwhile, on Nov. 11, 1977, the European Union's High Court of Justice in Luxembourg approved Affirmative Action programs giving women preferential treatment in the 15 European Union countries.

Let us agree that despite the evidences of a booming economy, the poor are suffering grievously, with children being born into desperate material and psychological poverty; for them the ideal of "equal opportunity for all" is a cruel joke. Many feel that the federal government has abandoned its guarantee to provide the minimum necessities for each American, so that the pace of this tragedy seems to be worsening daily. In addition to this, African-Americans have a legacy of slavery and unjust discrimination to contend with, and other minorities have also suffered from injustice. Women have their own peculiar history of being treated unequally in relevant ways. What is the answer to this national problem? Is it increased welfare? More job training? More support for education? Required licensing of parents to have children? Negative income tax? More support for families or for mothers with small children? All of these have merit and should be part of the national debate. But, my thesis is, however tragic the situation may be (and we may disagree on just how tragic it is), one policy is *not* a legitimate part of the solution and that is *reverse, unjust discrimination* against young white males. Strong Affirmative Action, which implicitly advocates reverse discrimination, while no doubt well intentioned, is morally heinous, asserting, by implication, that *two wrongs make a right*.

The *Two Wrongs Make a Right* Thesis goes like this: Because *some* whites once enslaved some blacks, the descendants of those slaves (some of whom may now enjoy high incomes and social status) have a right to opportunities and offices over better qualified whites who had nothing to do with either slavery or the oppression of blacks (and who may even have suffered hardship comparable to that of poor blacks). In addition, Strong Affirmative Action creates a new Hierarchy of the Oppressed: blacks get primary preferential treatment, women second, Native Americans third, Hispanics fourth, Handicapped fifth, and Asians sixth and so on until white males, no matter how needy or well qualified, must accept the leftovers. Naturally, combinations of oppressed classes (e.g., a one-eyed, black Hispanic female) trump all single classifications. The equal protection clause of the Fourteenth Amendment becomes reinterpreted as "Equal protection for all equals, but some equals are more equal than others."

Before analyzing arguments concerning Affirmative Action, I must define my terms.

By *Weak Affirmative Action* I mean policies that will increase the opportunities of disadvantaged people to attain social goods and offices. It includes such things as dismantling of segregated institutions, widespread advertisement to groups not previously represented in certain privileged positions, special scholarships for the disadvantaged classes (e.g., the poor, regardless of race or gender), and even using diversity or under-representation of groups with a history of past discrimination as a tie breaker when candidates for these goods and offices are relatively equal. The goal of *Weak Affirmative Action* is equal opportunity to compete, not equal results. We seek to provide each citizen regardless of race or gender a fair chance to the most favored positions in society. There is no more moral requirement to guarantee that 12% of professors are black than to guarantee that 85% of the players in the National Basketball Association are white.

By *Strong Affirmative Action* I mean preferential treatment on the basis of race, ethnicity or gender (or some other morally irrelevant criterion), discriminating in favor of underrepresented groups against overrepresented groups, aiming at roughly equal results. *Strong Affirmative Action* is *reverse discrimination*. It says it is right to do wrong to correct a wrong. This is the policy currently being promoted under the name of *Affirmative Action,* so I will use that term or "AA" for short throughout this essay to stand for this version of affirmative action. I will not argue for or against the principle of *Weak Affirmative Action*. Indeed, I think it has some moral weight. *Strong Affirmative Action* has none, or so I will argue.

This essay concentrates on AA policies with regard to race, but the arguments can be extended to cover ethnicity and gender. I think that if a case for Affirmative Action can be made it will be as a corrective to racial oppression. I will examine nine arguments regarding AA. The first six will be *negative,* attempting to show that the best arguments for Affirmative Action fail. The last three will be *positive* arguments for policies opposing Affirmative Action:

I. A Critique of Arguments for Affirmative Action

A. The Need for Role Models

This argument is straightforward. We all have need of role models, and it helps to know that others like us can be successful. We learn and are encouraged to strive for excellence by emulating our heroes and "our kind of people" who have succeeded.

In the first place it's not clear that role models of one's own racial or sexual type are necessary (let alone sufficient) for success. One of my heroes was Gandhi, an Indian Hindu, another was my grade school science teacher, Miss DeVoe, and another Martin Luther King, behind whom I marched in Civil Rights demonstrations. More important than having role models of one's "own type" is having genuinely good people, of whatever race or gender, to emulate. Our common humanity should be a sufficient basis for us to see the possibility of success in people of virtue and merit. To yield to the demand, however tempting it may be, for "role-models-just-like-us" is to treat people like means not ends. It is to elevate morally irrelevant particularity over relevant traits, such as ability and integrity. We don't need people exactly like us to find inspiration. As Steve Allen once quipped, "If I had to follow a role model exactly, I would have become a nun."

Furthermore, even if it is of some help to people with low self-esteem to gain encouragement from seeing others of their particular kind in successful positions, it is doubtful whether this is a sufficient reason to justify preferential hiring or reverse discrimination. What good is a role model who is inferior to other professors or physicians or business personnel? The best way to create role models is to promote people because they are the best qualified for the job. It is the violation of this fact that is largely responsible for the widespread whisper in the medical field (at least in New York), "Never go to a black physician under 40" (referring to the fact that AA has affected the medical system during the past twenty years). Fight the feeling how I will, I cannot help wondering on seeing a black or woman in a position of honor, "Is she in this position because she merits it or because of Affirmative Action?" Where Affirmative Action is the policy, the "figment of pigment" creates a stigma of undeservedness, whether or not it is deserved.[1]

Finally, entertain this thought experiment. Suppose we discovered that tall handsome white males somehow made the best role models for the most people, especially poor people. Suppose even large numbers of minority people somehow found inspiration in their sight. Would we be justified in hiring tall handsome white males over better qualified short Hispanic women, who were deemed less role-model worthy?[2]

B. The Compensation Argument

The argument goes like this: blacks have been wronged and severely harmed by whites. Therefore white society should compensate blacks for the injury caused them. Reverse discrimination in terms of preferential hiring, contracts, and scholarships is a fitting way to compensate for the past wrongs.[3]

This argument actually involves a distorted notion of compensation. Normally, we think of compensation as owed by a specific person A to another person B whom A has wronged in a specific way C. For example, if I have stolen your car and used it for a period of time to make business profits that would have gone to you, it is not enough that I return your car. I must pay you an amount reflecting your loss and my ability to pay. If I have made $5,000 and only have $10,000 in assets, it would not be possible for you to collect $20,000 in damages—even though that is the amount of loss you have incurred.

Sometimes compensation is extended to groups of people who have been unjustly harmed by the greater society. For example, the United States government has compensated the Japanese-Americans who were interred during the Second World War, and the West German government has paid reparations to the survivors of Nazi concentration camps. But here a specific people have been identified who were wronged in an identifiable way by the government of the nation in question.

On the face of it, demands by blacks for compensation do not fit the usual pattern. Southern states with Jim Crow laws could be accused of unjustly harming blacks, but it is hard to see that the United States government was involved in doing so. Much of the harm done to blacks was the result of private discrimination, not state action. So the Germany/U.S. analogy doesn't hold. Furthermore, it is not clear that all blacks were harmed in the same way or whether some were *unjustly* harmed or harmed more than poor whites and others (e.g., short people). Finally, even if identifiable blacks were harmed by identifiable social practices, it is not clear that most forms of Affirmative Action are appropriate to restore the situation. The usual practice of a financial payment seems more appropriate than giving a high level job to someone unqualified or only minimally qualified, who, speculatively, might have been better qualified had he not been subject to racial discrimination. If John is the star tailback of our college team with a promising professional future, and I accidentally (but culpably) drive my pickup truck over his legs, and so cripple him, John may be due compensation, but he is not due the tailback spot on the football team.

Still, there may be something intuitively compelling about compensating members of an oppressed group who are minimally qualified. Suppose that the Hatfields and the McCoys are enemy clans and some youths from the Hatfields go over and steal diamonds and gold from the McCoys, distributing it within the Hatfield economy. Even though we do not know which Hatfield youths did the stealing, we would want to restore the wealth, as far as possible, to the McCoys. One way might be to tax the Hatfields, but another might be to give preferential treatment in terms of scholarships and training programs and hiring to the McCoys.

This is perhaps the strongest argument for Affirmative Action, and it may well justify some weaker versions of AA, but it is doubtful whether it is sufficient to justify strong versions with quotas and goals and time tables in skilled positions. There are at least two reasons for this. First, we have no way of knowing how many people of any given group would have achieved some given level of competence had the world been different. This is especially relevant if my objections to the Equal Results Argument (below) are correct. Secondly, the normal criterion of competence is a strong prima facie consideration when the most important positions are at stake. There are three reasons for this: (1) treating people according to their merits respects them as persons, as ends in themselves, rather than as means to social ends (if we believe that individuals possess a dignity which deserves to be respected, then we ought to treat that individual on the basis of his or her merits, not as a mere instrument for social policy); (2) society has given people expectations that if they attain certain levels of excellence they will be awarded appropriately and (3) filling the most important positions with the best qualified

is the best way to ensure efficiency in job-related areas and in society in general. These reasons are not absolutes. They can be overridden.[4] But there is a strong presumption in their favor, so that a burden of proof rests with those who would override them.

At this point we get into the problem of whether innocent non-blacks should have to pay a penalty in terms of preferential hiring of blacks. We turn to that argument.

C. The Argument for Compensation from Those Who Innocently Benefited from Past Injustice

Young white males as innocent beneficiaries of unjust discrimination against blacks and women have no grounds for complaint when society seeks to level the tilted field. They may be innocent of oppressing blacks, other minorities, and women, but they have unjustly benefited from that oppression or discrimination. So it is perfectly proper that less qualified women and blacks be hired before them.

The operative principle is: He who knowingly and willingly benefits from a wrong must help pay for the wrong. Judith Jarvis Thomson puts it this way. "Many [white males] have been direct beneficiaries of policies which have downgraded blacks and women . . . and even those who did not directly benefit . . . had, at any rate, the advantage in the competition which comes of the confidence in one's full membership [in the community], and of one's right being recognized as a matter of course."[5] That is, white males obtain advantages in self-respect and self-confidence deriving from a racist/sexist system which denies these to blacks and women.

Here is my response to this argument: As I noted in the previous section, compensation is normally individual and specific. If A harms B regarding x, B has a right to compensation from A in regards to x. If A steals B's car and wrecks it, A has an obligation to compensate B for the stolen car, but A's son has no obligation to compensate B. Furthermore, if A dies or disappears, B has no moral right to claim that society compensate him for the stolen car—though if he has insurance, he can make such a claim to the insurance company. Sometimes a wrong cannot be compensated, and we just have to make the best of an imperfect world.

Suppose my parents, divining that I would grow up to have an unsurpassable desire to be a basketball player, bought an expensive growth hormone for me. Unfortunately, a neighbor stole it and gave it to little Michael, who gained the extra 13 inches—my 13 inches—and shot up to an enviable 6 feet 6 inches. Michael, better known as Michael Jordan, would have been a runt like me but for his luck. As it is he profited from the injustice, and excelled in basketball, as I would have done had I had my proper dose.

Do I have a right to the millions of dollars that Jordan made as a professional basketball player—the unjustly innocent beneficiary of my growth hormone? I have a right to something from the neighbor who stole the hormone, and it might be kind of Jordan to give me free tickets to the Bulls' basketball games, and remember me in his will. As far as I can see, however, he does not *owe* me anything, either legally or morally.

Suppose further that Michael Jordan and I are in high school together and we are both qualified to play basketball, only he is far better than I. Do I deserve to start in his position because I would have been as good as he is had someone not cheated me as a child? Again, I think not. But if being the lucky beneficiary of wrongdoing does not entail that Jordan (or the coach) owes me anything in regards to basketball, why should it be a reason to engage in preferential hiring in academic positions or highly coveted jobs? If minimal qualifications are not adequate to override excellence in basketball, even when the minimality is a consequence of wrongdoing, why should they be adequate in other areas?

D. The Diversity Argument

It is important that we learn to live in a pluralistic world, learning to get along with those of other races, conditions, and cultures, so we should have schools and employment situations as fully integrated as possible. In a shrinking world we need to appreciate each other's culture and specific way of looking at life. Diversity is an important symbol and educative device. Thus, proponents of AA argue, preferential treatment is warranted to perform this role in society.

Once again, there is some truth in these concerns. Diversity of ideas challenges us to scrutinize our own values and beliefs, and diverse customs have aesthetic and moral value, helping us to appreciate the novelty and beauty in life. Diversity may expand our moral horizons. But, again, while we can admit the value of diversity, it hardly seems

adequate to override the moral requirement to treat each person with equal respect. *Diversity for diversity's sake is moral promiscuity*, since it obfuscates rational distinctions, undermines treating individuals as ends, treating them, instead, as mere means (to the goals of social engineering), and, furthermore, unless those hired are highly qualified, the diversity factor threatens to become a fetish. At least at the higher levels of business and the professions, *competence* far outweighs considerations of diversity. I do not care whether the group of surgeons operating on me reflect racial or gender balance, but I do care that they are highly qualified. Neither do most football or basketball fans care whether their team reflects ethnic and gender diversity, but demand the best combination of players available. And likewise with airplane pilots, military leaders, business executives, and, may I say it, teachers and university professors. One need not be a white male to teach, let alone, appreciate Shakespeare, nor need one be black to teach, let alone appreciate, Alice Walker's *The Color Purple*.

There may be times when diversity may seem to be "crucial" to the well-being of a diverse community, such as for a police force. Suppose that white policemen tend to overreact to young black males and the latter group distrust white policemen. Hiring more less qualified black policemen, who would relate better to these youth, may have overall utilitarian value. But such a move, while we might make it as a lesser evil, could have serious consequences in allowing the demographic prejudices to dictate social policy. A better strategy would be to hire the best police, that is, those who can perform in a disciplined, intelligent manner, regardless of their race. A white policeman must be able to arrest a black burglar, even as a black policeman must be able to arrest a white rapist. The quality of the police man or woman, not their race or gender, is what counts.

On the other hand, if a black policeman, though lacking some of the formal skills of the white policeman, really is able to do a better job in the black community, this might constitute a case of merit, not Affirmative Action. As Stephen Kershnar points out, this is similar to the legitimacy of hiring Chinese men to act as undercover agents in Chinatown.[6]

E. The Equal Results Argument

Some philosophers and social scientists hold that human nature is roughly identical, so that on a fair playing field the same proportion from every race and ethnic group and both genders would attain to the highest positions in every area of endeavor. It would follow that any inequality of results itself is evidence for inequality of opportunity.

> History is important when considering governmental rules like Test 21 because low scores by blacks can be traced in large measure to the legacy of slavery and racism: segregation, poor schooling, exclusion from trade unions, malnutrition, and poverty have all played their roles. Unless one assumes that blacks are naturally less able to pass the test, the conclusion must be that the results are themselves socially and legally constructed, not a mere given for which law and society can claim no responsibility.
>
> The conclusion seems to be that genuine equality eventually requires equal results. Obviously blacks have been treated unequally throughout U.S. history, and just as obviously the economic and psychological effects of that inequality linger to this day, showing up in lower income and poorer performance in school and on tests than whites achieve. Since we have no reason to believe that differences in performance can be explained by factors other than history, equal results are a good benchmark by which to measure progress made toward genuine equality. (John Arthur, *The Unfinished Constitution* [Belmont, CA: Wadsworth Publishing Co., 1990], p. 238)

Sterling Harwood seems to support a similar theory when he writes, "When will [AA] end? When will affirmative action stop compensating blacks? As soon as the unfair advantage is gone, affirmative action will stop. The elimination of the unfair advantage can be determined by showing that the percentage of blacks hired and admitted at least roughly equaled the percentage of blacks in the population."[7]

Albert G. Mosley develops a similar argument. "Establishing Blacks' presence at a level commensurate with their proportion in the relevant labor market need not be seen as an attempt to actualize some valid prediction. Rather, given the impossibility of determining what level of representation Blacks would have achieved were it not for racial discrimination, the assumption of proportional representa-

tion is the only *fair* assumption to make. This is not to argue that Blacks should be maintained in such positions, but their contrived exclusion merits equally contrived rectification."[8] The result of a just society should be equal numbers in proportion to each group in the work force.

However, Arthur, Mosley, and Harwood fail even to consider studies that suggest that there are innate differences between races, sexes, and groups. If there are genetic differences in intelligence, temperament, and other qualities within families, why should we not expect such differences between racial groups and the two genders? Why should the evidence for this be completely discounted?

Mosley's reasoning is as follows: Since we don't know for certain whether groups proportionately differ in talent, we should presume that they are equal in every respect. So we should presume that if we were living in a just society, there would be roughly proportionate representation in every field (e.g., equal representation of doctors, lawyers, professors, carpenters, airplane pilots, basketball players, and criminals). Hence, it is only fair—productive of justice—to aim at proportionate representation in these fields.

But the logic is flawed. Under a situation of ignorance we should not presume equality or inequality of representation—but conclude that we *don't know* what the results would be in a just society. Ignorance doesn't favor equal group representation any more than it favors unequal group representation. It is neutral between them.

Consider this analogy. Suppose that you were the owner of a National Basketball Association team. Suppose that I and other frustrated white basketball players bring a class-action suit against you and all the other team owners, claiming that you have subtly and systematically discriminated against white and Asian basketball players who make up less than 20% of the NBA players. You reply that you and the other owners are just responding to individual merit, we respond that the discrimination is a function of deep prejudice against white athletes, especially basketball players, who are discouraged in every way from competing on fair terms with blacks who dominate the NBA. You would probably wish that the matter of unequal results was not brought up in the first place, but once it has been, would you not be in your rights to defend yourself by producing evidence, showing that *average* physiological differences exist between blacks and whites and Asians, so that we should not presume unjust discrimination?

Similarly, the proponents of the Doctrine of Equal Results open the door to a debate over average ability in ethnic, racial and gender groups. The proponent of equal or fair opportunity would just as soon downplay this feature in favor of judging people as individuals by their merit (hard though that may be). But if the proponent of AA insists on the Equal Results Thesis, we are obliged to examine the Equal Abilities Thesis, on which it is based—the thesis that various ethnic and gender groups all have the same distribution of talent on the relevant characteristic. With regard to cognitive skills we must consult the best evidence we have on average group differences. We need to compare average IQ scores, SAT scores, standard personality testing, success in academic and professional areas and the like. If the evidence shows that group differences are nonexistent, the AA proponent may win, but if the evidence turns out to be against the Equal Abilities Thesis, the AA proponent loses. Consider for a start that the average white and Asian scores 195 points higher on the SAT tests and that on virtually all IQ tests for the past seven or eight decades the average black IQ is 85 as opposed to the average white and Asian IQ at over 100, or that males and females differ significantly on cognitive ability tests. Females outperform males in reading comprehension, perceptual speed, and associative memory (ratios of 1.4 to 2.2), but males typically outnumber females among high scoring individuals in mathematics, science and social science (by a ratio of 7.0 in the top 1% of overall mathematics distribution).[9] The results of average GRE, LSAT, MCAT scores show similar patterns or significant average racial difference. The black scholar Glenn Loury notes, "In 1990 black high school seniors from families with annual incomes of $70,000 or more scored an average of 855 on the SAT, compared with average scores of 855 and 879 respectively for Asian-American and white seniors whose families had incomes between $10,000 and 20,000 per year."[10] Note, we are speaking about statistical averages. There are brilliant and retarded people in each group.

When such statistics are discussed many people feel uncomfortable and want to drop the subject. Perhaps these statistics are misleading, but then we need to look carefully at the total evidence. The proponent of equal opportunity urges us to get beyond racial and gender criteria in assignment of offices and opportunities and treat each person, not as an *average* white or black or female or male, but as a *person* judged on his or her own merits.

Furthermore, on the logic of Mosley and company, we should take aggressive AA against Asians and Jews since they are overrepresented in science, technology, and medicine, and we should presume that Asians and Jews are no more talented than average. So that each group receives its fair share, we should ensure that 12% of the philosophers in the United States are black, reduce the percentage of Jews from an estimated 15% to 2%—thus firing about 1,300 Jewish philosophers. The fact that Asians are producing 50% of Ph.D.s in science and math in this country and blacks less than 1% clearly shows, on this reasoning, that we are providing special secret advantages to Asians. By this logic, we should reduce the quota of blacks in the NBA to 12%.

But why does society have to enter into this results game in the first place? Why do we have to decide whether all difference is environmental or genetic? Perhaps we should simply admit that we lack sufficient evidence to pronounce on these issues with any certainty—but if so, should we not be more modest in insisting on equal results? Here's a thought experiment. Take two families of different racial groups, Green and Blue. The Greens decide to have only two children, to spend all their resources on them, and to give them the best possible education. The two Green kids respond well and end up with achievement test scores in the 99th percentile. The Blues fail to practice family planning and have 15 children. They can only afford 2 children, but lack of ability or whatever prevents them from keeping their family size down. Now they need help for their large family. Why does society have to step in and help them? Society did not force them to have 15 children. Suppose that the achievement test scores of the 15 children fall below the 25th percentile. They cannot compete with the Greens. But now enters AA. It says that it is society's fault that the Blue children are not as able as the Greens and that the Greens must pay extra taxes to enable the Blues to compete. No restraints are put on the Blues regarding family size. This seems unfair to the Greens. Should the Green children be made to bear responsibility for the consequences of the Blues' voluntary behavior?[11]

My point is simply that philosophers like Arthur, Harwood, and Mosley need to cast their net wider and recognize that demographics and child-bearing and -rearing practices are crucial factors in achievement. People have to take some responsibility for their actions. The equal results argument (or axiom) misses a greater part of the picture.

F. The "No One Deserves His Talents" Argument against Meritocracy

According to this argument, the competent do not deserve their intelligence, their superior character, their industriousness, or their discipline; therefore they have no right to the best positions in society; therefore it is not unjust to give these positions to less (but still minimally) qualified blacks and women. In one form this argument holds that since no one deserves anything, society may use any criteria it pleases to distribute goods. The criterion most often designated is social utility. Versions of this argument are found in the writings of John Arthur, John Rawls, Bernard Boxill, Michael Kinsley, Ronald Dworkin, and Richard Wasserstrom. Rawls writes, "No one deserves his place in the distribution of native endowments, any more than one deserves one's initial starting place in society. The assertion that a man deserves the superior character that enables him to make the effort to cultivate his abilities is equally problematic; for his character depends in large part upon fortunate family and social circumstances for which he can claim no credit. The notion of desert seems not to apply to these cases."[12] Michael Kinsley is even more adamant:

> Opponents of affirmative action are hung up on a distinction that seems more profoundly irrelevant: treating individuals versus treating groups. What is the moral difference between dispensing favors to people on their "merits" as individuals and passing out society's benefits on the basis of group identification?
>
> Group identifications like race and sex are, of course, immutable. They have nothing to do with a person's moral worth. But the same is true of most of what comes under the label "merit." The tools you need for getting ahead in a meritocratic society—not all of them but most: talent, education, instilled cultural values such as ambition—are distributed just as arbitrarily as skin color. They are fate. The notion that people somehow "deserve" the ad-

vantages of these characteristics in a way they don't "deserve" the advantage of their race is powerful, but illogical.[13]

It will help to put the argument in outline form.

1. Society may award jobs and positions as it sees fit as long as individuals have no claim to these positions.

2. To have a claim to something means that one has earned it or deserves it.

3. But no one has earned or deserves his intelligence, talent, education or cultural values which produce superior qualifications.

4. If a person does not deserve what produces something, he does not deserve its products.

5. Therefore better qualified people do not deserve their qualifications.

6. Therefore, society may override their qualifications in awarding jobs and positions as it sees fit (for social utility or to compensate for previous wrongs).

So it is permissible if a minimally qualified black or woman is admitted to law or medical school ahead of a white male with excellent credentials or if a less qualified person from an "underutilized" group gets a professorship ahead of an eminently better qualified white male. Sufficiency and underutilization together outweigh excellence.

My response: Premise 4 is false. To see this, reflect that just because I do not deserve the money that I have been given as a gift (for instance) does not mean that I am not entitled to what I get with that money. If you and I both get a gift of $100 and I bury mine in the sand for five years while you invest yours wisely and double its value at the end of five years, I cannot complain that you should split the increase 50/50 since neither of us deserved the original gift. If we accept the notion of responsibility at all, we must hold that persons deserve the fruits of their labor and conscious choices. Of course, we might want to distinguish moral from legal desert and argue that, morally speaking, effort is more important than outcome, whereas, legally speaking, outcome may be more important. Nevertheless, there are good reasons in terms of efficiency, motivation, and rough justice for holding a strong prima facie principle of giving scarce high positions to those most competent.

The attack on moral desert is perhaps the most radical move that egalitarians like Rawls and company have made against meritocracy, and the ramifications of their attack are far reaching. Here are some implications: Since I do not deserve my two good eyes or two good kidneys, the social engineers may take one of each from me to give to those needing an eye or a kidney—even if they have damaged their organs by their own voluntary actions; since no one deserves anything, we do not deserve pay for our labors or praise for a job well done or first prize in the race we win. The notion of moral responsibility vanishes in a system of levelling.

But there is no good reason to accept the argument against desert. We do act freely and, as such, we are responsible for our actions. We deserve the fruits of our labor, reward for our noble feats and punishment for our misbehavior.[14]

We have considered six arguments for Affirmative Action and have found no compelling case for Strong AA and only one plausible argument (a version of the compensation argument) for Weak AA. We must now turn to the arguments against Affirmative Action to see whether they fare any better.

◇

II. Arguments against Affirmative Action

A. Affirmative Action Requires Discrimination against a Different Group

Weak AA weakly discriminates against new minorities, mostly innocent young white males, and Strong Affirmative Action strongly discriminates against these new minorities. As I argued in I. 4, this discrimination is unwarranted, since, even if some compensation to blacks were indicated, it would be unfair to make innocent white males bear the whole brunt of the payments. Recently I had this experience. I knew a brilliant philosopher, with outstanding publications in first level journals, who was having difficulty getting a tenure-track position. For the first time in my life I offered to make a phone call on his behalf to a university to which he had applied. When I got the Chair of the Search Committee, he offered that the committee was under instructions from the Administration to hire a woman or a black. They had one of each on their short list, so they weren't even considering the applications of

white males. At my urging, he retrieved my friend's file, and said, "This fellow looks far superior to the two candidates we're interviewing, but there's nothing I can do about it." Cases like this come to my attention regularly. In fact, it is poor white youth who become the new pariahs on the job market. The children of the wealthy have little trouble getting into the best private grammar schools and, on the basis of superior early education, into the best universities, graduate schools, managerial and professional positions. Affirmative Action simply shifts injustice, setting blacks, Hispanics, Native Americans, Asians, and women against young white males, especially ethnic and poor white males. It makes no more sense to discriminate in favor of a rich black or female who had the opportunity of the best family and education available against a poor white, than it does to discriminate in favor of white males against blacks or women. It does little to rectify the goal of providing equal opportunity to all.

At the end of his essay supporting Affirmative Action, Albert Mosley points out that other groups besides blacks have been benefitted by AA, "women, the disabled, the elderly."[15] He's correct in including the elderly, for through powerful lobbies, such as the AARP, they do get special benefits, including Medicare, and may sue on the grounds of being discriminated against due to *Agism*, prejudice against older people. Might this not be a reason to reconsider Affirmative Action? Consider the sheer rough percentages of those who qualify for AA programs.

Group	Percentage in Population
1. Women	52%
2. Blacks	12%
3. Hispanics	9%
4. Native Americans	2%
5. Asians	4%
6. Physically & Mentally Disabled	10%
7. Welfare Recipients	6%
8. The Elderly	25% (est. Adults over 60)
9. Italians (in New York City)	3%
Totals	**123%**

The elderly can sue on the grounds of Agism, receive entitlements in terms of Social Security and

Medicare, and have the AARP lobbying on their behalf. Recently, it has been proposed that homosexuals be included in oppressed groups deserving Affirmative Action.[16] At Northeastern University in 1996 the faculty governing body voted to grant homosexuals Affirmative Action status at this university. How many more percentage points would this add? Several authors have advocated putting all poor people on the list.[17] And if we took handicaps seriously, would we not add ugly people, obese people, and, especially, short people, for which there is ample evidence of discrimination? How about left-handed people (about 9% of the population)— they can't play shortstop or third base and have to put up with a right-handedly biased world. The only group not on the list is that of white males. Are they, especially healthy, middle class young white males, becoming the new "oppressed class"? Should we add them to our list?

Respect for persons entails that we treat each person as an end in him or herself, not simply as a means to be used for social purposes. What is wrong about discrimination against blacks is that it fails to treat black people as individuals, judging them instead by their skin color not their merit. What is wrong about discrimination against women is that it fails to treat them as individuals, judging them by their gender, not their merit. What is equally wrong about *Affirmative Action* is that it fails to treat white males with dignity as individuals, judging them by *both their race and gender,* instead of their merit. *Current Strong Affirmative Action is both racist and sexist.*

B. Affirmative Action Encourages Mediocrity and Incompetence

A few years ago Rev. Jesse Jackson joined protesters at Harvard Law School in demanding that the law school faculty hire black women. Jackson dismissed Law School Dean Robert C. Clark's standard of choosing the best qualified person for the job as "cultural anemia." "We cannot just define who is qualified in the most narrow vertical academic terms," he said. "Most people in the world are yellow, brown, black, poor, non-Christian and don't speak English, and they can't wait for some white males with archaic rules to appraise them."[18] It might be noted that if Jackson is correct about the depth of cultural decadence at Harvard, blacks might be well advised to form and support their own more vital law schools and leave places like Harvard to their archaism.

At several universities, the administration has forced departments to hire members of minorities even when far superior candidates were available. Shortly after obtaining my Ph.D. in the late 1970s, I was mistakenly identified as a black philosopher (I had a civil rights record and was once a black studies major) and was flown to a major university, only to be rejected for a more qualified candidate when it was discovered that I was white.

Stories of the bad effects of Affirmative Action abound. The philosopher Sidney Hook writes that "at one Ivy League university, representatives of the Regional HEW[19] demanded an explanation of why there were no women or minority students in the Graduate Department of Religious Studies. They were told that a reading knowledge of Hebrew and Greek was presupposed. Whereupon the representatives of HEW advised orally: 'Then end those old fashioned programs that require irrele-vant languages. And start up programs on relevant things which minority group students can study without learning languages.'"[20]

Nicholas Capaldi notes that the staff of HEW itself was one-half women, three-fifths members of minorities, and one-half black—a clear case of racial over-representation.

In 1972 officials at Stanford University discovered a proposal for the government to monitor curriculum in higher education: the "Summary Statement . . . Sex Discrimination Proposed HEW Regulation to Effectuate Title IX of the Education Amendment of 1972" to "establish and use internal procedure for reviewing curricula, designed both to ensure that they do not reflect discrimination on the basis of sex and to resolve complaints concerning allegations of such discrimination, pursuant to procedural standards to be prescribed by the Director of the office of Civil Rights." Fortunately, Secretary of HEW Caspar Weinberger discovered the intrusion and assured Stanford University that he would never approve it.[21]

Government programs of enforced preferential treatment tend to appeal to the lowest possible common denominator. Witness the 1974 HEW Revised Order No. 14 on Affirmative Action expectations for preferential hiring: "Neither minorities nor female employees should be required to possess higher qualifications than those of the lowest qualified incumbents."

Furthermore, no test may be given to candidates unless it is *proved* to be relevant to the job.

No standard or criteria which have, by intent or effect, worked to exclude women or minorities as a class can be utilized, unless the institution can demonstrate the necessity of such standard to the performance of the job in question.

Whenever a validity study is called for . . . the user should include . . . an investigation of suitable alternative selection procedures and suitable alternative methods of using the selection procedure which have as little adverse impact as possible. . . . Whenever the user is shown an alternative selection procedure with evidence of less adverse impact and substantial evidence of validity for the same job in similar circumstances, the user should investigate it to determine the appropriateness of using or validating it in accord with these guidelines.[22]

At the same time Americans are wondering why standards in our country are falling and the Japanese and Koreans are getting ahead. Affirmative Action with its twin idols, Sufficiency of Qualification and Diversity, is the enemy of excellence. I will develop this thought in the next section.

C. An Argument from the Principle of Merit

Traditionally, we have believed that the highest positions in society should be awarded to those who are best qualified. The Koran states that "A ruler who appoints any man to an office, when there is in his dominion another man better qualified for it, sins against God and against the State." Rewarding excellence both seems just to the individuals in the competition and makes for efficiency. Note that one of the most successful acts of racial integration, the Brooklyn Dodgers' recruitment of Jackie Robinson in the late 1940s, was done in just this way, according to merit. If Robinson had been brought into the major league as a mediocre player or had batted .200, he would have been scorned and sent back to the minors where he belonged.

As mentioned earlier, merit is not an absolute value, but there are strong *prima facie* reasons for awarding positions on that basis, and it should enjoy a weighty presumption in our social practices.

In a celebrated article Ronald Dworkin says that "Bakke had no case" because society did not owe Bakke anything. That may be, but then why does it owe anyone anything? Dworkin puts the matter in Utility terms, but if that is the case, society may owe Bakke a place at the University of California/Davis, for it seems a reasonable rule-utilitarian principle that achievement should be rewarded in society. We generally want the best to have the best positions, the best qualified candidate to win the political office, the most brilliant and competent scientist to be chosen for the most challenging research project, the best qualified pilots to become commercial pilots, only the best soldiers to become generals. Only when little is at stake do we weaken the standards and content ourselves with sufficiency (rather than excellence)—there are plenty of jobs where "sufficiency" rather than excellence is required. Perhaps we have even come to feel that medicine or law or university professorships are so routine that they can be performed by minimally qualified people—in which case AA has a place.

Note! No one is calling for quotas or proportional representation of *underutilized* groups in the National Basketball Association where blacks make up 80% of the players. But, surely, if merit and merit alone reigns in sports, should it not be valued at least as much in education and industry?

The case for meritocracy has two pillars. One pillar is a deontological argument, which holds that we ought to treat people as ends and not merely means. By giving people what they deserve as *individuals* rather than as members of *groups,* we show respect for their inherent worth. If you and I take a test, and you get 95% of the answers correct, and I only get 50% correct, it would be unfair to you for both of us to receive the same grade, say an A, and even more unfair to give me a higher grade A+ than your B+. Although I have heard cases where teachers have been instructed to "race norm" grading (giving blacks and Hispanics higher grades for the same numerical scores), most proponents of AA stop short of advocating such a practice. But, I would ask them, what's really the difference between taking the overall average of a white and black and "race norming" it? If teachers shouldn't do it, why should administrators?

The second pillar for meritocracy is utilitarian. In the end, we will be better off by honoring excellence. We want the best leaders, teachers, policemen, physicians, generals, lawyers, and airplane pilots that we can possibly produce in society. So our program should be to promote equal opportunity, as much as is feasible in a free market economy, and reward people according to their individual merit.[23]

Conclusion

Let me sum up my discussion. The goal of the Civil Rights movement and of moral people everywhere has been justice for all, including equal opportunity. The question is: how best to get there. Civil Rights legislation removed the unjust legal barriers, opening the way towards equal opportunity, but it did not tackle the deeper causes that produce differential results. Weak Affirmative Action aims at encouraging minorities to strive for excellence in all areas of life, without unduly jeopardizing the rights of majorities. The problem of Weak Affirmative Action is that it easily slides into Strong Affirmative Action where quotas, "goals and timetables," "equal results"—in a word—*reverse discrimination*—prevail and are forced onto groups, thus promoting mediocrity, inefficiency, and resentment. Furthermore, AA aims at the higher levels of society—universities and skilled jobs, but if we want to improve our society, the best way to do it is to concentrate on families, children, early education, and the like, so all are prepared to avail themselves of opportunity.

Affirmative Action, on the one hand, is too much, too soon and on the other hand, too little, too late.

In addition to the arguments I have offered, Affirmative Action, rather than unite people of good will in the common cause of justice, tends to balkanize us into segregation-thinking. Professor Derrick Bell of Harvard Law School recently said that the African American Supreme Court Judge Clarence Thomas, in his opposition to Affirmative Action, "doesn't think black."[24] Does Bell really claim that there is a standard and proper "black" (and presumably a white) way of thinking? Ideologues like Bell, whether radical blacks like himself, or Nazis who advocate "think Aryan," both represent the same thing: cynicism about rational debate, the very antithesis of the quest for impartial truth and justice. People who believe in reason to resolve our differences will oppose this kind of balkanization of the races.

Martin Luther said that humanity is like a man mounting a horse who always tends to fall off on the other side of the horse. This seems to be the case with Affirmative Action. Attempting to redress the discriminatory iniquities of our history, our well-intentioned social engineers now engage in new forms of discriminatory iniquity and thereby think that they have successfully mounted the horse of racial harmony. They have only fallen off on the other side of the issue.[25]

Endnotes

1.   This argument is related to *The Need of Breaking Stereotypes Argument*. Society may simply need to know that there are talented blacks and women, so that it does not automatically assign them lesser respect or status. The right response is that hiring less qualified people is neither fair to those better qualified who are passed over nor an effective way to remove inaccurate stereotypes. If high competence is accepted as the criterion for hiring, then it is unjust to override it for purposes of social engineering. Furthermore, if blacks and women are known to hold high positions simply because of reverse discrimination, they will still lack the respect due to those of their rank.

2.   Stephen Kershnar suggested this point to me.

3.   For a good discussion of this argument see B. Boxill, "The Morality of Reparation," in *Social Theory and Practice* 2:1 (1972) and Albert G. Mosley in his and Nicholas Capaldi, *Affirmative Action: Social Justice or Unfair Preference?* (Rowman & Littlefield, 1996), p. 23–27.

4.   Merit sometimes maybe justifiably overridden by need, as when parents choose to spend extra earnings on special education for their disabled child rather than for their gifted child. Sometimes we may override merit for utilitarian purposes. E.g., suppose you are the best shortstop on a baseball team but are also the best catcher. You'd rather play shortstop, but the manager decides to put you at catcher because, while your friend can do an adequate job at short, no one else is adequate at catcher. It's permissible for you to be assigned the job of catcher. Probably, some expression of appreciation would be due you.

5.   Judith Jarvis Thomson, "Preferential Hiring," in Marshall Cohen, Thomas Nagel and Thomas Scanlon, eds., *Equality and Preferential Treatment* (Princeton: Princeton University Press, 1977).

6.   Stephen Kershnar pointed this out in written comments (December 22, 1997).

7.   Sterling Harwood, "The Justice of Affirmative Action," in Yearger Hudson and C. Peden, eds., *The Bill of Rights: Bicentennial Reflections* (Lewiston, NY: Edwin Mellen).

8. See Mosley, op cit., p. 28 and Bernard Boxill, *Blacks and Social Justice* (Rowman & Littlefield, 1984), whom Mosley quotes in his article, also defends this position.

9. Larry Hedges and Amy Nowell, "Sex Differences in Mental Test Scores, Variability, and Numbers of High-Scoring Individuals," *Science* 269 (July 1995), pp. 41–45. See Phillip E. Vernon's summary of the literature in *Intelligence: Heredity and Environment* (New York, 1979), Yves Christen, "Sex Differences in the Human Brain," in Nicholas Davidson, ed., *Gender Sanity* (Rowman & Littlefield, 1989) and T. Bouchard et al., "Sources of Human Psychological Differences: The Minnesota Studies of Twins Reared Apart," *Science* 250 (1990); Richard Herrnstein and Charles Murray, *The Bell Curve* (New York: Free Press, 1994); and Michael E. Levin, *Why Race Matters* (Westport, CT: Praeger, 1997), for support for the thesis of racial and gender differences. Although these matters are controversial, the evidence for average differences must be carefully considered before we accept the equal outcomes thesis. See also Arianna Stassinopoulos, *The Female Woman* (Davis-Poynter, 1973), p. 28f for corroboration of this thesis.

10. Glen Loury, "'Getting Involved' An Appeal for Greater Community Participation in the Public Schools," *Washington Post Education Review* (August 6, 1995). Stephan and Abigail Thernstrom, in *America in Black and White* (1997), offer the same statistics and add:

> Today's typical twelfth-grader scores no better on a reading test than the average white in the eighth grade, and is 5.4 years behind the typical white in science . . . blacks with a parent who graduated from college on average score below whites whose parents never finished high school. In a 1992 test of adult literacy and numeracy, the typical black college graduate performed only a shade better than the typical white high school graduate with no college, and far below the white college dropout." (p. 19)

11. Iddo Landau, "Are You Entitled to Affirmative Action?" *Applied Philosophy* 11 (Winter/Spring 1997) and Richard Kahlenberg, "Class Not Race" (*The New Republic*, April 3, 1995) advocate affirmative action on the basis of class or low income, not race or gender. I think this is an improvement, depending on how it is implemented, but it ignores family responsibility.

12. John Rawls, *A Theory of Justice* (Harvard University Press, 1971), p. 104. See Bernard Boxill, "The Morality of Preferential Hiring," *Philosophy and Public Affairs* 7:3 (1983), part of which is reprinted above.

13. Michael Kinsley, "Equal Lack of Opportunity," *Harper's* (June 1983).

14. My point does not depend on any particular theory of free will. One is reminded of Nozick's point that Rawls' professed aim of articulating the enormous worth of each individual seems contrary to the reductive determinism in his natural lottery argument.

15. Albert Mosley, op cit., p. 53.

16. J. Sartorelli, "The Nature of Affirmative Action, Anti-Gay Oppression, and the Alleviation of Enduring Harm," *International Journal of Applied Philosophy* 11:2 (1997).

17. For example, Iddo Landau, "Are You Entitled to Affirmative Action?", *International Journal of Applied Philosophy* 11:2 (1997), and Richard Kahlenberg, "Class Not Race," *The New Republic* (April 3, 1995).

18. *New York Times,* May 10, 1990.

19. HEW stands for the Federal Department of "Health, Education & Welfare."

20. Quoted by Nicholas Capaldi, *Out of Order: Affirmative Action and the Crisis of Doctrinaire Liberalism* (Buffalo, NY: Prometheus, 1985).

21. Capaldi, op cit., p. 95.

22. Capaldi, ibid. Michael Levin begins his book *Feminism and Freedom* (Transaction Press: 1987) with federal court case *Beckman v NYFD* in which 88 women who failed the New York City Fire Department's entrance exam in 1977 filed a class-action sex discrimination suit. The court found that the physical strength component of the test was not job-related, and thus a violation of Title VII of the Civil Rights Act, and ordered the city to hire 49 of the women. It further ordered the fire department to devise a special, less-demanding physical strength exam for women. Following EEOC guidelines if the passing rate for women is less than 80% that of the passing rate of men, the test is presumed invalid.

23. For further discussion of this point see my "Equality and Desert," *Philosophy* 72 (1997).

24. See L. Gordon Crovitz, "Borking Begins, but Mudballs Bounce Off Judge Thomas," *The Wall Street Journal* (July 17, 1991). Have you noticed the irony in this mudslinging at Judge Thomas? The same blacks and whites who oppose Judge Thomas, as not the best person for the job, are themselves the strongest proponents of Affirmative Action, which embraces the tenet that minimally qualified blacks and women should get jobs over white males.

25. Some of the material in this essay appeared in "The Moral Status of Affirmative Action," *Public Affairs Quarterly* 6:2 (1992). I have not had space to consider all the objections to my position or discuss the issue of freedom of association, which, I think, should be given much scope in private but not in public institutions. Barbara Bergmann (*In Defense of Affirmative Action* [New York: Basic Books, 1996], pp. 122–25) and others argue that we already offer preferential treatment for athletes and veterans, especially in university admissions, so, being consistent, we should provide it for women and minorities. My answer is that I am against giving athletic scholarships, and I regard scholarships to veterans as a part of a contractual relationship, a reward for service to one's country. But I distinguish entrance programs from actual employment. I don't think that veterans should be afforded special privilege in hiring practices, unless it be as a tie breaker.

I should also mention that my arguments from merit and respect apply more specifically to public institutions than private ones, where issues of property rights and freedom of association carry more weight.

My gratitude to Wallace Matson, Bill Shaw, Stephen Kershnar, Jim Landesman, Jeffrey Reiman, and Elliot Cohen for comments on earlier versions of this essay.

30. The Case against Pojman

ALBERT MOSLEY

Albert Mosley argues that Louis Pojman's main arguments against affirmative action hold only against straw positions that defenders of affirmative action have never held. Arguing that affirmative action is a policy designed to facilitate the inclusion of blacks and women and is not meant as an expression of racial or sexual superiority, he contends that this makes it quite different from Pojman's strong affirmative action, which he views as a form of reverse racism that would be wrong even if it were meant to correct a wrong.

Pojman's attack on policies that consider race or gender as important factors in determining the award of educational, employment, and investment opportunities, what he calls "strong affirmative action," is a textbook case of how to use the strawman fallacy. His characterization of "strong affirmative action" as "reverse, unjust discrimination against young white males" is his first strawman.[1] For, by definition, such a policy would be little more than a form of reverse racism, and would be wrong, even if it was meant to correct a wrong.

By beginning with this characterization, Pojman is able to ignore the significant disanalogies between racism and sexism, on the one hand, and so-called "preferential policies," on the other hand. Policies designed to facilitate the inclusion of blacks and women are meant not as an expression of the racial and sexual superiority of blacks and females over white males, but to correct for the belief in the racial superiority of whites and the gender superiority of males. White males are not construed as innately inferior, morally tainted, or in need of paternal guidance by blacks and women.

The fact that many white males feel threatened by demands for the inclusion of black, and women

is not because "strong affirmative action" simply reverses racist and sexist roles. Nonetheless, I believe the failure of blacks and women to appreciate the white male perspective is a serious moral shortcoming of the civil rights revolution. Too often, blacks and women have adopted a posture of moral superiority by default, without having sufficiently reflected on and cultivated their own efforts at practical judgments.

Pojman's second strawman is his reconstruction of the justification for "preferential policies" offered by its defenders:

> Because *some* whites once enslaved some blacks, the descendants of those slaves, some of whom may now enjoy high incomes and social status, have a right to opportunities and offices over better qualified whites who had nothing to do with either slavery or the oppression of blacks, and who may even have suffered hardship comparable to that of poor blacks.[2]

On this view of "strong affirmative action," while only *some* whites enslaved some blacks, *all* descendants of slaves are to be granted preferential status over *all* whites. By this, Pojman implies that being the descendant of a slave imparts a kind of genealogical privilege that trumps all other considerations, including injuries of class. This is a position

Reprinted from the *International Journal of Applied Philosophy* 12:2 (1998), pp. 161–168, by permission.

that I certainly have not taken, nor is it a position that any defender of preferential policies, to my knowledge, has ever advocated. And Pojman provides no citations to support his claim that this is a position advocated by anyone.

Having prepared the stage, he proceeds to a more detailed refutation of strawman arguments in favor of policies of inclusion. His first target is the argument that blacks and women need individuals from their group to serve as role models. He writes:

> This argument is straightforward. We all have need of role models, and it helps to know that others like us can be successful. We learn and are encouraged to strive for excellence by emulating our heroes and "our kind of people" who have succeeded.[3]

But, Pojman counters, role models should be those who are most competent, and, he claims, race and gender are irrelevant to determinations of competence.

> One of my heroes was Gandhi, an Indian Hindu, another was my grade school teacher, Miss DeVoe, and another Martin Luther King, behind whom I marched in Civil Rights demonstrations. More important than having role models of one's "own type" is having genuinely good people, of whatever race or gender, to emulate.[4]

Here Pojman takes his own ability to choose role models from the best examples that humanity has had to offer as exemplary of how all people should choose their role models. But we should note that the examples he provides are few and of a similar kind: nurturers and moral leaders. He does not tell us who were his role models in philosophy, politics, business, science, industry, exploration, warfare, literature, music, art, etc., because they undoubtedly would have been just like him, white males.

On the other hand, after centuries of theological, philosophical, scientific, and aesthetic arguments purporting to show that black people were cursed by God, cognitively and morally degenerate, and members of a species intermediate between apes and humans, there remains serious doubt by both blacks and whites that black people are capable of the kinds of achievements Pojman and other white males are able to take for granted. Taking our common profession as an example, David Hume denied that any other race but whites had developed credible civilizations:

> I am apt to suspect the negroes to be naturally interior to the whites. There scarcely ever was a civilised nation of that complexion, nor even an individual, eminent either in action or speculation. No ingenious manufactures amongst them, no arts, no sciences. On the other hand, the most rude and barbarous of the whites, such as the ancient Germans, the present Tartars, have still something eminent about them, in their valor, form of government, or some other particular. Such a uniform and constant difference could not happen, in so many countries and ages, if nature had not made an initial distinction between these breeds of men.[5]

And while Hume's work on the foundations of knowledge awoke Immanuel Kant from his "dogmatic slumber," Hume's opinions on the differences between the races reinforced Kant's view that skin color was an indelible sign of cognitive capacity. "So fundamental is the difference between [the black and white] races of man . . . it appears to be as great in regard to mental capacities as in color." Thus, "a clear proof that what [a Negro] said was stupid" is that "this fellow was quite black from head to foot."[6]

Clearly, it is not affirmative action that has created the stigma of undeservedness that Pojman calls the "figment of the pigment."[7] For centuries, the presumption has been that if a person is black, that in itself was evidence of his or her inherent incompetence and lack of potential. Given this historical legacy, it is not difficult to see how race might be a tacit factor in judgments of potential and actual performance, even by well-meaning contemporary philosophers.

I am sure that Pojman is aware of the legacy of degradation I have alluded to, and the effect that stereotypes promulgated by the most respected minds of an era might have in shaping the opportunities and orientations of the stereotyped. But he exhibits no inclination to explore this possibility, or even to acknowledge its existence and credibility. On the other hand, in opposing the "argument" that the underrepresentation of blacks and women is a legacy of racism and sexism, he shows no hesitation in citing the historical argument that there are "innate differences between races, sexes, and groups," such that we should expect groups to be represented differentially rather than proportionally in different areas.[8] Elaborating on this claim, he cites evidence that black high school seniors from families with annual incomes of $70,000 or more scored no higher on the SAT than white and Asian-Americans from families with incomes between $10,000 and $20,000, and concludes: "When such statistics are discussed many people feel uncomfortable and want to drop the subject. Perhaps these statistics are misleading, but then we need to look carefully at the total evidence."[9]

Of course, one explanation of this "fact" is the one offered by Hume and Kant, namely that blacks and women are simply not as smart as white men. This is the explanation that continues to be popular among neo-conservatives,[10] and is the explanation Pojman ever so gently orients the reader toward. But this is not the only explanation, despite its simplicity, accessibility, and imminence of its historical sources. An alternative, and I believe more plausible, explanation is simply that income is not a good measure of similar family circumstances.

Black families with incomes of $60,000 have less financial and real capital, on the average, than white families with incomes between $10,000 and $20,000. In comparing income and wealth between blacks and whites, Oliver and Shapiro write:

> The highest earning black households possess twenty-three cents of median net financial assets for every dollar held by high-income white households. One startling comparison reveals that poverty-level whites control nearly as many mean net financial assets as the highest-earning blacks, $26,683 to $28,310.[11]

This being the case, it should not be surprising that they would also have less capital (in terms of training and skills) as well. This lack of capital and wealth is a direct result of the appropriation of black wealth under slavery and the exclusion of blacks from the accumulation of wealth after slavery. The de facto and de jure use of government power reinforced social biases which impeded blacks and favored whites in the acquisition of financial assets, real property, and human capital as forms of wealth.

If policies of inclusion are defended as a means of correcting the underrepresentation of blacks and women, Pojman suggests that we should be equally concerned with correcting the underrepresentation of ugly people, fat people, left-handed people, and presumably people with bad breath and noxious body odor.[12] Other prominent contemporary philosophers, such as John Kekes, have advanced similar arguments:

> It is true that American Blacks, Indians, Hispanics, and women have suffered injustice as a group. But so have homosexuals, epileptics, the urban and the rural poor, the physically ugly, those whose careers were ruined by McCarthyism, prostitutes, the obese, and so forth. There is no good reason for selecting some of these groups over others for preferential treatment. The arguments given to justify preferential treatment apply equally to all.[13]

But this conclusion follows only if we take correcting every misfortune and disadvantage as the special responsibility of the state, another strawman position that leads unerringly to absurdity.

Because state action has been directly involved in leading to the present condition of blacks, native Americans, and women, the state has a special responsibility for contributing to the correction of that condition. But as a matter of historical fact, there were no state sanctioned laws and institutional practices preventing ugly people, fat people, or left-handed people from learning to read, acquiring property with good growth potential, or attending the best schools.

With regard to the role of state action, Pojman claims that though Southern states may be "accused of unjustly harming blacks, it is hard to see that the United States government was involved in doing so. Much of the harm done to blacks was the result of private discrimination, not state action."[14] But this is simply historical obfuscation, whether it be from malintent or mere ignorance. Even the arch opponent of affirmative action policies (both strong and weak), libertarian Richard Epstein, acknowledges the role of local and state governments in the North (as precedents for the *Plessy* decision), and the role of the federal government (Supreme Court rulings in *Dred Scott* and *Plessy*, National Labor Relations Board Support of racist unions, redlining, etc.) in accounting for the exclusion of blacks from participation in free-market opportunities. In both the North and the South, Epstein concludes:

> The police power exception to a wide range of constitutional protections was the vehicle that allowed local government to trample the ordinary rights of property and contract, which were as valuable to blacks as they were to whites.[15]

Even where identifiable individuals were harmed by some form of state action, Pojman argues that giving them preferential treatment for opportunities they are not most qualified for is inappropriate compensation.

> If John is the star tailback of our college team with a promising professional future, and I accidentally (but culpably) drive my pickup truck over his legs, and so cripple him, John may be due compensation, but he is not due the tailback spot on the football team.[16]

Again, Pojman uses an inappropriate analogy to construct a strawman substitute for the compensation argument. Of course, a cripple would not be able to play tailback because, being unable to run, the cripple lacks even minimal qualifications for the position. But if A and B were competing for the tailback position, and A not merely decreases, but successfully destroys B's ability to perform, then it certainly seems unjust that A would get the position by default.[17] On the other hand, if B is able to perform without unnecessary risk of injury, it would seem admirable and just to put him on the field instead of A, even if A were able to perform better at the position.

Pojman suggests that if A is more competent than B, this is in itself sufficient to award the position to A, irrespective of how this increased competency has been acquired. But people who use unjust tactics typically do so because they have formed "expectations that if they attain certain levels of excellence they will be awarded appropriately," irrespective of how they may have attained their immanence. Suppose A's parents covertly fed him steroids. Pojman's Michael Jordan parable suggests that the coach, upon learning of the fact, should not give A's position to the underperforming B.[18] Pojman seems unbothered by this prospect, as his argument exculpating unjust enrichment indicates. It seems that, for Pojman, efficient performance is not merely important, it is the most important factor that should shape our choices.

It follows that considerations of justice as well as diversity are, on Pojman's view, of less value than merit and efficiency:

> [C]ompetence far outweighs considerations of diversity. I do not care whether the group of surgeons operating on me reflect racial or gender balance, but I do care that they are highly qualified.[19]

And likewise with sports teams, pilots, military leaders, business executives and university professors. One wonders about the extent to which Pojman would be comforted by the skill of a Nazi doctor who had perfected his skills on Jewish prisoners.

Perhaps I am being unfair to Pojman, but one must question a position which elevates efficiency to such ultimate esteem. No defense of policies of inclusion that I know of has as a necessary corollary the lowering of standards of performance. But they typically do challenge many of the qualifications historically used to regulate access to training, jobs, and capital. It is a simple fact that those who have been excluded can develop their skills only if they are given the opportunities. Otherwise, it is a classic case of Catch-22. Black people are excluded because they are not among the best qualified and they are not among the best qualified because they have been excluded from opportunities to gain qualification. This is especially pernicious when the qualifications required have a suspect relationship to performance.

Pojman appears to follow in the footsteps of Thomas Malthus, defending those who have merit as being naturally more competent and prudent, while accounting for the growing number of the dispossessed in terms of their own inherent faults. His position suggests that sub-Saharan Africa has the greatest incidence of poverty in the world, and African Americans a disproportionate incidence of poverty in the United States, not because of centuries of enslavement, exploitation, and exclusion but because of their own diminished intelligence and faulty cultures. At best, it is the result of the interference of government in the workings of the free market. There is no acknowledgement that modern slavery was a creation of an unfettered free market seeking the most efficient means of exploiting the wealth of the new world.

Nor does Pojman show any appreciation of the thesis that both wage slavery and chattel slavery derive from a common source. Rather, he seeks to portray the progeny of the two kinds of slavery as in competition for the diminishing rewards and opportunities made possible by the market. As such, he views "strong affirmative action" as a policy that allows the progeny of chattel slavery to claim injuries that trump those of wage slavery. He thus makes policies of inclusion out to be merely the reverse of the policies of exclusion that preserved educational, employment, and investment opportunities for white males. Only now, it is the policy of "strong affirmative action" that is portrayed as preserving such opportunities for blacks.

"So," Pojman would have us ask, "should a black woman from a middle class family with an income of $70,000 be preferred for some opportunity over a 'better qualified' white male from a poor family with an income of $20,000?" as if an affirmative answer proves the moral absurdity of a policy of "strong affirmative action." Yet, as philosophical and legal analysis well teaches us, details are critical to the assessment of particular judgments. It is the circumstances that would determine whether such a choice was justified or unjustified.

Suppose the opportunity in question is that of membership in a union or employment on a police department that in the past excluded blacks and women as a matter of policy, and has continued to do so despite injunctions to desist. Suppose the opportunity in question is that of admission to a law school or trade organization that in the past excluded blacks and women as a matter of policy, and has continued to do so into the present. Suppose the opportunity in question is that of qualifying for a type of loan or promotion to a position that in the past excluded blacks and women as a matter of policy, and has continued to do so because of prevailing practice.

By adopting an ahistorical, context-independent perspective on the issue, Pojman and like neoconservatives construe policies of inclusion in a manner that makes them appear repugnant to our ordinary sense of morality and propriety. Neoconservatives condemn the preexisting tendency to discriminate, and the corrective is then portrayed as a new form of discrimination that is as reprehensible as the form it replaces. My aim has been to challenge this portrayal, and to show that policies of inclusion are not mirror images of racism and sexism.

One of the most effective of Pojman's strawmen is the portrayal of policies of inclusion as covert expressions of misguided egalitarianism. On this view, strong affirmative action is the attempt to guarantee the equal representation of every group in every profession. But this is a misrepresentation of the aim of affirmative action, another strawman. Affirmative action is not the attempt to guarantee the equal representation of every group in every profession. To do so would be absurd. Rather, affirmative action evolved in recognition that blacks and women were underrepresented in almost every category of achievement, that there was massive governmental complicity in enforcing such exclusions, and that exclusionary practices and their effects continued into the present. Groups protected under the 14th amendment and the Civil Rights Act of 1964 are indicative of those who, in the past, have been harmed as a result of legal and institutional practices designed to limit their access to rights and opportunities made available to others. It is a mistake to construe policies designed to increase access for such groups as deriving from the belief that all groups should be equally represented in every category of endeavor.

One of Pojman's principal objections to policies of inclusion construes them as contrary to the efficient functioning of the market. That the market helped produce the conditions now in need of correction and would tend to perpetuate those conditions if left unchecked is hidden behind the fiction of unmitigated good flowing from an unfettered free market. Affirmative action, whether weak or strong, need not deny the efficacy of a free market in order to insist that a free market economy has both costs and benefits. The question affirmative action forces us to confront is to what extent those costs and benefits have been color-coded and will be allowed to remain so. This is a matter not merely of efficiency, but of morality.

Endnotes

1. Louis Pojman, "The Case against Affirmative Action," *International Journal of Applied Philosophy* 12:1, 1998, p. 98.
2. Ibid.
3. Pojman, p. 99.
4. Ibid.
5. David Hume, "Of National Characters," in *Selected Essays* (Oxford University Press, 1993), n. 120, p. 360.
6. Immanuel Kant, *Observations on the Feeling of the Beautiful and Sublime,* trans. John T. Goldthwait (University of California Press, 1960), pp. 111–113.
7. Ibid.

8. Pojman, p. 104.

9. Pojman, p. 105.

10. See Richard Herrnstein and Charles Murray, *The Bell Curve: Intelligence and Class Structure in American Life* (New York: The Free Press, 1994).

11. Melvin Oliver and Thomas Shapiro, *Black Wealth/White Wealth* (Routledge, 1995), p. 101, chpt. 5 passim.

12. Pojman, p. 109.

13. John Kekes, "The Injustice of Affirmative Action Involving Preferential Treatment" in *Ethics: History, Theory, and Contemporary Issues*, ed. Steven Cahn and Peter Markie (New York: Oxford University Press, 1998), p. 883. See

also Michael Levin, "Is Racial Discrimination Special?" in *Journal of Value Inquiry* 15, 1981, pp. 232 ff.

14. Pojman, p. 100.

15. Richard Epstein, *Forbidden Grounds: The Case against Employment Discrimination Laws* (Cambridge: Harvard University Press, 1992), p. 115, chpt. 5 passim.

16. Pojman, p. 100.

17. Tanya Harding certainly expected to benefit from eliminating Nancy Kerrigan in the figure skating competitions. Though successful, she did not succeed by default.

18. Pojman, p. 102.

19. Pojman, p. 103.

---

31. *Affirmative Racism*

CHARLES MURRAY

Charles Murray argues that preferential treatment for blacks has actually worked against their interest by encouraging a new form of racism that tacitly accepts the view that blacks are temporarily less competent than whites. The problem with this new form of racism, Murray claims, is that it perpetuates the race-based inequality it seeks to eliminate.

A few years ago, I got into an argument with a lawyer friend who is a partner in a New York firm. I was being the conservative, arguing that preferential treatment of blacks was immoral; he was being the liberal, urging that it was the only way to bring blacks to full equality. In the middle of all this he abruptly said, "But you know, let's face it. We must have hired at least ten blacks in the last few years, and none of them has really worked out." He then returned to his case for still stronger affirmative action, while I wondered what it had been like for those ten blacks. And if he could make a remark like that so casually, what remarks would he be able to make some years down the road, if by that time it had been fifty blacks who hadn't "really worked out"?

My friend's comment was an outcropping of a new racism that is emerging to take its place alongside the old. It grows out of preferential treatment for blacks, and it is not just the much-publicized reactions, for example, of the white policemen or firemen who are passed over for promotion because of an affirmative action court order. The new racism that is potentially most damaging is located among the white elites—educated, affluent, and occupying the positions in education, business, and government from which this country is run. It currently focuses on blacks; whether it will eventually extend to include Hispanics and other minorities remains to be seen.

The new racists do not think blacks are inferior. They are typically longtime supporters of civil rights. But they exhibit the classic behavioral symptom of racism: They treat blacks differently from whites, because of their race. The results can be as concretely bad and unjust as any that the old racism produces. Sometimes the effect is that blacks are refused an education they otherwise could have gotten. Sometimes blacks are shunted into dead-end jobs. Always, blacks are denied the right to compete as equals.

From *The New Republic* (December 31, 1984). Reprinted by permission of *The New Republic* 1984, The New Republic, Inc.

The new racists also exhibit another characteristic of racism: They *think* about blacks differently from the way they think about whites. Their global view of blacks and civil rights is impeccable. Blacks must be enabled to achieve full equality They are still unequal, through no fault of their own (it is the fault of racism, the fault of inadequate opportunity, the legacy of history). But the new racists' local view is that the blacks they run across professionally are not, on the average, up to the white standard. Among the new racists, lawyers have gotten used to the idea that the brief a black colleague turns in will be less rehearsed and argued than the one they would have done. Businessmen expect that a black colleague will not read a balance sheet as subtly as they do. Teachers expect black students to wind up at the bottom of the class.

The new racists also tend to think of blacks as a commodity. The office must have a sufficient supply of blacks, who must be treated with special delicacy. The personnel problems this creates are more difficult than most because whites barely admit to themselves what's going on.

What follows is a foray into very poorly mapped territory. I will present a few numbers that explain much about how the process gets started. But the ways that the numbers get translated into behavior are even more important. The cases I present are composites constructed from my own observations and taken from firsthand accounts. All are based on real events and real people, stripped of their particularities. But the individual cases are not intended as evidence, because I cannot tell you how often they happen. They have not been the kind of thing that social scientists or journalists have wanted to count. I am writing this because so many people, both white and black, to whom I tell such stories know immediately what I am talking about. It is apparent that a problem exists. How significant is it? What follows is as much an attempt to elicit evidence as to present it.

As in so many of the crusades of the 1960s, the nation began with a good idea. It was called "affirmative action," initiated by Lyndon Johnson through Executive Order 11246 in September 1965. It was an attractive label and a natural corrective to past racism: actively seek out black candidates for jobs, college, or promotions, without treating them differently in the actual decision to hire, admit, or promote. The term originally evoked both the letter and the spirit of the order.

Then, gradually, affirmative action came to mean something quite different. In 1970 a federal court established the legitimacy of quotas as a means of implementing Johnson's executive order. In 1971 the Supreme Court ruled that an employer could not use minimum credentials as a prerequisite for hiring if the credentials acted as a "built-in headwind" for minority groups—even when there was no discriminatory intent and even when the hiring procedures were "fair in form." In 1972 the Equal Employment Opportunity Commission acquired broad, independent enforcement powers.

Thus by the early 1970s it had become generally recognized that a good-faith effort to recruit qualified blacks was not enough—especially if one's school depended on federal grants or one's business depended on federal contracts. Even for businesses and schools not directly dependent on the government, the simplest way to withstand an accusation of violating Title VII of the Civil Rights Act of 1964 was to make sure not that they had not just interviewed enough minority candidates, but that they had actually hired or admitted enough of them. Employers and admissions committees arrived at a rule of thumb: If the blacks who are available happen to be the best candidates, fine; if not, the best available black candidates will be given some sort of edge in the selection process. Sometimes the edge will be small; sometimes it will be predetermined that a black candidate is essential, and the edge will be very large.

Perhaps the first crucial place where the edge applies is in admission to college. Consider the cases of the following three students: John, William, and Carol, 17 years old and applying to college, are all equal on paper. Each has a score of 520 in the mathematics section of the Scholastic Aptitude Test, which puts them in the top third—at the 67th percentile—of all students who took the test. (Figures are based on 1983 data.)

John is white. A score of 520 gets him into the state university. Against the advice of his high school counselor, he applies to a prestigious school, Ivy U. where his application is rejected in the first cut—its average white applicant has math scores in the high 600s.

William is black, from a middle-class family who sent him to good schools. His score of 520 puts him at the 95th percentile of all blacks who took the test. William's high school counselor points out that he could probably get into Ivy U. William applies and is admitted—Ivy U. uses separate standards for admission of whites and blacks, and William is among the top blacks who applied.

Carol is black, educated at an inner city school, and her score of 520 represents an extraordinary achievement in the face of terrible schooling. An alumnus of Ivy U. who regularly looks for promising inner city candidates finds her, recruits her, and sends her off with a full scholarship to Ivy U.

When American universities embarked on policies of preferential admissions by race, they had the Carols in mind. They had good reason to be optimistic that preferential treatment would work—for many years, the best universities had been weighting the test scores of applicants from small-town public schools when they were compared against those of applicants from the top private schools, and had been giving special breaks to students from distant states to ensure geographic distribution. The differences in preparation tended to even out after the first year or so. Blacks were being brought into a long-standing and successful tradition of preferential treatment.

In the case of blacks, however, preferential treatment ran up against a large black-white gap in academic performance combined with ambitious goals for proportional representation. This gap has been the hardest for whites to confront. But though it is not necessary or even plausible to believe that such differences are innate, it is necessary to recognize openly that the differences exist. By pretending they don't, we begin the process whereby both the real differences and the racial factor are exaggerated.

The black-white gap that applies most directly to this discussion is the one that separates blacks and whites who go to college. In 1983, for example, the mean Scholastic Aptitude Test score for all blacks who took the examination was more than 100 points below the white score on both the verbal and the math sections. Statistically, it is an extremely wide gap. To convert the gap into more concrete terms, think of it this way: In 1983, the same Scholastic Aptitude Test math score that put a black at the 50th percentile of all blacks who took the test put him at the 16th percentile of all whites who took the test.

These results clearly mean we ought to be making an all-out effort to improve elementary and secondary education for blacks. But that doesn't help much now, when an academic discrepancy of this magnitude is fed into a preferential admissions process. As universities scramble to make sure they are admitting enough blacks, the results feed the new racism. Here's how it works:

In 1983, only 66 black students nationwide scored above 700 in the verbal section of the Scholastic Aptitude Test, and only 205 scored above 700 in the mathematics section. This handful of students cannot begin to meet the demand for blacks with such scores. For example, Harvard, Yale, and Princeton have in recent years been bringing an aggregate of about 270 blacks into each entering class. If the black students entering these schools had the same distribution of scores as that of the freshman class as a whole, then every black student in the nation with a verbal score in the 700s, and roughly 70 percent of the ones with a math score in the 700s, would be in their freshman classes.

The main problem is not that a few schools monopolize the very top black applicants, but that these same schools have much larger implicit quotas than they can fill with those applicants. They fill out the rest with the next students in line—students who would not have gotten into these schools if they were not black, who otherwise would have been showing up in the classrooms of the nation's less glamorous colleges and universities. But the size of the black pool does not expand appreciably at the next levels. The number of blacks scoring in the 600s on the math section in 1983, for example, was 1,531. Meanwhile, 31,704 nonblack students in 1983 scored in the 700s on the math section and 121,640 scored in the 600s. The prestige schools cannot begin to absorb these numbers of other highly qualified freshmen, and they are perforce spread widely throughout the system.

At schools that draw most broadly from the student population, such as the large state universities, the effects of this skimming produce a situation that confirms the old racists in everything they want most to believe. There are plenty of outstanding students in such student bodies (at the University of Colorado, for example, 6 percent of the freshmen in 1981 had math scores in the 700s and 28 percent had scores in the 600s), but the skimming process combined with the very small raw numbers means that almost none of them are black. What students and instructors see in their day-to-day experience in the classroom is a disproportionate number of blacks who are below the white average, relatively few blacks who are at the first rank. The image that the white student carries away is that blacks are less able than whites.

I am not exalting the SAT as an infallible measure of academic ability or pointing to test scores to try to convince anyone that blacks are performing below the level of whites. I am simply using them to explain what instructors and students already notice, and talk about, among themselves.

They do not talk openly about such matters. One characteristic of the new racism is that whites deny in public but acknowledge in private that there are significant differences in black and white academic performance. Another is that they dismiss the importance of tests when black scores are at issue, blaming cultural bias and saying that test scores are not good predictors of college performance. At the same time, they watch anxiously over their own children's test scores.

The differences in academic performance do not disappear by the end of college. Far from narrowing, the gap separating black and white academic achievement appears to get larger. Various studies, most recently at Harvard, have found that during the 1970s blacks did worse in college (as measured by grade point average) than their test scores would have predicted. Moreover, the black-white gap in the Graduate Record Examination is larger than the gap in the Scholastic Aptitude Test. The gap between black and white freshmen is a bit less than one standard deviation (the technical measure for comparing scores). Black and white seniors who take the Graduate Record Examination reveal a gap of about one and a quarter standard deviations.

Why should the gap grow wider? Perhaps it is an illusion—for example, perhaps a disproportionate number of the best black students never take the examination. But there are also reasons for suspecting that in fact blacks get a worse education in college than whites do. Here are a few of the hypotheses that deserve full exploration.

Take the situation of William—a slightly above-average student who, because he is black, gets into a highly competitive school. William studies very hard during the first year. He nonetheless gets mediocre grades. He has a choice. He can continue to study hard and continue to get mediocre grades, and be seen by his classmates as a black who cannot do very well. Or he can explicitly refuse to engage in the academic game. He decides to opt out, and his performance gets worse as time goes on. He emerges from college with a poor education and is further behind the whites than he was as a freshman.

If large numbers of other black students at the institution are in the same situation as William, the result can be group pressure not to compete academically. (At Harvard, it is said, the current term among black students for a black who studies like a white is "incognegro.") The response is not hard to understand. If one subpopulation of students is conspicuously behind another population and is visibly identifiable, then the population that is behind must come up with a good excuse for doing poorly. "Not wanting to do better" is as good as any.

But there is another crucial reason why blacks might not close the gap with whites during college: They are not taught as well as whites are. Racist teachers impeding the progress of students? Perhaps, but most college faculty members I know tend to bend over backward to be "fair" to black students—and that may be the problem. I suggest that inferior instruction is more likely to be a manifestation of the new racism than the old.

Consider the case of Carol, with outstanding abilities but deprived of decent prior schooling: She struggles the first year, but she gets by. Her academic skills still show the aftereffects of her inferior preparation. Her instructors diplomatically point out the more flagrant mistakes, but they ignore minor lapses, and never push her in the aggressive way they push white students who have her intellectual capacity. Some of them are being patronizing (she is doing quite well, considering). Others are being prudent: Teachers who criticize black students can find themselves being called racists in the classroom, in the campus newspaper, or in complaints to the administration.

The same process continues in graduate school. Indeed, because there are even fewer blacks in graduate schools than in undergraduate schools, the pressure to get black students through to the degree, no matter what, can be still greater. But apart from differences in preparation and ability that have accumulated by the end of schooling, the process whereby we foster the appearance of black inferiority continues. Let's assume that William did not give up during college. He goes to business school, where he gets his Master's degree. He signs up for interviews with the corporate recruiters. There are one hundred persons in his class, and William is ranked near the middle. But of the five blacks in his class, he ranks first (remember that he was at the 95th percentile of blacks taking the Scholastic Aptitude Test). He is hired on his first interview by his first-choice company, which also attracted the very best of the white students. He is hired alongside five of the top-ranking white members of the class.

William's situation as one of five blacks in a class of one hundred illustrates the proportions that prevail in business schools, and business schools are by no means one of the more extreme examples. The pool of black candidates for any given profession is a small fraction of the white pool. This works out to a 20-to-1 edge in business; it is even greater in most of the other professions. The result, when many hiring institutions are competing, is that a major gap between the abilities of new black and white employees in any given workplace is highly likely. Everyone needs to hire a few blacks, and the edge that "being black" confers in the hiring decision warps the sequence of hiring in such a way that a scarce resource (the blacks with a given set of qualifications) is exhausted at an artificially high rate, producing a widening gap in comparison with the remaining whites from which an employer can choose.

The more aggressively affirmative action is enforced, the greater the imbalance. In general, the first companies to hire can pursue strategies that minimize or even eliminate the difference in ability between the new black and white employees. IBM and Park Avenue law firms can do very well, just as Harvard does quite well in attracting the top black students. But the more effectively they pursue these strategies, the more quickly they strip the population of the best black candidates.

To this point I have been discussing problems that are more or less driven by realities we have very little hope of manipulating in the short term except by discarding the laws regarding preferential treatment. People do differ in acquiring abilities. Currently, acquired abilities in the white and black populations are distributed differently. Schools and firms do form a rough hierarchy when they draw from these distributions. The results follow ineluctably. The dangers they represent are not a matter of statistical probabilities, but of day-to-day human reactions we see around us.

The damage caused by these mechanistic forces should be much less in the world of work than in the schools, however. Schools deal in a relatively narrow domain of skills, and "talent" tends to be assigned specific meanings and specific measures. Workplaces deal in highly complex sets of skills, and "talent" consists of all sorts of combinations of qualities.

A successful career depends in large part upon finding jobs that elicit and develop one's strengths.

At this point the young black professional must sidestep a new series of traps laid by whites who need to be ostentatiously nonracist. Let's say that William goes to work for the XYZ Corporation, where he is assigned with another management trainee (white) to a department where much of the time is spent preparing proposals for government contracts. The white trainee is assigned a variety of scut work—proofreading drafts, calculating the costs of minor items in the bid, making photocopies, taking notes at conferences. William gets more dignified work. He is assigned portions of the draft to write (which are later rewritten by more experienced staff), sits in on planning sessions, and even goes to Washington as a highly visible part of the team to present the bid. As time goes on, the white trainee learns a great deal about how the company operates, and is seen as a go-getting young member of the team. William is perceived to be a bright enough fellow, but not much of a detail man and not really much of a self-starter.

Even if a black is hired under terms that put him on a par with his white peers, the subtler forms of differential treatment work against him. Particularly for any corporation that does business with the government, the new employee has a specific, immediate value purely because he is black. There are a variety of requirements to be met and rituals to be observed for which a black face is helpful. These have very little to do with the long-term career interests of the new employee; on the contrary, they often lead to a dead end as head of the minority-relations section of the personnel department.

Added to this is another problem that has nothing to do with the government. When the old racism was at fault (as it often still is), the newly hired black employee was excluded from the socialization process because the whites did not want him to become part of the group. When the new racism is at fault, it is because many whites are embarrassed to treat black employees as badly as they are willing to treat whites. Hence another reason that whites get on-the-job training that blacks do not: Much of the early training of an employee is intertwined with menial assignments and mild hazing. Blacks who are put through these routines often see themselves as racially abused (and when a black is involved, old-racist responses may well have crept in). But even if the black is not unhappy about the process, the whites are afraid that he is, and so protect him from it. There are many variations, all having the same effect: The black is denied an apprenticeship that the white has no way of escaping. Without serving the apprenticeship, there is no way of becoming part of the team.

Carol suffers a slightly different fate. She and a white woman are hired as reporters by a major newspaper. They both work hard, but after a few months there is no denying it: Neither one of them can write. The white woman is let go. Carol is kept on, because the paper cannot afford to have any fewer blacks than it already has. She is kept busy with reportorial work, even though they have to work around the writing problem. She is told not to worry—there's lots more to being a journalist than writing.

It is the mascot syndrome. A white performing at a comparable level would be fired. The black is kept on, perhaps to avoid complications with the Equal Employment Opportunity Commission (it can be very expensive to fire a black), perhaps out of a more diffuse wish not to appear discriminatory. Everybody pretends that nothing is wrong—but the black's career is at a dead end. The irony, of course, is that the white who gets fired and has to try something else has been forced into accepting a chance of making a success in some other line of work whereas the black is seduced into *not* taking the same chance.

Sometimes differential treatment takes an even more pernicious form: the conspiracy to promote a problem out of existence. As part of keeping Carol busy, the newspaper gives her some administrative responsibilities. They do not amount to much. But she has an impressive title on a prominent newspaper and she is black—a potent combination. She gets an offer from a lesser paper in another part of the country to take a senior editorial post. Her current employer is happy to be rid of an awkward situation and sends along glowing references. She gets a job that she is unequipped to handle—only this time, she is in a highly visible position, and within a few weeks the deficiencies that were covered up at the old job have become the subject of jokes all over the office. Most of the jokes are openly racist.

It is important to pause and remember who Carol is: an extremely bright young woman, not (in other circumstances) a likely object of condescension. But being bright is no protection. Whites can usually count on the market to help us recognize egregious career mistakes and to prevent us from being promoted too far from a career line that fits our strengths, and too far above our level of readiness. One of the most prevalent characteristics of white differential treatment of blacks has been to exempt blacks from these market considerations, substituting for them a market premium attached to race.

The most obvious consequence of preferential treatment is that every black professional, no matter how able, is tainted. Every black who is hired by a white-run organization that hires blacks preferentially has to put up with the knowledge that many of his coworkers believe he was hired because of his race; and he has to put up with the suspicion in his own mind that they might be right.

Whites are curiously reluctant to consider this a real problem—it is an abstraction, I am told, much less important than the problem that blacks face in getting a job in the first place. But black professionals talk about it, and they tell stories of mental breakdowns; of people who had to leave the job altogether; of long-term professional paralysis. What white would want to be put in such a situation? Of course it would be a constant humiliation to be resented by some of your coworkers and condescended to by others. Of course it would affect your perceptions of yourself and your self-confidence. No system that produces such side effects—as preferential treatment *must* do—can be defended unless it is producing some extremely important benefits.

And that brings us to the decisive question. If the alternative were no job at all, as it was for so many blacks for so long, the resentment and condescension are part of the price of getting blacks into the positions they deserve. But is that the alternative today? If the institutions of this country were left to their own devices now, to what extent would they refuse to admit, hire, and promote people because they were black? To what extent are American institutions kept from being racist by the government's intervention?

It is another one of those questions that are seldom investigated aggressively, and I have no evidence. Let me suggest a hypothesis that bears looking into: that the signal event in the struggle for black equality during the last thirty years, the one with real impact, was not the Civil Rights Act of 1964 or Executive Order 11246 or any other governmental act. It was the civil rights movement itself.

It raised to a pitch of acute and lasting discomfort the racial consciousness of the generations of white Americans who are now running the country. I will not argue that the old racism is dead at any level of society. I will argue, however, that in the typical corporation or in the typical admissions office, there is an abiding desire to be not-racist. This need not be construed as brotherly love. Guilt will do as well. But the civil rights movement did its job. I suggest that the laws and the court decisions and the continuing intellectual respectability behind preferential treatment are now holding many doors open to qualified blacks that would otherwise be closed.

Suppose for a moment that I am right. Suppose that, for practical purposes, racism would not get in the way of blacks if preferential treatment were abandoned. How, in my most optimistic view, would the world look different?

There would be fewer blacks at Harvard and Yale; but they would all be fully competitive with the whites who were there. White students at the state university would encounter a cross-section of blacks who span the full range of ability, including the top levels, just as whites do. College remedial courses would no longer be disproportionately black. Whites rejected by the school they wanted would quit assuming they were kept out because a less-qualified black was admitted in their place. Blacks in big corporations would no longer be shunted off to personnel-relations positions, but would be left on the mainline tracks toward becoming comptrollers and sales managers and chief executive officers. Whites would quit assuming that black colleagues had been hired because they were black. Blacks would quit worrying that they had been hired because they were black.

Would blacks still lag behind? As a population, yes, for a time, and the nation should be mounting a far more effective program to improve elementary and secondary education for blacks than it has mounted in the last few decades. But in years past virtually every ethnic group in America has at one time or another lagged behind as a population, and has eventually caught up. In the process of catching up, the ones who breached the barriers were evi-

dence of the success of that group. Now blacks who breach the barriers tend to be seen as evidence of the inferiority of that group.

And that is the evil of preferential treatment. It perpetuates an impression of inferiority. The system segments whites and blacks who come in contact with each other so as to maximize the likelihood that whites have the advantage in experience and ability. The system then encourages both whites and blacks to behave in ways that create self-fulfilling prophecies even when no real differences exist.

It is here that the new racism links up with the old. The old racism has always openly held that blacks are permanently less competent than whites. The new racism tacitly accepts that, in the course of overcoming the legacy of the old racism, blacks are temporarily less competent than whites. It is an extremely fine distinction. As time goes on, fine distinctions tend to be lost. Preferential treatment is providing persuasive evidence for the old racists, and we can already hear it *sotto voce:* "We gave you your chance, we let you educate them and push them into jobs they couldn't have gotten on their own and coddle them every way you could. And see: They still aren't as good as whites, and you are beginning to admit it yourselves." Sooner or later this message will be heard by a white elite that needs to excuse its failure to achieve black equality.

The only happy aspect of the new racism is that the corrective—to get rid of the policies encouraging preferential treatment—is so natural. Deliberate preferential treatment by race has sat as uneasily with America's equal-opportunity ideal [since 1965] as it did during the days of legalized segregation. We had to construct tortuous rationalizations when we permitted blacks to be kept on the back of the bus—and the rationalizations to justify sending blacks to the head of the line have been just as tortuous. Both kinds of rationalization say that sometimes it is all right to treat people of different races in different ways. For years, we have instinctively sensed this was wrong in principle but intellectualized our support for it as an expedient. I submit that our instincts were right. There is no such thing as good racial discrimination.

32. The Case for Affirmative Action

James P. Sterba

In Selection 32, James P. Sterba argues that once affirmative action is appropriately defined and the conditions for its morally justifiable application are set out, then we can answer the main objections that have been raised against it. In particular, he argues that given his account, the cases of affirmative action that Charles Murray cites would not be morally justified. To be justified, Sterba argues, affirmative action must be directed at candidates whose qualifications are such that when their selection or appointment is combined with a suitably designed educational enhancement program, they will normally turn out, within a reasonably short time, to be as qualified as, or even more qualified than, their peers. So if affirmative action is properly applied and carried out, it will not, as Murray argues, harm those who receive it.

Affirmative action with respect to women and minorities is a policy of preferring qualified women and minority candidates who have been disadvantaged by past injustices over equally or more qualified white male candidates who have not been similarly disadvantaged. In fact, it is generally the case that the white male candidates who are passed over by a policy of affirmative action have themselves benefited from past injustices suffered by women and minority candidates (e.g., unequal educational opportunities). To be justified, however, such a policy of affirmative action must favor only candidates whose qualifications are such that when their selection or appointment is combined with a suitably designed educational enhancement program, they will normally turn out, within a reasonably short time, to be as qualified as, or even more qualified than, their peers.[1] Such candidates have the potential to be as qualified as, or more qualified than, their peers, but that potential has not yet been actualized because of past injustices. Affirmative action, with its suitably designed educational enhancement program, purports to actualize just that potential. In this way, persons who receive affirmative action are like runners in a race who, for a time, are forced to compete at a disadvantage with the other runners—say, by having weights tied to their legs, but later are allowed to compete against those

other runners by first having the weights removed and then receiving some special assistance for an appropriate period of time so that the results of the race will turn out to be fair. Affirmative action, therefore, is a policy directed at only those women and minority candidates who are highly qualified yet, because of past discrimination and prejudice, are less qualified than they would otherwise be; it seeks to provide such candidates with a benefit that will nullify the effects of past injustices by enabling them to become as qualified as or more qualified than their peers.

It should be noted that what I defend as affirmative action is not captured by what Louis Pojman calls either strong or weak affirmative action. (See Selection 29.) Unfortunately, this sort of disagreement has characterized much of the debate about affirmative action: what critics attack is frequently not what defenders of affirmative action have defended.[2] Thus, it would seem that we can move this debate closer to a resolution if we can get more agreement on what we should call affirmative action. In this regard, I think that it is more appropriate for critics of affirmative action to take their definitions from those who defend affirmative action rather to come up with definitions of their own. In this way, critics of affirmative action (if there actually are any left, once we get straight about the most morally defensible form of affirmative action!) can then avoid missing their targets.[3]

In Hopwood v. Texas (see Selection 33), the U.S. Court of Appeals for the Fifth Circuit argued that

Reprinted from *Justice for Here and Now* (New York: Cambridge University Press, 1998), pp. 104–9, with additions.

an institution can only justifiably implement an affir-mation action program if it is designed simply to cor-rect for the past discrimination of just that institution. Evidence of discrimination in Texas's school system as a whole (As of May 1994, desegregation suits re-mained pending against more than forty Texas school districts, and at the time that the Hopwood plaintiffs filed suit, the U.S. Office of Civil Rights had not yet determined that the state had desegregated its schools sufficiently to comply with federal civil rights laws.) is not considered relevant to the issue of whether the affirmative action program of the Uni-versity of Texas Law School is justified, although most of the applicants to the law school had passed through this very educational system with its alleged inequalities. I contend, however, that this limit im-posed by the Hopwood court on the type of past dis-crimination required to justify an affirmative action program is far too narrow to be morally defensible.[4] From a moral, if not a legal, perspective, injustices and inequalities that occur earlier in an educational system can be appropriately corrected for by higher institutions using well-designed affirmative action programs. In fact, if these injustices and inequalities are not corrected for by some appropriate form of af-firmative action, there may be no remedy for them.

The Hopwood court was right in arguing that we shouldn't think that a person's race (or sex) con-trols his or her point of view.[5] Thus, the court cites the U.S. Supreme Court as holding that it is legally inappropriate to impute to women and minorities a different attitude about such issues as the federal budget, school prayer, voting, and foreign relations.[6] In this sense, we should all be color- and gender-blind. But it is quite a different thing for the Hop-wood court to restrict, in the way it has, the type of past discrimination that can be justified remedied. We cannot get beyond past injustices by artificially limiting our ability to correct for them.

I now propose to defend affirmative action, as I have defined it, by considering the various ways that it has been said to lead to injustice. According to its critics, affirmative action leads to injustice for the following reasons:

1. It is not required to compensate for unjust institutions of the distant past.

2. It harms those who receive it.

3. It is directed at the wrong people.

4. It is not directed at all of those who de-serve it.

5. It is unfair to the white males whom it dis-criminates against.

In support of the first objection, Christopher Morris argues that affirmative action is not required by the existence of unjust institutions in the distant past, such as American slavery, because compensation for past injustices is owed only to individuals who would have been better off except for those past in-justices.[7] With respect to individual African Ameri-cans living today, however, it is not true that they would have been better off if there had been no American slavery, because, given the contingencies of procreation, African Americans who are living today would not even have been born if their ances-tors had not been forcibly uprooted from Africa, en-slaved, and brought to this country. Of course, in the absence of American slavery and the racism it en-gendered, some Africans would surely have immi-grated to this country, but they would have done so more like other immigrants, and their contemporary descendants would be different individuals from present-day African Americans, who trace their his-tory through the practice of American slavery.

I think the best response to this objection is not to deny that most African Americans today are the product of American slavery and would not have existed without it, but only to point out that the injustices for which present-day African Americans deserve compensation are actually of more recent vintage.[8] For example, they are the injustices of poor housing, unequal education, job discrimination, in-adequate health and welfare programs, and an un-fair criminal justice system, all of which African Americans today would certainly be better off with-out. Of course, these current injustices do have their origins in the injustices of the past, particularly the institutions of American slavery and the Jim Crow law that succeeded it. The grounds that present-day African Americans can claim for compensation are not the injustices of the distant past, however, but rather the ongoing injustices that currently make them worse off as individuals—injustices that other contemporary Americans are responsible for and could do something about, in part by endorsing af-firmative action programs.

In support of the second objection, Charles Murray claims that affirmative action harms those who receive it by placing women and minorities into positions for which they are not qualified.[9] Murray cites examples, from his personal experience and the personal experiences of others, of women and minorities that were harmed in this way. In one example, a. black woman is hired for a position for which she lacks the qualifications, and as a result her responsibilities are reduced, making her job a dead-end position. Yet according to my earlier account, when affirmative action has such an effect, it is not justified. To be justified, affirmative action must be directed at candidates whose qualifications are such that when their selection or appointment is combined with a suitably designed educational enhancement program, they will normally turn out, within a reasonably short time, to be as qualified as, or even more qualified than, their peers. So if affirmative action is properly applied and carried out, it will not harm those who receive it.[10]

In support of the third objection, James Fishkin claims that affirmative action benefits the most qualified, who are actually the least deserving because they are the least discriminated against.[11] Yet the most qualified who benefit from affirmative action may not have been subjected to less discrimination; they may simply have resisted discrimination more vigorously. And even supposing that the most qualified were subject to less discrimination in the past, why wouldn't affirmative action be the appropriate response to the degree of discrimination to which they were subjected? If we assume that affirmative action is provided only to those candidates whose qualifications are such that when their selection or appointment is actually combined with a suitably designed educational enhancement program, they will normally turn out, within a reasonably short time, to be as qualified as or even more qualified than their peers, then affirmative action does seem to be appropriately directed at the most qualified candidates among those who have suffered from past discrimination. More severe forms of discrimination, whose effects upon a person's qualifications and potential are even more detrimental, would require correctives other than affirmative action, such as remedial education and job-training programs.

In support of the fourth objection, that affirmative action is not directed at all of those who deserve it, Carl Cohen claims that "compensatory affirmative action, if undertaken at all, must be undertaken for every person who qualifies on some reasonably objective standard, a standard free of racial (or sexual) orientation."[12] Robert Simon agrees, maintaining that there are candidates besides women and minorities who have suffered from discrimination and prejudice, or simply from being economically disadvantaged.[13] Cohen mentions Appalachian whites and impoverished Finns from upper Michigan as additional candidates for affirmative action.[14] Why should affirmative action not be directed at these people as well as at women and minorities?

Why not, indeed! Surely if other individuals have suffered comparable hardships from discrimination and prejudice, or from simply being economically disadvantaged, some remedy would be appropriate. So Cohen's and Simon's objection is not an objection to affirmative action per se, but rather an objection to affirmative action as a narrowly conceived rather than a broadly conceived program. In fact, Cohen's and Simon's analyses point to the need for a more broadly conceived affirmative action program.

It should be noted, however, that if affirmative action is to be extended in this way to remedy other injustices in society, it must become a larger program. The few positions that have been targeted for affirmative action candidates have been created with the idea of simply remedying injustices suffered by women and minorities. If we now wish to remedy other comparable injustices in society as well, we will need to create many more positions to deal with the increased scope of affirmative action. Properly understood, Cohen's and Simon's analyses point to the need for just such an expansion.

Nevertheless, there might be good moral grounds for using the law to correct for sexual and racial discrimination but not for discrimination against Appalachian whites and impoverished Finns from upper Michigan, given that sexual and racial discrimination are two of the deepest and most pervasive forms of discrimination in our society. The law, it may be argued, should not be thought to be the instrument for correcting every injustice, but only for the gravest and most pervasive injustices.

In support of the fifth objection, Barry Gross claims that affirmative action is unfair to white males because it deprives them of equal opportunity by selecting or appointing women or minority candidates over more qualified white male candidates. To help fix ideas, consider the following two programs. Program A hires qualified women and minority candidates over equally or more qualified white male candidates and then puts them through a six-month training program, after which it lets go any trainees who are not as qualified as, or more qualified than, anyone else in the hiring pool. Program B admits certain highly qualified women and minority candidates into a six-month training program for which white male candidates are not eligible, and then hires just those women and minority candidates who, after completing the program, are equally qualified as, or more qualified than, anyone else in the hiring pool. I take it that Gross would object to Program A because it involves hiring women and minority candidates who are less qualified, but he need not object to Program B, because he need not object to every attempt to compensate women and minorities for past discrimination, but only to programs (like Program A) that he believes to be unfair because they involve hiring less qualified women and minority candidates over more qualified white male candidates.

In response, Bernard Boxill denies that affirmative action is unfair to white males who are passed over for affirmative action candidates. After all, although these white males may not actually have discriminated against women and minorities themselves, Boxill argues that they have benefited from the discrimination of others—for example, through unequal educational opportunities. Hence, women and minorities do deserve compensation for this unjust discrimination, and, moreover, affirmative action seems to be an appropriate form of compensation. It also is difficult to understand how the opponent of affirmative action could object to attempts to remedy past discrimination like Program A while accepting attempts like Program B, given that they are so similar.

Of course, there are white males holding desirable positions in society who have benefited more from past discrimination than have the white males who would lose out to women or minority affirmative action candidates. So, ideally, an affirmative action program should be demanding sacrifices from these well-positioned white males as well. This could be done by requiring them to retire early, or by reducing their work week in order to avoid laying off affirmative action hires, or by allowing affirmative action considerations to take precedence over seniority rules when actual layoffs become necessary.[15] Maybe we could target, among others, white male college professors who have taught for more than twenty years. Yet while it would be morally preferable to place the burdens of affirmative action on those who have benefited most from past discrimination, when the political power to do so is lacking it would still be morally permissible to place the burden primarily on white males who are competing for jobs and positions with affirmative action candidates, given that they still have benefited from past discrimination, although not as much as others.[16]

In sum, I have argued that once affirmative action is appropriately defined and the conditions for its morally justifiable application are set out, then we can answer the main objections that have been raised against it. It also bears noting that the moral necessity of forms of affirmative action to deal with past discrimination is so strong that even in the face of stiff legal challenges to affirmative action in California and Texas, new forms of affirmative action such as Texas's ten percent plan and California's four percent plan have emerged to fill the albeit insufficient space permitted by the law.[17] Of course, these plans may not be called "affirmative action programs," but I think that a rose by any other name would smell as sweet.

Endnotes

1. For a defense of affirmative action that shows that treating people unequally (i.e., giving affirmative action to qualified women and minority candidates but not to qualified white male candidates) is compatible with treating them as equals, see Ronald Dworkin, *Taking Rights Seriously* (New York: Oxford University Press, 1977), chapter 9.
2. Once corrections are made for our different definitions of affirmative action, I think that there will be considerable agreement between Louis Pojman's view and my own, particularly because he seems willing to endorse all sorts of remedies for past discrimination although he doesn't want to call them "affirmative action."
3. Critics of affirmative action need to target the most morally defensible form of affirmative action if they really want to show that, however it is characterized, affirmative action is morally objectionable. In other words, critics of affirmative action need to address their strongest opponent.

4. It is even narrower than the U.S. Supreme Court itself defends. See the discussion in *Hopwood v. Texas* (Selection 33, p. 262–268).

5. Ibid.

6. Ibid.

7. Christopher Morris, "Existential Limits to the Rectification of Past Wrongs," *American Philosophy Quarterly* 21 (1984), pp. 175–182; Ellen Frankel Paul, "Set-Asides, Reparations, and Compensatory Justice," in John Chapman, ed., *Compensatory Justice* (New York: New York University Press, 1991), pp. 97–142; Thomas Schwartz, "Welfare Judgments and Future Generations," *Theory & Decisions* 11 (1979), pp. 181–94.

8. A few African Americans, particularly those who have come or whose ancestors have come from the Caribbean, are not the product of American slavery, but almost all African Americans have slavery of some sort in their background.

9. Charles Murray, "Affirmative Racism," Selection 31.

10. In the example cited from Murray, the black woman appears to lack the qualifications so that even "a suitably designed educational enhancement program" would not have resulted in her becoming, within a reasonably short time, as qualified as or even more qualified than their peers. For that reason, affirmative action was not justified in this case.

11. James Fishkin, *Justice, Equal Opportunity and the Family* (New Haven: Yale University Press, 1983), pp. 88, 89, 105.

12. Carl Cohen, *Naked Racial Preference* (Lanham, MD: Madison Books, 1995), p. 31.

13. Robert Simon, "Affirmative Action and Faculty Appointments," in Steven Cahn, ed., *Affirmative Action and the University* (Philadelphia: Temple University Press, 1993), pp. 93–121.

14. Cohen also suggests, however, that the inclusiveness of such an affirmative action program might lead to its abandonment. He writes: "If the complications grow excessive we may think it well to avoid the artificial inequalities likely to flow from inadequate data, or flaws in the compensatory calculation by refraining altogether from those calculations and again treating all applicants on the same footing" (*Naked Racial Preferences*, p. 31). But if this is Cohen's view, it would have the effect of simply freezing in place the effects of past injustices.

15. For a discussion of this issue, see Gertrude Ezorsky, *Racism and Justice* (Ithaca: Cornell University Press, 1991); Michel Rosenfeld, *Affirmative Action and Justice* (New Haven: Yale University Press, 1991); and Jeffrey Rosen, "Is Affirmative Action Doomed?" *The New Republic*, October 17, 1994.

16. In order to distribute the burdens of affirmative action programs more fairly, general revenues could be used, where appropriate, to defray the costs of whatever educational or training programs are required for implementing such programs.

17. See *New York Times*, November 11, 1999.

---

33. *Hopwood v. Texas*

UNITED STATES COURT OF APPEALS FOR THE FIFTH CIRCUIT (1996)

The issue before the court is whether the Fourteenth Amendment permits the University of Texas Law School to discriminate in favor of blacks and Mexican Americans by using race as a factor in its admissions. The U.S. Court of Appeals for the Fifth Circuit ruled that it does not. The appeals court ruled that achieving diversity is not a sufficient reason to justify an affirmative action program. According to the court, only the goal of remedying proven past racial discrimination at the law school itself would provide an adequate reason in this case for an affirmative action program. In July 1996, the U.S. Supreme Court announced that it would not hear an appeal of the Hopwood decision.

With the best of intentions, in order to increase the enrollment of certain favored classes of minority students, the University of Texas School of Law discriminates in favor of those applicants by giving substantial racial preferences in its admissions program. The beneficiaries of this system are blacks and Mexican Americans, to the detriment of whites and non-preferred minorities. The question we decide today is whether the Fourteenth Amendment permits the school to discriminate in this way.

We hold that it does not. The law school has presented no compelling justification, under the Fourteenth Amendment or Supreme Court precedent, that allows it to continue to elevate some races over others, even for the wholesome purpose of correcting perceived racial imbalance in the student body. "Racial preferences appear to 'even the score'. . . only if one embraces the proposition that our society is appropriately viewed as divided into races, making it right that an injustice rendered in the past to a black man should be compensated for by discriminating against a white." *City of Richmond v. J. A. Croson Co.*, (1989). . . .

------------------------------ ◇ ------------------------------

1

The University of Texas School of Law is one of the nation's leading law schools, consistently ranking in the top twenty. . . . Accordingly, admission to the law school is fiercely competitive, with over 4,000 applicants a year competing to be among the approximately 900 offered admission to achieve an entering class of about 500 students. Many of these applicants have some of the highest grades and test scores in the country.

Numbers are therefore paramount for admission. In the early 1990s, the law school largely based its initial admissions decisions upon an applicant's so-called Texas Index ("TI") number, a composite of undergraduate grade point average ("GPA") and Law School Aptitude Test ("LSAT") score. The law school used this number as a matter of administrative convenience in order to rank candidates and to predict, roughly, one's probability of success in law school. Moreover, the law school relied heavily upon such numbers to estimate the number of offers of admission it needed to make in order to fill its first-year class. . . .

Of course, the law school did not rely upon numbers alone. The admissions office necessarily exercised judgment in interpreting the individual scores of applicants, taking into consideration factors such as the strength of a student's undergraduate education, the difficulty of his major, and significant trends in his own grades and the undergraduate grades at his respective college (such as grade inflation). Admissions personnel also considered what qualities each applicant might bring to his law school class. Thus, the law school could consider an applicant's background, life experiences, and outlook. Not surprisingly, these hard-to-quantify factors were especially significant for marginal candidates. . . .

Because of the large number of applicants and potential admissions factors, the TI's administrative usefulness was its ability to sort candidates. For the class entering in 1992—the admissions group at issue in this case—the law school placed the typical applicant in one of three categories according to his TI scores: "presumptive admit," "presumptive deny," or a middle "discretionary zone." An applicant's TI category determined how extensive a review his application would receive.

Most, but not all, applicants in the presumptive admit category received offers of admission with little review. Professor Stanley Johanson, the Chairman of the Admissions Committee, or Dean Laquita Hamilton, the Assistant Dean for Admissions, reviewed these files and downgraded only five to ten percent to the discretionary zone because of weaknesses in their applications, generally a non-competitive major or a weak undergraduate education.

Applicants in the presumptive denial category also received little consideration. Similarly, these files would be reviewed by one or two professors, who could upgrade them if they believed that the TI score did not adequately reflect potential to compete at the law school. Otherwise, the applicant was rejected.

Applications in the middle range were subjected to the most extensive scrutiny. . . .

Blacks and Mexican Americans were treated differently from other candidates, however.[1] First, compared to whites and non-preferred minorities, the TI ranges that were used to place them into the three admissions categories were lowered to allow the law school to consider and admit more of them. In March 1992, for example, the presumptive TI admission score for resident whites and non-preferred minorities was 199. Mexican Americans and blacks needed a TI of only 189 to be presumptively admitted. The difference in the presumptive–deny ranges is even more striking. The presumptive denial score for "nonminorities" was 192; the same score for blacks and Mexican Americans was 179. . . .

According to the law school, 1992 resident white applicants had a mean GPA of 3.53 and an LSAT of 164. Mexican Americans scored 3.27 and 158; blacks scored 3.25 and 157. The category of "other minority" achieved a 3.56 and 160. . . . These disparate standards greatly affected a candidate's chance of admission. For example, by March 1992, because the presumptive denial score for whites was a TI of 192 or lower, and the presumptive admit TI for minorities was 189 or higher, a minority candidate with a TI of 189 or above almost certainly would be admitted, even though his score was considerably below the level at which a white candidate almost certainly would be rejected. . . . The stated purpose of this lowering of standards was to meet an "aspiration" of admitting a class consisting of 10% Americans and 5% blacks, proportions roughly comparable to the percentages of those races graduating from Texas colleges. . . .

Cheryl Hopwood, Douglas Carvell, Kenneth Elliott, and David Rogers (the "plaintiffs") applied for admission to the 1992 entering law school class. All four were white residents of Texas and were rejected. The plaintiffs were considered as discretionary zone candidates. Hopwood, with a GPA of 3.8 and an LSAT of 39 (equivalent to a three-digit LSAT of 160), had a TI of 199, a score barely within the presumptive–admit category for resident whites, which was 199 and up. She was dropped into the discretionary zone for resident whites (193 to 198), however, because Johanson decided her educational background overstated the strength of her GPA. . . .

2

The central purpose of the Equal Protection Clause "is to prevent the States from purposefully discriminating between individuals on the basis of race." . . . It seeks ultimately to render the issue of race irrelevant in governmental decisionmaking. . . . Accordingly, discrimination based upon race is highly suspect. "Distinctions between citizens solely because of their ancestry are by their very nature odious to a free people whose institutions are founded upon the doctrine of equality," and "racial discriminations are in most circumstances irrelevant and therefore prohibited. . . ." *Hirabayashi v. United States* (1943). Hence, "preferring members of any one group for no reason other than race or ethnic origin is discrimination for its own sake. This the Constitution forbids." *Regents of Univ. of Cal. v. Bakke* (1978), see also *Loving v. Virginia* (1967); *Brown v. Board of Educ.*, (1954). These equal protection maxims apply to all races. *Adarand Constructors v. Pena* (1995).

In order to preserve these principles, the Supreme Court recently has required that any govern-

mental action that expressly distinguishes between persons on the basis of race be held to the most exacting scrutiny. Furthermore, there is now absolutely no doubt that courts are to employ strict scrutiny when evaluating all racial classifications, including those characterized by their proponents as "benign" or "remedial." . . .

Strict scrutiny is necessary because the mere labeling of a classification by the government as "benign" or "remedial" is meaningless. As Justice O'Connor indicated in *Croson:*

> Absent searching judicial inquiry into the justifications for such race-based measures, there is simply no way of determining what classifications are "benign" or "remedial" and what classifications are in fact motivated by illegitimate notions of racial inferiority or simple racial politics. Indeed, the purpose of strict scrutiny is to "smoke out" illegitimate uses of race by assuring that the legislative body is pursuing a goal important enough to warrant use of a highly suspect tool. The test also ensures that the means chosen "fit" this compelling goal so closely that there is little or no possibility that the motive for the classification was illegitimate racial prejudice or stereotype.

Under the strict scrutiny analysis, we ask two questions: (1) Does the racial classification serve a compelling government interest, and (2) is it narrowly tailored to the achievement of that goal? . . .

Justice Powell's separate opinion in *Bakke* provided the original impetus for recognizing diversity as a compelling state interest in higher education. In that case, Allen Bakke, a white male, was denied admission to the Medical School of the University of California at Davis, a state-run institution. . . .

Under the medical school's admissions system, the white applicants, who comprised the majority of the prospective students, applied through the general admissions program. A special admissions program was reserved for members of "minority groups" or groups designated as "economically and/or educationally disadvantaged." The university set aside sixteen of the one hundred positions in the entering class for candidates from the special program.

The California Supreme Court struck down the program on equal protection grounds, enjoined any consideration of race in the admissions process, and ordered that Bakke be admitted. The United States Supreme Court affirmed in part and reversed in part in an opinion announced by Justice Powell. The

Court reached no consensus on a justification for its result, however. Six Justices filed opinions, none of which garnered more than four votes. The two major opinions—one four-Justice opinion by Justices Brennan, White, Marshall, and Blackmun and one by Justice Stevens in which Chief Justice Burger and Justices Stewart and Rehnquist joined—reflected completely contrary views of the law.

While Justice Powell found the program unconstitutional under the Equal Protection Clause and affirmed Bakke's admission, Justice Stevens declined to reach the constitutional issue and upheld Bakke's admission under title VI. Justice Powell also concluded that the California Supreme Court's proscription of the consideration of race in admissions could not be sustained. This became the judgment of the Court, as the four-Justice opinion by Justice Brennan opined that racial classifications designed to serve remedial purposes should receive only intermediate scrutiny. These Justices would have upheld the admissions program under this intermediate scrutiny, as it served the substantial and benign purpose of remedying past societal discrimination.

Hence, Justice Powell's opinion has appeared to represent the "swing vote," and though, in significant part, it was joined by no other Justice, it has played a prominent role in subsequent debates concerning the impact of *Bakke*. . . . Justice Powell reasoned that diversity is a sufficient justification for limited racial classification. He argued that diversity of minorities' viewpoints furthered "academic freedom," an interest under the Constitution. . . . As the Adarand Court states, the *Bakke* Court did not express a majority view and is questionable as binding precedent. . . .

Indeed, recent Supreme Court precedent shows that the diversity interest will not satisfy strict scrutiny. Foremost, the Court appears to have decided that there is essentially only one compelling state interest to justify racial classifications: remedying past wrongs. In *Croson*, the Court flatly stated that "unless [racial classifications] are strictly reserved for remedial settings, they may in fact promote notions of racial inferiority and lead to a politics of racial hostility." . . . Justice O'Connor, in her *Adarand*-vindicated dissent in Metro *Broadcasting*, joined by Justices Rehnquist, Scalia, and Kennedy, explained this position:

Modern equal protection has recognized only one [compelling state] interest: remedying the effects of racial discrimination. The interest

in increasing the diversity of broadcast viewpoints is clearly not a compelling interest. It is simply too amorphous, too insubstantial, and too unrelated to any legitimate basis for employing racial classifications.

. . . In short, there has been no indication from the Supreme Court other than Justice Powell's lonely opinion in *Bakke*, that the state's interest in diversity constitutes a compelling justification for governmental race-based discrimination. Subsequent Supreme Court case law strongly suggests, in fact, that it is not.

Within the general principles of the Fourteenth Amendment, the use of race in admissions for diversity in higher education contradicts, rather than furthers, the aims of equal protection. Diversity fosters, rather than minimizes, the use of race. It treats minorities as a group, rather than as individuals. It may further remedial purposes but, just as likely, may promote improper racial stereotypes, thus fueling racial hostility. The use of race, in and of itself, to choose students simply achieves a student body that looks different. Such a criterion is no more rational on its own terms than would be choices based upon the physical size or blood type of applicants. . . .

While the use of race per se is proscribed, state-supported schools may reasonably consider a host of factors—some of which may have some correlation with race—in making admissions decisions. The federal courts have no warrant to intrude on those executive and legislative judgments unless the distinctions intrude on specific provisions of federal law or the Constitution. A university may properly favor one applicant over another because of his ability to play the cello, make a downfield tackle, or understand chaos theory. An admissions process may also consider an applicant's home state or relationship to school alumni. Law schools specifically may look at things such as unusual or substantial extracurricular activities in college, which may be atypical factors affecting undergraduate grades. Schools may even consider factors such as whether an applicant's parents attended college or the applicant's economic and social background.

The assumption is that a certain individual possesses characteristics by virtue of being a member of a certain racial group. This assumption, however, does not withstand scrutiny. "The use of a racial characteristic to establish a presumption that the individual also possesses other, and socially relevant, characteristics, exemplifies, encourages, and legitimizes the mode of thought and behavior that underlies most prejudice and bigotry in modern America." Richard A. Posner, The *DeFunis* Case and the Constitutionality of Preferential Treatment of Racial Minorities (1974).

To believe that a person's race controls his point of view is to stereotype him. The Supreme Court, however, "has remarked a number of times, in slightly different contexts, that it is incorrect and legally inappropriate to impute to women and minorities 'a different attitude about such issues as the federal budget, school prayer, voting, and foreign relations.'" Michael S. Paulsen, Reverse Discrimination and Law School Faculty Hiring: The Undiscovered Opinion, 71 TEX. L. Rev. 993, 1000 (1993). "Social scientists may debate how peoples' thoughts and behavior reflect their background, but the Constitution provides that the government may not allocate benefits or burdens among individuals based on the assumption that race or ethnicity determines how they act or think." *Metro Broadcasting* (O'Connor, J., dissenting).[2]

Finally, the use of race to achieve diversity undercuts the ultimate goal of the Fourteenth Amendment: the end of racially motivated state action. Justice Powell's conception of race as a "plus" factor would allow race always to be a potential factor in admissions decisionmaking. While Justice Blackmun recognized the tension inherent in using race-conscious remedies to achieve a race-neutral society, he nevertheless accepted it as necessary. Several Justices who, unlike Justices Powell and Blackmun, are still on the Court, have now renounced toleration of this tension, however.[3] . . .

3

We now turn to the district court's determination that "the remedial purpose of the law school's affirmative action program is a compelling government objective." The plaintiffs argue that the court erred by finding that the law school could employ racial criteria to remedy the present effects of past discrimination in Texas's primary and secondary schools. The plaintiffs contend that the proper unit for analysis is the law school, and the state has shown no recognizable present effects of the law school's past discrimination. The law school, in response, notes Texas's well-documented history of discrimination in education and argues that its effects continue today at the law school, both in the level of educational

attainment of the average minority applicant and in the school's reputation.

In contrast to its approach to the diversity rationale, a majority of the Supreme Court has held that a state actor may racially classify where it has a "strong basis in the evidence for its conclusion that remedial action was necessary." Generally, "in order to justify an affirmative action program, the State must show there are 'present effects of past discrimination.'" . . .

The Supreme Court has "insisted upon some showing of prior discrimination by the governmental unit involved before allowing limited use of racial classifications in order to remedy such discrimination." *Wygant* (1977). In *Wygant*, the Court analyzed a collective bargaining agreement between a school board and a teachers union that allowed the board to give minorities preferential treatment in the event of layoffs. A plurality rejected the theory that such a program was justified because it provided minority role models. Such a claim was based upon remedying "societal discrimination," a rationale the Court consistently has rejected as a basis for affirmative action. Accordingly, the state's use of remedial racial classifications is limited to the harm caused by a specific state actor. . . .

The *Croson* Court further discussed how to identify the relevant past discriminator. Writing for the Court, Justice O'Connor struck down a minority business set-aside program implemented by the City of Richmond and justified on remedial grounds. While the district court opined that sufficient evidence had been found by the city to believe that such a program was necessary to remedy the present effects of past discrimination in the construction industry, the Court held:

> Like the "role model" theory employed in *Wygant*, a generalized assertion that there had been past discrimination in an entire industry provides no guidance for a legislative body to determine the precise scope of the injury it seeks to remedy. It "has no logical stopping point." "Relief" for such an ill-defined wrong could extend until the percentage of public contracts awarded to [minority businesses] in Richmond mirrored the percentage of minorities in the population as a whole.

. . . [However], one cannot conclude that the law school's past discrimination has created any current hostile environment for minorities. While the school once did practice de jure discrimination in denying admission to blacks, the Court in *Sweatt v. Painter* struck down the law school's program. Any other discrimination by the law school ended in the 1960s.

By the late 1960s, the school had implemented its first program designed to recruit minorities, and it now engages in an extensive minority recruiting program that includes a significant amount of scholarship money. The vast majority of the faculty, staff, and students at the law school had absolutely nothing to do with any discrimination that the law school practiced in the past.

In such a case, one cannot conclude that a hostile environment is the present effect of past discrimination. Any racial tension at the law school is most certainly the result of present social discrimination and, if anything, is contributed to, rather than alleviated by, the overt and prevalent consideration of race admissions. . . .

As we have noted, the district court accepted the law school's argument that past discrimination on the part of the Texas school system (including primary and secondary schools), reaching back perhaps as far as the education of the parents of today's students, justifies the current use of racial classifications.[4] No one disputes that Texas has a history of racial discrimination in education. We have already discussed, however, that the *Croson* Court unequivocally restricted the proper scope of the remedial interest to the state actor that had previously discriminated. 488 U.S. The district court squarely found that "in recent history, there is no evidence of overt officially sanctioned discrimination at the University of Texas." As a result, past discrimination in education, other than at the law school, cannot justify the present consideration of race in law school admissions. . . .

The district court also sought to find a remedial justification for the use of race and, at the same time, attempted to distinguish *Croson* using *United States v. Fordice* (1992). The court held that the law school had a compelling interest to "desegregate" the school through affirmative action. The reliance upon *Fordice* is misplaced, however. . . .

Fordice does not overrule *Croson*. The central holding of *Fordice* is that a state or one of its subdivisions must act to repudiate the continuing "policies or practices" of discrimination.[5] In other words, a state has an affirmative duty to remove policies, tied to the past, by which it continues to discriminate. The *Fordice* Court did not address, in any, a state actor's duty to counter the present effects of past discrimination that it did not cause.[6]

In sum, the law school has failed to show a compelling state interest in remedying the present effects of past discrimination sufficient to maintain the use of race in its admissions system. Accordingly, it is unnecessary for us to examine the district court's determination that the law school's admissions program was not narrowly tailored to meet the compelling interests that the district court erroneously perceived. . . .

In summary, we hold that the University of Texas School of Law may not use race as a factor in deciding which applicants to admit in order to achieve a diverse student body, to combat the perceived effects of a hostile environment at the law school, to alleviate the law school's poor reputation in the minority community, or to eliminate any present effects of past discrimination by actors other than the law school. Because the law school has proffered these justifications for its use of race in admissions, the plaintiffs have satisfied their burden of showing that they were scrutinized under an unconstitutional admissions system. The plaintiffs are entitled to reapply under an admissions system that invokes none of these serious constitutional infirmities. We also direct the district court to reconsider the question of damages, and we conclude that the proposed intervenors properly were denied intervention.

Endnotes

1. As blacks and Mexican Americans were the only two minority categories granted preferential treatment in admissions, it is inaccurate to say that the law school conducted separate admissions programs for "minorities" and "non-minorities." While the law school application form segregated racial and ethnic classification into seven categories—"Black/African American," "Native American," "Asian American," "Mexican American," "Other Hispanic" (meaning non-Mexican descent), "White," and "Other (describe)"—only American blacks and Mexican Americans received the benefit of the separate admissions track.

2. Thus, to put it simply, under the Equal Protection Clause

> the distribution of benefits and costs by government on racial or ethnic grounds is impermissible. Even though it is frequently efficient to sort people by race or ethnic origin, because racial or ethnic identity may be a good proxy for functional classifications, efficiency is rejected as a basis for governmental action in this context.

3. As professor Van Alstyne has argued:

> Rather, one gets beyond racism by getting beyond it now: by a complete, resolute, and credible commitment never to tolerate in one's own life—or in the life or practices of one's government—the differential treatment of other human beings by race. Indeed, that is the great lesson for government itself to teach: in all we do in life, whatever we do in life, to treat any person less well than another or to favor any more than another for being black or white or brown or red, is wrong. Let that be our fundamental law and we shall have a Constitution universally worth expounding.

4. The argument is that because the state discriminated in its primary and secondary school systems, the students' educational attainment was adversely affected, and this harm extended to their higher education, thus justifying giving current applicants a "plus" based on race. This rea-

soning is especially important in justifying benefits for Mexican Americans, as there is no evidence that the law school implemented de jure (or even de facto) discrimination against this group in its admissions process. Because this logic ignores the relevant actions in this case, i.e., discrimination by the law school, it is not necessary for us to examine the potential causational flaws in the argument.

5. In more detail, the *Fordice* Court said the following:

> If the State perpetuates policies and practices traceable to its prior system that continue to have segregative effects—whether by influencing student enrollment or by fostering segregation in other facets of the university system—and such policies are without sound educational justification and can be practicably eliminated, the State has not satisfied its burden of proving that it has dismantled its prior system.

6. In *Croson*, Justice O'Connor did argue that a state may act to prevent its powers from being used to support private discrimination. "[A] state or local subdivision, (if delegated the authority from the State) has the authority to eradicate the effects of private discrimination within its own legislative jurisdiction.") (emphasis added). Hence, a specific state actor can act to prevent the state from being used as a "passive participant" in private discrimination. This power does not create wide-ranging authority to remedy societal discrimination, however.

34. The Case against Hopwood

Reva B. Siegel

Reva B. Siegel argues that the Hopwood *court endorsed two contradictory conceptions of race in reaching its decision. In arguing that diversity is not a sufficient justification for affirmative action, the appeals court maintained that race is a morphological accident, of no more significance than a person's physical size or blood type. According to this view, race correlates with nothing that would be relevant to legitimate choice of applicants. However, in arguing for limiting affirmative action to correcting for the proven past discrimination of the particular social agents, the court allows that there can be significant racial differences in the absence of discrimination with which it would be illegitimate to interfere. According to this view, racial differences can be quite relevant to legitimate choice. In short, Siegel argues that the* Hopwood *court required the University of Texas Law School to assume that applicants from different racial backgrounds are both the same and different in the very same respect, which is impossible.*

The *Hopwood* opinion makes quite clear that, under prevailing Supreme Court opinions, remedying identifiable racial discrimination is a constitutionally compelling reason for adopting an affirmative action plan. At the same time it emphasizes that the Constitution only allows the use of affirmative action for remedial purposes in narrowly circumscribed circumstances. As the Fifth Circuit reads Supreme Court case law, affirmative action can be employed

From *Race and Representation,* edited by Robert Post and Michael Rogin (New York: Zone Books, 1998), pp. 43–48, 58–63. Reprinted with permission.

for the purpose of remedying the "present effects of past discrimination," but not for the purpose of "remedying the present effects of past *societal* discrimination."[1] Drawing on plurality opinions of the 1980s, the Fifth Circuit construes statements prohibiting the use of affirmative action to remedy societal discrimination to mean that "the state's use of remedial racial classifications is limited to [rectifying] the harm caused by a specific state actor."[2] Moreover, before a state actor can implement an affirmative action plan, "it 'must ensure that . . . it has strong evidence that remedial action is warranted'"[3]

The Fifth Circuit selectively discusses the justifications that various justices have advanced for restricting the remedial use of affirmative action to those circumstances where a state actor can show convincing evidence of prior acts of discrimination. The *Wygant* case from which the Fifth Circuit liberally quotes explains that affirmative action policies should be so limited to ensure that the policies do not unduly burden innocent people.[4] The Fifth Circuit's opinion does not mention this concern about burdening innocent parties, but it justifies the constitutional restrictions imposed on the remedial use of affirmative action by quoting a passage from the *Croson* case that explains why the government must supply evidence of prior discrimination before adopting an affirmative action plan:

> [A] generalized assertion that there had been past discrimination in an entire industry provides no guidance for a legislative body to determine the precise scope of the injury it seeks to remedy. It "has no logical stopping point." "Relief" for such an ill-defined wrong could extend until the percentage of public contracts awarded to [minority businesses] in Richmond mirrored the percentage of minorities in the population as a whole.[5]

Quoting *Croson*, the Fifth Circuit observes that "'an amorphous claim that there has been past discrimination in a particular industry cannot justify the use of an unyielding quota.' Such claims were based upon 'sheer speculation' about how many minorities would be in the . . . business absent past discrimination."[6]

Reasoning from these passages, the Fifth Circuit concludes that the district court erred in allowing the University of Texas Law School to employ an affirmative action policy to remedy discrimination in the state's educational system: "[A] remedy reaching all education within a state addresses a pu-

tative injury that is vague and amorphous. It has no logical stopping point.'"[7] As the Fifth Circuit acknowledges, in *Croson,* the Court did indicate that in appropriate circumstances, state or local government could rectify the effects of private discrimination within its own legislative jurisdiction, in order to avoid becoming a passive participant in private discrimination;[8] but the Fifth Circuit discounts this more expansive account of government's remedial authority,[9] insisting that a governmental unit can only rectify effects of discrimination which that particular governmental unit has caused. "[W]hen one state actor begins to justify racial preferences based upon the actions of other state agencies, the remedial actor's competence to determine the existence and scope of the harm and the appropriate reach of the remedy is called into question."[10] "Such boundless 'remedies' raise a constitutional concern beyond mere competence. *In this situation, an inference is raised that the program was the result of racial social engineering rather [than] a desire to implement a remedy.*"[11] The court then concludes that, despite the long history of overt discrimination in University of Texas Law School admissions,[12] such discrimination ended in the 1960s when the school implemented its first program designed to recruit minorities,[13] and further concludes that there are no present effects of the school's past discrimination of sufficient magnitude to warrant the school's use of affirmative action in admissions.[14]

What is the basis of the Fifth Circuit's "inference" that an affirmative action program at the University of Texas Law School designed to remedy the effects of discrimination in the state's educational system would be "the result of racial social engineering rather than a desire to implement a remedy"? As the Fifth Circuit analyzes it, the law school lacks information about the extent of such discrimination and would therefore have to proceed on the basis of assumptions about the degree to which the under-representation of minorities in the competitive applicant pool was attributable to discrimination. But the *Hopwood* court insists that no legitimately remedial affirmative action program can rest on such assumptions. Following the *Croson* opinion, the *Hopwood* opinion insists that there is no way of knowing how many racial minorities would participate in any given social endeavor in the absence of discrimination; making assumptions about such matters without proof is "'sheer speculation.'" In short, it is constitutionally impermissible to assume that in a world without discrimination minorities would participate in various social endeavors at the same rate as other social groups.[15] For the *Hopwood* court, affirmative action goals premised on assumptions about proportional participation raise "the inference that the program was the result of racial social engineering rather [than] a desire to implement a remedy." (The pejorative reference to social engineering derives from a famous article attacking affirmative action authored by Morris Abram, who objected to a new generation of "social engineers" in the leadership of the civil rights movement who believe that "the government's role [is] to bring about proportional representation."[16])

In the early days of the civil rights movement, the federal judiciary was confident that significant racial disparities had their roots in discrimination, but over the decades critics of civil rights law have energetically contested that assumption and courts have gradually retreated from it, requiring ever more detailed proof that social stratification is the product of discrimination perpetrated by the particular agent whose practices are contested.[17] The Supreme Court's opinion in *Croson* employed this body of antidiscrimination law to restrict constitutionally permissible uses of voluntary affirmative action,[18] and *Hopwood* in turn applied *Croson*'s reasoning with zeal. As the Fifth Circuit construes the Fourteenth Amendment, it is a violation of equal protection for a state actor to adopt a race-conscious remedy premised on the assumption that in a world without discrimination, African Americans and other minorities would participate in various social endeavors at the same rate as whites.

Hopwood's *Internal Contradictions and Underlying Preoccupations*

By this point it should be clear that the diversity and remedial sections of the *Hopwood* opinion are premised on two deeply conflicting conceptions of race. The diversity sections of the opinion assert that race is but a morphological accident, a matter of skin color, no more: "The use of race, in and of itself, to choose students simply achieves a student body that looks different. Such a criterion is no more rational on its own terms than would be choices based upon the physical size or blood

type of applicants."[19] On this view, race has no socially relevant content, and provides no basis for choosing among white and black applicants for admission to the law school. The Constitution forbids the University of Texas Law School from assuming that applicants of different racial backgrounds differ. But the remedial sections of the opinion make precisely the opposite assumption about race. Here the *Hopwood* opinion asserts that there *are* socially relevant differences among racial groups. It is "'sheer speculation'... how many minorities would be in [a] business absent past discrimination," and the Constitution forbids the University of Texas Law School from assuming that, in a world without discrimination, members of minority groups would participate and achieve in various social endeavors at the same rate as members of other groups. In short, the two sections of the opinion make diametrically opposing positive and normative claims about race. Indeed, if we distill the normative argument of the *Hopwood* opinion, we discover that the law school's affirmative action plan is unconstitutional because the Constitution forbids the law school from assuming that applicants of different racial backgrounds are different and because the Constitution forbids the law school from assuming that applicants of different racial backgrounds are the same. Thus, as the *Hopwood* opinion draws on the Supreme Court's recent equal protection cases, it reveals that these equal protection cases employ quite contradictory modes of reasoning about race.

It is clear enough that the racial rhetoric in the diversity sections of the *Hopwood* opinion is drawn from the civil rights tradition. This portion of the opinion turns concepts of racial "stereotyping" (and stigma) on the diversity rationale for affirmative action, drawing perhaps as well on academic criticisms of race and gender "essentialism."[20] But the racial rhetoric in the remedial sections of the *Hopwood* opinion seems to come from a very different source. Here the court reasons about race as a cultural phenomenon, drawing perhaps on commentators such as Nathan Glazer, Morris Abram, or Dinesh D'Souza, who analyze race as a form of ethnicity and explain racial status as a product of the cultural resources various groups bring to the task of assimilating to the norms of the dominant culture."[21] If we take seriously the justifications for restricting racial remedies spelled out in *Croson* and *Hopwood*, we confront a view of race-as-culture that seems in deep tension with the professed aims of colorblind constitutionalism.

The analysis of race-conscious remedies contained in the *Croson* and *Hopwood* opinions seems to distinguish between licit and illicit forms of racial stratification. The analysis begins from the premise that we can in fact distinguish between racial formations that are the product of discrimination and those that would exist in the world "absent discrimination." That racial stratification which state actors can prove is traceable to institutional acts of racial discrimination may be rectified by race-conscious remedies. But racial stratification that cannot be shown to be the product of such discrimination is licit—and protected by the Fourteenth Amendment of the United States Constitution. *Hopwood*'s injunction against "racial social engineering" bars the state from pursuing policies of race-conscious remediation that risk disturbing "natural" forms of racial stratification, that is, those racial distributions that arise from differences in tastes or talents among racial groups. (Note how equal protection doctrine restricting the remedial use of affirmative action is concerned about the risk that racial remedies might alter real differences among racial groups—*not* the risk that race discrimination might go unrectified.) If one follows the logic of concerns about proportional representation and racial social engineering expressed in *Croson* and *Hopwood,* it appears that strict scrutiny doctrines under the Fourteenth Amendment radically restrict the use of race-conscious remedies in order to protect and preserve real differences among racial groups. To say the least, this is a counterintuitive ambition for a body of law that embraces as its "ultimate goal" the purpose "'of eliminating entirely from governmental decisionmaking such irrelevant factors as a human being's race.'"[22] . . .

As we have seen, in *Croson* and *Adarand,* the Court adopted a strict scrutiny framework that elevates the standing of white plaintiffs to contest race-conscious remedies and suggests that their claims of race discrimination have much in common with the race discrimination that minorities suffer; the Court has thus given constitutional protection to the injuries whites suffer as members of a racial group, even as it refuses to construe the equal protection clause to redress the grievances they suffer as members of income or occupational groups adversely affected by government policies. In short, the Court has applied strict scrutiny in ways that would seem to reflect and reinforce the racial-group consciousness of white Americans. But the Court also insists that in applying strict scrutiny to affirmative action, it is protecting the minority beneficiaries of such programs from the racial hostility, stereotyping, and stigma that resentful whites may direct at them. Of course, the Court itself has played a role in encouraging the resentment of affirmative action which it then claims it must accommodate. Still, if we suppose that the Court is ultimately a majoritarian institution, perhaps it has taken the only leadership role it can in permitting race-conscious remedies as "suspect" social undertakings. As a majoritarian institution, the Court may well be persuaded that restricting race-conscious state action is the best way to ameliorate racial consciousness in the polity at large. The Court might well hold this view in good faith—even if the strategy it has adopted focuses on the symbolism of governmental action, while ignoring the ways that persisting racial stratification will itself perpetuate racial consciousness.

Given all this, one might conclude that the Court is indeed struggling to bring about the day "when race will become a truly irrelevant, or at least insignificant, factor"[23]—even if it has chosen contestable means for achieving this goal. But it becomes harder to credit the Court's claim that it is attempting to move the nation "beyond" race as one considers the racial privacy discourse the Court invokes to justify restrictions on affirmative action. Consider, for example, the race-conscious views and commitments that the Court has expressed when it differentiates legitimate forms of affirmative action from constitutionally illegitimate forms of "racial balancing. " As the Court has defined it, a race-conscious remedy is illegitimate "racial balancing" whenever such a remedy alleviates racial stratification that is the product of "societal discrimination" or disturbs racial formations that would naturally exist "absent unlawful discrimination."[24] In so reasoning, the Court has embraced a "thick" conception of race, expressing its view that, even in a world where there was no discrimination, there would *still* be occupational differences (and, presumably, income differences) among racial groups. More importantly, it has harnessed this view of race-as-culture to a normative discourse about the proper uses of state power, interpreting the Constitution to prohibit government from altering such natural racial differences. Whatever one thinks about the claim that there would be important racial differences in a world without race discrimination—and such claims must remain speculative because we have never inhabited such a world—they assume very different meaning as a foundation for a privacy discourse concerned with protecting such "natural" differences from governmental interference. When the Court, which generally espouses judicial deference, intervenes in the political process to prevent legislatures from disturbing racial stratification that is "merely" the product of societal discrimination and to prevent legislatures from altering cultural differences among racial groups that would naturally exist in a hypothetical world that has never existed, it seems safe to say that the Court is more involved in preserving the racial status quo than its claims about getting beyond race would seem to suggest.

But still, it can be objected, the Court has only intervened in the political process to inhibit *race-conscious* efforts to alleviate racial stratification; it has always allowed legislatures to use racially neutral means to attack the same problem.[25] Bearing this in mind, we could read the Court's use of racial privacy discourse as an ill-considered and ultimately incidental ground of objection to race-based state action. Whatever view of racial stratification the Court's embrace of racial privacy discourse would seem to express, the Court has, after all, voiced other objections to race-conscious remedies. As the Court and numerous critics of affirmative action have pointed out, such regulatory measures involve practices of racial group assignment that at this juncture of American history have become the site of heightened social conflict. Given the unstable social meaning of race-conscious remedies, the Court could reasonably conclude that the quest to ameliorate racial stratification would be better pursued by formally race-neutral means.

Suppose, then, that the Court were committed to eliminating racial stratification, but, for reasons of principle or pragmatism, believed that it was wrong for government to pursue this goal by race-conscious means. Having taken the unusual measure of intervening in the political process to invalidate race-conscious efforts to ameliorate racial stratification, the Court might then use its institutional authority to encourage legislatures to adopt racially neutral means of achieving the same end. If legislatures reformed educational, zoning, and criminal laws or any number of social welfare policies that affect the life prospects of minority communities, such racially neutral measures might promote integration of basic social institutions just as surely as affirmative action programs do—and without the kind of conflict that race-specific regulation now engenders.

But if the Court *permits* legislatures to ameliorate racial stratification by racially neutral means, it certainly does not employ its institutional authority to encourage them to do so. In the years since the demise of de jure segregation, minority plaintiffs have repeatedly brought law suits challenging racially neutral forms of state action that contribute to the racial stratification affirmative action redresses. The Court might have construed the equal protection clause to require heightened scrutiny of racially neutral policies that have a disparate impact on minority communities—an interpretation of the Fourteenth Amendment that would commit the moral authority of the equal protection clause to the alleviation of racial stratification, without requiring government to act by race-based means.[26] On this view, the constitutional guarantee of equal protection of the laws would require the state to govern impartially, constraining the state from enacting policies that significantly disadvantaged subordinate social groups, unless the state could articulate a weighty justification for adopting policies that aggravated the racial stratification of American society. But the Court does not treat racially neutral state action that aggravates racial stratification as raising significant equal protection concerns. Since the days of *Bakke*, the federal judiciary has reviewed challenges to drug-sentencing guidelines, residential zoning rules, and educational funding and districting policies that disparately burden minority communities on the presumption that such regulation is constitutional unless animated by discriminatory purpose; this is a quite restrictive standard, often defined as tantamount to malice or an intent to harm, which plaintiffs have great difficulty in proving and which the Court justifies as warranted by the deference courts owe to coordinate branches of government.[27] In short, the Court's willingness to intervene in the political process to restrict race-conscious initiatives intended to alleviate racial stratification utterly dissolves when it reviews racially neutral state action having a disparate impact on minorities; in these cases, concerns about the Court's position as a "counter-majoritarian" insti-tution suddenly assume preeminence. Thus, today doctrines of strict scrutiny function primarily, if not exclusively, to restrict race-conscious initiatives intended to alleviate racial stratification, while the Court treats the forms of racially neutral state action that continue to perpetuate racial stratification as presumptively race-neutral, and warranting only the most deferential review. This is the larger constitutional context in which colorblindness objections to race-conscious remedies deserve to be evaluated.

For several decades now the Court has ambivalently sanctioned affirmative action, while subjecting the policies to increasing restrictions. In deciding *Hopwood*, the Fifth Circuit ignored these signs of begrudging tolerance and imposed more severe restrictions on educational affirmative action than the Court has yet embraced; but, as we have seen, the Fifth Circuit derived the core, and conflicting, rationales for its decision from the Supreme Court's recent rulings on race-conscious remedies. In this sense, *Hopwood* is the fruit of the Court's recent rulings on race-conscious remedies.

Since the *Hopwood* decision, minority applications and admissions at the University of Texas Law School have fallen precipitously. The University of Texas Law School has now offered positions in the fall 1997 class to 11 African American students, down from 65 last year, and to 33 Hispanic students, down from 70 last year.[28] Early in the summer, there were no black students willing to attend, although at present, 4 African-American and 21 Hispanic students are planning to enroll in the first-year class of 494 students.[29] In short, it seems that the University of Texas Law School will have an entering class that is less than one percent black—no small achievement for an institution that was (once?) white by law.

If we consider the racial privacy rhetorics that accompany *Hopwood*'s use of colorblindness discourse—in particular, its condemnation of the law school's admission policy as "racial social engineering"—it is hard to view this result as an unintended by-product of the court's decision. . . .

◇

Endnotes

1. *Hopwood v. Texas* at 949 (emphasis added).
2. *Ibid.* at 950.
3. *Ibid.* at 950 (quoting *Wygant v. Board. of Education*, 476 U.S. 267, 277 [1986] [Powell, J., plurality opinion]).
4. The Fifth Circuit relies heavily on the Supreme Court's splintered opinion in *Wygant v. Jackson Board of Education*, 476 U.S. 267 (1985), where a plurality opinion by Justice Powell and a concurring opinion by Justice O'Connor repeatedly expressed these concerns. See *ibid.* at 276 (Powell, J., plurality opinion) : "No one doubts that there has been serious racial discrimination in this country. But as the basis for imposing discriminatory legal remedies that work against innocent people, societal discrimination is insufficient and over expansive. In the absence of particularized findings, a court could uphold remedies that are ageless in their reach into the past, and timeless in their ability to affect the future." See also *ibid.* at 287 (O'Connor, J., concurring in part and concurring in the judgment) (public employer may undertake an affirmative action program which furthers a "legitimate remedial purpose . . . by means that do not impose disproportionate harm on the interests, or unnecessarily trammel the rights, of innocent individuals directly and adversely affected by a plan's racial preference"); *ibid.* at 288 (endorsing the plurality's view that "a governmental agency's interest in remedying 'societal discrimination' that is, discrimination not traceable to its own actions,

cannot be deemed sufficiently compelling to pass constitutional muster under strict scrutiny" and citing Justice Powell's *Bakke* opinion for support).
5. *Hopwood*, 78 F.3d at 950 (quoting *Croson*, 488 U.S. 469, 498 [1989]).
6. *Ibid.* (quoting *Croson*, 488 U.S. at 499).
7. *Ibid.* at 950 (quoting *Wygant v. Board of Education*, 476 U.S. 267, 275 [1986] [Powell, J., plurality opinion]). For the same reasons, the court determines "that the University of Texas System is itself too expansive an entity to scrutinize for past discrimination." *Ibid.* at 951.
8. For the Supreme Court's discussion of this question, see *Croson*, 488 U.S. 469, 503–4 (1989); see also *ibid.* at 491–92, 509 (O'Connor, J., plurality opinion).
9. See *Hopwood*, 78 F.3d at 955 n.49.
10. *Ibid.* at 951.
11. *Ibid.* (emphasis added).
12. See text accompanying notes 12–23 above.
13. *Hopwood*, 78 F.3d at 953.
14. *Ibid.* at 952–56.
15. Objecting to the affirmative action plan challenged in the *Croson* case, the Supreme Court observed that "[it] rests upon the 'completely unrealistic' assumption that minorities will choose a particular trade in lockstep proportion to their representation in the local population," and quoted one of Justice O'Connor's opinions to the effect that "'it is completely unrealistic to assume that

individuals of one race will gravitate with mathematical exactitude to each employer or union absent unlawful discrimination.'" *Croson*, 488 U.S. at 507–8 (quoting *Sheet Metal Workers v. EEOC*, 478 U.S. 421, 494 [1986] [O'Connor, J., concurring in part and dissenting in part]).
16. See Morris B. Abram, "Affirmative Action: Fair Shakers and Social Engineers," *Harvard Law Review* 99 (1986): 1312, 1313.
17. For a discussion of the early race cases, see Vicki Schultz, "Telling Stories About Women and Work: Judicial Interpretations of Sex Segregation in the Workplace in Title VII Cases Raising the Lack of Interest Argument," *Harvard Law Review* 103 (1990): 1750, 1771–75. For an early and influential critique of the evidentiary presumptions of antidiscrimination law, see Glazer, 33–76 (arguing that judicial enforcement of the Civil Rights Act of 1964 had transformed its goal from "equal opportunity" to "statistical parity"). For a leading case in which the Supreme Court signaled that it was adopting a more cautious approach to the question of proving discrimination, see *Hazelwood School District v. United States*, 433 U.S. 299, 307–8 and n.13 (1977) ("Where gross statistical disparities can be shown, they alone in a proper case may constitute prima facie proof of a pattern or practice of discrimination" but "[w]hen special qualifications are required to fill particular jobs, comparisons to the general population [rather than to the smaller group of individuals who possess the necessary qualifications] may have little probative value").
18. In *Croson*, the Supreme Court invalidated Richmond's minority business set-aside program for city contracting, despite the fact that African Americans comprised half the city's population but minority businesses received only 0.67 percent of the city's prime construction contracts. See *Croson*, 488 U.S. at 479–80. According to the Court, the city's program was constitutionally defective, among other reasons, because the city had failed to gather evidence that would demonstrate that low minority participation in city-generated construction work was attributable to discrimination in the award of prime or subcontracts. When the city pointed to the fact that minority membership in the local contractors' associations was very low, the Court refused to infer that the absence of minority participation was attributable to discrimination: "There are numerous explanations for (this dearth of minority participation, including past societal discrimination in education and economic opportunities as well as both black and white career and entrepreneurial choices. Blacks may be disproportionately attracted to industries other than construction." *Ibid.* at 503. The Court held that before Richmond could adopt a remedial affirmative action plan, it would have to establish at least a prima facie case that there was discrimination in the bidding process, by demonstrating a discrepancy between the percentage of minority firms that received prime or subcontracts and the percentage of minority firms in the relevant market

that were qualified to undertake prime or subcontracting work in public construction projects. *Ibid.* at 501–2.
In so ruling, the Court applied law governing proof of a prima facie case of employment discrimination to the voluntary affirmative action context. As the Court itself acknowledged, this inquiry is designed to identify whether discrimination occurred in a transaction in which a particular agent was involved (relevant where the imposition of liability is concerned); it will not identify structural barriers to participation in the transaction in question—factors the Court referred to as "past societal discrimination in education and economic opportunities."
19. *Hopwood*, 78 F.3d at 945.
20. Feminist and antiracist arguments about "essentialism" are now being appropriated and transformed by opponents of race-conscious remedies, much as the color-blindness argument was. Initially, scholars analyzing gender and race stratification described how an observer's social status or position could influence her perception of social relationships, arguing that this kind of positional bias often results in "essentialist" claims—generalizations about group experience that reflect the experience of certain, socially privileged group members rather than the experience of all group members. By the late 1980s, the critique of essentialism was appropriated by critics who were not interested in problems of positional bias, but instead objected to the possibility of making *any* general claims about the distinctive situation, experience, or "voice" of groups that have suffered discrimination. Cf. Angela P. Harris, "Foreword: The Jurisprudence of Reconstruction," *California Law Review* 82 (1994): 741, 754–55 (describing the "essentialism" debate).
With this new focus, the critique made its way into Supreme Court jurisprudence, supplying a new basis for objecting to "benign," race-conscious civil rights measures (e.g., race-based preferences in the award of radio broadcast licenses; race-conscious design of voting districts). Not only did such race-based programs discriminate against white people; now they were also said to discriminate against people of color by making "stereotypical" assumptions about the perspectives or opinions of people of color. See, e.g., *Miller v. Johnson*, 515 U.S. 900, 911–12 (1995) ("When the State assigns voters on the basis of race, it engages in the offensive and demeaning assumption that voters of a particular race, because of their race, 'think alike, share the same political interests, and will prefer the same candidates at the polls.'") (quoting *Shaw v. Reno*, 509 U.S. 630, 646 [1993]); *Metro Broadcasting v. FCC*, 497 U.S. 547, 604 (1990) (O'Connor, J., dissenting) ("Such [race-based] policies may embody stereotypes that treat individuals as the product of their race, evaluating their thoughts and efforts—their very worth as citizens—according to a criterion barred to the Government by history and the Constitution.").
21. See, e.g., Michael Omi and Howard Winant, *Racial Formation in the United States From the 1960s to the 1990s*

(2d ed. New York, 1994), 16–23 (discussing group of scholars who analyze race as ethnicity in order to explain the relative ability of African Americans and immigrant ethnic groups to assimilate into American society); Dinesh D'Souza, *The End of Racism: Principles for a Multiracial Society* (New York, 1995) (arguing that the subordinate status of African Americans is better explained by cultural "pathologies" of the group than by theories that trace group status to genetic endowment or racial discrimination).

22. *Hopwood*, 78 F.3d at 948 (quoting *Croson*, 488 U.S. 469, 495 [1989] [O'Connor, J., plurality opinion] [quoting *Wygant v. Jackson Board of Education*, 476 U.S. 267, 320 (1986) (Stevens, J., dissenting)]).

23. *Adarand*, 515 U.S. at 229.

24. See, e.g., *Croson*, 488 U.S. 469, 507–8 (1989).

25. See, e.g., *ibid.* at 507–9.

26. During the 1970s, some federal courts were interpreting the Fourteenth Amendment in this fashion, but the Court decisively rejected this approach in *Washington v. Davis*, 426 U.S. 229 (1976). See Siegel, "Why Equal Protection No Longer Protects," 1133–34, 1144–45.

27. See *ibid.* at 1133–44.

28. See Jayne N. Suhler, "Texas Professional Schools See Few Minorities Decline in Fall Numbers Linked to Court Decision," *Dallas Morning News*, 5 June 1997, 1A.

29. See Karen Brandon, "In California, Minority Enrollments Falling at Leading Law Schools," *Chicago Tribune*, 6 July 1997; Suhler, 1A.

Suggestions for Further Reading

Anthologies

Cahn, Steven. *The Affirmative Action Debate.* New York: Routledge, 1995.

Cohen, Marshall, Thomas Nagel, and Thomas Scanlon. *Equality and Preferential Treatment.* Princeton, NJ: Princeton University Press, 1977.

Gould, Carol C., and Marx W. Wartofsky. *Women and Philosophy.* New York: G. P. Putnam & Sons, 1976.

Gross, Barry R. *Reverse Discrimination.* Buffalo, NY: Prometheus, 1976.

Alternative Views

Appiah, Anthony. *Color Consciousness.* Princeton: Princeton University Press, 1996.

Bergman, Barbara. *The Economic Emergence of Women.* New York: Basic Books, 1986.

Bower, William, and Derek Bok. *The Shape of the River.* Princeton: Princeton University Press, 1998.

Capaldi, Nicholas. *Out of Order: Affirmative Action and the Crisis of Doctrinaire Liberalism.* Buffalo, NY: Prometheus Press, 1985.

Cohen, Carl. *Naked Racial Preference.* Lanham, MD: Madison Books, 1995.

Ezorsky, Gertrude. *Racism and Justice: The Case for Affirmative Action.* Ithaca: Cornell University Press, 1991.

Fullinwider, Robert K. *The Reverse Discrimination Controversy.* Totowa, NJ: Rowman and Littlefield, 1980.

Nieli, Russell. *Racial Preference and Racial Justice.* Washington, DC: Ethics and Public Policy Center, 1991.

Rosenfeld, Michel. *Affirmative Action and Justice.* New Haven, CT: Yale University Press, 1991.

Sowell, Thomas. *Markets and Minorities.* New York: Basic Books, 1981.

Practical Applications

United States Commission on Civil Rights. *Toward an Understanding of Bakke.* Washington, DC: U.S. Government Printing Office, 1979.

Sexual Harassment

Introduction

Basic Concepts

The moral problem of sexual harassment is the problem of determining the nature of sexual harassment and how to avoid it. Actually, sexual harassment was not recognized by U.S. trial courts as an offense until the late 1970s, and it was only affirmed by the U.S. Supreme Court as an offense in the 1980s. The term *sexual harassment* itself was not even coined until the 1970s. So the moral problem of sexual harassment is one that many people have only recently come to recognize. Obviously, the Senate Judiciary Committee hearings on Anita Hill's charge that Clarence Thomas had sexually harassed her heightened people's awareness of this problem.

In 1980, the Equal Employment Opportunity Commission issued guidelines finding harassment on the basis of sex to be a violation of Title VII of the Civil Rights Act of 1964, labeling sexual harassment "unwelcome sexual advances, requests for sexual favors, and other verbal or physical conduct of a sexual nature" when such behavior occurred in any of three circumstances:

1. Where submission to such conduct is made either explicitly or implicitly a term or condition of an individual's employment.

2. Where submission to or rejection of such conduct by an individual is used as the basis for employment decisions affecting such an individual.

3. Where such conduct has the purpose or effect of unreasonably interfering with an individual's work performance or creating an intimidating, hostile, or offensive working environment.

In 1986, the U.S. Supreme Court in *Meritor Savings Bank v. Vinson* agreed with the EEOC, ruling that there could be two types of sexual harassment: harassment that conditions concrete employment benefits on granting sexual favors (often called the *quid pro quo* type) and harassment that creates a hostile or offensive work environment without affecting economic benefits (the hostile environment type). Nevertheless, the court made it quite difficult for a plaintiff to establish that either of these types of sexual harassment had occurred. For example, a polite verbal "no" does not suffice to show that sexual advances are unwelcome; a woman's entire conduct both in and outside the workplace is subject to appraisal determining whether or not she welcomed the advances. But isn't it odd that a woman should have to prove that an offer "If you don't sleep with me you will be fired" is unwelcomed? Moreover, if a woman rejects such an offer and is fired, unless she is a perfect employee, she will have difficulty proving that she was fired because she rejected the offer. Actually, in such a case, what the Supreme Court should have required is that the employer be able to show that a woman who rejects a sexual advance would still have been fired even if she had said yes.

U.S. courts have also made it difficult to classify work environments as hostile to women. In *Christoforou v. Ryder Truck Rental, Inc.*, a supervisor's actions of fondling a plaintiff's rear end and breasts, propositioning her and trying to force a kiss at a Christmas party were considered "too sporadic and innocuous" to support a finding of a hostile work environment. In *Rabidue v. Osceola Refining Co.*, a workplace where pictures of nude and scantily clad women abounded, including one, which hung on a wall for eight years, of a woman with a golf ball on her breasts and a man with his golf club, standing over her and yelling "fore," and where a co-worker, never disciplined despite repeated complaints, routinely referred to women as "whores," "cunts," and "pussy" was judged not sufficiently hostile an environment to constitute sexual harassment. At times, the courts seem to be appealing to the pervasiveness of certain forms of harassment as grounds for tolerating them. As though we should only prohibit wrongful acts if most people aren't doing them. At other times, the courts appear to be judging sexual harassment to be what men, but not women, say it is. What this shows is that the problem of avoiding sexual harassment is intimately tied to its definition, and women and men seem to disagree radically about what constitutes sexual harassment.

Alternative Views

In Selection 35, Barbara A. Gutek surveys the research that has been done on defining sexual harassment and determining how frequently it occurs. Gutek notes that a number of factors influence whether some behavior is classified as sexual harassment:

1. How intrusive and persistent the behavior is. (The more physically intrusive and persistent the behavior is, the more likely that it will be defined as sexual harassment.)

2. The nature of the relationship between the actors. (The better the actors know each other, the less likely the behavior will be labeled sexual harassment.)

3. The characteristics of the observer. (Men and people in authority are less likely to label behavior as sexual harassment.)

4. The inequality in the relationship. (The greater the inequality, the more likely the behavior will be labeled sexual harassment.)

Gutek contends that the frequency of sexual harassment in the workplace is relatively high. For example, the U.S. Merit System Protection Board found that 42 percent of the women responding to its study reported experiencing sexual harassment on the job within the previous two years. She seeks to explain this frequency as due to the fact that women are stereotypically identified as sexual objects in ways that men are not. She notes that women are stereotypically characterized as sexy, affectionate, and attractive, whereas men are stereotypically characterized as competent and active. These stereotypes, Gutek claims, spill over into the workplace, making it difficult for women to be perceived as fellow workers rather than sex objects, and these perceptions foster sexual harassment. It would seem, therefore, that eliminating the problem of sexual harassment from our society will require breaking down these stereotypes.

Unlike Gutek, Ellen Frankel Paul (Selection 36) argues that the problem of sexual harassment is overblown. She thinks sexual harassment has been exaggerated to include everything from rape to "looks." Paul argues that the extortion of sexual favors by a supervisor from a subordinate by threatening to penalize, fire, or fail to reward is sexual harassment, but she argues that a hostile working environment should be regarded as sexual harassment only when the "reasonable man" of tort law would find the working environment offensive. However, as one of Gutek's studies shows, reasonable men and reasonable women can disagree over what constitutes sexual harassment in the workplace. In this study, 67.2 percent of men as compared to 16.8 percent of women would be flattered if asked to have sex, while 15 percent of the men and 62.8 percent of the women said they would be insulted by such an offer. So the crucial question is: Whose perspective should be determinative?

In Selection 37, Nancy Davis notes that between 25 and 40 percent of female college students report they have been subjected to some sort of harassment from their instructors. She maintains that the frequency and seriousness of sexual harassment in the university are widely underestimated because of such factors as the unequal power between students and professors, traditional gender roles and expectations, popular academic fiction that portrays "co-eds" as lusty seducers of respectable male professors, and the reluctance of educators to "break ranks" with their colleagues. She also claims that when many women are faced with sexual harassment at the university, they tend to deal with the problem by dropping the course, not coming to office hours, changing their major, or even dropping out of school altogether—all with unfortunate consequences.

In Selection 38, James P. Sterba reviews the developments in sexual harassment law and proposes a definition of what is—or better, what should be—sexual harassment. He then offers a partial explanation of why sexual harassment happens in both civilian and military life. Finally, he sets out two positive norms, a principle of androgyny and a principle of desert, in addition to the negative norm that prohibits sexual harassment. We need to focus on these positive principles, he claims, in order to make progress toward reducing the frequency of sexual harassment.

Practical Application

In *Harris v. Forklift Systems Inc.* (Selection 39), the Supreme Court took an important step toward a more reasonable stance on sexual harassment. In this case, Teresa Harris worked as a rental manager at Forklift Systems. Charles Hardy, Forklift's president, told Harris on several occasions, in the presence of other employees, "You're a woman, what do you know?" and "We need a man as the rental manager." Again in front of others, he suggested that the two of them "go to the Holiday Inn to negotiate (Harris's) raise." Hardy occasionally asked Harris and other female employees to get coins from his front pants pockets. On other occasions, he threw objects on the ground in front of Harris and other women, and asked them to pick the objects up. He made sexual innuendos about Harris's and other women's clothing. On one occasion, while Harris was arranging a deal with one of Forklift's customers, Hardy asked Harris in front of other employees, "What did you do, promise some (sex) Saturday night?" Soon after, Harris quit her job at Forklift.

In this case, the Supreme Court struck down the district court's requirement that in order for sexual harassment to be established, Harris needed to show that Hardy's conduct had "seriously affected her psychological well-being." This was an important decision, but obviously it does not go far enough in specifying a reasonable standard for sexual harassment.

35. Understanding Sexual Harassment at Work

Barbara A. Gutek

Barbara A. Gutek surveys the research that has been done on defining sexual harassment and determining how frequently it occurs. She notes that several factors influence whether a behavior is classified as sexual harassment: (1) how intrusive and persistent the behavior is; (2) the nature of relationship between the actors; (3) the characteristics of the observer, and (4) the inequality in the relationship. Gutek contends that the frequency of sexual harassment in the workplace is relatively high. For example, the U.S. Merit System Protection Board found that 42 percent of the women responding to its study reported experiencing sexual harassment on the job within the previous two years. Gutek seeks to explain this frequency as due to the fact that women are stereotypically identified as sexual objects in ways that men are not.

I. Introduction

The topic of sexual harassment at work was virtually unstudied until the concern of feminists brought the issue to the attention of the public and researchers. Much of the research on sexual harassment addresses two complementary questions. (1) How do people define sexual harassment? (2) How common is it? Research on these issues provides useful background information for lawyers and policy makers interested in seeking legal redress for harassment victims, and ultimately in eradicating sexual harassment. . . .

The first issue, people's definitions of sexual harassment, shows the extent to which laws and regulations reflect broad public consensus. Knowing the frequency of sexual harassment—a workplace problem that had no name until the mid-1970s—is important for those seeking to establish laws and procedures to remedy the problem. Further, frequency or prevalence deserves study because sexual harassment has negative consequences for women workers and organizations. These two areas—definition and prevalence—are often studied independently, using different research subjects, research designs, and methods of data collection.

This article traces the development of research on sexual behavior in the workplace from its early emphasis on defining and documenting sexual harassment through other findings on sexual nonharassment. To understand sex at work, several frameworks or theories are discussed, with special emphasis on the concept of sex-role spillover.

The term *sexual behavior* will be used throughout this article to encompass the range of sexual behaviors, such as nonwork-related behavior with sexual content or overtones, found within the workplace and included in many research studies. Few studies attempt to limit themselves to legally liable sexual harassment. Thus, the term "sexual behavior" consists of behavior that is legally considered sexual harassment as well as nonharassing sexual behavior.

Finally, it should be noted that this article is not a review of the status of sexual harassment laws or legal practices. It is limited to the social science research which addresses issues relevant to sexual harassment policy and lawsuits.

II. The Discovery of Sexual Harassment

In the mid-1970s, sexuality in the workplace suddenly received considerable attention through the discovery of sexual harassment, which appeared to be relatively widespread and to have long-lasting, harmful effects on a significant number of working

From "Understanding Sexual Harassment at Work," *Notre Dame Journal of Law, Ethics and Public Policy* (1992). Reprinted by permission.

women. This "discovery" was somewhat counterintuitive, since some women were believed to benefit from seductive behavior and sexual behaviors at work, gaining unfair advantage and acquiring perks and privileges from their flirtatious and seductive behavior. The first accounts of sexual harassment were journalistic reports and case studies. Soon the topic was catapulted into public awareness through the publication of two important books. Lin Farley's book, *Sexual Shakedown: The Sexual Harassment of Women on the Job,* aimed to bring sexual harassment to public attention, create a household word, and make people aware of harassment as a social problem. Catharine MacKinnon's book, *Sexual Harassment of Working Women,* sought a legal mechanism for handling sexual harassment and compensating its victims. In a strong and compelling argument, MacKinnon contended that sexual harassment was primarily a problem for women, that it rarely happened to men, and therefore that it should be viewed as a form of sex discrimination. Viewing sexual harassment as a form of sex discrimination would make available to victims the same legal protection available to victims of sex discrimination. In 1980, the Equal Employment Opportunity Commission (EEOC) established guidelines consistent with MacKinnon's position and defined sexual harassment under Title VII of the 1964 Civil Rights Act as a form of unlawful sex-based discrimination. Several states have passed their own increasingly strong laws aimed at eliminating sexual harassment and legal scholars have sought additional avenues to recover damages incurred from sexual harassment. Various public and private agencies as well as the courts have seen a steady if uneven increase in sexual harassment complaints since the early 1980s.

The various guidelines and regulations define sexual harassment broadly. For example, the updated EEOC guidelines state that

> [u]nwelcome sexual advances, requests for sexual favors, and other verbal or physical conduct of a sexual nature constitute sexual harassment when (1) submission to such conduct is made either explicitly or implicitly a term or condition of an individual's employment or academic advancement, (2) submission to or rejection of such conduct by an individual is used as the basis for employment decisions, or academic decisions affecting such individual, or (3) such conduct has the pur-

pose or effect of reasonably interfering with an individual's work or academic performance or creating an intimidating, hostile, or offensive working or academic environment.

Researchers began serious study of sex at work only after Farley's and MacKinnon's books and two compendia of information on sexual harassment were in progress and generally after the EEOC had established guidelines in 1980. Not surprisingly, researchers were heavily influenced by these important developments in policy and law. These developments focused the concerns of researchers on the two specific issues mentioned above: definition of harassment and frequency of occurrence.

III. Defining Sexual Harassment

The first issue can be succinctly stated: "What constitutes sexual harassment?" For lawyers, the courts, personnel managers, ombudspersons, and others, this is perhaps the most important issue that they must face. If "it" is harassment, it is illegal; otherwise it is not. Researchers, aware of the problems in defining harassment and perhaps eager to contribute to the developments in law and policy, began to supply a spate of studies.

Studies concerned with the definition of sexual harassment come in two types. First are surveys of various populations of people who are asked to tell whether various acts constitute sexual harassment. Second are experimental studies in which students, employees, or managers are asked to rate one or more hypothetical situations in which aspects of the situation are varied along important dimensions. These experimental studies using a hypothetical situation, also known as the "paper people paradigm," come in two variants. In the first variant, subjects are asked to determine whether a particular scenario depicts an instance of sexual harassment. In the second variant, researchers examine the attributions of subjects to understand how subjects' interpretations of a scenario affect their use of the label, sexual harassment.

The strengths of the experimental research design—random assignment to conditions and manipulation of causal variables—allow researchers to make causal statements about what affects how people define sexual harassment. The weakness of the design is that the situation is invariably insufficiently "real": Subjects who have limited information and little appreciation of, or experience with, the subject matter may not respond the way people would in a real (rather than hypothetical) situation.

The survey studies show that sexual activity as a requirement of the job is defined as sexual harassment by about 81 percent to 98 percent of working adults, and similar results have been reported with students as subjects. Lesser forms of harassment such as sexual touching are not as consistently viewed as sexual harassment. For example, I found that 59 percent of men but 84 percent of women asserted that sexual touching at work is sexual harassment. A sizable minority (22 percent of men and 33 percent of women) considered sexual comments at work meant to be complimentary to be sexual harassment.

In contrast to the survey studies which often ask respondents to specify which of a set of actions constitutes harassment, in experimental studies, subjects are usually asked to rate how harassing some incident is, on a five-point or seven-point scale. Such a method makes it impossible to say what percentage of people consider any particular act or event harassment and results are usually reported as mean scores (on, say, a three-, five-, or seven-point scale). It should be noted that experimental studies are generally not concerned with the percentage of their subjects, usually students, who consider behavior X to be harassment, but instead address the factors or variables which affect whether or not some specified incident or act is labeled harassment.

The experimental studies show that except for the most outrageous and clearly inappropriate behavior, whether or not an incident is labeled harassment varies with several characteristics of the incident and the people involved. In these studies, the following variables make a difference: (1) the behavior in question, (2) the relationship between harasser and victim, (3) the sex of the harasser, (4) the sex and age of the victim, (5) the sex of the rater, and (6) the occupation of the person doing the rating. Another way of categorizing these factors is shown below: Characteristics of the behavior, nature of the relationship between the actors, characteristics of the observer/rater, and context factors all affect whether or not a particular act or event is considered sexual harassment.

Factors Affecting the Definition of Sexual Harassment

1. *Characteristics of the behavior.* The more physically intrusive and persistent the behavior, the more likely it is to be defined as sexual harassment by an observer.

2. *The nature of the relationship between actors.* The better the two actors know each other (friends, spouses, long-time co-workers) the less likely the behavior will be labeled sexual harassment by an observer.

3. *Characteristics of the observer.* Men and people in authority (e.g., senior faculty, senior managers) are less likely than others to label a behavior sexual harassment.

4. *Context factors.* The greater the inequality (in position, occupation, age), the more likely the behavior will be labeled sexual harassment by an observer. When the "recipient" of the behavior is low status or relatively powerless (female, young, poor), the behavior is more likely to be judged harassment than when the "recipient" is high status or relatively powerful.

The most important factor determining judgment of sexual harassment is the behavior involved. The experimental studies and survey studies yield the same pattern of findings: Explicitly sexual behavior and behavior involving implied or explicit threats are more likely to be perceived as harassment than other, less threatening or potentially complimentary behavior. Touching is also more likely to be rated as sexual harassment than comments, looks, or gestures. In addition, Weber-Burdin and Rossi concluded that the initiator's behavior is much more important than the recipient's behavior, although if a female recipient behaved seductively, college student raters may reduce the ratings of harassment.

The relationship between the two people is also important. The situation is considered more serious harassment when the initiator is a supervisor of the recipient rather than an equal or a subordinate or more serious if the person previously declined to date the harasser than if the two people had a prior dating relationship. The incident is more likely to be viewed as sexual harassment when a man is the harasser, a woman is the victim and when the female victim is young.

The person doing the rating makes a difference. The most important characteristic . . . is gender. When women are doing the rating, they define a wide variety of sexual behavior at work as sexual harassment, while men tend to rate only the more extreme behavior as harassment. Similarly, on a scale of Tolerance for Sexual Harassment (TSHI), college men reported more tolerance than women, that is, men objected less than women to sexual harassing behavior. In short, the finding that women apply a broader definition of sexual harassment then men is pervasive and widely replicated although not universally found. It is worth noting that at least one factor strongly associated with gender, sex-role identity, did not make much of a difference in people's judgments of sexual harassment. Powell, using a student sample, found that sex-role identity generally did not affect definition of sexual harassment although highly feminine subjects were somewhat more likely than others to label some behaviors sexual harassment and highly masculine male students were somewhat less likely than others to label insulting sexual remarks sexual harassment. In addition, organizational status seems to have an effect. Higher-level managers rating an incident are less likely to see it as serious harassment than middle-level or lower-level managers. In one study, faculty tended to view an incident as less serious than students whereas in another, there were no substantial differences in the ratings of faculty and students.

The experimental studies using attribution analysis probe an evaluator's thought processes as he or she makes a determination whether or not a particular scenario constitutes harassment. Pryor suggested that people are more likely to judge a man's behavior [to be] sexual harassment if his behavior is attributed to his enduring negative intentions toward the target woman. Such negative intentions can either reflect hostility or insensitivity to women. Pryor and Day found that the perspective people take in interpreting a social-sexual encounter affects their judgments of sexual harassment. This may help explain why men and women tend to differ in their judgments of sexual harassment, that is, men may take the man's (usually the initiator's) point of view whereas women are more likely to take the woman's (the victim in many experimental studies) point of view. In support of this view, Konrad and Gutek found that women's greater experience with sexual harassment helps to explain the sex differences in defining sexual harassment. In a similar vein, Kenig and Ryan came to the conclusion that men's and women's perceptions of sexual harassment reflect their self-interest. It is in men's self-interest to see relatively little sexual harassment because men are most often the offenders whereas it is in women's self-interest to see relatively more sexual harassment because women tend to be the victims in sexual harassment encounters.

Cohen and Gutek's analyses suggest that people may make different attributions depending on whether they view the initiator and recipient as friends. More specifically, they found that when student subjects were asked to evaluate an ambiguous, potentially mildly sexually harassing encounter, they tended to assume that the two participants were friends, perhaps dating partners, and that the behavior was welcome and complimentary rather than harassing. Similarly, student subjects were less likely to rate a behavior harassment if they knew that the parties [had] dated and were more likely to rate a behavior harassment if the woman recipient had . . . refused to date the male initiator. In the latter case, subjects may attribute the man's overture to his "enduring negative intentions" toward the woman since her prior refusal of a date presumably eliminates the explanation that he was unsure how she felt about him.

IV. Frequency of Sexual Harassment at Work

The other area of research that developed in response to legal and policy development was a documentation of the forms and prevalence of harassment experienced. In 1979, MacKinnon wrote: "The unnamed should not be taken for the nonexistent." Thus, providing a label and then a definition for sexual harassment was an important step in developing ways to measure the prevalence of sexual harassment.

The research on frequency of harassment focuses heavily but not exclusively on heterosexual encounters. It is often studied separate from the research on definition and employs a different research design, and different subjects. Research aiming to establish rates of harassment in a population must be concerned with drawing a representative sample from a known population in order to generalize results in that population.

The research on prevalence shows a broad range of rates, depending in part on the time frame used. The U.S. Merit System Protection Board's study found that 42 percent of the women respondents reported experiencing sexual harassment on the job within the previous two years. When the study was repeated several years later, the figure remained the same. In a Seattle, Washington, study of city employees, more than one-third of all respondents reported sexual harassment in the previous twenty-four months of employment. Dunwoody-Miller and Gutek found that 20 percent of California state civil service employees reported being sexually harassed at work in the previous five years. Reviewing the results from several different measures of prevalence . . . , Gutek suggested that up to 53 percent of women had been harassed sometime in their working life. The figures are higher in the military; two-thirds of women surveyed in a 1990 study said they had been sexually harassed.

Other studies using purposive or convenience samples generally show higher rates of harassment. In a study by the Working Women's Institute, 70 percent of the employed women respondents said they had experienced sexual harassment. . . . An early study of the readers of *Redbook* magazine found that 88 percent of those mailing in questionnaires had experienced sexual harassment. Schneider reported that more than two-thirds of her matched sample of lesbian and heterosexual working women had experienced unwelcome sexual advances within the previous year.

Because respondents in purposive or convenience samples can choose whether or not to respond, and participating in the study may require some expenditure of effort, researchers assume that people who have been harassed may be more motivated to participate. Thus, the incidence rates are likely to be somewhat inflated.

Although women of all ages, races, occupations, income levels, and marital statuses experience harassment, research suggests that young and unmarried women are especially vulnerable. Not surprisingly, most women are harassed by men, not by women. In addition, women in nontraditional jobs (e.g., truck driver, neurosurgeon, engineer, roofer) and in nontraditional industries such as the military

and mining are more likely to experience harassment than other women. These higher rates are over and above what is expected by their high amount of work contact with men. On the basis of the set of studies done so far, it seems likely that overall, from one-third to one-half of all women have been sexually harassed at some time in their working lives, although frequency rates in some types of work may be higher.

Sexual harassment at work has also been reported by men in several studies. The U.S. Merit System Protection Board's study found 15 percent of the men to be harassed by males or females at work. On the basis of men's reports of specific behavior, Gutek suggested that up to 9 percent of men could have been harassed by women sometime in their working lives. After a careful analysis of men's accounts of harassment, however, Gutek concluded that few of the reported incidents were sexual harassment as legally defined, and some of the incidents may not have even been considered sexual if the same behavior had been initiated by a man or by another woman who was considered a less desirable sexual partner by the man.

V. Frequency of Sexual Nonharassment

Several studies have also examined other kinds of sexual behavior at work, behavior that most people do not consider harassment, including comments or whistles intended to be compliments, quasi-sexual touching such as hugging or an arm around the shoulder, requests for a date or sexual activity often in a joking manner, and sexual jokes or comments that are not directed to a particular person. These other "nonharassing," less serious, and presumably nonproblematic behaviors are considerably more common than harassment. For example, Gutek found that 61 percent of men and 68 percent of women said that they had received at least one sexual comment that was meant to be complimentary sometime in their working lives. In addition, 56 percent of men and 67 percent of women reported that they had been the recipient of at least one sexual look or gesture that was intended to be complimentary. About eight out of every ten workers have been recipients of some kind of sexual overture that was intended [as] a compliment. Schneider found that 55 percent of a sample of heterosexual working women and 67 percent of a sample of lesbian working women reported that within the last year at work, someone had joked with them about their body or appearance. Other studies show similar findings. Dunwoody-Miller and Gutek reported that 76 percent of women and 55 percent of men indicated that as California state civil service employees, they had received complimentary comments of a sexual nature. Looks and gestures of a sexual nature that were meant as compliments were also common (reported by 67 percent of women and 47 percent of men).

Although men [are rarely] harassed, the amount of sexual behavior reported by them at work remains substantial. For example, Gutek found that men were more likely than women to say that they were sexually touched by an opposite-sex person on their job. According to Abbey, Davies, and Gottfried and Fasenfest, men are more likely than women to perceive the world in sexual terms. Also, men are more likely than women to mistake friendliness for seduction and find the office . . . a little too exciting with women around. This seems consistent with the common stimulus-response view that women's presence elicits sexual behavior from men. Reports from men, however, suggest that sex is present in male-dominated workplaces, whether or not women are actually present. This "floating sex" takes the form of posters, jokes, sexual metaphors for work, comments, obscene language, and the like. The relationship seems to be quite straightforward: the more men, the more sexualized the workplace. [That much] of this sexualization . . . is degrading . . . as well as sexual is what creates the "hostile" environment that government regulations aim to eliminate.

[Altogether,] the research on harassment and "nonharassment" shows that sexual behavior is so common at work that one might say that sex permeates work. An equally important conclusion . . . is that the legal behavior is considerably more common than the illegal sexual harassment. This finding is not surprising, but it is important; when some people first hear about sexual harassment, they may confuse it with the more common legal behavior at work which they, themselves, have seen and experienced. This confusion of nonthreatening legal behavior with sexual harassment can lead some to incorrectly denigrate women's complaints as prudish or overly sensitive.

VI. Impacts of Sexual Behavior at Work

Any behavior as common as sexual harassment and nonharassment at work is likely to have a wide variety of ramifications for the individuals involved. So far researchers have concentrated on identifying negative effects of sexual harassment to call attention to harassment as a social and workplace problem. But only scattered attempts have been made [to study] the impacts of other types of sexual behavior at work.

Sexual harassment has a variety of negative consequences for women. . . . In addition to the discomfort associated with the sexually harassing experiences and violation of physical privacy, women often find that their careers are interrupted. Up to 10 percent of women have quit a job because of sexual harassment. Others fear becoming victims of retaliation if they complain about the harassment, and some are asked to leave. For example, Coles found that among eighty-one cases filed with the California Department of Fair Employment and Housing between 1979 and 1983, almost half of the complainants were fired and another quarter quit out of fear or frustration.

Women may also experience lower productivity, less job satisfaction, reduced self-confidence, and a loss of motivation and commitment to their work and their employer. They may avoid men who are known harassers, even though contact with those men is important for their work. Thus, harassment constrains the potential for forming friendships or work alliances with male workers. Furthermore, women are likely to feel anger and resentment and even exhibit self-blame, which leads to additional stress. Crull and Cohen also stated that, while the implicit/overt types of harassment may not have the same direct repercussions as those of the explicit/overt types, all types of sexual harassment at work create high stress levels and serve as a hidden occupational hazard. Finally, sexual harassment helps to maintain the sex segregation of work when it is used to coerce women out of nontraditional jobs.

Besides affecting their work, sexual harassment affects women's personal lives in the form of physical and emotional illness and disruption of marriage or other relationships. . . . For example, Tangri, Burt, and Johnson reported that 33 percent of women said their emotional or physical condition became worse, and Gutek found that 15 percent of women victims . . . said their health was affected and another 15 percent said it damaged their relationships with men.

[Even] more intriguing . . . nonharassing sexual behavior also has negative work-related consequences for women workers, although even they are not always aware of them. For example, Gutek found that the experience of all kinds of sexual behavior, including remarks intended to be complimentary, was associated with lower job satisfaction among women. . . . In addition, women reported that they are not flattered, and in fact are insulted, by sexual overtures of all kinds from men. In one study, 62 percent of women said they would be insulted by a sexual proposition from a man at work. Another example, the office "affair," can have serious detrimental effects on a woman's credibility as well as her career, especially if the relationship is with a supervisor.

Men seem to suffer virtually no work-related consequences of sexual behavior at work. Less than 1 percent of men reported that they quit a job because of sexual harassment, and, in the course of discussing sexual incidents, not one man said he lost a job as a consequence of a sexual overture or request from a woman at work. In the same study, 67 percent of men said they would be flattered by sexual overtures from women. In addition, many men view a certain amount of sexual behavior as appropriate to the work setting, and, as noted above, are less likely to consider any given behavior as sexual harassment. In one study, 51 percent of the men who received overtures from women said they themselves were at least somewhat responsible for the incident. That men experience so few work-related consequences of sex at work is especially odd, since they report so much sexual behavior both that is directed at them by women and that seems to float throughout the workplace.

When men do report "consequences," they are personal rather than work-related, and again, they are viewed in a positive manner. Most often, they report dating relationships or affairs that they find enjoyable; for instance, "There was this little blonde who had the hots for me" or "I think she liked me. I

was young and she was married. She wasn't very happy with her husband."

VII. Understanding Sexual Behavior at Work

[M]ost studies of sexual behavior at work have been in response to the discovery of sexual harassment and policies developed to address harassment. Much of the research is descriptive and diverse, providing interesting information about sexual behavior at work, and useful information for policy makers and lawyers. Some researchers have begun to develop frameworks for studying sexual behavior at work.

One framework sometimes used to study harassment is the power perspective: that is, sexual harassment is an expression of power relationships, and women constitute a threat to men's economic and social standing. With that perspective, Lipman-Blumen viewed the women's "seductive" behavior as micro-manipulation, as a response to male control of social institutions—including the workplace and the academy—which she labeled macro-manipulation. Other researchers explicitly borrowed from the literature on rape. They contend that sexual harassment is analogous to rape: Power, not sexual drive, is the dominant motivation. They further contend that victims of rape and harassment experience similar effects.

In an attempt to explain their own findings on sexual harassment, Tangri, Burt, and Johnson developed three models: the natural/biological model, the organizational model, and the sociocultural model. The natural/biological model assumes that sexual harassment and other forms of sexual expression at work are simply manifestations of natural attraction between two people. According to Tangri, Burt, and Johnson, one version of this model suggests that because men have a stronger sex drive, they more often initiate sexual overtures at work [and] in other settings. The organizational model assumes that sexual harassment is the result of certain opportunity structures within . . . hierarchies. People in higher positions can use their authority (their legitimate power) and their status to coerce lower-status people into accepting a role of sex object or engaging in sexual interactions. The third model, the sociocultural model, "argues that sexual harassment reflects the larger society's differential distribution of power and status between the sexes." Harassment is viewed as a mechanism for maintaining male dominance over women. . . . Male dominance is maintained by patterns of male–female interaction as well as by male domination of economic and political matters. Tangri, Burt, and Johnson's analysis revealed that none of the three models could by itself offer an adequate explanation of their data on sexual harassment. Another model, emphasizing the effects of sex-role expectations in an organizational context, is called sex-role spillover. The following analysis builds on earlier research on this concept.

VIII. Sex-Role Spillover

Sex-role spillover denotes the carryover of gender-based expectations into the workplace. Among the characteristics assumed by many to be associated with femaleness (such as passivity, loyalty, emotionality, nurturance) is being a sex object. Women are assumed to be sexual and to elicit sexual overtures from men rather naturally. In a thirty-nation study of sex stereotypes, the characteristics of sexy, affectionate, and attractive were associated with femaleness. This aspect of sex-role spillover, the sex-object aspect, is most relevant to the study of sex at work.

Sex-role spillover occurs when women, more than men in the same work roles, are expected to be sex objects or are expected to project sexuality through their behavior, appearance, or dress. What is equally important is the fact that there is no strongly held comparable belief about men. For example, of the forty-nine items that were associated with maleness in at least nineteen of the twenty-five countries studied by Williams and Best, none was directly or indirectly related to sexuality. While it is generally assumed that men are more sexually active than women and men are the initiators in sexual encounters, the cluster of characteristics that are usually associated with the male personality do not include a sexual component. Rather the stereotype of men revolves around the dimension of competence and activity. It includes the belief that men are rational, analytic, assertive, tough, good at math and science, competitive, and make good leaders. The stereotype of men—the common view of the male personality—is the perfect picture of asexuality. Sex-role spillover thus introduces the view of women as sexual beings in the workplace, but it simply reinforces the view of men as organizational beings—"active, work-oriented." [Note also] these stereotypes of female characteristics and male characteristics have remained quite stable through the 1970s and into the 1980s.

The spillover of the female sex-role, including the sexual aspect, occurs at work for at least four reasons. First, gender is the most noticeable social characteristic: People immediately notice whether a person is a man or a woman. Second, men may feel more comfortable reacting to women at work in the same manner that they react to other women in their lives, and unless a woman is too young, old, or unattractive, that includes viewing her as a potential sexual partner. Third, women may feel comfortable reacting to men in a manner expected by the men—that is, conforming to the men's stereotype. Fourth, characteristics of work and sex roles may facilitate the carryover of sex role into work role. Sex roles remain relatively stable throughout our lives and permeate all domains of life. On the other hand, the work role may change many times and is specific to only one domain of life. Sex roles are also learned much earlier than are work roles, and they entail a wide variety of diffuse skills and abilities. Work roles, on the other hand, call for more specific skills and abilities.

The important point here is that being sexual and being a sex object are aspects of the female sex role that frequently are carried over to the workplace by both men and women. A variety of subtle pressures may encourage women to behave in a sexual manner at work, and this then confirms their supposedly essential sexual nature. Because it is expected, people notice female sexuality, and they believe it is normal, natural, an outgrowth of being female.

Unfortunately, women do not seem to be able to be sex objects and analytical, rational, competitive, and assertive at the same time because femaleness is viewed as "not-maleness," and it is the men who are viewed as analytic, logical, and assertive. [Even though] the model of male and female as polar opposites has been severely criticized on several grounds, a dichotomy is used by researchers and laypersons alike (for example, we speak of the "opposite" sex). This is an important part of sex-role spillover. [The] sexual aspects the female role [not only are] carried over to work, but also swamp or overwhelm a view of women as capable, committed workers. This is especially true in an environment where sexual jokes, innuendos, posters, and small talk are common. A recent study by Mohr and Zanna showed that sex-role traditional men exposed to sexually explicit material behaved in a significantly more sexual and obtrusive manner toward women than men who did not see sexually explicit material. As Kanter noted, a woman's perceived sexuality can "blot out" all other characteristics, particularly in a sexualized work environment. Thus, sex role interferes with and takes precedence over work role.

What is doubly troublesome about this inability to be sexual and a worker at the same time is that women are not the ones who usually choose between the two. A female employee might decide to be a sex object at work, especially if her career or job is not very important to her. More often, however, the working woman chooses not to be a sex object but may be so defined by male colleagues or supervisors anyway, regardless of her own actions. A woman's sexual behavior is noticed and labeled sexual even if it is not intended as such. To avoid being cast into the role of sex object, a woman may have to act completely asexual. Then she is subject to the charge of being a "prude," an "old maid," or "frigid," and in her attempt to avoid being a sex object, she is still stereotyped by her sexuality, or more accurately, by her perceived lack of sexuality.

The situation for men is entirely different. Benefiting from the stereotype of men as natural inhabitants of organizations—goal-oriented, rational, analytic, competitive, assertive, strong, or, . . . "active, work-oriented"—men may be able to behave in a blatantly sexual manner, seemingly with impunity. Even when a man goes so far as to say that he encourages overtures from women by unzipping his pants at work, he may escape being viewed as sexual or more interested in sex than work by supervisors and colleagues. While the image of women acting in a seductive manner and distracting men from work is viewed as a detriment to the organization, many executives know of men who are "playboys" and harassers, yet they may not see them as detriments to the organization. These men may hire the wrong women for the wrong reasons, make poor use of female human resources in the organization, squander the organization's resources in their quests for new sexual partners, and make elaborate attempts to impress potential sexual partners—all of this may escape the notice of employers. In short, men's sexual

behavior at work often goes unnoticed [for at least two reasons]. First, . . . there is no strongly recognized sexual component of the male sex role. Thus, men's sexual behavior is neither salient nor noticed. Second, perhaps sexual pursuits and conquests, jokes, and innuendos can be subsumed under the stereotype of the organizational man—goal-oriented, rational, competitive, and assertive—which are expected and recognized as male traits. Men may make sexual overtures in an assertive, competitive manner. Likewise, sexual jokes, metaphors, and innuendos may be seen as part of competitive male horseplay. Thus the traits of competitiveness, assertiveness, and goal orientation are noticed, while the sexual component is not. . . .

IX. The Spillover Perspective: Behaviors, Impacts, and Beliefs Concerning Sex at Work

How does the sex-role spillover perspective enrich our understanding of sex at work or integrate the diverse findings about sexual harassment? This perspective leads to an examination of both men's and women's behavior at work and stereotypes or beliefs about how men and women behave. . . . It helps to explain the apparent paradox that women are perceived as using sex to their advantage, while, in practice, they are hurt by sex at work. On the other hand, while men are not perceived as sexual at work, they may display [and benefit from] more sexual behavior.

Sex-role spillover is also useful in explaining why sexual harassment remained invisible for so long. In the absence of data on the subject, women were labeled as sexy, men as asexual. Sexual overtures including harassment were elicited by the sexy women; men who are normally active and work-oriented, "all-business," could be distracted by seductively behaving women, but these distractions were considered a trivial part of men's overall work behavior. If the woman felt uncomfortable with the situation, it was her problem. If she could not handle [it] and complained . . . , it was at least partially her fault. Men and women, including women victims, shared this belief. Thus a woman who complained might be labeled a troublemaker and be asked to leave. . . .

[Although] the spillover perspective is not incompatible with a power perspective, it falls short in accounting for hostile sexual coercion at work. To take an extreme (but not unknown) case, rape in the office [could hardly be considered] a spillover from externally imposed sex roles. Rather, it is best construed as aggression or power, and a power perspective of sexual harassment may be a better explanatory model.

X. Closing Remarks

Much of the research on sexual harassment was inspired by innovations and developments in law and policy, and . . . so far has focused primarily on two issues, definition and prevalence, although topics such as consequences to victims and conditions under which harassment occurs have also been studied.

Recently, Terpstra and his colleagues have engaged in . . . research in a new area: the factors that affect the outcome of decisions in sexual harassment cases. Terpstra and Baker studied Illinois state EEOC cases and examined the factors associated with the outcomes of sexual harassment charges; only 31 percent of formal charges (twenty of sixty-five cases) resulted in a settlement favorable to the complainant. Using the same set of EEOC cases, Terpstra and Cook found that employment-related consequences experienced by the complainant were the most critical factor in filing a charge. Other research, for example, on men who harass and the way men respond to women when sexually explicit material is or is not available, represent other new and important areas of research.

Overall, the research on sexual harassment and sex at work has provided data showing that many of the common beliefs about sexual behavior at work are false. The contribution of research toward understanding and explaining sex at work has been valuable. A domain of human behavior that was largely invisible a decade ago is now visible, numerous misconceptions have been uncovered, and some facts have been exposed as myths by researchers.

---

36. *Exaggerating the Extent of Sexual Harassment*

ELLEN FRANKEL PAUL

Ellen Frankel Paul argues that sexual harassment has been exaggerated to include everything from rape to "looks." She argues that the extortion of sexual favors by a supervisor from a subordinate by threatening to penalize, fire, or fail to reward is sexual harassment. But she argues that a hostile working environment should be regarded as sexual harassment only when the "reasonable man" of tort law would find the working environment offensive. She contends that given this understanding of sexual harassment, scatological jokes, leers, unwanted offers of dates, and other sexual annoyances would no longer have their day in court.

Women in American society are victims of sexual harassment in alarming proportions. Sexual harassment is an inevitable corollary to class exploitation; as capitalists exploit workers, so do males in positions of authority exploit their female subordinates. Male professors, supervisors, and apartment managers in ever increasing numbers take advantage of the financial dependence and vulnerability of women to extract sexual concessions.

Valid Assertions?

These are the assertions that commonly begin discussions of sexual harassment. For reasons that will be adumbrated below, dissent from the prevailing

From "Bared Buttocks and Federal Cases," *Society* (1991). Reprinted by permission.

view is long overdue. Three recent episodes will serve to frame this disagreement.

Valerie Craig, an employee of Y & Y Snacks, Inc., joined several co-workers and her supervisor for drinks after work one day in July 1978. Her supervisor drove her home and proposed that they become more intimately acquainted. She refused his invitation for sexual relations, whereupon he said that he would "get even" with her. Ten days [later] she was fired from her job. She soon filed a complaint of sexual harassment with the Equal Employment Opportunity Commission (EEOC), and the case wound its way through the courts. Craig prevailed, the company was held liable for damages, and she received back pay, reinstatement, and an order prohibiting Y & Y from taking reprisals against her in the future.

Carol Zabowicz, one of only two female forklift operators in a West Bend Co. warehouse, charged that her co-workers . . . from 1978 to 1982 sexually harassed her by such acts as: asking her whether she was wearing a bra; two of the men exposing their buttocks between ten and twenty times; a male co-worker grabbing his crotch and making obscene suggestions or growling; subjecting her to offensive and abusive language; and exhibiting obscene drawings with her initials on them. Zabowicz began to show symptoms of physical and psychological stress, necessitating several medical leaves, and she filed a sexual harassment complaint with the EEOC. The district court judge remarked that "the sustained, malicious, and brutal harassment meted out . . . was more than merely unreasonable; it was malevolent and outrageous." The company knew of the harassment and took corrective action only after the employee filed an EEOC complaint. The company was thus held liable, and Zabowicz was awarded back pay for the period of her medical absence, and a judgment that her rights were violated under the Civil Rights Act of 1964.

On September 17, 1990, Lisa Olson, a sports reporter for the *Boston Herald,* charged five football players of the just-defeated New England Patriots with sexual harassment for making sexually suggestive and offensive remarks to her when she entered their locker room to conduct a post-game interview. The incident amounted to nothing short of "mind rape," according to Olson. After vociferous lamentations in the media, the National Football League fined the team and its players $25,000 each. The National Organization for Women called for a

boycott of Remington electric shavers because the owner of the company, Victor Kiam, also owns the Patriots and . . . allegedly displayed insufficient sensitivity at the time . . . the episode occurred.

Utopian Treatment for Women

All these incidents are indisputably disturbing. In an ideal world—one far different from the one that we inhabit or are ever likely to inhabit—women would not be subjected to such treatment in the course of their work. Women (and men) would be accorded respect by co-workers and supervisors, their feelings would be taken into account, and their dignity would be left intact. For women to expect reverential treatment in the workplace is utopian, yet they should not have to tolerate outrageous, offensive sexual overtures and threats as they go about earning a living.

One question that needs to be pondered is: What kinds of undesired sexual behavior should women be protected against by law? That is, what kind of actions are deemed so outrageous and violate a woman's rights to such extent that the law should intervene, and what actions should be considered inconveniences of life, to be morally condemned but not adjudicated? A subsidiary question concerns the type of legal remedy appropriate for the wrongs that do require redress. Before directly addressing these questions, it might be useful to diffuse some of the hyperbole adhering to the sexual harassment issue.

Harassment Surveys

Surveys are one source of this hyperbole. If their results are accepted at face value, they lead to the conclusion that women are disproportionately victims of legions of sexual harassers. A poll by the Albuquerque *Tribune* found that nearly 80 percent of the respondents reported that they or someone they knew had been victims of sexual harassment. The Merit System Protection Board determined that 42 percent of the women (and 14 percent of men) working for the federal government had experienced some form of unwanted sexual attention between 1985 and 1987, with unwanted "sexual teasing" identified as the most prevalent form. A Defense Department survey found that 64 percent of women in the military (and 17 percent of the men) suffered "uninvited and unwanted sexual attention" within the previous year. The United Methodist Church established that 77 percent of its clergy-women experienced incidents of sexual harassment, with 41 percent of these naming a pastor or colleague as the perpetrator, and 31 percent mentioning church social functions as the setting.

A few caveats about polls in general, and these in particular . . . Pollsters looking for a particular social ill tend to find it, usually in gargantuan proportions. (What fate would lie in store for a pollster who concluded that child abuse, or wife beating, or mistreatment of the elderly had dwindled to the point of negligibility!) Sexual harassment is a notoriously ill-defined and almost infinitely expandable concept, including everything from rape to unwelcome neck massage, discomfiture on witnessing sexual overtures directed at others, yelling at and blowing smoke in the ears of female subordinates, and displaying pornographic pictures in the workplace. Defining sexual harassment, as the United Methodists did, as "any sexually related behavior that is unwelcome, offensive, or . . . fails to respect the rights of others," (makes] the concept broad enough to include everything from "unsolicited suggestive looks or leers [or] pressures for dates" to "actual sexual assaults or rapes." Categorizing everything from rape to "looks" as sexual harassment makes us all victims, a state of affairs satisfying to radical feminists, but not very useful for distinguishing serious injuries from the merely trivial.

Yet even if the surveys exaggerate the extent of sexual harassment, however defined, what they do reflect is a great deal of tension between the sexes. As women in ever-increasing numbers entered the workplace in the last two decades, as the women's movement challenged alleged male hegemony and exploitation with ever greater intemperance, and as women entered previously all-male preserves from the board rooms to the coal pits, it is lamentable, but should not be surprising, that this tension sometimes takes sexual form. Not that sexual harassment on the job, in the university, and in other settings is a trivial or insignificant matter, but a sense of proportion needs to be restored and, even more important, distinctions need to be made. In other words, sexual harassment must be de-ideologized. State-

ments that paint nearly all women as victims and all men and their patriarchal, capitalist system as perpetrators, are ideological fantasy. Ideology blurs the distinction between being injured—being a genuine victim—and merely being offended. An example is this statement by Catharine A. MacKinnon, a law professor and feminist activist:

> Sexual harassment perpetuates the interlocked structure by which women have been kept sexually in thrall to men and at the bottom of the labor market. Two forces of American society converge: men's control over women's sexuality and capital's control over employees' work lives. Women historically have been required to exchange sexual services for material survival, in one form or another. Prostitution and marriage as well as sexual harassment in different ways institutionalize this arrangement.

Such hyperbole needs to be diffused, and distinctions need to be drawn. Rape, a nonconsensual invasion of a person's body, is a crime clear and simple, a violation of the right to the physical integrity of the body (the right to life, as John Locke or Thomas Jefferson would have put it). Criminal law should and does prohibit rape. Whether it is useful to call rape "sexual harassment" is doubtful, for it makes the latter concept overly broad while trivializing the former.

Extortion of Sexual Favors

Intimidation in the workplace of the kind that befell Valerie Craig—that is, extortion of sexual favors by a supervisor from a subordinate by threatening to penalize, fire, or fail to reward—is what the courts term *quid pro quo* sexual harassment. Since the mid-1970s, the federal courts have treated this type of sexual harassment as a form of sex discrimination in employment proscribed under Title VII of the Civil Rights Act of 1964. A plaintiff who prevails against an employer may receive such equitable remedies as reinstatement and back pay, and the court can order the company to prepare and disseminate a policy against sexual harassment. Current law places principal liability on the company, not the harassing supervisor, even when higher management is unaware of the harassment and thus cannot take any steps to prevent it.

Quid pro quo sexual harassment is morally objectionable and analogous to extortion: The harasser extorts property (use of the woman's body) through the leverage of fear for her job. The victim of such behavior should have legal recourse, but serious reservations can be held about rectifying these injustices through the blunt instrument of Title VII. In egregious cases the victim is left less than whole (back pay will not compensate her for ancillary losses), and no prospect for punitive damages are offered to deter would-be harassers. Even more distressing about Title VII is that the primary target of litigation is not the actual harasser, but the employer. This places a double burden on a company. The employer is swindled by the supervisor because he spent his time pursuing sexual gratification and thereby impairing the efficiency of the workplace by mismanaging his subordinates, and the employer must endure lengthy and expensive litigation, pay damages, and suffer loss to its reputation. It would be fairer to both the company and the victim to treat sexual harassment as a tort—that is, as a private wrong or injury for which the court can assess damages. Employers should be held vicariously liable only when they know of an employee's behavior and do not try to redress it.

Defining Harassment Is Difficult

As for the workplace harassment endured by Carol Zabowicz—bared buttocks, obscene portraits, etc.—that too should be legally redressable. Presently, such incidents also fall under the umbrella of Title VII and are termed hostile environment sexual harassment, a category accepted later than *quid pro quo* and with some judicial reluctance. The main problem with this category is that it has proven too elastic: Cases have reached the courts based on everything from off-color jokes to unwanted, persistent sexual advances by co-workers. A new tort of sexual harassment would handle these cases better. Only instances above a certain threshold of egregiousness or outrageousness would be actionable. In other words, the behavior that the plaintiff found offensive would also have to be offensive to the proverbial "reasonable man" of the tort law. That is, the behavior would have to be objectively injurious rather than merely subjectively offensive. The defendant would be the actual harasser, not the company, unless it knew about the problem and failed to act. Victims of scatological jokes, leers, unwanted offers of dates, and other sexual annoyances would no longer have their day in court.

A distinction must be restored between morally offensive behavior and behavior that causes serious harm. Only the latter should fall under the jurisdiction of criminal or tort law. Do we really want legislators and judges delving into our most intimate private lives, deciding when a look is a leer, and when a leer is a Civil Rights Act offense? Do we really want courts deciding, as one recently did, whether a school principal's disparaging remarks about a female school district administrator was sexual harassment and, hence, a breach of Title VII, or merely the act of a spurned and vengeful lover? Do we want judges settling disputes such as the one that arose at a car dealership after a female employee turned down a male co-worker's offer of a date and his colleagues retaliated by calling her offensive names and embarrassing her in front of customers? Or another case in which a female shipyard worker complained of an "offensive working environment" because of the prevalence of pornographic material on the docks? Do we want the state to prevent or compensate us for any behavior that someone might find offensive? Should people have a legally enforceable right not to be offended by others? At some point, the price for such protection is the loss of both liberty and privacy rights.

No Perfect Working Environment Exists

Workplaces are breeding grounds of envy, personal grudges, infatuation, and jilted loves, and beneath a fairly high threshold of outrageousness, these travails should be either suffered in silence, complained of to higher management, or left behind as one seeks other employment. No one, female or male, can expect to enjoy a working environment that is perfectly stress-free, or to be treated always and by everyone with kindness and respect. To the extent that sympathetic judges have encouraged women to seek monetary compensation for slights and annoyances, they have not done them a great service. Women need to develop a thick skin in order to survive and prosper in the work force. It is patronizing to think that they need to be recompensed by male judges for seeing a few pornographic pictures on a wall. By their efforts to extend sexual harassment charges to even the most trivial behavior, the radical feminists send a message that women are not resilient enough to ignore the run-of-the-mill, churlish provocation from male co-workers. It is difficult to imagine a suit by a longshoreman complaining of mental stress due to the display of nude male centerfolds by female co-workers. Women cannot expect to have it both ways: equality where convenient, but special dispensations when the going gets rough. Equality has its price and that price may include unwelcome sexual advances, irritating and even intimidating sexual jests, and lewd and obnoxious colleagues.

Egregious acts—sexual harassment per se—must be legally redressable. Lesser but not trivial offenses, whether at the workplace or in other more social settings, should be considered moral lapses for which the offending party receives opprobrium,

disciplinary warnings, or penalties, depending on the setting and the severity. Trivial offenses, dirty jokes, sexual overtures, and sexual innuendoes do make many women feel intensely discomfited, but, unless they become outrageous through persistence or content, these too should be taken as part of life's annoyances. The perpetrators should be either endured, ignored, rebuked, or avoided, as circumstances and personal inclination dictate. Whether Lisa Olson's experience in the locker room of the Boston Patriots falls into the second or third category is debatable. The media circus triggered by the incident was certainly out of proportion to the event.

As the presence of women on road gangs, construction crews, and oil rigs becomes a fact of life, the animosities and tensions of this transition period are likely to abate gradually. Meanwhile, women should "lighten up," and even dispense a few risqué barbs of their own, a sure way of taking the fun out of it for offensive male bores.

---

37. *Sexual Harassment in the University*

NANCY ("ANN") DAVIS

Nancy Davis notes that between 25 and 40 percent of female college students report they have been subjected to some sort of harassment from their instructors. She maintains that the frequency and seriousness of sexual harassment in the university are widely underestimated. She also claims that when many women are faced with sexual harassment at the university, they tend to deal with the problem in ways that have unfortunate consequences for themselves.

The notion of sexual harassment entered public consciousness in the United States with the publication of a survey on sexual harassment in the workplace conducted by *Redbook* in 1976. More than 9,000 women responded to the survey, and almost nine out of ten reported experiencing some sort of sexual harassment on the job.[1] Unsurprisingly, these reve-

Reprinted from Steven M. Cahn, ed., *Morality, Responsibility, and the University* (1990), by permission of Temple University Press and the author.

lations stimulated a lot of discussion in the news media, the popular press, and academic journals.[2] At about the same time, sexual harassment was found by the courts to constitute a form of sex discrimination and thus to be illegal under the terms of Title VII of the 1964 Civil Rights Act, which prohibits discrimination on the basis of race, sex, religion, or national origin.[3] Shortly thereafter, the same sorts of protections were held to extend to the educational sphere.[4] Title IX of the Education Amendments Act of 1972 forbids sex discrimination in all public and private institutions that receive federal money from grants, loans, or contracts.

Though sexual harassment in the university began to receive attention in the media in the late 1970s, not until 1986 did educational institutions themselves really begin to sit up and take notice. In that year, in *Meritor Savings Bank FSB v. Vinson,* the courts held that it was possible for an employer to be found guilty under Title VII if an employee's harassing conduct created a "hostile environment" for the harassed employee, and it allowed individuals who were the victims of sexual harassment to sue employers that did not have a policy that clearly prohibited sexual harassment.[5] These findings have been held to be applicable to educational institutions, and though many institutions had initially been slow to react, most were not slow to draw the obvious moral, namely, that it was not just an individual harassing instructor who might be liable to prosecution but the university that employed that instructor as well.[6] Most educational institutions have formulated or are in the process of formulating policies concerning sexual harassment.

In addition to being illegal and in opposition to expressed policies of many (if not most) educational institutions, sexual harassment is condemned as unethical by the American Association of University Professors, and by many of the myriad professional organizations that most faculty members are associated with.[7] It is difficult to produce a comprehensive, uncontroversial definition of sexual harassment,[8] or a philosophically watertight account that explains just what it is about the different kinds of behavior that have been described as sexual harassment that makes them all of a piece unethical. Although, as we shall see, these difficulties pose problems for attempts to formulate fair and effective policies about sexual harassment, they pose no serious impediment to the achievement of consensus about the more blatant forms of sexual harassment. In the classic *quid pro quo* case in which an instructor puts unwelcome sexual pressure on a student and makes it clear that . . . academic evaluation or professional advancement [depends] on her yielding to that pressure, what the instructor does is obviously coercive, unjust, disrespectful, and discriminatory.[9] It is an abuse of power, a betrayal of trust, and inimical to the existence of a healthy educational environment in several ways.

Yet surveys conducted at college campuses around the nation reveal that a sizable proportion of female college students—somewhere between 25 percent and 40 percent—report they have been subjected to some sort of sexual harassment on the part of their instructors,[10] and anecdotal evidence provided by female students, faculty members, and administrators corroborates those findings. Surveys may be difficult to interpret and compare, for they do not all employ the same definition of sexual harassment, and anecdotal evidence must always be treated with caution, but it is clear that sexual harassment and other forms of sexually inappropriate behavior are no rarity in the university.[11] Any serious participant in higher education must be puzzled and distressed by this fact.

Commentators have identified many different . . . factors contributing to the prevalence of sexual harassment in the university. Some have emphasized that the university was and remains a male-dominated institution whose ground rules and procedures were fashioned by men. Traditionally, the influential teaching and administrative jobs in the university have been occupied by men, and it is men who have made the policies and interpreted the rules of university governance. Though things have changed considerably in the past decade or so, most of the senior faculty and administrative positions are still occupied by men. And women remain significantly in the minority in most, if not all, academic fields. This situation is thought, in itself, to be a problem. It is women, not men, who are almost always the victims of sexual harassment and men, not women, who are almost always the harassers.[12] And men are likely to both operate with a narrower notion of sexual harassment and have lower estimates of the incidence of sexual harassment on campus than women. They are also likelier to view the incidents of sexual harassment they acknowledge do occur as isolated personal incidents rather than as expressions of an institutional (or broader) problem. Commentators thus often cite the dearth of senior women and the associated inexperience and insensitivity of academic men as among the principal factors contributing to sexual harassment on campus. If women were less of a minority on campus or if they occupied positions of power that enabled them to have greater influence on rules, practices, and policies, then (it is thought) the incidence of sexual harassment on campus would decrease.

The women's movement and other associated movements have led many women—and many men—to question received gender stereotypes. But it is clear, nevertheless, that those stereotypes continue to exert a powerful influence on people's views about the relations between male professors and female students. Although it is a truism that social attitudes about status, gender, and sexuality frame people's expectations about "proper" relations between the sexes, most of us are blind to many of the effects of those attitudes, and implications of those expectations often go unnoticed.[13] Though fewer people may now regard liaisons between experienced and influential older men and inexperienced, comparatively powerless younger women as the ideal sort of relationship, such liaisons are still widely thought to be acceptable (if not simply normal). And the persistence of romanticized Pygmalionesque views of the educational process appears to legitimate such relations between male professors and female students. It is clear that gender stereotypes and associated differential social expectations contribute in a number of ways to the incidence of sexual harassment on campus.

Until we have a better understanding of why there has been so much sexual harassment in the university, we are not likely to be able to arrive at a solid understanding of what can or should be done to curtail it: The formulation of a cogent and successful sexual harassment policy thus requires more reflection on the factors that have contributed to the existence—or persistence—of sexual harassment in the university. Commentators are correct, I believe, in citing both the dearth of senior women in the university and the persistence of conventional gender expectations as significant contributing factors. . . .

It is clear that both the frequency and the seriousness of sexual harassment in the university are widely underestimated (even when sexual harassment is given its narrow interpretation and taken to refer only to such things as *quid pro quo* threats and actual sexual assault). There are a number of reasons why this is so. Personal, institutional, ideological, and societal factors all conspire to deter students from reporting incidents of sexual harassment and from taking concerted action to follow through with the reports of sexual harassment that they do make. If the data on sexual harassment are correct, it is clear that very few of the victims of sexual harassment in the workplace or in the university report it at all.[14] It is worth making clear what in the university context specifically discourages students from reporting sexual harassment.

Students and professors possess unequal power, influence, confidence, experience, and social standing.[15] And this inequality contributes to students'

fears of being ridiculed, disbelieved, punished, or thought incompetent if they come forward with reports of sexually inappropriate conduct on the part of their instructors. Fear of the humiliations that befall many of the women who report rape and other forms of sexual assault evidently makes many women wary of reporting sexual offenses, especially when—as is evidently true in cases of sexual harassment—the attacker is someone who is known to the accuser. The student who has been sexually harassed by her professor is in a particularly vulnerable position, especially if she is known to have had an ongoing personal association with him or has previously submitted to his coercion. The stereotype of the professor as brilliant, principled, and passionately dedicated to his work and to the educational growth of his students leads students to doubt that their allegations would be believed. After all, professors are widely regarded as respectable members of the community. Often enough, students lose confidence in their perceptions of their own actions: If they hadn't done something wrong, then why would this respectable citizen behave so bizarrely?[16] "Blame the victim" sensibilities pervade our society, and so it is not too hard to understand why a confused and distressed victim of sexual harassment would shoulder the blame herself, rather than attribute it to the distinguished, respectable, and (formerly) much-admired professor who was (or appeared to be) so generous with his time and concern.

There are also other factors that erode a woman's confidence, and make her fear that the instructor's harassing behavior must somehow be her fault.[17] Late adolescence and early adulthood are vulnerable and psychologically chaotic times. Among the many difficulties that college-age students face is the struggle to come to terms with their sexuality, and it is easy for them to be insecure in the midst of that process, unclear about their own desires and unsure about how to interpret (and deal with) the many conflicting and ambivalent desires that they have. Though both men and women undoubtedly undergo personal upheaval, their behavior does not meet with the same social interpretation or response, nor are men and women supposed to handle their ambivalences the same way. Men are expected to become more confident and hence more persistent in their pursuit of sexual relationships as they mature. The myth endures that women enjoy being the object of persistent male attentions and invitations but like to play "hard to get" and thus refuse invitations they really wish to accept: When a woman says "no," what she really means is "maybe" or "ask me again later." Since, moreover, women are taught to be polite and nonconfrontational, the woman who tries to act "decently" when confronted with an unwelcome sexual invitation/offer/threat may be seen as thereby expressing ambivalence, which, according to the foregoing myth, may be construed as an expression of interest. If the woman actually does feel ambivalent—she wants to refuse the invitation, but she feels some attraction to the man who has issued it—then she may guiltily believe that she "led him on" even when she said no. And so she may regard the instructor's sexually inappropriate behavior as her fault.[18]

Gender roles and social expectations affect perceptions in other ways as well. Traditionally, women have been judged by their appearance, and they have thus been obliged to devote considerable energy to the attempt to look "attractive," for except among the most wealthy, it was a woman's appearance and good (compliant) manners that were the principal determinant of whether or not she would attract a man and marry, which was essential for her economic security. Though economics have changed, the traditional view continues to exert an influence on people's thinking, and women still feel pressure to dress attractively and act politely. Yet a woman who is attractive is seen as open to, and perhaps as actually inviting, sexual responses from men. This perception, plus the myth that men's sexual self-control is so fragile that it can be overwhelmed by the presence of an attractive woman, contributes to the view that the women who are sexually harassed are those who "asked for it" (by being physically attractive, or attractively dressed).

Surveys make it clear that there is no correlation between a woman's being attractive (or "sexily" dressed) and her being sexually harassed. Sexual harassment, like rape, is primarily an issue of power, not sex. But the myth persists that it is a female student's appearance that is the cause of her instructor's sexually inappropriate behavior toward her. This myth influences female students' perceptions of both their own and their professors' conduct. And if, as she may well suppose, she bears responsibility for the instructor's behaving as he does, she is likely not to think of his conduct as being sexual harassment.[19]

Popular academic fiction has done a lot to perpetuate these myths, and a lot to reinforce unfortunate gender stereotypes. "Co-eds" are portrayed as lusty seducers of respectable male professors, who are often portrayed as hapless victims of those feminine wiles. One can conjecture that most college-age women have read a few of the standard academic novels and that those novels provide some of the background for their interpretation of their professors' conduct.[20]

Believing that her experience of sexual harassment is rare, believing, perhaps, the various myths surrounding the mechanics of male and female attraction, and being influenced by the myth-supporting academic fiction she reads in English courses, the sexually harassed student may believe that the whole thing is her fault. It is not something that she should report but something she should be ashamed of. And so her energies are likely to be spent trying to cope with or "manage" the incident, not reporting it or attempting to bring the sexual harasser to justice.[21]

The asymmetrical power and influence of students and professors not only affect the student's perception of whether or not her claims of sexual harassment would be believed, they also affect her perception of the risks involved in making such a report (even when she does not fear being disbelieved). The professor holds the power of evaluation, and often enough, the student sees him as gatekeeper to her desired career. If she displeases him, then—whether it is through the mechanism of letters of reference or the more informal workings of the "old boy network"—he may, she fears, ruin her career prospects.[22]

The structural organization of the university also serves to deter victims from reporting sexually inappropriate behavior. The myriad of departments, programs, divisions, and colleges may be quite daunting to an undergraduate, who may not understand the relations between them or be able easily to determine who has authority with respect to what.[23] Nor does it help that some of those people to whom a student might turn appear as confused and powerless as the student herself—or altogether uninterested. A student may summon up her courage to report an incident of sexual misconduct to a professor whom she feels she can trust, only to be told to report it to the department chair, whom she may not know at all. If the department chair has not been through this before or if the chair is overworked or less than sympathetic to her plight, then the student may be met with (what she interprets as) annoyance and indifference ("Well, what do you want me to do about it?") or referred to a dean, who may seem to the student a distant, busy, and daunting individual. The organization of the university, with its convoluted procedures and divisions of responsibility, is quotidian to experienced faculty members who understand the hierarchy and the system. But they may be intimidating to someone who does not understand them and who is already traumatized and alienated.

The attitudes of academics toward their colleagues and students and their views about their own intellectual mission and personal responsibilities may also serve to discourage students from reporting sexual harassment. What is perhaps more important, however, is that those attitudes clearly serve to deter faculty members who learn of a colleague's sexually inappropriate behavior from taking action on it. "Educators see themselves as a community of scholars bound together by common interests and goals."[24] They are reluctant to "break ranks," to do things that they perceive as disloyal or damaging to a colleague. In some cases this reluctance may be an expression of a long-standing liberal commitment to tolerance of difference or a manifestation of the desire to uphold academic freedom or respect the autonomy of one's colleagues.[25] In other cases, and less (ostensibly) nobly, it may be thought to stem from academics' desire to be left alone to get on with their own work, protect their own interests, or stay out of academic politics. But whatever the precise blend of factors (what might be called) the ideology of the faculty tends to support the stance of uninvolvement.

Untenured and nontenure-track faculty are in an especially precarious position. The accused senior colleague may wield a good deal of power in the university and in his particular academic field. If displeased or moved to seek retaliation, he may do things that place the untenured faculty member's job at risk. Female faculty members—who are statistically more likely to be untenured or not tenure-track and very much in the minority in their profession—may be particularly vulnerable. Both their professional success thus far and their professional future may well depend upon their being perceived as "good colleagues," people who happen to be female in a largely male context and profession and "don't make a fuss about it." Becoming involved with a sexual harassment case may call attention to a female instructor's gender in ways that make her uncomfortable and may place her in double jeopardy, for she may feel that she is being obliged to risk her own credibility, her good relations with her colleagues, and her own professional connections. And oddly enough, though there is no shortage of good motivations for helping a student who reports an incident of sexual misconduct—a desire to help and protect a student who is hurt and frightened and feels she has nowhere else to turn, the desire to uphold the express and tacit values of the institution, the perception of the need to show students that female faculty members can act with strength and integrity—the female instructor who is willing to assist a student who complains of sexual harassment may find her own motives impugned by resentful male colleagues. As an older woman (and therefore, as convention has it, a less-attractive woman) she may be accused of projecting her unfulfilled desires for male sexual attention onto the student, of being a harridan, or a lesbian who wants to get even with men, of being bitter about her own lack of academic success (which she wrongly and wrongfully attributes to being a woman), and so on.[26]

It is clear that both students' reluctance to come forward with complaints of sexual harassment and faculty members' disinclination to get involved when students do come forward contribute to an underestimation of the scope of the problem of sexual harassment in academia. It is not only the frequency with which sexually inappropriate behavior occurs that is underestimated, however, but the extent of the damage it causes as well. The explanation of why this is so is both complex and multifaceted.

Part of the explanation lies in the invisibility of much of the damage in question. It is easy to see the harm in an instructor's following through on a threat to take reprisals against a student who rejects his demands or in an instructor's tendering an unduly (though perhaps not deliberately or even consciously) harsh evaluation of the student who does not respond favorably to his sexual overtures. Those students are the victims of unfair academic evaluations, and both the professor's integrity and the integrity of the institution's grading practices are severely compromised by such behavior. But other harms—to the individual student, to other students, to the educational institution and to the society at large—are less obvious.

Many of the students who find themselves the recipients of unwelcome sexual overtures, remarks, or questions deal with the problem by "managing" it, and the most common form of management is avoidance: The student drops the course, ceases to attend the class, withdraws the application to be a lab assistant, quits coming to office hours, changes her major, or, in the most extreme cases, drops out of school altogether.[27] Though these avoidance tactics may effectively remove the opportunity for an instructor to engage in harassing behavior, they do so at a cost. The student who thinks she can avoid being sexually harassed by simply avoiding the professor in question may thereby be deprived of valuable academic and professional opportunities, and the pool of motivated and intelligent aspirants to the relevant profession is thus reduced. Though, on such a scenario, both the damage to the individual and the loss to society are real, they are largely undetectable. If the number of women in the profession is already low, then the temptation may be to suppose, for example, that "women just aren't interested in engineering" or that "most women just aren't able to do the sort of abstract thinking required for graduate-level physics," adding the insult of misdiagnosis to the injury of sexual harassment. Women who were in fact driven out of the profession by being robbed of the opportunity to pursue their studies in peace are deemed uninterested or incapable. And viewing these women as uninterested or incapable obviously has implications for how other female aspirants to such careers are likely to be viewed, and to view themselves.

Nor does the damage stop there. When a student is given grounds for wondering whether her instructor's academic interest and encouragement were motivated by his sexual interest in her, she may well come to doubt the legitimacy of her previous accomplishments: Perhaps her success thus far has owed more to sexual attributes that instructors found attractive than to her own hard work and ability. A good, serious, hardworking student may thus lose the sort of self-confidence that anyone needs to succeed in a competitive field, and that women especially need if they are to succeed in traditionally male professions that remain statistically (if not ideologically) male dominated. If, in addition, other students and instructors attribute the harassed student's academic success to sexual involvement with, or manipulation of, her instructors, then relationships with her peers and her other instructors (and with her own students, if she is a teaching assistant) may well be harmed, and suspicion may be cast on the success of other women. More subtly, both students and instructors may be drawn into a familiar form of overgeneralization and thus may come to harbor the suspicion that women's successes in the academic and professional fields in which they are a significant minority owe more to the women's skills at sexually manipulating those in power than to their hard work and ability. Generalized resentment of women or the unspoken background belief that women do not play fair or cannot "pull their own weight" may result, and this consequence may silently lead instructors to interact differently with male and female students and to approach them with different expectations. Given the insidious working of socialization, neither the students nor the instructors may be aware of the existence of such differential treatment; yet it may well be prejudicial and, ultimately, extremely detrimental. Again, both the existence of the harm and its causation are difficult to pin down in such cases and difficult to distinguish from the apparently statistically supported view that "women just aren't good at (or interested in) physics."

It should be clear from this discussion that sexual harassment (or, more broadly, sexually inappropriate behavior) can cause significant damage to the individuals who are its direct victims, to other women, and to the society at large. But it is hard to make the estimation of that damage more precise, for attempts to arrive at a more precise measure of the damage are complicated by the many other factors that make academic and professional success more difficult for women. It is not likely, after all, that a woman's first or only experience of sex discrimination will occur in a college lecture hall or in a professor's office, and it is plausible to suppose that a woman's prior experiences will influence how much damage will be done to her by an instructor's sexual harassment or other sexually inappropriate behavior. Prior experiences may both magnify the harm that is done to her by sexual harassment and, at the same time, diminish the possibility of perceiving that behavior as the cause of the harm. If women have routinely been victims of sex discrimination or societal sexist attitudes, then how can one say that it is the experience of sexual harassment in the university that is the cause of a woman's subsequent distress or the explanation of her decision to enter a "traditionally female" job or profession?[28]

Reflection on this problem suggests a connection between widespread ignorance about the extent of sexually inappropriate behavior in the university and the seriousness of the damage it may cause, and the difficulties involved in attempting to come up with a widely acceptable definition of sexual harass-

ment. In a society that many people would characterize as pervaded by sexist attitudes (if not actual sex discrimination) and in one in which there is disagreement about what constitutes (objectionable) sexism and what is merely a response to differences between men and women, it may be difficult, if not impossible, to reach a consensus about what constitutes sexual harassment. Any university policy that hopes to do any good must take note of this fact.

Endnotes

Acknowledgment: I wish to thank Susan Hobson-Panico, Thomas A. Stermitz, and S. Mickie Grover for their helpful discussion of some of the issues addressed in this essay.

1. Claire Saffran, "What Men Do to Women on the Job," *Redbook* (November 1976), pp. 149, 217–223; see p. 217: "In fact, nearly 9 out of 10 report that they have experienced one or more forms of unwanted attentions on the job. This can be visual (leering and ogling) or verbal (sexual remarks and teasing). It can escalate to pinching, grabbing and touching, to subtle hints and pressures, to overt requests for dates and sexual favors—with the implied threat that it will go against the woman if she refuses."

2. See, e.g., Karen Lindsay, "Sexual Harassment on the Job and How to Stop It," *Ms.* (November 1977), pp. 47–48, 50–51, 74–75, 78; Margaret Mead, "A Proposal: We Need Taboos on Sex at Work," *Redbook* (April 1978), pp. 31, 33, 38; Caryl Rivers, "Sexual Harassment: The Executive's Alternative to Rape," *Mother Jones* (June 1978), pp. 21–24, 28; Claire Saffran, "Sexual Harassment: The View From the Top," *Redbook* (March 1981), pp. 45–51. See also Constance Backhouse and Leah Cohen, *Sexual Harassment on the Job* (Englewood Cliffs, N.J.: Prentice-Hall, 1981), originally published in 1978 as *The Secret Oppression;* and Catherine A. MacKinnon, *Sexual Harassment of Working Women* (New Haven: Yale University Press, 1979).

Popular discussions of sexual harassment in academia include Adrienne Munich, "Seduction in Academe," *Psychology Today* (February 1978), pp. 82–84, 108; Anne Nelson, "Sexual Harassment at Yale," *Nation,* January 14, 1978, pp. 7–10; Lorenzo Middleton, "Sexual Harassment by Professors: An 'Increasingly Visible' Problem," *Chronicle of Higher Education,* September 15, 1980, pp. 1, 4–5; Noel Epstein, "When Professors Swap Good Grades for Sex," *Washington Post,* September 6, 1981, pp. C1, C4; Anne Field, "Harassment on Campus: Sex in a Tenured Position?" *Ms.* (September 1981), pp. 68, 70, 73, 100–102; Suzanne Perry, "Sexual Harassment on the Campuses: Deciding Where to Draw the Line," *Chronicle of Higher Education,* March 23, 1983, pp. 21–22.

3. In *Barnes v. Castle,* 561 F2d 983 (D.C. Cir. 1977), which held that sexual harassment is actionable as sex-based discrimination under Title VII and also extended some liability to an employer for the discriminatory acts of its supervisors.

4. *Alexander v. Yale University,* 549 F. Supp. 1 (D. Conn 1977), established sexual harassment as sex discrimination under Title IX.

5. *Meritor Savings Bank FSB v. Vinson,* 1206 S. Ct. 2399 (1986).

6. Thus both Title VII and Title IX apply when a student is sexually harassed by an instructor. Under Title IX, a student may have a cause of action against the individual instructor who sexually harassed her, and under Title VII, a cause of action against the university that employed that instructor. For relevant discussion, see Annette Gibbs and Robin B. Balthorpe, "Sexual Harassment in the Workplace and Its Ramifications for Academia," *Journal of College Student Personnel 23* (1982), 158–162.

7. See, for example, "Statement on Professional Ethics," adopted in 1966 (pp. 133–134 of the *AAUP Policy Documents and Reports,* Washington, D.C.: AAUP, 1984), which condemns "any exploitation for [a teacher's] private advantage" (p. 133); "A Statement of the Association's Council: Freedom and Responsibility" (pp. 135–136), adopted in 1970, which declares that "students are entitled to an atmosphere conductive to learning and to even-handed treatment in all aspects of the teacher-student relationship" (p. 135); and "Sexual Harassment: Suggested Policy and Procedures for Handling Complaints," (pp. 98–100), adopted in 1984, which states, "it is the policy of this institution that no member of the academic community may sexually harass another" (p. 99).

8. See, e.g., Eliza G. C. Collins and Timothy B. Blodgett, "Sexual Harassment . . . Some See It . . . Some Won't," *Harvard Business Review 59* (1981), 76–95; Phyllis L. Crocker, "An Analysis of University Definitions of Sexual Harassment," *Signs 8* (1983), 696–707; John Hughes and Larry May, "Sexual Harassment," *Social Theory and Practice 6* (1980), 249–280; Catherine A. MacKinnon, "Sexual Harassment: Its First Decade in Court," in her *Feminism*

Unmodified (Cambridge: Harvard University Press, 1987), pp. 103–116, 251–256; Rosemary Tong, "Sexual Harassment," in her *Women, Sex, and the Law* (Totowa, N.J.: Rowman and Littlefield, 1983).

9. There is some disagreement as to whether it is sex discrimination, but there can be no serious doubt that it is wrongful discrimination. Whether it follows through on the threat and whether or not she submits to it are irrelevant. See, e.g., Crocker, "Analysis of University Definitions," p. 704: "Once a student is propositioned, all her future interactions with, and evaluations by, the professor are tainted and suspect, whether a promise or threat was ever made or carried out."

10. See Phyllis L. Crocker, "Annotated Bibliography on Sexual Harassment in Education," *Women's Rights Law Reporter 7* (1982), 91–106. And see *Symposium on Sexual Harassment* in *Thought & Action 5*, (1989): 17–52, especially the essay by Anne Traux, "Sexual Harassment in Higher Education: What We've Learned," pp. 25–38, for an overview of surveys and results. Though a good deal of the sexual harassment on campus involves faculty members and administrators as victims, and some involves students as harassers, considerations of space and focus require that I confine this essay to the discussion of sexual harassment that involves students as victims and instructors as harassers. Discussion will also be confined to cases in which it is male instructors who are the harassers and female students who are the victims. As many commentators have observed, the cases in which a female instructor harasses a male student or a male instructor harasses a male student are few and far between. According to Traux, p. 25: "Nationally, about 95 percent of all sexual harassment reports involve men harassing females." See also Gibbs and Balthorpe, "Sexual Harassment in the Workplace"; MacKinnon, "Sexual Harassment: Its First Decade"; Tong, "Sexual Harassment"; Donna J. Benson and Gregg E. Thomson, "Sexual Harassment on a University Campus: The Confluence of Authority Relations, Sexual Interest, and Gender Stratification," *Social Problems 29* (1982), 236–251; Bernice Lott, Mary Ellen Reilly, and Dale R. Howard, "Sexual Assault and Harassment: A Campus Community Case Study," *Signs 8* (1982), 296–319.

11. Because . . . there is so much disagreement about what sorts of conduct constitute actual sexual harassment, and because *sexual harassment* is a legal term that is used to describe certain forms of legally proscribed sex discrimination, I prefer to use the broader (and vaguer) terms *sexually inappropriate behavior* and *sexual misconduct* whenever context and expression permit. If, as I shall argue, there are different kinds of sexually inappropriate behavior that may be wrong but are not (for various reasons) happily classified with the sorts of wrongful behavior that constitute blatant sexual harassment, then it may be misleading to use *sexual harassment* as omnivorously as many commentators—and the Equal Opportunity Commission—have done.

12. It is, of course, possible for a female professor to harass a male student or for a professor of one sex to harass a student of the same sex. But it is clear that the vast majority of harassers are men, and the vast majority of victims are women, and surveys suggest that the incidence of sexual harassment of male students by female instructors is indeed very small. It is of course possible for a female instructor to make a *quid pro quo* offer/threat to a male student. But the fact that women are a minority, both in the upper echelons of the teaching and administrative staff and in most departments, together with the familiar facts about gender expectations and status, suggests that such harassment will be rare. And subtler forms of sexually inappropriate behavior, which the perpetrator does not perceive as unwelcome or coercive, will probably be even rarer.

Involvements between older, established men and young women are accepted as normal, while those between older, established women and young, unestablished men clearly are not. Women who are involved in relationships with young, less-established men are generally the object of criticism, not admiration or even tolerance. In addition, since the determination of a woman's social status is held to depend heavily on the status of the male she is associated with, the attractions of such a relationship are likely not to be great: Whereas a female student may gain status by involvement with a male professor, a female professor forfeits status by involvement with a male student. If, as most commentators point out, sexual harassment is primarily an issue of power, not sex, there is considerably less incentive for a female faculty member to seek involvement with a male student, and considerably more disincentive. Finally, one can reasonably suppose that because women have long been in the minority in academia and have long been subject to various forms of sex discrimination and disparagement, they are likely to be more sensitive to the risks and problems that even well-intentioned relationships between persons of unequal power create. Whether it is accurate to say that gender is itself a form of hierarchy in a society that has been and continues to be so male-dominated (see MacKinnon, "Sexual Harassment: Its First Decade"), there are good reasons to recognize that, as things now stand, the problem of sexual harassment is almost always one of men harassing women. Though, in the abstract, the issue of sexual harassment—the exploitative use of power—is sex-neutral, if not sex-blind, in circumstances in which it is men who (by and large) possess the power, it is women who will (by and large) be the victims.

That both males and females can be the victims of sexually inappropriate behavior has sometimes—mistakenly—been thought to undercut the claim that sexual harassment is a form of sex discrimination. But the existence of cases in which a male student is victimized by a female instructor does nothing to undercut such a claim, for the effects of being so victimized may be different for men and women, and the background of long-standing and ongoing discrimination against women makes it plausible to suppose that the effects would indeed be different. People suppose that because wrongs are committed both in the case in which a male professor harasses a female student and in the case in which a female professor harasses a male student, they must be the same wrong. But this is not obviously a correct assumption. In both cases there is a wrongful abuse of power and authority, but in one case . . . there is also—because of the long-standing and ongoing discrimination against women—another wrong, namely, that of sex discrimination.

Nor does the existence of cases of single-sex harassment undercut the claim that sexual harassment is sex discrimination, unless one regards the obvious and widespread discrimination against homosexuals as some form of discrimination other than sex discrimination or construes sex discrimination so narrowly that conventional gender identity is seen as defining one's sex. Neither of these assumptions is plausible.

There are reasons for being uneasy at the characterization of sexual harassment as a form of sex discrimination. In some cases of sexually inappropriate behavior (which the Equal Opportunity Commission Guidelines would classify as sexual harassment), it is primarily an instructor's obvious disrespect, rather than the sexual cast of that disrespect, that seems more perspicuously identified as the thing that makes his actions wrong.

But the best reasons for uneasiness are probably pragmatic ones. Recent Supreme Court decisions have significantly weakened the scope of protections against racial discrimination (from Title VII and elsewhere); there is reason to suspect that sex discrimination protections will fare no better. They may even fare worse, for there is good reason to insist that there are no important ineliminable differences between persons of different races, but there are obviously differences between the sexes.

13. One has only to look at advertising or television sitcoms, or—as Billie Wright Dziech and Linda Weiner point out in *The Lecherous Professor* (Boston: Beacon Press, 1984)—watch teenagers interact in a shopping mall to be reminded how powerful and pervasive gender expectations are. See Benson and Thomson, "Sexual Harassment on a University Campus"; MacKinnon, *Sexual Harassment of Working Women*; MacKinnon, "Sexual Harassment: Its First Decade."

14. According to Traux, "Sexual Harassment in Higher Education," p. 26, "Of those harassed, not more than one in 10 actually report the harassment."

15. And as many would point out, women and men are not peers in these areas either.

16. To some degree, what medical ethicists have called "the fallacy of the generalization of expertise" is at work here. People who are thought to be successful or expert in one area are frequently—and unreasonably—thought to be successful or expert in others. Thus some people wrongly suppose that physicians are knowledgeable in matters of medical ethics (simply) because they are knowledgeable in medical matters, and others suppose that the good scholar of history (e.g.) must also be a good and decent person.

17. See Robert Shrank, "Two Women, Three Men on a Raft," *Harvard Business Review 55* (1977), 100–109 for an interesting discussion of how men may unreflectively work to undermine women's self-confidence.

18. Or she may think that she should "be complimented, not incensed, if confronted with male sexual interest" (see Benson and Thomson, "Sexual Harassment on a Campus," p. 237) and thus feel that she has no right to complain.

19. One woman interviewed by Collins and Blodgett ("Sexual Harassment," p. 93) said: "A lot of women hesitate to report sexual harassment because women: (1) don't think they'll be believed; (2) will be punished by smaller raises or cruddy jobs [the analogue in the university context: will be punished by lower grades or undeservedly harsh evaluations]; (3) will be ostracized by male and female employees [students and other instructors]; (4) will be accused of inviting the advance; (5) have guilt feelings that perhaps it was invited subconsciously; (6) fear publicity; (7) are unsure exactly what is harassment and what is just interaction of people."

20. Some of the novels that come to mind here are Joyce Carol Oates, *Them*; John Barth, *The End of the Road*; and Bernard Malamud, *Dubin's Lives*. See Dziech and Weiner, *The Lecherous Professor*, pp. 62–63, 68, 118.

21. See especially Benson and Thomson, "Sexual Harassment on Campus"; and Dziech and Weiner, *The Lecherous Professor*, chap. 4. Also relevant is Judith Berman Brandenburg, "Sexual Harassment in the University: Guidelines for Establishing a Grievance Procedure," *Signs 8* (1982), 321–336. See Mary P. Rowe, "Dealing with Sexual Harassment," *Harvard Business Review 59* (1981), 42–47, for a detailed set of proposed procedures for harassed employees that places more emphasis on "management" of sexual harassment in the workplace than on prevention or redress.

22. A quotation from Dziech and Weiner, *The Lecherous Professor*, p. 83, drives this point home. One pre-med student said: It's easy for someone else to say that I should do something about Dr. —, but how can I? He was the first person at — to take my work seriously. At least I think it's my work that made him notice me. He's the one who's pushing for me to get into med school. If I refuse him, then I ruin my whole life.

23. Material in this and the succeeding paragraph benefited from the discussion in chap. 2 of Dziech and Weiner, *The Lecherous Professor*.

24. Ibid., p. 49.

25. I do not mean to suggest that respect for academic freedom or one's colleagues' autonomy requires (or even

permits) a faculty member who learns of an incident of sexual harassment to ignore the student who reports it or otherwise discourage her from pressing her complaint. Neither academic freedom nor professional autonomy is absolute, and it is difficult to see what intellectually respectable academic purpose *is* served by the tolerance of sexual harassment. Of course, a faculty member who believes that some respectable academic purpose is served by tolerating a colleague's sexually inappropriate behav-

ior should be given the opportunity to explain his or her views. But such an opportunity can arise only if students are listened to and encouraged, not dissuaded from bringing their sexual harassment complaints forward in the first place.

26. See Dziech and Weiner, *The Lecherous Professor*, chap. 6.
27. See note 21.
28. The old adage that "defendants must take plaintiffs as they find them" is of some help here, but not much.

---

38. Understanding, Explaining, and Eliminating Sexual Harassment

JAMES P. STERBA

James P. Sterba reviews the developments in sexual harassment law, hoping to increase our understanding of what is, or better, what should be, sexual harassment. He then offers a partial explanation of why sexual harassment happens in both civilian and military life. He goes on to propose two positive norms, a Principle of Androgyny and a Principle of Desert, in addition to the negative one that prohibits sexual harassment. He claims we need to focus on these positive norms in order to make progress toward reducing the frequency of sexual harassment.

In 1998, the U.S. Supreme Court made four attempts to clarify sexual harassment law (*Oncale v. Sundowner Offshore Services, Inc., Burlington Industries, Inc. v. Ellerth, Faragher v. City of Boca Raton*, and *Gebser et al. v. Lago Vista Independent School District*). In 1998 as well, Judge Susan Webber Wright of the U.S. Court of Appeals for the Eighth Circuit dismissed the sexual harassment case of Paula Corbin Jones against President Clinton on the somewhat controversial grounds that even if Clinton as governor of Arkansas had done all Jones claimed he had done (i.e., summoned her from her convention post to his hotel suite, dropped his pants in front of Jones, asked her to "kiss it," touched her thigh and tried to kiss her on the neck, and despite apparently accepting her "no" for an answer, partially and momentarily blocked her exit for enough time to tell her that he knew her boss and that it would be best if the incident were kept between the two of them),

Clinton would not have sexually harassed Jones because she could not demonstrate any tangible job detriment or adverse employment action for her refusal to submit to Clinton's alleged advances. Thus, while the flurry of judicial activity in 1998 did increase the scope of sexual harassment law—sitting U.S. presidents are now liable for sexual harassment suits, as are grade school and high school teachers—unfortunately our understanding of the nature of sexual harassment has yet to achieve a comparable advance. Nor as yet do we have a very good explanation of why sexual harassment occurs as frequently as it does in our society.

Accordingly, in Part I of this chapter, I will review the developments in sexual harassment law, hoping to increase our understanding of what is—or better, what should be, sexual harassment. In Part II, I will offer a partial explanation of why sexual harassment happens in both civilian and military life. In Part III, I will determine what positive norms, in addition to the negative one that prohibits sexual harassment, we need to focus on in order to make progress toward reducing its frequency.

Reprinted from *Justice for Here and Now* (Cambridge, 1998), pp. 93–99, by permission with substantial additions.

Part I: Understanding Sexual Harassment

Sexual harassment was not recognized by U.S. trial courts as an offense until the late 1970s, and it was only affirmed by the U.S. Supreme Court as an offense in the 1980s. The term *sexual harassment* itself was not even coined until the 1970s. So the problem of sexual harassment is one that many people have only recently come to recognize. Obviously, the Senate Judiciary Committee hearings in 1991 on Anita Hill's charge that Clarence Thomas had sexually harassed her,[1] the U.S. Navy's Tailhook scandal in 1992, the Bob Packwood scandal in 1995, and more recently in 1997, Paula Jones's amended sexual harassment suit against President Clinton have all helped heighten people's awareness of this problem. (See Selections 20–24.)

In 1976, a federal district judge, in the first legal case using the term "sexual harassment," ruled that Diane Williams, a public information specialist at the U.S. Department of Justice who was dismissed after turning down her supervisor's sexual advances, had been harassed "based on sex" within the meaning of Title VII of the Civil Rights Act of 1964. Four years later, the Equal Employment Opportunity Commission issued guidelines finding harassment on the basis of sex to be a violation of Title VII of the Civil Rights Act of 1964 (see Selection 49), labeling sexual harassment as "unwelcome sexual advances, requests for sexual favors, and other verbal or physical conduct of a sexual nature when such behavior occurred in any of three circumstances:

1. Where submission to such conduct is made either explicitly or implicitly a term or condition of an individual's employment,

2. Where submission to or rejection of such conduct by an individual is used as the basis for employment decisions affecting such individual, or

3. Where such conduct has the purpose or effect of unreasonably interfering with an individual's work performance or creating an intimidating, hostile, or offensive working environment.

In 1986, the U.S. Supreme Court in *Meritor Savings Bank v. Vinson* (see Selection 51) unanimously agreed with the EEOC, ruling that there could be two types of sexual harassment: harassment that conditions concrete employment benefits on granting sexual favors (called the *quid pro quo* type) and harassment that creates a hostile or offensive work environment without affecting economic benefits (the *hostile environment* type). Nevertheless, the court made it quite difficult for a plaintiff to establish that either of these types of sexual harassment had occurred. For example, a polite verbal "no" does not suffice to show that sexual advances are unwelcome, and a woman's entire conduct both in and outside the workplace is subject to appraisal determining whether or not she welcomed the advances. For example, in the *Vinson* case, there was "voluminous testimony regarding Vinson's dress and personal fantasies," and in the Senate Judiciary Committee hearings, Anita Hill was not able to prevent intensive examination of her private life, although Clarence Thomas was able to declare key areas of his private life off limits, such as his practice of viewing and discussing pornographic films.

The Supreme Court also made it difficult to classify work environments as hostile to women unless the harassment is sufficiently severe or pervasive. Applying the Supreme Court's standard, a lower court, in *Christoforou v. Ryder Truck Rental*, judged a supervisor's actions of fondling a plaintiff's rear end and breasts, propositioning her, and trying to force a kiss at a Christmas party to be "too sporadic and innocuous" to support a finding of a hostile work environment.[2] Similarly, in *Rabidue v. Osceola Refining Co.*, a workplace where pictures of nude and scantily clad women abounded (including one, which hung on a wall for eight years, of a woman with a golf ball on her breasts and a man with his golf club standing over her and yelling "Fore!") and where a co-worker, never disciplined despite repeated complaints, routinely referred to women as "whores," "cunts," "pussies," and "tits," was judged by a lower court not to be a sufficiently hostile environment to constitute sexual harassment.[3] Notice, by contrast, that the U.S. Senate Arms Services Committee, in its hearings on homosexuals in the military, regarded an environment in which known homosexuals are simply doing their duty in the military to be too hostile an environment in which to ask male heterosexuals to serve.

Yet why should we accept the Supreme Court's characterization of sexual harassment, especially given its requirements of unwelcomeness and pervasiveness?[4] As the Supreme Court interprets sexual harassment, a person's behavior must be unwelcome in a fairly strong sense before it constitutes sexual harassment. But why should a woman have to prove that the offer "If you don't sleep with me, you will be fired" is unwelcome before it constitutes sexual harassment?[5] Isn't such an offer objectively unwelcome? Isn't it just the kind of offer that those in positions of power should not be making to their subordinates, an offer that purports to make their continuing employment conditional upon providing sexual favors? Surely, unless we are dealing with some form of legalized prostitution, and maybe not even then, such offers are objectively unwelcome.[6] Given, then, that such offers are objectively unwelcome, why is there any need to show that they are also subjectively unwelcome before regarding them as violations of Title VII of the Civil Rights Act? The requirement of subjective unwelcomeness is simply a gratuitous obstacle that makes the plaintiff's case far more difficult to prove than it should be.[7]

In addition, if the plaintiff is fired after refusing such an offer, the Supreme Court requires her to prove that the firing occurred because the offer was refused, which is very difficult to do unless one is a perfect employee. Wouldn't it be fairer to require the employer to prove that the plaintiff would have been fired even if she had said "yes" to the offer?[8] Of course, employers could avoid this burden of proof simply by not making any such offers in the first place.[9] But when they do make objectively unwelcome offers, why shouldn't the burden of proof be on them to show that any subsequent firing was clearly unrelated to the plaintiff's refusal of the offer? Fairness is particularly relevant in this context because we are committed to equal opportunity in the workplace, which requires employing women and men on equal terms. Accordingly, we must guard against imposing special burdens on women in the workplace when there are no comparable burdens imposed on men.[10]

The demand for equal opportunity in the workplace also appears to conflict with the Supreme Court's pervasiveness requirement for establishing a hostile environment. Citing a lower court, the Supreme Court contends that, to be actionable, sexual harassment "must be sufficiently severe or pervasive 'to alter the conditions of the [victim's] employment and create an abusive working environment.'"[11] But as this standard has been interpreted by lower courts, the pervasiveness of certain forms of harassment in the workplace has become grounds for tolerating them. In *Rabidue*, the majority argued that

> It cannot seriously be disputed that in some work environments, humor and language are rough hewn and vulgar. Sexual jokes, sexual conversations and girlie magazines abound. Title VII was not meant to or can change this. Title VIII is the federal court mainstay in the struggle for equal employment opportunity for the female workers of America. But it is quite different to claim that Title VII was designed to bring about a magical transformation in the social mores of American workers.[12]

The Supreme Court itself seems to sound a similar theme by emphasizing the application of Title VII to only extreme cases of sexual harassment as found in *Vinson*.

However, as the EEOC interprets Title VII, the law has a broader scope. It affords employees the right to work in an environment free from discriminatory intimidation, ridicule, and insult. According to the EEOC, sexual harassment violates Title VIII where conduct creates an intimidating, hostile, or offensive environment or where it unreasonably interferes with work performance. (See Selection 47.)

But how are we to determine what unreasonably interferes with work performance? In *Rabidue*, the majority looked to prevailing standards in the workplace to determine what was reasonable or unreasonable. Yet Justice Keith, in dissent, questioned this endorsement of the status quo, arguing that just as a Jewish employee can rightfully demand a change in her working environment if her employer maintains an anti-Semitic workforce and tolerates a workplace in which "kike" jokes, displays of Nazi literature, and anti-Jewish conversation "may abound," surely women can rightfully demand a change in the sexist practices that prevail in their working environments.[13] In *Henson v. Dundee*, the majority also drew an analogy between sexual harassment and racial harassment:

> Sexual harassment which creates a hostile or offensive environment for members of one sex is every bit the arbitrary barrier to sexual equality at the workplace that racial harassment is to racial equality. Surely, a requirement that a man or woman run a gauntlet of sexual abuse in return for the privilege of being al-

lowed to work and make a living can be as demeaning and disconcerting as the harshest of racial epithets.[14]

And this passage is also quoted approvingly by the Supreme Court in *Vinson*.

Moved by such arguments, the majority in *Ellison v. Brady* proposed that rather than looking to prevailing standards to determine what is reasonable, we should look to the standard of a reasonable victim, or given that most victims of sexual harassment are women—the standard of a reasonable woman.[15] They contend that this standard may be different from the standard of a "reasonable man." For example, what male superiors may think is "harmless social interaction" may be experienced by female subordinates as offensive and threatening.[16]

Nevertheless, if we are concerned to establish equal opportunity in the workplace, there should be no question about what standard of reasonableness to use here. It is not that of a reasonable woman, nor that of a reasonable man for that matter, but the standard of what is reasonable for everyone affected to accept. For equal opportunity is a moral requirement, and moral requirements are those which are reasonable for everyone affected to accept. This assumes that apparent conflicts over what is reasonable to accept—for example, conflicts between the standard of a reasonable woman and that of a reasonable man—are conflicts that can and should be resolved by showing that one of these perspectives is more reasonable than the other, or that some still other perspective is more reasonable still. However, at least in the context of sexual harassment, this standard of what is reasonable for everyone affected to accept will accord closely with the standard of a reasonable woman, given that once women's perspectives are adequately taken into account, the contrasting perspective of a reasonable man will be seen as not so reasonable after all.[17]

In its decision in *Harris v. Forklift Systems, Inc.* (1993), the Supreme Court took an important step toward a more reasonable stance on sexual harassment. (See Selection 53.) In this case, Teresa Harris worked as a rental manager at Forklift Systems. Charles Hardy, Forklift's president, said to Harris on several occasions, in the presence of other employees, "You're a woman, what do you know?" and "We need a man as the rental manager." Again in front of others, he suggested that the two of them "go to the Holiday Inn to negotiate [Harris's] raise."

Hardy occasionally asked Harris and other female employees to get coins from his front pants pockets. On other occasions, he threw objects on the ground in front of Harris and other women and asked them to pick the objects up. He made sexual innuendoes about Harris's and other women's clothing. On one occasion, while Harris was arranging a deal with one of Forklift's customers, Hardy asked her in front of other employees, "What did you do, promise some [sex] Saturday night?" Soon after, Harris quit her job at Forklift.

In this case, the Supreme Court struck down the district court's requirement that in order for sexual harassment to be established Harris needed to show that Hardy's conduct had "seriously affected her psychological well-being." This was an important decision, but obviously it does not go far enough in specifying a reasonable standard for sexual harassment.

It is also important to recognize here that achieving equal opportunity in the workplace will conflict, to some degree, with freedom of speech. Consider the case of *Robinson v. Jacksonville Shipyards*, in which a U.S. District Court upheld claims of sexual harassment on hostile work environment grounds and issued extensive remedial orders.[18] Plaintiff Lois Robinson was one of a very small number of female skilled craftworkers employed at the Shipyards—one of six women out of 832 craftworkers. Her allegations of sexual harassment centered around "the presence in the workplace of pictures of women in various stages of undress and in sexually suggestive or submissive poses, as well as remarks by male employees and supervisors which demean women." Although there was some evidence of several incidents in which the sexually suggestive pictures and comments were directed explicitly at Robinson, most were not.

In analyzing this case, Nadine Strossen, past president of the ACLU, argues that even sexually offensive speech should be protected unless it is explicitly directed at a particular individual or group of individuals.[19] Accordingly, Strossen endorses the ACLU's amicus brief in the *Robinson v. Jacksonville Shipyards* case, which considered the court's ban on the public display of sexually suggestive material without regard to whether the expressive activity was explicitly directed toward any employee as too broad. However, in light of the fact that Jacksonville Shipyards had itself banned all public displays of expressive activity except sexual materials, the amicus brief went on to favor the imposition of a workplace rule that would right the balance and permit the posting of other materials as well—materials critical of such sexual expression, as well as other political and religious or social messages that are currently banned. Such a rule would implement a "more speech" approach in an effort to counter offensive speech.

But would such a rule work? Would it succeed in protecting the basic interests of women, especially their right to equal opportunity in the workplace? It is not clear that it would be effective in male-dominated workplaces like Jacksonville Shipyards, where women are a tiny minority of the workforce, and so are likely to have their voices drowned out in the free market of expression that this rule would permit.

Nor does Strossen's distinction between offensive speech explicitly directed at a particular person or group and offensive speech that is not so directed seem all that useful, given that most sexual harassment is directed at women not because they are Jane Doe or Lois Robinson, but because they are women. So why should we distinguish between sexual harassment that is explicitly directed at a particular woman because she is a woman, and sexual harassment that is only directed at a particular woman because it is explicitly directed at all women? Of course, sexually harassing speech can be more or less offensive, and maybe its offensiveness does correlate, to some degree, with the manner in which that harassment is directed at women. Nevertheless, what is crucial here is that the offensiveness of sexually harassing speech becomes unacceptable when it undermines the equal opportunity of women in the workplace—that is, when it imposes special burdens on women in the workplace where there are no comparable burdens on men. It is at this point that justice demands that we impose whatever limitations on sexually harassing speech are needed to secure equal opportunity in the workplace.

Most recently, in *Oncale v. Sundowner Offshore Services, Inc.* (1998) the Supreme Court expanded the scope of sexual harassment to include same-sex sexual harassment even when the harasser is not homosexual. (See, Selection 54.) In this case, Joseph Oncale was working for Sundowner Offshore Services on a Chevron U.S.A. oil platform in the Gulf of Mexico. He was employed as a roustabout on an eight-man crew which included John Lyons, Danny Pippen and Brandon Johnson. Lyons, the crane operator, and Pip-

pen, the driller, had supervisory authority. On several occasions, Oncale was forcibly subjected to sex-related, humiliating actions against him by Lyons, Pippen, and Johnson in the presence of the rest of the crew. On one occasion, the men grabbed him in the company shower and forced a bar of soap between his buttocks and threatened to rape him. When he complained to the company's safety compliance clerk, Valent Hohen, about Lyons and Pippen's behavior, Hohen told Oncale that he was also being harassed by the two men himself. So Oncale quit, asking that his pink slip reflect that he "voluntarily left due to sexual harassment and verbal abuse."

The Supreme Court, seeking to end conflicting stances taken by lower courts in same-sex sexual harassment cases (some of which found sexual harassment in cases like Oncale's, while others held that same-sex sexual harassment could not be supported by Title VII of the Civil Rights Act, and still others held that same-sex sexual harassment is only actionable when the harasser is homosexual) held in a unanimous decision that nothing in Title VIII necessarily bars a claim of discrimination "because of . . . sex" merely because the plaintiff and the defendant (or the person charged with acting on behalf of the defendant) are of the same sex. In these same-sex cases of sexual harassment, as in the more standard different-sex cases, special burdens are imposed on the victims of sexual harassment where there are no comparable burdens imposed on others similarly situated. In Oncale's case, sexual taunts, threats, and abuse were directed at him because his appearance and behavior was judged not to be "masculine" enough by his harassers.

It is also important to see that while sexual harassers are usually either the same-sex or different-sex harassers, they can also be what has been called "equal opportunity sexual harassers," that is, harassers who target both men and women. (See Selection 30.) Moreover, some lower courts have argued that equal opportunity sexual harassment falls outside the scope of the protection of Title VII of the Civil Rights Act because such harassers do not limit their harassment to the members of one sex, and so their victims could not claim that they would not have been harassed "but for their sex." Fortunately, in the light of the *Oncale* decision, it should be possible to reinterpret the "because of . . . sex" restriction of Title VII in such a way that all three forms of sexual harassment are prohibited. This is because what is objectionable about all three forms of sexual harassers is that they engage in degrading and abusive sexual conduct that is chosen on the basis of or "because of" the sex of their victims.

Moreover, sexual harassers, whether they be same-sex, different-sex, or equal opportunity sexual harassers, typically impose special burdens on some when there are no comparable burdens imposed on others who are similarly situated, and this frequently is part of what is wrong with sexual harassment. Yet sexual harassment, understood as engaging in degrading and abusive sexual conduct that is chosen on the basis of the victim's sex, would still be wrong even if it were inflicted on everyone within the harasser's reach. Thus, the comparative harm that frequently results from sexual harassment does not exhaust its offensiveness.

Accordingly, drawing on the foregoing discussion, I offer the following definition of sexual harassment:

> **Sexual harassment** is objectively unwelcome sexual advances, requests for sexual favors. and other verbal or physical conduct of a sexual nature, which are determined to be both objectionable and actionable by the standard of what is reasonable for everyone affected to accept, and which usually, but not always, imposes a special burden on some individuals when there are no comparable burdens imposed on others who are similarly situated.

Sexual harassment so defined can clearly be of the quid pro quo or the hostile environment type, but given that these two types of sexual harassment share this common definition, their features will tend to overlap in particular cases, such as in the *Burlington Industries* case recently taken up by the Supreme Court.[20] Moreover, assuming that neither Kimberly Ellerth suffered any economic detriment from the vice president of Burlington Industries who harassed her nor Paula Jones from then-Governor Clinton, they still could have suffered from sexual harassment, according to my definition. It all depends on whether the sexual behavior to which they were allegedly exposed is both objectionable and actionable as determined by the standard of what is reasonable for everyone affected to accept. Of course, when the burdens imposed by sexual harassment are slight, they will presumably not be reasonably judged as legally actionable by everyone affected and so will not properly fall within the scope of the law.

Part II: Sexual Harassment in Civilian and Military Life

As is well known, there is a high incidence of sexual harassment in both civilian and military life. In research conducted by psychologists, 50 percent of women questioned in the civilian workplace said they had been sexually harassed. According to the U.S. Merit Systems Protection Board, within the federal government, 56 percent of 8,500 female civilian workers surveyed claimed to have experienced sexual harassment. According to the *National Law Journal,* 64 percent of women in "pink-collar" jobs reported being sexually harassed and 60 percent of 3000 women lawyers at 250 top law firms said that they had been harassed at some point in their careers. In a survey by *Working Women* magazine, 60 percent of high-ranking corporate women said they have been harassed; 33 percent more knew of others who had been.[21] Similarly, in a 1995 survey of 90,000 female soldiers, sailors, and fliers, 60 percent of the women said they had been sexually harassed. Only 47 percent of the Army women surveyed said that they believed their leaders were serious about putting a stop to sexual harassment.[22] According to another study, 66 percent of women in the military experienced at least one form of sexual harassment in the past year.[23] Another study found that 50 percent of women at the Naval Academy, 59 percent of women at the Air Force Academy, and 76 percent of women at the Military Academy experienced some form of sexual harassment at least twice a month.[24]

Yet despite the high incidence of sexual harassment in both civilian and military life, at least in the United States, there are some important differences that suggest somewhat different explanations of why sexual harassment is taking place in these contexts. The most important difference of this sort is the still widely expressed belief that women do not belong in the military. For example, 45 percent of first-year midshipmen expressed the view that women did not belong in the military and 38 percent of fourth-year midshipmen felt the same.[25] The same view can be found among the highest commanders in the U.S. military. For example, Air Force Chief General Merrill McPeak testified before the Senate Arms Services Committee in 1991 that if he had to choose between a qualified woman and a less qualified man to fill a combat role, he would go with the man. "I admit it does not make much sense, but that is the way I feel about it," McPeak responded.[26] Surely, it would be difficult to find a male CEO of a Fortune 500 company who would be willing to publicly express the same feelings as General McPeak about the suitability of employing qualified women.

There are, of course, some parallels in civilian life to this attitude toward women found in the military. For example, probably a significant number of the 863 craftworkers who worked along with the six women craftworkers at Jacksonville Shipyards in the case previously cited thought that the women did not belong there, either. But what is distinctive about the U.S. military is the degree to which the belief that women do not belong there is still widely and openly held. As another general put it,

> War is a man's work. Biological convergence on the battlefield (women serving in combat) would not only be dissatisfying in terms of what women could do, but it would be an enormous psychological distraction for the male, who wants to think that he's fighting for that woman somewhere behind, not up there in the same foxhole with him. It tramples the male ego. When you get right down to it, you have to protect the manhood of war.[27]

What I am suggesting is that this widely and openly held belief that women do not belong is distinctive of military life and helps explain the prevalence of sexual harassment there.

But what then explains the prevalence of sexual harassment in civilian life? Since at present there is no comparable widely and openly held belief that women don't belong in civilian life, or even in the civilian workplace, where women now occupy 50 percent of the labor force,[28] there must be another belief that supports the sexual harassment that occurs there. I suggest that is the belief that while women do belong in civilian life, it is still appropriate to treat them as sexual objects in ways that men are not to be treated, with the consequence that they are sexually subordinate to men. It is this belief, I think, which primarily fuels sexual harassment in civilian life. According to this belief, women are classified as having a lesser status than men and so are open to sexual harassment in ways that men are not. Of course, the belief that it is appropriate to treat women as sexual objects in ways that men are not, such that they are sexually subordinate to men, also functions in the military, but there, I think, sex-

ual harassment is more strongly supported by the belief that women just don't belong in the military.

Obviously, so far I have been seeking to explain the sexual harassment of ostensibly heterosexual women by ostensibly heterosexual men, which is the dominant form of different-sex sexual harassment. But what about same-sex and equal opportunity sexual harassment? Same-sex and equal opportunity sexual harassment are, I believe, best explained in a way analogous to the way I have sought to explain different-sex sexual harassment. In same-sex sexual harassment, either the harassers believe that their victims do not belong in some social setting, as was true in the *Oncale* case, or they believe their victims do belong but that it is still appropriate to treat them as sexual objects in ways that others (including the harasser) are not to be treated, as is standardly the case when the same-sex harasser is homosexual. Similarly, the same holds true of equal opportunity sexual harassers. Either equal opportunity sexual harassers believe that their particular victims do not belong in some social setting, or they believe that they do belong but that it is still appropriate to treat them as sexual objects in ways that others (including the harasser) are not to be treated.

Part III: The Need for Positive as well as Negative Norms

Suppose, then, that I am right that the high incidence of different-sex sexual harassment in civilian life is explained by the belief, held by many men and also women, that it is appropriate to treat women as sexual objects, and hence as sexually subordinate to men, and that the high incidence of different-sex sexual harassment in military life is explained by the fact that many men and women hold this same belief, but even more so by the fact that they also hold the belief that women just don't belong in the military. And suppose further that I am right that same-sex and equal opportunity sexual harassment can be similarly explained. What, then, can be done to rid society of the problem of sexual harassment? Obviously, sexual harassment law and the moral and legal theory that supports it are an attempt to rid society of this problem. This approach primarily tells men not to harass women and then tries to explain what constitutes sexual harassment. However, this approach is essentially negative. It tells men what not to do, not what to do. Of course, in most moral contexts, it is far easier to come up with negative norms than positive ones—easier to tell people what they should not be doing than what they should be doing. Nevertheless, when we can come up with appropriate positive norms, they can be helpful in ways that merely negative ones cannot. So what I am suggesting is that specifying some appropriate positive norms can help us to better rid ourselves of this social problem. Accordingly, I want to propose two positive norms for dealing with the problem of sexual harassment. The first is:

> The **Principle of Androgyny** (or **Equal Opportunity**), which requires that the traits desirable and distributable in society be equally open to both women and men or, in the case of virtues, equally expected of both women and men, other things being equal.

Why this principle? We all know that when we think stereotypically about men and women in our society, we come up with different lists of desirable traits and undesirable traits, such as the following:

Men	Women
Independent	**Dependent**
Competitive	Cooperative
Aggressive, assertive	Nurturant, caring
Unemotional, stoic, detached	Emotional
	Passive, nonviolent
Active, **violent**	**Concerned with appearances (vain)**
Unconcerned with appearances	**Submissive,** self-effacing
Dominant	**Indecisive**
Decisive	Seen as object (of beauty or sexual attraction)
Seen as subject	Neat
Sloppy	**Slut** or **nun**
Sexually active	Intuitive, **illogical**
Reasonable, rational, logical	In need of protection
Protective	Sensitive
Insensitive	

And if we assume that the traits in bold are obviously undesirable ones, then in addition to having quite different stereotypical traits associated with men and women in our society, we will also have more undesirable traits on the women's list than on the men's list. Such lists clearly reflect the gender roles and traits with which boys and girls, men and women are socialized into in society. In the past, the desirable gender traits stereotypically associated with men were thought to characterize mental health.[29] More recently, these same traits have been used to describe the successful corporate executive.[30] Accordingly, distinctive gender roles and traits have been used in these ways to favor men over women and heterosexuals over homosexuals. Nevertheless, there is good reason to think that the only morally defensible attitude we could take toward these gender roles and traits is expressed by the principle of androgyny (or equal opportunity). This is because for any stereotypical masculine role or trait that is desirable and distributable in society, we can always ask: Why shouldn't women who have the capability be able to fulfill that role or acquire that trait as well? And similarly, for any stereotypical feminine role or trait that is desirable and distributable in society, we can ask: Why shouldn't men who have the capability be able to fulfill that role or acquire that trait as well? And surely the answer to both of these questions is that there is no reason at all why both women and men shouldn't be able to fulfill those roles and acquire those traits. This means that the principle of androgyny (or equal opportunity) is the only norm that is morally defensible in this regard. It opposes enforced gender roles and traits in favor of requiring that the traits that are truly desirable and distributable in society be equally open to both women and men or, in the case of virtues, equally expected of both women and men, other things being equal.[31]

So characterized, the principle of androgyny (or equal opportunity) represents neither a revolt against so-called feminine virtues and traits nor their exaltation over so-called masculine virtues and traits.[32] This is because it does not view women's liberation as simply the freeing of women from the confines of traditional roles, which makes it possible for them to develop in ways heretofore reserved for men. Nor does it view women's liberation as simply the reevaluation and glorification of so-called feminine activities like housekeeping or mothering or so-called feminine modes of thinking as reflected in an ethic of caring. The first perspective ignores or devalues genuine virtues and desirable traits traditionally associated with women while the second ignores or devalues genuine virtues and desirable traits traditionally associated with men. In contrast, the principle of androgyny (or equal opportunity) seeks a broader-based norm for both women and men that combines virtues and desirable traits traditionally associated with women with virtues and desirable trails traditionally associated with men. For this reason, the principle of androgyny (or equal opportunity) is a common norm for both men (*andro-*) and women (*-gyne*).

So the principle of androgyny (or equal opportunity), by undermining enforced gender roles and traits, will also be undermining those very social structures that give rise to the problem of sexual harassment. Discrimination "because of . . . sex" will be much rarer when there is very little, possibly nothing at all, that is desirable and distributable that stereotypically characterizes men over women or homosexuals over heterosexuals. When people will have the chance to develop themselves in accord with their natural abilities and their free choices rather than socially imposed gender roles and traits, there will arise too many in-group differences and too many between-group similarities either with respect to women and men or with respect to homosexuals and heterosexuals to support anything like the existing practice of sexual harassment. The success of androgyny (or equal opportunity) will thus undercut the very possibility of sexual harassment.

The second positive norm I wish to propose is:

The **Principle of Desert,** which requires that we treat and evaluate people on the basis of their proper role- or job-related qualifications and excellences when this is appropriate or required.

Ideally, this principle would pick up where the principle of androgyny (or equal opportunity) left off. If we have been successful in following the principle of androgyny (or equal opportunity), then we would have been successful in developing ourselves on the basis of our natural abilities and free choices, and thus we would have had the chance to acquire the proper role- and job-related qualifications and excellences that accord with our natural abilities and free choices. Yet whether or not the principle of androgyny (or equal opportunity) has been followed, the principle of desert still requires that we treat and evaluate people on the basis of their proper role- or job-related qualifications and excellences when this is appropriate or required.

Now if women in the military were treated and evaluated according to this norm, it would surely undermine the belief that they do not belong there and thus drastically reduce the sexual harassment to which that belief gives rise. What most people do not realize is that the opening up of the military to women was not embarked upon as an effort to achieve social equality. Rather, the U.S. Defense Department turned to women into order to save the All-Volunteer Force.[33] The women drawn to military service were smarter and better educated than the men. For example, according to one study, over 90 percent of women recruited had high school diplomas, compared to 63 percent of the men, and women also scored ten points higher on service exams.[34] In addition, proportionately more female than male cadets have been selected as Rhodes and Marshall scholars, and proportionately more women entering West Point have been National Honor Society members and high school valedictorians and salutatorians in all but two years since integration in 1976.[35] As one Defense Department report put it, "The trade-off in today's recruiting market is between a high quality female and a low quality male."[36]

Of course, women have less upper body strength, but 32 percent of women have met or exceeded the minimum male test scores and 78 percent of women have qualified for "very heavy" military jobs after six months of weight lifting, jogging with 75-pound backpacks, and performing squats with 100-pound barrels on their shoulders.[37] Women's physiology also makes them more tolerant of G-forces than men and so more suitable as fighter pilots, one of the most prestigious jobs in the military.[38] Interestingly, in 1961 NASA invited women civilian pilots to join the race for space against the Russians, and the women began testing out extraordinary well. One woman, Mary Wallace Funk, who held several world records in flying, had beaten John Glenn on the stress tests, bicycle analysis tests, lung power tests, and Wally Schirra on vertigo while setting a record in the bicycle endurance and isolation tests; she lasted 10 hours and 30 minutes before hallucinating. But then, without explanation,

NASA canceled any further women's tests, and later in 1961, as Linda Bird Francke puts it, "Male astronauts rocketed into our history books."[39]

Of course, women are subject to pregnancy and motherhood, but statistically these have not been much of a problem in the military.[40] In fact, men suffer a higher absentee rate because of disciplinary problems and substance abuse.[41] So when women's strengths and weaknesses are taken into account compared to those of men, women turn out to be highly qualified for many combat and noncombat roles within the military and, in fact, qualified for many more combat roles than those in which they are allowed to serve. Accordingly, attending to women's proper role- or job-related qualifications should undermine the belief that they do not belong in the military and significantly reduce the sexual harassment to which that belief gives rise.

Similarly, attending to women's proper role- or job-related qualifications in civilian life should undermine the belief that it is appropriate to treat women as sexual objects in ways that men are not treated, such that they are sexually subordinate to men, as well as significantly reducing the sexual harassment to which that belief gives rise. In fact, it will simply not be possible for men to treat and evaluate women on the basis of their proper role- or job-related qualifications and excellences when this is appropriate or required and at the same time treat women as sexual objects, and hence as sexually subordinate to men. Nevertheless, treating and evaluating women on the basis of their proper role- or job-related qualifications and excellences when this is appropriate or required will sometimes require a certain degree of creative imagination. For example, Lani Guinier points out that New York City once used a height requirement favoring tall men to select for police officers. When standards changed and more women became police officers, it became apparent that often they were actually better at keeping the peace than their male counterparts in some situations. For example, in New York City housing projects, black and Puerto Rican women police officers chose to mentor rather than confront teenage boys, thereby offering them respect, and the young men, grateful for the attention from adults, reciprocated by checking their own behavior. And women of all colors have been found to be better at defusing domestic violence situations.[42] Furthermore, when the Los Angeles Police Department wanted to do

something about the problem of police abuse, the Christopher Commission Report told the city to hire more women. The commission found that women were not reluctant to use force, but that they were not nearly as likely to be involved in the use of excessive force. The women were also more communicative and more skillful at deescalating potentially violent situations. The report concluded that current approaches to policing underemphasize communication skills, sensitivity to cultural differences, and courteousness.[43] What this shows is that it not always easy to determine what are the proper role- or job-related qualifications. Assuming that these can be determined, however, treating and evaluating women on the basis of them when this is appropriate or required should help to undermine the belief that it is appropriate to treat women as sexual objects and hence as sexually subordinate to men, and should also significantly reduce the sexual harassment to which that belief gives rise.

In the case of homosexuals, because of the ability of many to hide their status as homosexuals, they have already been able to demonstrate their ability to perform well in all sorts of social roles and jobs from which they would be excluded if they were openly homosexual. With respect to homosexuals, therefore, the principle of desert demands that they be given what they deserve—that is, that they be treated and evaluated according to their proper role- or job-related qualifications and excellences.

Now it is sometimes argued that discrimination can be justified against homosexuals because they engage in forms of sexual intercourse that are not open to procreation. But heterosexuals also engage in those same forms of sexual intercourse, and they are not similarly discriminated against. In the United States, in fact, heterosexuals who can reproduce are allowed to marry other heterosexuals who are sterile with the blessings of both church and state, even though the relationships they form are no different from homosexual relationships with respect to their openness to procreation.[44] Correctly applying the principle of desert, therefore, should put an end to this discrimination against homosexuals.

Of course, more can and should be said about how we should apply the principle of desert to treat and evaluate people on the basis of their proper role- or job-related qualifications and excellences when this is appropriate or required, but hopefully I have said enough to indicate how endorsing both this principle and the principle of androgyny (or equal opportunity) will, in fact, help to undermine the existing practice of sexual harassment.

In sum, what I have tried to do in this paper is, first, provide a Definition of Sexual Harassment:

> **Sexual harassment** is objectively unwelcome sexual advances, requests for sexual favors, and other verbal or physical conduct of a sexual nature, which are determined to be both objectionable and actionable by the standard of what is reasonable for everyone affected to accept, and which usually, but not always, imposes a special burden on some individuals when there are no comparable burdens imposed on others who are similarly situated.

Second, I have tried to show how two fundamental beliefs help explain the high incidence of sexual harassment in military and civilian life respectively: the belief that women do not belong in the military and the belief that while women do belong in civilian life, it is still appropriate to treat them as sexual objects, and, hence, as such sexually subordinate to men. Third, I have suggested two positive norms we need to attend to, in addition to the negative one prohibiting sexual harassment, if we want to better rid society of this practice. Those norms are:

> The **Principle of Androgyny** (or **Equal Opportunity**), which requires that the traits that are truly desirable and distributable in society be equally open to both women and men or, in the case of virtues, equally expected of both women and men, other things being equal.

> The **Principle of Desert**, which requires that we treat and evaluate people on the basis of their proper role- or job-related qualifications and excellences when this is appropriate or required.[45]

Clearly, sexual harassment is a very difficult and troubling problem in our society, but dealing with it also provides us with an opportunity to rethink individually and collectively the roles of men and women in our society, which is one of the most important moral tasks we face.

Endnotes

1. In 1991, in response to these hearings of the Senate Judicial Committee, Congress amended the Civil Rights Act to allow victims to claim monetary damages in cases involving all kinds of intentional discrimination, including sexual harassment. As a result, the financial stakes in harassment cases rose dramatically. (*South Bend Tribune*, April 6, 1998)

2. *Christoforou v. Ryder Truck Rental.* 668 F. Supp.294 (S.D.N.Y. 1987).

3. *Rabidue v. Osceola Refining Co.* 805 F.2d 611, 620 (6th Cir. 1986).

4. In a recent study (see Selection 3), Barbara A. Gutek determined that a number of factors influence whether people tend to classify certain behavior as sexual harassment. They are: (1) How intrusive and persistent the behavior (the more physically intrusive and persistent the behavior is, the more likely that it will be defined as sexual harassment); (2) the nature of relationship between the actors (the better the actors know each other, the less likely the behavior will be labeled sexual harassment); (3) the characteristics of the observer (men and people in authority are less likely to label behavior as sexual harassment); and (4) the inequality in the relationship (the greater the inequality, the more likely the behavior will be labeled sexual harassment).

5. Obviously, most offers of this sort will be more subtle. If they are going to serve their purpose, however, their message must still be relatively easy to discern.

6. Even where there is legalized prostitution, such offers may still be objectively unwelcome because women would have wanted and could have reasonably expected a fairer, and thus better array of occupations open to them.

7. There is an analogous requirement of subjective consent in the law concerning rape that is similarly indefensible. See Susan Estrich, "Sex at Work," *Stanford Law Review* 43 (1991), pp. 813–861.

8. Nor should one be concerned that this suggestion would undercut an appropriate presumption of innocence. This is because the presumption of innocence is weaker for civil cases than for criminal cases. Thus, in a civil law sexual harassment case, the making of an objectively unwanted sexual offer and then firing the person who refused that offer should be sufficient grounds for removing that presumption.

9. Or they could simply not fire those to whom they make the offers.

10. Barbara Gutek contends that sexual harassment is caused by the fact that women are stereotypically identified as sexual objects in ways that men are not. She notes that women are stereotypically characterized as sexy,

affectionate, and attractive, whereas men are stereo-typically characterized as competent and active. These stereotypes, Gutek claims, spill over into the workplace, making it difficult for women to be perceived as fellow workers rather than sex objects, and it is these percep-tions that foster sexual harassment. (See Selection 3.) It would seem, therefore, that eliminating the problem of sexual harassment from our society will require breaking down these stereotypes. See my *Justice for Here and Now* (Cambridge, 1998), Chapter 4.

11. *Meritor Savings Bank v. Vinson.*

12. *Rabidue v. Osceola Refining Co.* 805 F.2d 611, 620 (6th Cir. 1986).

13. *Rabidue v. Osceola Refining Co.* 805 F.2d 611, 620 (6th Cir. 1986).

14. *Henson v. Dundee,* 682 F.2d 897, 904 (11th Cir. 1982).

15. *Ellison v. Brady,* 924 F.2d 872 (9th Cir. 1991).

16. As one of Getek's studies shows, reasonable men and reasonable women can disagree over what consti-tutes sexual harassment in the workplace. In this study, 67.2 percent of men as compared to 16.8 percent of women would be flattered if asked to have sex, while 15 percent of the men and 62.8 percent of the women said they would be insulted by such an offer. (See Selection 3.)

17. Of course, men in particular will have to make a con-siderable effort to arrive at this most reasonable perspec-tive, and it certainly will not be easy for them to attain it.

18. *Robinson v. Jacksonville Shipyards,* 760 F. Supp. 1486 (M.D. Fla. 1991).

19. Nadine Strossen, "Regulating Workplace Sexual Ha-rassment and Upholding the First Amendment—Avoiding a Collision," *Villanova Law Review* 37 (1992), p. 211–228.

20. It does seem reasonable to grant, however, that there is a stronger presumption of employee liability with re-spect to *quid pro quo* sexual harassment than hostile envi-ronment sexual harassment, if only because a company is normally presumed to be more responsible for those who occupy positions of power within it.

21. Cherly Gomez-Preston, *When No Means No* (New York: Carol Publishing Co., 1993), pp. 35–36. Ellen Bravo and Ellen Cassedy, *The 9 to 5 Guide to Combating Sex-ual Harassment* (New York: John Wiley and Sons, 1992), pp. 4–5: The problem is international as well as national. A three-year study of women in Estonia, Finland, Sweden, and the Soviet Union showed that nearly 50 percent of all working women experience sexual harassment. A survey released in 1991 by the Santama Group to Con-sider Sexual Harassment at Work showed that about 70 percent of Japanese women say they have experienced some type of sexual harassment on the job. See Susan Webb, *Step Forward* (New York: Master Media, 1991), pp. xiv, xvii.

22. *New York Times,* November 11, 1996, February 4, 1997.

23. Linda Bird Francke, *Ground Zero* (New York: Simon and Schuster, 1997), p. 157.

24. Ibid., p. 191.

25. Ibid., p. 187.

26. Ibid., p. 232.

27. Marysia Zalewski and Jane Parpart, *The "Man" Ques-tion in International Relations* (Boulder: Westview, 1998), p. 1.

28. *Time,* March 23, 1998, p. 49.

29. Beverly Walker, "Psychology and Feminism—If You Can't Beat Them, Join Them," in Dale Spender, ed., *Men's Studies Modified* (Oxford: Pergamon Press, 1981), pp. 112–114.

30. Debra Renee Kaufman, "Professional Women: How Real Are the Recent Gains?" in Janet A. Kourany, James P. Sterba and Rosemarie Tong, eds., *Feminist Philosophies,* 2nd ed. (Upper Saddle River: Prentice-Hall, 1999), pp. 189–202.

31. To distinguish traits of character that are virtues from those that are just desirable traits, we could define the class of virtues as those desirable and distributable traits that can be reasonably expected of both women and men. Admittedly, this is a restrictive use of the term *virtue.* In normal usage, the term *virtue* is almost synonymous with the term *desirable trait.* But there is good reason to focus on those desirable traits that can be justifiably inculcated in both women and men, and so for our purposes let us refer to this class of desirable traits as virtues.

32. For a valuable discussion and critique of these two viewpoints, see Iris Young, "Humanism, Gynocentrism, and Feminist Politics," *Women's Studies International Forum* 8 (1985), pp. 173–183.

33. Francke, *Ground Zero,* p. 16.

34. Ibid.

35. Ibid., p. 198.

36. Ibid., p. 16.

37. Ibid., p. 248.

38. Ibid., p. 236

39. Ibid., p. 226.

40. Ibid., p. 18.

41. Ibid., p. 16.

42. Lani Guinier, *Becoming Gentlemen* (Boston: Beacon, 1997), pp. 18–19.

43. *Report of the Independent Commission of the Los Angeles Police Department* (Christopher Commission, 1991).

44. John Corvino, *Same Sex* (Lanham: Rowman & Little-field, 1997), p. 6.

45. These two norms, of course, are not the only positive norms that are relevant to sexual harassment cases, al-though they are probably the most important ones. Other norms would provide guidance as to how romantic over-tures should be made so as to avoid sexual harassment.

39. Harris v. Forklift Systems, Inc.

SUPREME COURT OF THE UNITED STATES

The issue before the Supreme Court was whether a hostile work environment under Title VII of the Civil Rights Act of 1964 must cause serious harm to a reasonable person's psychological well-being. The Court unanimously ruled that behavior that fell short of seriously harming a reasonable person's psychological well-being could still be sexual harassment if in other ways it unreasonably interfered with a person's work environment.

. . . In this case we consider the definition of a discriminatorily "abusive work environment" (also known as a "hostile work environment") under Title VII of the Civil Rights Act of 1964.

Teresa Harris worked as a manager at Forklift Systems, Inc., an equipment rental company, from April 1985 until October 1987. Charles Hardy was Forklift's president.

The magistrate found that, throughout Harris's time at Forklift, Hardy often insulted her because of her gender and often made her the target of unwanted sexual innuendos. Hardy told Harris on several occasions, in the presence of other employees, "You're a woman, what do you know" and "We need a man as the rental manager"; at least once, he told her she was "a dumb ass woman." Again in front of others, he suggested that the two of them "go to the Holiday Inn to negotiate [Harris's] raise." Hardy occasionally asked Harris and other female employees to get coins from his front pants pocket. He threw objects on the ground in front of Harris and other women, and asked them to pick the objects up. He made sexual innuendos about Harris's and other women's clothing.

In mid-August 1987, Harris complained to Hardy about his conduct. Hardy said he was surprised that Harris was offended, claimed he was only joking, and apologized. He also promised he would stop, and based on this assurance Harris stayed on the job. But in early September, Hardy began anew: While Harris was arranging a deal with one of Forklift's customers, he asked her, again in front of other employees, "What did you do, promise the guy . . . some [sex] Saturday night?" On October 1, Harris collected her paycheck and quit.

Harris then sued Forklift, claiming that Hardy's conduct had created an abusive work environment for her because of her gender. The United States District Court for the Middle District of Tennessee, adopting the report and recommendation of the Magistrate, found this to be "a close case," but held that Hardy's conduct did not create an abusive environment. The court found that some of Hardy's comments "offended [Harris], and would offend the reasonable woman," but that they were not

> so severe as to be expected to seriously affect [Harris's] psychological well-being. A reasonable woman manager under like circumstances would have been offended by Hardy, but his conduct would not have risen to the level of interfering with that person's work performance.
>
> Neither do I believe that (Harris) was subjectively so offended that she suffered injury. . . . Although Hardy may at times have genuinely offended [Harris], I do not believe that he created a working environment so poisoned as to be intimidating or abusive to [Harris].

In focusing on the employee's psychological well-being, the District Court was following Circuit precedent.

We granted certiorari to resolve a conflict among the Circuits on whether conduct, to be actionable as "abusive work environment" harassment (no *quid pro quo* harassment issue is present here), must "seriously affect [an employee's] psychological well-being" or lead the plaintiff to "suffe[r] injury."

Title VII of the Civil Rights Act of 1964 makes it "an unlawful employment practice for an employer

... to discriminate against any individual with respect to his compensation, terms, conditions, or privileges of employment, because of such individual's race, color, religion, sex, or national origin." As we made clear in *Meritor Savings Bank v. Vinson* (1986), this language "is not limited to 'economic' or 'tangible' discrimination. The phrase 'terms, conditions, or privileges of employment' evinces a congressional intent 'to strike at the entire spectrum of disparate treatment of men and women' in employment," which includes requiring people to work in a discriminatorily hostile or abusive environment. When the workplace is permeated with "discriminatory intimidation, ridicule, and insult," that is "sufficiently severe or pervasive to alter the conditions of the victim's employment and create an abusive working environment," Title VII is violated.

This standard, which we reaffirm today, takes a middle path between making actionable any conduct that is merely offensive and requiring the conduct to cause a tangible psychological injury. As we pointed out in *Meritor*, "mere utterance of an ... epithet which engenders offensive feelings in an employee" does not sufficiently affect the conditions of employment to implicate Title VII. Conduct that is not severe or pervasive enough to create an objectively hostile or abusive work environment—an environment that a reasonable person would find hostile or abusive—is beyond Title VII's purview. Likewise, if the victim does not subjectively perceive the environment to be abusive, the conduct has not actually altered the conditions of the victim's employment, and there is no Title VII violation.

But Title VII comes into play before the harassing conduct leads to a nervous breakdown. A discriminatorily abusive work environment, even one that does not seriously affect employees' psychological well-being, can and often will detract from employees' job performance, discourage employees from remaining on the job, or keep them from advancing in their careers. Moreover, even without regard to these tangible effects, the very fact that the discriminatory conduct was so severe or pervasive that it created a work environment abusive to employees because of their race, gender, religion, or national origin offends Title VII's broad rule of workplace equality. The appalling conduct alleged in *Meritor*, and the reference in that case to environments "'so heavily polluted with discrimination as to destroy completely the emotional and psychological stability of minority group workers,'" merely present some especially egregious examples of harassment. They do not mark the boundary of what is actionable.

We therefore believe the District Court erred in relying on whether the conduct "seriously affect[ed] plaintiff's psychological well-being" or led her to "suffe[r] injury." Such an inquiry may needlessly focus the fact finder's attention on concrete psychological harm, an element Title VII does not require. Certainly Title VII bars conduct that would seriously affect a reasonable person's psychological well-being, but the statute is not limited to such conduct. So long as the environment would reasonably be perceived, and is perceived, as hostile or abusive, there is no need for it also to be psychologically injurious.

This is not, and by its nature cannot be, a mathematically precise test. We need not answer today all the potential questions it raises, nor specifically address the EEOC's new regulations on this subject. But we can say that whether an environment is "hostile" or "abusive" can be determined only by looking at all the circumstances. These may include the frequency of the discriminatory conduct; its severity; whether it is physically threatening or humiliating, or a mere offensive utterance; and whether it unreasonably interferes with an employee's work performance. The effect on the employee's psychological well-being is, of course, relevant to determining whether the plaintiff actually found the environment abusive. But while psychological harm, like any other relevant factor, may be taken into account, no single factor is required.

Forklift, while conceding that a requirement that the conduct seriously affect psychological well-being is unfounded, argues that the District Court nonetheless correctly applied the *Meritor* standard. We disagree. Though the District Court did conclude that the work environment was not "intimidating or abusive to [Harris]," it did so only after finding that the conduct was not "so severe as to be expected to seriously affect plaintiff's psychological well-being," and that Harris was not "subjectively so offended that she suffered injury." The District Court's application of these incorrect standards may well have influenced its ultimate conclusion, especially given that the court found this to be a "close case."

We therefore reverse the judgment of the Court of Appeals, and remand the case for further proceedings consistent with this opinion.

Suggestions for Further Reading

Bouchard, Elizabeth. *Everything You Need to Know about Sexual Harassment.* New York: Rosen, 1997.

Bravo, Ellen, and Ellen Cassedy. *The 9 to 5 Guide to Combating Sexual Harassment.* New York: Wiley, 1992.

Copeland, Lois, and Leslie R. Wolfe. *Violence against Women as Bias Motivated Hate Crime: Defining the Issues.* Washington, DC: Center for Women Policy Studies, 1991.

Dooling, Richard. *Blue Streak: Swearing, Free Speech, and Sexual Harassment.* New York: Random House, 1996.

Dziech, Billie Wright, and Linda Weiner. *The Lecherous Professor: Sexual Harassment on Campus.* Champaign: University of Illinois Press, 1992.

Gerdes, Louise I., ed. *Sexual Harassment: Current Controversies.* San Diego, CA: Greenhaven Press, 1999.

Hill, Anita. *Speaking Truth to Power.* New York: Doubleday, 1997.

Larkin, June. *Sexual Harassment: High School Girls Speak Out.* Toronto: Second Story Press, 1994.

McKenzie, Richard B. "The Thomas/Hill Hearings: A New Legal Harassment." *The Freeman,* January 1992. Available from the Foundation for Economic Education, Irvington-on-Hudson, NY 10533.

MacKinnon, Catharine A. *Sexual Harassment of Working Women: A Case of Sex Discrimination.* New Haven: Yale University Press, 1979.

Morris, Celia. *Bearing Witness: Sexual Harassment, Citizenship, Government.* New York: Little, Brown, 1994.

Paludi, Michele A., ed. *Sexual Harassment on College Campuses: Abusing the Ivory Power.* Albany: State University of New York Press, 1996.

Patai, Daphne, *Heterophobia: Sexual Harassment and the Future of Feminism.* Lanham, MD: Rowman & Littlefield, 1999.

Phelps, Timothy M., and Helen Winternitz. *Capital Games: Clarence Thomas, Anita Hill, and the Story of a Supreme Court Nomination.* Westport, CT: Hyperion, 1992.

Repa, Barbara Kate, and William Petrocelli. *Sexual Harassment on the Job.* Berkeley, CA: Nolo Press, 1992.

Riggs, Robert, Patricia Murrell, and JoAnn Cutting. *Sexual Harassment in Higher Education.* Washington, DC: George Washington University Press, 1993.

Stein, Laura W. *Sexual Harassment in America.* Westport, CT: Greenwood Publishing Group, 1999.

Sunrall, Amber Coverdale. *Sexual Harassment: Women Speak Out.* Freedom, CA: The Crossing Press, 1992.

Webb, Susan L. *Step Forward: Sexual Harassment in the Workplace: What You Need to Know!* 2d. ed. New York: MasterMedia, 1997.

Pornography

Introduction

Basic Concepts

The problem of pornography, as Catharine MacKinnon formulates it in Selection 40, is whether pornography should be prohibited for promoting discrimination and violence against women. But this has not been how the problem has been traditionally understood. In the Anglo-American legal tradition, pornography has always been identified with obscenity.[1] The test for obscenity set forth by the U.S. Supreme Court in *Roth v. United States* (1957) is "whether to the average person, applying contemporary community standards, the dominant theme of the material taken as a whole appeals to prurient interest." This test itself was an attempt to improve upon an 1868 test of obscenity that was taken over from English law. According to this earlier test, obscene materials are such that they have the tendency "to deprave and corrupt those whose minds are open to such immoral influences, and into whose hands a publication of this sort may fall." In *Roth v. United States*, the U.S. Supreme Court sought to remedy three defects in this 1868 test. First, the 1868 test permitted books to be judged obscene on the basis of isolated passages read out of context. In contrast, the Roth test requires

that material be judged as obscene only if "the dominant theme of the material taken as a whole" is so judged. Second, the 1868 test allowed the obscenity of a work to be determined by its likely effects on unusually susceptible persons. By contrast, the Roth test judges material to be obscene on the basis of its likely effect on the "average person." Third, the 1868 test posited standards of obscenity fixed for all time. By contrast, the Roth test only appeals to "contemporary community standards."

Yet despite these advantages of the Roth test, problems remained. First, who was the average person to whose prurience the obscene materials has to appeal? In *Miskin v. New York* (1966), the Supreme Court needed to apply its Roth test to books that described sadomasochistic sexual acts, fetishism, lesbianism, and male homosexuality. Since these works did not appeal to the prurient interest of the average person in the population at large, the Supreme Court reformulated its Roth test so that when "material is designed for and primarily disseminated to a clearly defined deviant sexual group, . . . the prurient-appeal requirement of the Roth test is satisfied if the dominant theme of the material taken as a whole appeals to the prurient interest in sex of the members of that group." Second, how was the Supreme Court to avoid the task of having to determine what are community standards for an endless number of obscenity cases? In *Miller v. California* (1973), the Supreme Court dealt with the problem by delegating and relativizing the task of determining contemporary community standards to local communities. Henceforth, the application of local community standards determines whether material appeals to prurient interest. Obviously, this puts a severe burden on national publishers who now have to take into account local community standards for any work they distribute. For example, when Larry C. Flynt routinely mailed a copy of his publication *Hustler* to a person who had ordered it by mail from a town in Ohio, he was subsequently tried for a violation of the Ohio obscenity statutes and sentenced to seven to twenty-five years in prison. So even with these improvements in the Supreme Court's test for obscenity, problems still remain.

Alternative Views

In Selection 40, Catharine MacKinnon takes an entirely new approach to pornography and obscenity. She sees pornography as a practice of sex discrimination, a violation of women's civil rights. She defines pornography "as the graphic sexually explicit subordination of women through pictures or words that also includes women dehumanized as sexual objects, things or commodities; enjoying pain or humiliation or rape; being tied up, cut up, mutilated, bruised, or physically hurt; in postures of sexual submission or servility or display; reduced to body parts, penetrated by objects or animals, or presented in scenarios of degradation, injury, torture; shown as filthy or inferior; bleeding, bruised or hurt in a context that makes these conditions sexual." By contrast, she defines erotica "as sexually explicit materials premised on equality." She argues that pornography is a harmful form of gender inequality that outweighs any social interest in

its protection by recognized First Amendment standards. She points to recent experimental research that shows that pornography causes harm to women through increasing men's attitudes and behavior of discrimination in both violent and nonviolent forms.

In Selection 41, Wendy Kaminer surveys the history of the feminist antiporn movement in North America from the late 1970s to the present. She notes how the movement became politically allied with the New Right in the 1980s; how it succeeded in passing antiporn legislation in Indianapolis in 1984, which was later declared unconstitutional by a federal appeals court; and how, most recently, it has mounted new legislative endeavors in the United States and Canada both at the state and national levels. Kaminer points out that the feminist case against pornography is based on a presumed link between pornography and sexual violence, but she questions how direct that link is and whether it depends on a blurring of the distinction between speech and conduct. She also suggests that alcohol and other substance abuse may have a more direct role in causing sexual violence. Accordingly, she argues that legislative endeavors other than banning pornography would be more likely to reduce sexual violence, and that the most likely legislative result of the feminist antiporn movement, given its political allegiance with the New Right, would be a broader censorship that would not serve feminist interests.

Kaminer further notes that the first application of the Supreme Court ruling in Canada against pornography was to prohibit the distribution of a small lesbian magazine. But Catharine MacKinnon has argued that this action by the Canadian custom authority was not, in fact, based on Canada's recent Supreme Court decision, but rather on a more long-standing practice of the custom authority that should have been disallowed in light of the

Court's recent decision.[2] Moreover, if enforcement of the Canadian Court's recent antiporn decision were actually to result in, say, a 25 percent drop in crimes of sexual violence in Canada, then, despite Kaminer's objections, it is difficult to see how this would not constitute sufficient justification for comparable judicial decisions in the United States.

Some opponents of any legal prohibition on pornography point to the Danish experience, where the legalization of pornography has not led to any increase in reported incidents of sexual assault against women. But even here the evidence is mixed because, for example, although the number of rapes reported to authorities has decreased over the years, it is estimated that the number of actual rapes has increased.

Practical Application

In *American Booksellers v. Hudnutt* (Selection 42), the federal judiciary ruled against an Indianapolis ordinance, contending that pornography which qualified as constitutionally protected speech could not be prohibited on the grounds that it caused harm to women. At the same time, the Court seemed to regard the issue of harm to women to be relevant when it argued that pornography did not harm those who cooperated in the production of pornography because they "generally have the capacity to protect themselves from participating in and being personally victimized by pornography." By contrast, the Supreme Court of Canada (Selection 43) judged that preventing harm to women is an acceptable grounds for restricting pornography, and that, moreover, restricting pornography would in fact prevent harm to women.

One explanation for the difference between the rules of the U.S. and Canadian courts is that, as MacKinnon points out, in sexist societies, it is difficult to recognize the harm that pornography causes women. Yet if MacKinnon is right, treating women equally in this regard will require a radical transformation of our society that will also affect the solutions to the other moral problems discussed in this anthology. Moreover, this radical transformation would be the kind that libertarians would be expected to champion since they are so concerned with preventing harm to others.

Endnotes

1. In ordinary usage, to call something obscene is to condemn that thing as blatantly disgusting, whereas to call something pornographic is simply to characterize it as sexually explicit. So in ordinary usage, unlike the law, it is an open question whether the pornographic is also obscene.

2. Catharine MacKinnon, "The First Amendment under Fire From the Left," in Adele Stan, ed., *Debating Sexual Correctness* (New York: Delta, 1995); pp. 116–117.

40. Pornography, Civil Rights, and Speech

CATHARINE MACKINNON

Catharine MacKinnon argues that pornography is a practice of sex discrimination and hence a violation of women's civil rights. According to MacKinnon, pornography celebrates and legitimizes rape, battery, sexual harassment, and the sexual abuse of children. More generally, it eroticizes the dominance and submission that is the dynamic common to them all. She argues for the constitutionality of city ordinances, which she has helped design, that prohibit pornography.

. . . There is a belief that this is a society in which women and men are basically equals. Room for marginal corrections is conceded, flaws are known to exist, attempts are made to correct what are conceived as occasional lapses from the basic condition of sex equality. Sex discrimination law has concentrated most of its focus on these occasional lapses. It is difficult to overestimate the extent to which this belief in equality is an article of faith for most people, including most women, who wish to live in self-respect in an internal universe, even (perhaps especially) if not in the world. It is also partly an expression of natural law thinking: If we are inalienably equal, we can't "really" be degraded.

This is a world in which it is worth trying. In this world of presumptive equality, people make money based on their training or abilities or diligence or qualifications. They are employed and advanced on the basis of merit. In this world of just deserts, if someone is abused, it is thought to violate the basic rules of the community. If it doesn't, victims are seen to have done something they could have chosen to do differently, by exercise of will or better judgment. Maybe such people have placed themselves in a situation of vulnerability to physical abuse. Maybe they have done something provocative. Or maybe they were just unusually unlucky. In such a world, if such a person has an experience, there are words for it. When they speak and say it, they are listened to. If they write about it, they will be published. If certain experiences are never spo-

ken about, if certain people or issues are seldom heard from, it is supposed that silence has been chosen. The law, including much of the law of sex discrimination and the First Amendment, operates largely within the realm of these beliefs.

Feminism is the discovery that women do not live in this world, that the person occupying this realm is a man, so much more a man if he is white and wealthy. This world of potential credibility, authority, security, and just rewards, recognition of one's identity and capacity, is a world that some people do inhabit as a condition of birth, with variations among them. It is not a basic condition accorded humanity in this society, but a prerogative of status, a privilege, among other things, of gender.

I call this a discovery because it has not been an assumption. Feminism is the first theory, the first practice, the first movement, to take seriously the situation of all women from the point of view of all women, both on our situation and on social life as a whole. The discovery has therefore been made that the implicit social content of humanism, as well as the standpoint from which legal method has been designed and injuries have been defined, has not been women's standpoint. Defining feminism in a way that connects epistemology with power as the politics of women's point of view, this discovery can be summed up by saying that women live in another world: specifically, a world of *not* equality, a world of inequality.

Looking at the world from this point of view, a whole shadow world of previously invisible silent abuse has been discerned. Rape, battery, sexual harassment, forced prostitution, and the sexual abuse of children emerge as common and systematic. We find that rape happens to women in all contexts, from the family, including rape of girls and babies, to students and women in the workplace, on the streets, at home, in their own bedrooms by men they do not know and by men they do know, by men they are married to, men they have had a social conversation with, and, least often, men they have never seen before. Overwhelmingly, rape is something that men do or attempt to do to women (44 percent of American women according to a recent study) at some point in our lives. Sexual harassment of women by men is common in workplaces and educational institutions. Based on reports in one study of the federal workforce, up to 85 percent of women will experience it, many in physical forms. Between a quarter and a third of women are battered in their homes by men. Thirty-eight percent of little girls are sexually molested inside or outside the family. Until women listened to women, this world of sexual abuse was *not spoken* of. It was the unspeakable. What I am saying is, if you *are* the tree falling in the epistemological forest, your demise doesn't make a sound if no one is listening. Women did not "report" these events, and overwhelmingly do not today, because no one is listening, because no one believes us. This silence does not mean nothing happened, and it does not mean consent. It is the silence of women of which Adrienne Rich has written, "Do not confuse it with any kind of absence."

Believing women who say we are sexually violated has been a radical departure, both methodologically and legally. The extent and nature of rape, marital rape, and sexual harassment itself were discovered in this way. Domestic battery as a syndrome, almost a habit, was discovered through refusing to believe that when a woman is assaulted by a man to whom she is connected, it is not an assault. The sexual abuse of children was uncovered, Freud notwithstanding, by believing that children were not making up all this sexual abuse. Now what is striking is that when each discovery is made, and somehow made real in the world, the response has been: It happens to men too. If women are hurt, men are hurt. If women are raped, men are raped. If women are sexually harassed, men are sexually harassed. If women are battered, men are battered. Symmetry must be reasserted. Neutrality must be reclaimed. Equality must be reestablished.

The only areas where the available evidence supports this, where anything like what happens to women also happens to men, involve children—little boys are sexually abused—and prison. The liberty of prisoners is restricted, their freedom restrained, their humanity systematically diminished, their bodies and emotions confined, defined, and regulated. If paid at all, they are paid starvation wages. They can be tortured at will, and it is passed off as discipline or as means to a just end. They become compliant. They can be raped at will, at any moment, and nothing will be done about it. When they scream, nobody hears. To be a prisoner means to be defined as a member of a group for whom the rules of what can be done to you, of what is seen as abuse of you, are reduced as part of the definition of your status. To be a woman is that kind of definition and has that kind of meaning.

Men *are* damaged by sexism. (By men I mean the status of masculinity that is accorded to males on the basis of their biology but is not itself biological.) But whatever the damage of sexism to men, the condition of being a man is not defined as subordinate to women by force. Looking at the facts of the abuses of women all at once, you see that a woman is socially defined as a person who, whether or not she is or has been, can be treated in these ways by men at any time, and little, if anything, will be done about it. This is what it means when feminists say that maleness is a form of power and femaleness is a form of powerlessness.

In this context, all of this "men too" stuff means that people don't really believe the things I have just said are true, though there really is little question about their empirical accuracy. The data are extremely simple, like women's pay figure of fifty-nine cents on the dollar. People don't really seem to believe that either. Yet there is no question of its empirical validity. This is the workplace story: What women do is seen as not worth much, or what is not worth much is seen as something for women to do. *Women* are seen as not worth much. . . . Now why are these basic realities of the subordination of women to men, for example, that only 7.8 percent of women have never been sexually assaulted, not effectively believed, not perceived as real in the face of all this evidence? Why don't *women* believe our own experiences? In the face of all this evidence, especially of systematic sexual abuse—subjection to violence with impunity is one extreme expression, although not the only one, of a degraded status—the view that basically the sexes are equal in this society remains unchallenged and unchanged. The day I got this was the day I understood its real message, its real coherence: *This is equality for us.*

I could describe this, but I couldn't explain it until I started studying a lot of pornography. In pornography, there it is, in one place, all of the abuses that women had to struggle so long even to begin to articulate, all the *unspeakable* abuse: the rape, the battery, the sexual harassment, the prostitution, and the sexual abuse of children. Only in pornography it is called something else: sex, sex, sex, sex, and sex, respectively. Pornography sexualizes rape, battery, sexual harassment, prostitution, and child sexual abuse; it thereby celebrates, promotes, authorizes, and legitimizes them. More generally, it eroticizes the dominance and submission that is the [common] dynamic. It makes hierarchy sexy and calls that "the truth about sex" or just a mirror of reality. Through this process pornography constructs what a woman is as what men want from sex. This is what pornography means.

Pornography constructs what a woman is in terms of its view of what men want sexually, such that acts of rape, battery, sexual harassment, prostitution, and sexual abuse of children become acts of sexual equality. Pornography's world of equality is a harmonious and balanced place. Men and women are perfectly complementary and perfectly bipolar. Women's desire to be fucked by men is equal to men's desire to fuck women. All the ways men love to take and violate women, women love to be taken and violated. The women who most love this are most men's equals, the most liberated; the most participatory child is the most grown-up, the most equal to an adult. Their consent merely expresses or ratifies these preexisting facts.

The content of pornography is one thing. There, women substantively desire dispossession and cruelty. We desperately want to be bound, battered, tortured, humiliated, and killed. Or, to be fair to the soft core, merely taken and used. This is erotic to the male point of view. Subjection itself, with self-determination ecstatically relinquished, is the content of women's sexual desire and desirability. Women are there to be violated and possessed, men to violate and possess us, either on screen or by camera or pen on behalf of the consumer. On a simple descriptive level, the inequality of hierarchy, of which gender is the primary one, seems necessary for sexual arousal to work. Other added inequalities identify various pornographic genres or subthemes, although they are always added through gender: age, disability, homosexuality, animals, objects, race (including anti-Semitism), and so on. Gender is never irrelevant.

What pornography *does* goes beyond its content: It eroticizes hierarchy, it sexualizes inequality. It makes dominance and submission into sex. Inequality is its central dynamic; the illusion of freedom coming together with the reality of force is central to its working. Perhaps because this is a bourgeois culture, the victim must look free, appear to be freely acting. Choice is how she got there. Willing is what she is when she is being equal. It seems equally important that then and there she actually be forced and that forcing be communicated on some level, even if only through still photos of her in postures of receptivity and access, available for penetration. Pornography in this view is a form of forced sex, a practice of sexual politics, an institution of gender inequality.

From this perspective, pornography is neither harmless fantasy nor a corrupt and confused misrepresentation of an otherwise natural and healthy sexual situation. It institutionalizes the sexuality of male supremacy, fusing the erotization of dominance and submission with the social construction of male and female. To the extent that gender is sexual, pornography is part of constituting the meaning of that sexuality. Men treat women as who they see women as being. Pornography constructs who that is. Men's power over women means that the way men see women defines who women can be. Pornography is that way. Pornography is not imagery in some relation to a reality elsewhere constructed. It is not a distortion, reflection, projection, expression, fantasy, representation, or symbol either. It is a sexual reality.

In Andrea Dworkin's definitive work, *Pornography: Men Possessing Women*, sexuality itself is a social construct gendered to the ground. Male dominance here is not an artificial overlay upon an underlying inalterable substratum of uncorrupted essential sexual being. Dworkin presents a sexual theory of gender inequality of which pornography is a constitutive practice. The way pornography produces its meaning constructs and defines men and women as such. Gender has no basis in anything other than the social reality its hegemony constructs. Gender is what gender means. The process that gives sexuality its male supremacist meaning is the same process through which gender inequality becomes socially real.

In this approach, the experience of the (overwhelmingly) male audiences who consume pornography is therefore not fantasy or simulation or catharsis but sexual reality, the level of reality on which sex itself largely operates. Understanding this dimension of the problem does not require noticing that pornography models are real women to whom, in most cases, something real is being done; nor does it even require inquiring into the systematic infliction of pornography and its sexuality upon women, although it helps. What matters is the way in which the pornography itself provides what those who consume it want. Pornography *participates* in its audience's eroticism by creating an accessible sexual object, the possession and consumption of which *is* male sexuality, as socially constructed; to be consumed and possessed as which, *is* female sexuality, as socially constructed; pornography is a process that constructs it that way.

The object world is constructed according to how it looks with respect to its possible uses. Pornography defines women by how we look according to how we can be sexually used. Pornography codes how to look at women, so you know what you can do with one when you see one. Gender is an assignment made visually, both originally and in everyday life. A sex object is defined on the basis of its looks, in terms of its usability for sexual pleasure, such that both the looking—the quality of the gaze, including its point of view—and the definition according to use become eroticized as part of the sex itself. This is what the feminist concept "sex object" means. In this sense, sex in life is no less mediated than in art. Men have sex with their image of a woman. It is not that life and art imitate each other; in this sexuality, they *are* each other.

To give a set of rough epistemological translations, to defend pornography as consistent with the equality of the sexes is to defend the subordination of women to men as sexual equality. What in the pornographic view is love and romance looks a great deal like hatred and torture to the feminist. Pleasure and eroticism become violation. Desire appears as lust for dominance and submission. The vulnerability of women's projected sexual availability, that acting we are allowed (that is, asking to be acted upon), is victimization. Play conforms to scripted roles. Fantasy expresses ideology, is not exempt from it. Admiration of natural physical beauty becomes objectification. Harmlessness becomes harm. Pornography is a harm of male supremacy made difficult to see because of its pervasiveness, potency, and, principally, because of its success in making the world a pornographic place. Specifically, its harm cannot be discerned, and will not be addressed, if viewed and approached neutrally, because it *is* so much of "what is." In other words, to the extent pornography succeeds in constructing social reality, it becomes invisible as harm. If we live in a world that pornography creates through the power of men in a male-dominated situation, the issue is not what the harm of pornography is, but how that harm is to become visible.

Obscenity law provides a very different analysis and conception of the problem of pornography. In 1973 the legal definition of obscenity became that which the average person, applying contemporary community standards, would find that, taken as a whole, appeals to the prurient interest; that which depicts or describes in a patently offensive way— you feel like you're a cop reading someone's *Miranda* rights—sexual conduct specifically defined by the applicable state law; and that which, taken as a whole, lacks serious literary, artistic, political, or scientific value. Feminism doubts whether the average person gender-neutral exists; has more questions about the content and process of defining what community standards are than it does about deviations from them; wonders why prurience counts but powerlessness does not and why sensibilities are better protected from offense than women are from exploitation; defines sexuality, and thus its violation and expropriation, more broadly than does state law; and questions why a body of law that has not in practice been able to tell rape from intercourse should, without further guidance, be entrusted with telling pornography from anything less. Taking the work "as a whole" ignores that which the victims of pornography have long known: Legitimate settings diminish the perception of injury done to those whose trivialization and objectification they contextualize. Besides, and this is a heavy one, if a woman is subjected, why should it matter that the work has other value? Maybe what redeems the work's value is what enhances its injury to women, not to mention that existing standards of literature, art, science, and politics, examined in a feminist light, are remarkably consonant with pornography's mode, meaning, and message. And finally—first and foremost, actually—although the subject of these materials is overwhelmingly women, their contents almost entirely made up of women's bodies, our invisibility has been such, our equation as a sex *with* sex has been such, that the law of obscenity has never even considered pornography a women's issue.

Obscenity, in this light, is a moral idea, an idea about judgments of good and bad. Pornography, by contrast, is a political practice, a practice of power and powerlessness. Obscenity is ideational and abstract; pornography is concrete and substantive. The two concepts represent two entirely different things. Nudity, excess of candor, arousal or excitement, prurient appeal, illegality of the acts depicted, and unnaturalness or perversion are all qualities that bother obscenity law when sex is depicted or portrayed. Sex forced on real women so that it can be sold at a profit and forced on other real women; women's bodies trussed and maimed and raped and made into things to be hurt and obtained and accessed, and this presented as the nature of women in a way that is acted on and acted out, over and over; the coercion that is visible and the coercion that has become invisible—this and more bothers feminists about pornography. Obscenity as such probably does little harm. Pornography is integral to attitudes and behaviors of violence and discrimination that define the treatment and status of half the population.

At the request of the city of Minneapolis, Andrea Dworkin and I conceived and designed a local human rights ordinance in accordance with our approach to the pornography issue. We define pornography as a practice of sex discrimination, a violation of women's civil rights, the opposite of sexual equality. Its point is to hold those who profit from and benefit from that injury accountable to those who are injured. It means that women's injury—our damage, our pain, our enforced inferiority—should outweigh their pleasure and their profits, or sex equality is meaningless.

We define pornography as the graphic sexually explicit subordination of women through pictures or words that also includes women dehumanized as sexual objects, things, or commodities; enjoying pain or humiliation or rape; being tied up, cut up, mutilated, bruised, or physically hurt; in postures of sexual submission or servility or display; reduced to body parts, penetrated by objects or animals, or presented in scenarios of degradation, injury, torture; shown as filthy or inferior; bleeding, bruised, or hurt in a context that makes these conditions sexual. Erotica, defined by distinction as not this, might be sexually explicit materials premised on equality. We also provide that the use of men, children, or transsexuals in the place of women is pornography. The definition is substantive in that it is sex-specific, but it covers everyone in a sex-specific way, so is gender neutral in overall design. . . .

This law aspires to guarantee women's rights consistent with the First Amendment by making visible a conflict of rights between the equality guaranteed to all women and what, in some legal sense, is now the freedom of the pornographers to make and sell, and their consumers to have access to, the materials this ordinance defines. Judicial resolution of this conflict, if the judges do for women what they have done for others, is likely to entail a balancing of the rights of women arguing that our lives and opportunities, including our freedom of speech and action, are constrained by—and in many cases flatly precluded by, in, and through—pornography, against those who argue that the pornography is harmless, or harmful only in part but not in the whole of the definition; or that it is more important to preserve the pornography than it is to prevent or remedy whatever harm it does.

In predicting how a court would balance these interests, it is important to understand that this ordinance cannot now be said to be either conclusively legal or illegal under existing law or precedent, although I think the weight of authority is on our side. This ordinance enunciates a new form of the previously recognized governmental interest in sex equality. Many laws make sex equality a governmental interest. Our law is designed to further the equality of the sexes, to help make sex equality real. Pornography is a practice of discrimination on the basis of sex, on one level because of its role in creating and maintaining sex as a basis for discrimination. It harms many women one at a time and helps keep all women in an inferior status by defining our subordination as our sexuality and equating that with our gender. It is also sex discrimination because its victims, including men, are selected for victimization on the basis of their gender. But for their sex, they would not be so treated.

The harm of pornography, broadly speaking, is the harm of the civil inequality of the sexes made invisible as harm because it has become accepted as the sex difference. Consider this analogy with race: If you see Black people as different, there is no harm to segregation; it is merely a recognition of that difference. To neutral principles, separate but equal was equal. The injury of racial separation to Blacks arises "solely because [they] choose to put that construction upon it." Epistemologically translated: How you see it is not the way it is. Similarly, if you see women as just different, even or especially if you don't know that you do, subordination will not look like subordination at all, much less like harm. It will merely look like an appropriate recognition of the sex difference.

Pornography does treat the sexes differently, so the case for sex differentiation can be made here. But men as a group do not tend to be (although some individuals may be) treated the way women are treated in pornography. As a social group, men are not hurt by pornography the way women as a social group are. Their social status is not defined as *less* by it. So the major argument does not turn on mistaken differentiation, particularly since the treatment of women according to pornography's dictates makes it all too often accurate. The salient quality of a distinction between the top and the bottom in a hierarchy is not difference, although top is certainly different from bottom; it is power. So the major argument is: Subordinate but equal is not equal.

Particularly since this is a new legal theory, a new law, and "new" facts, perhaps the situation of women it newly exposes deserves to be considered on its own terms. Why do the problems of 53 percent of the population have to look like somebody else's problems before they can be recognized as existing? Then, too, they can't be addressed if they do look like other people's problems, about which something might have to be done if something is done about these. This construction of the situation truly deserves inquiry. Limiting the justification for this law to the situation of the sexes would serve to limit the precedential value of a favorable ruling.

Its particularity aside, the *approach* to the injury is supported by a whole array of prior decisions that have justified exceptions to First Amendment guarantees when something that matters is seen to be directly at stake. What unites many cases in which speech interests are raised and implicated but not, on balance, protected, is harm, harm that counts. In some existing exceptions, the definitions are much more open-ended than ours. In some the sanctions are more severe, or potentially more so. For instance, ours is a civil law; most others, although not all, are criminal. Almost no other exceptions show as many people directly affected. Evidence of harm in other cases tends to be vastly less concrete and more conjectural, which is not to say that there is necessarily less of it. None of the previous cases addresses a

problem of this scope or magnitude—for instance, an eight-billion-dollar-a-year industry. Nor do other cases address an abuse that has such widespread legitimacy. Courts have seen harm in other cases. The question is, will they see it here, especially given that the pornographers got there first. I will confine myself here to arguing from cases on harm to people, on the supposition that, pornographers notwithstanding, women are not flags. . . .

To reach the magnitude of this problem on the scale it exists, our law makes trafficking in pornography—production, sale, exhibition, or distribution—actionable. Under the obscenity rubric, much legal and psychological scholarship has centered on a search for the elusive link between harm and pornography defined as obscenity. Although they were not very clear on what obscenity was, it was its harm they truly could not find. They looked high and low—in the mind of the male consumer, in society or in its "moral fabric," in correlations between variations in levels of antisocial acts and liberalization of obscenity laws. The only harm they have found has been harm to "the social interest in order and morality." Until recently, no one looked very persistently for harm to women, particularly harm to women through men. The rather obvious fact that the sexes *relate* has been overlooked in the inquiry into the male consumer and his mind. The pornography doesn't just drop out of the sky, go into his head, and stop there. Specifically, men rape, batter, prostitute, molest, and sexually harass women. Under conditions of inequality, they also hire, fire, promote, and grade women, decide how much or whether we are worth paying and for what, define and approve and disapprove of women in ways that count, that determine our lives.

If women are not just born to be sexually used, the fact that we are seen and treated as though that is what we are born for becomes something in need of explanation. If we see that men relate to women in a pattern of who they see women as being, and that forms a pattern of inequality, it becomes important to ask where that view came from or, minimally, how it is perpetuated or escalated. Asking this requires asking different questions about pornography than the ones obscenity law made salient.

Now I'm going to talk about causality in its narrowest sense. Recent experimental research on pornography shows that the materials covered by our definition cause measurable harm to women through increasing men's attitudes and behaviors of discrimination in both violent and nonviolent forms. Exposure to some of the pornography in our definition increases the immediately subsequent willingness of normal men to aggress against women under laboratory conditions. It makes normal men more closely resemble convicted rapists attitudinally, although as a group they don't look all that different from them to start with. Exposure to pornography also significantly increases attitudinal measures known to correlate with rape and self-reports of aggressive acts, measures such as hostility toward women, propensity to rape, condoning rape, and predicting that one would rape or force sex on a woman if one knew one would not get caught. On this latter measure, by the way, about a third of all men predict that they would rape, and half would force sex on a woman.

As to that pornography covered by our definition in which normal research subjects seldom perceive violence, long-term exposure still makes them see women as more worthless, trivial, nonhuman, and objectlike, that is, the way those who are discriminated against are seen by those who discriminate against them. Crucially, all pornography by our definition acts dynamically over time to diminish the consumer's ability to distinguish sex from violence. The materials work behaviorally to diminish the capacity of men (but not women) to perceive that an account of a rape is an account of a rape. The so-called sex-only materials, those in which subjects perceive no force, also increase perceptions that a rape victim is worthless and decrease the perception that she was harmed. The overall direction of current research suggests that the more expressly violent materials accomplish with less exposure what the less overtly violent—that is, the so-called sex-only materials—accomplish over the longer term. Women are rendered fit for use and targeted for abuse. The only thing that the research cannot document is which individual women will be next on the list. (This cannot be documented experimentally because of ethics constraints on the researchers—constraints that do not operate in life.) Although the targeting is systematic on the basis of sex, for individuals it is random. They are selected on a roulette basis. Pornography can no longer be said to be just a mirror. It does not just reflect the world or some people's perceptions. It *moves* them. It increases attitudes that are lived out, circumscribing the status of half the population.

What the experimental data predict will happen actually does happen in women's real lives. It's fairly frustrating that women have known for some time that these things do happen. As Ed Donnerstein, an experimental researcher in this area, often puts it, "We just quantify the obvious." It is women, primarily, to whom the research results have been the obvious, because we live them. But not until a laboratory study predicts that these things *will* happen do people begin to believe you when you say they *did* happen to you. There is no—*not any*—inconsistency between the patterns the laboratory studies predict and the data on what actually happens to real women. Show me an abuse of women in society, I'll show it to you made sex in the pornography. If you want to know who is being hurt in this society, go see what is being done and to whom in pornography and then go look for them in other places in the world. You will find them being hurt in just that way. We did in our hearings.

In our hearings women spoke, to my knowledge for the first time in history in public, about the damage pornography does to them. We learned that pornography is used to break women, to train women to sexual submission, to season women, to terrorize women, and to silence their dissent. It is this that has previously been termed "having no effect." The way men inflict on women the sex they experience through the pornography gives women no choice about seeing the pornography or doing the sex. Asked if anyone ever tried to inflict unwanted sex acts on them that they knew came from pornography, 10 percent of women in a recent random study said yes. Among married women, 24 percent said yes. That is a lot of women. A lot more don't know. Some [who do know] testified in Minneapolis. One wife said of her ex-husband, "He would read from the pornography like a textbook, like a journal. In fact when he asked me to be bound, when he finally convinced me to do it, he read in the magazine how to tie the knots." Another woman said of her boyfriend, "[H]e went to this party, saw pornography, got an erection, got me . . . to inflict his erection on. . . . There is a direct causal relationship there." One woman, who said her husband had rape and bondage magazines all over the house, discovered two suitcases full of Barbie dolls with rope tied on their arms and legs and with tape across their mouths. Now think about the silence of women. She said, "He used to tie me up and he tried those things on me." A therapist in private practice reported:

Presently or recently I have worked with clients who have been sodomized by broom handles, forced to have sex with over 20 dogs in the back seat of their car, tied up and then electrocuted on their genitals. These are children, [all] in the ages of 14 to 18, all of whom [have been directly affected by pornography,] [e]ither where the perpetrator has read the manuals and manuscripts at night and used these as recipe books by day or had the pornography present at the time of the sexual violence.

One woman, testifying that all the women in a group of ex-prostitutes were brought into prostitution as children through pornography, characterized their collective experience: "[I]n my experience there was not one situation where a client was not using pornography while he was using me or that he had not just watched pornography or that it was verbally referred to and directed me to pornography." "Men," she continued, "witness the abuse of women in pornography constantly and if they can't engage in that behavior with their wives, girlfriends or children, they force a whore to do it."

Men also testified about how pornography hurts them. One young gay man who had seen *Playboy* and *Penthouse* as a child said of such heterosexual pornography: "It was one of the places I learned about sex and it showed me that sex was violence. What I saw there was a specific relationship between men and women. . . . [T]he woman was to be used, objectified, humiliated, and hurt; the man was in a superior position, a position to be violent. In pornography I learned that what it meant to be sexual with a man or to be loved by a man was to accept his violence." For this reason, when he was battered by his first lover, which he described as "one of the most profoundly destructive experiences of my life," he accepted it.

Pornography also hurts men's capacity to relate to women. One young man spoke about this in a way that connects pornography—not the prohibition on pornography—with fascism. He spoke of his struggle to repudiate the thrill of dominance, of his difficulty finding connection with a woman to whom he is close. He said: "My point is that if women in a society filled by pornography must be wary for their physical selves, a man, even a man of good intentions, must be wary for his mind. . . . I do not want to be a mechanical, goose-stepping follower of the Playboy bunny, because that is what

I think it is. . . . [T]hese are the experiments a master race perpetuates on those slated for extinction." The woman he lives with is Jewish. There was a very brutal rape near their house. She was afraid; she tried to joke. It didn't work. "She was still afraid. And just as a well-meaning German was afraid in 1933, I am also very much afraid."

Pornography stimulates and reinforces, it does not cathect or mirror, the connection between one-sided freely available sexual access to women and masculine sexual excitement and sexual satisfaction. The catharsis hypothesis is fantasy. The fantasy theory is fantasy. Reality is: Pornography conditions male orgasm to female subordination. It tells men what sex means, what a real woman is, and codes them together in a way that is behaviorally reinforcing. This is a real five-dollar sentence, but I'm going to say it anyway: Pornography is a set of hermeneutical equivalences that work on the epistemological level. Substantively, pornography defines the meaning of what a woman is seen to be by connecting access to her sexuality with masculinity through orgasm. What pornography means *is* what it does.

So far, opposition to our ordinance centers on the trafficking provision. This means not only that it is difficult to comprehend a group injury in a liberal culture—that what it *means* to be a woman is defined by this and that it is an injury for all women, even if not for all women equally. It is not only that the pornography has got to be accessible, which is the bottom line of virtually every objection to this law. It is also that power, as I said, is when you say something, it is taken for reality. If you talk about rape, it will be agreed that rape is awful. But rape is a conclusion. If a victim describes the facts of a rape, maybe she was asking for it or enjoyed it or at least consented to it, or the man might have thought she did, or maybe she had had sex before. It is now agreed that there is something wrong with sexual harassment. But describe what happened to you, and it may be trivial or personal or paranoid, or maybe you should have worn a bra that day. People are against discrimination. But describe the situation of a real woman, and they are not so sure she wasn't just unqualified. In law, all these disjunctions between women's perspective on our injuries and the standards we have to meet go under dignified legal rubrics like burden of proof, credibility, defenses, elements of the crime, and so on. These standards all contain a definition of what a woman is in terms of what sex is and the low value placed on us through it. They reduce injuries done to us to authentic expressions of who we are. Our silence is written all over them. So is the pornography.

We have as yet encountered comparatively little objection to the coercion, force, or assault provisions of our ordinance. I think that's partly because the people who make and approve laws may not yet see what they do as that. They *know* they use the pornography as we have described it in this law, and our law defines that, the reality of pornography, as a harm to women. If they suspect that they might on occasion engage in or benefit from coercion or force or assault, they may think that the victims won't be able to prove it—and they're right. Women who charge men with sexual abuse are not believed. The pornographic view of them is: They want it; they all want it. When women bring charges of sexual assault, motives such as veniality or sexual repression must be invented, because we cannot really have been hurt. Under the trafficking provision, women's lack of credibility cannot be relied on to negate the harm. There's no woman's story to destroy, no credibility-based decision on what happened. The hearings establish the harm. The definition sets the standard. The grounds of reality definition are authoritatively shifted. Pornography is bigotry, *period*. We are now—in the world pornography has decisively defined—having to meet the burden of proving, once and for all, for all of the rape and torture and battery, all of the sexual harassment, all of the child sexual abuse, all of the forced prostitution, *all* of it that the pornography is part of and that is part of the pornography, that the harm *does happen* and that when it happens it looks like this. Which may be why all this evidence never seems to be enough.

It is worth considering what evidence has been enough when other harms involving other purported speech interests have been allowed to be legislated against. By comparison to our trafficking provision, analytically similar restrictions have been allowed under the First Amendment, with a legislative basis far less massive, detailed, concrete, and conclusive. Our statutory language is more ordinary, objective, and precise and covers a harm far narrower than the legislative record substantiates. Under *Miller,* obscenity was allowed to be made criminal in the name of the "danger of offending the sensibilities of unwilling recipients, or exposure to juveniles." Under our law, we have direct evidence of harm, not just a conjectural danger, that unwilling women in considerable numbers are not simply offended in their sensibilities, but are violated in their persons and restricted in their options. Obscenity law also suggests that the applicable standard for legal adequacy in measuring such connections may not be statistical certainty. The Supreme Court has said that it is not their job to resolve empirical uncertainties that underlie state obscenity legislation. Rather, it is for them to determine whether a legislature could reasonably have determined that a connection might exist between the prohibited material and harm of a kind in which the state has legitimate interest. Equality should be such an area. The Supreme Court recently recognized that prevention of sexual exploitation and abuse of children is, in its words, "a governmental objective of surpassing importance." This might also be the case for sexual exploitation and abuse of women, although I think a civil remedy is initially more appropriate to the goal of empowering adult women than a criminal prohibition would be.

Other rubrics provide further support for the argument that this law is narrowly tailored to further a legitimate governmental interest consistent with the goals underlying the First Amendment. Exceptions to the First Amendment—you may have gathered from this—exist. The reason they exist is that the harm done by some speech outweighs its expressive value, if any. In our law a legislature recognizes that pornography, as defined and made actionable, undermines sex equality. One can say—and I have—that pornography is a causal factor in violations of women; one can also say that women will be violated so long as pornography exists; but one can also say simply that pornography violates women. Perhaps this is what the woman had in mind who testified at our hearings that for her the question is not just whether pornography causes violent acts to be perpetrated against some women. "Porn is already a violent act against women. It is our mothers, our daughters, our sisters, and our wives that are for sale for pocket change at the newsstands in this country." *Chaplinsky v. New Hampshire* recognized the ability to restrict as "fighting words" speech which "by [its] very utterance inflicts injury." Perhaps the only reason that pornography has not been "fighting words"—in the sense of words that by their utterance tend to incite immediate breach of the peace—is that women have seldom fought back, yet.

Some concerns that are close to those of this ordinance underlie group libel laws, although the differences are equally important. In group libel law, as Justice Frankfurter's opinion in *Beauharnais* illustrates, it has been understood that an individual's treatment and alternatives in life may depend as much on the reputation of the group to which that person belongs as on their own merit. Not even a partial analogy can be made to group libel doctrine without examining the point made by Justice Brandeis and recently underlined by Larry Tribe: Would more speech, rather than less, remedy the harm? In the end, the answer may be yes, but not under the abstract system of free speech, which only enhances the power of the pornographers while doing nothing substantively to guarantee the free speech of women, for which we need civil equality. The situation in which women presently find ourselves with respect to the pornography is one in which more *pornography* is inconsistent with rectifying or even counterbalancing its damage through speech, because so long as the pornography exists in the way it does there *will not be more speech by women*. Pornography strips and devastates women of credibility, from our accounts of sexual assault to our everyday reality of sexual subordination. We are stripped of authority and reduced and devalidated and silenced. Silenced here means that the purposes of the First Amendment, premised upon conditions presumed and promoted by protecting free speech, do not pertain to women because they are not our conditions. Consider them: Individual self-fulfillment—how does pornography promote our individual self-fulfillment? How does sexual inequality even permit it? Even if she can form words, who listens to a woman with a penis in her mouth? Facilitating consensus—to the extent pornography does so, it does so one-sidedly by silencing protest over the injustice of sexual subordination. Participation in civic life—central to Professor Meiklejohn's theory—how does pornography enhance women's participation in civic life? Anyone who cannot walk down the street or even lie down in her own bed without keeping her eyes cast down and her body clenched against assault is unlikely to have much to say about the issues of the day, still less will she become Tolstoy. Facilitating change—*this law* facilitates the change that existing First Amendment theory had been used to throttle. Any system of freedom of expression that does not address a problem where the free speech of men silences the free speech of women, a real conflict between speech interests as well as between people, is not serious about securing freedom of expression in this country.

For those of you who still think pornography is only an idea, consider the possibility that obscenity law got one thing right. Pornography is more actlike than thoughtlike. That pornography, in a feminist view, furthers the idea of the sexual inferiority of women, which is a political idea, doesn't make the pornography itself a political idea. One can express the idea a practice embodies. That does not make that practice an idea. Segregation expresses the idea of the inferiority of one group to another on the basis of race. That does not make segregation an idea. A sign that says "Whites Only" is only words. Is it therefore protected by the First Amendment? Is it not an act, a practice, of segregation because what it means is inseparable from what it does? *Law* is only words.

The issue here is whether the fact that words and pictures are the central link in the cycle of abuse will immunize that entire cycle, about which we cannot do anything without doing something about the pornography. As Justice Stewart said in *Ginsburg*, "When expression occurs in a setting where the capacity to make a choice is absent, government regulation of that expression may coexist with and *even implement* First Amendment guarantees." I would even go so far as to say that the pattern of evidence we have closely approaches Justice Douglas's requirement that "freedom of expression can be suppressed if, and to the extent that, it is so closely brigaded with illegal action as to be an inseparable part of it." Those who have been trying to separate the acts from the speech—that's an act, that's an act, there's a law against that act, regulate that act, don't touch the speech—notice here that the illegality of the acts involved doesn't mean that the speech that is "brigaded with" it *cannot* be regulated. This is when it *can* be.

I take one of two penultimate points from Andrea Dworkin, who has often said that pornography is not speech for women, it is the silence of women. Remember the mouth taped, the woman gagged, "Smile, I can get a lot of money for that." The smile is not her expression, it is her silence. It is not her expression not because it didn't happen, but because it *did* happen. The screams of the women in pornography are silence, like the screams of Kitty Genovese, whose plight was misinterpreted by some onlookers as a lovers' quarrel. The flat expressionless voice of the woman in the New Bedford gang rape, testifying, is silence. She was raped as men cheered and watched, as they do in and with the pornography. When women resist and men say, "Like this, you stupid bitch, here is how to do it" and shove their faces into the pornography, this "truth of sex" is the silence of women. When they say, "If you love me, you'll try," the enjoyment we fake, the enjoyment we learn is silence. Women who submit because there is more dignity in it than in losing the fight over and over live in silence. Having to sleep with your publisher or director to get access to what men call speech is silence. Being humiliated on the basis of your appearance, whether by approval or disapproval, because you have to look a certain way for a certain job, whether you get the job or not, is silence. The absence of a woman's voice, everywhere that it cannot be heard, is silence. And anyone who thinks that what women say in pornography is women's speech—the "Fuck me, do it to me, harder," all of that—has never heard the sound of a woman's voice.

The most basic assumption underlying First Amendment adjudication is that, socially, speech is free. The First Amendment says Congress shall not abridge the freedom of speech. Free speech, get it, *exists*. Those who wrote the First Amendment *had* speech—they wrote the Constitution. *Their* problem was to keep it free from the only power that realistically threatened it: the federal government. They designed the First Amendment to prevent government from constraining that which, if unconstrained by government, was free, meaning *accessible to them*. At the same time, we can't tell much about the intent of the framers with regard to the question of women's speech, because I don't think we crossed their minds. It is consistent with this analysis that their posture toward freedom of speech tends to presuppose that whole segments of the population are not systematically silenced socially, prior to government action. If everyone's power were equal to theirs, if this were a nonhierarchical society, that might make sense. But the place of pornography in the inequality of the sexes makes the assumption of equal power untrue.

This is a hard question. It involves risks. Classically, opposition to censorship has involved keeping government off the backs of people. Our law is about getting some people off the backs of other people. The risks that it will be misused have to be measured against the risks of the status quo. Women will never have that dignity, security, compensation that is the promise of equality so long as the pornography exists as it does now. The situation of women suggests that the urgent issue of our freedom of speech is not primarily the avoidance of state intervention as such, but getting affirmative access to speech for those to whom it has been denied.

41. Feminists against the First Amendment

Wendy Kaminer

Wendy Kaminer surveys the history of the feminist antiporn movement in North America from the late 1970s to the present. She points out that the feminist case against pornography is based on a presumed link between pornography and sexual violence, but she questions how direct that link is and whether it depends on a blurring of the distinction between speech and conduct. She also suggests that alcohol and other substance abuse may have a more direct role in causing sexual violence, and argues that the most likely legislative result of the feminist antiporn movement, given its political allegiance with the New Right, would be a broader censorship that would not serve feminist interests.

Despite efforts to redevelop it, New York's 42nd Street retains its underground appeal, especially for consumers of pornography. What city officials call "sex-related uses"—triple-X video (formerly book) stores, peep shows, and topless bars—have declined in number since their heyday in the 1970s, and much of the block between Seventh and Eighth avenues is boarded up, a hostage to development. New sex businesses—yuppie topless bars and downscale lap-dancing joints (don't ask)—are prospering elsewhere in Manhattan. But Peepland (MULTI-VIDEO BOOTHS! NUDE DANCING GIRLS!) still reigns, and Show World, a glitzy sex emporium, still anchors the west end of the block, right around the corner from *The New York Times*.

In the late 1970s I led groups of suburban women on tours through Show World and other 42nd Street hot spots, exposing them, in the interests of consciousness-raising, to pornography's various genres: Nazi porn, nurse porn, lesbian porn, bondage porn—none of it terribly imaginative. The women didn't exactly hold hands as they ventured down the street with me, but they did stick close together; traveling en masse, they were not so conspicuous as individuals. With only a little less discomfort than resolve, they dutifully viewed the pornography.

This was in the early days of the feminist antiporn movement, when legislative strategies against pornography were mere gleams in the eye of the feminist writer Andrea Dworkin, when it seemed possible to raise consciousness about pornography without arousing demands for censorship. That pe-

riod of innocence did not last long. By 1981 the New Right had mounted a nationwide censorship campaign to purge schools and public libraries of sex education and other secular-humanist forms of "pornography." Sex education was "filth and perversion," Jerry Falwell announced in a fundraising letter that included, under the label "Adults Only. Sexually Explicit Material," excerpts from a college health text. By the mid-1980s right-wing advocates of traditional family values had co-opted feminist antiporn protests—or, at least, they'd co-opted feminist rhetoric. The feminist attorney and law professor Catharine MacKinnon characterized pornography as the active subordination of women, and Phyllis Schlafly wrote, "Pornography really should be defined as the degradation of women."

Pornography as Sex Discrimination

Of course, while feminists blamed patriarchy for pornography, moral majoritarians blamed feminism and other humanist rebellions. The alliance between feminists and the far right was not ideological but political. In 1984 antiporn legislation devised by Andrea Dworkin and Catharine MacKinnon, defining pornography as a violation of women's civil rights, was introduced in the Indianapolis city council by an anti-ERA activist, passed with the support of the right, and signed into law by the Republican mayor, William Hudnutt.

With the introduction of this bill, a new legislative front opened in the war against pornography, alienating civil-libertarian feminists from their more censorious sisters, while appealing to populist

Reprinted from *The Atlantic Monthly,* November 1992, by permission of the publisher and the author.

concerns about declining moral values. By calling for the censorship of pornography, some radical feminists found their way into the cultural mainstream—and onto the margins of First Amendment law.

The legislation adopted in Indianapolis offered a novel approach to prohibiting pornography that had all the force of a semantic distinction: Pornography was not simply speech, Catharine MacKinnon suggested, but active sex discrimination, and thus was not protected by the First Amendment. (In her 1989 book *Toward a Feminist Theory of the State,* MacKinnon characterized pornography as "a form of forced sex.") Regarding pornography as action, defining it broadly as any verbal or visual sexually explicit material (violent or not) that subordinates women, presuming that the mere existence of pornography oppresses women, the Indianapolis ordinance gave any woman offended by any arguably pornographic material the right to seek an order prohibiting it, along with damages for the harm it presumably caused. In other words, any woman customer browsing in a bookstore or patrolling one, glancing at a newsstand or a triple-X video store, was a potential plaintiff in a sex discrimination suit. Given all the literature, films, and videos on the mass market that could be said to subordinate women, this ordinance would have created lots of new business for lawyers—but it did not stand. Within a year of its enactment, [Dworkin and MacKinnon's] law was declared unconstitutional by a federal appeals court in a decision affirmed by the U.S. Supreme Court.

The feminist antiporn movement retreated from the legislative arena and passed out of public view in the late 1980s, only to re-emerge with renewed strength on college campuses. College professors following fashions in poststructuralism asserted that legal principles, like those protecting speech, were mere rhetorical power plays: Without any objective, universal merit, prevailing legal ideals were simply those privileged by the mostly white male ruling class. The dominant poststructural dogma of the late 1980s denied the First Amendment the transcendent value that the liberal belief in a marketplace of ideas has always awarded it.

◇

Massachusetts Mischief

This unlikely convergence of First Amendment critiques from multiculturalists, poststructuralists, and advocates of traditional family values, recently combined with high-profile rape and harassment cases and women's abiding concern with sexual violence, buoyed the feminist antiporn movement. This year it reemerged on the national and local scene with renewed legislative clout. The presumption that pornography oppresses women and is a direct cause of sexual violence is the basis for bills introduced in the U.S. Senate and the Massachusetts legislature. Last June the Senate Judiciary Committee passed the Pornography Victims' Compensation Act, which would make producers, distributors, exhibitors, and retailers convicted of disseminating material adjudged obscene liable for damages to victims of crimes who could claim that the material caused their victimization. The Massachusetts legislature held hearings on a much broader antiporn bill, closely modeled on the Indianapolis ordinance. Disarmingly titled "An Act to Protect the Civil Rights of Women and Children," the Massachusetts bill would not only make purveyors of pornography liable for crimes committed by their customers; it would also allow any woman, whether or not she has been the victim of a crime, to sue producers, distributors, exhibitors, or retailers of any sexually explicit visual material that subordinates women. (The exclusion of verbal "pornography" from the antitrafficking provision would protect the likes of Norman Mailer, whom many feminists consider a pornographer, so long as his works are not adapted for the screen.) What this bill envisions is that the First Amendment would protect only that speech considered sexually correct.

The feminist case against pornography is based on the presumption that the link between pornography and sexual violence is clear, simple, and inexorable. The argument is familiar: Censorship campaigns always blame unwanted speech for unwanted behavior; Jerry Falwell once claimed that sex education causes teenage pregnancy, just as feminists claim that pornography causes rape. One objection to this assertion is that it gives rapists and batterers an excuse for their crimes, and perhaps even a "pornography made me do it" defense.

The claim that pornography causes rape greatly oversimplifies the problem of sexual violence. We can hardly say that were it not for pornography, there would be no rape or battering. As feminists opposed to antiporn legislation have pointed out, countries in which commercial pornography is illegal—Saudi Arabia, for example—are hardly safe havens for women.

This is not to deny that there probably is some link between violence in the media and violence in real life, but it is complicated, variable, and difficult to measure. Not all hate speech is an incantation; not all men are held spellbound by pornography. Poststructural feminists who celebrate subjectivism should be among the first to admit that different people respond to the same images differently. All we can confidently claim is that the way women are imagined is likely to have a cumulative effect on the way they're treated, but that does not mean any single image is the clear and simple cause of any single act.

The Dworkin-MacKinnon bill, however, did more than assume that pornography causes sex discrimination and other crimes against women. It said that pornography *is* violence and discrimination: the active subordination of women (and it assumed that we can all agree on what constitutes subordination). MacKinnon and her followers deny that prohibiting pornography is censorship, because they effectively deny that pornography is speech—and that is simply Orwellian. The line between speech and behavior is sometimes blurred: Dancing nude down a public street is one way of expressing yourself which may also be a form of disorderly conduct. But if pornography is sex discrimination, then an editorial criticizing the president is treason.

Most feminists concerned about pornography are probably not intent on suppressing political speech, but the legislation they support, like the Massachusetts antiporn bill, is so broad, and its definition of pornography so subjective, that it would be likely to jeopardize sex educators and artists more than it would hard-core pornographers, who are used to operating outside the law. Feminist legislation makes no exception for "pornography" in which some might find redeeming social value; it could, for example, apply in the case of a woman disfigured by a man who had seen too many paintings by Willem de Kooning. "If a woman is subjected," Catharine MacKinnon writes, "why should it matter that the work has other value?"

With this exclusive focus on prohibiting material that reflects incorrect attitudes toward women, antiporn feminists don't deny the chilling effect of censorship; they embrace it. Any speech that subordinates women—any pornography—is yelling "Fire!" in a crowded theater, they say, falling back on a legal canard. But that's true only if, just as all crowds are deemed potential mobs, all men are deemed potential abusers whose violent impulses are bound to be sparked by pornography. It needs to be said, by feminists, that efforts to censor pornography reflect a profound disdain for men. Catharine MacKinnon has written that "pornography works as a behavioral conditioner, reinforcer and stimulus, not as idea or advocacy. It is more like saying 'kill' to a trained guard dog—and also the training process itself." That's more a theory of sexuality than of speech: Pornography is action because all men are dogs on short leashes.

This bleak view of male sexuality condemns heterosexuality for women as an exercise in wish fulfillment (if only men weren't all dogs) or false consciousness (such as male-identified thinking). True feminism, according to MacKinnon, unlike liberal feminism, "sees sexuality as a social sphere of male power of which forced sex is paradigmatic." With varying degrees of clarity, MacKinnon and Dworkin suggest that in a context of pervasive, institutionalized inequality, there can be no consensual sex between men and women: We can never honestly distinguish rape from intercourse.

An Esoteric Debate

A modified version of this message may well have particular appeal to some college women today, who make up an important constituency for the antiporn movement. In their late teens and early twenties, these women are still learning to cope with sexuality, in a violent and unquestionably misogynistic world. Feminism on campus tends to focus on issues of sexuality, not of economic equity. Anxiety about date rape is intense, along with anxiety about harassment and hate speech. Understanding and appreciating the First Amendment is a lot less evident, and concern about employment discrimination seems somewhat remote. It's not hard to understand why: College women in general haven't experienced overt repression of opinions and ideas or many problems in the workplace, but from childhood they've known what it is to fear rape. In the age of AIDS, the fear can be crippling.

Off campus the antiporn feminist critique of male sexuality and heterosexuality for women has little appeal, but it is not widely known. MacKinnon's theoretical writings are impenetrable to readers who lack familiarity with poststructural jargon and the patience to decode sentences like this: "If objectivity is the epistemological stance of which women's

sexual objectification is the social process, its imposition the paradigm of power in the male form, then
the state will appear most relentless in imposing the
male point of view, when it comes closest to achieving its highest formal criterion of distanced aper-
spectivity." Dworkin is a much more accessible
polemicist, but she is also much less visible outside
feminist circles. Tailored, with an air of middle-class
respectability and the authority of a law professor, MacKinnon looks far less scary to mainstream
Americans than her theories about sexuality, which
drive the antiporn movement, might sound.

If antipornography crusades on the right reflect grassroots concern about changing sexual
mores and the decline of the traditional family, anti-
pornography crusades on the feminist left reflect the
concerns and perceptions of an educated elite. In
the battle for the moral high ground, antiporn feminists claim to represent the interests of a racially
diverse mixture of poor and working class women
who work in the pornography industry—and they
probably do represent a few. But many sex-industry
workers actively oppose antiporn legislation (some
feminists would say they have been brainwashed
by patriarchy or actually coerced), and it's not at all
clear that women who are abused in the making of
pornography would be helped by forcing it deeper
underground; working conditions in an illegal business are virtually impossible to police. It's hard to
know how many other alleged victims of pornography feel represented by the antiporn movement,
and I know of no demographic study of the movement's active members.

Leaders of the feminist antiporn movement,
however, do seem more likely to emerge from academia and the professions than from the streets or
battered women's shelters. Debra Robbin, a former
director of the New Bedford Women's Center, one of
the first shelters in Massachusetts, doesn't believe
that "women on the front lines," working with victims of sexual violence, will "put much energy into
a fight against pornography." Activists don't have
time: "They can barely leave their communities to
go to the statehouses to fight for more funding." The
poor and working-class women they serve would
say, "Yeah, pornography is terrible, but I don't have
food on my table." Carolin Ramsey, the executive
director of the Massachusetts Coalition of Battered
Women Service Groups, says that the pornography
debate "doesn't have a lot to do with everyday life
for me and the women I'm serving." She explains,
"Violence in the home and the streets that directly

threatens our lives and our families is more pressing than a movie. Keeping my kids away from
drugs is more important than keeping them away
from literature."

Ramsey is sympathetic to antiporn feminists
("there's room in the movement for all of us"), and
she believes that "violence in the media contributes
to violence in real life." Still, she considers the pornography debate "esoteric" and "intellectual" and
feels under no particular pressure from her con-
stituents to take a stand against pornography.

If censoring pornography is the central feminist
issue for Catharine MacKinnon, it is a peripheral issue for activists like Robbin and Ramsey. Robbin in
particular does not believe that eliminating pornography would appreciably lessen the incidence
of sexual abuse. David Adams, a co-founder and
the executive director of Emerge, a Boston counseling center for male batterers, believes that only a minority of his clients (perhaps 10 to 20 percent) use
hard-core pornography. He estimates that half may
have substance-abuse problems, and adds that alcohol seems more directly involved in abuse than
pornography. Adams agrees with feminists that
pornography is degrading to women but does not
support legislation regulating it, because "the legislation couldn't work and would only open the door
to censorship."

What might work instead? Emerge conducts
programs in Boston and Cambridge public schools
on violence, aimed at both victims and perpetrators.
"There's a lot of violence in teen relationships,"
Adams observes. Debra Robbin wishes that women
in the antiporn movement would "channel their energies into funding battered women's shelters and
rape-crisis centers."

Reforming the criminal-justice system is also a
priority for many women concerned about sexual
violence. Antistalking laws could protect many more
women than raids on pornographic video stores are
ever likely to; so could the efficient processing of
cases against men who abuse women.

Sensationalism as an Organizing Tool

Why do some women channel their energies into a
fight against pornography? Antiporn legislation has
the appeal of a quick fix, as Robbin notes. And, she

adds, "there's notoriety to be gained from protesting pornography." The "harder work"—promoting awareness and understanding of sexual violence, changing the way children are socialized, and helping women victims of violence—is less sensationalist and less visible.

Sensationalism, however, is an organizing tool for antiporn feminists. If questions about the effects of pornography seem intellectual to some women involved in social-service work, the popular campaign against pornography is aggressively anti-intellectual. Although advocates of First Amendment freedoms are stuck with intellectual defenses of the marketplace of ideas, antiporn feminists whip up support for their cause with pornographic slide shows comprising hard-core pictures of women being tortured, raped, and generally degraded. Many feminists are equally critical of the soft-core porn movies available at local video stores and on cable TV, arguing that the violence in pornography is often covert (and they include mainstream advertising images in their slide shows). But hard-core violence is what works on the crowd. Feminist rhetoric often plays on women's worst fears about men: "Pornography tells us that there but for the grace of God go us," Gail Dines, a sociology professor at Wheelock College, exclaimed during her recent slide show at Harvard, as she presented photographs of women being brutalized.

Dines's porn show was SRO, its audience some 300 undergraduates who winced and gasped at the awful slides and cheered when Dines pointed to a pornographic picture of a woman and said, "When I walk down the street, what they know about me is what they know about her!" She warned her mostly female audience that pornographers have "aggressively targeted college men." She seemed preoccupied with masturbation. Part of the problem of pornography, she suggested, is that men use it to masturbate, and "women weren't put on this world to facilitate masturbation." She advised a student concerned about the presence of *Playboy* in the college library that library collections of pornography aren't particularly worrisome, because men are not likely to masturbate in libraries.

In addition to condemnations of male sexuality, Dines offered questionable horror stories about pornography's atrocities, like this: Rape vans are roaming the streets of New York. Women are dragged into the vans and raped on camera; when their attackers sell the rape videos in commercial outlets, the women have no legal recourse.

A story like this is impossible to disprove (how do you prove a negative?), but it should probably not be taken at face value, as many students in Dines's audience seemed to take it. William Daly, the director of New York City's Office of Midtown Enforcement, which is responsible for monitoring the sex industry in New York, has never heard of rape vans; almost anything is possible on 42nd Street, but he is skeptical that rape vans are a problem. Part of Dines's story, however, is simply untrue: Under New York State privacy law, says Nan Hunter, a professor of law at Brooklyn Law School, women could seek damages for the sale of the rape videos, and also an injunction against their distribution.

It would be difficult even to raise questions about the accuracy of the rape-van story, however, in the highly emotional atmosphere of a slide show; you'd be accused of not believing the women. Just as slides of bloody fetuses pre-empt rational debate about abortion, pornographic slide shows pre-empt argumentative questions and rational consideration of First Amendment freedoms, the probable effect of efforts to censor pornography, and the actual relationship between pornography and violence.

A Pornographic Culture?

Does pornography cause violence against women, as some feminists claim? Maybe, in some cases, under some circumstances involving explicitly violent material. Readers interested in the social-science debate should see both the report of the Attorney General's Commission on Pornography, which found a link between pornography and violence against women, and the feminist writer Marcia Pally's "Sense and Censorship," published by Americans for Constitutional Freedom and the Freedom to Read Foundation. In addition to the equivocal social-science data, however, we have the testimony of women who claim to have been brutalized by male consumers of pornography. Antiporn feminists generally characterize pornography as a "how to" literature on abusing women, which men are apparently helpless to resist. But evidence is mainly anecdotal: At a hearing . . . on the antiporn bill in the Massachusetts legislature, several women told awful, lurid tales of sexual abuse, said to have been inspired by pornography. Like a TV talk show, the Attorney General's commission presented testimony from pornography's alleged victims, which may or may not have been true. It's difficult to cross-examine a sobbing self-proclaimed victim; you either take her testimony at face value or you don't.

Still, many people don't need reliable, empirical evidence about a link between pornography and behavior to believe that one exists. When feminists talk about pornography, after all, they mean a wide range of mainstream media images—Calvin Klein ads, Brian De Palma films, and the endless stream of TV shows about serial rapist stranglers and housewives who moonlight as hookers. How could we not be affected by the routine barrage of images linking sex and violence and lingerie? The more broadly pornography is defined, the more compelling are assertions about its inevitable effect on behavior, but the harder it is to control. How do we isolate the effects of any particular piece of pornography if we live in a pornographic culture?

Narrowly drawn antiporn legislation, which legislators are most likely to pass and judges most likely to uphold, could not begin to address the larger cultural problem of pornography. Feminists themselves usually claim publicly that they intend to prohibit only hard-core pornography, although on its face their legislation applies to a much broader range of material. But if you accept the feminist critique of sexism in the media, hard-core porn plays a relatively minor role in shaping attitudes and behavior. If feminists are right about pornography, it is a broad social problem, not a discrete legal one: [It] is not a problem the law can readily solve, unless perhaps we suspend the First Amendment entirely and give feminists the power to police mainstream media, the workplace, and schools.

The likelihood that feminists would not be the ones to police 42nd Street should antiporn legislation pass is one reason that many feminists oppose the antiporn campaign. If society is as sexist as Andrea Dworkin and Catharine MacKinnon claim, it is not about to adopt a feminist agenda when it sets out to censor pornography. The history of antiporn campaigns in this country is partly a history of campaigns against reproductive choice and changing roles for men and women. The first federal obscenity legislation, known as the Comstock Law, passed in 1873, prohibited the mailing of not only dirty pictures but also contraceptives and information about abortion. Early in this century Margaret Sanger and the sex educator Mary Ware Dennett were prosecuted for obscenity violations. Recently the New Right campaign against socially undesirable literature has focused on sex education in public schools.

Antiporn activists on the right consider feminism and homosexuality (which they link) to be threats to traditional family life (which, in fact, they are). In Canada a landmark Supreme Court ruling . . . [that] adopted a feminist argument against pornography was first used to prohibit distribution of a small lesbian magazine, which a politically correct feminist would be careful to label erotica.

Gay and lesbian groups, as well as advocates of sex education and the usual array of feminists and nonfeminist civil libertarians, actively oppose antipornography legislation. Some state National Organization for Women chapters—New York, California, and Vermont—have taken strong anticensorship stands, but at the national level NOW has not taken a position in the pornography debate. President Patricia Ireland would like to see pornography become socially unacceptable, "like smoking," but is wary of taking legal action against it, partly because she's wary of "giving people like Jesse Helms the power to decide what we read and see." But for major, national feminist organizations, like NOW and the NOW Legal Defense and Education Fund, the pornography debate is a minefield to be carefully avoided. Pornography is probably the most divisive issue feminists have faced since the first advocates of the ERA, in the 1920s, squared off against advocates of protective labor legislation for women. Feminists for and against antiporn legislation are almost as bitterly divided as pro-choice activists and members of Operation Rescue.

Renewed concern about abortion rights may drain energy from the antiporn movement. Feminists may awaken to the danger that antipornography laws will be used against sex educators and advocates of choice. (A gag rule on family-planning clinics may have made some feminists more protective of the First Amendment.) Politicians courting women voters may find that antiporn legislation alienates more feminists than it pleases. Still, censorship campaigns will always have considerable appeal. Like campaigns to reinstate the death penalty, they promise panaceas for profound social pathologies. They make their case by exploiting the wrenching anecdotal testimony of victims: Politicians pushing for the death penalty hold press conferences flanked by mothers of murdered children, just as feminists against pornography spotlight raped and battered women.

Rational argument is no match for highly emotional testimony. But it may be wishful thinking to believe that penalizing the production and distribution of hard-core pornography would have much effect on sexual violence. It would probably have little effect even on pornography, given the black market. It would, however, complicate campaigns to distribute information about AIDS, let alone condoms, in the public schools. It would dis-

tract us from the harder, less popular work of reforming sexual stereotypes and roles, and addressing actual instead of metaphorical instruments of violence. The promise of the antiporn movement is the promise of a world in which almost no one can buy pornography and almost anyone can buy a gun.

42. *American Booksellers v. Hudnutt*

United States District Court and Court of Appeals

The issue before the federal judiciary was whether the Indianapolis ordinance that sought to prohibit pornography as a practice that discriminated against women was restricting speech rather than conduct—and, if it was restricting speech, whether it was restricting speech that was protected by the First Amendment to the U.S. Constitution. The federal judiciary ruled that the ordinance was indeed restricting speech protected by the First Amendment rather than conduct.

Indianapolis enacted an ordinance defining "pornography" as a practice that discriminates against women. "Pornography" is to be redressed through the administrative and judicial methods used for other discrimination. . . .

"Pornography" under the ordinance is "the graphic sexually explicit subordination of women, whether in pictures or in words, that also includes one or more of the following:
1. Women are presented as sexual objects who enjoy pain or humiliation; or
2. Women are presented as sexual objects who experience sexual pleasure in being raped; or
3. Women are presented as sexual objects tied up or cut up or mutilated or bruised or physically hurt, or as dismembered or truncated or fragmented or severed into body parts; or
4. Women are presented as being penetrated by objects or animals; or
5. Women are presented in scenarios of degradation, injury, abasement, torture, shown as filthy or inferior, bleeding, bruised, or hurt in a context that makes these conditions sexual; or
6. Women are presented as sexual objects for domination, conquest, violation, exploitation, possession, or use, or through postures

or positions of servility or submission or display.". . .

First Amendment Requirements

This Ordinance cannot be analyzed adequately without first recognizing this: The drafters of the Ordinance have used what appears to be a legal term of art, "pornography," but have in fact given the term a specialized meaning which differs from the meanings ordinarily assigned to that word in both legal and common parlance. In Section 16-3(v) (page 6), the Ordinance states:

Pornography shall mean the sexually explicit subordination of women, graphically depicted, whether in pictures or in words, that includes one or more of the following:

There follows. . . a listing of five specific presentations of women in various settings which serve as examples of "pornography" and as such further define and describe that term under the Ordinance.

As is generally recognized, the word "pornography" is usually associated, and sometimes synonymous, with the word, "obscenity." "Obscenity" not only has its own separate and specialized meaning in the law, but in laymen's use also, and it is a much broader meaning than the definition given the word "pornography" in the Ordinance which is at issue in this action. There is thus a considerable risk of confusion in analyzing this Ordinance unless care and precision are used in that process.

The Constitutional analysis of this Ordinance requires a determination of several underlying issues: First, the Court must determine whether the Ordinance imposes restraints on speech or behavior (content versus conduct); if the Ordinance is found to regulate speech, the Court must next determine whether the subject speech is protected or not protected under the First Amendment; if the speech . . . regulated by this Ordinance is protected speech under the Constitution, the Court must then decide whether the regulation is constitutionally permissible . . . based on a compelling state interest justifying the removal of such speech from First Amendment protections.

Do the Ordinances Regulate Speech or Behavior (Content or Conduct)?

It appears to be central to the defense of the Ordinance by defendants that the Court accept their premise that the City-County Council has not attempted to regulate speech, let alone protected speech. Defendants repeat throughout their briefs the incantation that their Ordinance regulates conduct, not speech. They contend (one senses with a certain sleight of hand) that the production, dissemination, and use of sexually explicit words and pictures is the actual subordination of women and not an expression of ideas deserving of First Amendment protection. . . .

Defendants claim support for their theory by analogy, arguing that it is an accepted and established legal distinction that has allowed other courts to find that advocacy of a racially "separate but equal" doctrine in a civil rights context is protected speech under the First Amendment though "segregation" is not constitutionally protected behavior. Accordingly, defendants characterize their Ordinance here as a civil rights measure, through which they seek to prevent the distribution, sale, and exhibition of "pornography," as defined in the Ordinance, in order to regulate and control the underlying unacceptable conduct.

The content-versus-conduct approach espoused by defendants is not persuasive, however, and is contrary to accepted First Amendment principles. Accepting as true the City-County Council's finding that pornography conditions society to subordinate women, the means by which the Ordinance attempts to combat this sex discrimination is nonetheless through the regulation of speech.

For instance, the definition of pornography, the control of which is the whole thrust. . . , states that it is "the sexually explicit subordination of women, graphically *depicted,* whether in *pictures* or in *words,* that includes one or more of the following:" (emphasis supplied) and the following five descriptive subparagraphs begin with . . . , *Women are presented. . . .*"

The unlawful acts and discriminatory practices regulated by this Ordinance are set out in Section 16-3(g):

> (4) Trafficking in pornography: the production, sale, exhibition, or distribution of pornography. . . .
> (5) Coercion into pornographic performance: coercing, intimidating or fraudulently inducing any person . . . into performing for pornography . . .
> (6) Forcing pornography on a person: . . . .
> (7) Assault or physical attack due to pornography: the assault, physical attack, or injury of any woman, man, child or transsexual in a way that is directly caused by specific pornography. . .

Section (7), *supra,* goes on to provide a cause of action in damages against the perpetrators, makers, distributors, sellers, and exhibitors of pornography and injunctive relief against the further exhibition, distribution or sale of pornography.

In summary, therefore, the Ordinance establishes through the legislative findings that pornography causes a tendency to commit these various harmful acts, and outlaws the pornography (that is, the "depictions"), the activities involved in the production of pornography, and the behavior caused by or resulting from pornography

Thus, though the purpose of the Ordinance is cast in civil rights terminology—"to prevent and prohibit all discriminatory practices of sexual subordination or inequality through pornography" . . . —it is clearly aimed at controlling the content of the speech and ideas that the City-County Council has found harmful and offensive. Those words and pictures which depict women in sexually subordinate roles are banned by the Ordinance. Despite defendants' attempt to redefine offensive speech as harmful action, the clear wording of the Ordinance discloses that they seek to control speech, and those restrictions must be analyzed in light of applicable constitutional requirements and standards.

Is the Speech Regulated by the Ordinance Protected or Unprotected Speech under the First Amendment?

The First Amendment provides that government shall make no law abridging the freedom of speech. However, "the First and Fourteenth Amendments have never been thought to give absolute protection to every individual to speak whenever or wherever he pleases or to use any form of address in any circumstances that he chooses." *Cohen v. California* (1971). Courts have recognized only a "relatively few categories of instances," . . . where the government may regulate certain forms of individual expression. The traditional categories of speech subject to permissible government regulation include "the lewd and obscene, the profane, the libelous, and the insulting or 'fighting' words—those which by their very utterance inflict injury or tend to incite an immediate breach of the peace." *Chaplinsky v. State of New Hampshire* (1942). In addition, the Supreme Court has recently upheld legislation prohibiting the dissemination of material depicting children engaged in sexual conduct. *New York v. Ferber* (1982).

Having found that the Ordinance at issue here seeks to regulate speech (and not conduct), the next question before the Court is whether the Ordinance, which seeks to restrict the distribution, sale, and exhibition of "pornography" as a form of sex discrimination against women, falls within one of the established categories of speech subject to permissible government regulation, that is, speech deemed to be unprotected by the First Amendment.

It is clear that this case does not present issues relating to profanity, libel, or "fighting words." In searching for an analytical "peg," the plaintiffs argue that the Ordinance most closely resembles obscenity, and is, therefore, subject to the requirements set forth in *Miller v. California* (1973). . . . But the defendants admit that the scope of the Ordinance is not limited to the regulation of legally obscene ma-

terial as defined in *Miller*. . . . In fact, defendants concede that the "pornography" they seek to control goes beyond obscenity, as defined by the Supreme Court and excepted from First Amendment protections. Accordingly, the parties agree that the materials . . . in the restrictions set out in the Ordinance include to some extent what have traditionally been protected materials.

The test under *Miller* for determining whether material is legal obscenity is:

> (a) whether "the average person, applying contemporary community standards" would find that the work, taken as a whole, appeals to the prurient interest. . . . ; (b) whether the work depicts or describes, in a patently offensive way, sexual conduct specifically defined by the applicable state law; and (c) whether the work, taken as a whole, lacks serious literary, artistic, political, or scientific value. . . .

It is obvious that this three-step test is not directly applicable to the present case, because, as has been noted, the Ordinance goes beyond legally obscene material in imposing its controls. The restrictions in the Indianapolis ordinance reach what has otherwise traditionally been regarded as protected speech under the *Miller* test. Beyond that, the Ordinance does not speak in terms of a "community standard" or attempt to restrict the dissemination of material that appeals to the "prurient interest." Nor has the Ordinance been drafted in a way to limit only distributions of "patently offensive" materials. Neither does it provide for the dissemination of works which, though "pornographic," may have "serious literary, artistic, political or scientific value." Finally, the Ordinance does not limit its reach to "hard-core sexual conduct," though conceivably "hard-core" materials may be included in its proscriptions.

Because the Ordinance spans so much more . . . in its regulatory scope than merely "hard-core" obscenity by limiting the distribution of "pornography," the proscriptions in the Ordinance intrude with defendants' explicit approval into areas of otherwise protected speech. Under ordinary constitutional analysis, that would be sufficient grounds to overturn the Ordinance, but defendants argue that this case is not governed by any direct precedent, that it raises a new issue for the Court and even though the Ordinance regulates protected speech, it does so in a constitutionally permissible fashion.

Does Established First Amendment Law Permit the Regulation Provided for in the Ordinance of Otherwise Protected Speech?

In conceding that the scope of this Ordinance extends beyond constitutional limits, it becomes clear that what defendants actually seek by enacting this legislation is a newly defined class of constitutionally unprotected speech, labeled "pornography" and characterized as sexually discriminatory.

Defendants vigorously argue that *Miller* is not the "'constitutional divide' separating protected from unprotected expression in this area." . . . Defendants point to three cases which allegedly support their proposition that *Miller* is not the exclusive guideline for disposing of pornography/obscenity cases, and that the traditional obscenity test should not be applied in the present case. . . .

Defendants first argue that the Court must use the same reasoning applied by the Supreme Court in *New York v. Ferber* . . . which upheld a New York statute prohibiting persons from promoting child pornography by distributing material which depicted such activity, and carve out another similar exception to protected speech under the First Amendment.

Defendants can properly claim some support for their position in *Ferber*. There the Supreme Court allowed the states "greater leeway" in their regulation of pornographic depictions of children in light of the State's compelling interest in protecting children who, without such protections, are extraordinarily vulnerable to exploitation and harm. The court stated in upholding the New York statute:

> The prevention of sexual exploitation and abuse of children constitutes a government objective of surpassing importance. The legislative findings accompanying passage of the New York laws reflect this concern: . . . .

The Supreme Court continued in *Ferber* by noting that the *Miller* standard for legal obscenity does not satisfy the unique concerns and issues posed by child pornography where children are involved; it is irrelevant, for instance, that the materials sought to be regulated contain serious literary, artistic, political, or scientific value. In finding that some speech, such as that represented in depictions of child pornography, is outside First Amendment protections, the *Ferber* court stated:

> When a definable class of material . . . bears so heavily and pervasively on the welfare of children engaged in its production, we think the balance of competing interests is clearly struck and that it is permissible to consider these materials as without the protection of the First Amendment.

Defendants, in the case at bar, argue that the interests of protecting women from sex-based discrimination are analogous to and every bit as compelling and fundamental as those which the Supreme Court upheld in *Ferber* for the benefit of children. But *Ferber* appears clearly distinguishable from the instant case on both the facts and law.

As has already been shown, the rationale applied by the Supreme Court in *Ferber* appears intended to apply solely to child pornography cases. In *Ferber*, the court recognized "that a state's interest in 'safeguarding the physical and psychological well-being of a minor' is 'compelling.'". . . Also, the obscenity standard in *Miller* is appropriately abandoned in child pornography cases because it "[does] not reflect the State's particular and more compelling interest in prosecuting those who promote the sexual exploitations of children." . . . Since a state's compelling interest in preventing child pornography outweighs an individual's First Amendment rights, the Supreme Court held that "the states are entitled to greater leeway in the regulation of pornographic depictions of children.". . .

In contrast, the case at bar presents issues more far reaching than those in *Ferber*. Here, the City-County Council found that the distribution, sale, and exhibition of words and pictures depicting the subordination of women is a form of sex discrimination and as such is appropriate for governmental regulation. The state has a well-recognized interest in preventing sex discrimination, and, defendants argue, it can regulate speech to accomplish that end.

But the First Amendment gives primacy to free speech and any other state interest (such as the interest of sex-based equality under law) must be so compelling as to be fundamental; only then can it be deemed to outweigh the interest of free speech. This Court finds no legal authority or public policy argument which justifies so broad an incursion into First Amendment freedoms as to allow that which defendants attempt to advance here. *Ferber* does not open the door to allow the regulation contained in the Ordinance for the reason that adult women as a group do not, as a matter of public policy or applicable law, stand in need of the same type of protection which has long been afforded children. This is true even of women who are subject to the sort of inhuman treatment defendants have described and documented to the Court in support of this Ordinance. The Supreme Court's finding in *Ferber* of the uncontroverted state interest in "safeguarding the physical and psychological well-being of a minor" and its resultant characterization of that interest as "compelling," . . . is an interest that inheres to children and is not an interest which is readily transferable to adult women as a class. Adult women generally have the capacity to protect themselves from participating in and being personally victimized by pornography, which makes the State's interest in safeguarding the physical and psychological well-being of women by prohibiting "the sexually explicit subordination of women, graphically depicted, whether in pictures or in words" not so compelling as to sacrifice the guarantees of the First Amendment. In any case, whether a state interest is so compelling as to be a fundamental interest sufficient to warrant an exception from constitutional protections, therefore, surely must turn on something other than mere legislative dictate, which issue is discussed more fully further on in this Opinion. . . .

The second case relied upon by defendants to support their contention that *Miller* is not controlling in the present case is *FCC v. Pacifica Foundation* . . . (1978). According to defendants, *Pacifica* exemplifies the Supreme Court's refusal to make obscenity the sole legal basis for regulating sexually explicit conduct.

In *Pacifica,* the Supreme Court was faced with the question of whether a broadcast of patently offensive words dealing with sex and excretion may be regulated on the basis of their content. . . . The Court held that this type of speech was not entitled to absolute constitutional protection in every context. . . . Since the context of the speech in *Pacifica* was broadcasting, it was determined only to be due "the most limited First Amendment protection." The reason for such treatment was two-fold:

First, the broadcast media have established a uniquely pervasive presence in all the lives of all Americans. Patently offensive, indecent material presented over the airwaves confronts the citizen, not only in public, but also in the privacy of the home, where the individual's

right to be left alone plainly outweighs the First Amendment rights of an intruder.

Second, broadcasting is uniquely accessible to children, even those too young to read. . . .

Although the defendants correctly point out that the Supreme Court did not use the traditional obscenity test in *Pacifica,* this Court is not persuaded that the rule enunciated there is applicable to the facts of the present case. The Ordinance does not attempt to regulate the airwaves; in terms of its restrictions, it is not even remotely concerned with the broadcast media. The reasons for the rule in *Pacifica,* that speech in certain contexts should be afforded minimal First Amendment protection, are not present here, since we are not dealing with a medium that "invades" the privacy of the home. In contrast, if an individual is offended by "pornography," as defined in the Ordinance, the logical thing to do is avoid it, an option frequently not available to the public with material disseminated through broadcasting.

In addition, the Ordinance is not written to protect children from the distribution of pornography, in contrast to the challenged FCC regulation in *Pacifica.* Therefore, the peculiar state interest in protecting the "well-being of its youth," . . . does not underlie this Ordinance and cannot be called upon to justify a decision by this Court to uphold the Ordinance.

The third case cited by defendants in support of their proposition that the traditional obscenity standard in *Miller* should not be used to overrule the Ordinance is *Young v. American Mini Theatres, Inc.* . . . (1976). In *Young* the Supreme Court upheld a city ordinance that restricted the location of movie theatres featuring erotic films. The Court, in a plurality opinion, stated that "[e]ven though the First Amendment protects communication in this area from total suppression, we hold that the State may legitimately use the content of these materials as the basis for placing them in a different classification from other motion pictures." . . . The Court concluded that the city's interest in preserving the character of its neighborhoods justified the ordinance which required that adult theaters be separated, rather than concentrated, in the same areas as it is permissible for other theaters to do without limitation. . . .

Young is distinguishable from the present case because we are not here dealing with an attempt by the City-County Council to restrict the time, place, and manner in which "pornography" may be distributed. Instead, the Ordinance prohibits completely the sale, distribution, or exhibition of material depicting women in a sexually subordinate role, at all times, in all places and in every manner.

The Ordinance's attempt to regulate speech beyond one of the well-defined exceptions to protected speech under the First Amendment is not supported by other Supreme Court precedents. The Court must, therefore, examine the underlying premise of the Ordinance: That the State has so compelling an interest in regulating the sort of sex discrimination imposed and perpetuated through "pornography" that it warrants an exception to free speech.

Is Sex Discrimination a Compelling State Interest Justifying an Exception to First Amendment Protections?

It is significant to note that the premise of the Ordinance is the sociological harm, *i.e.,* the discrimination, which results from "pornography" to degrade women as a class. The Ordinance does not presume or require specifically defined, identifiable victims for most of its proscriptions. The Ordinance seeks to protect adult women, as a group, from the diminution of their legal and sociological status as women, that is, from the discriminatory stigma which befalls women *as women* as a result of "pornography." On page one of the introduction to defendants' *Amicus Brief,* counsel explicitly argues that the harm which underlies this legislation is the "harm to the treatment and *status* of women . . . on the basis of sex.". . .

This is a novel theory advanced by the defendants, an issue of first impression in the courts. If this Court were to accept defendants' argument—that the State's interest in protecting women from the humiliation and degradation which comes from being depicted in a sexually subordinate context is so compelling as to warrant the regulation of otherwise free speech to accomplish that end—one wonders what would prevent the City-County Council (or any other legislative body) from enacting protections for other equally compelling claims against exploitation and discrimination as are presented here. Legislative bodies, finding support here, could also enact legislation prohibiting other unfair expression—the publication and distribution of racist material, for instance, on the grounds that it causes racial discrimination,[1] or legislation prohibit-

ing ethnic or religious slurs on the grounds that they cause discrimination against particular ethnic or religious groups, or legislation barring literary depictions which are uncomplimentary or oppressive to handicapped persons on the grounds that they cause discrimination against that group of people, and so on. If this Court were to extend to this case the rationale in *Ferber* to uphold the Amendment, it would signal so great a potential encroachment upon First Amendment freedoms that the precious liberties reposed within those guarantees would not survive. The compelling state interest, which defendants claim gives constitutional life to their Ordinance, though important and valid as that interest may be in other contexts, is not so fundamental an interest as to warrant a broad intrusion into otherwise free expression.

Defendants contend that pornography is not deserving of constitutional protection because its harms victimize all women. It is argued that "pornography" not only negatively affects women who risk and suffer the direct abuse of its production, but also, those on whom violent pornography is forced through such acts as compelled performances of "dangerous acts such as being hoisted upside down by ropes, bound by ropes and chains, hung from trees and scaffolds or having sex with animals. . . . " It is also alleged that exposure to pornography produces a negative impact on its viewers, causing in them an increased willingness to aggress toward women, *ibid*. . . . , and experience self-generated rape fantasies, increases in sexual arousal and a rise in the self-reported possibility of raping. . . . In addition, it causes discriminatory attitudes and behavior toward all women. . . . The City-County Council, after considering testimony and social research studies, enacted the Ordinance in order to "combat" pornography's "concrete and tangible harms to women.". . .

Defendants rely on *Paris Adult Theatre I v. Slaton* . . . (1973) to justify their regulation of "pornography." In that case the Supreme Court held "there are legitimate state interests at stake in stemming the tide of commercialized obscenity . . . [that] include the interest of the public in the quality of life and the total community environment, the tone of commerce in the great city centers, and, possibly, . . . public safety itself.". . .

The Georgia Legislature had determined that in that case exposure to obscene material adversely affected men and women, that is to say, society as a whole. Although the petitioners argued in that case that there was no scientific data to conclusively prove that proposition, the Court said, "[i]t is not for us to resolve empirical uncertainties underlying state legislation, save in the exceptional case where that legislation plainly impinges upon rights protected by the constitution itself." . . .

Based on this reasoning, defendants argue that there is more than enough "empirical" evidence in the case at bar to support the City-County Council's conclusion that "pornography" harms women in the same way obscenity harms people, and, therefore, this Court should not question the legislative finding. As has already been acknowledged, it is not the Court's function to question the City-County Council's legislative finding. The Court's solitary duty is to ensure that the Ordinance accomplishes its purpose without violating constitutional standards or impinging upon constitutionally protected rights. In applying those tests, the Court finds that the Ordinance cannot withstand constitutional scrutiny.

It has already been noted that the Ordinance does not purport to regulate legal obscenity, as defined in *Miller.* Thus, although the City-County Council determined that "pornography" harms women, this Court must and does declare the Ordinance invalid without being bound by the legislative findings because "pornography," as defined

and regulated in the Ordinance, is constitutionally protected speech under the First Amendment and such an exception to [its] protections is constitutionally unwarranted. This Court cannot legitimately embark on judicial policy making, carving out a new exception to the First Amendment simply to uphold the Ordinance, even when there may be many good reasons to support legislative action. To permit every interest group, especially those who claim to be victimized by unfair expression, their own legislative exceptions to the First Amendment so long as they succeed in obtaining a majority of legislative votes in their favor demonstrates the potentially predatory nature of what defendants seek through this Ordinance and defend in this lawsuit.

It ought to be remembered by defendants and all others who would support such a legislative initiative that, in terms of altering sociological patterns, much as alteration may be necessary and desirable, free speech, rather than being the enemy, is a long-tested and worthy ally. To deny free speech in order to engineer social change in the name of accomplishing a greater good for one sector of our society erodes the freedoms of all and, as such, threatens tyranny and injustice for those subjected to the rule of such laws. The First Amendment protections presuppose the evil of such tyranny and prevent a finding by this Court upholding the Ordinance. . . .

Endnote

1. In *Beauharnais v. Illinois* . . . the Supreme Court upheld an Illinois libel statute prohibiting the dissemination of materials promoting racial or religious hatred and which tended to produce a breach of the peace and riots. It has been recognized that "the rationale of that decision turns quite plainly on the strong tendency of the prohibited utterances to cause violence and disorder." *Collin v. Smith* (7th Cir. 1978). The Supreme Court has recognized breach of the peace as the traditional justification for upholding a criminal libel statute. *Beauharnais* . . . Therefore, a law preventing the distribution of material that causes racial discrimination, an attitude, would be upheld under this analysis. Further, the underlying reasoning of the *Beauharnais* opinion, that the punishment of libel raises no constitutional problems, has been questioned in many recent cases. . . .

43. *Donald Victor Butler v. Her Majesty the Queen*

THE SUPREME COURT OF CANADA

The issue before the Supreme Court of Canada was that of determining whether and to what extent Parliament may legitimately criminalize obscenity. The Court ruled that the criminalization of obscenity accorded with the Canadian Charter of Rights and Freedom. In particular, the material to be suppressed depicted women "as sexual playthings, hysterically and instantly responsive to male sexual demands" and was produced simply for economic profit. The Court ruled that just as in the case of hate propaganda, it need not require conclusive social science evidence of harm to women before justifying prohibition. The Court judged that "a reasonable apprehension of harm" sufficed. The Court further judged that less intrusive legislation would not be as effective in preventing harm to women.

This appeal [challenges] the constitutionality of the obscenity provisions of the *Criminal Code, . . .* s. 163. They are attacked on the ground that they contravene . . . the *Canadian Charter of Rights and Freedoms.* The case requires the Court to address one of the most difficult and controversial of contemporary issues, . . . determining whether, and to what extent, Parliament may legitimately criminalize obscenity. [We] begin with a review of the facts that gave rise to this appeal, as well as of the proceedings in the lower courts.

Facts and Proceedings

In August 1987, the appellant, Donald Victor Butler, opened the Avenue Video Boutique located in Winnipeg, Manitoba. The shop sells and rents "hardcore" videotapes and magazines as well as sexual paraphernalia. Outside the store is a sign that reads:

> Avenue Video Boutique; a private members only adult video/visual club. Notice: If sex-oriented material offends you, please do not enter. No admittance to persons under 18 years.

On August 21, 1987, the City of Winnipeg Police entered the appellant's store with a search warrant and seized [its] inventory. The appellant was charged with 173 counts in the first indictment: 3 counts of selling obscene material . . . 41 counts of possessing obscene material for the purpose of distribution . . . 128 counts of possessing obscene material for the purpose of sale . . . and 1 count of exposing obscene material to public view. . .

On October 19, 1987, the appellant reopened the store at the same location. As a result of a police operation a search warrant was executed on October 29, 1987, resulting in the arrest of an employee, Norma McCord. The appellant was arrested at a later date.

A joint indictment was laid against the appellant doing business as Avenue Video Boutique and Norma McCord. The joint indictment contains 77 counts: . . . 2 counts of selling obscene material, . . . 73 counts of possessing obscene material for the purpose of distribution, . . . 1 count of possessing obscene material for the purpose of sale . . . and 1 count of exposing obscene material to public view. . . .

The trial judge convicted the appellant on eight counts relating to eight films. Convictions were entered against the co-accused McCord with respect to two counts relating to two of the films. Fines of $1,000 per offence were imposed on the appellant. Acquittals were entered on the remaining charges.

The Crown appealed the 242 acquittals with respect to the appellant and the appellant cross-appealed the convictions. The majority of the Manitoba Court of Appeal allowed the appeal of the Crown and entered convictions for the appellant with respect to all of the counts, Twaddle and Helper J. J. A. dissenting. . . .

In reaching the conclusion that legislation proscribing obscenity is a valid objective that justifies some encroachment of the right to freedom of expression, I am persuaded in part that such legislation may be found in most free and democratic societies. As Nemetz C. J. B. C. aptly pointed out in *R. v. Red Hot Video,* . . . for centuries democratic societies have set certain limits to freedom of expression. He cited . . . the following passage of Dickson J. A. . . . in *R. v. Great West News Ltd.*:

> All organized societies have sought in one manner or another to suppress obscenity. The right of the state to legislate to protect its moral fibre and well-being has long been recognized, with roots deep in history. It is within this frame that the Courts and Judges must work.

The advent of the *Charter* did not have the effect of dramatically depriving Parliament of a power that it has historically enjoyed. It is also noteworthy that the criminalization of obscenity was considered to be compatible with the *Canadian Bill of Rights*. As Dickson J. A. stated in *R. v. Prairie Schooner News Ltd.* . . . :

> Freedom of speech is not unfettered either in criminal law or civil law. The *Canadian Bill of Rights* was intended to protect, and does protect, basic freedoms of vital importance to all Canadians. It does not serve as a shield behind which obscene matter may be disseminated without concern for criminal consequences. The interdiction of the publications which are the subject of the present charges in no way trenches upon the freedom of expression which the *Canadian Bill of Rights* assures.

. . . Finally . . . the burgeoning pornography industry renders the concern even more pressing and substantial than when the impugned provisions were first enacted. [Therefore,] the objective of avoiding the harm associated with the dissemination of pornography in this case is sufficiently pressing and substantial to warrant some restriction on full exercise of the right to freedom of expression. The analysis of whether the measure is proportional to the objective must . . . be undertaken in light of the conclusion that the objective of the impugned section is valid only insofar as it relates to the harm to society associated with obscene materials. Indeed, the section as interpreted in previous decisions and in these reasons is fully consistent with that objective. The objective of maintaining conventional standards of propriety, independently of any harm to society, is no longer justified in light of the values of individual liberty that underlie the *Charter*. This, then, being the objective of s. 163, which [is] pressing and substantial, I must now determine whether the section is rationally connected and pro-

portional to this objective. As outlined above, s. 163 criminalizes the exploitation of sex, and sex and violence, when, on the basis of the community test, it is undue. The determination of when such exploitation is undue is directly related to the immediacy of a risk of harm to society that is reasonably perceived as arising from its dissemination. . . .

The proportionality requirement has three aspects:

1. the existence of a rational connection between the impugned measures and the objective;

2. minimal impairment of the right or freedom; and

3. a proper balance between the effects of the limiting measures and the legislative objective.

In assessing whether the proportionality test is met . . . keep in mind the nature of expression that has been infringed. In the *Prostitution Reference* . . . Dickson C. J. wrote:

> When a *Charter* freedom has been infringed by state action that takes the form of criminalization, the Crown bears the heavy burden of justifying that infringement. Yet the expressive activity, as with any infringed *Charter* right, should also be analysed in the particular context of the case. Here, the activity to which the impugned legislation is directed is expression with an economic purpose. It can hardly be said that communications regarding an economic transaction of sex for money lie at, or even near, the core of the guarantee of freedom of expression.

The values that underlie the protection of freedom of expression relate to the search for truth, participation in the political process, and individual self-fulfillment. The Attorney General for Ontario argues that, of these, only "individual self-fulfillment," and only in its most base aspect, that of physical arousal, is engaged by pornography. . . . [C]ivil liberties groups argue that pornography forces us to question conventional notions of sexuality and thus launches us into an inherently political discourse. In their factum, the B. C. Civil Liberties Association adopts a passage from R. West, "The Feminist-Conservative Anti-Pornography Alliance and the 1986 Attorney General's Commission on Pornography Report." . . . :

Good pornography has value because it validates women's will to pleasure. It celebrates female nature. It validates a range of female sexuality that is wider and truer than that legitimated by the non-pornographic culture. Pornography when it is good celebrates both female pleasure and male rationality.

A proper application of the test should not suppress what West refers to as "good pornography." The objective of the impugned provision is not to inhibit the celebration of human sexuality. However, it cannot be ignored that the realities of the pornography industry are far from the picture which the B. C. Civil Liberties Association would have us paint. Shannon J., in *R. v. Wagner* . . . , describes the materials more accurately when he observed:

Women, particularly, are deprived of unique human character or identity and are depicted as sexual playthings, hysterically and instantly responsive to male sexual demands. They worship male genitals and their own value depends upon the quality of their genitals and breasts.

In my view, the kind of expression that is sought to be advanced does not stand on equal footing with other kinds of expression that directly engage the "core" of the freedom of expression values. This conclusion is further buttressed by the fact that the targeted material is expression that is motivated, in the overwhelming majority of cases, by economic profit. This Court held in *Rocket v. Royal College of Dental Surgeons of Ontario* . . . that an economic motive for expression means that restrictions on the expression might "be easier to justify than other infringements."

I will now turn to an examination of the three basic aspects of the proportionality test.

Rational Connection

The message of obscenity that degrades and dehumanizes is analogous to that of hate propaganda. As the Attorney General of Ontario has argued . . . , obscenity wields the power to wreak social damage in that a significant portion of the population is humiliated by its gross misrepresentations.

Accordingly, the rational link between s. 163 and the objective of Parliament relates to the actual causal relationship between obscenity and the risk of harm to society at large. On this point, it is clear that the literature of the social sciences remains subject to controversy. In *Fringe Product Inc.* . . . Charron Dist. Ct. J. considered numerous written reports and works and heard six days of testimony from experts who endeavoured to describe the status of the social sciences with respect to the study of the effects of pornography. Charron Dist. Ct. J. reached the conclusion that the relationship between pornography and harm was sufficient to justify Parliament's intervention. This conclusion is not supported unanimously.

The recent conclusions of the Fraser Report . . . could not postulate any causal relationship between pornography and the commission of violent crimes, the sexual abuse of children, or the disintegration of communities and society. . . .

While a direct link between obscenity and harm to society may be difficult, if not impossible, to establish, it is reasonable to presume that exposure to images bears a causal relationship to changes in attitudes and beliefs. The Meese Commission Report . . . concluded in respect of sexual violent material:

The available evidence strongly supports the hypothesis that substantial exposure to sexually violent materials . . . bears a causal relationship to antisocial acts of sexual violence and, for some subgroups, possibly to unlawful acts of sexual violence.

Although we rely for this conclusion on significant scientific empirical evidence, we feel it worthwhile to note the underlying logic of the conclusion. The evidence says simply that the images that people are exposed to bear a causal relationship to their behavior. This is hardly surprising. What would be surprising would be to find otherwise, and we have not so found. We have not, of course, found that the images people are exposed to are a greater cause of sexual violence than all or even many other possible causes. . . . Nevertheless, it would be strange indeed if graphic representations of a form of behavior, especially in a form that almost exclusively portrays such behavior as desirable, did not have at least some effect on patterns of behavior.

In the face of inconclusive social science evidence, the approach adopted . . . in *Irwin Toy* is instructive. In that case, the basis for the legislation was that television advertising directed at young children is *per se* manipulative. The Court made it clear that in choosing its mode of intervention, it is sufficient that Parliament had a *reasonable basis:*

> In the instant case, the Court is called on to assess competing social science evidence respecting the appropriate means for addressing the problem of children's advertising. The question is whether the government had a reasonable basis, on the evidence tendered, for concluding that the ban on all advertising directed at children impaired freedom of expression as little as possible given the government's pressing and substantial objective.
>
> . . . The Court also recognized that the government was afforded a margin of appreciation to form legitimate objectives based on somewhat inconclusive social science evidence.

Similarly, . . . the absence of proof of a causative link between hate propaganda and hatred of an identifiable group was discounted as a determinative factor in assessing the constitutionality of the hate literature provisions of the *Criminal Code.* Dickson C. J. stated:

> First, to predicate the limitation of free expression upon proof of actual hatred gives insufficient attention to the severe psychological trauma suffered by members of those identifiable groups targeted by hate propaganda. Second, it is clearly difficult to prove a causative link between a specific statement and hatred of an identifiable group.

McLachlin J. (dissenting) expressed it as follows:

> To view hate propaganda as "victimless" in the absence of any proof that it moved its listeners to hatred is to discount the wrenching impact it may have on members of the target group. . . . Moreover, it is simply not possible to assess [precisely] the effects that expression of a particular message will have on all those who are ultimately exposed to it.

The American approach on the necessity of a causal link between obscenity and harm to society was set out by Burger C. J. in *Paris Adult Theatre* . . . :

> Although there is no conclusive proof of a connection between antisocial behavior and obscene material, the legislature . . . could

quite reasonably determine that such a connection does or might exist. . . .

I am in agreement with Twaddle J. A. who expressed the view that Parliament was entitled to have a "reasoned apprehension of harm" resulting from the desensitization of individuals exposed to materials that depict violence, cruelty, and dehumanization in sexual relations.

Accordingly . . . there is a sufficiently rational link between the criminal sanction, which demonstrates our community's disapproval of the dissemination of materials that potentially victimize women and restricts the negative influence that such materials have on changes in attitudes and behaviour, . . .

———◇———

Minimal Impairment

In determining whether less intrusive legislation may be imagined, this Court stressed in the *Prostitution Reference* . . . that it is not necessary that the legislative scheme be the "perfect" scheme, but that it be appropriately tailored *in the context of the infringed right.* . . . Furthermore, in *Irwin Toy*, Dickson C. J., Lamer and Wilson J. J. stated:

> While evidence exists that other less intrusive options reflecting more modest objectives were available to the government, there is evidence establishing the necessity of a ban to meet the objectives the government had reasonably set. This Court will not, in the name of minimal impairment, take a restrictive approach to social science evidence and require legislatures to choose the least ambitious means to protect vulnerable groups. . . .

There are several factors that contribute to the finding that the provision minimally impairs the freedom which is infringed.

First, the impugned provision does not proscribe sexually explicit erotica without violence that is not degrading or dehumanizing. It is designed to catch material that creates a risk of harm to society. It might be suggested that proof of actual harm should be required. It is apparent from [that] above that it is sufficient . . . for Parliament to have a reasonable basis for concluding that harm will result and this requirement does not demand actual proof of harm.

Second, materials [with] scientific, artistic or literary merit are not captured by the provision. As discussed above, the Court must be generous in [applying] the "artistic defence." For example, in certain cases, materials such as photographs, prints, books and films that may undoubtedly be produced with some motive for economic profit may nonetheless claim the protection of the *Charter* insofar as their defining characteristic is . . . aesthetic expression and thus represent the artist's attempt at individual fulfillment. The existence of an accompanying economic motive does not of itself deprive a work of significance as an example of individual artistic or self-fulfillment.

Third, in considering whether the provision minimally impairs the freedom in question, it is legitimate for the Court to take into account Parliament's past abortive attempts to replace the definition with one that is more explicit. In *Irwin Toy,* our Court recognized that it is legitimate to [consider] the fact that earlier laws and proposed alternatives were thought to be less effective than the legislation [now] being challenged. The attempt to provide exhaustive instances of obscenity has been shown to be destined to fail. . . . [The] only practicable alternative is to strive toward a more abstract definition of obscenity that is contextually sensitive and responsive to progress in the knowledge and understanding of the phenomenon to which the legislation is directed. . . . [The] standard of "undue exploitation" is therefore appropriate. The intractable nature of the problem and the impossibility of precisely defining a notion that is inherently elusive makes the possibility of a more explicit provision remote. In this light, it is appropriate to question whether, and at what cost, greater legislative precision can be demanded.

Fourth, while the discussion in this appeal has been limited to the definition portion of s. 163, I would note that the impugned section . . . has been held by this Court not to extend its reach to the private use or viewing of obscene materials. *R. v. Rioux* . . . unanimously upheld the finding of the Quebec Court of Appeal that s. 163 . . . does not include the private viewing of obscene materials. Hall J. affirmed the finding of Pratte J.:

> . . . I would therefore say that showing obscene pictures to a friend or projecting an obscene film in one's own home is not in itself a crime nor is it enough to establish in-

tention of circulating them nor help to prove such an intention. . . .

This Court also cited with approval the words of Hyde J.:

> Before I am prepared to hold that private use of written matter or pictures within an individual's residence may constitute a criminal offence, I require a much more specific text of law than we are now dealing with. It would have been very simple for Parliament to have included the word "exhibit" in this section if it had wished to cover this situation. . . .

Accordingly, it is only the public distribution and exhibition of obscene materials which is in issue here.

Finally, I wish to address the arguments of the interveners, Canadian Civil Liberties Association and Manitoba Association for Rights and Liberties, that the objectives of this kind of legislation may be met by alternative, less intrusive measures. First, it is submitted that reasonable time, manner and place restrictions would be preferable to outright prohibition. I am of the view that this argument should be rejected. Once it has been established that the objective is the avoidance of harm caused by the degradation which many women feel as "victims" of the message of obscenity, and of the negative impact exposure to such material has on perceptions and attitudes towards women, it is untenable to argue that these harms could be avoided by placing restrictions on access to such material. Making the materials more difficult to obtain by increasing their cost and reducing their availability does not achieve the same objective. Once Parliament has reasonably concluded that certain acts are harmful to certain groups in society and to society in general, it would be inconsistent, if not hypocritical, to argue that such acts could be committed in more restrictive conditions. The harm sought to be avoided would remain the same in either case.

It is also submitted that there are more effective techniques to promote the objectives of Parliament. For example, if pornography is seen as encouraging violence against women, there are certain activities which discourage it—counselling rape victims to charge their assailants, provision of shelter and assistance for battered women, campaigns for laws against discrimination on the grounds of sex, education to increase the sensitivity of law enforcement agencies and other governmental authorities. In addition, it is submitted that education is an underused response.

It is noteworthy that many of the above suggested alternatives are in the form of *responses* to the harm engendered by negative attitudes against women. The role of the impugned provision is to control the dissemination of the very images that contribute to such attitudes. Moreover, it is true that there are additional measures which could alleviate the problem of violence against women. However, given the gravity of the harm, and the threat to the values at stake, I do not believe that the measure chosen by Parliament is equalled by the alternatives which have been suggested. Education, too, may offer a means of combating negative attitudes to women, just as it is currently used as a means of addressing other problems dealt with in the *Code*. However, there is no reason to rely on education alone. It should be emphasized that this is in no way intended to deny the value of other educational and counselling measures to deal with the roots and effects of negative attitudes. Rather, it is only to stress the arbitrariness and unacceptability of the claim that such measures represent the sole legitimate means of addressing the phenomenon. Serious social problems such as violence against women require multipronged approaches by government. Education and legislation are not alternatives but complements in addressing such problems. There is nothing in the *Charter* which requires Parliament to choose between such complementary measures.

Balance Between Effects of Limiting Measures and Legislative Objective

The final question to be answered in the proportionality test is whether the [law's] effects so severely trench on a protected right that the legislative objective is outweighed by the infringement. The infringement on freedom of expression is confined to a measure designed to prohibit the distribution of sexually explicit materials accompanied by violence and those without violence that are degrading or dehumanizing. As . . . already concluded, this kind of expression lies far from the core of the guarantee of freedom of expression. It appeals only to the most base aspect of individual fulfillment and is primarily economically motivated.

The objective of the legislation, on the other hand, is of fundamental importance in a free and democratic society. It is aimed at avoiding harm, which Parliament has reasonably concluded will be caused directly or indirectly, to individuals, groups such as women and children, and . . . to society as a whole, by the distribution of these materials. It thus seeks to enhance respect for all members of society, and nonviolence and equality in their relations with each other.

I therefore conclude that the restriction on freedom of expression does not outweigh the importance of the legislative objective.

Suggestions for Further Reading

Anthologies

Copp, David, and Susan Wendell. *Pornography and Censorship*. Buffalo: Prometheus Press, 1983.

Donnerstein, Edward, Daniel Linz, and Steven Penrod. *The Question of Pornography*. New York: Free Press, 1987.

Dwyer, Susan. *The Problem of Pornography*. Belmont: Wadsworth Publishing, 1995.

Wekesser, Carol. *Pornography: Opposing Viewpoints*. San Diego: Greenhaven Press, 1997.

Alternative Views

Dworkin, Andrea. *Pornography: Men Possessing Women*. New York: Perigee, 1981.

Griffin, Susan. *Pornography and Silence*. New York: Harper & Row, 1981.

Juffer, Jane. *At Home with Pornography*. New York: New York University Press, 1998.

Lovelace, Linda, with Mike McGrady. *Ordeal*. New York: Berkeley Books, 1980.

MacKinnon, Catharine. *Only Words*. Cambridge: Harvard University Press, 1993.

Soble, Alan. *Pornography.* New Haven: Yale University Press, 1986.

Practical Applications

Report of the Attorney General's Commission on Pornography. Washington, DC: Government Printing Office, 1986.

MacKinnon, Catharine, and Andrea Dworkin. *In Harm's Way: The Pornography Civil Rights Hearings.* Cambridge: Harvard University Press, 1998.

Section VIII
Hate Speech

Introduction

Basic Concepts

Hate speech is any form of expression that is racist, sexist, heterosexist, or otherwise denigrating and offensive to someone or some group of people. The moral problem of hate speech concerns whether such expression should be prohibited in whole or in part. In recent years, there has been an increase in the reported incidents of hate speech on college and university campuses across the United States. At the University of Michigan, racist leaflets were distributed in dorms, and white students painted themselves black and placed rings in their noses at "jungle parties." Also at Michigan, a student walked into a classroom and saw written on the blackboard: "A mind is a terrible thing to waste—especially on a nigger." At Purdue University, a counselor found "Death Nigger" scratched on her door. At Dartmouth College, a black professor was called "a cross between a welfare queen and a bathroom attendant" and the *Dartmouth Review* purported to quote a black student, "Dese boys be sayin' that we be comin' here to Dartmut an' not takin' the classics. . . ." At Brown University, an African student found a note under her door saying, "This room is for coloreds only." At the University of Wisconsin, white male students trailed African-American female students shouting, "I've never tried a nigger before." At Northwest Missouri State University, white supremacists distributed flyers stating, "The Knights of the Ku Klux Klan are Watching You." Responding to such incidents, colleges and universities across the country have taken steps to prohibit hate speech. At Stanford University, the following speech code was adopted:

(1) Stanford is committed to the principles of free inquiry and free expression. Students have the right to hold and vigorously defend and promote their opinions, thus entering them into the life of the University, there to flourish or wither according to their merits. Respect for this right requires that students tolerate even expression of opinions which they find abhorrent. Intimidation of students by other students in their exercise of this right, by violence or threat of violence, is therefore considered to be a violation of the Fundamental Standard.

(1) Stanford is also committed to principles of equal opportunity and nondiscrimination. Each student has the right to equal access to a Stanford education, without discrimination on the basis of sex, race, color, handicap, religion, sexual orientation, or national and ethnic origin. Harassment of students on the basis of any of these characteristics tends to create a hostile environment that makes access to education for those subjected to it

less than equal. Such discriminatory harassment is therefore considered to be a violation of the Fundamental Standard.

(3) This interpretation of the Fundamental Standard is intended to clarify the point at which protected free expression ends and prohibited discriminatory harassment begins. Prohibited harassment includes discriminatory intimidation by threats of violence, and also includes personal vilification of students on the basis of their sex, race, color, handicap, religion, sexual orientation, or national and ethnic origin.

(4) Speech or other expression constitutes harassment by vilification if it:
   (a) is intended to insult or stigmatize an individual or a small number of individuals on the basis of their sex, race, color, handicap, religion, sexual orientation, or national and ethnic origin; and
   (b) is addressed directly to the individual or individuals whom it insults or stigmatizes; and
   (c) makes use of "fighting" words or nonverbal symbols. In the context of discriminatory harassment, "fighting" words or nonverbal symbols are words, pictures, or symbols that, by virtue of their form, are commonly understood to convey direct and visceral hatred or contempt for human beings on the basis of their sex, race, color, handicap, religion, sexual orientation, and national and ethnic origin.

The Stanford speech code was more limited in scope than either the University of Michigan or the University of Wisconsin speech codes, both of which were declared unconstitutional in 1989 and 1991, respectively. But in 1995 the Stanford speech code was itself declared unconstitutional by Justice Peter Stone of the California Superior Court (see Selection 48). However, this hardly settles the matter from either a legal

or a moral perspective. From a legal perspective, the unwillingness of the U.S. judiciary to balance free speech concerns against concerns for equality or equal opportunity sets it apart from all other liberal democracies. So it may be that the U.S. legal system is out of touch here with its own liberal democratic traditions. And from a moral perspective, what is important is not what this or that court has decided with respect to prohibiting hate speech, but whether good moral arguments can be given for or against such a prohibition—hence, the importance of the readings in this section, which take up both the legal and moral arguments for and against prohibiting hate speech.

Alternative Views

In Selection 44, Gerald Gunther argues against Stanford's speech code and other similar university codes. He contends that university campuses should exhibit greater, not less, freedom of expression than prevails in society at large. He further argues that the "fighting words" exception to the First Amendment protection of freedom of speech is not broad enough to justify Stanford's speech code. In fact, some legal scholars have argued that the Supreme Court's fighting words exception has been so qualified over the years that it no longer restricts free speech at all.[1] In agreement with Gunther, Alan Dershowitz (Selection 45) argues that the use of speech codes may also turn out to be counterproductive and end up restricting the freedom of expression of those who now support the speech codes. Nadine Strossen points out that this frequently has been the case in the past. For example, the British Race Relations Act of 1965, which was supposed to restrict racist speech, was later used to prosecute black power leaders.[2]

In support of such codes, Charles Lawrence III (Selection 46) argues that the landmark *Brown v. Board of Education* Supreme Court decision disestablished racial desegregation by regulating speech as well as conduct. He further questions whether the Fourteenth Amendment's equal protection clause, on which the Brown decisions relied, prohibits only governmental and not private discrimination, and he illustrates the considerable harm racial hate speech can cause by its connection to continuing patterns of racism. By analogy with the Brown decisions, Lawrence concludes that Stanford's and other similar speech codes are justified. According to Lawrence, we cannot accept the Brown decisions as most people do and also reject limited speech codes like Stanford's.

In Selection 47, Katharine Bartlett and Jean O'Barr argue that the hate speech debate has tended to focus on the most visible forms of racism while ignoring other more subtle discriminatory practices that pervade college campuses. For example, Bartlett and O'Barr contrast the different standards of behavior that are appropriate for men and women students. Thus, for men but not for women, it is appropriate to pass gas, belch in public, spit loudly on the ground, consume particularly large quantities, and sit in undignified positions with legs apart. By contrast, it is appropriate for women to use submissive gestures such as inappropriate smiling when making a serious statement or asking a question, or averting their eyes, especially when dealing with men, and to laugh prettily and convincingly at the male behaviors that are inappropriate for women if they want to be one of the guys. Although these more subtle forms of discrimination are not as egregious as those in discussions of hate speech, Bartlett and O'Barr contend that they may play an even larger role in establishing the subordination of members of certain groups on college campuses.

Practical Applications

The issue before the Superior Court of California was whether Stanford University's Speech Code violated the First Amendment of the U.S. Constitution (Selection 48). Judge Stone found that it did, in fact, violate the First Amendment because it was overbroad and restricted speech beyond fighting words. In addition, Stone found the defendants' claim that they were proscribing conduct, not speech, to be without merit. The judge further found that although the First Amendment protection of speech does not, in general, apply to private institutions, it does in California because of a 1992 law called Leonard's Law. In arguing for the appropriateness of applying the First Amendment protection of speech at Stanford University, Stone contended that the university, with all its resources, should be able to fight hate speech with more speech of its own. Although it may be true that Stanford as a whole may have resources to fight hate speech, individual victims of hate speech may lack the necessary resources and so may be deprived of the chance to benefit from the educational opportunities at Stanford as long as hate speech is protected. In Selection 49, the ACLU proposes a course of action for reconciling free speech with equal opportunity.

Obviously, the moral problem of hate speech is connected to the other moral problems discussed in this anthology (see Sections VII, IX, and X) that address different aspects of the general question of how free people should be. So it should be helpful in determining your position on the problem of hate speech to see how it relates to acceptable solutions to these other moral problems.

Endnotes

1. Nadine Strossen, "Regulating Racist Speech: A Modest Proposal?" *Duke University Law Review* (1990), pp. 508–514.

2. Ibid., p. 556.

44. No Speech Code

GERALD GUNTHER

Gerald Gunther argues against Stanford's speech code and other similar university codes. He contends that university campuses should exhibit greater, not less, freedom of expression than prevails in society at large. He further argues that the "fighting words" exception to the First Amendment protection of freedom of speech is not broad enough to justify Stanford's speech code.

I am deeply troubled by current efforts—however well-intentioned—to place new limits on freedom of expression at this and other campuses. Such limits are not only incompatible with the mission and meaning of a university; they also send exactly the wrong message from academia to society as a whole. University campuses should exhibit greater, not less, freedom of expression than prevails in society at large.

Proponents of new limits argue that historic First Amendment rights must be balanced against "Stanford's commitment to the diversity of ideas and persons." Clearly, there is ample room and need for vigorous University action to combat racial and other discrimination. But curbing freedom of speech is the wrong way to do so. The proper answer to bad speech is usually more and better speech—not new laws, litigation, and repression.

Lest it be thought that I am insensitive to the pain imposed by expressions of racial or religious hatred, let me say that I have suffered that pain and empathize with others under similar verbal assault. My deep belief in the principles of the First Amendment arises in part from my own experiences.

I received my elementary education in a public school in a very small town in Nazi Germany. There I was subjected to vehement anti-Semitic remarks from my teacher, classmates and others—"Judensau," Jew pig, was far from the harshest. I can assure you that they hurt. More generally, I lived in a country where ideological orthodoxy reigned and where the opportunity for dissent was severely limited.

The lesson . . . drawn from my childhood in Nazi Germany and my happier adult life in this country is the need to walk the sometimes difficult path of denouncing the bigots' hateful ideas with all my power, yet at the same time challenging any community's attempt to suppress hateful ideas by force of law.

Obviously, given my own experience, I do *not* quarrel with the claim that words *can* do harm. But I firmly deny that a showing of harm suffices to deny First Amendment protection, and I insist on the elementary First Amendment principle that our Constitution usually protects even offensive, harmful expression.

That is why—at the risk of being thought callous or doctrinaire—I feel compelled to speak out against the attempt by some members of the Stanford community to enlarge the area of forbidden speech under the Fundamental Standard. Such proposals, in my view, seriously undervalue the First Amendment and far too readily endanger its precious content. Limitations on free expression beyond those established by law should be eschewed in an institution committed to diversity and the First Amendment.[1]

In explaining my position, I will avoid extensive legal arguments. Instead, I want to speak from the heart, on the basis of my own background and of my understanding of First Amendment Principles—principles supported by an even larger number of scholars and Supreme Court justices, especially since the days of the Warren Court.

Among the core principles is that any official effort to suppress expression must be viewed with the

Reprinted by permission of *Stanford Lawyer* and the author. Adapted from two letters to the chair of the Student Conduct Legislative Council, dated March 10 and May 1, 1989, and published in *Stanford University Campus Report* on March 15 and May 3, respectively.

greatest skepticism and suspicion. Only in very narrow, urgent circumstances should government or similar institutions be permitted to inhibit speech. True, there are certain categories of speech that may be prohibited; but the number and scope of these categories has steadily shrunk over the last fifty years. Face-to-face insults are one such category; incitement to immediate illegal action is another. But opinions expressed in debates and arguments about a wide range of political and social issues should not be suppressed simply because of disagreement with those views, with the content of the expression.

Similarly, speech should not and cannot be banned simply because it is "offensive" to substantial parts or a majority of a community. The refusal to suppress offensive speech is one of the most difficult obligations the free speech principle imposes upon all of us; yet it is also one of the First Amendment's greatest glories—indeed it is a central test of a community's commitment to free speech.

The Supreme Court's 1989 decision to allow flag-burning as a form of political protest, in *Texas v. Johnson,* warrants careful pondering by all those who continue to advocate campus restraints on "racist speech." As Justice Brennan's majority opinion in *Johnson* reminded, "If there is a bedrock principle underlying the First Amendment, it is that the Government may not prohibit the expression of an idea simply because society finds the idea itself offensive or disagreeable." In refusing to place flag-burning outside the First Amendment, moreover, the *Johnson* majority insisted (in words especially apt for the "racist speech" debate): "The First Amendment does not guarantee that other concepts virtually sacred to our Nation as a whole—such as the principle that discrimination on the basis of race is odious and destructive—will go unquestioned in the marketplace of ideas. We decline, therefore, to create for the flag an exception to the joust of principles protected by the First Amendment."

Campus proponents of restricting offensive speech are currently relying for justification on the Supreme Court's allegedly repeated reiteration that "fighting words" constitute an exception to the First Amendment. Such an exception has indeed been recognized in a number of lower court cases. However, there has only been *one* case in the history of the Supreme Court in which a majority of the Justices has ever found a statement to be a punishable resort to "fighting words." That was *Chaplinsky v. New Hampshire,* a nearly fifty-year-old case involving words that would very likely not be found punishable today.

More significant is what has happened in the nearly half-century since: Despite repeated appeals to the Supreme Court to recognize the applicability of the "fighting words" exception by affirming challenged convictions, the Court has in every instance refused. One must wonder about the strength of an exception that, while theoretically recognized, has for so long not been found apt in practice. Moreover, the proposed Stanford rules are *not* limited to face-to-face insults to an addressee, and thus go well beyond the traditional, albeit fragile, "fighting words" exception.

The phenomenon of racist and other offensive speech that Stanford now faces is not a new one in the history of the First Amendment. In recent decades, for example, well-meaning but in my view misguided majorities have sought to suppress not only racist speech but also antiwar and antidraft speech, civil rights demonstrators, the Nazis and the Ku Klux Klan, and left-wing groups.

Typically, it is people on the extremes of the political spectrum (including those who advocate overthrow of our constitutional system and those who would not protect their opponents' right to dissent were they the majority) who feel the brunt of repression and have found protection in the First Amendment; typically, it is well-meaning people in the majority who believe that their "community standards," their sensibilities, their sense of outrage, justify restraints.

Those in power in a community recurrently seek to repress speech they find abhorrent; and their efforts are understandable human impulses. Yet freedom of expression—and especially the protection of dissident speech, the most important function of the First Amendment—is an antimajoritarian principle. Is it too much to hope that, especially on a university campus, a majority can be persuaded of the value of freedom of expression and of the resultant need to curb our impulses to repress dissident views?

The principles to which I appeal are not new. They have been expressed, for example, by the most distinguished Supreme Court justices ever since the beginning of the Court's confrontations with First Amendment issues nearly seventy years ago. These principles are reflected in the words of so imperfect a First Amendment defender as Justice Oliver Wendell Holmes: "If there is any principle of the

Constitution that more imperatively calls for attachment than any other, it is the principle of free thought—not free thought for those who agree with us but freedom for the thought that we hate."

This is the principle most elaborately and eloquently addressed by Justice Louis D. Branders, who reminded us that the First Amendment rests on a belief "in the power of reason as applied through public discussion" and therefore bars "silence coerced by law—the argument of force in its worst form."

This theme, first articulated in dissents, has repeatedly been voiced in majority opinions in more recent decades. It underlies Justice Douglas's remark in striking down a conviction under a law banning speech that "stirs the public to anger": "A function of free speech [is] to invite dispute. . . . Speech is often provocative and challenging. That is why freedom of speech [is ordinarily] protected against censorship or punishment."

It also underlies Justice William J. Brennan's comment about our "profound national commitment to the principle that debate on public issues should be uninhibited, robust, and wide-open, and that it may well include vehement, caustic, and sometimes unpleasantly sharp attacks"—a comment he followed with a reminder that constitutional protection "does not turn upon the truth, popularity, or social utility of the ideas and beliefs which are offered."

These principles underlie as well the repeated insistence by Justice John Marshall Harlan, again in majority opinions, that the mere "inutility or immorality" of a message cannot justify its repression, and that the state may not punish because of "the underlying content of the message." Moreover, Justice Harlan, in one of the finest First Amendment opinions on the books, noted, in words that Stanford would ignore at its peril at this time:

"The constitutional right of free expression is powerful medicine in a society as diverse and populous as ours. To many, the immediate consequence of this freedom may often appear to be only verbal tumult, discord and even offensive utterance. These are, however, within established limits, in truth necessary side effects of the broader enduring values which the process of open debate permits us to achieve. That the air may at times seem filled with verbal cacophony is, in this sense, not a sign of weakness but of strength."

In this same passage, Justice Harlan warned that a power to ban speech merely because it is offensive is an "inherently boundless" notion, and added that "we think it is largely because the governmental officials cannot make principled distinctions in this area that the Constitution leaves the matters of taste and style so largely to the individual." The Justice made these comments while overturning the conviction of an antiwar protester for "offensive conduct." The defendant has worn, in a courthouse corridor, a jacket bearing the words "Fuck the Draft." It bears noting, in light of the ongoing campus debate, that Justice Harlan's majority opinion also warned that "we cannot indulge in the facile assumption that one can forbid particular words without also running the substantial risk of suppressing ideas in the process."

I restate these principles and repeat these words for reasons going far beyond the fact that they are familiar to me as a First Amendment scholar. I believe—in my heart as well as my mind—that these principles and ideals are not only established but right. I hope that the entire Stanford community will seriously reflect upon the risks to free expression, lest we weaken hard-won liberties at Stanford and, by example, in this nation.

◇

Endnote

1. These comments were directed at a proposal later withdrawn in the face of criticism to prohibit not only "personal abuse" but also "defamation of groups"—expression "that by accepted community standards pejoratively characterizes persons or groups on the basis of personal or cultural differences."

45. Speech Codes and Diversity

ALAN DERSHOWITZ

Alan Dershowitz argues that the use of speech codes may turn out to be counterproductive and end up restricting the freedom of expression of those who now support speech codes.

There is now a debate among pundits over whether the "political correctness" movement on college and university campuses constitutes a real threat to intellectual freedom or merely provides conservatives with a highly publicized opportunity to bash the left for the kind of intolerance of which the right has often been accused.

My own sense, as a civil libertarian whose views lean to the left, is that the "P.C." movement is dangerous and that it is also being exploited by hypocritical right wingers.

In addition to being intellectually stifling, the P.C. movement is often internally inconsistent. Among its most basic tenets are (1) the demand for greater "diversity" among students and faculty members; and (2) the need for "speech codes," so that racist, sexist, and homophobic ideas, attitudes, and language do not "offend" sensitive students.

Is it really possible that the bright, well-intentioned students (and faculty) who are pressing the "politically correct" agenda do not realize how inherently self-contradictory these two basic tenets really are? Can they be blind to the . . . reality that true diversity of viewpoints is incompatible with speech codes that limit certain diverse expressions and attitudes?

I wonder if most of those who are pressing for diversity really want it. What many on the extreme left seem to want is simply more of their own: more students and faculty who think like they do, vote like they do, and speak like they do. The last thing they want is a truly diverse campus community with views that are broadly reflective of the multiplicity of attitudes in the big, bad world outside of the ivory towers.

How many politically correct students are demanding—in the name of diversity—an increase in the number of Evangelical Christians, National Rifle Association members, and Right to Life advocates? Where is the call for more anticommunist refugees from the Soviet Union, [more] Afro-Americans who oppose race-specific quotas, and [more] women who are antifeminist?

Let's be honest: The demand for diversity is at least in part a cover for a political power grab by the left. Most of those who are recruited to provide politically correct diversity—Afro-Americans, women, gays—are thought to be supporters of the left. And historically, the left—like the right—has not been a bastion of diversity.

Now the left—certainly the extreme left that has been pushing hardest for political correctness—is behind the demands for speech codes. And if they were to get their way, these codes would not be limited to racist, sexist, or homophobic *epithets*. They would apply as well to politically incorrect *ideas* that are deemed offensive by those who would enforce the codes. Such ideas would include criticism of affirmative action programs, opposition to rape-shield laws, advocacy of the criminalization of homosexuality, and defense of pornography.

I have heard students argue that the expression of such ideas—both in and out of class, both by students and professors—contributes to an atmosphere of bigotry, harassment, and intolerance, and that it makes it difficult for them to learn.

The same students who insist that they be treated as adults when it comes to their sexuality, drinking, and school work beg to be treated like children when it comes to politics, speech, and controversy. They whine to Big Father and Mother—the president or provost of the university—to "protect" them from offensive speech, instead of themselves trying to combat it in the marketplace of ideas.

Reprinted by permission of *Harvard Law Record* and the author.

Does this movement for political correctness—this intolerance of verbal and intellectual diversity—really affect college and university students today? Or is it, as some argue, merely a passing fad, exaggerated by the political right and the media?

It has certainly given the political right—not known for its great tolerance of different ideas—a heyday. Many hypocrites of the right, who would gladly impose their own speech codes if *they* had the power to enforce *their* way, are selectively wrapping themselves in the same First Amendment they willingly trash when it serves their political interest to do so.

But hypocrisy aside—since there is more than enough on both sides—the media is not exaggerating the problem of political correctness. It is a seri-ous issue on college and university campuses. As a teacher, I can feel a palpable reluctance on the part of many students—particularly those with views in neither extreme and those who are anxious for peer acceptance—to experiment with unorthodox ideas, to make playful comments on serious subjects, to challenge politically correct views, and to disagree with minority, feminist, or gay perspectives.

I feel this problem quite personally, since I happen to agree—as a matter of substance—with most "politically correct" positions. But I am appalled at the intolerance of many who share my substantive views. And I worry about the impact of politically correct intolerance on the generation of leaders we are currently educating.

---

46. *Regulating Racist Speech on Campus*

CHARLES R. LAWRENCE III

In support of speech codes, Charles Lawrence argues that the landmark Brown v. Board of Education *Supreme Court decisions disestablished racial desegregation by regulating speech as well as conduct. He further questions whether the equal protection clause of the Fourteenth Amendment on which the Brown decisions relied prohibits only governmental and not private discrimination, and he illustrates the considerable harm racial hate speech can cause through its connection to continuing patterns of racism. By analogy with the Brown decisions, Lawrence concludes that Stanford's and other similar speech codes are justified.*

Racist incidents occur at the University of Michigan, University of Massachusetts–Amherst, University of Wisconsin, University of New Mexico, Columbia University, Wellesley College, Duke University, and University of California–Los Angeles. (*Ms.* Magazine, October 1987)

The campus ought to be the last place to legislate tampering with the edges of First Amendment protections.

University of Michigan:
"Greek Rites of Exclusion": Racist leaflets distributed in dorms; white students paint them-selves black and place rings in their noses at "jungle parties." (*The Nation*, July 1987)

Silencing a few creeps is no victory if the price is an abrogation of free speech. Remember, censorship *is an ugly word too.*

Northwest Missouri State University:
White Supremacists distribute flyers stating: "The Knights of the Ku Klux Klan are Watching You." (Klanwatch Intelligence Report No. 42, February 1988 [*Klanwatch*])

Kansas University:
KKK members speak. (*Klanwatch*)

Temple University:
White Student Union formed. (*Klanwatch*)

Reprinted by permission of *Duke University Law Review* and the author.

Stanford University:
Aryan Resistance literature distributed.
(*Klanwatch*)

Stockton State College (New Jersey):
Invisible Empire literature distributed.
(*Klanwatch*)

Memphis State University:
Bomb threats at Jewish Student Union.
(*Klanwatch*)

Arizona State University:
Shot fired at Hillel Foundation building.
(*Klanwatch*)

The harm that censors allege will result unless speech is forbidden rarely occurs.

Dartmouth College:
Black professor called "a cross between a welfare queen and a bathroom attendant" and the *Dartmouth Review* purported to quote a Black student, "Dese boys be sayin' that we be comin' here to Dartmut an' not takin' the classics." (*The Nation,* February 27, 1989)

Yes, speech is sometimes painful. Sometimes it is abusive. That is one of the prices of a free society.

Purdue University:
Counselor finds "Death Nigger" scratched on her door. (*The Nation,* February 27, 1989)

More speech, not less, is the proper cure for offensive speech.

Smith College:
African student finds message slipped under her door that reads, "African Nigger do you want some bananas? Go back to the Jungle." (*New York Times,* October 19, 1988)

Speech cannot be banned simply because it is offensive.

University of Michigan:
Campus radio station broadcasts a call from a student who "joked": "Who are the most famous black women in history? Aunt Jemima and Mother Fucker." (*The Nation,* February 27, 1989)

Those who don't like what they are hearing or seeing should try to change the atmosphere through education. That is what they will have to do in the real world after they graduate.

University of Michigan:
A student walks into class and sees this written on the blackboard: "A mind is a terrible thing to waste—especially on a nigger." (*Chicago Tribune,* April 23, 1989)

People of color, women, and gays and lesbians owe their vibrant political movements in large measure to their freedom to communicate. If speech can be banned because it offends someone, how long will it be before the messages of these groups are themselves found offensive?

Stanford University:
"President Donald Kennedy refused yesterday to consider amnesty for students who took over his office last week. . . . Kennedy insisted that the probe of violations of the Stanford behavior code go forward. The students [who were demanding more minority faculty and ethnic studies reforms] consider the prospect of disciplinary action unfair in view of Stanford's decision earlier this year not to punish two white students who defaced a poster of 19th century composer Ludwig von Beethoven to portray a stereotypical black face, then tacked it up in a predominantly black dormitory The two incidents differ sharply, Kennedy said. The poster was admittedly racially offensive. But its defacement probably was protected by constitutional freedoms. However, the office takeover was clearly a violation of Stanford's policy against campus disruption." (*San Francisco Chronicle,* May 25, 1989)

Now it's the left that is trying to restrict free speech. Though the political labels have shifted, the rationale is the same: Our adversaries are dangerous and therefore should not be allowed to speak.

In recent years, university campuses have seen a resurgence of racial violence and a corresponding rise in the incidence of verbal and symbolic assault and harassment to which Blacks and other traditionally subjugated groups are subjected. The events listed above were gathered from newspaper and magazine reports of racist incidents on campuses. The accompanying italicized statements criticizing proposals to regulate racism on campus were garnered from conversations, debates, and panel discussions at which I was present. Some were recorded verbatim and are exact quotes; others paraphrase the sentiment expressed. I have heard some version of each of these arguments many times over. These incidents are but a small sampling of the hate speech to which minorities are subjected on a daily basis on our nation's college campuses. There is a heated debate in the civil liberties community concerning the proper response to incidents of racist speech on campus. Strong disagreements have arisen between those individuals who believe that racist speech such as that described above should be regulated by the university or some public body and those individuals who believe that racist expression should be protected from all public regulation. At the center of the controversy is a tension between the constitutional values of free speech and equality. Like the debate over affirmative action in university admissions, this issue has divided old allies and revealed unrecognized or unacknowledged differences in the experience, perceptions, and values of members of long-standing alliances. It also has caused considerable soul searching by individuals with longtime commitments to both the cause of political expression and the cause of racial equality.

I write this chapter from within the cauldron of this controversy. I make no pretense of dispassion or objectivity, but I do claim a deep commitment to the values that motivate both sides of the debate. I have spent the better part of my life as a dissenter. As a high school student I was threatened with suspension for my refusal to participate in a civil defense drill, and I have been a conspicuous consumer of my First Amendment liberties ever since. I also have experienced the injury of the historical, ubiquitous, and continuous defamation of American racism. I grew up with Little Black Sambo and Amos and Andy, and I continue to receive racist tracts in the mail and shoved under my door. As I struggle with the tension between these constitutional values, I particularly appreciate the experience of both belonging and not belonging that gives to African Americans and other outsider groups a sense of duality. W. E. B. DuBois—scholar and founder of the National Association for the Advancement of Colored People (NAACP)—called the gift and burden inherent in the dual, conflicting heritage of all African Americans their "second-sight."[1]

The double consciousness of groups outside the ethnic mainstream is particularly apparent in the context of this controversy. Blacks know and value

the protection the First Amendment affords those of us who must rely on our voices to petition both government and our neighbors for redress of grievances. Our political tradition has looked to "the word,"[2] to the moral power of ideas, to change the system when neither the power of the vote nor that of the gun were available. This part of us has known the experience of belonging and recognizes our common and inseparable interest in preserving the right of free speech for all. But we also know the experience of the outsider. The framers excluded us from the protection of the First Amendment. The same Constitution that established rights for others endorsed a story that proclaimed our inferiority. It is a story that remains deeply ingrained in the American psyche. We see a different world than that seen by Americans who do not share this historical experience. We often hear racist speech when our white neighbors are not aware of its presence.

It is not my purpose to belittle or trivialize the importance of defending unpopular speech against the tyranny of the majority. There are very strong reasons for protecting even racist speech. Perhaps the most important reasons are that it reinforces our society's commitment to the value of tolerance, and that by shielding racist speech from government regulation, we are forced to combat it as a community. These reasons for protecting racist speech should not be set aside hastily, and I will not argue that we should be less vigilant in protecting the speech and associational rights of speakers with whom most of us would disagree.

But I am deeply concerned about the role that many civil libertarians have played, or the roles we have failed to play, in the continuing, real-life struggle through which we define the community in which we live. I fear that by framing the debate as we have—as one in which the liberty of free speech is in conflict with the elimination of racism—we have advanced the cause of racial oppression and placed the bigot on the moral high ground, fanning the rising flames of racism. Above all, I am troubled that we have not listened to the real victims, that we have shown so little empathy or understanding for their injury, and that we have abandoned those individuals whose race, gender, or sexual orientation provokes others to regard them as second-class citizens. These individuals' civil liberties are most directly at stake in the debate. In this [reading] I focus on racism. Although I will not address violent pornography and homophobic hate speech directly,

I will draw on the experience of women and gays as victims of hate speech where they operate as instructive analogues.

I have set two goals in constructing this [essay]. The first goal is limited and perhaps overly modest, but it is nonetheless extremely important: I will demonstrate that much of the argument for protecting racist speech is based on the distinction that many civil libertarians draw between direct, face-to-face racial insults, which they think deserve First Amendment protection, and all other fighting words, which they find unprotected by the First Amendment. I argue that the distinction is false, that it advances none of the purposes of the First Amendment, and that the time has come to put an end to the ringing rhetoric that condemns all efforts to regulate racist speech, even narrowly drafted provisions aimed at racist speech that results in direct, immediate, and substantial injury.

I also urge the regulation of racial epithets and vilification that do not involve face-to-face encounters—situations in which the victim is part of a captive audience and the injury is experienced by all members of a racial group who are forced to hear or see these words. In such cases, the insulting words are aimed at an entire group with the effect of causing significant harm to individual group members.

My second goal is more ambitious and more indeterminate. I propose several ways in which the traditional civil liberties position on free speech does not take into account important values expressed elsewhere in the Constitution. Further, I argue that even those values the First Amendment itself is intended to promote are frustrated by an interpretation that is acontextual and idealized, by presupposing a world characterized by equal opportunity and the absence of societally created and culturally ingrained racism.

Brown v. Board of Education: A Case About Regulating Racist Speech

The landmark case of *Brown v. Board of Education* is not one we normally think of as concerning speech. As read most narrowly, the case is about the rights of Black children to equal educational opportunity. But *Brown* can also be read more broadly to articulate a principle central to any substantive understanding of the equal protection clause, the foundation on which all antidiscrimination law rests. This is the principle of equal citizenship. Under that

principle, "Every individual is presumptively entitled to be treated by the organized society as a respected, responsible, and participating member."[3] The principle further requires the affirmative disestablishment of societal practices that treat people as members of an inferior or dependent caste, as unworthy to participate in the larger community. The holding in *Brown*—that racially segregated schools violate the equal protection clause—reflects the fact that segregation amounts to a demeaning, caste-creating practice. The prevention of stigma was at the core of the Supreme Court's unanimous decision in *Brown* that segregated public schools are inherently unequal. Observing that the segregation of Black pupils "generates a feeling of inferiority as to their status in the community,"[4] Chief Justice Earl Warren recognized what a majority of the Court had ignored almost sixty years earlier in *Plessy v. Ferguson*.[5] The social meaning of racial segregation in the United States is the designation of a superior and an inferior caste, and segregation proceeds "on the ground that colored citizens are . . . inferior and degraded."[6]

The key to this understanding of *Brown* is that the practice of segregation, the practice the Court held inherently unconstitutional, was *speech. Brown* held that segregation is unconstitutional not simply because the physical separation of Black and white children is bad or because resources were distributed unequally among Black and white schools. *Brown* held that segregated schools were unconstitutional primarily because of the *message* segregation conveys—the message that Black children are an untouchable caste, unfit to be educated with white children. Segregation serves its purpose by conveying an idea. It stamps a badge of inferiority upon Blacks, and this badge communicates a message to others in the community, as well as to Blacks wearing the badge, that is injurious to Blacks. Therefore, *Brown* may be read as regulating the content of racist speech. As a regulation of racist speech, the decision is an exception to the usual rule that regulation of speech content is presumed unconstitutional.

The Conduct/Speech Distinction

Some civil libertarians argue that my analysis of *Brown* conflates speech and conduct. They maintain that the segregation outlawed in *Brown* was discriminatory conduct, not speech, and the defamatory message conveyed by segregation simply was an incidental by-product of that conduct. This position is often stated as follows: "Of course segregation conveys a message, but this could be said of almost all conduct. To take an extreme example, a murderer conveys a message of hatred for his victim. But we would not argue that we cannot punish the murder—the primary conduct—merely because of this message, which is its secondary by-product."[7] The Court has been reluctant to concede that the First Amendment has any relevance whatsoever in examples like this one, because the law would not be directed at anything resembling speech or at the views expressed. In such a case the regulation of speech is truly incidental to the regulation of the conduct.

These same civil libertarians assert that I suggest that all conduct with an expressive component should be treated alike—namely, as unprotected speech. This reading of my position clearly misperceives the central point of my argument. I do not contend that *all* conduct with an expressive component should be treated as unprotected speech. To the contrary, my suggestion that *racist* conduct amounts to speech is premised upon a unique characteristic of racism—namely its reliance upon the defamatory message of white supremacy to achieve its injurious purpose. I have not ignored the distinction between the speech and conduct elements of segregation, although, as the constitutional scholar Lawrence Tribe explained, "Any particular course of conduct may be hung almost randomly on the 'speech' peg or the 'conduct' peg as one sees fit."[8] Rather, my analysis turns on that distinction; I ask the question of whether there is a purpose to outlawing segregation that is unrelated to its message and conclude that the answer is no.

If, for example, John W. Davis, counsel for the Board of Education of Topeka, Kansas, had been asked during oral argument in *Brown* to state the board's purpose in educating Black and white children in separate schools, he would have been hard pressed to answer in a way unrelated to the purpose of designating Black children as inferior. If segregation's primary goal is to convey the message of white supremacy, then *Brown's* declaration that segregation is unconstitutional amounts to a regulation of the message of white supremacy. Properly understood, *Brown* and its progeny require that the systematic group defamation of segregation be disestablished. Although the exclusion of Black children from white schools and the denial of educational resources and association that accompany exclusion can be characterized as conduct, these particular instances of conduct are concerned primarily with communicating the idea of white supremacy. The nonspeech elements are by-products of the main message rather than the message being simply a by-product of unlawful conduct.

The public accommodations provisions of the Civil Rights Act of 1964[9] illuminate why laws against discrimination also regulate racist speech. The legislative history and the Supreme Court's opinions upholding the act establish that Congress was concerned that Blacks have access to public accommodations to eliminate impediments to the free flow of interstate commerce, but this purpose could have been achieved through a regime of separate but equal accommodations. Title II of the Civil Rights Act goes farther; it incorporates the principle of the inherent inequality of segregation and prohibits restaurant owners from providing separate places at the lunch counter for "whites" and "coloreds." Even if the same food and the same service are provided, separate but equal facilities are unlawful. If the signs indicating separate facilities remain in place, then the statute is violated despite proof that restaurant patrons are free to disregard the signs. Outlawing these signs graphically illustrates my point that antidiscrimination laws are primarily regulations of the content of racist speech.

In the summer of 1966, Robert Cover and I were working as summer interns with C. B. King in Albany, Georgia. One day we stopped for lunch at a take-out chicken joint. The establishment was housed in a long diner-like structure with an awning extending from each of two doors in the side of the building. A sign was painted at the end of each awning. One said White, the other Colored. Bob and I entered the "white" side together, knowing we were not welcome to do so. When the proprietor took my order, I asked if he knew the signs on his awnings were illegal under Title II of the Civil Rights Act of 1964. He responded, "People can come in this place through any door they want to." What this story makes apparent is that the signs themselves violate the antidiscrimination principle even when the conduct of denial of access is not present.

Another way to understand the inseparability of racist speech and discriminatory conduct is to view individual racist acts as part of a totality. When viewed in this manner, white supremacists' conduct or speech is forbidden by the equal protection clause. The goal of white supremacy is not achieved by individual acts or even by the cumulative acts of a group, but rather it is achieved by the institutionalization of the ideas of white supremacy. The institutionalization of white supremacy within our culture has created conduct on the societal level that is greater than the sum of individual racist acts. The racist acts of millions of individuals are mutually reinforcing and cumulative because the status quo of institutionalized white supremacy remains long after deliberate racist actions subside.

Professor Kendall Thomas describes the way in which racism is simultaneously speech (a socially constructed meaning or idea) and conduct by asking us to consider the concept of "race" not as a noun but as a verb. He notes that race is a social construction. The meaning of "Black" or "white" is derived through a history of acted-upon ideology. Moreover, the cultural meaning of race is promulgated through millions of ongoing contemporaneous speech/acts. Thus, he says, "We are raced." The social construction of race is an ongoing process.[10]

It is difficult to recognize the institutional significance of white supremacy or how it *acts* to harm, partially because of its ubiquity. We simply do not see most racist conduct because we experience a world in which whites are supreme as simply "the world." Much racist conduct is considered unrelated to race or regarded as neutral because racist conduct maintains the status quo . . . of the world as we have known it. Catharine MacKinnon has observed that "To the extent that pornography succeeds in constructing social reality, it becomes invisible as harm." Thus, pornography "is more act-like than thought-like."[11] This truth about gender discrimination is equally true of racism.

Just because one can express the idea or message embodied by a practice such as white supremacy does not necessarily equate that practice with the idea. Slavery was an idea as well as a practice, but the Supreme Court recognized the inseparability of idea and practice in the institution of slavery when it held the enabling clause of the Thirteenth Amendment [gave] Congress . . . the power to pass "all laws necessary and proper for abolishing all badges and incidents of slavery in the United States."[12] This understanding also informs the regulation of speech/conduct in the public accommodations provisions of the Civil Rights Act of 1964 discussed above. When the racist restaurant or hotel owner puts a Whites Only sign in his window, his sign is more than speech. Putting up the sign is more than an act excluding Black patrons who see the sign. The sign is part of the larger practice of segregation and white supremacy that constructs and maintains a culture in which nonwhites are excluded from full citizenship. The inseparability of the idea and practice of racism is central to *Brown's* holding that segregation is inherently unconstitutional.

Racism is both 100 percent speech and 100 percent conduct. Discriminatory conduct is not racist unless it also conveys the message of white supremacy—unless it is interpreted within the culture to advance the structure and ideology of white supremacy. Likewise, all racist speech constructs the social reality that constrains the liberty of nonwhites because of their race. By limiting the life opportunities of others, this act of constructing meaning also makes racist speech conduct.

The Public/Private Distinction

There are critics who would contend that *Brown* is inapposite because the equal protection clause only restricts government behavior, while the First Amendment protects the speech of private persons. They say, "Of course we want to prevent the state from defaming Blacks, but we must continue to be vigilant about protecting speech rights, even of racist individuals, from the government. In both cases our concern must be protecting the individual from the unjust power of the state."

At first blush, this position seems persuasive, but its persuasiveness relies upon the mystifying properties of constitutional ideology. In particular, I refer to the state action doctrine. Roughly stated,

> The [state action] doctrine holds that although someone may have suffered harmful treatment of a kind that one might ordinarily describe as a deprivation of liberty or a denial of equal protection of the laws, that occurrence excites no constitutional concern unless the proximate active perpetrators of the harm include persons exercising the special authority or power of the government of a state.[13]

By restricting the Fourteenth Amendment's application to discrimination implicating the government, the state action rule immunizes private discriminators from constitutional scrutiny In so doing, it leaves untouched the largest part of the vast system of segregation in the United States. The *Civil Rights Cases*[14] in which this doctrine was firmly established stands as a monument preserving American racial discrimination. Although the origin of state action is textual, countervailing values of privacy, freedom of association, and free speech all have been used to justify the rule's exculpation of private racism.

For example, it is argued that a white family's decision to send its children to private school or to move to a racially exclusive suburb should be accorded respect in spite of the Fourteenth Amendment's requirement of nondiscrimination because these decisions are part of the right to individual familial autonomy. In this way, the state action rule's rather arbitrary limit on the scope of the antidiscrimination principle is transformed into a right of privacy—which is presented as the constitutional embodiment of an affirmative, neutral, and universally shared value. A new and positive image emerges—an image that has been abstracted from its original context.

In the abstract, the right to make decisions about how we will educate our children or with whom we will associate is an important value in American society. But when we decontextualize by viewing this privacy value in the abstract, we ignore the way it operates in the real world. We do not ask ourselves, for example, whether it is a value to which all people have equal access. And we do not inquire about who has the resources to send their children to private school or move to an exclusive suburb. The privacy value, when presented as an ideal, seems an appropriate limitation on racial justice because we naively believe that everyone has an equal stake in this value.

I do not mean to suggest that privacy or autonomy has no normative value; there is some point at which the balance ought to be struck in its favor *after full consideration of the inequities that might accompany that choice.* What is objectionable about the privacy language that I am discussing here is that it ignores inequities and assumes we all share equally in the value being promoted.

The Supreme Court's treatment of the abortion controversy provides the most striking example of the fact that the right of autonomous choice is not shared by rich and poor alike. In *Roe v. Wade,* the Court declared in no uncertain terms that the right of privacy "is broad enough to encompass a woman's decision whether or not to terminate her pregnancy."[15] Yet, in *Harris v. McRae,* the Court with equal

certainty asserted, "It simply does not follow that a woman's freedom of choice carries with it a constitutional entitlement to the financial resources to avail herself of the full range of protected choices."[16]

The argument that distinguishes private racist speech from the government speech outlawed by *Brown* suffers from the same decontextualizing ideology. If the government is involved in a joint venture with private contractors to engage in the business of defaming Blacks, should it be able to escape the constitutional mandate that makes that business illegal simply by handing over the copyright and the printing presses to its partners in crime? I think not. And yet this is the essence of the position that espouses First Amendment protection for those partners.

In an insightful article considering the constitutional implications of government regulation of pornography, legal scholar Frank Michelman observed that the idea of state action plays a crucial if unspoken role for judges and civil libertarians who favor an absolute rule against government regulation of private pornographic publications (or racist speech), even when that expression causes "effects fairly describable . . . as deprivations of liberty and denials of equal protection of the laws."[17] He noted that judges and civil libertarians would not balance the evils of private subversions of liberty and equal protection against the evils of government censorship because "the Constitution, through the state action doctrine, in effect tells them not to." Michelman suggests that [this] doctrine, by directing us to the text of the Fourteenth Amendment, diverts our attention from the underlying issue—whether we should balance the evils of private deprivations of liberty against the government deprivations of liberty that may arise out of state regulations designed to avert . . . private deprivations.

A person who responds to the argument that *Brown* mandates the abolition of racist speech by reciting the state action doctrine fails to consider that the alternative to regulating racist speech is infringement of the claims of Blacks to liberty and equal protection. The best way to constitutionally protect these competing interests is to balance them directly. To invoke the state action doctrine is to circumvent our value judgment as to how these competing interests should be balanced.

The deference usually given to the First Amendment values in this balance is justified using the argument that racist speech is unpopular speech, that like the speech of civil rights activists, pacifists, and religious and political dissenters, it is in need of special protection from majoritarian censorship. But for over three hundred years, racist speech has been the liturgy of the leading established religion of the United States, the religion of racism. Racist speech remains a vital and regrettably popular characteristic of the U.S. vernacular. It must be noted that there has not yet been satisfactory retraction of the government-sponsored defamation in the slavery clauses,[18] the *Dred Scott* decision,[19] the Black codes, the segregation statutes, and countless other group libels. The injury to Blacks is hardly redressed by deciding the government must no longer injure our reputation if one then invokes the First Amendment to ensure that racist speech continues to thrive in an unregulated private market.

Consider, for example, the case of *McLaurin v. Oklahoma State Regents*,[20] in which the University of Oklahoma graduate school, under order by a federal court to admit McLaurin, a Black student, designated a special seat, roped off from other seats, in each classroom, the library, and the cafeteria. The Supreme Court held that this arrangement was unconstitutional because McLaurin could not have had an equal opportunity to learn and participate if he was humiliated and symbolically stigmatized as an untouchable. Would it be any less injurious if all McLaurin's classmates had shown up at class wearing blackface? Should this symbolic speech be protected by the Constitution? Yet, according to a *Time* magazine report, in the fall of 1988 at the University of Wisconsin, "Members of the Zeta Beta Tau fraternity staged a mock slave auction, complete with some pledges in blackface."[21] More recently, at the same university, white male students trailed Black female students shouting, "I've never tried a nigger before."[22] These young women were no less severely injured than was McLaurin simply because the university did not directly sponsor their assault. If the university fails to protect them in their right to pursue their education free from this kind of degradation and humiliation, then surely there are constitutional values at stake.

It is a very sad irony that the first instinct of many civil libertarians is to express concern for possible infringement of the assailants' liberties while barely noticing the constitutional rights of the assailed. Shortly after *Brown*, many Southern communities tried to escape the mandate of desegregation by closing public schools and opening private

(white) academies. These attempts to avoid the Fourteenth Amendment through the privatization of discrimination consistently were invalidated by the courts. In essence, the Supreme Court held that the defamatory message of segregation would not be insulated from constitutional proscription simply because the speaker was a nongovernment entity.

The Supreme Court also has indicated that Congress may enact legislation regulating private racist speech. In upholding the public accommodations provisions of Title II of the Civil Rights Act of 1964 in *Heart of Atlanta Motel v. United States*,[23] the Court implicitly rejected the argument that the absence of state action meant that private discriminators were protected by First Amendment free speech and associational rights. Likewise in *Bob Jones University v. United States*,[24] the Court sustained the Internal Revenue Service decision to discontinue tax-exempt status for a college with a policy against interracial dating and marriage. The college framed its objection in terms of the free exercise of religion, arguing its policy was religiously motivated, but the Court found that the government had "a fundamental, overriding interest in eradicating racial discrimination in education" that "substantially outweighs whatever burden denial of tax benefits" placed on the college's exercise of its religious beliefs.[25] It is difficult to believe that the university would have fared any better under free speech analysis or if the policy had been merely a statement of principle rather than an enforceable disciplinary regulation. Regulation of private racist speech also has been held constitutional in the context of prohibition of race-designated advertisements for employees, home sales, and rentals.

Thus *Brown* and the antidiscrimination law it spawned provide precedent for my position that the content regulation of racist speech is not only permissible but may be required by the Constitution in certain circumstances. This precedent may not mean that we should advocate the government regulation of all racist speech, but it should give us pause in assuming absolutist positions about regulations aimed at the message or idea such speech conveys. If we understand *Brown*—the cornerstone of the civil rights movement and equal protection doctrine—correctly, and if we understand the necessity of disestablishing the system of signs and symbols that signal Blacks' inferiority, then we should not proclaim that all racist speech that stops short of physical violence must be defended.

Racist Speech as the Functional Equivalent of Fighting Words

Much recent debate over the efficacy of regulating racist speech has focused on the efforts by colleges and universities to respond to the burgeoning incidents of racial harassment on their campuses. At Stanford, where I teach, there has been considerable controversy over whether racist and other discriminatory verbal harassment should be regulated and what form any regulation should take. Proponents of regulation have been sensitive to the danger of inhibiting expression, and the current regulation (which was drafted by my colleague Tom Grey) manifests that sensitivity. It is drafted somewhat more narrowly than I would have preferred, leaving unregulated hate speech that occurs in settings where there is a captive audience, but I largely agree with this regulation's substance and approach. I include it here as one example of a regulation of racist speech that I would argue violates neither First Amendment precedent nor principle. The regulation reads as follows:

Fundamental Standard Interpretation: Free Expression and Discriminatory Harassment

1. Stanford is committed to the principles of free inquiry and free expression. Students have the right to hold and vigorously defend and promote their opinions, thus entering them into the life of the University, there to flourish or wither according to their merits. Respect for this right requires that students tolerate even expression of opinions that they find abhorrent. Intimidation of students by other students in their exercise of this right, by violence or threat of violence, is therefore considered . . . a violation of the Fundamental Standard.

2. Stanford is also committed to principles of equal opportunity and nondiscrimination. Each student has the right to equal access to a Stanford education, without discrimination on the basis of sex, race, color, handicap, religion, sexual orientation, or national and ethnic origin. Harassment of students on the basis of any of these characteristics tends to create a hostile environment that makes access to education for those subjected to it less than equal. Such discriminatory harassment is therefore considered to be a violation of the Fundamental Standard.

3. This interpretation of the Fundamental Standard is intended to clarify the point at which protected free expression ends and prohibited discriminatory harassment begins. Prohibited harassment includes discriminatory intimidation by threats of violence, and also includes personal vilification of students on the basis of their sex, race, color, handicap, religion, sexual orientation, or national and ethnic origin.

4. Speech or other expression constitutes harassment by vilification if it:
   a. is intended to insult or stigmatize an individual or a small number of individuals on the basis of their sex, race, color, handicap, religion, sexual orientation, or national and ethnic origin; and
   b. is addressed directly to the individual or individuals whom it insults or stigmatizes; and
   c. makes use of "fighting" words or nonverbal symbols.

   In the context of discriminatory harassment, "fighting" words or nonverbal symbols are words, pictures, or symbols that, by virtue of their form, are commonly understood to convey direct and visceral hatred or contempt for human beings on the basis of their sex, race, color, handicap, religion, sexual orientation, and national and ethnic origin.[26]

This regulation and others like it have been characterized in the press as the work of "thought police," but the rule does nothing more than prohibit intentional face-to-face insults, a form of speech that is unprotected by the First Amendment. When racist speech takes the form of face-to-face insults, catcalls, or other assaultive speech aimed at an individual or a small group of persons, then it falls within the "fighting words" exception to First Amendment protection. The Supreme Court has held that words that "by their very utterance inflict injury or tend to incite an immediate breach of the peace"[27] are not constitutionally protected.

Face-to-face racial insults, like fighting words, are undeserving of First Amendment protection for two reasons. The first reason is the immediacy of the injurious impact of racial insults. The experience of being called "nigger," "spic," "Jap," or "kike" is like receiving a slap in the face. The injury is instantaneous. There is neither an opportunity for intermediary reflection on the idea conveyed nor an opportunity for responsive speech. The harm to be avoided is both clear and present. The second reason that racial insults should not fall under protected speech relates to the purpose underlying the First Amendment. The purpose of the First Amendment is to foster the greatest amount of speech. Racial insults disserve that purpose. Assaultive racist speech functions as a preemptive strike. The racial invective is experienced as a blow, not a proffered idea, and once the blow is struck, it is unlikely that dialogue will follow. Racial insults are undeserving of First Amendment protection because the perpetrator's intention is not to discover truth or initiate dialogue, but to injure the victim.

The fighting words doctrine anticipates that the verbal slap in the face of insulting words will provoke a violent response, resulting in a breach of the peace. When racial insults are hurled at minorities, the response may be silence or flight rather than a fight, but the preemptive effect on further speech is the same. Women and minorities often report that they find themselves speechless in the face of discriminatory verbal attacks. This inability to respond is not the result of oversensitivity among these groups, as some individuals who oppose protective regulation have argued. Rather it is the product of several factors, all of which evidence the nonspeech character of the initial preemptive verbal assault. The first factor is that the visceral emotional response to personal attack precludes speech. Attack produces an instinctive, defensive psychological reaction. Fear, rage, shock, and flight all interfere with any reasoned response. Words like "nigger," "kike," and "faggot" produce physical symptoms that temporarily disable the victim, and the perpetrators often use these words with the intention of producing this effect. Many victims do not find words of response until well after the assault, when the cowardly assaulter has departed.

A second factor that distinguishes racial insults from protected speech is the preemptive nature of such insults—words of response to such verbal attacks may never be forthcoming because speech is usually an inadequate response. When one is personally attacked with words that denote one's subhuman status and untouchability, there is little, if anything, that can be said to redress either the emotional or reputational injury. This is particularly true when the message and meaning of the epithet resonates with beliefs widely held in society. This preservation of widespread beliefs is what makes the face-to-face racial attack more likely to preempt speech than other fighting words do. The racist name caller is accompanied by a cultural chorus of equally demeaning speech and symbols. Segregation and other forms of racist speech injure victims because of their dehumanizing and excluding message. Each individual message gains its power because of the cumulative and reinforcing effect of countless similar messages that are conveyed in a society where racism is ubiquitous.

The subordinated victims of fighting words also are silenced by their relatively powerless position in society. Because of the significance of power and position, the categorization of racial epithets as fighting words provides an inadequate paradigm; instead one must speak of their functional equivalent. The fighting words doctrine presupposes an encounter between two persons of relatively equal power who have been acculturated to respond to face-to-face insults with violence: The fighting words doctrine is a paradigm based on a white male point of view. It captures the "macho" quality of male discourse. It is accepted, justifiable, and even praiseworthy when "real men" respond to personal insult with violence. (Presidential candidate George Bush effectively emulated the most macho—and not coincidentally most violent—of movie stars, Clint Eastwood, when he repeatedly used the phrase, "Read my lips!" Any teenage boy will tell you the subtext of this message: "I've got nothing else to say about this and if you don't like what I'm saying we can step outside.") The fighting words doctrine's responsiveness to this male stance in the world and its blindness to the cultural experience of women is another example of how neutral principles of law reflect the values of those who are dominant.

Black men also are well aware of the double standard that our culture applies in responding to insult. Part of the culture of racial domination through violence—a culture of dominance manifested historically in thousands of lynchings in the South and more recently in the racial violence at Howard Beach and Bensonhurst—is the paradoxical expectation on the part of whites that Black males will accept insult from whites without protest, yet will become violent without provocation. These expectations combine two assumptions: First, that Blacks as a group—and especially Black men—are more violent; and second, that as inferior persons, Blacks have no right to feel insulted. One can imagine the response of universities if Black men started to respond to racist fighting words by beating up white students.

In most situations, minorities correctly perceive that a violent response to fighting words will result in a risk to their own life and limb. This risk forces targets to remain silent and submissive. This response is most obvious when women submit to sexually assaultive speech or when the racist name caller is in a more powerful position—the boss on the job or a member of a violent racist group. Certainly, we do not expect the Black woman crossing the Wisconsin campus to turn on her tormentors and pummel them. Less obvious, but just as significant, is the effect of pervasive racial and sexual violence and coercion on individual members of subordinated groups, who must learn the survival techniques of suppressing and disguising rage and anger at an early age.

One of my students, a white gay male, related an experience that is quite instructive in understanding the fighting words doctrine. In response to my request that students describe how they experienced the injury of racist speech, Michael told a story of being called "faggot" by a man on a subway. His description included all of the speech-inhibiting elements I have noted. . . . He found himself in a state of semishock, nauseous, dizzy, unable to muster the witty, sarcastic, articulate rejoinder he was accustomed to making. He was instantly aware of the recent spate of gay bashing in San Francisco and that many of these incidents had escalated from verbal encounters. Even hours later when the shock subsided and his facility with words returned, he realized that any response was inadequate to counter the hundreds of years of societal defamation that one word—*faggot*—carried with it. Like the word *nigger* and unlike the word *liar*, it is not sufficient to deny the truth of the word's application, to say, "I am not a faggot." One must deny the truth of the word's meaning, a meaning shouted from the rooftops by the rest of the world a million times a day. The complex response "Yes, I am a member of the group you despise and [I reject] the degraded meaning of the word you use. . . " is not effective in a subway encounter. Although many of us constantly and in myriad ways seek to counter the lie spoken in the meaning of hateful words like *nigger* and *faggot*, it is a nearly impossible burden to

bear when one is ambushed by a sudden, face-to-face hate speech assault.

But there was another part of my discussion with Michael that is equally instructive. I asked if he could remember a situation when he had been verbally attacked with reference to his being a white male. Had he ever been called a "honkey," a "chauvinist pig," or "mick"? (Michael is from a working-class Irish family in Boston.) He said that he had been called some version of all three and that although he found the last one more offensive than the first two, he had not experienced—even in that subordinated role—the same disorienting powerlessness he had experienced when attacked for his membership in the gay community. The question of power, of the context of the power relationships within which speech takes place, and the connection to violence must be considered as we decide how best to foster the freest and fullest dialogue within our communities. Regulation of face-to-face verbal assault in the manner contemplated by the proposed Stanford provision will make room for more speech than it chills. The provision is clearly within the spirit, if not the letter, of existing First Amendment doctrine.

The proposed Stanford regulation, and indeed regulations with considerably broader reach, can be justified as necessary to protect a captive audience from offensive or injurious speech. Courts have held that offensive speech may not be regulated in public forums such as streets and parks where listeners may avoid the speech by moving on or averting their eyes,[28] but the regulation of otherwise protected speech has been permitted when the speech invades the privacy of unwilling listeners' homes or when unwilling listeners cannot avoid the speech.[29] Racist posters, flyers, and graffiti in dorms, classrooms, bathrooms, and other common living spaces would fall within the reasoning of these cases. Minority students should not be required to remain in their rooms to avoid racial assault. Minimally, they should find a safe haven in their dorms and other common rooms that are a part of their daily routine. I would argue that the university's responsibility for ensuring these students receive an equal educational opportunity provides a compelling justification for regulations that ensure them safe passage in all common areas. Black, Latino, Asian, or Native American students should not have to risk being the target of racially assaulting speech every time they choose to walk across campus. The regulation of vilifying speech that cannot be anticipated or avoided would not preclude announced speeches and rallies where minorities and their allies would have an opportunity to organize counterdemonstrations or avoid the speech altogether.

Knowing the Injury and Striking the Balance: Understanding What Is at Stake in Racist Speech Cases

I argued in the last section that narrowly drafted regulations of racist speech that prohibit face-to-face vilification and protect captive audiences from verbal and written harassment can be defended within the confines of existing First Amendment doctrine. Here I argue that many civil libertarians who urge that the First Amendment prohibits any regulation of racist speech have given inadequate attention to the testimony of individuals who have experienced injury from such speech. These civil libertarians fail to comprehend both the nature and extent of the injury inflicted by racist speech. I further urge that understanding the injury requires reconsideration of the balance that must be struck between our concerns for racial equality and freedom of expression.

The arguments most commonly advanced against the regulation of racist speech go something like this: We recognize that minority groups suffer pain and injury as the result of racist speech, but we must allow this hate mongering for the benefit of society as a whole. Freedom of speech is the lifeblood of our democratic system. It is a freedom that enables us to persuade others to our point of view. Free speech is especially important for minorities because often it is the only vehicle for rallying support for redress of their grievances. Even though we do not wish anyone to be persuaded that racist lies are true, we cannot allow the public regulation of racist invective and vilification because any prohibition broad enough to prevent racist speech would catch in the same net forms of speech that are central to a democratic society.

Whenever we argue that racist epithets and vilification must be allowed, not because we would condone them ourselves but because of the potential danger the precedent of regulation would pose for the speech of all dissenters, we are balancing our concern for the free flow of ideas and the democratic process with our desire for equality. This kind of categorical balance is struck whenever we frame any rule—even an absolute rule. [We must] be conscious of the nature and extent of injury to both concerns when we engage in this kind of balancing. In this case, we must place on one side of the balance the nature and extent of the injury caused by racism. We must also consider whether the racist speech we propose to regulate is advancing or retarding the values of the First Amendment.

Understanding the Injury Inflicted by Racist Speech

There can be no meaningful discussion about how to reconcile our commitment to equality and our commitment to free speech until we acknowledge that racist speech inflicts real harm and that this harm is far from trivial. I should state that more strongly: To engage in a debate about the First Amendment and racist speech without a full understanding of the nature and extent of the harm of racist speech risks making the First Amendment an instrument of domination rather than a vehicle of liberation. Not everyone has known the experience of being victimized by racist, misogynist, or homophobic speech, and we do not share equally the burden of the societal harm it inflicts. Often we are too quick to say we have heard the victims' cries when we have not; we are too eager to assure ourselves we have experienced the same injury and therefore can make the constitutional balance without danger of mismeasurement. For many of us who have fought for the rights of oppressed minorities, it is difficult to accept that by underestimating the injury from racist speech we too might be implicated in the vicious words we would never utter. Until we have eradicated racism and sexism and no longer share in the fruits of those forms of domination, we cannot legitimately strike the balance without hearing the protest of those who are dominated. My plea is simply that we listen to the victims.

Members of my own family were involved in a recent incident at a private school in Wilmington, Delaware, that taught me much about both the nature of the injury racist speech inflicts and the lack of understanding many whites have of that injury.

A good Quaker school dedicated to a deep commitment to and loving concern for all the members of its community, Wilmington Friends School also became a haven for white families fleeing the court-ordered desegregation of the Wilmington public schools. In recent years, the school strove to meet its commitment to human equality by enrolling a small (but significant) group of minority students and hiring an even smaller number of Black faculty and staff. My sister Paula, a gifted, passionate, and dedicated teacher, was the principal of the lower school. Her sons attended the high school. My brother-in-law, John, teaches geology at the University of Delaware. He is a strong, quiet, loving man, and he is white. My sister's family had moved to Wilmington, shouldering the extra burdens and anxieties borne by an interracial family moving to a town where, not long ago, the defamatory message of segregation graced the doors of bathrooms and restaurants. Within a year they had made a place as well-loved and respected members of the community, particularly the school community, where Paula was viewed as a godsend and my nephews made many good friends.

In May of their second year in Wilmington, an incident occurred that shook the entire school community but was particularly painful to my sister's family and others who [were] the objects of hateful speech. In a letter to the school community explaining a decision to expel four students, the school's headmistress described the incident as follows:

On Sunday evening, May 1, four students in the senior class met by prearrangement to paint the soccer kickboard, a flat rectangular structure, approximately 8 ft. by 25 ft., standing in the midst of the Wilmington Friends School playing fields. They worked for approximately one hour under bright moonlight and then went home.

What confronted students and staff the following morning, depicted on the kickboard, were racist and anti-Semitic slogans and, most disturbing of all, threats of violent assault against one clearly identified member of the senior class. The slogans written on the kickboard included "Save the land, join the Klan," and "Down with Jews"; among the drawings were at least twelve hooded Ku Klux Klansmen, Nazi swastikas, and a burning cross. The most frightening and disturbing depictions, however, were those that threatened violence against one of our senior Black students. He was drawn, in a cartoon figure, identified by his name, and his initials, and by the name of his mother. Directly to the right of his head

was a bullet, and farther to the right was a gun with its barrel directed toward the head. Under the drawing of the student, three Ku Klux Klansmen were depicted, one of whom was saying that the student "dies." Next to the gun was a drawing of a burning cross under which was written "Kill the Tarbaby."[30]

When I visited my sister's family a few days after this incident, the injury they had suffered was evident. The wounds were fresh. My sister, a care giver by nature and vocation, was clearly in need of care. My nephews were quiet. Their faces betrayed the aftershock of a recently inflicted blow and a newly discovered vulnerability. I knew the pain and scars were no less enduring because the injury had not been physical. And when I talked to my sister, I realized the greatest part of her pain came not from the incident itself, but rather from the reaction of white parents who had come to the school in unprecedented numbers to protest the offending students' expulsion. "It was only a prank." "No one was physically attacked." "How can you punish these kids for mere words, mere drawings." Paula's pain was compounded by the failure of these people with whom she lived and worked to recognize that she had been hurt, to understand in even the most limited way the reality of her pain and that of her family.

Many people called the incident "isolated." But Black folks know that no racial incident is "isolated" in the United States. That is what makes the incidents so horrible, so scary. It is the knowledge that they are *not* the isolated unpopular speech of a dissident few that makes them so frightening. These incidents are manifestations of a ubiquitous and deeply ingrained cultural belief system, an American way of life. Too often in recent months, as I have debated this issue with friends and colleagues, I have heard people speak of the need to protect "offensive" speech. The word offensive is used as if we were speaking of a difference in taste, as if I should learn to be less sensitive to words that "offend" me. I cannot help but believe that those people who speak of offense—those who argue that this speech must go unchecked—do not understand the great difference between offense and injury. They have not known the injury my sister experienced, have not known the fear, vulnerability, and shame experienced by the Wisconsin students described at the beginning of this [reading]. There is a great difference between the offensiveness of words that you would rather not hear because they are labeled dirty, im-polite, or personally demeaning and the *injury* inflicted by words that remind the world that you are fair game for physical attack, that evoke in you all of the millions of cultural lessons regarding your inferiority that you have so painstakingly repressed, and that imprint upon you a badge of servitude and subservience for all the world to see. It is instructive that the chief proponents of restricting people who inflict these injuries are women and people of color, and there are few among these groups who take the absolutist position that any regulation of this speech is too much.

Again, *Brown v. Board of Education* is a useful case for our analysis. *Brown* is helpful because it articulates the nature of the injury inflicted by the racist message of segregation. When one considers the injuries identified in the *Brown* decision, it is clear that racist speech causes tangible injury, and it is the kind of injury for which the law commonly provides, and even requires, redress.

Psychic injury is no less an injury than being struck in the face, and it often is far more severe. *Brown* speaks directly to the psychic injury inflicted by racist speech in noting that the symbolic message of segregation affected "the hearts and minds" of Negro children "in a way unlikely ever to be undone."[31] Racial epithets and harassment often cause deep emotional scarring and feelings of anxiety and fear that pervade every aspect of a victim's life. Many victims of hate propaganda have experienced physiological and emotional symptoms, such as rapid pulse rate and difficulty in breathing.

A second injury identified in *Brown*, and present in my example, is reputational injury. As Professor Tribe has noted, "Libelous speech was long regarded as a form of personal assault . . . that government could vindicate . . . without running afoul of the constitution."[32] Although *New York Times v. Sullivan* and its progeny have subjected much defamatory speech to constitutional scrutiny—on the reasoning that "debate on public issues should be uninhibited, robust and wide-open"[33] and should not be "chilled" by the possibility of libel suits— these cases also demonstrate a concern for balancing the public's interest in being fully informed with the competing interest of defamed persons in vindicating their reputation.

The interest of defamed persons is even stronger in racial defamation cases than in the *Sulli-*

van line of cases. The *Sullivan* rule protects statements of fact that are later proven erroneous. But persons who defame a racial group with racial epithets and stereotyped caricatures are not concerned that they may have "guessed wrong" in attempting to ascertain the truth. The racial epithet is the expression of a widely held belief. It is invoked as an assault, not as a statement of fact that may be proven true or false. Moreover, if the *Sullivan* rule protects erroneous speech because of an ultimate concern for the discovery of truth, then the rule's application to racial epithets must be based on an acceptance of the possible "truth" of racism, a position that, happily, most First Amendment absolutists are reluctant to embrace. Furthermore, the rationale of *Sullivan* and its progeny is that public issues should be vigorously debated and that, as the Supreme Court held in *Gertz v. Robert Welch, Inc.,* there is "no such thing as a false idea."[34] But are racial insults ideas? Do they encourage wide-open debate?

Brown is a case about group defamation. The message of segregation was stigmatizing to Black children. To be labeled unfit to attend school with white children injured the reputation of Black children, thus foreclosing employment opportunities and the right to be regarded as respected members of the body politic. An extensive discussion on the constitutionality or efficacy of group libel laws is beyond the scope of this [reading], and it must suffice to note that although *Beauharnais v. Illinois,*[35] which upheld an Illinois group libel statute, has fallen into disfavor with some commentators, *Brown* remains an instructive case. By identifying the inseparability of discriminatory speech and action in the case of segregation, where the injury is inflicted by the meaning of the segregation, *Brown* limits the scope of *Sullivan. Brown* reflects the understanding that racism is a form of subordination that achieves its purposes through group defamation.

The third injury identified in *Brown* is the denial of equal educational opportunity. *Brown* recognized that even where segregated facilities are materially equal, Black children did not have an equal opportunity to learn and participate in the school community if they bore the additional burden of being subjected to the humiliation and psychic assault that accompanies the message of segregation. University students bear an analogous burden when they are forced to live and work in an environment where at any moment they may be subjected to denigrating verbal harassment and assault. The testimony of nonwhite students about the detrimental effect of racial harassment on their academic performance and social integration in the college community is overwhelming. A similar injury is recognized and addressed in the requirement of Title VII of the Civil Rights Act that employers maintain a nondiscriminatory, nonhostile work environment and in federal and state regulations prohibiting sexual harassment on campuses as well as in the workplace.

All three of these very tangible, continuing, and often irreparable forms of injury—psychic, reputational, and the denial of equal educational opportunity—must be recognized, accounted for, and balanced against the claim that a regulation aimed at the prevention of these injuries may lead to restrictions on important First Amendment liberties.

The Other Side of the Balance: Does the Suppression of Racial Epithets Weigh for or against Speech?

In striking a balance, we also must think about what we are weighing on the side of speech. Most Blacks—unlike many white civil libertarians—do not have faith in free speech as the most important vehicle for liberation. The First Amendment coexisted with slavery, and we still are not sure it will protect us to the same extent that it protects whites. It often is argued that minorities have benefited greatly from First Amendment protection and therefore should guard it jealously. We are aware that the struggle for racial equality has relied heavily on the persuasion of peaceful protest protected by the First Amendment, but experience also teaches us that our petitions often go unanswered until protests disrupt business as usual and require the self-interested attention of those persons in power.

Paradoxically, the disruption that renders protest speech effective usually causes it to be considered undeserving of First Amendment protection. Note the cruel irony in the news story cited at the beginning of this [essay] that describes the Stanford president's justification for prosecuting students engaged in a peaceful sit-in for violation of the university's Fundamental Standard: The protesting students were punished, but the racist behavior the students were protesting went unpunished. This lack of symmetry was justified on the grounds that punishment might violate the bigots' First Amendment rights—a particularly ironic result given Pro-

fessor Derrick Bell's observation that it was Black students' civil rights protests that underlay the precedents on which white students . . . established their First Amendment rights in school and university settings. As in so many other areas, a policy that Blacks paid the price for is used against them and on behalf of whites. Once one begins to doubt the existence of a symmetry between official reactions to racism and official reactions to protests against racism, the absolutist position loses credence: It becomes difficult . . . to believe that fighting to protect speech rights for racists will ensure our own speech rights. Our experience is that the American system of justice has never been symmetrical where race is concerned. No wonder we see equality as a precondition of free speech and place more weight on that side of the balance aimed at the removal of the badges and incidents of slavery that continue to flourish in our culture.

Blacks and other people of color are equally skeptical about the absolutist argument that even the most injurious speech must remain unregulated because in an unregulated marketplace of ideas the best ideas will rise to the top and gain acceptance. Our experience tells us the opposite. We have seen too many demagogues elected by appealing to U.S. racism. We have seen too many good, liberal politicians shy away from the issues that might brand them as too closely allied with us. The American marketplace of ideas was founded with the idea of the racial inferiority of nonwhites as one of its chief commodities, and ever since the market opened, racism has remained its most active item in trade.

But it is not just the prevalence and strength of the idea of racism that make the unregulated marketplace of ideas an untenable paradigm for those individuals who seek full and equal personhood for all. The real problem is that the idea of the racial inferiority of nonwhites infects, skews, and disables the operation of a market (like a computer virus, sick cattle, or diseased wheat). It trumps good ideas that contend with it in the market. It is an epidemic that distorts the marketplace of ideas and renders it dysfunctional.

Racism is irrational. Individuals do not embrace or reject racist beliefs as the result of reasoned deliberation. For the most part, we do not even recognize the myriad ways in which the racism that pervades our history and culture influences our beliefs. But racism is ubiquitous. We are all racists. Often we fail to see it because racism is so woven into our culture that it seems normal. In other words, most of our racism is unconscious. So it must have been with the middle-aged, white, male lawyer who thought he was complimenting a Mexican-American law student of mine who had applied for a job with his firm. "You speak very good English," he said. But she was a fourth-generation Californian, not the stereotypical poor immigrant he unconsciously imagined she must be.

The disruptive and disabling effect on the market of an idea that is ubiquitous and irrational, but seldom seen or acknowledged, should be apparent. If the community is considering competing ideas about providing food for children, shelter for the homeless, or abortions for pregnant women, and the choices made among the proposed solutions are influenced by the idea that some children, families, or women are less deserving of our sympathy because they are racially inferior, then the market is not functioning as either John Stuart Mill or Oliver Wendell Holmes envisioned it. In the term used by constitutional theorist John Ely, there is a "process defect."[36]

Professor Ely coined the term *process defect* in the context of developing a theory to identify instances in which legislative action should be subjected to heightened judicial scrutiny under the equal protection clause. Ely argued that the courts should interfere with the normal majoritarian political process when the defect of prejudice bars groups subject to widespread vilification from participation in the political process and causes governmental decision makers to misapprehend the costs and benefits of their actions. This same process defect that excludes vilified groups and misdirects the government operates in the marketplace of ideas. Mill's vision of truth emerging through competition in the marketplace of ideas relies on the ability of members of the body politic to recognize "truth" as serving their interest and to act on that recognition.[37] As such, this vision depends on the same process that James Madison referred to when he described his vision of a democracy in which the numerous minorities within society would form coalitions to create majorities with overlapping interests through pluralist wheeling and dealing.[38] Just as the defect of prejudice blinds white voters to interests that overlap with those of vilified minorities, it also blinds them to the "truth" of an idea or the efficacy of solutions associated with that vilified group. And just as prejudice causes governmental decision makers to misapprehend the costs and benefits of their actions, it also causes all of us to misapprehend the value of ideas in the market.

Prejudice that is unconscious or unacknowledged causes the most significant distortions in the market. When racism operates at a conscious level, opposing ideas may prevail in open competition for the rational or moral sensibilities of the market participant. But when individuals are unaware of their prejudice, neither reason nor moral persuasion will likely succeed.

Racist speech also distorts the marketplace of ideas by muting or devaluing the speech of Blacks and other despised minorities. Regardless of intrinsic value, their words and ideas become less salable in the marketplace of ideas. An idea that would be embraced by large numbers of individuals if it were offered by a white individual will be rejected or given less credence if its author belongs to a group demeaned and stigmatized by racist beliefs.

An obvious example of this type of devaluation is the Black political candidate whose ideas go unheard or are rejected by white voters, although voters would embrace the same ideas if they were championed by a white candidate. Once again, the experience of one of my gay students provides a paradigmatic example of how ideas are less acceptable when their authors are members of a group that has been victimized by hatred and vilification. Bob had not "come out" when he first came to law school. During his first year, when issues relating to heterosexism came up in class or in discussions with other students, he spoke to these issues as a sympathetic "straight" white male student. His arguments were listened to and taken seriously. In his second year, when he had come out and his classmates knew that he was gay, he found that he was not nearly as persuasive an advocate for his position as when he was identified as straight. He was the same person saying the same things, but his identity gave him less authority. Similarly, Catharine MacKinnon argues that pornography causes women to be taken less seriously as they enter the public arena.[39] Racial minorities have the same experiences on a daily basis as they endure the microaggression of having their words doubted, or misinterpreted, or assumed to be without evidentiary support, or when their insights are ignored and then appropriated by whites who are assumed to have been the original authority.

Finally, racist speech decreases the total amount of speech that reaches the market by coercively silencing members of those groups who are its targets. I noted earlier in this [reading] the ways in which racist speech is inextricably linked with racist conduct. The primary purpose and effect of the speech/conduct that constitutes white supremacy is the exclusion of nonwhites from full participation in the body politic. Sometimes the speech/conduct of racism is direct and obvious. When the Klan burns a cross on the lawn of a Black person who joined the NAACP or exercised the right to move to a formerly all-white neighborhood, the effect of this speech does not result from the persuasive power of an idea operating freely in the market. It is a threat; a threat made in the context of a history of lynchings, beatings, and economic reprisals that made good on earlier threats; a threat that silences a potential speaker. Such a threat may be difficult to recognize because the tie between the speech and the threatened act is unstated. The tie does not need to be explicit because the promised violence is systemic. The threat is effective because racially motivated violence is a well-known historical and contemporary reality. The threat may be even more effective than a phone call that takes responsibility for a terrorist bomb attack and promises another, a situation in which we easily recognize the inextricable link between the speech and the threatened act. The Black student who is subjected to racial epithets, like the Black person on whose lawn the Klan has burned a cross, is threatened and silenced by a credible connection between racist hate speech and racist violence. Certainly the recipients of hate speech may be uncommonly brave or foolhardy and ignore the system of violence in which this abusive speech is only a bit player. But it is more likely that we, as a community, will be denied the benefit of many of their thoughts and ideas.

Again MacKinnon's analysis of how First Amendment law misconstrues pornography is instructive. She notes that in concerning themselves only with government censorship, First Amendment absolutists fail to recognize that whole segments of the population are systematically silenced by powerful private actors. "As a result, [they] cannot grasp that the speech of some silences the speech of others in a way that is not simply a matter of competition for airtime."[40]

. . . We must embark upon the development of a First Amendment jurisprudence that is grounded in the reality of our history and contemporary experience, particularly the experiences of the victims of oppression. We must eschew abstractions of First Amendment theory that proceed without attention to the dysfunction in the marketplace of ideas created by racism and unequal access to that market.

We must think hard about how best to launch legal attacks against the most assaultive and indefensible forms of hate speech. Good lawyers can create exceptions and narrow interpretations limiting the harm of hate speech without opening the floodgates of censorship. We must weigh carefully and critically the competing constitutional values expressed in the First and Fourteenth Amendments.

A concrete step in this direction is the abandonment of overstated rhetorical and legal attacks on individuals who conscientiously seek to frame a public response to racism that preserves our First Amendment liberties. I have ventured a second step . . . by suggesting that the regulation of certain face-to-face racial vilification on university campuses may be justified under current First Amendment doctrine as an analogy to the protection of certain classes of captive audiences. Most important, we must continue this discussion—one in which victims of racist speech are heard. We must be as attentive to the achievement of the constitutional ideal of equality as we are to the ideal of untrammeled expression. There can be no true free speech where there are still masters and slaves.

◇

Epilogue

"Eeny, meeny, miney, mo."

It is recess time at the South Main Street School. It is 1952, and I am nine. Eddie Becker, Muck Makowski, John Thomas, Terry Flynn, Howie Martin, and I are standing in a circle, each with our right foot thrust forward. The toes of our black, high-top Keds sneakers touch, forming a tight hub of white rubber at the center, our skinny blue-jeaned legs extending like spokes from the hub. Heads bowed, we are intently watching Muck, who is hunkered down on one knee so that he can touch our toes as he calls out the rhyme. We are enthralled and entranced by the drama of this boyhood ritual, this customary pregame incantation. It is no less important than the game itself.

But my mind is not on the ritual. I have lost track of the count that will determine whose foot must be removed from the hub, who will no longer have a chance to be a captain in this game. I hardly feel Muck's index finger as it presses through the rubber to my toes. My mind is on the rhyme. I am the only Black boy in this circle of towheaded pre-pubescent males. Time stands still for me. My palms are sweaty and I feel a prickly heat at the back of my neck. I know that Muck will not say the word.

"Catch a tiger by the toe."

The heads stay down. No one looks at me. But I know that none of them is picturing the capture of a large striped animal. They are thinking of me, imagining my toe beneath the white rubber of my Keds sneaker—my toe attached to a large, dark, thick-lipped, burr-headed American fantasy/nightmare.

"If he hollers let him go."

Tigers don't holler. I wish I could right now.

My parents have told me to ignore this word that is ringing unuttered in my ears. "You must not allow those who speak it to make you feel small or ugly," they say. They are proud, Mississippi-bred Black professionals and longtime political activists; oft-wounded veterans of the war against the racist speech/conduct of Jim Crow and his many relations, they have, on countless occasions, answered the bad speech/conduct of racism with the good speech/conduct of their lives—representing the race; being smarter, cleaner, and more morally upright than white folk to prove that Black folk are equal, are fully human—refuting the lies of the cul-

tural myth that is American racism. "You must know that it is their smallness, their ugliness of which this word speaks," they say.

I am struggling to heed their words, to follow their example, but I feel powerless before this word and its minions. In a moment's time it has made me an other. In an instant it has rebuilt the wall between my friends' humanity and my own, the wall that I have so painstakingly disassembled.

I was good at games, not just a good athlete, but a strategist, a leader. I knew how to make my teammates feel good about themselves so that they played better. It just came naturally to me. I could choose up a team and make the members feel like family. When other folks felt good, I felt good too. Being good at games was the main tool I used to knock down the wall I'd found when I came to this white school in this white town. I looked forward to recess because that was when I could do the most damage to the wall. But now this rhyme, this word, had undone all my labors.

"Eeny, meeny, miney, mo."

I have no memory of who got to be captain that day or what game we played. I just wished Muck had used "One potato, two potato. . . ." We always used that at home.

Endnotes

1. W. E. B. DuBois, *The Souls of Black Folk,* 16–17 (1953).
2. V. Harding, *There Is a River,* 82 (1981).
3. Karst, "Citizenship, Race and Marginality," 30 *Wm. & Mary L. Rev 1,* 1 (1988).
4. 347 U.S. at 494.
5. 163 U.S. 537 (1896).
6. Id. at 560 (J. Harlan, dissenting).
7. See, e.g., Strossen, "Regulating Racist Speech on Campus: A Modest Proposal?" *Duke L. J.* 484 at 541–543 (1990).
8. L. Tribe, *American Constitutional Law* §12–7 at 827 (2d ed. 1988).
9. 42 U.S.C. §2000A (1982).
10. K. Thomas, comments at Frontiers of Legal Thought Conference, Duke Law School (Jan. 26, 1990).
11. C. MacKinnon, *Toward a Feminist Theory of the State,* 204 (1989).
12. *Jones v. Alfred H. Mayer Co.,* 392 U.S. 409, 439 (1968) (upholding Congress's use of the "badge of servitude" idea to justify federal legislation prohibiting racially discriminatory practices by private persons).

13. Michelman, "Conceptions of Democracy in American Constitutional Argument: The Case of Pornography Regulation," 56 *Tenn. L. Rev.* 291, 306 (1989).
14. 109 U.S. 3 (1883).
15. 410 U.S. 113 (1973).
16. 448 U.S. 297, 316 (1980).
17. See Michelman, *supra* note 14, at 306–307.
18. U.S. Const. Art. 1, §2, cl. 3 and §9, cl. 1; art. IV, §2, cl. 3.
19. *Dred Scott v. Sanford,* 60 U.S. (19 How.) 393 (1857).
20. 339 U.S. 637 (1950).
21. "A Step Toward Civility," *Time,* May 1, 1989, at 43.
22. Id.
23. *Heart of Atlanta Motel, Inc. v. United States,* 379 U.S. 241, 258 (1964); see also *Roberts v. United States Jaycees,* 468 U.S. 609, 624 (1984) (Court upheld the public accommodations provision of the Minnesota Human Rights Act).
24. 461 U.S. 574, 595 (1983).
25. 461 U.S. At 604.
26. Interpretation of the Fundamental Standard defining when verbal or nonverbal abuse violates the student conduct code adopted by the Stanford University Student

Conduct Legislative Council, March 14, 1990. "SCLC Offers Revised Reading of Standard," *Stanford Daily,* Apr. 4, 1990, §1, col. 4.

It is important to recognize that this regulation is not content-neutral. It prohibits "discriminatory harassment" rather than just plain harassment, and it regulates only discriminatory harassment based on "sex, race, color, handicap, religion, sexual orientation, and national and ethnic origin." It is arguably viewpoint neutral with respect to these categories, although its reference to "words . . . that, by virtue of their form, are commonly understood to convey direct and visceral hatred or contempt" probably means that there will be many more epithets that refer to subordinated groups than words that refer to superordinate groups covered by the regulation.

27. *Chaplinsky v. New Hampshire,* 315 U.S. 568, 572(1942).

28. See *Cohen v. California,* 403 U.S. 15, 21 (1971) (holding that the state could not excise, as offensive conduct, particular epithets from public discourse); *Erznoznik v. City of Jacksonville,* 433 U.S. 205, 209 (1975) (overturning a city ordinance that deterred drive-in theaters from showing movies containing nudity).

29. See *Kovacks v. Cooper,* 336 U.S. 77, 86 (1949) (right to free speech not abridged by city ordinance outlawing use of sound trucks on city streets); *Federal Communications Comm'n. v. Pacific Found.,* 438 U.S. 726, 748 (1978) (limited First Amendment protection of broadcasting that extends into privacy of home); *Rowan v. United States Post Office Dep't,* 397 U.S. 728, 736 (1790) (unwilling recipient of sexually arousing material had right to instruct Postmaster General to cease mailings to protect recipient from unwanted communication of "ideas").

30. Letter from Dulany O. Bennett to parents, alumni, and friends of the Wilmington Friends School (May 17, 1988).

31. 347 U.S. at 494.

32. L. Tribe, *supra* note 9, at 861.

33. 376 U.S. 254, 270.

34. 418 U.S. 323, 339 (1974).

35. 343 U.S. 250 (1952).

36. J. Ely, *Democracy and Distrust,* 103–104, 135–179 (1980).

37. J. S. Mill, *On Liberty,* ch. 2 (1859).

38. J. Madison, *The Federalist No. 51,* at 323–324 (C. Rossiter ed. 1961).

39. MacKinnon, "Not a Moral Issue," 2 *Yale L. & Pol'y Rev.* 321, 325–326, 335 (1984).

40. C. MacKinnon, *supra* note 12, at 206.

---

47. The Chilly Climate on College Campuses: An Expansion of the Hate Speech Debate

KATHARINE T. BARTLETT AND JEAN O'BARR

Katharine Bartlett and Jean O'Barr argue that the hate speech debate has focused on the most visible forms of racism while ignoring other, more subtle, discriminatory practices that pervade college campuses. Although these more subtle forms of discrimination are not as egregious as those usually focused on in discussions of hate speech, Bartlett and O'Barr contend that they may play an even larger role in establishing the subordination of members of certain groups on college campuses.

Reports of the kind of outrageous, blatantly racist, sexist, or heterosexist events which are the subject of the powerful debate about "hate speech" regulations[1] have become increasingly frequent in the late 1980s and early 1990s. Few colleges can claim to have remained free of such events, which include verbal assaults in various public and "private" settings, defacement of posters and walls with swastikas, nude caricatures, and "KKK" signatures, and other sorts of repeated harassment based on the sex, race, or sexual lifestyle of particular individuals or groups.

Reprinted by permission of *Duke University Law Review* and the authors.

In addition to these very visible incidents of blatant racial, sexual, and homophobic vilification, however, there are even more common, everyday types of behaviors that also disempower members of subordinated groups. These behaviors are so ordinary, so numerous, and so pervasive as to be taken almost entirely for granted by victims and victimizers alike. The hate speech debate focuses only on the most visible forms of racism and thus misses these more subtle discriminatory practices that pervade our current cultural milieu. In this comment, we show, through an exploration of sexism on college campuses, how the hate speech debate is incomplete, and how its terms may even stymie a full analysis of the wider range of subordinating behaviors that characterize racism, sexism, and heterosexism on college campuses in this country. Based upon this analysis, we argue in favor of branching out from a focus on the regulation of blatant forms of racist, sexist, and heterosexist harassment, toward a more multifaceted set of campus strategies.

Everyday Oppressions

In an effort to bring the everyday oppression of campus sexism into question, Roberta Hall and Bernice Sandler of the Project on the Status and Education of Women of the Association of American Colleges have catalogued more than thirty-five of these behaviors in two reports, *The Classroom Climate: A Chilly One for Women?* and *Out of the Classroom: A Chilly Campus Climate for Women?*[2] Examples of some of these behaviors convey a sense of how common and potentially devastating they are:

- When faculty members ask questions in class, "they mak[e] eye contact with men more often than with women, so that individual men students are more likely to feel recognized and encouraged to participate in class";[3]

- Faculty members use tones that communicate interest, and "assum[e] a posture of attentiveness (for example, leaning forward) when men speak," but a patronizing or impatient tone and inattentive posture (such as looking at the clock) when talking with women;[4]

- Faculty members call directly on men students more often than on women students, and are more likely to probe a male student's response to help the student work toward a fuller answer or explanation;[5]

- Faculty members call men students by name more often than women students, and credit comments and ideas to men but not to women;[6]

- Faculty members "wait longer for men than for women to answer a question before going on to another student," and are more likely to interrupt a woman student;[7]

- Faculty members "ask women students questions that require factual answers . . . while asking men ['higher order'] questions that demand personal evaluation and critical thinking";[8]

- Faculty members give longer and more complete responses to the questions of men students than to those of women students;[9]

- Faculty members "spontaneously offer to write letters of reference for men students but not for equally competent women students," and invite men, but not women, students to share authorships, accompany them on professional trips, and meet recognized scholars outside the department;[10]

- Female athletes' accomplishments go relatively unnoticed, as compared to men's sports, which are the focus of discussion and praise;[11]

- "Women are expected to perform stereotypically 'feminine' roles in conjunction with social events and cooperative housing arrangements—such as preparing food and cleaning up—while men make tapes, provide entertainment or do maintenance work";[12]

- Women are asked questions by faculty members, admissions staff and financial aid officers that question their seriousness of purpose, their need for educational credentials, and their actual or potential marital or parental status, that men are not asked.[13]

Not surprisingly, women minority students, older women students, lesbians, and disabled women are especially affected by these forms of behavior that devalue them both as women and as members of another outsider group. Moreover, the combination of sex and race, age, sexual preference, or disability may inspire additional forms of prejudice and subordination. Thus, for example, the silence of an African American woman may be perceived as "sullenness," whereas the silence of an Asian, Hispanic, or Native American woman may be perceived as "passivity."[14] Older women are viewed as bored, economically dependent spouses who have nothing better to do with their time and are often patronized by faculty members and other students.[15] Disabled women students are often overlooked, excluded, or dismissed; concepts are over-explained, or delivered in an overtly loud or patronizing tone.[16] Disabled women are presumed to be asexual beings, who do not date and who will never assume marital or family roles.[17]

The harm caused by these behaviors, like the harm caused by more blatant forms of sexist expression, is very real. Researchers on sex difference in language have identified patterns of women's speech that appear to correspond to the devaluation that women experience in relation to their male peers. Robin Lakoff was one of the first to identify a number of "hedges" common to women's speech that tend to convert declarative sentences into ambiguous, uncertain statements.[18] These hedges include hesitations and false starts ("I think . . . I was wondering. . . "); high pitch; "tag" questions ("This is really important, don't you think?"); a questioning intonation in making a statement; excessive use of qualifiers ("Don't you think that maybe sometimes . . . "); and other speech forms that are excessively polite and deferential ("This is probably not important, but . . .").[19] Women also tend to use more submissive gestures, such as inappropriate smiling when making a serious statement or asking a question, or averting their eyes, especially when dealing with men.[20]

These responses reflect the lower status and power that many women feel as a result of the behaviors described above.[21] They are also self-perpetuating, for they put women at a disadvantage in a classroom environment where assertion, clarity, and confidence are rewarded, and thus reinforce the attitudes of faculty and peers that women need not be taken seriously.[22]

The gendered nature of women's responses is apparent from the fact that they are more likely to be construed as signs of weakness or lack of proficiency than arguably analogous behaviors by men.

> For example, a woman student who "breaks down and cries" because of academic pressure is likely to be seen as "unstable," whereas a male student who, for the same reason, "goes out and gets drunk" is simply "blowing off steam." The man is welcomed back as "one of the guys," the woman—avoided—or advised to "get out of the kitchen if she can't take the heat."[23]

Other forms of sexism also take forms that are not widely understood as sexism. Take, for example, "red light district" (or "Bourbon Street") parties historically given by some fraternities at Duke University and elsewhere. Women attend the parties dressed as prostitutes in scanty clothing, allegedly to be "picked up" by men. These parties are understood as "just good, clean fun." They are sexy, provocative fantasies that release "normal" male energies "without harm." Everyone can have a good time. In fact, of course, such events eroticize the objectification of women. Women existing to serve men comes to stand for "good, clean fun." In such an example, injury based upon gender derives not from overt attacks and explicit messages of hate. Injury derives, instead, from eroticizing women's subordination to men. This process of definition implicates basic social patterns and explanatory frameworks—indeed, matters of fundamental identity for both women and men. For this reason, efforts by women's groups to eliminate these parties have been long, tedious, and contentious.

The difficulty of identifying, and communicating about, these issues can be seen in another Duke example. At a recent discussion in a dormitory unit, attended by women and men, the topic was acquaintance rape. The group asked a Women's Studies teacher to attend as a resource person. One of the men, whose previous comments indicated that he was sympathetic to changing the practices surrounding date rape at fraternity functions, offered this explanation for why such rapes occur. It is, he said, like driving home when you are drunk at 2 A.M. You come to a red light. You don't want anyone to think you're a softie, so you just go through it. All the guys do. The men and women listening to his account agreed with him—he had found a good image. Both the gendered nature of the image—woman/red light, hard/soft, the role of alcohol, the salience of peer pressure, ignoring established laws and conventions, the equating of woman and object, to name but a few—and its harmful implications, escaped all present. When cognitive systems about sexuality are operating in this way, getting outside them to expose their sexism—their inherent inequality—proves a formidable task.

Sexual harassment provides yet another set of examples. Although many campuses, in compliance with the law, now have student-faculty committees to hear sexual harassment cases, most committees are underutilized, in part because the victims of sexual harassment are conditioned to experience their harassment as "normal"—the way things are and will always be. Indeed, when a professor, or a graduate student in a position of authority, "comes on" to a female student or a female staff member or a female professor, she is supposed to be flattered. Her femininity is being affirmed; she is considered attractive by someone who counts. She is desirable. Such advances are dismissed, at worst, as trivial, something that women with a good sense of humor take in stride—certainly not a sign of deep sexism. The sexism, of course, is that the woman is affirmed only as an object of someone else's pleasure. She is expected to be pleased, grateful, and giving. The professional penalty for failing these expectations is sometimes high.

It is even more difficult to recognize the sexism of less overt forms of harassment. A recent classroom exercise in the introductory Women's Studies class at Duke enabled some students to do so. In this class, students were asked to commit gender role violations—to do something they considered inappropriate for themselves and then to analyze how they and their observers felt and explain why. Here are excerpts from a student report of violations and the reactions:

> I am on a varsity team, so I spend a considerable amount of time in and around the gym every day. I therefore come into contact with more sweaty guys than anyone could ever want to. One thing, or two things, actually, that I notice many of them seem to do, *very publicly*, is scratch their crotches and spit loudly on the ground. It never seems to bother them how many people are around, or if a passerby has to step out of their way to avoid

a stream of spit. Personally, I'm not very fond of these two common traits, but even if disgusting, what upsets me most is that they are perfectly acceptable behavior for athletic men, but not women.[24]

Most of my friends are men and while I adore them and appreciate my privileged status as one of the guys, I am often amazed and frequently disgusted by the activities I observe in their presence. Furthermore, I realize that I'm only one of the guys as long as I laugh (prettily and convincingly) at their antics, but should I repeat them myself, I immediately become a girl who has overstepped her bounds. Specifically, I am referring to that boundary between men's bodies, which make noises, have needs and drives, and women's bodies, which are not allowed any of these things. Of the many functions available, I chose those three that were either the most uncommon to women, the most offensive to me/uncomfortable for me to do, or the most obvious violation of gender roles: spitting, passing gas, and consuming particularly large quantities of food.[25]

Their shock and difficulty in dealing with my crudeness was expected, as not only were they disgusted, but I was as well. I was embarrassed and confused that I had so rudely followed my instinct and belched in public. My embarrassment stemmed from the values and manners which had been so deeply ingrained in my character. These values caused me to react by apologizing for my actions. However it was actually my apology which caused me to be confused. I could not understand why I was apologizing for something which guys praise one another for doing publicly.[26]

The particular gender norm that I violated seems to come from the fact that it is acceptable for men to do "whatever" they want. . . . [M]en are allowed the luxury of sitting in undignified positions, sitting with their legs apart, or slouched down, and cursing, and other like behavior, whereas women are not. Partially this must come from the fact that our society is ingrained with the idea that whatever men do is of course "right" or "correct."[27]

If a person can be made to control their own body by an external force (even if this external force acts through internal restraints) then has not this control actually been removed from the individual? Furthermore, this process of suppression has insidious implications for the position of women in our society, for once a person's body can be controlled, how difficult is it to prevent the expression of their mind, and then their social and political need?[28]

I've noticed that men tend to re-arrange themselves directly as an assertion of their superiority; in debates, when they cannot think of a good response (as if to say "yeah, but do you have one of these?") or in the midst of bragging (as if such an acknowledgement is corroborating evidence that his story is true).[29]

Formal definitions of harassment don't cover behaviors like these; it is hard to imagine how they could, without instituting a kind of Orwellian nightmare. It is *these ordinary, everyday* types of behaviors, however, that condition women to accept the limits placed on their social and cultural possibilities on an ordinary, everyday basis.

The Problem of Deniability

An important part of the problem we are describing is that the forms of more subtle, sexist degradation that women experience on college campuses are easily, and often, denied. This deniability is one very important reason why sexism remains an elusive target. There is a widespread belief that women in America—at least white women—have "made it." Sure, sexism used to exist, the story goes: Opportunities for women used to be limited, and there are still some old fogeys around who continue to think of women in old-fashioned, stereotypical ways. But the legal barriers have been removed, allowing full participation in society achieved by women. Equal rights have been won. Any failures that women now experience are failures of the individual, or private choices not to pursue one's full potential.[30] The institutions are clean.

The possibility exists, of course, that the very advances women have made in legal terms are countered culturally by a rise in misogyny at the individual level. In other words, the eradication of formal, visible, undesirable forms of sexism might cause a rise in the incidence and intensity of the informal, invisible, and deniable behaviors which undermine women's sense of self-value and women's opportunities.

Whether the incidence of everyday oppression is growing, the everyday behaviors we have discussed are easy to ignore. Because of their very ordinariness, these behaviors are less precise and more difficult to describe than the more extreme forms of abuse. In addition, these behaviors take enormously varied forms, which we are only now beginning to specify in any comprehensive way. They are subject to endless mutation; as one behavior is recognized as sexist, racist, or heterosexist, it may be suppressed, only to take a different, less recognizable form.[31] Moreover, these behaviors tend to be subtle and unconscious,[32] not openly hostile or mean-minded, and are sometimes [taken up] by members of the victimized groups themselves. For these reasons, even apart from whatever free speech issues might be implicated, few would argue that these behaviors can be the subject of effective, formal regulation. At most, critics argue that their identification and education about them can lead to self-regulation and eventual voluntary modification.

A focus on verbal and symbolic abuse has the unintended consequence of further reinforcing the invisibility of these everyday forms of oppression. First, by comparison, these behaviors seem so trivial, so harmless, so ordinary. How can white women, or blacks, complain of "insensitive," offhand classroom remarks or petty slights, in a world where skinheads shout "nigger" at a black man waiting to use a public telephone, or posters go up celebrating the massacre of Montreal feminists?

Second, this focus on regulation reinforces a conceptualization of racism, sexism, and heterosexism as blatant and intentional with specific perpetrators and specific victims. This conceptualization, while accurate with respect to some forms of verbal or symbolic assault, makes it more difficult to recognize and respond to the kind of racist, sexist, or heterosexist behaviors that are subtle, unknowing, and without a single clear perpetrator or intended victim. Where this conceptualization prevails, a remark which is not meant as insulting or derogating is seen as harmless, or worse, trivial.[33] The victim comes to be viewed as the problem. The question shifts from "How do we eradicate racist, sexist, and heterosexist behaviors?" to "Why do some people have to be so sensitive?"

A focus on blatant, intentional acts of verbal or symbolic abuse also enhances the likelihood that those holding such unconscious prejudices will respond with resentment and annoyance to calls to improve the campus atmosphere for members of subordinated groups.[34] The cry becomes: "We do not do *these awful things* at this university: We are civilized people. *I* certainly am not a racist; would not do these things. And I don't know anyone else who would. What's the big deal all about?"

In this way, everyday behaviors are legitimated by their separation from the more blatantly assaultive behaviors that have become the rallying point for regulatory action. Defining the readily definable—trading grades for sexual favors is sexual harassment; shouting "cunts" at a group of women protesting for greater campus security against rape demeans and defames women; and so on—leaves untouched, even sanitizes, the remaining activities.[35] As a result, the pervasive behaviors that devalue individuals based upon their race, sex, and sexual lifestyle implicitly are disassociated from more blatant behaviors, and the nonregulatory alternatives that might be effective against these multiple forms of oppression remain unexplored.

Many forms of regulation, of course, necessarily leave some set of undesirable practices untouched and thus, in some sense, affirmed. The effect of not regulating the overt behaviors condones *these* behaviors, as well as the covert ones.[36] One might argue that in this area, as in others, the best way to attack many problems is "one step at a time." Distinctions between what the law forbids and what it does not, however, usually turn on the extent of the harm caused. It seems at least plausible that subtle, everyday forms of sexist oppression on college campuses are every bit as harmful as those caused by more blatant forms of oppression.[37] Indeed, the invisibility of these everyday behaviors and these everyday harms may make them all the more insidious. For this reason, it is crucial that any attempt to eradicate the more blatant examples of racism, sexism, and heterosexism simultaneously combats the validation of the remainder.

If there is a silver lining to the blatant, egregious forms of hateful harassment, it is that they help to make the underlying forms of prejudice undeniable. Incidents directed specifically against women, although fewer in number, serve the same purpose with respect to sexism. The problem is that we are in danger of getting stuck on these more dramatic examples and thereby failing to deal with the more subtle, daily forms of oppression that may play an even larger role in establishing the subordi-

nation of members of certain groups on college campuses. Recognizing that the everyday may be as oppressive as the extraordinary is essential to any meaningful transformation of the campus climate.

How might colleges and universities stimulate awareness of all those behaviors that denigrate members of subordinated groups? The simple fact that we know less about the ordinary daily forms of discrimination means that we have fewer intellectual and political tools to bring to bear on the very discussion of them. Strategies, however, are urgently needed and these strategies must be sufficiently diverse that no one single variety of degrading practices is taken for the whole problem. To take just a few examples, many universities have widely disseminated the contents of the reports upon which we have relied heavily in this comment.[38] Others have designed workshops for faculty, administrators, and students to generate awareness of these issues.[39] At least two universities have used these materials as part of classroom curricula.[40] Still other universities have initiated their own research on the campus environment at their own institutions.[41]

One recent example of a productive campus program was a mock date rape trial staged at Duke University on April 12, 1990.[42] Date rape is one of those events which is "everyday," in comparison to the more dramatic and less common instances of stranger rape that occur on college campuses. Like other more common forms of sexual oppression, its boundaries are blurred, its harm unappreciated, and its dimensions misunderstood. At the mock trial, not only students but also college faculty and administrators played roles, lending support to the message that date rape is a problem to be taken seriously on campus. A local prosecutor and well-known defense attorney played the parts of counsel. A balanced script made it clear that date rape is a complicated phenomenon, with two points of view representing conflicting, and overlapping, social norms. The event was promoted by clever advertisements in the student newspaper, that sketched out chronologically the (all-too-familiar) alternative accounts of what led to the eventual charge of rape. After the trial—attended by over 250 students—the audience divided up into six groups to deliberate as juries about the guilt or innocence of the defendant. Such events, legitimized by the support and participation of well-placed university administrators and student groups, bring hidden everyday dilemmas involving sexual oppression out into the open, where they can be revealed, taken seriously, and debated in a setting which is both real and yet controlled. They not only educate the university population about a pervasive campus problem, but also inform many women that their concerns and perspectives are important to the university.

Most of all, universities must be pressed to throw their moral weight around. Since universities cannot be neutral, they must attend to how their actions affirm some perspectives as "regular" and marginalize others as "special."[43] Curricular reforms must reflect a commitment to diverse cultural and racial experiences. Universities must support student organizations and facilitate cultural events and other campus programs to help eliminate the alien environment in which many students find themselves. Moreover, university administrators should publicly identify and condemn specific, objectionable behaviors—those that are subtle and unintentional as well as blatant and egregious, and those that cannot be legally regulated as well as those that can. This public practice must be continual and ongoing, not sporadic or only in response to the most overt and repulsive events. Moreover, strategies for change must be sensitive to the range of individuals whose attitudes and behaviors require attention. Strategies that generate only guilt will impede constructive communication, as will strategies that generate backlash by those who feel no guilt.[44] We all are implicated by the racism, sexism, and homophobia in our universities. Only strategies that produce greater self-awareness by *all* members of the university community will enable climate changes conducive to genuine understanding between individuals whose diversity we are both required, and privileged, to respect.

Endnotes

1. See Charles Lawrence, "If He Hollers, Let Him Go: Regulating Racist Speech on Campus," 1990 *Duke L.J.* 431; Nadine Strossen, "Regulating Racist Speech: A Modest Proposal?" 1990 *Duke L.J.* 484; see also Mari J. Matsuda, "Public Response to Racist Speech: Considering the Victim's Story," 87 *Mich. L. Rev.* 2320 (1989).

2. See Roberta M. Hall and Bernice R. Sandler, "The Classroom Climate: A Chilly One for Women?" (Project on the Status and Education of Women 1982) [hereinafter R. Hall and B. Sandler, "Classroom Climate"]; Roberta M. Hall and Bernice R. Sandler, "Out of the Classroom: A Chilly Campus Climate for Women?" (Project on the Status and Education of Women 1984) [hereinafter R. Hall and B. Sandler, "Out of the Classroom"].

3. R. Hall and B. Sandler, "Classroom Climate," supra note 2, at 7. This, and other behaviors, have been documented even at women's colleges that have recently become co-educational. See Edward B. Fiske, "Lessons," *N.Y. Times,* Apr. 11, 1990, at B8, col. 1 (reporting experiences at Wheaton College).

4. R. Hall and B. Sandler, "Classroom Climate," supra note 2, at 7.

5. Id. at 8.

6. Id.

7. Id. at 8–9.

8. Id. at 9.

9. Id.

10. Id. at 11.

11. R. Hall and B. Sandler, "Out of the Classroom," supra note 2, at 10.

12. Id.

13. Id. at 6–7.

14. Id. at 12.

15. Id.

16. Id.

17. Id. at 13. By this criticism, we do not mean to endorse dating, or the assumption of marital or family roles, as the female norm. The point is, rather, that a particular norm is assumed with respect to disabled women that is restrictive for many of them.

18. Robin Lakoff, *Language and Woman's Place* 53 (1975). For a comprehensive, annotated bibliography of the wealth of research in this area, see Cheris Kramarae, Barrie Thorne, and Nancy Henley, "Sex Similarities and Differences in Language, Speech, and Nonverbal Communication: An Annotated Bibliography," in *Language, Gender, and Society* 151 (Barrie Thorne, Cheris Kramarae, and Nancy Henley eds. 1983).

19. R. Lakoff, supra note 18, at 53; see also R. Hall and B. Sandler, "Classroom Climate," supra note 2, at 9–10; John Conley, William O'Barr, and E. Allen Lind, "The Power of Language: Presentational Style in the Courtroom," 1978 *Duke L.J.* 1375, 1379–80 (poor and uneducated most likely to use speech that conveys a lack of forcefulness). For a riveting narrative illustrating the use of subordinate speech patterns by a welfare recipient client in an administrative hearing concerning charges of welfare fraud, see Lucie White, "Subordination, Rhetorical Survival Skills, and Sunday Shoes: Notes on the Hearing of Mrs. G.," 38 *Buffalo L. Rev.* 1, 21–32 (1990).

20. R. Hall and B. Sandler, "Classroom Climate," supra note 2, at 9–10.

21. William O'Barr and Bowman Atkins, "'Women's Language' or 'Powerless Language'?" in *Women and Language in Literature and Society* 93, 102–104 (Sally McConnell-Ginet, Ruth Borker, and Nelly Furman eds. 1980) (finding greater correlation between use of "women's language" and lower social status than with gender per se).

22. These values are perhaps most evident in law school classrooms, which are seen as the training ground for a profession in which assertiveness and confidence are critically important. A survey of 765 law students from five different law schools revealed that male students volunteer in class significantly more often than female students, that the rate of women's participation decreases over time while the rate of men's participation remains constant, and that women students feel more insecure than male students. See Taunya Lovell Banks, "Gender Bias in the Classroom," 38 *J Legal Educ.* 137, 141–142 (1988). A study of 667 Boalt Hall students, which corroborated these findings, also concluded that women law students with comparable entrance qualifications attained lower grades than their male peers, and had much lower self-esteem. See Suzanne Homer and Lois Schwartz, "Admitted but Not Accepted: Outsiders Take an Inside Look at Law School," 5 *Berkeley Women's L.J.* 1, 28–31, 33–34, 37–44 (1989–90). Virtually all of the work in this area has reached consistent conclusions. See Stephanie M. Wildman, "The Question of Silence: Techniques to Ensure Full Class Participation," 38 *J. Legal Educ.* 147 (1988); "Gender, Legal Education, and the Legal Profession: An Empirical Study of Stanford Law Students and Graduates," 40 *Stan. L. Rev.* 1209, 1239 (1988) (showing men law students at Stanford more likely than women to ask questions and volunteer answers in class); see also Catherine Weiss and Louise Melling, "The Legal Education of Twenty Women," 40 *Stan. L. Rev.* 1299, 1333–45 (1988) (describing experiences of twenty women law students at Yale Law School, including their disproportionate silencing in the classroom and their alienation from the classroom).

23. R. Hall and B. Sandler, "Out, of the Classroom," supra note 2, at 3.

24. Comment by Kerry Dolan.

25. Comment by Janice Jensen.

26. Name withheld upon request.

27. Comment by Kerry Dolan.

28. Comment by Janice Jensen.

29. Comment by Lucy Mochman.

30. Elinor Lenz and Barbara Myerhoff express this point of view in their best-seller, The *Feminization of America: How Women's Values Are Changing Our Public and Private Lives* 248–49 (1985) ("The process of feminization has shown us the way to achieve a balanced and humane society . . . [whether we achieve such a society] will be determined by our response to this unprecedented opportunity for individual and social change."). In a powerful critique

of this book, Catharine Hantzis both challenges the claim that gender justice is a completed agenda, and examines how the premature celebration of women's equality leads women to adapt to rather than resist their oppression. See Catharine Hantzis, "Is Gender Justice a Completed Agenda?" 100 *Harv. L. Rev.* 690 (1987).

31. This phenomenon is captured by what Richard Delgado, in the context of racism, calls the "Law of Racial Thermodynamics: Racism is neither created nor destroyed." Richard Delgado, "When a Story Is just a Story: Does Voice Really Matter?" 76 *Va. L. Rev.* 95, 106 (1990). Although this phenomenon, to the best of our knowledge, has not yet been scientifically documented, it rings true to many members of "outsider" groups, who find that the identification and suppression of one form of oppression leads to the emergence and growth of another.

32. Professor Lawrence, himself, has contributed some of the most sophisticated scholarship about the unconscious aspects of racism. See Charles Lawrence, "The Id, the Ego, and Equal Protection: Reckoning with Unconscious Racism," 39 *Stan. L. Rev.* 317 (1987); see also Lawrence, supra note 1, at 468–470. Regulation seems a particularly ineffective weapon against verbal and symbolic acts driven by unconscious hate and prejudice.

33. Darryl Brown in an excellent student note on racism in the university has demonstrated the extent to which this "perpetrator perspective" is reflected in the law of race discrimination. See Note, "Racism and Race Relations in the University," 76 *Va. L. Rev.* 295, 309 (1990). Brown argues that this perspective "conceptualizes racism as a discrete and specific act, an act committed by one individual, group, or institution against another whose injury can be identified," and thus "ignores the possibility that 'race' is structural and interstitial, that it can be the root of injury even when not traceable to a specific intention or action." Id. at 309–310.

34. See Id. at 310. Brown writes:.

> [A]n understanding of racism limited to the perpetrator perspective, helps to explain vocal resentment of whites to charges of racism and provides insight into allegations that the term "racism" has been so misused and overused that it has lost its meaning. When whites conceive of "racism" as requiring an intentional racist motive for which they deserve personal blame for a personal fault, they get angry because they know they had no racist intent. They plead that they were misunderstood, or that blacks are "oversensitive."

Id. at 310–311 (footnote omitted). The following line in a Letter to the Editor of the Duke student newspaper illustrates this infuriated (and infuriating) attitude: "I am sick of a bunch of whining women who place blame for social evils on the nearest scapegoat, and I am tired of these women pointing their fingers at me and all other males." Tony Leung, "Don't Assign Blame for Rape So Quickly," *Chronicle*, Mar. 28, 1990, at 8, col. 3–4.

35. A similar criticism has been made by feminists in relation to pornography and rape. See e.g., Catharine A. MacKinnon, *Feminism Unmodified: Discourses on Life and Law* 162 (1987) (in carving out and prohibiting a limited number of types of pornography, obscenity law authorizes and legitimizes the rest); Katharine T. Bartlett, "Porno-Symbolism: A Response to Professor McConahay," *Law and Contemp. Probs.*, Winter 1988, at 71, 73 (by "rendering unacceptable the most extreme forms of pornography, [society] legitimizes the remainder"); Frances Olsen, "Statutory Rape: A Feminist Critique of Rights Analysis," 63 *Tex. L. Rev.* 387, 427 (1984) ("Censuring the most blatant and oppressive manifestations of sexual aggression may make its more subtle, everyday forms actually seem more acceptable.")

36. We thank Professor Tom Grey for this point.

37. See Note, supra note 33, at 323.

38. See "Selected Activities Using 'The Classroom Climate: A Chilly One for Women?'" (Project on the Status and Education of Women 1984) (reporting dissemination strategies at the University of Delaware, Michigan State University, Pennsylvania State University, California State University at Northridge, Harvard University, and Rutgers University).

39. Id. at 2–3 (describing programs and workshops at the University of Maine at Orono, Bangor Community College, American University, Northeastern Illinois University, and the University of Nebraska, Lincoln).

40. The University of Texas at El Paso, for example, used "The Classroom Climate," supra note 2, in an upper division course, "Women, Power and Politics," both to sensitize students to campus climate issues and to teach research [methods and] design." Id. at 3. At Denison University, these materials were used to generate discussion and paper assignments based upon the student's own experiences. Id.

41. These universities include Bowling Green State University, the University of Delaware, Rhode Island College, Massachusetts Institute of Technology, and the University of Maryland. Id. at 3–4.

42. The mock trial was based upon an original play written by Rebecca Patton, Duke Law School Class of 1991, and presented by the Duke Rape and Sexual Assault Task Force and the Interfraternity Council.

43. See Lawrence, supra note 1, at 473–475.

44. Darryl Brown makes this point specifically with respect to strategies toward ending campus racism. Note, supra note 33, at 333–334.

---

48. *Corry v. Stanford University*

THE SUPERIOR COURT OF CALIFORNIA

The issue before the Superior Court of California was whether Stanford University's speech code violated the First Amendment of the U.S. Constitution. Judge Stone found that it did, in fact, violate the First Amendment because it was overbroad and restricted speech beyond "fighting words." In addition, Judge Stone found the defendants' claim that they were proscribing conduct, not speech, to be without merit. The judge further found that although the First Amendment protection of speech does not, in general, apply to private institutions, it does in California because of a law passed in 1992.

To summarize the parties' arguments, defendants in this case maintain that the type of speech that the speech code proscribes is not protected under the Constitution. Defendants argue that the speech code only proscribes "fighting words," which are constitutionally permissible under the case of *Chaplinsky v. New Hampshire* (1942).

Plaintiffs, on the other hand, maintain that this speech code is a violation of their First Amendment rights to free speech under the U.S. Constitution. Relying on the case of *R.A.V. v. City of St. Paul* (1992), plaintiffs argue that defendants' speech code seeks to prohibit speech on the basis of its content and therefore is constitutionally impermissible.

It must be noted, however, that the "First and Fourteenth Amendments safeguard the rights of free speech and assembly by limitations on state action, not on action by the owner of private property . . ."

The protections of the First Amendment prevent abridgment of speech by state actors only. In this case, however, defendants are private parties. The Supreme Court has declined to characterize private universities as state actors even though the "universities were publicly funded, publicly regulated, and performed a public function, and even though other nexus existed between the state and the university." Accordingly, defendants argue that since they are private parties, the First Amendment protects their speech rights, and does not prohibit them from doing anything at all.

In response, however, plaintiffs maintain that California Education Code §94367 (hereinafter, "the Leonard Law") allows a private university student to have the same right to exercise his or her right to free speech on campus as he or she enjoys off campus. This code section specifically allows a private student to commence a civil action for any violations thereof. It is plaintiffs' position that this code section enables them to take action against defendants' speech code, despite the fact that Stanford is a private party.

However, defendants maintain that even if the speech code infringes upon plaintiffs' protected speech off campus, the Leonard Law's command that Stanford must tolerate such speech on its campus would violate Stanford's First Amendment right to be free of State regulation with respect to its speech. Accordingly, it is defendants' position that the Leonard Law would be unconstitutional as applied to defendants' speech code in a number of ways.

In summarizing the parties' arguments, therefore, a two-part analysis is necessary for a proper determination of this motion. The first issue involves the constitutionality of defendants' speech code. The Court must first decide whether the speech code abridges speech which the U.S. Constitution seeks to protect outside of campus. If the answer is "no," then the analysis ends and plaintiffs' motion for a preliminary injunction should be denied. On the other hand, if it is determined that the speech code is unconstitutional, then the second step of the analysis must be discussed: the constitutionality of the Leonard Law. This Court must then decide whether this code section violates defendants' constitutional rights. If so, then this code section would be unconstitutional and inapplicable to the defendants. If, on the other hand, the Court finds that the code section is constitutional and ap-

plicable to the defendants, then this section would give the Court access to Stanford even though it is a private party and plaintiffs' motion for a preliminary injunction should be granted.

This Court will address the two-part analysis separately below.

I. The Constitutionality of Defendants' Speech Code

A. Constitutionality under Chaplinsky and Later Line of Cases

Defendants argue that the speech code proscribes only gutter epithets that are fighting words, and that under *Chaplinsky v. New Hampshire* (1942) such words are not subject to constitutional protection. In *Chaplinsky*, the Supreme Court upheld a conviction under New Hampshire speech statute which prohibited offensive or annoying words on public streets. The Court, basing its decision on the state court's narrow interpretation of the statute, held that "fighting words," those words "which by their very utterance inflict injury or tend to incite an immediate breach of the peace," did not enjoy First Amendment protection.

The court reasoned that the statute had been appropriately applied to Mr. Chaplinsky, who had called a city official a "God-damned racketeer" and a "damned Fascist," since his words would have "likely provoked the average person to retaliate, and thereby cause a breach of the peace." In this case, defendants argue that their speech code comports with the standard set forth in *Chaplinsky*, since the speech code explicitly sets out the fighting words test in its regulations.

Defendants further argue that this speech code is "meant to insure that no idea as such is proscribed, and accordingly it does not prohibit the expression of any view, however racist, sexist, homophobic, or blasphemous in content." Rather, defendants state that the speech code "draws the line at fighting words. . . ." Such an argument is persuasive since vilifying a student with racial epithets, for example, would clearly have the effect of likely provoking the average person to retaliate and of inflicting injury by their very utterance. If phrases such as "God damned racketeer" and "damned Fascist" are "no essential part of any exposition of ideas . . .," then certainly words which the defendants seek to proscribe (such as "damned nigger," etc.) should not enjoy constitutional protection.

Plaintiffs' gravamen, however, does not lie with any desire to vilify another student with "gutter epithets." Instead, it appears that plaintiffs' complaint rests on the argument that defendants' speech code, as drawn, goes beyond fighting words and, in effect, proscribes the expression of particular ideas and constitutionally protected speech. Plaintiffs partly base this claim on the rationale that the *Chaplinsky* holding has now been significantly narrowed to apply to only fighting words whose "utterance is likely to lead to immediate violence." Such a claim, if valid, would undermine the constitutionality of the speech code since, as plaintiffs argue, it prohibits "insults" and "offensive speech," not just "words that make people fight."

Plaintiffs' argument has merit. A review of authority reveals that there has been an apparent narrowing of the *Chaplinsky* doctrine. For example, in *Terminiello v. Chicago* (1949), the Supreme Court reversed petitioner's conviction under a breach of the peace ordinance which the trial court had interpreted to include speech which "stirs the public anger [or] invites dispute," as well as speech which creates a disturbance. Although the petitioner's criticism of political and racial groups had caused several disturbances among spectators, the court found that such words, "unless shown likely to produce a clear and present danger of serious substantive evil that rises far above public inconvenience, annoyance, or unrest," could not be proscribed.

In *Terminiello*, the Supreme Court reasoned that speech which "stirs the audience to anger" or "invites dispute" is protected under the First Amendment.

Additionally, in the case of *Gooding v. Wilson* (1972), the Supreme Court reversed petitioner's conviction under a Georgia abusive language statute after he had threatened and insulted two police officers. The Supreme Court found that even though the statute regulated only language which inflicts injury or affects the "sensibilities" of the hearer, it did not meet the requirements of the fighting words doctrine because it was not limited to words that "tend to cause an immediate breach of the peace." The Court found the statute was not limited to words that would have a direct tendency to cause acts of violence by the person to whom, individually, the remark was addressed.

Thereafter, in *Lewis v. City of New Orleans* (1974), the Supreme Court remanded a conviction under a Louisiana statute that banned the use of obscene language toward any police officer in the line of duty. Even though the state court held that the law prohibited only "fighting words," the Supreme Court found that, in light of *Gooding,* the statute was unconstitutionally overbroad since "obscene" and "opprobrious" words regulated under the statute "may well have conveyed anger and frustration without provoking a violent reaction from an officer."

More recently, in the case of *UWM Post v. Board of Regents of U. of Wisconsin* (1991), the Court stated that "since *Chaplinsky,* the Supreme Court has narrowed and clarified the scope of the fighting words doctrine . . . to include only words which tend to incite an immediate breach of the peace."[1] In addition to limiting the scope of the fighting words to words which tend to incite an immediate breach of the peace, it appears that a more stringent definition of "breach of the peace" has been set forth. Referring to the *Gooding* case, the Supreme Court stated that "in order to constitute fighting words, speech must not only breach decorum but also must tend to bring the addressee to fisticuffs." Consequently, in *UWM Post*, the Court found that since the elements of the *UWM* Rule did not require that "the regulated speech, by its very utterance, tend to incite violent reaction, the rule [went] beyond the . . . scope of the fighting words doctrine."

In sum, therefore, based upon the line of cases following *Chaplinsky*, it appears that the Court has, in effect, narrowed the *Chaplinsky* definition of fighting words to eliminate the "inflict injury" prong of the test. As such, under this narrowed version of *Chaplinsky*, defendants' speech code presumably proscribes more than "fighting words" as defined in subsequent case law. On its face, the speech code prohibits words which will not only cause people to react violently, but also cause them to feel insulted or stigmatized. As discussed above, however, defendants cannot proscribe speech that merely hurts the feelings of those who hear it.

The speech code also punishes words that "are commonly understood to convey" hatred and contempt on the basis of race, religion, etc. Clearly, this focuses upon the content of the words. All that is required under the speech code is that the words convey a message of hatred and contempt, not that they will likely cause an imminent breach of the peace. By proscribing certain words, without even considering their context, i.e., whether under a given situation there will be a breach of the peace, defendants' speech code fails to meet the "fighting words" standard as set forth under *Chaplinsky* and the later line of cases. As written, the speech code clearly punishes students for words which may not cause an imminent breach of the peace, but instead merely "conveys a message of hatred and contempt." To this extent, the speech code is overbroad since it is conceivable that a student could be punished for speech that did not (and would not) result in immediate violence. As a result, due to its overbreadth, defendants' speech code cannot pass constitutional scrutiny.

B. Constitutionality under *R.A.V. v. City of St. Paul*

1. The Claims of the Parties. Even assuming, arguendo, that all the expressions under the speech code are proscribable under the "fighting words" doctrine, under *R.A.V. v. City of St. Paul* (1992), the speech code would still be unconstitutional if it proscribes speech on the basis of the content the speech addresses.

Plaintiffs claim this is exactly what defendants' speech code does. Plaintiffs argue that the speech code, similar to the ordinance in *R.A.V.,* is an impermissible content-based regulation, since it does not proscribe all fighting words, but only those that are based on sex, race, color, and the like. Plaintiffs state that such "hostility" or "favoritism" toward the underlying message . . . is unconstitutional. "The First Amendment forbids such selective incorporation."

Defendants, on the other hand, argue that *R.A.V.* is not applicable here since, unlike the ordinance in *R.A.V.,* defendants' speech code is directed toward conduct (discriminatory harassment), not speech. Discriminatory harassment, defendants assert, includes personal vilification by means of fighting words/gutter epithets. Defendants, citing *R.A.V.* and *Wisconsin v. Mitchell* (1993), contend that where a regulation is directed toward conduct, the expression can be "swept up incidentally" without violating First Amendment rights.

2. The Case of R.A.V. In *R.A.V.,* the Supreme Court struck down a St. Paul "bias motivated hate crime" ordinance which made it a misdemeanor to place on private or public property a symbol which one knows, or has reasonable grounds to know, arouses anger in others on the basis of race, color, creed, religion or gender.

The majority accepted the Minnesota Supreme Court's construction of the ordinance as only applying to fighting words, an area of speech traditionally unprotected. Nevertheless, the Court found the ordinance unconstitutional since it did not proscribe all fighting words, but only those based on the categories listed in the ordinance.

The Court reasoned that such selectivity created the very real possibility that "the city was seeking to handicap the expression of particular ideas," and not fighting words in general. The Court did hold that the government could still prohibit fighting words so long as the proscription was unrelated to the distinct message contained in the expression. Thus, as the majority noted, libel could be proscribed, but not libel only critical of the government.

In the case at hand, a close examination of defendants' speech code reveals that plaintiffs' position is compelling. Similar to the ordinance in *R.A.V.,* defendants' speech code only proscribes a select class of fighting words: insults aimed at sex, race, color, handicap, sexual orientation, national or ethnic origin. Here, the same dangers the majority warned against exist. Defendants' speech code singles out a limited type of proscribable expression for a broad range of proscribable expression. Fighting words directed toward race and the like are punishable, yet those directed toward political affiliation, for example, are not. As plaintiffs note, "Insults, no matter how vicious or severe, are permissible unless they are addressed to one of the specified disfavored groups." Defendants, it would appear, have prohibited certain expression based on the underlying message. This is the type of content-based regulation the Court in *R.A.V.* found impermissible under the First Amendment.

3. Whether Defendants' Speech Code Falls Under an Exception . . . Whether Defendants' Speech Code Is Directed Toward Conduct. Although conceptually similar to the fourth exception enumerated in *R.A.V.,* a brief discussion is warranted since defendants raise this point separately. Defendants, as mentioned earlier, claim that their speech code is directed at prohibiting discriminatory harassment and not speech per se.

The Court in *R.A.V.* stated that its holding did not preclude regulation of subcategories of proscribable speech when such regulations are aimed at conduct. Thus, as the Court noted, sexual derogatory fighting words can be banned from the workplace because it would produce a violation of Title VII's general prohibition against sexual discrimination, a particular type of conduct. In essence, such words would be "swept up incidentally within the reach of a statute aimed at conduct rather than speech."

As it can be discerned from the above analysis, the Court, however, found the St. Paul ordinance was not directed toward conduct, but sought to prohibit certain fighting words. Similarly, as plaintiffs note, there is little evidence in the record which indicates defendants' speech code is aimed at conduct. Examination of the speech code reveals no mention of conduct or harassment as being proscribed. Rather, what is addressed is the prohibition of a certain category of expression which may result in a breach of the peace. Speech, in this respect, is not swept up incidentally, but is the aim of the proscription. It appears, therefore, that defendants' claim is without merit.

C. Conclusion

In conclusion, defendants' speech code cannot withstand the analysis and the holding in *R.A.V.* The speech code prohibits speech based on the content of the underlying expression and is not directed at conduct. It punishes those who express views on the disfavored subjects of race, gender, and the like, yet permits fighting words which do not address these topics. For these reasons, therefore, defendants' speech code appears to be in violation of the principles of the First Amendment.

◇

II. The Applicability and Constitutionality of Education Code §94367 ("The Leonard Law")

The next step in the analysis is a determination of whether the Court has standing to take action against Stanford, who is a private party. The pro-

tections of the First Amendment prevent abridgement of speech by state actors. Defendants state that as private parties, the First Amendment protects their speech rights and does not prohibit them from doing anything at all. The "First and Fourteenth Amendments safeguard the rights of free speech and assembly by limitation on state action, not on action by the owner of private property . . .

In response, however, plaintiffs argue that the courts have standing to take action against defendants through the enforcement of the Leonard Law. Specifically, this code section states as follows:

> (a) No private postsecondary educational institution shall make or enforce any rule subjecting any student to disciplinary sanctions solely on the basis of conduct that is speech or other communication that, when engaged in outside the campus or facility of a private postsecondary institution, is protected from governmental restriction by the First Amendment to the United States Constitution or Section 2 of Article 1 of the California Constitution. (b) Any student enrolled in a private postsecondary institution that has made or enforced any rule in violation of subdivision (a) may commence a civil action to obtain appropriate injunctive and declaratory relief as determined by the court. Upon motion, a court may award attorney's fees to a prevailing plaintiff in a civil action pursuant to this section.

Pursuant to this statute, a private university student has the same right to exercise his or her right to free speech on campus as he or she enjoys off campus. The Leonard Law specifically allows a private student to commence a civil action for any violation of this code section. As such, it is plaintiffs' position that the court has standing to take action against defendants in this case through the application of §94367.

Since it has been determined in Section I that the speech code is unconstitutional, the next step in the analysis is the applicability and constitutionality of Education Code §94367. It is defendants' position that even assuming that plaintiffs' fighting words are protected speech off campus, with the effect that §94367 requires Stanford to permit them on campus, Education Code §94367 would be unconstitutional as applied to defendants' speech code.

Defendant Stanford's Rights of Association

The First Amendment protects the freedom of association. Case law indicates that the State offends the right of free association by preventing an association from effectuating "its basic goals" of "high ethical standards" by preventing an association from "excluding individuals with ideologies or philosophies different from those of its existing members," or by preventing an association from "protecting [itself] 'from intrusion by those with adverse political principles'." Indeed, there "can be no clearer example of an intrusion into the inherent structure or affairs of an association than a regulation that forces the group to accept members it does not desire." Defendants maintain that this is particularly true when the association is a university: "The freedom of a university to make its own judgments as to education includes the selection of its student body."

Defendants argue that to the extent that the Leonard Law prohibits Stanford from implementing its speech code by proscribing fighting words/gutter epithets on its campus, and from disciplining or excluding students who vilify others, the Leonard Law offends Stanford's right of freedom of association.

Expressive associational rights derive from the Court's recognition that the ability to associate with others is crucial to effective advocacy. "By collective efforts individuals can make their views known, when, individually, their voices would be faint or lost." In determining whether to extend First Amendment expressive association rights to organizations, the crucial inquiry for the Court has been whether enforcement of the legislation in question would substantially alter a group's activities. That is, the organization must be able to prove that its ability to advocate effectively the specific expressive viewpoints of the organization will be compromised. "The Court thus looks at the connection between the membership and the message." As such, a court will refuse to protect an association's expressive rights unless the association is "organized for specific expressive purposes," but there must also exist a logical nexus between the discriminatory practices of the group and its purpose or message.

With respect to the expressive associational rights of defendants, this Court must first determine the "specific expressive purpose" for which the University was founded. Plaintiffs submit that the mission of the University is to provide its students with a comprehensive liberal arts education in which controversial ideas and presuppositions are subject to academic scrutiny, challenged by others in an effort to expand the critical reasoning skill of its students. Stanford is committed to the principles of free inquiry and free expression. Students have a "right to hold and vigorously defend and promote their opinions . . . . Respect for this right requires that students tolerate even expression of opinions which they find abhorrent."

Plaintiffs' position is that the defendants have not exhibited any logical nexus between their express purposes and the unconstitutional and illegal practices—the denial of First Amendment protected speech—in which they engage. Plaintiffs argue that not only is the enforcement of the speech code inconsistent with the specific express purposes of the University, but defendants have failed to proffer any arguments that the application of the Leonard Law will compromise the ability of the University to express its alleged concern with the "principles of equal opportunity and nondiscrimination." The membership of the University is not co-extensive with the message it may wish to promulgate. Where "allowing Blacks to march with the KKK would change the primary message which the KKK advocates," allowing students who may disagree with University dogma will not extinguish the message of the University. Unlike the Ku Klux Klan, defendant Stanford is an organization where the membership and message are not co-extensive.

It appears that in cases such as this, where a party claims that it is being forced to accept members that it does not desire, the pertinent question is whether admitting the undesired members will affect the ability of the original members to express the views on which the organization was founded. For example, in *Board of Directors of Rotary Int'l v. Rotary Club* (1987), the Court held that California could force Rotary Clubs to admit women because the Court did not find enough evidence "to demonstrate that admitting women . . . will affect in any significant way the existing members' ability to carry out their various purposes."

Similarly, in this case, it does not appear that defendants' ability to express their views will be significantly impaired by the application of Education Code §94367. As plaintiffs point out, defendant Stanford is a major international institution, well funded, with access to numerous alternative means of conveying its views that the speech prohibited by the speech code is offensive and intolerable. Therefore, by denying defendants the ability to discipline (expel) students for violation of the speech code, defendants' ability to express its message is not impaired because defendants retain numerous alternative means of expressing their views.

Defendants have not satisfied any of the legal prerequisites to claiming First Amendment protection under expressive associational rights. Plaintiffs argue that the case of *Pruneyard Shopping Center v. Robins* (1980) is directly on point. In *Pruneyard,* appellant private shopping center owner sought protection from Zionist picketers on precisely the same grounds on which defendants petition this Court—alleging that a private property owner has a First Amendment right of expressive association not to be forced by the State to use its property as a forum for the speech of others with whom it may disagree. In finding the California law constitutional, the Court distinguished expressly its prior ruling in *Wooley v. Maynard* (1977), in which it found unconstitutional a New Hampshire law requiring that all vehicles display the State motto, "Live Free or Die." In doing so, the Court distinguished between a State compelling a private actor to disseminate the State's ideology for the express purpose that it be read by the public—the *Wooley* issue—and a State compelling a private actor to allow speech of any content, irrespective of its conformity with State dogma—the *Pruneyard* issue.

More specifically, the Court distinguished *Pruneyard* on three grounds. First, the shopping center, by the owner's own choice, was not limited to the personal use of the appellant. The center was organized as an establishment open to the public to come and go as they please. Hence, the Court concluded that there was no likelihood that the views of the petitioner would be construed as those of the appellant. Second, no specific message was directed by the State. Accordingly, the fears of government viewpoint discrimination at issue in *Wooley* were nonexistent. Finally, the Court found that appellant could disavow any connection with the message proffered by petitioners by posting signs to that effect in the center.

Plaintiffs argue that the facts in this case are indistinguishable from *Pruneyard.* First, defendant Stanford University is not limited to the personal use of defendants, but rather opens up its campus and admissions process to the general public.[2] Furthermore, the public access and large size of the University confirm the assertion that the views expressed by any of its students will not be construed to represent those of the University. Additionally, defendants could easily disclaim any such wrongful attribution of a student's expressions for those of the University. Identical to the *Pruneyard* situation, plaintiffs validly argue that California does not dictate any specific message through the Leonard Law, a situation which eliminates any concerns over government-sponsored viewpoint discrimination.

In sum, therefore, the crucial inquiry in determining whether defendants' First Amendment rights are offended by the Leonard Law is whether there exists a nexus between the express purposes of the group and the activity which it seeks to continue (i.e., suppressing student speech rights). The determination includes analysis of various factors: whether there is a concern of State-sponsored viewpoint discrimination, whether observers are likely to construe the offensive speech as an endorsement by the University of such views, and whether the University has adequate means at its disposal by which to rebut or separate itself from the offensive message. As discussed above, in analyzing these factors, no sufficient nexus exists here which would affect defendants' rights of association. For these reasons, defendants' contention that the Leonard Law is unconstitutional since it infringes upon its First Amendment rights of association is unpersuasive.

III. Conclusion

In summary, based upon the above analysis, the following conclusion is reached: First, defendants' speech code does violate plaintiffs' First Amendment rights since the speech code proscribes more than just fighting words as defined in *Chaplinsky* and the later lines of case law. To this extent, therefore, defendants' speech code is overbroad. In addition, however, the speech code also targets the content of certain speech. Similar to the ordinance in *R.A.V.,* the speech code is an impermissible content-based regulation since it does not proscribe all fighting words, but only those which are based upon sex, race, color, and the like. Accordingly, the speech code is unconstitutional not only due to its overbreadth but also due to its content-based restrictions.

Second, since defendants are private parties, the only means by which the Court can have standing to take action against the defendants is through the enforcement of Education Code §94367 (the

"Leonard Law"). In this case, Education Code §94367 does apply and proscribe defendants' speech code. For these reasons, plaintiffs' motion for a preliminary injunction should therefore be granted.

Endnotes

1. It must be noted that the *Chaplinsky* court originally set out a two-part definition for fighting words: (1) words which by their very utterance inflict injury; and (2) words which by their very utterance tend to inflict an immediate breach of the peace.

2. Additionally, it is important to note that a shopping center is located on the University campus. This, too, appears to be a location where the Code applies; the Stanford Shopping Center is a very similar forum to that in *Pruneyard*.

49. *Free Speech and Bias on College Campuses*
ACLU POLICY STATEMENT[1]

Preamble

The significant increase in reported incidents of racism and other forms of bias at colleges and universities is a matter of profound concern to the ACLU. Some have proposed that racism, sexism, homophobia, and other such biases on campus must be addressed in whole or in part by restrictions on speech. The alternative to such restrictions, it is said, is to permit such bias to go unremedied and to subject the targets of such bias to a loss of equal educational opportunity. The ACLU rejects both these alternatives and reaffirms its traditional and unequivocal commitment both to free speech and to equal opportunity.

Policy

1. Freedom of thought and expression are indispensable to the pursuit of knowledge and the dialogue and dispute that characterize meaningful education. All members of the academic community have the right to hold and to express views that others may find repugnant, offensive, or emotionally distressing. The ACLU opposes all campus regulations which interfere with the freedom of professors, students, and administrators to teach, learn, discuss, and debate or to express ideas, opinions, or feelings in classroom, public, or private discourse.[2]

2. The ACLU has opposed and will continue to oppose and challenge disciplinary codes that reach beyond permissible boundaries into the realm of protected speech, even when those codes are directed at the problem of bias on campus.[3]

3. This policy does not prohibit colleges and universities from enacting disciplinary codes aimed at restricting acts of harassment, intimidation, and invasion of privacy.[4] The fact that words may be used in connection with otherwise actionable conduct does not immunize such conduct from appropriate regulation.[5] As always, however, great care must be taken to avoid applying such provisions overbroadly to protected expression. The ACLU will continue to review such college codes and their application in specific situations on a case-by-case basis under the principles set forth in this policy and in Policy 72.[6]

4. All students have the right to participate fully in the educational process on a nondiscriminatory basis. Colleges and universities have an affirmative obligation to combat racism, sexism, homophobia, and other forms of bias, and a responsibility to provide equal opportunities through education. To address these responsibilities and obligations, the ACLU advocates the following actions by colleges and universities:

    a. to utilize every opportunity to communicate through its administrators, faculty, and students its commitment to the elimination of all forms of bigotry on campus;

    b. to develop comprehensive plans aimed at reducing prejudice, responding promptly to incidents of bigotry and discriminatory harassment, and protecting students from any such further incidents;

    c. to pursue vigorously efforts to attract enough minorities, women, and members of other historically disadvantaged groups as students, faculty members, and administrators to alleviate isolation and to ensure real integration and diversity in academic life;

    d. to offer and consider whether to require all students to take courses in the history and meaning of prejudice, including racism, sexism, and other forms of invidious discrimination;[7]

    e. to establish new-student orientation programs and continuing counseling programs that enable students of different races, sexes, religions, and sexual orientations to learn to live with each other outside the classroom;

    f. to review and, where appropriate, revise course offerings as well as extracurricular programs in order to recognize the contributions of those whose art, music, literature, and learning have been insufficiently reflected in the curriculum of many American colleges and universities;

    g. to address the question of *de facto* segregation in dormitories and other university facilities; and

    h. to take such other steps as are consistent with the goal of ensuring that all students have an equal opportunity to do their best work and to participate fully in campus life.

This policy is issued in connection with, and is intended as an interpretation and enhancement of, the binding resolution on racist speech adopted at the 1989 Biennial Conference. That resolution provides:

> The ACLU should undertake educational activities to counter incidents of racist, sexist, anti-Semitic, and homophobic behavior (including speech) on school campuses and should encourage school administrators to speak out vigorously against such incidents. At the same time the ACLU should undertake educational activities to counter efforts to limit or punish speech on university campuses.

Endnotes

1. Adopted by ACLU National Board of Directors, without dissent, on October 13, 1990.

2. See generally ACLU Policy Nos. 60, 63, 65, 71.

3. The ACLU to date has opposed overbroad student speech codes adopted by the University of Connecticut, University of Michigan, University of Wisconsin, and the University of California.

4. Although "harassment," "intimidation," and "invasion of privacy" are imprecise terms susceptible of impermissibly overbroad application, each term defines a type of conduct which is legally proscribed in many jurisdictions when directed at a specific individual or individuals and when intended to frighten, coerce, or unreasonably harry or intrude upon its target. Threatening telephone calls to a minority student's dormitory room, for example, would be proscribable conduct under the terms of this policy. Expressive behavior which has no other effect than to create an unpleasant learning environment, however, would not be the proper subject of regulation. See also Policy No. 316.

5. For example, intimidating phone calls, threats of attack, extortion, and blackmail are unprotected forms of conduct which include an element of verbal or written expression.

6. In determining whether a university disciplinary code impermissibly restricts protected speech, there must be

a searching analysis both of the language of the code and the manner in which it is applied. Many factors, which are heavily fact-oriented, must be considered, including time, place, pattern of conduct and, where relevant, the existence of an authority relationship between speaker and target.

7. All courses and programs must be taught consistent with the principles prescribed in ACLU Policy 60.

Suggestions for Further Reading

Anthologies

Matsuda, Mari J., Charles R. Lawrence, III, and Richard Delgado. *Words That Wound.* Boulder, CO: Westview, 1993.

Whillock, Rita Kirk, and David Slayden. *Hate Speech.* London: Sage Publications, 1995.

Basic Concepts

Walker, Samuel. *Hate Speech: The History of an American Controversy.* Lincoln: University of Nebraska Press, 1994.

Alternative Views

Abel, Richard. *Speaking Respect, Respecting Speech.* Chicago: University of Chicago, 1998.

Fish, Stanley. *There's No Such Thing as Free Speech, and It's a Good Thing, Too.* Oxford: Oxford University Press, 1994.

Hentoff, Nat. *Free Speech for Me—But Not for Thee.* New York: HarperCollins, 1992.

Lamarche, Gary. *Speech and Equality.* New York: New York University Press, 1996.

MacKinnon, Catherine. *Only Words.* Cambridge: Harvard University Press, 1993.

Rauch, Jonathan. *Kindly Inquisitors: New Attacks on Free Thought.* Chicago: University Press of Chicago, 1993.

Shiell, Timothy. *Campus Hate Speech on Trial.* Topeka: University of Kansas Press, 1998.

Sunstein, Cass. *Democracy and the Problem of Free Speech.* New York: Free Press, 1993.

Section IX

Gay and Lesbian Rights

Introduction

Basic Concepts

The prohibition of homosexuality has ancient roots, but its enforcement has usually been haphazard at best because acts between consenting adults make it hard to find a complainant. Even so, twenty-four states and the District of Columbia still have statutes prohibiting homosexual acts. Penalties range from three months in prison or one year's probation to life imprisonment.

Moreover, these statutes prohibit *sodomy*, which involves more than just homosexuals. For example, the Georgia statute whose constitutionality was upheld by the Supreme Court in *Bowers v. Hardwick* holds that "a person commits the offense of sodomy when he performs or submits to any sexual act involving the sex organs of one person and the mouth or anus of another." Sodomy is defined broadly here because the main complaint against homosexual acts—that they are unnatural—also applies to a range of other acts. More specifically, the complaint applies to oral and anal intercourse between heterosexuals, masturbation, and bestiality, as well as homosexual acts.

Now we must understand what is considered unnatural about these acts. One sense of *natural* refers to what is found in nature as contrasted with what is artificial or the product of human artifice. In this sense, homosexuality would seem natural: It is found in virtually every human society. But even if homosexuality is understood to be a product of a certain type of upbringing or socialization and hence artificial, that would hardly seem grounds for condemning it: Much human behavior has a similar origin.

Another sense of natural refers to what is common or statistically normal as contrasted with what is uncommon or statistically abnormal. In this sense, homosexuality would not be natural: Most people are not homosexuals, even though one study found that about half of all American males have engaged in homosexual acts at some time in their lives. But being unnatural in this sense could not be grounds for condemning homosexuality because many traits we most value in people are also statistically abnormal and, hence, unnatural in this sense.

Still another sense of natural refers to a thing's proper function; it is this sense of natural that is frequently used to condemn homosexuality. If we maintain that the proper function of human sexual organs is simply procreation, then any use of those organs for any other purpose would be unnatural. Thus, homosexuality, contraception, masturbation, and bestiality would all be unnatural. But clearly the proper function of human sexual organs is not limited to procreation. These organs are also used to express love and provide pleasure for oneself and others. Given that our sexual organs can be properly used for these other purposes, we would need to argue that every use of these organs must serve their procreative function if we are to be able to condemn homosexuality. No nontheologically based argument has succeeded in establishing this conclusion.[1] Moreover, once we grant that, for example, contraception and masturbation can be morally permissible, no ground seems to be left, based on the proper functioning of our sexual organs, for denying that homosexuality can be morally permissible as well.

Alternative Views

In Selection 50, John Finnis sets out the following argument against homosexuality:

1. In masturbating as in being masturbated or sodomized, one disintegrates oneself in two ways: (a) by treating one's body as an instrument for one's own gratification and (b) by making one's choosing self the quasi-slave of one's experiencing self.

2. By so doing one is not actualizing or experiencing a common good.

3. Marriage with its twofold goals of procreation and friendship is a common good.

4. Marriage is a common good that can be experienced in the orgasmic union of the reproductive organs of a man and a woman united in commitment to that good.

5. This common good makes husband and wife a biological and a personal unit.

6. The common good of friends who are not and cannot be married has nothing to do

with procreation and hence their procreative organs cannot make them a biological and a personal unit.

7. Hence, homosexual acts cannot actualize the common good of friendship.

8. Nor is such conduct the participation in some intelligible good because it is not focused on the exercise of a skill but rather on the satisfaction of a desire for one's own pleasure.

9. Such conduct is also deeply hostile to the self-understanding of those members of the community who are committed to real marriage with its shared responsibilities.

10. For this reason, a political community is justified in denying the validity of such conduct, and in taking appropriate steps to discourage it.

The thrust of Finnis's argument is directed not only at homosexual acts, but also at heterosexual masturbation and sodomy, bestiality, and contraception. For Finnis, all of these acts are wrong for the same reason. So, if we accept Finnis's argument, we cannot consistently allow for the moral permissibility of some of these acts but not of others; the moral permissibility of all of these acts must stand or fall together.

In Selection 51, Martha Nussbaum criticizes Finnis for assuming without argument that the purpose of homosexual acts is always the instrumental use of another person's body for one's own gratification. She contends that both the past and the present provide ample evidence against this assumption. Nussbaum also criticizes Finnis for assuming without argument that the only type of community that a sexual relationship can create is a procreative community. Again, she contends that both the past and the present provide ample evidence against this assumption.

In Selection 52, Richard D. Mohr surveys various ways in which homosexuals are discriminated against in our society. Mohr cites

---

[1]Clearly if there is to be freedom of religion, a nontheologically based argument is needed here.

one study in which 90 percent of gays and lesbians report that they have been victimized because of their sexual orientation. Mohr argues that being gay or lesbian is not a matter of choice, making it difficult, if not impossible to change one's sexual orientation. Obviously, then, what sodomy statutes demand of homosexuals is that they not act as they are. A difficult charge indeed! Moreover, it is a charge that does not appear to be supported by a defensible account of what is wrong with homosexual behavior.

While opposing antisodomy laws, Carl Horowitz (Selection 53) contends that those who decide to live openly as homosexuals should accept the disapproval of those around them. He further contends that although the homosexual rights movement began as an acceptable demand for the state not to interfere with private homosexual behavior, it has evolved into an unacceptable demand for the state to act on behalf of public homosexual behavior. But it is not clear whether Horowitz endorses the same legal rights for homosexuals as for heterosexuals—for example, the right to marriage, the right to job opportunities, and the right to child custody and adoption. On the one hand, Horowitz does require that homosexuals have the same legal rights to noninterference as heterosexuals. On the other hand, he holds that homo-sexuals should not expect to be treated equally. But shouldn't the equal treatment that homosexuals expect be the same legal rights that heterosexuals enjoy?

Practical Applications

An important Supreme Court case dealing with homosexuality is *Bowers v. Hardwick* (1986). In this case, the issue before the Court was whether the Georgia sodomy statute violates the federal Constitution. In delivering the opinion of the court, Justice White argues that the statute does not because the Constitution does not confer a fundamental right on homosexuals to engage in sodomy. While in previous cases, the Constitution was interpreted to confer a right to decide whether or not to beget or bear a child and a right not to be convicted for possessing and reading obscene material in the privacy of one's home, White argues that the Constitution cannot analogously be interpreted to confer a fundamental right on homosexuals to engage in sodomy. Justice Burger concurs, stressing the ancient roots of sodomy statutes. Justice Blackmun, joined by Justices Brennan and Marshall, argues that notwithstanding the ancient roots of prohibitions against homosexuality, a right to be let alone that is the underpinning of previous court decisions justifies in this case a right to engage in sodomy at least in the privacy of one's home.

In this case, the majority of the Supreme Court seemed to reach its conclusion by interpreting previous decisions in an excessively literal manner in much the same way that the majority of the court ruled in *Olmstead v. United States* (1928) that warrantless wiretapping did not violate Fourth Amendment prohibitions against search and seizure because the framers of the amendment were not explicitly prohibiting this method of obtaining incriminating evidence. Just as it later repudiated its ruling in *Olmstead*, the Supreme Court in *Romer v. Evans* (Selection 53) recently struck down Colorado's Amendment 2 for imposing a disability on homosexuals—a decision that appears to be at least a partial repudiation of *Bowers v. Hardwick*.

In one of the most important court decisions on gay and lesbian rights to date, the Supreme Court of Vermont unanimously ruled that the Common Benefits Clause of the Vermont Constitution requires that same-sex couples not be deprived of the benefits and protections extended to opposite-sex couples

(Selection 54). The court left it to the Legislature either to legalize gay marriages, which no state has yet done, or to adopt a domestic partnership law that would be the most sweeping in the country. Across the country the campaign to legalize gay and lesbian marriages has inspired a vigorous opposition. Since the prospect arose in a Hawaii case in 1991, nearly thirty states have passed laws against gay and lesbian marriages. But gay and lesbian rights advocates say it is not clear whether those laws will stand against challenges similar to the successful challenge raised against the marriage law in Vermont.

It is also important to note that adherents of all three of our political ideals generally tend to favor granting homosexuals the same rights as heterosexuals. Libertarians favor this view because to do otherwise would deny homosexuals important basic liberties. Welfare liberals favor this view because to do otherwise would deny homosexuals fundamental fairness. Socialists favor this view because to do otherwise would deny homosexuals basic equality.

---

50. *Homosexual Conduct Is Wrong*

JOHN FINNIS

John Finnis argues against homosexuality on the grounds that it involves treating one's body as an instrument for one's own gratification rather than actualizing or experiencing a common good. He also argues that because homosexual conduct is deeply hostile to the self-understanding of those members of the community who are committed to real marriage with its shared responsibilities, a political community is justified in taking appropriate steps to discourage it.

The underlying thought is on the following lines. In masturbating, as in being masturbated or sodomized, one's body is treated as instrumental for the securing of the experiential satisfaction of the conscious self. Thus one disintegrates oneself in two ways, (1) by treating one's body as a mere instrument of the consciously operating self, and (2) by making one's choosing self the quasi-slave of the experiencing self which is demanding gratification. The worthlessness of the gratification, and the disintegration of oneself, are both the result of the fact that, in these sorts of behavior, one's conduct is not the actualizing and experiencing of a real common good. Marriage, with its double blessing— procreation and friendship—is a real common good. Moreover, it is a common good that can be both actualized and experienced in the orgasmic union of the reproductive organs of a man and a woman united in commitment to that good. Conjugal sexual activity, and—as Plato and Aristotle and Plutarch and Kant all argue—*only* conjugal activity is free from the shamefulness of instrumentalization that is found in masturbating and in being masturbated or sodomized.

At the very heart of the reflections of Plato, Xenophon, Aristotle, Musonius Rufus, and Plutarch on the homoerotic culture around them is the very deliberate and careful judgment that homosexual *conduct* (and indeed all extramarital sexual gratification) is radically incapable of participating in, or actualizing, the common good of friendship. Friends who engage in such conduct are following a natural

---

Reprinted from the legal depositions from the trial in Colorado on the constitutionality of Amendment 2.

impulse and doubtless often wish their genital conduct to be an intimate expression of their mutual affection. But they are deceiving themselves. The attempt to express affection by orgasmic nonmarital sex is the pursuit of an illusion. The orgasmic union of the reproductive organs of husband and wife really unites them biologically (and their biological reality is part of, not merely an instrument of, their *personal* reality); that orgasmic union therefore can actualize and allow them to experience their real common good—their marriage with the two goods, children and friendship, which are the parts of its wholeness as an intelligible common good. But the common good of friends who are not and cannot be married (man and man, man and boy, woman and woman) has nothing to do with their having children by each other, and their reproductive organs cannot make them a biological (and therefore a personal) unit. So their genital acts together cannot do what they may hope and imagine.

In giving their considered judgment that homosexual conduct cannot actualize the good of friendship, Plato and the many philosophers who followed him intimate an answer to the questions why it should be considered shameful to use, or allow another to use, one's body to give pleasure, and why this use of one's body differs from one's bodily participation in countless other activities (e.g., games) in which one takes and/or gets pleasure. Their response is that pleasure is indeed a good, when it is the experienced aspect of one's participation in some intelligible good, such as a task going well, or a game or a dance or a meal or a reunion. Of course, the activation of sexual organs with a view to the pleasures of orgasm is sometimes spoken of as if it were a game. But it differs from real games in that its point is not the exercise of skill; rather, this activation of reproductive organs is focused upon the body precisely as a source of pleasure for one's consciousness. So this is a "use of the body" in a strongly different sense of "use." The body now is functioning not in the way one, as a bodily person, acts to instantiate some other intelligible good, but precisely as providing a service to one's consciousness, to satisfy one's desire for satisfaction.

This disintegrity is much more obvious when masturbation is solitary. Friends are tempted to think that pleasuring each other by some forms of mutual masturbation could be an instantiation or actualization or promotion of their friendship. But that line of thought overlooks the fact that if their friendship is

not marital . . . activation of their reproductive organs cannot be, in reality, an instantiation or actualization of their friendship's common good. In reality, whatever the generous hopes and dreams with which the loving partners surround their use of their genitals, *that use* cannot express more than is expressed if two strangers engage in genital activity to give each other orgasm, or a prostitute pleasures a client, or a man pleasures himself. Hence, Plato's judgment, at the decisive moment of the *Gorgias*, that there is no important distinction in essential moral worthlessness between solitary masturbation, being sodomized as a prostitute and being sodomized for the pleasure of it. . . .

Societies such as classical Athens and contemporary England (and virtually every other) draw a distinction between behavior found merely (perhaps extremely) offensive (such as eating excrement) and behavior to be repudiated as destructive of human character and relationships. Copulation of humans with animals is repudiated because it treats human sexual activity and satisfaction as something appropriately sought in a manner that, like the coupling of animals, is divorced from the expressing of an intelligible common good—and so treats human bodily life, in one of its most intense activities, as merely animal. The deliberate genital coupling of persons of the same sex is repudiated for a very similar reason. It is not simply that it is sterile and disposes the participants to an abdication of responsibility for the future of humankind. Nor is it simply that it cannot *really* actualize the mutual devotion that some homosexual persons hope to manifest and experience by it; nor merely that it harms the personalities of its participants by its disintegrative manipulation of different parts of their one personal reality. It is also that it treats human sexual capacities in a way that is deeply hostile to the self-understanding of those members of the community who are willing to commit themselves to real marriage [even one that happens to be sterile] in the understanding that its sexual joys are not mere instruments or accompaniments to, or mere compensation for the accomplishments of marriage's responsibilities, but rather are the *actualizing and experiencing* of the intelligent commitment to share in those responsibilities. . . .

This pattern of judgment, both widespread and sound, concludes as follows. Homosexual orientation—the deliberate willingness to promote and engage in homosexual acts—is a standing denial of the intrinsic aptness of sexual intercourse to actualize and give expression to the exclusiveness and open-ended commitment of marriage as something good in itself. All who accept that homosexual acts can be a humanly appropriate use of sexual capacities must, if consistent, regard sexual capacities, organs, and acts as instruments to be put to whatever suits the purposes of the individual "self" who has them. Such an acceptance is commonly (and in my opinion rightly) judged to be an active threat to the stability of existing and future marriages; it makes nonsense, for example, of the view that adultery is per se (and not merely because it may involve deception), and in an important way, inconsistent with conjugal love. A political community that judges that the stability and educative generosity of family life is of fundamental importance to the community's present and future can rightly judge that it has a compelling interest in denying that homosexual conduct is a valid, humanly acceptable choice and form of life, and in doing whatever it properly can, as a community with uniquely wide but still subsidiary functions, to discourage such conduct.

---

51. *Homosexual Conduct Is Not Wrong*

MARTHA NUSSBAUM

Martha Nussbaum criticizes John Finnis for assuming without argument that the purpose of homosexual acts is always the instrumental use of another person's body for one's own gratification. Nussbaum also criticizes Finnis for assuming without argument that the only type of community that a sexual relationship can create is a pro-creative community.

Finnis's arguments against homosexuality set themselves in a tradition of "natural law" argumentation that derives from ancient Greek traditions. The term "law of nature" was first used by Plato in his *Gorgias*. The approach is further developed by Aristotle, and, above all, by the Greek and Roman Stoics, who are usually considered to be the founders of natural law argumentation in the modern legal tradition, through their influence on Roman law. This being so, it is worth looking to see whether those traditions did in fact use "natural law" arguments to rule homosexual conduct morally or legally substandard.

Plato's dialogues contain several extremely moving celebrations of male–male love, and judge this form of love to be, on the whole, superior to male–female love because of its potential for spirituality and friendship. The *Symposium* contains a series of speeches, each expressing conventional views about this subject that Plato depicts in an appealing light. The speech by Phaedrus points to the military advantages derived by including homosexual couples in a fighting force: Because of their intense love, each will fight better, wishing to show himself in the best light before his lover. The speech of Pausanias criticizes males who seek physical pleasure alone in their homosexual relationships, and praises those who seek in sex deeper spiritual communication. Pausanias mentions that tyrants will sometimes promulgate the view that same-sex relations are shameful in order to discourage the kind of community of dedication to political liberty that such relations foster. The speech of Aristophanes holds that all human beings are divided halves of formerly whole beings, and that sexual desire is the pursuit of one's lost other half; he points out that the superior people in any society are those whose lost "other half" is of the same sex—especially the male–male pairs—since these are likely to be the strongest and most warlike and civically minded

Reprinted from the legal depositions from the trial in Colorado on the constitutionality of Amendment 2.

people. Finally, Socrates's speech recounts a process of religious-mystical education in which male–male love plays a central guiding role and is a primary source of insight and inspiration into the nature of the good and beautiful.

Plato's *Phaedrus* contains a closely related praise of the intellectual, political, and spiritual benefits of a life centered around male–male love. Plato says that the highest form of human life is one in which a male pursues "the love of a young man along with philosophy," and is transported by passionate desire. He describes the experience of falling in love with another male in moving terms, and defends relationships that are mutual and reciprocal over relationships that are one-sided. He depicts his pairs of lovers as spending their life together in the pursuit of intellectual and spiritual activities, combined with political participation. (Although no marriages for these lovers are mentioned, it was the view of the time that this form of life does not prevent its participants from having a wife at home, whom they saw only rarely and for procreative purposes.)

Aristotle speaks far less about sexual love than does Plato, but it is evident that he too finds in male–male relationships the potential for the highest form of friendship, a friendship based on mutual well-wishing and mutual awareness of good character and good aims. He does not find this potential in male–female relationships, since he holds that females are incapable of good character. Like Pausanias in Plato's *Symposium*, Aristotle is critical of relationships that are superficial and concerned only with bodily pleasure; but he finds in male–male relationships—including many that begin in this way—the potential for much richer developments.

The ideal city of the Greek Stoics was built around the idea of pairs of male lovers whose bonds gave the city rich sources of motivation for virtue.

Although the Stoics wished their "wise man" to eliminate most passions from his life, they encouraged him to foster a type of erotic love that they defined as "the attempt to form a friendship inspired by the perceived beauty of young men in their prime." They held that this love, unlike other passions, was supportive of virtue and philosophical activity.

Furthermore, Finnis's argument . . . against homosexuality is a bad moral argument by any standard, secular or theological. First of all, it assumes that the purpose of a homosexual act is always or usually casual bodily pleasure and the instrumental use of another person for one's own gratification. But this is a false premise, easily disproved by the long historical tradition I have described and by the contemporary lives of real men and women. Finnis offers no evidence for this premise, or for the equally false idea that procreative relations cannot be selfish and manipulative. Second, having argued that a relationship is better if it seeks not casual pleasure but the creation of a community, he then assumes without argument that the only sort of community a sexual relationship can create is a "procreative community." This is, of course, plainly false. A sexual relationship may create, quite apart from the possibility of procreation, a community of love and friendship, which no religious tradition would deny to be important human goods. Indeed, in many moral traditions, including those of Plato and Aristotle, the procreative community is ranked beneath other communities created by sex, since it is thought that the procreative community will probably not be based on the best sort of friendship and the deepest spiritual concerns. That may not be true in a culture that values women more highly than ancient Greek culture did; but the possibility of love and friendship between individuals of the same sex has not been removed by these historical changes.

52. Prejudice and Homosexuality

RICHARD D. MOHR

Richard D. Mohr begins by noting that although gays are a significant percentage of the American population, they are characterized by stereotypes based on false generalizations. He cites one study in which 90 percent of gays and lesbians report that they have been victimized because of their sexual orientation. Mohr also questions whether a correct understanding of Christianity would condemn homosexuality, and he denies that any argument from nature supports such a condemnation. He further argues that if gays were socially accepted, society would be enriched and a step closer to its goal of "liberty and justice for all."

Who are gays anyway? A 1993 *New York Times*–CBS poll found that only one-fifth of Americans suppose that they have a friend or family member who is gay or lesbian. This finding is extraordinary given the number of practicing homosexuals in America. In 1948, Alfred Kinsey published a study of the sex lives of 12,000 white males. Its method was so rigorous that it set the standard for subsequent statistical research across the social sciences, but its results shocked the nation: Thirty-seven percent of the men had at least one homosexual experience to orgasm in their adult lives; an additional thirteen percent had homosexual fantasies to orgasm; four percent were exclusively homosexual in their practices; another five percent had virtually no heterosexual experience, and nearly one fifth had at least as many homosexual as heterosexual experiences. Kinsey's 1953 study of the sex lives of 8,000 women found the occurrence of homosexual behavior at about half the rates for men.

Every second family in the country has a member who is essentially homosexual and many more people regularly have homosexual experiences. Who are homosexuals? They are your friends, your minister, your teacher, your bank teller, your doctor, your mail carrier, your officemate, your roommate, your congressional representative, your sibling, parent, and spouse. They are we. We are everywhere, virtually all ordinary, virtually all unknown.

Ignorance about gays, however, has not stopped people from having strong opinions about them. The void which ignorance leaves has been filled with stereotypes. Society holds two oddly contradictory groups of antigay stereotypes. One revolves around an individual's allegedly confused gender identity: Lesbians are females who want to be, or at least look and act like, men—bull dykes, diesel dykes; while gay men are males who want to be, or at least look and act like, women—queens, fairies, nances, limp-wrists, nellies, sissies, aunties. These stereotypes of mismatches between biological sex and socially defined gender provide the materials through which lesbians and gay men become the butts of ethnic-like jokes. These stereotypes and jokes, though derisive, basically view gays as ridiculous: "How do you identify a bull dyke?" Answer: "She kick-starts her vibrator and rolls her own tampons." Or, "How many fags does it take to change a light bulb?" Answer: "Eight—one to replace it and seven to scream 'Faaaaaabulous!'"

The other set of stereotypes revolves around gays as a pervasive sinister conspiratorial threat. The core stereotype here is that of the gay person—especially gay man—as child molester, and more generally as sex-crazed maniac. Homosexuality here is viewed as a vampire-like corruptive contagion. These stereotypes carry with them fears of the very destruction of family and civilization itself. Now, that which is essentially ridiculous can hardly have such a staggering effect. Something must be afoot.

Sense can be made of this incoherent amalgam if the nature of stereotypes is clarified. Stereotypes are not simply false generalizations from a skewed sample of cases examined. Admittedly, false generalizing plays some part in the stereotypes society holds about gays and other groups. If, for instance, one takes as one's sample gay men who are in psychiatric hospitals or prisons, as was done in nearly all early investigations, not surprisingly one will probably find them to be of a crazed or criminal cast. Such false generalizations, though, simply confirm beliefs already held on independent grounds, ones that likely led the investigator to the prison and psychiatric ward to begin with. Evelyn Hooker, who in the late 1950s carried out the first rigorous studies of nonclinical gay men, found that psychiatrists, when presented with case files including all the standard diagnostic psychological profiles—but omitting indications of sexual orientation—were unable to distinguish gay files from nongay ones, even though they believed gay men to be crazy and supposed themselves to be experts in detecting craziness. These studies proved a profound embarrassment to the psychiatric establishment, the financial well-being of which has been substantially enhanced by "curing" allegedly insane gays. The studies led the way to the American Psychiatric Association's finally, in 1973, dropping homosexuality from its registry of mental illnesses. Nevertheless, the stereotype of gays as sick continues apace in the mind of America.

False generalizations help maintain stereotypes, they do not form them. As the story of Hooker's discoveries shows, stereotypes have a life beyond facts; their origins lie in a culture's ideology—the general system of beliefs by which it lives—and they are sustained across generations by diverse cultural transmissions, hardly any of which, including slang and jokes, even purport to have a scientific basis. Stereotypes, then, are not the products of bad science, but reflections of society's conception of itself.

On this understanding, it is easy to see that stereotypes about gays as gender-confused reinforce still powerful gender roles in society. If, as these stereotypes presume and condemn, one is free to choose one's social roles independently of one's biological sex, many guiding social divisions, both domestic and commercial, might be threatened. Blurred would be the socially sex-linked distinctions between breadwinner and homemaker, boss and secretary, doctor and nurse, protector and protected, even God and His world. The accusations "fag" and "dyke" serve in significant part to keep women in their place and to prevent men from breaking ranks and ceding away theirs.

The stereotypes of gays as civilization destroyers function to displace (possibly irresolvable) social problems from their actual source to a remote and (society hopes) manageable one. For example, the stereotype of child molester functions to give the traditionally defined family unit a false sheen of innocence. It keeps the unit from being examined too closely for incest, child abuse, wife-battering, and the terrorizing of women and children by a father's constant threats. The stereotype teaches that the problems of the family are not internal to it, but external.

One can see these cultural forces at work in society's and the media's treatment of current reports of violence, especially domestic violence. When a husband kills his wife or a father rapes his daughter—regular Section B fare even in major urban papers—this is never taken by reporters, columnists, or pundits as evidence that there is something wrong with heterosexuality or with traditional families. These issues are not even raised. But when a homosexual child molestation is reported, it is taken as confirming evidence of the way homosexuals are. One never hears of "heterosexual murders," but one regularly hears of "homosexual" ones.

If this account of stereotypes holds, society has been profoundly immoral. For its treatment of gays is a grand-scale rationalization, a moral sleight-of-hand. The problem is not that society's usual standards of evidence and procedure in decision making have been misapplied to gays, rather when it comes to gays, the standards themselves have simply been ruled out of court and disregarded in favor of mechanisms that encourage unexamined fear and hatred.

Partly because lots of people suppose they don't know any gay people and partly through the maintaining of stereotypes, society at large is unaware of the many ways in which gays are subject to discrimination in consequence of widespread fear and hatred. Contributing to this social ignorance of discrimination is the difficulty for gay people, as an invisible minority, even to complain of discrimination. For if one is gay, to register a complaint would suddenly target oneself as a stigmatized person, and so, especially in the absence of any protection against discrimination, would simply invite additional discrimination. So, discrimination against gays, like rape, goes seriously underreported. Even so, known discrimination is massive.

Annual studies by the National Gay and Lesbian Task Force have consistently found that more than ninety percent of gay men and lesbians have been victims of violence or harassment in some form on the basis of their sexual orientation. Greater than one in five gay men and nearly one in ten lesbians have been punched, hit, or kicked; a quarter of all gays have had objects thrown at them; a third have been chased; a third have been sexually harassed, and fourteen percent have been spit on, all just for being perceived to be gay.

The most extreme form of antigay violence is queer-bashing—where groups of young men target a person who they suppose is a gay man and beat and kick him unconscious and sometimes to death amid a torrent of taunts and slurs. Few such cases with gay victims reach the courts. Those that do are marked by inequitable procedures and results. Frequently judges will describe queer-bashers as "just All-American Boys." A District of Columbia judge handed suspended sentences to queer-bashers whose victim had been stalked, beaten, stripped at knife point, slashed, kicked, threatened with castration, and pissed on, because the judge thought the bashers were good boys at heart—they went to a religious prep school. In 1989, a judge in Dallas handed a sentence he acknowledged as light to the eighteen-year-old murderer of two gay men, because the murderer had killed them in a gay cruising zone, where the judge said they might be molesting children. The judge thereby justified a form of vigilantism that bears an eerie resemblance to the lynching of black men on the grounds that they might molest white women. Indeed, queer-bashing has the same function that past lynchings of blacks had—to keep a whole stigmatized group in line. As with lynchings, society has routinely averted its eyes, giving its permission or even tacit approval to violence and harassment.

Police and juries will simply discount testimony from gays; they frequently construe assaults on and murders of gays as "justified" self-defense. The killer simply claims his act was an understandably panicked response to a sexual overture. Alternatively, when guilt seems patent, juries will accept highly implausible "diminished capacity" defenses, as in the case of Dan White's 1978 assassination of openly gay San Francisco city councilman Harvey Milk. Hostess Twinkies made him do it, or so the successful defense went. These inequitable procedures collectively show that the life and liberty of gays, like those of blacks, simply count for less than the life and liberty of members of the dominant culture.

The equitable rule of law is the heart of an orderly society. The collapse of the rule of law for gays shows that society is willing to perpetrate the worst possible injustices against them. As the ethnic and religious wars in the former Yugoslavia have made clear, there is only a difference in degree between the collapse of the rule of law and systematic extermination of members of a population simply for having some group status. In the Nazi concentration camps, gays were forced to wear pink triangles as identifying badges, just as Jews were forced to wear yellow stars. In remembrance of that collapse of the rule of law, the pink triangle has become the chief symbol of the gay rights movement.

Gays are also subject to widespread discrimination in employment. Governments are leading offenders here. They do a lot of discriminating themselves, require that others do it, and set precedents favoring discrimination in the private sector. Lesbians and gay men are barred from serving in the armed forces. The federal government has also denied gays employment in the CIA, FBI, National Security Agency, and the state department. The government refuses to give security clearances to gays and so forces the country's considerable private sector military and aerospace contractors to fire employees known to be gay and to avoid hiring those perceived to be gay. State and local governments regularly fire gay teachers, policemen, firemen, social workers, and anyone else who has contact with the public. Further, state licensing laws (though frequently honored only in the breech) officially bar gays from a vast array of occupations and professions—everything from doctors, lawyers, accountants, and nurses to hairdressers, morticians, even used car dealers.

Gays are subject to discrimination in a wide variety of other ways, including private-sector employment, public accommodations, housing, insurance of all types, custody, adoption, and zoning regulations that bar "singles" or "nonrelated" couples from living together. A 1988 study by the congressional Office of Technology Assessment found that a third of America's insurance companies openly admit that they discriminate against lesbians and gay men. In nearly half the states, same-sex sexual behavior is illegal, so that the central role of sex to meaningful life is officially denied to lesbians and gay men.

Illegality, discrimination, and the absorption by gays of society's hatred of them all interact to impede and, for some, block altogether the ability of gay men and lesbians to create and maintain significant personal relations with loved ones. Every facet of life is affected by discrimination. Only the most compelling reasons could justify it.

Many people think society's treatment of gays is justified because they think gays are extremely immoral. To evaluate this claim, different senses of "moral" must be distinguished. Sometimes by "morality" is meant the values generally held by members of a society—its mores, norms, and customs. On this understanding, gays certainly are not moral: Lots of people hate them, and social customs are designed to register widespread disapproval of gays. The problem here is that this sense of morality is merely a descriptive one. On this understanding, every society has a morality—even Nazi society, which had racism and mob rule as central features of its "morality" understood in this sense. What is needed in order to use the notion of morality to praise or condemn behavior is a sense of morality that is prescriptive or normative.

As the Nazi example makes clear, that a belief or claim is descriptively moral does not entail that it is normatively moral. A lot of people in a society saying something is good, even over aeons, does not make it so. The rejection of the long history of socially approved and state-enforced slavery is another good example of this principle at work. Slavery would be wrong even if nearly everyone liked it. So consistency and fairness require that one abandon the belief that gays are immoral simply because most people dislike or disapprove of gays.

Furthermore, recent historical and anthropological research has shown that opinion about gays has been by no means universally negative. It has varied widely even within the larger part of the Christian era and even within the Church itself. There are even societies—current ones—where homosexual behavior is not only tolerated but is a universal compulsory part of male social maturation. Within the last thirty years, American society has undergone a grand turnabout from deeply ingrained, near total condemnation to near total acceptance on two emotionally charged "moral" or "family" issues—contraception and divorce. Society holds its current descriptive morality of gays not because it has to, but because it chooses to.

If popular opinion and custom are not enough to ground moral condemnation of homosexuality, perhaps religion can. Such arguments usually proceed along two lines. One claims that the condemnation is a direct revelation of God, usually through the Bible. The other claims to be able to detect condemnation in God's plan as manifested in nature; homosexuality (it is claimed) is "contrary to nature."

One of the more remarkable discoveries of recent gay research is that the Bible may not be as univocal in its condemnation of homosexuality as many have believed. Christ never mentions homosexuality. Recent interpreters of the Old Testament have pointed out that the story of Lot at Sodom is probably intended to condemn inhospitality rather than homosexuality. Further, some of the Old Testament condemnations of homosexuality seem simply to be ways of tarring those of the Israelites' opponents who happen to accept homosexual practices when the Israelites themselves did not. If so, the condemnation is merely a quirk of history and rhetoric rather than a moral precept.

What does seem clear is that those who regularly cite the Bible to condemn an activity like homosexuality do so by reading it selectively. Do ministers who cite what they take to be condemnations of homosexuality in Leviticus maintain in their lives all the hygienic and dietary laws of Leviticus? If they cite the story of Lot at Sodom to condemn homosexuality, do they also cite the story of Lot in the Cave to praise incestuous rape? It seems then not that the Bible is being used to ground condemnations of homosexuality as much as society's dislike of homosexuality is being used to interpret the Bible.

Even if a consistent portrait of condemnation could be gleaned from the Bible, what social significance should it be given? One of the guiding principles of society, enshrined in the Constitution as a check against the government, is that decisions affecting social policy are not made on religious grounds. The Religious Right has been successful in stymieing sodomy-law reform, in defunding gay safe-sex literature and gay art, and in blocking the introduction of gay materials into school curriculums. If the real ground of the alleged immorality invoked by governments to discriminate against gays is religious (as it seems to be in these cases), then one of the major commitments of our nation is violated. Religious belief is a fine guide around which a person might organize his own life, but an awful instrument around which to organize some-one else's life.

People also try to justify society's treatment of gays by saying they are unnatural. Though the ac-cusation of unnaturalness looks whimsical, when applied to homosexuality, it is usually delivered with venom of forethought. It carries a high emotional charge, usually expressing disgust and evincing queasiness. Probably it is nothing but an emotional charge. For people get equally disgusted and queasy at all sorts of things that are perfectly natural, yet that could hardly be fit subjects for moral condem-nation. Two typical examples in current American culture are some people's responses to mothers' suckling in public and to women who do not shave body hair. Similarly people fling the term "unnat-ural" against gays in the same breath and with the same force as when they call gays "sick" and "gross." When people have strong emotional reac-tions, as they do in these cases, without being able to give good reasons for them, they are thought of not as operating morally, but as being obsessed and manic. So the feelings of disgust that some people have toward gays will hardly ground a charge of immorality.

When "nature" is taken in technical rather than ordinary usages, it also cannot ground a charge of homosexual immorality. When unnatural means "by artifice" or "made by humans," it can be pointed out that virtually everything that is good about life is unnatural in this sense. The chief fea-ture that distinguishes people from other animals is people's very ability to make over the world to meet their needs and desires. Indeed people's well-being depends on these departures from nature. On this understanding of human nature and the natural, ho-mosexuality is perfectly unobjectionable; it is simply a means by which some people adapt nature to fulfill their desires and needs.

Another technical sense of natural is that some-thing is natural and so, good, if it fulfills some function in nature. On this view, homosexuality is unnatural because it violates the function of genitals, which is to produce babies. One problem with this view is that lots of bodily parts have lots of functions and just because some one activity can be fulfilled by only one organ (say, the mouth for eating), this activ-ity does not condemn other functions of the organ to immorality (say, the mouth for talking, licking stamps, blowing bubbles, or having sex). So the pos-sible use of the genitals to produce children does not, without more, condemn the use of the genitals for other purposes, say, achieving ecstasy and intimacy.

The functional view of nature will only provide a morally condemnatory sense to the unnatural if a thing that might have many uses has but one proper function to the exclusion of other possible functions. But whether this is so cannot be established simply by looking at the thing. For what is seen is all its possible functions. The notion of function seemed like it might ground moral authority, but instead it turns out that moral authority is needed to define proper function.

Some people try to fill in this moral authority by appeal to the "design" or "order" of an organ, saying, for instance, that the genitals are designed for the purpose of procreation. But these people cheat intellectually if they do not make explicit who the designer and orderer is. If the "who" is God, we are back to square one—holding others accountable to one's own religious beliefs.

Further, ordinary moral attitudes about child-bearing will not provide the needed supplement which would produce a positive obligation to use the genitals for procreation. Though there are local exceptions, society's general attitude toward a child-less couple is that of pity not censure—even if the couple could have children. The pity may be an unsympathetic one, that is, not registering a course one would choose for oneself, but this does not make it a course one would require of others. The couple who discovers they cannot have children are viewed not as having thereby had a debt cancelled, but rather as having to forgo some of the richness of life, just as a quadriplegic is viewed not as absolved from some moral obligation to hop, skip, and jump, but as missing some of the richness of life. Consis-tency requires then that, at most, gays who do not or cannot have children are to be pitied rather than condemned. What is immoral is the willful prevent-ing of people from achieving the richness of life. Immorality in this regard lies with those social cus-toms, regulations, and statutes that prevent lesbians and gay men from establishing blood or adoptive families, not with gays themselves.

Many gays would like to raise or foster children—perhaps those alarming number of gay kids who have been beaten up and thrown out of their "families" for being gay. And indeed many les-bian and gay male couples are now raising robust, happy families where children are the blessings of adoption, artificial insemination, or surrogacy. The country is experiencing something approaching a gay and lesbian baby boom.

Sometimes people attempt to establish authority for a moral obligation to use bodily parts in a certain fashion simply by claiming that moral laws are natural laws and vice versa. On this account, inanimate objects and plants are good in that they follow natural laws by necessity, animals follow them by instinct, and persons follow them by a rational will. People are special in that they must first discover the laws that govern them. Now, even if one believes the view—dubious in the post-Newtonian, post-Darwinian world—that natural laws in the usual sense (e = mc^2, for instance) have some moral content, it is not at all clear how one is to discover the laws in nature that apply to people.

On the one hand, if one looks to people themselves for a model—and looks hard enough—one finds amazing variety, including homosexual relations as a social ideal (as in upper-class fifth-century Athens) and even as socially mandatory (as in some Melanesian initiation rites today). When one looks to people, one is simply unable to strip away the layers of social custom, history, and taboo in order to see what's really there to any degree more specific than that people are the creatures that make over their world and are capable of abstract thought. That this is so should raise doubts that neutral principles are to be found in human nature that will condemn homosexuality

On the other hand, if one looks to nature apart from people for models, the possibilities are staggering. There are fish that change sex over their lifetimes: Should we "follow nature" and be operative transsexuals? Orangutans, genetically our next of kin, live completely solitary lives without social organization of any kind among adults: Ought we to "follow nature" and be hermits? There are many species where only two members per generation reproduce: Shall we be bees? The search in nature for people's purpose far from finding sure models for action is likely to leave one morally rudderless.

But (it might also be asked) aren't gays willfully the way they are? It is generally conceded that if sexual orientation is something over which an individual—for whatever reason—has virtually no control, then discrimination against gays is presumptively wrong, as it is against racial and ethnic classes.

Attempts to answer the question whether or not sexual orientation is something that is reasonably thought to be within one's own control usually

appeal simply to various claims of the biological or "mental" sciences. But the ensuing debate over genes, hormones, hypothalamuses, twins, early childhood development, and the like is as unnecessary as it is currently inconclusive. All that is needed to answer the question is to look at the actual experience of lesbians and gay men in current society and it becomes fairly clear that sexual orientation is not likely a matter of choice.

On the one hand, the "choice" of the gender of a sexual partner does not seem to express a trivial desire which might as easily be fulfilled by a simple substitution of the desired object. Picking the gender of a sex partner is decidedly dissimilar, that is, to such activities as picking a flavor of ice cream. If an ice cream parlor is out of one's flavor, one simply picks another. And if people were persecuted, threatened with jail terms, shattered careers, loss of family and housing and the like for eating, say, rocky road ice cream, no one would ever eat it. Everyone would pick another easily available flavor. That gay people abide in being gay even in the face of persecution suggests that being gay is not a matter of easy choice.

On the other hand, even if establishing a sexual orientation is not like making a relatively trivial choice, perhaps it is relevantly like making the central and serious life-choices by which individuals try to establish themselves as being of some type or having some occupation. Again, if one examines gay experience, this seems not to be the general case. For one virtually never sees anyone setting out to become a homosexual, in the way one does see people setting out to become doctors, lawyers, and bricklayers. One does not find gays-to-be picking some end—"At some point in the future, I want to become a homosexual"—and then setting about planning and acquiring the ways and means to that end, in the way one does see people deciding that they want to become lawyers, and then sees them plan what courses to take and what sort of temperaments, habits, and skills to develop in order to become lawyers. Typically gays-to-be simply find themselves having homosexual encounters and yet, at least initially, resisting quite strongly the identification of being homosexual. Such a person even very likely resists having such encounters, but ends up having them anyway. Only with time, luck, and great personal effort, but sometimes never, does the person gradually come to accept her or his orientation, to view it as a given material condition of life, coming as materials do with certain capacities and limitations. The person begins to act in accordance with his or her orientation and its capacities, seeing its actualization as a requisite for an integrated personality and as a central component of personal well-being. As a result, the experience of coming out to oneself has for gays the basic structure of a discovery, not the structure of a choice. And far from signaling immorality, coming out to others affords one of the few remaining opportunities in ever more bureaucratic, technological, and socialistic societies to *manifest* courage.

How would society at large be changed if gays were socially accepted? Suggestions to change social policy with regard to gays are invariably met with claims that to do so would invite the destruction of civilization itself: After all, isn't that what did Rome in? Actually, Rome's decay paralleled not the flourishing of homosexuality but its repression under the later Christianized emperors. Predictions of American civilization's imminent demise have been as premature as they have been frequent. Civilization has shown itself to be rather resilient here, in large part because of the country's traditional commitments to respect for privacy, to individual liberties, and especially to people minding their own business. These all give society an open texture and the flexibility to try out things to see what works. And because of this, one now need not speculate about what changes reforms in gay social policy might bring to society at large. For many reforms have already been tried.

Half the states have decriminalized lesbian and gay male sex acts. Can you guess which of the following states still have sodomy laws: Wisconsin, Minnesota; New Mexico, Arizona; Vermont, New Hampshire; Nebraska, Kansas? One from each pair does and one does not have sodomy laws. And yet one would be hard pressed to point out any substantial social differences between the members of each pair. (If you're interested: It's the second of each pair with them.) Empirical studies have shown that there is no increase in other crimes in states that have decriminalized.

Neither has the passage of legislation barring discrimination against gays ushered in the end of civilization. Nearly a hundred counties and municipalities, including some of the country's largest cities (like Chicago and New York City) have passed such statutes, as have eight states: Wisconsin, Connecticut, Massachusetts, Hawaii, New Jersey, Vermont, California, and Minnesota. Again, no more

brimstone has fallen in these places than elsewhere. Staunchly antigay cities, like Miami and Houston, have not been spared the AIDS crisis.

Berkeley, California, followed by a couple dozen other cities including New York, has even passed "domestic partner" legislation giving gay couples at least some of the same rights to city benefits as are held by heterosexually married couples, and yet Berkeley has not become more weird than it already was. A number of major universities (like Stanford and the University of Chicago) and respected corporations (like Levi Strauss and Company, the Montefiore Medical Center of New York, and Apple Computer, Inc.) are also following Berkeley's lead.

Seemingly hysterical predictions that the American family would collapse if such reforms would pass proved false, just as the same dire predictions that the availability of divorce would lessen the ideal and desirability of marriage proved unfounded. Indeed if current discrimination, which drives gays into hiding and into anonymous relations, ended, far from seeing gays destroying American families, one would see gays forming them.

Virtually all gays express a desire to have a permanent lover. But currently society and its discriminatory impulse make gay coupling very difficult. It is difficult for people to live together as couples without having their sexual orientation perceived in the public realm and becoming targets for discrimination. Life in hiding is a pressure-cooker existence not easily shared with another. Members of nongay couples are asked to imagine what it would take to erase every trace of their own sexual orientation for even just one week.

Even against oppressive odds, gays have shown an amazing tendency to nest. And those gay couples who have survived the odds show that the structure of more usual couplings is not a matter of destiny, but of personal responsibility. The so-called basic unit of society turns out not to be a unique immutable atom, but can adopt different parts, be adapted to different needs, and even be improved. Gays might even have a thing or two to teach others about divisions of labor, the relation of sensuality and intimacy, and the stages of development in such relations.

If discrimination ceased, gay men and lesbians would enter the mainstream of the human community openly and with self-respect. The energies that the typical gay person wastes in the anxiety of leading a day-to-day existence of systematic disguise would be released for use in personal flourishing. From this release would be generated the many spin-off benefits that accrue to a society when its individual members thrive.

Society would be richer for acknowledging another aspect of human diversity. Families with gay members would develop relations based on truth and trust rather than lies and fear. And the heterosexual majority would be better off for knowing that they are no longer trampling their gay friends and neighbors.

Finally, and perhaps paradoxically, in extending to gays the rights and benefits reserved for its dominant culture, America would confirm its deeply held vision of itself as a morally progressing nation, a nation itself advancing and serving as a beacon for others—especially with regard to human rights. The words with which our national pledge ends—"with liberty and justice for all"—are not a description of the present, but a call for the future. America is a nation given to a prophetic political rhetoric that acknowledges that morality is not arbitrary and that justice is not merely the expression of the current collective will. It is this vision that led the black civil rights movement to its successes. Those senators and representatives who opposed that movement and its centerpiece, the 1964 Civil Rights Act, on obscurantist grounds, but who lived long enough and were noble enough came in time to express their heartfelt regret and shame at what they had done. It is to be hoped and someday to be expected that those who now grasp at anything to oppose the extension of that which is best about America to gays will one day feel the same.

---

53. *Homosexuality's Legal Revolution*

CARL F. HOROWITZ

While opposing antisodomy laws, Carl Horowitz contends that homosexuals who decide to live openly as homosexuals should accept the disapproval of those around them. He further contends that while the homosexual rights movement began as an acceptable demand for the state not to interfere with private homosexual behavior, it has evolved into an unacceptable demand for the state to interfere on behalf of public homosexual behavior.

Last April, a brief series of events occurred in a Madison, Wisconsin, restaurant that spoke volumes about the current character of the homosexual rights movement. An employee of the Espresso Royal Cafe asked two women—presumably lesbians—to refrain from passionately kissing as they sat at a window table. Madison's gay community was not amused. The very next day, about 125 homosexual demonstrators showed up on the premises, and conducted a "kiss-in" for several minutes. A spokeswoman for the protesters, Malvene Collins, demanded, "You say gays and lesbians cannot show affection here? Why not here but in every other restaurant in Madi-

son?" The establishment's chastised owner, Donald Hanigan, assured the crowd, "I regret that this incident ever happened. I want all of you to come in here every day."[1]

In October, several dozen homosexual males, many dressed in women's clothing, openly hugged and kissed in a terminal of Seattle-Tacoma Airport, and handed out condoms and leaflets to travelers. Matt Nagel, spokesman for the Seattle chapter of a new homosexual organization, Queer Nation, seemed to sum up the feeling among militants in the local homosexual community. "We're going to homophobic bars, we're going to pack them, we're going to be openly affectionate, we're going to dance together and make it uncomfortable for all the straight people there."[2]

Reprinted from the *Freeman* with permission of the Foundation for Economic Education, Inc.

At the same time in Chicago, six homosexual couples staged a "kiss-in" at the cosmetics counter of a Bloomingdale's department store until they were escorted out by security guards. Far from being deterred, the couples shortly went down to the cafeteria of a nearby office building, where they resumed their public display of affection.[3]

A Bid for Legitimacy

After some two decades of confrontation, the homosexual rights movement is consolidating its bid for legitimacy. The phrase "Out of the closet, and into the streets" sounds quaint. That battle has already been won. Openly homosexual adults are certainly in the streets—and in stores, airports, and "homophobic" bars. Openly gay television characters, each with handsome, well-scrubbed looks, populate daytime and evening drama. Gay-oriented news programming is available on radio and television. Homosexual activists have all but completed their campaign to persuade the nation's educational establishment that homosexuality is normal "alternative" behavior, and thus any adverse reaction to it is akin to a phobia, such as fear of heights, or an ethnic prejudice, such anti-Semitism.[4]

The movement now stands on the verge of fully realizing its use of law to create a separate homosexual society paralleling that of the larger society in every way, and to intimidate heterosexuals uncomfortable about coming into contact with it. Through aggressive lobbying by such gay organizations as the Human Rights Campaign Fund, the Lambda Legal Defense and Education Fund, and the National Gay and Lesbian Task Force, the first part of that mission has enjoyed enormous success. About 90 counties and municipalities now have ordinances banning discrimination on the basis of gender orientation. There are roughly 50 openly gay public officials, up from less than a half-dozen in 1980.[5]

Gay couples increasingly receive the full benefits of marriage, if not through state recognition of homosexual marriage ceremonies, then through enactment of domestic partnership laws.[6] The State of California recently took a big step toward legalization of such marriages: This December it announced that "nontraditional" families, including homosexual couples, could formally register their unions as "unincorporated nonprofit associations."[7] Divorced gay parents are receiving with increasing frequency the right to custody of natural children. Gay adults without children are increasingly receiving the right to adopt them. Aspiring homosexual clergy are demanding—and receiving—the right to be ordained. Openly gay teachers are teaching in public schools. Homosexual soldiers, aware that their sexual orientation is grounds for expulsion from the military, openly declare their proclivities.

A Federal gay rights bill is the ultimate prize, and homosexual activists are blunt and resolute in pursuing such legislation. For example, Jeff Levi, spokesman for the National Gay and Lesbian Task Force, remarked at a press conference coinciding with the national gay march on Washington in October 1987:

> . . . we are no longer seeking just a right to privacy and a protection from wrong. We also have a right—as heterosexual Americans already have—to see government and society affirm our lives. . . . Until our relationships are recognized in the law—through domestic partner legislation or the definition of beneficiaries, for example—until we are provided with the same financial incentives in tax law and government programs to affirm our family relationships, then we will not have achieved equality in American society.[8]

Yet homosexual activists know that this legal revolution will never succeed without the unpleasant task of coercing heterosexuals into masking their displeasure with homosexuality. It is thus not enough merely to break down all existing barriers to homosexual affection being expressed through marriage, childrearing, or employment. The law must additionally be rewritten to make it as difficult as possible for heterosexuals to avoid contact with such displays, or to show discomfort toward them.

This two-edged approach would create a world in which stringent laws at all levels, aggressively enforced and strictly interpreted, force business owners to refuse to discriminate against the openly homosexual in patronage, leasing, and hiring. Removing overtly homosexual patrons from a bar, an airport, or any other public space would result in heavy fines and even jail sentences against property owners or their employees (or in lieu of these sanctions, mandatory purgation). Derogatory remarks directed at homosexuals, even with sexuality only incidental, would likewise result in criminal penalties.

1990: A Pivotal Year

The year 1990 was pivotal for the homosexual legal revolution. The states of Massachusetts and Wisconsin in the late 1980s had enacted laws forbidding discrimination against homosexuals. The victories would come quickly now, especially at the local level. In March, the City of Pittsburgh voted to include sexual orientation as a right protected under the City Code. In October, Stanford University allowed homosexual couples to qualify for university student housing. In November, voters in San Francisco, buoyed by a heavy turnout of that city's large gay population, produced a "lavender sweep," not only passing Proposition K, a city initiative to allow homosexuals to register as domestic partners at City Hall (a similar measure was defeated in 1989), but electing two openly lesbian candidates to the City Board of Supervisors, and an openly homosexual male candidate to the Board of Education.

Voters in Seattle refused to repeal an existing gender orientation ordinance. Congress did its part early in the year by overwhelmingly passing the Hate Crimes Statistics Act (or Hate Crimes Act), which requires the Justice Department to publish hate crime statistics according to classifications that include sexual orientation.[9]

This agenda would likely have been even further realized with Michael Dukakis as President. In 1988, his Presidential campaign organization placed an advertisement in a New York homosexual newspaper, pledging, "As President, I will fight for Federal legislation to add a prohibition against discrimination based on sexual orientation to the existing protections of the 1964 Civil Rights Act."[10] Rank-and-file pressure on even a centrist Democratic Presidential candidate would be difficult to fend off. Rule 5C of the National Democratic Party currently states: "With respect to groups such as . . . lesbians and gay men . . . each state party shall develop and submit party outreach programs for such groups identified in their plans, including recruitment, education and training, in order to receive full participation by such groups in the delegate-selection process and at all levels of party affairs."

For close to 20 years, old-time party regulars have been walking on eggshells on this issue, praying it would go away, yet never really having the stomach for open conflict. Now the day of reckoning looms. Democratic candidates and party officials opposing this recent requirement (none dare call it a quota) must be willing either silently to watch the slow disintegration of their party, or to speak out and face de facto expulsion. It is therefore not surprising that all candidates for the Democratic Party Presidential nomination in 1988, in response to a questionnaire circulated by the National Gay and Lesbian Task Force, promised to support a Federal gay rights bill.

Republicans offer only little more resistance. The few . . . who do speak out against the homosexual lobby—most notably, U.S. Representative William Dannemeyer of California—enjoy little support from their party.[11] One need only remember how reluctantly and belatedly Congress acted merely to reprimand U.S. Representative Barney Frank, Massachusetts Democrat, for aiding a male roommate in running a prostitution service from the basement of his Washington, D.C., townhouse. One need only remember also how quickly a Bush White House official, Doug Wead, who circulated a memorandum complaining of the high visibility of gay activists at the Hate Crimes Act signing ceremony, was fired from his post.

"Gay Civil Rights"

The homosexual lobby speaks of itself as struggling for "civil rights." "The gay community's goal is integration—just as it was with Martin Luther King," argues homosexual activist and San Francisco Board of Supervisors President Harry Britt.[12] Yet, underneath the surface, gay civil rights seems analogous to Black "civil rights" *after* Reverend King's death. Far from seeking integration with the heterosexual world, it vehemently avoids it. More important, the movement seeks to win sinecures through the state, and over any objections by "homophobic" opposition. With a cloud of a heavy fine or even a jail sentence hanging over a mortgage lender, a rental agent, or a job interviewer who might be discomforted by them, homosexuals under these laws can win employment, credit, housing, and other economic entitlements. Heterosexuals would have no right to discriminate against homosexuals, but apparently, not vice versa. Libertarians as well as traditionalists ought to be troubled by this.

Consider a recent controversy in Madison, Wisconsin, as noted earlier, a national bastion of "enlightened" attitudes. Three single women had recently moved into the same apartment, and one announced that she was a lesbian. The other two, not unreasonably, asked her to move. The lesbian filed a grievance with the local Human Rights Board, and, predictably, won. The shock came in the punishment. The two heterosexual women had to pay $1,500 in "damages" to the lesbian, send her a public letter of apology, attend a two-hour "briefing" on homosexuality (conducted, needless to say, by homosexuals), and submit to having their living arrangements monitored for two years.[13]

With such laws in effect, this outcome would not be so much played out as simply avoided. Let one hypothetical example suffice, one that no doubt *has* been played out regularly, and that goes a long way in explaining why in any metropolitan area gays tend to cluster in a few neighborhoods.

A man enters an apartment rental office, inquiring about a vacancy. He openly indicates he is a homosexual, or at least implies as much through certain mannerisms. For good measure, he brings along his lover. The rental manager fudges, clears his throat, and says, "Well, er, several people are looking at the apartment. Call me later." An hour later, a second man, alone, walks in. He does not announce his sexuality. Who gets the apartment?

In the absence of gay protectionism, and assuming equal incomes, the manager (sighing with relief) would probably award the apartment to the second applicant. Gay militants would cry, "Discrimination!"—and miss the point. Discrimination based on sexual orientation is fundamentally different from that based on race. Homosexuality constitutes a behavioral, not a genetic trait. It is within the moral right of a landlord, job interviewer, banker, or anyone else performing a "gatekeeper" function to discourage economically risky behavior, sexual or otherwise. Libertarian columnist Doug Bandow articulates this:

> The point is, homosexuals have no right to force others to accept or support their lifestyle. Certainly government has no business discriminating against them: Antisodomy laws, for instance, are a vicious intrusion in the most

intimate form of human conduct. And gays who pay taxes have as much right to government services and employment as anyone else.

> But someone who decides to live openly as a homosexual should accept the disapproval of those around him. For many Americans still believe that there is a fundamental, unchangeable moral code by which men are to live. . . .

> Using government to bludgeon homophobics into submission is even more intolerant than the original discrimination.[14]

Under normal circumstances, the rental manager would not want to lease to gays who, once moved in, might tell their friends that the neighborhood could have possibilities as a "gay" one. Word-of-mouth travels fast within their world. Beyond a certain "tipping-point," many heterosexual residents near and within the complex, rather than risk feeling stigmatized, would choose to move. Their places largely would be taken by overt homosexuals.

In fact this is exactly how neighborhoods such as Castro (San Francisco), West Hollywood (formerly part of Los Angeles, now separately incorporated largely due to gay pressure), the West Village (New York City), and Dupont Circle (Washington, D.C.) all rapidly developed reputations as "gay neighborhoods," and how large sections of Martha's Vineyard, Fire Island, and Rehoboth Beach became "gay resorts."[15] The tipping-point principle also applies to public facilities such as restaurants. At the Grapevine Cafe in Columbus, Ohio, for example, heterosexual customers stopped coming when the clientele became heavily gay.[16]

What would happen with a sexual orientation law in place? The rental manager knows that if he turns down an openly homosexual applicant, he risks prosecution. Any rejection can serve as proof of discriminatory intent, even with factors such as length of employment, income, and previous tenant record taken into account.[17] In response to such a fear, the manager, though reluctantly, is likely to award the apartment to the homosexual.

For gay activists, therein lies the payoff. By codifying into law "protection" of homosexual mannerisms, they can intimidate gatekeepers into providing job security and housing for the openly homosexual. Thus, without necessarily mentioning anything about quotas or, for that matter, homosexuality, law in the United States is increasingly mandating *homosexual affirmative action.*[18] Such law has the same intent as the recently vetoed Kennedy-Hawkins Civil Rights Act.

Sexual Schism

If the homosexual rights movement is in large measure an affirmative action strategy, certain consequences should be evident, all of which already are on their way to being entrenched. Most obviously, American culture is experiencing a sexual schism as deep as any racial one. There are other damaging ramifications.

First, wherever such laws exist, they will attract homosexuals to the jurisdictions enacting them. Common sense dictates that any community laying out the welcome mat for homosexuality lays it for homosexuals, implicitly telling others to kindly step aside. Aside from legal protection, there is political strength in concentrated numbers. Most aspiring elected officials in San Francisco, for example, must now pay homage to the achievement of local gays, and show up at gay events. As Proposition K coordinator Jean Harris remarked following the November elections, "We've shocked the world and made history with this lavender sweep. . . . It's clear that if you don't get the support of the gay-lesbian community you're going to be in trouble."[19] While the homosexual voting bloc will never be a majority in any city, even San Francisco, it can wield enormous veto power over the objections of all other blocs.

Second, having learned the power of the gatekeeper role, many homosexuals will seek to become gatekeepers themselves. It takes no great stretch of imagination, for example, to understand that the growing number of college administrations severely punishing antigay harassment (even if such "harassment" takes no more sinister a form than a satirical campus newspaper editorial or cartoon) has much to do with the growing number of college administrators and faculty who are themselves homosexual (and possibly were hired on that very basis).[20] Nor does it take much imagination to understand that gay employers have more reason than ever to favor homosexuals in their hiring and promotion practices.

Third, these laws will create market bottlenecks. Heterosexuals and even "closeted" homosexuals will be at a competitive disadvantage for jobs and housing. For them, prices will be higher and wages lower than in the absence of such "safeguards." This is especially significant since gay culture is visible in high-cost cities such as New York and San Francisco.

Gays view economic victories to be won here, and few have been as resounding as the *Braschi* decision.[21] In July 1989, the New York State Court of Appeals ruled that a gay lover had the right to stay in his deceased partner's rent-controlled apartment because he qualified as a member of the partner's family, a decision recently upheld by the Appellate Division of the State Supreme Court. "We conclude that the term 'family,'" the lower court argued, "should not be rigidly restricted to those people who have formalized their relationship by obtaining, for instance, a marriage certificate or an adoption order. . . A more realistic, and certainly equally valid, view of a family includes two adult lifetime partners whose relationship is long term and characterized by an emotional and financial commitment and interdependence."[22]

Gay activists understandably were elated at this imprimatur for homosexual marriage; they know household economics. Homosexual couples defined as "married" could reduce not only their housing costs, but also their income taxes (by filing jointly), pensions, and insurance premiums. They also would qualify for paid medical leave, spousal bereavement leave, and other employee benefits. At this writing, the San Francisco chapter of the American Civil Liberties Union is considering suing several locally based corporations that deny benefits to their homosexual employees' partners.[23]

Fourth, the new legalism will increase heterosexual anger—and even violence—toward homosexuals. Reports of "gay bashing" (the real kind) simultaneous with increased homosexual visibility cannot be a coincidence. What economist Thomas Sowell[24] and psychologist Stephen Johnson[25] have each revealed about racial affirmative action can apply to sexual affirmative action as well; unprotected groups, lacking recourse through rule of law, may resort to violence against innocent members of protected groups. Those who make it their bailiwick to monitor every incident of petty harassment of gays are impervious to any possibility that when laws force heterosexuals to bottle up dialogue, their feelings may erupt in more destructive ways. *Gay bashing, then, is in some measure a product of the very laws designed to punish it.*

The Language of Victimhood

The radical homosexual movement seeks centralization of state power in the name of "civil rights." What began as a demand for the state not to interfere [with] private homosexual behavior has evolved into a demand for the state to intercede on behalf of public homosexual behavior. In so doing, the movement has advanced further into the same totalitarian netherworld that various Black and feminist movements also have come to occupy. In each case, activists proclaim "victim" status, malign the intentions of critics, and demand government entitlements that necessarily discriminate against others. "Once upon a time," syndicated columnist Paul Greenberg writes in *The Washington Times,* "civil rights were unifying and universal—a way to open society to the claims of individual merit. Now 'civil rights' becomes a code word for dividing society into competing, resentful groups."[26]

Gay militants know the cue-card language of victimhood. For example, Gara LaMarche and William B. Rubenstein write in *The Nation,* "The targets of the 1950s witch hunts were both Communists and other leftists, labeled 'subversives,' and homosexuals, labeled 'sexual perverts.' Today, as the cold war mentality collapses, enemies are again being found at home, but this time lesbians and gay men are leading the list."[27] With former President Ronald Reagan and Cardinal John O'Connor leading the list of personages in the "McCarthy" role, the authors can make believe this really is the 1950s.

Just as opposing current racial and ethnic civil rights orthodoxies inevitably invites being labelled "racist" and "ethnocentric," opposing the current homosexual orthodoxy almost guarantees being denounced as "homophobic." One is simply not free to not pay tribute to them. The few people willing to toe the line pay the consequences. Pete Hamill, hardly an ally of the hard Right, knows this too well. Having written a column in the August 1990 *Esquire* sharply critical of those aggressively politicizing their homosexuality (though with genuine warmth for his homosexual friends), he was subsequently subject to constant attack by ACT-UP (AIDS Coalition to Unleash Power) and other homosexual gendarmes.[28] When early in 1990, Martin Luther King III remarked in a speech in Poughkeepsie, New York, that "something must be wrong" with homosexuals, enraged gay leaders demanded (and got) an apology.

Heterosexuals need not even fire the first shot to invoke gay wrath. When a pair of Queer Nation activists disrupted the airing of the December 14, 1990, segment of *The Arsenio Hall Show,* they insisted that the host explain why so few of his guests were gay. Unappeased by Hall's assurance that many are, the activists continued their on-camera ranting for about 10 minutes. Hall, of course, must now bear the onus as a "homophobe."[29]

Gay activists may incessantly speak of their "rights," yet oddly care little for those of others. Articles in *Outweek,* a year-old tabloid dedicated to exposing homosexual liaisons (real or imagined) of public figures believed otherwise to be heterosexual, routinely call for removing freedom of speech from anyone alleged to be "homophobic."[30] A placard at a recent gay rights march in Washington read, "BAN HOMOPHOBIA, NOT HOMOSEXUALITY."[31] Radical homosexuals apparently do not reciprocate when it comes to the First Amendment.

The most shameful example of the gays' civil rights double standard . . . was their temporarily successful attempt to blackball Andy Rooney, longtime humorist of CBS's *60 Minutes* program. The details of the saga—Rooney's allegedly antigay comments on a CBS news special reviewing the events of 1989;[32] the subsequent storm of protest by gay militants; Rooney's explanation to them in the form of a letter to and an interview with a national gay newspaper, the *Advocate;* the anti-Black comments falsely attributed to Rooney in the interview; and his three-month suspension without pay from CBS—are well-known.[33]

[The] interview was a pure frame-up [and] homosexual militants routinely make hate-filled denunciations of "straights." More ominous is how quickly CBS moved to institute damage control, choosing to take the word of a gay cub reporter, lacking any tape of the interview, over that of Mr. Rooney, a loyal and popular CBS employee for some four decades. This is how CBS, which now hires a homosexual group to conduct "gay sensitivity seminars" for its news personnel, responded to its fear of a lawsuit or a boycott of network sponsors. The network's action was an indication of how readily small businesses might capitulate under a federal gay civil rights law.

Rooney . . . was reinstated on *60 Minutes* before the three months, but no thanks to any good graces from CBS top brass. Give the credit instead to Rooney's supportive *60 Minutes* colleagues and the show's falling Nielsen ratings. Yet Rooney, chastened, had to issue a public apology prior to re-instatement, one that virtually forfeited his right to say "offensive" things about gays in the future, ironic since his job requires being cantankerously peevish. Free speech lost.

Homosexual militants also have little use for the right to privacy save their own. They view any public figure's possible homosexual behavior as grist for voyeuristic public consumption. The mere existence of a spurious scandal sheet like *Outweek* ought to outrage the sensibilities of all individual-ists. The hypocrisy of it all begs a comparison. Sup-pose the *National Enquirer* or some other general circulation gossip magazine exposed as homosexu-als the same celebrities that *Outweek* does. Homo-sexual activists would properly see this as character assassination. Yet . . . when a homosexual publica-tion engages in the identical practice, it is creating "positive gay role models."[34]

"Now, the idea that one must be either in the closet or out of it is an invention of those who would politicize sex and abolish privacy," Thomas Short writes in *National Review*. "They wrongly make what-ever is not publicly proclaimed seem secret, furtive. This dichotomy of being either in the closet or out of it should not exist. . . . We all have some secrets to keep."[35] Homosexual radicals do not keep sexual se-crets. Since a homosexual act is political, even the most casual encounter by an otherwise heterosexual person must be made public, at whatever cost to that person. *Outweek,* and the mentality to which it caters, is more than indiscreet; it is totalitarian.

The Growing Threat of Violence

There is something about encountering homosex-uality in its militant and pugnacious form that touches a deep, almost reflexive anger, even among most heterosexual liberals. That is why attempts at "mainstreaming" gay culture, even when holding an olive branch, are bound to fail. One of the sad-dest books to appear in recent years is *After the Ball: How America Will Conquer Its Fear and Hatred of Gays in the 90s.*[36] Authors Marshall Kirk and Hunter Madsen, both homosexual, advocate a national cam-paign to cheerfully "sell" gay culture. They suggest, for example, that gay organizations buy up adver-tising space in "straight" newspapers with pictures of historical figures such as Alexander the Great, asking, "Did you know he was gay?"

Kirk and Madsen, like their surlier compatriots, fail to grasp that public homosexuality strikes at both a heterosexual's fear of loss of sexual identity and sense of belonging to a family. For even in this age of artificial insemination, families are not sus-tainable without heterosexuality. No matter how much the homosexual activist naively protests, "Gays are people, too," such a plea will receive in re-turn grudging respect, and little else.

In a summary piece for *Newsweek*'s March 12, 1990, cover story, "The Future of Gay America," Jonathan Alter revealed a rare understanding of this dynamic.[37] He notes, "'Acting gay' often involves more than sexual behavior itself. Much of the dis-like for homosexuals centers not on who they are or what they do in private, but on so-called affec-tations—'swishiness' in men, the 'butch' look for women—not directly related to the more private sex act." Quite rightly so—one doubts if more than a tiny fraction of heterosexuals have even *inadver-tently* witnessed a homosexual act. Alter then gets to the core of the issue. "Heterosexuals," he writes, "tend to argue that gays can downplay these char-acteristics and 'pass' more easily in the straight world than Blacks can in a white world. . . . This may be true, but it's also irrelevant. For most gays those traits aren't affectations but part of their iden-tities; attacking their swishiness is the same as at-tacking *them*."

Yet if gays, through their carefully practiced "gay" mannerisms, know fully well they are antag-onizing many heterosexuals, then why do they dis-play them? Is it not in part to make heterosexuals sweat?[38] By aggressively politicizing these traits, and demanding that those objecting must grin and bear it, they are in a sense restricting heterosexual free-dom of speech. Male and even female opposition to persons with these traits is slowly taking a nasty turn, moving from violence of language to violence of fists. And yet, given the emerging legal climate, one discovers within oneself a disquieting empathy with the inchoate rage behind such acts.

Most heterosexuals are reasonably libertarian; an October 1989 Gallup Poll indicated that by a 47-to-36 margin (with the remainder undecided), Americans prefer legalization of homosexual rela-tions between consenting adults.[39] This is all to the good. Antisodomy laws serve no purpose but to intimidate people out of private, consensual acts. On the other hand, the brazen, *open* display of ho-mosexuality—as if to taunt, to tease, to maliciously sow confusion into sexual identities—is something most heterosexuals do not handle gracefully. With an unofficial government mandate for preferential treatment, it is not difficult to imagine a backlash. When homosexual lawyer-artist William Dobbs plastered explicit homosexual artwork throughout the Yale University campus back in 1989, he was not simply making a homoerotic statement; he was daring "homophobes" to remove the art, and risk suspension or expulsion from the university.[40] Those having little to lose may accept his dare—and it may be people like Dobbs as well as such art that gets torn up.

Should a sober discussion of the possibilities for heterosexual violence be forbidden? Nobody in a *rational* state of mind would seek to emulate the exploits of "skinheads" or the late San Francisco Supervisor Dan White. Yet let readers here imagine themselves in that Madison restaurant or Seattle airport, being witness to mass displays of homosexual kissing, and feeling utterly helpless to evince the slightest disapproval. Wouldn't such a scenario provoke an impulse, however fleeting and irrational, to do bodily harm? Doesn't the knowledge that the law is now stacked against even nonviolent disapproval ("hate crimes") merely add to the likelihood of a conflagration?

The principal motive of the gay movement is coming into focus with each passing month: to bait heterosexuals' less morally sturdy side, goading them into verbal or (better) physical assaults against the openly homosexual. That way, cries of homosexual victimhood would carry even more self-fulfilling prophecy, so much the better to vilify heterosexuals.

Gay militants aren't hesitant about admitting to such motives. Some want nothing less than war in the streets. Homosexual playwright and ACT-UP founder Larry Kramer recently called upon a gay audience to take gun practice for use in eventual combat against police and gay-bashers. "They hate us anyway," he rationalized. A cover of a recent issue of *Outweek* displayed a lesbian pointing a gun at the reader, with the headline, "Taking Aim at Bashers," while another cover announced, "We Hate Straights."[41] Even "mainstream" gay leaders, such as Urvashi Vaid, executive director of the National Gay and Lesbian Task Force, endorse such tactics, whatever the loss of potential supporters.[42]

The crowning legacy of the new gay legalism may yet be widespread violence, a violence brought on by state inhibition of rational dialogue at the behest of gay radicals, and in the name of "sensitivity." That alone is enough reason to oppose it.

Endnotes

1. "Gay Rights Protesters Win Right to Kiss," *The Washington Times*, April 18, 1990.
2. Joyce Price, "Queer Nation Decides It's Time to Bash Back," *The Washington Times*, October 15, 1990.
3. Price, "Queer Nation."
4. One of the best arguments that homosexuality is not simply a statistical aberration, but a behavioral abnormality, can be found in Steven Goldberg, "Is Homosexuality Normal?" *Policy Review*, Summer 1982, pp. 119–38.
5. "The Future of Gay America," *Newsweek*, March 12, 1990, pp. 21–22.
6. "Gay Measure Stirs Florida," *The Washington Times*, August 24, 1990.
7. Tupper Hall, "Gay Couples Allowed to File as 'Nonprofit' Associations," *The Washington Times*, December 17, 1990.
8. Jeff Levi, speech to National Press Club, October 10, 1987.
9. The term "hate crime," in the hands of the homosexual lobby, is so vague that even an accidental epithet could qualify as an offense. For example, of the 462 anti-homosexual "hate crimes" committed in Virginia in 1987, 423—over 90 percent—involved mere name calling. See

Patrick Buchanan, "The Real Victims of Hate Crimes," *The Washington Times*, March 7, 1990. The National Gay and Lesbian Task Force (NGLTF), in its own estimate of hate crimes committed nationwide in 1988, admitted that 77 percent were verbal. In fact, the origin of the legislation lay in a 1985 NGLTF presentation before the National Institute of Justice. See Congressman William Dannemeyer, *Shadow in the Land: Homosexuality in America* (San Francisco: Ignatius Press, 1989), pp. 71–75. Congressman Dannemeyer's book is the best currently available on the homosexual lobby.
10. Advertisement in the *New York Native*, April 18, 1988.
11. See Dannemeyer, *Shadow in the Land*.
12. Quoted in *Newsweek*, "The Future of Gay America," p. 21.
13. Phyllis Schlafly, "A Choice, Not an Echo in California," *The Washington Times*, March 2, 1990.
14. Doug Bandow, "Government as God," in *The Politics of Plunder: Misgovernment in Washington* (New Brunswick, NJ: Transaction, 1990), pp. 18–20.
15. Even sympathetic observers of this process admit that public identification of a neighborhood as "gay" induces nongays to move out. See Manuel Castells and Karen

Murphy, "Cultural Identity and Urban Structure: The Spatial Organization of San Francisco's Gay Community," in Norman I. and Susan S. Fainstein, eds., *Urban Policy Under Capitalism* (Beverly Hills, CA: Sage Publications, 1982), pp. 237–59. For a decidedly unsympathetic (and highly personal) account of how the process works in resort communities, see Midge Decter, "The Boys on the Beach," *Commentary*, September 1980, pp. 35–48.

16. James N. Baker and Shawn D. Lewis, "Lesbians: Portrait of a Community," *Newsweek*, March 12, 1990, p. 24.

17. For evidence of this, see Dannemeyer, *Shadow in the Land*, p. 70.

18. For example, gay activists have now convinced the courts that having AIDS qualifies as a condition covered by Federal handicap discrimination laws. *Shuttleworth v. Broward County*, 41 FEP Cases 406 (S.D. Fla. 1986); *Thomas v. Atascadero Unified School District*, 662 F. Supp. 376 (C.D. Cal. 1987).

19. Valerie Richardson, "Gay Voters Claim Biggest Victory in San Francisco," *The Washington Times*, November 9, 1990.

20. At Harvard University, for example, the administration quickly suspended a student who removed a sign from an empty table in a dining hall indicating that it was reserved for a campus homosexual organization. Leave aside the absurd notion that a lunch table ought to be reserved for any particular sexual group, and the absence of malice on the part of the student (who simply sought a vacant seat in an otherwise crowded room). This student's suspension could only have come about either because the administrators meting out the punishment were radical homosexuals or because they were heterosexual but feared crossing swords with campus homosexuals.

In a sad coda to this incident, the suspended student later committed suicide. See Thomas Sowell, "Call of the Woolly Pulpit," *The Washington Times*, December 7, 1990.

21. *Braschi v. Stahl Associates Co.*, 74 N.Y. 2d 201.

22. Dennis Hevesi, "Court Extends 'Family' Rule to Rent-Stabilized Units," *The New York Times*, December 6, 1990.

23. Richardson, "Gay Voters Claim Biggest Victory."

24. Thomas Sowell, "Affirmative Action: A Worldwide Disaster," *Commentary*, December 1989, pp. 21–41; see also Sowell, *Preferential Policies, An International Perspective* (New York: William Morrow, 1990).

25. Stephen Johnson, "Reverse Discrimination and Aggressive Behavior," *Journal of Psychology*, January 1980, pp. 11–19; Johnson, "Consequences of Reverse Discrimination," *Psychological Reports*, December 1980, pp. 1035–1038.

26. Paul Greenberg, "Decline and Fall of Civil Rights," *The Washington Times*, November 8, 1990.

27. Gara LaMarche and William B. Rubenstein, "The Love That Dare Not Speak," *The Nation*, November 5, 1990, p. 524.

28. Pete Hamill, "Confessions of a Heterosexual," *Esquire*, August 1990, pp. 55–57.

29. "Gay Protesters Confront Arsenio Hall," *The Washington Times*, December 17, 1990.

30. Quoted in Andrew Sullivan, "Gay Life, Gay Death," *The New Republic*, December 27, 1990, p. 24. That Sullivan, an ally of the homosexual legal revolution, is alarmed over the totalitarianism inherent in such pronouncements should be taken seriously; he supports—on conservative grounds, no less—legalizing homosexual marriage. See Sullivan, "Here Comes the Groom," *The New Republic*, August 28, 1989, pp. 20–22.

31. David Rieff, "The Case Against Sensitivity," *Esquire*, November 1990, p. 124.

32. Here was Rooney's "antigay" remark: "Many of the ills which kill us are self-induced." They include "too much alcohol, too much food, drugs, homosexual unions, and cigarettes." Given that at the time of that statement over 50,000 persons already had died of AIDS, Rooney would hardly qualify as anything other than a bearer of unpleasant truth.

33. For good interpretations of this episode, see Eric Breindel, "The Andy Rooney Affair" *Commentary*, May 1990, pp. 56–57; Cal Thomas, "Silence from the Pluralism Corner," *The Washington Times*, March 12, 1990.

34. The evidence suggests that increased social tolerance of homosexuality does not necessarily lead to homosexuals themselves being happier. See Martin S. Weinberg and Colin J. Williams, *Male Homosexuals* (New York: Oxford University Press, 1974); Samuel McCracken, "Are Homosexuals Gay?" *Commentary*, January 1979, pp. 19–29.

35. Thomas Short, "Gay Rights or Closet Virtues?" *National Review*, September 17, 1990, pp. 43–44.

36. Marshall Kirk and Hunter Madsen, *After the Ball: How America Will Conquer Its Fear and Hatred of Gays in the 90s* (Garden City, NY: Doubleday, 1989).

37. Jonathan After, "Degrees of Discomfort," *Newsweek*, March 12, 1990, p. 27.

38. This is the position taken in McCracken, "Are Homosexuals Gay?" pp. 27–28.

39. The Gallup Report, Report No. 289 (Princeton, NJ: The Gallup Poll, October 1989), p. 13.

40. "The Future of Gay America," pp. 22–23.

41. See Sullivan, "Gay Life, Gay Death," p. 25.

42. "The Future of Gay America," p. 23.

54. Baker v. Vermont (1999)

SUPREME COURT OF VERMONT

The issue before the Supreme Court of Vermont is whether its state constitution permits it to exclude same-sex couples from the benefits and protections that its laws provide opposite-sex married couples. The court unanimously concluded that the Common Benefits Clause of the Vermont Constitution—which reads, "That government is, or ought to be, instituted for the common benefit, protection, and security of the people, nation, or community, and not for the particular emolument or advantage of any single person, family or sets of persons, who are a part only of that community"—requires that same-sex couples not be deprived of the benefits and protections extended to opposite-sex couples.

Present: AMESTOY, C. J., DOOLEY, MORSE, JOHNSON and SKOGLUND, JJ.

May the State of Vermont exclude same-sex couples from the benefits and protections that its laws provide to opposite-sex married couples? That is the fundamental question we address in this appeal, a question that the Court well knows arouses deeply-felt religious, moral, and political beliefs. Our constitutional responsibility to consider the legal merits of issues properly before us provides no exception for the controversial case. The issue before the Court, moreover, does not turn on the religious or moral debate over intimate same-sex relationships, but rather on the statutory and constitutional basis for the exclusion of same-sex couples from the secular benefits and protections offered married couples.

We conclude that under the Common Benefits Clause of the Vermont Constitution, which, in pertinent part, reads,

> That government is, or ought to be, instituted for the common benefit, protection, and security of the people, nation, or community, and not for the particular emolument or advantage of any single person, family, or set of persons, who are a part only of that community,

plaintiffs may not be deprived of the statutory benefits and protections afforded persons of the opposite sex who choose to marry. We hold that the State is constitutionally required to extend to same-sex couples the common benefits and protections that flow from marriage under Vermont law. Whether this ultimately takes the form of inclusion within the marriage laws themselves or a parallel "domestic partnership" system or some equivalent statutory alternative, rests with the Legislature. Whatever system is chosen, however, must conform with the constitutional imperative to afford all Vermonters the common benefit, protection, and security of the law.

Plaintiffs are three same-sex couples who have lived together in committed relationships for periods ranging from four to twenty-five years. Two of the couples have raised children together. Each couple applied for a marriage license from their respective town clerk, and each was refused a license as ineligible under the applicable state marriage laws. Plaintiffs thereupon filed this lawsuit against defendants—the State of Vermont, the Towns of Milton and Shelburne, and the City of South Burlington—seeking a declaratory judgment that the refusal to issue them a license violated the marriage statutes and the Vermont Constitution. . . .

We typically look to a variety of sources in construing our Constitution, including the language of the provision in question, historical context, case-law development, the construction of similar provisions in other state constitutions, and sociological materials. The Vermont Constitution was adopted with little recorded debate and has undergone remarkably little revision in its 200-year history. Recapturing the meaning of a particular word or phrase as understood by a generation more than two centuries removed from our own requires, in some respects, an immersion in the culture and materials of the past more suited to the work of professional historians than courts and lawyers. The responsibility of the Court, however, is distinct from that of the historian, whose interpretation of past thought and actions necessarily informs our analysis of current issues but cannot alone resolve them. Out of the shifting and complicated kaleidoscope of events, social forces, and ideas that culminated in the Vermont Constitution of 1777, our task is to distill the essence, the motivating ideal of the framers. The challenge is to remain faithful to that historical ideal, while addressing contemporary issues that the framers undoubtedly could never have imagined.

We first focus on the words of the Constitution themselves, for, as Chief Justice Marshall observed, "although the spirit of an instrument, especially of a constitution, is to be respected not less than its letter, yet the spirit is to be collected chiefly from its words." One of the fundamental rights included in Chapter I of the Vermont Constitution of 1777, entitled "A Declaration of Rights of the Inhabitants of the State of Vermont," the Common Benefits Clause as originally written provided:

> That government is, or ought to be, instituted for the common benefit, protection, and security of the people, nation or community; and not for the particular emolument or advantage of any single man, family or set of men, who are a part only of that community; and that the community hath an indubitable, unalienable and indefeasible right, to reform, alter or abolish government, in such manner as shall be, by that community, judged most conducive to the public weal.

The first point to be observed about the text is the affirmative and unequivocal mandate of the first section, providing that government is established for the common benefit of the people and community as a whole. Unlike the Fourteenth Amendment, whose origin and language reflect the solicitude of a dominant white society for an historically-oppressed African-American minority (no state shall "deny" the equal protection of the laws), the Common Benefits Clause mirrors the confidence of a homogeneous, eighteenth-century group of men aggressively laying claim to the same rights as their peers in Great Britain or, for that matter, New York, New Hampshire, or the Upper Connecticut River Valley. . . . The same assumption that all the people should be afforded all the benefits and protections bestowed by government is also reflected in the second section, which prohibits not the denial of rights to the op-

pressed, but rather the conferral of advantages or emoluments upon the privileged.

The words of the Common Benefits Clause are revealing. While they do not, to be sure, set forth a fully-formed standard of analysis for determining the constitutionality of a given statute, they do express broad principles which usefully inform that analysis. Chief among these is the principle of inclusion. As explained more fully in the discussion that follows, the specific proscription against governmental favoritism toward not only groups or "set[s] of men," but also toward any particular "family" or "single man," underscores the framers' resentment of political preference of any kind. The affirmative right to the "common benefits and protections" of government and the corollary proscription of favoritism in the distribution of public "emoluments and advantages" reflect the framers' overarching objective "not only that everyone enjoy equality before the law or have an equal voice in government but also that everyone have an equal share in the fruits of the common enterprise." Thus, at its core the Common Benefits Clause expressed a vision of government that afforded every Vermonter its benefit and protection and provided no Vermonter particular advantage. . . .

We look next to the government's purpose in drawing a classification that includes some members of the community within the scope of the challenged law but excludes others. Consistent with Article 7's guiding principle of affording the protection and benefit of the law to all members of the Vermont community, we examine the nature of the classification to determine whether it is reasonably necessary to accomplish the State's claimed objectives.

We must ultimately ascertain whether the omission of a part of the community from the benefit, protection and security of the challenged law bears a reasonable and just relation to the governmental purpose. Consistent with the core presumption of inclusion, factors to be considered in this determination may include: (1) the significance of the benefits and protections of the challenged law; (2) whether the omission of members of the community from the benefits and protections of the challenged law promotes the government's stated goals; and (3) whether the classification is significantly underinclusive or overinclusive. . . .

With these general precepts in mind, we turn to the question of whether the exclusion of same-sex couples from the benefits and protections incident to marriage under Vermont law contravenes Article 7. The first step in our analysis is to identify the nature of the statutory classification. As noted, the marriage statutes apply expressly to opposite-sex couples. Thus, the statutes exclude anyone who wishes to marry someone of the same sex.

Next, we must identify the governmental purpose or purposes to be served by the statutory classification. The principal purpose the State advances in support of the excluding same-sex couples from the legal benefits of marriage is the government's interest in "furthering the link between procreation and child rearing." The State has a strong interest, it argues, in promoting a permanent commitment between couples who have children to ensure that their offspring are considered legitimate and receive ongoing parental support. The State contends, further, that the Legislature could reasonably believe that sanctioning same-sex unions "would diminish society's perception of the link between procreation and child rearing . . . [and] advance the notion that fathers or mothers . . . are mere surplusage to the functions of procreation and child rearing." The State argues that since same-sex couples cannot conceive a child on their own, state-sanctioned same-sex unions "could be seen by the Legislature to separate further the connection between procreation and parental responsibilities for raising children." Hence, the Legislature is justified, the State concludes, "in using the marriage statutes to send a public message that procreation and child rearing are intertwined."

Do these concerns represent valid public interests that are reasonably furthered by the exclusion of same-sex couples from the benefits and protections that flow from the marital relation? It is beyond dispute that the State has a legitimate and long-standing interest in promoting a permanent commitment between couples for the security of their children. It is equally undeniable that the State's interest has been advanced by extending formal public sanction and protection to the union, or marriage, of those couples considered capable of having children, i.e., men and women. And there is no doubt that the overwhelming majority of births today continue to result from natural conception between one man and one woman. . . .

It is equally undisputed that many opposite-sex couples marry for reasons unrelated to procreation, that some of these couples never intend to have children, and that others are incapable of having

children. Therefore, if the purpose of the statutory exclusion of same-sex couples is to "further the link between procreation and child rearing," it is significantly under-inclusive. The law extends the benefits and protections of marriage to many persons with no logical connection to the stated governmental goal.

Furthermore, while accurate statistics are difficult to obtain, there is no dispute that a significant number of children today are actually being raised by same-sex parents, and that increasing numbers of children are being conceived by such parents through a variety of assisted-reproductive techniques. See D. Flaks, et al., Lesbians Choosing Motherhood: A Comparative Study of Lesbian and Heterosexual Parents and Their Children, 31 Dev. Psychol. (1995) (citing estimates that between 1.5 and 5 million lesbian mothers resided with their children in United States between 1989 and 1990, and that thousands of lesbian mothers have chosen motherhood through donor insemination or adoption); G. Green and F. Bozett, Lesbian Mothers and Gay Fathers, in Homosexuality: Research Implications for Public Policy (J. Gonsiorek et al. eds., 1991) (estimating that numbers of children of either gay fathers or lesbian mothers range between six and fourteen million); C. Patterson, Children of the Lesbian Baby Boom: Behavioral Adjustment, Self-Concepts, and Sex Role Identity, in Lesbian and Gay Psychology (B. Greene et al. eds., 1994) (observing that although precise estimates are difficult, number of families with lesbian mothers is growing); E. Shapiro & L. Schultz, Single-Sex Families: The Impact of Birth Innovations Upon Traditional Family Notions, 24 J. Fam. L. (1985) ("[I]t is a fact that children are being born to single-sex families on a biological basis, and that they are being so born in considerable numbers").

Thus, with or without the marriage sanction, the reality today is that increasing numbers of same-sex couples are employing increasingly efficient assisted-reproductive techniques to conceive and raise children. The Vermont Legislature has not only recognized this reality, but has acted affirmatively to remove legal barriers so that same-sex couples may legally adopt and rear the children conceived through such efforts (allowing partner of biological parent to adopt if in child's best interest without reference to sex). The State has also acted to expand the domestic relations laws to safeguard the interests of same-sex parents and their children when such couples terminate their domestic relationship.

Therefore, to the extent that the State's purpose in licensing civil marriage was, and is, to legitimize children and provide for their security, the statutes plainly exclude many same-sex couples who are no different from opposite-sex couples with respect to these objectives. If anything, the exclusion of same-sex couples from the legal protections incident to marriage exposes their children to the precise risks that the State argues the marriage laws are designed to secure against. In short, the marital exclusion treats persons who are similarly situated for purposes of the law, differently.

The State also argues that because same-sex couples cannot conceive a child on their own, their exclusion promotes a "perception of the link between procreation and child rearing," and that to discard it would "advance the notion that mothers and fathers . . . are mere surplusage to the functions of procreation and child rearing." Apart from the bare assertion, the State offers no persuasive reasoning to support these claims. Indeed, it is undisputed that most of those who utilize non-traditional means of conception are infertile married couples, and that many assisted-reproductive techniques involve only one of the married partner's genetic material, the other being supplied by a third party through sperm, egg, or embryo donation. The State does not suggest that the use of these technologies undermines a married couple's sense of parental responsibility, or fosters the perception that they are "mere surplusage" to the conception and parenting of the child so conceived. Nor does it even remotely suggest that access to such techniques ought to be restricted as a matter of public policy to "send a public message that procreation and child rearing are intertwined." Accordingly, there is no reasonable basis to conclude that a same-sex couple's use of the same technologies would undermine the bonds of parenthood, or society's perception of parenthood.

The question thus becomes whether the exclusion of a relatively small but significant number of otherwise qualified same-sex couples from the same legal benefits and protections afforded their opposite-sex counterparts contravenes the mandates of Article 7. It is, of course, well settled that statutes are not necessarily unconstitutional because they fail to extend legal protection to all who are similarly situated. Courts have upheld underinclusive statutes out of a recognition that, for reasons of pragmatism or administrative convenience, the legislature may choose to address problems incrementally. The State does not contend, however, that the same-sex exclusion is necessary as a matter of pragmatism or administrative convenience. We turn, accordingly, from the principal justifications advanced by the State to the interests asserted by plaintiffs. . . .

While the laws relating to marriage have undergone many changes during the last century, largely toward the goal of equalizing the status of husbands and wives, the benefits of marriage have not diminished in value. On the contrary, the benefits and protections incident to a marriage license under Vermont law have never been greater. They include, for example, the right to receive a portion of the estate of a spouse who dies intestate and protection against disinheritance through elective share provisions; preference in being appointed as the personal representative of a spouse who dies intestate; the right to bring a lawsuit for the wrongful death of a spouse; the right to bring an action for loss of consortium; the right to workers' compensation survivor benefits; the right to spousal benefits statutorily guaranteed to public employees, including health, life, disability, and accident insurance; the opportunity to be covered as a spouse under group life insurance policies issued to an employee; the opportunity to be covered as the insured's spouse under an individual health insurance policy; the right to claim an evidentiary privilege for marital communications; homestead rights and protections; the presumption of joint ownership of property and the concomitant right of survivorship; hospital visitation and other rights incident to the medical treatment of a family member; and the right to receive, and the obligation to provide, spousal support, maintenance, and property division in the event of separation or divorce. . . .

While other statutes could be added to this list, the point is clear. The legal benefits and protections flowing from a marriage license are of such significance that any statutory exclusion must necessarily be grounded on public concerns of sufficient weight, cogency, and authority that the justice of the deprivation cannot seriously be questioned. Considered in light of the extreme logical disjunction between the classification and the stated purposes of the law—protecting children and "furthering the link between procreation and childrearing"—the exclusion falls substantially short of this standard. The laudable governmental goal of promoting a commitment between married couples to promote the security of their children and the community as a whole provides no reasonable basis for denying the legal benefits and protections of marriage to same-sex couples, who are no differently situated with respect to this goal than their opposite-sex counterparts. Promoting a link between procreation and childrearing similarly fails to support the exclusion. We turn, accordingly, to the remaining interests identified by the State in support of the statutory exclusion.

The State asserts that a number of additional rationales could support a legislative decision to exclude same-sex partners from the statutory benefits and protections of marriage. Among these are the State's purported interests in "promoting childrearing in a setting that provides both male and female role models," minimizing the legal complications of surrogacy contracts and sperm donors, "bridging differences" between the sexes, discouraging marriages of convenience for tax, housing or other benefits, maintaining uniformity with marriage laws in other states, and generally protecting marriage from "destabilizing changes." The most substantive of the State's remaining claims relates to the issue of childrearing. It is conceivable that the Legislature could conclude that opposite-sex partners offer advantages in this area, although we note that child-development experts disagree and the answer is decidedly uncertain. The argument, however, contains a more fundamental flaw, and that is the Legislature's endorsement of a policy diametrically at odds with the State's claim. In 1996, the Vermont General Assembly enacted, and the Governor signed, a law removing all prior legal barriers to the adoption of children by same-sex couples. At the same time, the Legislature provided additional legal protections in the form of court-ordered child support and parent-child contact in the event that same-sex parents dissolved their "domestic relationship." In light of these express policy choices, the State's arguments that Vermont public policy favors opposite-sex over same-sex parents or disfavors the use of artificial reproductive technologies, are patently without substance. . . .

Thus, viewed in the light of history, logic, and experience, we conclude that none of the interests asserted by the State provides a reasonable and just basis for the continued exclusion of same-sex couples from the benefits incident to a civil marriage license under Vermont law. Accordingly, in the faith that a case beyond the imagining of the framers of our Constitution may, nevertheless, be safely anchored in the values that infused it, we find a constitutional obligation to extend to plaintiffs the common benefit, protection, and security that Vermont law provides opposite-sex married couples. It remains only to determine the appropriate means and scope of relief compelled by this constitutional mandate.

It is important to state clearly the parameters of today's ruling. Although plaintiffs sought injunctive and declaratory relief designed to secure a marriage license, their claims and arguments here have focused primarily upon the consequences of official exclusion from the statutory benefits, protections, and security incident to marriage under Vermont law. While some future case may attempt to establish that—notwithstanding equal benefits and protections under Vermont law—the denial of a marriage license operates per se to deny constitutionally protected rights, that is not the claim we address today.

We hold only that plaintiffs are entitled under Chapter I, Article 7, of the Vermont Constitution to obtain the same benefits and protections afforded by Vermont law to married opposite-sex couples. We do not purport to infringe upon the prerogatives of the Legislature to craft an appropriate means of addressing this constitutional mandate, other than to note that the record here refers to a number of potentially constitutional statutory schemes from other jurisdictions. These include what are typically referred to as "domestic partnership" or "registered partnership" acts, which generally establish an alternative legal status to marriage for same-sex couples, impose similar formal requirements and limitations, create a parallel licensing or registration scheme, and extend all or most of the same rights and obligations provided by the law to married partners. . . .

The judgment of the superior court upholding the constitutionality of the Vermont marriage statutes under Chapter I, Article 7 of the Vermont Constitution is reversed. The effect of the Court's decision is suspended, and jurisdiction is retained in this Court, to permit the Legislature to consider and enact legislation consistent with the constitutional mandate described herein.

DOOLEY, J., concurring.

. . . This is a concurrence and not a dissent. I agree with the majority that the consequence of limiting marriage to a man and woman is the exclusion of these plaintiffs, and many persons similarly situated, from numerous rights, benefits, and duties that government and society provide to—and impose on—married persons. However we might have described marriage in relation to the very limited government that was created by our Constitution, the complexity of the current system of government-created benefits and burdens has made civil marriage a modern-day emolument, a government recognized and supported special status for which these plaintiffs are not eligible. . . .

Vermont's legal climate differs considerably from that in other jurisdictions where courts have held that lesbians and gay men are not a suspect classification. Indeed, the federal analysis of the rights of lesbians and gay men almost always starts with Bowers v. Hardwick (1986), a decision that reflects a legal climate quite hostile to those rights. Bowers upheld a Georgia conviction for sodomy based on a sex act committed by two males in the bedroom of defendant's home. It held that, for due process purposes, individuals do not have "a fundamental right to engage in homosexual sodomy.". . .

Since 1992, it has generally been the policy of Vermont to prohibit discrimination based on sexual orientation. This includes discrimination based on "male or female homosexuality." Thus, I believe our "legal climate" is vastly different from that in Bowers, where, after considering that twenty-four states had criminalized sodomy between consenting adults, the United States Supreme Court concluded that there was no fundamental right, deeply rooted in the Nation's history, to engage in such conduct. My point here is simply that the rationale in federal decisions for withholding a more searching scrutiny does not apply in Vermont. . . .

JOHNSON, J., concurring in part and dissenting in part.

Forty years ago, in reversing a decision that had denied injunctive relief for the immediate desegregation of publicly owned parks and recreational facilities in Memphis, Tennessee, a unanimous United States Supreme Court stated:

The basic guarantees of our Constitution are warrants for the here and now and, unless there is an overwhelming compelling reason, they are to be promptly fulfilled.

Plaintiffs come before this Court claiming that the State has unconstitutionally deprived them of the benefits of marriage based solely upon a discriminatory classification that violates their civil rights. They ask the Court to remedy the unlawful discrimination by enjoining the State and its municipalities from denying them the license that serves to identify the persons entitled to those benefits. The majority agrees that the Common Benefits Clause of the Vermont Constitution entitles plaintiffs to obtain the same benefits and protections as those bestowed upon married opposite-sex couples, yet it declines to give them any relief other than an exhortation to the Legislature to deal with the problem. I concur with the majority's holding, but I respectfully dissent from its novel and truncated remedy, which in my view abdicates this Court's constitutional duty to redress violations of constitutional rights. I would grant the requested relief and enjoin defendants from denying plaintiffs a marriage license based solely on the sex of the applicants.

The majority declares that the issue before this Court does not turn on the heated moral debate over intimate same-sex relationships, and further, that this Court has a constitutional responsibility to consider the legal merits of even controversial cases. Yet, notwithstanding these pronouncements, the majority elects to send plaintiffs to an uncertain fate in the political caldron of that very same moral debate. And to what end? Passing this case on to the Legislature will not alleviate the instability and uncertainty that the majority seeks to avoid, and will unnecessarily entangle this Court in the Legislature's efforts to accommodate the majority's mandate within a "reasonable period of time."

In 1948, when the California Supreme Court struck down a state law prohibiting the issuance of a license authorizing interracial marriages, the Court did not suspend its judgment to allow the Legislature an opportunity to enact a separate licensing scheme for interracial marriages. Indeed, such a mandate in that context would be unfathomable to us today. Here, we have held that the State has unconstitutionally discriminated against plaintiffs, thereby depriving them of civil rights to which they are entitled. Like the Hawaii Circuit Court, which rejected the State's reasons for excluding same-sex couples from marriage, we should simply enjoin the State from denying marriage licenses to plaintiffs based on sex or sexual orientation. That remedy would provide prompt and complete relief to plaintiffs and create reliable expectations that would stabilize the legal rights and duties of all couples. . . .

◇

Suggestions for Further Reading

Anthologies

Baird, Robert, and Katherine Baird. *Homosexuality: Debating the Issues*. Amherst: Prometheus Books, 1995.

Batchelor, Edward, Jr. *Homosexuality and Ethics*. New York: Pilgrim Press, 1980.

Dudley, William. *Homosexuality—Opposing Viewpoints*. San Diego: Greenhaven Press, 1993.

Rolefl, Tamara. *Gay Rights*. San Diego: Greenhaven Press, 1997.

Basic Concepts

"Survey on the Constitutional Right to Privacy in the Context of Homosexual Activity." *Miami Law Review* (1986), pp. 521–657.

Alternative Views

du Mas, Frank M. *Gay Is Not Good*. Nashville, Tenn.: Thomas Nelson Publishers, 1979.

Finnis, John. "Law, Morality, and 'Sexual Orientation,'" *Notre Dame Law Review*, 1994.

Friedman, Richard. *Male Homosexuality*. New Haven, CT: Yale University Press, 1988.

Harrigan, J. *Homosexuality: The Test Case for Christian Ethics*. Mahwah, N.J.: Paulist Press, 1988.

Hoagland, Sarah. *Lesbian Ethics*. Palo Alto: Institute of Lesbian Studies, 1988.

Kaplan, Morris. *Sexual Justice*. New York: Routledge, 1997.

Malloy, Edward A. *Homosexuality and the Christian Way of Life*. Lanham, Md.: University Press of America, 1981.

Mohr, Richard D. *Gays/Justice*. New York: Columbia University Press, 1988.

Nussbaum, Martha. "Platonic Love and Colorado Law: The Relevance of Ancient Greek Norms to Modern Sexual Controversies," *Virginia Law Review*, 1994.

Ruse, Michael. *Homosexuality*. Oxford: Basil Blackwell, 1988.

Thomas, Laurence, and Michael Levin. *Sexual Orientation*. Lanham: Rowman & Littlefield, 1999.

Section X

Gun Control

Introduction

Basic Concepts

Americans own about 150–200 million firearms. Fifty percent of American households contain guns and half of these homes contain the estimated 70 million handguns currently in private hands. Each year, approximately 38,000 Americans are killed with firearms. Of this number, 19,000 are suicides, 18,000 are homicides, and the remaining 2,000 are gun accidents. By comparison, in 1990, twenty-two people were killed in Great Britain with handguns, thirteen in Sweden, ninety-one in Switzerland, eighty-seven in Japan, ten in Australia, and sixty-eight in Canada. In addition, 40,000 gun-related injuries, whether intentional or accidental, are inflicted upon Americans each year. Meanwhile in any given year, there are up to one million crimes committed involving guns. According to recent surveys, 68 percent of Americans believe that firearms laws should be stricter, 80 percent favor handgun registration, and 93 percent favor the seven-day waiting period for handgun purchases initially required by the Brady Bill (see Selection 60). But public opinion has only minimally been reflected in legislation in the United States. The National Rifle Association has been particularly effective in defeating legislation that it opposes. But what is the right thing to do here? Does morality favor gun control or oppose it? This is the moral problem of gun control, and its resolution requires weighing the arguments for and against gun control set out in this section.

Alternative Views

In their study of King County, Washington, Arthur Kellerman and Donald Reay (Selection 55) found that there are forty-three suicides, criminal homicides, or accidental deaths involving guns kept at home for every case of a homicide for self-protection. In addition, they found that over 80 percent of the homicides occurred during arguments or altercations. In light of their findings, Kellerman and Reay raise the question of whether keeping firearms in the home increases a family's protection or places it at greater risk.

In Selection 56, Gary Kleck and Marc Gertz argue that the U.S. National Crime Victimization Survey underestimates the number of gun defenses each year at 80,000–82,000, in part because it is a nonanonymous survey conducted by a branch of the federal government. Kleck and Gertz claim that their own privately conducted anonymous survey accurately estimates the number of gun defenses at 2.1–2.5 million a year. They argue that this number of gun defenses is plausible given that it would mean that only 3 percent of the 93 million

426

Americans who have access to guns would have been involved in a gun defense each year. The conclusion that Kleck and Gertz want us to endorse is that the benefits of this number of gun defenses justifies the risks of gun ownership that the Kellerman and Reay study brought to light.

In Selection 57, Philip J. Cook and Jens Ludwig report on conducting a gun defense survey of their own similar to the Gary Kleck and Marc Gertz gun defense survey which arrived at a figure of 3.1 million gun defenses each year. But Cook and Ludwig then raise objections both to their own survey and to Kleck and Gertz's. They point out that this figure for gun defenses conflicts with other data we have about the number of robberies and assaults that occur each year. They also point out that there is a serious problem of false positives given the small number of those who are actually surveyed who do report a defensive gun use.

Looking at another aspect of the problem of gun control, Franklin E. Zimring and Gordon Hawkins argue in Selection 58 that the use of firearms in assault and robbery is the single environmental feature of American society most clearly linked to the extraordinary death rate from interpersonal violence in the United States. Using international comparisons, they show that while the United States is similar to many other industrial countries in its crime rate, it has a much higher rate of lethal violence. According to Zimring and Hawkins, the greater availability of guns in the United States is a contributory cause of this higher rate of lethal violence. Zimring and Hawkins argue that the use of guns as opposed to other weapons in assaults effects certain mechanical and social changes in the nature of assaults that increase death rates. For example, studies have shown that gun attacks were five times as likely to kill as knife attacks.

Daniel D. Polsby and Don B. Kates, Jr. (Selection 59) argue against the instrumental theory of America's higher homicide rate, a view they associate with Zimring and Hawkins. According to this view, the higher homicide rate is due to the higher incidence of firearms in the United States. Polsby and Kates claim that a better explanation can be found in the perpetrator theory, which accounts for the higher incidence of firearms in terms of the motives, intentions, and risk-taking preferences of the Americans who engage in lethal violence. For instance, Polsby and Kates point out that 70–80 percent of murderers have criminal records and that years before European countries adopted the restrictive firearms policies most of them have today, they already enjoyed very low rates of violent crime. Their restrictive firearms policies did not tame a violent culture, as gun control advocates hope to achieve in the United States. But how does this finding show that a more restrictive handgun control policy could not achieve this effect in the United States?

Practical Applications

In 1993, after much opposition, the Brady Bill (Selection 60) was enacted into law. The bill was named for James S. Brady, who was shot by John Hinckley, Jr. during an assassination attempt on President Ronald Reagan. Brady was seriously wounded and suffered permanent debilitating injuries. He and his wife have actively lobbied for gun control.

The Brady Bill requires a five-day waiting period. In a concession to the NRA, the bill expired in 1998 after states were able to computerize their criminal records for instant checks of gun purchasers. Obviously, the key question here and elsewhere is: How free should people be? In particular, should people be free to own and carry handguns for self-defense, and how is this freedom related to others that people have or should have?

55. Protection or Peril? An Analysis of Firearm-Related Deaths in the Home

Arthur L. Kellerman and Donald T. Reay

In their study of King County, Washington, Arthur Kellerman and Donald Reay found that there are forty-three suicides, criminal homicides, or accidental deaths involving guns kept at home for every case of a homicide for self-protection. In addition, they found that over 80 percent of the homicides occurred during arguments or altercations. In light of their findings, Kellerman and Reay raise the question of whether keeping firearms in the home increases a family's protection or places it at greater risk.

There are approximately 120 million guns in private hands in the United States. About half of all the homes in America contain one or more firearms. Although most persons who own guns keep them primarily for hunting or sport, three-quarters of gun owners keep them at least partly for protection. One-fifth of gun owners identify "self-defense at home" as their most important reason for having a gun.

Risks of Guns in the Home

Keeping firearms in the home carries associated risks. These include injury or death from unintentional gunshot wounds, homicide during domestic quarrels, and the ready availability of an immediate, highly lethal means of suicide. To understand better the epidemiology of firearm-related deaths in the home, we studied all the gunshot deaths that occurred in King County, Washington, between 1978 and 1983. We were especially interested in characterizing the gunshot deaths that occurred in the residence where the firearm involved was kept.

Adapted from Arthur L. Kellerman and Donald T. Reay, "Protection or Peril? An Analysis of Firearm-Related Deaths in the Home." The complete article, with references and graphics, can be found in *The New England Journal of Medicine* 314 (24): 1557–60. Reprinted with permission.

King County, Washington (1980 census population 1,270,000), contains the cities of Seattle (population 494,000) and Bellevue (population 74,000), as well as a number of smaller communities. The county population is predominantly urban (92 percent) and white (88.4 percent), with smaller Black (4.4 percent) and Asian (4.3 percent) minorities. All violent deaths in King County are investigated by the office of the medical examiner.

We systematically reviewed the medical examiner's case files to identify every firearm-related death that occurred in the county between January 1, 1978, and December 31, 1983. In addition to general demographic information, we obtained specific data regarding the manner of death, the scene of the incident, the circumstances, the relationship of the suspect to the victim, the type of firearm involved, and the blood alcohol level of the victim at the time of autopsy. When records were incomplete, corroborating information was obtained from police case files and direct interviews with the original investigating officers.

Types of Gunshot Deaths

Gunshot deaths involving the intentional shooting of one person by another were considered homicides. Self-protection homicides were considered "justifiable" if they involved the killing of a felon during the commission of a crime; they were considered "self-defense" if that was the determination of the investigating police department and the King

County prosecutor's office. All homicides resulting in criminal charges and all unsolved homicides were considered criminal homicides.

The circumstances of all homicides were also noted. Homicides committed in association with another felony (e.g., robbery) were identified as "felony homicides." Homicides committed during an argument or fight were considered "altercation homicides." Those committed in the absence of either set of circumstances were termed "primary homicides."

Deaths from self-inflicted gunshot wounds were considered suicides if they were officially certified as such by Donald T. Reay, . . . the medical examiner. Unintentional self-inflicted gunshot wounds were classified as accidental. Although the medical examiner's office considers deaths involving the unintentional shooting of one person by another as homicide, we classified these deaths as accidental for our analysis. Deaths [with uncertainties] about the circumstances or motive were identified as "undetermined."

Over the six-year interval, the medical examiner's office investigated 743 deaths from firearms (9.75 deaths per 100,000 person-years). This total represented 22.7 percent of all violent deaths occurring in King County during this period, excluding traffic deaths. Firearms were involved in 45 percent of all homicides and 49 percent of all suicides in King County—proportions lower than the national averages of 61 and 57 percent, respectively. Guns accounted for less than 1 percent of accidental deaths and 5.7 percent of deaths in which the circumstances were undetermined.

Of the 743 deaths from firearms noted during this six-year period, 473 (63.7 percent) occurred inside a house or dwelling, and 398 (53.6 percent) occurred in the home where the firearm involved was kept. Of these 398 firearm deaths, 333 (83.7 percent) were suicides, 50 (12.6 percent) were homicides, and 12 (3 percent) were accidental gunshot deaths. The precise manner of death was undetermined in three additional cases involving self-inflicted gunshot wounds.

In 265 of the 333 cases of suicide (80 percent), the victim was male. A blood ethanol test was positive in 86 of the 245 suicide victims tested (35 percent) and showed a blood ethanol level of 100 mg per deciliter or more in 60 of the 245 (24.5 percent). Sixty-eight percent of the suicides involved handguns. In eight cases, the medical examiner's case files specifically noted that the victim had acquired the firearm within two days of committing suicide.

The victim was male in thirty of the fifty homicide deaths (60 percent). A blood ethanol test was positive in twenty-seven of forty-seven homicide victims tested (5 percent) and showed a blood ethanol level of 100 mg per deciliter or more in ten of the victims (21 percent). Handguns were involved in thirty-four of these deaths (68 percent).

Forty-two homicides (84 percent) occurred during altercations in the home, including seven that were later determined to have been committed in self-defense. Two additional homicides involving the shooting of burglars by residents were considered legally "justifiable." Forty-one homicides (82 percent) resulted in criminal charges against a resident of the house or apartment in which the shooting occurred.

Four of the twelve accidental deaths involved self-inflicted gunshot wounds. All twelve victims were male. A blood ethanol test in the victims was positive in only two cases. Eleven of these accidental deaths involved handguns.

Excluding firearm-related suicides, sixty-five deaths occurred in the house where the firearm involved was kept. In two of these cases, the victim was a stranger to the persons living in the house, whereas in twenty-four cases (37 percent), the victim was an acquaintance or friend. Thirty-six gunshot victims (55 percent) were residents of the house in which the shooting occurred, including twenty-nine who were victims of homicide. Residents were most often shot by a relative or family member (eleven cases), their spouse (nine cases), a roommate (six cases), or themselves (seven cases).

Household Members at Risk

Guns kept in King County homes were involved in the deaths of friends or acquaintances 12 times as often as in those of strangers. Even after the exclusion of firearm-related suicides, guns kept at home were involved in the death of a member of the household 18 times more often than in the death of a stranger. For every time a gun in the home was involved in a "self-protection" homicide, we noted 1.3 accidental gunshot deaths, 4.6 criminal homicides, and 37 firearm-related suicides.

We found the home to be a common location for deaths related to firearms. During our study period, almost two-thirds of the gunshot deaths in King County occurred inside a house or other dwelling. Over half these incidents occurred in the residence in which the firearm involved was kept. Few involved acts of self-protection.

Less than 2 percent of homicides nationally are considered legally justifiable. Although justifiable homicides do not include homicides committed in self-defense, the combined total of both in our study was still less than one-fourth the number of criminal homicides involving a gun kept in the home. A majority of these homicide victims were residents of the house or apartment in which the shooting occurred.

More than 80 percent of the homicides noted during our study occurred during arguments or altercations. Susan Baker has observed that in cases of assault, people tend to reach for the most lethal weapon readily available. Easy access to firearms may therefore be particularly dangerous in households prone to domestic violence.

of our cases, and we do not know how long before death any suicide victim planned his or her attempt. However, given the high case-fatality rate associated with suicide attempts involving firearms, it seems likely that easy access to guns increases the probability that an impulsive suicide attempt will end in death.

Detectable concentrations of ethanol were found in the blood of a substantial proportion of the victims tested. This suggests that ethanol may be an independent risk factor for gunshot death. Although this hypothesis is compatible with the known behavioral and physiologic effect of ethanol, the strength of this association remains to be defined.

There are many reasons [why] people own guns. Unfortunately, our files rarely identified why the firearm involved had been kept in the home. We cannot determine, therefore, whether guns kept for protection were more or less hazardous than guns kept for other reasons.

Guns and Suicide

We found the most common form of firearm-related death in the home to be suicide. Although previous authors have correlated regional suicide rates with estimates of firearm density, the precise nature of the relation between gun availability and suicide is unclear. The choice of a gun for suicide may involve a combination of impulse and the close proximity of a firearm. Conversely, the choice of a gun may simply reflect the seriousness of a person's intent. If suicides involving firearms are more a product of the easy availability of weapons than of the strength of intent, limiting access to firearms will decrease the rate of suicide. If the opposite is true, suicidal persons will only work harder to acquire a gun or kill themselves by other means. For example, although the elimination of toxic coal gas from domestic gas supplies in Great Britain resulted in a decrease in successful suicide attempts, a similar measure in Australia was associated with increasing rates of suicide by other methods.

A study of thirty survivors of attempts to commit suicide with firearms suggests that many of them acted on impulse. Whether this observation applies to nonsurvivors as well is unknown. The recent acquisition of a firearm was noted in only eight

Self-Defense Handguns Outnumber Long Guns

We did note, however, that handguns were far more commonly involved in gunshot deaths in the home than shotguns or rifles. The single most common reason for keeping firearms given by owners of handguns, unlike owners of shoulder weapons, is "self-defense at home." About 45 percent of the gun-owning households nationally own handguns. If the proportion of homes containing handguns in King County is similar to this national average, then these weapons were 2.6 times more likely to be involved in a gunshot death in the home than were shotguns and rifles combined.

Several limitations of this type of analysis must be recognized. Our observations are based on a largely urban population and may not be applicable to more rural communities. Also, various rates of suicide and homicide have been noted in other metropolitan counties. These differences may reflect variations in social and demographic composition as well as different patterns of firearm ownership.

Mortality studies like ours do not include cases in which burglars or intruders are wounded or frightened away by a firearm's use or display. Cases in which would-be intruders may have purposely avoided a house known to be armed are also not identified. We did not report the total number or extent of nonlethal firearm injuries involving guns kept in the home. A complete determination of firearm risks versus benefits would require that these figures be known.

The home can be a dangerous place. We noted forty-three suicides, criminal homicides, or acciden-

tal gunshot deaths involving a gun kept in the home for every case of homicide for self-protection. In the light of these findings, it may reasonably be asked whether keeping firearms in the home increases a family's protection or places it in greater danger. Given the unique status of firearms in American society and the national toll of gunshot deaths, it is imperative that we answer this question.

56. Armed Resistance to Crime

GARY KLECK AND MARC GERTZ

Gary Kleck and Marc Gertz argue that the National Crime Victimization Survey underestimates the number of gun defenses each year in the United States at 80,000–82,000, in part because it is a nonanonymous survey which is conducted by a branch of the federal government. In contrast, Kleck and Gertz claim that their own privately conducted anonymous survey accurately estimates the number of gun defenses at 2.1–2.5 million a year.

However consistent the evidence may be concerning the effectiveness of armed victim resistance, there are some who minimize its significance by insisting that it is rare. This assertion is invariably based entirely on a single source of information, the National Crime Victimization Survey (NCVS).

Data from the NCVS imply that each year there are only about 68,000 defensive uses of guns in connection with assaults and robberies, or about 80,000 to 82,000 if one adds in uses linked with household burglaries. These figures are less than one-ninth of the estimates implied by the results of at least thirteen other surveys, most of which have been previously reported. The NCVS estimates imply that about 0.09 of 1% of U.S. households experience a defensive gun use (DGU) in any one year, compared to the Mauser survey's estimate of 3.79% of households over a five-year period, or about 0.76% in any

one year, assuming an even distribution over the five-year period, and no repeat uses.

The strongest evidence that a measurement is inaccurate is that it is inconsistent with many other independent measurements or observations of the same phenomenon; indeed, some would argue that this is ultimately the *only* way of knowing that a measurement is wrong. Therefore, one might suppose that the gross inconsistency of the NCVS-based estimates with all other known estimates, each derived from sources with no known flaws even remotely substantial enough to account for nine-to-one, or more, discrepancies, would be sufficient to persuade any serious scholar that the NCVS estimates are unreliable.

Equally important, those who take the NCVS-based estimates seriously have consistently ignored the most pronounced limitations of the NCVS for estimating DGU frequency. The NCVS is a non-anonymous national survey conducted by a branch of the federal government, the U.S. Bureau of the Census. Interviewers identify themselves to Rs [respondents] as federal government employees, even displaying, in face-to-face contacts, an identification

Reprinted from the *Journal of Criminal Law and Criminology* (1995) by permission of Northwestern University School of Law.

card with a badge. Rs are told that the interviews are being conducted on behalf of the U.S. Department of Justice, the law enforcement branch of the federal government. As a preliminary to asking questions about crime victimization experiences, interviewers establish the address, telephone number, and full names of all occupants, age twelve and over, in each household they contact. In short, it is made very clear to Rs that they are, in effect, speaking to a law enforcement arm of the federal government, whose employees know exactly who the Rs and their family members are, where they live, and how they can be recontacted.

Even under the best of circumstances, reporting the use of a gun for self-protection would be an extremely sensitive and legally controversial matter for either of two reasons. As with other forms of forceful resistance, the defensive act itself, regardless of the characteristics of any weapon used, might constitute an unlawful assault or at least the R might believe that others, including either legal authorities or the researchers, could regard it that way. Resistance with a gun also involves additional elements of sensitivity. Because guns are legally regulated, a victim's possession of the weapon, either in general or at the time of the DGU, might itself be unlawful, either in fact or in the mind of a crime victim who used one. More likely, lay persons with a limited knowledge of the extremely complicated law of either self-defense or firearms regulation are unlikely to know for sure whether their defensive actions or their gun possession was lawful.

It is not hard for gun-using victims interviewed in the NCVS to withhold information about their use of a gun, especially since they are *never directly asked whether they used a gun for self-protection.* They are asked only general questions about whether they did anything to protect themselves. In short, Rs are merely given the opportunity to volunteer the information that they have used a gun defensively. All it takes for an R to conceal a DGU is to simply refrain from mentioning it, i.e., to leave it out of what may be an otherwise accurate and complete account of the crime incident.

Further, Rs in the NCVS are not even asked the general self-protection question unless they already independently indicated that they had been a victim of a crime. This means that any DGUs associated with crimes the Rs did not want to talk about would remain hidden. It has been estimated that the NCVS may catch less than one-twelfth of spousal assaults and one-thirty-third of rapes, thereby missing nearly all DGUs associated with such crimes.

The NCVS was not designed to estimate how often people resist crime using a gun. It was designed primarily to estimate national victimization levels; it incidentally happens to include a few self-protection questions which include response categories covering resistance with a gun. Its survey instrument has been carefully refined and evaluated over the years to do as good a job as possible in getting people to report illegal things which *other* people have done *to* them. This is the exact opposite of the task which faces anyone trying to get good DGU estimates—to get people to admit controversial and possibly illegal things which the *Rs themselves have done.* Therefore, it is neither surprising, nor a reflection on the survey's designers, to note that the NCVS is singularly ill-suited for estimating the prevalence or incidence of DGU. It is not credible to regard this survey as an acceptable basis for establishing, in even the roughest way, how often Americans use guns for self-protection.

◇

The National Self-Defense Survey

The present survey is the first survey ever devoted to the subject of armed self-defense. It was carefully designed to correct all of the known correctable or avoidable flaws of previous surveys which critics have identified. We use the most anonymous possible national survey format, the anonymous random digit dialed telephone survey. We did not know the identities of those who were interviewed, and made this fact clear to the Rs. We interviewed a large nationally representative sample covering all adults, age eighteen and over, in the lower forty-eight states and living in households with telephones. We asked DGU questions of all Rs in our sample, asking them separately about both their own DGU experiences and those of other members of their households. We used both a five-year recall period and a one-year recall period. We inquired about uses of both handguns and other types of guns and excluded occupational uses of guns and uses against animals. Finally, we asked a long series of detailed questions designed to establish exactly what Rs did with their guns; for example, if they had confronted other humans, and how had each DGU connected to a specific crime or crimes. . . .

Questions about the details of DGU incidents permitted us to establish whether a given DGU met all of the following qualifications for an incident to be treated as a genuine DGU: (1) the incident involved defensive action against a human rather than an animal, but not in connection with police, military, or security guard duties; (2) the incident involved actual contact with a person, rather than merely investigating suspicious circumstances, etc.; (3) the defender could state a specific crime which he thought was being committed at the time of the incident; (4) the gun was actually used in some way—at a minimum it had to be used as part of a threat against a person, either by verbally referring to the gun (e.g., "get away—I've got a gun") or by pointing it at an adversary. We made no effort to

assess either the lawfulness or morality of the Rs' defensive actions.

The most technically sound estimates presented in Table I are those based on the shorter one-year recall period that rely on Rs' firsthand accounts of their own experiences (person-based estimates). These estimates appear in the first two columns. They indicate that each year in the U.S. there are about 2.2 to 2.5 million DGUs of all types by civilians against humans, with about 1.5 to 1.9 million of the incidents involving use of handguns.

These estimates are larger than those derived from the best previous surveys, indicating that technical improvements in the measurement procedures have . . . *increased* rather than decreased estimates of the frequency that DGUs occur. Defensive gun use

Table 1. Civilian Defensive Gun Use, U.S., 1988–1993[1]

Recall Period:		Past Year			
Base:		*Person*		*Household*	
Gun Types:		*All Guns*	*Handguns*	*All Guns*	*Handguns*
Persons/	A:[2]	2,549,862	1,893,079	1,540,405	1,072,434
Households	B:[2]	2,163,519	1,545,371	1,325,918	896,945
Annual Uses	A:	2,549,862	1,893,079	1,540,405	1,072,434
	B:	2,163,519	1,545,371	1,325,918	896,945
Recall Period:		Past Five Years			
Base:		*Person*		*Household*	
Gun Types:		*All Guns*	*Handguns*	*All Guns*	*Handguns*
Persons/	A:[2]	6,374,655	5,099,724	3,782,767	2,885,822
Households	B:[2]	5,717,872	4,442,941	3,353,794	2,515,345
Annual Uses	A:	1,884,348	1,442,941	1,158,283	515,345
	B:	1,683,342	888,588	1,029,615	505,069

[1] Defensive uses of guns against humans by civilians (i.e., excluding uses by police officers, security guards, or military personnel).
[2] A estimates are based on all reported defensive gun uses reported in the survey; B estimates are based on only cases with no indications that the case might not be a genuine defensive gun use.
Population Bases: Estimated resident population, age eighteen and over, U.S., April, 1993: 190,538,000; estimated households (assuming the 1992–1993 percentage increase was the same as the 1991–1992 increase): 97,045,525 (U.S. Bureau of the Census, 1993, at 17, 55).

is thus just another specific example of a commonplace pattern in criminological survey work, which includes victimization surveys, self-report surveys of delinquency, surveys of illicit drug use, etc.: the better the measurement procedures, the higher the estimates of controversial behaviors.

Are these estimates plausible? Could it really be true that Americans use guns for self-protection as often as 2.1 to 2.5 million times a year? The estimate may seem remarkable in comparison to expectations based on conventional wisdom, but it is not implausibly large in comparison to various gun-related phenomena. There are probably over 220 million guns in private hands in the U.S., implying that only about 1% of them are used for defensive purposes in any one year—not an impossibly high fraction. In a December 1993 Gallup survey, 49% of U.S. households reported owning a gun, and 31% of adults reported personally owning one. These figures indicate that there are about 47.6 million households with a gun, with perhaps 93 million, or 49% of the adult U.S. population, living in households with guns, and about 59.1 million adults personally owning a gun. Again, it hardly seems implausible that 3% (2.5 million/93 million) of the people with immediate access to a gun could have used one defensively in a given year.

Huge numbers of Americans not only have access to guns, but the overwhelming majority of gun owners, if one can believe their statements, are willing to use a gun defensively. In a December 1989 national survey, 78% of American gun owners stated that they would not only be willing to use a gun defensively in some way, but would be willing to *shoot* a burglar. The percentage willing to use a gun defensively in *some* way, though not necessarily by shooting someone, would presumably be even higher than this.

Nevertheless, having access to a gun and being willing to use it against criminals is not the same as actually doing so. The latter requires experiencing a crime under circumstances in which the victim can get to, or already possesses, a gun. We do not know how many such opportunities for crime victims to use guns defensively occur each year. It would be useful to know how large a fraction of crimes with direct offender-victim contact result in a DGU. Unfortunately, a large share of the incidents covered by our survey are probably outside the scope of incidents that realistically are likely to be reported to either the NCVS or police. If the DGU incidents reported in the present survey are not entirely a subset within the pool of cases covered by the NCVS, one cannot meaningfully use NCVS data to estimate the share of crime incidents which result in a DGU. Nevertheless, in a ten-state sample of incarcerated felons interviewed in 1982, 34% reported having been "scared off, shot at, wounded or captured by an armed victim." From the criminals' standpoint, this experience was not rare.

How could such a serious thing happen so often without becoming common knowledge? This phenomenon, regardless of how widespread it really is, is largely an invisible one as far as governmental statistics are concerned. Neither the defender/victim nor the criminal ordinarily has much incentive to report this sort of event to the police, and either or both often have strong reasons *not* to do so. Consequently, many of these incidents never come to the attention of the police, while others may be reported but without victims' mentioning their use of a gun. And even when a DGU is reported, it will not necessarily be recorded by the police, who ordinarily do not keep statistics on matters other than DGUs resulting in a death, since police record-keeping is largely confined to information helpful in apprehending perpetrators and making a legal case for convicting them. Because such statistics are not kept, we cannot even be certain that a large number of DGUs are *not* reported to the police.

The health system cannot shed much light on this phenomenon either, since very few of these incidents involve injuries. In the rare case where someone is hurt, it is usually the criminal, who is unlikely to seek medical attention for any but the most life-threatening gunshot wounds, as this would ordinarily result in a police interrogation. Physicians in many states are required by law to report treatment of gunshot wounds to the police, making it necessary for medically treated criminals to explain to police how they received their wounds.

Finally, it is now clear that virtually none of the victims who use guns defensively tell interviewers about it in the NCVS. Our estimates imply that only about 3% of DGUs among NCVS Rs are reported to interviewers. Based on other comparisons of alternative survey estimates of violent events with NCVS estimates, this high level of underreporting is eminently plausible. Colin Loftin and Ellen J. Mackenzie reported that rapes might be thirty-three times as frequent as NCVS estimates indicate, while spousal violence could easily be twelve times as high.

There is no inherent value to knowing the exact number of DGUs any more than there is any value to knowing the exact number of crimes which are committed each year. The estimates in Table I are at best only rough approximations, which are probably too low. It is sufficient to conclude from these numbers that DGU is very common, far more common than has been recognized to date by criminologists or policy makers, and certainly far more common than one would think based on any official sources of information.

There is little legitimate reason to continue accepting the NCVS estimates of DGU frequency as even approximately valid. The gross inconsistencies between the NCVS and all other sources of information make it reasonable to suppose that all but a handful of NCVS victims who had used a gun for protection in the reported incidents refrained from mentioning this gun use. In light of evidence on the injury-preventing effectiveness of victim gun use, in some cases where the absence of victim injury is credited to either nonresistance or some unarmed form of resistance, the absence of injury may have actually been due to resistance with a gun, which the victim failed to mention to the interviewer. . . .

Since as many as 400,000 people a year use guns in situations where the defenders claim that they "almost certainly" saved a life by doing so, this re-sult cannot be dismissed as trivial. If even one-tenth of these people are accurate in their stated perceptions, the number of lives saved by victim use of guns would still exceed the total number of lives taken with guns. It is not possible to know how many lives are actually saved this way, for the simple reason that no one can be certain how crime incidents would have turned out had the participants acted differently than they actually did. But surely this is too serious a matter to simply assume that practically everyone who says he believes he saved a life by using a gun was wrong.

This is also too serious a matter to base conclusions on silly statistics comparing the number of lives taken with guns with the number of criminals *killed* by victims. Killing a criminal is not a benefit to the victim, but rather a nightmare to be suffered for years afterward. Saving a life through DGU would be a benefit, but this almost never involves killing the criminal; probably fewer than 3,000 criminals are lawfully killed by gun-wielding victims each year, representing only about 1/1000 of the number of DGUs, and less than 1% of the number of purportedly lifesaving DGUs. Therefore, the number of justifiable homicides cannot serve as even a rough index of life-saving gun uses. Since this comparison does not involve any measured benefit, it can shed no light on the benefits and costs of keeping guns in the home for protection.

57. Guns in America

PHILIP J. COOK AND JENS LUDWIG

Philip J. Cook and Jens Ludwig conducted a gun defense survey of their own similar to the Gary Kleck and Marc Gertz gun defense survey, arriving at a figure of 3.1 million gun defenses each year. But they raise some objections both to their own survey and to Kleck and Gertz's, possibly the most serious of which is the problem of false positives, given the small number of those actually surveyed who do report a defensive gun use.

The United States is unique among wealthy nations in its vast private inventory of firearms. The nearly 200 million guns in private hands are used in part for recreation, mostly hunting and target shooting. But what engenders the most public controversy over firearms is their use against people during either the commission of or defense against crime.

Gun advocates regard firearms as an important crime deterrent and source of protection, while control advocates denounce guns for the damage they do in the hands of criminals. What both groups can agree on is that widespread ownership of firearms has an important impact on the quality of life in America.

To learn more about the role of firearms, the National Institute of Justice (NIJ) sponsored—through a grant to the Police Foundation—[and conducted] a nationally representative telephone survey in 1994 on private ownership and use of firearms by American adults. . . .

Gun Ownership

Prevalence

According to conventional wisdom, about half of American households own guns, a belief affirmed by a long series of national polls dating back to 1959.[1] Yet data from the 1994 telephone survey (National Survey of Private Ownership of Firearms—

NSPOF) indicate that just 35 percent (plus or minus 1.3 percent) of households own guns. This estimate may be somewhat off the mark but not by much. Conventional wisdom appears out of date. . . .

Defensive Gun Uses

NSPOF Estimates

Private citizens sometimes use their guns to scare off trespassers and fend off assaults. Such defensive gun uses (DGUs) are sometimes invoked as a measure of the public benefits of private gun ownership. On the basis of data from the Bureau of Justice Statistics' National Crime Victimization Survey (NCVS), one would conclude that defensive uses are rare indeed, about 108,000 per year. But other surveys yield far higher estimates of the number of DGUs. Most notable has been a much publicized estimate of 2.5 million DGUs, based on data from a 1994 telephone survey conducted by Florida State University professors Gary Kleck and Mark Gertz.[2] The 2.5 million figure has been picked up by the press and now appears regularly in newspaper articles, letters to the editor, editorials, and even Congressional Research Service briefs for public policymakers.

The NSPOF survey is quite similar to the Kleck and Gertz instrument and provides a basis for replicating their estimate. Each of the respondents in the NSPOF was asked the question, "Within the past 12 months, have you yourself used a gun, even if it was not fired, to protect yourself or someone else, or for the protection of property at home, work, or elsewhere?" Answers in the affirmative were followed with "How many different times did you use a gun,

Reprinted from *Guns in America* (1997), the National Institute of Justice, U.S. Department of Justice. Notes renumbered.

even if it was not fired, to protect yourself or property in the past 12 months?" Negative answers to the first DGU question were followed by "Have you *ever* used a gun to defend yourself or someone else?" (emphasis in original). Each respondent who answered yes to either of these DGU questions was asked a sequence of 30 additional questions concerning the most recent defensive gun use in which the respondent was involved, including the respondent's actions with the gun, the location and other circumstances of the incident, and the respondent's relationship to the perpetrator.

Forty-five respondents reported a defensive gun use in 1994 against a person (exhibit 1). Given the sampling weights, these respondents constitute 1.6 percent of the sample and represent 3.1 million adults. Almost half of these respondents reported multiple DGUs during 1994, which provides the basis for estimating the 1994 DGU incidence at 23 million. This surprising figure is caused in part by a few respondents reporting large numbers of defensive gun uses during the year; for example, one woman reported 52!

A somewhat more conservative NSPOF estimate is shown in the column of exhibit 1 that reflects the application of the criteria used by Kleck and Gertz to identify "genuine" defensive gun uses. Respondents were excluded on the basis of the most recent DGU description for any of the following reasons: the respondent did not see a perpetrator; the respondent could not state a specific crime that was involved in the incident; or the respondent did not actually display the gun or mention it to the perpetrator.

Applying those restrictions leaves 19 NSPOF respondents (0.8 percent of the sample), representing 1.5 million defensive users. This estimate is directly comparable to the well-known estimate of Kleck and Gertz, shown in the last column of exhibit 1. While the NSPOF estimate is smaller, it is statistically plausible that the difference is due to sampling error. Inclusion of multiple DGUs reported by half of the 19 NSPOF respondents increases the estimate to 4.7 million DGUs.

Some Troubling Comparisons

If the DGU numbers are in the right ballpark, millions of attempted assaults, thefts, and break-ins were foiled by armed citizens during the 12-month period. According to these results, guns are used far more often to defend against crime than to perpetrate crime. (Firearms were used by perpetrators in 1.07 million incidents of violent crime in 1994, according to NCVS data.)

Thus, it is of considerable interest and importance to check the reasonableness of the NSPOF estimates before embracing them. Because respondents were asked to describe only their most recent defensive gun use, our comparisons are conservative, as they assume only one defensive gun use per defender. The results still suggest that DGU estimates are far too high.

For example, in only a small fraction of rape and robbery attempts do victims use guns in self-defense. It does not make sense, then, that the NSPOF estimate of the number of rapes in which a woman defended herself with a gun was more than the to-

Exhibit 1. Defensive Gun Use (DGU) Estimates for One-Year Recall Period (1994)—Comparison of NSPOF with Kleck and Gertz Estimates

1 Year	NSPOF Estimates		Kleck and Gertz
	All DGUs Against Persons (N = 45)	DGUs Meeting Kleck and Gertz Criteria* (N = 19)	(N = 66)
Estimated number of defenders (in millions)	3.1	1.5	2.5
Estimated number of DGUs (in millions)	23.0	4.7	n.a.

*In their 1995 DGU study, Kleck and Gertz presented estimates based on only the DGU reports that met certain criteria (see text).

Exhibit 2. Defensive Gun Uses
Compared to Total Crime Counts (1994)

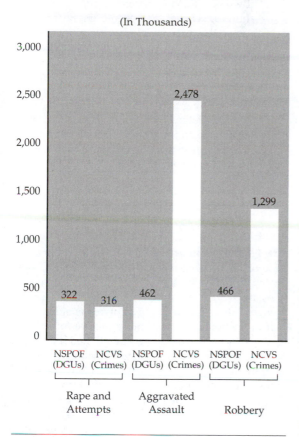

(In Thousands)

Source: Bureau of Justice Statistics, *Criminal Victimization, 1994: National Crime Victimization Survey,* April 1996, NCJ 158022.

tal number of rapes estimated from NCVS (exhibit 2). For other crimes listed in exhibit 2, the results are almost as absurd: the NSPOF estimate of DGU robberies is 36 percent of all NCVS-estimated robberies, while the NSPOF estimate of DGU assaults is 19 percent of all aggravated assaults. If those percentages were close to accurate, crime would be a risky business indeed!

NSPOF estimates also suggest that 130,000 criminals are wounded or killed by civilian gun defenders. That number also appears completely out of line with other, more reliable statistics on the number of gunshot cases.[3]

The evidence of bias in the DGU estimates is even stronger when one recalls that the DGU estimates are calculated using only the most recently reported DGU incidents of NSPOF respondents; as noted, about half of the respondents who reported a DGU indicated two or more in the preceding year. Although there are no details on the circumstances of those additional DGUs, presumably they are similar to the most recent case and provide evidence for additional millions of violent crimes foiled and perpetrators shot.

False Positives

Regardless of which estimates one believes, only a small fraction of adults have used guns defensively in 1994. The only question is whether that fraction is 1 in 1,800 (as one would conclude from the NCVS) or 1 in 100 (as indicated by the NSPOF estimate based on Kleck and Gertz's criteria).

Any estimate of the incidence of a rare event based on screening the general population is likely to have a positive bias. The reason can best be explained by use of an epidemiological framework.[4] Screening tests are always subject to error, whether the "test" is a medical examination for cancer or an interview question for DGUs. The errors are either "false negatives" or "false positives." If the latter tend to outnumber the former, the population prevalence will be exaggerated.

The reason this sort of bias can be expected in the case of rare events boils down to a matter of arithmetic. Suppose the true prevalence is 1 in 1,000. Then out of every 1,000 respondents, only 1 can possibly supply a "false negative," whereas any of the 999 may provide a "false positive." If even 2 of the 999 provide a false positive, the result will be a positive bias—regardless of whether the one true positive tells the truth.

Respondents might falsely provide a positive response to the DGU question for any of a number of reasons:

- They may want to impress the interviewer by their heroism and hence exaggerate a trivial event.

- They may be genuinely confused due to substance abuse, mental illness, or simply less-than-accurate memories.

- They may actually have used a gun defensively within the last couple of years but falsely report it as occurring in the previous year—a phenomenon known as "telescoping."

Of course, it is easy to imagine the reasons why that rare respondent who actually did use a gun defensively within the time frame may have decided not to report it to the interviewer. But again, the arithmetic dictates that the false positives will likely predominate.

In line with the theory that many DGU reports are exaggerated or falsified, we note that in some of these reports, the respondents' answers to the followup items are not consistent with respondents' reported DGUs. For example, of the 19 NSPOF respondents meeting the more restrictive Kleck and Gertz DGU criteria (exhibit 1), 6 indicated that the circumstance of the DGU was rape, robbery, or attack—but then responded "no" to a subsequent question: "Did the perpetrator threaten, attack, or injure you?"

The key explanation for the difference between the 108,000 NCVS estimate for the annual number of DGUs and the several million from the surveys discussed earlier is that NCVS avoids the false-positive problem by limiting DGU questions to persons who first reported that they were crime victims. Most NCVS respondents never have a chance to answer the DGU question, falsely or otherwise.

Unclear Benefits and Costs from Gun Uses

Even if one were clever enough to design a questionnaire that would weed out error, a problem in interpreting the result would remain. Should the number of DGUs serve as a measure of the public benefit of private gun possession, even in principle? When it comes to DGUs, is more better? That is doubtful, for two kinds of reasons:

- First, people who draw their guns to defend themselves against perceived threats are not necessarily innocent victims; they may have started fights themselves or they may simply be mistaken about whether the other persons really intended to harm them. Survey interviewers must take the respondent's word for what happened and why; a competent police investigation of the same incident would interview all parties before reaching a conclusion.

- Second and more generally, the number of DGUs tells us little about the most important effects on crime of widespread gun ownership. When a high percentage of homes, vehicles, and even purses contain guns, that presumably has an important effect on the behavior of predatory criminals. Some may be deterred or diverted to other types of crime. Others may change tactics, acquiring a gun themselves or in some other way seeking to preempt gun use by the intended victim.[5] Such consequences presumably have an important effect on criminal victimization rates but are in no way reflected in the DGU count.

---◇---

Conclusions

The NSPOF provides the most complete data available on the private stock of firearms in the United States, including the kinds of guns owned, by whom they are owned, and for what purpose they were acquired. When asked, handgun owners usually gave self-protection as their primary motive for owning guns, while long-gun owners mentioned hunting or target shooting. Other findings support the conclusion that handguns are much more likely than long guns to be kept unlocked and ready for use in the home and to be carried in public; they are much less likely to be used in sporting activities. Despite those differences, demographic and socioeconomic patterns of firearm ownership in 1994 were similar for handguns and long guns; in fact, most handgun owners also owned one or more long guns.

A fair conclusion is that the more fundamental divide is not between handgun and long-gun owners but between those who own guns and those who do not. Those who like guns, have some experience with them, and have the means to obtain them tend to keep several for various purposes. But most of the adult public turns elsewhere for recreation and protection against crime.

Over time, the relative importance of self-protection and sport as motivations for gun acquisition and use has changed. Perhaps as a result of the increasing urbanization of America, the overall prevalence of gun ownership appears to be declining, as is participation in hunting. Proportionately fewer households owned firearms in 1994 than was true in the 1960s and 1970s, and the younger cohorts are entering into gun ownership at slower rates than previous ones. When people do acquire guns now, the motivation is more likely self-defense than in the past: The mix of new firearms sold in 1994 was equally divided between handguns and long guns, whereas 25 years earlier twice as many long guns were sold.[6]

The NSPOF does not provide much evidence on whether consumers who buy guns for protection against crime get their money's worth. The NSPOF-based estimate of millions of DGUs each year greatly exaggerates the true number, as do other estimates based on similar surveys. Much debated is whether the widespread ownership of firearms deters crime or makes it more deadly—or perhaps both—but the DGU estimates are not informative in this regard.

For other purposes, the NSPOF is a reliable reference. Such information is vital to the evaluation of the ongoing debate over government regulation of gun transactions, possession, and use.

Endnotes

1. For example, the December 1993 Gallup Poll estimated that 49 percent of households possessed a gun.
2. Kleck and Gertz, 1995.
3. In 1994 about 17,000 people were shot dead in criminal assaults and justifiable homicides. Given what we know about the case fatality rate, fewer than 100,000 non-fatal gunshot woundings were known to the police. (See Cook, P. J., "The Case of the Missing Victims," *Journal of Quantitative Criminology*, 1985.) Presumably, the true number of justifiable shootings was just a fraction of this total.

4. Hemenway, D., "Survey Research and Self-defense Gun Use: An Explanation of Extreme Overestimates," Harvard Injury Control Center Discussion Paper, 1996.
5. Cook, P. J., "The Technology of Personal Violence." In M. Tonry (ed.), *Crime and Justice: A Review of Research* (Vol. 14), Chicago: University of Chicago Press, 1–71, 1991.
6. Cook. P. J., "Notes on the Availability and Prevalence of Firearms," *American Journal of Preventive Medicine*, 9 Supp: 33–38, May/June 1993.

---

58. Crime Is Not the Problem

FRANKLIN E. ZIMRING AND GORDON HAWKINS

Franklin E. Zimring and Gordon Hawkins argue that the use of firearms in assault and robbery is the single environmental feature of American society that is most clearly linked to the extraordinary death rate from interpersonal violence in the United States. Using international comparisons, they show that while the United States is similar to many other industrial countries in its crime rate, it has a much higher rate of lethal violence. According to Zimring and Hawkins, the greater availability of guns in the United States contributes to this higher rate of lethal violence.

Los Angeles and Sydney

Los Angeles is the second largest city in the United States with a 1992 population estimated at 3.6 million

From *Crime Is Not the Problem: Lethal Violence in America* by Franklin Zimring and Gordon Hawkins, copyright © (1997) by Oxford University Press, Inc. Used by permission of Oxford University Press, Inc.

for its crime statistics reporting unit. It is a multiracial, multicultural city on the Pacific Coast with a crime rate that by most accounts is its most serious civic problem. Sydney, Australia, is also a city of 3.6 million located on the Pacific Coast of the continent. While multicultural by Australian standards, the ethnic and language mixture falls far short of that in Los Angeles. Crime in Sydney is a serious annoyance, but not a major threat to the continued viability of the city or to the health and welfare of its citizens.

Figure 1 compares the volume of four crimes reported by the police in Sydney and Los Angeles by expressing the number of offenses in Sydney as a percentage of the Los Angeles crime volume. Since the population of the two cities is the same, the crime volume comparison is also a crime rate comparison. The theft category reported at the far left of Figure 1 includes most forms of stealing that are unaggravated by elements that the law regards as increasing the gravity of the offense. This is the most common offense reported in all cities, and the two jurisdictions under review are no exception. Sydney reports just over 90,000 theft incidents, roughly three-quarters of the volume reported in Los Angeles.

Burglary is an aggravated form of theft where the offender breaks and enters private property in order to steal. The crime statistics for Sydney report the offense under two headings: breaking and entering a dwelling, and breaking and entering a building that is not a dwelling. The volume of such crimes in Sydney during 1992 exceeded 63,000, about 10 percent more than the number of burglaries reported in Los Angeles.

The pattern noted for burglary contrasts sharply with robbery, the other major category of aggravated property crime. Robbery is defined as the taking of property from the person of another by force or by the threat of force. In 1992 Los Angeles reported 39,508 robberies while Sydney reported 4,942, one-eighth the Los Angeles rate. The ratio of burglaries to robberies in Los Angeles is just under 3 to 2; the ratio of burglaries to robberies in Sydney is greater than 12 to 1.

The final crime category reported in Figure 1 is for homicides resulting from intentional injury. There were fifty-three such offenses reported by the police in Sydney during 1992, a crime volume equal to 5 percent of the 1,094 homicides reported by the Los Angeles police that same year. The difference between the two cities in rates of criminal homicide exceeds an order of magnitude. The citizens of Sydney can thus live with their high crime rate in relative comfort because they are not dying from it in large numbers.

The major statistical conclusion one draws from an inspection of Figure 1 is that the nature of the comparison between Sydney and Los Angeles depends on what is being compared. For theft and burglary the two cities are quite similar. For robbery and homicide they are vastly dissimilar.

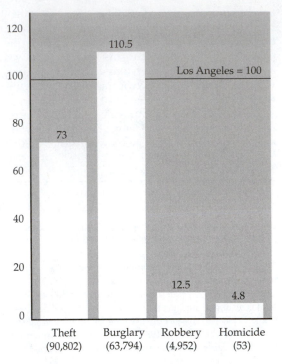

Figure 1. Sydney Crime Volume Compared with Los Angeles, 1992. *Source:* U.S. Department of Justice, Federal Bureau of Investigation, 1992; New South Wales Bureau of Criminal Statistics 1992.

The substantive conclusion to be drawn from this statistical pattern can be stated in two ways. It seems beyond dispute that what separates the two cities is not the amount of crime they experience, but the character of the crime they experience. But the point can be put more sharply than that: What is distinctive and threatening in Los Angeles is not a crime problem but a violence problem.

◇

New York City and London

New York City is the largest city in the United States with a population at 7 million. London has a city population of 6.6 million. Figure 2 shows London crime rates per 100,000 using New York City rates as a standard for comparison. The statistical comparison in Figure 2 is even more surprising than that concerning Los Angeles and Sydney, and to the same

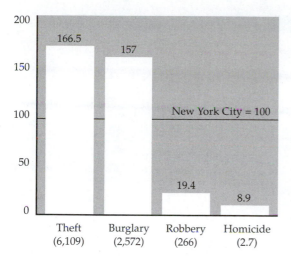

Figure 2. London Crime Rates (per 100,000) Compared with New York City, 1990. *Source:* U.S. Department of Justice, Federal Bureau of Investigation, 1990; London Research Centre 1993.

effect. London has more theft than New York City and a rate of burglary 57 percent higher. But the robbery rate in London is less than one-fifth the robbery rate in New York City and the homicide rate in London is less than one-tenth the New York City figure.

The total number of offenses per 100,000 citizens in Figure 2 is higher in London than in New York City. If total crime rates were the problem, Londoners should live in fear or New Yorkers in relative complacency. They have the same magnitude of crime. But with death rates eleven times as high as London, the population of New York City is far from comfortable. Lethal violence is New York City's distinctive problem, not crime, and lower rates of general theft are no consolation for huge death toll differences.

If readers are wondering whether these data are selective and misleading crime rates, or are numbers that are produced by the peculiarities of different reporting systems, the next set of comparisons should provide some reassurance that our city comparisons are part of a broad and consistent pattern.

Twenty Countries

We can show clearly that America's special problem is violence and not crime by comparing the results of a twenty-nation survey of citizens about the rate at which they were victims of crime with World Health Organization data on death from assaults for the same nations. Figure 3 shows the violent death rates for each group of five nations with the highest crime levels, then the next two highest, and finally the lowest crime categories.

There are several indications that a country's crime rate is substantially independent of its rate of lethal violence. First, the variation in violent death rate is quite large within the separate crime rate categories. Within the group of highest crime nations, the homicide rates vary by a factor of eleven, in the next group by a factor of five, in the third group by a factor of three, and in the lowest crime group by a factor of eight. In contrast, the median homicide rates for the four different crime categories are clustered between 1.3 and 2.2. So knowing which crime rate category a country belongs in does not tell one anything much about what rate of violent death that country suffers.

And knowing a country's violent death rate does not predict much about its crime rate. The lowest death rate country (England) has a crime rate just over average. The next lowest violence nation is Japan, which has the lowest crime rate also. The third lowest death rate country is the Netherlands in the highest crime rate group. The pattern is just as opaque at the top of the violence distribution. The most violent country, the United States, has a high crime rate as well. The next most violent country, Northern Ireland, is in the lowest crime rate group.

This data set provides a multinational example of the central point that lethal violence is the crucial problem in the United States. It shows the United States clustered with other industrial countries in crime rate, but head and shoulders above the rest in violent death.

It also suggests that lethal violence might be the best predictor of citizen fear on a transnational basis. Where would you rather live when examining the map of Figure 3? In England with its high crime rate and 0.5 deaths per 100,000 or in Northern Ireland with a much lower crime rate and nine times the death rate?) Your money or your life?

Judging from Figure 3, the United States has about the same rate of crime and prevalence of criminality as the Netherlands and Australia. But ours is by far the most dangerous country to live in. We currently have a Netherlands-size crime problem and a king-size violence problem that threatens the

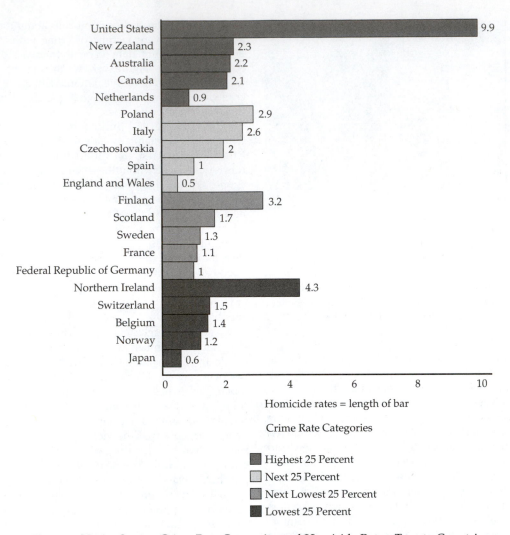

Homicide rates = length of bar

Crime Rate Categories

■ Highest 25 Percent
□ Next 25 Percent
▨ Next Lowest 25 Percent
■ Lowest 25 Percent

Figure 3. Victim Survey Crime Rate Categories and Homicide Rates, Twenty Countries.
Source: van Dijk and Mayhew 1993 (victim survey crime rates);
World Health Organization 1990 (homicide rates).

social organization of our cities. Which problem is at the root of citizen fear in the United States? Which problem should we try to solve? . . .

◇

Firearms and Lethal Violence

When discussing American lethal violence with any foreign criminologist, guns are always the first factor to be mentioned as an explanation of the distinc-

tively high rates of death in the United States. What sets the foreign criminologists' comments apart from our American colleagues' is not the unanimity with which they focus on guns, however, because this topic is inevitably mentioned by American criminologists as well. But our foreign colleagues are frequently unwilling to discuss any other feature of American society or government *except* gun ownership and use. In Europe or Japan, any mention of social, demographic, or economic factors as a cause of homicide is commonly regarded as an evasion of the most obvious reason why American violence is specially dangerous. This singular preoccupation with guns and gun use overstates the degree to which U.S. lethal violence can be explained by a single cause, but not by much. Firearms use is so prominently associated with the high death rate from violence that starting with any other topic would rightly be characterized as an intentional evasion.

This section discusses the role of firearms use in explaining the high rate of lethal interpersonal violence in the United States. This is but one element of a complex set of issues that concerns that relationship between guns and violence in the United States. Self-inflicted and accidental gunshot cases are excluded from this analysis. We will not discuss general patterns of gun ownership and use in this [section] or survey the many different types of control strategy that might reduce gun violence. The central concern here is whether and to what extent our distinctive patterns of gun use explain the high death rates from American violence.

The first part of the analysis discusses the way in which the topic and method of this study push firearms to a position of central importance. The second part examines what we call global approaches to firearms as a contributing cause to lethal violence. The third part sets out a variety of different explanations for why firearms use increases the death rate from violence and surveys what is known about each of those mechanisms. A concluding part talks about issues of causation, in discussions of the relationship between gun use and lethal violence.

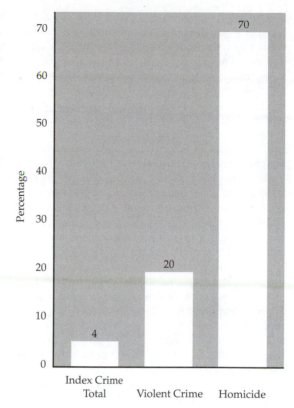

Figure 4. The Prevalence of Firearms Use in Three Crime Categories, United States, 1993.
Source: U.S. Department of Justice, Federal Bureau of Investigation, 1993.

Why Guns?

There are two features of our approach that put special emphasis on gun use: the emphasis on lethal violence and the frequent use of cross-national comparisons. Figure 4 shows the special connection between gun use and deadly violence in the United States by comparing the proportion of police-reported gun use in total index felonies, violent felonies in the crime index, and killings resulting from intentional injury.

The estimates presented in the figure probably understate gun use in index and violent felonies recorded because gun use is not reported for forcible rape and cannot be assessed for noncontact property crime. But . . . the 4 percent estimate for the proportion of total index offenses involving guns confirms what the National Rifle Association has

been insisting upon for some time: only a very small proportion of all criminal offenses in the United States are known to involve guns. If all crimes are of equally serious concern to citizens and policy makers, the low prevalence of firearms in serious crime would be a significant reason to look for other instrumentalities and approaches when attempting to reduce crime.

What the middle bar shows is that when the crimes analyzed are restricted to those that threaten or inflict bodily injury—homicide, rape, robbery, and aggravated assault—the proportion of gun involvement increases fivefold, from 4 to 20 percent. When the subject of the inquiry shifts again to criminal injuries that take life, the prevalence of guns jumps again, this time rising to 70 percent. A shorthand way of communicating the importance of the shift to lethal violence as the focus of inquiry is this: if crime is nominated as the problem, guns are involved in one of every twenty-five cases; if lethal violence is nominated as the problem, then guns are implicated in seven of every ten cases.

The contrast between the one-in-five share of violent felonies committed with guns and the 70 percent gun share for American homicide makes guns appear very much more important when the focus shifts from all violence to lethal violence; this contrast also provides a preliminary basis for concluding that attacks with guns are more dangerous than attacks with other weapons. The 20 percent share of violent crime committed with guns in the United States is significant, but very far from cornering the market. The majority of robberies, rapes, and criminal assaults are committed with personal force, knives, or blunt objects. Even the elimination of all firearms incidents would leave a very high volume of violent offenses. But the 70 percent of all lethal attacks committed with firearms represents a statistical dominance that is difficult to ignore or to minimize. Guns alone account for more than twice as much homicide in the United States as all other means combined.

And the contrasting percentage of gun use for lethal and nonlethal violence also provides circumstantial evidence that guns are far more dangerous than any other instruments when used in violent assaults. If 25 percent of all aggravated assaults produce 70 percent of the lethal outcomes, then that 25 percent of gun attacks are seven times more likely to produce death on the average than the 80 percent of all serious assault that does not involve guns and that cumulatively accounts for only 30 percent of all killings. These are only preliminary indications, because gun attacks may be the product of different motives and situations from attacks employing other means. But the dominance of gun cases in the whole of the lethal violence category makes firearms use a necessary first step in the explanation of American lethal violence.

While solely domestic statistics implicate firearms as a dominant cause of American lethal violence, the sort of international statistical comparison that we have used as a primary tool in earlier analysis also calls attention to firearms. No large industrial democracy other than the United States reports firearms as the cause of a majority of its homicides. Thus, scholars engaging in international comparison are confronted with two extraordinary distinctions between homicide in the United States and in

the rest of the developed Western world: very much higher rates of homicide in the United States, and a uniquely high percentage of gun use in U.S. violence. Concluding that the elevated gun use is a cause of the distinctively high homicide experience seems natural.

One example of this reasoning from a statistical comparison may be found in an essay by Ronald V. Clarke and Pat Mayhew, "The British Gas Suicide Story and Its Criminological Implications." Clarke and Mayhew compare homicide rates per one million population for England and Wales and the United States for firearms, handguns (also counted in the firearms category), and all means other than firearms. Their results are set out in a table, which is reproduced here as Table 1.

All forms of homicide are more frequent in the United States than in England and Wales. Killings by all means other than guns occur in the United States at a rate per million population that is 3.7 times the nongun homicide rate reported in England and Wales. But homicides by handguns occur in the United States at a rate per million population that is 175 times as great. This comparison leads the authors to conclude that "there is little doubt that limiting the availability of firearms in the United States would have a substantial effect on homicide and probably also on other violent crime."

Even though this conclusion cannot be established solely from population statistics of the sort presented in Table 1, the tendency to reach it is inevitable when both the magnitude of gun use and the aggregate death toll differences are that high. The fact that homicide rates with handguns in the United States are 175 times as high as in Great Britain may be only coincidental to the large difference in total homicide rates between the two countries. But few who have studied these international differences are willing to accept the coincidence hypothesis. Instead, those who analyze American violence by first making international comparisons tend to be adamant in their belief that gun use is a major explanation of the elevated death toll from violence. As we have said, it is hard to get them to consider anything else.

And the obvious conclusion about the relationship between firearms and lethal violence in the United States is also the correct one. High levels of gun use in assault and robbery are a very important contributory cause to elevated U.S. death rates from violence. While the magnitude of the difference that can be attributed solely to gun use cannot

Table 1. Gun and Nongun Homicides, England and Wales and the United States, 1980–1984

	Homicides		Average annual rate per one million population[a]		England and Wales to United States ratio
Type of murder	England and Wales	United States	England and Wales	United States	
All gun[b]	213	63,218	.86	54.52	1 to 63.4
Handgun[b]	57	46,553	.23	40.15	1 to 174.6
Nongun[b]	2,416	41,354	9.75	35.67	1 to 3.7
Total[c]	2,629	104,572	10.61	90.19	1 to 8.5

[a]Annual average population for 1980–1984: United States, 231.9 million; England and Wales, 49.55 million.
[b]Figures for the United States involved some extrapolation from homicides for which weapon was known.
[c]Figures for England and Wales relate to offenses currently recorded as homicide.
Source: Clarke and Mayhew 1988, Table 2, p. 107.

be determined with precision, as much as half of the difference between American and European homicide rates may be explained by differential resort in the United States to the most lethal of the commonly used instruments of violence. . . .

The Causes of Differential Lethality

Guns may cause increases in the death rate from assault in a variety of different ways. The use of guns as opposed to other weapons in assault may be associated with both mechanical and social changes in violent assault that can increase death rates. Among the mechanical or instrumentality aspects of gun use that can increase death rates are: the greater injurious impact of bullets, the longer range of firearms; and the greater capacity of firearms for executing multiple attacks. Among the features in social setting related to gun use are: the need to use more lethal instruments of assault in situations where an attacker fears that his adversary may have a gun, the need to sustain or intensify a deadly assault because an opponent possesses or is using firearms, and the increased willingness to use guns and other lethal weapons in personal conflict because such weapons are used generally. All of these aspects may increase the lethality of assaults committed with guns, but by no means to the same degree. There are also two social impacts of gun possession and use

that can lower death rates: the deterrence of assaults because of fear of gun-owning victims and the prevention of attempted assaults by an armed victim.

Instrumentality Effects

Of all the possible ways that gun use increases the deadliness of attacks, the theory that gunshot wounds inflict more damage than other methods of personal attacks is considered the most important and has been the subject of the most research.

The early debate about the influence of guns on deaths from assault involved different theories of the types of intention that produced assaults that lead to death. Marvin Wolfgang in his landmark study of homicide doubted that the weapon used in an attack made much difference in the chance that a death would result since so many different weapons could produce death if an attacker tried hard enough (Wolfgang 1958). Zimring responded to this assertion with a study of knife and gun assaults and killings in Chicago (Zimring 1968).

Zimring's data suggested that many homicides were the result of attacks apparently conducted with less than a single-minded intent to kill. Unlike the Wolfgang study where only fatal attacks were examined, the first Zimring study compared fatal and nonfatal gun and knife assaults in Chicago over four police periods. The study found that 70 percent of all gun killings in Chicago were the result of attacks that resulted in only one wound to the victim, and most attacks with guns or knives that killed a victim looked quite similar to the knife and gun attacks that did not kill (Zimring 1968). From this data, Zimring argued that most homicides were the result of ambiguously motivated assaults, so that the offender would risk his victim's death, but usually did not press on until death was assured.

Under such circumstances, the capacity of a weapon to inflict life-threatening injury would have an important influence on the death rate from assault. The 1968 Chicago study found that gun attacks were about five times as likely to kill as knife attacks, and this ratio held when the comparison was controlled for the number of wounds inflicted and the specific location of the most serious wound (Zimring 1968). Since knives were the next most deadly frequently used method of inflicting injury in attacks, the large difference in death rate suggested that substituting knives or other less dangerous instruments for guns would reduce the death rate from assault.

This weapon dangerousness comparison was first reported for Chicago in 1968 and has been replicated in other sites. Follow-up studies have shown that a difference in weapon as subtle as firearm caliber can double the death rate from gun assaults. The summary conclusion from this line of research can be simply stated: the objective dangerousness of a weapon used in violent assaults appears to be a major influence on the number of victims who will die from attacks. This "instrumentality effect" is the major documented influence of guns on death rate.

The use of guns in robbery is different from their use in wounding since the weapon is not necessarily used to inflict harm. Because robberies with guns frighten their victims into complying with the robbers' demands more than other robberies, a smaller number of gun robberies result in woundings than personal force robberies and robberies with knives. Still, the greater dangerousness of guns when fired more than compensates for the lower number of wounds. For street robberies and those that take place in commercial establishments, the death rate for every 1000 gun robberies is about three times that generated by robberies at knife point and about ten times the death rate from robberies involving personal force.

Another way of estimating the impact of gun use on the dangerousness of robbery is to focus on the prevalence of gun use in fatal and nonfatal robbery incidents. Figure 5 contrasts the firearms share of robberies and robbery killings in the United States for 1992.

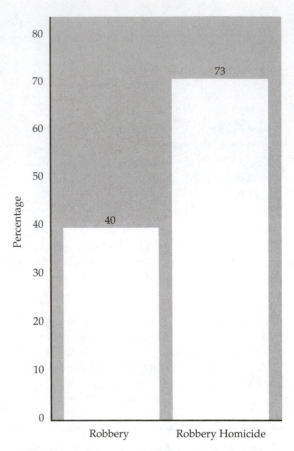

Figure 5. Firearms Use in U.S. Robbery and Robbery Homicide, 1992. *Source:* U.S. Department of Justice, Federal Bureau of Investigation, 1992.

The contrast in Figure 5 is about half that noted between violent crime and homicide in Figure 4. Firearms are responsible for 40 percent of robberies and 73 percent of all robbery killings in the United States, so that the apparent death rate from gun robbery nationwide is four times that of nongun robberies in the aggregate. The data onNew York City robbery . . . estimate a 10-to-1 difference in death rate.

The death rate comparison in Figure 5 is subject to at least two qualifications. In the first place, the difference in death rate noted in the figure already takes into account whatever savings of life results from the lower rate of resistance to gun-using robbers. So the difference in death rate from gun robbery as a result of the greater injury potential of bullet wounds may be larger than the 4-to-1 ratio derived from the data in Figure 5.

The second qualification cuts in the opposite direction. Many of the robberies committed with guns involve commercial entities and other relatively well-defended robbery targets. These robberies might involve a greater risk of injury or death that is to some degree independent of the weapon used by the robber. The switch to knives or blunt instruments in such cases might lead to a higher rate of victim injury or death than is generated by other types of knife and blunt instrument robbery. Of course, some of these difficult target robberies might not be committed if firearms were not available. So the calculus of comparison between gun robberies and other types of robbery is both multidimensional and complex.

There is one sense in which what we call global gun-versus-nongun comparisons in robbery are less problematic than global comparisons involving assault. Because persons committing assault intend to injure, the weapons they select may be probative of their intention to risk a lethal outcome. Since robbery involves only the threat of force, the choice of weapon may not directly reflect an intention to do harm and the choice of more dangerous weapons may not as closely reflect a more serious intention to injure. The robber may not intend any harm at the point of choosing weapons, and differences in total death rate may thus reflect only instrumentality effects. . . .

Social Factors

The mechanical factors just discussed are characteristics of guns that may influence the death rate from attacks committed with firearms. What we call social factors are the many ways in which a social environment where many people possess and use firearms in interpersonal assault may have an influence on the extent to which assaults lead to fatal conclusions. There are at least three different theories as to how a social environment of high gun use can increase killings and at least two theories about how a social environment of extensive gun ownership and use might reduce violent deaths. But precise and specific empirical evaluation of theories about social and environmental effects is not easy.

One way in which a social environment of frequent gun assaults can increase the death rate from assault is by making those engaged in physical combat resort to more lethal instruments of assault and also to continue and intensify an assault because an opponent is armed. A social environment of frequent

gun use multiplies the number of cases where both sides in a conflict possess lethal weapons. This should increase the death rate from both gun and knife attacks by motivating more sustained application of lethal force because of the counterforces risked if the attacker desists too soon.

One common feature of a two-way gun fight is that each combatant is unwilling to stop shooting until it seems clear that his opponent is incapable of shooting back. For this reason, it seems likely that the death rate from bilateral gun fights will be much higher than in situations where one party is armed with a gun and the other party has no deadly weapon. An attack where only one participant uses lethal force should be less likely to produce death because the combatant who controls the lethal force can stop pressing his attack without risking being shot or stabbed.

A second environmental influence closely related to the problem of bilateral lethal force is the way in which fear that others may have guns may motivate people to arm themselves with deadlier weapons than they might otherwise feel would be necessary for either self-defense or attack. When approaching a conflict in which guns are believed to be present, a potential combatant is more likely to feel it necessary to arm himself with a knife or a gun. The irony here is that one element that may increase the use of firearms in combat is a fear of guns in the hands of others. In this way increases in gun use can, in many social settings, become self-fulfilling prophecies.

A third effect of an environment where gun use is frequent that might increase mortality rates from assault is that a high frequency of gun use might lead citizens to expect that firearms are used in interpersonal conflict. On this theory, an increase in gun use would occur, not only out of fear, but out of social habit as the widespread practice of carrying guns and using them to resolve conflicts. The use of a gun in many serious conflicts may no longer be regarded as deviant behavior. This could increase gun use over time substantially. We know of no way to directly measure the extent of this type of legitimation of the use of deadly force, but it is an influence that could be of considerable significance.

There are two current theories about how a social environment of frequent gun use might reduce the death toll from criminal violence: self-defense and deterrence. The self-defense theory argues that a larger number of firearms produces a larger proportion of gun ownership and self-defense gun use.

Potential crime victims will use guns to prevent or thwart attack and thus reduce the death toll—at least among nonoffenders—from assault. The extent of this direct self-defense dividend from high gun ownership is the subject of a lively debate.

One major methodological problem with measuring self-defense is that asking persons in a survey whether they have used a gun to prevent a criminal act produces self-serving statements that cannot be verified. *Each* party to an argument that turned violent is likely to regard the other party as a criminal aggressor, and to think that his own use of force was permissible self-defense. When talking to only one of two combatants, the story one is likely to hear is that a crime was prevented by a gun even though the respondent's opponent would swear that in fact a crime was committed by the person representing himself as the victim. Official police statistics on assault involve an umpire's decision made by police about the culpability of the parties. But survey research cannot generate a valid test of the allegations of a self-serving respondent.

A final theory of social influence argues that widespread gun ownership and use deters criminal assault because would-be offenders recognize the high probability that a criminal attack will be met with lethal force. The probability of substantial across-the-board crime reduction from this kind of armed citizen deterrence is emphasized frequently by opponents of gun control legislation in the United States. And it has been associated with legislative proposals to loosen restrictions on carrying concealed guns. Indeed one small city in Georgia passed an ordinance requiring citizen possession of firearms for which the stated rationale was deterrence.

The measurement of the types of social impact that have been outlined in this section is difficult and some of the most important social influences are the most difficult to assess empirically. The degree to which widespread ownership and use of guns leads to the expectation that they will be used in personal assaults could have a substantial impact on the amount of lethal violence experienced in a society incrementally over a long period of time. But the rigorous empirical assessment of this would be practically impossible to execute because it would be a process taking place gradually over decades without any specific landmarks to be the focus of evaluation. Yet the potential importance of this factor in determining a society's rate of lethal interpersonal violence is not smaller merely because it is not susceptible to rigorous measurement.

Some of the theories of social influence outlined above can be tested in relatively straightforward ways. The quantity and quality of self-defense uses of firearms can be assessed using police statistics and, to a lesser extent, surveys. Police statistics can provide a minimum estimate of incidents of citizen self-defense where a neutral factfinder affirms that the person using the force was not to blame for the event. Survey reports of self-defense can be useful in defining issues even if the factual accounts in the survey cannot be verified. When surveys show that 70 percent of all claimed incidents of crime prevention concern the offense of aggravated assault, the criminologist can pay specific attention to assault and homicide statistics in studying the influence of gun ownership and use on crime.

Another opportunity for straightforward evaluation is the comparison of multiple-wounding and case-fatality rates in one- and two-way gun battles. That sort of specific assessment would be a logical next step in the epidemiological research into intentional injury that is in progress in the United States.

There are a number of hypotheses that cannot be isolated and separately measured. If high gun ownership environments are associated with higher-than-average proportionate use of guns in assault, is this because would-be attackers are afraid their opponents may be armed or is it another manifestation of a general social expectation that it is permissible to use guns in certain types of social conflict? If the widespread availability of handguns prevents some lethal attacks but also increases the death rate from attacks, how can these two countervailing tendencies be isolated and measured?

To some extent, the difficulties of isolating each element of gun influence for individual assessment are intractable, but the precise measure of individual influences on death rates may also be relatively unimportant. From a social policy standpoint, the sort of global assessment that was discussed earlier may tell us all that we have to know because it provides an estimate of the magnitude of the net effect of variations in gun use over time and cross-nationally.

The major problem with many such global estimates by themselves, however, is the issue of causal ordering. But once the mechanical ways in which gun use increases the death rate from assault have been identified and measured, it may be possible to approach the sort of global estimates discussed earlier with more confidence that variations in gun use are, for the most part, independent variables in the equation and that variations in homicide rates are, again for the most part, the dependent variables. If so, a large positive correlation between percentage firearms use in homicide and rates of homicide over time tells us that mechanical and social elements that accompany increases in gun use have a much greater elevating influence on death rates than any restraining influence that may be concurrent. If lethal violence is the focus of social concern, such an aggregate conclusion may be more important than the precise assessment of the impact of specific aspects of firearms use.

Firearms Use as Contributing Cause

The use of firearms in assault and robbery is the single environmental feature of American society that is most clearly linked to the extraordinary death rate from interpersonal violence in the United States. But the strength of this relationship does not mean that firearms ownership and use has a simple, invariable, or independent influence on homicide rates. In this section, we consider the question of the causal connection between gun use and lethality. We do this not only because it is an important issue in relation to firearms and lethal violence, but also because reflecting on the questions of causation that arise in connection with firearms teaches us an important lesson about the role of many other environmental influences on the incidence of lethal violence.

The American debate about guns has produced one of the few causal critiques ever to appear on a bumper sticker: the famous "Guns don't kill people, people kill people." Behind the strong sentiment that inspired this and a multitude of related appeals lies an important logical point. Firearms ownership and use is neither a necessary nor a sufficient cause of violent death in the United States. Firearms are not a necessary cause of killings because of the wide array of alternative methods of killing that are available ranging from the strangler's hands to car bombs. Even in the United States in 1996, nearly 30 percent of all killings did not involve guns. Moreover, the widespread availability of firearms is not a sufficient condition for intentional homicide by a wide margin. One-half of all American households own guns and it is estimated that one-quarter of all households own a handgun—the weapon used in three-

quarters of all gun homicides. Yet only a small fraction of all gun owners become gun attackers. The logical point here is that guns do not become dangerous instruments of attack if they are not used in an attack.

If gun use is neither a necessary nor a sufficient cause of violent death, what is the proper descriptive label for the role gun use plays in deaths due to intentional injury? The most accurate label for the role of firearms in those cases of death and injury from intentional attacks in which they are used is *contributing cause.* Even where the availability of a gun plays no important role in the decision to commit an assault, the use of a gun can be an important contributing cause in the death and injury that results from gun attacks. When guns are used in a high proportion of such attacks, the death rate from violent attack will be high. Current evidence suggests that a combination of the ready availability of guns and the willingness to use maximum force in interpersonal conflict is the most important single contribution to the high U.S. death rate from violence. Our rate of assault is not exceptional; our death rate from assault is exceptional.

The role of gun use as a contributing cause means that the net effect of firearms on violence will depend on the interaction of gun availability with other factors that influence the rate of violent assaults in a society and the willingness of people to use guns in such assaults. So the precise contribution of firearms to the death toll from violence is contingent on many other factors that may influence the number and character of violent attacks.

Some implications of this contingency deserve emphasis. Introducing 10,000 loaded handguns into a social environment where violent assault is a rare occurrence will not produce a large number of additional homicide deaths unless it also increases the rate of assault. The percentage increase in homicide might be considerable if guns become substitutes for less lethal weapons. But the additional number of killings would be small because of the low rate of attack. Introducing 10,000 handguns into an environment where rates of attack and willingness to use handguns in attack are both high is a change that would produce many more additional deaths. The net effect of guns depends on how they are likely to be used.

One corollary of viewing guns as an interactive and contributing cause to intentional homicide is that societies with low rates of violent assault will pay a lower price if they allow guns to be widely available than will societies with higher rates of violence. The sanguine sound bite encountered in American debates about guns is: "An armed society is a polite society" (Handgun Control Inc. 1995). This does not seem particularly plausible to us, but it seems likely that only a very polite society can be heavily armed without paying a high price.

The United States of the 1990s is far from that polite society. Our considerable propensity for violent conflict would be a serious societal problem even if gun availability and use were low. But the very fact that the United States is a high-violence environment makes the contribution of gun use to the death toll from violence very much greater. When viewed in the light of the concept of contributing causation, the United States has both a violence problem and a gun problem, and each makes the other more deadly.

59. *American Homicide Exceptionalism*

DANIEL D. POLSBY AND DON B. KATES, JR.

The United States has a similar crime rate to other industrial countries but a much higher homicide rate. Daniel D. Polsby and Don B. Kates, Jr. argue against the instrumental theory of America's higher homicide rate, which claims that it results from the higher incidence of firearms in the United States, in favor of the perpetrator theory, which explains the phenomenon in terms of the motives, intentions, and risk-taking preferences of the Americans who engage in lethal violence. Polsby and Kates point out, for instance, that 70–80 percent of murderers have criminal records.

Introduction

The standard account of America's homicide problem, championed in one way or another by many prominent criminologists, has now received its classic statement by Franklin Zimring and Gordon Hawkins. G7 countries, except for Japan, have quite similar crime rates; indeed, their experience with many types of crime seems to have been quite parallel since at least the middle of the twentieth century.[1] All experienced a roughly coincidental surge of larcenies, burglaries, and assaults as each of their postwar baby booms matured into late adolescence; all of them had to cope, and, like America, are still learning to cope, with people using marijuana, cocaine, and other illegal psychoactive drugs; all have had to endure the cultural despoilments and occasionally deliberate depravity of television, rock 'n' roll music, and Hollywood movies; all have grown

rich, interdependent, and (in some respects, anyway) strikingly similar since the end of the Second World War. But in one very obvious and tragic way America is an outlier. Its murder rate is one of the highest in the world.[2]

According to the instrumentality theory of American homicide exceptionalism, the explanation cannot possibly be that America has more crime and not more criminals because it does not ("crime is not the problem").[3] Rather, the finger of blame points where Zimring and George Newton, and former U.S. Attorney General Ramsey Clark, pointed it thirty years ago: guns.[4] The lethality of interpersonal violence is dictated by the lethality of the instrumentalities at the disposal of antagonists.[5] Guns are hard to get legally in most of the civilized world nowadays: indeed, in Japan, which experiences fewer murders in an average year than does the United States in a few weeks,[6] guns are all but impossible to come by; whereas in America semiautomatic pistols and rifles and powerful shotguns can be had from sporting goods stores with, at most, a few days' waiting.[7] At gun shows and in private transactions, even these minimal restrictions are

Daniel D. Polsby, American Homicide Exceptionalism, 69, *University of Colorado Law Review* 969 (98). Reprinted with permission.

either inapplicable or are ignored.[8] More than forty percent and perhaps half of American households have guns in them, and in many cases more than one gun.[9] There are far more guns in the United States than there are microwave ovens,[10] automobiles,[11] dogs or cats,[12] nearly as many guns as there are people.[13] Virtually all of these firearms are privately owned.[14] Few are required to be, and even fewer actually are, registered to their owners. If an American is overcome with rage, or with any other urgent reason for wishing to arm himself, chances are he will be able to outfit himself with a gun forthwith. If he does, he will have a means of inflicting wounds that are about an order of magnitude more likely to result in a victim's death than would be knife wounds or blunt trauma. Elsewhere in the rich countries of the world, people are equally as criminally inclined as Americans, as prone to abuse alcohol and each other, but because they cannot readily get their hands on powerful weapons like guns, as Americans can and do, they experience homicide rates only a fraction of those seen here. Or so the argument goes.

The case for this interpretation of experience has seemed so powerful to American opinion leaders that dissenting views have very nearly been swept from public view and relegated to the pages of *Guns and Ammo* or, occasionally, *National Review*.[15] Broadcasters and cable networks have lately been running unanswered public service announcements blaming handguns for the deaths of ten children per day, and there is virtual unanimity among newspapers and mass-circulation magazines that not only is the instrumentality theory correct, but that its correctness is a scientific fact, like Newton's Laws of Motion or Quantum Theory, beyond worthwhile discussion.

There is, however, very deep public acceptance of an interpretation of experience that is in tension with an instrumentality theory of American homicide exceptionalism. Perpetrator theories, as we call them, focus on the motives, intentions, and risk-taking preferences of individuals instead of on the tools ("instrumentalities") that they have selected to carry on their activities. No one should need to be reminded that Americans do believe in human perversity as well as in the connection between perversity and crime. In virtually every part of the country there has been broad political support for large public investments in prisons that no longer advertise rehabilitation as a product they can dependably de-

liver. Americans are far more supportive of the death penalty than people in other rich countries. Americans are fully prepared to disown public officials who espouse liberal penological philosophies—for example, on the use of prison furloughs or conjugal visitation, as behavioral incentives—and to embrace back-to-the-future, get-tough approaches to prison administration such as chain gangs. These are largely symbolic gestures: what they symbolize is a belief that human perversity exists, and that the proper social response to this perversity is punishment, not therapy.

Though they are not, strictly speaking, logically inconsistent, there are very important conceptual and practical differences between perpetrator theories and instrumentality theories. Theoretically, they see causation in opposite ways: instrumentality theory posits that "gun causes homicide," while perpetrator theory interprets human transactions with lethal outcomes as tending to flow from perpetrators' intentions, either to kill or to run a conscious risk of killing a victim. Instrumentality theory sees guns as an explanation, whereas perpetrator theory sees guns as something that need to be explained (that is, by the recklessness or murderousness of an offender).

More importantly, there is a large practical difference between these two theories. The strong form of instrumentality theory—the sort championed by Zimring and Hawkins—comes close to denying the relevance of criminal justice policy either as an explanation for given rates of homicide or as a tool for changing those rates. Suppose, for example, it is proposed to drive down the homicide rate. Increasing the harshness or certainty of punishment for murder and manslaughter would be barking up the wrong tree if excess undesirable behavior is not seen as a part of the problem. Incapacitative detention (such as "three strikes and you're out" or "truth in sentencing") would be seen as at best a marginal address to the problem unless one were prepared to tolerate much larger prison populations and much more type-I error (that is, falsely supposing the dangerousness of a potential offender).[16] Even changes in the numbers or tactics of police might be thought beside the point. All these interventions aim to change the incentives to commit crimes by application of the straightforward utilitarian technique of altering the likelihood of apprehension or the painfulness of consequences. But if crime is not the problem, such changes might be largely inapposite.

And of course in this theory, crime is *not* ordinarily seen as the problem: "most homicides result from non-criminal social relations";[17] murderers "are good citizens who [only] kill each other"[18] because a gun was available in a moment of ungovernable fury— "previously law abiding citizens committing impulsive gun-murders while engaged in arguments with family members or acquaintances;"[19] "[t]hat gun in the closet to protect against burglars will most likely be used to shoot a spouse in a moment of rage. . . . *The problem is you and me—law-abiding folks.*"[20]

> Murder is a crime of passion. Few murders are premeditated. The tragedy is that the rifle was standing there in the closet when the son was seized by fury and shot his father, or the pistol was by the bed during a drunken argument and the husband shot his wife.[21]

In this rendering of the problem, the solution, if there is one at all, must revolve around regulating guns: "gun control." Zimring and Hawkins are firmly in this camp, for despite their aversions to the need for "a diversified portfolio of countermeasures to lethal violence,"[22] they are as clear currently as in previous animadversions[23] on the subject that gun control is the *sine qua non* of lowering homicide rates,[24] without which no program for reducing lethal violence can even be taken seriously.[25]

The strong form of perpetrator theory, on the other hand, is completely to the contrary. It holds that, theoretically and practically, instrumentality regulation could have at most a small peripheral value. If a person intends to kill someone, or is willing to risk a killing for the sake of making a credible threat to kill, then chances are he will try to get a gun. Once he is determined to use a gun criminally, making *that* also a crime is a meaningless, no-value-added gesture; regardless of weapons laws, there will always be enough guns floating around in any modern society to supply the comparatively few persons who want to kill or at least to embrace the risk of killing. As a retired English police official, Colin Greenwood, put the matter:

> At first glance it may seem odd, or even perverse, to suggest that statutory controls on the private ownership of firearms are irrelevant to the problem of armed crime, yet that is precisely what the evidence shows. Armed crime and violent crime generally are products of ethnic and social factors unrelated to the availability of any particular type of weapon. The

numbers of firearms required [to arm criminals are minute in comparison to the overall number in private hands], and these are supplied no matter what controls are instituted. Controls have had serious effects on legitimate users of firearms, but there is no case either in the history of this country [England] or in the experience of other countries, in which controls have been shown to have restricted the flow of weapons to criminals or in any way to have reduced armed crime.[26]

These models imply two quite different regulatory responses. If crime is not the problem, then one should focus efforts where the real problem is—on deadly attacks, rather than on crime. But if deadly attacks are simply a part of an undifferentiated packet of high-risk behaviors that are engaged in by a small and discrete sub-population ("criminals"), then one should expect payoffs, in the form of lower homicide rates and less crime generally, by proceeding in the old-fashioned way, with more intensive and more effective policing and more credible threats of prosecution and imprisonment. It matters which theory is more nearly correct, though both could perfectly well be true (and, to a degree, both certainly are). Even instrumentality theory doubters (for example, the present authors) will affirm that there are at least *some* "instrumentality homicides." Even the set of most highly-motivated and capable killers would surely find that other weapons could only incompletely substitute for guns; there must surely be some killings by gunshot that would never have resulted if the perpetrator had been armed only with a bludgeon or a knife. But even if one could enumerate instrumentality homicides with certainty (which would disclose whether instrumentality homicides were a large or a small percentage of the total), one would still have to consider the other side of the question—the social utility of private firearms possession. It is only by the trick of assigning that utility some value approaching zero that instrumentality theory generates its accustomed policy prescription. . . .

I. *Inferences from Abroad*

Summarizing the foreign experience with crime and lethal violence, Zimring and Hawkins write: "If general levels of crime determine the rate of lethal violence, then increases or decreases in crime should result in parallel increases or decreases in lethal violence."[27] Such parallel fluctuation does not, however, occur. Take thirty years of data from the G7 countries. The proposition bears out in the United States, Canada, and Italy (all of which experienced significant increases in theft and homicide between 1960 and 1990), but proves false in Japan (where theft increased, but very little, and an already low murder rate declined substantially) and glaringly false in England,[28] France, and Germany (where theft increased and homicide rates declined or did not change).[29] Can we trust these data? Beyond a certain point it is unnecessary to do so: as Zimring and Hawkins argue, the basic story emerges from the rough cut: property crimes have gone up in all the rich countries since the baby-boom generation began edging into its mid-teens, but murder rates have risen, fallen, or stayed the same.

Now consider the victimization rates (they argue) for various crimes (robbery, assault, all violent offenses, and property offenses) in twelve to eighteen countries including the United States. For property crimes between 1988 and 1991, one finds the victimization experience of the United States at the high end of the distribution, essentially tied with such countries as Spain, Canada, the Netherlands, New Zealand, and Australia.[30] For "all violent offenses" during the same period, the United States is again at the high end of the distribution, tied with Canada, New Zealand, and Poland and significantly behind Australia.[31] For robbery rates (with 1991 as the for instance), again the United States victimization numbers are at the high end, along with Italy, Australia, England, Canada, and Czechoslovakia but well behind Poland.[32] For assault, the United States is distinctly a second-class power. Canada, Australia, and New Zealand lead the league; America is back in the *peloton* tied with Finland, Poland, and the Netherlands.[33]

These numbers depict a fairly straightforward story. The United States, like other Anglophone countries, is a pretty tough town, near but not all the way at the head of the class for most categories of crime. It is not, as Zimring and Hawkins point out, very different-looking from comparison countries until one looks at lethal outcomes measures. "What separates the United States from the rest of the industrial Western world . . . is [its] relatively small number of life-threatening attacks, usually shootings. . . ."[34] Here, America is in a class by itself.

It remains to be established, however, what all this information means. The question begged by these data, the implication that we are plainly invited to draw from them, is that *a priori* one should expect a certain uniformity in the relationship between crime rates to lethality rates when comparing the United States and other countries. But this implication lies well beyond either logic or experience. Perhaps American robbers and assaulters are simply a deadlier lot than Australians, Frenchmen, Englishmen (and so on), better armed because they are prepared to be more violent than their foreign counterparts. Though plenty of evidence can be adduced to the effect that the United States is rather like other industrialized countries, there is plenty of other evidence that in fact the United States is rather *unlike* other industrialized countries. Consider, for example, the case of rape—a crime that seldom involves the use of a gun.[35] The United States has far higher rates of rape than other industrialized countries: for example, it is anywhere from thirteen to twenty-three times higher than the English rate;[36] almost five times the French rate;[37] almost six times the German rate;[38] and *thirty times* the Japanese rate.[39] All of these measurements approximate the homicide rate disparities that show up when the United States is compared with these other countries.

It would be a treat to hear an instrumentality-based explanation for American rape exceptionalism, but the point that is illustrated by disparity is too important to be let stand as a joky debater's taunt. There are large differences between Americans and the populations of foreign countries, even English-speaking countries with many superficial similarities. American rates of non-firearms homicide are far higher than homicide rates *from all causes* in England and Japan,[40] a circumstance that supports the inference that *murder rates in the United States would be many times higher than English or Japanese rates even if every civilian firearm in this country suddenly vanished in a puff of smoke.* The United States records more non-firearms murders than there are murders from all causes in Western Europe and Japan combined, territories more than half again as populous as the United States.

The culture here, at least in some crucial aspects, is quite different from anything found in other rich countries of the world. These differences far transcend the question of firearms and how they are distributed. They dictate how young men will answer narcissistic injuries and territorial affronts, and what one may or may not do in order to get money or drugs or sex (and so on). One should hardly be surprised to see big differences from one place to another in what sorts of behavior will get one arrested, how various categories of crime are defined, when violence, including killing, is most to be expected, and whom we should expect to be involved. American criminals and those of England, France, and so on, cannot usefully be compared directly without a far more detailed account than is presently available concerning their similarities and differences. Without such an account, the instrumentality theory of American homicide exceptionalism is reduced to a tendentious assumption. Demand for firearms on account of their lethality could be all one could ask for to explain the unusual prevalence of firearms homicide in the United States. . . .

A crucial link in the instrumentality story of American homicide exceptionalism is the proposition that firearms availability turns ordinary citizens into circumstantial candidates for the state penitentiary: "[T]he majority of homicide victims die not as a result of criminal activity, but because of arguments between people who know each other";[41] [T]he social processes that generate arguments that result in homicides are not distinctively criminal in most cases";[42] "[They arise] out of arguments and other social encounters between acquaintances";[43] "[M]ost homicides result from noncriminal social relations";[44] "Most of the circumstances that generate homicide are not property crimes involving strangers, but arguments among acquaintances that nobody would regard as distinctively criminal until the attack began."[45]

Similarly, most murderers are "neither felons nor crazy," but just "people involved in family fights and fights over jobs and money, and people who are sad or depressed"[46]—"previously law abiding citizens committing impulsive gun-murders while engaged in arguments with family members or acquaintances."[47]

There can be little question that criminals equipped with guns are more dangerous than those without. But it does not follow, and in fact it is not true, that law-abiding people who possess guns are likewise more socially dangerous. There has now accumulated a good deal of direct evidence concerning the identity and background of murderers, that makes it evident that the "plain folks" account can no longer be wrapped in the mantle of science.[48] Murderers are not plain folks. Neither, for the most part, are their victims. To the extent that killings are

the product of arguments, it should be borne in mind that only arguments between a certain sort of antagonist are likely to have a mortal outcome.

It has long been clear that murderers are, in comparison with the general population, disproportionately likely to have significantly subaverage intelligence, suffer from insanity or brain damage, alcoholism or substance abuse, or combinations of these problems. Numerous American, Canadian, and European studies find that people with impaired cognitive capacity, mental illness, or a history of substance abuse are several times more likely to engage in violent crime in general than are ordinary citizens.[49] Murderers exhibit this same predisposition:

> Although there is some controversy [about the distinctiveness of murderers from other criminals], it has long been suspected that homicidal behavior might result from brain dysfunction associated with impaired ability to regulate goal-directed activity and modulate impulsive response. These neurological risk factors include abnormalities in brain functioning, pre- and perinatal influences, history of head injury, delayed psychomotor and speech development, and learning difficulties.[50]

> An early onset of alcohol abuse is one of the hallmarks of Type II alcoholism, a condition that has been related to the propensity for impulsive, violent crimes under intoxication. Substance abuse also may be a part of an adult lifestyle among violent and impulsive offenders.[51]

> [Among violent and nonviolent Finnish criminals] the homicidal group tended to differ from the other groups in cruelty to animals during childhood, had an earlier onset of alcohol abuse [than either of the other groups] and a higher prevalence of drug dependence than those in the nonviolent groups, and had experienced over three times more physical abuse than offenders in the nonviolent group. . . . These results are congruent with earlier research findings. . . .[52]

An American review of homicide studies notes that the "research literature on characteristics of those who murder yields a profile of offenders that indicates many have histories of committing personal violence in childhood against other children, siblings, and small animals."[53]

From the 1960s to date, national and local studies document that seventy to eighty percent of all murderers have formal adult criminal records.[54] Prior to an uptick in the mid 1980s, minors—who practically never have adult records—had committed ten percent of murders; more recently minors' "market share" has been over fifteen percent.[55] Of those killers who are old enough to have adult records, ninety percent or more do. Most of these criminals are not even thirty years old, but in their few adult years have averaged four major felony arrests over a six-year crime career.[56] (By contrast, something like eighty-five percent of the population has never been arrested even once.)[57] Based on a national sample of prison interviews, the Bureau of Justice Statistics estimates that in the 1980s, about 13,200 murders were committed while the offender was on parole or probationary release for a prior felony conviction.[58] At the time they committed murder, eleven percent of killers had been released on bail or recognizance while awaiting trial for some previous offense.[59]

These formal criminal records, moreover, represent only the proverbial tip of the iceberg. Many of these individuals have prior crime histories which are unknown because either they were not caught[60] or their crime record was as a juvenile and hence is confidential and, perhaps in addition, expunged.[61] One of the few studies to obtain access to juvenile records, that of David Kennedy and his colleagues at Harvard's Kennedy School, analyzed Boston-area juvenile gun and knife murders for the years 1990 to 1994. In their less than twenty-one years of life, the 125 killers in this sample had had an average 9.7 prior arrests—three arrests for prior murders, hundreds for prior gun crimes and nongun violent felonies, and even more for drug and property crimes.[62] It is a safe bet that many adult murderers' juvenile records would supplement and extend their average of four adult major felony arrests. It is not a mistake of the ordinary sort but rather an extravagant falsification of reality to claim, as some researchers have, that such individuals "would be considered law-abiding citizens prior to their pulling the trigger."[63]

Furthermore, not even the small fraction of murderers without a prior criminal record—ten percent or so of the total—can accurately be characterized as "law-abiding citizens." A few fit that characterization, but many will have come to the attention of the police repeatedly for matters, such as domestic battery, in which, as a matter of custom, arrests have

been sparingly made. Studies show "most family murders are prefaced by [the killer's] long history of assaults";[64] in ninety percent of cases, the police had been called to the same address at least once within the preceding two years; the median number of prior police calls to that address was five during that period.[65] But none of those five or more disturbance calls may have ended in an arrest. True, perhaps as many as seventy to seventy-five percent of domestic homicide offenders have previously been arrested.[66] Significantly, however, domestic murderers may have a long history of brutalizing within the family yet only have a record for attacking others outside the family. Massachusetts data show that seventy-five percent of adult wife-batterers have a prior crime record, but half their prior violence arrests were for attacks on nonfamily members.[67]

"[W]ith comparatively few exceptions, homicide reflects a long-standing pattern [of the murderers' prior similar] behavior."[68] Because homicide, even among the most "at risk" populations, remains relatively rare, one cannot reverse the assertion that "most killers were criminals" and pretend to know which individuals, among the population of likely candidates, actually will go on to commit murder.[69] But murderers remain a highly unusual and aberrant population. Recognizing this is the key to understanding why arguments between murderers have a relatively high risk of deadly issue, but arguments between "plain folks," even well-armed plain folks, almost never have a lethal outcome.

At least with respect to their criminal history, it is evident that victims more resemble their killers than they do the population generally. David Kennedy found that Boston-area juveniles who murdered other juveniles averaged 9.7 prior criminal arraignments in Massachusetts courts, compared with their victims' average of 9.5 criminal arraignments.[70] "Probation officers said it was rare to lose a kid to gun violence who had not previously been on probation, and the dark joke among gang officers was whether it would be ethical to (get rich by) tak[ing] out life insurance on certain kids."[71] At least sixty percent of those homicides were by or among gang members. "This is a conservative estimate, since [it did not include] cases in which the circumstances were unknown or ambiguous. . . ."[72] Philip Cook and John Laub found that, nationally, guns are used in eighty-eight percent of adult and juvenile gang murders.[73] Typical of findings in local studies across the nation are that seventy-one percent of minors wounded in Los Angeles drive-by shoot-ings "were documented members of violent street gangs";[74] that eighty percent of homicides in Wash-ington, D.C., are "drug-related"; that nearly seventy percent of admittees in 1994 through 1996 at a ma-jor Maryland trauma center who had been shot, knifed, or beaten tested positive for alcohol, co-caine, opiates, marijuana, amphetamines, or phen-cyclidine and many were substance-dependent;[75] and that eighty-four percent of 1990 homicide vic-tims in Philadelphia had crime records or showed antemortem use of illegal substances (or both). In addition, the Rand Foundation study, "Homicide in Harlem," estimated that "the great majority of both perpetrators and victims of assaults and murders had previous arrests, probably over eighty percent or more."[76] A study of gunshot wounds reported to the Charlotte, North Carolina, Police Department in 1992 and 1993 found that seventy-one percent of adult victims had criminal records. In Chicago, the Police Detective Bureau reports that nearly two-thirds of victims (as compared with three-quarters of apprehended perpetrators) have adult arrest records.[77]

The murder wave that began in the mid 1980s affected only a very narrow band of the American population. Through most of that decade, nearly all of the country continued to decompress from the baby-boomer crime wave that peaked before 1980. Rates of victimization by persons over age twenty-five, regardless of race, declined more or less con-tinuously from 1980 onward.[78] But between 1985 and 1990, the murder rate among young African-American males increased extremely. The victimiza-tion rate for black males in their middle and late teens nearly tripled in those years, from 37.4 in 100,000 to 105.3 in 100,000. For men between ages twenty and twenty-four, it more than doubled (from 63.1 in 100,000 to 140.7 in 100,000). The victimization rate for the population as a whole is less than 10 in 100,000.

The crucial thing is not that many murders arise out of arguments, but who is doing the argu-ing. Everyone experiences interpersonal conflict in one way or another and at one time or another, but it is exceptionally rare for such antagonisms to lead to mortal consequences unless at least one of the disputants has a life history of crime (often irra-tionally violent), mental disorder, or substance abuse. The mystery of why, contrary to all common experience, arguments lead to murder disappears when we realize who the participants in these par-ticular arguments are: drug dealers versus customers or competitors; co-members of criminal gangs or rival gangs; and abusive men versus the women and children they have brutalized on countless prior occasions.

IV. International Comparisons

Two distinct issues are broached by the instrumen-tality theory of American homicide exceptionalism. One is how the distribution of firearms is related to crime, murder, and so on. The other is how regu-latory laws are related to the distribution of fire-arms. For many years, confusion between these two propositions has been a stable feature of firearms policy discourse,[79] but the two questions are quite distinct. People's persistent refusal to obey, for ex-ample, anti-pornography laws, anti-narcotics laws, or highway speed limits (especially in wide-open, empty places like the Dakotas) should serve as a re-minder that passing a law is one thing and getting people to obey it is another. Indeed, compliance with any law will certainly be inflected by a number of variables.

First and most conventionally, people calculate the probability of being apprehended if they dis-obey a law and the severity of the punishment if they are apprehended. This is usually called the general deterrence principle: severity of punish-ment discounted by probability of apprehension. The general deterrence principle predicts that, other things equal, one should see less and less compli-ance with any given law as it becomes more and more difficult for authorities to detect violations or as it becomes more and more difficult to persuade juries to punish people who are caught. But a num-ber of other factors must certainly be as important, if not more important, to compliance. For example, people cannot be expected to obey a law they do not know about.[80] Then there is the matter of institu-tional respect: other things equal, one would expect less obedience of a law among people who did not respect the jurisdiction of the enacting authority than among people who did.[81] Convenience is often im-portant: one should expect to see more obedience to a law where it is easy to obey than where it is diffi-cult.[82] People certainly calculate how obedience to a law will likely impinge on their own private welfare:

heroin addicts, fearful of withdrawal, are less likely to obey narcotics laws than otherwise similar people who have never touched heroin. Finally, a "self-reputation" for law-abidingness is important to most individuals.[83] People engaged in arrantly illegal behavior commonly tell themselves face-saving, self-justifying stories (it's not really illegal; everybody does it; I have a right; I am only re-claiming a patrimony which was stolen, by the cap-italists or the Elders of Zion or whoever).

The moral of this story is that one must sup-pose that compliance with prohibitory gun control laws (for illustration, a national law banning hand-guns) would be uneven in any heterogeneous population. One would expect the most rapid com-pliance by handgun owners who did not think they actually needed a handgun for anything and who respected the authority of the national government to prohibit such weapons. One would expect rela-tively lower levels of compliance among people who were convinced they needed a strong form of self-defense (especially people who, rightly or wrongly, distrusted the police) and who were either outright contemptuous of law or adroit at making up self-justifications for noncompliance with it. The second category by definition includes more criminals and sociopaths than the first. Assuming compliance with gun control laws does, over some period of time, lead to appreciably fewer weapons being in circula-tion, it would seem to be obvious—axiomatic—that throughout this period of transition, criminals and sociopaths must be increasingly well-armed, in rela-tion to the population as a whole—and even more so in relation to the most law-abiding tail of the dis-tribution. The instrumentality theory must offer some sort of justification for believing that the rela-tionship between firearms distribution and crime, lethal outcomes, or any other variable output will approximate a monotonic function over a twenty- or thirty-year period of time, so that in each succes-sive period in which one observes fewer firearms diffused among the population, one also observes, or tends to observe, less homicide, suicide, and other serious violence.

There is no such direct evidence, but indirect evidence might arguably be derived by comparing the experience of the United States and that of other countries. Compare the (relatively) high homicide (or suicide) rate in Seattle, Washington (where hand-gun control is lax), and the relatively low rates in Vancouver, B.C., (where it is strict): res ipsa loquitur.[84]

Compare London with New York and see how, with similar rates of burglary and assault, gun-happy New York outstrips gun-controlled London in terms of lethal outcomes.[85] Do not such cross-sectional comparisons offer strong evidence that gun control policies actually do work?

It is a standard move in instrumentality the-ory argumentation to offer international or cross-cultural comparisons to establish the proposition that American homicide exceptionalism is essen-tially explained by American gun laws or the lack of them.[86] But it is far from obvious what one can learn from this technique without controlling for relevant differences in the populations being compared. After all, differences in gun control laws—and, for that matter, differences in the ac-tual distribution of firearms, which is a different and surely far more important matter—are seldom going to be the main differences between a pair of cities each in different country. Without adequately ac-counting for other variables, most obviously, differ-ences in their demographic makeup, these sorts of comparisons run the risk of degenerating into mere tendentiousness.

Indeed, one indication of the loose fit between gun control laws and homicide rates can be drawn from historical experience. American homicide ex-ceptionalism long antedated modern gun control laws. Years before European countries adopted the restrictive firearms policies that most of them have today,[87] they enjoyed very low rates of violent crime.[88] In the absence of prohibitory legislation, England and continental Europe were important markets for so-called pocket pistols (small, light-caliber hand-guns), which were fabricated in innumerable small factories all over Europe,[89] and in the years preced-ing the First World War, at least a million .32 caliber Browning pocket pistols, and a hundred thousand .25 caliber pistols, were shipped to Europe from the United States.[90] These countries' gun control laws were nothing like as strict as American laws during this period,[91] though American rates of criminal violence, then as now, were far higher than Euro-pean rates. It is an anachronism to locate American homicide exceptionalism primarily in national dif-ferences in firearms regulation. As historian Eric Monkkonen has pointed out:

> Virtually every analysis put forward to explain the [comparatively] very high United States homicide rate has been ahistorical. . . . Had

they been proposed as historical, they would have foundered quickly for the explanatory inadequacy of these "pet" theories becomes immediately apparent in a historical context.[92]

It is, moreover, an historical solecism to hold the English nation up as an exemplar of peaceable law-abidingness or, for that matter, of the effectiveness of gun control laws as a means of controlling homicide and other crime. During the Middle Ages, in fact, England without guns may have had a murder rate more than double the current American murder rate.[93] The "English were noted throughout Europe for their turbulence and proclivity to violence."[94] It was not until the nineteenth century that England began to assume its modern reputation for peacefulness, and by the time it adopted restrictive gun control legislation, the Firearms Act of 1920,[95] England ranked among the world's most placid nations. Yet prior to 1920, the principal gun control law in the country was that policemen would not carry firearms.

English and European gun control originated as a reaction, not to crime, but to the political violence which racked the continent after the First World War.[96] Weimar Germany adopted similar laws for similar reasons about the same time.[97] The laws were enacted in order to cope with the violence, yet (although one cannot, of course, be certain) it seems fair to observe that statutory gun control measures did not obviously have much of a pacifying effect either on crime or political violence. The United States and Switzerland (another country where household firearms have always been encouraged) have suffered far less from assassination, terrorism, and political violence than have England or continental Europe through most of the twentieth century.

Moreover, England and Europe have seen ordinary apolitical violent crime increase over the past seventy years, to as great or even a greater extent than has the United States (although of course from much lower base levels).[98] "No matter how one approaches the figures," Colin Greenwood wrote in the early 1970s, "one is forced to the rather startling conclusion that the use of firearms in crime" in England "was very much less" before 1920 "when there were no controls of any sort and when anyone, convicted criminal or lunatic, could buy any type of firearm without restriction. Half a century of strict controls has ended, perversely, with a far greater use of this class of weapon in crime than ever before."[99] Since then, violent crime, and particularly firearms

crime, has so steadily increased that ever increasing numbers of English police are being armed.[100]

Greenwood is not to be read as arguing that it is advisable to allow lunatics and criminals to purchase firearms. The point is, rather, that relatively little irregular behavior with firearms can be attributed to people with innocuous life histories, whereas those from whom one has most to fear, criminals and lunatics, have relatively little compunction about defying or evading laws, gun control laws among them, meant to control their behavior.

◇

V. Implications for Public Policy

The connection between guns and American homicide exceptionalism becomes explicit only in the population of criminals. That is why crime *is* after all the problem, and why changing the subject to homicidal violence, on the pretext that killing is a stochastic property of armed populations that are not in other respects predisposed to violence, is seriously misleading. The challenge for public policy is not how to further burden the lives of the innocuous many but rather how to manage the antisocial behavior of the toxic few. What one can learn from the experience of other countries that would help attain this objective is pervasively questionable. Obviously foreign countries will have quite different rules of police practice and criminal procedure than those applicable in the United States; both as a formal legal (or constitutional) matter and as a matter of sociology, authorities are differently constrained, and undoubtedly in most cases less constrained, than their United States counterparts. It follows that the crime-control (or violence-control) lessons one could possibly learn by studying (for example) Japan or Italy are going to be of limited applicability in the United States unless we are able also to import the people, customs, traditions, criminal procedures, shared habits of mind, and social organization of Japan or Italy. One would probably do better, in the long run, presuming that institutions *cannot* be transplanted from one culture to another than presuming that they can.[101]

That is not to deny that it makes common sense to prohibit people with histories of violence or crime from possessing guns. Even though it is difficult to catch someone in unlawful possession of guns (or anything else small enough to conceal), no one will deny that police ought to arrest such a person if, perchance, they should encounter one. But that is not a strategy that suggests trying to limit access to firearms by the risky few through controlling the behavior of the harmless many, whose possession of firearms raises their murder risk not at all in statistical terms, and their suicide risk, at most, very little.[102] There is after all,

> no evidence anywhere to show that reducing the availability of firearms *in general* likewise

reduces their availability to persons with criminal intent, or that persons with criminal intent would not be able to arm themselves under any set of general restrictions on firearms.[103]

Perhaps one can agree, in the end, that it is not crime, but criminals that really are the problem. But this is a semantic quibble that leaves the conversation precisely where it was before Zimring and Hawkins's latest contribution.

Endnotes

1. *See* Franklin E. Zimring & Gordon Hawkins, *Crime Is Not the Problem: Lethal Violence in America* 27–33 (1997).

2. *See id.* at 8 fig. 1.3.

3. *Id.; see also* Franklin E. Zimring & Gordon Hawkins, *The Citizen's Guide to Gun Control* 13–20 (1987) [hereinafter *Citizen's Guide*].

4. *See Citizen's Guide, supra* note 3.

5. *See id.* at 15–16.

6. *See* Zimring & Hawkins, *supra* note 1, at 7–8.

7. *See e.g.,* Colo. Rev. Stat. § 12-26.5-103 (requiring only an instant criminal background check on the firearms purchaser); Cal. Penal Code § 12076 (West 1991).

8. *See* Melvin Claxton & William Gaines, "Fire Sale: America's Unchecked Gun Market," *Chi. Trib.,* Dec. 29, 1997, at A1.

9. *See* Gary Kleck, *Point Blank: Guns and Violence in America* 17–64 (1991).

10. *See* Bureau of the Census, U.S. Dep't of Com., *Statistical Abstract of the United States* 1997: *National Data Book* 728 tbl.1207 (1997).

11. *See id.* at 627 tbl.1009.

12. *See id.* at 255 tbl.412.

13. *See id.* at 28 tbl.26.

14. *See* Gary Kleck, *Targeting Guns: Firearms and Their Control* 96–97 tbl.3.1 (1997).

15. *See, e.g.,* Daniel Polsby, "The Closed American Mind: From the Hip," *National Review,* Mar. 24, 1997, at 33.

16. *See* Franklin E. Zimring & Gordon Hawkins, *Incapacitation: Penal Confinement and the Restraint of Crime* (1995).

17. Zimring & Hawkins, *supra* note 1, at 61. The quoted language is taken from a rhetorical question, which the authors answer thus: "The social processes that generate arguments that result in homicides are not distinctively criminal in most cases." *Id.* Compare the following self-description given by a group devoted solely to anti-gun advocacy, the Violence Policy Center:

> [T]he majority of homicide victims die not as a result of criminal activity, but because of arguments between people who know each other. The reality of firearms violence is that it stems not from "guns in the wrong hands," but from the virtually unregu-

lated distribution of an inherently dangerous consumer product. . . .

Violence Policy Center, *About the Violence Policy Center* (n.d.).

18. National Coalition to Ban Handguns, *A Shooting Gallery Called America* (n.d.) [hereafter National Coalition].

19. John Lindsay, *The Case for Federal Firearms Control* 22 (1973). *A Shooting Gallery Called America* cites *The Case for Federal Firearms Control* in further asserting that "each year" thousands of "gun murders [are] done by law-abiding citizens who might have *stayed* law-abiding if they had not *possessed* firearms." National Coalition, *supra* note 18 (emphasis in original); and "that most murders are committed by previously law-abiding citizens where the killer and the victim are related or acquainted." *Id.*

20. David Kairys, "A Carnage in the Name of Freedom," *Phila. Inquirer,* Sept. 12, 1988 (emphasis added).

21. Ramsey Clark, *Crime in America* 108 (1970); *see also* Editorial, "Run Down, Gunned Down," *Wash. Post,* Mar. 4, 1994, at A22; George Edwards, "Murder and Gun Control," *Wayne L. Rev.* 1335 (1972). In this regard, Dee Helfgott, the coordinator of Coalition for Handgun Control of Southern California, Inc., stated:

> Most murders (seventy-three percent) are committed impulsively by previously law abiding citizens during arguments with family members or acquaintances. . . . A readily available gun is what turns an assault into a murder. The handgun, often kept in the home for self-defense, is six times as likely to be used against a family member as it is to be used against an intruder.

Hearings before the Subcomm. on Crime of the Comm. on the Judiciary, 94th Cong. 1774 (1975) (statement of Dee Helfgott, Coordinator, Coalition for Handgun Control of Southern California, Inc.).

22. Zimring & Hawkins, *supra* note 1, at 190.

23. *See, e.g., Citizen's Guide, supra* note 3; Norval Morris & Gordon Hawkins, *An Honest Politician's Guide to Gun Control* (1969); George Newton & Franklin Zimring, *Firearms and Violence in American Life* (1969); Franklin

Zimring, *Fun and Games with Guns and Statistics*, 1968 *Wis. L. Rev.* 1113.

24. *See* Zimring & Hawkins, *supra* note 1, at 199.

25. *See id.* at 201.

26. Colin Greenwood & Joseph Magaddino, "Comparative Cross-Cultural Statistics," in *Restricting Handguns* 39 (Don Kates ed., 1979). At the time this was written, Greenwood held the rank of Chief Inspector of the West Yorkshire Constabulary. He retired as a Chief Superintendent. *See also* Colin Greenwood, *Firearms Control: A Study of Armed Crime and Firearms Control in England and Wales* (1972) [hereinafter *Firearms Control*].

27. Zimring & Hawkins, *supra* note 1, at 21.

28. *Not*, apparently, "the United Kingdom," which consists also of Northern Ireland and Scotland.

29. *See* Zimring & Hawkins, *supra* note 1, at 27–28.

30. *See id.* at 35–35.

31. *Id.* at 37.

32. *See id.* at 38.

33. *See id.* at 38–39.

34. *Id.* at 50.

35. Only 10% of rapes involve the perpetrators using a firearm. *See* Patsy A. Klaus & Marshall Deberry, "The Crime of Rape," Bureau of Justice Statistics Bull., Mar. 1985, at 4 tbl.11.

36. Based on Interpol Statistics for the year 1984, the American rape rate was 13.2 times greater than that of England and Wales. *See* Carol A. Kalish, Bureau of Justice Statistics, Special Rep.: International Crime Rates 3, tbl.4 (May 1988). Based on 1988 survey evidence, the U.S. victimization rate for sexual assault was 23 times greater than the England/Wales rate. *See* Jan J. M. van Dijk, "On the Uses of Local, National and International Crime Surveys," in *Australian Institute of Criminology, International Trends in Crime: East Meets West* 137, 147, fig. 6 (1992). Despite the practice of some modern unisex rape statutes, it is not clear that "sexual assault" always or even usually equals "rape"; either or both may be intended to include forcible sodomy as well. But "sexual assault" evidently does mean serious predation of some kind since van Dijk contradistinguishes it from mere "sexual incidents," also covered by the survey. *See id.*

37. *See* John Kaplan et al., *Criminal Law* 29 (1996).

38. *See id.*

39. *See id.*

40. *See* Bureau of Justice Statistics, *Sourcebook of Criminal Justice Statistics* 319 tbl.3.11 (1996); *see also* United Nations, 1995 *Demographic Yearbook* (1995).

41. Violence Policy Center, *supra* note 17; *see also* Josh Sugarmann & Kristen Rand, *Cease Fire: A Comprehensive Strategy to Reduce Firearms Violence* 4 (1994) ("The majority of firearm murder stems from arguments that turn deadly because of ready access to a firearm."); Josh Sugarmann, "The NRA Is Right—But We Still Need to Ban Handguns," *Wash. Monthly*, June 1987, at 11 ("[M]ost handgun murderers are not caused by predatory strangers. Hand-

gun violence is usually the result of people being angry, drunk, careless, or depressed—who just happen to have a handgun around.").

42. Zimring & Hawkins, *supra* note 1, at 61.

43. *Id.* at 16.

44. *Id.* at 61.

45. *Id.* at 78.

46. Deane Calhoun, "From Controversy to Prevention: Building Effective Firearm Policies," *Inj. Prevention Network Newsl.*, Winter 1989–90, at 15.

47. Lindsay, *supra* note 19; *see also* National Coalition, *supra* note 18 (citing Lindsay and asserting that "each year" thousands of "gun murders [are] done by law-abiding citizens who might have *stayed* law-abiding if they had not possessed firearms" (emphasis in original) and "that most murders are committed by previously law-abiding citizens where the killer and the victim are related or acquainted"); Edwards, *supra* note 21.

48. *See* Calhoun, *supra* note 101 (Most murderers "are neither felons nor crazy," but rather "people involved in family fights and fights over jobs and money, and people who are sad or depressed."); Katherine Kaufer Christoffel, "Toward Reducing Pediatric Injuries from Firearms: Charting a Legislative and Regulatory Course," 88 *Pediatrics* 294, 300 (1991) ([M]ost shootings are not committed by felons or mentally ill people, but are acts of passion that are committed using a handgun that is owned for home protection."); Daniel W. Webster et al. "Reducing Firearms Injuries," *Issues in Sci. & Tech.*, Spring 1991, at 73 ("[M]ost [murderders] would be considered law-abiding citizens prior to their pulling the trigger.").

49. See Sheilah Hodgins, "Mental Disorder, Intellectual Deficiency, and Crime," 49 *Archives of Gen. Psychiatry* 476 (1992), for a collection and analysis of particular studies.

50. Pekka Santilla & Jaana Haapasalo, "Neurological and Psychological Risk Factors Among Young Homicidal, Violent, and Nonviolent Offenders in Finland," 1 *Homicide Stud.* 234 (1997). The authors continue:

> For example, Lewis et al. (1985) found that in a small sample of nine homicidal offenders, neurological impairment was present in several subjects. In a study comparing juvenile murderers with other violent delinquents and nonviolent delinquents, Lewis et al. (1988) showed that the murderers did not differ from the other violent delinquents on neuropsychiatric variables but that they were more impaired neuropsychiatrically than the nonviolent offenders (also, see Nestor, 1992). Support for neurological abnormalities in association with violent behavior has been found in extensive reviews of the literature.

Id. (some citations omitted).

51. *Id.* at 237 (citations omitted).

52. *Id.* at 247 (citations omitted). Though we have generally deleted the citations, the quoted language included references to ten different studies or literature reviews. In

the Finnish study, however, differences between violent offenders and murderers were found to be somewhat less marked than in some of the earlier studies.

53. Ronald M. Holmes & Stephen T. Holmes, *Murder in America* 8–9 (1994).

54. *See, e.g.,* D. Mulvihill et al., *Crimes of Violence: Report of the Task Force on Individual Acts of Violence* 532 (1969) (data run of murder arrestees nationally over a four-year period in the mid 1960s found 74.7% to have had prior arrest(s) for violent felony or burglary); Federal Bureau of Investigation, United States Dep't of Justice, *Uniform Crime Report* 38 (1971) (in data run of murder arrestees over a one-year period 77.9% had priors). In two Bureau of Justice Statistics special reports covering late 1980s national samples, 76.7% of murder arrestees had criminal histories as did 78% of defendants in murder prosecutions. *See* Bureau of Justice Statistics, U.S. Dep't of Justice, *Special Rep.: Murder in Families* 5 tbl.7 (1994); Bureau of Justice Statistics, U.S. Dep't of Justice, *Special Rep.: Murder in Large Urban Counties,* 1988 (1993); *see also* R. Narloch, Cal. Bureau of Criminal Statistics, *Criminal Homicide in California* 53–54 (1973); A. Swersey & E. Enloe, *Homicide in Harlem* 17 (1975) ("We estimate that the great majority of both perpetrators and victims of assaults and murders had previous arrests, probably over 80% or more.").

55. "After a long plateau at around 10 percent, the juvenile share of homicide arrests started climbing in the mid-1980s, [peaking at] 17 percent by 1994." Cook & Laub, *supra* note 75.

56. *See* Federal Bureau of Investigation, U.S. Dep't of Justice, *Uniform Crime Report* 42 (1975).

57. *See* Mark Cooney, "The Decline of Elite Homicide," 35 *Criminology* 381 (1997).

58. *See* Bureau of Justice Statistics, U.S. Dep't of Justice, *Special Rep.: Probation and Parole Violators in State Prison* (Aug. 1995) (surveying state prison inmates in 1991).

59. *See* DiIulio, *supra* note 50, at 16.

60. "[M]ost violent acts escape the attention of authorities and are thus not made a part of official written records. . . ." Gary Kleck, "Policy Lessons from Recent Gun Control Research," *L. & Contemp. Probs.,* Winter 1986, at 35, 40.

61. *See* T. Markus Funk & Daniel D. Polsby, "Some Distributional Consequences of Expunging Juvenile Delinquency Records: The Problem of Lemons," 52 *Wash. U. J. Urb. & Contemp. L.* 161 (1997).

62. *See* Kennedy et al., *supra* note 77, at 159–60.

63. Webster et al., *supra* note 103.

64. Murray A. Straus, "Domestic Violence and Homicide Antecedents," 62 *Bull. N.Y. Acad. Med.* 446, 454 (1986).

65. *See id.* at 457.

66. *See* Kleck, *supra* note 115, at 41.

67. *See* David M. Kennedy, "Pulling Levers: Chronic Offenders, High-Crime Settings, and a Theory of Prevention," 31 *Val. U. L. Rev.* 455 (1997) ("[D]omestic violence offenders, at least those who come to the attention of

the criminal justice system, tend to have robust [prior] offending histories.").

68. Straus, *supra* note 119, at 450.

69. *See, e.g.,* Lane, *supra* note 28, at 324, 341–53.

70. *See* Kennedy et al., *supra* note 117, at 159.

71. *Id.* at 158.

72. *Id.* at 162.

73. *See* Cook & Laub, *supra* note 75, at 13.

74. H. Range Hutson et al., "Adolescents and Children Injured or Killed in Drive-By Shootings in Los Angeles," 330 *New Eng. J. Med.* 324, 325 (1994).

75. *See* Carl A. Soderstrom et al., "Psychoactive Substance Use Disorders Among Seriously Injured Trauma Center Patients," 277 *JAMA* 1769, 1771 (1997). Other trauma care center studies disgustedly characterize urban knife and bullet wounds as "a chronic recurrent disease peculiar to unemployed, uninsured law breakers." R. Stephen Smith et al., "Recidivism in an Urban Trauma Center," 127 *Archives of Surgery* 668, 670 (1992) (describing the conclusions in D. W. Sims et al., "Urban Trauma: A Chronic, Recurrent Disease," 29 *J. Trauma* 940 (1989); M. C. Morrisey et al., "The Incidence of Recurrent Penetrating Wound Trauma in an Urban Trauma Center," 31 *J. Trauma* 1536 (1991)).

76. Swersey & Enloe, *supra* note 109.

77. *See* Chicago Police Department, *supra* note 74, at 21.

78. *See* Bureau of the Census, U.S. Dep't of Com., *Statistical Abstract of the United States: National Data Book* 1995, at 202 tbl.314 (1995).

79. *See, e.g.,* Frank Zimring, "Is Gun Control Likely to Reduce Violent Killings?" 35 *U. Chi. L. Rev.* 721 (1968).

80. *Cf.* Lambert v. California, 355 U.S. 225 (1957) (holding that the defendant's ignorance of a felon registration law did excuse failure to comply because the "criminal act" was "wholly passive").

81. *See* Tom Tyler, *Why People Obey the Law* 60 (1990).

82. Many more people in Chicago signed up for their auto registration stickers once it became possible to do so over the telephone rather than waiting in a long line at City Hall.

83. *See* Tyler, *supra* note 136.

84. *See* John Sloan et al., "Firearms Regulation and Rates of Suicide," 322 *New Eng. J. of Med.* 369, 369–73 (1990); John Sloan et al., "Handgun Regulations, Crime, Assaults, and Homicide: A Tale of Two Cities," 319 *New Eng. J. of Med.* 1256, 1256–62 (1988).

85. *See* Zimring & Hawkins, *supra* note 1, at 44–50.

86. *See, e.g.,* Susan Baker, "Without Guns Do People Kill People?" 75 *Am. J. Pub. Health* 587 (1985); Charles M. Callahan & Frederick P. Rivara, "Urban High School Youth and Handguns: A School-Based Survey," 267 *JAMA* 3038, 3042 (1992); Judith Cohen Dolins & Katherine Kaufer Christoffel, "Reducing Violent Injuries: Priorities for Pediatrician Advocacy," 94 *Pediatrics* 638, 648 (1994). . . .

87. Much of continental Europe (but not Switzerland or England) had severely restricted firearms ownership

during the long period of autocracy prior to the French Revolution. *See* Lee Kennett & James LaVerne Anderson, *The Gun in America: The Origins of a National Dilemma,* 3–34 (1975); Don B. Kates, Jr., "Handgun Prohibition and the Original Meaning of the Second Amendment," 82 *Mich. L. Rev.* 203, 233 (1983) (France). By the late-nineteenth century, however, autocracy had largely been replaced with at least semi-popular government in western Europe, with French-style universal military service, "and much of the restrictive arms legislation was rescinded." Kennett & Anderson, *supra,* at 32 (citing particularly a French-language source for France). See *Firearms Control, supra* note 26, at ch. 1, for a review of late-nineteenth century European law.

88. *See generally Firearms Control, supra* note 26, chs. 1–3; "Critical Review," *supra* note 28; "Historical Trends," *supra* note 28; Eric Monkkonen, "Diverging Homicide Rates: England and the United States," in *Violence in America, supra* note 28; Frank Morn, "Firearms Use and Police: An Historic Evolution of American Values," in *Firearms and Violence, supra* note 57, at 496–501.

89. Ian Hogg, *German Pistols and Revolvers,* 1871–1945 (Harrisburg, Stackpole, 1971) (listing, inter alia, Becker & Hollander of Suhl and Stendawerke G.m.b.H, at 10. . .).

90. Raymond Caranta, "Pre-WWII Pocket Pistols," in *Gun Digest—1997,* at 140 (Ken Warner ed.).

91. *See* Editorial, "The Menace of the Pistol," *Boston Advertiser,* 1910, *reprinted in* 2 *American Institute of Criminal Law* 23, 93 (1911). For the nineteenth- and twentieth-century development of "Saturday Night Special" and other American handgun bans or licensing schemes, see Don B. Kates, "Toward a History of Handgun Prohibition in the United States," *in Restricting Handguns* 7 (Don B. Kates ed., 1979).

92. Monkkonen, *supra* note 143, at 81–82.

93. *See* Lane, *supra* note 28.

94. John Wood Osborne, *The Silent Revolution* 9 (1970); *cf.* David Wooton, "Disarming the English," *London Rev. Books,* July 21, 1994, at 20 ("I cannot now stir a mile from my own house after sunset without one or two servants with blunderbusses," wrote Horace Walpole in 1782, "a footpad or a highwayman might be around any turn in the road.").

95. 10 & 11 Geo. 5, ch. 43 (current version within Firearms Act, 1968, ch. 27).

96. *See* Kennett & Anderson, *supra* note 142, at 33; Malcolm, *supra* note 56; *see also* Don B. Kates, *Guns, Murders and the Constitution: A Realistic Assessment of Gun Control* 39 (1990) [hereinafter *Guns, Murders and the Constitution*]:

> The different purposes of [post World War I] European versus American laws are evidenced by their diametrically opposite patterns: many of the "Saturday Night Special" laws American states enacted to deal with 19th century crime banned all but standard military-issue revolvers (i.e. the very expensive large, heavy Colt). In stark contrast, such military caliber arms were the first guns banned in post-WWI Europe, the purpose being to disarm restive former soldiers and the para-military groups they formed.

Id.

97. *See* Daniel Polsby & Don Kates, "Of Holocausts and Gun Control," 75 *Wash. U. L. Q.* 1237, 1240 (1998).

98. *See* David B. Kopel, *The Samurai, the Mountie and the Cowboy* (1992); "Critical Review," *supra* note 28; "Historical Trends," *supra* note 28.

99. *Firearms Control, supra* note 26, at 243.

100. *See Guns, Murders and the Constitution, supra* note 151, at 40; Kopel *supra* note 153, at 91–93. "[I]n 1974 the American rate was 40 times the English; 15 years . . . later, the American rate was only ten times greater." *Guns, Murders and the Constitution, supra* note 151, at 40. Though this convergence reflects some decrease in American homicide, it is primarily due to a steady increase in English homicide.

101. See discussion and sources cited in Mayer Freed & Daniel Polsby, "Just Cause for Termination Rules and Economic Efficiency," 38 *Emory L. J.* 1097, 1140 (1989).

102. *See* Kleck, *supra* note 9, at 223–68; Lawrence Southwick, "Do Guns Cause Crime? Does Crime Cause Guns? A Granger Test," 25 *Atlantic Econ. J.* 256, 262–65 (1997).

103. Wright et al., *supra* note 57, at 138.

60. The Brady Bill

CONGRESS OF THE UNITED STATES

To provide for a waiting period before the purchase of a handgun, and for the establishment of a national instant criminal background check system to be contacted by firearms dealers before the transfer of any firearm.

Sec. 102. Federal Firearms Licensee Required to Conduct Criminal Background Check Before Transfer of Firearm to Non-Licensee

(a) INTERIM PROVISION
   (1) IN GENERAL—Section 922 of Title 18, U.S. Code, is amended by adding at the end the following:
   (s) (1) Beginning on the date that is 90 days after the date of enactment of this subsection and ending on the day before the date that is 60 months after such date of enactment, it shall be unlawful for any licensed importer, licensed manufacturer, or licensed dealer to sell, deliver, or transfer a handgun to an individual who is not licensed under section 923, unless—
   (A) after the most recent proposal of such transfer by the transferee—
      (i) the transferor has—
         (I) received from the transferee a statement of the transferee containing the information described in paragraph (3),
         (II) verified the identity of the transferee by examining the identification document presented;
         (III) within 1 day after the transferee furnishes the statement, provided notice of the contents of the statement to the chief law enforcement officer of the place of residence of the transferee, and
         (IV) within 1 day after the transferee furnishes the statement, transmitted a copy of the statement to the chief law enforcement officer of the place of residence of the transferee; and
      (ii) (I) 5 business days (meaning days on which State offices are open) have elapsed from the date the transferor furnished notice of the contents of the statement to the chief law enforcement officer, during which period the transferor has not received information from the chief law enforcement officer that receipt or possession of the handgun by the transferee would be in violation of Federal, State, or local law; or
         (II) the transferor has received notice from the chief law enforcement officer that the officer has no information indicating that receipt or possession of the handgun by the transferee would violate Federal, State, or local law;
   (B) the transferee has presented to the transferor a written statement, issued by the chief law enforcement officer of the place of residence of the transferee during the 10-day period ending on the date of the most recent proposal of such transfer by the transferee, stating that the transferee requires access to a handgun because of a threat to the life

of the transferee or of any member of the household of the transferee;

(C) (i) the transferee has presented to the transferor a permit that—

    (I) allows the transferee to possess or acquire a handgun; and

    (II) was issued not more than 5 years earlier by the State in which the transfer is to take place; and

  (ii) the law of the State provides that such a permit is to be issued only after an authorized government official has verified that the information available to such official does not indicate that possession of a handgun by the transferee would be in violation of the law;

(D) the law of the State requires that, before any licensed importer, licensed manufacturer, or licensed dealer completes the transfer of a handgun to an individual who is not licensed under section 923, an authorized government official verify that the information available to such official does not indicate that possession of a handgun by the transferee would be in violation of law;

(E) the Secretary has approved the transfer under section 5812 of the Internal Revenue Code of 1986; or

(F) on application of the transferor, the Secretary has certified that compliance with subparagraph (A)(i)(III) is impracticable because—

  (i) the ratio of the number of law enforcement officers of the State in which the transfer is to occur to the number of square miles of land area of the State does not exceed 0.0025;

  (ii) the business premises of the transferor at which the transfer is to occur are extremely remote in relation to the chief law enforcement officer; and

  (iii) there is an absence of telecommunications facilities in the geographical area in which the business premises are located.

(2) A chief law enforcement officer to whom a transferor has provided notice pursuant to paragraph (1)(A)(i)(III) shall make a reasonable effort to ascertain within 5 business days whether receipt or possession would be in violation of the law, including research in whatever State and local record-keeping systems are available and in a national system designated by the Attorney General.

(3) The statement referred to in paragraph (1)(A)(i)(I) shall contain only—

(A) the name, address, and date of birth appearing on a valid identification document (as defined in section 1028(d)(1)) of the transferee containing a photograph of the transferee and a description of the identification used;

(B) a statement that the transferee—

  (i) is not under indictment for, and has not been convicted in any court of, a crime punishable by imprisonment for a term exceeding 1 year;

  (ii) is not a fugitive from justice;

  (iii) is not an unlawful user of or addicted to any controlled substance (as defined in section 102 of the Controlled Substances Act);

  (iv) has not been adjudicated as a mental defective or been committed to a mental institution;

  (v) is not an alien who is illegally or unlawfully in the United States;

  (vi) has not been discharged from the Armed Forces under dishonorable conditions; and

  (vii) is not a person who, having been a citizen of the United States, has renounced such citizenship;

(C) the date the statement is made; and

(D) notice that the transferee intends to obtain a handgun from the transferor.

(4) Any transferor of a handgun who, after such transfer, receives a report from a chief law enforcement officer containing information that receipt or possession of the handgun by the transferee violates Federal, State, or local law shall, within 1 business day after receipt of such request, communicate any information related to the transfer that the

transferor has about the transfer and the transferee to—

(A) the chief law enforcement officer of the place of business of the transferor; and

(B) the chief law enforcement officer of the place of residence of the transferee.

(5) Any transferor who receives information, not otherwise available to the public, in a report under this subsection shall not disclose such information except to the transferee, to law enforcement authorities, or pursuant to the direction of a court of law.

(6) (A) Any transferor who sells, delivers, or otherwise transfers a handgun to a transferee shall retain the copy of the statement of the transferee with respect to the handgun transaction, and shall retain evidence that the transferor has complied with subclauses (III) and IV) of paragraph (1)(A)(i) with respect to the statement.

(B) Unless the chief law enforcement officer to whom a statement is transmitted under paragraph (1)(A)(i)(IV) determines that a transaction would violate Federal, State, or local law—

(i) the officer shall, within 20 business days after the date the transferee made the statement on the basis of which the notice was provided, destroy the statement, any record containing information derived from the statement, and any record created as a result of the notice required by paragraph (1)(A)(i)(III);

(ii) the information contained in the statement shall not be conveyed to any person except a person who has a need to know in order to carry out this subsection; and

(iii) the information contained in the statement shall not be used for any purpose other than to carry out this subsection.

(C) If a chief law enforcement officer determines that an individual is ineligible to receive a handgun and the individual requests the officer to provide the reason for such determination, the officer shall provide such reasons to the indi-

vidual in writing within 20 business days after receipt of the request.

(7) A chief law enforcement officer or other person responsible for providing criminal history background information pursuant to this subsection shall not be liable in an action at law for damages—

(A) for failure to prevent the sale or transfer of a handgun to a person whose receipt or possession of the handgun is unlawful under this section; or

(B) for preventing such a sale or transfer to a person who may lawfully receive or possess a handgun.

(8) For purposes of this subsection, the term "chief law enforcement officer" means the chief of police, the sheriff, or an equivalent officer or the designee of any such individual.

(9) The Secretary shall take necessary actions to ensure that the provisions of this subsection are published and disseminated to licensed, dealers, law enforcement officials, and the public.

(2) HANDGUN DEFINED.—Section 921(a) of title 18, United States Code, is amended by adding, at the end the following: (29) The term "handgun" means—

(A) a firearm which has a short stock and is designed to be held and fired by the use of a single hand; and

(B) any combination of parts from which a firearm described in subparagraph (A) can be assembled.

(b) PERMANENT PROVISION.—Section 922 of title 18, United States Code, as amended by subsection (a)(1), is amended by adding at the end the following:

(1) Beginning on the date that is 40 days after the Attorney General notifies licensees under section 103(d) of the Brady Handgun Violence Prevention Act that the national instant criminal background check system is established, a licensed importer, licensed manufacturer, or licensed dealer shall not transfer a firearm to any other person who is not licensed under this chapter, unless—

(A) before the completion of the transfer, the licensee contacts the national instant criminal background check system established under section 103 of that Act;

(B) (i) the system provides the licensee with a unique identification number; or

(ii) three business days (meaning a day on which State offices are open) have elapsed since the licensee contacted the system, and the system has not notified the licensee that the receipt of a firearm by such other person would violate subsection (g) or (n) of this section; and

(C) the transferor has verified the identity of the transferee by examining a valid identification document (as defined in section 1028(d)(1) of this title) of the transferee containing a photograph of the transferee.

(2) If receipt of a firearm would not violate section 922 (g) or (n) or State law, the system shall—

(A) assign a unique identification number to the transfer;

(B) provide the licensee with the number; and

(C) destroy all records of the system with respect to the call (other than the identifying number and the date the number was assigned) and all records of the system relating to the person or the transfer.

(3) Paragraph (1) shall not apply to a firearm transfer between a licensee and another person if—

(A) (i) such other person has presented to the licensee a permit that—

(I) allows such other person to possess or acquire a firearm; and

(II) was issued not more than 5 years earlier by the State in which the transfer is to take place; and

(ii) the law of the State provides that such a permit is to be issued only after an authorized government official has verified that the information available to such official does not indicate that possession of a firearm by such other person would be in violation of law;

(B) the Secretary has approved the transfer under section 5812 of the Internal Revenue Code of 1986; or

(C) on application of the transferor, the Secretary has certified that compliance with paragraph (1)(A) is impracticable because—

(i) the ratio of the number of law enforcement officers of the State in which the transfer is to occur to the number of square miles of land area of the State does not exceed 0.0025;

(ii) the business premise of the licensee at which the transfer is to occur are extremely remote in relation to the chief law enforcement officer (as defined in subsection (s)(8)); and

(iii) there is an absence of telecommunications facilities in the geographical area in which the business premises are located.

(4) If the national instant criminal background check system notifies the licensee that the information available to the system does not demonstrate that the receipt of a firearm by such other person would violate subsection (g) or (n) or State law, and the licensee transfers a firearm to such other person, the licensee shall include in the record of the transfer the unique identification number provided by the system with respect to the transfer.

(5) If the licensee knowingly transfers a firearm to such other person and knowingly fails to comply with paragraph (1) of this subsection with respect to the transfer and, at the time such other person most recently proposed the transfer, the national instant criminal background check system was operating and information was available to the system demonstrating that receipt of a firearm by such other person would violate subsection (g) or (n) of this section or State law, the Secretary may, after notice and opportunity for a hearing, suspend for not more than 6 months or revoke any license issued to the licensee under section 923, and may impose on the licensee a civil fine of not more than $5,000.

(6) Neither a local government nor an employee of the Federal Government or of any State or

local government, responsible for providing information to the national instant criminal background check system shall be liable in an action at law for damages—

(A) for failure to prevent the sale or transfer of a firearm to a person whose receipt or possession of the firearm is unlawful under this section; or

(B) for preventing such a sale or transfer to a person who may lawfully receive or possess a firearm.

(c) PENALTY—Section 924(a) of title 18, United States Code, is amended—

(1) in paragraph (1), by striking "paragraph (2) or (3) of"; and

(2) by adding at the end the following:

"(5) Whoever knowingly violates subsection (s) or (t) of section 922 shall be fined not more than $1,000, imprisoned for not more than 1 year, or both."

Sec. 103. National Instant Criminal Background Check System

(a) DETERMINATION OF TIMETABLES.—Not later than 6 months after the date of enactment of this Act, the Attorney General shall—

(1) determine the type of computer hardware and software that will be used to operate the national instant criminal background check system and the means by which State criminal records systems and the telephone or electronic device of licensees will communicate with the national system;

(2) investigate the criminal records system of each State and determine for each State a timetable by which the State should be able to provide criminal records on an on-line capacity basis to the national system; and

(3) notify each State of the determinations made pursuant to paragraphs (1) and (2).

(b) ESTABLISHMENT OF SYSTEM.—Not later than 60 months after the date of the enactment of this Act, the Attorney General shall establish a national instant criminal background check system that any licensee may contact, by telephone or by other electronic means in addition to the telephone, for information, to be supplied immediately, on whether receipt of a firearm by a prospective transferee would violate section 922 of title 18, United States Code, or State law.

Suggested Readings

Anthologies

Nisbet, Lee. *The Gun Control Debate.* Buffalo: Prometheus Books, 1990.

Roleff, Tamara. *Gun Control.* San Diego: Greenhaven Press, 1997.

Alternative Views

Clark, Robert. *Deadly Force: The Lure of Violence.* Springfield: Charles C Thomas, 1988.

Diaz, Tom. *Making a Killing: The Business of Guns in America.* New York: New Press, 1999.

Halbrook, Stephen. *That Every Man Be Armed.* Oakland: Independence Institute, 1990.

Kleck, Gary. *Targeting Guns.* New York: Aldine de Gruyter, 1997.

Lott, John. *More Guns, Less Crime.* Chicago: University of Chicago, 1998.

Prothrow-Stith, Deborah. *Deadly Consequences.* New York: HarperCollins, 1991.

Practical Applications

National Rifle Association of America (NRA) www.nra.org.

Handgun Control Inc. www.handguncontrol.org.

Section XI

Animal Liberation and Environmental Justice

Introduction

Basic Concepts

The problem of animal liberation and environmental justice has begun to attract widespread public attention. Beginning with the 1973 publication of Peter Singer's article, "Animal Liberation," in the *New York Review of Books,* followed by the publication two years later of his book of the same title, people have become increasingly concerned with two of the most serious forms of exploitation: animal experimentation and factory farming.

Animal experimentation is a big business, involving 60 to 100 million animals a year. Two experiments alone—the rabbit-blinding Draize eye test and the LD50 toxicity test designed to find the lethal dose for 50 percent of a sample of animals—cause the deaths of more than 5 million animals per year in the United States alone. In factory farming, millions of animals are raised in such a way that their short lives are dominated by pain and suffering. Veal calves are put in narrow stalls and tethered with a chain so that they cannot turn around, lie down comfortably, or groom themselves. They are fed a totally liquid diet to promote rapid weight gain, and they are given no water

because thirsty animals eat more than those who drink water.

In recent years, environmental concern has focused on a myriad of problems from acid rain to the destruction of rainforests and the ozone layer. For example, the acidity of rainfall over the northeastern United States has quadrupled since 1900. Moreover, in 1995, some 12,350 square miles of Brazilian rainforest—an area larger than Belgium—was reduced to ashes, and over the past decade, ozone levels over Antarctica have diminished by 50 percent. In many cases, resolving these problems will require extensive programs and international cooperation. For example, in the Montreal protocol of 1987, dozens of nations agreed to cut their chlorofluorocarbon emissions (which are thought to be the major cause of ozone depletion) in half by the end of the century, and several countries and the major chlorofluorocarbon manufacturers have more recently announced their intentions to eliminate the chemicals by that deadline.

At the most general level, the problem of animal liberation and environmental concern raises the question of what should be our policies for treating animals and preserving the environment, or alternatively, what is the moral status of nonhuman living things. One possible answer is that nonhuman living things have no independent moral status at all; their moral status depends completely on the impact they have on human welfare. Another possible answer is that nonhuman living things have an independent moral status such that their welfare has to be weighed against, and at least sometimes outweigh, considerations of human welfare.

Obviously, supporters of animal liberation favor the view that animals have independent moral status, but they disagree as to the grounds for this independent moral status. Some claim that animals have independent moral status because taking their welfare into account would maximize overall utility. Others claim that the independent moral status of animals rests on a nonutilitarian foundation.

This conflict among supporters of animal liberation reflects a general conflict among utilitarians and nonutilitarians on a wide range of practical problems (see the General Introduction to this anthology). With respect to this problem, however, supporters of animal liberation cannot rely on some form of a Kantian theory to reach an acceptable resolution because most animals are incapable of forming either an actual or hypothetical contract with human beings for the purpose of securing their common welfare. Kantian theory, however, is only a means to a goal, which is to achieve a fair resolution of morally relevant interests. Consequently, if nonhuman living things do have morally relevant interests, then to achieve that goal, some means other than Kantian theory will have to be employed.

This is not to say that Kantian theory is not useful for achieving a fair resolution of conflicts when only human interests pertain. In fact, it would seem that a fair resolution of conflicts among human and nonhuman interests would mirror a fair resolution of conflicts among purely human interests. For example,

if a utilitarian (or a nonutilitarian) resolution were fair when only human interests are taken into account, a utilitarian (or a nonutilitarian) resolution would seem to be fair when both human and nonhuman interests are considered.

With respect to environmental concern, supporters do not agree that all nonhuman living things have independent moral status. Those who maintain that only sentient beings have independent moral status attempt to ground human concern for other living things on the impact they have on the welfare of sentient beings. Accordingly, to resolve the problem of animal liberation and environmental concern, we must determine which living beings have independent moral status and what sort of justification best accounts for that status.

Alternative Views

In Selection 61, Peter Singer argues for the independent moral status of animals by comparing the bias against animals, which he calls "speciesism," with biases against blacks and women. According to Singer, the grounds we have for opposing racism and sexism are also grounds for opposing speciesism because all forms of discrimination run counter to the principle of equal consideration. Racists violate this principle by giving greater weight to the interests of members of their own race in cases of conflict; sexists violate this principle by favoring the interests of their own specific sex; and speciesists violate this principle by allowing the interests of their own species to override the greater interests of other species.

Animals have interests, Singer maintains, because they have a capacity for suffering and enjoyment. According to the principle of equal consideration, there is no justification for regarding the pain animals feel as less important than the same amount of pain (or pleasure) humans feel. As for the practical requirements of this view, Singer contends that we cannot go astray if we give the same respect to the lives of animals that we give to the lives of humans at a similar mental level. In the end, Singer thinks, this requires a utilitarian weighing of both human and animal interests.

Singer's view has been challenged on grounds that utilitarianism does not ultimately support a strong case for animal rights for several reasons. First of all, by Singer's own admission, it is permissible to eat farm animals, typically cattle and sheep, that are reared and killed without suffering. Second, Singer's objection to the suffering inflicted on animals in factory farms can be overcome by reforming the practices used on such farms rather than by requiring that we become vegetarians. Third, a radical turn to vegetarianism would probably result in the elimination of most farm animals as we know them because they certainly cannot survive in the wild. This would seriously disrupt and/or eliminate many industries and social practices, resulting in significant disutility.

Responding to these criticisms in an article in the *New York Review of Books*, Singer makes two points. He first claims that adopting vegetarianism would improve people's general health, eliminate Third World poverty, and create new and beneficial industries and social practices. Second, Singer claims that in political campaigning, opposition to the current techniques of factory farming is not taken seriously unless one is also a committed vegetarian. According to Singer, only vegetarians can silence that invariable objection to reforming our treatment of animals: But don't you eat them?

Nevertheless, Singer's response turns on the political effectiveness of being a vegetarian and the effects vegetarianism would have on human welfare rather than its effects on animal welfare. However, it is in terms of animal welfare that the case for animal rights must ultimately be made.

Kathryn George argues in Selection 62 that the ethical vegetarianism endorsed by Singer is partial to adult males and to people living in developed countries rather than those living in developing or underdeveloped countries. This is because for all those not living in developed countries, ethical vegetarianism is so burdensome that they are exempt from its requirements. But if most people are exempt from the requirements of ethical vegetarianism, in what sense is it an ideal? George argues that it is not. She further argues that the way diets are supplemented in developed countries by fortifying foods so as to make it easier to be a vegetarian are not part of a sustainable food production. So they cannot serve as a way of making vegetarianism morally required for more people. What is morally required, according to George, is semivegetarianism, with continued moderate food fortification and preservation.

In Selection 63, Paul W. Taylor argues that all living beings have independent moral status. He grounds his view on two central claims: (1) that each individual organism is a teleological center of life, pursuing its own good in its own way, and (2) that whether we are concerned with standards of merit or with the concept of inherent worth, there is no ground for believing that humans by their very nature are superior to other species. Taylor's argument for his second claim is similar to the argument used in the General Introduction to support morality against rational egoism. Both claim that their view represents a non–question-begging solution.

The main difficulty with Taylor's view is how we are to weigh human welfare against the good of other living beings if we were to grant that human beings are not superior to other species. In a later book that develops the argument of this essay, Taylor distinguishes between basic and nonbasic interests of living beings, but because he doesn't hold that the basic interests always have priority over nonbasic interests, it is difficult to know how decisions should be made when there is conflict between human and nonhuman interests.

In Selection 64, James P. Sterba seeks to resolve a central debate in contemporary environmental ethics between those who defend an anthropocentric ethics and those who defend a nonanthropocentric ethics by showing that when the most morally defensible versions of each of these perspectives are laid out, they do not lead to different practical recommendations. He develops a set of principles for weighing human against nonhuman welfare, contending that it should be acceptable to defenders of both anthropocentric and nonanthropocentric environmental ethics. Obviously, the crucial question is whether these principles do represent common ground between these opposing perspectives and whether they can be effectively applied.

In Selection 65, Karen Warren raises an important challenge to mainstream environmental ethics. The challenge is that such mainstream ethics have failed to recognize that the domination of nature is rooted in the domination of women, or at least has failed to recognize that both forms of domination are interconnected. To elucidate this connection, Warren claims that at least within the dominant Western culture, the following argument is sanctioned:

1. Women are identified with nature and the realm of the physical; men are identified with the "human" and the realm of the mental. (For example, naturist language describes women as cows, foxes, chicks, serpents, bitches, beavers, old bats, pussy-cats, cats, bird-brains, hare-brains. Sexist language feminizes and sexualizes Nature: Nature is raped, mastered, conquered, controlled, mined. Her "secrets" are "penetrated" and her "womb" is put into the services of the "man of science." "Virgin timber" is felled, cut down."Fertile soil"

is tilled and land that lies "fallow" is "barren," useless.)

2. Whatever is identified with nature and the realm of the physical is inferior to whatever is identified with the "human" and the realm of the mental; or, conversely, the latter is superior to the former.

3. Thus, women are inferior to men; or, conversely, men are superior to women.

4. For any X and Y, if X is superior to Y, then X is justified in subordinating Y.

5. Thus, men are justified in subordinating women.

Warren points out that there is a "logic of domination" to this argument. It begins with a *claim of difference*. It then moves from a claim of difference to a *claim of superiority* and then from a claim of superiority to a *claim of subordination* or *domination*. Warren contends that this same logic of domination is common to all forms of domination and so is used to support, for example, racism, classism, and ageism, as well as sexism and naturism (Warren's term for the domination of nature). If Warren is correct, it follows that if one is against any one of these forms of domination, one should be against them all.

Practical Applications

The next two selections come from the only federal law in the United States pertaining to the treatment of animals. The provisions of the Animal Welfare Act (Selection 66) pertain only to the transportation of animals and the treatment of animals for research and experimentation. The Act does not mention the treatment of animals in factory farms. The amendments to the Animal Welfare Act (Selection 67) passed in 1985 represent a considerable strengthening of the original Act. Specifically, the amendments call for a national data bank that will list the results of all animal experiments and thus prevent needless repetition. All laboratories using live animals are also required, under the amendments, to set up animal-care committees and submit to annual inspections. Facilities that house dogs must let them exercise, and those that house primates must provide for their "psychological well-being." Unfortunately, the implementation of these amendments is currently held up by the federal budget office.

In *Tennessee Valley Authority v. Hill* (Selection 68), the issue before the Supreme Court was whether the Endangered Species Act of 1973 prohibited the completion of a dam whose operation would destroy the habitat of the snail darter, an endangered species; the dam was virtually complete and Congress continued to appropriate large sums of money to the project even after the congressional appropriations committees were apprised of the project's apparent impact on the snail darter's survival. The Court held that the act did prohibit the dam's completion because its language and the debate that led to its passage required that its provisions be applied without exceptions. Immediately after this court deci-sion, however, Congress amended the act to provide a "review" process that would relax the protection accorded endangered species in some circumstances. In the case of the snail darter, protection was relaxed because it was possible to transport snail darters to another river. Additional populations of snail darters were found in other rivers. An interesting sidelight to this case, however, was that an interim economic study found that the dam was a pork barrel construction project. Its benefits to the Tennessee economy could have been achieved in less costly ways while the natural state of the river was preserved.

Although there is no denying that existing federal laws that protect animals and the environment are quite limited in scope, it seems clear that any solution to the problem of animal liberation and environmental concern that gives independent moral status to all living beings, or even just to all sentient beings will, if implemented, have a significant impact on the way we live and work and, accordingly, on how we are able to solve the other practical problems discussed in this anthology.

61. All Animals Are Equal

PETER SINGER

Peter Singer begins his defense of animal liberation by comparing the bias against animals with biases against blacks and women, arguing that all of these forms of discrimination, violate the principle of equal consider-ation. According to this principle, there is no justification for regarding the pain that animals feel as less important than the same amount of pain (or pleasure) felt by humans.

"Animal Liberation" may sound more like a parody of other liberation movements than a serious objective. The idea of "The Rights of Animals" actually was once used to parody the case for women's rights. When Mary Wollstonecraft, a forerunner of today's feminists, published her *Vindication of the Rights of Women* in 1792, her views were widely regarded as absurd, and before long an anonymous publication appeared entitled *A Vindication of the Rights of Brutes*. The author of this satirical work (now known to have been Thomas Taylor, a distinguished Cambridge philosopher) tried to refute Mary Wollstonecraft's arguments by showing that they could be carried one stage further. If the argument for equality was sound when applied to women, why should it not be applied to dogs, cats, and horses? The reasoning seemed to hold for these "brutes" too; yet to hold that brutes had rights was manifestly absurd; therefore the reasoning by which this conclusion had been reached must be unsound, and if unsound when applied to brutes, it must also be unsound when applied to women, since the very same arguments had been used in each case.

In order to explain the basis of the case for the equality of animals, it will be helpful to start with an examination of the case for the equality of women. Let us assume that we wish to defend the case for women's rights against the attack by Thomas Taylor. How should we reply?

One way in which we might reply is by saying that the case for equality between men and women cannot validly be extended to nonhuman animals. Women have a right to vote, for instance, because they are just as capable of making rational decisions about the future as men are; dogs, on the other hand, are incapable of understanding the significance of voting, so they cannot have the right to vote. There are many other obvious ways in which men and women resemble each other closely, while humans and animals differ greatly. So, it might be said, men and women are similar beings and should have similar rights, while humans and nonhumans are different and should not have equal rights.

The reasoning behind this reply to Taylor's analogy is correct up to a point, but it does not go far enough. There *are* important differences between humans and other animals, and these differences must give rise to *some* differences in the rights that each have. Recognizing this obvious fact, however, is no barrier to the case for extending the basic principle of equality to nonhuman animals. The differences that exist between men and women are equally undeniable, and the supporters of Women's Liberation are aware that these differences may give rise to different rights. Many feminists hold that women have the right to an abortion on request. It does not follow that since these same feminists are campaigning for equality between men and women they must support the right of men to have abortions too. Since a man cannot have an abortion, it is meaningless to talk of his right to have one. Since a dog can't vote, it is meaningless to talk of its right to vote. There is no reason why either Women's Liberation or Animal Liberation should get involved in such nonsense. The extension of the basic principle of equality from one group to another does not imply that we must treat both groups in exactly the same way, or grant exactly the same rights to both groups. Whether we should do so will depend on the nature of the members of the two groups. The basic principle of equality does not require equal or identical *treatment*; it requires equal *consideration*. Equal consideration for

From *Animal Liberation* (New York: New York Review, 1975), pp. 1–22. Reprinted by permission of Peter Singer.

different beings may lead to different treatment and different rights.

So there is a different way of replying to Taylor's attempt to parody the case for women's rights, a way that does not deny the obvious differences between humans and nonhumans but goes more deeply into the question of equality and concludes by finding nothing absurd in the idea that the basic principle of equality applies to so-called "brutes." At this point such a conclusion may appear odd; but if we examine more deeply the basis [for] our opposition to discrimination on grounds of race or sex ultimately, we will see that we would be on shaky ground if we were to demand equality for Blacks, women, and other groups of oppressed humans while denying equal consideration to nonhumans. To make this clear we need to see first exactly why racism and sexism are wrong.

When we say that all human beings, whatever their race, creed, or sex, are equal, what is it that we are asserting? Those who wish to defend hierarchical, inegalitarian societies have often pointed out that by whatever test we choose it simply is not true that all humans are equal. Like it or not we must face the fact that humans come in different shapes and sizes; they come with different moral capacities, different intellectual abilities, different amounts of benevolent feeling and sensitivity to the needs of others, different abilities to communicate effectively, and different capacities to experience pleasure and pain. In short, if the demand for equality were based on the actual equality of all human beings, we would have to stop demanding equality.

Still, one might cling to the view that the demand for equality among human beings is based on the actual equality of the different races and sexes. Although, it may be said, humans differ as individuals there are no differences between the races and sexes *as such*. From the mere fact that a person is Black or a woman we cannot infer anything about that person's intellectual or moral capacities. This, it may be said, is why racism and sexism are wrong. The white racist claims that whites are superior to Blacks, but this is false—although there are differences among individuals, some Blacks are superior to some whites in all of the capacities and abilities that could conceivably be relevant. The opponent of sexism would say the same: A person's sex is no guide to his or her abilities, and this is why it is unjustifiable to discriminate on the basis of sex.

The existence of individual variations that cut across the lines of race or sex, however, provides us with no defense at all against a more sophisticated opponent of equality, one who proposes that, say, the interests of all those with IQ scores below 100 be given less consideration than the interests of those with ratings over 100. Perhaps those scoring below the mark would, in this society, be made the slaves of those scoring higher. Would a hierarchical society of this sort really be so much better than one based on race or sex? I think not. But if we tie the moral principle of equality to the factual equality of the different races or sexes, taken as a whole, our opposition to racism and sexism does not provide us with any basis for objecting to this kind of inegalitarianism.

There is a second important reason why we ought not to base our opposition to racism and sexism on any kind of actual equality, even the limited kind that asserts that variations in capacities and abilities are spread evenly between the different races and sexes: We can have no absolute guarantee that these capacities and abilities really are distributed evenly, without regard to race or sex, among human beings. So far as actual abilities are concerned there do seem to be certain measurable differences between both races and sexes. These differences do not, of course, appear in each case, but only when averages are taken. More important still, we do not yet know how much of these differences is really due to the different genetic endowments of the different races and sexes, and how much is due to poor schools, poor housing, and other factors that are the result of past and continuing discrimination. Perhaps all of the important differences will eventually prove to be environmental rather than genetic. Anyone opposed to racism and sexism will certainly hope that this will be so, for it will make the task of ending discrimination a lot easier; nevertheless it would be dangerous to rest the case against racism and sexism on the belief that all significant differences are environmental in origin. The opponent of, say, racism who takes this line will be unable to avoid conceding that *if* differences in ability do after all prove to have some genetic connection with race, racism would in some way be defensible.

Fortunately there is no need to pin the case for equality to one particular outcome of a scientific investigation. The appropriate response to those who claim to have found evidence of genetically based differences in ability between the races or sexes is not to stick to the belief that the genetic explanation must be wrong, whatever evidence to the contrary may turn up: Instead we should make it quite clear that the claim to equality does not depend on intelligence, moral capacity, physical strength, or similar matters of fact. Equality is a moral idea, not an assertion of fact. There is no logically compelling reason for assuming that a factual difference in ability between two people justifies any difference in the amount of consideration we give to their needs and interests. *The principle of the equality of human beings is not a description of an alleged actual equality among humans: It is a prescription of how we should treat humans.*

Jeremy Bentham, the founder of the reforming utilitarian school of moral philosophy, incorporated the essential basis of moral equality into his system of ethics by means of the formula: "Each to count for one and none for more than one." In other words, the interests of every being affected by an action are to be taken into account and given the same weight as the like interests of any other being. A later utilitarian, Henry Sidgwick, put the point in this way: "The good of any one individual is of no more importance, from the point of view (if I may say so) of the Universe, than the good of any other." More recently leading figures in contemporary moral philosophy have shown a great deal of agreement in specifying as a fundamental presupposition of their moral theories some similar requirement which operates so as to give everyone's interests equal consideration—although these writers generally cannot agree on how this requirement is best formulated.[1]

It is an implication of this principle of equality that our concern for others and our readiness to consider their interests ought not depend on what they are like or on what abilities they may possess. Precisely what this concern or consideration requires us to do may vary according to the characteristics of those affected by what we do: Concern for the well-being of a child growing up in America would require that we teach him to read; concern for the well-being of a pig may require no more than that we leave him alone with other pigs in a place where there is adequate food and room to run freely. But the basic element—the taking into account of the interests of the being, whatever those interests may be—must, according to the principle of equality, be extended to all beings, Black or white, masculine or feminine, human or nonhuman.

Thomas Jefferson, who was responsible for writing the principle of the equality of men into the American Declaration of Independence, saw this point. It led him to oppose slavery even though he

was unable to free himself fully from his slaveholding background. He wrote in a letter to the author of a book that emphasized the notable intellectual achievements of Negroes in order to refute the then common view that they had limited intellectual capacities:

> Be assured that no person living wishes more sincerely than I do, to see a complete refutation of the doubts I have myself entertained and expressed on the grade of understanding allotted to them by nature, and to find that they are on a par with ourselves . . . but whatever be their degree of talent it is no measure of their rights. Because Sir Isaac Newton was superior to others in understanding, he was not therefore lord of the property or person of others.[2]

Similarly when in the 1850s the call for women's rights was raised in the United States a remarkable Black feminist named Sojourner Truth made the same point in more robust terms at a feminist convention:

> . . . they talk about this thing in the head; what do they call it? ["Intellect," whispered someone near by.] That's it. What's that got to do with women's rights or Negroes' rights? If my cup won't hold but a pint and yours holds a quart, wouldn't you be mean not to let me have my little half-measure full?[3]

It is on this basis that the case against racism and the case against sexism must both ultimately rest; and it is in accordance with this principle that the attitude that we may call "speciesism," by analogy with racism, must also be condemned. Speciesism—the word is not an attractive one, but I can think of no better term—is a prejudice or attitude of bias toward the interests of members of one's own species and against those of members of other species. It should be obvious that the fundamental objections to racism and sexism made by Thomas Jefferson and Sojourner Truth apply equally to speciesism. If possessing a higher degree of intelligence does not entitle one human to use another for his own ends, how can it entitle humans to exploit nonhumans for the same purpose?[4]

Many philosophers and other writers have proposed the principle of equal consideration of interests, in some form or other, as a basic moral principle; but not many of them have recognized that this principle applies to members of other species as well as to our own. Jeremy Bentham was one of the few who did realize this. In a forward-looking passage written at a time when Black slaves had been freed by the French but in the British dominions were still being treated in the way we now treat animals, Bentham wrote:

> The day *may* come when the rest of the animal creation may acquire those rights which never could have been withholden from them but by the hand of tyranny. The French have already discovered that the blackness of the skin is no reason why a human being should be abandoned without redress to the caprice of a tormentor. It may one day come to be recognized that the number of the legs, the villosity of the skin, or the termination of the *os sacrum* are reasons equally insufficient for abandoning a sensitive being to the same fate. What else is it that should trace the insuperable line? Is it the faculty of reason, or perhaps the faculty of discourse? But a full-grown horse or dog is beyond comparison a more rational, as well as a more conversable animal, than an infant of a day or a week or even a month, old. But suppose they were otherwise, what would it avail? The question is not, Can they *reason?* nor Can they *talk?* but, *Can they suffer?*[5]

In this passage Bentham points to the capacity for suffering as the vital characteristic that gives a being the right to equal consideration. The capacity for suffering—or more strictly, for suffering and/or enjoyment or happiness—is not just another characteristic like the capacity for language or higher mathematics. Bentham is not saying that those who try to mark "the insuperable line" that determines whether the interests of a being should be considered happen to have chosen the wrong characteristic. By saying that we must consider the interests of all beings with the capacity for suffering or enjoyment Bentham does not arbitrarily exclude from consideration any interests at all—as those who draw the line with reference to the possession of reason or language do. The capacity for suffering and enjoyment is *a prerequisite for having interests at all*, a condition that must be satisfied before we can speak of interests in a meaningful way. It would be nonsense to say that it was not in the interests of a stone to be kicked along the road by a schoolboy. A stone does not have interests because it cannot suffer. Nothing that we can do to it could possibly make any difference to its welfare. A mouse, on the other hand, does have an interest in not being kicked along the road, because it will suffer if it is.

If a being suffers there can be no moral justification for refusing to take that suffering into consideration. No matter what the nature of the being, the principle of equality requires that its suffering be counted equally with the like suffering—in so far as rough comparisons can be made—of any other being. If a being is not capable of suffering, or of experiencing enjoyment or happiness, there is nothing to be taken into account. So the limit of sentience (using the term as a convenient if not strictly accurate shorthand for the capacity to suffer and/or experience enjoyment) is the only defensible boundary of concern for the interests of others. To mark this boundary by some other characteristic like intelligence or rationality would be to mark it in an arbitrary manner. Why not choose some other characteristic, like skin color?

The racist violates the principle of equality by giving greater weight to the interests of members of his own race when there is a clash between their interests and the interests of those of another race. The sexist violates the principle of equality by favoring the interests of his own sex. Similarly the speciesist allows the interests of his own species to override the greater interests of members of other species. The pattern is identical in each case.

Most human beings are speciesists. . . . Ordinary human beings—not a few exceptionally cruel or heartless humans, but the overwhelming majority of humans—take an active part in, acquiesce in, and allow their taxes to pay for practices that require the sacrifice of the most important interests of members of other species in order to promote the most trivial interests of our own species.

There is, however, one general defense of these practices . . . that needs to be disposed of. . . . It is a defense which, if true, would allow us to do anything at all to nonhumans for the slightest reason, or for no reason at all, without incurring any justifiable reproach. This defense claims that we are never guilty of neglecting the interests of other animals for one breathtakingly simple reason: They have no interests. Nonhuman animals have no interests, according to this view, because they are not capable of suffering. By this is not meant merely that they are not capable of suffering in all the ways that humans are—for instance, that a calf is not capable of suffering from the knowledge that it will be killed in six months time. That modest claim is, no doubt, true;

but it does not clear humans of the charge of speciesism, since it allows that animals may suffer in other ways—for instance, by being given electric shocks, or being kept in small, cramped cages. The defense I am about to discuss is the much more sweeping, although correspondingly less plausible, claim that animals are incapable of suffering in any way at all; that they are . . . unconscious automata, possessing neither thoughts nor feelings nor a mental life of any kind.

Although . . . the view that animals are automata was proposed by the seventeenth-century French philosopher René Descartes, to most people, then and now, it is obvious that if, for example, we stick a sharp knife into the stomach of an unanesthetized dog, the dog will feel pain. That this is so is assumed by the laws in most civilized countries which prohibit wanton cruelty to animals. Readers whose common sense tells them that animals do suffer may prefer to skip the next few paragraphs . . . since they do nothing but refute a position which they do not hold. Implausible as it is, though, for the sake of completeness this skeptical position must be discussed.

Do animals other than humans feel pain? How do we know? Well, how do we know if anyone, human or nonhuman, feels pain? We know that we ourselves can feel pain. We know this from the direct experiences of pain that we have when, for instance, somebody presses a lighted cigarette against the back of our hand. But how do we know that anyone else feels pain? We cannot directly experience anyone else's pain, whether that "anyone" is our best friend or a stray dog. Pain is a state of consciousness, a "mental event," and as such it can never be observed. Behavior like writhing, screaming, or drawing one's hand away from the lighted cigarette is not pain itself; nor are the recordings a neurologist might make of activity within the brain observations of pain itself. Pain is something that we feel, and we can only infer that others are feeling it from various external indications.

In theory, we *could* always be mistaken when we assume that other human beings feel pain. It is conceivable that our best friend is really a very cleverly constructed robot, controlled by a brilliant scientist so as to give all the signs of feeling pain, but really no more sensitive than any other machine. We can never know, with absolute certainty, that this is not the case. But while this might present a puzzle for philosophers, none of us has the slight-est real doubt that our best friends feel pain just as we do. This is an inference, but a perfectly reasonable one, based on observations of their behavior in situations in which we would feel pain, and on the fact that we have every reason to assume that our friends are beings like us, with nervous systems like ours that can be assumed to function as ours do, and to produce similar feelings in similar circumstances.

If it is justifiable to assume that other humans feel pain as we do, is there any reason why a similar inference should be unjustifiable in the case of other animals?

Nearly all the external signs that lead us to infer pain in other humans can be seen in other species, especially [those] most closely related to us—other species of mammals, and birds. Behavioral signs—writhing, facial contortions, moaning, yelping, or other forms of calling, attempts to avoid the source of pain, appearance of fear at the prospect of its repetition, and so on—are present. In addition, we know that these animals have nervous systems very like ours, which respond physiologically as ours do when the animal is in circumstances in which we would feel pain: an initial rise of blood pressure, dilated pupils, perspiration, an increased pulse rate, and, if the stimulus continues, a fall in blood pressure. Although humans have a more developed cerebral cortex than other animals, this part of the brain is concerned with thinking functions rather than with basic impulses, emotions, and feelings. These impulses, emotions, and feelings are located in the diencephalon, which is well developed in many other species of animals, especially mammals and birds.[6]

We also know that the nervous systems of other animals were not artificially constructed to mimic the pain behavior of humans, as a robot might be artificially constructed. The nervous systems of animals evolved as our own did, and in fact the evolutionary history of humans and other animals, especially mammals, did not diverge until the central features of our nervous systems were already in existence. A capacity to feel pain obviously enhances a species' prospects of survival, since it causes members of the species to avoid sources of injury. It is surely unreasonable to suppose that nervous systems which are virtually identical physiologically, have a common origin and a common evolutionary function, and result in similar forms of behavior in similar circumstances should actually operate in an entirely different manner on the level of subjective feelings.

It has long been accepted as sound policy in science to search for the simplest possible explanation of whatever it is we are trying to explain. Occasionally it has been claimed that it is for this reason "unscientific" to explain the behavior of animals by theories that refer to the animal's conscious feelings, desires, and so on—the idea being that if the behavior in question can be explained without invoking consciousness or feelings, that will be the simpler theory. Yet we can now see that such explanations, when placed in the overall context of the behavior of both human and nonhuman animals, are far more complex than their rivals. We know from our own experience that explanations of our own behavior that did not refer to consciousness and the feeling of pain would be incomplete; it is simpler to assume that the similar behavior of animals with similar nervous systems is to be explained in the same way than to try to invent some other explanation for the behavior of nonhuman animals as well as an explanation for the divergence between humans and nonhumans in this respect.

The overwhelming majority of scientists who have addressed themselves to this question agree. Lord Brain, one of the most eminent neurologists of our time, has said:

I personally can see no reason for conceding mind to my fellow men and denying it to animals. . . . I at least cannot doubt that the interests and activities of animals are correlated with awareness and feeling in the same way as my own, and which may be, for aught I know, just as vivid.[7]

While the author of a recent book on pain writes:

Every particle of factual evidence supports the contention that the higher mammalian vertebrates experience pain sensations at least as acute as our own. To say that they feel less because they are lower animals is an absurdity; it can easily be shown that many of their senses are far more acute than ours—visual acuity in certain birds, hearing in most wild animals, and touch in others; these animals depend more than we do today on the sharpest possible awareness of a hostile environment. Apart from the complexity of the cerebral cortex (which does not directly perceive pain) their nervous systems are almost identical to ours and their reactions to pain remarkably similar, though lacking (so far as we know) the philosophical and moral overtones. The emotional element is all too evident, mainly in the form of fear and anger.[8]

In Britain, three separate expert government committees on matters relating to animals have accepted the conclusion that animals feel pain. After noting the obvious behavioral evidence for this view, the Committee on Cruelty to Wild Animals said:

. . . we believe that the physiological, and more particularly the anatomical, evidence fully justifies and reinforces the commonsense belief that animals feel pain.

And after discussing the evolutionary value of pain they concluded that pain is "of clear-cut biological usefulness" and this is "a third type of evidence that animals feel pain." They then went on to consider forms of suffering other than mere physical pain, and added that they were "satisfied that animals do suffer from acute fear and terror." In 1965, British government [reports] on experiments on animals, and on the welfare of animals under intensive farming methods, agreed with this view, concluding that animals are capable of suffering both from straightforward physical injuries and from fear, anxiety, stress, and so on.[9]

That might well be thought enough to settle the matter; but there is one more objection that needs to be considered. There is, after all, one behavioral sign that humans have when in pain which nonhumans do not have. This is a developed language. Other animals may communicate with each other, but not, it seems, in the complicated way we do. Some philosophers, including Descartes, have thought it important that while humans can tell each other about their experience of pain in great detail, other animals cannot. (Interestingly, this once neat dividing line between humans and other species has now been threatened by the discovery that chimpanzees can be taught a language.)[10] But as Bentham pointed out long ago, the ability to use language is not relevant to the question of how a being ought to be treated—unless that ability can be linked to the capacity to suffer, so that the absence of a language casts doubt on the existence of this capacity.

This link may be attempted in two ways. First, there is a hazy line of philosophical thought, stemming perhaps from some doctrines associated with influential philosopher Ludwig Wittgenstein, that maintains we cannot meaningfully attribute states of consciousness to beings without language. This position seems to me very implausible. Language may be necessary for abstract thought, at some level anyway; but states like pain are more primitive, and have nothing to do with language.

The second and more easily understood way of linking language and the existence of pain is to say that the best evidence that we can have that another creature is in pain is when he tells us that he is. This is a distinct line of argument, for it is not being denied that a non–language-user conceivably *could* suffer, but only that we could ever have sufficient reason to *believe* that he is suffering. Still, this line of argument fails too. As Jane Goodall has pointed out in her study of chimpanzees, *In the Shadow of Man,* when it comes to the expressions of feelings and emotions language is less important than in other areas. We tend to fall back on nonlinguistic modes of communication such as a cheering pat on the back, an exuberant embrace, a clasp of the hands, and so on. The basic signals we use to convey pain, fear, anger, love, joy, surprise, sexual arousal, and many other emotional states are not specific to our own species.[11]

Charles Darwin made an extensive study of this subject, and the book he wrote about it, *The Expression of the Emotions in Man and Animals,* notes countless nonlinguistic modes of expression. The statement "I am in pain" may be one piece of evidence for the conclusion that the speaker is in pain, but it is not the only possible evidence, and since people sometimes tell lies, not even the best possible evidence.

Even if there were stronger grounds for refusing to attribute pain to those who do not have a language, the consequences of this refusal might lead us to reject the conclusion. Human infants and young children are unable to use language. Are we to deny that a year-old child can suffer? If not, language cannot be crucial. Of course, most parents understand the responses of their children better than they understand the responses of other animals; but this is just a fact about the relatively greater knowledge that we have of our own species, and the greater contact we have with infants, as compared to animals. Those who have studied the behavior of other animals, and those who have pet animals, soon learn to understand their responses as well as we understand those of an infant, and sometimes

better. Jane Goodall's account of the chimpanzees she watched is one [example], but the same can be said of those who have observed species less closely related to our own. Two among many possible examples are Konrad Lorenz's observations of geese and jackdaws, and N. Tinbergen's extensive studies of herring gulls.[12] Just as we can understand infant human behavior in the light of adult human behavior, so we can understand the behavior of other species in the light of our own behavior—and sometimes we can understand our own behavior better in the light of the behavior of other species.

So to conclude: There are no good reasons, scientific or philosophical, for denying that animals feel pain. If we do not doubt that other humans feel pain we should not doubt that other animals do so too.

Animals can feel pain. As we saw earlier, there can be no moral justification for regarding the pain (or pleasure) that animals feel as less important than the same amount of pain (or pleasure) felt by humans. But what exactly does this mean, in practical terms? To prevent misunderstanding I shall spell out what I mean a little more fully.

If I give a horse a hard slap across its rump with my open hand, the horse may start, but it presumably feels little pain. Its skin is thick enough to protect it against a mere slap. If I slap a baby in the same way, however, the baby will cry and presumably does feel pain, for its skin is more sensitive. So it is worse to slap a baby than a horse, if both slaps are administered with equal force. But there must be some kind of blow . . . perhaps a blow with a heavy stick . . . that would cause the horse as much pain as we cause a baby by slapping it with our hand. That is what I mean by "the same amount of pain" and if we consider it wrong to inflict that much pain on a baby for no good reason then we must, unless we are speciesists, consider it equally wrong to inflict the same amount of pain on a horse for no good reason.

There are other differences between humans and animals that cause other complications. Normal adult human beings have mental capacities which will, in certain circumstances, lead them to suffer more than animals would in the same circumstances. If, for instance, we decided to perform extremely painful or lethal scientific experiments on normal adult humans, kidnapped at random from public parks for this purpose, every adult who entered a park would become fearful that he would be kidnapped. The resultant terror would be a form of suffering additional to the pain of the experiment. The same experiments performed on nonhuman animals would cause less suffering since the animals would not have the anticipatory dread of being kidnapped and experimented upon. This does not mean, of course, that it would be right to perform the experiment on animals, but only that there is a reason, which is *not* speciesist, for preferring to use animals rather than normal adult humans, if the experiment is to be done at all. Note, however, that this same argument gives us a reason for preferring to use human infants—orphans perhaps—or retarded humans for experiments, rather than adults, since infants and retarded humans would also have no idea of what was going to happen to them. So far as this argument is concerned nonhuman animals and infants and retarded humans are in the same category; and if we use this argument to justify experiments on nonhuman animals we have to ask ourselves whether we are also prepared to allow experiments on human infants and retarded adults; and if we make a distinction between animals and these humans, on what basis can we do it, other than a barefaced—and morally indefensible—preference for members of our own species?

There are many areas in which the superior mental powers of normal adult humans make a difference: anticipation, more detailed memory, greater knowledge of what is happening, and so on. Yet these differences do not all point to greater suffering on the part of the normal human being. Sometimes an animal may suffer more because of his more limited understanding. If, for instance, we are taking prisoners in wartime we can explain to them that while they must submit to capture, search, and confinement they will not otherwise be harmed and will be set free at the conclusion of hostilities. If we capture a wild animal, however, we cannot explain that we are not threatening its life. A wild animal cannot distinguish an attempt to overpower and confine from an attempt to kill; the one causes as much terror as the other.

It may be objected that comparisons of the sufferings of different species are impossible to make, and that for this reason when the interests of animals and humans clash the principle of equality gives no guidance. It is probably true that comparisons of suffering between members of different species cannot be made precisely, but precision is not essential. Even if we were to prevent the inflic-

tion of suffering on animals only when it is quite certain that the interests of humans will not be affected to anything like the extent that animals are affected, we would be forced to make radical changes in our treatment of animals that would involve our diet, the farming methods we use, experimental procedures in many fields of science, our approach to wildlife and to hunting, trapping, and the wearing of furs, and areas of entertainment like circuses, rodeos, and zoos. As a result, a vast amount of suffering would be avoided.

So far I have said a lot about the infliction of suffering on animals, but nothing about killing them. This omission has been deliberate. The application of the principle of equality to the infliction of suffering is, in theory at least, fairly straightforward. Pain and suffering are bad and should be prevented or minimized, irrespective of the race, sex, or species of the being that suffers. How bad a pain is depends on how intense it is and how long it lasts, but pains of the same intensity and duration are equally bad, whether felt by humans or animals.

The wrongness of killing a being is more complicated. I have kept, and shall continue to keep, the question of killing in the background because in the present state of human tyranny over other species the more simple, straightforward principle of equal consideration of pain or pleasure is a sufficient basis for identifying and protesting all the major abuses of animals that humans practice. Nevertheless, it is necessary to say something about killing.

Just as most humans are speciesists in their readiness to cause pain to animals when they would not cause a similar pain to humans for the same reason, so most humans are speciesists in their readiness to kill other animals when they would not kill humans. We need to proceed more cautiously here, however, because people hold widely differing views about when it is legitimate to kill humans, as the continuing debates over abortion and euthanasia attest. Nor have moral philosophers been able to agree on exactly what it is that makes it wrong to kill humans, and under what circumstances killing a human being may be justifiable.

Let us consider first the view that it is always wrong to take an innocent human life. We may call this the "sanctity of life" view. People who take this view oppose abortion and euthanasia. They do not usually, however, oppose the killing of nonhumans—so perhaps it would be more accurate to describe this view as the "sanctity of *human* life" view.

The belief that human life, and only human life, is sacrosanct is a form of speciesism. To see this, consider the following example.

Assume that, as sometimes happens, an infant has been born with massive and irreparable brain damage. The damage is so severe that the infant can never be any more than a "human vegetable," unable to talk, recognize other people, act independently of others, or develop a sense of self-awareness. The parents of the infant, realizing that they cannot hope for any improvement in their child's condition and being in any case unwilling to spend, or ask the state to spend, the thousands of dollars that would be needed annually for proper care of the infant, ask the doctor to kill the infant painlessly.

Should the doctor do what the parents ask? Legally, he should not, and in this respect the law reflects the sanctity of life view. The life of every human being is sacred. Yet people who would say this about the infant do not object to the killing of nonhuman animals. How can they justify their different judgments? Adult chimpanzees, dogs, pigs, and many other species far surpass the brain-damaged infant in their ability to relate to others, act independently, be self-aware, and any other capacity that could reasonable be said to give value to life. With the most intensive care possible, there are retarded infants who can never achieve the intelligence level of a dog. Nor can we appeal to the concern of the infant's parents, since they themselves, in this imaginary example (and in some actual cases), do not want the infant kept alive.

The only thing that distinguishes the infant from the animal, in the eyes of those who claim it has a "right to life," is that it is, biologically, a member of the species *Homo sapiens,* whereas chimpanzees, dogs, and pigs are not. But to use *this* difference as the basis for granting a right to life to the infant and not to the other animals is, of course, pure speciesism.[13] It is exactly the kind of arbitrary difference that the most crude and overt kind of racist uses in attempting to justify racial discrimination.

This does not mean that to avoid speciesism we must hold that it is as wrong to kill a dog as it is to kill a normal human being. The only position that is irredeemably speciesist is the one that tries to make the boundary of the right to life run exactly parallel to the boundary of our own species. Those who hold the sanctity of life view do this because while distinguishing sharply between humans and other animals they allow no distinctions to be made within our own species, objecting to the killing of the severely retarded and the hopelessly senile as strongly as they object to the killing of normal adults.

To avoid speciesism we must allow that beings which are similar in all relevant respects have a similar right to life—and mere membership in our own biological species cannot be a morally relevant criterion for this right. Within these limits we could still hold that, for instance, it is worse to kill a normal adult human, with a capacity for self-awareness, and the ability to plan for the future and have meaningful relations with others, than it is to kill a mouse, which presumably does not share all of these characteristics; or we might appeal to the close family and other personal ties which humans have but mice do not have to the same degree; or we might think that it is the consequences for other humans, who will be put in fear of their own lives, that make the crucial difference; or we might think it is some combination of these factors, or other factors altogether.

Whatever criteria we choose, however, we will have to admit that they do not follow precisely the boundary of our own species. We may legitimately hold that there are some features of certain beings which make their lives more valuable than those of other beings; but there will surely be some nonhuman animals whose lives, by any standards, are more valuable than the lives of some humans. A chimpanzee, dog, or pig, for instance, will have a higher degree of self-awareness and a greater capacity for meaningful relations with others than a severely retarded infant or someone in a state of advanced senility. So if we base the right to life on these characteristics we must grant these animals a right to life as good as, or better than, such retarded or senile humans.

Now this argument cuts both ways. It could be taken as showing that chimpanzees, dogs, and pigs, along with some other species, have a right to life and we commit a grave moral offense whenever we kill them, even when they are old and suffering and our intention is to put them out of their misery. Alternatively one could take the argument as showing that the severely retarded and hopelessly senile have no right to life and may be killed for quite trivial reasons, as we now kill animals.

Since the focus of this [reading] is on ethical questions concerning animals and not on the morality of euthanasia I shall not attempt to settle this issue finally. I think it is reasonably clear, though, that while both of the positions just described avoid speciesism, neither is entirely satisfactory. What we need is some middle position which would avoid speciesism but would not make the lives of the retarded and senile as cheap as the lives of pigs and dogs now are, nor make the lives of pigs and dogs so sacrosanct that we think it wrong to put them out of hopeless misery. What we must do is bring nonhuman animals within our sphere of moral concern and cease to treat their lives as expendable for whatever trivial purposes we may have. At the same time, once we realize that the fact that a being is a member of our own species is not in itself enough to make it always wrong to kill that being, we may come to reconsider our policy of preserving human lives at all costs, even when there is no prospect of a meaningful life or of existence without terrible pain.

I conclude, then, that a rejection of speciesism does not imply that all lives are of equal worth. While self-awareness, intelligence, the capacity for meaningful relations with others, and so on are not relevant to the question of inflicting pain—since pain is pain, whatever other capacities, beyond the capacity to feel pain, the being may have—these capacities may be relevant to the question of taking life. It is not arbitrary to hold that the life of a self-aware being, capable of abstract thought, of planning for the future, of complex acts of communication, and so on, is more valuable than the life of a being without these capacities. To see the difference between the issues of inflicting pain and taking life, consider how we would choose within our own species. If we had to choose to save the life of a normal human or a mentally defective human, we would probably choose to save the life of the normal human; but if we had to choose between preventing pain in the normal human or the mental defective—imagine that both have received painful but superficial injuries, and we only have enough painkiller for one of them—it is not nearly so clear how we ought to choose. The same is true when we consider other species. The evil of pain is, in itself, unaffected by the other characteristics of the being that feels the pain; the value of life is affected by these other characteristics.

Normally this will mean that if we have to choose between the life of a human being and the life of another animal we should choose to save the life of the human; but there may be special cases in which the reverse holds true, because the human being in question does not have the capacities of a normal human being. So this view is not speciesist, although it may appear to be at first glance. The preference, in normal cases, for saving a human life over the life of an animal when a choice *has* to be made is a preference based on the characteristics that normal humans have, and not on the mere fact that they are members of our own species. This is why when we consider members of our own species who lack the characteristics of normal humans we can no longer say their lives are always to be preferred to those of other animals. . . . In general, though, the question of when it is wrong to kill (painlessly) an animal is one to which we need give no precise answer. As long as we remember that we should give the same respect to the lives of animals as we give to the lives of those humans at a similar mental level, we shall not go far wrong.

Endnotes

1. For Bentham's moral philosophy, see his *Introduction to the Principles of Morals and Legislation,* and for Sidgwick's see *The Methods of Ethics* (the passage quoted is from the seventh edition, p. 382). As examples of leading contemporary moral philosophers who incorporate a requirement of equal consideration of interests, see R. M. Hare, *Freedom and Reason* (New York: Oxford University Press, 1963) and John Rawls, *A Theory of Justice* (Cambridge: Harvard University Press, Belknap Press, 1972). For a brief account of the essential agreement on this issue between these and other positions, see R. M. Hare, "Rules of War and Moral Reasoning," *Philosophy and Public Affairs,* vol. 1, no. 2 (1972).

2. Letter to Henri Gregoire, February 25, 1809.

3. Reminiscences by Francis D. Gage, from Susan B. Anthony, *The History of Woman Suffrage,* vol. 1; the passage is to be found in the extract in Leslie Tanner, ed., *Voices from Women's Liberation* (New York: Signet, 1970).

4. I owe the term "speciesism" to Richard Ryder.

5. *Introduction to the Principles of Morals and Legislation,* chapter 17.

6. Lord Brian, "Presidential Address," in C. A. Keele and R. Smith, eds., *The Assessment of Pain in Men and Animals* (London: Universities Federation for Animal Welfare, 1962).

7. Ibid., p. 11.

8.   Richard Serjeant, *The Spectrum of Pain* (London: Hart-Davis, 1969), p. 72.

9.   See the reports of the Committee on Cruelty to Wild Animals (Command Paper 8268, 1951), paragraphs 36–42; the Departmental Committee on Experiments on Animals (Command Paper 2641, 1965), paragraphs 179–182; and the Technical Committee to Enquire into the Welfare of Animals Kept under Intensive Livestock Husbandry Systems (Command Paper 2836, 1965), paragraphs 26–28 (London: Her Majesty's Stationery Office).

10. One chimpanzee, Washoe, has been taught the sign language used by deaf people, and acquired a vocabulary of 350 signs. Another, Lana, communicates in structured sentences by pushing buttons on a special machine. For a brief account of Washoe's abilities, see Jane van Lawick-Goodall, *In the Shadow of Man* (Boston: Houghton Mifflin, 1971), pp. 252–254; and for Lana, see *Newsweek*, 7 January, 1974, and *New York Times*, 4 December 1974.

11. *In the Shadow of Man*, p. 225; Michael Peters makes a similar point in "Nature and Culture," in Stanley and Roslind Godlovitch and John Harris, eds., *Animals, Men and Morals* (New York: Taplinger Publishing Co., 1972).

12. Konrad Lorenz, *King Solomon's Ring* (New York: T. Y. Crowell, 1952); N. Tinbergen, *The Herring Gull's World*, rev. ed. (New York: Basic Books, 1974).

13. I am here putting aside religious views, for example the doctrine that all and only humans have immortal souls, or are made in the image of God. Historically these views have been very important, and no doubt are partly responsible for the idea that human life has a special sanctity. Logically, however, these religious views are unsatisfactory, since a reasoned explanation of why it should be that all humans and no nonhumans have immortal souls is not offered. This belief too, therefore, comes under suspicion as a form of speciesism. In any case, defenders of the "sanctity of life" view are generally reluctant to base their position on purely religious doctrines, since these doctrines are no longer as widely accepted as they once were.

---◇---

62. *Ethical Vegetarianism Is Unfair to Women and Children*

Kathryn Paxton George

Kathryn George argues that the ethical vegetarianism endorsed by Singer is partial to adult males and to people living in developed countries rather than those living in developing or underdeveloped countries. The reason is that for all those not living in developed countries, ethical vegetarianism is so burdensome that they are exempt from its requirements. She goes on to argue that supplementing diets in developed countries by fortifying foods to make it easier to be a vegetarian are not part of a sustainable food production, so they cannot serve as a way of making vegetarianism morally required for more people.

Vegetarianism has been promoted by a variety of authorities as both humanitarian and healthful. Not only should people avoid harming animals by eating them, but we can also avoid the harmful effects of high-fat diets by avoiding meat, eggs, and dairy products. The claim that vegetarian diets are health-ful is separate from the claim that such diets are morally required, but these ideas do influence one another. I am going to suggest here that the apparent safety and benefits of vegetarian diets for adult males has led some philosophers, especially Peter Singer and Tom Regan, to assume that the adult male body is considered the normal *human* body. Assuming facts about this male human norm, they derive a general moral rule demanding ethical vegetarianism for everyone regardless of age, sex, or environment. I will refer to these arguments as the

Reprinted from *Earth Ethics* 2nd ed. by James P. Sterba (Englewood Cliffs, NJ: Prentice-Hall, 1995), by permission of Prentice-Hall Inc.

"Regan-Singer arguments." I will show that their assumption about the male norm is mistaken, and their call for ethical vegetarianism results in ageism, sexism, and classism. The Regan-Singer arguments for ethical vegetarianism rely on the *Principle of Equality,* but as I will show, if all animals are equal, women and children become less equal than men. That logical outcome will show that their arguments are incoherent and fail. Finally, the standard against which risk is presumed to be measured is arbitrarily assumed to be the adult male body.

First, let's review the moral claims. Singer, Regan, and virtually all other philosophers defending the moral status of animals claim that animals are the moral equals of humans and that we may not kill them for food. According to Peter Singer (1975, 1990), we may not use their products unless we could be sure that these products are obtained under painless conditions. Singer's utilitarian position would permit some people to eat animals or their products if they have a strong welfare-interest (say, for reasons of ill health), but these would be *exceptional cases.* Singer's reasons are apparently similar to those offered by Tom Regan (1983). Regan's rights position allows certain people to consume meat as exceptional cases based on what he calls the *Liberty Principle:*

> Provided that all those involved are treated with respect, and assuming that no special considerations obtain, any innocent individual has the right to act to avoid being made worse off even if doing so harms other innocents (1983, p. 333).

Being made to starve or suffer a significant decline in health and vigor would make a person worse-off, and Regan accedes that if some humans have a strong welfare-interest in consuming meat or animal products, this would excuse them from a duty to be vegetarians. But Regan clearly thinks most people do not fall into such a category. He briefly discusses protein complementation and then dismisses the argument from nutrition:

> Certain amino acids are essential for our health. Meat isn't. We cannot, therefore, defend meat-eating on the grounds that we will ruin our health if we don't eat it or even that we will run a very serious risk of doing so if we abstain (1983, p. 337).

Traditional moral theories used by Regan and Singer assume the moral equality of persons regard-

less of age, sex, race, and so forth. This assumption is called the *Principle of Equality.* Without the Principle of Equality, Tom Regan and Peter Singer cannot begin to make an argument for the rights and welfare of animals. Rights-holders deserve equal treatment, and the rules generated by the moral system should be impartial and nondiscriminatory concerning aspects about the rights-holders that they cannot change by choice. No particular group of people should bear a very much greater burden than others in attempting to keep the moral rule. That can mean that society should eliminate moral, social, or legal constraints that will cause people to suffer an increased burden in their attempts to function in society, at least as far as possible. For example, the Principle of Equality is the underlying reason that our society provides ramps and elevators for those who cannot use stairs. And because we subscribe to the Principle of Equality, we believe it is wrong to punish criminal offenders of one race more harshly that those of another. Nondiscrimination is the attempt by fair-minded people to affirm the equal worth of each member of the moral community. No single group can simply assume that its own practices are the only right ones, or even the best ones. If the rule prescribing ethical vegetarian diets is truly impartial, it should not require greater or very much greater burdens for some groups because of aspects about themselves that cannot be changed and that are thought to be neutral to the interests served by the rule.

Having set out a brief exposition of the foundations for ethical vegetarianism, I will now present a critical examination of this proposed moral rule. My claim is that the rule is partial to adult males and that, probably unwittingly, no one has noticed that the rule systematically imposed greater burdens on women and children. Second, the rule unfairly penalizes people who live in certain kinds of economic and environmental circumstances. My critique takes three tacks: (1) Regan and Singer (probably unwittingly) assume that there is no significant difference in the nutritional needs of males, females, children, and the elderly. To make their moral arguments, these scholars rely on conclusions drawn from nutritional studies done on adult males in industrialized countries. In addition, they do not consider studies citing the limitations of such diets for other age groups and for many women. Instead, the male body is assumed to be the norm for all. Women, children, and others are referred to in the scientific literature as "nutritionally vulnerable" with respect to certain vitamins and minerals such as iron, calcium, vitamin D and zinc. All current arguments for ethical vegetarianism treat such nutritional vulnerability as an *exception* rather than as a norm. But, the very fact that the majority is regarded as a mere exception suggests that the ideal is skewed in favor of a group in power. A hidden assumption in the moral argument is that *being less vulnerable is good*, simply because one is *stronger*, and *being vulnerable is bad* or, at least not as good, because one is *weaker*. But that is a bald argument for power rather than for justice or moral virtue. So, the traditional moral theories fail on grounds of arbitrariness; i.e., the mere imposition of power through acceptance of a false belief. And, the theories become incoherent for their failure to treat all members of the moral community impartially. (2) The requirement of ethical vegetarianism is also inconsistent and classist because it presupposes a society largely structured on wealth generated from unsustainable environmental, agricultural, and industrial practices. But most people in the world live in ethnic, cultural, economic, and environmental circumstances where this supposed ethical ideal poses much more serious health risks than it does for people in the United States, Europe, and other rich countries. But being richer does not automatically make people more moral. (3) Attempts to correct inequities by requiring supplementation for women and children exacerbate rather than resolve the problem of unfairness.

The first criticism will show that Regan-Singer become incoherent because they cannot consistently apply the Principle of Equality. Neither Singer nor Regan considers the different nutritional needs of adults versus infants and children and men versus women, although these differences are well documented in the medical and nutrition literature. Infants and young children have higher energy, vitamin, and mineral needs than adults do because they are continuously growing and adding new tissue to their bodies. Nationally recognized nutrition authority Dr. Johanna T. Dwyer of Tufts University Schools of Medicine and Nutrition writes:

> Vegetarianism in children deserves special attention because diets that sustain adults in good health are not necessarily appropriate for infants, young children, or adolescents (1993b, p. 171).

Phyllis B. Acosta of Florida State University's Department of Nutrition and Food Science states her concerns in stronger terms:

> Eating practices that promote health in the adult may have detrimental effects on growth and health status of the infant and young child (1998, p. 872).

Adolescents also need diets that are dense in nutrients per kilocalorie because they undergo the pubertal growth spurt. "Sex differences in nutrient needs become especially pronounced during adolescence" (Dwyer 1993a, p. 258). The onset of menstruation in females increases their iron needs, and the need for protein increases because the body size is increasing rapidly (Dwyer 1993a). Because bone mass is being accumulated, calcium needs remain higher until about age 25. The recommended daily allowances (RDAs) are "considerably higher for adolescents than they are for younger children or adults, especially if they are expressed on a nutrients-per-calorie basis" (Dwyer 1993a, p. 257). Pregnant adult women have greater protein, calcium, iron, vitamin C, vitamin D, vitamin E, thiamin, riboflavin, niacin, vitamin B-6, folate, vitamin B-12, phosphorus, magnesium, zinc, selenium, and iodide needs than adult males, and breastfeeding women have requirements that are higher still for almost all of these nutrients (National Research Council 1989). People over age 50 have different requirements for several nutrients as reflected in the RDAs (National Research Council 1989; Munro et al. 1987).

In pregnant women, "certain dietary practices that restrict or prohibit the consumption of an important source of nutrients, such as avoidance of all animal foods or of vitamin D-fortified milk, increase the risk of inadequate nutrient intake" (Institute of Medicine 1990, p. 18). Pregnant vegan women may be at greater nutritional risk for "inadequate weight gain, low protein intake, inadequate iron intake with resulting anemias, low calcium, zinc, and vitamin B-12 intakes, and in some instances low vitamin D, zinc and iodide intakes" (Dwyer 1991, pp. 75–76). Because the health of a fetus depends upon the health of the individual woman carrying it, these factors may pose a fetal risk as well. In some cases, nutritional deficiency in a woman at the time of conception can seriously impair fetal development or the health of a breast-feeding child (e.g., folic acid deficiency; vitamin B-12 deficiency) (Institute of Medicine 1990).

Women and children are more likely to suffer iron deficiency than adult males even in industrialized societies. Only a few years ago, marginal iron levels in women were not regarded with much alarm by physicians and nutritionists. Recently, however, it has been found that iron plays a vital role in childhood development and maintenance of the central nervous system, organ function, and immune function (Dallman 1989). Researchers usually categorized their test subjects as "normal," "iron deficient," or "iron deficient anemic," where iron deficiency is a state preceding anemia. In a review of 45 studies, Hercberg and Galan (1989) note that iron deficiency has "effects on skeletal muscle, cardiac muscle, brain tissue, liver tissue, gastrointestinal tractus [sic], body temperature relation, [and] DNA synthesis [because] iron participates in a wide variety of biochemical processes.... The key liabilities of tissue iron deficiency, even at a mild degree relate to decrease in intellectual performance, and in physical capacity during exercise, alteration of temperature regulation, [and] immune function" (p. 63; see also Dallman 1989; Parks and Wharton 1989; Scrimshaw 1991). Moreover, the effects of diets without adequate available sources of iron in infancy and young childhood cannot be compensated for by later improvements and/or later supplementation, and "maternal mortality, prenatal and perinatal infant death and prematurity are significantly increased" for iron deficiency in pregnancy (Scrimshaw 1991, p. 50; see also Dallman 1989; Oski 1993; Walter et al. 1989).

Women are particularly sensitive to iron deficiency because of periodic blood loss at menses and during pregnancy (Scrimshaw 1991; Hercberg and Galan 1992). Because iron carries oxygen to body cells, anemia causes reduction in capacity to perform work, reduction in mental acuity, greater vulnerability to other kinds of illnesses, and a variety of other symptoms. A significant number of women become iron deficient during pregnancy even when they eat iron-rich foods including meat (Bothwell et al. 1989), and nutritionists have expressed concern that because vegetarian diets restrict nutrient sources further, vegetarian diets may not provide adequate iron (Dwyer 1991). Although pregnant "vegan women [in the U.S.] can meet increased needs for most nutrients during pregnancy by diet alone ... iron needs rise so much after the second trimester that supplements are usually needed since plant sources of iron are less bioavailable than heme iron" (Dwyer and Loew 1994, p. 91). The point about supplements is important because these are more commonly available in industrialized environments.

Vegans reject dairy products and that significantly reduces sources of calcium. Most of the concern centers on bone health among women and children. Continued inadequacy of calcium in the diet is thought to be a major contributing factor to osteoporosis (Dawson-Hughes 1991; Matkovic et al. 1979; Rodysill 1987), and milk is still recommended as the best source of calcium: "The calcium in milk and milk products is well-absorbed, whereas that in most plant sources is either poorly or negligibly available" (Allen 1986, p. 7). Osteoporosis is a major concern for post-menopausal women because it causes bone loss and fractures, particularly of the hip, forearm, and vertebrae. Women are at much greater risk for this disease than men. Although men are not completely exempt, their generally denser skeletons and testosterone levels prevent its occurrence until quite late in life (Johns Hopkins Medical Institutions 1994a, b).

But the time to prevent osteoporosis appears to be in childhood and adolescence. Peak bone mass is built then and the better it is built, the more bone there will be. Then, when bone loss begins it will take a longer time to reach a stage of severe depletion. Young women have already built almost all of their bone by about age 17 with some new bone formation perhaps continuing into the twenties (Dawson-Hughes 1991). By age 30 many women begin to lose bone (Rodysill 1987). In women "over the first several years after menopause, the skeleton undergoes a period of accelerated mineral loss in the process of adapting to declining concentrations of estrogen. After this period of adjustment, the rate of bone loss declines and remains fairly constant" (Dawson-Hughes 1991).

The nutritional evidence suggests that the best candidates for vegetarianism and veganism are young, adult, healthy males living in industrialized cultures. Males have generally larger skeletons and so have a lower risk of osteoporosis in late middle and old age. Adult males have higher iron levels than females and are at much less risk of anemia in adolescence and adulthood because they do not have periodic blood loss with menstruation and childbirth. They do not have protein, vitamin, or mineral stresses from feeding a rapidly growing fetus or a nursing infant, nor are they unduly stressed by their own growth requirements, as most of their growth is accomplished.

Do these facts mean that women and children in the United States cannot be healthy vegetarians?

No, it does not. Dwyer (1991) and Dwyer and Loew (1994) maintain that all risks for vegans in the United States can be overcome with a well-planned and well-supplemented diet. What does "well-planned" mean? Here I quote more fully the context of Dwyer's (1991) statement:

> For those who wish to progress to a vegan diet that includes no animal foods whatsoever, additional care in dietary planning is needed. In addition to iron and zinc, unplanned vegan diets are often low in kilocalories, calcium, and are always low in vitamin B-12 and vitamin D unless supplementary sources of these vitamins are provided, since plant foods contain no known sources of these vitamins. The assistance of a registered dietitian is helpful, since a good deal of skill in planning and familiarity with unconventional food sources is needed by omnivores who wish to alter their dietary intakes in this way. Certainly, if the individual in question is an infant, child, pregnant or lactating woman, over 65 years of age, recovering from an illness, or a chronic sufferer of a disease, dietetic consultation is highly advisable in order to incorporate these additional considerations into dietary planning and to avoid or circumvent adverse nutritional consequences. Several good articles are available to guide counseling efforts for vulnerable groups . . . (pp. 82–83).

Ethical vegetarianism does not pose insurmountable risk of harm in industrialized societies. But if the harms can be overcome only by imposing a significantly greater burden on some groups while granting health benefits to others, then the standard against which the risk is measured must surely be unfair. Moralists like Regan and Singer claim anyone can be an ethical vegetarian with no extra special burden. Their norm identifies physical strength in maintaining health on a particular diet as *morally good*. But morality is a matter of *will* and *choice*, not physical strength. Women and children are treated as outliers, exceptions, and "vulnerable groups," who do not fit expected norms. However, scientifically, there is no ideal "human" body, but only real men, women, and children.

What kind of response might Regan or Singer make to my criticisms? It is really no use attacking the facts. They are too well substantiated. To be fair, those defending vegetarianism from traditional

moral theories would say that anyone who needs to eat milk, eggs, or meat should not be required to abstain. But Singer and Regan assume or argue that these people will be *exceptional cases*. That is, their bodily needs fall outside the usual or expected norm. Regan's (1983) animal rights position allows certain people to consume meat as exceptional cases (p. 333). He says that any humans having a strong welfare-interest in consuming meat or animal products would be *excused* from a duty to be vegetarians. People who live in an environment where vegetables and grains cannot be grown (such as the arctic) would be excused. Regan clearly thinks most persons do not or would not (ideally) fall into such a category, and he does not notice that his exceptions are granted along gender and age lines. If all human beings had a male physiology, then the argument that Regan and Singer make for ethical vegetarianism would be valid. But because humans have many different physiologies roughly identifiable by age groups and sex, that premise is false and their arguments are invalid. Women, children, and others who do not fit these norms are excused whenever they have different requirements. But they are excused because they are "vulnerable," i.e., *weaker*.

Here is the core of my objection: Who are these others that traditionalists like Regan and Singer think may be excused? They are the vast majority of the *world's* population. And, if women, infants and children, the elderly, and people who live almost everywhere else besides western societies are *routinely* excused for doing what would normally be considered wrong, in practice this relegates them to a *moral underclass* of beings who, because of their natures or cultures, are not capable of being fully moral. They are *physiologically* barred from "doing the right thing" because they are not "being the right thing." The structure of this ethical thinking degrades the reality and human worth of these groups of people who do not fit.

After considering the nutritional facts, Regan or Singer might answer that the vegetarian ideal is not a moral ideal for women, children, and others who would be exempt because of the burden of risk. It is simply an ideal for males, one among a plurality of ideals. There are several problems with this reply, however. First, women and children are being exempted or excused because of their vulnerability, that is to say, their supposed physical weakness. But this so-called weakness is weakness *only* in comparison with an arbitrarily established standard of strength, one peculiar ability of the male body. But men and women have a variety of different kinds of strengths and weaknesses. In this case the Regan-Singer standard favors males in a world where males have the most social and political power as well. Second, positing a plurality of ideals tied to physical differences implies a kind of essential male nature and an essential female nature that is divisive of the implementation of the Principle of Equality. Morality should focus on what one can will and choose rather than on aspects of the self that one cannot change.

My second general criticism of the Regan-Singer arguments is that they assume a social standard largely structured on wealth generated from unsustainable environmental, agricultural, and industrial practices. Women, children, and people who live in other cultures and environments should conform their ethical behavior as if they have the same kind of bodies as adult males living in wealthy countries. Making judgments about whether other people can reasonably choose to be vegetarians and excusing the others is quite unfair. From a white middle-class college professor's perspective, American or Western society may appear quite homogeneous. The education level is high, food is available in great variety, is plentiful and fortified; the unemployed have Food Stamps; supplements seem readily available. These are conditions of great wealth by world standards, and they make vegetarianism reasonably safe. But, setting aside conditions outside the United States, a significant number of Americans do not have access to adequate food or nutritional information, and they are defined by their economic class. For example, many inner city residents cannot buy vegetables—there is no supermarket nearby (Kozol 1988). Shall we simply excuse them then? But there really is something quite arrogant about excusing all of these people from attaining the ideal; it supposes the richer are better. They are not. They are just luckier.

Ethical vegetarians might respond to these criticisms in still another way. In industrialized societies supplements are readily available and they are effective. Women and children should use them to make their risk minimal (Varner 1994). Essentially, this is a "separate but equal" or "special rights" argument. Women and men have separate but "equal" needs. Thus, ethical vegetarianism would not denigrate the moral equality of women (or children) because their requirements are "separate but equally valid."

This counter argument is flawed for two reasons. First, even if risks for vegetarians were equalized, burdens would not be. Western adult male vegetarians have many fewer burdens to bear, while women and child vegetarians must work harder to be "equal" simply because of their age or sex. Adult males rarely suffer anemia; they do not lose iron through periodic menstruation; they do not carry fetuses in their bodies or nurse infants; their growth is completed and they almost always have larger skeletons than females and so have a much lower incidence of osteoporosis. Supplements are expensive, some are best prescribed by a physician to avoid overdose, they are usually not covered by insurance, and they may increase a vegetarian woman's personal and psychological worries (Herbert and Subak-Sharpe 1990; Ossell 1993).

Second, the arbitrary adult male norm remains. Even if it is not too risky for a middle-class infant, child, adolescent, pregnant, lactating, perimenopausal, post-menopausal female, or elderly person to be an ethical vegetarian, that judgment will surely be made from a biased perspective—one that assesses the risk from the standpoint of the supposed male norm. Women, children, and seniors are being told to fix, mend, or correct their imperfect bodies as necessary (by supplementation, fortified foods, or eating in special ways) to meet a vegetarian ideal that is much less burdensome for adult men. A moral demand that these groups use supplementation again negates the life and value of those who do not fit a norm based on the male body (cf. Tuana 1993).

Regan or Singer might also make a third sort of response to my criticisms: Many nutritionists believe that obligatory vegans—that is vegetarians by circumstance of not having meat or dairy available—in "developing" countries have a poor health status attributable to "environmental factors (such as lack of medical care, vaccination, education, and sanitation) rather than solely to diet" (Dwyer and Loew 1994, p. 88). That is, if we could improve those background conditions to a level similar to the United States, then supplemented vegan diets would constitute little risk in those places, too. We might conclude that the risks would then be equalized (although burdens would not be equalized) among the sexes and ages, at least in theory.

My response is that the fundamental problem of bias would still remain, but even if we set that problem aside, the program comes at a cost to humans and animals. Vegan and vegetarian diets are lower in risk in Western nations when individuals have access to education, medical care, and sufficient resources to buy proper foods and supplements. Most importantly, these diets pose less risk in our culture largely because much of our food is fortified. We tend to think of our food as "naturally" protecting us. And it does! A diet consisting of the worst junk food is unlikely to result in pellagra or beriberi in the United States because virtually all flours are vitamin B fortified. Vitamin D is added to milk and is perhaps the single most important factor in the reduction of the incidence of rickets in children and osteomalacia in women and adolescents (Sanders and Reddy 1994).

In many parts of the world, beriberi, pellagra, rickets, scurvy, kwashikor, megaloblastic anemia, and iron deficiency are still endemic (Scrimshaw 1990), although the incidence has declined this century and the severity of the affected is usually less marked. Our food system protects us against these diseases, but that protection depends on food preservation, transportation, fortification, variety, and plenty—a system that also includes some unsustainable agricultural and environmental practices inconsistent with environmental goals. The industrialized food system has alleviated human suffering on one hand and caused environmental damage on the other. Exporting safe vegan or vegetarian diets to the rest of the developing world would require exporting our food system with even more fortification of cereals and other foods, greater processing of foods such as egg substitutes, calcium-fortified soy products, and so forth. Fortification and food processing presuppose a complex industrialized food system, with research biochemistry, food processing plants, mines to produce supplements, quality control bureaucracies, food preservation techniques, refrigeration, shipping, and perhaps even chemical-dependent agriculture. A sophisticated research scientific and industrial complex with vitamin and mineral factories able to synthesize supplements without using animal products would be needed. For that, research biochemistry and chemistry labs are necessary, mines for extraction of raw materials, and a network of universities to train scientists, and so forth. All of these aspects of our food systems have environmental consequences, many or most of which are at odds with environmental goals. Environmental goals aim at reduction of some industrialized food production, but if one wishes to simultaneously encourage vegetarian diets, then a return to whole foods and unsupplemented or less supplemented diets may be necessary. Downscaling industrialized food production may mean that cereals and infant formulas may not be iron-fortified, milk may not have vitamin D added (if dairy is consumed), soy milk may not be calcium-fortified, and vitamin B-12 may be unavailable for vegans. Very likely, human suffering would increase. Such circumstances would place even greater burdens on women, children, and others unless diets are adjusted to personal physiology and consumption of animal flesh and animal products continues in moderation.

De-industrialization of agriculture and the scientific food production process suggests that at least some animal agriculture and fishing should be maintained to assure that infants, children, adolescents, the elderly, pregnant and lactating women have good sources of iron, zinc, and vitamin B-12 (meat/flesh of animals), calcium and B-12 (dairy), vitamin D (eggs and fatty fish). And as I have said, even an industrialized food system places discriminatory burdens on these groups, despite mitigation by supplementation. While we should, of course, encourage the worldwide availability of health care and good nutrition, the concomitant requirement of ethical vegetarianism may defeat environmental sustainability. The best course seems to be a middle ground such as semi-vegetarianism with moderate continued food fortification and preservation. A strict moral censure of meat eating will be hard-pressed to escape the exploitation of the earth, of nonindustrialized cultures, and of the animals it seeks to spare. It is more likely to preserve class distinctions and discrimination than to dissipate them. Nutritional education, medical care, and dietary supplements should, of course, be made available to those who want and need them. Agreeing to these facts and values does not, however, commit us to the ethical vegetarian ideal. It would, at most, commit us to improving conditions for all human and nonhuman animals depending on ecosystem impacts and cultural conditions.

Finally, *individuals* should not consider themselves responsible for being vegetarians or nonvegetarians per se. Moral decisions about what to eat should be made in social, political, and temporal contexts. In my view eating groups constitute contexts. For example, most people around the world eat as members of families where women are the primary food preparers for relatives of mixed ages and sexes. Preparing different meals for adult males due to ethical considerations would very likely burden women disproportionately. Therefore, eating in the context of such families should permit semi-vegetarian meals for all. For example, are you eating at home with your children? If so, eat semi-vegetarian. Are you living at home with an aging parent? Eat semi-vegetarian. On the other hand, if an adult, healthy male between the ages of 20 and 50 is out of town (not eating with young children), catching a dinner alone in a restaurant, he should eat vegetarian. If one were an adult woman in the same situation, things are less clear. Is she pregnant or could she become pregnant, nursing a child, at risk for anemia or osteoporosis, etc.? If so, then she may choose to eat semi-vegetarian or not, depending upon her own health circumstances and the availability of fortified food in her culture. If she is alone and does not have these burdens or risks, then in a culture such as ours she should eat vegetarian. The context of with whom, where, and when one is eating is the most important factor in a day-to-day decision about what it is right to eat.

◇

References

Acosta, Phyllis B. 1988. Availability of essential amino acids and nitrogen in vegan diets. *American Journal of Clinical Nutrition* 48: 868–74.

Allen, Lindsay H. 1986. Calcium and osteoporosis. *Nutrition Today* 21 (May/June): 6–10.

Bothwell, T. H., R. D. Baynes, B. J. MacFarlane, and A. P. MacPhail. 1989. Nutritional iron requirements and food iron absorption. *Journal of Internal Medicine* 226: 357–65.

Dallman, Peter R. 1989. Iron deficiency: Does it matter? *Journal of Internal Medicine* 226: 5 (November): 367–72.

Dawson-Hughes, Bess. 1991. Calcium supplementation and bone loss: A review of controlled clinical trials. *American Journal of Clinical Nutrition* 54 (supplement): 274S–80S.

Dwyer, Johanna T. 1988. Health aspects of vegetarian diets. *American Journal of Clinical Nutrition* 48: 712–38.

———. 1991. Nutritional consequences of vegetarianism. *Annual Reviews in Nutrition* 11: 61–9.

———. 1993a. Nutrition and the adolescent. In Robert M. Suskind and Leslie Lewinter-Suskind, *Textbook of Pediatric Nutrition*, 2nd ed., 257–64. New York: Raven Press.

———. 1993b. Vegetarianism in children. In Patricia M. Queen and Carol E. Lang, eds., *Handbook of Pediatric Nutrition*, 171–86. Gaithersburg, MD: Aspen Publishers.

———, and Franklin M. Loew. 1994. Nutritional risks of vegan diets to women and children: Are they preventable? *Journal of Agricultural and Environmental Ethics* 7:1 87–109.

Freeland-Graves, Jeanne. 1988. Mineral adequacy of vegetarian diets. *American Journal of Clinical Nutrition* 48: 859–62.

George, Kathryn Paxton. 2000. *Animal, Vegetable, or Woman? A Feminist Critique of Ethical Vegetarianism*. Ithaca, NY: SUNY Press, forthcoming.

Gussow, Joan Dye. 1994. Ecology and vegetarian considerations: Does environmental responsibility demand the elimination of livestock? *American Journal of Clinical Nutrition* 59 (supplement): 1110S–1116S.

Hercberg, Serge, and Pilar Galan. 1989. Biochemical effects of iron deprivation. *Acta Paediatrica Scandinavica* 361 (supplement): 63–70.

Herbert, Victor, and Genell J. Subak-Sharpe, eds. 1990. *The Mount Sinai School of Medicine Complete Book of Nutrition*. New York: St. Martin's Press.

Institute of Medicine. 1991. *Nutrition during Lactation*. Subcommittee on Nutrition during Lactation, Committee on Nutritional Status during Pregnancy and Lactation, Food and Nutrition Board, National Academy of Sciences. Washington, DC: National Academy Press.

———. 1990. *Nutrition during Pregnancy*. Subcommittee on Nutritional Status and Weight Gain during Pregnancy, Subcommittee on Dietary Intakes and Nutrient Supplements during Pregnancy, Committee on Nutritional Status during Pregnancy and Lactation, Food and Nutrition Board, National Academy of Sciences. Washington, DC: National Academy Press.

Johns Hopkins Medical Institutions. 1994a. Calcium: Maximizing its benefit. *The Johns Hopkins Medical Letter: Health after 50* 5: 12 (February): 4–5.

———. 1994b. Osteoporosis: No sex discrimination. *Johns Hopkins Medical Letter: Health after 50* 6: 1 (March): 3.

Kozol, Jonathan. 1988. *Rachel and Her Children: Homeless Families in America*. New York: Crown.

Lappé, Frances Moore. 1971. *Diet for a Small Planet*. New York: Ballantine.

———. 1982. *Diet for a Small Planet* 10th ed. New York: Ballantine.

Lewis, Stephen. 1994. An opinion on the global impact of meat consumption. *American Journal of Clinical Nutrition* 59 (supplement): 1099S–1102S.

Matkovic, Velimir K., K. Kostial, I. Simonovic, R. Buzina, A. Broderac, and B. E. C. Nordin. 1979. Bone status and fracture rates in two regions of Yugoslavia. *American Journal of Clinical Nutrition* 32: 540–49.

Munro, Hamish N., Paulo M. Suter, and Robert M. Russell. 1987. Nutritional requirements of the elderly. *Annual Review of Nutrition* 7: 23–49.

National Research Council. 1989. *Recommended Dietary Allowances* 10th ed. Subcommittee on the Tenth Edition of the RDAs, Food and Nutrition Board, Commission on Life Sciences. Washington, DC: National Academy Press.

Oski, Frank A. 1993. Current concepts: Iron deficiency in infancy and childhood. *New England Journal of Medicine* 329(3): 190–93.

Ossell, Joanne. 1993. *Food Analyst Plus: A Complete Nutritional Analysis Software.* CD-ROM. Hopkins, MN: Hopkins Technology.

Parks, Y. A., and B. A. Wharton. 1989. Iron deficiency and the brain. *Acta Paediatrica Scandinavica* 361 (supplement): 71–77.

Regan, Tom. 1983. *The Case for Animal Rights.* Berkeley: University of California Press.

Rodysill, Kirk J. 1987. Postmenopausal osteoporosis: Intervention and prophylaxis: A review. *Journal of Chronic Diseases* 40(8): 743–60.

Sanders, T. A. B., and Sheela Reddy. 1994. Vegetarian diets and children. *American Journal of Clinical Nutrition* 59 (supplement): S1176–S1181.

Scrimshaw, Nevin S. 1991. Iron deficiency. *Scientific American* (October): 46–52.

Singer, Peter. 1975. *Animal Liberation.* New York: Avon.

———. 1990. *Animal Liberation* 2nd ed. New York: Random House.

Truesdell, Delores D., E. N. Whitney, and P. B. Acosta. 1984. Nutrients in vegetarian foods. *Journal of the American Dietetic Association* 84: 28–35.

Tuana, Nancy. 1993. *The Less Nobel Sex: Scientific, Religious, and Philosophical Conceptions of Woman's Nature.* Bloomington: Indiana University Press.

Varner, Gary. 1994. In defense of the vegan ideal. *Journal of Agricultural and Environmental Ethics* 7(1): 29–40.

Walter, T., I. De Andraca, P. Chadud, and C. G. Perales. 1989. Iron deficiency anemia: Adverse effects on infant psychomotor development. *Pediatrics* 84: 7–17.

63. *The Ethics of Respect for Nature*

Paul W. Taylor

According to Paul W. Taylor, the ethics of respect for nature is made up of three elements: a belief system, an ultimate moral attitude, and a set of rules of duty and standards of character. The belief system is said to justify the adoption of the attitude of respect for nature , which in turn requires a set of rules and standards of character. Two central elements of the belief system are (1) that each individual organism is a teleological center of life, pursuing its own good in its own way, and (2) that whether we are concerned with standards of merit or with the concept of inherent worth, the claim that humans by their very nature are superior to other species is groundless.

Human-Centered and Life-Centered Systems of Environmental Ethics

In this paper I show how the taking of a certain ultimate moral attitude toward nature, which I call

"respect for nature," has a central place in the foundations of a life-centered system of environmental ethics. I hold that a set of moral norms (both standards of character and rules of conduct) governing human treatment of the natural world is a rationally grounded set if and only if, first, commitment to those norms is a practical entailment of adopting the attitude of respect for nature as an ultimate moral attitude, and second, the adopting of that attitude on the part of all rational agents can itself be justified. When the basic characteristics of the attitude of

From "The Ethics of Respect for Nature," *Environmental Ethics* (1986), pp. 197–218. Reprinted by permission of the publisher. Notes renumbered.

respect for nature are made clear, it will be seen that a life-centered system of environmental ethics need not be holistic or organicist in its conception of the kinds of entities that are deemed the appropriate objects of moral concern and consideration. Nor does such a system require that the concepts of ecological homeostasis, equilibrium, and integrity provide us with normative principles from which could be derived (with the addition of factual knowledge) our obligations with regard to natural ecosystems. The "balance of nature" is not itself a moral norm, however important may be the role it plays in our general outlook on the natural world that underlies the attitude of respect for nature. I argue that finally it is the good (well-being, welfare) of individual organisms, considered as entities having inherent worth, that determines our moral relations with the Earth's wild communities of life.

In designating the theory . . . as life centered, I intend to contrast it with all anthropocentric views. According to the latter, human actions that affect the natural environment and its nonhuman inhabitants are right (or wrong) by either of two criteria: They have consequences that are favorable (or unfavorable) to human well-being, or they are consistent (or inconsistent) with the system of norms that protect and implement human rights. From this human-centered standpoint it is to humans and only to humans that all duties are ultimately owed. We may have responsibilities *with regard to* the natural ecosystems and biotic communities of our planet, but these responsibilities are in every case based on the contingent fact that our treatment of those ecosystems and communities of life can further the realization of human values and/or human rights. We have no obligation to promote or protect the good of nonhuman living things, independently of this contingent fact.

A life-centered system of environmental ethics is opposed to human-centered ones precisely on this point. From the perspective of a life-centered theory, we have prima facie moral obligations that are owed to wild plants and animals themselves as members of the Earth's biotic community. We are morally bound (other things being equal) to protect or promote their good for *their* sake. Our duties to respect the integrity of natural ecosystems, to preserve endangered species, and to avoid environmental pollution stem from the fact that these are ways in which we can help make it possible for wild species populations to achieve and maintain a healthy existence in a natural state. Such obligations

are due those living things out of recognition of their inherent worth. They are entirely additional to and independent of the obligations we owe to our fellow humans. Although many of the actions that fulfill one set of obligations also fulfill the other, two different grounds of obligation are involved. Their well-being, as well as human well-being, is something to be realized *as an end in itself*.

If we were to accept a life-centered theory of environmental ethics, a profound reordering of our moral universe would take place. We would begin to look at the whole of the Earth's biosphere in a new light. Our duties with respect to the "world" of nature would be seen as making prima facie claims on us to be balanced against our duties with respect to the "world" of human civilization. We could no longer simply take the human point of view and consider the effects of our actions exclusively from the perspective of our own good.

The Good of a Being and the Concept of Inherent Worth

What would justify acceptance of a life-centered system of ethical principles? In order to answer this it is first necessary to make clear the fundamental moral attitude that underlies and makes intelligible the commitment to live by such a system. It is then necessary to examine the considerations that would justify any rational agent's adopting that moral attitude.

Two concepts are essential to the taking of a moral attitude of the sort in question. A being which does not "have" these concepts, that is, which is unable to grasp their meaning and conditions of applicability, cannot be said to have the attitude as part of its moral outlook. These concepts are, first, that of the good (well-being, welfare) of a living thing, and second, the idea of an entity possessing inherent worth. I examine each concept in turn.

(1) Every organism, species population, and community of life has a good of its own which moral agents can intentionally further or damage by their actions. To say that an entity has a good of its own is simply to say that, without reference to any *other* entity, it can be benefited or harmed. One can act in its overall interest or contrary to its overall interest, and environmental conditions can be good for it (advantageous to it) or bad for it (disadvantageous to it). What is good for an entity is what "does

it good" in the sense of enhancing or preserving its life and well-being. What is bad for an entity is something that is detrimental to its life and well-being.[1]

We can think of the good of an individual non-human organism as consisting in the full development of its biological powers. Its good is realized to the extent that it is strong and healthy. It possesses whatever capacities it needs to successfully cope with its environment and so preserve its existence throughout the various stages of the normal life cycle of its species. The good of a population or community of such individuals consists in the population or community maintaining itself from generation to generation as a coherent system of genetically and ecologically related organisms whose average good is at an optimum level for the given environment. (Here *average good* means that the degree of realization of the good of *individual organisms* in the population or community is, on average, greater than would be the case under any other ecologically functioning order of interrelations among those species populations in the given ecosystem.)

The idea of a being having a good of its own . . . does not entail that the being must have interests or take an interest in what affects its life for better or for worse. We can act in a being's interest or contrary to its interest without its being interested in what we are doing to it in the sense of wanting or not wanting us to do it. It may, indeed, be wholly unaware that favorable and unfavorable events are taking place in its life. [Trees], for example, have no knowledge or desires or feelings. Yet it is undoubtedly the case that trees can be harmed or benefited by our actions. We can crush their roots by running a bulldozer too close to them. We can see to it that they get adequate nourishment and moisture by fertilizing and watering the soil around them. Thus we can help or hinder them in the realization of their good. It is the good of trees themselves that is thereby affected. We can similarly act so as to further the good of an entire tree population of a certain species (say, all the redwood trees in a California valley) or the good of a whole community of plant life in a given wilderness area, just as we can do harm to such a population or community.

When construed in this way, the concept of a being's good is not coextensive with sentience or the capacity for feeling pain. William Frankena has argued for a general theory of environmental ethics in which the ground of a creature's being worthy of moral consideration is its sentience. I have offered some criticisms of this view elsewhere, but the full refutation of such a position . . . finally depends on the positive reasons for accepting a life-centered theory of the kind I am defending in this essay.[2]

It should be noted further that I am leaving open the question of whether machines—in particular, those which are not only goal-directed, but also self-regulating—can properly be said to have a good of their own.[3] Since I am concerned only with human treatment of wild organisms, species populations, and communities of life as they occur in our planet's natural ecosystems, it is to those entities alone that the concept "having a good of its own" will here be applied. I am not denying that other living things, whose genetic origin and environmental conditions have been produced, controlled, and manipulated by humans for human ends, do have a good of their own in the same sense as do wild plants and animals. It is not my purpose in this essay, however, to set out or defend the principles that should guide our conduct with regard to their good. It is only insofar as their production and use by humans have good or ill effects upon natural ecosystems and their wild inhabitants that the ethics of respect for nature comes into play.

(2) The second concept essential to the moral attitude of respect for nature is the idea of inherent worth. We take that attitude toward wild living things (individuals, species populations, or whole biotic communities) when and only when we regard them as entities possessing inherent worth. Indeed, it is only because they are conceived in this way that moral agents can think of themselves as having validly binding duties, obligations, and responsibilities that are *owed* to them as their *due*. I am not at this juncture arguing why they *should* be so regarded; I consider it at length below. But so regarding them is a presupposition of our taking the attitude of respect toward them and accordingly understanding ourselves as bearing certain moral relations to them. This can be shown as follows:

What does it mean to regard an entity that has a good of its own as possessing inherent worth? Two general principles are involved: the principle of moral consideration and the principle of intrinsic value.

According to the principle of moral consideration, wild living things are deserving of the concern and consideration of all moral agents simply in virtue of their being members of the Earth's community of life. From the moral point of view their good must be taken into account whenever it is affected for better or worse by the conduct of rational agents. This holds no matter what species the creature belongs to. The good of each is to be accorded some value and so acknowledged as having some weight in the deliberations of all rational agents. Of course, it may be necessary for such agents to act in ways contrary to the good of this or that particular organism or group of organisms in order to further the good of others, including the good of humans. But the principle of moral consideration prescribes that, with respect to each being an entity having its own good, every individual is deserving of consideration.

The principle of intrinsic value states that, regardless of what kind of entity it is in other respects, if it is a member of the Earth's community of life, the realization of its good is something *intrinsically* valuable. This means that its good is prima facie worthy of being preserved or promoted as an end in itself and for the sake of the entity whose good it is. Insofar as we regard any organism, species population, or life community as an entity with inherent worth, we believe that it must never be treated as if it were a mere object or thing whose entire value lies in being instrumental to the good of some other entity. The well-being of each is judged to have value in and of itself.

Combining these two principles, we can now define what it means for a living thing or group of living things to possess inherent worth. To say that it possesses inherent worth is to say that its good is deserving of the concern and consideration of all moral agents, and that the realization of its good has intrinsic value, to be pursued as an end in itself and for the sake of the entity whose good it is.

The duties owed to wild organisms, species populations, and communities of life in the Earth's natural ecosystems are grounded on their inherent worth. When rational, autonomous agents regard such entities as possessing inherent worth, they place intrinsic value on the realization of their good and so hold themselves responsible for performing actions that will have this effect and for refraining from actions having the contrary effect.

The Attitude of Respect for Nature

Why should moral agents regard wild living things in the natural world as possessing inherent worth?

To answer this question we must first take into account the fact that, when rational, autonomous agents subscribe to the principles of moral consideration and intrinsic value and so conceive of wild living things as having that kind of worth, such agents are *adopting a certain ultimate moral attitude toward the natural world.* This is the attitude I call "respect for nature." It parallels the attitude of respect for persons in human ethics. When we adopt the attitude of respect for persons as the proper (fitting, appropriate) attitude to take toward all persons as persons, we consider the fulfillment of the basic interests of each individual to have intrinsic value. We thereby make a moral commitment to live a certain kind of life in relation to other persons. We place ourselves under the direction of a system of standards and rules that we consider validly binding on all moral agents as such.[4]

Similarly, when we adopt the attitude of respect for nature as an ultimate moral attitude we make a commitment to live by certain normative principles. These principles constitute the rules of conduct and standards of character that are to govern our treatment of the natural world. This is, first, an *ultimate* commitment because it is not derived from any higher norm. The attitude of respect for nature is not grounded on some other, more general, or more fundamental attitude. It sets the total framework for our responsibilities toward the natural world. It can be justified, as I show below, but its justification cannot consist in referring to a more general attitude or a more basic normative principle.

Second, the commitment is a *moral* one because it is understood to be a disinterested matter of principle. It is this feature that distinguishes the attitude of respect for nature from the set of feelings and dispositions that comprise the love of nature. The latter stems from one's personal interest in and response to the natural world. Like the affectionate feelings we have toward certain individual human beings, one's love of nature is nothing more than the particular way one feels about the natural environment and its wild inhabitants. And just as our love for an individual person differs from our respect for all persons as such (whether we happen to love them or not), so love of nature differs from respect for nature. Respect for nature is an attitude we believe all moral agents ought to have simply as moral agents, regardless of whether or not they also love nature. Indeed, we have not truly taken the attitude of respect for nature ourselves unless we believe this. To put it in a Kantian way, to adopt the attitude of respect for nature is to take a stance that one wills it to be a universal law for all rational beings. It is to hold that stance categorically, as being validly applicable to every moral agent without exception, irrespective of whatever personal feelings toward nature such an agent might have or might lack.

Although the attitude of respect for nature is, in this sense, a disinterested and universalizable attitude, anyone who does adopt it has certain steady, more or less permanent dispositions. These dispositions, which are themselves to be considered disinterested and universalizable, comprise three interlocking sets: dispositions to seek certain ends, dispositions to carry on one's practical reasoning and deliberation in a certain way, and dispositions to have certain feelings. We may accordingly analyze the attitude of respect for nature into the following components. (a) The disposition to aim at, and to take steps to bring about, as final and disinterested ends, the promoting and protecting of the good of organisms, species populations, and life communities in natural ecosystems. (These ends are "final" in not being pursued as means to further ends. They are "disinterested" in being independent of the self-interest of the agent.) (b) The disposition to consider actions that tend to realize those ends to be prima facie obligatory *because* they have that tendency. (c) The disposition to experience positive and negative feelings toward states of affairs in the world *because* they are favorable or unfavorable to the good of organisms, species populations, and life communities in natural ecosystems.

The logical connection between the attitude of respect for nature and the duties of a life-centered system of environmental ethics can now be made clear. Insofar as one sincerely takes that attitude and so has the three sets of dispositions, one will at the same time be disposed to comply with certain rules of duty (such as nonmaleficence and noninterference) and with standards of character (such as fairness and benevolence) that determine the obligations and virtues of moral agents with regard to the Earth's wild living things. We can say that the actions one performs and the character traits one develops in fulfilling these moral requirements are the way one *expresses* or *embodies* the attitude in one's conduct and character. In his famous essay, "Justice as Fairness," John Rawls describes the rules of the duties of human morality (such as fidelity, gratitude, honesty, and justice) as "forms of conduct in which recognition of others as persons is manifested."[5] I hold that the rules of duty governing our treatment of the natural world and its inhabitants are forms of conduct in which the attitude of respect for nature is manifested.

The Justifiability of the Attitude of Respect for Nature

I return to the question posed earlier, which has not yet been answered: Why *should* moral agents regard wild living things as possessing inherent worth? I now argue that the only way we can answer this question is by showing how adopting the attitude of respect for nature is justified for all moral agents. Let us suppose that we were able to establish that there are good reasons for adopting the attitude, reasons which are intersubjectively valid for every rational agent. If there are such reasons, they would justify anyone's having the three sets of dispositions mentioned above as constituting what it means to have the attitude. Since these include the disposition to promote or protect the good of wild living things as a disinterested and ultimate end, as well as the disposition to perform actions for the reason that they tend to realize that end, we see that such dispositions commit a person to the principles of moral consideration and intrinsic value. To be disposed to further, as an end in itself, the good of any entity in nature just because it is that kind of entity, is to be disposed to give consideration to *every* such entity and to place intrinsic value on the realization of its good. Insofar as we subscribe to these two principles we regard living things as possessing inherent worth. Subscribing to the principles is what it *means* to so regard them. To justify the attitude of respect for nature, then, is to justify commitment to these principles and thereby to justify regarding wild creatures as possessing inherent worth.

We must keep in mind that inherent worth is not some mysterious sort of objective property belonging to living things that can be discovered by empirical observation or scientific investigation. To ascribe inherent worth to an entity is not to describe it by citing some feature discernible by sense perception or inferable by inductive reasoning. Nor is there a logically necessary connection between the concept of a being having a good of its own and the concept of inherent worth. We do not contradict ourselves by asserting that an entity that has a good of its own lacks inherent worth. In order to show that such an entity "has" inherent worth we must give good reasons for ascribing that kind of value to it (placing that kind of value upon it, conceiving of it to be valuable in that way). Although it is humans (persons, valuers) who must do the valuing, for the ethics of respect for nature, the value so ascribed is not a human value. That is to say, it is not a value derived from considerations regarding human well-being or human rights. It is a value that is ascribed to nonhuman animals and plants themselves, independently of their relationship to what humans judge to be conducive to their own good.

Whatever reasons, then, justify our taking the attitude of respect for nature as defined above are also reasons that show why we *should* regard the living things of the natural world as possessing inherent worth. We saw earlier that, since the attitude is an ultimate one, it cannot be derived from a more fundamental attitude nor shown to be a special case of a more general one. On what sort of grounds, then, can it be established?

The attitude we take toward living things in the natural world depends on the way we look at them, on what kind of beings we conceive them to be, and on how we understand the relations we bear to them. Underlying and supporting our attitude is a certain *belief system* that constitutes a particular world view or outlook on nature and the place of human life in it. To give good reasons for adopting the attitude of respect for nature, then, we must first articulate the belief system which underlies and supports that attitude. If it appears that the belief system is internally coherent and well ordered, and if, as far as we can now tell, it is consistent with all known scientific truths relevant to our knowledge of the object of the attitude (which in this case includes the whole set of the Earth's natural ecosystems and their communities of life), then there remains the task of indicating why scientifically informed and rational thinkers with a developed capacity of reality awareness can find it acceptable as a way of conceiving of the natural world and our place in it. To the extent we can do this we provide at least a reasonable argument for accepting the belief system and the ultimate moral attitude it supports.

I do not hold that such a belief system can be *proven* to be true, either inductively or deductively.

As we shall see, not all of its components can be stated in the form of empirically verifiable propositions. Nor is its internal order governed by purely logical relationships. But the system as a whole, I contend, constitutes a coherent, unified, and rationally acceptable "picture" or "map" of a total world. By examining each of its main components and seeing how they fit together, we obtain a scientifically informed and well-ordered conception of nature and the place of humans in it.

This belief system underlying the attitude of respect for nature I call (for want of a better name) "the biocentric outlook on nature." Since it is not wholly analyzable into empirically confirmable assertions, it should not be thought of as simply a compendium of the biological sciences concerning our planet's ecosystems. It might best be described as a philosophical world view, to distinguish it from a scientific theory or explanatory system. However, one of its major tenets is the great lesson we have learned from the science of ecology: the interdependence of all living things in an organically unified order whose balance and stability are necessary conditions for the realization of the good of its constituent biotic communities.

Before turning to an account of the main components of the biocentric outlook, it is convenient here to set forth the overall structure of my theory of environmental ethics as it has now emerged. The ethics of respect for nature is made up of three basic elements: a belief system, an ultimate moral attitude, and a set of rules of duty and standards of character. These elements are connected with each other in the following manner. The belief system provides a certain outlook on nature which supports and makes intelligible an autonomous agent's adopting, as an ultimate moral attitude, the attitude of respect for nature. It supports and makes intelligible the attitude in the sense that, when an autonomous agent understands its moral relations to the natural world in terms of this outlook, it recognizes the attitude of respect to be the only *suitable* or *fitting* attitude to take toward all wild forms of life in the Earth's biosphere. Living things are now viewed as *the appropriate objects of the attitude of respect* and are accordingly regarded as entities possessing inherent worth. One then places intrinsic value on the promotion and protection of their good. As a consequence of this, one makes a moral commitment to abide by a set of rules of duty and to fulfill (as far as one can by one's own efforts) certain standards of good character. Given one's adoption of the attitude of respect, one makes that moral commitment because one considers those rules and standards to be validly binding on all moral agents. They are seen as embodying forms of conduct and character structures in which the attitude of respect for nature is manifested.

This three-part complex which internally orders the ethics of respect for nature is symmetrical with a theory of human ethics grounded on respect for persons. Such a theory includes, first, a conception of oneself and others as persons, that is, as centers of autonomous choice. Second, there is the attitude of respect for persons as persons. When this is adopted as an ultimate moral attitude it involves the disposition to treat every person as having inherent worth or "human dignity." Every human being, just in virtue of her or his humanity, is understood to be worthy of moral consideration, and intrinsic value is placed on the autonomy and well-being of each. This is what Kant meant by conceiving of persons as ends in themselves. Third, there is an ethical system of duties which are acknowledged to be owed by everyone to everyone. These duties are forms of conduct in which public recognition is given to each individual's inherent worth as a person.

This structural framework for a theory of human ethics is meant to leave open the issue of consequentialism (utilitarianism) versus nonconsequentialism (deontology). That issue concerns the particular kind of system of rules defining the duties of moral agents toward persons. Similarly, I am leaving open [here] the question of what particular kind of system of rules defines our duties with respect to the natural world.

The Biocentric Outlook on Nature

The biocentric outlook on nature has four main components. (1) Humans are thought of as members of the Earth's community of life, holding that membership on the same terms as apply to all the nonhuman members. (2) The Earth's natural ecosystems as a totality are seen as a complex web of interconnected elements, with the sound biological functioning of each being dependent on the sound biological functioning of the others. (This is the component referred to above as the great lesson that the science of ecology has taught us.) (3) Each individual organism is conceived of as a teleological center of life, pursuing its own good in its own way. (4) Whether we are concerned with standards of merit or with the concept of inherent worth, the claim that humans by their very nature are superior to other species is a groundless claim and, in the light of elements (1), (2), and (3) above, must be rejected as nothing more than an irrational bias in our own favor. . . .

The Denial of Human Superiority

This fourth component of the biocentric outlook on nature is the single most important idea in establishing the justifiability of the attitude of respect for nature. Its central role is due to the special relationship it bears to the first three components of the outlook. This relationship will be brought out after the concept of human superiority is examined and analyzed.[6]

In what sense are humans alleged to be superior to other animals? We are different from them in having certain capacities that they lack. But why should these capacities be a mark of superiority? From what point of view are they judged to be signs of superiority and what sense of superiority is meant? After all, various nonhuman species have capacities that humans lack. There is the speed of a cheetah, the vision of an eagle, the agility of a monkey. Why should not these be taken as signs of *their* superiority over humans?

One answer . . . is that these capacities are not as *valuable* as the human capacities that are claimed to make us superior. Such uniquely human characteristics as rational thought, aesthetic creativity, autonomy and self-determination, and moral freedom, it might be held, have a higher value than the capacities found in other species. Yet we must ask: valuable to whom, and on what grounds?

The human characteristics mentioned are all valuable to humans. They are essential to the preservation and enrichment of our civilization and culture. Clearly it is from the human standpoint that they are being judged to be desirable and good. It is not difficult here to recognize a begging of the question. Humans are claiming human superiority from a strictly human point of view, that is, from a point of view in which the good of humans is taken as the standard of judgment. All we need to do is to look at the capacities of nonhuman animals (or plants, for that matter) from the standpoint of *their* good to find a contrary judgment of superiority. The speed of the cheetah, for example, is a sign of its superiority to humans when considered from the standpoint of the good of its species. If it were as slow a runner as a human, it would not be able to survive. And so for all the other abilities of nonhumans which further their good but which are lacking in humans. In each case the claim to human superiority would be rejected from a nonhuman standpoint.

When superiority assertions are interpreted in this way, they are based on judgments of *merit*. To judge the merits of a person or an organism one must apply grading or ranking standards to it. (As I show below, this distinguishes judgments of merit from judgments of inherent worth.) Empirical investigation then determines whether it has the "good-making properties" (merits) in virtue of which it fulfills the standards being applied. In the case of humans, merits may be either moral or nonmoral. We can judge one person to be better than (superior to) another from the moral point of view by applying certain standards to their character and conduct. Similarly, we can appeal to nonmoral criteria in judging someone to be an excellent piano player, a fair cook, a poor tennis player, and so on. Different social purposes and roles are implicit in the making of such judgments, providing the frame of reference for the choice of standards by which the nonmoral merits of people are determined. Ultimately such purposes and roles stem from a society's way of life as a whole. Now a society's way of life may be thought of as the cultural form given to the realization of human values. Whether moral or nonmoral standards are being applied, then, all judgments of people's merits finally depend on human values. All are made from an exclusively human standpoint.

The question that naturally arises at this juncture is: Why should standards that are based on human values be assumed to be the only valid criteria of merit and hence the only true signs of superiority? This question is especially pressing when humans are being judged superior in merit to nonhumans. [A] human being may be a better mathematician than a monkey, but the monkey may be a better tree climber than a human being. If we humans value mathematics more than tree climbing, that is because our conception of civilized life makes the development of mathematical ability more desirable than the ability to climb trees. But is it not unreasonable to judge non-

humans by the values of human civilization, rather than by values connected with what it is for a member of *that* species to live a good life? If all living things have a good of their own, it makes sense to judge the merits of nonhumans by standards derived from *their* good. To use only standards based on human values is already to commit oneself to holding that humans are superior to nonhumans, which is the point in question.

A further logical flaw arises in connection with the widely held conviction that humans are *morally* superior beings because they possess, while others lack, the capacities of a moral agent (free will, accountability, deliberation, judgment, practical reason). This view rests on a conceptual confusion. As far as moral standards are concerned, only beings that have the capacities of a moral agent can properly be judged to be *either* moral (morally good) or immoral (morally deficient). Moral standards are simply not applicable to beings that lack such capacities. Animals and plants cannot therefore be said to be morally inferior in merit to humans. Since the only beings that can have moral merits *or be deficient in such merits* are moral agents, it is conceptually incoherent to judge humans as superior to nonhumans on the ground that humans have moral capacities while nonhumans don't.

Up to this point I have been interpreting the claim that humans are superior to other living things as a grading or ranking judgment regarding their comparative merits. There is, however, another way of understanding the idea of human superiority. According to this interpretation, humans are superior to nonhumans not as regards their merits but as regards their inherent worth. Thus the claim of human superiority is to be understood as asserting that all humans, simply in virtue of their humanity, have *a greater inherent worth* than other living things.

The inherent worth of an entity does not depend on its merits.[7] To consider something as possessing inherent worth, we have seen, is to place intrinsic value on the realization of its good. This is done regardless of whatever particular merits it might have or might lack, as judged by a set of grading or ranking standards. In human affairs, we are all familiar with the principle that one's worth as a person does not vary with one's merits or lack of merits. The same can hold true of animals and plants. To regard such entities as possessing inherent worth entails disregarding their merits and deficiencies, whether they are being judged from a human standpoint or from the standpoint of their own species.

The idea of one entity having more merit than another, and so being superior to it in merit, makes perfectly good sense. Merit is a grading or ranking concept, and judgments of comparative merit are based on the different degrees to which things satisfy a given standard. But what can it mean to talk about one thing being superior to another in inherent worth? In order to get at what is being asserted in such a claim it is helpful first to look at the social origin of the concept of degrees of inherent worth.

The idea that humans can possess different degrees of inherent worth originated in societies having rigid class structures. Before the rise of modern democracies with their egalitarian outlook, one's membership in a hereditary class determined one's social status. People in the upper classes were looked up to, while those in the lower classes were looked down upon. In such a society one's social superiors and social inferiors were clearly defined and easily recognized.

Two aspects of these class-structured societies are especially relevant to the idea of degrees of inherent worth. First, those born into the upper classes were deemed more worthy of respect than those born into the lower orders. Second, the superior worth of upper class people had nothing to do with their merits nor did the inferior worth of those in the lower classes rest on their lack of merits. One's superiority or inferiority entirely derived from a social position one was born into. The modern concept of a meritocracy simply did not apply. One could not advance into a higher class by any sort of moral or nonmoral achievement. Similarly, an aristocrat held his title and all the privileges that went with it just because he was the eldest son of a titled nobleman. Unlike the bestowing of knighthood in contemporary Great Britain, one did not earn membership in the nobility by meritorious conduct.

We who live in modern democracies no longer believe in such hereditary social distinctions. Indeed, we would wholeheartedly condemn them on moral grounds as fundamentally unjust. We have come to think of class systems as a paradigm of social injustice, it being a central principle of the democratic way of life that among humans there are no superiors and no inferiors. Thus we have rejected the whole conceptual framework in which people are judged to have different degrees of inherent worth. That idea is incompatible with our notion of

human equality based on the doctrine that all humans, simply in virtue of their humanity, have the same inherent worth. (The belief in universal human rights is one form that this egalitarianism takes.)

The vast majority of people in modern democracies, however, do not maintain an egalitarian outlook when it comes to comparing human beings with other living things. Most people consider our own species to be superior to all other species and this superiority is understood to be a matter of inherent worth, not merit. There may exist thoroughly vicious and depraved humans who lack all merit. Yet because they are human they are thought to belong to a higher class of entities than any plant or animal. That one is born into the species *Homo sapiens* entities one to have lordship over those who are one's inferiors, namely, those born into other species. The parallel with hereditary social classes is very close. Implicit in this view is a hierarchical conception of nature according to which an organism has a position of superiority or inferiority in the Earth's community of life simply on the basis of its genetic background. The "lower" orders of life are looked down upon and it is considered perfectly proper that they serve the interests of those belonging to the highest order, namely humans. The intrinsic value we place on the well-being of our fellow humans reflects our recognition of their rightful position as our equals. No such intrinsic value is to be placed on the good of other animals, unless we choose to do so out of fondness or affection for them. But their well-being imposes no moral requirement on us. In this respect there is an absolute difference in moral status between ourselves and them.

This is the structure of concepts and beliefs that people are committed to insofar as they regard humans to be superior in inherent worth to all other species. I now wish to argue that this structure of concepts and beliefs is completely groundless. If we accept the first three components of the biocentric outlook and from that perspective look at the major philosophical traditions which have supported that structure, we find it to be at bottom nothing more than the expression of an irrational bias in our own favor. The philosophical traditions themselves rest on very questionable assumptions or else simply beg the question. I briefly consider three of the main traditions to substantiate the point. These are classical Greek humanism, Cartesian dualism, and the Judeo-Christian concept of the Great Chain of Being.

The inherent superiority of humans over other species was implicit in the Greek definition of man as a rational animal. Our animal nature was identified with "brute" desires that need the order and restraint of reason to rule them (just as reason is the special virtue of those who rule in the ideal state). Rationality was then seen to be the key to our superiority over animals. It enables us to live on a higher plane and endows us with a nobility and worth that other creatures lack. This familiar way of comparing humans with other species is deeply ingrained in our Western philosophical outlook. The point to consider here is that this view does not actually provide an argument *for* human superiority but rather makes explicit the framework of thought that is implicitly used by those who think of humans as inherently superior to nonhumans. The Greeks who held that humans, in virtue of their rational capacities, have a kind of worth greater than any nonrational being, never looked at rationality as but one capacity of living things among many others. But when we consider rationality from the standpoint of the first three elements of the ecological outlook, we see that its value lies in its importance for *human* life. Other creatures achieve their species-specific good without the need of rationality, although they often make use of capacities that humans lack. So the humanistic outlook of classical Greek thought does not give us a neutral (non–question-begging) ground on which to construct a scale of degrees of inherent worth possessed by different species of living things.

The second tradition, centering on the Cartesian dualism of soul and body, also fails to justify the claim to human superiority. That superiority is supposed to derive from the fact that we have souls while animals do not. Animals are mere automata and lack the divine element that makes us spiritual beings. I will not go into the now familiar criticisms of this two-substance view. I only add the point that, even if humans are composed of an immaterial, unextended soul and a material, extended body, this in itself is not a reason to deem them of greater worth than entities that are only bodies. Why is a soul substance a thing that adds value to its possessor? Unless theological reasoning is offered here (which many, including, myself, would find unacceptable on epistemological grounds), no logical connection is evident. An immaterial something that thinks is better than a material something that doesn't think only if thinking itself has value, either intrinsically or instrumentally. Now it is intrinsically valuable to humans alone, who value it as an end in itself, and it is instrumentally valuable to those who benefit from it, namely humans.

For animals that neither enjoy thinking for its own sake nor need it for living the kind of life for which they are best adapted, it has no value. Even if "thinking" is broadened to include all forms of consciousness, there are still many living things that can do without it and yet live what is, for their species, a good life. The anthropocentricity underlying the claim to human superiority runs throughout Cartesian dualism.

A third major source of the idea of human superiority is the Judeo-Christian concept of the Great Chain of Being. Humans are superior to animals and plants because their Creator has given them a higher place on the chain. It begins with God at the top, and then moves to the angels, who are lower than God but higher than humans, then to humans, positioned between the angels and the beasts (partaking of the nature of both), and then on down to the lower levels occupied by nonhuman animals, plants, and finally inanimate objects. Humans, being "made in God's image," are inherently superior to animals and plants by virtue of their being closer (in their essential nature) to God.

The metaphysical and epistemological difficulties with this conception of a hierarchy of entities are, in my mind, insuperable. Without entering into this matter here, I point out that if we are unwilling to accept the metaphysics of traditional Judaism and Christianity, we are again left without good reasons for holding to the claim of inherent human superiority.

The foregoing considerations (and others like them) leave us with but one ground for the assertion that a human being, regardless of merit, is a higher kind of entity than any other living thing. This is the mere fact of the genetic makeup of the species *Homo sapiens*. But this is surely irrational and arbitrary. Why should the arrangement of genes of a certain type be a mark of superior value, especially when this fact about an organism is taken by itself, unrelated to any other aspect of its life? We might just as well refer to any other genetic makeup as a ground of superior value. Clearly we are confronted here with a wholly arbitrary claim that can only be explained as an irrational bias in our own favor.

That the claim is nothing more than a deepseated prejudice is brought home to us when we look at our relation to other species in the light of the first three elements of the biocentric outlook. Those elements taken conjointly give us a certain overall view of the natural world and of the place of humans in it. When we take this view we come to understand other living things, their environmental conditions, and their ecological relationships in such a way as to awake in us a deep sense of our kinship with them as fellow members of the Earth's community of life. Humans and nonhumans alike are viewed together as integral parts of one unified whole in which all living things are functionally interrelated. Finally, when our awareness focuses on the individual lives of plants and animals, each is seen to share with us the characteristic of being a teleological center of life striving to realize its own good in its own unique way.

As this entire belief system becomes part of the conceptual framework by which we understand and perceive the world, we come to see ourselves as bearing a certain moral relation to nonhuman forms of life. Our ethical role in nature takes on a new significance. We begin to look at other species as we look at ourselves, seeing them as beings which have a good they are striving to realize just as we have a good we are striving to realize. We accordingly develop the disposition to view the world from the standpoint of their good as well as from the standpoint of our own good. Now if the groundlessness of the claim that humans are inherently superior to other species were brought clearly before our minds, we would not remain intellectually neutral toward that claim but would reject it as fundamentally at variance with our total world outlook. In the absence of any good reasons for holding it, the assertion of human superiority would then appear simply as the expression of an irrational and self-serving prejudice that favors one particular species over several million others.

Rejecting the notion of human superiority entails its positive counterpart: the doctrine of species impartiality. One who accepts that doctrine regards all living things as possessing inherent worth—the *same* inherent worth, since no one species has been shown to be either "higher" or "lower" than any other. Now we saw earlier that, insofar as one thinks of a living thing as possessing inherent worth, one considers it to be the appropriate object of the attitude of respect and believes that attitude to be the only fitting or suitable one for all moral agents to take toward it.

Here, then, is the key to understanding how the attitude of respect is rooted in the biocentric outlook on nature. The basic connection is made through the denial of human superiority. Once we reject the claim that humans are superior either in merit or in worth to other living things, we are ready to adopt the attitude of respect. The denial of human superiority is itself the result of taking the perspective on nature built into the first three elements of the biocentric outlook.

Now the first three elements of the biocentric outlook, it seems clear, would be found acceptable to any rational and scientifically informed thinker who is fully "open" to the reality of the lives of nonhuman organisms. Without denying our distinctively human characteristics, such a thinker can acknowledge the fundamental respects in which we are members of the Earth's community of life and in which the biological conditions necessary for the realization of our human values are inextricably linked with the whole system of nature. In addition, the conception of individual living things as teleological centers of life simply articulates how a scientifically informed thinker comes to understand them as the result of increasingly careful and detailed observations. Thus, the biocentric outlook recommends itself as an acceptable system of concepts and beliefs to anyone who is clear-minded, unbiased, and factually enlightened, and who has a developed capacity of reality awareness with regard to the lives of individual organisms. This is as good a reason for making the moral commitment involved in adopting the attitude of respect for nature as any theory of environmental ethics could possibly have.

Moral Rights and the Matter of Competing Claims

I have not asserted anywhere in the foregoing account that animals or plants have moral rights. This omission was deliberate. I do not think that the reference class of the concept, bearer of moral rights, should be extended to include nonhuman living things. My reasons for taking this position, however, go beyond the scope of this paper. I believe I have been able to accomplish many of the same ends which those who ascribe rights to animals or plants wish to accomplish. There is no reason, more-over, why plants and animals, including whole species populations and life communities, cannot be accorded *legal* rights under my theory. To grant them legal protection could be interpreted as giving them legal entitlement to be protected, and this would be a means by which a society that subscribed to the ethics of respect for nature could give public recognition to their inherent worth.

There remains the problem of competing claims, even when wild plants and animals are not thought of as bearers of moral rights. If we accept the bio-centric outlook and accordingly adopt the attitude of respect for nature as our ultimate moral attitude, how do we resolve conflicts that arise from our re-spect for persons in the domain of human ethics and our respect for nature in the domain of environ-mental ethics? This is a question that cannot ade-quately be dealt with here. My main purpose in this paper has been to try to establish a base point from which we can start working toward a solution to the problem. I have shown why we cannot just begin with an initial presumption in favor of the interests of our own species. It is after all within our power as moral beings to place limits on human population and technology with the deliberate intention of sharing the Earth's bounty with other species. That such sharing is an ideal difficult to realize even in an approximate way does not take away its claim to our deepest moral commitment.

Endnotes

1. The conceptual links between an entity *having* a good, something being good *for* it, and events doing good *to* it are examined by G. H. Von Wright in *The Varieties of Goodness* (New York: Humanities Press, 1963), chaps. 3 and 5.

2. See W. K. Frankena, "Ethics and the Environment," in K. E. Goodpaster and K. M. Sayre, eds., *Ethics and Problems of the 21st Century* (Notre Dame: University of Notre Dame Press, 1979), pp. 3–20. I critically examine Frankena's views in "Frankena on Environmental Ethics," *Monist* (1981): 237–243.

3. In the light of considerations set forth in Daniel Den-nett's *Brainstorms: Philosophical Essays on Mind and Psy-chology* (Montgomery, Vt.: Bradford Books, 1978), it is advisable to leave this question unsettled at this time. When machines are developed that function in the way our brains do, we may well come to deem them proper subjects of moral consideration.

4. I have analyzed the nature of this commitment of hu-man ethics in "On Taking the Moral Point of View," *Mid-west Studies in Philosophy*, vol. 3, *Studies in Ethical Theory* (1978), pp. 35–61.

5. John Rawls, "Justice as Fairness," *Philosophical Review* 67 (1958): 183.

6. My criticisms of the dogma of human superiority gain independent support from a carefully reasoned essay by R. and V. Routley showing the many logical weaknesses in arguments for human-centered theories of environ-mental ethics. R. and V. Routley, "Against the Inevitabil-ity of Human Chauvinism," in K. E. Goodpaster and K. M. Sayre, eds., *Ethics and Problems of the 21st Century* (Notre Dame: University of Notre Dame Press, 1979), pp. 36–59.

7. For this way of distinguishing between merit and in-herent worth, I am indebted to Gregory Vlastos, "Justice and Equality," in R. Brandt, ed., *Social Justice* (Englewood Cliffs, N.J.: Prentice-Hall, 1962), pp. 31–72.

64. Environmental Justice

James P. Sterba

James P. Sterba seeks to resolve a central debate in contemporary environmental ethics between those who defend anthropocentric ethics and those who defend nonanthropocentric ethics by showing that when the most morally defensible versions of each of these perspectives are laid out, they do not lead to different practical recommendations. In this way he hopes to show how it is possible for defenders of anthropocentric and nonanthropocentric environmental ethics, despite their theoretical disagreement concerning whether humans are superior to members of other species, to agree on a common set of principles for achieving environmental justice.

A central debate, if not the most central debate, in contemporary environmental ethics is between those who defend anthropocentric ethics and those who defend nonanthropocentric ethics. This debate pits deep ecologists like George Sessions against reform or shallow ecologists like John Passmore.[1] It divides biocentric egalitarians like Paul Taylor from social ecologists like Murray Bookchin.[2] In this paper I propose to go some way toward resolving this debate by showing that when the most morally defensible versions of each of these perspectives are laid out, they do not lead to different practical requirements. In this way I hope to show how it is possible for defenders of anthropocentric and nonanthropocentric environmental ethics, despite their theoretical disagreement concerning whether humans are superior to members of other species, to agree on a common set of principles for achieving environmental justice.

Nonanthropocentric Environmental Ethics

Consider first the nonanthropocentric perspective. In support of this perspective it can be argued that we have no non–question-begging grounds for re-

From "Violence against Nature," in *Social Philosophy Today,* ed. Creighton Peden and Yeager Hudson (1993). Reprinted by permission. Material added and notes renumbered in this edition.

garding the members of any living species as superior to the members of any other. It allows that the members of species differ in a myriad of ways, but argues that these differences do not provide grounds for thinking that the members of any one species are superior to the members of any other. In particular, it denies that the differences between species provides grounds for thinking that humans are superior to the members of other species. Of course, the nonanthropocentric perspective recognizes that humans have distinctive traits that members of other species lack, like rationality and moral agency. It just points out that the members of nonhuman species also have distinctive traits that humans lack, like the homing ability of pigeons, the speed of the cheetah, and the ruminative ability of sheep and cattle.

Nor will it do to claim that the distinctive traits humans have are more valuable than the distinctive traits members of other species possess because there is no non—question-begging standpoint from which to justify that claim. From a human standpoint, rationality and moral agency are more valuable than any distinctive trait found in nonhuman species, since, as humans, we would not be better off if we were to trade in those traits for the distinctive traits found in nonhuman species. Yet the same holds true of nonhuman species. Pigeons, cheetahs, sheep, and cattle would not be better off if they were to trade in their distinctive traits for the distinctive traits of other species.

Of course, the members of some species might be better off if they could retain the distinctive traits of their species while acquiring one or another of the distinctive traits possessed by some other species. For example, we humans might be better off if we could retain our distinctive traits while acquiring the ruminative ability of sheep and cattle. But many of the distinctive traits of species cannot be even imaginatively added to the members of other species without substantially altering the original species. For example, in order for the cheetah to acquire the distinctive traits possessed by humans, presumably it would have to be so transformed that its paws became something like hands to accommodate its humanlike mental capabilities, thereby losing its distinctive speed, and ceasing to be a cheetah. So possessing distinctively human traits would not be good for the cheetah. And with the possible exception of our nearest evolutionary relatives, the same holds true for the members of other species: They would not be better off having distinctively human traits. Only in fairy tales and in the world of Disney can the members of nonhuman species enjoy a full array of distinctively human traits. So there would appear to be no non–question-begging perspective from which to judge that distinctively human traits are more valuable than the distinctive traits possessed by other species. Judged from a non–question-begging perspective, we would seemingly have to regard the members of all species as equals.[3]

Nevertheless, regarding the members of all species as equals still allows for human preference in the same way that regarding all humans as equals still allows for self-preference.

First of all, human preference can be justified on grounds of defense. Thus, we have

A Principle of Human Defense: Actions that defend oneself and other human beings against harmful aggression are permissible even when they necessitate killing or harming animals or plants.[4]

This principle is strictly analogous to the principle of self-defense that applies in human ethics and permits actions in defense of oneself or other human beings against harmful human aggression.[5] In the case of human aggression, however, it will sometimes be possible to effectively defend oneself and other human beings by first suffering the aggression and then securing adequate compensation later. Since in the case of nonhuman aggression this is unlikely to obtain, more harmful preventive actions such as killing a rabid dog or swatting a mosquito will be justified.

Second, human preference can also be justified on grounds of preservation. Accordingly, we have

A Principle of Human Preservation: Actions that are necessary for meeting one's basic needs or the basic needs of other human beings are permissible even when they require aggressing against the basic needs of animals and plants.

Now needs, in general, if not satisfied, lead to lacks or deficiencies with respect to various standards. The basic needs of humans, if not satisfied, lead to lacks or deficiencies with respect to a standard of a decent life. The basic needs of animals and plants, if not satisfied, lead to lacks or deficiencies with respect to a standard of a healthy life.[6]

In human ethics, there is no principle that is strictly analogous to this Principle of Human Preservation. There is a principle of self-preservation in human ethics that permits actions that are necessary for meeting one's own basic needs or the basic needs of other people, even if this requires *failing to meet* (through an act of omission) the basic needs of still other people. For example, we can use our resources to feed ourselves and our family, even if this necessitates failing to meet the basic needs of people in Third World countries. But, in general, we don't have a principle that allows us to aggress against (through an act of commission) the basic needs of some people in order to meet our own basic needs or the basic needs of other people to whom we are committed or happen to care about. Actually, the closest we come to permitting aggressing against the basic needs of other people in order to meet our own basic needs or the basic needs of people to whom we are committed or happen to care about is our acceptance of the outcome of life and death struggles in lifeboat cases, where no one has an antecedent right to the available resources. For example, if you had to fight off others in order to secure the last place in a lifeboat for yourself or for a member of your family, we might say that you justifiably aggressed against the basic needs of those whom you fought to meet your own basic needs or the basic needs of the member of your family. . . .

Now the principle of human preservation does not permit aggressing against the basic needs of humans even if it is the only way to meet our own basic needs or the basic needs of other human beings. Rather, this principle is directed at a different range of cases in which we can meet our own basic needs and the basic needs of other humans simply by aggressing against the basic needs of nonhuman living beings. With respect to these cases, the principle of human preservation permits actions that are necessary for meeting one's own basic needs or the basic needs of other human beings even when they require aggressing against the basic needs of individual animals and plants or even of whole species or ecosystems.

Of course, we could envision an even more permissive principle of human preservation, one that would permit us to aggress against the basic needs of both humans and nonhumans to meet our own basic needs or the basic needs of other human beings. But while adopting such a principle by permitting cannibalism would clearly reduce the degree of predation of humans on other species, and so would be of some benefit to other species, it would clearly be counterproductive to meeting basic human needs. This is because implicit nonaggression pacts based on a reasonable expectation of a comparable degree of altruistic forbearance from fellow humans have been enormously beneficial and probably were necessary for the survival of the human species. So it is difficult to see how it would be in the interest of humans to forgo such benefits when they can easily meet their basic needs by simply aggressing against the basic needs of the members of nonhuman species. Of course, we may be required to meet our basic needs by aggressing against the basic needs of the members of some nonhuman species rather than others, for example, in order to protect endangered species. But while some such qualifications may be morally required, they will not undermine the general moral acceptability of the principle of human preservation even if we were to adopt a nonanthropocentric perspective.[7]

Nevertheless, preference for humans can go beyond bounds, and the bounds that are compatible with a nonanthropocentric perspective are expressed by the following:

> *A Principle of Disproportionality:* Actions that meet nonbasic or luxury needs of humans are prohibited when they aggress against the basic needs of animals and plants.

This principle is strictly analogous to a principle in human ethics that prohibits meeting some people's nonbasic or luxury needs by aggressing against the basic needs of other people.[8]

Without a doubt, the adoption of such a principle with respect to nonhuman nature would significantly change the way we live our lives. Such a principle is required, however, if there is to be any

substance to the claim that the members of all species are equal. We can no more consistently claim that the members of all species are equal and yet aggress against the basic needs of some animals or plants whenever this conflicts with our own nonbasic or luxury needs than we can consistently claim that all humans are equal and yet aggress against the basic needs of some other human beings whenever this conflicts with our nonbasic or luxury needs.[9] Consequently, if species equality is to mean anything, it must be that the basic needs of the members of nonhuman species trump the nonbasic needs of humans in these cases of conflict.

So while a nonanthropocentric perspective allows a degree of preference for the members of the human species, it also significantly limits that preference.

Nevertheless, animal liberationists may wonder about the further implications of this nonanthropocentric perspective for the treatment of animals. Obviously, a good deal of work has already been done on this topic. Initially, philosophers thought that humanism could be extended to induce animal liberation and eventually environmental concern.[10] Then Baird Callicott argued that animal liberation and environmental concern were as opposed to each other as they were to humanism.[11] The resulting conflict Callicott called "a triangular affair." Agreeing with Callicott, Mark Sagoff contended that any attempt to link animal liberation and environmental concern would lead to "a bad marriage and a quick divorce."[12] Yet more recently, such philosophers as Mary Ann Warren have tended to play down the opposition between animal liberation and environmental concern, and even Callicott now thinks he can bring the two back together again.[13] There are good reasons for thinking that such a reconciliation is possible.

Right off, it would be good for the environment if people generally, especially people in the First World, adopted a more vegetarian diet of the sort that animal liberationists are recommending. This is because a good portion of livestock production today consumes grains that could be more effectively used for direct human consumption. For example, 90 percent of the protein, 99 percent of the carbohydrate, and 100 percent of the fiber value of grain is wasted by cycling it through livestock, and currently 64 percent of the U.S. grain crop is fed to livestock.[14] So by adopting a more vegetarian diet, people generally, and especially people in the First World, could significantly reduce the amount of farmland that has to be kept in production to feed the human population. This, in turn, could have beneficial effects on the whole biotic community by eliminating the amount of soil erosion and environmental pollutants that result from raising livestock. For example, it has been estimated that 85 percent of U.S. topsoil lost from cropland, pasture, range land, and forest land is directly associated with raising livestock.[15]

But even though a more vegetarian diet seems in order, it is not clear that the interests of farm animals would be well served if all of us became complete vegetarians. Sagoff assumes that in a completely vegetarian human world people would continue to feed farm animals as before.[16] But it is not clear that we would have any obligation to do so. Moreover, in a completely vegetarian human world, we would probably need about half of the grain we now feed livestock to meet people's nutritional needs, particularly in Second and Third World countries. There simply would not be enough grain to go around. And then there would be the need to conserve cropland for future generations. So in a completely vegetarian human world, it seems likely that the population of farm animals would be decimated, relegating many of the farm animals that remain to zoos. On this account, it would seem to be more in the interest of farm animals generally that they be maintained under healthy conditions, and then killed relatively painlessly and eaten, rather than that they not be maintained at all. So a completely vegetarian human world would not seem to serve the interest of farm animals.

Nor, it seems, would it be in the interest of wild species who no longer have their natural predators not to be hunted by humans. Of course, where possible, it may be preferable to reintroduce natural predators. But this may not always be possible because of the proximity of farm animals and human populations, and then if action is not taken to control the populations of wild species, disaster could result for the species and their environments. For example, deer, rabbits, squirrels, quails, and ducks reproduce rapidly, and in the absence of predators can quickly exceed the carrying capacity of their environments. So it is in the interest of certain wild species and their environments that humans intervene periodically to maintain a balance. Of course, there will be many natural environments where it is in the interest of the environment and the wild animals that inhabit it to be simply left alone. But here,

too, animal liberation and environmental concern would not be in conflict. For these reasons, animal liberationists would have little reason to object to the proposed three principles for a nonanthropocentric environmental ethics.

Anthropocentric Environmental Ethics

But suppose we were to reject the central argument of the nonanthropocentric perspective and deny that the members of all species are equal. We might claim, for example, that humans are superior because, through culture, they "realize a greater range of values" than members of nonhuman species; or we might claim that humans are superior in virtue of their "unprecedented capacity to create ethical systems that impart worth to other life-forms."[17] Or we might offer some other grounds for human superiority.[18] Suppose, then, we adopt this anthropocentric perspective. What follows?

First of all, we will still need a principle of human defense. However, there is no need to adopt a different principle of human defense from the principle favored by a nonanthropocentric perspective. Whether we judge humans to be equal or superior to the members of other species, we will still want a principle that allows us to defend ourselves and other human beings from harmful aggression, even when this necessitates killing or harming animals or plants.

Second, we will also need a principle of human preservation. But here, too, there is no need to adopt a different principle from the principle of human preservation favored by a nonanthropocentric perspective. Whether we judge humans to be equal or superior to the members of other species, we will still want a principle that permits actions that are necessary for meeting our own basic needs or the basic needs of other human beings, even when this requires aggressing against the basic needs of animals and plants.

The crucial question is whether we will need a different principle of disproportionality. If we judged humans to be superior to the members of other species, will we still have grounds for preferring in this way the basic needs of animals and plants over the nonbasic or luxury needs of humans?

Here it is important to distinguish between two degrees of preference that we noted earlier. First, we could prefer the basic needs of animals and plants over the nonbasic or luxury needs of humans when to do otherwise would involve *aggressing against* (by an act of commission) the basic needs of animals and plants. Second, we could prefer the basic needs of animals and plants over the nonbasic or luxury needs of humans when to do otherwise would involve simply *failing to meet* (by an act of omission) the basic needs of animals and plants.

Now in human ethics when the basic needs of some people are in conflict with the nonbasic or luxury needs of others, the distinction between failing to meet and aggressing against basic needs seems to have little moral force. In such conflicting cases, both ways of not meeting basic needs are objectionable.[19]

But in environmental ethics, whether we adopt an anthropocentric or a nonanthropocentric perspective, we would seem to have grounds for morally distinguishing between the two cases, favoring the basic needs of animals and plants when to do otherwise would involve *aggressing against* those needs in order to meet our own nonbasic or luxury needs, but not when it would involve simply *failing to meet* those needs in order to meet our own nonbasic or luxury needs. This degree of preference for the members of the human species would be compatible with the equality of species insofar as members of nonhuman species also fail to meet the basic needs of members of the human species.

Even so, this theoretical distinction would have little practical force since most of the ways that we have of preferring our own nonbasic needs over the basic needs of animals and plants actually involve aggressing against their basic needs to meet our own nonbasic or luxury needs rather than simply failing to meet their basic needs.[20]

Yet even if most of the ways we have of preferring our own nonbasic or luxury needs do involve aggressing against the basic needs of animals and plants, wouldn't human superiority provide grounds for making such sacrifices? Or put another way, shouldn't human superiority have more theoretical and practical significance than I am allowing? Not, I claim, if we are looking for the most morally defensible position to take.

For consider: The claim that humans are superior to the members of other species, if it can be justified at all, is something like the claim that a person came in first in a race where others came in second, third, fourth, and so on. It would not imply that the members of other species are without intrinsic value. In fact, it would imply just the opposite—that the members of other species are also intrinsically valuable although not as intrinsically valuable as humans, just as the claim that a person came in first in a race implies that the persons who came in second, third, fourth, and so on are also meritorious, although not as meritorious as the person who came in first.

This line of argument draws further support once we consider that many animals and plants are superior to humans in one respect or another—e.g., the sense of smell of the wolf, the acuity of sight of the eagle, or the photosynthetic power of plants. So any claim of human superiority must [recognize] excellences in nonhuman species, even for excellences that are superior to their corresponding human excellences. In fact, it demands that recognition.

Moreover, if the claim of human superiority is to have any moral force, it must rest on non–question-begging grounds. Accordingly, we must be able to give a non–question-begging response to the nonanthropocentric argument for the equality of species. Yet for any such argument to be successful, it would have to recognize the intrinsic value of the members of nonhuman species. Even if it could be established that human beings have greater intrinsic value, we would still have to recognize that nonhuman nature has intrinsic value as well. So the relevant question is: How are we going to recognize the presumably lesser intrinsic value of nonhuman nature?

Now if human needs, even nonbasic or luxury ones, are always preferred to even the basic needs of the members of nonhuman species, we would not be giving any recognition to the intrinsic value of nonhuman nature. But what if we allowed the nonbasic or luxury needs of humans to trump the basic needs of nonhuman nature half the time, and half the time we allowed the basic needs of nonhuman nature to trump the nonbasic or luxury needs of humans. Would that be enough? Certainly, it would be a significant advance over what we are presently doing. For what we are presently doing is meeting the basic needs of nonhuman nature, at best, only when it serves our own needs or the needs of those we are committed to or happen to care about, and that does not recognize the intrinsic value of nonhuman nature at all. A fifty-fifty arrangement would be an advance indeed. But it would not be enough.

The reason it would not be enough is that the claim that humans are superior to nonhuman nature no more supports the practice of aggressing against the basic needs of nonhuman nature to satisfy our own nonbasic or luxury needs than the claim that a person came in first in a race would support the practice of aggressing against the basic needs of those who came in second, third, fourth and so on to satisfy the nonbasic or luxury needs of the person who came in first. A higher degree of merit does not translate into a right of domination, and to claim a right to aggress against the basic needs of nonhuman nature in order to meet our own nonbasic or luxury needs is clearly to claim a right of domination. All that we would be justified in doing, I have argued, is not meeting the basic needs of nonhuman nature when this conflicts with our nonbasic or luxury needs. What we are not justified in doing is aggressing against the basic needs of nonhuman nature when this conflicts with our nonbasic or luxury needs. But this is no more than is justified assuming the equality of species.

In sum, whether we endorse anthropocentric or nonanthropocentric environmental ethics, we should favor the very same principles: a Principle of Human Defense, a Principle of Human Preservation, and a Principle of Disproportionality as I have interpreted them. Taken together these three principles strike the right balance between concerns of human welfare and the welfare of nonhuman nature.

Of course, the practical implications of these three principles would include proposals for conserving existing resources, particularly nonrenewable ones, proposals for converting to renewable resources, proposals for redistributing resources to meet basic needs of both humans and nonhumans, and proposals for population control, all implemented principally by educational changes and by changes in the tax and incentive structures of our society. In the longer work from which this paper is drawn, I go on to discuss these practical proposals in more detail. In this paper, I have sought to provide the nonanthropocentric and anthropocentric grounding for such proposals in a common set of conflict resolution principles that are required for achieving environmental justice.

Endnotes

1. See John Passmore, *Man's Responsibility for Nature* (London: Charles Scribner's Sons, 1974) and George Sessions and Bill Devall, *Deep Ecology* (Salt Lake City: Glibb Smith, 1985).
2. See Paul Taylor, *Respect for Nature* (Princeton: Princeton University Press, 1987) and Murray Bookchin, *The Ecology of Freedom* (Montreal: Black Rose Books, 1991). It is also possible to view Passmore as pitted against Taylor and Bookchin as pitted against Sessions, but however one casts the debate, those who defend an anthropocentric ethics are still opposed to those who defend a nonanthropocentric ethics.
3. I am assuming here that either we treat humans as superior overall to other living things or we treat them as equal overall to other living things. Accordingly, if there is no self-evident or non–question-begging grounds for claiming that humans are superior overall to other living things, then, I claim that we should treat humans as equal overall to all other living things.
4. For the purposes of this [reading], I will follow the convention of excluding humans from the class denoted by "animals."
5. Of course, one might contend that no principle of human defense applies in human ethics because either "nonviolent pacifism" or "nonlethal pacifism" is the most morally defensible view. However, I have argued elsewhere that this is not the case, and that still other forms

of pacifism more compatible with just war theory are also more morally defensible than either of these forms of pacifism. See Selection 76.
6. For further discussion of basic needs, see *How to Make People Just* (Totowa, N.J.: Rowman & Littlefield, 1988), pp. 45–50.
7. It should be pointed out that the principle of human preservation does not support an unlimited right of procreation. In fact, the theory of justice presupposed here gives priority to the basic needs of existing beings over the basic needs of future possible beings, a supposition that should effectively limit (human) procreation.
8. This principle is clearly acceptable to welfare liberals and socialists, and it can even be shown to be acceptable to libertarians. See Selection 4.
9. Of course, libertarians have claimed that we can recognize that people have equal basic rights while failing to meet, but not aggressing against, the basic needs of other human beings. However, I have argued that this claim is mistaken. See Selection 4.
10. Peter Singer's *Animal Liberation* (New York: New York Review, 1975) inspired this view.
11. Baird Callicott, "Animal Liberation: A Triangular Affair," *Environmental Ethics* (1980), 311–328.
12. Mark Sagoff, "Animal Liberation and Environmental Ethics: Bad Marriage, Quick Divorce," *Osgood Hall Law Journal* (1984), 297–307.

13. Mary Ann Warren, "The Rights of the Nonhuman World," in *Environmental Philosophy*, edited by Robert Elliot and Arran Gare (London, 1983), 109–134, and Baird Callicott, *In Defense of the Land Ethic* (Albany: SUNY Press, 1989), chapter 3.

14. *Realities for the 90's* (Santa Cruz, 1991), p. 4.

15. Ibid., p. 5.

16. Mark Sagoff, op. cit., pp. 301–305.

17. Holmes Rolston, *Environmental Ethics* (Philadelphia: Temple University Press, 1988), pp. 66–68; Murray Bookchin., op. cit., p. xxxvi.

18. See the discussion of possible grounds of human superiority in Taylor, pp. 135–152 and in Byran Norton, *Why Preserve Natural Variety?* (Princeton: Princeton University Press, 1987), 135–150.

19. This is clearly true for welfare liberals and socialists, and it can even be shown to be true for libertarians because most failings to meet the basic needs of others really turn out to be acts of aggressing against the basic needs of others. See *How to Make People Just*, chapter 7.

20. The same holds true in human ethics where most of the ways that we have of preferring our own nonbasic needs over other humans actually involve aggressing against their needs to meet our own nonbasic or luxury needs rather than simply failing to meet them. See the previous note.

◇

65. *The Power and the Promise of Ecological Feminism*

KAREN J. WARREN

Karen Warren challenges mainstream environmental ethics to recognize that the domination of nature is rooted in the domination of women, or at least has failed to recognize that both these forms of domination are interconnected. According to Warren, women are identified with nature and the realm of the physical, while men are identified with the "human" and the realm of the mental. On the basis of this identification, Warren argues that women are judged inferior to men and their subordination to men is taken to be thereby justified. She calls the argumentative move from a claim of difference to a claim of superiority to a claim of domination the "logic of domination."

Ecological feminism (ecofeminism) has begun to receive a fair amount of attention lately as an alternative feminism and environmental ethic. Since Francoise d'Eaubonne introduced the term *ecofeminisme* in 1974 to bring attention to women's potential for bringing about an ecological revolution, the term has been used in a variety of ways. As I use the term here, ecological feminism is the position that there are important connections—historical, experiential, symbolic, and theoretical—between the domination of women and the domination of nature, an understanding of which is crucial to both feminism and environmental ethics. I argue that the promise and power of ecological feminism is that *it provides a distinctive framework both for reconceiving feminism and for developing an environmental ethic which takes seri-* ously connections between the domination of women and the domination of nature. I do so by discussing the nature of a feminist ethic and the ways in which ecofeminism provides a feminist and environmental ethic. I conclude that any feminist theory *and* any environmental ethic which fails to take seriously the twin and interconnected dominations of women and nature is at best incomplete and at worst simply inadequate.

◇

Feminism, Ecological Feminism, and Conceptual Frameworks

Whatever else it is, feminism is at least the movement to end sexist oppression. It involves the elimination of any and all factors that contribute to the continued and systematic domination or subordination

Reprinted from *Environmental Ethics* (1990) by permission of the author.

of women. While feminists disagree about the nature of and solutions to the subordination of women, all feminists agree that sexist oppression exists, is wrong, and must be abolished.

A "feminist issue" is any issue that contributes in some way to understanding the oppression of women. Equal rights, comparable pay for comparable work, and food production are feminist issues whenever an understanding of them contributes to an understanding of the continued exploitation or subjugation of women. Carrying water and searching for firewood are feminist issues wherever and whenever women's primary responsibility for these tasks contributes to their lack of full participation in decision making, income producing, or high status positions engaged in by men. What counts as a feminist issue, then, depends largely on context, particularly the historical and material conditions of women's lives.

Environmental degradation and exploitation are feminist issues because an understanding of them contributes to an understanding of the oppression of women. In India, for example, both deforestation and reforestation through the introduction of a monoculture species tree (e.g., eucalyptus) intended for commercial production are feminist issues because the loss of indigenous forests and multiple species of trees has drastically affected rural Indian women's ability to maintain a subsistence household. Indigenous forests provide a variety of trees for food, fuel, fodder, household utensils, dyes, medicines, and income-generating uses, while monoculture species forests do not. Although I do not argue for this claim here, a look at the global impact of environmental degradation on women's lives suggests important respects in which environmental degradation is a feminist issue.

Feminist philosophers claim that some of the most important feminist issues are *conceptual* ones: These issues concern how one conceptualizes such mainstay philosophical notions as reason and rationality, ethics, and what it is to be human. Ecofeminists extend this feminist philosophical concern to nature. They argue that, ultimately, some of the most important connections between the domination of women and the domination of nature are conceptual. To see this, consider the nature of conceptual frameworks.

A *conceptual framework* is a set of *basic* beliefs, values, attitudes, and assumptions which shape and reflect how one views oneself and one's world. It is a socially constructed lens through which we perceive ourselves and others. It is affected by such factors as gender, race, class, age, affectional orientation, nationality, and religious background.

Some conceptual frameworks are oppressive. An *oppressive conceptual framework* is one that explains, justifies, and maintains relationships of domination and subordination. When an oppressive conceptual framework is *patriarchal*, it explains, justifies, and maintains the subordination of women by men.

I have argued elsewhere that there are three significant features of oppressive conceptual frameworks: (1) value-hierarchical thinking, i.e., "up-down" thinking which places higher value, status, or prestige on what is "up" rather than on what is "down"; (2) value dualisms, i.e., disjunctive pairs in which the disjuncts are seen as oppositional (rather than as complementary) and exclusive (rather than as inclusive), and which place higher value (status, prestige) on one disjunct rather than the other (e.g., dualisms which give higher value or status to that which has historically been identified as "mind," "reason," and "male" than to that which has historically been identified as "body," "emotion," and "female"); and (3) logic of domination, i.e., a structure of argumentation which leads to a justification of subordination.

The third feature of oppressive conceptual frameworks is the most significant. A logic of domination is not *just* a logical structure. It also involves a substantive value system, since an ethical premise is needed to permit or sanction the "just" subordination of that which is subordinate. This justification typically is given on grounds of some alleged characteristic (e.g., rationality) which the dominant (e.g., men) have and the subordinate (e.g., women) lack.

Contrary to what many feminists and ecofeminists have said or suggested, there may be nothing *inherently* problematic about "hierarchical thinking" or even "value-hierarchical thinking" in contexts other than contexts of oppression. Hierarchical thinking is important in daily living for classifying data, comparing information, and organizing material. Taxonomies (e.g., plant taxonomies) and biological nomenclature seem to require *some* form of "hierarchical thinking." Even "value-hierarchical thinking" may be quite acceptable in certain contexts. (The same may be said of "value dualisms" in nonoppressive contexts.) For example, suppose it is true that what is unique about humans is our conscious capacity to radically reshape our social environments (or "societies"), as Murray Bookchin suggests. Then one could truthfully say that humans are better equipped to radically reshape their environments than are rocks or plants—a "value-hierarchical" way of speaking.

The problem is not simply *that* value-hierarchical thinking and value dualisms are used, but *the way* in which each has been used *in oppressive conceptual frameworks* to establish inferiority and to justify subordination.[1] It is the logic of domination, *coupled* with value-hierarchical thinking and value dualisms, which "justifies" subordination. What is explanatorily basic, then, about the nature of oppressive conceptual frameworks is the logic of domination.

For ecofeminism, that a logic of domination is explanatorily basic is important for at least three reasons. First, without a logic of domination, a description of similarities and differences would be just that: a description of similarities and differences. Consider the claim, "Humans are different from plants and rocks in that humans can (and plants and rocks cannot) consciously and radically reshape the communities in which they live; humans are similar to plants and rocks in that they are both members of an ecological community." Even if humans are "better" than plants and rocks with respect to the conscious ability of humans to radically transform communities, one does not *thereby* get any *morally* relevant distinction between humans and nonhumans, or an argument for the domination of plants and rocks by humans. To get *those* conclusions one needs to add at least two powerful assumptions, viz., (A2) and (A4) in argument A below:

A1 Humans do, and plants and rocks do not, have the capacity to consciously and radically change the community in which they live.

A2 Whatever has the capacity to consciously and radically change the community in which it lives is morally superior to whatever lacks this capacity.

A3 Thus, humans are morally superior to plants and rocks.

A4 For any X and Y, if X is morally superior to Y, then X is morally justified in subordinating Y.

A5 Thus, humans are morally justified in subordinating plants and rocks.

Without the two assumptions that *humans are morally superior* to (at least some) nonhumans, (A2), and that *superiority justifies subordination*, (A4), all one has is some difference between humans and some nonhumans. This is true *even if* that difference is given in terms of superiority. Thus, it is the logic of domination, (A4), which is the bottom line in ecofeminist discussions of oppression.

Second, ecofeminists argue that, at least in Western societies, the oppressive conceptual framework which sanctions the twin dominations of women and nature is a patriarchal one characterized by all three features of an oppressive conceptual framework. Many ecofeminists claim that, historically, within at least the dominant Western culture, a patriarchal conceptual framework has sanctioned the following argument B:

B1 Women are identified with nature and the realm of the physical; men are identified with the "human" and the realm of the mental.

B2 Whatever is identified with nature and the realm of the physical is inferior to ("below") whatever is identified with the "human" and the realm of the mental; or, conversely, the latter is superior to ("above") the former.

B3 Thus, women are inferior to ("below") men; or, conversely, men are superior to ("above") women.

B4 For any X and Y, if X is superior to Y, then X is justified in subordinating Y.

B5 Thus, men are justified in subordinating women.

If sound, argument B establishes *patriarchy*, i.e., the conclusion given at (B5) that the systematic domination of women by men is justified. But according to ecofeminists, (B5) is justified by just those three features of an oppressive conceptual framework identified earlier: value-hierarchical thinking, the assumption at (B2); value dualisms, the assumed dualism of the mental and the physical at (B1) and the assumed inferiority of the physical vis-á-vis the mental at (B2); and a logic of domination, the assumption at (B4), the same as the previous premise (A4). Hence, according to ecofeminists, insofar as an oppressive patriarchal conceptual framework has functioned historically (within at least dominant Western culture) to sanction the twin dominations of women and nature (argument B), both argument B and the patriarchal conceptual framework, from whence it comes, ought to be rejected.

Of course, the preceding does not identify which premises of B are false. What is the status of premises (B1) and (B2)? Most, if not all, feminists claim that (B1), and many ecofeminists claim that (B2), have been assumed or asserted within the dominant Western philosophical and intellectual tradition.[2] As such, these feminists assert, as a matter of historical fact, that the dominant Western philosophical tradition has assumed the truth of (B1) and (B2). Ecofeminists, however, either deny (B2) or do not affirm (B2). Furthermore, because some ecofeminists are anxious to deny any historical identification of women with nature, some ecofeminists deny (B1) when (B1) is used to support anything other than a strictly historical claim about what has been asserted or assumed to be true within patriarchal culture—e.g., when (B1) is used to assert that women properly are identified with the realm of nature and the physical.[3] Thus, from an ecofeminist perspective, (B1) and (B2) are properly viewed as problematic though historically sanctioned claims: They are problematic precisely because of the way they have functioned historically in a patriarchal conceptual framework and culture to sanction the dominations of women and nature.

What *all* ecofeminists agree about, then, is the way in which the *logic of domination* has functioned historically within patriarchy to sustain and justify the twin dominations of women and nature.[4] Since *all* feminists (and not just ecofeminists) oppose patriarchy, the conclusion given at (B5), all feminists (including ecofeminists) must oppose at least the logic of domination, premise (B4), on which argument B rests—whatever the truth-value status of (B1) and (B2) *outside* of a patriarchal context.

That *all* feminists must oppose the logic of domination shows the breadth and depth of the ecofeminist critique of B: It is a critique not only of the three assumptions on which this argument for the domination of women and nature rests, viz., the assumptions at (B1), (B2), and (B4); it is also a critique of patriarchal conceptual frameworks generally, i.e., of those oppressive conceptual frameworks which put men "up" and women "down," allege some way in which women are morally inferior to men, and use that alleged difference to justify the subordination of women by men. Therefore, ecofeminism is necessary to *any* feminist critique of patriarchy, and, hence, necessary to feminism (a point I discuss again later).

Third, ecofeminism clarifies why the logic of domination, and any conceptual framework which gives rise to it, must be abolished in order both to make possible a meaningful notion of difference which does not breed domination and to prevent feminism from becoming a "support" movement based primarily on shared experiences. In contemporary society, there is no one "woman's voice," no *woman* (or *human*) *simpliciter*: Every woman (or human) is a woman (or human) of some race, class, age, affectional orientation, marital status, regional or national background, and so forth. Because there are no "monolithic experiences" that all women share, feminism must be a "solidarity movement" based on shared beliefs and interests rather than a "unity in sameness" movement based on shared experiences and shared victimization. In the words of Maria Lugones, "Unity—not to be confused with solidarity—is understood as conceptually tied to domination."

Ecofeminists insist that the sort of logic of domination used to justify the domination of humans by gender, racial or ethnic, or class status is also used to justify the domination of nature. Because eliminating a logic of domination is part of a feminist critique—whether a critique of patriarchy, white supremacist culture, or imperialism—ecofeminists insist that *naturism* is properly viewed as an integral part of any feminist solidarity movement to end sexist oppression and the logic of domination which conceptually grounds it.

Ecofeminism Reconceives Feminism

The discussion so far has focused on some of the oppressive conceptual features of patriarchy. As I use the phrase, the "logic of traditional feminism" refers to the location of the conceptual roots of sexist oppression, at least in Western societies, in an oppressive patriarchal conceptual framework characterized by a logic of domination. Insofar as other systems of oppression (e.g., racism, classism, ageism, heterosexism) are also conceptually maintained by a logic of domination, appeal to the logic of traditional feminism ultimately locates the basic conceptual interconnections among *all* systems of oppression in the logic of domination. It thereby explains at a *conceptual* level why the eradication of sexist oppression requires the eradication of the other forms of oppression. It is by clarifying this conceptual connection between systems of oppression that a movement to end sexist oppression—traditionally the special turf of feminist theory and practice—leads to a reconceiving of feminism as *a movement to end all forms of oppression.*

Suppose one agrees that the logic of traditional feminism requires the expansion of feminism to include other social systems of domination (e.g., racism and classism). What warrants the inclusion of nature in these "social systems of domination"? Why must the logic of traditional feminism include the abolition of "naturism" (i.e., the domination or oppression of nonhuman nature) among the "isms" feminism must confront? The conceptual justification for expanding feminism to include ecofeminism is twofold. One basis has already been suggested: By showing that the conceptual connections between the dual dominations of women and nature are located in an oppressive and, at least in Western societies, patriarchal conceptual framework characterized by a logic of domination, ecofeminism explains how and why feminism, conceived as a movement to end sexist oppression, must be expanded and reconceived as also a movement to end naturism. This is made explicit by the following argument C:

C1 Feminism is a movement to end sexism.

C2 But sexism is conceptually linked with naturism (through an oppressive conceptual framework characterized by a logic of domination).

C3 Thus, feminism is (also) a movement to end naturism.

Because, ultimately, these connections between sexism and naturism are conceptual—embedded in an oppressive conceptual framework—the logic of traditional feminism lends to the embrace of ecological feminism.

The other justification for reconceiving feminism to include ecofeminism has to do with the concepts of gender and nature. Just as conceptions of gender are socially constructed, so are conceptions of nature. Of course, the claim that women and nature are social constructions does not require anyone to deny that there are actual humans and actual trees, rivers, and plants. It simply implies that *how* women and nature are conceived is a matter of historical and social reality. These conceptions vary cross-culturally and by historical time period. As a result, any discussion of the "oppression or domination of nature" involves reference to historically specific forms of social domination of nonhuman nature by humans, just as discussion of the "domination of women" refers to historically specific forms of social domination of women by men. Although I do not argue for it here, an ecofeminist defense of the historical connections between the dominations of women and of nature, claims (B1) and (B2) in argument B, involves showing that within patriarchy the feminization of nature and the naturalization of women have been crucial to the historically successful subordinations of both.

If ecofeminism promises to reconceive traditional feminism in ways which include naturism as a legitimate feminist issue, does ecofeminism also promise to reconceive environmental ethics in ways which are feminist? I think so. This is the subject of the remainder of the paper.

Climbing from Ecofeminism to Environmental Ethics

Many feminists and some environmental ethicists have begun to explore the use of first-person narrative as a way of raising philosophically germane issues in ethics often lost or underplayed in mainstream philosophical ethics. Why is this so? What is it about narrative which makes it a significant resource for theory and practice in feminism and environmental ethics? Even if appeal to first-person narrative is a helpful literary device for describing ineffable experience or a legitimate social science methodology for documenting personal and social history, how is first-person narrative a valuable vehicle of argumentation for ethical decision making and theory building? One fruitful way to begin answering these questions is to ask them of a particular first-person narrative.

Consider the following first-person narrative about rock climbing:

> For my very first rock climbing experience, I chose a somewhat private spot, away from other climbers and onlookers. After studying "the chimney," I focused all my energy on making it to the top. I climbed with intense determination, using whatever strength and skills I had to accomplish this challenging feat.

By midway I was exhausted and anxious. I couldn't see what to do next—where to put my hands or feet. Growing increasingly more weary as I clung somewhat desperately to the rock, I made a move. It didn't work. I fell. There I was, dangling midair above the rocky ground below, frightened but terribly relieved that the belay rope had held me. I knew I was safe. I took a look up at the climb that remained. I was determined to make it to the top. With renewed confidence and concentration, I finished the climb to the top.

On my second day of climbing, I rappelled down about 200 feet from the top of the Palisades at Lake Superior to just a few feet above the water level. I could see no one—not my belayer, not the other climbers, no one. I unhooked slowly from the rappel rope and took a deep cleansing breath. I looked all around me—really looked—and listened. I heard a cacophony of voices—birds, trickles of water on the rock before me, waves lapping against the rocks below. I closed my eyes and began to feel the rock with my hands—the cracks and crannies, the raised lichen and mosses, the almost imperceptible nubs that might provide a resting place for my fingers and toes when I began to climb. At that moment I was bathed in serenity. I began to talk to the rock in an almost inaudible, child-like way, as if the rock were my friend. I felt an overwhelming sense of gratitude for what it offered me—a chance to know myself and the rock differently, to appreciate unforeseen miracles like the tiny flowers growing in the even tinier cracks in the rock's surface, and to come to know a sense of *being in relationship* with the natural environment. It felt as if the rock and I were silent conversational partners in a longstanding friendship. I realized then that I had come to care about this cliff which was so different from me, so unmovable and invincible, independent and seemingly indifferent to my presence. I wanted to be with the rock as I climbed. Gone was the determination to conquer the rock, to forcefully impose my will on it; I wanted simply to work respectfully with the rock as I climbed. And as I climbed, that is what I felt. I felt myself *caring* for this rock and feeling thankful that climbing provided the opportunity for me to know it and myself in this new way.

There are at least four reasons why use of such a first-person narrative is important to feminism and environmental ethics. First, such a narrative gives voice to a felt sensitivity often lacking in traditional analytical ethical discourse, viz., a sensitivity to conceiving of oneself as fundamentally "in relationship with" others, including the nonhuman environment. It is a modality which *takes relationships themselves seriously*. It thereby stands in contrast to a strictly reductionist modality that takes relationships seriously only or primarily because of the nature of the *relators* or parties to those relationships (e.g., relators conceived as moral agents, right holders, interest carriers, or sentient beings). In the rock-climbing narrative above, it is the climber's relationship with the rock she climbs which takes on special significance—which is itself a locus of value—in addition to whatever moral status or moral considerability she or the rock or any other parties to the relationship may also have.[5]

Second, such a first-person narrative gives expression to a variety of ethical attitudes and behaviors often overlooked or underplayed in mainstream Western ethics, e.g., the difference in attitudes and behaviors toward a rock when one is "making it to the top" and when one thinks of oneself as "friends with" or "caring about" the rock one climbs.[6] These different attitudes and behaviors suggest an ethically germane contrast between two different types of relationship humans or climbers may have toward a rock: an imposed conqueror-type relationship, and an emergent caring-type relationship. This contrast grows out of, and is faithful to, felt, lived experience.

The difference between conquering and caring attitudes and behaviors in relation to the natural environment provides a third reason why the use of first-person narrative is important to feminism and environmental ethics: It provides a way of conceiving of ethics and ethical meaning as *emerging out of* particular situations moral agents find themselves in, rather than as being *imposed on* those situations (e.g., as a derivation or instantiation of some predetermined abstract principle or rule). This emergent feature of narrative centralizes the importance of *voice*. When a multiplicity of cross-cultural *voices* are centralized, narrative is able to give expression to a range of attitudes, values, beliefs, and behaviors which may be overlooked or silenced by imposed ethical meaning and theory. As a reflection of and on felt, lived experiences, the use of narrative in ethics provides a stance from which ethical discourse can be held accountable to the historical, material, and social realities in which moral subjects find themselves.

Lastly, and for our purposes perhaps most importantly, the use of narrative has argumentative significance. Jim Cheney calls attention to this feature of narrative when he claims, "To contextualize ethical deliberation is, in some sense, to provide a narrative or story, from which the solution to the ethical dilemma emerges as the fitting conclusion." Narrative has argumentative force by suggesting *what counts* as an appropriate conclusion to an ethical situation. One ethical conclusion suggested by the climbing narrative is that what counts as a proper ethical attitude toward mountains and rocks is an attitude of respect and care (whatever that turns out to be or involve), not one of domination and conquest.

In an essay entitled "In and Out of Harm's Way: Arrogance and Love," feminist philosopher Marilyn Frye distinguishes between "arrogant" and "loving" perception as one way of getting at this difference in the ethical attitudes of care and conquest. Frye writes:

> The loving eye is a contrary of the arrogant eye.
>
> The loving eye knows the independence of the other. It is the eye of a seer who knows that nature is indifferent. It is the eye of one who knows that to know the seen, one must consult something other than one's own will and interests and fears and imagination. One must look at the thing. One must look and listen and check and question.
>
> The loving eye is one that pays a certain sort of attention. This attention can require a discipline but not a self-denial. The discipline is one of self-knowledge, knowledge of the scope and boundary of the self. . . . In particular, it is a matter of being able to tell one's own interests from those of others and of knowing where one's self leaves off and another begins. . . .
>
> The loving eye does not make the object of perception into something edible, does not try to assimilate it, does not reduce it to the size of the seer's desire, fear, and imagination, and hence does not have to simplify. It knows the complexity of the other as something which will forever present new things to be known. The science of the loving eve would favor The Complexity Theory of Truth [in contrast to The Simplicity Theory of Truth] and presuppose The Endless Interestingness of the Universe.

According to Frye, the loving eye is not an invasive, coercive eve which annexes others to itself, but one which "knows the complexity of the other as something which will forever present new things to be known."

When one climbs a rock as a conqueror, one climbs with an arrogant eye. When one climbs with a loving eye, one constantly "must look and listen and check and question." One recognizes the rock as something very different, something perhaps totally indifferent to one's own presence, and finds in that difference joyous occasion for celebration. One knows "the boundary of the self," where the self— the "I," the climber—leaves off and the rock begins. There is no fusion of two into one, but a complement of two entities *acknowledged* as separate, different, independent, yet *in relationship;* they are in relationship *if only* because the loving eye is perceiving it, responding to it, noticing it, attending to it.

An ecofeminist perspective about both women and nature involves this shift in attitude from "arrogant perception" to "loving perception" of the nonhuman world. Arrogant perception of nonhumans by humans presupposes and maintains *sameness* in such a way that it expands the moral community to those beings who are thought to resemble (be like, similar to, or the same as) humans in some morally significant way. Any environmental movement or ethic based on arrogant perception builds a moral hierarchy of beings and assumes some common denominator of moral considerability in virtue of which like beings deserve similar treatment or moral consideration and unlike beings do not. Such environmental ethics are or generate a "unity in sameness." In contrast, "loving perception" presupposes and maintains *difference*—a distinction between the self and other, between human and at least some nonhumans—in such a way that perception of the other as other is an expression of love for one who/which is recognized at the outset as independent, dissimilar, different. As Maria Lugones says, in loving perception, "Love is seen not as fusion and erasure of difference but as incompatible with them." "Unity in sameness" alone is an *erasure of difference.*

"Loving perception" of the nonhuman natural world is an attempt to understand what it means *for humans* to care about the nonhuman world, a world *acknowledged* as being independent, different, perhaps even indifferent to humans. Humans are different from rocks in important ways, even if they are also both members of some ecological community. A moral community based on loving perception of oneself *in relationship with* a rock, or with the natural environment as a whole, is one which acknowledges and respects difference, whatever "sameness" also exists. The limits of loving perception are determined only by the limits of one's (e.g., a person's, a community's) ability to respond lovingly (or with appropriate care, trust, or friendship)—whether it is to other humans or to the nonhuman world and elements of it.

If what I have said so far is correct, then there are very different ways to climb a mountain, and *how* one climbs it and *how* one narrates the experience of climbing it matter ethically. If one climbs with "arrogant perception," with an attitude of "conquer and control," one keeps intact the very sorts of thinking that characterize a logic of domination and an oppressive conceptual framework. Since the oppressive conceptual framework which sanctions the domination of nature is a patriarchal one, one also thereby keeps intact, even if unwittingly, a patriarchal conceptual framework. Because the dismantling of patriarchal conceptual frameworks is a feminist issue, *how* one climbs a mountain and *how* one narrates—or tells the story—about the experience of climbing also are *feminist issues*. In this way, ecofeminism makes visible why, at a conceptual level, environmental ethics is a feminist issue.

---◇---

Conclusion

I have argued in this paper that ecofeminism provides a framework for a distinctively feminist and environmental ethic. Ecofeminism grows out of the felt and theorized about connections between the domination of women and the domination of nature. As a contextualist ethic, ecofeminism refocuses environmental ethics on what nature might mean, morally speaking, *for* humans, and on how the relational attitudes of humans to others—humans as well as nonhumans—sculpt both what it is to be human and the nature and ground of human responsibilities to the nonhuman environment. Part of what this refocusing does is to take seriously the voices of women and other oppressed persons in the construction of that ethic.

A Sioux elder once told me a story about his son. He sent his seven-year-old son to live with the child's grandparents on a Sioux reservation so that he could "learn the Indian ways." Part of what the grandparents taught him was how to hunt the four-leggeds of the forest. As I heard the story, the boy was taught, "to shoot your four-legged brother in his hind area, slowing it down but not killing it. Then, take the four-legged's head in your hands, and look into his eyes. The eyes are where all the suffering is. Look into your brother's eyes and feel his pain. Then, take your knife and cut the four-legged under his chin, here, on his neck, so that he dies quickly. And as you do, ask your brother, the four-legged, for forgiveness for what you do. Offer also a prayer of thanks to your four-legged kin for offering his body to you just now, when you need food to eat and clothing to wear. And promise the four-legged that you will put yourself back into the earth when you die, to become nourishment for the earth, and for the sister flowers, and for the brother deer. It is appropriate that you should offer this blessing for the four-legged and, in due time, reciprocate in turn with your body in this way, as the four-legged gives life to you for your survival." As I reflect on that story, I am struck by the power of the environ-mental ethic that grows out of and takes seriously narrative, context, and such values and relational attitudes as care, loving perception, and appropriate reciprocity, and doing what is appropriate in a given situation—however that notion of appropriateness eventually gets filled out. I am also struck by what one is able to see, once one begins to explore some of the historical and conceptual connections between the dominations of women and of nature. A *re-conceiving* and *re-visioning* of both feminism and environmental ethics, is, I think, the power and promise of ecofeminism.

---◇---

Endnotes

1. It may be that in contemporary Western society, which is so thoroughly structured by categories of gender, race, class, age, and affectional orientation, that there simply is no meaningful notion of "value-hierarchical thinking" which does not function in an oppressive context. For the purposes of this paper, I leave that question open.

2. Many feminists who argue for the historical point that claims (B1) and (B2) have been asserted or assumed to be

true within the dominant Western philosophical tradition do so by discussion of that tradition's conceptions of reason, rationality, and science. For a sampling of the sorts of claims made within that context, see "Reason, Rationality, and Gender," ed. Nancy Tuana and Karen J. Warren, a special issue of the American Philosophical Association's *Newsletter on Feminism and Philosophy* 88, no. 2 (March 1989): 17–71. Ecofeminists who claim that (B2) has been assumed to be true within the dominant Western philosophical tradition include: Gray, *Green Paradise Lost;* Griffin, *Woman and Nature: The Roaring Inside Her;* Merchant, *The Death of Nature;* Ruether, *New Woman/New Earth.* For a discussion of some of these ecofeminist historical accounts, see Plumwood, "Eco-feminism." While I agree that the historical connections between the domination of women and the domination of nature is a crucial one, I do not argue for that claim here.

3. Ecofeminists who deny (B1) when (B1) is offered as anything other than a true, descriptive, historical claim about patriarchal culture often do so on grounds that an objectionable sort of biological determinism, or at least harmful female sex-gender stereotypes, underlie (B1). For a discussion of this "split" among those ecofeminists ("nature feminists") who assert and those ecofeminists ("social feminists") who deny (B1) as anything other than a true historical claim about how women are described in patriarchal culture, see Griscom, "On Healing the Nature/History Split."

4. I make no attempt here to defend the historically sanctioned truth of these promises.

5. Suppose . . . that a necessary condition for the existence of a moral relationship is that at least one party to the relationship is a moral being (leaving open for our purposes what counts as a "moral being"). If this is so, then the Mona Lisa cannot properly be said to have or stand in a moral relationship with the wall on which she hangs, and a wolf cannot have or properly be said to have or stand in a moral relationship with a moose. Such a necessary-condition account leaves open the question whether *both* parties to the relationship must be moral beings. The point here is simply that however one resolves *that* question, recognition of the relationships themselves as a locus of value is a recognition of a source of value that is different from and not reducible to the values of the "moral beings" in those relationships.

6. It is interesting to note that the image of being friends with the Earth is one which cytogeneticist Barbara McClintock uses when she describes the importance of having "a feeling for the organism," "listening to the material [in this case the corn plant]," in one's work as a scientist. See Evelyn Fox Keller, "Women, Science, and Popular Mythology," in *Machina Ex Dea: Feminist Perspectives on Technology,* ed. Joan Rothschild (New York: Pergamon Press, 1983), and Evelyn Fox Keller, *A Feeling For the Organism: The Life and Work of Barbara McClintock* (San Francisco: W. H. Freeman, 1983).

66. *From the Animal Welfare Act*
CONGRESS OF THE UNITED STATES

Sec. 13. The Secretary shall promulgate standards to govern the humane handling, care, treatment, and transportation of animals by dealers, research facilities, and exhibitors. Such standards shall include minimum requirements with respect to handling, housing, feeding, watering, sanitation, ventilation, shelter from extremes of weather and temperatures, adequate veterinary care, including the appropriate use of anesthetic, analgesic, or tranquilizing drugs, when such use would be proper in the opinion of the attending veterinarian of such research facilities, and separation by species when the Secretary finds such separation necessary for the humane handling, care, or treatment of animals. In promulgating and enforcing standards established pursuant to this section, the Secretary is authorized and directed to consult experts, including outside consultants where indicated. Nothing in this Act shall be construed as authorizing the Secretary to promulgate rules, regulations, or orders with regard to design, outlines, guidelines, or performance of actual research or experimentation by a research facility as determined by such research facility: *Provided* That the Secretary shall require, at least annually, every research facility to show that professionally acceptable standards governing the care, treatment, and use of animals, including appropriate use of anesthetic, analgesic, and tranquilizing drugs, during experimentation are being followed by the research facility during actual research or experimentation.

67. Amendments to the Animal Welfare Act

Congress of the United States

The bill amends the Animal Welfare Act as follows:

1. Expands the definition of the term *research facility* to include each department, agency or instrumentality of the United States which uses animals for research or experimentation; defines the term *Federal agency* to mean any Executive agency from which a research facility has received or may receive Federal funds to support the conduct of research, experimentation, or testing involving the use of animals; and, makes it clear that the definition of "animal" is the same as that provided under the current Act.

2. Deletes the language stating that minimum requirements be applied to the standards promulgated by the Secretary of Agriculture to govern the humane handling, care, treatment, and transportation of animals by dealers, research facilities and exhibitors; adds exercise for dogs as a standard; and, allows the Secretary to make exceptions to the standards, but only when such exceptions are specified by the research protocol.

3. Requires the Secretary to promulgate standards for research facilities, including requirements for animal care, treatment, and practices in experimental procedures, to ensure that animal pain and distress are minimized. Requires each research facility, in its annual statement of compliance, to provide the Secretary of Agriculture with assurances that such standards are being followed. Also requires the research facility to provide annual training sessions for personnel involved with animal care and treatment.

4. Provides that any State (or political subdivision of that State) may promulgate standards in addition to those promulgated by the Secretary.

5. Mandates the establishment and makeup of an animal research committee of three or more members within each research facility. Makes it unlawful for any member of the committee to release trade secrets or confidential information. The committee must make inspections at least semiannually of all animal study areas of the research facility and file an inspection report which must remain on file at the research facility for three years. The committee must notify, in writing, the Animal and Plant Health Inspection Service (APHIS) of the Department of Agriculture and the funding Federal agency of any unacceptable conditions that are not corrected despite notification. Federal support for a particular project can be suspended or revoked for continued failure by a research facility to comply with the standards of animal care, treatment, or practices; such suspension or revocation may be appealed.

6. The inspection results of the animal research committee must be available to the Department of Agriculture's inspectors for review during inspection. These inspectors must forward to APHIS and the funding Federal agency any inspection records of the committee which include reports of any deficient conditions of animal care or treatment and any deviations of research practices from the originally approved proposal that adversely affect animal welfare.

7. Prohibits the Secretary from promulgating rules, regulations, or orders that may require a research facility to disclose trade secrets or commercial or financial information which is privileged or confidential.

8. Mandates the establishment of an information service on improved methods of animal experimentation at the National Agricultural Library. . . .

68. Tennessee Valley Authority v. Hill

SUPREME COURT OF THE UNITED STATES

The issue before the Supreme Court was whether the Endangered Species Act of 1973 prohibited the completion of a dam whose operation would destroy the habitat of the snail darter, an endangered species. The dam was virtually completed, and Congress had continued to appropriate large sums of money to the project even after congressional appropriations committees were apprised of the apparent impact on the snail darter's survival. Chief Justice Burger, delivering the opinion of the Court, held that the Endangered Species Act did prohibit the completion of the dam because the language of the act and the history that led to its passage required that its provisions be applied without exceptions.

We begin with the premise that operation of the Tellico Dam will either eradicate the known population of snail darters or destroy their critical habitat. Petitioner does not now seriously dispute this fact. . . . The Secretary of the Interior is vested with exclusive authority to determine whether a species such as the snail darter is "endangered" or "threatened" and to ascertain the factors which have led to such a precarious existence. . . . Congress has authorized— indeed commanded—the Secretary to "issue such regulations as he deems necessary and advisable to provide for the conservation of such species.". . . As we have seen, the Secretary promulgated regulations which declared the snail darter an endangered species whose critical habitat would be destroyed by creation of the Tellico Dam. Doubtless petitioner would prefer not to have these regulations on the books, but there is no suggestion that the Secretary exceeded his authority or abused his discretion in issuing the regulations. Indeed, no judicial review of the Secretary's determinations has ever been sought and hence the validity of his actions are not open to review in this Court. . . .

[It is] curious . . . that the survival of a relatively small number of three-inch fish among all the countless millions of species extant would require the permanent halting of a virtually completed dam for which Congress has expended more than $100 million. The paradox is not minimized by the fact that Congress continued to appropriate large sums of public money for the project, even after congressional Appropriations Committees were apprised of its apparent impact on the survival of the snail darter. We conclude, however, that the explicit provisions of the Endangered Species Act require precisely that result. . . .

. . . By 1973, when Congress held hearings on what would later become the Endangered Species Act of 1973, it was informed that species were still being lost at the rate of about one per year, . . . and "the pace of disappearance of species" appeared to be "accelerating." Moreover, Congress was also told that the primary cause of this trend was something other than the normal process of natural selection:

> [M]an and his technology has [*sic*] continued at an ever-increasing rate to disrupt the natural ecosystem. This has resulted in a dramatic rise in the number and severity of the threats faced by the world's wildlife. The truth in this is apparent when one realizes that half of the recorded extinctions of mammals over the past 2,000 years have occurred in the most recent 50-year period. . . .

That Congress did not view these developments lightly was stressed by one commentator:

> The dominant theme pervading all Congressional discussion of the proposed [Endangered Species Act of 1973] was the overriding need *to devote whatever effort and resources were necessary* to avoid further diminution of national and worldwide wildlife resources. Much of the testimony at the hearings and much debate was devoted to the biological problem of extinction. Senators

and Congressmen uniformly deplored the irreplaceable loss to aesthetics, science, ecology, and the national heritage should more species disappear. . . .

The legislative proceedings in 1973 are . . . replete with expressions of concern over the risk that might lie in the loss of *any* endangered species. Typifying these sentiments is the Report of the House Committee on Merchant Marine and Fisheries on . . . a bill that contained the essential features of the subsequently enacted Act of 1973; in explaining the need for the legislation, the Report stated:

> As we homogenize the habitats in which these plants and animals evolved, and as we increase the pressure for products that they are in a position to supply (usually unwillingly) we threaten their—and our own—genetic heritage.
>
> *The value of this genetic heritage is, quite literally, incalculable.*
>
> From the most narrow possible point of view, *it is in the best interest of mankind to minimize the losses of genetic variations.* The reason is simple: They are potential resources. They are keys to puzzles which we cannot solve, and may provide answers to questions which we have not yet learned to ask.
>
> To take a homely, but apt, example: One of the critical chemicals in the regulation of ovulations in humans was found in a common plant. Once discovered, and analyzed, humans could duplicate it synthetically, but had it never existed—or had it been driven out of existence before we knew its potentialities—we would never have tried to synthesize it in the first place.
>
> Who knows, or can say, what potential cures for cancer or other scourges, present or future, may lie locked up in the structures of plants which may yet be undiscovered, much less analyzed . . . Sheer self-interest impels us to be cautious. . . .

As the examples cited here demonstrate, Congress was concerned about the *unknown* uses that endangered species might have and about the *unforeseeable* place such creatures may have in the chain of life on this planet. . . .

. . . Representative Dingell provided an interpretation of what the Conference bill would require, making it clear that the mandatory provisions . . . were not casually or inadvertently included:

> . . . A recent article . . . illustrates the problem which might occur absent this new language in the bill. It appears that the whooping cranes of this country, perhaps the best known of our endangered species, are being threatened by Air Force bombing activities along the gulf coast of Texas. Under existing law, the Secretary of Defense has some discretion as to whether or not he will take the necessary action to see that this threat disappears. . . . [O]nce the bill is enacted, [the Secretary of Defense] *would be required to take the proper steps.* . . .
>
> Another example . . . [has] to do with the continental population of grizzly bears which may or may not be endangered, but which is surely threatened. . . . Once this bill is enacted, the appropriate Secretary, whether of Interior, Agriculture or whatever, *will have to take action* to see that this situation is not permitted to worsen, and that these bears are not driven to extinction. The purposes of the bill included the conservation of the species and of the ecosystems upon which they depend, and *every agency of government is committed* to see that those purposes are carried out. . . . [T]he agencies of Government can no longer plead that they can do nothing about it. *They can, and they must. The law is clear.* . . .

Notwithstanding Congress's expression of intent in 1973, we are urged to find that the continuing appropriations for Tellico Dam constitute an implied repeal of the 1973 Act, at least insofar as it applies to the Tellico Project. In support of this view, TVA points to the statements found in various House and Senate Appropriations Committees' Reports. . . . Since we are unwilling to assume that these latter Committee statements constituted advice to ignore the provisions of a duly enacted law, we assume that these Committees believed that the Act simply was not applicable in this situation. But even under this interpretation of the Committees' actions, we are unable to conclude that the Act has been in any respect amended or repealed. . . .

. . . The starting point in this analysis must be the legislative proceedings leading to the 1977 appropriations since the earlier funding of the dam occurred prior to the listing of the snail darter as an endangered species. In all successive years, TVA confidently reported to the Appropriations Committees that efforts to transplant the snail darter appeared to be successful; this surely gave those Committees some basis for the impression that there was no direct conflict between the Tellico Project and the Endangered Species Act. Indeed, the special appropriation for 1978 of $2 million for transplantation of endangered species supports the view that the Committees saw such relocation as the means whereby collision between Tellico and the Endangered Species Act could be avoided. . . .

. . . Here we are urged to view the Endangered Species Act "reasonably," and hence shape a remedy "that accords with some modicum of common sense and the public weal." . . . But is that our function? We have no expert knowledge on the subject of endangered species, much less do we have a mandate from the people to strike a balance of equities on the side of the Tellico Dam. Congress has spoken in the plainest of words, making it abundantly clear that the balance has been struck in favor of affording endangered species the highest of priorities, thereby adopting a policy which it described as "institutionalized caution."

Our individual appraisal of the wisdom or unwisdom of a particular course consciously selected by the Congress is to be put aside in the process of interpreting a statute. Once the meaning of an enactment is discerned and its constitutionality determined, the judicial process comes to an end. We do not sit as a committee of review, nor are we vested with the power of veto. The lines ascribed to Sir Thomas More by Robert Bolt are not without relevance here:

> The law, Roper, the law. I know what's legal, not what's right. And I'll stick to what's legal. . . . I'm *not* God. The currents and eddies of right and wrong, which you find such plain-sailing, I can't navigate, I'm no voyager. But in the thickets of the law, oh there I'm a forester. . . . What would you do? Cut a great road through the law to get after the Devil? . . . And when the last law was down, and the Devil turned round on you—where would you hide, Roper, the laws all being flat? This country's planted thick with laws from coast to coast—Man's laws, not God's—and if you cut them down . . . d'you really think you could stand upright in the winds that would blow then? . . . Yes, I'd give the Devil benefit of law, for my own safety's sake.
> —R. Bolt, *A Man for All Seasons*

We agree with the Court of Appeals that . . . the commitment to the separation of powers is too fundamental for us to pre-empt congressional action by judicially decreeing what accords with "common sense and the public weal." Our Constitution vests such responsibilities in the political branches.

Suggestions for Further Reading

Anthologies

Armstrong, Susan, and Richard Botzler. *Environmental Ethics*. 2nd ed. New York: McGraw Hill, 1998.

Regan, Tom, and Peter Singer (eds.). *Animal Rights and Human Obligation*. Englewood Cliffs, N.J.: Prentice-Hall, 1976.

Sterba, James P. *Earth Ethics*. 2nd ed. Upper Saddle River, NJ: Prentice-Hall, 2000.

Alternative Views

Attfield, Robin. *Environmental Philosophy*. Aldershot: Avebury, 1994.

Carruthers, Peter. *The Animals Issue*. Cambridge: Cambridge University Press, 1992.

DesJardins, Joseph. *Environmental Ethics*. 2nd ed. Belmont: Wadsworth Publishing Co., 1997.

Dombrowski, Daniel A. *The Philosophy of Vegetarianism*. Amherst, MA: University of Massachusetts Press, 1984.

Frey, R. G. *Rights, Killing and Suffering*. Oxford, England: Basil Blackwell, 1983.

Hargrove, Eugene. *The Foundations of Environmental Ethics*. Englewood Cliffs, NJ: Prentice-Hall, 1988.

Marrietta, Don. *For People and the Planet*. Philadelphia: Temple University Press, 1995.

Plumwood, Val. *Feminism and the Mastery of Nature.* London: Routledge, 1993.

Rachels, James. *Created from Animals.* Oxford: Oxford University Press, 1990.

Regan, Tom. *The Case for Animal Rights.* Berkeley: University of California Press, 1984.

Singer, Peter. *Animal Liberation* (rev. ed.). New York: New York Review, 1990.

Stone, Christopher D. *Earth and Other Ethics.* New York: Harper & Row, 1987.

Taylor, Paul W. *Respect for Nature.* Princeton: Princeton University Press, 1986.

Practical Applications

Akers, Keith. *A Vegetarian Sourcebook.* New York: G. P. Putnam and Sons, 1983.

Boas, Max, and Steve Chain. *Big Mac: The Unauthorized Story of McDonald's.* New York: New American Library, 1976.

Gore, Al. *Earth in the Balance.* New York: Houghton Mifflin, 1992.

Singer, Peter. *Ethics into Actions* (Lanham, MD: Rowman & Littlefield, 1998).

Swanson, Wayne, and George Schultz. *Prime Rip.* Englewood Cliffs, NJ: Prentice-Hall, 1982.

Section XII

Punishment and Responsibility

Introduction

Basic Concepts

The problem of punishment and responsibility is the problem of who should be punished and of what their punishment should consist. It is a problem of punishment *and* responsibility because determining who should be punished and what their punishment should consist of involves an assessment of responsibility. However, before discussing alternative justifications for assigning punishment, it is important to first clarify the concepts of punishment and responsibility.

Let us begin with the concept of punishment. Consider the following definition:

> **a** Punishment is hardship inflicted on an offender by someone entitled to do so.

This definition certainly seems adequate for many standard cases of punishment. For example, suppose you pursue and capture a young man who has just robbed a drugstore. The police then arrive and arrest the fellow. He is tried, convicted, and sentenced to two years in prison. Surely it would seem that a sentence of two years in prison in this case would constitute punishment, and obviously the sentence meets the conditions of (a).

But suppose we vary the example a bit. Suppose that, as before, you pursue the robber, but this time he gets away and in the process drops the money he took from the drugstore which you then retrieve. Suppose further that two eyewitnesses identify you as the robber, and you are arrested by the police, tried, and sentenced to two years in prison. Surely we would like to say that in this example it is you who is being punished, albeit unjustly; however, according to (a), this is not the case. For according to this definition, punishment can only be inflicted on offenders, and you are not an offender. But this simply shows that (a) is too narrow a definition of punishment. There clearly are cases, like our modified example, in which we can truly say that nonoffenders, that is, innocent people, are being punished. Accordingly, an acceptable definition of punishment should allow for such cases.

Let us consider, then, the following definition of punishment, which does allow for the possibility that nonoffenders can be punished:

> **b** Punishment is hardship inflicted on a person by someone entitled to do so.

Although (b) clearly represents an advance over (a) in that it allows for the possibility that innocent people can be punished, serious difficulties remain. For according to (b), paying taxes is punishment, as is civil commitment of mentally ill persons who have not committed any offense. And even though we may have good reasons for opposing taxation and even good reasons for opposing civil commitment, it is usually not because we regard such impositions as punishments. Clearly, then, a definition of punishment that includes paying taxes and civil commitment as punishments is simply too broad; what is needed is a definition that is narrower than (b) but broader than (a).

Consider the following possibility:

    c Punishment is hardship inflicted on a person who is found guilty of an offense by someone entitled to do so.

This definition, like (b), allows that innocent people can be punished, because it is possible that a person can be found guilty by some procedure or other without really being guilty. Yet (c), unlike (b), does not allow that just any hardship imposed by someone entitled to do so is punishment. Rather, only a hardship imposed *for an offense* can be a punishment.

But is this definition adequate? It would seem not. According to (c), paying a $5 parking ticket or suffering a 15-yard penalty in a football game are both punishments. Yet in both cases the hardship imposed lacks the moral condemnation and denunciation that is characteristic of punishment. This suggests the following definition:

    d Punishment is hardship involving moral condemnation and denunciation inflicted on a person who is found guilty of an offense by someone entitled to do so.

Examples like the $5 parking ticket and the 15-yard penalty indicate that we need to distinguish between punishments proper, which satisfy the conditions of (d), and mere penalties, which only satisfy the conditions of (c).

When we impose mere penalties, we are claiming that a person has done something wrong, perhaps even something morally wrong, but, because of the insignificant nature of the offense, we don't attempt to determine whether the person is morally blameworthy for so acting. Because we do not make this determination, we do not go on to morally condemn and denounce those we penalize. By contrast, when we impose punishments proper, we do make such a determination and, as a consequence, we do condemn and denounce those we penalize.

Turning to the concept of responsibility, we find that this concept is employed in a variety of different but related ways. For example, in everyday usage, we say that people are responsible for their actions if they could have acted otherwise than they did. In making this claim, we usually assume that people could have acted otherwise than they did in two respects. First, we assume that they could have acted otherwise if they had the ability to do so; for example, as presumably most varsity athletes have even when they play badly. Second, we assume that people could have acted otherwise if they had the opportunity to do so; for example, as you or I might have, even if we lacked the relevant ability, when, by chance, we were substituted in some varsity game and performed miserably. Thus, we can say that people are responsible for their actions if they had the ability and opportunity to act otherwise than they did.

Lawyers, however, usually approach the concept of responsibility differently. They are typically concerned with determining whether people have *mens rea*, which translated means "a guilty mind." When people are said to have *mens rea*, they are held responsible for their actions.

Mens rea is said to involve three conditions:

1. Knowledge of circumstances
2. Foresight of consequences
3. Voluntariness

The first condition of *mens rea* is said to be absent when, for example, you didn't know the gun was loaded, or you didn't know the person you shot breaking into your home was a plainclothes police officer operating on a false lead. In such a case, lawyers would say you lacked *mens rea* because you lacked the knowledge of the relevant circumstances. The second condition of *mens rea* is said to be absent when, for example, you had no reason to suspect the person you shot would be wandering behind your target in a fenced-off range. In such a case, lawyers would say you lacked *mens rea* because you lacked foresight of the relevant consequences. The third condition of *mens rea* is said to be absent when, for example, you are having an epileptic fit or being attacked by a swarm of bees. This third condition is the least understood of the three conditions of *mens rea.*

But actually this weakness of the lawyer's *mens rea* notion of responsibility with respect to its third condition seems to be the strength of the everyday notion. This is because the everyday notion of responsibility is an unpacking of what it is for an action to be voluntary. Consequently, if we put the two notions together, we arrive at the following more adequate analysis.

People are responsible for their action if they have:

1. Knowledge of circumstances
2. Foresight of consequences
3. The ability and opportunity to act otherwise than they did

Armed with a clearer understanding of the notions of punishment and responsibility, we should be in a better position to examine alternative justifications for assigning punishment in a society.

Forward-Looking and Backward-Looking Views

There are basically two kinds of justification for punishment: forward-looking and backward-looking. Forward-looking justifications maintain that punishment is justified because of its relationship to what *will occur.* Backward-looking justifications maintain that punishment is justified because of its relationship to what *has occurred.* An example of a forward-looking justification would be the claim that punishment is justified because it deters or reforms persons from crime. An example of a backward-looking justification would be the claim that punishment is justified because it fits or is proportionate to a crime or is applied to a person who is responsible for a crime. Those who adopt forward-looking justifications for punishment view punishment from the point of view of a social engineer seeking to produce certain good consequences in society. By contrast, those who adopt backward-looking justifications view punishment from the point of view of a stern balancer seeking to achieve a moral balance between punishment and the crime.

Karl Menninger provides us with a forceful example of a forward-looking justification for punishment—one that is directed at the reform of the offender (Selection 69). Menninger criticizes the existing criminal justice system as ineffective at preventing crime, grounded as it is on a theory of human motivation that fails to recognize the similarities between the motives of offenders and nonoffenders. In its place, Menninger advocates a therapeutic treatment program that would detain offenders, and possibly potential offenders, until they are reformed. Thus, Menninger would replace vengeful punishment—which he regards as itself a crime—with humanitarian reform.

One prerequisite for the justification of Menninger's system of humanitarian reform that is not generally recognized is that the opportunities open to offenders for leading a good life must be reasonably adequate, or at least arguably just and fair. If this is not the case, there would be little justification for asking criminal offenders to live their lives within the bounds of the legal system. Nor for that matter could we expect any attempt at implementing a system of reform like Menninger's to be generally effective in a society characterized by basic social and economic injustices. In such a society, criminal offenders who perceive these injustices will have a strong moral reason to resist any attempt to turn them into law-abiding citizens.

Richard B. Brandt (Selection 70), however, argues that a system of punishment similar to the actual systems found in the United States and Great Britain can be justified on utilitarian or forward-looking grounds. Such a system would be justified, Brandt claims, because it would secure the good consequences of both reform and deterrence. Yet C. S. Lewis (Selection 71) claims that the goals of both reform and deterrence are opposed to a fundamental requirement of justice: giving people what they deserve. Obviously, if Lewis's critique is sound, it presents a serious difficulty for both Menninger's and Brandt's views, as well as for any other forward-looking view.

Obviously, raising difficulties for forward-looking justifications for punishment is not the same as directly defending backward-looking justifications, thus the importance of the attempt by Edmund L. Pincoffs (Selection 72) to provide us with such a defense.

Pincoffs begins by setting out the following three principles that he claims are characteristic of the traditional backward-looking justification for punishment:

1. The only acceptable reason for punishing a person is that he or she has committed a crime.

2. The only acceptable reason for punishing a person in a given manner and degree is that the punishment is equal to the crime.

3. Whoever commits a crime must be punished in accordance with his or her desert.

Pincoffs claims that the underlying rationale for these principles can be expressed as follows:

a A proper justification for punishment is one that justifies it to the criminal.

b Punishment is justified because the criminal has willed the punishment he or she now suffers.

But how can criminals be said to will their own punishment if they do not like or want to be punished? One possible answer, which seems consistent with Pincoffs's analysis, is that criminals, by deliberately violating the rights of others (e.g., by harming others in some way), imply that they think it is reasonable for them to do so. But if this were the case, it would be reasonable for anyone else in similar circumstances to do the same. As a result, criminals would be implicitly conceding that it is all right for others to violate their rights by punishing them, and in this sense they could be said to will their own punishment.

In response to such a defense of a backward-looking justification for punishment, supporters of the forward-looking view might claim that the above principles and their underlying rationale are only proximate answers to the question of why punishment is justified, the ultimate answer to which is still given by the forward-looking view. Since Pincoffs's principles and their underlying rationale do not seem to be compatible with Menninger's system of humanitarian reform, such a response does imply that the ultimate forward-looking justification for punishment is to be found more in general deterrence, as in Brandt's system, than in humanitarian reform. But even if this were the case, the ultimate justification for punishment would still be forward-looking.

To meet this response, supporters of a backward-looking view need to show why Pincoffs's principles and their underlying rationale cannot be subsumed under a forward-looking justification. This might be done by showing that Pincoffs's principles and their underlying rationale can be grounded in a social contract theory of corrective justice analogous to the social contract theory of distributive justice discussed in Section I. Because many philosophers believe that a social contract theory of distributive justice conflicts with forward-looking goals, it should be possible to argue that a social contact theory of corrective justice does the same.[1]

Practical Applications

Obviously, a crucial area for the application of forward-looking and backward-looking views is capital punishment. Ernest van den Haag (Selection 73) argues that although we don't know for sure whether capital punishment deters would-be offenders, the greater severity of capital punishment still gives us reason to expect more deterrence from it. Accordingly, van den Haag maintains that the burden of proof is on opponents of capital punishment to show why the greater severity of capital punishment does not lead to more deterrence. In Selection 74, Jeffrey Reiman attempts to meet van den Haag's challenge. He maintains that greater severity in and of itself does not mean more deterrence; a less severe punishment might suffice to deter a particular crime. Moreover, Reiman argues if greater severity were al-

ways justified on grounds of producing more deterrence, then torturing criminals to death would be justified because torturing criminals to death is clearly a more severe punishment than simply executing them. Since van den Haag presumably does not want to endorse torturing criminals to death, he must reject one or more of the premises on which his argument for capital punishment is based.

In 1976 the U.S. Supreme Court (Selection 75) examined the question of whether capital punishment violates the Eighth Amendment prohibition of cruel and unusual punishment. The majority of the Court held that it does not violate that prohibition. In support of its ruling, the majority maintained that capital punishment does not offend contemporary standards of decency as shown by recent legislation in this area. But on the harder question of whether capital punishment is contrary to human dignity and so lacks either a forward-looking or a backward-looking justification, the Court simply deferred to state legislatures. That left the Court with the easier task of deciding whether the procedures for imposing capital punishment, as provided by the Georgia statute that was under review, were capricious and arbitrary. On this score the Court found no reason to fault the Georgia statute.

In more recent cases, however, the Court has gone beyond this purely procedural issue and ruled that the imposition of capital punishment for rape (*Coker v. Georgia*) and on anyone who did not fire a fatal shot or intend the death of a victim (*Locket v. Ohio*) would be unconstitutional. Given that the Court has not seen fit to defer to the judgment of state legislatures in these matters, it is not clear why the Court should continue to defer to their judgment with regard to the question of whether capital punishment can be supported by an adequate forward-looking or backward-looking justification.

In any case, once you have faced that question yourself and worked out a theory of corrective justice, you will still not know exactly how to apply that theory unless you also know how just the distribution of goods and resources is in your society. This is because, regardless of whether you adopt an essentially forward- or backward-looking theory of corrective justice, you will need to know what economic crimes—that is, crimes against property—should be punished according to your theory; and in order to know that, you will need to know what demands are placed on the available goods and resources by solutions to the other problems discussed in this anthology. Of course, some crimes (e.g., many cases of murder and rape) are crimes against people rather than property. And presumably these crimes would be proscribed by your theory of corrective justice independent of the solutions to other contemporary moral problems. Nevertheless, because most crimes are crimes against property, the primary application of your theory will still depend on solutions to the other moral problems discussed in this anthology. In particular, you will need to know to what extent goods and resources can legitimately be expended for military purposes—which just happens to be the moral problem taken up in the next section of this anthology.

Endnote

1. James P. Sterba, "Retributive Justice," *Political Theory* (1977); "Social Contract Theory and Ordinary Justice," *Political Theory* (1981); "Is There a Rationale for Punishment?" *American Journal of Jurisprudence* (1984); "A Rational Choice Justification for Punishment," *Philosophical Topics* (1990).

---

69. The Crime of Punishment

KARL MENNINGER

Karl Menninger argues that the reason crime is so difficult to eradicate is that it serves the needs of offenders and nonoffenders alike. In fact, according to Menninger, the motives of offenders and nonoffenders are quite similar; what distinguishes serious offenders is simply a greater sense of helplessness and hopelessness in the pursuit of their goals. Menninger concludes that we must find better ways to enable people to realize their goals. Menninger also argues that punishment as a vengeful response to crime does not work because crime is an illness requiring treatment by psychiatrists and psychologists. Thus, Menninger finds vengeful punishment itself to be a crime.

Few words in our language arrest our attention as do "crime," "violence," "revenge," and "injustice."

We abhor crime; we adore justice; we boast that we live by the rule of law. Violence and vengefulness we repudiate as unworthy of our civilization, and we assume this sentiment to be unanimous among all human beings.

Yet crime continues to be a national disgrace and a worldwide problem. It is threatening, alarming, wasteful, expensive, abundant, and apparently increasing! In actuality it is decreasing in frequency of occurrence, but it is certainly increasing in visibility and the reactions of the public to it.

Our system for controlling crime is ineffective, unjust, expensive. Prisons seem to operate with revolving doors—the same people going in and out and in and out. *Who cares?*

Our city jails and inhuman reformatories and wretched prisons are jammed. They are known to be unhealthy, dangerous, immoral, indecent, crime-breeding dens of iniquity. Not everyone has smelled them, as some of us have. Not many have heard the groans and the curses. Not everyone has seen the hate and despair in a thousand blank, hollow faces. But, in a way, we all know how miserable prisons are. *We want them to be that way.* And they are. *Who cares?*

Professional, big-time criminals prosper as never before. Gambling syndicates flourish. White-collar crime may even exceed all others but goes undetected in [most] cases. We are all being robbed and we know who the robbers are. They live nearby. *Who cares?*

The public filches millions of dollars worth of food and clothing from stores, towels and sheets from hotels, jewelry and knick-knacks from shops. The public steals, and the same public pays it back in higher prices. *Who cares?*

Time and time again somebody shouts about this state of affairs, just as I am shouting now. The magazines shout. The newspapers shout. The television and radio commentators shout (or at least they "deplore"). Psychologists, sociologists, leading jurists, wardens, and intelligent police chiefs join the chorus. Governors and mayors and Congressmen are sometimes heard. They shout that the situation is bad, bad, bad, and getting worse. Some suggest that we immediately replace obsolete procedures with scientific methods. A few shout contrary sentiments. Do the clear indications derived from scientific discovery for appropriate changes continue to fall on deaf ears? Why is the public so long-suffering, so apathetic and thereby so continuingly self-destructive? How many Presidents (and other citizens) do we have to lose before we do something?

The public behaves as a sick patient does when a dreaded treatment is proposed for his ailment. We all know how the aching tooth may suddenly quiet down in the dentist's office, or the abdominal pain disappear in the surgeon's examining room. Why should a sufferer seek relief and shun it? Is it merely the fear of pain of the treatment? Is it the fear of unknown complications? Is it distrust of the doctor's ability? All of these, no doubt.

But, as Freud made so incontestably clear, the sufferer is always somewhat deterred by a kind of subversive, internal opposition to the work of cure. He suffers on the one hand from the pains of his affliction and yearns to get well. But he suffers at the same time from traitorous impulses that fight against the accomplishment of any change in himself, even recovery! Like Hamlet, he wonders whether it may be better after all to suffer the familiar pains and aches associated with the old method than to face the complications of a new and strange, even though possibly better way of handling things.

The inescapable conclusion is that society secretly *wants* crime, *needs* crime, and gains definite satisfactions from the present mishandling of it! We condemn crime; we punish offenders for it; but we need it. The crime and punishment ritual is a part of our lives. We need crimes to wonder at, to enjoy vicariously, to discuss and speculate about, and to publicly deplore. We need criminals to identify ourselves with, to envy secretly, and to punish stoutly. They do for us the forbidden, illegal things we *wish* to do and, like scapegoats of old, they bear the burdens of our displaced guilt and punishment—"the iniquities of us all."

We have to confess that there is something fascinating for us all about violence. That most crime is not violent we know but we forget, because crime is not a breaking, a rupturing, a tearing—even when it is quietly done. To all of us crime seems like violence.

The very word "violence" has a disturbing, menacing quality. . . . In meaning it implies something dreaded, powerful, destructive, or eruptive. It is something we abhor—or do we? Its first effect is to startle, frighten—even to horrify us. But we do not always run away from it. For violence also intrigues us. It is exciting. It is dramatic. Observing it and sometimes even participating in it gives us acute pleasure.

The newspapers constantly supply us with tidbits of violence going on in the world. They exploit its dramatic essence often to the neglect of conservative reporting of more extensive but less violent damage—the flood disaster in Florence, Italy, for example. Such words as crash, explosion, wreck, assault, raid, murder, avalanche, rape, and seizure evoke pictures of eruptive devastation from which we cannot turn away. The headlines often impute violence metaphorically even to peaceful activities. Relations are "ruptured," a tie is "broken," arbitration "collapses," a proposal is "killed."

Meanwhile on the television and movie screens there constantly appear for our amusement scenes of fighting, slugging, beating, torturing, clubbing, shooting, and the like which surpass in effect anything that the newspapers can describe. Much of this violence is portrayed dishonestly; the scenes are only semirealistic; they are "faked" and romanticized.

Pain cannot be photographed; grimaces indicate but do not convey its intensity. And wounds—unlike violence—are rarely shown. This phony quality of television violence in its mentally unhealthy aspect encourages irrationality by giving the impression to the observer that being beaten, kicked, cut, and stomped, while very unpleasant, are not very painful or serious. For after being slugged and beaten the hero rolls over, opens his eyes, hops up, rubs his cheek, grins, and staggers on. The *suffering* of violence is a part both the TV and movie producers *and* their audience tend to repress.

Although most of us *say* we deplore cruelty and destructiveness, we are partially deceiving ourselves. We disown violence, ascribing the love of it to other people. But the facts speak for themselves. We do love violence, all of us, and we all feel secretly guilty for it, which is another clue to public resistance to crime-control reform.

The great sin by which we all are tempted is the wish to hurt others, and this sin must be avoided if we are to live and let live. If our destructive energies can be mastered, directed, and sublimated, we can survive. If we can love, we can live. Our destructive energies, if they cannot be controlled, may destroy our best friends, as in the case of Alexander the Great, or they may destroy supposed "enemies" or innocent strangers. Worst of all—from the standpoint of the individual—they may destroy us.

Over the centuries of man's existence, many devices have been employed in the effort to control these innate suicidal and criminal propensities. The earliest of these undoubtedly depended upon fear—fear of the unknown, fear of magical retribution, fear of social retaliation. These external devices were replaced gradually with the law and all its machinery, religion and its rituals, and the conventions of the social order.

The routine of life formerly required every individual to direct much of his aggressive energy against the environment. There were trees to cut down, wild animals to fend off, heavy obstacles to remove, great burdens to lift. But the machine has gradually changed all of this. Today, the routine of life, for most people, requires no violence, no fighting, no killing, no life-risking, no sudden supreme exertion: occasionally, perhaps, a hard pull or a strong push, but no tearing, crushing, breaking, forcing.

And because violence no longer has legitimate and useful vents or purposes, it must *all* be controlled today. In earlier times, its expression was often a virtue; today, its control *is* the virtue. The control involves symbolic, vicarious expressions of violence—violence modified; "sublimated," as Freud called it, "neutralized," as Hartmann described it. Civilized substitutes for direct violence are the objects of daily search by all of us. The common law and the Ten Commandments, traffic signals and property deeds, fences and front doors, sermons and concerts, Christmas trees and jazz bands— these and a thousand other things exist today to help in the control of violence.

My colleague Bruno Bettelheim thinks we do not properly educate our youth to deal with their violent urges. He reminds us that nothing fascinated our forefathers more. The *Iliad* is a poem of violence. Much of the Bible is a record of violence. Our penal system and many methods of childrearing express violence—"violence to suppress violence." And, he concludes [in the article "Violence: A Neglected Mode of Behavior"]: "We shall not be able to deal intelligently with violence unless we are first ready to see it as a part of human nature, and then we shall come to realize the chances of discharging violent tendencies are now so severely curtailed that their regular and safe draining-off is not possible anymore."

Why aren't we all criminals? We all have the impulses; we all have the provocations. But becoming civilized, which is repeated ontologically in the process of social education, teaches us what we may do with impunity. What then evokes or permits the breakthrough? Why is it necessary for some to bribe their consciences and do what they do not approve of doing? Why does all sublimation sometimes fail and overt breakdown occur in the controlling and managing machinery of the personality? Why do we sometimes lose self-control? Why do we "go to pieces"? Why do we explode?

These questions point up a central problem in psychiatry. Why do some people do things they do not want to do? Or things we do not want them to do? Sometimes crimes are motivated by a desperate need to act, to do *something* to break out of a state of passivity, frustration, and helplessness too long endured, like a child who shoots a parent or a teacher after some apparently reasonable act. Granting the universal presence of violence within us all, controlled by will power, conscience, fear of punishment, and other devices, granting the tensions and the temptations that are also common to us all, why do the mechanisms of self-control fail so completely in some individuals? Is there not some pre-existing defect, some moral or cerebral weakness, some gross deficiency of common sense that lets some people tumble or kick or strike or explode, while the rest of us just stagger or sway?

When a psychiatrist examines many prisoners, writes [Seymour] Halleck [in *Psychiatry and the Dilemmas of Crime*], he soon discovers how important in the genesis of the criminal outbreak is the offender's previous *sense of helplessness or hopelessness*. All of us suffer more or less from infringement of our personal freedom. We fuss about it all the time; we strive to correct it, extend it, and free ourselves from various oppressive or retentive forces. We do not want others to push us around, to control us, to dominate us. We realize this is bound to happen to some extent in an interlocking, interrelated society such as ours. No one truly has complete freedom. But restriction irks us.

The offender feels this way, too. He does not want to be pushed around, controlled, or dominated. And because he often feels that he is thus oppressed (and actually is) and because he does lack facility in improving his situation without violence, he suffers more intensely from feelings of helplessness.

Violence and crime are often attempts to escape from madness; and there can be no doubt that some mental illness is a flight from the wish to do the violence or commit the act. Is it hard for the reader to believe that suicides are sometimes committed to forestall the committing of murder? There is no doubt of it. Nor is there any doubt that murder is sometimes committed to avert suicide.

Strange as it may sound, many murderers do not realize whom they are killing, or, to put it another way, that they are killing the wrong people. To be sure, killing anybody is reprehensible enough, but the worst of it is that the person who the killer

thinks should die (and he has reasons) is not the person he attacks. Sometimes the victim himself is partly responsible for the crime committed against him. It is this unconscious (perhaps sometimes conscious) participation in the crime by the victim that has long held up the very humanitarian and progressive-sounding program of giving compensation to victims. The public often judges the victim as well as the attacker.

Rape and other sexual offenses are acts of violence so repulsive to our sense of decency and order that it is easy to think of rapists in general as raging, ovesexed, ruthless brutes (unless they are conquering heroes). Some rapists are. But most sex crimes are committed by undersexed rather than oversexed individuals, often undersized rather than oversized, and impelled less by lust than by a need for reassurance regarding an impaired masculinity. The unconscious fear of women goads some men with a compulsive urge to conquer, humiliate, hurt, or render powerless some available sample of womanhood. Men who are violently afraid of their repressed but nearly emergent homosexual desires, and men who are afraid of the humiliation of impotence, often try to overcome these fears by violent demonstrations.

The need to deny something in oneself is frequently an underlying motive for certain odd behavior—even up to and including crime. Bravado crimes, often done with particular brutality and ruthlessness, seem to prove *to the doer* that "I am no weakling! I am no sissy! I am no coward. I am no homosexual! I am a tough man who fears nothing." The Nazi storm troopers, many of them mere boys, were systematically trained to stifle all tender emotions and force themselves to be heartlessly brutal.

Man perennially seeks to recover the magic of his childhood days—the control of the mighty by the meek. The flick of an electric light switch, the response of an automobile throttle, the click of a camera, the touch of a match to a skyrocket—these are keys to a sudden and magical display of great power induced by the merest gesture. Is anyone already so blasé that he is no longer thrilled at the opening of a door specially for him by a magic-eye signal? Yet for a few pennies one can purchase a far more deadly piece of magic—a stored explosive and missile encased within a shell which can be ejected from a machine at the touch of a finger so swiftly that no eye can follow. A thousand yards away something falls dead—a rabbit, a deer, a beautiful mountain sheep, a sleeping child, or the President of the United States. Magic! Magnified, projected power. "Look what I can do. I am the greatest!"

It must have come to every thoughtful person, at one time or another, in looking at the revolvers on the policemen's hips, or the guns soldiers and hunters carry so proudly, that these are instruments made for the express purpose of delivering death to someone. The easy availability of these engines of destruction, even to children, mentally disturbed people, professional criminals, gangsters, and even high school girls is something to give one pause. The National Rifle Association and its allies have been able to kill scores of bills that have been introduced into Congress and state legislatures for corrective gun control since the death of President Kennedy. Americans still spend about $2 billion on guns each year.

Fifty years ago, Winston Churchill declared that the mood and temper of the public in regard to crime and criminals is one of the unfailing tests of the civilization of any country. Judged by this standard, how civilized are we?

The chairman of the President's National Crime Commission, Nicholas Katzenbach, declared . . . that organized crime flourishes in the United States because enough of the public wants its services, and most citizens are apathetic about its impact. It will continue uncurbed as long as Americans accept it as inevitable and, in some instances, desirable.

Are there steps that we can take which will reduce the aggressive stabs and self-destructive lurches of our less well-managing fellow men? Are there ways to prevent and control the grosser violations, other than the clumsy traditional maneuvers which we have inherited? These depend basically upon intimidation and slow-motion torture. We call it punishment, and justify it with our "feeling." We know it doesn't work.

Yes, there *are* better ways. There are steps that could be taken; some *are* taken. But we move too slowly. Much better use . . . could be made of the members of my profession and other behavioral scientists than having them deliver courtroom pronunciamentos. The consistent use of a diagnostic clinic would enable trained workers to lay what they can learn about an offender before the judge who would know best how to implement the recommendation.

This would no doubt lead to a transformation of prisons, if not to their total disappearance in their present form and function. Temporary and permanent detention will perhaps always be necessary for a few, especially the professionals, but this could be more effectively and economically performed with new types of "facility" (that strange, awkward word for institution).

I assume it to be a matter of common and general agreement that our object in all this is to protect the community from a repetition of the offense by the most economical method consonant with our other purposes. Our "other purposes" include the desire to prevent these offenses from occurring, to reclaim offenders for social usefulness, if possible, and to detain them in protective custody, if reclamation is *not* possible. But how?

The treatment of human failure or dereliction by the infliction of pain is still used and believed in by many nonmedical people. "Spare the rod and spoil the child" is still considered wise counsel by many.

Whipping is still used by many secondary schoolmasters in England, I am informed, to stimulate study, attention, and the love of learning. Whipping was long a traditional treatment for the "crime" of disobedience on the part of children, pupils, servants, apprentices, employees. And slaves were treated for centuries by flogging for such offenses as weariness, confusion, stupidity, exhaustion, fear, grief, and even overcheerfulness. It was assumed and stoutly defended that these "treatments" cured conditions for which they were administered.

Meanwhile, scientific medicine was acquiring many new healing methods and devices. Doctors can now transplant organs and limbs; they can remove brain tumors and cure incipient cancers; they can halt pneumonia, meningitis, and other infections; they can correct deformities and repair breaks and tears and scars. But these wonderful achievements are accomplished on *willing* subjects, people who voluntarily ask for help by even heroic measures. And the reader will be wondering, no doubt, whether doctors can do anything with or for people who *do not want* to be treated at all, in any way! Can doctors cure willful aberrant behavior? Are we to believe that crime is a *disease* that can be reached by scientific measures? Isn't it merely "natural meanness" that makes all of us do wrong things at times even when we "know better"? And are not self-control, moral stamina, and will power the things needed? Surely there is no medical treatment for the lack of those!

Let me answer this carefully, for much misunderstanding accumulates here. [With] the prevalent understanding of the words, crime is *not* a disease. Neither is it an illness, although I think it *should* be! It *should* be treated, and it could be; but it mostly isn't.

These enigmatic statements are simply explained. Diseases are undesired states of being which have been described and defined by doctors, usually given Greek or Latin appellations, and treated by long-established physical and pharmacological formulae. Illness, on the other hand, is best defined as a state of impaired functioning of such a nature that the public expects the sufferer to repair to the physician for help. The illness may prove to be a disease; more often it is only vague and nameless misery; but something which doctors, not lawyers, teachers, or preachers, are supposed to be able and willing to help.

When the community begins to look upon the expression of aggressive violence as the symptom of an illness or as indicative of illness, it will be because it believes doctors can do something to correct such a condition. At present, some better-informed individuals do believe and expect this. However angry at or sorry for the offender, they want him "treated" in an effective way so that he will cease to be a danger to them. And they know that the traditional punishment, "treatment-punishment," will not effect this.

What *will*? What effective treatment is there for such violence? It will surely have to begin with motivating or stimulating or arousing in a cornered individual the wish and hope and intention to change his methods of dealing with the realities of life. Can this be done by education, medication, counseling, training? I would answer *yes*. It can be done successfully, in a majority of cases, if undertaken in time.

The present penal system and the existing legal philosophy do not stimulate or even expect such a change to take place in the criminal. Yet change is what medical science always aims for. The prisoner, like the doctor's other patients, should emerge from his treatment experience a different person, differently equipped, differently functioning, and headed in a different direction than when he began treatment.

It is natural for the public to doubt that this can be accomplished with criminals. But remember that the public *used* to doubt that change could be effected in the mentally ill. No one a hundred years ago believed mental illness to be curable. Today *all* people know (or should know) that *mental illness is curable* in the great majority of instances and that the prospects and rapidity of cure are directly related to the availability and intensity of proper treatment.

The forms and techniques of psychiatric treatment used today number in the hundreds. No one patient requires or receives all forms, but each patient is studied with respect to his particular needs, basic assets, interests, and special difficulties. A therapeutic team may embrace a dozen workers—as in a hospital setting—or it may narrow down to the doctor and the spouse. Clergymen, teachers, relatives, friends, and even fellow patients often participate informally but helpfully in the process of readaptation.

All of the participants in this effort to bring about a favorable change in the patient—i.e., in his vital balance and life program—are imbued with what we may call a *therapeutic attitude*. This is one in direct antithesis to attitudes of avoidance, ridicule, scorn, or punitiveness. Hostile feelings toward the subject, however justified by his unpleasant and even destructive behavior, are not in the curriculum of therapy or in the therapist. This does not mean that therapists approve of the offensive and obnoxious behavior of the patient; they distinctly disapprove of it. But they recognize it as symptomatic of continued imbalance and disorganization, which is what they are seeking to change. They distinguish between disapproval, penalty, price, and punishment.

Doctors charge fees; they impose certain "penalties" or prices, but they have long since put aside primitive attitudes of retaliation toward offensive patients. A patient may cough in the doctor's face or vomit on the office rug; a patient may curse or scream or even struggle in the extremity of his pain. But these acts are not "punished." Doctors and nurses have no time or thought for inflicting unnecessary pain even on patients who may be difficult, disagreeable, provocative, and even dangerous. It is their duty to care for them, to try to make them well, and to prevent them from doing themselves or others harm. This requires love, not hate. This is the deepest meaning of the therapeutic attitude. Every doctor knows it; every worker in a hospital or clinic knows it (or should).

There is another element in the therapeutic attitude. It is the quality of hopefulness. If no one believes that the patient can get well, if no one—not even the doctor—has any hope, there probably won't be any recovery. Hope is just as important as love in the therapeutic attitude.

"But you were talking about the mentally ill," readers may interject, "those poor, confused, bereft, frightened individuals who yearn for help from you doctors and nurses. Do you mean to imply that will-fully perverse individuals, our criminals, can be similarly reached and rehabilitated? Do you really believe that effective treatment of the sort you visu-alize can be applied to people *who do not want any help,* who are so willfully vicious, so well aware of the wrongs they are doing, so lacking in penitence or even common decency that punishment seems the only thing left?"

Do I believe there is effective treatment for of-fenders, and that they *can* be changed? *Most certainly and definitely I do.* Not all cases, to be sure; there are also some physical afflictions which we can-not cure at the moment. Some provision has to be made for incurables—pending new knowledge— and these will include some offenders. But I believe the majority of them would prove to be curable. The willfulness and the viciousness of offenders are part of the thing for which they have to be treated. These must not thwart the therapeutic attitude.

It is simply not true that most of them are "fully aware" of what they are doing, nor is it true that they want no help from anyone, although some of them say so. Prisoners are individuals: Some want treatment, some do not. Some don't know what treatment is. Many are utterly despairing and hope-less. Where treatment is made available in insti-tutions, many prisoners seek it even with the full knowledge that doing so will not lessen their sen-tences. In some prisons, seeking treatment by pris-oners is frowned upon by the officials.

Various forms of treatment are even now being tried in some progressive courts and prisons over the country—educational, social, industrial, reli-gious, recreational, and psychological treatments. Socially acceptable behavior, new work-play oppor-tunities, new identity and companion patterns all help toward community reacceptance. Some parole officers and some wardens have been extremely in-genious in developing these modalities of rehabili-tation and reconstruction—more than I could list here even if I knew them all. But some are trying. The secret of success in all programs, however, is the replacement of the punitive attitude with a thera-peutic attitude.

Offenders with propensities for impulsive and predatory aggression should not be permitted to live among us unrestrained by some kind of social control. *But the great majority of offenders, even "crim-inals," should never become prisoners if we want to "cure" them.*

There are now throughout the country many citizens' action groups and programs for the pre-vention and control of crime and delinquency. With such attitudes of inquiry and concern, the public could acquire information (and incentive) leading to a change of feeling about crime and criminals. It will discover how unjust is much so-called "justice," how baffled and frustrated many judges are by the ossified rigidity of old-fashioned, obsolete laws and state constitutions which effectively prevent the in-troduction of sensible procedures to replace useless, harmful ones.

I want to proclaim to the public that things are not what it wishes them to be, and will only become so if it will take an interest in the matter and assume some responsibility for its own self-protection.

Will the public listen?

If the public does become interested, it will re-alize that we must have more facts, more trial proj-ects, more checked results. It will share the dismay of the President's Commission in finding that no one knows much about even the incidence of crime with any definiteness or statistical accuracy.

The average citizen finds it difficult to see how any research would in any way change his mind about a man who brutally murders his children. But just such inconceivably awful acts most dramati-cally point up the need for research. Why should— how can—a man become so dreadful as that in our culture? How is such a man made? Is it comprehen-sible that he can be born to become so depraved?

There are thousands of questions regarding crime and public protection which deserve scien-tific study. What makes some individuals maintain their interior equilibrium by one kind of distur-bance of the social structure rather than by another kind, one that would have landed him in a hospi-tal? Why do some individuals specialize in certain types of crime? Why do so many young people reared in areas of delinquency and poverty and bad example never become habitual delinquents? (Per-haps this is a more important question than why some of them do.)

The public has a fascination for violence, and clings tenaciously to its yen for vengeance, blind and deaf to the expense, futility, and dangerousness of the resulting penal system. But we are bound to hope that this will yield in time to the persistent, penetrating light of intelligence and accumulating scientific knowledge. The public will grow increasingly ashamed of its cry for retaliation, its persistent demand to punish. This is its crime, *our* crime against criminals—and, incidentally, our crime against ourselves. For before we can diminish our sufferings from the ill-controlled aggressive assaults of fellow citizens, we must renounce the philosophy of punishment, the obsolete, vengeful penal attitude. In its place we would seek a comprehensive constructive social attitude—therapeutic in some instances, restraining in some instances, but preventive in its total social impact.

In the last analysis this becomes a question of personal morals and values. No matter how glorified or how piously disguised, vengeance as a human motive must be personally repudiated by each and every one of us. This is the message of old religions and new psychiatries. Unless this message is heard, unless we, the people—the man on the street, the housewife in the home—can give up our delicious satisfactions in opportunities for vengeful retaliation on scapegoats, we cannot expect to preserve our peace, our public safety, or our mental health.

---

70. *A Utilitarian Theory of Punishment*

RICHARD B. BRANDT

Richard B. Brandt argues that a system of punishment similar to that found in the United States and Great Britain can be justified on utilitarian or forward-looking grounds. He rejects the view that a utilitarian theory cannot approve of any excuses for criminal liability. He also denies that a utilitarian theory must approve of occasionally punishing the innocent provided the theory is understood in an extended sense to require a principle of equal distribution.

The ethical foundations of the institution and principles of criminal justice require examination just as do the ethical foundations of systems of economic distribution. In fact, the two problems are so similar that it is helpful to view either one in the light of conclusions reached about the other. It is no accident that the two are spoken of as problems of "justice," for the institution of criminal justice is essentially a mode of allocating welfare (or "illfare," if we prefer). Also, just as economic return can be regarded as a reward for past services, the punishment of criminals can be regarded as punishment for past disservices. Moreover, just as a major reason for differences in economic reward is to provide motivation for promoting the public welfare by industrious effort, so a major reason for a system of punishment for criminals is to give motivation for not harming the public by crime. The two topics, then, are very similar; but they are also sufficiently different to require separate discussion. . . .

The broad questions to be kept in the forefront of discussion are the following: (1) What justifies anyone in inflicting pain or loss on an individual on account of his past acts? (2) Is there a valid general principle about the punishments proper for various acts? (Possibly there should be no close connection between offense and penalty; perhaps punishment should be suited to the individual needs of the criminal, and not to his crime.) (3) What kinds of defense should excuse from punishment? An answer to these questions would comprise prescriptions for the broad outlines of an ideal system of criminal justice. . . .

Abridged from *Ethical Theory* (Prentice-Hall, 1959), pp. 480, 489–495, 503–505. Reprinted by permission of Richard B. Brandt. Notes renumbered.

The Utilitarian Theory of Criminal Justice

. . . It is convenient to begin with the utilitarian theory. Since we have tentatively concluded that an "extended" rule-utilitarianism is the most tenable form of theory, we shall have this particular type of theory in mind. For present purposes, however, it would make no difference, except at two or three points where we shall make note of the fact, if we confined our attention to a straight rule-utilitarian principle. There is no harm in thinking of the matter in this way. . . .

The essence of the rule-utilitarian theory, we recall, is that our actions, whether legislative or otherwise, should be guided by a set of prescriptions, the conscientious following of which by all would have maximum net expectable utility. As a result, the utilitarian is not, just as such, committed to any particular view about how anti-social behavior should be treated by society—or even to the view that society should do anything at all about immoral conduct. It is only the utilitarian principle *combined* with statements about the kind of laws and practices which will maximize expectable utility that has such consequences. Therefore, utilitarians are free to differ from one another about the character of an ideal system of criminal justice; some utilitarians think that the system prevalent in Great Britain and the United States essentially corresponds to the ideal, but others think that the only system that can be justified is markedly different from the actual systems in these Western countries. We shall concentrate our discussion, however, on the more traditional line of utilitarian thought which holds that roughly the actual system of criminal law, say in the United States, is morally justifiable, and we shall follow roughly the classic exposition of the reasoning given by Jeremy Bentham[1]—but modifying this freely when we feel amendment is called for. At the end of the [reading] we shall look briefly at a different view.

Traditional utilitarian thinking about criminal justice has found the rationale of the practice, in the United States, for example, in three main facts. (Those who disagree think the first two of these "facts" happen not to be the case.) (1) People who are tempted to misbehave, to trample on the rights of others, to sacrifice public welfare for personal gain, can usually be deterred from misconduct by fear of punishment, such as death, imprisonment, or fine. (2) Imprisonment or fine will teach malefactors a lesson; their characters may be improved, and at any rate a personal experience of punishment will make them less likely to misbehave again. (3) Imprisonment will certainly have the result of physically preventing past malefactors from misbehaving during the period of their incarceration.

In view of these suppositions, traditional utilitarian thinking has concluded that having laws forbidding certain kinds of behavior on pain of punishment, and having machinery for the fair enforcement of these laws, is justified by the fact that it maximizes expectable utility. Misconduct is not to be punished just for its own sake; malefactors must be punished for their past acts, according to law, as a way of maximizing expectable utility.

The utilitarian principle, of course, has implications for decisions about the severity of punishment to be administered. Punishment is itself an evil, and hence should be avoided where this is consistent with the public good. Punishment should have precisely such a degree of severity (not more or less) that the probable disutility of greater severity just balances the probable gain in utility (less crime because of the more serious threat). The cost, in other words, should be counted along with the value of what is bought; and we should buy protection up to the point where the cost is greater than the protection is worth. How severe will such punishment be? Jeremy Bentham had many sensible things to say about this. Punishment, he said, must be severe enough so that it is to no one's advantage to commit an offense even if he receives the punishment; a fine of $10 for bank robbery would give no security at all. Further, since many criminals will be undetected, we must make the penalty heavy enough in comparison with the prospective gain from crime that a prospective criminal will consider the risk hardly worth it, even [when] it is not certain he will be punished at all. Again, the more serious offenses should carry the heavier penalties, not only because the greater disutility justifies the use of heavier penalties . . . to prevent them, but also because criminals should be motivated to commit a less serious rather than a more serious offense. Bentham thought the prescribed penalties should allow for some variation at the discretion of the judge, so that the actual suffering caused should roughly be the same in all cases; thus, a heavier fine will be imposed on a rich man than on a poor man.

Bentham also argued that the goal of maximum utility requires that certain facts should *excuse* from culpability, for the reason that punishment in such cases "must be inefficacious." He listed as such (1) the fact that the relevant law was passed only after the act of the accused, (2) that the law had not been made public, (3) that the criminal was an infant, insane, or was intoxicated, (4) that the crime was done under physical compulsion, (5) that the agent was ignorant of the probable consequences of his act or was acting on the basis of an innocent misapprehension of the facts, such that the act the agent thought he was performing was a lawful one, and (6) that the motivation to commit the offense was so strong that no threat of law could prevent the crime. Bentham also thought that punishment should be remitted if the crime was a collective one and the number of the guilty so large that great suffering would be caused by its imposition, or if the offender held an important post and his services were important for the public, or if the public or foreign powers would be offended by the punishment; but we shall ignore this part of his view.

Bentham's account of the logic of legal "defenses" needs amendment. What he should have argued is that *not* punishing in certain types of cases (cases where such defenses as those just indicated can be offered) reduces the amount of suffering imposed by law and the insecurity of everybody, and that failure to impose punishment in these types of case will cause only a negligible increase in the incidence of crime.

How satisfactory is this theory of criminal justice? Does it have any implications that are far from being acceptable when compared with concrete justified convictions about what practices are morally right?[2]

Many criminologists . . . would argue that Bentham was mistaken in his facts: The deterrence value of [the] threat of punishment, they say, is much less than he imagined, and criminals are seldom reformed by spending time in prison. If these contentions are correct, then the ideal rules for society's treatment of malefactors are very different from what Bentham thought, and from what actual practice is today in the United States. To say all this, however, is not to show that the utilitarian *principle* is incorrect, for in view of these facts presumably the attitudes of a "qualified" person would not be favorable to criminal justice as practiced today. Utilitarian theory might still be correct, but its im-

plications would be different from what Bentham thought—and they might coincide with justified ethical judgments. We shall return to this.

The whole utilitarian approach, however, has been criticized on the ground that it ought not in consistency to approve of *any* excuses from criminal liability.[3] Or at least, it should do so only after careful empirical inquiries. It is not obvious, it is argued, that we increase net expectable utility by permitting such defenses. At the least, the utilitarian is committed to defend the concept of "strict liability." Why? Because we could get a more strongly deterrent effect if everyone knew that *all behavior* of a certain sort would be punished, irrespective of mistaken supposals of fact, compulsion, and so on. The critics admit that knowledge that all behavior of a certain sort will be punished will hardly deter from crime the insane, persons acting under compulsion, persons acting under erroneous beliefs about facts, and others, but, as Professor Hart points out, it does not follow from this that general knowledge that certain acts will always be punished will not be salutary.

[But the] utilitarian has a solid defense against charges of this sort. We must bear in mind (as the critics do not) that the utilitarian principle, *taken by itself, implies nothing whatever* about whether a system of law should excuse persons on the basis of certain defenses. What the utilitarian does say is that, when we *combine* the principle of utilitarianism with *true* propositions about a certain thing or situation, then we shall come out with true statements about obligations. The utilitarian is certainly not committed to saying that one will derive true propositions about obligations if one starts with *false* propositions about fact or about what will maximize welfare, or with *no* such propositions at all. Therefore the criticism sometimes made (for example, by Hart), that utilitarian theory does not render it "obviously" or "necessarily" the case that the recognized excuses from criminal liability should be accepted as excusing from punishment, is beside the point. Moreover, in fact the utilitarian can properly claim that we do have excellent reason for believing that the general public would be no better motivated to avoid criminal offenses than it now is, if the insane and others were also punished along with intentional wrong-doers. Indeed, he may reasonably claim that the example of punishment of these individuals could only have a hardening effect—like public executions. Furthermore, the utilitarian can point out that abolition of the standard exculpating excuses would lead to serious insecurity. Imagine the pleasure of driving an automobile if one knew one could be executed for running down a child whom it was absolutely impossible to avoid striking! One certainly does not maximize expectable utility by eliminating the traditional excuses. In general, then, the utilitarian theory is not threatened by its implications about exculpating excuses.

It might also be objected against utilitarianism that it cannot recognize the validity of *mitigating* excuses (which presumably have the support of "qualified" attitudes). Would not consequences be better if the distinction between premeditated and impulsive acts were abolished? The utilitarian can reply that people who commit impulsive crimes, in the heat of anger, do not give thought to legal penalties; they would not be deterred by a stricter law. Moreover, such a person is unlikely to repeat his crime, so that a mild sentence saves an essentially good man for society.[4] Something can also be said in support of the practice of judges in giving a milder sentence when a person's temptation is severe: At least the *extended* rule-utilitarian can say, in defense of the practice of punishing less severely the crime of a man who has had few opportunities in life, that a judge ought to do what he can to repair inequalities in life, and that a mild sentence to a man who has had few opportunities is one way of doing this. There are, then, utilitarian supports for recognizing the mitigating excuses. . . .

Another popular objection to the utilitarian theory is that the utilitarian must approve of prosecutors or judges occasionally withholding evidence known to them, for the sake of convicting an innocent man, if the public welfare really is served by so doing. Critics of the theory would not deny that there *can* be circumstances where the dangers are so severe that such action is called for; they only say that utilitarianism calls for it all too frequently. Is this criticism justified? Clearly, the utilitarian is not committed to advocating that a provision should be written into the *law* so as to permit punishment of persons for crimes they did not commit if to do so would serve the public good. Any such provisions would be a shattering blow to public confidence and security. The question is only whether there should be an informal moral rule to the same effect, for the guidance of judges and prosecutors. Will the rule-utilitarian necessarily be committed to far too sweeping a moral rule on this point? We must recall that he is not in the position of the act-utilitarian, who must say that an innocent man must be punished if in *his particular case* the public welfare would be served by his punishment. The rule-utilitarian rather asserts only that an innocent man should be punished if he falls within a class of cases such that net expectable utility is maximized if *all* members of the class are punished, taking into account the possible disastrous effects on public confidence if it [knows] that judges and prosecutors are guided by such a rule. Moreover, the "extended" rule-utilitarian has a further reason for not punishing an innocent man unless he has had more than his equal share of the good things of life already; namely, that there is an obligation to promote equality of welfare, whereas severe punishment is heaping "illfare" on one individual person. When we take these considerations into account, it is *not* obvious that the rule-utilitarian (or the "extended" rule-utilitarian) is committed to action that we are justifiably convinced is immoral.[5] . . .

Utilitarianism and Reform

Some thinkers today believe that criminal justice in Great Britain and the United States is in need of substantial revision. If we agree with their proposals, we have even less reason for favoring the retributive principles; but we must also question the traditional utilitarian emphasis on deterrence as the primary function of the institution of criminal justice.

Their proposal, roughly, is that we should extend, to all criminal justice, the practices of juvenile courts and institutions for the reform of juvenile offenders. Here, retributive concepts have been largely discarded at least in theory, and psychiatric treatment and programs for the prevention of crime by means of slum clearance, the organization of boys' clubs, and so forth, have replaced even deterrence as guiding ideas for social action.

The extension of these practices to criminal justice as a whole would work somewhat as follows: First, the present court procedure would be used to determine whether an offense has actually been committed. Such procedure would necessarily include ordinary rules about the admission of evidence, trial by jury, and the exculpating justifications and excuses for offenses (such as wrong suppositions about the facts). Second, if an accused were adjudged guilty, decisions about his treatment would then be in the hands of the experts, who would determine what treatment was called for and when the individual was ready for return to normal social living. The trial court might, of course, set some maximum period during which such experts would have a right to control the treatment of the criminal. What the experts would do would be decided by the criminal's condition; it would be criminal-centered treatment, not crime-centered treatment.

One might object to this proposal that it overlooks the necessity of disagreeable penalties for crime, in order to deter prospective criminals effectively. But it is doubtful whether threats of punishment have as much deterrent value as is often supposed. Threats of punishment will have little effect on morons, or on persons to whom normal living offers few prospects of an interesting existence.[6] Moreover, persons from better economic or social circumstances will be deterred sufficiently by the prospect of conviction in a public trial and being at the disposal of a board for a period of years.

Such proposals have their difficulties. For instance, would the police be as safe as they are if criminals knew that killing a policeman would be no more serious in its consequences than the crime for which the policeman was trying to arrest them? However, there is much factual evidence for answering such questions, since systems of criminal justice along such lines are already in operation in some parts of the world, in particular among the Scandinavian countries. In fact, in some states the actual practice is closer to the projected system than one might expect from books on legal theory.

Another objection that many would raise is that psychiatry and criminology have not yet advanced far enough for such weighty decisions about the treatment of criminals to be placed in their hands. The treatment of criminals might vary drastically depending on the particular theoretical predilections of a given theorist, or on his personal likes and dislikes. One can probably say as much, or more, however, about the differences between judges in their policies for picking a particular sentence within the range permitted by law.

An institution of criminal justice operating on such basic principles would come closer to our views about how parents should treat their children, or teachers their students, than the more traditional practices of criminal justice today.

We should repeat that this view about the ideal form for an institution of criminal justice is not in conflict with utilitarianism; in fact, it is utilitarian in outlook. The motivation behind advocating it is the thought that such a system would do more good. It differs from the kind of institution traditionally advocated by utilitarians like Bentham only in making different factual assumptions, primarily about the deterrence value of threat of imprisonment, and the actual effect of imprisonment on the attitudes of the criminal.

Endnotes

1. In *Principles of Morals and Legislation.*
2. Act-utilitarians face special problems. For instance, if I am an act-utilitarian and serve on a jury, I shall work to get a verdict that will do the most good, irrespective of the charges of the judge, and of any oath I may have taken to give a reasonable answer to certain questions on the basis of the evidence presented—unless I think my doing so will have indirect effects on the institution of the jury, public confidence in it, and so on. This is certainly not what we think a juror should do. Of course, neither a juror nor a judge can escape his prima facie obligation to do what good he can; this obligation is present in some form in every theory. The act-utilitarian, however, makes this the whole of one's responsibility.
3. See H. L. A. Hart, "Legal Responsibility and Excuses," in Sidney Hook (ed.), *Determinism and Freedom* (New York: New York University Press, 1958), pp. 81–104; and David Braybrooke, "Professor Stevenson, Voltaire, and the Case of Admiral Byng," *Journal of Philosophy*, LIII (1956), 787–796.
4. The utilitarian must admit that the same thing is true for many deliberate murders; and probably he should also admit that some people who commit a crime in the heat of anger would have found time to think had they known that a grave penalty awaited them.
5. In any case, a tenable theory of punishment must approve of punishing persons who are *morally* blameless. Suppose someone commits treason for moral reasons. We may have to say that his deed is not reprehensible . . . and might even (considering the risk he took for his principles) be morally admirable. Yet we think such persons must be punished no matter what their motives; people cannot be permitted to take the law into their own hands.
6. It is said that picking pockets was once a capital offense in England and hangings were public, in order to get the maximum deterrent effect. But hangings in public had to be abolished, because such crimes as picking pockets were so frequent during the spectacle! See N. F. Cantor, *Crime, Criminals, and Criminal Justice* (New York: Henry Holt & Company, Inc., 1932).

71. A Critique of the Humanitarian Theory of Punishment

C. S. LEWIS

C. S. Lewis argues that the humanitarian theory of punishment is not in the interests of the criminal. According to Lewis, this is because the theory is concerned with the goals of reform and deterrence and not the requirements of justice. Hence, it permits the violation of the criminal's rights as a way of promoting these goals. Moreover, Lewis claims, deciding what promotes reform and deterrence, unlike deciding what is required by justice, seems best left to experts. Yet these experts, Lewis argues, even with the best of intentions, may act "as cruelly and unjustly as the greatest tyrants."

In England we have lately had a controversy about Capital Punishment. I do not know whether a murderer is more likely to repent and make a good end on the gallows a few weeks after his trial or in the prison infirmary thirty years later. I do not know whether the fear of death is an indispensable deterrent. I need not [here] decide whether it is a morally permissible deterrent. Those are questions which I propose to leave untouched. My subject is not Capital Punishment in particular, but that theory of punishment in general which the controversy showed to be almost universal among my fellow countrymen. It may be called the Humanitarian theory. Those who hold it think that it is mild and merciful. In this I believe that they are seriously mistaken. I believe that the "Humanity" which it claims is a dangerous illusion and disguises the possibility of cruelty and injustice without end. I urge a return to the traditional or Retributive theory not solely, not even primarily, in the interests of society, but in the interests of the criminal.

According to the Humanitarian theory, to punish a man because he deserves it, and as much as he deserves, is mere revenge, and, therefore, barbarous and immoral. It is maintained that the only legitimate motives for punishing are the desire to deter others by example or to mend the criminal. When

this theory is combined, as frequently happens, with the belief that all crime is more or less pathological, the idea of mending tails off into that of healing or curing and punishment becomes therapeutic. Thus it appears at first sight that we have passed from the harsh and self-righteous notion of giving the wicked their deserts to the charitable and enlightened one of tending the psychologically sick. What could be more amiable? One little point which is taken for granted in this theory needs, however, to be made explicit. The things done to the criminal, even if they are called cures, will be just as compulsory as they were in the old days when we called them punishments. If a tendency to steal can be cured by psychotherapy, the thief will no doubt be forced to undergo the treatment. Otherwise, society cannot continue.

[T]his doctrine, merciful though it appears, really means that each one of us, from the moment he breaks the law, is deprived of the rights of a human being.

The reason is this: The Humanitarian theory removes from Punishment the concept of Desert. But the concept of Desert is the only connecting link between punishment and justice. It is only as deserved or undeserved that a sentence can be just or unjust. I do not here contend that the question "Is it deserved?" is the only one we can reasonably ask about a punishment. We may very properly ask whether it is likely to deter others and to reform the criminal. But neither of these two last questions is a question about justice. There is no sense in talking about a "just deterrent" or a "just cure." We demand of a

From "The Humanitarian Theory of Punishment," *Res Judicatae* (1953), pp. 224–230. Reprinted by permission of the *Melbourne University Law Review* and the Trustee for the C. S. Lewis Estate.

deterrent not whether it is just but whether it will deter. We demand of a cure not whether it is just but whether it succeeds. Thus when we cease to consider what the criminal deserves and consider only what will cure him or deter others, we have tacitly removed him from the sphere of justice altogether; instead of a person, a subject of rights, we now have a mere object, a patient, a "case."

The distinction will become clearer if we ask who will be qualified to determine sentences when sentences are no longer held to derive their propriety from the criminal's deservings. On the old view the problem of fixing the right sentence was a moral problem. Accordingly, the judge who did it was a person trained in jurisprudence: trained, that is, in a science which deals with rights and duties, and which, in origin at least, was consciously accepting guidance from the Law of Nature, and from Scripture. We must admit that in the actual penal code of most countries at most times these high originals were so much modified by local custom, class interests, and utilitarian concessions, as to be very imperfectly recognizable. But the code was never in principle, and not always in fact, beyond the control of the conscience of the society. And when (say, in eighteenth-century England) actual punishments conflicted too violently with the moral sense of the community, juries refused to convict and reform was finally brought about. This was possible because, so long as we are thinking in terms of Desert, the propriety of the penal code, being a moral question, is a question on which every man has the right to an opinion, not because he follows this or that profession, but because he is simply a man, a rational animal enjoying the Natural Light. But all this is changed when we drop the concept of Desert. The only two questions we may now ask about a punishment are whether it deters and whether it cures. But these are not questions on which anyone is entitled to have an opinion simply because he is a man. He is not entitled to an opinion even if, in addition to being a man, he should happen also to be a jurist, a Christian, and a moral theologian. For they are not questions about principle but about matter of fact; and for such *cuiquam in sua arte credendum*. Only the expert "penologist" (let barbarous things have barbarous names), in the light of previous experiment, can tell us what is likely to deter: Only the psychotherapist can tell us what is likely to cure. It will be in vain for the rest of us, speaking simply as men, to say, "but this punishment is hideously unjust,

hideously disproportionate to the criminal's deserts." The experts with perfect logic will reply, "but nobody was talking about deserts. No one was talking about *punishment* in your archaic vindictive sense of the word. Here are the statistics proving that this treatment deters. Here are the statistics proving that this other treatment cures. What is your trouble?"

The Humanitarian theory, then, removes sentences from the hands of jurists whom the public . . . is entitled to criticize and places them in the hands of technical experts whose special sciences do not even [use] such categories as rights or justice. . . . [S]ince this transference results from an abandonment of the old idea of punishment, and, therefore, of all vindictive motives, it will be safe to leave our criminals in such hands. I will not . . . comment on the simple-minded view of fallen human nature which such a belief implies. Let us rather remember that the "cure" of criminals is to be compulsory; and let us then watch how the theory actually works in the mind of the Humanitarian. The immediate starting point of this article was a letter I read in [a leftist weekly]. The author [pleaded] that a certain sin, now treated by our laws as a crime, should henceforward be treated as a disease. And he complained that under the present system the offender, after a term in gaol, was simply let out to return to his original environment where he would probably relapse. What he complained of was not the shutting up but the letting out. On his remedial view of punishment the offender should . . . be detained until he was cured. And of course the official straighteners are the only people who can say when that is. The first result of the Humanitarian theory is, therefore, to substitute for a definite sentence (reflecting to some extent the community's moral judgment on the degree of ill-desert involved) an indefinite sentence terminable only by the word of those experts—and they are not experts in moral theology or . . . the Law of Nature—who inflict it. Which of us, if he stood in the dock, would not prefer to be tried by the old system?

It may be said that by the continued use of the word *punishment* and the use of the verb "inflict" I am misrepresenting Humanitarians. They are not punishing, not inflicting, only healing. But do not . . . be deceived by a name. To be taken without consent from my home and friends; to lose my liberty; to undergo all those assaults on my personality that modern psychotherapy knows how to deliver; to be remade after some pattern of "normality" hatched in a Viennese laboratory to which I never professed allegiance; to know that this process will never end until either my captors have succeeded or I have grown wise enough to cheat them with apparent success—who cares whether this is called Punishment or not? That it includes most of the elements for which any punishment is feared—shame, exile, bondage, and years eaten by the locust—is obvious. Only enormous ill-desert could justify it; but ill-desert is the very conception which the Humanitarian theory has thrown overboard.

If we turn from the curative to the deterrent justification of punishment we shall find the new theory even more alarming. When you punish a man *in terrorem,* make of him an " example" to others, you are admittedly using him as a means to an end; someone else's end. This, in itself, would be a very wicked thing to do. On the classical theory of Punishment it was of course justified on the ground that the man deserved it. That was assumed to be established before any question of "making him an example" arose. You then, as the saying is, killed two birds with one stone; in the process of giving him what he deserved you set an example to others. But take away desert and the whole morality of the punishment disappears. Why, in Heaven's name, am I to be sacrificed to the good of society in this way?—unless, of course, I deserve it.

But that is not the worst. If the justification of exemplary punishment is not to be based on desert but solely on its efficacy as a deterrent, it is not absolutely necessary that the man we punish should even have committed the crime. The deterrent effect demands that the public should draw the moral, "If we do such an act we shall suffer like that man." The punishment of a man actually guilty whom the public think innocent will not have the desired effect; the punishment of a man actually innocent will, provided the public think him guilty. But every modern State has powers which make it easy to fake a trial. When a victim is urgently needed for exemplary purposes and a guilty victim cannot be found, all the purposes of deterrence will be equally served by the punishment (call it "cure" if you prefer) of an innocent victim, provided that the public can be cheated into thinking him guilty. It is no use to ask me why I assume that our rulers will be so wicked. The punishment of an innocent, that is, an undeserving, man is wicked only if we grant the traditional view that righteous punishment means deserved punishment. Once we have abandoned that criterion, all punishments have to be justified, if at all, on other grounds that have nothing to do with desert. Where the punishment of the innocent can be justified on those grounds (and it could in some cases be justified as a deterrent) it will be no less moral than any other punishment. Any distaste for it on the part of a Humanitarian will be merely a hang-over from the Retributive theory.

It is, indeed, important to notice that my argument so far supposes no evil intentions on the part of the Humanitarian and considers only what is involved in the logic of his position. My contention is that good men (not bad men) consistently acting upon that position would act as cruelly and unjustly as the greatest tyrants. They might in some respects act even worse. Of all tyrannies a tyranny sincerely exercised for the good of its victims may be the most oppressive. It may be better to live under robber barons than under omnipotent moral busybodies. The robber baron's cruelty may sometimes sleep, his cupidity may at some point be satiated; but those who torment us for our own good will torment us without end for they do so with the approval of their own conscience. They may be more likely to go to Heaven yet at the same time likelier to make a Hell of earth. Their very kindness stings with intolerable insult. To be "cured" against one's will and cured of states which we may not regard as disease is to be put on a level with those who have not yet reached the age of reason or those who never will; to be classed with infants, imbeciles, and domestic animals. But to be punished, however severely, because we have deserved it, because we "ought to have known better," is to be treated as a human person made in God's image.

In reality, however, we must face the possibility of bad rulers armed with a Humanitarian theory of punishment. A great many popular blueprints for a Christian society are merely what the Elizabethans called "eggs in moonshine" because they assume that the whole society is Christian or that the Christians are in control. This is not so in most contemporary States. Even if it were, our rulers would still be fallen men, and, therefore, neither very wise nor very good. As it is, they will usually be unbelievers. And since wisdom and virtue are not the only or the commonest qualifications for a place in the government, they will not often be even the best unbelievers. The practical problem of Christian politics is not that of drawing up schemes for a Christian society, but that of living as innocently as we can with unbelieving fellow-subjects under unbelieving rulers who will never be perfectly wise and good and who will sometimes be very wicked and very foolish. And when they are wicked the Humanitarian theory of punishment will put in their hands a finer instrument of tyranny than wickedness ever had before. For if crime and disease are to be regarded as the same thing, it follows that any state of mind which our masters choose to call "disease" can be treated as crime and compulsorily cured. It will be vain to plead that states of mind which displease government need not always involve moral turpitude and do not therefore always deserve forfeiture of liberty. For our masters will not be using the concepts of Desert and Punishment but those of disease and cure. We know that one school of psychology already regards religion as a neurosis. When this particular neurosis becomes inconvenient to government, what is to hinder government from proceeding to "cure" it? Such "cure" will, of course, be compulsory; but under the Humanitarian theory it will not be called by the shocking name of Persecution. No one will blame us for being Christian, no one will hate us, no one will revile us. The new Nero will approach us with the silky manners of a doctor, and though all will be in fact as compulsory as the *tunica molesta* or Smithfield or Tyburn, all will go on within the unemotional therapeutic sphere where words like *right* and *wrong* or *freedom* and *slavery* are never heard. And thus when the command is given, every prominent Christian in the land may vanish overnight into Institutions for the Treatment of the Ideologically Unsound, and it will rest with the expert gaolers to say when (if ever) they are to re-emerge. But it will not be persecution. Even if the treatment is painful, even if it is life-long, even if it is fatal, that will be only a regrettable accident; the intention was purely therapeutic. Even in ordinary medicine there were painful operations and fatal operations; so in this. But because they are "treatment," not punishment, they can be criticized only by fellow experts and on technical grounds, never by men as men and on grounds of justice.

That is why I think it essential to oppose the Humanitarian theory of punishment, root and branch, wherever we encounter it. It carries on its front a semblance of mercy which is wholly false. That is how it can deceive men of good will. The error began, perhaps, with Shelley's statement that the distinction between mercy and justice was invented in the courts of tyrants. It sounds noble, and was indeed the error of a noble mind. But the distinction is essential. The older view was that mercy "tempered" justice, or (on the highest level of all) that mercy and justice had met and kissed. The essential act of mercy was to pardon; and pardon in its very essence involves the recognition of guilt, and ill-desert in the recipient. If crime is only a disease which needs cure, not sin which deserves punishment, it cannot be pardoned. How can you pardon a man for having a gumboil or a club foot? But the Humanitarian theory wants simply to abolish Justice and substitute Mercy for it. This means that you start being "kind" to people before you have considered their rights, and then force upon them supposed kindnesses which they in fact had a right to refuse, and finally kindnesses which no one but you will recognize as kindnesses and which the recipient will feel as abominable cruelties. You have overshot the mark. Mercy, detached from Justice, grows unmerciful. That is the important paradox. As there are plants which will flourish only in mountain soil, so it appears that Mercy will flower only when it grows in the crannies of the rock of Justice: Transplanted to the marshlands of mere Humanitarianism, it becomes a man-eating weed, all the more dangerous because it is still called by the same name as the mountain variety. But we ought long ago to have learned our lesson. We should be too old now to be deceived by those humane pretensions that have served to usher in every cruelty of the revolutionary period in which we live. These are the "precious balms" that will "break our heads."

There is a fine sentence in Bunyan: "It came burning hot into my mind, whatever he said, and however he flattered, when he got me home to his house, he would sell me for a slave." There is a fine couplet, too, in John Ball:

Beware ere ye be woe
Know your friend from your foe.

One last word. You may ask why I sent this to an Australian periodical. The reason is simple . . . : I can get no hearing for it in England.

72. Classical Retributivism

EDMUND L. PINCOFFS

Edmund L. Pincoffs begins by setting out three principles that, he holds, express the essence of a Kantian retributive theory of punishment. He then claims that the underlying rationale for these principles is to provide a justification of the punishment to the criminal on the grounds that she has willed the punishment she now suffers. Pincoffs concludes by noting two difficulties for the retributive theory of punishment that he has not addressed: how to make punishment equal to the crime and how to distinguish punishment from revenge.

I.

The classification of Kant as a retributivist[1] is usually accompanied by a reference to some part of the following passage from the *Rechtslehre*, which is worth quoting at length.

> Juridical punishment can never be administered merely as a means for promoting another good either with regard to the criminal himself or to civil society, but must in all cases be imposed only because the individual on whom it is inflicted *has committed a crime*. For one man ought never to be dealt with merely as a means subservient to the purpose of another, nor be mixed up with the subjects of real right. Against such treatment his inborn personality has a right to protect him, even though he may be condemned to lose his civil personality. He must first be found guilty and *punishable* before there can be any thought of drawing from his punishment any benefit for himself or his fellow-citizens. The penal law is a categorical imperative; and woe to him who creeps through the serpent-windings of utilitarianism to discover some advantage that may discharge him from the justice of punishment, or even from the due measure of it, according to the Pharisaic maxim: "It is better that *one* man should die than the whole

people should perish." For if justice and righteousness perish, human life would no longer have any value in the world. . . .

> But what is the mode and measure of punishment which public justice takes as its principle and standard? It is just the principle of equality, by which the pointer of the scale of justice is made to incline no more to the one side than the other. It may be rendered by saying that the undeserved evil which any one commits on another, is to be regarded as perpetrated on himself. Hence it may be said: "If you slander another, you slander yourself; if you steal from another, you steal from yourself; if you strike another, you strike yourself; if you kill another, you kill yourself." This is the Right of RETALIATION (*jus talionis*); and properly understood, it is the only principle which in regulating a public court, as distinguished from mere private judgment, can definitely assign both the quality and the quantity of a just penalty. All other standards are wavering and uncertain; and on account of other considerations involved in them, they contain no principle conformable to the sentence of pure and strict justice.[2]

Obviously we could mull over this passage for a long time. What, exactly, is the distinction between the Inborn and the Civil Personality? How is the Penal Law a Categorical Imperative: by derivation from one of the five formulations in the *Grundlegung*, or as a separate formulation? But we are on the trail of the traditional retributive theory of punishment and do not want to lose ourselves in niceties. There are two main points in this passage to which we should give particular attention:

From *The Rationale of Legal Punishment* (1966), pp. 2–16. Reprinted by permission of Humanities Press, Inc., Atlantic Highlands, N.J., 07716.

i. The only acceptable reason for punishing a man is that he has committed a crime.

ii. The only acceptable reason for punishing a man in a given manner and degree is that the punishment is "equal" to the crime for which he is punished.

These propositions, I think it will be agreed, express the main points of the first and second paragraphs respectively. Before stopping over these points, let us go on to a third. It is brought out in the following passage from the *Rechtslehre*, which is also often referred to by writers on retributivism.

> Even if a civil society resolved to dissolve itself with the consent of all its members—as might be supposed in the case of a people inhabiting an island resolving to separate and scatter themselves throughout the whole world—the last murderer lying in prison ought to be executed before the resolution was carried out. This ought to be done [so] that everyone may realize the desert of his deeds, and that bloodguiltiness may not remain upon the people; for otherwise they will all be regarded as participators in the murder as a public violation of justice.[3]

It is apparent from this passage that, [as far] as the punishment of death for murder is concerned, the punishment awarded not only may but must be carried out. If it must be carried out "so that everyone may realize the desert of his deeds," then punishment for deeds other than murder must be carried out too. We will take it, then, that Kant holds that:

iii. Whoever commits a crime must be punished in accordance with his desert.

Whereas (i) tells us what kind of reason we must have *if* we punish, (iii) now tells us that we must punish *whenever* there is desert of punishment. Punishment, Kant tells us elsewhere, is "The *juridical* effect or consequence of a culpable act of Demerit."[4] Any crime is a culpable act of demerit, in that it is an "*intentional* transgression—that is, an act accompanied with the consciousness that it is a transgression."[5] This is an unusually narrow definition of crime, since crime is not ordinarily limited to intentional acts of transgression but may also include unintentional ones, such as acts done in ignorance of the law, and criminally negligent acts. However, Kant apparently leaves room for "culpable acts of demerit" outside of the category of crime. These he

calls "faults," which are unintentional transgressions of duty; but "are nevertheless imputable to a person."[6] I can only suppose, though it is a difficulty in the interpre-tation of the *Rechtslehre,* that when Kant says that punishment must be inflicted "only because he has committed a crime," he is not including in "crime" what he would call a fault. Crime would, then, refer to any *intentional* imputable transgressions of duty and these are what must be punished as involving ill desert. The difficulties involved in the definition of crime as the transgression of duty, as opposed to the mere violation of a legal prohibition, will be taken up later.

Taking the three propositions we have isolated as expressing the essence of the Kantian retributivistic position, we must now ask a direct and obvious question. What makes Kant hold this position? Why does he think it apparent that consequences should have *nothing to do* with the decision whether, and how, and how much to punish? There are two directions any answer to this question might follow. One would lead us into an extensive excursus on the philosophical position of Kant, the relation of this to his ethical theory, and the relation of his general theory of ethics to his philosophy of law. It would, in short, take our question as one about the consistency of Kant's position concerning the justification of punishment with the whole of Kantian philosophy. This would involve discussion of Kant's reasons for believing that moral laws must be universal and categorical in virtue of their form alone, and divorced from any empirical content; of his attempt to make out a moral decision-procedure based on an "empty" categorical imperative; and, above all, of the concept of freedom as a postulate of practical reason, and as the central concept of the philosophy of law. This kind of answer, however, we must forego here; for while it would have considerable interest in its own right, it would lead us astray from our purpose, which is to understand as well as we can the retributivist position, not as a part of this or that philosophical system but for its own sake. It is a position taken by philosophers with diverse philosophical systems; we want to take another direction, then, in our answer. Is there any *general* (nonspecial, nonsystematic) reason why Kant rejects consequences in the justification of punishment?

Kant believes that consequences have nothing to do with the justification of punishment partly because of his assumptions about the *direction* of justification; and these assumptions are . . . also to be found underlying the thought of Hegel and Bradley.

Justification is not only *of* something, it is also *to* someone: It has an addressee. Now there are important confusions in Kant's and other traditional justifications of punishment turning on the question what the "punishment" *is* which is being justified. . . . But if we are to feel the force of the retributivist position, we can no longer put off the question of the addressee of justification.

To whom is the Kantian justification of punishment directed? The question may seem a difficult one to answer, since Kant does not consider it himself as a separate issue. Indeed, it is not the kind of question likely to occur to a philosopher of Kant's formalistic leanings. A Kantian justification or rationale stands, so to speak, on its own. It is a structure which can be examined, tested, probed by any rational being. Even to speak of the addressee of justification has an uncomfortably relativistic sound, as if only persuasion of A or B or C is possible, and proof impossible. Yet, in practice, Kant does not address his proffered justification of punishment so much to any rational being (which, to put it otherwise, is to address it not at all), as to the being most affected: the criminal himself.

It is the criminal who is cautioned not to creep through the serpent-windings of utilitarianism. It is the criminal's rights which are in question in the debate with Beccaria over capital punishment. It is the criminal we are warned not to mix up with property or things: the "subjects of Real Right." In the *Kritik der Praktischen Vernunst*, the intended direction of justification becomes especially clear.

> Now the notion of punishment, as such, cannot be united with that of becoming a partaker of happiness; for although he who inflicts the punishment may at the same time have the benevolent purpose of directing this punishment to this end, yet it must be justified in itself as punishment, that is, as mere harm, so that if it stopped there, and the person punished could get no glimpse of kindness hidden behind this harshness, he must yet admit that justice was done him, and that his reward was perfectly suitable to his conduct. In every punishment, as such, there must first be justice, and this constitutes the essence of the notion. Benevolence may, indeed, be united with it, but the man who has deserved punishment has not the least reason to reckon upon this.[7]

Since this matter of the direction of justification is central in our understanding of traditional ret-

ributivism, and not generally appreciated, it will be worth our while to pause over this paragraph. Kant holds here, as he later holds in the *Rechtslehre*, that once it has been decided that a given "mode and measure" of punishment is justified, then "he who inflicts punishment" may do so in such a way as to increase the long-term happiness of the criminal. This could be accomplished, for example, by using a prison term as an opportunity for reforming the criminal. But Kant's point is that reforming the criminal has nothing to do with justifying the infliction of punishment. It is not inflicted because it will give an opportunity for reform, but because it is merited. The passage does not need my gloss; it is transparently clear. Kant wants the justification of punishment to be such that the criminal "who could get no glimpse of kindness behind this harshness" would have to admit that punishment is warranted.

Suppose we tell the criminal, "We are punishing you for your own good." This is wrong because it is then open to him to raise the question whether he deserves punishment, and what you consider good to be. If he does not deserve punishment, we have no right to inflict it, especially in the name of some good of which the criminal may not approve. So long as we are to treat him as rational—a being with dignity—we cannot force our judgements of good upon him. This is what makes the appeal to supposedly good consequences "wavering and uncertain." They waver because the criminal has as much right as anyone to question them. They concern ends which he may reject, and means which he might rightly regard as unsuited to the ends.

In the "Supplementary Explanations of the Principles of Right" of the *Rechtslehre*, Kant distinguishes between "punitive justice (*justitia punitiva*), in which the ground of the penalty is moral (*quia peccatum est*)," and "punitive *expediency,* the foundation of which is merely pragmatic (*ne peccetur*) as being grounded on the experience of what operates most effectively to prevent crime." Punitive justice, says Kant, has an "entirely distinct place (*locus justi*) in the topical arrangement of the juridical conceptions." It does not seem reasonable to suppose that Kant makes this distinction merely to discard punitive expediency entirely, that he has no concern at all for the *ne peccetur.* But he does hold that there is no place for it in the justification of punishment proper: For this can only be to show the criminal that the punishment is just.

How is this to be done? The difficulty is that on the one hand the criminal must be treated as a rational being, an end in himself; but on the other hand the justification we offer him cannot be allowed to appear as the opening move in a rational discussion. It cannot turn on the criminal's acceptance of some premise which, as a rational being, he has a perfect right to question. If the end in question is the well-being of society, we are assuming that the criminal will not have a different view of what that well-being consists in, and we are telling him that he should sacrifice himself *to* that end. As a rational being, he can question whether any end we propose is a good end. And we have no right to demand that he sacrifice himself to the public well-being, even supposing he agrees with us on what that consists in. No man has a duty, in Kant's view, to be benevolent.[8]

The way out of the quandary is to show the criminal that we are not inflicting the punishment on him for some questionable purpose of our own choice, but that he, as a free agent, has exercised *his* choice in such a way as to make the punishment a necessary consequence. "His own evil deed draws the punishment upon himself."[9] The undeserved evil which anyone commits on another, is to be regarded as perpetuated on himself."[10] But may not the criminal rationally question this asserted connection between crime and punishment? Suppose he wishes to regard the punishment *not* as "drawn upon himself" by his own "evil deed?" Suppose he argues that no good purpose will be served by punishing him? But this line of thought leads into the "serpent-windings of utilitarianism," for if it is good consequences that govern, then justice goes by the board. What may not be done to him in the name of good consequences? What proportion would remain between what he has done and what he suffers?[11]

But punishment is *inflicted*. To tell the criminal that he "draws it upon himself" is all very well, only how do we justify *to ourselves* the infliction of it? Kant's answer is found early in the *Rechtslehre*.[12] There he relates punishment to crime *via* freedom. Crime consists in compulsion or constraint of some kind: a hindrance of freedom.[13] If it is wrong that freedom should be hindered, it is right to block this hindrance. But to block the constraint of freedom it is necessary to apply constraint. Punishment is a "hindering of a hindrance of freedom." Compulsion of the criminal is, then, justified only to the extent that it hinders his compulsion of another.

But how are we to understand Kant here? Punishment comes after the crime. How can it hinder [it]? The reference cannot be to the hindrance of future crime, or Kant's doctrine reduces to a variety of utilitarianism. The picture of compulsion versus compulsion is clear enough, but how are we to apply it? Our answer must be somewhat speculative, since there is no direct answer to be found in the *Rechtslehre*. The answer must begin from yet another extension of the concept of a crime. For the crime cannot consist merely in an act. What is criminal is acting in accordance with a wrong maxim—a maxim which would, if made universal, destroy freedom. The adoption of the maxim is criminal. Should we regard punishment, then, as the hindrance of a wrong maxim? But how do we hinder a maxim? We show, exhibit, its wrongness by taking it at face value. If the criminal has adopted it, he is claiming that it can be universalized. But if it is universalized it warrants the same treatment of the criminal as he has accorded to his victim. So if he murders he must be executed; if he steals we must "steal from" him.[14] What we do to him he willed, in willing, to adopt his maxim as universalizable. To justify the punishment to the criminal is to show him that the compulsion we use on him proceeds according to the same rule by which he acts. This is how he "draws the punishment upon himself." In punishing, we are not adopting his maxim but demonstrating its logical consequences if universalized: We show the criminal *what* he has willed. This is the positive side of the Kantian rationale of punishment.

II.

Hegel's version of this rationale has attracted more attention, and disagreement, in recent literature. It is the Hegelian metaphysical terminology that is partly responsible for the disagreement and that has stood in the way of an understanding of the retributivist position. The difficulty turns around the notions of "annulment of crime" and punishment as the "right" of the criminal. Let us consider "annulment" first.

In the *Philosophie des Rechts*[15] Hegel tells us that

Abstract right is a right to coerce, because the wrong which transgresses it is an exercise of force against the existence of my freedom in an external thing. The maintenance of this existent against the exercise of force therefore itself takes the form of an external act and an exercise of force annulling the force originally brought against it.[16]

Holmes complains that by the use of his logical apparatus, involving the negation of negations (or annulment), Hegel professes to establish what is only a mystic (though generally felt) bond between wrong and punishment.[17] Hastings Rashdall asks how any rational connection can be shown between the evil of the pain of punishment, and the twin evils of the suffering of the victim and the moral evil which "pollutes the offender's soul," unless appeal is made to the probable good consequences of punishment. The notion that the "guilt" of the offense must be, in some mysterious way, wiped out by the suffering of the offender does not seem to provide it.[18] Crime, which is an evil, is apparently to be "annulled" by the addition to it of punishment, which is another evil. How can two evils yield a good?[19]

But in fact Hegel is following the *Rechtslehre* quite closely here, and his doctrine is very near to Kant's. In the notes taken at Hegel's lectures,[20] we find Hegel quoted as follows:

If crime and its annulment . . . are treated as if they were unqualified evils, it must, of course, seem quite unreasonable to will an evil merely because "another evil is there already.". . . But it is not merely a question of an evil or of this, that, or the other good; the precise point at issue is wrong, and the righting of it. . . . The various considerations which are relevant to punishment as a phenomenon and to the bearing it has on the particular consciousness, and which concern its effects (deterrent, reformative, etcetera) on the imagination, are an essential topic for examination in their place, especially in connection with modes of punishment, but all these considerations presuppose as their foundation the fact that punishment is inherently and actually just. In discussing this matter the only important things are, first, that crime is to be annulled, not because it is the producing of an evil, but because it is the infringing of the right as right, and secondly, the question of what that positive existence is which crime possesses and which must be annulled; it is this existence which is the real evil to be removed, and the essential point is the question of where it lies. So long as the concepts here at issue are not clearly apprehended, confusion must continue to reign in the theory of punishment.[21]

While this passage is not likely to dethrone confusion, it does bring us closer to the basically Kantian heart of Hegel's theory. To "annul crime" should be read "right wrong." Crime is a wrong which consists in an "infringement of the right as right."[22] It would be unjust, says Hegel, to allow crime, which is the invasion of a right, to go unrequited. For to allow this is to admit that the crime is "valid": that is, that it is not in conflict with justice. But this is what we do not want to admit, and the only way of showing this is to pay back the deed to the agent: Coerce the coercer. For by intentionally violating his victim's rights, the criminal in effect claims that the rights of others are not binding on him; and this is to attack *das Recht* itself: the system of justice in which there are rights which must be respected. Punishment not only keeps the system in balance, it vindicates the system itself.

Besides talking about punishment's "annulment" of crime, Hegel has argued that it is the "right of the criminal." The obvious reaction to this is that it is a strange justification of punishment which makes it someone's right, for it is at best a strange kind of right which no one would ever want to claim! McTaggart's explanation of this facet of Hegel's theory is epitomized in the following quotation:

What, then, is Hegel's theory? It is, I think, briefly this: In sin, man rejects and defies the moral law. Punishment is pain inflicted on him because he has done this, and in order that he may, by the fact of his punishment, be forced into recognizing as valid the law which he rejected in sinning, and so repent of his sin— really repent, and not merely be frightened out of doing it again.[23]

If McTaggart is right, then we are obviously not going to find in Hegel anything relevant to the justification of legal punishment, where the notions of sin and repentance are out of place. And this is the conclusion McTaggart of course reaches. "Hegel's view of punishment," he insists, "cannot properly be applied in jurisprudence, and . . . his chief mistake regarding it lay in supposing that it could."[24]

But though McTaggart may be right in emphasizing the theological aspect of Hegel's doctrine of punishment, he is wrong in denying it a jurisprudential aspect. In fact, Hegel is only saying what Kant emphasized: That to justify punishment to the criminal is to show him that *he* has chosen to be treated as he is being treated.

The injury (the penalty) which falls on the criminal is not merely *implicitly* just—as just, it is *eo ipso* his implicit will, an embodiment of his freedom, his right; on the contrary, it is also a right *established* within the criminal himself, that is, in his objectively embodied will, in his action. The reason for this is that his action is the action of a rational being and this implies that it is something universal and that by doing it the criminal has laid down a law which he has explicitly recognized in his action and under which in consequence he should be brought as under his right.[25]

To accept the retributivist position, then, is to accept a thesis about the burden of proof in the justification of punishment. Provided we make the punishment "equal" to the crime it is not up to us to justify it to the criminal, beyond pointing out to him that it is what he willed. It is not that he initiated a chain of events likely to result in his punishment, but that in willing the crime he willed that he himself should suffer in the same degree as his victim. But what if the criminal simply wanted to commit his crime and get away with it (break the window and run, take the funds and retire to Brazil, kill but live)? Suppose we explain to the criminal that *really* in willing to kill he willed to lose his life; and, unimpressed, he replies that *really* he wished to kill and save his skin. The retributivist answer is that to the extent that the criminal understands freedom and justice he will understand that his punishment was made inevitable by his own choice. No moral theory can hope to provide a justification of punishment which will seem such to the criminal merely as a nexus of passions and desires. The retributivist addresses him as a rational being, aware of the significance of his action. The burden of proof, the retributivist would argue, is on the theorist who would not start from this assumption. For to assume from the beginning that the criminal is not rational is to treat him, from the beginning, as merely a "harmful animal."

What is involved in the action of the criminal is not only the concept of crime, the rational aspect present in crime as such whether the individual wills it or not, the aspect which the state has to vindicate, but also the abstract rationality of the individual's *volition*. Since that is so, punishment is regarded as containing the criminal's right and hence by being pun-

ished he is honored as a rational being. He does not receive this due of honor unless the concept and measure of his punishment are derived from his own act. Still less does he receive it if he is treated as a harmful animal who has to be made harmless, or with a view to deterring and reforming him.[26]

To address the criminal as a rational being aware of the significance of his action is to address him as a person who knows that he has not committed a "bare" act; to commit an act is to commit oneself to the universalization of the rule by which one acted. For a man to complain about the death sentence for murder is as absurd as for a man to complain that when he pushed down one tray of the scales, the other tray goes up; whereas the action, rightly considered, is of pushing down *and* up. "The criminal gives his consent already by his very act."[27] "The Eumenides sleep, but crime awakens them, and hence it is the very act of crime which vindicates itself."[28]

F. H. Bradley's contribution to the retributive theory of punishment adds heat but not much light. The central, and best-known, passage is the following:

> If there is any opinion to which the man of uncultivated morals is attached, it is the belief in the necessary connection of punishment and guilt. Punishment is punishment, only where it is deserved. We pay the penalty because we owe it, and for no other reason; and if punishment is inflicted for any other reason whatever than because it is merited by wrong, it is a gross immorality, a crying injustice, an abominable crime, and not what it pretends to be. We may have regard for whatever considerations we please—our own convenience, the good of society, the benefit of the offender; we are fools, and worse, if we fail to do so. Having once the right to punish, we may modify the punishment according to the useful and the pleasant; but these are external to the matter, they cannot give us a right to punish, and nothing can do that but criminal desert. This is not a subject to waste words over; if the fact of the vulgar view is not palpable to the reader, we have no hope, and no wish, to make it so.[29]

Bradley's sympathy with the "vulgar view" should be apparent. And there is at least a seeming variation between the position he expresses here and that we have attributed to Kant and Hegel. For Bradley can be read here as leaving an open field for utilitarian reasoning, when the question is how and how much to punish. Ewing interprets Bradley this way, and argues at some length that Bradley is involved in an inconsistency.[30] However, it is quite possible that Bradley did not mean to allow kind and quantity of punishment to be determined by utilitarian considerations. He could mean, as Kant meant, that once punishment is awarded, then "it" (what the criminal must suffer: time in jail, for example) may be made use of for utilitarian purposes. But, it should by this time go without saying, the retributivist would then wish to insist that we not argue backward from the likelihood of attaining these good purposes to the rightness of inflicting the punishment.

Bradley's language is beyond question loose when he speaks, in the passage quoted, of our "modifying" the punishment, "having once the right to punish." But when he says that "we pay the penalty because we owe it, and for no other reason," Bradley must surely be credited with the insight that we may owe more or less according to the gravity of the crime. The popular view, he says, is "that punishment is justice; that justice implies the giving what is due."[31] And "punishment is the complement of criminal desert; is justifiable only so far as deserved."[32] If Bradley accepts this popular view, then Ewing must be wrong in attributing to him the position that kind and degree of punishment may be determined by utilitarian considerations.[33]

III.

Let us sum up traditional retributivism, as we have found it expressed in the paradigmatic passage we have examined. We have found no reason in Hegel or Bradley to take back or qualify importantly the *three propositions* we found central in Kant's retributivism:

i. The only acceptable reason for punishing a man is that he has committed a crime.

ii. The only acceptable reason for punishing a man in a given manner and degree is that the punishment is "equal" to the crime.

iii. Whoever commits a crime must be punished in accordance with his desert.

To these propositions should be added *two underlying assumptions:*

i. An assumption about the direction of justification: to the criminal.

ii. An assumption about the nature of justification: To show the criminal that it is he who has willed what he now suffers.

Though it may have been stated in forbidding metaphysical terms, traditional retributivism cannot be dismissed as unintelligible, or absurd, or implausible.[34] There is no obvious contradiction in it; and there are no important disagreements among the philosophers we have studied over what it contends. Yet in spite of the importance of the theory, no one has yet done much more than sketch it in broad strokes. If, as I have surmised, it turns mainly on an assumption concerning the direction of justification, then this assumption should be explained and defended.

And the key concept of "desert" is intolerably vague. What does it mean to say that punishment must be proportionate to what a man *deserves*? This seems to imply, in the theory of the traditional retributivists, that there is some way of measuring desert, or at least of balancing punishment against it. How this measuring or balancing is supposed to be done, we will discuss later. What we must recognize here is that there are alternative criteria of "desert," and that it is not always clear which of these the traditional retributivist means to imply.

When we say of a man that he "deserves severe punishment" how, if at all, may we support our position by arguments? What kind of considerations tend to show what a man does or does not deserve? There are at least two general sorts: those which tend to show that what he has done is a member of a class of action which is especially heinous; and those which tend to show that his doing of this action was, in (or because of) the circumstances, particularly wicked. The argument that a man deserves punishment may rest on the first kind of appeal alone, or on both kinds. Retributivists who rely on the first sort of consideration alone would say that anyone who would do a certain sort of thing, no matter what the circumstances may have been, deserves punishment. Whether there are such retributivists I do not know. Kant, because of his insistence on *intention* as a necessary condition of committing a crime, clearly wishes to bring in considerations of the second sort as well. It is not, on his view, merely *what* was done, but the intention of the agent which must be taken into account. No matter what the intention, a man cannot commit a crime deserving punishment if his deed is not a transgression. But if he does commit a transgression, he must do so intentionally to commit a crime; and all crime is deserving of punishment. The desert of the crime is a factor both of the seriousness of the transgression, considered by itself, and the degree to which the intention to transgress was present. If, for Kant, the essence of morality consists in knowingly acting from duty, the essence of immorality consists in knowingly acting against duty.

The retributivist can perhaps avoid the question of how we decide that one crime is morally more heinous than another by hewing to his position that no such decision is necessary so long as we make the punishment "equal" to the crime. To accomplish this, he might argue, it is not necessary to argue to the *relative* wickedness of crimes. But at best this leaves

us with the problem how we *do* make punishments equal to crimes, a problem which will not stop plaguing retributivists. And there is the problem *which* transgressions, intentionally committed, the retributivist is to regard as crimes. Surely not every morally wrong action!

And how is the retributivist to fit in appeals to punitive expediency? None of our authors denies that such appeals may be made, but where and how do they tie into punitive justice? It will not do simply to say that justifying punishment to the criminal is one thing, and justifying it to society is another. Suppose we must justify in both directions at once? And who are "we" anyway—the players of which roles, at what stage of the game? And has the retributivist cleared himself of the charge, sure to arise, that the theory is but a cover for a much less commendable motive than respect for justice: elegant draping for naked revenge?

Endnotes

1. . . . [S]ince in our own time there are few defenders of retributivism, the position is most often referred to by writers who are opposed to it. This does not make for clarity. In the past few years, however, there has been an upsurge of interest, and some good articles have been written. Cf. esp. J. D. Mabbott, "Punishment," *Mind,* XLVIII (1939), pp. 152–167; C. S. Lewis, "The Humanitarian Theory of Punishment," *20th Century* (Australian), March, 1949; C. W. K. Mundle, "Punishment and Desert," *The Philosophical Quarterly,* IV (1954), pp. 216–228; A. S. Kaufman, "Anthony Quinton on Punishment," *Analysis,* October, 1959; and K. G. Armstrong, "The Retributivist Hits Back," *Mind,* LXX (1961), pp. 471–490.
2. *Rechtslehre.* Part Second, 49, E. Hastie translation, Edinburgh, 1887, pp. 195–197.
3. Ibid., p. 198. Cf. also the passage on p. 196 beginning "What, then, is to be said of such a proposal as to keep a Criminal alive who has been condemned to death. . . ."
4. Ibid., Prolegomena, General Divisions of the Metaphysic of Morals, IV. (Hastie, p. 38).
5. Ibid., p. 32.
6. Ibid., p. 32.
7. Book I, Ch. I, Sec. VIII, Theorem IV, Remark 11 (T. K. Abbott translation, 5th ed., revised, London, 1898, p. 127).
8. *Rechtslehre.*
9. "Supplementary Explanation of The Principles of Right," V.
10. Cf. long quote from the *Rechtslehre,* above.
11. How can the retributivist allow utilitarian considerations even in the administration of the sentence? Are we

not then opportunistically imposing our conception of good on the convicted man? How did we come by this right, which we did not have when he stood before the bar awaiting sentence? Kant would refer to the loss of his "Civil Personality"; but what rights remain with the "Inborn Personality," which is not lost? How is human dignity modified by conviction of crime?
12. Introduction to The Science of Right, General Definitions and Divisions, D. Right is Joined with the Title to Compel. (Hastie, p. 47).
13. This extends the definition of crime Kant has given earlier by specifying the nature of an imputable transgression of duty.
14. There are serious difficulties in the application of the "Principle of Equality" to the "mode and measure" of punishment. This will be considered. . . .
15. I shall use this short title for the work with the formidable double title of *Naturrecht und Stattswissenschaft in Grundrisse; Grundlinien der Philosophie des Rechts (Natural Law and Political Science in Outline: Elements of the Philosophy of Right).* References will be to the T. M. Knox translation (*Hegel's Philosophy of Right,* Oxford, 1942).
16. *Philosophie des Rechts,* Sect. 93 (Knox, p. 67).
17. O. W. Holmes, Jr., *The Common Law,* Boston, 1881, p. 42.
18. Hastings Rashdall, *The Theory of Good and Evil,* 2nd. Edn., Oxford, 1924, vol. 1, pp. 285–286.
19. G. E. Moore holds that, consistently with his doctrine of organic wholes, they might; or at least they might yield that which is less evil than the sum of the constituent evils. This indicates for him a possible vindication of the

Retributive theory of punishment. (*Principia Ethica*, Cambridge, 1903, pp. 213–214).
20. Included in the Knox translation.
21. Knox translation, pp. 69–70.
22. There is an unfortunate ambiguity in the German word *Recht,* here translated as "right." The word can mean either that which is a right or that which is in accordance with the law. So when Hegel speaks of "infringing the right as right" it is not certain whether he means a right as such or the law as such, or whether, in fact, he is aware of the ambiguity. But to say that the crime infringes the law is analytic, so we will take it that Hegel uses *Recht* here to refer to that which is right. But what the criminal does is not merely to infringe a right, but "the right (*das recht*) as right," that is, to challenge by his action the whole system of rights. (On "*Recht,*" Cf. J. Austin, *The Province of Jurisprudence Determined* [London, Library of Ideas Edition, 1954], Note 26, pp. 285–288 esp. pp. 287–288.)
23. J. M. E. McTaggart, *Studies in The Hegelian Cosmology,* Cambridge, 1901, Ch. V, p. 133.
24. Ibid., p. 145.
25. Op Cit., Sect. 100 (Hastie, p. 70).
26. Ibid., Lecture-notes on Sect. 100, Hastie, p. 71.
27. Ibid., Addition to Sect. 100, Hastie, p. 246.
28. Ibid., Addition to Sect. 101, Hastie, p. 247. There is something ineradicably *curious* about retributivism. We keep coming back to the metaphor of the balance scale. Why is the metaphor powerful and at the same time strange? Why do we agree so readily that "the assassination" cannot "trammel up the consequence," that "even-handed justice commends the ingredients of our poisoned chalice to our own lips?"
29. F. H. Bradley, *Ethical Studies,* Oxford, 1952, pp. 26–27.
30. A. C. Ewing, *The Morality of Punishment,* London, 1929, pp. 41–42.
31. Op. Cit., p. 29.
32. Ibid., p. 30.
33. Op. Cit., p. 41.
34. Or, more ingeniously, "merely logical," the "elucidation of the use of a word"; answering the question, "When (logically) *can* we punish?" as opposed to the question answered by the utilitarians, "When (morally) *may* or *ought* we to punish?" (Cf. A. M. Quinton, "On Punishment," *Analysis,* June, 1954, pp. 133–142.)

73. *Deterrence and Uncertainty*

Ernest van den Haag

Ernest van den Haag argues that although we don't know for sure whether capital punishment deters would-be offenders, the greater severity of capital punishment still gives us reason to expect more deterrence from it. Accordingly, van den Haag maintains that the burden of proof is on opponents of capital punishment to show why the greater severity of capital punishment does not lead to more deterrence.

. . . If we do not know whether the death penalty will deter others [in a uniquely effective way], we are confronted with two uncertainties. If we impose the death penalty, and achieve no deterrent effect thereby, the life of a convicted murderer has been expended in vain (from a deterrent viewpoint). There is a net loss. If we impose the death sentence and thereby deter some future murderers, we spared the lives of some future victims (the prospective murderers gain too; they are spared punishment because they were deterred). In this case, the death penalty has led to a net gain, unless the life of a convicted murderer is valued more highly than that of the unknown victim, or victims (and the nonimprisonment of the deterred nonmurderer).

The calculation can be turned around, of course. The absence of the death penalty may harm no one and therefore produce a gain—the life of the convicted murderer. Or it may kill future victims of murderers who could have been deterred, and thus produce a loss—their life.

Reprinted with permission of the publisher from the *Journal of Criminal Law, Criminology and Police Science,* vol. 60, no. 2 (1969).

To be sure, we must risk something certain— the death (or life) of the convicted man, for something uncertain—the death (or life) of the victims of murderers who may be deterred. This is in the nature of uncertainty—when we invest, or gamble, we risk the money we have for an uncertain gain. Many human actions, most commitments—including marriage and crime—share this characteristic with the deterrent purpose of any penalization, and with its rehabilitative purpose (and even with the protective).

More proof is demanded for the deterrent effect of the death penalty than is demanded for the deterrent effect of other penalties. This is not justified by the absence of other utilitarian purposes such as protection and rehabilitation; they involve no less uncertainty than deterrence.[1]

Irrevocability may support a demand for some reason to expect more deterrence than revocable penalties might produce, but not a demand for more proof of deterrence. . . . The reason for expecting more deterrence lies in the greater severity, the terrifying effect inherent in finality. Since it seems more important to spare victims than . . . murderers, the burden of proving that the greater severity inherent in irrevocability adds nothing to deterrence lies on those who oppose capital punishment. Proponents of the death penalty need show only that there is no more uncertainty about it than about greater severity in general.

The demand that the death penalty be proved more deterrent than alternatives cannot be satisfied any more than the demand that six years in prison be proved to be more deterrent than three. But the uncertainty that confronts us favors the death penalty as long as [it] might save future victims of murder. This effect is as plausible as the general idea that penalties have deterrent effects which increase with their severity. Though we have no proof of the positive deterrence of the penalty, we also have no proof of zero, or negative effectiveness. I believe we have no right to risk additional future victims of murder for the sake of sparing convicted murderers; on the contrary, our moral obligation is to risk the possible ineffectiveness of executions. However rationalized, the opposite view appears to be motivated by the simple fact that executions are more subjected to social control than murder. However, this applies to all penalties and does not argue for the abolition of any.

Endnote

1. Rehabilitation or protection are of minor importance in our actual penal system (though not in our theory). We confine many people who do not need rehabilitation and against whom we do not need protection (e.g., the exasperated husband who killed his wife); we release many unrehabilitated offenders against whom protection is needed. Certainly rehabilitation and protection are not, and deterrence is, the main actual function of legal punishment, if we disregard nonutilitarian purposes.

74. Civilization, Safety, and Deterrence

JEFFREY H. REIMAN

Jeffrey Reiman maintains that greater severity in and of itself does not mean more deterrence. Moreover, Reiman argues if greater severity were always justified on grounds of producing more deterrence, then torturing criminals to death would be justified because torturing criminals to death is clearly a more severe punishment than simply executing them.

. . . By placing execution alongside torture in the category of things we will not do to our fellow human beings even when they deserve them, we broadcast the message that totally subjugating a person to the power of others *and* confronting him with the advent of his own humanly administered demise is too horrible to be done by civilized human beings to their fellows even when they have earned it: too horrible to do, and too horrible to be capable of doing. And I contend that broadcasting this message loud and clear would in the long run contribute to the general detestation of murder and be, to the extent to which it worked itself into the hearts and minds of the populace, a deterrent. In short, refusing to execute murderers though they deserve it both reflects and continues the taming of the human species that we call civilization. Thus, I take it that the abolition of the death penalty, though it is a just punishment for murder, is part of the civilizing mission of modern states. . . .

. . . I said that judging a practice too horrible to do even to those who deserve it does not exclude the possibility that it could be justified if necessary to avoid even worse consequences. Thus, were the death penalty clearly proven a better deterrent to the murder of innocent people than life in prison, we might have to admit that we had not yet reached a level of civilization at which we could protect ourselves without imposing this horrible fate on murderers, and thus we might have to grant the necessity of instituting the death penalty. But

this is far from proven. The available research by no means clearly indicates that the death penalty reduces the incidence of homicide more than life imprisonment does. . . .

Conceding that it has not been proven that the death penalty deters more murders than life imprisonment, van den Haag has argued that neither has it been proven that the death penalty does *not* deter more murders, and thus we must follow common sense which teaches that the higher the cost of something, the fewer people will choose it, and therefore at least some potential murderers who would not be deterred by life imprisonment will be deterred by the death penalty. Van den Haag writes:

> . . . our experience shows that the greater the threatened penalty, the more it deters.
>
> . . . Life in prison is still life, however unpleasant. In contrast, the death penalty does not just threaten to make life unpleasant—it threatens to take life altogether. This difference is perceived by those affected. We find that when they have the choice between life in prison and execution, 99 percent of all prisoners under sentence of death prefer life in prison. . . .
>
> From this unquestioned fact a reasonable conclusion can be drawn in favor of the superior deterrent effect of the death penalty. Those who have the choice in practice. . . fear death more than they fear life in prison. . . . If they do, it follows that the threat of the death penalty, all other things equal, is likely to deter more than the threat of life in prison. One is most deterred by what one fears most. From which it follows that whatever statistics fail, or do not fail, to show, the death

From Jeffrey H. Reiman, "Justice, Civilization, and the Death Penalty: Answering van den Haag." *Philosophy and Public Affairs*, vol. 14 (Spring 1985). Excerpt, pp. 141–147, reprinted with permission of Princeton University Press.

penalty is likely to be more deterrent than any other.[1]

Those of us who recognize how common sensical it was, and still is, to believe that the sun moves around the earth, will be less willing than Professor van den Haag to follow common sense here, especially when it comes to doing something awful to our fellows. Moreover, there are good reasons for doubting common sense on this matter. Here are four:

1. From the fact that one penalty is more feared than another, it does not follow that the more feared penalty will deter more than the less feared, unless we know that the less feared penalty is not fearful enough to deter everyone who can be deterred— and this is just what we don't know with regard to the death penalty. Though I fear the death penalty more than life in prison, I can't think of any act that the death penalty would deter me from that an equal likelihood of spending my life in prison wouldn't deter me from as well. Since it seems to me that whoever would be deterred by a given likelihood of death would be deterred by an *equal* likelihood of life behind bars, I suspect that the commonsense argument only seems plausible because we evaluate it unconsciously assuming that potential criminals will face larger likelihoods of death sentences than of life sentences. If the likelihoods were equal, . . . where life imprisonment was improbable enough to make it too distant a possibility to worry much about, a similar low probability of death would have the same effect. After all, we are undeterred by small likelihoods of death every time we walk the streets. And if life imprisonment were sufficiently probable to pose a real deterrent threat, it would pose as much of a deterrent threat as death. And this is just what most of the research we have on the comparative deterrent impact of execution versus life imprisonment suggests.

2. In light of the fact that roughly 500 to 700 suspected felons are killed by the police in the line of duty every year, and the fact that the number of privately owned guns in [the United States] is substantially larger than the number of households. . . , it must be granted that anyone contemplating committing a crime *already* faces a substantial risk of ending up dead. . . . It's hard to see why anyone *who is not already deterred by this* would be deterred by the addition of the more distant risk of death after apprehension, conviction, and appeal. Indeed, this suggests that people consider risks in a much cruder way than van den Haag's appeal to common sense suggests—which should be evident to anyone who contemplates how few people use seatbelts (14 percent of drivers, on some estimates), when it is widely known that wearing them can spell the difference between life (outside prison) and death.

3. Van den Haag has maintained that deterrence does not work only by means of cost-benefit calculations made by potential criminals. It works also by the lesson about the wrongfulness of murder that is slowly learned in a society that subjects murderers to the ultimate punishment.[2] But if I am correct in claiming that the refusal to execute even those who deserve it has a civilizing effect, then the refusal to execute also teaches a lesson about the wrongfulness of murder. My claim here is admittedly speculative, but no more so than van den Haag's to the contrary. [My] view has the added virtue of accounting for the failure of research to show an increased deterrent effect from executions *without having to deny the plausibility of van den Haag's commonsense argument that at least some additional potential murders will be deterred by the prospect of the death penalty*. If there is a deterrent effect from *not executing*, then . . . while executions will deter some murderers, this effect will be balanced by the weakening of the deterrent effect of not executing, such that no net reduction in murders will result. And this . . . also disposes of van den Haag's argument that, in the absence of knowledge one way or the other on the deterrent effect of executions, we should execute murderers rather than risk the lives of innocent people whose murders might have been

deterred. . . . If there is a deterrent effect of not executing, it follows that we risk innocent lives either way. And if this is so, it seems that the only reasonable course of action is to refrain from imposing what we know is a horrible fate.

4. Those who still think that van den Haag's commonsense argument for executing murderers is valid will find that the argument proves more than they bargained for. Van den Haag maintains that, in the absence of conclusive evidence on the relative deterrent impact of the death penalty versus life imprisonment, we must follow common sense and assume that if one punishment is more fearful than another, it will deter some potential criminals not deterred by the less fearful punishment. Since people sentenced to death will almost universally try to get their sentences changed to life in prison, it follows that death is more fearful than life imprisonment, and thus . . . will deter some additional murderers. Consequently, we should institute the death penalty to save the lives these additional murderers would have taken. But, since people sentenced to be tortured to death would surely try to get their sentences changed to simple execution, the same argument proves that death-by-torture will deter still more potential murderers. Consequently, we should institute death-by-torture to save the lives these additional murderers would have taken. Anyone who accepts van den Haag's argument is then confronted with a dilemma: Until we have conclusive evidence that capital punishment is a greater deterrent to murder than life imprisonment, he must grant *either* that we should not follow common sense and not impose the death penalty; *or* we should follow common sense and torture murderers to death. In short, either we must abolish the electric chair or reinstitute the rack. Surely, this is the *reductio ad absurdum* of van den Haag's commonsense argument.

◇

Endnotes

1. Ernest van den Haag and John P. Conrad, *The Death Penalty: A Debate* (New York: Plenum Press, 1983), pp. 68–69.

2. Ibid., p. 63.

75. Gregg v. Georgia

SUPREME COURT OF THE UNITED STATES

The issue before the Supreme Court of the United States was whether capital punishment violates the Eighth Amendment's prohibition of cruel and unusual punishment. The majority of the Court held that it does not violate this prohibition because capital punishment (1) accords with contemporary standards of decency, (2) may serve some deterrent or retributive purpose that is not degrading to human dignity, and (3) is no longer arbitrarily applied in the case of the Georgia law under review. Dissenting Justice Brennan argued that (1) through (3) do not suffice to show that capital punishment is constitutional; it would further have to be shown that capital punishment is not degrading to human dignity. Dissenting Justice Marshall objected to the majority's decision on the grounds that capital punishment is not necessary for deterrence and that a retributive purpose for it is not consistent with human dignity. He also contended that contemporary standards of decency with respect to capital punishment are not based on informed opinion.

We address initially the basic contention that the punishment of death for the crime of murder is, under all circumstances, "cruel and unusual" in violation of the Eighth and Fourteenth Amendments of the Constitution. . . .

The Court on a number of occasions has both assumed and asserted the constitutionality of capital punishment. In several cases that assumption provided a necessary foundation for the decision, as the Court was asked to decide whether a particular method of carrying out a capital sentence would be allowed to stand under the Eighth Amendment. But until *Furman v. Georgia* (1972), the Court never confronted squarely the fundamental claim that the punishment of death always, regardless of the enormity of the offense or the procedure followed in imposing the sentence, is cruel and unusual punishment in violation of the Constitution. Although this issue was presented and addressed in *Furman*, it was not resolved. . . . Four Justices would have held that capital punishment is not unconstitutional *per se*; two Justices would have reached the opposite conclusion; and three Justices, while agreeing that the statutes then before the Court were invalid as applied, left open the question whether such punishment may ever be imposed. We now hold that the punishment of death does not invariably violate the Constitution. . . .

It is clear from the foregoing precedents that the Eighth Amendment has not been regarded as a static concept. As Mr. Chief Justice Warren said, in an oft-quoted phrase, "[t]he Amendment must draw its meaning from the evolving standards of decency that mark the progress of a maturing society." . . . Thus, an assessment of contemporary values concerning the infliction of a challenged sanction is relevant to the application of the Eighth Amendment. As we develop below more fully, this assessment does not call for a subjective judgment. It requires, rather, that we look to objective indicia that reflect the public attitude toward a given sanction.

But our cases also make clear that public perceptions of standards of decency with respect to criminal sanctions are not conclusive. A penalty also must accord with "the dignity of man," which is the "basic concept underlying the Eighth Amendment." This means, at least, that the punishment not be "excessive." When a form of punishment in the abstract (in this case, whether capital punishment may ever be imposed as a sanction for murder) rather than in the particular (the propriety of death as a penalty to be applied to a specific defendant for a specific crime) is under consideration, the inquiry into "excessiveness" has two aspects. First, the punishment must not involve the unnecessary and wanton infliction of pain. Second, the punishment must not be grossly out of proportion to the severity of the crime.

Of course, the requirements of the Eighth Amendment must be applied with an awareness of the limited role to be played by the courts. This does not mean that judges have no role to play, for the

Eighth Amendment is a restraint upon the exercise of legislative power. . . .

But, while we have an obligation to insure that constitutional bounds are not overreached, we may not act as judges as we might as legislators.

> Courts are not representative bodies. They are not designed to be a good reflex of a democratic society. Their judgment is best informed, and therefore most dependable, within narrow limits. Their essential quality is detachment, founded on independence. History teaches that the independence of the judiciary is jeopardized when courts become embroiled in the passions of the day and assume primary responsibility in choosing between competing political, economic and social pressures. *Dennis v. United States* (1951)

Therefore, in assessing a punishment selected by a democratically elected legislature against the constitutional measure, we presume its validity. We may not require the legislature to select the least severe penalty possible so long as the penalty selected is not cruelly inhumane or disproportionate to the crime involved. And a heavy burden rests on those who would attack the judgment of the representatives of the people.

This is true in part because the constitutional test is intertwined with an assessment of contemporary standards and the legislative judgment weighs heavily in ascertaining such standards. "[I]n a democratic society legislatures, not courts, are constituted to respond to the will and consequently the moral values of the people." *Furman v. Georgia.* The deference we owe to the decisions of the state legislatures under our federal system, is enhanced where the specification of punishments is concerned, for "these are peculiarly questions of legislative policy." *Gore v. United States.* . . . A decision that a given punishment is impermissible under the Eighth Amendment cannot be reversed short of a constitutional amendment. The ability of the people to express their preference through the normal democratic processes, as well as through ballot referenda, is shut off. Revisions cannot be made in the light of further experience.

. . . We now consider specifically whether . . . death for the crime of murder is a *per se* violation of the Eighth and Fourteenth Amendments to the Constitution. We note first that history and precedent strongly support a negative answer to this question.

The imposition of the death penalty for the crime of murder has a long history of acceptance both in the United States and in England. The common-law rule imposed a mandatory death sentence on all convicted murderers. And the penalty continued to be used into the twentieth century by most American States, although the breadth of the common-law rule was diminished, initially by narrowing the class of murders to be punished by death and subsequently by widespread adoption of laws expressly granting juries the discretion to recommend mercy.

It is apparent from the text of the Constitution itself that the existence of capital punishment was accepted by the Framers. At the time the Eighth Amendment was ratified, capital punishment was a common sanction in every State. Indeed, the First Congress of the United States enacted legislation providing death as the penalty for specific crimes. . . .

For nearly two centuries, this Court, repeatedly and often expressly, has recognized that capital punishment is not invalid *per se.* . . .

Four years ago, the petitioners in *Furman* and its companion cases predicated their argument primarily on the asserted proposition that standards of decency had evolved to the point where capital punishment no longer could be tolerated. The petitioners in those cases said, in effect, that the evolutionary process had come to an end, and that standards of decency required that the Eighth Amendment be construed finally as prohibiting capital punishment for any crime regardless of its depravity and impact on society. This view was accepted by two Justices. Three others were unwilling to go so far; focusing on the procedures by which convicted defendants were selected for the death penalty rather than on the actual punishment inflicted, they joined in the conclusion that the statutes before the Court were constitutionally invalid.

The petitioners . . . before the Court today renew the "standards of decency" argument, but developments . . . since *Furman* have undercut substantially the assumptions on which their argument rested. Despite the continuing debate, dating back to the nineteenth century, over the morality and utility of capital punishment, it is now evident that a large proportion of American society continues to regard it as an appropriate and necessary criminal sanction.

The most marked indication of society's endorsement of the death penalty for murder is the legislative response to *Furman*. The legislatures of at least thirty-five States have enacted new statutes that provide for the death penalty for at least some crimes that result in the death of another person. And the Congress of the United States, in 1974, enacted a statute providing the death penalty for aircraft piracy that results in death. These recently adopted statutes have attempted to address the concerns expressed by the Court in *Furman* primarily (i) by specifying the factors to be weighed and the procedures to be followed in deciding when to impose a capital sentence, or (ii) by making the death penalty mandatory for specified crimes. But all of the post-*Furman* statutes make clear that capital punishment itself has not been rejected by the elected representatives of the people. . . .

As we have seen, however, the Eighth Amendment demands more than that a challenged punishment be acceptable to contemporary society. The Court also must ask whether it comports with the basic concept of human dignity at the core of the Amendment. Although we cannot "invalidate a category of penalties because we deem less severe penalties adequate to serve the ends of penology," the sanction imposed cannot be so totally without penological justification that it results in the gratuitous infliction of suffering.

The death penalty is said to serve two principal social purposes: retribution and deterrence of capital crimes by prospective offenders.

In part, capital punishment is an expression of society's moral outrage at particularly offensive conduct. This function may be unappealing to many, but it is essential in an ordered society that asks its citizens to rely on legal processes rather than self-help to vindicate their wrongs.

> The instinct for retribution is part of the nature of man, and channeling that instinct in the administration of criminal justice serves an important purpose in promoting the stability of a society governed by law. When people begin to believe that organized society is unwilling or unable to impose upon criminal offenders the punishment they "deserve," then there are sown the seeds of anarchy—of self-help, vigilante justice, and lynch law. *Furman v. Georgia*.

"Retribution is no longer the dominant objective of the criminal law," but neither is it a forbidden objective nor one inconsistent with our respect for the dignity of men. Indeed, the decision that capital punishment may be the appropriate sanction in extreme cases is an expression of the community's belief that certain crimes are themselves so grievous an affront to humanity that the only adequate response may be the penalty of death.

Statistical attempts to evaluate the worth of the death penalty as a deterrent to crimes by potential offenders have occasioned a great deal of debate. The results simply have been inconclusive. As one opponent of capital punishment has said:

> [A]fter all possible inquiry, including the probing of all possible methods of inquiry, we do not know; and for systematic and easily visible reasons cannot know; what the truth about this "deterrent" effect may be. . . .
>
> The inescapable flaw is . . . that social conditions in any state are not constant through time, and that social conditions are not the same in any two states. If an effect were observed (and the observed effects, one way or another, are not large) then one could not at all tell whether any of this effect is attributable to the presence or absence of capital punishment. A "scientific"—that is to say, a soundly based—conclusion is simply impossible, and no methodological path out of this tangle suggests itself. C. Black, *Capital Punishment: The Inevitability of Caprice and Mistake* 25–26 (1974).

Although some of the studies suggest that the death penalty may not function as a significantly greater deterrent than lesser penalties, there is no convincing empirical evidence either supporting or refuting this view. We may nevertheless assume safely that there are murderers, such as those who act in passion, for whom the threat of death has little or no deterrent effect. But for many others, the death penalty undoubtedly is a significant deterrent. There are carefully contemplated murders, such as murder for hire, where the possible penalty of death may well enter into the cold calculus that precedes the decision to act. And there are some categories of murder, such as murder by a life prisoner, where other sanctions may not be adequate.

The value of capital punishment as a deterrent of crime is a complex factual issue the resolution of which properly rests with the legislatures, which can evaluate the results of statistical studies in terms of their own local conditions and with a flexibility of approach that is not available to the courts. . . .

In sum, we cannot say that the judgment of the Georgia Legislature that capital punishment may be necessary in some cases is clearly wrong. Considerations of federalism, as well as respect for the ability of a legislature to evaluate, in terms of its particular State, the moral consensus concerning the death penalty and its social utility as a sanction, require us to conclude, in the absence of more convincing evidence, that the infliction of death as a punishment for murder is not without justification and thus is not unconstitutionally severe.

Finally, we must consider whether the punishment of death is disproportionate in relation to the crime for which it is imposed. There is no question that death as a punishment is unique in its severity and irrevocability. When a defendant's life is at stake, the Court has been particularly sensitive to insure that every safeguard is observed. But we are concerned here only with the imposition of capital punishment for the crime of murder, and when a life has been taken deliberately by the offender, we cannot say that the punishment is invariably disproportionate to the crime. It is an extreme sanction, suitable to the most extreme of crimes.

We hold that the death penalty is not a form of punishment that may never be imposed, regardless of the circumstances of the offense, regardless of the character of the offender, and regardless of the procedure followed in reaching the decision to impose it.

We now consider whether Georgia may impose the death penalty on the petitioner in this case. . . .

The basic concern of *Furman* centered on those defendants who were being condemned to death capriciously and arbitrarily. Under the procedures before the Court in that case, sentencing authorities were not directed to give attention to the nature or circumstances of the crime committed or the [defendant's] character or record. . . . Left unguided, juries imposed the death sentence in a way that could only be called freakish. The new Georgia sentencing procedures, by contrast, focus the jury's attention on the particularized nature of the crime and the particularized characteristics of the individual defendant. While the jury is permitted to consider any aggravating or mitigating circumstances, it must find and identify at least one statutory aggravating factor before it may impose a penalty of death. In this way the jury's discretion is channeled. No longer can a jury wantonly and freakishly impose the death

sentence; it is always circumscribed by legislative guidelines. In addition, the review function of the Supreme Court of Georgia affords additional assurance that the concerns that prompted our decision in *Furman* are not present to any significant degree in the Georgia procedure applied here.

For the reasons expressed in this opinion, we hold that the statutory system under which Gregg was sentenced to death does not violate the Constitution. Accordingly, the judgment of the Georgia Supreme Court is affirmed. . . .

Mr. Justice *Brennan*, dissenting.[1]

The Cruel and Unusual Punishments Clause "must draw its meaning from the evolving standards of decency that mark the progress of a maturing society." The opinions of Mr. Justice Stewart, Mr. Justice Powell, and Mr. Justice Stevens today hold that "evolving standards of decency" require focus not on the essence of the death penalty itself but primarily upon the procedures employed by the State to single out persons to suffer the penalty of death. Those opinions hold further that, so viewed, the Clause invalidates the mandatory infliction of the death penalty but not its infliction under sentencing procedures that Mr. Justice Stewart, Mr. Justice Powell, and Mr. Justice Stevens conclude adequately safeguard against the risk that the death penalty was imposed in an arbitrary and capricious manner.

In *Furman v. Georgia*, I read "evolving standards of decency" as requiring focus on the essence of the death penalty itself and not primarily or solely on the procedures under which the determination to inflict the penalty upon a particular person was made. . . .

This Court inescapably has the duty, as the ultimate arbiter of the meaning of our Constitution, to say whether, when individuals condemned to death stand before our Bar, "moral concepts" require us to hold that the law has progressed to the point where we should declare that the punishment of death, like punishments on the rack, the screw, and the wheel, is no longer morally tolerable in our civilized society. My opinion in *Furman v. Georgia* concluded that our civilization and the law had progressed to this point and that therefore the punishment of death, for whatever crime and under all circumstances, is "cruel and unusual" in violation of the Eighth and Fourteenth Amendments of the Constitution. I shall not again canvass the reasons that led to that conclusion. I emphasize only that foremost among the "moral concepts" recognized in our cases and inherent in the Clause is the primary moral principle that the State, even as it punishes, must treat its citizens in a manner consistent with their intrinsic worth as human beings—a punishment must not be so severe as to be degrading to human dignity. A judicial determination whether the punishment of death comports with human dignity is therefore not only permitted but compelled by the Clause.

. . . Death for whatever crime and under all circumstances "is truly an awesome punishment. The calculated killing of a human being by the State involves, by its very nature, a denial of the executed person's humanity. . . . An executed person has indeed 'lost the right to have rights.'" Death is not only an unusually severe punishment, unusual in its pain, in its finality, and in its enormity, but it serves no penal purpose more effectively than a less severe punishment; therefore the principle inherent in the Clause that prohibits pointless infliction of excessive punishment when less severe punishment can adequately achieve the same purposes invalidates the punishment. . . .

Mr. Justice *Marshall,* dissenting.

. . . My sole purposes here are to consider the suggestion that my conclusion in *Furman* has been undercut by developments since then, and briefly to evaluate the basis for my Brethren's holding that the extinction of life is a permissible form of punishment under the Cruel and Unusual Punishments Clause.

In *Furman* I concluded that the death penalty is constitutionally invalid for two reasons. First, the death penalty is excessive. And second, the American people, fully informed as to the purposes of the death penalty and its liabilities, would in my view reject it as morally unacceptable.

Since the decision in *Furman,* the legislatures of thirty-five States have enacted new statutes authorizing the imposition of the death sentence for certain crimes, and Congress has enacted a law providing the death penalty for air piracy resulting in death. I would be less than candid if I did not acknowledge that these developments have a significant bearing on a realistic assessment of the moral acceptability of the death penalty to the American people. But if the constitutionality of the death penalty turns, as I have urged, on the opinion of an *informed* citizenry, then even the enactment of new death statutes cannot be viewed as conclusive. In *Furman,* I observed that the American people are largely unaware of the information critical to a judgment on the morality of the death penalty, and concluded that if they were better informed they would consider it shocking, unjust, and unacceptable. A recent study, conducted after the enactment of the post-*Furman* statutes, has confirmed that the American people know little about the death penalty, and that the opinions of an informed public would differ significantly from those of a public unaware of the consequences and effects of the death penalty.

Even assuming, however, that the post-*Furman* enactment of statutes authorizing the death penalty renders the prediction of the views of an informed citizenry an uncertain basis for a constitutional decision, the enactment of those statutes has no bearing whatsoever on the conclusion that the death penalty is unconstitutional because it is excessive. An excessive penalty is invalid under the Cruel and Unusual Punishments Clause "even though popular sentiment may favor" it. The inquiry here, then, is simply whether the death penalty is necessary to accomplish the legitimate legislative purposes in punishment, or whether a less severe penalty—life imprisonment—would do as well.

The two purposes that sustain the death penalty as nonexcessive in the Court's view are general deterrence and retribution. In *Furman,* I canvassed the relevant data on the deterrent effect of capital punishment. The state of knowledge at that point, after literally centuries of debate, was summarized as follows by a United Nations Committee:

> It is generally agreed between the retentionists and abolitionists, whatever their opinions about the validity of comparative studies of deterrence, that the data which now exist show no correlation between the existence of capital punishment and lower rates of capital crime.

The available evidence, I concluded in *Furman,* was convincing that "capital punishment is not necessary as a deterrent to crime in our society."

The Solicitor General in his *amicus* brief in these cases relies heavily on a study by Isaac Ehrlich, reported a year after *Furman,* to support the contention that the death penalty does deter murder. . . .

. . . Ehrlich found a negative correlation between changes in the homicide rate and changes in execution risk. His tentative conclusion was that for the period from 1933 to 1967 each additional execution in the United States might have saved eight lives.

The methods and conclusions of the Ehrlich study have been severely criticized on a number of grounds. . . .

. . . Analysis of Ehrlich's data reveals that all empirical support for the deterrent effect of capital punishment disappears when the five most recent years are removed from his time series—that is to say, whether a decrease in the execution risk corresponds to an increase or a decrease in the murder rate depends on the ending point of the sample period. This finding has cast severe doubts on the reliability of Ehrlich's tentative conclusions. . . .

The Ehrlich study, in short, is of little, if any, assistance in assessing the deterrent impact of the death penalty. The evidence I reviewed in *Furman* remains convincing, in my view, that "capital punishment is not necessary as a deterrent to crime in our society." The justification for the death penalty must be found elsewhere.

The other principal purpose said to be served by the death penalty is retribution. The notion that retribution can serve as a moral justification for the sanction of death finds credence in the opinion of my Brothers Stewart, Powell, and Stevens, and that of my Brother White in *Roberts v. Louisiana.* It is this notion that I find to be the most disturbing aspect of today's unfortunate decisions.

The concept of retribution is a multifaceted one, and any discussion of its role in the criminal law must be undertaken with caution. On one level, it can be said that the notion of retribution or reprobation is the basis of our insistence that only those who have broken the law be punished, and in this sense the notion is quite obviously central to a just system of criminal sanctions. But our recognition that retribution plays a crucial role in determining who may be punished by no means requires approval of retribution as a general justification for punishment. It is the question whether retribution can provide a moral justification for punishment—in particular, capital punishment—that we must consider. . . .

The . . . contentions—that society's expression of moral outrage through the imposition of the death penalty pre-empts the citizenry from taking the law into its own hands and reinforces moral values—are not retributive in the purest sense. They are essentially utilitarian in that they portray the death penalty as valuable because of its beneficial results. These justifications for the death penalty are inadequate because the penalty is, quite clearly I think, not necessary to the accomplishment of those results.

There remains for consideration, however, what might be termed the purely retributive justification for the death penalty—that the death penalty is appropriate, not because of its beneficial effect on society, but because the taking of the murderer's life is itself morally good. . . .

The mere fact that the community demands the murderer's life in return for the evil he has done cannot sustain the death penalty for . . . "The Eighth Amendment demands more than that a challenged punishment be acceptable to contemporary society." To be sustained under the Eighth Amendment, the death penalty must "compor[t] with the basic concept of human dignity at the core of the Amendment"; the objective in imposing it must be "[consistent] with our respect for the dignity of [other] men." Under these standards, the taking of life "because the wrongdoer deserves it" surely must fall, for such a punishment has at its very basis the total denial of the wrongdoer's dignity and worth.

The death penalty, unnecessary to promote the goal of deterrence or to further any legitimate notion of retribution, is an excessive penalty forbidden by the Eighth and Fourteenth Amendments. I respectfully dissent from the Court's judgment upholding the sentences of death imposed upon the petitioners in these cases.

Endnote

1. [This opinion applies also to No. 75-5706, *Proffitt v. Florida, post,* p. 242, and No. 75-5394, *Jurek v Texas, post,* p. 262.]

Suggestions for Further Reading

Anthologies

Acton, H. B. *The Philosophy of Punishment.* London: Macmillan & Co., 1969.

Adams, David. *Philosophical Problems in the Law.* Belmont, CA: Wadsworth Publishing Co., 1996.

Altman, Andrew. *Arguing About Law.* Belmont, CA: Wadsworth Publishing Co., 1996.

Ezorsky, Gertrude. *Philosophical Perspectives on Punishment.* Albany: State University of New York Press, 1972.

Feinberg, Joel, and Hyman Gross. *Philosophy of Law.* Belmont, CA: Wadsworth Publishing Co., 1980.

Gorr, Michael, and Sterling Harwood. *Crime and Punishment.* Boston: Jones and Bartlett, 1995.

Murphy, Jeffrie G. *Punishment and Rehabilitation.* Belmont, CA: Wadsworth Publishing Co., 1984.

Basic Concepts

Golding, Martin P. *Philosophy of Law.* Englewood Cliffs: Prentice-Hall, 1975.

Richards, David A. J. *The Moral Criticism of Law.* Belmont, CA: Dickenson Publishing Co., 1977.

The Forward-Looking and Backward-Looking Views

Adams, Robert. *The Abuses of Punishment.* New York: St. Martin's Press, 1998.

Andenaes, Johannes. *Punishment and Deterrence.* Ann Arbor: The University of Michigan Press, 1974.

Gross, Hyman. *A Theory of Criminal Justice.* New York: Oxford University Press, 1979.

Menninger, Karl. *The Crime of Punishment.* New York: The Viking Press, 1968.

Montague, Philip. *Punishment as Societal Defense.* Lanham, MD: Rowman & Littlefield, 1995.

Murphy, Jeffrie G. *Retribution, Justice and Therapy.* Boston: D. Reidel Publishing Co., 1979.

Packer, Herbert. *The Limits of the Criminal Sanction.* Stanford: Stanford University Press, 1968.

Von Hirsh, Andrew. *Doing Justice.* New York: Hill and Wang, 1976.

Practical Application

Bedau, Hugo. *The Death Penalty in America.* New York: Oxford University Press, 1996.

Black, Charles L., Jr. *Capital Punishment.* New York: W. W. Norton & Co., 1974.

——— . "Reflections on Opposing the Penalty of Death." *St. Mary's Law Journal* (1978), pp. 1–12.

Prejean, Helen. *Dead Man Walking.* New York: Random House, 1993.

van den Haag, Ernest. *Punishing Criminals.* Lanham, MD: University Press of America, 1991.

War and Humanitarian Intervention

Introduction

Basic Concepts

The problem of war and humanitarian intervention is simply the problem of determining the moral limits of the international use of force. *Just war theories* attempt to specify what these moral limits are. Such theories have two components: a set of criteria that establishes a right to go to war (*jus ad bellum*), and a set of criteria that determines legitimate conduct in war (*jus in bello*). The first set of criteria can be grouped under the label "just cause," the second under "just means."

Consider the following specification of just cause:

1. There must be substantial aggression.

2. Nonbelligerent correctives must be either hopeless or too costly.

3. Belligerent correctives must be neither hopeless nor too costly.

This specification of just cause excludes the criterion of legitimate authority, which has had a prominent place in just war theories. This criterion is excluded because it has the character of a second-order requirement; it is a requirement that must be satisfied whenever there is a question of group action with respect to any moral problem whatsoever. For example, with respect to the problem of the distribution of goods and resources in a society, we can certainly ask who has the (morally legitimate) authority to distribute or redistribute goods and resources in a society. But before we ask such questions with respect to particular moral problems, it is important to understand first what are the morally defensible solutions to these problems because a standard way of identifying morally legitimate authorities is by their endorsement of such solutions. With respect to the problem of war and humanitarian intervention, we first need to determine the nature and existence of just causes before we try to identify morally legitimate authorities by their endorsement of such causes.

Assuming that there are just causes, just war theorists go on to specify just means. Consider the following specification of just means:

1. The harm inflicted on the aggressor must not be disproportionate to the aggression.

2. Harm to innocents should not be directly intended as an end or a means.

The first criterion is a widely accepted requirement of just means. The second criterion is also widely accepted and contains the main requirement of the doctrine of double effect (see the introduction to Section III). Many philosophers seem willing to endorse the application of the doctrine in this context given that those to whom the doctrine applies are generally recognized to be persons with full moral status.

To evaluate these requirements of just war theory, we need to determine to what degree they can be supported by the moral approaches to practical problems presented in the General Introduction. Of course, one or more of these approaches may ultimately favor the pacifist position, but assuming that these approaches favored some version of a just war theory, which version would that be?

Obviously, a utilitarian approach would have little difficulty accepting the requirement of just cause and requirement (1) on just means because these requirements can be interpreted as having a utilitarian backing. However, this approach would only accept requirement (2) on just means conditionally, because occasions would surely arise when violations of this requirement would maximize net utility.

Unlike a utilitarian approach, an Aristotelian approach is relatively indeterminate in its requirements. All that is certain, as I have interpreted the approach, is that it would be absolutely committed to requirement (2) on just means.[1] Of course, the other requirements on just cause and just means would be required by particular versions of this approach.

A Kantian approach is distinctive in that it seeks to combine and compromise both the concern of a utilitarian approach for maximal net utility and the concern of an Aristotelian approach for the proper development of each individual.[2] In its hypothetical choice situation, persons would clearly favor the requirement of just cause and requirement (1) on just means, although they would not interpret them in a strictly utilitarian fashion.

Yet what about the requirement (2) on just means? Because persons behind a veil of ignorance would not be committed simply to what-

ever maximizes net utility, they would want to put a stricter limit on the harm that could be inflicted on innocents in defense of a just cause than could be justified on utilitarian grounds alone. This is because persons behind a veil of ignorance would be concerned not only with what maximizes net utility, but also with the distribution of utility to particular individuals. Persons imagining themselves to be ignorant of what position they are in would be particularly concerned that they might turn out to be in the position of those who are innocent, and, consequently, they would want strong safeguards against harming those who are innocent, such as requirement (2) on just means.

Yet even though persons behind a veil of ignorance would favor differential restriction on harm to innocents, they would not favor an absolute restriction on intentional harm to innocents. They would recognize as exceptions to such a restriction cases where intentional harm to innocents is either:

1. Trivial (e.g., stepping on someone's foot to get out of a crowded subway).

2. Easily reparable (e.g., lying to a temporarily depressed friend to keep her from committing suicide).

3. Sufficiently outweighed by the consequences of the action (e.g., shooting one of two hundred civilian hostages to prevent in the only way possible the execution of all two hundred).

Accordingly, while persons behind a veil of ignorance would favor requirement (2) on just means, their commitment to this requirement would also have to incorporate the above exceptions. Even so, these exceptions are far more limited than those that would be tolerated by a utilitarian approach.

In sum, a Kantian approach would strongly endorse the requirement of just cause and requirements (1) and (2) on just means. Yet its commitment to requirement (2) on just means would fall short of the absolute commitment that is characteristic of an Aristotelian approach to practical problems.

It is clear, therefore, that our three moral approaches to practical problems differ significantly with respect to their requirements for a just war theory. A utilitarian approach strongly endorses the requirement of just cause and requirement (1) on just means, but only conditionally endorses requirement (2) on just means. An Aristotelian approach endorses requirement (2) on just means as an absolute requirement, but is indeterminate with respect to the other requirements of just war theory. Only a Kantian approach strongly endorses all of the basic requirements of a traditional just war theory, although it does not regard requirement (2) on just means as an absolute requirement. Fortunately for traditional just war theory, there are good reasons for favoring a Kantian approach over the other two moral approaches to practical problems.

One reason for favoring a Kantian over a utilitarian approach is that its requirements are derived from a veil of ignorance decision procedure that utilitarians and Kantians alike recognize to be fair. It is not surprising, therefore, to find such utilitarians as John Harsanyi and R. M. Hare simply endorsing this decision procedure and then trying to show that the resulting requirements would maximize utility.[3] Yet we have just seen how the concern of persons behind a veil of ignorance with the distribution of utility would lead them to impose a stricter limit on the harm that could be inflicted on innocents in defense of a just cause than could be justified on grounds of maximizing utility alone. At least with respect to just war theory, therefore, a utilitarian approach and a Kantian approach differ significantly in their practical requirements.

Utilitarians who endorse this decision procedure are faced with a difficult choice: give up

their commitment to this decision procedure or modify their commitment to utilitarian goals. Utilitarians cannot easily choose to give up their commitment to this decision procedure because the acceptability of utilitarianism as traditionally conceived has always depended on showing that fairness and utility rarely conflict, and that when they do, it is always plausible to think that the requirements of utility are morally overriding. Consequently, when a fair decision procedure significantly conflicts with utility—which it is not plausible to think can always be morally overridden by the requirements of utility—that procedure exposes the inadequacy of a utilitarian approach to practical problems.

These reasons for favoring a Kantian over a utilitarian approach to practical problems are also reasons for favoring an Aristotelian approach, because an Aristotelian approach is also concerned with fairness and the distribution of utility to particular individuals. Nevertheless, there are other reasons for favoring a Kantian approach over an Aristotelian approach.

One reason is that a Kantian approach does not endorse any absolute requirements. In particular, a Kantian approach does not endorse an absolute requirement not to intentionally harm innocents. A Kantian approach recognizes that if the harm is trivial, easily reparable, or sufficiently outweighed by the consequences, such harm can be morally justified.

Another reason for favoring a Kantian approach over an Aristotelian is that a Kantian approach is determinate in its requirements; it actually leads to a wide range of practical recommendations. By contrast, an Aristotelian approach lacks a deliberative procedure that can produce agreement with respect to practical requirements. This is evident because supporters of this approach tend to endorse radically different practical requirements. In this regard, the veil of ignorance decision procedure employed by a Kantian approach appears to be just the sort of morally defensible device needed to achieve determinate requirements.

Finally, the particular requirements of just war theory endorsed by a Kantian approach are further supported by the presence of analogous requirements for related areas of conduct. Thus, the strong legal prohibitions that exist against punishing the innocent provide support for the strong prohibition against harming innocents expressed by requirement (2) on just means. This is the type of correspondence we would expect from an adequate moral theory; requirements in one area of conduct would be analogous to those in related areas of conduct.

Alternative Views

In the first selection (Selection 76), James P. Sterba argues that when pacifism and just war theory are given their most morally defensible interpretations, they can be reconciled both in theory and practice. He argues that the most morally defensible form of pacifism is antiwar pacifism (which prohibits participation in all wars) rather than nonviolent pacifism (which prohibits any use of violence against other human beings) or nonlethal pacifism (which prohibits any use of lethal force against other human beings). He also argues that when just war theory is given its most morally defensible interpretation, it favors a strong just means prohibition against intentionally harming innocents and favors the use of belligerent means only when such means (1) minimize the loss and injury to innocent lives overall; (2) threaten innocent lives only to prevent the loss of innocent lives; and (3) threaten or take the lives of unjust aggressors when it is the only way to prevent serious injury to innocents. He contends that the few wars and large scale conflicts that meet these stringent requirements of just

war theory (e.g., India's military action against Pakistan in Bangladesh and the Tanzanian incursion into Uganda during the rule of Idi Amin) are the only wars and large-scale conflicts to which antiwar pacifists cannot justifiably object. He calls the view that emerges from this reconciliation "just war pacifism."

In Selection 77, Michael Walzer argues in favor of humanitarian intervention whenever cruelty and suffering are extreme and no local forces are capable of putting an end to them. In such situations, Walzer maintains that anyone who can should intervene, but that wealthy and powerful states have an obligation to do so. Walzer notes that some of these interventions will allow one to enter a country, get the job done, and leave relatively quickly. But others will not allow this, and virtually all such interventions will require putting one's soldiers at risk.

By contrast, Barbara Conry argues in Selection 78 that a U.S. military intervention is generally not a viable solution to regional conflicts. In the first place, she argues, in the vast majority of cases such interventions do not work because the altruism of those intervening cannot usually outlast the nationalism or self-interest of the parties in the conflict. Second, she argues that it is virtually impossible for such interventions to be impartial; an intervening power almost always ends up siding with one or the other party in the conflict. Third, she claims that such interventions give rise to anti-American sentiment based on the north–south conflict between the rich and the poor, and they constitute a drain on U.S. resources.

Thus, while Walzer thinks that interventions in regional conflicts motivated by altruism can and should be undertaken, Conry thinks that only those relatively few interventions that are also motivated by national interest can and should be undertaken.

Practical Applications

The readings in this section have already suggested a number of practical solutions to the problem of war and humanitarian intervention. In Selection 79, Kofi A. Annan, the current Secretary General of the United Nations, surveys the history of United Nations interventions in internal armed conflict, focusing on the recent interventions in Somalia, Rwanda, and Bosnia and Herzegovina. Annan notes the successes and failures associated with these interventions, but, in general, he favors a greater role for the United Nations in enforcing international norms of human rights.

Nevertheless, it is important to recognize that a solution to the problem of war and humanitarian intervention cannot stand alone; it requires solutions to the other practical problems discussed in this anthology as well. For example, a solution to the problem of the distribution of income and wealth may show that it is morally illegitimate to increase military security by sacrificing the basic needs of the less advantaged members of a society rather than by sacrificing the nonbasic needs of the more advantaged members of the society. Accordingly, it is impossible to reach a fully adequate solution to this or any other practical problem discussed in this anthology without solving the other practical problems as well.

Endnotes

1. See General Introduction.
2. See General Introduction.
3. See John Harsanyi, *Rational Behavior and Bargaining Equilibrium in Games and Social Situations* (Cambridge: Cambridge University Press, 1977), and R. M. Hare, "Justice and Equality," in *Justice: Alternative Political Perspectives*, ed. James P. Sterba (Belmont, CA: Wadsworth Publishing Co., 1991).

76. Reconciling Pacifists and Just War Theorists

JAMES P. STERBA

James P. Sterba argues that when pacifism and just war theory are given their most morally defensible interpreta-tions, they can be reconciled both in theory and practice. He argues that the most morally defensible form of pacifism is antiwar pacifism rather than nonviolent pacifism or nonlethal pacifism. He also argues that when just war theory is given its most morally defensible interpretation, it favors a strong just means prohibition against intentionally harming innocents and favors the use of belligerent means only when such means (1) minimize the loss and injury to innocent lives overall, (2) threaten innocent lives only to prevent the loss of innocent lives, and (3) threaten or take the lives of unjust aggressors when it is the only way to prevent serious injury to innocents. Sterba contends that the few wars and large-scale conflicts that meet these stringent requirements of just war theory are the only wars and large-scale conflicts to which antiwar pacifists cannot justifiably object.

Traditionally pacifism and just war theory have rep-resented radically opposed responses to aggression. Pacifism has been interpreted to rule out any use of violence in response to aggression. Just war the-ory has been interpreted to permit a measured use of violence in response to aggression. It has been thought that the two views might sometimes agree in particular cases—for example, that pacifists and just war theorists might unconditionally oppose nu-clear war, but beyond that it has been generally held that the two views lead to radically opposed recom-mendations. In this paper, I hope to show that this is not the case. I will argue that pacifism and just war theory, in their most morally defensible inter-pretations, can be substantially reconciled both in theory and practice.

In traditional just war theory there are two basic elements: an account of just cause and an account of just means. Just cause is usually specified as follows:

1. There must be substantial aggression;

2. Nonbelligerent correctives must be either hopeless or too costly; and

3. Belligerent correctives must be neither hopeless nor too costly.

Needless to say, the notion of substantial aggression is a bit fuzzy, but it is generally understood to be the

type of aggression that violates people's most fun-damental rights. To suggest some specific examples of what is and is not substantial aggression, usually the taking of hostages is regarded as substantial aggression while the nationalization of particular firms owned by foreigners is not so regarded. But even when substantial aggression occurs, frequently nonbelligerent correctives are neither hopeless nor too costly. And even when nonbelligerent correc-tives are either hopeless or too costly, in order for there to be a just cause, belligerent correctives must be neither hopeless nor too costly.

Traditional just war theory assumes, however, that there are just causes and goes on to specify just means as imposing two requirements:

1. Harm to innocents should not be directly intended as an end or a means.

2. The harm resulting from the belligerent means should not be disproportionate to the particular defensive objective to be attained.

While the just means conditions apply to each de-fensive action, the just cause conditions must be met by the conflict as a whole.

It is important to note that these requirements of just cause and just means are not essentially about war at all. Essentially, they constitute a theory of just defense that can apply to war but can also apply to a wide range of defensive actions short of war. Of course, what needs to be determined is whether these requirements can be justified. Since just war theory is usually opposed to pacifism, to secure a non–question-begging justification for the theory and its requirements we need to proceed as much as possible from premises that are common to pacifists and just war theorists alike. The difficulty here is that there is not just one form of pacifism but many. So we need to determine which form of pacifism is most morally defensible.

Now when most people think of pacifism they tend to identify it with a theory of nonviolence. We can call this view "nonviolent pacifism." It maintains that:

> Any use of violence against other human beings is morally prohibited.

It has been plausibly argued, however, that this form of pacifism is incoherent. In a well-known article, Jan Narveson rejects nonviolent pacifism as incoherent because it recognizes a right to life yet rules out any use of force in defense of that right. The view is incoherent, Narveson claims, because having a right entails the legitimacy of using force in defense of that right at least on some occasions.

Given the cogency of objections of this sort, some have opted for a form of pacifism that does not rule out all violence but only lethal violence. We can call this view "nonlethal pacifism." It maintains that

> Any lethal use of force against other human beings is morally prohibited.

In defense of nonlethal pacifism, Cheyney Ryan has argued that there is a substantial issue between the pacifist and the nonpacifist concerning whether we can or should create the necessary distance between ourselves and other human beings in order to make the act of killing possible. To illustrate, Ryan cites George Orwell's reluctance to shoot at an enemy soldier who jumped out of a trench and ran along the top of a parapet half-dressed and holding up his trousers with both hands. Ryan contends that what kept Orwell from shooting was that he couldn't think of the soldier as a thing rather than a fellow human being.

However, it is not clear that Orwell's encounter supports nonlethal pacifism. For it may be that what kept Orwell from shooting the enemy soldier was not his inability to think of the soldier as a thing rather than a fellow human being but rather his inability to think of the soldier who was holding up his trousers with both hands as a threat or a combatant. Under this interpretation, Orwell's decision not to shoot would accord well with the requirements of just war theory.

Let us suppose, however, that someone is attempting to take your life. Why does that permit you, the defender of nonlethal pacifism might ask, to kill the person making the attempt? The most cogent response, it seems to me, is that killing in such a case is not evil, or at least not morally evil, because anyone who is wrongfully engaged in an attempt upon your life has already forfeited his or her right to life by engaging in such aggression.[1] So, provided that you are reasonably certain that the aggressor is wrongfully engaged in an attempt upon your life, you would be morally justified in killing, assuming that it is the only way of saving your own life.

There is, however, a form of pacifism that remains untouched by the criticisms I have raised against both nonviolent pacifism and nonlethal pacifism. This form of pacifism neither prohibits all violence nor even all uses of lethal force. We can call the view "antiwar pacifism" because it holds that

> Any participation in the massive use of lethal force in warfare is morally prohibited.[2]

In defense of antiwar pacifism, it is undeniable that wars have brought enormous amounts of death and destruction in their wake and that many of those who have perished in them are noncombatants or innocents. In fact, the tendency of modern wars has been to produce higher and higher proportions of noncombatant casualties, making it more and more difficult to justify participation in such wars. At the same time, strategies for nonbelligerent conflict resolution are rarely intensively developed and explored before nations choose to go to war, making it all but impossible to justify participation in such wars.

To determine whether the requirements of just war theory can be reconciled with those of antiwar pacifism, however, we must consider whether we should distinguish between harm intentionally inflicted on innocents and harm whose infliction on innocents is merely foreseen. On the one hand, we could favor a uniform restriction against the infliction of harm on innocents that ignores the intended/foreseen distinction. On the other hand, we could favor a differential restriction that is more severe against the intentional infliction of harm upon innocents but is less severe against the infliction of harm that is merely foreseen. What needs to be determined, therefore, is whether there is any rationale for favoring this differential restriction on harm over a uniform restriction. . . .

Let us first examine the question from the perspective of those suffering the harm. Initially, it might appear to matter little whether the harm would be intended or just foreseen by those who cause it. From the perspective of those suffering harm, it might appear that what matters is simply that the overall amount of harm be restricted irrespective of whether it is foreseen or intended. But consider—don't those who suffer harm have more reason to protest when the harm is done to them by agents who are directly engaged in causing harm to them than when the harm is done incidentally by agents whose ends and means are good? Don't we have more reason to protest when we are being used by others than when we are affected by them only incidentally?

Moreover, if we examine the question from the perspective of those causing harm, additional support for this line of reasoning can be found. For it would seem that we as agents have more reason to protest a restriction against foreseen harm than we have reason to protest a comparable restriction against intended harm. This is because a restriction against foreseen harm limits our actions when our ends and means are good whereas a restriction against intended harm only limits our actions when our ends or means are evil or harmful, and it would seem that we have greater grounds for acting when both our ends and means are good than when they are not. Consequently, because we have more reason to protest when we are being used by others than when we are being affected by them only incidentally, and because we have more reason to act when both our ends and means are good than when they are not, we should favor the foreseen/intended distinction that is incorporated into just means.

It might be objected, however, that at least sometimes we could produce greater good overall by violating the foreseen/intended distinction of just means and acting with the evil means of intentionally harming innocents. On this account, it might be argued that it should be permissible at least sometimes to intentionally harm innocents in order to achieve greater good overall.

Now it seems to me that this objection is well taken insofar as it is directed against an absolute restriction upon intentional harm to innocents. It seems

clear that there are exceptions to such a restriction when intentional harm to innocents is:

1. Trivial (for example, as in the case of stepping on someone's foot to get out of a crowded subway);

2. Easily reparable (for example, as in the case of lying to a temporarily depressed friend to keep him from committing suicide); or

3. Greatly outweighed by the consequences of the action, especially to innocent people (for example, as in the case of shooting one of two hundred civilian hostages to prevent in the only way possible the execution of all two hundred).

Yet while we need to recognize these exceptions to an absolute restriction upon intentional harm to innocents, there is good reason not to permit simply maximizing good consequences overall because that would place unacceptable burdens upon particular individuals. More specifically, it would be an unacceptable burden on innocents to allow them to be intentionally harmed in cases other than the exceptions we have just enumerated. So allowing for these exceptions, we would have reason to favor a differential restriction against harming innocents that is more severe against the intentional infliction of harm upon innocents but is less severe against the infliction of harm upon innocents that is merely foreseen. Again, the main grounds for this preference is that we would have more reason to protest when we are being used by others than when we are being affected by them only incidentally, and more reason to act when both our ends and means are good than when they are not.

So far, I have argued that there are grounds for favoring a differential restriction on harm to innocents that is more severe against intended harm and less severe against foreseen harm. I have further argued that this restriction is not absolute so that when the evil intended is trivial, easily reparable, or greatly outweighed by the consequences, intentional harm to innocents can be justified. Moreover, there is no reason to think that antiwar pacifists would reject either of these conclusions. Antiwar pacifists are opposed to any participation in the massive use of lethal force in warfare, yet this need not conflict with the commitment of just war theorists to a differential but nonabsolute restriction on harm to innocents as a requirement of just means.[3] Where just war theory goes wrong, according to antiwar pacifists, is not in its restriction on harming innocents but rather in its failure to adequately determine when belligerent correctives are too costly to constitute a just cause or lacking in the proportionality required by just means. According to antiwar pacifists, just war theory provides insufficient restraint in both of these areas. Now to evaluate this criticism, we need to consider a wide range of cases where killing or inflicting serious harm on others in defense of oneself or others might be thought to be justified, beginning with the easiest cases to assess from the perspectives of antiwar pacifism and the just war theory and then moving on to cases that are more difficult to assess from these perspectives.

Case 1. Only the intentional or foreseen killing of an unjust aggressor would prevent one's own death.[4] This case clearly presents no problems. In the first place, antiwar pacifists adopted their view because they were convinced that there were instances of justified killing. And, in this case, the only person killed is an unjust aggressor. So surely antiwar pacifists would have to agree with just war theorists that one can justifiably kill an unjust aggressor if it is the only way to save one's life.

Case 2. Only the intentional or foreseen killing of an unjust aggressor and the foreseen killing of one innocent bystander would prevent one's own death and that of five other innocent people.[5] In this case, we have the foreseen killing of an innocent person as well as the killing of the unjust aggressor, but since it is the only way to save one's own life and the lives of five other innocent people, antiwar pacifists and just war theorists alike would have reason to judge it morally permissible. In this case, the intended life-saving benefits to six innocent people is judged to outweigh the foreseen death of one innocent person and the intended or foreseen death of the unjust aggressor.

Case 3. Only the intentional or foreseen killing of an unjust aggressor and the foreseen killing of one innocent bystander would prevent the death of five other innocent people. In this case, even though we lack the justification of self-defense, saving the lives of five innocent people in the only way possible still provides antiwar pacifists and just war theorists with sufficient grounds for granting the moral permissibility of killing an unjust aggressor, even when the killing of an innocent bystander is foreseen. Here the intended life-saving benefits to five innocent people

would still outweigh the foreseen death of one innocent person and the intended or foreseen death of the unjust aggressor.

Case 4. Only the intentional or foreseen killing of an unjust aggressor and the foreseen killing of five innocent people would prevent the death of two innocent people. In this case, neither antiwar pacifists nor just war theorists would find the cost and proportionality requirements of just war theory to be met. Too many innocent people would have to be killed to save too few. Here the fact that the deaths of the innocents would be merely foreseen does not outweigh the fact that we would have to accept the deaths of five innocents and the death of the unjust aggressor in order to be able to save two innocents.

Notice that up to this point in interpreting these cases, we have simply been counting the number of innocent deaths involved in each case and opting for whichever solution minimized the loss of innocent lives that would result. Suppose, however, that an unjust aggressor is not threatening the lives of innocents but only their welfare or property. Would the taking of the unjust aggressor's life in defense of the welfare and property of innocents be judged proportionate? Consider the following case.

Case 5. Only the intentional or foreseen killing of an unjust aggressor would prevent serious injury to oneself and/or five other innocent people. Since in this case the intentional or foreseen killing of the unjust aggressor is the only way of preventing serious injury to oneself and five other innocent people, then, by analogy with Cases 1 through 3, both antiwar pacifists and just war theorists alike would have reason to affirm its moral permissibility. Of course, if there were any other way of stopping unjust aggressors in such cases short of killing them, that course of action would clearly be required. Yet if there is no alternative, the intentional or foreseen killing of the unjust aggressor to prevent serious injury to oneself and/or five other innocent people would be justified.

In such cases, the serious injury could be bodily injury, as when an aggressor threatens to break one's limbs, or it could be serious psychological injury, as when an aggressor threatens to inject mind-altering drugs, or it could be a serious threat to property. Of course, usually where serious injury is threatened, there will be ways of stopping aggressors short of killing them. Unfortunately, this is not always possible.

In still other kinds of cases, stopping an unjust aggressor would require indirectly inflicting serious harm, but not death, upon innocent bystanders. Consider the following cases.

Case 6. Only the intentional or foreseen infliction of serious harm upon an unjust aggressor and the foreseen infliction of serious harm upon one innocent bystander would prevent serious harm to oneself and five other innocent people.

Case 7. Only the intentional or foreseen infliction of serious harm upon an unjust aggressor and the foreseen infliction of serious harm upon one innocent bystander would prevent serious harm to five other innocent people.

In both of these cases, serious harm is indirectly inflicted upon one innocent bystander in order to prevent greater harm from being inflicted by an unjust aggressor upon other innocent people. In Case 6, we also have the justification of self-defense, which is lacking in Case 7. Nevertheless, with regard to both cases, antiwar pacifists and just war theorists should agree that preventing serious injury to five or six innocent people in the only way possible renders it morally permissible to inflict serious injury on an unjust aggressor, even when the serious injury of one innocent person is a foreseen consequence. In these cases, by analogy with Cases 2 and 3, the foreseen serious injury of one innocent person and the intended or foreseen injury of the unjust aggressor should be judged proportionate given the intended injury-preventing benefits to five or six other innocent people.

Up to this point there has been the basis for general agreement among antiwar pacifists and just war theorists as to how to interpret the proportionality requirement of just means, but in the following case this no longer obtains.

Case 8. Only the intentional or foreseen killing of an unjust aggressor and the foreseen killing of one innocent bystander would prevent serious injuries to the members of a much larger group of people.

The interpretation of this case is crucial. In this case, we are asked to sanction the loss of an innocent life to prevent serious injuries to the members of a much larger group of people. Unfortunately, neither antiwar pacifists nor just war theorists have explicitly considered this case. Both antiwar pacifists and just war theorists agree that we can inflict serious injury on an unjust aggressor and an innocent bystander to prevent greater injury to other innocent people, as in Cases 6 and 7, and that one can even intentionally or indirectly kill an unjust aggressor to

prevent serious injury to oneself or other innocent people as in Case 5. Yet neither antiwar pacifists nor just war theorists have explicitly addressed the question of whether we can indirectly kill an innocent bystander in order to prevent serious injuries to the members of a much larger group of innocent people. Rather they have tended to confuse Case 8 with Case 5, where it is agreed that one can justifiably kill an unjust aggressor to prevent serious injury to oneself and/or five other innocent people. In Case 8, however, one is doing something quite different: One is killing an innocent bystander in order to prevent serious injury to the members of a much larger group of people.

Now this kind of trade-off is not accepted in standard police practice. Police officers are regularly instructed not to risk innocent lives simply to prevent serious injury to other innocents. Nor is there any reason to think that a trade-off that is unacceptable in standard police practice would be acceptable in larger scale conflicts. Thus, for example, even if the Baltic republics could have effectively freed themselves from the Soviet Union by infiltrating into Moscow several bands of saboteurs who would then attack several military and government installations in Moscow, causing an enormous loss of innocent lives, such trade-offs would not have been justified. Accordingly, it follows that if the proportionality requirement of just war theory is to be met, we must save more innocent lives than we cause to be lost, we must prevent more injuries than we bring about, and we must not kill innocents, even indirectly, simply to prevent serious injuries to ourselves and others. Moreover, even when our lives and the lives of others are being threatened, we must save more innocent lives than we cause to be lost.

Of course, sometimes our lives and well-being are threatened together. Or better, if we are unwilling to sacrifice our well-being then our lives are threatened as well. Nevertheless, if we are justified in our use of lethal force to defend ourselves in cases where we will indirectly kill innocents, it is because our lives are also threatened, not simply our well-being. And the same holds for when we are defending others.

What this shows is that the constraints imposed by just war theory on the use of belligerent correctives are actually much more severe than antiwar pacifists have tended to recognize. In determining when belligerent correctives are too costly to constitute a just cause or lacking in the proportionality required by just means, just war theory under its most morally defensible interpretation:

1. Allows the use of belligerent means against unjust aggressors only when such means minimize the loss and injury to innocent lives overall;

2. Allows the use of belligerent means against unjust aggressors to indirectly threaten innocent lives only to prevent the loss of innocent lives, not simply to prevent injury to innocents; and

3. Allows the use of belligerent means to directly or indirectly threaten or even take the lives of unjust aggressors when it is the only way to prevent serious injury to innocents.

Now it might be objected that all that I have shown through the analysis of the above eight cases is that killing in defense of oneself or others is morally permissible, not that it is morally required or morally obligatory. That is true. I have not established any obligation to respond to aggression with lethal force in these cases, but only that it is morally permissible to do so. For one thing, it is difficult to ground an obligation to use lethal force on self-defense alone, as would be required in Case 1 or in one version of Case 5. Obligations to oneself appear to have an optional quality that is absent from obligations to others. In Cases 2, 3, and 5 through 7, however, the use of force would prevent serious harm or death to innocents, and here I contend it would be morally obligatory if either the proposed use of force required only a relatively small personal sacrifice from us or if we were fairly bound by convention or a mutual defense agreement to come to the aid of others. In such cases, I think we can justifiably speak of a moral obligation to kill or seriously harm in defense of others.

Another aspect of Cases 1 through 3 and 5 through 7 to which someone might object is that it is the wrongful actions of others that put us into situations where I am claiming that we are morally justified in seriously harming or killing others. But for the actions of unjust aggressors, we would not be in situations where I am claiming that we are morally permitted or required to seriously harm or kill.

Yet doesn't something like this happen in a wide range of cases when wrongful actions are performed? Suppose I am on the way to the bank to deposit money from a fundraiser, and someone accosts me and threatens to shoot if I don't hand over the money. If I do hand over the money, I would be forced to do something I don't want to do, something that involves a loss to myself and others. But surely it is morally permissible for me to hand over the money in this case. And it may even be morally required for me to do so if resistance would lead to the shooting of others in addition to myself. So it does seem that bad people, by altering the consequences of our actions, can alter our obligations as well. What our obligations are under nonideal conditions are different from what they would be under ideal conditions. If a group of thugs comes into this room and make it very clear that they intend to shoot me if each of you doesn't give them one dollar, I think, and I would hope that you would also think, that each of you now has an obligation to give the thugs one dollar when before you had no such obligation. Likewise, I think that the actions of unjust aggressors can put us into situations where it is morally permissible or even morally required for us to seriously harm or kill when before it was not.

Now it might be contended that antiwar pacifists would concede the moral permissibility of Cases 1–3 and 5–7 but still maintain that any participation in the massive use of lethal force in warfare is morally prohibited. The scale of the conflict, antiwar pacifists might contend, makes all the difference. Of course, if this simply means that many large-scale conflicts will have effects that bear no resemblance to Cases 1–3 or 5–7, this can hardly be denied. Still, it is possible for some large-scale conflicts to bear a proportionate resemblance to the above cases. For example, it can be argued plausibly that India's military action against Pakistan in Bangladesh and the Tanzanian incursion into Uganda during the rule of Idi Amin resemble Cases 3, 5, or 7 in their effects upon innocents.[6] What this shows is that antiwar pacifists are not justified in regarding every participation in the massive use of lethal force in warfare as morally prohibited. Instead, antiwar pacifists must allow that, at least in some real-life cases, wars and other large-scale military operations both have been and will be morally permissible.

This concession from antiwar pacifists, however, needs to be matched by a comparable concession from just war theorists themselves, because too frequently they have interpreted their theory in morally indefensible ways. When just war theory is given a morally defensible interpretation, I have argued that the theory favors a strong just means prohibition against intentionally harming innocents. I have also argued that the theory favors the use of belligerent means only when such means (1) minimize the loss and injury to innocent lives overall; (2) threaten innocent lives only to prevent the loss of innocent lives, not simply to prevent injury to innocents; and (3) threaten or even take the lives of unjust aggressors when it is the only way to prevent serious injury to innocents.

Obviously, just war theory, so understood, is going to place severe restrictions on the use of belligerent means in warfare. In fact, most of the actual uses of belligerent means in warfare that have occurred turn out to be unjustified. For example, the U.S. involvement in Nicaragua, El Salvador, and Panama; the Soviet Union's involvement in Afghanistan; and Israeli involvement in the West Bank and the Gaza Strip all violate the just cause and just means provisions of just war theory as I have defended them. Even the recent U.S.-led war against Iraq violated both the just cause and just means provisions of just war theory.[7] In fact, one strains to find examples of justified applications of just war theory in recent history. Two examples I have already referred to are India's military action against Pakistan in Bangladesh and the Tanzanian incursion into Uganda during the rule of Idi Amin. But after mentioning these two examples it is difficult to go on. What this shows is that when just war theory and antiwar pacifism are given their most morally defensible interpretations, both views can be reconciled. In this reconciliation, the few wars and large-scale conflicts that meet the stringent requirements of just war theory are the only wars and large-scale conflicts to which antiwar pacifists cannot justifiably object.[8] We can call the view that emerges from this reconciliation "just war pacifism." It is the view which claims that due to the stringent requirements of just war theory, only very rarely will participation in a massive use of lethal force in warfare be morally justified. It is the view on which I rest my case for the reconciliation of pacifism and just war theory.[9]

Endnotes

1. Alternatively, one might concede that even in this case killing is morally evil, but still contend that it is morally justified because it is the lesser of two evils.

2. For two challenging defenses of this view, see Duane L. Cady, *From Warism to Pacifism* (Philadelphia: Temple University Press, 1989), and Robert L. Holmes, *On War and Morality* (Princeton: Princeton University Press, 1989).

3. This is because the just means restrictions protect innocents quite well against the infliction of intentional harm.

4. By an "unjust aggressor" I mean someone who the defender is reasonably certain is wrongfully engaged in an attempt upon her life or the lives of other innocent people.

5. What is relevant in this case is that the foreseen deaths are a relatively small number (one in this case) compared to the number of innocents whose lives are saved (six in this case). The primary reason for using particular numbers in this case and those that follow is to make it clear that at this stage of the argument no attempt is being made to justify the large-scale killing that occurs in warfare.

6. Although there is a strong case for India's military action against Pakistan in Bangladesh and the Tanzanian incursion into Uganda during the rule of Idi Amin, there are questions that can be raised about the behavior of Indian troops in Bangladesh following the defeat of the Pakistanian forces and about the regime Tanzania put in power in Uganda.

7. The just cause provision was violated because the extremely effective economic sanctions were not given enough time to work. It was estimated that when compared to past economic blockades, the blockade against Iraq had a near 100 percent chance of success if given about a year to work. (See the *New York Times,* January 14, 1991.) The just means provision was violated because the number of combatant and noncombatant deaths was disproportionate. As many as 120,000 Iraqi soldiers were killed, according to U.S. intelligence sources.

8. Of course, antiwar pacifists are right to point out that virtually all wars that have been fought have led to unforeseen harms and have been fought with less and less discrimination as the wars progressed. Obviously, these are considerations that in just war theory must weigh heavily against going to war.

9. Of course, more needs to be done to specify the requirements of just war pacifism. One fruitful way to further specify these requirements is to appeal to a hypothetical social contract decision procedure as has been done with respect to other practical problems. Here I have simply tried to establish the defensibility of just war pacifism without appealing to any such procedure. Yet once the defensibility of just war pacifism has been established, such a decision procedure will prove quite useful in working out its particular requirements.

77. The Politics of Rescue

MICHAEL WALZER

Michael Walzer argues in favor of humanitarian intervention whenever cruelty and suffering are extreme and no local forces are capable of putting an end to them. In such situations, Walzer maintains that anyone who can should intervene, but that wealthy and powerful states also have an obligation to do so. Walzer notes that some of these interventions will allow one to enter a country, get the job done, and leave relatively quickly. But others will not allow this, and virtually all such interventions will require putting one's soldiers at risk.

To intervene or not?—this should always be a hard question. Even in the case of a brutal civil war or a politically induced famine or the massacre of a local minority, the use of force in other people's countries should always generate hesitation and anxiety. So it does today among small groups of concerned people, some of whom end up supporting, some resisting interventionist policies. But many governments and many more politicians seem increasingly inclined to find the question easy: The answer is *not!* Relatively small contingents of soldiers will be sent to help out in cases where it isn't expected that they will have to fight—thus the United States in Somalia, the Europeans in Bosnia, the French in Rwanda. The aim in all these countries (though we experimented briefly with something more in Mogadishu) is not to alter power relations on the ground, but only to ameliorate their consequences—to bring food and medical supplies to populations besieged and bombarded, for example, without interfering with the siege or bombardment.

This might be taken as a triumph for the old principle of nonintervention, except that the reasons on which the principle is based, which I will rehearse in a moment, do not appear to be the reasons that move governments and politicians today. They are not focused on the costs of intervention or, for that matter, of nonintervention to the men and women whose danger or suffering poses the question, but only on the costs to their own soldiers and to themselves, that is, to their political standing at home. No doubt, governments must think about

such things: Political leaders have to maintain their domestic support if they are to act effectively abroad. But they must also *act effectively abroad* when the occasion demands it, and they must be able to judge the urgency of the demand in the appropriate moral and political terms. The ideology of the cold war once provided a set of terms, not in fact always appropriate to the cases at hand, but capable of overriding domestic considerations. In the aftermath of the cold war, no comparable ideology has that capacity. The question "To intervene or not?" gets answered every day, but with no sign that the judgments it requires are actually being made.

What about "Humanitarian Intervention"?

I am going to focus on the arguments for and against "humanitarian intervention," for this is what is at issue in the former Yugoslavia, the Caucasus, parts of Asia, much of Africa. Massacre, rape, ethnic cleansing, state terrorism, contemporary versions of "bastard feudalism," complete with ruthless warlords and lawless bands of armed men: These are the acts and occasions that invite us, or require us, to override the presumption against moving armies across borders and using force inside countries that have not threatened or attacked their neighbors. There is no external aggression to worry about, only domestic brutality, civil war, political tyranny, ethnic or religious persecution. When should the world's agents and powers (the United Nations, the European Community, the Pan American Alliance, the Organization

Reprinted from *Dissent* (Winter 1995) by permission of publisher and author.

of African Unity, the United States) merely watch and protest? When should they protest and then intervene?

The presumption against intervention is strong; we (on the left especially) have reasons for it, which derive from our opposition to imperial politics and our commitment to self-determination, even when the process of self-determination is something less than peaceful and democratic. Ever since Roman times, empires have expanded by intervening in civil wars, replacing "anarchy" with law and order, overthrowing supposedly noxious regimes. Conceivably, this expansion has saved lives, but only by creating in the process a "prison-house of nations," whose subsequent history is a long tale of prison revolts, brutally repressed. So it seems best that people who have lived together in the past and will have to do so in the future should be allowed to work out their difficulties without imperial assistance, among themselves. The resolution won't be stable unless it is locally grounded; there is little chance that it will be consensual unless it is locally produced.

Still, nonintervention is not an absolute moral rule: Sometimes, what is going on locally cannot be tolerated. Hence the practice of "humanitarian intervention"—much abused, no doubt, but morally necessary whenever cruelty and suffering are extreme and no local forces seem capable of putting an end to them. Humanitarian interventions are not justified for the sake of democracy or free enterprise or economic justice or voluntary association or · any other of the social practices and arrangements that we might hope for or even call for in other people's countries. Their aim is profoundly negative in character: to put a stop to actions that, to use an old-fashioned but accurate phrase, "shock the conscience" of humankind. There are some useful, and to my mind justified, contemporary examples: India in East Pakistan, Tanzania in Uganda, Vietnam in Cambodia. Interventions of this sort are probably best carried out by neighbors, as in these three cases, since neighbors will have some understanding of the local culture. They may also, however, have old scores to settle or old (or new) ambitions to dominate the neighborhood. If we had more trust in the effectiveness of the United Nations or the various regional associations, we could require international or at least multilateral endorsement, cooperation, and constraint. I will consider this possibility later on. It might be a way of controlling the economi-

cally or politically self-aggrandizing interventions of single states. For now, though, the agent-of-last-resort is anyone near enough and strong enough to stop what needs stopping.

But that's not always easy. On the standard view of humanitarian intervention (which I adopted when writing *Just and Unjust Wars* almost twenty years ago), the source of the inhumanity is conceived as somehow external and singular in character: a tyrant, a conqueror or usurper, or an alien power set over against a mass of victims. The intervention then has an aim that is simple as well as negative: Remove the tyrant (Pol Pot, Idi Amin), set the people free (Bangladesh), and then get out. Rescue the people in trouble from their troublers, and let them get on with their lives. Help them, and then leave them to manage as best they can by themselves. The test of a genuinely humanitarian intervention, on this view, is that the intervening forces are quickly in and out. They do not intervene and then stay put for reasons of their own, as the Vietnamese did in Cambodia.

But what if the trouble is internal, the inhumanity locally and widely rooted, a matter of political culture, social structures, historical memories, ethnic fear, resentment, and hatred? Or what if the trouble follows from state failure, the collapse of any effective government, with results closer to Hobbes's than to Kropotkin's predictions—not quite a "war of all against all" but a widely dispersed, disorganized, and murderous war of some against some? No doubt, there are still identifiable evil-doers, but now, let's say, they have support at home, reserves, evil-doers in waiting: What then? And what if there are overlapping sets of victims and victimizers, like the Somalian clans and warlords or, perhaps, the religious/ethnic/national groupings in Bosnia? In all these cases, it may well happen that the quick departure of the intervening forces is followed immediately by the reappearance of the conditions that led to intervention in the first place. Give up the idea of an external and singular evil, and the "in and out" test is very hard to apply.

We are extraordinarily dependent on the victim/ victimizer, good guys/bad guys model. I am not sure that any very forceful intervention is politically possible without it. One of the reasons for the weakness of the United Nations in Bosnia has been that many of its representatives on the ground do not believe that the model fits the situation they have to confront. They are not quite apologists for the Serbs, who have (rightly) been condemned in many United Nations resolutions, but they do not regard the Serbs as wholly "bad guys" or as the only "bad guys" in the former Yugoslavia. And that has made it difficult for them to justify the measures that would be necessary to stop the killing and the ethnic cleansing. Imagine that they took those measures, as (in my view) they should have done: Wouldn't they also have been required to take collateral measures against the Croats and Bosnian Moslems? In cases like this one, the politics of rescue is certain to be complex and messy.

It is much easier to go into a place like Bosnia than to get out, and the likely costs to the intervening forces and the local population are much higher than in the classic humanitarian interventions of the recent past. That is why American politicians and military officers have insisted that there must be an exit strategy before there can be an intervention. But this demand is effectively an argument against intervening at all. Exit strategies can rarely be designed in advance, and a public commitment to exit within such and such a time would give the hostile forces a strong incentive to lie low and wait. Better to stay home than to intervene in a way that is sure to fail.

Where the policies and practices that need to be stopped are widely supported, sustained by local structures and cultures, any potentially successful intervention is not going to meet the "in and out" test. It is likely to require a much more sustained challenge to conventional sovereignty: a long-term military presence, social reconstruction, what used to be called "political trusteeship" (since few of the locals—at least, the locals with power—can be trusted), and along the way, making all this possible, the large-scale and reiterated use of force. Is anyone ready for this? The question is especially hard for people on the left who are appalled by what happened or is happening in Bosnia, say, or Rwanda, but who have long argued, most of us, that the best thing to do with an army is to keep it at home. Even those who supported humanitarian interventions in the past have emphasized the moral necessity of a rapid withdrawal, leaving any ongoing use of force to indigenous soldiers.

Now this moral necessity seems to have become a practical, political necessity. Hence the general search for a quick fix, as in President Clinton's proposal (never very vigorously pursued) to "bomb the Serbs, arm the Bosnians." I would have supported both these policies, thinking that they might produce a local solution that, however bloody it turned out to be, could not be worse than what was happening anyway. But what if the quick fix failed, brought on an ever more brutal civil war, with no end in sight? Would we be ready then for a more direct and long-lasting military intervention—and if so, with what sort of an army? Under whose direction? With what weapons systems, what strategy and tactics, what willingness to take casualties and to impose them?

◇

Putting Soldiers at Risk

This last question is probably the crucial one in making intervention increasingly difficult and unlikely. It is very hard these days, in the Western democracies, to put soldiers at risk. But humanitarian interventions and peacekeeping operations are first of all military acts directed against people who are already using force, breaking the peace. They will be ineffective unless there is a willingness to accept the risks that naturally attach to military acts—to shed blood, to lose soldiers. In much of the world, bloodless intervention, peaceful peacekeeping is a contradiction in terms: If it were possible, it wouldn't be necessary. Insofar as it is necessary, we have to acknowledge the real status and function of the men and women whom we send to do the job. Soldiers are not like Peace Corps volunteers or Fulbright scholars or USIA musicians and lecturers—who should not, indeed, be sent overseas to dangerous places. Soldiers are destined for dangerous places, and they should know that (if they don't, they should be told).

This is not to say that soldiers should be sent recklessly into danger. But acknowledging their status and function poses the question that must be answered before they are sent anywhere, at the moment their mission is being defined: Is this a cause for which we are prepared to see American soldiers die? If this question gets an affirmative, then we cannot panic when the first soldier or the first significant number of soldiers, like the eighteen infantrymen in Somalia, are killed in a firefight. The Europeans in Bosnia, it has to be said, didn't even wait to panic: They made it clear from the beginning that the soldiers they sent to open roads and transport supplies were not to be regarded as *soldiers* in any usual sense; these were grown-up Boy Scouts doing good deeds. But this is a formula for failure. The soldiers who were not soldiers became, in effect, hostages of the Serbian forces that controlled the roads, subject to attack if anyone challenged that control. And the European governments became in turn the opponents of any such challenge.

Should we put soldiers at risk in faraway places when our own country is not under attack or threatened with attack (not Maine or Georgia or Oregon) and when national interests, narrowly understood, are not at stake? I am strongly inclined, sometimes, to give a positive answer to this question (whether volunteers or conscripts should bear these risks is too complicated to take up here). The reason is simple enough: All states have an interest in global stability and even in global humanity, and in the case of wealthy and powerful states like ours, this interest is seconded by obligation. No doubt, the "civilized" world is capable of living with grossly uncivilized behavior in places like East Timor, say— offstage and out of sight. But behavior of that kind, unchallenged, tends to spread, to be imitated or reiterated. Pay the moral price of silence and callousness, and you will soon have to pay the political price of turmoil and lawlessness nearer home.

[T]hese successive payments are not inevitable, but they come in sequence often enough. We see the sequence most clearly in Hannah Arendt's description of how European brutality in the colonies was eventually carried back to Europe itself. But the process can work in other ways too, as when terrorist regimes in the Third World imitate one another (often with help from the First World), and waves of desperate refugees flee to countries where powerful political forces, not yet ascendant, want only to drive them back. How long will decency survive *here*, if there is no decency *there*? Now obligation is seconded by interest.

As already acknowledged, interest and obligation together have often provided an ideology for imperial expansion or cold war advance. So it's the political right that has defended both, while the left has acquired the habit of criticism and rejection. But in this postimperial and post–cold war age, these positions are likely to be reversed or, at least, confused. Many people on the right see no point in intervention today when there is no material or, for that matter, ideological advantage to be gained. "What's Bosnia to them or they to Bosnia/that they should weep for her?" And a small but growing number of people on the left now favor intervening,

here or there, driven by an internationalist ethic. They are right to feel driven. Internationalism has always been understood to require support for, and even participation in, popular struggles. Liberation should always be a local initiative. In the face of human disaster, however, internationalism has a more urgent meaning. It's not possible to wait; anyone who can take the initiative should do so. Active opposition to massacre and massive deportation is morally necessary; its risks must be accepted.

◇

Enduring the Intervention

Even the risk of a blocked exit and a long stay. These days, for reasons we should probably celebrate, countries in trouble are no longer viewed as imperial opportunities. Instead, the metaphors are ominous: They are "bogs" and "quagmires." Intervening armies won't be defeated in these sticky settings, but they will suffer a slow attrition—and show no quick or obvious benefits. How did the old empires ever get soldiers to go to such places, to sit in beleaguered encampments, to fight an endless round of small, wearying, unrecorded battles? Today, when every death is televised, democratic citizens (the soldiers themselves or their parents) are unlikely to support or endure interventions of this kind. And yet, sometimes, they ought to be supported and endured. Consider: If some powerful state or regional alliance had rushed troops into Rwanda when the massacres first began or as soon as their scope was apparent, the terrible exodus and the cholera plague might have been avoided. But the troops would still be there, probably, and no one would know what had not happened.

Two forms of long-lasting intervention, both associated in the past with imperial politics, now warrant reconsideration. The first is a kind of trusteeship, where the intervening power actually rules the country it has "rescued," acting in trust for the inhabitants, seeking to establish a stable and more or less consensual politics. The second is a kind of protectorate, where the intervention brings some local group or coalition of groups to power and is then sustained only defensively to ensure that there is no return of the defeated regime or the old lawlessness and that minority rights are respected. Rwanda might have been a candidate for trusteeship; Bosnia for a protectorate.

These are arrangements that are hard to recommend and that would, no doubt, be hard to justify in today's political climate. The lives they saved would be speculative and statistical, not actual lives; only disasters that *might have* occurred (but how can we be sure?) would be avoided. This is rescue-in-advance, and it will be resisted by those local elites who believe that the need for rescue will never arise if they are allowed to take charge—or who are prepared to take charge at any cost. The very idea of a "failed state" will seem patronizing and arrogant to a group like, say, the Rwandan Patriotic Front, which hasn't yet had a chance to succeed. Nor is the history of trusteeships and protectorates particularly encouraging: The contemporary horror of the Sudanese civil war, for example, is no reason to forget the oppressiveness of the old "Anglo-Egyptian Sudan." Nonetheless, given what is now going on in Southeast Europe and Central Africa, morally serious people have to think again about the human costs and benefits of what we might call "standing interventions." Haiti today [October 1994] might provide a test case, since the U.S.-led, multinational force serves as the protector of the restored Aristide government—and that role is likely to be an extended one.

Which States Should Intervene?

Who will, who should, do the "standing" and pay the price of the possible but often invisible victories? This is no doubt the hardest question, but it isn't, curiously, the one that has attracted the most attention. The public debate has had a different focus—as if there were (as perhaps there once were) a large number of states eager to intervene. So the question is: Who can authorize and constrain these interventions, set the ground rules and the time frame, worry about their strategies and tactics? The standard answer on the left, and probably more widely, is that the best authority is international, multilateral—the U.N. is the obvious example. Behind this preference is an argument something like Rousseau's argument for the general will: In the course of a democratic decision procedure, Rousseau claimed, the particular interests of the different parties will cancel each other out, leaving a general interest untainted by particularity. As with individuals in domestic society, so with states in international society: If all of them are

consulted, each will veto the self-aggrandizing proposals of the others.

But this isn't a wholly attractive idea, for its result is very likely to be stalemate and inaction, which cannot always be the general will of international society. It is possible, of course, that some coalition of states, cooperating for the sake of shared (particular) interests, will have its way; or that stalemate will free the U.N.'s bureaucracy to pursue a program of its own. Multilateralism is no guarantee of anything. It may still be better than the unilateral initiative of a single powerful state—though in the examples with which I began, India, Vietnam, and Tanzania, local powers, did not do entirely badly; none of their interventions, with the possible exception of the last, would have been authorized by the U.N. In practice, we should probably look for some concurrence of multilateral authorization and unilateral initiative—the first for the sake of moral legitimacy, the second for the sake of political effectiveness—but it's the initiative that is essential.

Can we assume that there are states ready to take the initiative and sustain it? In Somalia, the United States made the undertaking but was unprepared for the long haul (perhaps the long haul was not called for in this case—no one is reporting today on conditions in the Somalian countryside, so we don't know). Bosnia provides a classic example of a serial rejection of the undertaking: Everyone deplored the war and the ethnic cleansing; no one was prepared to stop them—and no one is prepared now to reverse their effects. Similarly, the African states and the Western powers stood by and watched the Rwandan massacres. (Remember the Biblical injunction: "Do not stand idly by the blood of thy neighbor." The Rwandans, it turned out, had no local or global neighbors until they were dying by the thousands on foreign soil and on television.)

It seems futile to say what is also obvious: that some states should be prepared to intervene in some cases. It is probably equally futile to name the states and the cases, though that is what I mean to do, on the principle that even futility is improved when it is made less abstract. The European Community or, at least, the French and British together (the Germans were disqualified by their aggression in World War II) ought to have intervened early on in Bosnia. The Organization of African Unity, with the financial help of Europeans and Americans, should have intervened early on in Rwanda. (I concede that the Nigerian-led intervention in Liberia is not an entirely happy precedent, though it has probably slowed the killing.) The United States should have intervened in Haiti months before it did, though the probably necessary protectorate would best have been undertaken by a coalition of Central American and Caribbean states. It is harder to say who should have stopped the killing in southern Sudan or East Timor: There isn't always an obvious candidate or a clear responsibility. It is also hard to say how responsibility passes on, when the obvious candidates refuse its burdens. Should the United States, as the world's only or greatest "great power," be nominated agent-of-last-resort? With the transportation technology at our command, we are probably near enough, and we are certainly strong enough, to stop what needs stopping in most of the cases I have been discussing (though not in all of them at once).

But no one really wants the United States to become the world's policeman, even of-last-resort, as we would quickly see were we to undertake the role. Morally and politically, a division of labor is better, and the best use of American power will often be to press other countries to do their share of the work. Still, we will, and we should be, more widely involved than other countries with fewer resources. Sometimes, the United States should take the initiative; sometimes we should help pay for and even add soldiers to an intervention initiated by somebody else. In many cases, nothing at all will be done unless we are prepared to play one or the other of these parts—either the political lead or a combination of financial backer and supporting player. Old and well-earned suspicions of American power must give way now to a wary recognition of its necessity. (A friend comments: You would stress the wariness more if there were a Republican president. Probably so.)

Many people on the left will long for a time when this necessary American role is made unnecessary by the creation of an international military force. But this time, though it will obviously come before the much heralded leap from the realm of necessity to the realm of freedom, is still a long way off. Nor would a U.N. army with its own officers, capable of acting independently in the field, always find itself in the right fields (that is, the killing fields). Its presence or absence would depend on decisions of a Security Council likely to be as divided and uncertain as today, still subject to great-power veto and severe budgetary constraints. The useful role played by the U.N. in Cambodia (organizing and supervising elections) suggests the importance of strengthening its hand. But it wasn't the U.N. that overthrew Pol Pot and stopped the Khmer Rouge massacres. And so long as we can't be sure of its ability and readiness to do that, we will have to look for and live with unilateral interventions. It is a good thing, again, when these are undertaken by local powers like Vietnam; most often, however, they will depend on global powers like the United States and (we can hope) the European Community

Despite all that I have said so far, I don't mean to abandon the principle of nonintervention—only to honor its exceptions. It is true that right now there are a lot of exceptions. One reads the newspaper these days shaking. The vast numbers of murdered people; the men, women, and children dying of disease and famine willfully caused or easily preventable; the masses of desperate refugees—none of these are served by reciting high-minded principles. Yes, the norm is not to intervene in other people's countries; the norm is self-determination. But not for *these* people, the victims of tyranny, ideological zeal, ethnic hatred, who are not determining anything for themselves, who urgently need help from outside.

And it isn't enough to wait until the tyrants, the zealots, and the bigots have done their filthy work and then rush food and medicine to the ragged survivors. Whenever the filthy work can be stopped, it should be stopped. And if not by us, the supposedly decent people of this world, then by whom?

78. The Futility of U.S. Intervention in Regional Conflicts

Barbara Conry

Barbara Conry argues that U.S. military intervention is generally not a viable solution to regional conflicts. In the first place, she argues, in the vast majority of cases such interventions do not work because the altruism of those intervening cannot usually outlast the nationalism or self-interest of the parties in the conflict. Second, she argues that it is virtually impossible for such interventions to be impartial. Third, she claims that such interventions give rise to anti-American sentiment based on the north–south conflict between the rich and the poor, and they constitute a drain on U.S. resources.

The threat of tensions escalating into superpower confrontations helped stifle regional conflicts for many years, but age-old disputes across the globe have exploded since the end of the Cold War, and regional conflicts are on the rise. The "World Military and Social Expenditures" report counted an unprecedented twenty-nine "major" wars in 1992. ("Major" meant a war that involved one or more governments and killed at least 1,000 people in the year.) An informal *Time* magazine study a number of years ago revealed that approximately twenty wars were likely to be under way at any given time, but a [February 7] 1993 *New York Times* study identified forty-eight wars in progress (defined as two organized sides fighting and causing casualties). Although such precise numbers are not often cited, there is widespread agreement that regional conflicts, driven by religion, nationalism, and political and economic disputes, are rising dramatically and will continue to do so.

American Desire to Intervene

"Regional conflict" is difficult to define precisely, and experts use the term in a variety of ways. For the purpose of this analysis, the term will mean all armed upheaval, either cross-border or internecine, that affects a limited area but has little direct impact on the security of the rest of the world. The definition is necessarily broad, applicable to wars between established sovereign states, such as the Iran-Iraq conflict in the 1980s; internal strife in the absence of a functioning government, as in Somalia; a dispute between a sovereign government and an armed group within its borders, as in Sudan; or a conflict that involves both sovereign states and external nonstate parties, as in the former Yugoslavia.

In the age of mass communication, the entire world often witnesses the human tragedy associated with regional wars. Americans who are accustomed to basic human rights, relative stability, and freedom are often moved by distressing media images of remote war-torn regions. Those tragedies inspire in many Americans a sincere desire—even a sense that it is the duty of the United States—to alleviate the suffering. There is also widespread conviction that we have the means to do so. Since the American triumph in the Cold War and the successful expulsion of the world's fourth largest army [Iraq's] from Kuwait with so few allied casualties, Americans and foreigners alike have tended to assume that the U.S. military is capable of managing regional conflagrations whenever it chooses to do so.

In reality, U.S. military intervention is generally not a viable solution to regional conflicts and should not be undertaken except in the rare instances in which American national security is at stake. In most

Abridged from Barbara Conry, "The Futility of U.S. Intervention in Regional Conflicts," *Cato Institute Policy Analysis*, May 19, 1994. Reprinted by permission of the Cato Institute, Washington, DC.

cases regional conflicts cannot be helped—and may well be exacerbated—by the intervention of outside parties. U.S. intervention can be especially counterproductive, since it often intensifies smaller, less powerful countries' (the very nations most likely to be involved in regional conflicts) fears of America's hegemonic intentions. Militarily, too, the United States is ill suited to suppress regional conflicts, in which warring forces frequently rely on guerrilla warfare, street fighting, and other tactics that are not easily met by America's high-tech war machine. Retired British diplomat Jonathan Clarke has pointed out that

> America's adversaries know full well that they are uncompetitive on a "First World" battlefield. Their response, like that of the Massachusetts Minuteman confronting that British Redcoat, is to lower the threshold of war to prevent the full range of American advanced weaponry and electronic wizardry from operating. The result is that Americans enter today's messy Third World battles not as odds-on favorites but on level terms.

Indeed, it was precisely that type of warfare that prevented the United States from achieving its objectives in both Vietnam and Somalia—proving that the most powerful military in the world is far from invincible.

Not only does inappropriate military intervention fail to reconcile regional conflicts, it also has negative consequences for the United States. There can be significant political costs, ranging from diminished American credibility as the result of an unsuccessful mission to resentment on the part of foreign governments and populations of Washington's meddling in their affairs. More serious, injudicious military intervention can create threats to national security where none previously existed, stoking the fires of anti-Americanism, jeopardizing the lives of U.S. troops, and ultimately undermining our ability to protect vital national interests in the event of a direct threat. . . .

Idealism in Intervention

In the absence of a clear and defensible strategic rationale for intervention in regional conflicts, a smattering of idealistic justifications has emerged. In the past, idealism sometimes served as a fig leaf for more mundane motives. During the Gulf War, for instance, President Bush invoked such notions as the preservation of the new world order, protection of sovereignty, and a stance against "naked aggression" to obscure the harsher truth that he was deploying U.S. troops primarily to protect economic interests—American access to gulf oil. The idealistic arguments were essential to gain the support of those who are uncomfortable with the notion of war for self-interest yet accept war as a tragic but necessary sacrifice for the sake of altruistic objectives. For some people, humanitarian reasons or the advancement of various moral principles are in themselves adequate justification for U.S. military involvement in regional wars.

Democracy, human rights, national self-determination, and humanitarian assistance are the most common rationales for military intervention where no threat to national security exists. All are admirable ideals. Yet military interventions based on such ideals are even more problematic than those that are at least rhetorically rooted in national security, and intervention is usually an ineffective way to advance ideals. If anything, coercion tends to make a mockery of the very principle it was intended to defend. As Paul W. Schroeder of the United States Institute of Peace argued in the *Washington Quarterly,* "The more the lesson desired is inflicted by external armed force, the less the experience of defeat and failure is likely to be internalized in a useful way and lead to the kind of durable change desired."

Military intervention for reasons unrelated to American security also forces the United States to embrace inherently hypocritical policies. Because it is impossible for the United States to intervene in every instance in which American principles are offended, the necessary selection process inevitably gives priority to some conflicts while marginalizing others. As Robert Oakley, President Clinton's special envoy to Somalia, said, "The international community is not disposed to deploying 20, 40, 60,000 military forces each time there is an internal crisis in a failed state." To take action in some cases and not others does not make for consistent policy.

If the United States were to declare genocide in Bosnia sufficient grounds for American military intervention, for example, it would be blatantly hypocritical to ignore the (clearer and considerably more severe) genocide in Sudan. Similarly capricious was

Washington's determination that the breakdown of the Somali government merited U.S. intervention, while officials ignored the crisis in Rwanda after the apparent assassination of President Habyarimana on April 6, 1994 (100,000 were said to have been killed in the first two weeks of fighting alone) except to evacuate Americans from the area. Likewise, demands that U.S. troops protect democracy in Haiti are incongruous in light of Washington's quiet indifference toward the suspension of democracy in Algeria when Muslim extremists were poised to win elections in 1992. The inconsistency and hypocrisy of those policies are evidence of the weakness of intervention on the basis of nebulous principles.

A History of Failure

The United States should also avoid military intervention in regional conflicts because, in the vast majority of cases, it does not work. In fact, it usually aggravates the situation. Even if a consensus were to develop that global stability or any other objective should be pursued by all viable means, military intervention would remain an unwise course in most cases. It rarely achieves its purpose and often has the perverse effect of obstructing, rather than advancing, what it seeks to achieve. (American peacekeepers in Lebanon in 1983, for example, were an aggravating rather than a stabilizing force.) Intervention usually harms American interests as well. The most compelling arguments against American intervention are its ineffectiveness and the harm it causes all parties involved.

The ability of military action to achieve political objectives in the modern era is very limited. "Beware of the facile assumption that wars are fightable and winnable again. Beware of the illusion that there is a military solution to every geopolitical problem," warns journalist Theo Sommer. Many deeply rooted political and economic problems are impervious to military solutions.

Lack of Endurance

Intervening powers are at a disadvantage because their stake in the outcome is usually far smaller than that of the primary combatants. In the former Yu-

goslavia, for example, Bosnian Muslims, Croats, and Serbs are fighting out of nationalism, which they perceive as closely related to their very existence as states (or as distinct cultures). Nationalism in that case is an ideal for which many people are prepared to kill and die. Outside parties that become involved for essentially altruistic reasons are not prepared to fight with the same intensity or endurance. Altruism and nationalism simply do not inspire equal determination.

Moreover, the American public is renowned for its unwillingness to sustain heavy casualties in remote regional wars. American support for military action abroad tends to decline dramatically at the prospect of an extended occupation that will entail significant U.S. casualties. The erosion of public support usually leads to the erosion of congressional support, resulting in serious divisions within the government that is supposed to be directing the intervention. With leadership divided, there is little chance for success. The military, already operating under handicaps inherent to intervention, is virtually assured of failure. As political scientist Richard Falk has commented, "It is not that intervention can *never* work but that it will almost never succeed unless a costly, prolonged occupation is an ingredient of the commitment."

The failure of interventionism is not merely a post–Cold War phenomenon. During the Cold War it may have been easier to "sell" an intervention because Soviet influence in a regional conflict was always a potential, if indirect, threat to American security. Nevertheless, in the instances in which Washington deemed the threat sufficient to warrant intervention, the track record was poor. The pinnacle of failed Cold War intervention—at immense cost to the United States—may have been Vietnam, but it certainly was not the only failure. In Korea there were 137,000 American casualties in a war that ended in stalemate; there were a number of other, smaller but equally ineffectual interventions in conflicts in Africa and Central America during the Cold War as well. In all instances Americans bore significant human and economic costs, yet their sacrifices brought no lasting substantive gain and made little sense, even when rivalry with the Soviet Union was a factor. Similar sacrifices would make even less sense today in the absence of a superpower challenger.

The Vietnam disaster greatly diminished Washington's enthusiasm for military involvement overseas. Ronald Reagan tentatively resumed foreign adventurism, most notably by sending U.S. Marines to Beirut, Lebanon, as "impartial" peacekeepers in the Lebanese civil war. American interests in the outcome of the Lebanese war were remote at best, and Reagan's foray into the conflict was unproductive. The costs, however, were great—especially to the 241 Marines killed in their barracks by a suicide bomber, who clearly did not consider American involvement impartial.

The Impossibility of Impartiality

Indeed, U.S. involvement was not impartial. The presence of U.S. troops strengthened the position of the Christian-dominated regime of President Amin Geymayel at the expense of the other factions. The Lebanon debacle underscores a larger problem. It is exceedingly difficult for any outside party, acting alone or in concert with others, to remain impartial during an armed conflict, no matter how sincere the intention. That point was painfully proven once again in Mogadishu [Somalia] ten years after Beirut.

When President Bush sent U.S. troops to Somalia in 1992, he cited a humanitarian reason: to feed the starving Somali population. Civil order had broken down, and warring factions were using starvation as a weapon against innocent people. Despite the simple and narrow focus of the mission, the United States eventually found itself party to the civil war. Under the auspices of the United Nations, American troops were engaged for several months in a manhunt for "warlord" Mohammad Farah Aideed, culminating in a ferocious firefight on October 3, 1993, that cost the lives of eighteen Army Rangers. The search for Aideed was futile and, in the end, abandoned. In an ironic twist of events, a U.S. military plane carried "political leader" Aideed to a peace conference in Ethiopia only weeks after U.S. troops gave up their search.

Nothing substantial was accomplished. While it is true that Somalis were no longer starving, the worst of the famine was over before American troops arrived. According to many sources, some regions of Somalia were actually producing an agricultural surplus at the time the United States intervened. "Mission creep" transformed the objective from easing starvation to "nation building," and no substantive progress was made toward that goal. Street fighting diminished for a time, but even before the American

withdrawal in March 1994 it began to resume. Again, the costs have been tremendous: American, U.N., and Somali lives; scarce economic resources ($1.3 billion for the United States alone); and American credibility were all squandered in the unsuccessful mission. . . .

Yankee Go Home

Another cost of military intervention is a rise in anti-American sentiment, which was evident throughout the Cold War in Africa and Latin America and more recently in Somalia. When U.S. Marines made their dramatic landing in Mogadishu in December 1992, the Somalis greeted them with cheers. Less than a year later, on October 3, 1993, eighteen Americans died in a single day at the hands of Somalis. Hatred of the United States was unmistakable, particularly in the gruesome and widely published photograph of smiling Somalis dragging the corpse of an American soldier through the streets. Despite the apparent goodwill at the beginning of the mission, American involvement was violently resented once the United States became part of the war.

Similar ill will greeted U.S. soldiers when they attempted to land in Haiti as part of a U.N. force assisting the implementation of the Governors Island accord. Given the long history of U.S. interference in Haitian domestic affairs, the resistance should not have been surprising. The United States has meddled so much there—American troops occupied Haiti for nearly twenty years beginning in 1915, and Washington has frequently granted or withheld financial assistance in crude attempts to influence Haiti's domestic affairs—that U.N. secretary-general Boutros Boutros-Ghali initially rejected American participation in the peacekeeping force. Only after President Clinton threatened to withdraw American support for the agreement did the United Nations reluctantly accept a U.S. contingent. Faced with violent opposition to the American presence, which occurred soon after the massacre of U.S. troops in Mogadishu, the Clinton administration ordered the ships not to land. (The most powerful country in the world's lack of will to confront opposition described as a few hundred "thugs" also did significant damage to American credibility.)

Anti-Americanism in Haiti and Somalia should not be dismissed lightly. The Pentagon has identified north–south conflict—the "haves" versus the "have-nots"—as a serious future problem for the United States. In a study entitled "Terrorism Futures," religious, ethnic, and regional conflicts were cited as probable sources of terrorism in the next decade. At the beginning of the study in late 1991, researchers anticipated that religious extremism would be the gravest threat. The unexpected conclusion, though, was that an "us versus them" mentality would be a more alarming threat, pitting "fanatics from impoverished countries" against wealthier nations.

In view of the likelihood that the Third World, or the south, will be the site of many future conflicts, American intervention could provide the impetus for an era of divisive north–south confrontation. An interventionist policy could also make the United States a high-priority target for terrorists and other disgruntled factions. The flaring of hostility toward American military personnel in Somalia may be an omen of that danger.

Creating New Problems

Interventionism also jeopardizes U.S. vital interests in other ways. The most obvious threat is to the lives of American soldiers sent into the conflict. Once troops have been deployed, it becomes a vital interest to ensure their security. If they are in danger or if troops have been taken hostage, the United States has a responsibility to protect them. It was for that reason that President Clinton announced March 31, 1994, as the date for withdrawal from Somalia and, at the same time, took what appeared to be the contradictory action of sending several thousand additional troops to Mogadishu. To guarantee the security of the troops already there, additional forces had to be deployed. The intervention had created a threat to U.S. interests where there had previously been none.

Other, more abstract, threats arise from interventionism as well. The argument has been made that American credibility, like American soldiers, constitutes a vital interest that must be protected at all costs. Owen Harries, editor of the *National Interest*, made this argument with reference to American interests in Bosnia:

> At the beginning of the Bosnian crisis there was, in my opinion, no significant American

interest at stake . . . But that was then. In the meantime, the Clinton administration has managed to create a serious national interest in Bosnia where none before existed: an interest, that is, in the preservation of this country's prestige and credibility.

Harries goes on to say that American credibility is not merely a matter of national self-respect or patriotism. It is a vital interest with implications for national security. "For the greater one's prestige, the less necessary it is to resort to force and other forms of coercion in order for one's will to be effective—and vice versa," he says.

Intervention in regional wars is a distraction and a drain on resources. Diverting time, money, and manpower from areas that have a significant impact on national security to peripheral nonsecurity interests is never desirable. But in the event of a crisis that affects U.S. vital interests, it is downright dangerous. It is difficult for the United States to be well prepared to protect national security when its military resources are diffused all over the globe and are configured to participate in nebulous peacekeeping or peace enforcement operations.

Unnecessary interventions also waste another very important and readily depleted resource: public support for U.S. military operations. Failed military missions engender tremendous public skepticism about future operations. Although that caution may serve a useful purpose in keeping troops out of other regional conflicts, it may be dangerous in the event of a genuine threat to national security. The American people's support is essential to the success of military operations. Lack of public support when vital interests are at stake could weaken U.S. resolve—and therefore jeopardize our ability—to protect those interests. . . .

The United States should avoid regional intervention except in cases in which there is a direct and substantial threat to national security or American vital interests. No matter how superficially appealing the rationale, military intervention in regional conflicts generally does not work and often creates threats to U.S. security where none previously existed. In this era of proliferating regional wars, the United States must resist the impulse to intervene. To do otherwise is to invite further tragedy, increasing the suffering not only of the combatants but of the American people as well.

79. Peacekeeping, Intervention, and National Sovereignty in Internal Armed Conflict

KOFI A. ANNAN

Kofi A. Annan, the current Secretary General of the United Nations, surveys the history of the United Nations interventions with respect to internal armed conflict, focusing particularly on the recent interventions in Somalia, Rwanda, and Bosnia and Herzegovina. He notes the successes and failures associated with these interventions, but, in general, he favors a greater role for the United Nations in enforcing international norms of human rights.

The United Nations faces moral dilemmas as a matter of course. In the broadest sense, there is the gap between the ideals set out in the U.N. Charter—which we take as a moral imperative—and the realities of what the organization can actually achieve. With limited resources for the fight to eradicate poverty, we cannot possibly satisfy the needs of all who turn to us for help. Moreover, given the often harsh political facts of member states' interests and relations, the United Nations can respond to only some threats to the peace while other emergencies are left to unfold, untreated by the salve of international action.

If these are the dilemmas of inaction, the United Nations also encounters moral quandaries when it does act, when it does become present on the ground, carrying out its diverse work for peace, development, and human rights. Nowhere is this more true than when the organization is called on to deal with internal armed conflicts. These are often the most intractable of situations, and the United Nations is usually summoned when all other efforts have failed. Moreover, these sorts of conflicts often do not lend themselves to the traditional peacekeeping treatment. They are typically fought between regular armies and irregular forces or among irregular forces. Many involve more than two parties or groups, often accountable to no one. The distinction between combatants and civilians is often blurred, and child soldiers are not uncommon. Nations find themselves facing questions about the cohesion of

their societies and even their very ability to endure as functioning states. Civilians are not only caught in the cross fire but are often the targets of violence; denied food, shelter, and dignity; and subject to suffering less likely to occur in more conventional wars between the armies of two states. These circumstances require a coordinated political, military, and humanitarian response. The resultant intertwining of mandates and personnel is not without complications; indeed, the record of the international community in meeting this challenge is mixed.

Recent years have seen United Nations interventions succeed in helping several troubled nations make the difficult transition from conflict to reconciliation, reconstruction, and long-term development. Elsewhere, however, the organization has become embroiled in circumstances that scarred its credibility and moral stature. In an era of loosening restraints—on sovereignty, on military intervention, and most of all on the behavior of armed individuals—the United Nations has drawn many lessons from these experiences. The organization has come a long way in determining what it can and cannot do to save lives and promote peace.

Evolving Notions of Sovereignty

Respect for the fundamental sovereignty, territorial integrity, and political independence of states is a cornerstone of the international system, one of the most important building blocks of global stability, security, and progress. The founders of the United Nations enshrined this principle in Article 2, paragraph 7, of

Reprinted from *Hard Choices* (1998). Edited by Jonathan Moore, by permission of Rowman & Littlefield.

the United Nations Charter, which states, "Nothing contained in the present Charter shall authorize the United Nations to intervene in matters which are essentially within the domestic jurisdiction of any state." That stricture is just as relevant today; violations of sovereignty remain violations of the global order.

However, the understanding of sovereignty is undergoing a significant transformation. Satellite communication, environment degradation, and the globalization of markets are just a few of the contemporary phenomena that are bringing into question the extent of state authority. The starving child on television screens around the world has generated global constituencies and pressure for action that governments cannot ignore. The implications of human rights abuses and refugee and other migratory flows for international peace and security are forcing us to take a fresh look at sovereignty from a different perspective: sovereignty as a matter of responsibility, not just power.

This idea predates the interdependence among nations that characterizes the current era. The United Nations' joint responsibility to member states and to their citizens is reflected in the first words of the preamble of the charter: "We the peoples of the United Nations." In 1948, shortly after the adoption of the Universal Declaration of Human Rights, the United Nations General Assembly debated its right to express concern about the apartheid system in South Africa and reached a historic decision: the principle of international concern for human rights took precedence over the claim of noninterference in internal affairs. In the decades that followed, outside support for the antiapartheid movement within South Africa—in the form of trade sanctions and arms embargoes, global public awareness campaigns, and other measures intended to isolate the apartheid regime—played a crucial role in the eventual triumph over racism and the establishment of democratic rule. It is no exaggeration to say that this effort of moral suasion helped shape the conscience of the international community.

On many issues and in many of the world's disputes and conflicts, governments or other parties are adamantly opposed to any third-party or United Nations intervention, and sovereignty is the first line of defense. But let us also remember that nations routinely accept restrictions on their sovereignty in order to cooperate with others in the pursuit of various common global goods. States that are party to

the major international human rights covenants have chosen to make themselves accountable to treaty bodies that monitor adherence to these instruments. Environmental agreements, such as the Montreal Protocol on Substances That Deplete the Ozone Layer (1987), and disarmament texts, such as the Chemical Weapons Convention (1997) and the Convention on the Prohibition of Antipersonnel Mines (1997), likewise place limits on the actions and autonomy of individual states, constraints that are accepted in view of the larger benefits at stake.

What *is* different today, particularly since the end of the Cold War, is the rapidity with which the balance is shifting: away from indifference, away from acceptance of what might be called the misuses of sovereignty, and toward greater moral engagement, toward an international community based on shared norms and standards and a willingness to uphold those basic values. Each of my immediate predecessors commented on this trend. Javier Pérez de Cuéllar wrote in 1991, "It is now increasingly felt that the principle of non-interference with the essential domestic jurisdiction of States cannot be regarded as a protective barrier behind which human rights could be massively or systematically violated with impunity." Boutros Boutros-Ghali, in *An Agenda for Peace*, his 1992 report on preventive diplomacy, peacekeeping, and postconflict peace building, wrote, "The time of absolute and exclusive sovereignty . . . has passed; its theory was never matched by reality." Today, I say that the sovereignty of states can constitute an essential bulwark against intimidation or coercion, but it must not be allowed to obstruct effective action to address problems that transcend borders or to secure human dignity.

◇

The Changing Face of Military Intervention

The evolution in thinking about sovereignty has been one of the major factors behind the profound changes in United Nations peace operations since the late 1980s. Another, of course, was the end of the Cold War. With the end of ideological and superpower rivalry, the potential for consensus in the Security Council made possible much that had not been possible before and created an impetus for the international community to extend its reach. As a result, military interventions grew dramatically in both number and scope, and our responsibilities became more varied than even the most prophetic among us would have dared predict.

In most of the earliest, "traditional" peacekeeping operations, United Nations military forces were interposed between belligerent parties, principally to monitor a cease-fire and/or to report on the implementation of the peace agreement that had brought them there. The United Nations still performs these functions successfully in Cyprus and on the Golan Heights. But in recent years the international community has mandated the United Nations to undertake additional assignments, most commonly in the aftermath of internal conflicts, as opposed to wars between sovereign nations. Many of these operations are consent based, in which the U.N. has been asked to monitor and help implement comprehensive peace agreements. The United Nations has performed tasks as varied as organizing elections, demobilizing and reintegrating former combatants, and repatriating and resettling refugees and displaced persons. It has helped rebuild economic and social infrastructures; it has protected the delivery of humanitarian aid; it has monitored respect for human rights.

In these cases, the parties themselves temporarily cede a degree of sovereignty to the United Nations for the life of the peace agreement. The value of such "road maps" for reconciliation and peace is indisputable, as successful operations in Cambodia, El Salvador, Mozambique, and Namibia testify; they provide not only a precise timetable and detailed set of objectives but also a template against which compliance can be measured. In Angola it has proven more difficult to fully implement the peace agreement owing to the recalcitrance of one of the parties involved, but this point should not obscure the considerable progress that has been made thus far.

More difficult have been cases in which the United Nations has been called on to intervene in conflicts without the full and reliable consent of all the relevant parties. Clearly, civil wars and other internal situations arise that are on one level internal but that also have international dimensions: the risk that hostilities will spill across borders, flows of refugees, crimes against humanity, and other violations of international humanitarian law. In response, the Security Council has adopted resolutions and embarked on operations that have set precedents and helped redefine the ideas of sovereignty, military in-

tervention, and humanitarian action. Thus, in April 1991, the Security Council adopted Resolution 688 concerning the situation in Northern Iraq which for the first time recognized that a humanitarian emergency and massive population displacement could constitute a threat to international peace and security. Since then, the United Nations has acted in the following countries.

Somalia

Faced with conflict, famine, obstacles to the distribution of humanitarian assistance, and a complete breakdown of supervening authority, the Security Council (in Resolution 794 of 3 December 1992) authorized member states "to use all necessary means to establish as soon as possible a secure environment for humanitarian relief operations"—a rare use of military force for largely humanitarian goals. With no functioning government to grant consent for such an operation, the council invoked the enforcement provisions of Chapter VII of the U.N. Charter, the first time this was done to deal with a conflict confined within a state's borders. Months later, when a United Nations peacekeeping force took command of the mission from the United States–led multinational Unified Task Force (UNITAF), the mandate set out in Resolution 814 of 26 March 1993 included enforcement powers for disarmament as well as the delivery of humanitarian relief. UNOSOM II also had a mandate to help rebuild the nation, although no one expected this could be done coercively. That it failed to fulfill completely this ambitious mandate highlights the dangers of trying to mix peacekeeping and peace enforcement, especially in the absence of a coherent or solidly supported international policy. The humanitarian goals of the mission were largely accomplished, but the unhappy ending of UNOSOM II has in the eyes of some observers been the main cause of the Security Council's hesitancy to authorize any operation like it since.

Former Yugoslavia

The involvement of the United Nations in the conflicts in the former Yugoslavia began as a classic case of peacemaking and peacekeeping but then became much, much more. For the first time since the Nuremberg and Tokyo tribunals were set up following World War II, the Security Council established a tribunal to investigate and prosecute alleged war crimes. In the former Yugoslav Republic of Macedonia, the organization deployed its first "preventive" force on the borders of that country to help insulate against the spread of fighting from neighboring states. In Croatia, United Nations peacekeepers serving with the U.N. Transnational Administration for Eastern Slavonia, Baranja, and Western Sirmium (UNTAE) were assigned the rarely undertaken task of administering a disputed territory. With the weight of a 5,000-strong mechanized peacekeeping force and the watchful eyes of NATO behind it, the U.N. oversaw—in one of the most successful multifaceted peacekeeping operations in its history—the peaceful restoration of Croatian sovereignty while creating the conditions necessary for the maintenance of the region's multiethnic character. But it was the situation in Bosnia and Herzegovina that posed the greatest, most novel, and most disturbing challenges; these are discussed in greater detail below.

Rwanda

Rwanda is in many respects the intervention that did *not* happen, at least in the crucial early weeks of the crisis. Occurring so soon after the troubled operation in Somalia, the violence was left to unfold, which it did with ferocious speed and intensity, sparing not even children and the elderly and intruding on sanctuaries such as churches and hospitals. I have said on many occasions that a force of even modest size and means could have prevented much of the killing, but the opposite course was taken: a reduction in the size of the United Nations force that was already in place to police an earlier peace agreement. The international community is still coming to terms with that decision, with that failure to mount an adequate response to the genocide that ensued. Eventually, the United Nations became deeply involved in the search for peace in Rwanda and the surrounding region. Unique aspects of the organization's response included efforts to cope with the militarization of refugee camps in what was then eastern Zaire; the decision of the Security Council to authorize a French-led multinational intervention known as Operation Turquoise; the dispatch of a human rights field operation; and the creation by the Security Council of an international war crimes tribunal, only the second such body established since World War II.

If intervention can work, if intervention has become more grand in design and accomplished in its

outcomes, it is also true that these new, multidimensional interventions also encounter more obstacles and greater complexities, not to mention the risk of outright failure. A change in quantity, as has been said, produces a change in quality. Add one atom of oxygen to hydrogen oxide, and you have water. Add humanitarian assistance to a military operation, and you change the quality of a mission. Introduce outside players to an internal situation, and you change the quality of a mission. With lives and the integrity of the United Nations at stake, we must be ever vigilant to the dangers involved in such developments.

The U.N. Involvement in Bosnia and Herzegovina

When war erupted in Bosnia and Herzegovina in 1992, United Nations peacekeepers were thrust into a theater of operations where there was no peace to keep; humanitarian personnel were dispatched to a situation in which the denial of humanitarian assistance became an instrument of war and the inhumane practice of "ethnic cleansing" a central aim; and the international community was quickly immersed in a complex debate concerning mandates, political will, impartiality, the use (and nonuse) of force, and other wrenching questions. That debate, fervent throughout the war, has continued even after the signing of the Dayton Peace Agreement and has had significant implications for the ongoing use of one of the organization's most prized assets: its moral authority.

Mandates

The United Nations peacekeeping force dispatched to Bosnia-Herzegovina was not sent to end the war or to intervene on behalf of one side or another. Rather, the Security Council deployed a mission whose mandate was initially limited to delivering humanitarian aid and whose pattern of deployment and style of conduct reflected this aim. Subsequent resolutions asked the same force to contain the conflict through measures such as an arms embargo and a "no-fly zone" and to promote prospects for obtaining an overall settlement, for example, by negotiating local cease-fires. However, because the nature of the conflict, including "ethnic cleansing" and concentration camps, seemed to call for something more ambitious; because the operation's name, the United Nations Protection Force (UNPROFOR), suggested that something more militarily assertive was intended to be done; because of ambiguities and contradictions in the approach settled on by the Security Council; and unavoidably because of the actions of the parties to the conflict in Bosnia and Herzegovina, the force quickly ran into ethical and operational problems that affected its performance and credibility.

One such problem concerned the Security Council's apparently limited objective of alleviating the humanitarian consequences of the conflict. When the council operates in a principally humanitarian mode, it raises concerns that humanitarianism is being used to contain only the most visible ramifications of a crisis or as a substitute for the political and possibly military action and long-term commitment necessary to address the root causes of a crisis. This approach has serious consequences for relief actors and any troops deployed to assist a relief endeavor, as well as for the council itself as a body capable of responding effectively to threats to international peace and security.

A second dilemma arose with the confluence of humanitarian and military personnel and tasks. Some humanitarian organizations fear that military action makes their job more difficult and tarnishes their image as a disinterested party. This problem is especially acute when humanitarian issues become linked in negotiations with political and military issues. However, some of the same groups feel they have the right to take whatever action they deem necessary and that United Nations forces must be available to protect them in the course of doing so. That cannot be. There must be coordination; the military, political, and humanitarian components of an operation must each ensure that none of them takes an initiative that might compromise the others.

A third dilemma involved the U.N.'s response to ethnic cleansing. The Commission on Human Rights held its first-ever emergency session to condemn the practice. The Security Council created the first international criminal tribunal since the Nuremberg and Tokyo war crimes panels were established following World War II. The United Nations High Commissioner for Refugees (UNHCR), however, in fulfilling *its* mandate of protecting refugees and displaced persons by conveying to safety people who otherwise would have been forcibly expelled from their homes and/or murdered, was accused of abetting ethnic

cleansing. The response to this charge is clear: saving the lives of people in jeopardy had to take precedence. And, indeed, the UNHCR was criticized for both not doing enough and doing too much to evacuate populations. The conundrum underscores the difficulty of putting relief actors on the front lines, not just physically but politically.

Consent

In addition to a practicable mandate, the consent of the parties is another prerequisite for successful peacekeeping and military intervention. Consent means more than having a government and/or factional leaders agree to the presence of the United Nations peacekeepers and mediators. It is a commitment to the path of negotiation and dialogue, an admission that armed force has failed, that there is no military solution to the prevailing circumstances. Consent can come from exhaustion on the part of combatants and noncombatants or from the calculation that more is to be gained at the negotiating table than on the battlefield. The international community can also nurture consent through the use of positive inducements. In the short term, such inducements might include the provision of medical care or quick-impact projects to rehabilitate local infrastructure; over the longer term, the international community could offer financial and technical assistance for transforming a guerrilla group into a legitimate political party and for facilitating former combatants' reintegration into society. But the will to reconciliation and peace cannot be imposed. Absent a genuine interest by the parties themselves in a settlement, there are limits to what outsiders can accomplish. There is no doubting the international community's patience—witness longstanding involvements in Cyprus, Jerusalem, Kashmir, and the Golan Heights. But one can also ask whether it is ethically sound for the international community to expend resources and political will coaxing recalcitrant parties into negotiations, or becoming involved prematurely on the ground, where there is little chance of compliance and prospects for success somewhere else are not as daunting.

In Bosnia and Herzegovina the consent of the parties, when it came, tended to be hard-won and short-lived. Cease-fires were agreed to and immediately breached. Humanitarian aid convoys were blocked despite guarantees of safe passage. Such difficulties occurred largely because consent, particularly on the part of the Bosnian Serb side, would pose a hindrance to war aims. With the imposition of United Nations sanctions against the Bosnian Serb party, the question of consent became even more troublesome. And when the Security Council declared it would protect six "safe areas"—cities under siege by the Bosnian Serbs—UNPROFOR was obliged to cooperate and negotiate daily with a party on whom it was also expected to call air strikes in certain circumstances. The result was that Bosnian Serb leaders largely withdrew their consent and cooperation from UNPROFOR, declaring that they were applying their own "sanctions" to the United Nations in response to United Nations sanctions on them. UNPROFOR thus found itself obstructed, targeted by all sides, denied resupply, restricted in its movements, and subjected to constant criticism.

Impartiality

The impartiality of the United Nations enables it to enter war zones and other conflict areas and be accepted by the parties as good-faith interlocutor, as a presence for humanitarian objectives and peace. In conventional or internal conflicts, this principle is fundamental; the U.N. cannot afford to become part of the problem. In Bosnia and Herzegovina, that stance was tested to the extreme. One side suffered the overwhelming majority of casualties and atrocities and was often outraged by the decisions of the international community. One side was a recognized member state of the United Nations, which expected the organization to defend its interests. One side was the principal aggressor and therefore the primary target of sanctions and military force used by the international community. Peacekeepers, representing the will of the international community, were themselves scorned, taken hostage, attacked, and killed. Unfortunately, impartiality in the execution of the mandate was sometimes misconstrued as unthinking, or even amoral, neutrality between the warring parties.

In the face of illegal behavior (including violations of international humanitarian law), the Security Council is capable of granting a mandate that addresses the problem—and is therefore not impartial—and deploying an operation with the means to achieve this mandate. At the same time, the mandate must be implemented impartially and fairly, "without fear or favor." If the U.N. has both the assets and the political backing to do the job, this will make it part of the solution rather than part of the problem. The lesson of Somalia, Bosnia, and Rwanda

is that the U.N. must be clear about the problems facing it in discharging a mandate; the lengths to which we are prepared to go to overcome them; the means required; and the risks, costs, and moral dilemmas that will inevitably accompany any course of action or inaction in such difficult situations.

The Use, or Threat of Use, of Force

Can the international community spill blood to save lives and itself remain spotless? Can humanitarian objectives be fulfilled at the point of a gun? Can they be fulfilled at all if the guns are instead pointed at the humanitarians? These are not easy questions, but they arose repeatedly in Bosnia and Herzegovina.

Confronted with a lack of consent from all sides in the conflict but particularly by the Bosnian Serb party, UNPROFOR's mandate was gradually enlarged to include elements of enforcement. But peacekeeping derives from one set of assumptions and objectives and peace enforcement from another; mixing the two creates an untenable position for the force sent out to square the circle. UNPROFOR's resort to force, for example, caused it to be seen as a party to the conflict, thereby jeopardizing the cooperation necessary for it to fulfill its primary objective: to deliver emergency aid. Others criticized the force for *not* pursuing a war, for what was regarded as a woeful reluctance to use the enforcement powers granted to it.

Quite apart from whether UNPROFOR was a peace enforcement operation is the question of credibility in the use, and threat of use, of force. When the Security Council designated the safe areas, the secretary general offered options ranging from 7,600 to 34,000 troops to deter attacks against them. Member states chose the minimum option, and even then they only provided troops to reach the required level after more than a year. The gap between intent and action, between rhetoric and reality, was especially pronounced and contributed to the debacle that ensued when Srebrenica was overrun. The fall of Srebrenica—the inability of the United Nations to keep a designated safe area safe and to avert a human rights tragedy—has stained the record of the United Nations and will make it difficult for the international community to act in the future as a moral force. However, it must not be forgotten that the Security Council resolutions proclaiming the safe areas never asked the United Nations to either "protect" or "defend" them, merely to "deter attacks" by its presence. When the presence of the troops proved inadequate to deter attacks, they did not have the means to protect or defend the areas.

Effectiveness in the use of force is not only a matter of numbers; legitimacy is credibility's necessary counterpart. A military intervention with legitimacy—for example, in the form of a United Nations mandate representing the universal will of the international community—can win broad-based political support but without credibility may be unable to achieve its objectives. A credible force might get short-term results but without legitimacy may be unable to sustain long-term support. Together, credibility and legitimacy are mutually reinforcing, as was demonstrated when NATO played a lead role in monitoring implementation of the Dayton Peace Agreement.

Should the United Nations have used greater force in Bosnia and Herzegovina? A massive military intervention early in the conflict may have curbed or even prevented fighting not only in Bosnia and Herzegovina but elsewhere in the former Yugoslavia. It is likewise possible that no intervention at all might have allowed the parties to exhaust themselves sooner, also sparing the region prolonged bloodletting and destruction. Either of these courses of action might have had the opposite effect—namely, more violence, not less, and other unforeseen and possibly bloody consequences. Between these poles lies the intervention that did happen, which for all its shortcomings and difficulties succeeded in feeding and housing millions of people, assisting with the country's reconstruction, and laying the groundwork for peace negotiations.

Ultimately, member states must decide whether they want to give the U.N. the capacity for limited peace enforcement, as proved effective in the case of UNTAES. Whereas some believe such operations are better delegated to regional organizations and non-U.N. coalitions, these alternatives are not always available, and the United Nations pays a price in terms of moral authority and influence if it consistently declines to mount such operations itself.

Selectivity

The involvement of the United Nations in the former Yugoslavia dominated the organization's agenda in the peace and security field and distorted its peacemaking and peacekeeping efforts at the expense of other parts of the world. At the time of peak deployment in August 1995, the former Yugoslavia

accounted for nearly 70 percent of peacekeepers worldwide and more than two-thirds of peacekeeping costs. Many member states and others expressed concern that other conflicts and trouble spots failed to receive a commitment of action and resources commensurate with the unfolding tragedy. For each member of the Security Council, this is a matter of national interest and political will, of course, and also of media selectivity. But it is also a moral issue in that it prompts the world public to question the organization's universality. The United Nations cannot be everywhere, but it must be willing and able to respond to fair claims—large and small, within and beyond its leading members' spheres of interest—for its involvement.

The Vital Role of the Third Party amid Conflict and Suffering

The founders of the United Nations included a wealth of activist language in the charter: "to save succeeding generations from the scourge of war . . . to unite our strength . . . to employ international machinery . . . to take effective collective measures." These words constitute a rejection of indifference. They send a message of engagement, of international solidarity, of action instead of apathy in the face of hatred, bloodshed, and deprivation. They reflect a belief in the constructive, corrective power of human agency—the power of light over darkness.

The philosopher Edmund Burke once wrote, "The only thing necessary for the triumph of evil is for good men to do nothing." In heeding Burke's words, in trying to do our utmost for the common good, moral dilemmas have been and will continue to be a prominent part of the landscape. As we have seen in Bosnia and Herzegovina and elsewhere, of all United Nations activities, military interventions in internal armed conflicts are particularly fraught with vexing choices and questions. But as we also saw in Rwanda in 1994, where a modest intervention at the right moment could have saved many lives and a larger one could perhaps even have prevented the genocide, inaction has grave perils of its own. Aggressors and tyrants thrive on passivity, a culture of impunity prevails, and the moral standing of the international community (a dubious concept to some but not to me) suffers grave damage. It seems to me far better to accept the risk of error or failure than to remain on the sidelines; there is no purity in the abstract, and only disgrace and worse in retreat toward some imaginary safe harbor.

I entered office as secretary general stressing not only the United Nations' political and diplomatic considerations, not only its legal obligations, not only its fiscal limitations, but above all the moral

dimension of its work. At its best the United Nations can be a courageous third party that brings hope to victims and succor to the needy and that rouses the collective conscience of humankind. For all its shortcomings and constraints, the organization has compiled a solid record of achievement in this regard. We must nurture and sustain the moral vision that has made this possible.

Suggestions for Further Reading

Anthologies

Sterba, James P. *The Ethics of War and Nuclear Deterrence.* Belmont, CA: Wadsworth, 1985.

Wakin, Malham. *War, Morality and the Military Profession.* Boulder: Westview Press, 1979.

Winters, Paul. *Interventionism.* San Diego: Greenhaven Press, 1995.

Basic Concepts

Cady, Duane. *From Warism to Pacifism.* Philadelphia: Temple University Press, 1989.

Holmes, Robert. *On War and Morality.* Princeton: Princeton University Press, 1989.

Walters, LeRoy. *Five Classic Just-War Theories.* Ann Arbor: University Microfilms, 1971.

Walzer, Michael. *Just and Unjust Wars.* New York: Basic Books, 1994.

Alternative Views

Adelman, Howard. "The Ethics of Humanitarian Intervention." *Public Affairs Quarterly* (1992): 61–87.

Brzezinski, Zbigniew. "Selective Global Commitment." *Foreign Affairs* (1992): 1–20.

Falk, Richard. "Recycling Interventionism." *Journal of Peace Research* (1992): 129–134.

Hehir, Bryan. "Intervention: From Theories to Cases." *Ethics and International Affairs* (1995): 1–14.

Hoffmann, Stanley, with James P. Sterba. *The Ethics and Politics of Humanitarian Intervention.* Notre Dame: University of Notre Dame Press, 1996.

Laberge, Pierre. "Humanitarian Intervention: Three Ethical Positions." *Ethics and International Affairs* (1995): 14–36.

Lopez, George, and Nancy Myers. *Peace and Security.* Lanham, MD: Rowman & Littlefield, 1997.

Luper-Foy, Steven. "Intervention and Refugees." *Public Affairs Quarterly* (1992): 45–60.

Phillips, Robert, and Duane Cady. *Humanitarian Intervention: Just War vs. Pacifism.* Lanham: Rowman & Littlefield, 1995.

Pogge, Thomas. "An Institutional Approach to Humanitarian Intervention." *Public Affairs Quarterly* (1992): 89–103.

Powell, Colin. "U.S. Forces: Challenges Ahead." *Foreign Affairs* (1992): 32–45.